Dear Chris,

Many Thanks for all of your support, including as a founder member of Bread Action, which will become the _only_ place for bread response.

Cheers,

Stewart

23.11.03

Butterworths Data Security Law & Practice

Butterworths Data Security Law & Practice

Stewart Room
Partner, Field Fisher Waterhouse LLP

Members of the LexisNexis Group worldwide

United Kingdom	LexisNexis, a Division of Reed Elsevier (UK) Ltd, Halsbury House, 35 Chancery Lane, London, WC2A 1EL, and London House, 20–22 East London Street, Edinburgh EH7 4BQ
Australia	LexisNexis Butterworths, Chatswood, New South Wales
Austria	LexisNexis Verlag ARD Orac GmbH & Co KG, Vienna
Benelux	LexisNexis Benelux, Amsterdam
Canada	LexisNexis Canada, Markham, Ontario
China	LexisNexis China, Beijing and Shanghai
France	LexisNexis SA, Paris
Germany	LexisNexis Deutschland GmbH, Munster
Hong Kong	LexisNexis Hong Kong, Hong Kong
India	LexisNexis India, New Delhi
Italy	Giuffrè Editore, Milan
Japan	LexisNexis Japan, Tokyo
Malaysia	Malayan Law Journal Sdn Bhd, Kuala Lumpur
New Zealand	LexisNexis NZ Ltd, Wellington
Poland	Wydawnictwo Prawnicze LexisNexis Sp, Warsaw
Singapore	LexisNexis Singapore, Singapore
South Africa	LexisNexis Butterworths, Durban
USA	LexisNexis, Dayton, Ohio

First published in 2009

© Reed Elsevier (UK) Ltd 2009

Published by LexisNexis

All rights reserved. No part of this publication may be reproduced in any material form (including photocopying or storing it in any medium by electronic means and whether or not transiently or incidentally to some other use of this publication) without the written permission of the copyright owner except in accordance with the provisions of the Copyright, Designs and Patents Act 1988 or under the terms of a licence issued by the Copyright Licensing Agency Ltd, Saffron House, 6–10 Kirby Street, London EC1N 8TS. Applications for the copyright owner's written permission to reproduce any part of this publication should be addressed to the publisher.

Warning: The doing of an unauthorised act in relation to a copyright work may result in both a civil claim for damages and criminal prosecution.

Crown copyright material is reproduced with the permission of the Controller of HMSO and the Queen's Printer for Scotland. Parliamentary copyright material is reproduced with the permission of the Controller of Her Majesty's Stationery Office on behalf of Parliament. Any European material in this work which has been reproduced from EUR-lex, the official European Communities legislation website, is European Communities copyright.

Information Commissioner's Office material is reproduced with the permission of the Information Commissioner's Office.

A CIP Catalogue record for this book is available from the British Library.

ISBN 978-1-4057-4479-9

Typeset by Letterpart Ltd, Reigate, Surrey

Printed and bound in Great Britain by CPI Antony Rowe, Chippenham and Eastbourne

Visit LexisNexis at www.lexisnexis.co.uk

Preface and Acknowledgements

This book is the final instalment in a trilogy of books about information law that I have written, with the others being 'Data Protection and Compliance in Context' (December 2006) and 'Email: Law, Practice and Compliance' (December 2008). Although I can no longer be sure of the exact date when I commenced work on this instalment, it was definitely before the FSA announced that it had fined Nationwide Building Society £980,000 for the loss of a laptop computer containing account-holder data, because I remember making copious notes on the chapter outline about how this fine provided concrete proof of the emergence of the regulatory bear market for data security. This was about ten months before the news of the loss of the HMRC data disks hit the headlines. Since then the legal framework for data security has changed beyond all recognition. And fines for poor data security have now exceeded £3,000,000, with the expectation being that they will continue their rapid rise.

The trigger for the decision to make one of the books about data security was 'What price privacy?', a report published by the Information Commissioner in May 2006, which made his case for the introduction of prison sentences for 'data theft', which is a crime under section 55 of the Data Protection Act 1998. The report was another landmark event in the establishment of the regulatory bear market, but my interest was much closer and much more personal, as I happened to be defending the case referred to at paragraph 5.19 of the report. In September 2007, following two years of criminal litigation, a not guilty plea and a two-week trial, my clients were acquitted of all counts of data theft, which totals over 300 within over 150 summonses. This case, together with my next one, which was an appeal against an enforcement notice served by the Information Commissioner ordering laptop encryption, taught me just how complex the law in this area actually is. Yes, data security is about data protection law, but it is about much more than that. It is an area of the law that is particularly fraught with difficulty for the regulators.

So I have tried to bring together here as much of law on data security as I could, albeit I have deliberately stayed away from analysing laws of evidence and rules of criminal and civil procedure. I have covered the government's post-HMRC law reform agenda, which, although initially impressive has now lost momentum; there is still a substantial regulatory deficit between the powers that the Information Commissioner considers are required for effective regulation and those that have been granted.

Preface and Acknowledgements

Due to the close proximity of the next general election I think it would also be useful to consider the Conservatives' thinking; any lawyer worth their salt would advise their clients to consider the consequences of a change of government when a general election is looming. With this being the case I have touched upon the Conservatives' proposals for change at chapter 1, but, unfortunately, they came too late for me to consider them properly here. However, to ensure that the arguments are at least properly recorded for future analysis this book benefits from the views of Baroness Neville-Jones, Shadow Security Minister and National Security Adviser to the Leader of the Opposition. I am deeply grateful to Baroness Neville-Jones and her Chief of Staff, Mark Phillips, for their contributions and assistance.

My research has also brought me into close contact with many security professionals, technical experts, interested Parliamentarians, vendors of security technologies, security consultants and a number of the thought leaders in this area. I will credit some of them shortly.

These contacts have impressed upon me the fact that we are facing unprecedented challenges in the area of data security. The consensus of professional opinion seems to be that the UK is under sustained and serious attack from cyber-criminals and terrorists; senior police officers, politicians and other experts openly acknowledge this, both publicly and sometimes under the Chatham House Rule at industry conferences. Data security is a topic of utmost national importance.

We also face the challenge of data mishandling, with HMRC being the principal reference for government and the public sectors and the main catalyst for change. Yet, there is irony here; in data security terms, HMRC was a relatively benign event. Yes, it was massive in terms of numbers of people affected, but there is no evidence that it caused them any discernable damage. The only real damage that was done was to the trust relationship between the government and the people. People in the know seem to be in broad agreement that HMRC was a picnic compared to the damage that could be done by a real data disaster. Of course, it needs to be stressed that the private sector suffers just as much from data mishandling. The only difference between the public sector and the private sector is the fact that the public sector is currently subject to stronger regulation and greater transparency obligations.

Another prominent consideration is the effect of technological change and business process evolution. Exciting innovations, such as Cloud Computing and Software as a Service, pose new own challenges for data security and data handling. So do globalisation and the state of the economy.

Sadly, there is a sense of low morale within the community of data security professionals. The nature of the job and factors beyond their control, such as the need for cutbacks, cost saving and head count reductions, means that they are working under significant stress and pressure, more than ever before. Security can be, both literally and figuratively, a thankless task. Adding to the stress of the security professional is the increase in regulation. The case for a tougher regulatory framework was properly made and it has been accepted by all the main political parties, with a clear consensus that the Information Commissioner's powers should be strengthened, with penalties for transgressions increased. However, it is critical that regulation remains proportionate.

Preface and Acknowledgements

Thus, the development of the regulatory regime will need careful attention over the next couple of years. Regulation must achieve compliance and reasonable sanctions must be imposed to punish and deter non-compliance, but regulators must also be careful to avoid creating unnecessary market distortions. The Information Commissioner must have sufficient tools to do his job, but at the same time it is important that he encourages positive messages, cooperation with data controllers and a sense of partnership. Data controllers need comfort that they can approach regulators for advice and assistance, without fear that they will trigger a process that leads ultimately to their punishment or sanction. This is a very complex problem, but there are solutions. An amnesty could work, as could the legal separation of the regulatory responsibility for punishment from the regulatory responsibility for developing and achieving best practice. There is nothing in the Data Protection Directive that binds the UK to only one regulator for data protection.

The biggest threats to our data security are complacency, a lack of proper investment and the loss or shortage of professionalism and expertise however, not errant or over zealous exercise of regulatory powers. At the moment we are winning the battle with those who desire to do our systems and data harm, but it will be the unenviable task of the next government, whoever that may be, to achieve much more with much less. It is an adage in the security industry that the more you tighten your perimeter security the more you increase the insider threat. It is also an adage that the attackers go after low hanging fruit, moving quickly away from secure branches to less secure ones. The point here is the threat landscape is constantly evolving and changing. Standing still on data security means falling behind the threats and challenges.

So it is vitally important that we ensure a ready supply of security professionals for the future. The Obama administration has appreciated the seriousness of the skills gap in this area and so it is fostering interest in security jobs and careers, by running competitions in schools and colleges. Planning needs to start quickly on a scheme for the UK, to ensure that schools and universities deliver a constant supply of properly educated young adults to the economy, who are capable of maintaining our security. This needs a long-term vision and real political commitment.

There are many negative messages here, but it is important not to lose perspective. The UK is lucky to have a strong and deep seam of professionalism and expertise in the field of data security, with a stable democracy and legal regime. The scientific, academic and technical professions make an immense contribution to the security of our nation's systems. This is complimented by huge expertise in the private sector, with a strong, innovative and creative IT industry and consulting sector. There is a healthy community of professional and membership organisations, with active, informed and interested groups of members and recognised qualifications. We also have the benefit of a strong civil service and engagement and professionalism in the law enforcement community. It is these professionals that I now thank and acknowledge.

First, I would like to thank those who have made the greatest input to this book, those who have given me most of their time over the past three years. These include the very excellent Mike Pritchard at EMC, who has been a constant source of insight, help, support and friendship. Next, massive thanks go to Jonathan Bamford, the Assistant Information Commissioner, who has

Preface and Acknowledgements

kindly appeared at a series of industry conferences arranged by my firm, to spread the word about Privacy Enhancing Technologies, Privacy by Design and other critical initiatives of the Information Commissioner. Jonathan has kindly provided an introductory piece for this book, giving the regulator's view on the issues. Next, Philippe Renaudiere, the European Commission's Data Protection Officer, who, like Jonathan, has attended our conferences in London, to explain the EU view on PETs, and who has opened doors in Brussels. Next, Malcolm Marshall, Partner and Head of Information Protection Services at KPMG LLP, who, along with his colleagues, has provided me with a fast-track introduction into the sciences and disciplines of risk assessment and risk management for data security. Malcolm has also provided an introductory piece, giving his expert view on the issues. Next, my friends at RSA, The Security Division of EMC, who have given me hundreds of hours of exposure to security technologies. Among a very large cast I should thank Chris Johnson, Chris Bridgland, Paul Briault, Adam Bangle, Gil Litvin, Ian Williams, Andrew Moloney and Liz Kelly. There are also some ex-RSA people, such as Richard Turner (now CEO of Clearswift), Tim Pickard (now with Mimecast) and Ian Irvine who also deserve mention. Next, my good friend, Ed Gibson, Chief Cyber Security Advisor at Microsoft, who has given me unrestricted access to the Microsoft CISO Council and countless introductions. Finally, I wish to pay special tribute to Lte. General Sir Edmund Burton, who wrote the report into the loss of the MoD laptops and who is the Chairman of IAAC. Sir Edmund has been unstinting with his time, advice and encouragement and he has also graced this book writing the Foreword. Sir Edmund's report should be required reading for all security professionals. I also strongly encourage people to familiarise themselves with Sir Edmund's six principles for improving practices for data security, which he is communicating through regular keynote speeches to security professionals.

Within the community of security professionals I would like to thank Professor Howard A. Schmidt (President, Information Security Forum), who has also provided an expert view on the issues, Owen Pengelly (Head, Central Sponsor for Information Assurance, Cabinet Office), Nick Coleman (author of the Coleman Report, Independent Review of Government Information Assurance), Dr Guy Bunker (author of Data Leaks for Dummies), Dr Steve Marsh (Cabinet Office), Georgia Venetsanakos, Lynn Collier (Hitachi Data Systems), Nick Caley, Chi-Chi Liang (Symantec), Dr James Lyne (Sophos), Teresa Pa (Accenture), Clive Blackwell (Royal Holloway, University of London), Bill Sillett (Financial Services Authority), Andrew Watson (Metropolitan Police), Lee Newcomb (Capgemini), Bill Hey (Brit Insurance), Simon Holman (Nestle), Iain Sutherland (Information Security Solutions), Tony Dyhouse (QinetiQ), Geoff Harris (ISSA), Bryan Glick (Computing Magazine), Paul Fisher (SC Magazine), James Chappell (Detica) and Julian Parkin (Barclays Bank). Thanks also to Professor Dr Ian Walden at the Centre for Commercial Law Studies, Queen Mary.

Within Parliament I would also like to Lord Harris of Haringey and The Earl of Erroll.

Within my client base many thanks go to Heather MacRae, Sara Wain-Heapy, Peter Aitken and Martin Bradley (Marks & Spencer), Lucy McGrath (BBC) and Stephen Deadman (Vodafone).

Preface and Acknowledgements

At Field Fisher Waterhouse LLP I would like to thank all of my partners, with special thanks going to the Technology Law Group (Michael Chissick, Paul Barton, Andy Lucas, Simon Briskman, Eduardo Ustaran, David Naylor, Nick Holland, Hamish Sandison, Marcus Turle, Katrina Dick and Belinda Doshi), Mark Abell, Matthew Lohn, Chris Wormald, Stephen Gibbs, Duncan Black and Tony Lewis. Also, thanks to James Seadon, Antonis Patrikios, Victoria Hordern, Michelle Levin, Brian Davidson, Nick Fidducia, Nadine Bhantoe and Victoria Seaward, for help with research. Thanks too to Paul Heywood, Paul Edney and Rachel Thompson.

Thanks to Kischa Cook, for her help with the US issues.

Thanks also to Stewart Dresner (Privacy Laws and Business), Caroline Gould (Society for Computers and Law) and Linda Lynch (RSA).

At my publishers, very special thanks to Cara Annett, Sally Jones and Kate Nulty.

But, most of all, my heartfelt thanks to my darling wife Samantha and my lovely daughter Annabel, without whom nothing would be possible, or worth doing.

I also commend Computer Aid International, a UK registered charity and the world's largest provider of professionally refurbished PCs to the not-for-profit organisations in the developing world. CAI's aim is to reduce poverty through practical ICT solutions. To date CAI has provided over 150,000 fully refurbished PCs – donated by UK employers and individuals – to where they are most needed in schools, hospitals and not-for-profit organisations in over 100 developing countries. All computers, servers and laptops received and processed by CAI will have all of their data and programs removed. All hard disks are overwritten as standard and at no cost. CAI uses Blancco data wiping software, which is approved by the US Department of Defence and by the UK's CESG. Any hard disk that cannot be overwritten will be destroyed. By donating your unwanted IT equipment to CAI you will be complying with the Waste Electrical and Electronic Equipment (WEEE) Directive. CAI has been approved by the Environment Agency to operate as an Authorised Approved Treatment Facility (AATF) for WEEE.

I have tried to state the law at 31 August 2009. All mistakes are my own. This book will be regularly updated at www.breachaction.co.uk, our service for responding to security breaches and data loss.

Stewart Room
Hadley Wood, London
16 October 2009

Foreword

Lte. General Sir Edmund Burton

A series of serious security breaches occurred during the period 2007–2008. These were investigated independently at the direction of ministers and the reports were published, together, on 30 June 2008 in parallel with a comprehensive report (the Data Handling Review), sponsored by the Cabinet Secretary (Sir Gus O'Donnell).

Although the incidents that led to the reviews of data losses, and the reports that followed, attracted major press interest, the theme of Information Assurance (IA) had been a continuing challenge for government departments since 2001. The following chronology illustrates some of the key milestones:

- CESG Review — 2001
- E-envoy appointed as Central Sponsor for IA — 2002
- CSIA secretariat set up — 2002
- Launch of National IA Strategy — 2003
- Launch of Transformational Government Strategy — 2005
- IAAC launch of ID Assurance programme — 2006
- National IA Strategy updated — 2007
- Serial breaches of information/data security — 2007/8
- Major reviews and action led by Cabinet Office — 2008
- Publication of National Security Strategy — 2008
- Publication of National Cyber Security Strategy — 2009
- Publication of Digital Britain — 2009

This summary invites the question 'Why has it taken so long to implement the National IA strategies?'

Informal polls at conferences attended by specialists and non-executive directors in late 2008 indicated that few had read the reports published earlier that summer. An understanding of the importance of these issues to the UK, to Government, to the private sector and to every citizen – and a working knowledge of appropriate behaviour – is critical to our success as a vigorous, expanding, information and knowledge based economy.

A brief explanation for this widespread lack of engagement may be attributable to the following factors:

Foreword

Understanding:

- Information and data are not yet formally acknowledged to be key business assets, with potential vulnerabilities. Consequently, they are not properly exploited or appropriately protected.

- The significance of the growing interdependencies within and between government departments, and between government departments and their principal ICT service providers, is not understood. Identifying and managing these risks is crucial for both parties. Failures in service availability, integrity or confidentiality have operational and reputational impacts on both. Risks must be jointly identified, with appropriate measures taken in contracts, governance and training, in order to ensure that they are properly addressed.

- Most of the losses have resulted from a significant lack of understanding of the key issues and effective leadership, from executive boards, through business units, down to the level of individual users. This indicates an urgent need for a national approach to education and training, in order to achieve the essential change in corporate and personal behaviour and processes. Despite the current pressures on budgets, adequate funds must be made available for investment in educating the leadership and providing training in re-invigorated processes.

People:

- This undertaking represents a major culture change. Success in building a society and an economy in which data and information are key assets rests not only on a sound understanding of the potential opportunities and risks, but also on the behaviour of people and organisations. These will need to adapt, acknowledging the distinct differences in approach to information and the use of web-related technologies across the generations. There may well be a case for developing a generally accepted 'Information Highway Code' that can shape legislation, regulation, the behaviour of the institutions of state, executive boards, programme and project management teams and users. Underpinning all of this should be an ethical approach to the use, by government and private sectors, of personal and business data in a manner that is appropriate to an innovative 21st Century democracy.

Technology:

- The scale of investment in technology has resulted in a wide range of 'Privacy Enhancing Technologies' becoming available to users. These benefit from R&D undertaken by government and private sectors. There is no shortage of technologies; but their capabilities and limitations must be understood and they must be used and safeguarded intelligently, and upgraded systematically.

Processes:

- This represents a national scale, transformational change activity, taking account of major business interdependencies, demanding effective collaboration across boundaries, and the active engagement of executive and

Foreword

non-executive board members, leading effectively and by example. The quality, commitment and vigour of the leadership will dictate the pace and effectiveness of the change.

- The approach must be joint: that is to say that it must engage both public and private sectors in a corporate approach. Many of the risks are shared. So must be the approach to their mitigation. An effective approach will embody formal assessment processes, which should employ recognised 'Good Practice', including the contractual guidance issued by the Office of Government Commerce (OGC) and the use of proven Assurance Maturity Models. These maturity models will provide a rigorous source of data for executive boards, as they review Information Risk, with regular reports provided through internal audit processes and set out in statements of internal control.

- A formal approach to the assessment of performance needs to be backed by a formal code of discipline, which can deliver fairness and justice within and across public and private sector boundaries. The Data Protection Act 1998, updated as the need arises, will continue to provide a helpful framework for tackling breaches. Its principles are commendably simple, but are still not sufficiently widely understood.

This comprehensive book is an invaluable reference providing a stimulus for the development of existing legislation and regulation that will, with the appropriate education and leadership, enable the UK to exploit the opportunities of the Information Age, using information and data, safely, within an appropriate ethical framework.

Lte. General Sir Edmund
Author of the Report into the Loss of MOD Personal Data
and Chairman of IAAC

Expert Views

The Regulator's View – Jonathan Bamford

The amount of personal information that is generated and held about us as part of everyday life has grown massively since data protection laws first started to be conceived back in the late 1970s. The risk to personal information was more limited back then. Collecting and retaining information was expensive, storage devices were cumbersome and limited whilst access to information was provided only to a small number of people. Today the challenge of protecting personal information is of a different magnitude and the need for proper safeguards has never been greater. Adopting appropriate security measures has always been one of the cornerstones of data protection regulation. Minimising personal information and affording it proper security be it at the human, organisational or technical level are essential aspects of the law.

An increasing variety of tools are available to organisations to help them achieve compliance. These include using privacy impact assessments, deploying privacy enhancing technologies and making sure that an organisation's culture and governance reflects a respect for personal information from top to bottom. This 'privacy by design' approach ensures that protection is built in from first principles not ignored or bolted on as an inadequate and expensive afterthought.

High profile security breaches have shown how vulnerable personal information can be and how protecting it cannot be left to chance. This is not just a matter for the enlightened who see adopting proper safeguards as good for their business and good for those with whom they do business. It is a requirement of the law and those who handle our personal information need to understand and comply with its provisions.

Jonathan Bamford
Assistant Information Commissioner

Expert Views

The Corporate and Academic View – Professor Howard A. Schmidt

The security of sensitive data and the systems within which they are processed and stored is a mission-critical issue for many organisations. As well as being an asset, data can be a liability if they are not accorded sufficient protections. In the United States and the United Kingdom there are literally thousands of government departments, public authorities, educational establishments, healthcare providers, profit-making companies and others that can attest to this fact; suffering a security breach or data loss can cause data controllers serious, negative consequences, ranging from brand damage right the way through to severe regulatory action. Breach notification legislation, which started in California and which is now being embedded in Europe and further afield provides one of the mechanisms through which serious incidents will come to public attention.

Of course, security breaches and data loss are not new phenomena; they are as old as the hills, predating the invention of the computer and the mass adoption of new technologies. Yet we now seem to be more concerned about these topics than ever before. Why is this?

There are a series of factors at play here. As Stewart Room points out, the number and volume of data processing operations are increasing exponentially year-on-year, which means that the number of security incidents will increase correspondingly. And the more incidents there are the more that will come to public attention, which drives other concerns and interests. Prominent with these are the political interest and the press interest, which feed off one another. Naturally, these factors drive greater public awareness, leading, ultimately to law reform and tougher regulatory responses. As such, the interest in data security is never going to go away. Yes, it may wax and wane, but it will always be mission-critical. Data controllers who forget or overlook these facts are likely to pay a heavy price eventually.

It is essential that data controllers get to grips with the process of law reform and advancements in types and forms of regulation. Things are moving very quickly in this area, as the law seeks to keep up with the threats to data and systems, which are constantly evolving and changing in nature. In two years the UK's legal regime for data security has moved from a relatively supine position to being one of the strongest in the world.

This book is to be warmly welcomed for providing the first clear account of data security law in the UK. The breadth of coverage is truly impressive, bringing in areas of the law which many people will not have considered before. I am sure that it will be of great benefit to every member of the community of professionals working in data security to whom I heartily commend it.

Professor Howard A. Schmidt
President & CEO, Information Security Forum Ltd
Former White House Cyber Security Advisor
Former CSO Microsoft and Former VP/CISO eBay Inc.

Expert Views

The Consultant's View – Malcolm Marshall

Never before has data privacy been so high on the business agenda. A series of high profile incidents and a changing legal and regulatory landscape mean that simple errors by members of staff or suppliers can have serious brand and regulatory implications. A momentary lapse of concentration while sending an email, or careless disposal of old equipment, can now have consequences that are far beyond the imagination of the person responsible.

Anyone who has worked in the security and privacy fields knows that data has been going missing since the days of punched cards and earlier. But the public's understanding of the issue and their expectations of the level of care with which personal data is handled have changed. We now live in a world of almost zero tolerance. Fifteen years ago it was not unusual for me to find myself trying to persuade a client that storing back-up tapes in the IT manager's garage was a long way short of ideal. I'm pleased to say that it's a long time since I have had such a conversation. However, as standards have increased and regulators have taken more aggressive positions many now find that practices that were acceptable a year ago could be perceived by the media and regulators as negligent.

Global research conducted by KPMG's Data Loss Barometer team shows the number of people reported to be affected by data breaches increasing substantially over the past three years (www.datalossbarometer.com). The media coverage has helped to increase the public's awareness of the sensitivity of personal data held by governments and businesses and their expectation of the care with which this information should be treated has grown.

Against the background of changing public, government and regulatory expectations Stewart Room's new book is an important and timely guide to navigating what he describes as the UK's regulatory bear market. The change in regulatory landscape has been most apparent in the financial services sector with headline grabbing fines against some trusted household names. But businesses operating outside financial services need to understand the changing landscape. Further increases in regulatory scope and power will mean that understanding the legislation, regulation and recent case studies will help all businesses to reduce their risk of brand damage or serious infringements of the law.

Having seen Stewart in action with clients I'm very pleased that he is now sharing his knowledge and insights in the subject with a wider audience. The book will be of great interest and relevance to privacy, security, risk and compliance professionals as well as lawyers and data controllers. This is a rapidly evolving area and to reflect this Stewart will be updating the online editions regularly – we can be certain that good practice and the legal and regulatory requirement will not stand still. I hope that the reader enjoys the benefit of reading it in order to prevent a serious breach occurring and not to defend themselves after the event.

Malcolm Marshall
Partner, KPMG LLP
Head of Information Protection Services

The Conservatives' Position

Baroness Neville-Jones

Since HMRC lost the records of 25 million people in November 2007, data security has become one of the most prominent issues for debate amongst academics, legal professionals, politicians, civil servants and businesses alike. Unfortunately the passionate nature of this debate has not yet been matched by significant improvements in either the approach of organisations to the collection of data or to their handling of it.

Across Whitehall there have been at least eight other high profile data loss incidents since the HMRC scandal. Most recently, from the Opposition Benches in the House of Lords, I had to respond to the loss of sensitive Joint Intelligence Committee assessments. The scale of the problem is unlikely to be better in the private sector – it is just that the reporting requirements are lesser. Yet, without having completely rectified the causes of these lapses, some still advocate the greater collection and concentration of data.

The main argument advanced in support of this – that better efficiency will be achieved by these new technologies and that the technologies themselves can diminish risk overall – is hardly complete. It ignores two key considerations. First, that the efficiencies brought about by technology do not of themselves alter the fundamental point that the individual is the rightful owner of personal information, and the state and private sector merely possessors with the obligation to behave as responsible custodians. Secondly – and something which is a characteristic of all instances of data loss – that human error is always a (if not the) key contributor to data insecurity. Technology has not and will not replace the human element in any organisation.

If it is accepted that the public and private sectors are merely possessors of information and should act as responsible custodians, it follows that the regulatory regime for data security in both sectors needs to be robust. At the moment there is an ongoing debate about the remit and powers of the Information Commissioner's Office. In this book, Stewart Room makes clear that there is a substantial regulatory gap between the regime that the Information Commissioner considers is required and the one that the government will allow. I have suggested that the office of the Information Commissioner should emerge as one of the most important offices of state of the

Conservatives' Position

twenty-first century. To do so, the regulations and laws the Office champions must also keep pace with and be up to the challenges posed by twenty-first century technologies and processes.

It would be foolish, however, simply to imagine that a strong and top-down regulatory regime will alone solve the problem of data insecurity. Human error is a function of working practice, of workplace culture and of mindset. People must be instilled with their obligations and duties as possessors of information. Given the speed with which computer and network systems permit data sharing and processing, data security must become embedded in workplace culture – as instinctive as looking after cash on the person. Should the Information Commissioner's Office and other Information Assurance bodies decide to partner with government and the private sector to fix the problem through practical assistance rather than by merely imposing standards and requirements from outside, there is scope for the regulatory regime actively to propagate best practice. Until that time this book, as the first and long overdue guide to data security law and best practice, will make a significant contribution to advancing an understanding of the subject and spreading the culture we need.

Baroness Neville-Jones DCMG
Shadow Security Minister and National Security Adviser to the Leader of the Opposition

Contents

Preface and Acknowledgements .... *v*
Foreword by Lte. General Sir Edmund Burton .... *xi*
Expert Views .... *xv*
    The Regulator's View – Jonathan Bamford .... *xv*
    The Corporate and Academic View – Professor Howard A. Schmidt .. *xvi*
    The Consultant's View – Malcolm Marshall .... *xvii*
    The Conservatives' Position – Baroness Neville-Jones .... *xix*
Table of Abbreviations .... *xxix*
Table of Statutes .... *xxxiii*
Table of Statutory Instruments .... *xxxvii*
Table of European Legislation .... *xxxix*
Table of Cases .... *xliii*

Chapter 1 Key themes and issues 1
Central themes 2
    The current cycle of development of data security law 2
    The creation of the 'regulatory bear market' for
        data security in the UK 3
    The trajectory of the law – more disputes and litigation 4
HMRC – what happened? 6
    Chronological summary 7
    The key findings – Poynter 11
    The key findings – IPCC 13
    Recommendations 13
    HMRC aftermath and conclusions – trust in government damaged 14
    The government's reforms 15
    Regulatory consequences – the HMRC enforcement notice 15
The regulatory dynamic within data security law 16
    The Information Commissioner's campaign for more powers 17
What price privacy? 20
    The section 55 offence 21
    Background to the campaign for custodial penalties 23

Contents

The Commissioner's findings and submissions 25
Reaction to the report 26
The Criminal Justice and Immigration Act 2008 –
    privacy v the press 26
'What price privacy?' – Was it all worth it? 30
Law reform – completing the post-HMRC agenda 31

Chapter 2 Confidentiality, privacy and technology 37
What are 'data'? 38
Confidentiality, privacy and technology 39
    Confidentiality 39
        Parameters of the duty of confidence 40
        Information that has the necessary quality of confidence 41
        How the duty of confidence arises 41
        Liability in negligence for failing to implement appropriate
            security controls to protect confidential information
            from misuse 48
        Remedies for misappropriation of confidential information 50
        Privacy and human rights 50
    Data protection 54
        How the security principle relates to the other principles 54
        The international aspects of data protection law 55
        The development of data protection law in Europe 56
        Key aims and objectives of data protection law 61
        Personal data and processing 62
        Special categories of processing (sensitive personal data) 66
        Protected personal information 66
        The main actors 67
        The regulatory mechanisms 70
        The general rules on lawfulness and legitimacy and the
            data protection principles 71
        The security principle – guarding against security breaches
            and data loss 72
        Ensuring the reliability of employees 77
        Ensuring the reliability of data processors 86
        The state of technological development 99
        Remedies for breach of the security obligation 104
    Communications privacy 110
        Regulators' obligation to ensure security 110
        The Communications Directives of 1997, 2002 and 2006 111
        The transposition of the 2002 Directive 115

Computer Misuse Act 1990 124
    The territorial scope of the Act 124
    Section 1 offence – unauthorised access to computer material 126
    Section 2 offence 132
    Section 3 offence 133
    Overcoming security controls 135
Electronic signatures 136
    Types of electronic signatures 137
    Advanced electronic signatures 137
    Legal effect of electronic signatures 139
    Accreditation and supervision 140
    Liability for reliance upon a qualified certificate 140
    The transposition of the Directive 141

Chapter 3 Companies, corporate governance and financial services 145
Companies 145
    Companies and transparency 147
    Companies and corporate governance 149
Financial services 153
    EU Directives 153
    Financial Services and Markets Act 2000 164
    FSA Handbook 166
    Payment Card Industry Data Security Standard (PCI DSS) 173

Chapter 4 Considerations for the public sector 177
The intensity of regulation of data security in the public sector 177
Transformational Government – more technology, more data
    processing and more risk 178
Security considerations within public sector records management 179
    Freedom of Information Act 2000 179
    Data Protection Act 1998 180
    Codes of practice for records management 180
Public authorities with responsibility for aspects of data security 181
    Central Sponsor for Information Assurance (CSIA) 181
    The National Technical Authority for
        Information Assurance (CESG) 182
    Centre for the Protection of National Infrastructure (CPNI) 185
    Office of Cyber Security (OCS) and Cyber Security
        Operations Centre (CSOC) 185
Major reports and policy statements 185
    Consequences for the private sector 187
    National Information Assurance Strategy, June 2007 187

Contents

Data Handling Review, December 2007 to June 2008 188
National Security Strategy, March 2008 194
Data Handling Review, June 2008 194
Coleman Report, June 2008 195
National Risk Register, November 2008 197
HMG Security Policy Framework, December 2008 199
National Security Strategy Updated, June 2009 211
Cyber Security Strategy, June 2009 212
Digital Britain, June 2009 213
Civil Service Management Code 214
Contracting with the private sector 215
Data security in the NHS 223
   Information systems and technology within the NHS 224
   Electronic records and data security 225
   Codes of Practice, Procedures and Reviews – but is it
     an information policy? 227
   The Information Commissioner's position 231
   The Google alternative 233
Data security in the police service 235
   ACPO/ACPOS Information Systems Community
     Security Policy 235
   Code of Practice on the Management of
     Police Information 235
Data protection at the Ministry of Defence 239
   Report into the Loss of MOD Personal Data, April 2008 239
   MOD Action Plan 249
   Burton and the Information Commissioner 249

Chapter 5 Official secrets, regulatory and professional secrecy 251
Official secrets 251
   Official Secrets Act 1911 251
   Official Secrets Act 1920 252
   Official Secrets Act 1989 253
Examples of other public sector laws for secrecy 261
   Commissioners for Revenue and Customs Act 2005 261
   Identity Cards Act 2006 262
Professional secrecy laws for regulators 263
   Data Protection Act 1998 263
   Financial services 264
   Communications Act 2003 266
Professional secrecy rules for professionals 267
Press Complaints Commission 270

Contents

Chapter 6 Regulation and enforcement 271
Law as a relay race – the cycle of development 271
Who are the regulators? 272
    Other regulators 272
    Self regulation and the contractual control mechanism 272
    Data subjects as regulators 273
    The State's obligation to regulate itself 273
    Shoring up regulation 273
General principles of regulation – regulating the regulators 273
    Reports on better, more balanced regulation 274
    Legislative and Regulatory Reform Act 2006 277
    Regulatory Enforcement and Sanctions Act 2008 281
The focus of the Information Commissioner and the
    Financial Services Authority 282
    Information Commissioner's focus 282
    FSA's focus 283
    Who should regulate the financial services sector? 284
The creation of the regulatory bear market 285
    The FSA's public statements 285
    The Information Commissioner's public statements 289
    Impact of regulators' statements and interventions –
        consequences for regulation 324
Regulation and enforcement under the Data Protection Act 1998 324
    The Information Commissioner's regulatory and
        enforcement strategy 324
    The scheme within the Data Protection Act 1998 325
    Enforcement notices 326
    Information notices 337
    Inspections 340
    Monetary penalties (fining data controllers) 352
    Criminal proceedings against those who threaten the security of
        personal data 357
    Regulation and enforcement by the data subject 357
    Responding to and challenging regulatory action 359
    Enforcement action taken by the Information Commissioner 362
Regulation and enforcement under the Financial Services and
    Markets Act 2000 367
    The FSA's Financial Crime Sector Team 368
    The scheme under the Financial Services and Markets Act 2000 368
    Investigations 369
    Disciplinary measures 371

Contents

Decision Procedure and Penalties Manual (DEPP) 371
Enforcement action taken by the FSA 375
The trajectory of the law – carrots, sticks and more disputes 376

Chapter 7 Breach notification 377
Breach notification and the Data Protection Act 1998 378
    Fair processing (transparency) 379
    Registration and notification (transparency) 380
    Subject access (transparency) 381
    Information notices (transparency) 382
    Human rights issues 383
The Information Commissioner's position on breach notification 384
    The House of Lords report on 'Personal Internet
      Security', August 2007 384
    Written evidence to the House of Commons Home Affairs
      Committee inquiry into the Surveillance Society,
      November 2007 385
    The House of Commons report on 'Protection of
      Private Data', January 2008 386
    The Information Commissioner's guidance, March 2008 387
    The Thomas-Walport Data Sharing Review, July 2008 394
    RSA Conference Europe 396
    Data Handling Review – taking stock, taking action 399
The government's position on breach notification 400
    The House of Lords report on 'Personal Internet
      Security', August 2007 400
    The House of Commons report on 'Protection of
      Private Data', January 2008 403
    The Coleman Report on 'Protecting Government
      Information', June 2008 403
    The 'Data Handing Review', December 2007 to June 2008 404
    HMG Security Policy Framework 406
The EU's position on breach notification 406
    European Commission's proposal, November 2007 407
    European Parliament debate and amendments, September 2008 410
    European Commission's amended proposal, November 2008 413
    Article 29 Working Party opinion, February 2009 415
    Council's Common Position, February 2009 417
    Commission Communication, February 2009 420
    European Parliament debate and vote, May 2009 420
    Composite view of the EU proposals for breach notification 422
    The Privacy Laws and Business survey of European regulators 425

Contents

The Financial Services Authority's position on breach notification 426
Breach notification in the United States 427
   Breach notification rules at State level 428
   FTC initiatives for breach notification 430
   Other initiatives and Federal rules 433
   Breach notification in California 434
Breach notification under the ISO 27000 series 437

Chapter 8 Privacy Enhancing Technologies (PETs) 439
Data protection law – reacting to technological threats 439
Control mechanisms within data protection law 441
   The geographical control mechanism 442
   The contractual control mechanism 442
   Refocusing on the technological control mechanism 443
Examples of PETs 444
   Encryption 444
Definitions of PETs and scope of the initiative 447
   PETs for compliance with the data protection principles generally 447
   'White Paper for Decision-Makers' 451
   EU position on PETs 453
   Further clarification of the risks to personal data and the core
      philosophies of data protection 453
   The Commission's definition of PETs 454
   The Commission's objectives 455
   The economic benefits of PETs – promoting the EU IT industry 458
   Follow-up 458
   Legal effect 458
Functionality and accreditation 459
'Privacy by Design' 460

Appendix A FSA and ICO enforcement action 463

**Appendix B Transposition of Articles 16 and 17 of the
Data Protection Directive** 507

Appendix C Precedents 555
Example checklist for handling a data security
   breach (non-exhaustive) 555
Example incident response checklist for handling loss of
   laptop computer (short form, non-exhaustive) 560
Example breach notification letter to Information Commissioner 562
Example breach notification letter to data subject 563
Example data protection clauses for employment contract 564

Contents

Example information and communications systems
   security policy (short form, non-exhaustive) 565
Example of seventh data protection principle clauses for
   data processor contract (short form, non-exhaustive) 570
Example of pre-contractual due diligence for
   engagement of data processor (short form, non-exhaustive) 573

Appendix D Core resources 577
Data Protection Act 1998 (as amended) 577
Regulation of Investigatory Powers Act 2000, Part I, Chapter I 707
Computer Misuse Act 1990 741
Official Secrets Act 1989 759
Communication from the Commission to the European Parliament
   and the Council on Promoting Data Protection by
   Privacy Enhancing Technologies (PETs) –
   Brussels, 2.5.2007, COM(2007) 228 final 777
HMG Security Policy Framework, Version 2.0, May 2009 787
Data Handling Procedures in Government:
   Final Report, June 2008 845
Cross Government Actions: Mandatory Minimum Measures 885
FSA report 'Data Security in Financial Services: Firms'
   controls to prevent data loss by their employees
   and third-party suppliers', April 2008 893
ICO 'Guidance on data security breach management', March 2008 995
ICO 'Notification of Data Security Breaches to the
   Information Commissioner's Office', March 2008 1001
ICO 'Data Protection Guidance Note: privacy
   enhancing technologies (PETs)', V2.0, March 2007 1005

Index 1009

Table of Abbreviations

ACPO/ ACPOS	=	Association of Chief Police Officers/Association of Chief Police Officers in Scotland
AFPAA	=	Armed Forces Personnel Administration Agency
APEC	=	Asia-Pacific Economic Operation
ARTD	=	Army Recruiting and Training Division
ATRA	=	Army Training and Recruitment Agency
B&C	=	Benefits and Credits Business Unit of HMRC
BCS	=	British Computer Society
BPSS	=	Baseline Personnel Security Standard
BS	=	British Standard
CA 2006	=	Companies Act 2006
CAN SPAM	=	Controlling the Assault of Non Solicited Pornography and Marketing Act 2003
CAPS	=	CESG Assisted Products Services
CBI	=	Confederation of British Industry
CCTM	=	Claims Tested Mark
CERT	=	Computer Emergency Response Team
CESG	=	Communications-Electronics Security Group, The National Technical Authority for Information Assurance
CFA	=	Capita Financial Administrators Ltd
CIFAS	=	The UK's Fraud Prevention Service
CIO	=	Chief Information Officer
CJIA 2008	=	Criminal Justice and Immigration Act 2008
CLAS	=	CESG Listed Adviser Scheme
CNI	=	Critical National Infrastructure
COBIT	=	Control Objectives for Information and related Technology
ComSO	=	Communications Security Officer
COPPA	=	Children's Online Privacy Protection Act 1998
COTS	=	Commercial-Off-The-Shelf

Table of abbreviations

CPNI	=	Centre for the Protection of National Infrastructure
CRCA 2005	=	Commissioners for Revenue and Customs Act 2005
CRD	=	Capital Requirements Directive
CSIA	=	Central Sponsor for Information Assurance, now known as Information Security & Assurance
CSOC	=	Cyber Security Operations Centre
CSP	=	Community Security Policy
CSSR	=	Councils with Social Services Responsibilities
CTAS	=	CESG Tailored Assurance Service
DCA	=	Department of Constitutional Affairs
DCI	=	Defence Council Instruction
DCR	=	Detailed Care Record
DEPP	=	Decision Procedure and Penalties Manual
DHR	=	Data Handling Review
DPA 1998	=	Data Protection Act 1998
DPP	=	Director of Public Prosecutions
DSO	=	Departmental Security Officer
DSSO	=	Defence Security Standards Organisation
DSU	=	Departmental Security Unit
DTR	=	Disclosure Rules and Transparency Rules, FSA Handbook
DVA	=	Defence Vetting Agency
DVLA	=	Department of Vehicle Licensing Agency
ECHR	=	European Court of Human Rights
EDPS	=	European Data Protection Supervisor
EDS	=	Electronic Data Systems
EEA	=	European Economic Area
EECMA	=	European Electronic Communications Market Authority
EESC	=	European Economic and Social Committee
EG	=	Enforcement Guide
EHR	=	Electronic Health Records
ENISA	=	European Network and Information Security Agency
FACTA	=	Fair and Accurate Credit Transactions Act 2003
FCID	=	Financial Crime & Intelligence Division
FCO	=	Foreign and Commonwealth Office
FOI	=	Freedom of Information
FRC	=	Financial Reporting Council
FSA	=	Financial Services Authority
FSMA 2000	=	Financial Services and Markets Act 2000

Table of abbreviations

FTC	=	Federal Trade Commission
GCHQ	=	Government Communications Headquarters
GLB	=	Gramm-Leach-Bliley Act
GovCERTUK	=	CESG Computer Emergency Response Team
GPMS	=	Government Protective Marking Scheme
GSOL	=	Get Safe Online
HHS	=	Health and Human Services
HIPPA	=	Health Insurance Portability and Accountability Act 1996
HMRC	=	Her Majesty's Revenue and Customs
IA	=	Information Assurance
IAAC	=	Information Assurance Advisory Council
IAG	=	Information Age Government
ICO	=	Information Commissioner's Office
ICT	=	Information and Communication Technologies
IMS	=	Information Management Solutions
IPCC	=	Independent Police Complaints Commission
IPS	=	Identity and Passport Service
ISACA	=	Information Systems Audit and Controls Association
IS&A	=	Information Security & Assurance, the new name for CSIA
ISF	=	Information Security Forum
ISM Code	=	Information Security Management: NHS Code of Practice
ISMS	=	Information Security Management System
ISP	=	Internet Service Provider
ISSA	=	Information Systems Security Association
ISSP	=	Institute of Information Security Professionals
ITSO	=	Information Technology Security Officer
KTN	=	Cyber Security Knowledge Transfer Network
LAND	=	UK Land forces (military)
MDU	=	Medical Defence Union
MOD	=	Ministry of Defence
MOPI	=	Management of Police Information
NAO	=	National Audit Office
NCRS	=	NHS Care Records Service
NHS CRS	=	NHS Care Records Service
NPIA	=	National Policing Improvement Agency
NRA	=	National Regulatory Authority
OA	=	Office Automation
OCS	=	Office of Cyber Security

Table of abbreviations

OFCOM	=	Office of Communications
OFT	=	Office of Fair Trading
OGC	=	Office of Government Commerce
OSA	=	Official Secrets Acts
PA-DSS	=	Payment Application Data Security Standard
PCI DSS	=	Payment Card Industry Data Security Standard
PCI PED	=	PIN Entry Device Security Requirements
PECR	=	Privacy and Electronic (EC) Directive Regulations 2003
PET	=	Privacy Enhancing Technology
PFI	=	Private Finance Initiative
PHR	=	Personal Health Record
PIAB	=	Police Information Assurance Board
PICOS	=	Privacy and Identity Management for Community Services
PJHQ	=	Permanent Joint Headquarters
PNC	=	Police National Computer
PPP	=	Public Private Partnership
PRIMELIFE	=	Privacy and identity management in Europe for life
PRIN	=	Principles for Business, FSA Handbook
RIPA 2000	=	Regulation of Investigatory Powers Act 2000
RAF	=	Royal Air Force
RMADS	=	Risk Management and Accreditation Documentation Set
RN	=	Royal Navy
RTD	=	Research, Technological Development
SCR	=	Summary Care Record
SEPA	=	Single European Payment Area
SIRO	=	Senior Information Risk Owner
SIS	=	Security Intelligence Service
SO	=	Official Committee on Security
SPOC	=	Single Points of Contact
SPVA	=	Service Personnel and Veterans Agency
SYSC	=	Senior Management, Arrangements, Systems and Controls, FSA Handbook
TAFMIS	=	Training Administration and Financial Management Information System
TLB	=	Top Level Budget
UN	=	United Nations
VCDS	=	Vice Chief of Defence Staff
WAPI	=	World Association of Private Investigators

Table of Statutes

Paragraph references printed in **bold** type indicate where the Statute is set out in part or in full.

	PARA
Access to Personal Files Act 1987	
s 26	2.15
Commissioners for Revenue and Customs Act 2005	
s 18	**5.19**, 5.20
19	**5.19**
Communications Act 2003	
s 393	**5.28**
Companies Act 2006	
Pt 10 Ch 2 (ss 170–181)	3.1
s 172(1)	3.1
(2)	3.1
173	3.1
174	**3.1**
178	3.1
386	**3.2**
387	**3.2**
1138	**3.2**
Computer Misuse Act 1990	2.7, 2.124, 2.138, 5.4
s 1	**2.127**, 2.130, 2.134
(1)	2.131
(a)	2.128
(c)	2.133
2	2.131, 2.132, **2.134**
3	2.131, **2.135**, 2.137
(2)	2.136
4	**2.125**
5	**2.126**
9	2.125
17(2)	**2.129**, 2.130, 2.132
(3), (4)	**2.129**, 2.130
(5)	**2.131**, 2.132
(6)	**2.137**
(8)	**2.136**
(10)	2.135
Criminal Justice Act 1967	
s 8	2.130

	PARA
Criminal Justice and Court Services Act 2000	
Sch 7	
Pt II	
para 98	2.134
Criminal Justice and Immigration Act 2008	1.45, 1.46, 6.16, 6.19, 6.38, 6.53, 6.67, 6.90, 6.159, 7.16, 7.43
s 77	1.24, **1.40**, 6.100
144	1.24, 6.151
Criminal Justice and Public Order Act 1994	1.35
Data Protection Act 1984	1.35
Data Protection Act 1998	1.1, 1.5, 1.20, 1.24, 1.25, 1.31, 1.36, 1.43, 1.45, 2.1, 2.2, 2.11, 2.15, 2.16, 2.17, 2.20, 2.30, 2.32, 2.36, 2.45, 2.76, 2.84, 3.1, 3.22, 3.27, 4.5, 4.19, 4.21, 4.22, 4.23, 4.24, 4,45, 4.52, 4.53, 4.68, 4.77, 4.94, 4.95, 6.4, 6.35, 6.39, 6.46, 6.53, 6.54, 6.62, 6.66, 6.84, 6.86, 6.94, 6.97, 6.105, 6.121, 6.166, 6.171, 6.181, 7.6, 7.8, 7.16, 7.18, 7.20, 7.37, 7.42, 7.43, 7.90, 7.109, 8.3, 8.8, 8.10, 8.14
s 1	2.83, 2.95
(1)	2.26, 2.27, 2.28, 2.29, 2.33, 2.34
(e)	2.25
(2)	**2.29**
2	2.31, 7.32
3	1.33, 2.92, 6.122

Table of Statutes

	PARA
Data Protection Act 1998—*contd*	
s 4	2.46, 6.59
(1)	6.67
(4)	6.48, 6.67
Pt II (ss 7–15)	7.3
s 7	2.62, 6.164, 8.11
(1)(b)	7.9
(6)(a)	2.3
10	2.44, 6.99, 6.162, 6.164
11	2.44, 6.99
13	**2.91**, 2.92, 2.93, 2.98, 4.18, **6.109**, 6.110, 6.163, 6.164, 7.25, 7.27
(1)	2.97
(2)(a)	2.94, 2.97
Pt III (ss 16–26)	2.83, 7.3
s 16(1)	7.7
17	7.7
18(2)	7.7
20	7.7
21	7.7
29	7.3
36	2.23
Pt V (ss 40–50)	7.3
s 40	1.9, 1.27, 1.28, 6.64, 6.72, 6.99, 6.102, 6.104, 6.106, 6.107, 6.146, 6.168, 7.34
(1)	**6.103**
(2)	**6.103**, 6.109, 6.110, 6.111, 7.25
(6)	**6.113**
(7)	6.70, **6.114**
(8)	6.70, **6.113**
41(1)	6.115
(2)	6.115, 6.116
41A	**6.138**
(2)(c)	6.140, 6.141, 6.142
(5)	6.144, 6.150
(9)	6.141
(10), (11)	6.142
41B	6.144
41C	6.147
42	6.89, 6.99, 6.123, 6.161, 6.164, 7.12
43	6.73, 6.92, 6.99, 6.101, 6.122, 7.12
(1)	6.123, 6.124, 6.125, **7.11**
(4)	6.126
(6)	6.124
44	6.99, 6.101, 6.122
47	1.29, 6.19, 6.93, **6.119**, 6.168, 6.169, 6.174, 6.176, 7.12
(1), (2)	6.128
48	6.70, 6.116, 6.144
(3)	6.70, 6.124
49	6.117
(1), (2)	6.116
50	6.68, 6.89, 6.93, 6.130
51	2.37, 2.59, 6.1, **6.21**, 7.13
(2)	6.63

	PARA
Data Protection Act 1998—*contd*	
s 51 (7)	6.92
52(2)	1.32, 6.32
54A	6.49
(1)	6.68
(4)	6.68
55	1.9, 1.26, 1.32, 1.35, 1.38, 1.40, 1.42, 1.44, 2.4, 2.7, 6.67, 6.99, 6.100, 6.159, 6.174
(1)	1.33, 6.31
(2)(a)(i), (ii)	1.33
(b), (c)	1.33, 1.34
(d)	1.33
(3)	6.31
(4)	1.34, 6.31
(5)–(8)	1.34
55A	6.100, 6.151, **6.152**, **6.153**, 7.44
(3A)	**6.146**, 6.158
55B	6.151, **6.154**
55C	6.151, **6.155**, **6.183**
55D	6.151, **6.156**
55E	6.151, **6.157**
56(1)	**2.62**
(5), (6)	**2.62**
59	2.6, **5.22**
61	1.29, 6.119, **6.120**, 6.170, 6.182
68	2.27
Sch 1	2.79
Pt I	**2.46**
Pt II	
para 2(2)	7.5
(3)	7.4
(d)	8.5
9	**2.47**, 2.66
10	**2.47**, 2.66
11	**2.47**, 2.66, 2.80
(a), (b)	2.68
12	**2.47**, 2.66
(a)(i), (ii)	2.67
(b)	2.67
Sch 2	7.5
Sch 3	7.5
Sch 9	6.68, 6.92, 6.93, 6.99, 6.101, 6.124, 6.139, 6.143, 6.145, 6.149, 6.174, 6.182
para 1(1)	6.130
(3)	6.134
2	6.131, 6.132
4, 5	6.134
6, 7	6.135
8, 9	6.134
12	6.136
Electronic Communications Act 2000	
s 7, 8	**2.148**
Enterprise Act 2002	7.34
Pt 8 (ss 210–236)	6.70

Table of Statutes

	PARA
Enterprise Act 2002—*contd*	
s 237	2.6
Financial Services and Markets Act 2000	3.28, 6.67
s 1	3.26, 6.22
2	**3.26, 6.22**, 6.23
(2)(d)	6.177, 6.178
6	**3.27**
33	6.179
54	6.179
66	6.179
89A-G	3.3
89o	3.7
138	6.180
150	6.180
153	6.180
157	6.180
Pt XI (ss 165–177)	6.179, 6.181
s 165	**6.181**
166	6.69, 6.179, **6.182**
170–177	3.182
Pt XIV (ss 205–211)	6.183
s 380	6.179
382	6.179
Freedom of Information Act 2000	1.26, 4.94, 6.93
s 1	2.3
41	2.3
46	4.4
54	6.88
Health and Social Care Act 2001	
s 60	4.71
Human Rights Act 1998	1.31, 2.11, 2.59, 7.13, 7.43, 8.11
s 2, 3	2.14
6	2.14, 4.1
8(3)(b)	2.94
Identity Cards Act 2006	1.43
s 27	2.6, **5.20**
44	5.20
Intelligence Services Act 1994	
s 5	5.14
7	5.14
Interception of Communications Act 1985	2.108
Legislative and Regulatory Reform Act 2006	6.13, 6.104
s 1(3)	6.14
2(3)	6.14
21	6.14
(2)	6.63
22	6.14, 6.63

	PARA
Legislative and Regulatory Reform Act 2006—*contd*	
s 22 (2), (3)	6.16
National Audit Act 1983	
s 8(1), (2)	**1.11**
Occupiers' Liability Act 1957	2.73
s 2(4)(b)	2.71, 2.81
Official Secrets Act 1911	4.61, 5.2
s 1	**5.3**
2	5.5, 5.6
Official Secrets Act 1920	4.61, 5.2, 5.6
s 1	5.4
Official Secrets Act 1989	4.61, 5.2, 5.6, 7.3
s 1	5.15, 5.16
(1)	5.7, 5.9, 5.10, 5.14
(2)	5.7
(3)	5.9
(6)–(8)	5.7
2	5.15, 5.16
(4)	5.11
3	5.15, 5.16
(1), (2)	5.12
4	5.9, 5.10, 5.13, 5.14, 5.16
5(3)	5.16
6(1), (2)	5.15
(5)	5.15
7	5.7
(3)(a)	5.10
8	**5.17**
13(1)	5.8, 5.9
Patents Act 1977	
s 2	**2.85**
Police Act 1996	
s 53	4.84
53A	4.83, 4.84
Police Act 1997	
s 39	4.82
39A	4.82
Police Act 2007	
s 28	4.82
28A	4.82
73	4.82
Private Security Industry Act 2001	6.3
Regulation of Investigatory Powers Act 2000	2.58, 2.59, 2.61, 2.107
Pt I Ch 1 (ss 1–20)	2.108
s 1	**2.108**
(2)	2.117
(3)	**2.118**, 2.119
(6)	**2.117**
2(1)	**2.109, 2.110**
(2)	**2.112**, 2.113
(5)	**2.112**
(7)	**2.114**, 2.115
(8)	**2.115**

XXXV

Table of Statutes

	PARA
Regulation of Investigatory Powers Act 2000—*contd*	
s 2 (9)	**2.111**
3(1)–(5)	2.116
4	2.116
(2)	**2.56**
5	2.116, 5.14
12	**2.120**
Pt II (ss 26–48)	2.116
Pt III (ss 49–56)	2.8, 2.122
s 50(1), (2)	2.8
(3)	2.8
(c)	2.9
(5)–(9)	2.8
51(4), (5)	2.9
53(1)	2.9

	PARA
Regulation of Investigatory Powers Act 2000—*contd*	
s 53 (2)–(4)	2.9
(5)	2.9
56(1)	2.8
81(1)	**2.111**, 2.112
Regulatory Enforcement and Sanctions Act 2008	6.13
s 39(2)	6.19
46	6.19
50	6.19
Rehabilitation of Offenders Act 1974	2.62
Security Service Act 1989	
s 3	5.14

OTHER JURISDICTIONS
USA

	PARA
American Recovery and Reinvestment Act 2009	7.103
Children's Online Privacy Protection Act 1998	7.97
Controlling the Assault of Non-Solicited Pornography and Marketing Act 2003	7.97
E-Government Act 2002	6.44
Fair and Accurate Credit Transaction Act of 2003	2.18
s 111	7.102
114	7.99

	PARA
Fair Credit Reporting Act 1970	7.97
Federal Reserve Act 1913	
s 19(b)	7.102
Financial Services Modernization Act of 1999	2.18, 7.97
s 30(a)	7.106
Health Insurance Portability and Accountability Act of 1996	2.18, 7.97
Sarbanes-Oxley Act 2002	7.101
Telemarketing and Consumer Fraud and Abuse Prevention Act 2003	7.97

Table of Statutory Instruments

Paragraph references printed in **bold** type indicate where the Statutory Instrument is set out in part or in full.

	PARA
Communications Act 2003 (Maximum Penalty and Disclosure of Information) Order 2005, SI 2005/3469	5.28
Data Protection (Notification and Notification Fees) Regulations 2000, SI 2000/188	
reg 12	7.7
Electronic Signatures Regulations 2002, SI 2002/318	2.139
reg 3, 4	2.148
Information Tribunal (Enforcement Appeals) Rules 2005, SI 2005/14	6.114, 6.116
Legislative and Regulatory Reform Code of Practice (Appointed Day) Order 2007, SI 2007/3548	6.15
Privacy and Electronic Communications (EC Directive) Regulations 2003, SI 2003/2426	2.107
reg 5, 6	**2.123**
Regulation of Investigatory Powers (Maintenance of Interception Capability) Order 2002, SI 2002/1931	2.120
Schedule Pt II	**2.121**
Telecommunications (Lawful Business Practice) (Interception of Communications) Regulations 2000, SI 2000/2699	2.1, 2.56, 2.107, 2.119
reg 2	2.57

	PARA
Telecommunications (Lawful Business Practice) (Interception of Communications) Regulations 2000, SI 2000/2699—*contd*	
reg 3	**2.57**, 2.58

Table of European Legislation

Paragraph references printed in **bold** type indicate where the Legislation is set out in part or in full.

PARA

PRIMARY LEGISLATION
CONVENTIONS

Convention for the Protection of Individuals with regard to Automatic Processing of Personal Data (Strasbourg, 28 January 1981) 2.18, 8.1
    art 7 .... **2.19**
Convention on Cybercrime (Budapest, 23 November 2001)
    art 2 .... **2.138**
European Convention for the Protection of Human Rights and Fundamental Freedoms (Rome, 4 November 1950)
    art 8 ... **2.14**, 2.15, 2.20, 2.41, 2.54, 2.94, 2.95, 2.108, 4.1, 7.13, 8.1
    (2) 2.55, 2.99, 2.106
    10(2) 5.10

SECONDARY LEGISLATION
DECISIONS

Commission Decision 2001/497/EC 2.82
Commission Decision 2002/16/EC
    Recital (11), (12) **2.82**

PARA
Commission Decision 2004/915/EC 2.82

DIRECTIVES

Commission Directive 2003/124/EC 3.19
Commission Directive 2003/125/EC 3.19
Commission Directive 2004/72/EC 3.19
Commission Directive 2006/73/EC (the 'level 2' Directive) 3.16, 3.33, 5.26, 6.183
    art 5(2) **3.17**, 3.32
    (3) 3.32
    13(1) **3.17**
    (2)(a) **3.17**
    14 .... **3.17**
    16(1)(f) **3.17**
Council Directive 78/660/EEC (Fourth Company Law Directive) 3.6, 3.8

Table of European Legislation

	PARA
Council Directive 83/349/EEC (Seventh Company Law Directive)	3.6
European Parliament and Council Directive 95/46/EC (Data Protection Directive)	1.3, 1.4, 1.5, 1.6, 2.2, 2.15, 2.16, 2.19, 2.26, 2.34, 2.38, 2.40, 2.47, 2.85, 2.93, 2.96, 6.54, 7.87, 8.19, 8.20, 8.23, 8.27
Recital (2)	2.95
(7)	2.95
(10), (11)	2.95
(30)	8.5
(33)	8.5
(58)	8.5
(70)	8.5
art 1	**6.21**
2(a)	**2.22**, 2.33
(b)	**2.24**
(c)	**2.25**
(c)	8.5
3(1)	2.18
8(1)	2.31
16	2.17, **2.19**, 2.84, 2.101, 8.3
17	2.17, **2.19**, 2.101, 8.3
(1)	2.84
22	6.99
23	2.91, 2.92, 2.94, 6.99
24	6.99
25	2.21, 8.4
(6)	2.39
26	2.21, 8.4
28	2.37, 2.45, **6.21**, 6.68, 6.99
European Parliament and Council Directive 97/66/EC (Telecommunications Privacy Directive)	2.101, 2.107, 2.108
art 4	**2.19, 2.102**
5	**2.19, 2.102**
(1)	2.105, 2.106
(2)	2.106
14(1)	2.106
European Parliament and Council Directive 1999/93/EC (Electronic Signatures Directive)	
Recital (4)	2.139
(11)	2.139
(20)	2.139
art 2(1), (2)	2.140
(4)–(6)	2.141
(9)–(11)	2.141
(13)	2.146
3(2), (3)	2.146
5	**2.145**
(1), (2)	2.148
6	**2.147**
Annex I	2.141, **2.142**
Annex II	2.141, **2.143**
Annex III	2.141, **2.144**
European Parliament and Council Directive 2000/12/EC art 1.1(a)	3.25
European Parliament and Council Directive 2000/46/EC (Electronic Money Directive)	3.25
art 7	**3.25**
European Parliament and Council Directive 2002/21/EC (Framework Directive)	7.57
art 8.4(f)	2.100
European Parliament and Council Directive 2002/22/EC (Universal Service Directive)	7.58, 7.76, 7.84, 7.85
European Parliament and Council Directive 2002/58/EC (Electronic Communications Privacy Directive)	2.100, 7.1, 7.44, 7.64, 7.76, 7.84, 7.85, 7.88, 7.108, 8.19
art 1(1)	7.65
2	7.73, **7.78**
(b)	**2.105**
(d)	**2.105**
(h)	8.5
(i)	7.70
3	7.65, **7.79**
4	**2.19, 2.103**, 2.123, 7.57, **7.58**, 7.63, 7.65, 7.71
(1)	**7.68**
(2)	8.5
(3)	**7.66**, 7.68, **7.69**, 7.70, **7.80**
(4)	**7.67**, 7.68, 7.70, **7.80**
(5)	**7.80**
5	**2.19, 2.103**, 2.107, 2.123
(1)	2.105, 2.106, 2.112
(2)	2.106
(3)	2.105, 2.106
8	7.65
10, 11	7.65
15(1)	**2.106**
European Parliament and Council Directive 2003/6/EC (Market Abuse Directive)	
Recital (2)	3.19
(10)	3.19
art 1(1)	3.19
(2)	**3.20**
2, 3	**3.19**
5	3.20
European Parliament and Council Directive 2003/71/EC (Prospectus Directive)	3.5
art 1(1)	3.21
5(1)	3.21
European Parliament and Council Directive 2004/39/EC (the 'level 1' Directive) (Market in Financial Instruments Directive)	3.33, 6.183
art 13	3.17

Table of European Legislation

	PARA
European Parliament and Council Directive 2004/39/EC (the 'level 1' Directive) (Market in Financial Instruments Directive)—*contd*	
art 13 (2)	**3.16**
(4)	3.32
(5)	**3.16**, 3.32
25(5)	**3.18**
54	**5.26**
European Parliament and Council Directive 2004/109/EC (Transparency Obligations Directive)	3.6
art 6(1)	**3.4**
21(2)	**3.4**
25	**5.25**
European Parliament and Council Directive 2005/60/EC (Third EU Money Laundering Directive)	
art 2	3.22
8	3.22
20	3.22
28	3.22
30	3.22
European Parliament and Council Directive 2006/24/EC (Communications Data Retention Directive)	2.101
art 7	**2.19, 2.104**
European Parliament and Council Directive 2006/43/EC (Audit Directive)	3.6
art 23(1)	**5.29**
36(2), (3)	**5.27**
41	**3.8, 3.9**
European Parliament and Council Directive 2006/48/EC (Banking Consolidation Directive)	
art 4(22)	**3.14**
22	**3.14**
(1)	3.32
102–105	**3.14**
Annex V	3.32
para 2	**3.14**
12, 13	**3.14**
Annex X	
Pt 3	**3.15**
European Parliament and Council Directive 2006/49/EC (Capital Adequacy Directive)	**3.14**, 3.32
European Parliament and Council Directive 2007/64/EC (Payment Services Directive)	
Recital (32)	3.24
art 1(2)	**3.23**
3	**3.23**
22	**5.24**
55(2)	3.24

	PARA
European Parliament and Council Directive 2007/64/EC (Payment Services Directive)—*contd*	
art 56(2)	3.24
57(1)(a)	3.24
(2)	3.24
61(1)	3.24
Annex	**3.23**

REGULATIONS

Commission Regulation 2273/2003/EC	3.19
Commission Regulation 809/2004/EC Recital (31)	3.21
Commission Regulation 2006/2004/EC	7.58, 7.76, 7.84, 7.85
Commission Regulation 1287/2006/EC	**3.16**, 5.26, 6.183
art 12(1)(a)–(d)	**3.18**
European Parliament and Council Regulation 45/2001/EC	8.19, 8.23

RECOMMENDATIONS

Commission Recommendation 2007/657/EC arts 7–12	3.5

OTHER
COMMON POSITIONS

Statement of the Council's Reason: Common Position adopted by the Council on 16 February 2009 with a view to the adoption of a Directive of the European Parliament and of the Council amending Directive 2002/22/EC on universal service and users' rights relating to electronic communications networks, Directive 2002/58/EC concerning the processing of personal data and the protection of privacy in the electronic communications sectors and Regulation (EC) No 2006/2004 on consumer protection cooperation, 16497/1/0, page 5 (Amending Directive) 7.76, 7.83
Recital (47) 7.77
(51) 7.77

xli

Table of Cases

A

PARA

A v B (a company) [2002] EWCA Civ 337, [2003] QB 195, [2002] 2 All ER 545, [2002] 3 WLR 542, [2002] 2 FCR 158, [2002] 1 FLR 1021, 12 BHRC 466, [2002] IP & T 512, [2002] 17 LS Gaz R 36, [2002] NLJR 434, (2002) Times, 13 March, [2002] EMLR 371, [2002] All ER (D) 142 (Mar) 2.14
AMF International Ltd v Magnet Bowling Ltd [1968] 2 All ER 789, [1968] 1 WLR 1028, 66 LGR 706, 112 Sol Jo 522 .... 2.71, 2.81
Airey v Ireland (Application 6289/73) (1979) 2 EHRR 305, ECtHR 2.15
Alfa Laval Cheese Systems Ltd v Wincanton Engineering Ltd [1990] FSR 583 .... 2.7
Argyll (Duchess of) v Duke of Argyll [1967] Ch 302, [1965] 1 All ER 611, [1965] 2 WLR 790 .... 2.5
Ashburton (Lord) v Pape [1913] 2 Ch 469, 82 LJ Ch 527, [1911–13] All ER Rep 708, 57 Sol Jo 644, 109 LT 381, 29 TLR 623, CA 2.6
A-G v Barker [1990] 3 All ER 257, CA 2.4
A-G v Blake (Jonathan Cape Ltd third party) [2001] 1 AC 268, [2000] 4 All ER 385, [2000] 2 All ER (Comm) 487, [2000] 3 WLR 625, [2000] IP & T 1261, [2000] NLJR 1230, [2000] 32 LS Gaz R 37, 144 Sol Jo LB 242, [2001] 1 LRC 260, [2000] EMLR 949, [2000] All ER (D) 1074, HL 2.4, 2.5, 5.7
A-G v Observer Ltd, A-G v Times Newspapers Ltd [1990] 1 AC 109, [1988] 3 WLR 776, [1988] NLJR 296, [1990] LRC (Const) 938, sub nom A-G v Guardian Newspapers Ltd (No 2) [1988] 3 All ER 545, HL 2.5, 2.7
A-G's Reference (No 1 of 1991) [1993] QB 94, [1992] 3 All ER 897, [1992] 3 WLR 432, 157 JP 258, 136 Sol Jo LB 197, CA 2.128

B

B v A County Council [2006] EWCA Civ 1388, [2006] 3 FCR 568, [2007] 1 FLR 1189, [2007] Fam Law 292, 150 Sol Jo LB 1571, [2006] All ER (D) 270 (Nov) 2.11
Bloomstein v Railway Executive [1952] 2 All ER 418, 96 Sol Jo 496 .... 2.70
Bolam v Friern Hospital Management Committee [1957] 2 All ER 118, [1957] 1 WLR 582, 101 Sol Jo 357, 1 BMLR 1 .... 2.87
British Telecommunications plc v Rodrigues, EAT (854/92) (1995, unreported) 2.63

C

Campbell v Mirror Group Newspapers Ltd [2002] EWCA Civ 1373, [2003] QB 633, [2003] 1 All ER 224, [2003] 2 WLR 80, [2002] IP & T 944, (2002) Times, 16 October, [2003] EMLR 39, [2002] All ER (D) 177 (Oct); revsd [2004] UKHL 22, [2004] 2 AC 457, [2004] 2 All ER 995, [2004] 2 WLR 1232, [2004] IP & T 764, [2004] 21 LS Gaz R 36, [2004] NLJR 733, (2004) Times, 7 May, 148 Sol Jo LB 572, 16 BHRC 500, [2005] 1 LRC 397, [2004] All ER (D) 67 (May) 1.43, 2.14, 2.24, 2.93

Table of Cases

PARA

Caparo Industries plc v Dickman [1990] 2 AC 605, [1990] 1 All ER 568,
  [1990] 2 WLR 358, [1990] BCLC 273, [1990] BCC 164, 134 Sol Jo 494,
  [1990] 12 LS Gaz R 42, [1990] NLJR 248, [1991] LRC (Comm) 460, HL 2.11, 2.93
Coco v AN Clark (Engineers) Ltd [1968] FSR 415, [1969] RPC 41 .... 2.3, 2.7
Copland v UK (2007) 45 EHRR 37 .... 2.54
Corporate Officer of the House of Commons v Information Comr [2008] EWHC
  1084 (Admin), [2009] 3 All ER 403, [2008] NLJR 751, (2008) Times, 22 May,
  [2008] All ER (D) 217 (May) 2.4, 4.4
Creation Records Ltd v News Group Newspapers (1997) 141 Sol Jo LB 107,
  [1997] EMLR 444 .... 2.4, 2.6, 2.7

D

DPP v Bignell [1998] 1 Cr App Rep 1, 161 JP 541, [1998] Crim LR 53, ITCLR
  27, DC 2.131, 4.91
DPP v Lennon [2006] EWHC 1201 (Admin), 170 JP 532, 170 JPN 934, 150 Sol Jo
  LB 667, [2006] All ER (D) 147 (May) 2.136
Douglas v Hello! Ltd [2005] EWCA Civ 595, [2006] QB 125, [2005] 4 All ER 128,
  [2005] 3 WLR 881, [2005] 2 FCR 487, [2005] IP & T 1057,
  [2005] 28 LS Gaz R 30, [2005] NLJR 828, (2005) Times, 24 May,
  [2005] EMLR 609, [2005] All ER (D) 280 (May); revsd in part sub nom
  OBG Ltd v Allan; Douglas v Hello! Ltd (No 3); Mainstream Properties Ltd v
  Young [2007] UKHL 21, [2008] 1 AC 1, [2007] 4 All ER 545, [2008] 1 All ER
  (Comm) 1, [2007] 2 WLR 920, (2007) Times, 3 May, 151 Sol Jo LB 674,
  [2007] EMLR 325, [2008] 1 LRC 279, [2007] All ER (D) 44 (May) 2.5, 2.6
Dunford and Elliott Ltd v Johnson and Firth Brown Ltd [1977] 1 Lloyd's Rep 505,
  [1978] FSR 143, 121 Sol Jo 53, [1976] LS Gaz R 1060, CA 2.6
Durant v Financial Services Authority [2003] EWCA Civ 1746, [2004] FSR 573,
  [2004] IP & T 814, (2004) Times, 2 January, [2003] All ER (D) 124 (Dec) 2.23, 2.25,
    2.84, 6.1

E

Eckersley v Binnie (1987) 18 ConLR 1, CA 2.87
Ellis v DPP [2001] EWHC Admin 362, [2001] All ER (D) 190 (May) 2.129
English and American Insurance Co Ltd v Herbert Smith and Co [1988] FSR 232,
  [1987] NLJ Rep 148 .... 2.6, 2.7

F

Franchi v Franchi [1967] RPC 149 .... 2.4
Francome v Mirror Group Newspapers Ltd [1984] 2 All ER 408, [1984] 1 WLR
  892, 128 Sol Jo 484, CA 2.6, 2.7
Franklin v Giddins [1978] Qd R 72 .... 2.6
Fraser v Evans [1969] 1 QB 349, [1969] 1 All ER 8, [1968] 3 WLR 1172, 112 Sol Jo
  805, CA 2.5
Froom v Butcher [1976] QB 286, [1975] 3 All ER 520, [1975] 3 WLR 379,
  [1975] RTR 518, [1975] 2 Lloyd's Rep 478, 119 Sol Jo 613, CA 2.52

G

Gartside v Outram (1856) 26 LJ Ch 113, 3 Jur NS 39, 5 WR 35, 28 LTOS 120 .... 2.4
Glass v United Kingdom (Application 61827/00) [2004] 1 FCR 553, [2004] 1 FLR
  1019, [2004] Fam Law 410, 77 BMLR 120, (2004) Times, 11 March, [2004]
  All ER (D) 166 (Mar), ECtHR 2.15

	PARA
Green v Fibreglass Ltd [1958] 2 QB 245, [1958] 2 All ER 521, [1958] 3 WLR 71, 102 Sol Jo 472	2.70

H

HRH Prince of Wales v Associated Newspapers Ltd [2006] EWCA Civ 1776, [2008] Ch 57, [2007] 2 All ER 139, [2007] 3 WLR 222, [2008] IP & T 583, (2006) Times, 28 December, [2008] EMLR 121, [2006] All ER (D) 335 (Dec)	2.4
Halford v United Kingdom (Application 20605/92) (1997) 24 EHRR 523, [1997] IRLR 471, [1998] Crim LR 753, [1997] 94 LS Gaz R 24, 3 BHRC 31, ECtHR	2.54, 2.108
Haseldine v CA Daw & Son Ltd [1941] 2 KB 343, [1941] 3 All ER 156, 111 LJKB 45, 165 LT 185, 58 TLR 1, CA	2.69
Hedley Byrne & Co Ltd v Heller & Partners Ltd [1964] AC 465, [1963] 2 All ER 575, [1963] 3 WLR 101, [1963] 1 Lloyd's Rep 485, 107 Sol Jo 454, HL	2.93
Hellewell v Chief Constable of Derbyshire [1995] 4 All ER 473, [1995] 1 WLR 804, [1995] 07 LS Gaz R 35	2.7
Holmes, Re [2004] EWHC 2020 (Admin), [2005] 1 All ER 490, [2005] 1 WLR 1857, [2005] 1 Cr App Rep 229, (2004) Times, 28 October, [2004] All ER (D) 111 (Aug)	2.134

I

Ikarian Reefer, The. See National Justice Cia Naviera SA v Prudential Assurance Co Ltd, The Ikarian Reefer	
IRC v National Federation of Self Employed and Small Businesses [1982] AC 617, [1981] 2 All ER 93, [1981] 2 WLR 722, [1981] STC 260, 55 TC 133, 125 Sol Jo 325, HL	2.6

J

Johnson v Medical Defence Union [2007] EWCA Civ 262, [2007] 3 CMLR 181, 96 BMLR 99, (2007) Times, 10 April, [2007] All ER (D) 464 (Mar)	2.24, 2.30, 2.93, 6.110, 7.27

L

L v Finland (Application 20511/03) (2008) 48 EHRR 740, [2008] ECHR 20511/03, ECtHR	2.15
Leander v Sweden (Application 9248/81) (1987) 9 EHRR 433, ECtHR	2.15
Lindqvist (Criminal proceedings against): C-101/01 [2004] QB 1014, [2003] ECR I-12971, [2004] All ER (EC) 561, [2004] 2 WLR 1385, [2004] IP & T 469, (2003) Times, 13 November, [2003] All ER (D) 77 (Nov), ECJ	2.24, 2.95
Lion Laboratories Ltd v Evans [1985] QB 526, [1984] 2 All ER 417, [1984] 3 WLR 539, 128 Sol Jo 533, CA	2.4
Lips v Older [2004] EWHC 1686 (QB), [2004] All ER (D) 168 (Jun)	2.51
LSG-Gesellschaft zur Wahrnehmung von Leistungsschutzrechten GmbH v Tele2 Telecommunication GmbH, C-557/07, 19 February 2009, ECJ	2.99

M

McKennitt v Ash [2006] EWCA Civ 1714, [2007] 3 WLR 194, [2008] IP & T 703, (2006) Times, 20 December, [2007] EMLR 113, [2006] All ER (D) 200 (Dec)	2.14

Table of Cases

	PARA
McKinnon v Government of the USA [2008] UKHL 59, [2008] 4 All ER 1012, (2008) Times, 6 August, 152 Sol Jo (no 31) 29, [2008] All ER (D) 394 (Jul)	2.125, 2.126
Mars UK Ltd v Teknowledge Ltd [2000] FSR 138, [1999] IP & T 26, (1999) Times, 23 June, (1999) Independent, 1 July, [1999] All ER (D) 600	2.7
Morris v West Hartlepool Steam Navigation Co Ltd [1956] AC 552, [1956] 1 All ER 385, [1956] 1 WLR 177, [1956] 1 Lloyd's Rep 76, 100 Sol Jo 129, HL	2.87
Morton v William Dixon Ltd 1909 SC 807, Ct of Sess	2.87
Mosley v News Group Newspapers Ltd [2008] EWHC 1777 (QB), [2008] NLJR 1112, [2008] All ER (D) 322 (Jul)	2.5, 2.95
Murray v Express Newspapers plc [2008] EWCA Civ 446, [2008] 3 WLR 1360, [2008] NLJR 706, (2008) Times, 12 May, [2008] EMLR 399, [2008] All ER (D) 70 (May), sub nom Murray v Big Pictures (UK) Ltd [2008] 3 FCR 661, [2008] 2 FLR 599, [2008] Fam Law 732	2.14

N

National Justice Cia Naviera SA v Prudential Assurance Co Ltd, sub nom The Ikarian Reefer [1993] 2 Lloyd's Rep 68, [1993] FSR 563, [1993] 2 EGLR 183, [1993] 37 EG 158n; revsd [1995] 1 Lloyd's Rep 455, CA 2.72
Niemietz v Germany (Application 13710/88) (1992) 16 EHRR 97, ECtHR 2.54

O

OBG Ltd v Allan; Douglas v Hello! Ltd (No 3); Mainstream Properties Ltd v Young. See Douglas v Hello! Ltd
Odievre v France (Application 42326/98) [2003] 1 FCR 621, 14 BHRC 526, ECtHR 2.15

P

Peck v United Kingdom (2003) 36 EHRR 41, [2003] EMLR 15 .... 2.14
Pickard v Smith (1861) 10 CBNS 470, 142 ER 535, [1861–73] All ER Rep 204, 4 LT 470 .... 2.70
Practice Direction (Citation of Authorities) [2001] 1 WLR 2001, [2001] 1 Lloyd's Rep 725 .... 2.12

Q

Quinton v Peirce [2009] EWHC 912 (QB), [2009] All ER (D) 229 (Apr) 2.93

R

R (on the application of Stone) v South East Coast Strategic Health Authority [2006] EWHC 1668 (Admin), [2006] All ER (D) 144 (Jul) 2.4
R v Bow Street Metropolitan Stipendiary Magistrate, ex p United States Government [2000] 2 AC 216, [1999] 4 All ER 1, [1999] 3 WLR 620, [2000] 1 Cr App Rep 61, [1999] Crim LR 970, [1999] IP & T 77, [1999] NLJR 1406, HL 2.128
R v E [2004] EWCA Crim 1243, [2004] 1 WLR 3279, [2004] 2 Cr App Rep 484, [2004] 21 LS Gaz R 35, 148 Sol Jo LB 537, [2004] All ER (D) 253 (Apr), sub nom R v E (Admissibility: Covert listening device) (2004) Times, 27 May 2.113
R v G [2003] UKHL 50, [2004] 1 AC 1034, [2003] 4 All ER 765, [2003] 3 WLR 1060, [2004] 1 Cr App Rep 237, 167 JP 621, [2004] Crim LR 369, [2003] 43 LS Gaz R 31, (2003) Times, 17 October, [2004] 2 LRC 546, [2003] All ER (D) 257 (Oct) 1.34

Table of Cases

PARA

R v Governor of Brixton Prison, ex p Levin [1997] AC 741, [1997] 3 All ER 289, [1997] 3 WLR 117, [1998] 1 Cr App Rep 22, [1997] Crim LR 891, [1997] 30 LS Gaz R 28, [1997] NLJR 990, 141 Sol Jo LB 148, HL 2.126
R v Hardy [2002] EWCA Crim 3012, [2003] 1 Cr App Rep 494, [2003] Crim LR 394, (2002) Times, 18 November, [2002] All ER (D) 464 (Oct) 2.113
R v North and East Devon Health Authority, ex p Coughlan (Secretary of State for Health and another intervening) [2001] QB 213, [2000] 3 All ER 850, [2000] 2 WLR 622, 97 LGR 703, [1999] Lloyd's Rep Med 306, 51 BMLR 1, [1999] 31 LS Gaz R 39, 2 CCL Rep 285, 143 Sol Jo LB 213, [1999] All ER (D) 801, CA 4.18
R v Ponting [1985] Crim LR 318 .... 5.6
R v Rooney [2006] EWCA Crim 1841, [2006] All ER (D) 158 (Jul) 1.33, 4.91
R v Shayler [2001] EWCA Crim 1977, [2001] 1 WLR 2206, [2001] 40 LS Gaz R 40, 145 Sol Jo LB 235, [2001] All ER (D) 99 (Sep); affd [2002] UKHL 11, [2003] 1 AC 247, [2002] 2 All ER 477, [2002] 2 WLR 754, [2002] 17 LS Gaz R 34, (2002) Times, 22 March, [2002] All ER (D) 320 (Mar) 5.7, 5.10
R v Stanford [2006] EWCA Crim 258, [2006] 1 WLR 1554, [2006] 2 Cr App Rep 91, [2006] 09 LS Gaz R 30, (2006) Times, 7 February, 150 Sol Jo LB 162, [2006] All ER (D) 14 (Feb) 2.108
Robb v Green [1895] 2 QB 315, 59 JP 695, 64 LJQB 593, 14 R 580, 44 WR 25, [1895–9] All ER Rep 1053, 39 Sol Jo 653, 73 LT 15, 11 TLR 517, CA 2.6
Rotaru v Romania (Application 28341/95) (2000) 8 BHRC 449, ECtHR 2.15

S

Salomon v Customs and Excise Comrs [1967] 2 QB 116, [1966] 3 All ER 871, [1966] 3 WLR 1223, [1966] 2 Lloyd's Rep 460, 110 Sol Jo 833, CA 2.84
Salsbury v Woodland [1970] 1 QB 324, [1969] 3 All ER 863, [1969] 3 WLR 29, 113 Sol Jo 327, CA 2.69
Saltman Engineering Co Ltd v Campbell Engineering Co Ltd [1963] 3 All ER 413n, 65 RPC 203, CA 2.5
Schering Chemicals Ltd v Falkman Ltd [1982] QB 1, [1981] 2 All ER 321, [1981] 2 WLR 848, 125 Sol Jo 342, CA 2.4
Seager v Copydex Ltd [1967] 2 All ER 415, [1967] 1 WLR 923, [1967] RPC 349, 111 Sol Jo 335, CA 2.5, 2.12
Shelley Films Ltd v Rex Features Ltd [1994] EMLR 134 .... 2.6, 2.7
Smith v Lloyds TSB Bank Plc [2005] EWHC 246 (Ch), [2005] IP & T 646, [2005] All ER (D) 358 (Feb) 2.24
Swinney v Chief Constable of Northumbria Police [1997] QB 464, [1996] 3 All ER 449, [1996] 3 WLR 968, [1996] NLJR 878, CA 2.12

T

Terrapin Ltd v Builders' Supply Co (Hayes) Ltd [1960] RPC 128, CA 2.7

V

Vitof Ltd v Altoft [2006] EWHC 1678 (Ch), [2006] All ER (D) 139 (Jul) 2.7
Von Hannover v Germany (Application 59320/00) (2004) 16 BHRC 545, [2004] EMLR 379, ECtHR 1.43
Von Hannover v Germany (2006) 43 EHRR 7 .... 2.14

W

Ward v The Ritz Hotel (London) [1992] PIQR P315, CA 2.50, 2.51, 4.18

Table of Cases

	PARA
Westminster City Council v Croyalgrange Ltd [1986] 2 All ER 353, [1986] 1 WLR 674, 84 LGR 801, 83 Cr App Rep 155, 150 JP 449, [1986] Crim LR 693, 130 Sol Jo 409, [1986] LS Gaz R 2089, [1986] NLJ Rep 491, HL	2.133
Whiteford v Hunter [1950] WN 553, 94 Sol Jo 758, HL	2.87
Wilkinson v Rea Ltd [1941] 1 KB 688, [1941] 2 All ER 50, 110 LJKB 389, 165 LT 156, CA	2.70
Woodward v Hastings Corpn [1945] KB 174, [1944] 2 All ER 565, 43 LGR 29, 109 JP 41, 114 LJKB 211, 218, 172 LT 16, 61 TLR 94, CA	2.70
Wright v Cheshire County Council [1952] 2 All ER 789, 51 LGR 14, 116 JP 555, 96 Sol Jo 747, [1952] 2 TLR 641, CA	2.86

X

X and Y v Netherlands (Application 8978/80) (1985) 8 EHRR 235, ECtHR 2.15

Z

Z v Finland (Application 22009/93) (1997) 25 EHRR 371, 45 BMLR 107, ECtHR 2.15
Zezev v Governor of Brixton Prison [2002] EWHC 589 (Admin), [2002] 2 Cr App Rep 515 .... 2.126, 2.136

Chapter 1
KEY THEMES AND ISSUES

1.1 The recent history of data security law has been very turbulent, reflecting the crashing and disruptive manner in which the topic of data security first forced itself into the UK mass consciousness, on 20 November 2007. On this date the government revealed that a regional office under the control of Her Majesty's Revenue and Customs (HMRC) had lost two data disks containing an unencrypted copy of the entire Child Benefit database[1]. The data on these disks related to 25 million individuals.

The story of HMRC is well known, due to the press and media coverage it generated[2], the political reaction and the formal inquiries and investigations that were launched. The scale of the data loss was truly massive and at the date of publication of this book it still ranks as one of the world's largest incidents, in terms of numbers of people affected[3]. It also has the dubious distinction of attracting a government reward of £20,000 for the return of the disks[4] despite one political party valuing their worth to criminals at £1.5bn[5]. The findings of the official investigations are discussed in more depth later in this chapter.

The consequences of HMRC have been profound. Since news of the story broke there have been a series of major developments in data security law and practice. These include a number of very important amendments to the Data Protection Act 1998 and the emergence of new rules and philosophies for 'best practice' in the handling of data in many key areas (such as financial services, electronic communications and the public sector). HMRC has also encouraged the principal regulators for data security, the Information Commissioner and the Financial Services Authority, further along the path from 'light touch' to more interventionist strategies.

[1] For an account of the Chancellor of the Exchequer's statement to Parliament, see 'Point-by-point: Darling statement', BBC, 20 November 2007: http://news.bbc.co.uk/1/hi/uk_politics/7104115.stm.
[2] For an accessible, short chronology, see 'Timeline: Child benefits records loss', BBC, 25 June 2008: http://news.bbc.co.uk/1/hi/uk_politics/7104368.stm.
[3] For a comprehensive database of US data security breaches, including information about numbers of persons affected see www.datalossdb.org.
[4] '£20,000 reward offered for discs', BBC, 5 December 2007: http://news.bbc.co.uk/1/hi/uk_politics/7128851.stm.

1.1 Key themes and issues

[5] 'Discs worth £1.5bn to criminals', BBC, 28 November 2007: http://news.bbc.co.uk/1/hi/uk_politics/7117291.stm.

CENTRAL THEMES

1.2 There are three central themes within this book:

- The current cycle of development of data security law began in 2003, in the United States.
- In the UK the current cycle of development has resulted in the creation of a 'regulatory bear market'.
- The trajectory of the law is towards more disputes and litigation.

Thus, a new legal framework for data security is being created. However, this reform agenda is not yet complete, so practitioners will need to closely monitor further developments.

The current cycle of development of data security law

1.3 The current cycle of development of data security law began in 2003. The significance of 2003 lies in the fact that it was the year that California introduced the world's first breach notification law. Breach notification laws oblige data controllers to give notice of data security breaches to people affected. Some versions also require notification to regulators and other public authorities.

The importance of the Californian law cannot be overstated, as breach notification laws have arguably done more than any other legal development to encourage improvements in practices for data security. They have codified and institutionalised the need for transparency in the handling of serious data security breaches[1]; they feed a seemingly insatiable press and media appetite for news of security breaches and they stand as testament to the political interest in this field. Collectively these outcomes have resulted in news of security breaches also capturing the public imagination. As regards the political dimension, California opened the floodgates to the introduction of breach notification legislation in the vast majority of the States of the US, indicating that these laws are 'vote winners' within the electorate. Not surprisingly progress towards similar legislation is now very well advanced in the EU, having obtained the near universal support of the EU Institutions, Member States and national regulators for data protection.

In its truest sense breach notification acts as a regulatory transparency mechanism, which coupled with its 'name and shame' component, acts as a strong deterrent against bad practice. Notably, transparency equips the regulators with information that enables them to begin investigations, which can lead to enforcement action and, ultimately, the imposition of sanctions. Breach notification also adds legal and moral impetus to calls for the introduction of other transparency mechanisms, particularly inspections and audits. And in a purely chronological sense breach notification is the most significant legal development in data security law since the adoption of the EU Data Protection Directive[2] in 1995.

[1] California calls this 'personal data breach'.
[2] Directive 95/46/EC.

1.4 In this sense California's law was a watershed moment, representing the start of significant transitions in thinking about data security law and regulation.

In addition to all of these consequences the Californian law also put the spotlight on encryption, because its breach notification obligation extends only to security breaches involving unencrypted personal information[1]. This has contributed to encryption becoming an obligatory de facto 'Privacy Enhancing Technology' (PET). So it is that a failure to employ encryption will always expose the data controller to the potential wrath of the regulatory bear market.

For all of these reasons 2003 marks the beginning of the cycle of development of the law that is discussed in this book. With this task in mind this book relies heavily on the use of chronologies and the presentation of extracts from the source materials that data security lawyers will use in daily practice. The law is bound to become clearer over time, evolving through new legislation, case law and regulatory trends, but for the medium term at least the law will continue to be found in a hotchpotch of primary resources including the kinds of press releases, speeches, reports and regulatory guidance that are discussed here. Unfortunately, but perhaps not surprisingly, it is soon discovered that there are many ambiguities and uncertainties in the law, as well as contradictions. Yet despite these distractions it is still possible to detect the true trajectory of the law.

[1] The meaning of 'personal information' in the Californian legislation is much narrower than the meaning of 'personal data' under the Data Protection Directive.

The creation of the 'regulatory bear market' for data security in the UK

1.5 Most of us are familiar with the central characteristics of financial bear markets. A financial bear market may be considered to be one where negative sentiment reigns supreme. Pessimism about current affairs, or the state of the economy, leads to a sustained fall in the value of stock markets, as we have experienced during the global economic crisis. It is the opposite of a bull market, where sentiment is good and stock markets are rising.

There is much evidence to suggest that we have entered a regulatory bear market for data security. This regulatory bear market is one where the main regulators, the Information Commissioner and the Financial Services Authority, are very pessimistic about the state of data security within regulated organisations[1].

1.5 Key themes and issues

The Information Commissioner is also very pessimistic about the ability of UK data protection laws to properly regulate compliance[2]. In fact, the Information Commissioner is of the opinion that things are so bad that new laws are needed (to provide for the threat of gaol sentences, the imposition of fines, more invasive inspection powers and, of course, breach notification) to improve things. Collectively, this represents a damning indictment of data security practices and the law's ability to cope. 'Tougher' regulation is and will continue to be one of the defining characteristics of the regulatory bear market.

[1] 'NHS told to tighten data security', BBC, 25 May 2009: http://news.bbc.co.uk/1/hi/uk/8066609.stm.
[2] The Information Commissioner's concerns are not limited to the Data Protection Act 1998, but extend also to the adequacy of the Data Protection Directive. See, also, the Rand Europe report 'Review of the European Data Protection Directive', May 2009: http://www.ico.gov.uk/upload/documents/library/data_protection/detailed_specialist_guides/review_of_eu_dp_directive.pdf.

Tougher regulation to meet a changing threat landscape

1.6 The toughening of sanctions and regulators' attitudes represents a radical shift in thinking on data security law. In the field of data protection the law is moving quickly from what the Information Commissioner considers is a relatively toothless regime to one with considerable bite. This new approach to data security law is one that reflects and responds to the challenges as they currently stand, which are markedly different to the ones first anticipated by the original law makers back in the 1950s and 1960s. They are also very different to those of the 1970s, 1980s and of the first half of the 1990s[1]. Prominent within these new challenges are cyber-threats and those associated with increased use of the internet and advanced data processing techniques. Likewise, the economic value of information to criminals seems to have risen along with the information society, giving offences like common fraud and blackmail a new lease of life[2]. It is noticeable that one of the main goals of data security regulation for the financial services sector is the prevention of financial crime.

[1] It is significant that the data protection regime in Europe is built upon the Data Protection Directive, which itself is built on legal instruments first compiled in the early 1970s. Since the adoption of the Data Protection Directive the world of data processing has changed beyond compare, a point that is recognised in the Rand Europe report. In a press release announcing the Rand Europe report the Information Commissioner said 'The Directive is showing its age. Modern approaches to regulation mean that laws must concentrate on the real risks that people face in the modern world, must avoid unnecessary burdens, and must work well in practice': http://www.ico.gov.uk/upload/documents/pressreleases/2009/rand_report_120509.pdf.
[2] 'Blackmail fear over lost RAF data', BBC, 25 May 2009: http://news.bbc.co.uk/1/hi/uk/8066586.stm.

The trajectory of the law – more disputes and litigation

1.7 The regulatory bear market for data security will lead inevitably to more legal disputes and more litigation. This is not necessarily a bad thing; HMRC vindicated the many dire warnings about data security issued by the Information Commissioner and the Financial Services Authority. Increased incidents of disputes between the regulator and the regulated and more litigation between data subjects and data controllers (and between controllers and data processors) may help to improve the development of the law, perhaps through the creation of more case law, which is distinctly lacking in this area.

Factors that point to more disputes and litigation

1.8

- Despite the intensity of the post-HMRC focus on data handling and data security, it is inevitable that many data controllers will continue to breach the law. Those that do so in a serious manner are bound to face tougher responses and stronger sanctions in the years ahead, which will naturally extend to civil and criminal litigation in appropriate cases.
- Although the regulators can quite legitimately claim that they have performed very well in recent years, it is inevitable that they will make mistakes or fall into error during the performance of their regulatory duties. It is easy to foresee how litigation could arise over the use of inspection or fining powers for example.
- Transparency has been put back at the very heart of the new legal framework for data security, through the introduction of breach notification rules and proposals for inspections. These transparency mechanisms will lead to more security incidents coming to the attention of the regulators, leading naturally to more enforcement action and a consequent increase in the number of disputes and litigation.
- Related to this is the press and media interest. Due to the seemingly insatiable demand for news of data security incidents, the work of the regulators will be kept firmly in the spotlight. This may result in pressure for tougher action, leading to more disputes and litigation.
- The political dimension may also result in pressure for tougher action, with the same consequences.
- The regulators, particularly the Information Commissioner, may also be trapped by their own rhetoric. For example, in the course of making a case for new powers and penalties the Information Commissioner and his office have both resorted to dramatic and emotive language on occasions. The constant communication of negative messages and promises of a tougher approach create their own expectations about future strategy from which it will be very hard for the regulators to pull back.
- Similarly, the rising appreciation within the wider community of rights and obligations relating to information and security will generate its own pressures leading to more litigation between data subjects and data controllers and between controllers and processors.

All of these factors contribute to an increased likelihood of more disputes and more litigation, which will be one of the defining characteristics of the regulatory bear market. In this kind of environment no organisation can feel immune from the threat of formal legal action. Indeed it is already the case

1.8 *Key themes and issues*

that some of the UK's largest, or best known, or richest or most powerful organisations have felt the effects of a new, more interventionalist approach to data security regulation. Recent enforcement action taken by the Information Commissioner and the Financial Services Authority is considered in Chapter 6 and Appendix A.

HMRC – WHAT HAPPENED?

1.9 There have been two official investigations into HMRC, one conducted by Keiran Poynter[1] and the other conducted by the Independent Police Complaints Commission (IPCC)[2]. Both investigations published reports in June 2008, the contents of which are required reading for practitioners. These reports supported the service of an enforcement notice by the Information Commissioner under the Data Protection Act 1998, s 40.

While the Poynter and the IPCC investigations were carried out concurrently and in cooperation with each other, their focus and aims were different. The IPCC focused on whether any criminal conduct had been committed by HMRC staff under the Data Protection Act 1998, s 55, or disciplinary offences, while Poynter was concerned with the organisational, managerial and procedural aspects at HMRC.

The investigations found that there was no single cause for the loss of the disks. Rather, as the Poynter Report concluded, it was attributable to an 'unfortunate catalogue of inter-locking factors which in their totality triggered the events which unfolded'[3]. At the heart of the problem were inherent institutional deficiencies within HMRC, including ineffective practices and procedures, a lack of adequate training or guidance on policy and a lack of accountability for leadership and data ownership. As the IPCC report states at the outset 'corporate data handling was clearly woefully inadequate' and that such failings 'meant that an event like this was certain to happen – the only question being when'[4].

[1] 'Review of information security at HM Revenue and Customs Final report', Kieran Poynter, June 2008: http://www.hm-treasury.gov.uk/d/poynter_review250608.pdf.
[2] 'IPCC independent investigation report into loss of data relating to Child Benefit', IPCC, June 2008: http://www.ipcc.gov.uk/final_hmrc_report_25062008.pdf.
[3] Poynter Report, paragraph II.2.
[4] 'IPCC independent investigation report into loss of data relating to Child Benefit', Gary Garland, June 2008 at pages 4 and 5.

1.10 The other party involved in the data loss, but which was not specifically investigated by either Poynter or the IPCC, was the National Audit Office (NAO). The NAO's role is to scrutinise public spending on behalf of Parliament by auditing the accounts of central government departments and agencies and other public bodies. The NAO has a statutory right of access to documents and information. The National Audit Act 1983, s 8 provides:

'**8.— Right to obtain documents and information.**
(1)   Subject to subsection (2) below and except in relation to an examination under section 6 above in respect of the Welsh Ministers or the National Assembly for Wales Commission, the Comptroller and Auditor General

shall have a right of access at all reasonable times to all such documents as he may reasonably require for carrying out any examination under section 6 or 7 above and shall be entitled to require from any person holding or accountable for any such document such information and explanation as are reasonably necessary for that purpose.

(2) Subsection (1) above applies only to documents in the custody or under the control of the department, authority or body to which the examination relates.'

Chronological summary

1.11 The Poynter Report found that the loss of the disks was directly linked to an external audit of the Child Benefit Office, carried out by the NAO in March 2007. It was at this time that disks containing data downloaded from the Child Benefit database were first transferred to the NAO. Poynter believes that it was this series of events that set a precedent for the subsequent actions of the parties in October 2007.

March 2007 audit – the creation of a precedent

1.12 In March 2007 the NAO decided that it would 'independently sample' the Child Benefit database. To facilitate this, the NAO required specific data from the database, from which it intended to select its own samples for auditing purposes. The request for the data was made by NAO 'Employee 2', the lead auditor, and fell to 'Employee D', a business manager at HMRC, to deal with. Employee D worked in the Benefits and Credits Business Unit (B&C) and was one of two designated Single Points of Contact (SPOC) within HMRC for the March 2007 audit.

Employee D stated in an internal email to a superior colleague, 'Employee A', who was a senior HMRC official at B&C and the primary SPOC, that 'I've done a lot of digging and we can supply the majority of his [NAO Employee 2's] demands, at nil cost (Compliance have just recently done a 100% scan on live load so they could use that). If this hadn't been available it would have cost a fortune and have taken weeks'[1].

The 100% scan to which Employee D referred is a complete download of the data contained in the Child Benefit database, which is provided to the Claimant Compliance Business Unit (the Compliance Team) at HMRC every six months by Information Management Solutions (IMS), another part of HMRC. IMS was responsible for copying the data to the disks.

Several members of HMRC staff did query why such a large volume of data was to be provided to the NAO, but these queries were not escalated. This failing was attributable to operational concerns over costs and resources, which took priority, and a general lack of understanding at HMRC of policies and procedures. This meant that the appropriate level of authorisation to release such a large amount of sensitive information was not sought. 'Employee F', a member of IMS, stated during an interview that he had

1.12 Key themes and issues

suggested, as an alternative, that he could provide a small number of randomly selected records, as had been done in previous audits. In an emailed response to this suggestion sent on 12 March 2007 Employee D said:

> 'NAO are entitled to go where ever and have access to anything – without exception. They are a governing body and have absolute right to visit any part of our organisation and view any records/information we hold. As this information currently exists there are no cost implications to us in this instance, we cannot refuse them access. Employee A, Process Owner of Tax Credits and Child Benefit, is fully aware of the current position regarding the audit and supports this request for the information.'

[1] As quoted in the Poynter Report, paragraph IV.14 from an email sent by Employee D to Employee A (copied to Employee B) dated 5 March 2007.

1.13 Employee D's misunderstanding of the NAO's power was identified by Poynter as a factor that directly contributed to the loss of the disks. This attitude of deference to the NAO later informed other employees' opinions and dictated their actions in the October 2007 audit.

However, it does appear that Employee D did consult Employee A about the release of the data to the NAO and that there was a discussion about the availability of the 100% scan. They both recalled that Employee A suggested providing a sample of 12 records to the NAO. Employee A said in interviews that this was the only authorisation that he gave and that he was not aware that a complete copy of the 100% scan was to be given to the NAO in either March 2007 or October 2007. In his report Poynter states that he 'has found no further evidence to clarify the point but has no reason to doubt the veracity of Employee A's statement'[1].

Despite the lack of explicit authorisation to release anything other than 12 records, on 12 March Employee D sent an email to her colleagues 'Employee H' and 'Employee E' (an Assistant Director in the Compliance Team) responding to a query from Employee H. In this email Employee D stated:

> 'I was told there had been a 100% system scan carried out recently for Compliance ... I asked Employee F to get an extract for me, and following further enquiries ... we were told there were "some concerns" regarding confidentiality and the need to get security clearance before any information could be handed over. Hence my email. Hope this clears things up Employee H ...'[2]

Whether the issue of security clearance was resolved, and on whose authority, is still unclear. However, Poynter identifies that the lack of a 'clearly assigned data owner or guardian from which to seek this authorisation'[3] was a factor that directly contributed to the loss of the data. This issue was raised by Employee E in an email to Employee D:

> 'this data is originally Child Benefit Office data and not [Compliance Team] data. If NAO want this they should go to [IMS] for this and not to [the Compliance Team]. The fact that we may have the data is neither here nor there ... It is not just a question of "NAO can have anything", it is a question of them obtaining from the correct source.'[4]

HMRC – what happened? **1.15**

Employee E had clearly raised genuine concerns, so it is very unfortunate that he had no further involvement in the March 2007 audit. Not only did he press the issue of data ownership and the need to seek the appropriate (and correct) levels of authorisation, his assessment more accurately reflects the NAO's powers of access to information than that of Employee D.

1 The Poynter Report, paragraph IV.18.
2 As quoted in the IPCC Report, paragraph 132.
3 The Poynter Report, paragraph II.22.
4 As quoted in the Poynter Report paragraph IV.19, taken from an email from Employee E to Employee D and Employee H (copied to Employee B).

1.14 On 13 March 2007 the sample of 12 Child Benefit records was provided to Employee 2 at the NAO.

Following a review of the sample, Employee 2 wrote to 'Employee B' at HMRC asking whether the data could be divided into two categories and whether the address, bank and parent details could be removed to reduce the size of the file, as such information was not needed for audit purposes. However, as before, concerns over costs and operational issues took precedence over security and data protection considerations, so Employee 2's request was rejected by Employee D.

The lack of clarity as to accountability and data ownership was again the source of confusion, as Employee D directed Employee 2 to raise his concerns 'regarding data extracts etc' with the Compliance Team and a second business unit known as 'KAI'. Unfortunately the 100% scan data was not discussed at the appropriate meeting so neither the methods of manipulating the data to meet the NAO's requirements, nor the possibility of redaction were discussed.

Nevertheless, Employee D explained in an email to Employee A and Employee B, that '… regarding the data extract. It's all been sorted now … We have agreed that any information we hold needs to be put to more than one use if at all possible'. Employee A later stated that he took no action in relation to this email as he believed that Employee D was referring to the sample of 12 records and that at the meeting 'the compliance people whose data set this is … are going to talk about how to chop it down', further indicating the confusion surrounding responsibility and ownership of the data.

Removal of the disks off-site

1.15 On 15 March 2007 Employee 2 was handed two disks containing the 100% scan. Although Employee 2 travelled to HMRC's premises with the intention of removing the disks off-site, few within HMRC had contemplated this and certainly no one in a senior position ever knew that this had occurred. Employee F, Employee B and 'Employee J' did discuss the removal of the data off-site and their concerns about the risks involved in various telephone conversations and email exchanges between 14 and 16 March 2007, but again they failed to voice their concerns at a high enough level. The attitude was that Employee 2 was a 'trusted source' and therefore HMRC staff did not expect

1.15 Key themes and issues

there to be any restrictions on the data being removed from the building on portable media. This time, the disks were returned to HMRC on the successful completion of the audit in April 2007.

October 2007 audit

1.16 In September 2007 during the preparation phase of the November 2007 audit, 'Employee C', a Senior Executive Officer in B&C, was appointed as the SPOC in place of Employee D. However, save for a few initial emails, Employee C was excluded from all later email communications relating to the 100% scan. As a result, issues were not escalated to a more senior level or to the primary SPOC, Employee A, and there was no single person coordinating the NAO's request for information.

This audit was being governed by a new audit strategy document. While this did include a 'call for greater reliance on substantive work completed by the auditors'[1] it did not explicitly state that the NAO would require a full extract of the Child Benefit database. When Employee 2 was later questioned following the loss of the disks, he explained that he requested the full scan of the database as his request for a reduced or redacted version had been rejected out of hand in March 2007; therefore he felt that he had no other option.

Confusion over ownership of the data and failure to identify clear chains of authority marred the October audit and were significant contributing factors in the resultant data loss. In email correspondence with Employee 2 on 18 September, Employee E stated that the 100% data scan would be available in early October and that Employee 2 should contact Employee J to discuss 'how you might exploit this scan'[2]. In a later interview, Employee E said that he intended his email to be merely introductory. He felt that the request should be made to IMS, as he was not in a position to authorise the release of such data. Furthermore, when Employee 2 sent the subsequent request to Employee J it referred to copies of the 'data scans being carried out in early October 2007', not an exploitation of the data as suggested by Employee E.

Due to the precedent set in March 2007, Employee J accepted the email request from Employee 2 as confirmation that he should provide the requested data and so he requested copies of the entire Child Benefit database from the relevant department without seeking further authorisation. After a period of delay caused by technical issues and security concerns, which were again left unresolved, a copy of the 100% scan was burnt to two disks and was put in the 'tax post', the 'non-documented' HMRC internal mail system. Then disaster struck: the disks did not reach their intended destination.

Later that month on 24 October, further copies of the disks were sent to Employee 2 at the NAO via a secure postal service. The use of the secure postal system had more to do with the need for expediency rather than security as no one involved in the creation or distribution of the further copies

HMRC – *what happened?* **1.17**

thought to encrypt the disks or use other technological security measures. On 8 November the loss was eventually reported and on 20 November the government went public.

1   IPCC Report, paragraph 156.
2   IPCC Report, paragraph 161.

The key findings – Poynter

Specific factors directly contributing to the loss

1.17

> 'The data loss incident arose following a sequence of communication failures between junior HMRC officials and between them and the NAO. The loss was entirely avoidable and the fact that it could happen points to serious institutional deficiencies at HMRC.'[1]

The above conclusion is hardly surprising following a review of the facts, even as briefly summarised here. Although the investigation found no evidence 'of malice or knowing disregard for policy or procedure'[2], Poynter identifies two major institutional deficiencies from which the other, more specific, issues stemmed. It is clear from the above account that information security was simply not a management priority, while Poynter's more detailed analysis also revealed that 'HMRC had an organisational design which was unnecessarily complex and crucially, did not clearly focus on management accountability'[3].

The specific factors that directly contributed to the loss of the Child Benefit data are:

- The provision of the full 100% scan to the NAO and the removal of the data from HMRC's premises in March 2007, which set a precedent and created the conditions for the later loss to occur.
- That only an informal SPOC protocol existed between the NAO and HMRC, which was not widely publicised throughout the organisations or documented in any detail. Failure to clarify and adhere to the protocol prevented HMRC from managing the information flow to the NAO.
- Staff at HMRC focused on operational issues of costs and resources at the expense of concerns for the security risks.
- The failure to identify and further investigate other data redaction options due to poor communication and misunderstandings between the parties and internally within HMRC.
- That the staff at HMRC did not consider it necessary to seek approval for the release of the data. This is due to several factors including:
    - The misconception that the NAO had absolute authority to access any information held by HMRC.
    - The staff's lack of knowledge of HMRC guidance and the failure to establish clear lines of management accountability and data ownership, which meant that staff did not think it necessary to escalate the issues to a higher level.

1.17 *Key themes and issues*

- Failure of the NAO to communicate its information requirements in any detail.
- The use of insecure methods of data transfer and insufficient levels of technological security measures to protect the data, particularly given its highly sensitive nature and the portability of the media.

[1] The Poynter Report, paragraph I.4.
[2] The Poynter Report, paragraph II.2.
[3] The Poynter Report, paragraph I.5.

The general institutional factors

1.18 Poynter also identified institutional factors, which 'created the environment in which the data loss could occur'. Although HMRC had wide ranging and detailed guidance and policies in place, staff failed to follow them in either audit of 2007, as they were too generic and lacked 'sufficient procedural detail to guide staff in the specific circumstances'[1]. Indeed, the report goes on to state that some of the policies, including the policies dealing with removable media, were in draft form or were guidance for developing policy rather than defining the actual procedures to be followed. Furthermore, due to the lack of training and awareness of the existence of the policies few members of staff recognised the importance of information security or their general responsibilities in this regard.

[1] The Poynter Report, paragraph V.6.

The 'Wider Review'

1.19 The terms of reference which governed the Poynter investigation and subsequent report were wide enough to include a more general review of information management within HMRC. In this 'Wider Review' section of the report Poynter concludes that the loss of the two disks was symptomatic of wider problems within the organisation. Some of the conclusions of the Wider Review mirrored those expressed above, such as that the information security policies were inadequate and not suitable for operational use by staff on a daily basis. Other findings can be summarised as follows:

- At the time of the loss the management at HMRC failed to prioritise information security.
- Within HMRC, the organisational structure and the lack of clear accountability and chains of command precluded effective information management even if it was a priority for the senior figures.
- In merging two distinct entities, the Inland Revenue and HM Customs and Excise, to form HMRC, a complex and fragmented organisation was created which made implementing information security difficult.
- HMRC's operating processes are dictated by a paper-based approach rather than digital technologies.

HMRC – what happened? **1.21**

The key findings – IPCC

1.20 The findings of the IPCC's report reflect its focus on whether there was any criminality in the actions of HMRC staff. The report heavily criticises HMRC saying that its processes for data handling were 'woefully inadequate'[1], but it is categorical in its conclusion that there was no evidence of misconduct or criminality by any member of staff. The report blames institutional failings and echoes Poynter's findings that:

- There was no coherent system for handling data.
- Staff failed to appreciate the importance of secure data handling.
- A 'muddle through' ethos, that relied on common sense and informal policies based on past practices, dictated staff's day to day routine largely due to the failure of HMRC to provide adequate supporting training or guidance.

The report further concludes that in providing the 100% scan rather than a redacted version and by failing to ensure a safe and secure method of transfer there was probably a breach of the third and seventh data protection principles of the Data Protection Act 1998, which hold respectively that data processing should be relevant and not excessive and that data must be afforded appropriate technical and organisational protective measures. However, the report is quick to point out that such breaches were caused by the staff's lack of awareness and the absence of formal, well documented procedures rather than any criminal wrongdoing.

[1] IPCC Report, page 5.

Recommendations

The Poynter Report

1.21 The aim of the Poynter Report was to conduct a full root and branch review of the data handling practices of HMRC. The recommendations therefore reflect this, in both number (45 in total) and scope and include both specific recommendations, such as a wide ranging training programme, the appointment of a Director of Data Security and Data Guardians and increasing the visibility of senior managers, and in the longer term setting a 'new direction of travel'.

At the heart of the recommendations is the aim of introducing an information management strategy that represents a fundamental departure from the existing processes. The report identifies that the various departments within HMRC and the products that they offer (for example Child Benefit, PAYE and National Insurance) currently operate as discrete businesses with their own processes and systems, which each create a separate customer record. Therefore an individual is likely to have a number of customer records in his name. The report emphasises that the fragmented nature of this data creates inefficiencies and increases the security risk.

1.21 Key themes and issues

The report therefore advocates a 'trust' based model of data handling whereby HMRC moves away from accepting responsibility for collecting and maintaining customer data towards a strategy where customers entrust their data to HMRC on the basis that the organisation will ensure its security whilst the customer retains the responsibility for updating and maintaining the records. Although this model is widely used within the private sector, for example in online banking systems, it is a fairly radical step in relation to a government department. However, it is fully aligned with the government's aim of introducing transformational government and a seamless, single point of contact for customers.

This strategy will not be accomplished overnight and the report recognises that it will involve radical overhauls of the current system, which will not come cheaply. However the need to avoid further security breaches and the benefits of improved efficiency, information security, customer service and data integrity mean that such recommendations are essential steps for HMRC.

The IPCC Report

1.22 The recommendations of the IPCC report are far fewer in number and are much narrower in scope. There were only six in total and they focused on short-term, quick win changes such as reviewing the security controls and protocols, developing a data security strategy, a training programme and a communication strategy and reviewing and developing its role and responsibilities as a data controller.

HMRC aftermath and conclusions – trust in government damaged

1.23 HMRC is widely considered to have damaged the psychological bonds of trust between the Labour government and the citizen. Thus, repairing and regaining the public's trust was one of the most prominent stated aims of the government's response to HMRC. For example, the interim report of the Data Handling Review observed that 'the Government's ability to deliver and improve public services relies on high levels of public trust'.

In this context it is highly significant that the story broke at a time when the political climate in the UK was changing, following the decision of the Prime Minister, Gordon Brown, not to go ahead with the much anticipated autumn 2007 general election. In crude terms the Conservatives were in the ascendancy, overtaking Labour in the opinion polls. Therefore, the political climate in November 2007 guaranteed that HMRC would become a very big issue. This dimension is illustrated by the fact that the Chancellor of the Exchequer and the Prime Minister both felt it necessary to apologise for the loss of the disks, which in political terms was hugely embarrassing. The Liberal Democrats, for instance, said that HMRC rendered the Chancellor of Exchequer's position 'nearly untenable'[1].

---

[1] 'Darling's role nearly untenable', BBC, 25 November 2007: http://news.bbc.co.uk/1/hi/uk_politics/7112109.stm.

The government's reforms

1.24 HMRC therefore placed the onus on the government to implement reforms and to be fair, the government responded quickly, with the major developments being:

- The Prime Minister announced that there would be a government-wide review of data handling and that the Information Commissioner would be given powers to 'spot check' the public sector for compliance. The 'Data Handling Review', headed by Sir Gus O'Donnell, got down to work straightaway, publishing an interim report[1] in December 2007 and its final report[2] in June 2008.
- The Criminal Justice and Immigration Act 2008 amended the Data Protection Act 1998 to introduce the monetary penalties regime, which will give the Information Commissioner the power to fine organisations guilty of substantial breaches of the Act[3]. Another amendment sets the foundations for the introduction of custodial penalties for the criminal offence of unlawful obtaining of personal data[4] under the Data Protection Act 1998, s 55, or 'data theft' as it is colloquially known.
- Following a public consultation the Ministry of Justice officially endorsed the Information Commissioner's guidance on the handling of data security incidents[5].
- The Coroners and Justice Bill, announced in the Queen's Speech in December 2008, will put the Information Commissioner's right to spot check the public sector on a statutory footing[6].

[1] Data Handling Procedures in Government: Interim Progress Report, Cabinet Office, December 2007.
[2] Data Handling Procedures in Government: Final Report, Cabinet Office, June 2008.
[3] See the Criminal Justice and Immigration Act 2008, s 144. Regulations are required to bring the monetary penalties regime into effect.
[4] See the Criminal Justice and Immigration Act 2008, s 77.
[5] Response to the Data Sharing Review Report, Ministry of Justice, 24 November 2008, recommendation 11.
[6] See the Coroners and Justice Bill, s 156. In July 2009 the government partially accepted the case for spot checks of the private sector, through an amendment that will allow the Information Commissioner to designate classes of private sector data controllers for this purpose.

Regulatory consequences – the HMRC enforcement notice

1.25 As regards the regulatory consequences, the Poynter and IPCC reports were shared with the Information Commissioner, who served an enforcement notice on HMRC in June 2008, confirming the IPCC's opinion that HMRC had breached the third and seventh data protection principles in the Data Protection Act 1998. As a result HMRC was forced to give undertakings that it would, within 36 months, use its best endeavours to implement the 45 recommendations contained in the Poynter Report and to provide annual reports on its progress. The fact that there was a need to serve an enforcement notice is a damning indictment of the failings at HMRC. It also indicates that the Information Commissioner is doubtful that HMRC will deliver upon its obligations without the continuing threat of further enforcement action and possible criminal proceedings.

1.26 *Key themes and issues*

THE REGULATORY DYNAMIC WITHIN DATA SECURITY LAW

1.26 The existence of the regulatory bear market was confirmed by the Financial Services Authority (FSA) in March 2006, when it fined Capita Financial Administrators £300,000, for security weaknesses that exposed Capita and its investors to a risk of fraud[1]. The use of a fining scheme within regulation leaves no ambiguity about the regulator's willingness to take strong action. Until that point the FSA's position had been largely confined to spelling out policy[2].

The Information Commissioner arrived at data security a little later than the FSA, with the publication of 'What price privacy? The unlawful trade in confidential personal information' in May 2006[3]. This report is about the criminal obtaining, disclosure and sale of personal data, which are all offences under the Data Protection Act 1998, s 55. These offences are colloquially known as 'data theft'. The report is discussed in more detail later in this chapter.

Thus, in 2006 the FSA and the Information Commissioner were focused on very different parts of the data security continuum; the FSA was focused on the failure of systems for data security, for which it had shown a willingness to impose large fines, whereas the Information Commissioner was focused on a specialised form of criminal activity, which he considered was deserving of gaol sentences. This tells us a great deal about the trajectory of the law and the inevitability of conflicts between the regulator and the regulated, which will include both criminal and civil litigation.

However, in early 2007 the regulators' focus converged on the Nationwide Building Society, which had the sorry misfortune of facing two sets of enforcement action; in February the FSA fined Nationwide £980,000, following the loss of an unencrypted laptop computer, and in March the Information Commissioner obtained informal undertakings from Nationwide after finding that it had breached the Data Protection Act 1998, by failing to properly dispose of confidential waste papers containing personal data.

Interestingly, the joining of the regulators' focus reveals evidence of rivalry as well as cooperation. For example, in a report titled 'Data protection powers and penalties. The case for amending the Data Protection Act 1998'[4], published in December 2007, only a matter of weeks after the government revealed the loss of the HMRC disks, the Information Commissioner's Office (ICO) compared its powers to those of the FSA and other regulators, with unfavourable results[5].

---

[1] 'The weaknesses in systems and controls contributed to a small number of actual and attempted frauds that appear to have been carried out by a small number of colluding CFA staff. The value of the actual frauds was £328,341 and the value of the attempted frauds was £1,552,259. CFA took prompt action to ensure that its clients did not suffer a financial loss as a result. Nevertheless, the control failings were serious. The FSA is particularly concerned that: first, the initial instances of fraud were discovered by clients rather than by CFA. Had these clients not alerted CFA, there remained a material risk that it would not have identified the frauds or taken action to assess and revise its controls, which it has now done; and second, that the cumulative impact of the individual failings

The regulatory dynamic within data security law **1.27**

represented a significant risk to the FSA objective of reducing the risk of financial crime.' FSA Capita Financial Administrators Final Notice, 16 March 2006.
2 The FSA points to 2003 as the start of its focus on data security. In the FSA Capita Financial Administrators Final Notice, 16 March 2006, the FSA said 'the reduction of financial crime is one of the FSA's four statutory objectives and the profile of identity theft has increased significantly in recent years. In December 2003 the FSA issued its discussion paper DP26 "Developing our Policy on Fraud and Dishonesty". There have also been numerous high-profile articles in the national and trade press, FSA speeches and papers as well as guidance from industry organisations'.
3 Throughout 2004 and 2005 the ICO's main focus was freedom of information. The Freedom of Information Act 2000 came into force in January 2005.
4 http://www.ico.gov.uk/upload/documents/library/corporate/detailed_specialist_guides/data_protection_powers_penalties_v1_dec07.pdf.
5 In this context it is worth considering the Hampton Report, which is discussed in Chapter 6. This report identified the main powers of regulators, saying at paragraph 2.76 that 'Regulators have several different tools available when businesses are non-compliant. Individual powers vary from regulator to regulator, but most regulators can: issue warning letters; issue enforcement notices, which require businesses to do or not do particular things. Non-compliance with such notices is usually a criminal offence; or prosecute businesses'. This describes in general terms the powers of the Information Commissioner. The report then goes on to say at paragraph 2.77 that 'in addition, some regulators can: order businesses to cease trading immediately, or close premises; or issue administrative penalties'.

The Information Commissioner's campaign for more powers

1.27 The publication of 'The case for amending the Data Protection Act 1998' was not the Information Commissioner's first statement on the adequacy of his powers; in the 18 months leading up to HMRC the Commissioner made many public statements ruing the inadequacies of the Data Protection Act 1998 and calling for an increase in his powers.

Key events in the Information Commissioner's campaign for new powers and penalties are discussed in more detail in Chapter 6, but in outline the Information Commissioner's position has been that the enforcement regime within the Data Protection Act 1998 is not fit for purpose. A sense of the Information Commissioner's position can be found in evidence given to the House of Commons Justice Committee in December 2007[1], when the Commissioner said:

> 'At the moment, we have the power to serve an enforcement notice, but if I can paraphrase the law, an enforcement notice says, "You have got it wrong, do not do it again", and only if they do it again, in explicit breach of our enforcement notice, only then is it a criminal offence. That is a long drawn-out process which, going back to the earlier metaphor, involves bolting doors after horses have disappeared.'[2]

Prior to the amendment of the Data Protection Act 1998 by the Criminal Justice and Immigration Act 2008 the principal component of the enforcement regime was the enforcement notice. Enforcement notices are discussed in more detail in Chapter 6, but to summarise, the Data Protection Act 1998, s 40 gives the Information Commissioner the power to serve an enforcement notice when he is of the opinion that the data controller has contravened, or is contravening, the data protection principles.

1.27 Key themes and issues

[1] 'Protection of Private Data' First Report of Session 2007–08.
[2] This answer was given in response to a question from Mrs Morgan, who recalled that in earlier evidence to the Home Affairs Select Committee the Information Commissioner 'lamented your lack of any real teeth in this field'. The Information Commissioner did not challenge this assessment of his evidence.

Enforcement notice – a toothless regime or a counter-productive stance?

1.28 One of the Information Commissioner's main complaints about enforcement notices is that they do not contain sufficient deterrent effect. Connecting this to the regulatory bear market, the Commissioner has been as negative about enforcement notices as he has been about the state of compliance at data controllers[1].

There are many grounds to criticise the enforcement notice regime in the Data Protection Act 1998, but does this mean that it is as toothless as the Information Commissioner implies? An alternative view is that enforcement notices are powerful sanctions if used properly, containing a series of built-in deterrents. In the vast majority of cases enforcement notices should be able to achieve the Information Commissioner's core regulatory objectives[2]. They might also have the potential to achieve just as much as the new fining and inspection powers.

If this is true, then the Information Commissioner's stance on the enforcement notice power may have been counter-productive, acting to neutralise many of its deterrent effects in the eyes of data controllers, who could be forgiven for thinking that s 40 is a damp squib, one that they should not fear. The Information Commissioner's position might have fostered this impression[3].

[1] However, there is evidence that the ICO has found enforcement notices to be effective. The Information Commissioner told the House of Commons Home Affairs Committee that 'we took a very strong line against that; we served an enforcement notice and that activity has now stopped. We are vigilant, Mr Winnick, to deal with those sorts of problems as they surface'. 'A Surveillance Society', Fifth Report of Session 2007–08, Volume II, Oral and written evidence.
[2] In 'the case for amending the Data Protection Act' the ICO repeatedly gives reminders of the fact that it will use its new powers infrequently. This seems to imply that the enforcement notice will remain the primary enforcement power in most cases.
[3] 'At the moment our only real stick is an enforcement notice which says "Do not do it again" '. Richard Thomas, evidence to Home Affairs Committee, 'A Surveillance Society', Fifth Report of Session 2007–08, Volume II, Oral and written evidence.

1.29 The key features within enforcement notices that give them deterrent effect are:

- They can be structured so as to give controllers only a limited period of time to comply. The Data Protection Act 1998 gives the Information Commissioner the power to impose a 28-day time period for compliance, which can be truncated in serious cases.
- Dealing with enforcement notices can be very disruptive, time-consuming and costly.
- The failure to comply with an enforcement notice is a criminal offence[1].

- Directors, managers and similar officers can be personally prosecuted for the crimes committed by their organisations[2].

A 28-day time period for compliance, or shorter, can pose considerable managerial and operational problems for data controllers, even those who are working at best practice levels, with properly functioning incident management teams etc. Managing the process after receipt of an enforcement notice can be fraught with difficulty, particularly in a large organisation, because the issues that have to be addressed are many in number and are generally complex. For example, the notice will have to be viewed from a legal perspective, from an executable/deliverables perspective, from a financial perspective, from the political perspective (where the controller is in the public sector, or connected with the public sector)[3], from the shareholder perspective (particularly in listed companies) and so on. Dealing with these kinds of issues quickly absorbs considerable time and resources that can make 28 days look like an impossibly short period of time.

[1] See the Data Protection Act 1998, s 47.
[2] See the Data Protection Act 1998, s 61.
[3] See, for example, 'Firm "broke rules" over data loss', BBC, 22 August 2008: http://news.bbc.co.uk/1/hi/uk_politics/7575989.stm.

1.30 The core point here is that enforcement notices can – and very often do – set tough deadlines for compliance and it is the threat of tough deadlines that gives enforcement notices a deterrent effect. Tough deadlines for complex work involving complex issues are the ones that cause controllers the most amount of disruption, usually with immediate, direct and substantial financial consequences. Indeed, used properly it should be possible for the Information Commissioner to serve an enforcement notice that has financial consequences for the controller that are similar to monetary penalties.

The deterrent effect of personal criminal liability is obvious. Indeed it is common knowledge within the data security industry and related professions that nothing concentrates a director's or manager's mind as much as the threat of personal liability. In the public sector a criminal conviction arising from a data security issue will be at best very career damaging and at worst career destroying.

Thus, while the trajectory of the law on enforcement powers is clear, it would be a mistake for controllers to regard enforcement notices as being a damp squib. Depending upon the circumstances of the case they can be the very opposite, as many controllers will be able to testify to. For example, many of the data controllers who have already been through the mill of regulatory action for data security breaches will be able to confirm that they have been put to very considerable expense in correcting the deficiencies that the Information Commissioner's Office drew to their attention. In some cases they have even been put to multi-million pound expense.

1.31 *Key themes and issues*

Was the campaign successful?

1.31 While there is no doubt that the Information Commissioner attracted good publicity and many favourable hearings within parts of government and Parliament, the best assessment would be that by the time of HMRC nothing concrete had been achieved and there seemed to be little prospect for change in the short to medium term[1]. Against this background HMRC seemed to provide the Information Commissioner with a unique opportunity to force home his call for new powers once-and-for-all, a fact that was fully appreciated and very skilfully exploited.

In light of the government's reforms it must be concluded that the Information Commissioner and his Office have come out of HMRC very well indeed, with their prestige and powers heightened. All of the post-HMRC reforms identified earlier have benefited the Commissioner, whose influence is now felt all over the security agenda, whether this be in the creation of new legislation or the many new initiatives for best practice such as data sharing, privacy by design, privacy enhancing technologies, privacy impact assessments and encryption.

The period since HMRC has also highlighted the effectiveness of the Information Commissioner's law making powers, which, broadly speaking, arise under the Data Protection Act 1998 and the Human Rights Act 1998. The Information Commissioner truly is one of the most important law making bodies in the field of data security law, with an influence that is second only to Parliament and arguably even greater than the courts'. A good illustration of these powers is provided by the Ministry of Justice's endorsement of the ICO's guidance on the handling of data security breaches and breach notification.

None of this would have happened but for HMRC. HMRC vindicated the Information Commissioner, as already mentioned. In effect, the Information Commission was able to claim the moral, political and legal high ground, thereby increasing the momentum for reform. However, there is still much more to be achieved, as the reform agenda has not been completed.

[1] For example in October 2007 the government gave its response to 'Personal Internet Security', ruling out breach notification legislation.

WHAT PRICE PRIVACY?

1.32 As mentioned earlier, the Information Commissioner's first substantial piece of work on data security was his report 'What price privacy? The unlawful trade in confidential personal information', which was published in May 2006. This report is about the illegal trade in personal information.

The essence of the report is that there is a 'pervasive and widespread industry' trading in unlawfully obtained data. Because this activity represents 'so serious a threat to individual privacy'[1] the Commissioner considered that Parliament should introduce custodial penalties for those convicted.

In summary, the Commissioner found that at the heart of the industry were investigative journalists and private investigators. Of course, by extension the clients of private investigators were implicated, which includes law firms, insurance companies, finance companies, accountancy firms, public authorities (particularly Council Tax departments) and those individuals with particular motivations, such as divorcing. This was an interesting focus, reminding us that despite the prominence of e-crime and cyber crime activities there still remains a considerable human element within security breaches and 'data theft' (the colloquialism for section 55 offences).

The report itself was a special report to Parliament, submitted under the power granted to the Commissioner by the Data Protection Act 1998, s 52(2). Section 52(2) provides that the Commissioner 'may from time to time lay before each House of Parliament such other reports with respect to those functions as he thinks fit'. 'What price privacy?' constituted the first use of this power by the Information Commissioner.

1   'What price privacy? The unlawful trade in confidential personal information', 10 May 2006, HC 1056. Quotations taken from the foreword from the Information Commissioner p 3.

The section 55 offence

1.33 Protecting personal information and the privacy of individuals are the cornerstones of the Data Protection Act 1998. Data Protection Act 1998, s 55 criminalises the practice of obtaining personal information without the consent of the data controller, which is often done by deception, through the practice known as 'blagging' or through bribing corrupt officials in public or private organisations.

Section 55(1) states that it is an offence for a person, knowingly or recklessly, without the consent of the data controller, to obtain or disclose personal data or the information contained in personal data, or to procure the disclosure to another person of the information contained in personal data. The distinction between personal data and information contained in personal data is an important one, for, as held in *R v Rooney*[1], it is not necessary to disclose the identity of the individual to whom the information relates, as it is sufficient that the information is contained in personal data. In this instance the appeal court upheld the defendant's conviction because in disclosing that her sister's ex-partner had moved to an 'address in Tunstall', she had, contrary to s 55, unlawfully disclosed information contained in personal data.

The defences to the offence are set out in s 55(2), as amended by the Criminal Justice and Immigration Act 2008, s 78. Therefore it will not be an offence to obtain, disclose or procure such information without the consent of the data controller if it can be shown that:

- It was necessary for the prevention or detection of crime (s 55(2)(a)(i)).
- It was required or authorised by statute, rule of law or court order (s 55(2)(a)(ii)).

1.33　*Key themes and issues*

- The offender acted in the reasonable belief that he had a right in law to act as he did (s 55(2)(b)).
- The offender acted in the reasonable belief that he would have had the consent of the data controller if the data controller had known of the act and the circumstances surrounding it and for the 'special purposes'[2], with a view to the publication by any person of any journalistic, literary or artistic material, and in the reasonable belief that in the particular circumstances the obtaining, disclosing or procuring was justified as being in the public interest (s 55(2)(c) as amended by the Criminal Justice and Immigration Act 2008, s 78).
- In the particular circumstances, the obtaining, disclosing or procuring was justified as being in the public interest (s 55(2)(d)).

[1] [2006] EWCA Crim 1841.
[2] See the Data Protection Act 1998, s 3 for the definition of special purposes.

1.34 Section 55(4) to (8) makes it an offence to sell or offer to sell personal data which has been (or which is subsequently) obtained or procured knowingly or recklessly, without the consent of the data controller. Subsection (6) specifically states that an advertisement indicating that personal data may be available for sale constitutes an offer to sell data, thereby avoiding the jurisprudence that an advert is generally considered to be an invitation to treat rather than an offer to sell.

Until 2003, it was thought that the standard of recklessness in the defences in s 55(2)(b) and (c) introduced an objective test. However, in 2003 the House of Lords, in *R v G*[1], rejected the notion of objective recklessness, which had dominated English Jurisprudence for 12 years. Following this judgment a defendant may only be said to have acted recklessly if they acted with knowledge of the risks and if, in the circumstances known to the defendant, they had known that taking such risks was unjustified. In relation to the section 55 offences, the adoption of a subjective test of recklessness is favourable. Under the previous position it was not inconceivable to envisage a situation where an employee held an honest belief that they were justified in disclosing the confidential information, but that such belief was objectively unreasonable when viewed in the surrounding circumstances. The subjective test certainly brings the law in to line with the Department of Constitutional Affairs' statement in its consultation document 'Increasing penalties for deliberate and wilful misuse of personal data' that[2]:

> 'We want to make it absolutely clear that this does not mean penalising front-line public sector staff who, while sharing data for legitimate reasons, make an error of judgement in what are often marginal and complex cases ... Likewise a staff member who is deceived into giving out information will not be guilty of an offence.'

The offences under s 55 are some of the primary offences under the Act, the others being processing data without a register entry, enforced subject access, breach of an enforcement notice and obstruction of or failing to assist in the execution of a warrant. However, the offences as originally enacted did not carry a custodial sentence, a position which, according to the Information Commissioner in his foreword to 'What price privacy?', is unacceptable:

'When cases involving the unlawful procurement or sale of confidential personal information come before the courts, convictions often bring no more than a derisory fine or a conditional discharge. Low penalties devalue the data protection offence in the public mind and mask the true seriousness of the crime, even within the judicial system. They likewise do little to deter those who seek to buy or supply confidential information that should rightly remain private.'

1   [2003] UKHL 50, [2004] 1 AC 1034.
2   CP9/06.

Background to the campaign for custodial penalties

1.35 The Information Commissioner's drive to stem the trade of personal data is far from a new idea. A report to the Departmental Committee on Privacy, chaired by the Rt Hon Kenneth Younger[1] in 1972, called for greater regulation of the private investigator industry, in the form of a licensing regime, in order to promote privacy. However, a specific offence of disclosing personal information without consent was omitted from the Data Protection Act 1984 and was not introduced until 10 years later, following a number of well-publicised, high-profile breaches of privacy[2].

Despite the Information Commissioner's Office actively pursuing convictions under s 55, the trade in confidential information was far from stemmed. In fact, at the start of the twenty-first century the illicit trade in information and the accompanying threat to privacy became a hot topic in the media, with a number of well-publicised cases of unlawfully obtaining, disclosing or procuring confidential information, including those reported in the House of Commons Select Committee on Culture, Media and Sport's Fifth Report of Session 2002–03[3]:

- In January 2002 The Guardian reported that a solicitor's employee had, allegedly prompted by The Sun, stolen sensitive documents relating to a murder case and sold them onto The Sun, The Daily Mirror and The Express.
- In September 2002 The Guardian reported that a private detective agency called 'Southern Investigations' had been found to be selling information from police sources to various tabloid newspapers and that there was a 'black market' for such information.
- In January 2003 The Times reported that the HR directorate at the Inland Revenue had admitted that there was evidence that some employees had sold confidential information from tax returns to unnamed outside agencies.

The Select Committee's report focused on the intrusion of privacy by the media. In highlighting a consistent practice of 'improper and intrusive gathering of data' the report revealed worrying signs of the media's appetite for confidential information in order to make a story. In summarising oral evidence given by the editors of The Sun and The News of the World, Ms Rebekah Wade and Mr Andrew Coulson respectively, the report concluded that:

1.35 *Key themes and issues*

'it appears clear that, when they feel it is demanded by the "public interest", the editors of The Sun and The News of the World remain ready to make payments to the police in exchange for information. As far as [the Select Committee is] aware this practice is illegal for both parties and there is no public interest defence that a jury could legitimately take into account.'[4]

[1] Cmnd. 5012 London, 1972, HMSO.
[2] Section 55 evolved from and expanded on the offences that were introduced into the 1984 Act by the Criminal Justice and Public Order Act 1994. The offences under the 1984 Act were extremely restrictive as they were closely tied to registration, which was the fundamental premise under the 1984 Act. Consequently, what is now the data controller, could only be prosecuted if the disclosure was contrary to the organisation's entry on the register. However, although the amendments under the 1998 Act made the offences more workable and effective, the Commissioner argued in 'What price privacy?' that in failing to introduce a custodial sentence, that they did not go far enough.
[3] Culture, Media and Sport Committee – Privacy and media intrusion, Volume 1, 23 May 2003, page 36, paragraph 93.
[4] Culture, Media and Sport Committee – Privacy and media intrusion, Volume 1, 23 May 2003, page 39, paragraph 92.

1.36 The report made a total of 34 recommendations many of which centred around amendments that should be made to the Code of Conduct which governs the press (including an explicit ban on payments to the police for information and intermediaries instructed to obtain confidential information from public and private bodies[1]) or recommended courses of action for the Press Complaints Committee or other supervisory bodies. However the report was unequivocal that 'it is for the Information Commissioner to make sure that all public and commercial entities are aware of their responsibilities under the Data Protection Act and put in place adequate training, guidance and other mechanisms to ensure those responsibilities are fulfilled'[2].

Furthermore, during the same period a number of government initiatives were seeking to increase both the number and size of public databases holding individuals' confidential information whilst improving the accessibility to the data for those that have legitimate purposes. The aim, whether related to the National Identity Register under the ID cards project, transformational government or the NHS Connecting for Health Business Plan,[3] is to create a seamless service of 'joined-up public services and joined-up computer systems'[4] across a number of departments. However, such initiatives will inevitably provide opportunities for the criminally minded to seek to profit in illegitimate ways. The success of all of these initiatives depends on the public's implicit trust in the databases' security and in the ability of the government to keep the information private. The illicit trade in personal data does nothing but undermine such trust, particularly when public entities, albeit often as the innocent victim of blagging offences, are involved.

It is against this background that 'What price privacy?' should be viewed.

[1] Culture, Media and Sport Committee – Privacy and media intrusion, Volume 1, 23 May 2003, page 28, paragraph 63.iii.
[2] Culture, Media and Sport Committee – Privacy and media intrusion, Volume 1, 23 May 2003, page 38, paragraph 97.
[3] NHS Connecting for Health Business Plan 2005–2006, www.connectingforhealth.nhs.uk/publications.

⁴ 'What price privacy?', foreword from the Information Commissioner page 3 referring to the Cabinet Office, 'Transformational Government – Enabled by Technology' Cm 6683, November 2005.

The Commissioner's findings and submissions

1.37 At the heart of the report was evidence that the Commissioner had obtained through two operations:

- In November 2002 the Devon and Cornwall Constabulary raided premises in Surrey in connection with suspected misuse of data from the Police National Computer (PNC). Documents listing vehicle registration numbers were discovered that were obtained via unlawful vehicle checks carried out by corrupt officials within the Driver and Vehicle Licensing Agency (DVLA). This information was supplied to the Information Commissioner by the police.
- As a result of the raid in November 2002 the Information Commissioner launched an investigation into data protection offences, Operation Motorman. The documents seized from the premises of a private detective contained data unlawfully obtained from BT accounts (including itemised telephone bills, ex-directory telephone numbers and details of 'Friends and Family' telephone numbers and frequently dialled numbers), the PNC and DVLA (including details of registered keepers of vehicles and driving licence details). Further documents (including invoices, ledgers and workbooks) found at the property detailed who had requested the information, how much they were charged and what information was provided to them.

Much of this data was being provided to journalists working for national newspapers and magazines. In fact the investigation unearthed records indicating that information had been supplied to 305 named journalists. Therefore, although the report acknowledged that the buyers of unlawfully obtained information include insurance companies and creditors, much of the focus of the report, the Commissioner's follow up report 'What price privacy now?'[1] and subsequent commentary, centred on the press and media's use of such data.

¹ 'What price privacy now? The first six months' progress in halting the unlawful trade in confidential personal information', 13 December 2006, HC 36.

1.38 The central recommendation in 'What price privacy?' was that a custodial sentence of up to six months for summary convictions and up to two years for persons convicted by indictment should be introduced. Other recommendations included that:

- The Press Complaints Committee should take a much stronger stance in the involvement of the press in the trade of personal information.
- The Association of British Investigators should unequivocally condemn any activity that breaches the Data Protection Act 1998, s 55 and expel any member found guilty of an offence under that section.

1.38 *Key themes and issues*

The Commissioner, with the intention of stifling the demand for confidential personal data, also issued a wider, more general warning to all businesses and individuals obtaining, supplying or buying personal information, that they 'should restrict themselves to information which they are confident has been lawfully obtained. Otherwise, it is only a matter of time before they find themselves charged with this offence. It is in line with the Information Commissioner's new regulatory Strategy to prosecute such "commercial" offenders more actively'[1].

[1] 'What price privacy?', page 30, paragraph 7.10.

Reaction to the report

1.39 The government's initial reaction to the report was very positive. The Department of Constitutional Affairs launched a public consultation[1] proposing the introduction of custodial sentences, which followed the Commissioner's recommendation to the letter. Later on, in February 2007, the Department of Constitutional Affairs (DCA) issued a press release which stated:

> 'For the first time courts will be able to jail people who trade in – or deliberately misuse – the personal data of others, in a move to crack down on the illegal trade in personal information announced by the Department of Constitutional Affairs today ... Lord Falconer, Secretary of State for Constitutional Affairs and Lord Chancellor, said: "We are determined to do all we can to stamp out this intrusive and illegal trade." '

Thus, it seemed that the introduction of custodial penalties was a racing certainty. Indeed, in the follow-up report 'What price privacy now?', which came six months after the initial report and which followed the DCA's consultation, the Commissioner was able to point to 'significant and encouraging' progress having being made.

[1] Department of Constitutional Affairs Consultation Paper, 'Increasing penalties for deliberate and wilful misuse of personal data', 24 July 2006.

The Criminal Justice and Immigration Act 2008 – privacy v the press

1.40 The government introduced the amending provisions in the Criminal Justice and Immigration Bill, but the amendments in the Act, which received Royal Assent in May 2008, looked very different to those that were contemplated by both the Information Commissioner and the Department of Constitutional Affairs, in that they only go as far as introducing a power for the Secretary of State to increase the penalties for section 55 offences in individual cases. To understand the extent to which the amending provisions were watered down, it is worth considering how they first appeared within the Criminal Justice and Immigration Bill, when introduced in the Commons in June 2007:

> '75 Imprisonment for unlawfully obtaining etc. personal data
> (1)   Section 60 of the Data Protection Act 1998 (c. 29) (penalties for offences under Act) is amended as follows.

(2) In subsection (2) (offences under Act punishable by fine) for "other than section 54A" substitute "other than sections 54A and 55".
(3) After subsection (3) insert—
"(3A) A person guilty of an offence under section 55 is liable—
- (a) on summary conviction, to imprisonment for a term not exceeding 12 months or to a fine not exceeding the statutory maximum or to both;
- (b) on conviction on indictment, to imprisonment for a term not exceeding two years or to a fine or to both.

(3B) In the application of subsection (3A)(a)—
- (a) in England and Wales, in relation to an offence committed before the commencement of section 282(1) of the Criminal Justice Act 2003 (increase in sentencing powers of magistrates' court from 6 to 12 months for certain offences triable either way),
- (b) in Scotland, until the commencement of section 45(1) of the Criminal Proceedings etc. (Reform) (Scotland) Act 2007 (increase in sentencing powers from 6 to 12 months), and
- (c) in Northern Ireland,

the reference to 12 months is to be read as a reference to 6 months."'

However, the Criminal Justice and Immigration Act 2008, s 77 provides:

'77 Power to alter penalty for unlawfully obtaining etc. personal data
(1) The Secretary of State may by order provide for a person who is guilty of an offence under section 55 of the Data Protection Act 1998 (c. 29) (unlawful obtaining etc. of personal data) to be liable—
- (a) on summary conviction, to imprisonment for a term not exceeding the specified period or to a fine not exceeding the statutory maximum or to both,
- (b) on conviction on indictment, to imprisonment for a term not exceeding the specified period or to a fine or to both.

(2) In subsection (1)(a) and (b) "specified period" means a period provided for by the order but the period must not exceed—
- (a) in the case of summary conviction, 12 months (or, in Northern Ireland, 6 months), and
- (b) in the case of conviction on indictment, two years.

(3) The Secretary of State must ensure that any specified period for England and Wales which, in the case of summary conviction, exceeds 6 months is to be read as a reference to 6 months so far as it relates to an offence committed before the commencement of section 282(1) of the Criminal Justice Act 2003 (c. 44) (increase in sentencing powers of magistrates' courts from 6 to 12 months for certain offences triable either way).

(4) Before making an order under this section, the Secretary of State must consult—
- (a) the Information Commissioner,
- (b) such media organisations as the Secretary of State considers appropriate, and
- (c) such other persons as the Secretary of State considers appropriate.

(5) An order under this section may, in particular, amend the Data Protection Act 1998.'

1.41 *Key themes and issues*

1.41 So, what caused government to pull back? The answer was the press and media lobby; in looking to tackle the illicit trade in personal information the Information Commissioner pitted himself against the press and media, which is undoubtedly an extremely powerful adversary, particularly within the corridors of Whitehall. With the benefit of hindsight, it was obvious that the Commissioner's proposals would meet with strong press and media resistance. The fact that 'What price privacy now?' named and shamed over 30 press and media companies could only act to harden the resolve of the opposition.

In the run-up to Royal Assent the battle between the Information Commissioner and the press and media took a most unexpected course, when the Commissioner issued a press release titled 'Don't water down penalties for blaggers stealing personal information, says Information Commissioner'[1], which implored government not to pull back from the proposed amendments:

> 'The Information Commissioner, Richard Thomas, is today issuing a stark call to politicians to resist attempts to water down new penalties for deliberate breaches of people's health, financial and other personal details. He is also publishing new guidance for organisations to help them in the event of an accidental data breach.
>
> The ICO has welcomed the government's commitment to deter the unlawful trade in procuring personal information. Clause 76 of the Criminal Justice and Immigration Bill, which is currently going through Parliament, will enable courts to impose a custodial sentence on those convicted of existing offences of buying or selling personal data. This is the government's first legislative opportunity after recent data losses to demonstrate its seriousness in safeguarding people's personal information.
>
> Richard Thomas, Information Commissioner, said: "I am pleased that government is now taking data protection, and the need to prevent security breaches, more seriously. But there have been powerful last-ditch efforts to get clause 76 removed from the Criminal Justice and Immigration Bill. There has been widespread support for the government's decision to strengthen the law and – if data protection is to be taken seriously – it is vital that the government and other parties should stand firm against any possible amendments. I am determined to stop the pernicious illegal market in personal information which our reports exposed.
>
> Losing half the country's child benefit records looks to have been a serious mistake, but at least it was accidental. If there is a change of heart on legislation aimed at deliberate security breaches, the government will find it hard to convince people that measures aimed at preventing data loss need to be taken seriously. I know there are concerns in some quarters of the media, but – with a powerful public interest defence – responsible journalists have nothing to fear." '

[1] Don't water down penalties for blaggers stealing personal information, says Information Commissioner', 1 April 2008: http://www.ico.gov.uk/upload/documents/pressreleases/2008/section_55.pdf.

1.42 Needless to say, the press and media lobby won the day and the amending provisions were watered down. However, the Information Commissioner was able to put a positive gloss on the outcome in a subsequent press release[1]:

'The prospect of unlimited fines has not deterred people from engaging in the illegal market in personal information. The government had recognised that a custodial sentence – included in its Criminal Justice and Immigration Bill – was needed to deter those who steal data.

The Information Commissioner is pleased that the government has apparently resisted substantial pressure to abandon clause 76 of the Criminal Justice and Immigration Bill. Although of course we would have preferred the clause to have remained unchanged, we understand that the Justice Secretary will be able to introduce prison sentences if illegal activity continues. Our aim has always been to deter and this will now be a powerful Sword of Damocles hanging over the heads of anyone involved in obtaining personal data. The Information Commissioner strongly values press freedom and freedom of speech, and hopes that all journalists will steer well clear of the sort of practices which – in the words of one newspaper – will "poison the well for all journalism".

Stealing people's personal details remains a serious criminal offence. The ICO will continue to educate and inform to help protect the public's personal information, working constructively with the key organisations whose databases are most at risk from the blaggers. We will be watching the blagging market closely, will prosecute any case supported by evidence and will highlight any future breaches of Section 55 of the Data Protection Act to Ministers and to Parliament.'

In addition to watering down the amendment, the Criminal Justice and Immigration Act 2008 also introduced a new defence into the Data Protection Act 1998, s 55 for the benefit of the press and media:

'**78 New defence for purposes of journalism and other special purposes**

In section 55(2) of the Data Protection Act 1998 (c. 29) (defences against offence of unlawfully obtaining etc. personal data) after "it," at the end of paragraph (c) insert—
"(ca)   that he acted—
   (i)   for the special purposes,
   (ii)   with a view to the publication by any person of any journalistic, literary or artistic material, and
   (iii)   in the reasonable belief that in the particular circumstances the obtaining, disclosing or procuring was justified as being in the public interest,".'

[1] 'ICO statement on Section 55 offences', 3 April 2008: http://www.ico.gov.uk/upload/documents/pressreleases/2008/section_55_statement.pdf.

1.43 The resistance of the press and media to the amendments may not be surprising, but when viewed in isolation the custodial sentence proposed by the Information Commissioner was not inflammatory. It was consistent with custodial sanctions for misuse of personal information that were already on the statute books, including the recently enacted Identity Cards Act 2006, which provides for similar sentences of up to two years' imprisonment if information from the National Identity Register is unlawfully disclosed. Furthermore, the amendments were not seeking to introduce new criminal offences nor to 'threaten legitimate and responsible journalism'[1], because the press already enjoyed a strong public interest defence under the 1998 Act. As the Information Commissioner stated in his conclusion to 'What price privacy now?', 'Freedom of speech is not freedom to break the law by bribery or deception where there is no public interest justification'[2]. However despite this, the press and media organisations' argument that custodial sentences would have a 'chilling effect' on investigative journalism won over and the balance was tipped away from the individual's rights of privacy towards freedom of expression and of the press.

The reaction of the legislature, although not wholly surprising, is contrary to the judiciary's stance on encroachment of the press onto the private rights of the individual. The legislature's retreat in the face of the media's opposition must be considered against the European and the English courts' moves to expand the sphere of privacy into the public arena, for example by holding that photographs taken in public places may still be part of the private interest of the individual (see, for example *Campbell v Mirror Group Newspapers Ltd*[3] and *Von Hannover v Germany*[4] and subsequent cases).

[1] Information Commissioner's Office Briefing to the House of Lords Report Stage – Illegal trade in personal data, Clause 76 and proposed New Clauses – 23 April 2008.
[2] 'What price privacy now?', page 27.
[3] [2004] UKHL 22, [2004] 2 AC 457, [2004] 2 All ER 995.
[4] (2004) 16 BHRC 545, [2004] EMLR 379.

'What price privacy?' – Was it all worth it?

1.44 In responding to 'What price privacy?', the World Association of Private Investigators (WAPI), stated that although its governing council is 'committed to compliance with all law and regulation' it is concerned that the Information Commissioner is 'targeting the investigation sector while crime through fraud and identity theft continues to soar. In that context WAPI has called on the Information Commissioner to press Parliament for lawful access to data in appropriate situations instead of targeting investigators'[1].

This charge may not be without foundation. The Information Commissioner has repeatedly maintained that there is a 'pernicious and extensive trade in personal data' yet there is very little evidence within the Commissioner's annual reports to Parliament to support this statement; these reports indicate that only a handful of prosecutions are brought under the Data Protection Act 1998, s 55 each year. Although, it cannot be denied that a custodial sentence would act as a greater deterrent than the penalties which are currently handed down, the Commissioner's zeal in focusing his attention and resources on this issue is questionable. Another perspective is that the Commissioner has bigger fish to fry, as HMRC and other high-profile data losses have proved, and that he has therefore failed to focus on the most significant threats.

While these may be fair criticisms, there is an alternative view. As indicated earlier there is considerably more within the threat landscape than e-crime and cyber crime. The 'human element' within data security breaches, whether this be blagging, bribes or mere negligence, is just as important to understand and to tackle. Indeed, the HMRC data loss was just as much about human failure as anything else. In this sense it can be said that 'What price privacy?' has drawn attention to a critical risk area. The fact that the Commissioner has not mounted many prosecutions might be attributable more to resource constraints than anything else.

Furthermore, 'What price privacy?' should be viewed in its correct chronological context. The report was submitted to Parliament prior to the loss of the HMRC disks and while there were many indicators to render such a loss foreseeable, the fact remains that the Information Commissioner had to deal with the threats as he understood them to be at the time. In May 2006 the Information Commissioner was in possession of compelling evidence of the illegal trade in personal data and it was his statutory duty to tackle it. In this sense the Commissioner's focus on blagging and similar ills was perfectly understandable.

[1] 'What price privacy now?', page 18.

LAW REFORM – COMPLETING THE POST-HMRC AGENDA

1.45 In para 1.1 of this chapter it was observed that the consequences of the loss of the HMRC data disks have been profound; these include a series of very important amendments to the Data Protection Act 1998. These amendments, which are summarised in para 1.24 of this chapter, are:

- The monetary penalties regime introduced by the Criminal Justice and Immigration Act 2008. This is discussed in more detail in Chapter 6.
- The custodial penalties regime, provision for which was also introduced by the Criminal Justice and Immigration Act 2008. The amendments are set out in para 1.40 of this chapter.
- The compulsory inspection regime, which is contained in the Coroners and Justice Bill. Again, this is discussed in more detail in Chapter 6.

While it is only fair to say that post-HMRC the government was quick to embrace law reform, it is also true that the initial momentum has not been maintained. At the date of publication of this book 18 months have passed since the Criminal Justice and Immigration Act 2008 received Royal Assent and 12 months since the Coroners and Justice Bill was announced in the Queen's Speech; the monetary penalties and custodial penalties regimes have not been brought into effect and the Coroners and Justice Bill is just that, a Bill, not an Act.

Even when the government's law reform agenda is completed the legal framework for data security (and for data protection generally) will look very different from the one that the Information Commissioner's Office has been arguing for since 2006. In other words there will be a substantial regulatory deficit between the regime that the ICO considers is required and the one that the government will allow.

Of course, we cannot ignore the fact that there will be a General Election very soon, with the possibility of a Conservative government. So, how will the legal framework look under a Conservative government? Will the Conservatives complete the process of law reform commenced by the government in the

1.45 *Key themes and issues*

aftermath of HMRC? How much of the Information Commissioner's case for law reform will the Conservatives accept?

A very good indication of the Conservatives' intentions was provided by Baroness Neville-Jones, the Shadow Security Minister, in a speech to the 'Information Assurance for the Public Sector' Conference on 16 June 2009[1]:

> 'We should take the opportunity of overhauling law and practice in the area of data collection actually to strengthen the office of Information Commissioner. The outgoing holder of the office, Richard Thomas, has said, and I quote, that his "powers, sanctions and resources – fixed in another era – are now wholly inadequate. The ICO has made clear for some time that a stronger approach is required to help prevent unacceptable information handling". He asserts that "at last" the Commissioner will be able to impose substantial penalties for deliberate or reckless breaches and will have new powers to undertake inspections and audits of data controllers. And these powers have had to be wrenched out of a reluctant Executive as the result of major, embarrassing and damaging losses of sensitive personal information. In Richard Thomas's words "it is unfortunate that it has taken calamity to convince the government that we need stronger powers, resources and sanctions". This calamity was, of course, the loss of 25 million child benefit records by HMRC in 2007. There is a related point here, which is that the Office must be staffed adequately to meet current and future roles. Richard Thomas has said in terms that the ICO does not have the financial or staff resources to complete all its work. This must be remedied.'

If these words leave any doubt about the Conservatives' intentions, Baroness Neville-Jones' concluding remarks will remove them:

> 'It leads to the unavoidable conclusion that that the Information Commissioner should emerge as one of the important offices of state in the twenty first century.'

[1] http://www.conservatives.com/News/Speeches/2009/06/Pauline_Nevilles-Jones_Is_information_about_me_really_mine.aspx.

1.46 The Conservatives' plans were fleshed out in a report titled 'Reversing the Rise of the Surveillance State – 11 Measures to Protect Personal Privacy and Hold Government to Account'[1], launched on 21 September 2009 by Dominic Grieve QC, Shadow Justice Secretary, and Eleanor Laing, Shadow Justice Minister. Among other things, the report confirms the Conservatives' intentions to scrap the ID Card database and ContactPoint (the database built under powers in the Children Act 2004), but as far as data security and regulation and enforcement are concerned, the key provisions are:

- The Information Commissioner's successors will be appointed by Parliament, not the Ministry of Justice, thereby increasing the independence of the Commissioner.
- The Commissioner's audit powers will be strengthened.
- Privacy Impact Assessments will be made compulsory for all new legislation and government measures involving data collection and data sharing.
- Each government department will have to nominate a Minister and senior civil servant as being responsible for data security.

- The Commissioner will be tasked to develop best practice standards, following consultation with the private sector. This will include the creation of a kite mark system for best practice.

Putting Parliament in charge of the appointment of the Information Commissioner, rather than government, is certainly a positive move as far as independence is concerned (and is consistent with themes that have developed in the wake of the MPs' expenses scandal), albeit there was never any sense that the last Commissioner, Richard Thomas, lacked independence or felt compromised by his Office.

As regards the Conservatives' plans for audits, the key announcement was that 'the Information Commissioner will be required to audit government departments and other public bodies, on a rotating annual basis, and granted the powers required to discharge these functions. These will include ad hoc powers of inspection and financial penalties for the deliberate, reckless or grossly negligent management of data'. The report then goes on to reference the Conservatives' position on the Coroners and Justice Bill.

There is a subtle, but important, difference between the Conservatives' position and the government's on audits and inspections. Under the Coroners and Justice Bill as presently formulated the Information Commissioner will be given the power to carry out inspections of government departments, not a duty to do so; the Conservatives are saying that the Commissioner shall be obliged to carry out audits. This should improve the government's performance, but, of course, the Commissioner will need additional resources. Furthermore, if the phrase 'ad hoc' is to be taken to mean that 'unannounced' audits are on the cards, that will render the Conservatives' plans more in line with the Commissioner's proposals for inspections, again representing a considerable improvement on the scheme within the Coroners and Justice Bill. However, it is not clear that the Conservatives intend to go that far.

The Conservatives also commit themselves to bringing the monetary penalty regime established by the Criminal Justice and Immigration Act 2008 into effect. It may be possible to argue that this commitment represents an advance on the government's position, in the sense that the strength of the government's commitment is questionable in light of the delay that has passed since the Criminal Justice and Immigration Act 2008 achieved Royal Assent, but on the key point, that monetary penalties are required within an appropriate scheme of regulation, the government and the opposition are aligned on the point of principle.

[1] http://www.conservatives.com/News/News_stories/2009/09/Reversing_the_rise_of_the_surveillance_state.aspx.

1.47 The Conservatives' plans for Privacy Impact Assessments are:

'Require Privacy Impact Assessments of any proposals for new legislation or other measures that involve data collection or sharing at the earliest opportunity. Require government to consult the Information Commissioner on the PIA and publish his findings.'

1.47 *Key themes and issues*

This is certainly an advance over the government's position, which is currently contained in the Data Handling Review and HMG Security Policy Framework. It will undoubtedly act to strengthen the Information Commissioner's power and influence, putting him in a critical position during the legislative process.

The Conservatives' plans for best practice are:

> 'We would promote a relationship of dialogue, as well as accountability, between government departments and the Information Commissioner. The Information Commissioner would be tasked with issuing best practice guidance to departments on a range of issues, including data minimisation, data encryption, the length of time appropriate for data retention and requirements for ensuring data security in public sector contractual arrangements with third parties.'

This plan will have profound consequences; it acts to increase the Information Commissioner's power at the expense of Parliament and government. However, the Conservatives, if they form the next government, will have to be careful in the formulation of the new regime. Taking the encryption issue as an example, there are ambiguities in the Commissioner's present strategy. Likewise in the Commissioner's approach to breach notification, which may have the unintended consequence of encouraging data controllers to bury bad news. The Commissioner's enforcement strategies will also require review.

As regards the consultation with the private sector, the report says:

> 'As part of an ongoing review, we will engage in consultation with the private sector on further measures that are necessary and appropriate for data security. In particular, a Conservative government would task the Information Commissioner to consult with business on the viability of establishing an industry-wide data security kite mark, which would be voluntary but serve as a mark of best practice.'

The ideas behind the consultation process are sound and it would certainly help to improve the development of practice if the Commissioner was obliged to draw upon the skills of sector experts. As regards kite marks, there is already a kite mark scheme for information security management systems, within ISO 27001, but this has only a narrow focus; more work needs to be done in the field of best practice kite marks. Indeed, as discussed in Chapter 8, there is already a clear case for an accreditation scheme for Privacy Enhancing Technologies (PETs); at the moment the only kite mark scheme for technologies is provided by the CESG, for the public sector only; the private sector will benefit tremendously from kite marking for PETs.

1.48 If the Conservatives' plans are measured against Baroness Neville-Jones' ambition to see the ICO emerge as one of the important offices of State, then it would be fair to conclude that they set some of the foundations for achieving this. If properly thought through they should result in improvements in practices for data security in government and the public sector, in a benign and helpful way. However, the Conservatives' plans are still embryonic. In particular, they may wish to focus some thought on the question 'who regulates the regulators?', because while the ICO has done a lot of very good work over the past three years, its performance has not been perfect, or flawless. A critical task for the Conservatives will be to discover, understand and correct the fault lines in regulation, wherever they exist.

It is also worth spending some time on the issues that have not been covered in the Conservatives' proposals. They do not address the Commissioner's call for a new criminal offence of serious non-compliance with the data protection principles; this was one of the landmark proposals to government made by the Commissioner in the wake of HMRC. They do not address the issue of breach notification; a mature system for breach notification, brought in through legislation, not regulatory guidance, is a fundamental component of a mature plan for improving practices. They do not reveal the Conservatives' full thinking on improving performance in the private sector.

On this final point, of course it must be remembered that first and foremost the Conservatives' plans are about data handling in government, but they did touch upon the private sector:

> 'The focus of this report has remained data security in the public sector, in light of the growing concerns about the rise of a surveillance state. The relationship between the individual and the private sector is different. Data is more often shared on a voluntary – rather than coercive – basis and business is generally better at safeguarding personal data. However, there is increasing concern in this area, following high profile data breaches. In January 2009, it emerged that the online recruitment company, Monster, had been attacked by hackers who accessed a range of confidential information.
>
> In general, at least for commercial reputational reasons, companies have strong incentives to manage personal data securely and responsibly. However, the Data Protection Act is long and unwieldy. The Act informs organisations of their obligations, but offers little by way of guidance on how to go about securing this data. This presents a particular burden for smaller businesses.
>
> As part of an ongoing review, we will engage in consultation with the private sector on further measures that are necessary and appropriate for data security. In particular, a Conservative government would task the Information Commissioner to consult with business on the viability of establishing an industry-wide data security kite mark, which would be voluntary but serve as a mark of best practice.'

One of the central points within this extract is that business is generally better at safeguarding personal data. The empirical evidence that the private sector is better at safeguarding personal data is not available, but the US experience following the introduction of breach notification does not support the conclusion that has been drawn. The reference to the Monster data loss is well placed, but it is only the tip of a very big iceberg; there is much, freely available evidence of bad practice in the private sector being very widespread. Indeed, the Information Commissioner's enforcement activities imply that the private sector is just as bad as the public sector. The FSA's enforcement actions support this point, albeit it is recognised that the FSA has no vires to act in the public sector. The Conservatives are correct to say that brand and reputational effects should act to improve performance in the private sector, but, sadly, the reality seems to be very different. The introduction of breach notification

1.48 *Key themes and issues*

legislation should change the impression that the private sector is a better custodian of personal data than the public sector, but widespread opposition to such legislation for the private sector can be anticipated.

In conclusion, the Conservatives' proposals should result in improvements in data handling in government. If implemented in full they will result in a considerable enhancement of the Information Commissioner's powers.

Chapter 2

CONFIDENTIALITY, PRIVACY AND TECHNOLOGY

2.1 In the previous chapter it was mentioned that data security law is contained in a hotchpotch of primary resources. This chapter, along with Chapters 3 and 4, attempts to identify some of the key resources and why they may be relevant. This chapter is about confidentiality, privacy and technology. Chapter 3 is about companies, corporate governance and financial services. Chapter 4 is about the public sector. The laws discussed here apply in both the public and private sectors.

The categories of resources that need to be considered include the following:

- Primary and subordinate legislation, like the Data Protection Act 1998 and the Telecommunications (Lawful Business Practice) (Interception of Communications) Regulations 2000, SI 2000/2699. Much of the law has European origins.
- Case law. While there is a very healthy body of case law in the field of confidentiality and privacy, case law about the Data Protection Act 1998 is thin on the ground.
- Reports of Parliamentary inquiries in related areas. Essential reading includes the reports into the Surveillance Society, Personal Internet Security and Protection of Personal Data.
- The official reports that have been commissioned into security breaches, data handling and information assurance. Essential reading includes the Poynter and IPCC inquiries into HMRC, the Burton report, the Thomas-Walport report, the Data Handling Review and the Coleman report.
- Industry and professional standards for best practice, such as ISO 27000 series, PCI DSS and COBIT[1].
- Reports of regulatory proceedings. The Information Commissioner in particular has been prolific in his enforcement activities for data security in recent years, which provides a substantial body of authority on regulatory trends and attitudes.
- Official guidance, published by the regulators, government departments and public bodies. This will include materials published by the Article 29 Working Party, the EU expert group for data protection.
- Reports into threats and vulnerabilities. Some of the larger consultancy companies and IT companies publish regular surveys and reviews about

2.1 Confidentiality, privacy and technology

>discovered and emerging threats. Companies like KPMG, RSA, The Security Division of EMC, and Symantec are excellent sources of information about threats and vulnerabilities. Professional bodies such as Information Assurance Advisory Council (IAAC), Information Security Forum (ISF), Information Systems Audit and Controls Association (ISACA), Information Systems Security Association (ISSA), Institute of Information Security Professionals (ISSP), Cyber Security Knowledge Transfer Network (KTN), Microsoft CISO Council and Jericho Forum also make very valuable contributions to knowledge and the development of best practice.

- Contributions from practitioners and academics.

Collectively these resources enable a holistic view of the state of data security law and the measures that need to be adopted for the management of data security. Some sources provide very detailed insight, but the level at which a particular practitioner needs to understand any particular resources depends on their position. Lawyers, for example, will be expected to have a broad understanding of all of the source material. Security professionals and IT professionals will have more specialised knowledge of the technical issues. Of course, practitioners' visions need to extend beyond the silos of their own areas of specialism and expertise, but, unfortunately, this is too often not the case, a failing that contributes to organisational weaknesses, which provides a fertile environment for security breaches and data loss.

Wherever possible, extracts from primary resources are supplied, for easy reference if required, together with supporting URLs for freely available online resources.

[1] See http://www.isaca.org/Template.cfm?Section=COBIT6&Template=/TaggedPage/TaggedPageDisplay.cfm&TPLID=55&ContentID=7981.

WHAT ARE 'DATA'?

2.2 The focus of this book is data security law. For these purposes data include digital information processed by, or intended to be processed by computers, computer-controller equipment and electronic communications systems. The Data Protection Directive[1] and the Data Protection Act 1998 also share the idea that data includes information that is processed by computers etc, but they prefer to focus their attentions on the processing of personal data, which can encompass information held in paper documents and non-electronic/digital form. Thus, data security law will also extend to paperwork and similar.

The reach of data security law will also extend to information held in machines, or intended to be read by machines, that operate mechanically, without the need for computers. For example, old microfiche records may be said to contain data, despite the fact that they may never come into contact with computers or the digital environment; if those data are confidential, whether as private information or otherwise, an obligation to keep them safe will arise, irrespective of the application of the Data Protection Act 1998. Another example would be old-fashioned photographic film containing confidential images.

Data security law and practice focuses on much more than data and their processing systems however. The nature of the wider environment within which data are held is a critical consideration, extending the focus of law and practice to issues such as the physical security of the premises within which computers are located, or the systems for the physical transportation of processing equipment and storage media. The identity and character of the people using and accessing data are also key considerations, bringing into play issues concerning the recruitment, employment and disengagement of workers and contractors. Thus, it can be said that the focus of data security law and practice is broad and deep. It is certainly greater than the focus of the Data Protection Act 1998, where for many practitioners the law starts and ends.

1   Directive 95/46/EC.

CONFIDENTIALITY, PRIVACY AND TECHNOLOGY

Confidentiality

2.3 A duty of confidence can arise in contract or in equity. If a contract contains an express or implied confidentiality clause it will be enforceable by the party to whom the duty of confidence is owed, on the basis of the terms agreed, subject to any limitations set by the courts.

A duty of confidence will arise in equity if:

- The information has the necessary quality of confidence.
- The information is disclosed in circumstances that give rise to a duty of confidence.
- There is actual or anticipated misuse of the information by the person owing the duty. This might take the form of disclosure of the information to a third party without the consent or permission of the person or entity to whom that duty is owed[1], or through actual misuse of the information by the person owing the duty.

The underlying reason why the courts enforce duties of confidence is that it would be unconscionable for the person under a duty to misuse information that has been imparted in confidence. For this reason the Freedom of Information Act 2000 provides an absolute exemption from the Act's 'general right of access'[2] for information provided in confidence[3], if that disclosure would be actionable. Similarly, the subject access regime in the Data Protection Act 1998 contains exceptions for confidential information[4].

If a security breach affects confidential information, whether resulting from negligence, recklessness or a deliberate attack, it might be possible for the beneficiary of the duty to bring an action for any resulting loss. Thus, the law of confidence and any associated issues arising under the law of negligence should always be considered by the data controller during the development of

2.3 Confidentiality, privacy and technology

its systems for data security and in the aftermath of a security breach. Consequently, the controller should take steps to identify all confidential information within its custody, power or control. The controller that carries out this exercise soon discovers that personal data (within the meaning of the Data Protection Act 1998) forms only a part of the confidential information within its possession.

1 See *Coco v AN Clark (Engineers) Ltd* [1968] FSR 415, [1969] RPC 41. The judgment of Megarry J is considered to be the classic statement of the law of confidence.
2 Freedom of Information Act 2000, s 1.
3 Freedom of Information Act 2000, s 41.
4 Data Protection Act 1998, s 7(6)(a).

Parameters of the duty of confidence

2.4 The following are key parameters of the law of confidence:

1 The duty of confidence is not an absolute duty. Where the public interest favours the disclosure of confidential information to a third party such disclosure will not be actionable by the beneficiary of the duty[1]. This explains why the police, for example, are able to seize confidential materials during the course of criminal investigations. Similarly, the Data Protection Act 1998, s 55, as amended by the Criminal Justice and Immigration Act 2008, contains a public interest defence to the non-consensual obtaining, disclosure or sale of personal information. A recent example of the public interest overcoming confidentiality is provided by the High Court decision confirming the decisions of the Information Commissioner and the Information Tribunal ordering the disclosure of information about MPs' expenses claims[2].
2 Leaving aside cases where the duty of confidence arises through express contractual terms, confidentiality will not attach to petty, trivial or useless information[3]. In the Spycatcher case Lord Goff said that 'the second limiting principle is that the duty of confidence applies neither to useless information, nor to trivia'.
3 The general rule is that confidentiality will not attach to information that is in the public domain. Again, in the Spycatcher case Lord Goff said that 'in particular, once it has entered what is usually called the public domain (which means no more than that the information in question is so generally accessible that, in all the circumstances, it cannot be regarded as confidential) then, as a general rule, the principle of confidentiality can have no application to it'. However, where the duty of confidence arises under express contractual terms, it can survive past the point when the information itself has ceased to be confidential[4].
4 Information does not have to be completely secret for it to be confidential[5]. Many people may have knowledge of the information without affecting its confidential status.
5 An action for breach of confidence can only be brought if there is actual or potential misuse of the information.

Confidentiality, privacy and technology **2.6**

1 See, for example *Gartside v Outram* (1856) 26 LJ Ch 113 for an account of the iniquity rule. See also *R (on the application of Stone) v South East Coast Strategic Health Authority* [2006] EWHC 1668 (Admin) and *Lion Laboratories v Evans* [1985] QB 526, [1984] 2 All ER 417, which concern the prevention of harm to the public.
2 See *Corporate Officer of the House of Commons v Information Comr* [2008] EWHC 1084 (Admin), [2009] 3 All ER 403. In the course of the subsequent MPs' expenses scandal the police decided that they would not investigate the leak of expenses information to The Telegraph newspaper, as the leak was considered to be in the public interest. See, for example 'MPs' expenses: police will not investigate leaks to media', The Guardian, 19 May 2009: http://www.guardian.co.uk/global/2009/may/19/expenses-leak-police.
3 Where there are express contractual terms imposing a duty of confidence even useless, petty or trivial information can be protected from misuse.
4 See, for example *Attorney-General v Barker* [1990] 3 All ER 257 and *Attorney-General v Blake (Jonathan Cape Ltd third party)* [2001] 1 AC 268, [2000] 4 All ER 385.
5 See, for example *HRH Prince of Wales v Associated Newspapers Ltd* [2006] EWCA 1776, *Schering Chemicals Ltd v Falkman Ltd* [1982] QB 1, [1981] 2 All ER 321, *Creation Records Ltd v News Group Newspapers* [1997] EMLR 444 and *Franchi v Franchi* [1967] RPC 149.

Information that has the necessary quality of confidence

2.5 Information that may be considered to have the necessary quality of confidence includes official secrets[1] (in the sense of government information), private information[2] (including personal data) and trade secrets[3] (in the sense of commercial information).

1 See, for example *Attorney-General v Observer Ltd (No 2)* [1990] 1 AC 109, [1988] 3 All ER 545 (the 'Spycatcher' case). See also *Attorney-General v Blake (Jonathan Cape Ltd third party)* [2001] 1 AC 268, [2000] 4 All ER 385.
2 See, for example *Argyll (Duchess of) v Duke of Argyll* [1967] Ch 302, [1965] 1 All ER 611, a case that was concerned with marital relationships. For a more recent example, see *Mosley v News Group Newspapers Ltd* [2008] EWHC 1777 (QB), which concerned extra-marital sexual relationships.
3 See, for example *Saltman Engineering Co Ltd v Campbell Engineering Co Ltd* [1963] 3 All ER 413n, 65 RPC 203, or *Seager v Copydex Ltd* [1967] 2 All ER 415, [1967] 1 WLR 923, or *Fraser v Evans* [1969] 1 QB 349, [1969] 1 All ER 8. For a more recent example, see *Douglas v Hello! Ltd* [2005] EWCA Civ 595, [2006] QB 125.

How the duty of confidence arises

2.6 As mentioned above, a duty of confidence can arise in contract or in equity. In the latter situation the circumstances as a whole must be considered in order to determine whether a duty arises. Typically, a duty of confidentiality can arise in:

- Professional relationships, such as between lawyer and client, or doctor and patient.
- Partnership arrangements.
- Employer-employee relationships.
- Principal-agent relationships.
- Trustee-beneficiary relationships.
- Company-director relationships.
- Marital relationships, sexual relationships and other close personal relationships.

2.6 Confidentiality, privacy and technology

This list is merely illustrative, but the examples given are all connected by the fact that a reasonable person would regard them as involving a duty of confidence[1].

A duty of confidence can also arise:

- Where information with the necessary quality of confidence is obtained or received by a public authority acting pursuant to a statutory duty or power[2].
- Where such information is obtained or received by improper or surreptitious means[3].
- Where such information is obtained or received by mistake[4].

In all of these situations the recipient of the confidential information must have notice of the fact that the information is confidential, although this can include constructive knowledge, such as arises when the recipient deliberately turns a blind eye to the issue of confidentiality. If the recipient obtains the information through surreptitious means, it will be very difficult, if not impossible, for them to assert that they did not have notice.

[1] See, for example *Dunford and Elliott Ltd v Johnson and Firth Brown Ltd* [1978] FSR 143.
[2] See, for example the Data Protection Act 1998, s 59, which imposes a duty of confidence on the Information Commissioner in respect of personal information and business information received during the performance of his duties. See also the Enterprise Act 2002, s 237. See also the Identity Cards Act 2006, s 27. See also *IRC v National Federation of Self-Employed and Small Businesses Ltd* [1982] AC 617, [1981] 2 All ER 93.
[3] See *Ashburton (Lord) v Pape* [1913] 2 Ch 469 (defendant surreptitiously obtained copies of letters passing between plaintiff and his solicitor). See also *Francome v Mirror Group Newspapers Ltd* [1984] 2 All ER 408, [1984] 1 WLR 892 (information obtained through interception of telecommunications), or *Franklin v Giddins* [1978] Qd R 72 (trespasser stealing budwood cuttings for a new strain of nectarine), or *Robb v Green* [1985] 2 QB 315 (employee copies employer's customer list), or *Shelley Films Ltd v Rex Features Ltd* [1994] EMLR 134 (surreptitious photographs of costume design), or *Creation Records Ltd v News Group Newspapers* [1997] EMLR 444 (photographs of a photo shoot for album cover), or *Douglas v Hello! Ltd* [2005] EWCA Civ 595, [2006] QB 125 (surreptitious photographs taken at a celebrity wedding).
[4] See, for example *English and American Insurance Co Ltd v Herbert Smith and Co* [1988] FSR 232 (barrister instructed by the plaintiff mistakenly returning their papers to the defendant's solicitors).

THE DUTY AND OVERCOMING ENCRYPTION

2.7 An interesting question is whether the presence of encryption renders the underlying information confidential. As a starting point it would seem that if a person goes to the lengths of encrypting information the information must have a quality about it that is deserving of protection. However, there is no authority in law that holds that the mere presence of encryption renders the underlying information confidential. In the case of *Mars UK Ltd v Teknowledge Ltd*[1], which concerned a coin discriminator mechanism for the sorting of coins in coin operated machines, the defendant reverse engineered the mechanism, a process that required the decryption of encrypted program code. One of the questions before the court was whether the presence of encryption put the defendant on notice that the encrypted information was confidential. As Jacob J put it, the plaintiff's 'proposition [was] this:'

'that if the reverse engineer, working on an article which he has come by lawfully, discovers that the maker put in some form of encryption, then he is put on notice that the maker regards what is encrypted is confidential. So the encrypted information is to be regarded in law as a trade secret and treated as such. It is unlawful, being a breach of confidence, for anyone, without lawful excuse, to de-cipher the code.'

Jacob J's analysis and holding was as follows:

'I turn to examine whether the authorities support Mars' contentions. I begin with the well-known formulation of the case of action in breach of confidence by Megarry J. in Coco v. A.N. Clark (Engineers) Ltd [1969] R.P.C. 41 at 47.

First, the information itself, in the words of Lord Greene MR in the Saltman case on p.215, must "have the necessary quality of confidence about it." Secondly, that information must have been imparted in circumstances importing an obligation of confidence. Thirdly there must be an unauthorised use of that information to the detriment of the party communicating it.

This formulation has received high approval, e.g. through Lord Griffiths in Spycatcher (AG v. Guardian Newspapers Ltd (No. 2)) [1990] 1 A.C. 109 at 168.

So, starting with the first requirement, does the encrypted information in the Cashflow, have the "necessary quality of confidence"? I think the answer is clearly "no". The Cashflow is on the market. Anyone can buy it. And anyone with the skills to de-encrypt has access to the information. The fact that only a few have those skills is, as it seems to me, neither here nor there. Anyone can acquire the skills and anyway, a buyer is free to go to a man who has them. Mars suggest that the owner, although he owns the machine, does not own the information within it. That is too glib. What the owner has is the full right of ownership. With that goes an entitlement "to dismantle the machine to find out how it works and tell anyone he pleases" (a right recognised by Morritt J. in Alfa Laval Cheese Systems Ltd v. Wincanton Engineering Ltd [1990] F.S.R. 583).

In so holding, I am of course not saying that were anyone to steal the information direct from Mars, thus saving themselves reverse engineering and de-encryption, would not be liable for breach of confidence. The un-encrypted information remains confidential in the sense that in that form it has never been published. It is the sort of information which, if illegitimately taken, can give rise to the "springboard" (Roxburgh J.'s graphic adjectival noun in Terrapin Ltd v. Builders Supply Co. (Hayes) Ltd [1960] R.P.C. 128) type of the action for breach of confidence. The law of confidence merely prevents a party from taking a leap forwards by by-passing "special labours in respect of the product in order to discover its secret" (Francis Gurry, Breach of Confidence (1984)).

I turn to the second requirement, that of communication in circumstances importing an obligation of confidence. Mars say that such circumstances are to be inferred from the fact that the student of the Cashflow finds encryption. They say the fact of encryption is equivalent to a notice saying "confidential—you may not de-encrypt". And they go on to say that if such an express notice were given, the examiner of the machine would come under a duty of confidence. I think they are wrong on both counts. As pure matter of common sense I cannot see why the mere fact of encryption makes that which is encrypted confidential or why anyone who de-encrypts something in code, should necessarily be taken to be receiving information in confidence. He will

2.7 Confidentiality, privacy and technology

appreciate that the source of the information did not want him to have access, but that is all. He has no other relationship with that source. Nor do the circumstances have an analogy with eavesdropping or secret long-lens photography (see Laws J. in Hellewell v. Chief Constable of Derbyshire [1995] 1 W.L.R. 804 at 807) or telephone tapping. In that sort of case the snooper not only knows he is prying into other people's business but he has used some surreptitious means to do so. There is nothing surreptitious in taking a thing apart to find out how it is made.

In so holding I am applying the "reasonable man" test suggested by Megarry J. in Coco at page 48:

"It seems to me that if the circumstances are such that any reasonable man standing in the shoes of the recipient of the information would have realised that upon reasonable grounds the information was being given to him in confidence, then that should suffice to impose upon him the equitable obligation of confidence."

Megarry J. was contemplating a case of an actual transfer of information from one man to another: this case is just about finding out information from a product on the market. I do not think doing that would be regarded as anything other than fair game for competitors.

I should mention here part of the speech of Lord Goff in Spycatcher (Attorney General v. Guardian Newspapers [1990] 1 A.C. 109 at 281) for it was heavily relied upon by Mars:

"I start with the broad general principle (which I do not intend in any way to be definitive) that a duty of confidence arises when confidential information comes to the knowledge of a person (the confidant) in circumstances where he has notice, or is held to have agreed, that the information is confidential, with the effect that it would be just in all the circumstances that he should be precluded from disclosing the information to others. I have used the word "notice" advisedly, in order to avoid the (here unnecessary) question of the extent to which actual knowledge is necessary; though I of course understand knowledge to include circumstances where the confidant has deliberately closed his eyes to the obvious. The existence of this broad principle reflects the fact that there is such a public interest in the maintenance of confidences, that the law will provide remedies for their protection."

I realise that, in the vast majority of cases, in particular those concerned with trade secrets, the duty of confidence will arise from a transaction or relationship between the parties—often a contract. in which event the duty may arise by reason of either an express or an implied term of that contract. It is in such cases as these that the expressions "confider" and "confidant" are perhaps most aptly employed.... But it is well settled that a duty of confidence may arise in equity independently of such cases; and I have expressed the circumstances in which the duty arises in broad terms, not merely to embrace those cases where a third party receives information from a person who is under a duty of confidence in respect of it, knowing that it has been disclosed by that person to him in breach of his duty of confidence, but also to include certain situations, beloved of law teachers—where an obviously confidential document is wafted by an electric fan out of a window into a crowded street, or where an obviously confidential document, such as a private diary, is dropped in a public place, and is then picked up by a passer-by.

Mars rely upon Lord Goffs reference to an "obviously confidential document" fortuitously coming into the hands of a non-intended recipient. English and American Insurance Co. Ltd v. Herbert Smith [1988] F.S.R. 232 is an actual example of that. But this case is in no way comparable. The recipient (the customer) is an intended recipient of the article containing the information.... There is nothing obviously confidential about the machine he gets. There is no marking "confidential" and indeed there is not even any indication of encryption. By the time one gets to find out about the encryption it is, in my judgment, far too late to impose a duty of confidence. I do not think even an express statement would work to override the buyer's entitlement to find out how his machine worked.

Mars relied upon three other cases, namely Francome v. Mirror Group Newspapers Ltd [1984] 1 W.L.R. 892; Creation Records Ltd v. News Group Newspapers Ltd [1997] E.M.L.R. 444 and Shelley Films Ltd v. Rex Features Ltd [1994] E.M.L.R. 134. None of them come near to assisting their case. Francome was a case of eavesdropping by illegal phone tapping. No-one suggested that what was said in private was other than confidential or that the recipients of the information in the illegal phonetaps did not know this. The defence, such as it was, was iniquity. Creation was a case where, on the evidence, a photographer had got himself to a place where he should not have been (and knew he should not have been). The owner of a Cashflow is in no way in an analogous position. Shelley was much the same.

In the result I unhesitatingly reject Mars' claim based on breach of confidence.'

There seems to be little reason to disagree with the proposition that the mere presence of encryption does not render the underlying information confidential. After all, it is clear from the authorities that equity does not extend the obligation of confidence to trivia. However, a person who overcomes encryption without the permission of the controller who applied it in the first place will always face difficulties explaining their position; equity works on the conscience and the conscience must be taken to know that one of the reasons why a controller applies encryption to information is to keep it safe from unauthorised access and misuse. In other words, the presence of encryption can be regarded as being a clear indicator of both the nature of the underlying information and the mindset of the data controller[2]. As a result, a person who overcomes encryption must be said to be running a risk of breaching confidence, albeit it is true to observe, as Jacob J alluded to, that it is impossible to be sure of the encrypted information's true character until the information is decrypted. If the information is itself personal data within the meaning of the Data Protection Act 1998 overcoming encryption may also be a criminal offence under s 55. And if the information is held inside a computer, overcoming encryption might constitute a criminal offence under the Computer Misuse Act 1990.

1   [2000] FSR 138.
2   See, for example *Vitof Ltd v Altoft* [2006] EWHC 1678 (Ch), a case that considers the relationship between encryption and confidentiality. The trial judge observed that 'the Amended Particulars of Claim pleads that the PDFM source code constitutes information confidential to Vitof. It is common ground that source code is normally kept confidential, and that in the present case Mr Altoft encrypted the PDFM source code when sending it to Mr Chiovitti'.

OVERCOMING ENCRYPTION AND THE REGULATION OF INVESTIGATORY POWERS ACT 2000

2.8 As encryption is a clear indicator of secrecy, it is not surprising that law enforcement agencies will want the key, if they come about 'protected

2.8 Confidentiality, privacy and technology

information' during the course of an investigation. The Regulation of Investigatory Powers Act 2000 (RIPA 2000) defines protected information as:

'any electronic data which, without the key to the data–
(a) cannot, or cannot readily, be accessed, or
(b) cannot, or cannot readily, be put into an intelligible form;'[1]

RIPA 2000, Pt III, titled 'investigation of electronic data protected by encryption etc' contains a complete framework for the making of orders requiring the compulsory decryption of encrypted information. Section 49 enables public authorities, such as law enforcement agencies and HMRC, to serve 'disclosure notices' on any person holding the key to encryption, if decryption and subsequent disclosure of the decrypted information would be in the interests of national security, the prevention or detection of crime or in the UK's economic interests.

The effect of a disclosure notice is set out in s 50, which explains that a person in possession of both the encrypted information and the key who receives a s 49 notice is entitled to 'use any key in his possession to obtain access to the information or to put it in intelligible form' and 'shall be required, in accordance with the notice imposing the requirement, to make of a disclosure of the information in an intelligible form'[2]. Thus, it would seem that the utility of s 49 notices is obtaining disclosure of intelligible, ie, decrypted, material, not disclosure of the encryption keys themselves.

However, s 50(2) goes on to say that the recipient of a disclosure notice may deliver up the key itself, rather than the information in a decrypted form, while s 50(3) says that the recipient of the notice 'shall be required' to deliver up 'any key to the protected information that is in his possession at a relevant time' if (a) they are not in possession of the protected information, or (b) they are incapable of disclosing the information in an intelligible form because they do not possess the right key, or (c) if the disclosure notice itself gives a 'direction under section 51' for disclosure of the key itself. However, these requirements are subject to a limiting factor, for proportionality, which is contained in s 50(5) and (6). Section 50(5) says that 'it shall not be necessary, for the purpose of complying with the requirement, for the person given notice to make a disclosure of any keys in addition to those the disclosure of which is, alone, sufficient to enable the person to whom they are disclosed to obtain access to the information to put it into an intelligible form', while s 50(6) says that if the person receiving the notice is in possession of multiple keys they 'may select which of the keys, or combination of keys, to disclose for the purpose of complying with that requirement'. These limiting provisions aside, s 50(7) then says that if the person chooses to comply with a disclosure notice through the delivery of keys they 'shall not be taken to have complied with the disclosure requirement by the disclosure of a key unless he has disclosed every key to the protected information that is in his possession at a relevant time'.

Section 50(8) and (9) cater for the situation where the recipient of the notice is in possession of protected information but not the key. In this situation the effect of the disclosure notice is to require the disclosure of 'any information that would facilitate the obtaining of the key or the putting of the protected information into an intelligible form'.

1 Regulation of Investigatory Powers Act 2000, s 56(1).
2 Regulation of Investigatory Powers Act 2000, s 50(1).

2.9 As just mentioned, s 50(3)(c) requires a person receiving a disclosure notice to deliver the key, if the notice includes a direction under s 51. Section 51 directions can be given if 'there are special circumstances of the case which mean that the purposes for which it was believed necessary to impose the requirement in question would be defeated, in whole or in part, if the direction were not given' and 'the giving of the direction is proportionate to what is sought to be achieved by prohibiting any compliance with the requirement in question otherwise than by the disclosure of the key itself'[1]. The factors that have to be considered prior to the making of a direction under s 51 are set out in s 51(5) and include 'any adverse effect that the giving of the direction might have on a business carried on by the person on whom the disclosure requirement is imposed'.

The consequences of non-compliance with a disclosure notice are set out in s 53. Under s 53(1) 'a person to whom a section 49 notice has been given is guilty of an offence if he knowingly fails, in accordance with the notice, to make the disclosure required by virtue of the giving of the notice'. In order to cater for false assertions of non-possession of a key, s 53 includes a presumption of possession, which is rebuttable by the recipient of the disclosure notice, which has the effect of reversing the burden of proof. Section 53(2), which contains the presumption, says:

'(2) In proceedings against any person for an offence under this section, if it is shown that that person was in possession of a key to any protected information at any time before the time of the giving of the section 49 notice, that person shall be taken for the purposes of those proceedings to have continued to be in possession of that key at all subsequent times, unless it is shown that the key was not in his possession after the giving of the notice and before the time by which he was required to disclose it.'

The reversal of the burden of proof is contained in s 53(3), which says:

'(3) For the purposes of this section a person shall be taken to have shown that he was not in possession of a key to protected information at a particular time if–
 (a) sufficient evidence of that fact is adduced to raise an issue with respect to it; and
 (b) the contrary is not proved beyond a reasonable doubt.'

The defences to a charge of non-compliance are contained in s 53(4):

'(4) In proceedings against any person for an offence under this section it shall be a defence for that person to show–
 (a) that it was not reasonably practicable for him to make the disclosure required by virtue of the giving of the section 49 notice before the time by which he was required, in accordance with that notice, to make it; but
 (b) that he did make that disclosure as soon after that time as it was reasonably practicable for him to do so.'

2.9 Confidentiality, privacy and technology

The penalties on conviction are contained in s 53(5). The maximum penalty on conviction in the Crown Court is five years' imprisonment for national security cases and two years' imprisonment in other cases. The court can also impose a fine, which can be a standalone penalty or combined with a sentence of imprisonment.

1   See the Regulation of Investigatory Powers Act 2000, s 51(4).

Implications for data security law and practice and encryption key management

2.10 The disclosure notice procedure illustrates once again the limitations of confidentiality and privacy, demonstrating that data controllers will be required to remove security controls in serious cases. From the perspective of best practice, this also demonstrates the importance of the controller implementing strategies for key management. Controllers should also keep in mind, when considering their key management strategies, that directors and officers of businesses, as well as employees, can be prosecuted for non-compliance with a disclosure notice.

Liability in negligence for failing to implement appropriate security controls to protect confidential information from misuse

2.11 A critical issue for data controllers is, leaving aside any considerations arising under the Data Protection Act 1998 or the Human Rights Act 1998, will they be liable if, through their failure to apply appropriate security controls, someone misappropriates confidential information? There are three scenarios within this consideration:

- Confidential information could be deliberately misappropriated by an insider, perhaps a rogue employee or an onsite contractor.
- The information could be 'lost' through the negligence of an insider, perhaps by leaving a file of confidential papers on the train[1], or in a pub.
- The information could be misappropriated by an outsider, perhaps through a cyber attack or through 'blagging' (in the sense described by the Information Commissioner in 'What price privacy?') or similar.

If the duty of confidence arises through express contractual terms the parties will be free to reach their own agreement on the consequences that flow from a security breach. However, if the duty of confidence arises in equity the position is more complex, because the equitable duty of confidence is designed to prevent misuse of the information by the person under the duty of confidence, which is different to an obligation to take reasonable care of the data.

These issued were litigated in *B v A County Council*[2], a case about adoption proceedings. The claimants were seeking to adopt a child, but through the negligence of the local authority their identities were disclosed to the birth family, who embarked upon a course of harassment of the claimants. It was held that the local authority owed a duty of care to the claimants in negligence, to prevent the disclosure of the information, which was confidential, due to the parties being in a special relationship in the sense described in *Caparo Industries plc v Dickman*³.

1   'Secret terror files left on train', BBC, 11 June 2008: http://news.bbc.co.uk/1/hi/uk/7449255.stm.
2   [2006] EWCA Civ 1388, [2006] 3 FCR 568.
3   [1990] 2 AC 605, [1990] 1 All ER 568.

2.12 Thus, a case based on a failure to take reasonable care of confidential information should be presented as a negligence claim, rather than a breach of confidence claim as Buxton LJ explained:

> 'Since the claimants in my view have a right of action in negligence, it would therefore merely unduly complicate the case to descend into the law of confidence, as the judge rightly concluded. That makes it unnecessary to form any concluded view on a further formidable difficulty that the claimants would face. As the respondents correctly urged in this connexion, the fault of the defendants consisted of the careless release, not the intentional or deliberate misuse, of the confidential information. That is a relevant distinction because the law of breach of confidence depends on the equitable obligation of a person in possession of information to which he knows confidence attaches not to use that information for his own benefit: a principle best summarised by Denning MR in Seager v Copydex [1967] 1 WLR 923 at p 931E. That analysis does not extend to the acts of a merely negligent handler of information, who does not act for his own benefit, however much what he does may damage the owner of the information. Mr Blunt sought to meet that objection by showing us a decision previously unknown to me, Swinney v Chief Constable of Northumbria [1997] QB 464, where this court, on a very late application to amend pleadings, held that it was arguable that a party could claim damages for the merely negligent disclosure of information about him. As a decision on arguability the case is not binding on us, and under the terms of the Practice Direction (Citation of Authorities) [2001] 1 WLR 2001 should not have been cited to us, since it was not relied on as presenting a new principle or extending the present law. I would however be remiss if I did not say that I see no basis for the relief proposed separate from liability in contract or in negligence. I would respectfully adopt the as yet unpublished view of the leading authority in this field:
>
> "There is a distinction between an equitable duty of confidentiality and a duty to take care to prevent confidential information or documents from falling into the hand of someone else. The former is an obligation of conscience, which requires the recipient not to misuse the information or documents. The latter is a duty of a different character and is not an automatic concomitant of the former. In the absence of a relevant contract, it will only arise if there is a special relationship between the parties giving rise to a duty of care under the law of negligence." '

In conclusion, the effect of *B v A County Council* is that a data controller can be liable in negligence to the beneficiary of a duty of confidence for damage they suffer as a result of the controller failing to take reasonable care of the confidential information, provided that the beneficiary and controller are in a close relationship, the damage resulting from the loss is foreseeable and it would be fair, just and reasonable to hold the controller liable.

2.13 Confidentiality, privacy and technology

Remedies for misappropriation of confidential information

2.13 *B v A County Council* establishes that a data controller under a duty of confidence can be liable for the loss of confidential information if the loss is attributable to negligence, but what liability attaches to a person who misappropriates confidential information, whether an insider or an outsider?

As previously indicated, a person who obtains confidential information through surreptitious or improper means will be bound by the duty of confidence, which means that they will be liable to the full range of remedies that are open to the beneficiary of the duty, including injunctions, orders for destruction, orders for delivery-up and damages. In appropriate cases the beneficiary of the duty could also obtain a search order.

Privacy and human rights

2.14 Article 8 of the European Convention on Human Rights provides that:

'1. Everyone has the right to respect for his private and family life, his home and his correspondence.
2. There shall be no interference by a public authority with the exercise of this right except such as is in accordance with the law and is necessary in a democratic society in the interests of national security, public safety or the economic well-being of the country, for the prevention of disorder or crime, for the protection of health or morals, or for the protection of the rights and freedoms of others.'

The Convention has been incorporated into our domestic law by the Human Rights Act 1998. Human Rights Act 1998, s 2 requires courts and tribunals to have regard to decisions of the European Court of Human Rights, s 3 requires courts to interpret legislation so as to render it compatible with the Convention rights and s 6 requires public authorities, including courts and tribunals, to act compatibly with the Convention rights.

This combination of legal obligations has resulted in the courts extending the law of confidence to cover private information, so that where a person has a reasonable expectation of privacy it will amount to a breach of confidence if their privacy is interfered with. For example, in the case of *A v B (a company)*[1], a Court of Appeal case concerning a footballer's extra marital relationships, Lord Woolf held that 'a duty of confidence will arise whenever the party subject to the duty is in a situation where he either knows or ought to know that the other person can reasonably expect his privacy to be protected'. In the case of *Campbell v Mirror Group Newspapers Ltd*[2], a House of Lords case concerning the publication of photographs showing Naomi Campbell in the street outside a building used for Narcotics Anonymous meetings, Lord Hope explained that 'a duty of confidence will arise whenever the party subject to the duty is in a situation where he knows or ought to know that the other person can reasonably expect his privacy to be protected'.

Confidentiality, privacy and technology 2.15

Other landmark cases that have contributed to setting the boundaries of the right of privacy include:

- *Peck v United Kingdom*[3], which concerns the sharing of CCTV footage showing a suicide attempt in a high street.
- *Von Hannover v Germany*[4], which concerns long-lens photography, specifically photographs of Princess Caroline of Monaco in public places.
- *McKennitt v Ash*[5], which concerns the publication of falsehoods in an unauthorised biography.
- *Murray v Express Newspapers plc*[6], which concerns the taking of photographs of an author's child in a public place.

[1] [2002] EWCA Civ 337, [2003] QB 195.
[2] [2004] UKHL 22, [2004] 2 AC 457.
[3] (2003) 36 EHRR 41, [2003] EMLR 15.
[4] (2006) 43 EHRR 7.
[5] [2006] EWCA Civ 1714, [2007] 3 WLR 194.
[6] [2008] EWCA Civ 446, [2008] 3 WLR 1360.

THE OBLIGATION TO KEEP PRIVATE INFORMATION SAFE

2.15 Private information that is subject to a duty of confidence will be subject to the same security considerations as arise for other kinds of confidential information as a result of the *B v A County Council* and *Swinney* cases, which are discussed above. If the information also constitutes personal data it will be subject to the security obligations within the seventh data protection principle, which is discussed later.

In the case of *L v Finland*[1], a decision of the European Court of Human Rights, it was held that article 8 of the European Convention on Human Rights does place a positive obligation on the State to take positive steps to keep confidential data safe from unauthorised access.

From 1987 L was an outpatient at an eye clinic, where she was being treated for a HIV-related condition. In 1989 she started part-time work at the clinic. In 1992 she began to suspect that her colleagues at the clinic were aware of her condition, because staff had free access to the patient register, which contained information on diagnoses and treatment. Subsequently, the system was amended, following a complaint from L, so as to allow access to only those persons involved in the patient's treatment. Later, L requested an investigation into who had identified her files, but the investigation was inconclusive, because the system only retained log files for the last five accesses. As a result of the investigation the system was later amended, to retain log files of all accesses. L then sued for compensation, on the grounds that the clinic had failed to keep her data safe from unauthorised access, but she was unsuccessful. Thus, she brought a claim before the European Court of Human Rights. All of the material events occurred before the adoption of the Data Protection Directive.

The Court upheld L's claim, holding as follows:

2.15 Confidentiality, privacy and technology

'The hospital was a public hospital for whose acts the State is responsible for the purposes of the Convention (see Glass v. the United Kingdom, no. 61827/00, § 71, ECHR 2004-II). The processing of information relating to an individual's private life comes within the scope of Article 8 § 1 (see Rotaru v. Romania [GC], no. 28341/95, § 43, ECHR 2000-V, Leander v. Sweden, judgment of 26 March 1987, Series A no. 116, § 48). Personal information relating to a patient undoubtedly belongs to his or her private life. Article 8 is therefore applicable in the instant case. Indeed, this has not been contested by the parties.

Although the object of Article 8 is essentially that of protecting the individual against arbitrary interference by the public authorities, it does not merely compel the State to abstain from such interference: in addition to this primarily negative undertaking, there may be positive obligations inherent in an effective respect for private or family life (see Airey v. Ireland, judgment of 9 October 1979, Series A no. 32, p. 17, § 32). These obligations may involve the adoption of measures designed to secure respect for private life even in the sphere of the relations of individuals between themselves (see X and Y v. the Netherlands, judgment of 26 March 1985, Series A no. 91, p.11, § 23; Odièvre v. France [GC], no. 42326/98, ECHR 2003-III).

The Court observes that it has not been contended before it that there was any deliberate unauthorised disclosure of the applicant's medical data such as to constitute an interference with her right to respect for her private life. Nor has the applicant challenged the fact of compilation and storage of her medical data. She complains rather that there was a failure on the part of the hospital to guarantee the security of her data against unauthorised access, or, in Convention terms, a breach of the State's positive obligation to secure respect for her private life by means of a system of data protection rules and safeguards. The Court will examine the case on that basis, having regard in particular to the fact that in the domestic proceedings the onus was on the applicant to prove the truth of her assertion.

The protection of personal data, in particular medical data, is of fundamental importance to a person's enjoyment of his or her right to respect for private and family life as guaranteed by Article 8 of the Convention. Respecting the confidentiality of health data is a vital principle in the legal systems of all the Contracting Parties to the Convention. It is crucial not only to respect the sense of privacy of a patient but also to preserve his or her confidence in the medical profession and in the health services in general. The above considerations are especially valid as regards protection of the confidentiality of information about a person's HIV infection, given the sensitive issues surrounding this disease. The domestic law must afford appropriate safeguards to prevent any such communication or disclosure of personal health data as may be inconsistent with the guarantees in Article 8 of the Convention (see Z v. Finland, judgment of 25 February 1997, Reports of Judgments and Decisions 1997-I, §§ 95–96).

The Court notes that at the beginning of the 1990s there were general provisions in Finnish legislation aiming at protecting sensitive personal data. The Court attaches particular relevance to the existence and scope of the Personal Files Act of 1987 (see paragraph 19 above). It notes that the data controller had to ensure under section 26 that personal data were appropriately secured against, among other things, unlawful access. The data controller also had to make sure that only the personnel treating a patient had access to his or her patient record.

Undoubtedly, the aim of the provisions was to secure personal data against the risk of unauthorised access. As noted in Z v. Finland, the need for sufficient guarantees is particularly important when processing highly intimate and sensitive data, as in the instant case, where, in addition, the applicant worked in the same hospital where she was treated. The strict application of the law would therefore have constituted a substantial safeguard for the applicant's right secured by Article 8 of the Convention, making it possible, in particular, to police strictly access to any disclosure of health records.

However, the County Administrative Board found that, as regards the hospital in issue, the impugned health records system was such that it was not possible to retroactively clarify the use of patient records as it revealed only the five most recent consultations and that this information was deleted once the file had been returned to the archives. Therefore, the County Administrative Board could not determine whether information contained in the patient records of the applicant and her family had been given to or accessed by an unauthorised third person (see paragraph 10 above). This finding was later upheld by the Court of Appeal following the applicant's civil action. The Court for its part would also note that it is not in dispute that at the material time the prevailing regime in the hospital allowed for the records to be read also by staff not directly involved in the applicant's treatment.

It is to be observed that the hospital took ad hoc measures to protect the applicant against unauthorised disclosure of her sensitive health information by amending the patient register in summer 1992 so that only the treating personnel had access to her patient record and the applicant was registered in the system under a false name and social security number (see paragraph 7 above). However, these mechanisms came too late for the applicant.

The Court of Appeal found that the applicant's testimony about the events, such as her colleagues' hints and remarks beginning in 1992 about her HIV infection, was reliable and credible. However, it did not find firm evidence that her patient record had been unlawfully consulted (see paragraph 15 above).

The Court notes that the applicant lost her civil action because she was unable to prove on the facts a causal connection between the deficiencies in the access security rules and the dissemination of information about her medical condition. However, to place such a burden of proof on the applicant is to overlook the acknowledged deficiencies in the hospital's record keeping at the material time. It is plain that had the hospital provided a greater control over access to health records by restricting access to health professionals directly involved in the applicant's treatment or by maintaining a log of all persons who had accessed the applicant's medical file, the applicant would have been placed in a less disadvantaged position before the domestic courts. For the Court, what is decisive is that the records system in place in the hospital was clearly not in accordance with the legal requirements contained in section 26 of the Personal Files Act, a fact that was not given due weight by the domestic courts.

The Government have not explained why the guarantees provided by the domestic law were not observed in the instant hospital. The Court notes that it was only in 1992, following the applicant's suspicions about an information leak, that only the treating clinic's personnel had access to her medical records. The Court also observes that it was only after the applicant's complaint to the County Administrative Board that a retrospective control of data access was established (see paragraph 11 above).

Consequently, the applicant's argument that her medical data were not adequately secured against unauthorised access at the material time must be upheld.

2.15 Confidentiality, privacy and technology

> The Court notes that the mere fact that the domestic legislation provided the applicant with an opportunity to claim compensation for damages caused by an alleged unlawful disclosure of personal data was not sufficient to protect her private life. What is required in this connection is practical and effective protection to exclude any possibility of unauthorised access occurring in the first place. Such protection was not given here.
>
> The Court cannot but conclude that at the relevant time the State failed in its positive obligation under Article 8 § 1 of the Convention to ensure respect for the applicant's private life.
>
> There has therefore been a violation of Article 8 of the Convention.'

Of course, since the adoption of the Data Protection Directive the kind of complaints made by L have been regulated by the Finnish equivalent of the Data Protection Act 1998 and so will be subject to direct security obligations under the equivalent of the seventh data protection principle. This should not disguise the importance of this case however, as it confirms that security controls have to be implemented also for compliance with article 8. Seeing that article 8 has been transposed into our domestic law through the amendment of the law of confidence, L reinforces the jurisprudence in *B v A County Council*, to the effect that confidential data should be protected by appropriate security controls. The implications of this conclusion for data controllers are considerable; they must apply seventh data protection principle-style security controls to all of their confidential data, not just to their personal data.

[1] Application No. 20511/03, 17 July 2008, (2008) 48 EHRR 740.

Data protection

2.16 The international regulatory regime for data protection provides one of the cornerstones of data security law and practice, because at the heart of data protection law there is a key principle that requires data controllers to keep personal data safe and secure. In the UK the Data Protection Act 1998, which transposes the Data Protection Directive, provides at the seventh data protection principle:

> 'Appropriate technical and organisational measures shall be taken against unauthorised or unlawful processing of personal data and against accidental loss or destruction of, or damage to, personal data.'

How the security principle relates to the other principles

2.17 There are eight data protection principles within the Data Protection Act 1998. Compliance with the seventh principle, which together with its statutory interpretation transposes articles 16 and 17 of the Directive, is often a pre-requisite to compliance with the others. For example, consider the situation where malicious code gets past the firewall and other perimeter security controls; depending upon the technologies deployed and the organisation's practices, policies and procedures this may or may not constitute a breach of the seventh data protection principle. If that code causes personal

Confidentiality, privacy and technology **2.18**

data to be deleted or altered that may put the organisation in breach of the third data protection principle or the fourth principle, which are concerned with the adequacy and accuracy of personal data respectively.

These factors combined with the very broad scope of the legislation render data protection law an essential area of study for practitioners in the field of data security.

The international aspects of data protection law

2.18 Within Europe the national data protection laws of most countries are harmonised in accordance with Directives issued by the European Union and the provisions of a Council of Europe treaty[1]. Outside of Europe data protection laws have been adopted in the APEC region[2] and in countries including Argentina, Australia, Canada and New Zealand. There are also a number of international schemes and cooperation agreements that are designed to overcome differences in legal systems. These include the US Safe Harbor scheme[3] for imports of personal data from Europe and the EU 'white list'[4] of countries outside of Europe that provide adequate legal protection for personal data.

Europe and the United States have taken different paths to approximately the same position. One of the key distinctions between the European and US regimes is the 'omnibus' approach to data protection taken in Europe[5], which contrasts with the sectoral approach in the US[6]. The European approach has undoubtedly captured more acts of data processing within regulation, but the US could argue that it has taken a more risk-based – and therefore a more proportionate – approach. While important, these distinctions are starting to be of less importance. Europe has to admit that the US has taken the leadership in breach notification laws and in many other areas Europe is following the US example. The tougher approach to penalties and sanctions in the UK that has emerged in recent years is very influenced by the US position.

At this stage in the development of data protection law, the similarities in the laws of Europe and the US are arguably now greater than the difficulties. In terms of the trajectory of data security law, the European and US regimes are very likely to continue their convergence, particularly where the law's focus is cybercrime.

[1] Convention for the Protection of Individuals with regard to Automatic Processing of Personal Data, Strasbourg, 28.1.1981.
[2] See the APEC Privacy Framework 2004.
[3] http://www.export.gov/safeharbor/.
[4] For the current white list see http://ec.europa.eu/justice_home/fsj/privacy/thridcountries/index_en.htm.
[5] Article 3.1 of the Data Protection Directive provides that 'This Directive shall apply to the processing of personal data wholly or partly by automatic means, and to the processing otherwise than by automatic means of personal data which form part of a filing system or are intended to form part of a filing system'.
[6] For examples of relevant US legislation, including the Fair and Accurate Credit Transaction Act (FACTA), Financial Services Modernisation Act (Gramm-Leech-Bliley) and Health Insurance Portability and Accountability Act (HIPAA) see the Privacy Rights Clearing House website: http://www.privacyrights.org/index.htm.

2.19 *Confidentiality, privacy and technology*

The development of data protection law in Europe

2.19 The dominant legal instrument in European data protection law is the EU's Data Protection Directive[1]. This Directive forms the basis of the national data protection laws within all of the EU member states. The other important legal instrument is the Council of Europe Data Protection Convention, 1981[2].

The Directive and the Convention 'harmonise' national laws of the EU and Council of Europe Member States. This means that national data protection laws across Europe have the same aims and objectives. The harmonisation process does not result in national laws being exactly the same in either their wording or priorities however; there are many disparities between national laws built upon these instruments, including in the areas of enforcement, penalties and sanctions, which renders pan-European compliance a very complex problem for data controllers working across international boundaries.

The harmonised approach to data protection in Europe commenced in the late 1960s and the first legal instruments were created in 1973[3] and 1974[4]. These instruments were built around a series of key principles, an approach that has been followed by all subsequent instruments, albeit with increasing levels of detail. In 1981 the development of European data protection law achieved increased momentum with the Data Protection Convention, Europe's first and only Treaty in this area. The Convention dominated the legal landscape until 1995, when the Data Protection Directive was adopted by the EU. Since then the Directive has been dominant, but it should not be forgotten that the Convention is still binding law for those countries that have ratified it.

Data security has always been one of the data protection principles, with roots that can be traced right back to 1973. Table 2.1 shows the evolution of the data security principle through all of the major legal instruments.

Table 2.1 The evolution of the data security principle	
1973 Resolution	8. Precautions should be taken against any abuse or misuse of information. Electronic data banks should be equipped with security systems which bar access to the data held by them to persons not entitled to obtain such information, and which provide for the detection of misdirection of information, whether intentional or not. 9. Access to the information stored should be confined to persons who have a valid reason to know it. The operating staff of electronic data banks should be bound by rules of conduct aimed at preventing the misuse of data and, in particular, by rules of professional secrecy.

1974 Resolution	6. Precautions should be taken against any abuse or misuse of information. For this reason: a. everyone concerned with the operation of electronic data processing should be bound by rules of conduct aimed at preventing the misuse of data and in particular by a duty to observe secrecy; b. electronic data banks should be equipped with security systems which bar access to the data held by them to persons not entitled to obtain such information and which provide for the detection of misdirections of information, whether intentional or not. 7. Access to information that may not be freely communicated to the public should be confined to the persons whose functions entitle them to take cognisance of it in order to carry out their duties.
1981 Convention	Article 7 – Data security Appropriate security measures shall be taken for the protection of personal data stored in automated data files against accidental or unauthorised destruction or accidental loss as well as against unauthorised access, alteration or dissemination.
1995 Directive	Article 16 Confidentiality of processing Any person acting under the authority of the controller or of the processor, including the processor himself, who has access to personal data must not process them except on instructions from the controller, unless he is required to do so by law. Article 17 Security of processing 1. Member States shall provide that the controller must implement appropriate technical and organizational measures to protect personal data against accidental or unlawful destruction or accidental loss, alteration, unauthorized disclosure or access, in particular where the processing involves the transmission of data over a network, and against all other unlawful forms of processing. Having regard to the state of the art and the cost of their implementation, such measures shall ensure a level of security appropriate to the risks represented by the processing and the nature of the data to be protected.

2.19 Confidentiality, privacy and technology

	2. The Member States shall provide that the controller must, where processing is carried out on his behalf, choose a processor providing sufficient guarantees in respect of the technical security measures and organizational measures governing the processing to be carried out, and must ensure compliance with those measures. 3. The carrying out of processing by way of a processor must be governed by a contract or legal act binding the processor to the controller and stipulating in particular that: – the processor shall act only on instructions from the controller, – the obligations set out in paragraph 1, as defined by the law of the Member State in which the processor is established, shall also be incumbent on the processor. 4. For the purposes of keeping proof, the parts of the contract or the legal act relating to data protection and the requirements relating to the measures referred to in paragraph 1 shall be in writing or in another equivalent form.
1997 Directive[5]	Article 4 Security 1. The provider of a publicly available telecommunications service must take appropriate technical and organisational measures to safeguard security of its services, if necessary in conjunction with the provider of the public telecommunications network with respect to network security. Having regard to the state of the art and the cost of their implementation, these measures shall ensure a level of security appropriate to the risk presented. 2. In case of a particular risk of a breach of the security of the network, the provider of a publicly available telecommunications service must inform the subscribers concerning such risk and any possible remedies, including the costs involved. Article 5 Confidentiality of the communications 1. Member States shall ensure via national regulations the confidentiality of communications by means of a public telecommunications network and publicly available telecommunications services. In particular, they shall prohibit listening, tapping, storage or other kinds of interception or surveillance of communications, by others than users, without the consent of the users concerned, except when legally authorised, in accordance with Article 14(1).

	2. Paragraph 1 shall not affect any legally authorised recording of communications in the course of lawful business practice for the purpose of providing evidence of a commercial transaction or of any other business communication.
2002 Directive[6]	Article 4 Security 1. The provider of a publicly available electronic communications service must take appropriate technical and organisational measures to safeguard security of its services, if necessary in conjunction with the provider of the public communications network with respect to network security. Having regard to the state of the art and the cost of their implementation, these measures shall ensure a level of security appropriate to the risk presented. 2. In case of a particular risk of a breach of the security of the network, the provider of a publicly available electronic communications service must inform the subscribers concerning such risk and, where the risk lies outside the scope of the measures to be taken by the service provider, of any possible remedies, including an indication of the likely costs involved. Article 5 Confidentiality of the communications 1. Member States shall ensure the confidentiality of communications and the related traffic data by means of a public communications network and publicly available electronic communications services, through national legislation. In particular, they shall prohibit listening, tapping, storage or other kinds of interception or surveillance of communications and the related traffic data by persons other than users, without the consent of the users concerned, except when legally authorised to do so in accordance with Article 15(1). This paragraph shall not prevent technical storage which is necessary for the conveyance of a communication without prejudice to the principle of confidentiality. 2. Paragraph 1 shall not affect any legally authorised recording of communications and the related traffic data when carried out in the course of lawful business practice for the purpose of providing evidence of a commercial transaction or of any other business communication.

2.19 Confidentiality, privacy and technology

	3. Member States shall ensure that the use of electronic communications networks to store information or to gain access to information stored in the terminal equipment of a subscriber or user is only allowed on condition that the subscriber or user concerned is provided with clear and comprehensive information in accordance with Directive 95/46/EC, inter alia about the purposes of the processing, and is offered the right to refuse such processing by the data controller. This shall not prevent any technical storage or access for the sole purpose of carrying out or facilitating the transmission of a communication over an electronic communications network, or as strictly necessary in order to provide an information society service explicitly requested by the subscriber or user.
2006 Directive[7]	Article 7 Data protection and data security Without prejudice to the provisions adopted pursuant to Directive 95/46/EC and Directive 2002/58/EC, each Member State shall ensure that providers of publicly available electronic communications services or of a public communications network respect, as a minimum, the following data security principles with respect to data retained in accordance with this Directive: (a) the retained data shall be of the same quality and subject to the same security and protection as those data on the network; (b) the data shall be subject to appropriate technical and organisational measures to protect the data against accidental or unlawful destruction, accidental loss or alteration, or unauthorised or unlawful storage, processing, access or disclosure; (c) the data shall be subject to appropriate technical and organisational measures to ensure that they can be accessed by specially authorised personnel only; and (d) the data, except those that have been accessed and preserved, shall be destroyed at the end of the period of retention.

[1] Directive 95/46/EC of the European Parliament and of the Council of 24 October 1995 on the protection of individuals with regard to the processing of personal data and on the free movement of such data.
[2] Convention for the Protection of Individuals with regard to Automatic Processing of Personal Data, CETS No.: 108, 28 January 1981.
[3] Resolution (73) 22 on the protection of the privacy of individuals vis-à-vis electronic data banks in the private sector.
[4] Resolution (74) 29 on the protection of the privacy of individuals vis-à-vis electronic data banks in the public sector.
[5] Directive 97/66/EC of the European Parliament and of the Council of 15 December 1997 concerning the processing of personal data and the protection of privacy in the telecommunications sector.

6   Directive 2002/58/EC of the European Parliament and of the Council of 12 July 2002 concerning the processing of personal data and the protection of privacy in the electronic communications sector (Directive on privacy and electronic communications).
7   Directive 2006/24/EC of the European Parliament and of the Council of 15 March 2006 on the retention of data generated or processed in connection with the provision of publicly available electronic communications services or of public communications networks and amending Directive 2002/58/EC.

Key aims and objectives of data protection law

2.20 The initial focus of data protection was the protection of fundamental rights and freedoms, particularly privacy. The right to privacy is a fundamental human right within Europe, which is found within article 8 of the European Convention on Human Rights, as discussed earlier.

In many respects data protection laws can be considered to be modified privacy laws, in the sense that they prescribe particular rules on privacy for the world of data processing and electronic communications. When initially formulated by the Council of Europe in 1973 they were immediately innovative, as they extended privacy protections, albeit in a modified way, into the private sector; this was innovative because article 8 refers only to the activities of public authorities.

Since 1981 the law has had an additional focus, namely the maintenance of transborder data flows, that is the movement of personal data across national boundaries. These two interests can often be considerably opposed, meaning that data protection laws are intended to have a balancing effect. In other words, data protection laws are regulatory in nature[1] in that they are intended to control the behaviours of those who control the processing and those who work for them. In the event of non-compliance the law must apply appropriate sanctions and penalties. The individuals whose data are processed are also given direct rights over the controller, which they can enforce in court.

From the perspective of data security law, data protection's interest lies in the controller implementing sufficient measures to keep personal data safe and secure. In this sense the law imposes a security burden on the controller, but this is part of the price to be paid for the right to process personal data.

1   The regulatory nature of data protection law is reflected in the long title to the Data Protection Act 1998, which is 'An Act to make new provision for the regulation of the processing of information relating to individuals, including the obtaining, holding, use or disclosure of such information'.

SECURITY CONSIDERATIONS FOR THE GLOBAL PROCESSOR

2.21 Finally, its worth noting that a very special feature of the European data protection regime is the position it takes on the quality of the laws of non-European, third countries. Unless an exemption applies, Europe proceeds on the basis that the laws of third countries do not provide adequate protection for personal data[1]. This means that Europe places a general embargo over data exports from Europe.

2.21 Confidentiality, privacy and technology

This approach is clearly anachronistic, perhaps pointing to the prejudices of less enlightened times. In the field of data security, where European-based data controllers have demonstrated a propensity to suffer data security breaches that rival those of their US brethren, there are considerable doubts about the efficacy and reliability of this geographical control mechanism. However, for the time being at least that is the position taken by European data protection law. This imposes a substantial burden on controllers operating on the global stage, as they have to take special care to ensure that their non-European operations meet the requirements of the laws of their European establishments. As can be seen in Appendix B, there are considerable variances in the details of the security rules imposed across Europe, a factor that multinationals often overlook.

[1] See articles 25 and 26 of the Data Protection Directive.

Personal data and processing

2.22 So it is that European data protection laws regulate the processing of personal data by data controllers, but what is meant by personal data and processing?

At the heart of the Data Protection Directive's definition of personal data is the idea that the data must relate to an identifiable living individual. Article 2(a) of the Data Protection Directive provides:

> ' "personal data" shall mean any information relating to an identified or identifiable natural person ("data subject"); an identifiable person is one who can be identified, directly or indirectly, in particular by reference to an identification number or to one or more factors specific to his physical, physiological, mental, economic, cultural or social identity;'

If data do not meet these requirements, they will not be regulated by data protection law, irrespective of how otherwise important, confidential or sensitive they are. Anonymous data are also not regulated, nor are those relating to companies and public authorities.

It is a deeply unsatisfying fact of data protection law that there remains much confusion about the extent of the meaning of personal data. While remaining uncertainty about the status of data such as IP addresses may be understandable and explainable by the inevitable lag between technological developments and their regulation, the position is actually much worse, as there is still confusion about the meaning of the core concepts at the very heart of the definition[1].

[1] Opinion 4/2007 on the concept of personal data, Article 29 Working Party, WP 136, 20 June 2007: http://ec.europa.eu/justice_home/fsj/privacy/docs/wpdocs/2007/wp136_en.pdf.

DURANT AND THE MEANING OF PERSONAL DATA

2.23 In this country the meaning of personal data has been examined by the Court of Appeal in the leading case of *Durant v Financial Services Authority*[1].

Durant has injected two new concepts into the meaning of personal data, namely focus and biographical significance, the net effect of which is to require an effect on privacy for data to constitute personal data. Lord Justice Auld explained:

> 'It follows from what I have said that not all information retrieved from a computer search against an individual's name or unique identifier is personal data within the Act. Mere mention of the data subject in a document held by a data controller does not necessarily amount to his personal data. Whether it does so in any particular instance depends on where it falls in a continuum of relevance or proximity to the data subject as distinct, say, from transactions or matters in which he may have been involved to a greater or lesser degree. It seems to me that there are two notions that may be of assistance. The first is whether the information is biographical in a significant sense, that is, going beyond the recording of the putative data subject's involvement in a matter or an event that has no personal connotations, a life event in respect of which his privacy could not be said to be compromised. The second is one of focus. The information should have the putative data subject as its focus rather than some other person with whom he may have been involved or some transaction or event in which he may have figured or have had an interest, for example, as in this case, an investigation into some other person's or body's conduct that he may have instigated. In short, it is information that affects his privacy, whether in his personal or family life, business or professional capacity.'

Leaving aside the many complex questions that Durant's privacy-filter generates, it is clear that the meaning of personal data is intended to have very wide effect. In a practical sense the meaning of personal data draws in every public sector and private sector organisations that own or make use of computers as well as literally hundreds of millions of people who benefit from the law through their status as data subjects. Of course, an individual can be a data controller in their own right, albeit processing for purely domestic purposes is exempt from regulation[2].

1   [2003] EWCA Civ 1746, [2004] FSR 573.
2   Data Protection Act 1998, s 36.

THE MEANING OF PROCESSING

2.24 The broad effect of data protection law is also underpinned by the definition of processing, which is contained in article 2(b) of the Data Protection Directive[1]. This provides:

> ' "processing of personal data" ("processing") shall mean any operation or set of operations which is performed upon personal data, whether or not by automatic means, such as collection, recording, organization, storage, adaptation or alteration, retrieval, consultation, use, disclosure by transmission, dissemination or otherwise making available, alignment or combination, blocking, erasure or destruction;'

This definition identifies that processing can be undertaken by automated or non-automated means. This means that processing also includes the many by-products of computer use, including hard copies of data, as well as manual processing operations that are preliminary to automatic processing[2].

2.24 Confidentiality, privacy and technology

1   See also the *Bodil Lindqvist* case [2004] QB 1014, [2003] ECR I-12971.
2   However, see *Johnson v Medical Defence Union* [2007] EWCA Civ 262, [2007] 3 CMLR 181, which draws a difficult and novel distinction between the mental, human elements of computer use and data selection and the automated processing operations performed by computers. See also *Smith v Lloyds TSB Bank Plc* [2005] EWHC 246 (Ch) and, in contrast to *Johnson v Medical Defence Union*, see the judgment of Lord Phillips MR in *Campbell v Mirror Group Newspapers Ltd* [2002] EWCA Civ 1373, [2003] QB 633, where he said that 'While neither activity in itself may sensibly amount to processing, if that activity is carried on by, or at the instigation of, a "data controller", as defined, and is linked to automated processing of the data, we can see no reason why the entire set of operations should not fall within the scope of the legislation. On the contrary, we consider that there are good reasons why it should' (the Court of Appeal's decision was overturned by the House of Lords, but on different grounds).

REGULATION OF HIGHLY STRUCTURED PAPER FILES

2.25 An important innovation within the Data Protection Directive over the Convention was the extension of protections to a certain kind of non-automated processing, which the Directive calls a 'personal data filing system'. This is defined in article 2(c), in the following terms:

> ' "personal data filing system" ("filing system") shall mean any structured set of personal data which are accessible according to specific criteria, whether centralized, decentralized or dispersed on a functional or geographical basis;'

This definition clearly points to the need for structure within a personal data filing system, thereby ruling out protection of random documents[1]. However, in the UK the law has been extended to include within the meaning of data unstructured paper files held by the public sector, which effectively extends the protection of the law to random pieces of paper held by the public sector[2].

1   The equivalent filing system within the Data Protection Act 1998 is known as a 'relevant filing system'. This is defined in the Data Protection Act 1998, s 1(1) as 'any set of information relating to individuals to the extent that, although the information is not processed by means of equipment operating automatically in response to instructions given for that purpose, the set is structured, either by reference to individuals or by reference to criteria relating to individuals, in such a way that specific information relating to a particular individual is readily accessible'. See the judgment of Auld LJ in *Durant v Financial Services Authority* [2003] EWCA Civ 1746, [2004] FSR 573.
2   See the meaning of 'data' within the Data Protection Act 1998, s 1(1)(e), introduced by the Freedom of Information Act 2000.

THE STRUCTURE OF THE DEFINITIONS WITHIN THE DATA PROTECTION ACT 1998

2.26 The structure of the definitions in the Data Protection Act 1998 is slightly different to the approach taken by the Directive. The definition section in the Act has as its foundation the concept of data, which is not separately defined in the Directive. Data Protection Act 1998, s 1(1) provides as follows:

The meaning of data

2.27

' "data" means information which—
- (a) is being processed by means of equipment operating automatically in response to instructions given for that purpose,
- (b) is recorded with the intention that it should be processed by means of such equipment,
- (c) is recorded as part of a relevant filing system or with the intention that it should form part of a relevant filing system,
- (d) does not fall within paragraph (a), (b) or (c) but forms part of an accessible record as defined by section 68; or
- (e) is recorded information held by a public authority and does not fall within any of paragraphs (a) to (d)[1];'

These definitions show that data extends to information that is processed by computers and computer controlled equipment, 'manual' data which are intended to be processed by computers (etc), manual data that are contained in highly structured files, manual data that forms part of an accessible record[2] and manual data held by public authorities that are not held in structured files.

[1] Subsection (e) was inserted by the Freedom of Information Act 2000 and does not arise from the Directive.
[2] See the definition in the Data Protection Act 1998, s 68, which includes health records, educational records and certain local authority records, such as housing records.

The meaning of personal data

2.28 The next concept is personal data, which is defined in s 1(1) in the following terms:

' "personal data" means data which relate to a living individual who can be identified—
- (a) from those data, or
- (b) from those data and other information which is in the possession of, or is likely to come into the possession of, the data controller,

and includes any expression of opinion about the individual and any indication of the intentions of the data controller or any other person in respect of the individual;'

The meaning of processing

2.29 Next, is the definition of processing in s 1(1):

' "processing", in relation to information or data, means obtaining, recording or holding the information or data or carrying out any operation or set of operations on the information or data, including—
- (a) organisation, adaptation or alteration of the information or data,
- (b) retrieval, consultation or use of the information or data,
- (c) disclosure of the information or data by transmission, dissemination or otherwise making available, or

2.29 *Confidentiality, privacy and technology*

(d) alignment, combination, blocking, erasure or destruction of the information or data;'

The definition of processing is supplemented by the following definitions of obtaining, recording, using and disclosing contained in s 1(2):

'(2) In this Act, unless the context otherwise requires—
(a) "obtaining" or "recording", in relation to personal data, includes obtaining or recording the information to be contained in the data, and
(b) "using" or "disclosing", in relation to personal data, includes using or disclosing the information contained in the data.'

Johnson and the meaning of processing

2.30 The meaning of processing was considered by the Court of Appeal in the case of *Johnson v Medical Defence Union*[1]. What happened in this case was that a doctor working at the MDU selected information from electronic and other files, which she summarised in a new document. All of the information concerned the claimant, who complained that the selection of the information was unfair. However, the Court of Appeal on a majority decision held that the selection of the information did not constitute processing within the meaning of the Data Protection Act 1998, because the selection was a purely mental endeavour.

[1] [2007] EWCA Civ 262, [2007] 3 CMLR 181.

Special categories of processing (sensitive personal data)

2.31 The Directive applies more stringent rules to the processing of some special categories of personal data. These special categories of personal data are listed in article 8.1, which says that 'Member States shall prohibit the processing of personal data revealing racial or ethnic origin, political opinions, religious or philosophical beliefs, trade-union membership, and the processing of data concerning health or sex life'. The Data Protection Act 1998 refers to the special categories of personal data as 'sensitive personal data'[1].

[1] Data Protection Act 1998, s 2. This expands the special categories to include personal data relating to criminal offences and proceedings.

Protected personal information

2.32 Protected personal information is a new kind of personal data that arises from the government's Data Handling Review. The final report[1], published in June 2008, identifies a technical need for this addition, because the definition of sensitive personal data 'excludes important aspects of information that require high levels of protection'. The report explains[2]:

'The Data Protection Act defines "personal data" and "sensitive personal data". While the Government will continue to process all personal data in accordance with Data Protection Act requirements, neither is suitable for an administrative definition of information attracting certain technical protection. While all personal information is of value, the right technical level of protection varies significantly within the "personal data" category. "Sensitive personal data" is so specific as to exclude important aspects of information that require high levels of protection. As a result, this work has, with input from the Information Commissioner, specified an intermediate category of information, referred to as "protected personal information".

This definition relates to any material that links an identifiable individual with information that, if released, would put them at significant risk of harm or distress, or alternatively any source of information relating to 1000 or more individuals that is not in the public domain, even if the information about an individual is not considered likely to cause harm or distress. As in other areas, this is a minimum baseline. Departments will often wish to apply protection to smaller data sets depending on their risk assessment and the context in which information is kept.'

The concept of protected personal data has not been introduced into the Data Protection Act 1998 despite the many opportunities for amendment that have been open to the government in recent years. However, this should not distract from the importance of its introduction within the Data Handling Review, which has created an expectation about the behaviour of government departments. Furthermore, the fact that the Information Commissioner contributed to the development of the concept is highly significant and for the purposes of best practice it is likely that the Commissioner will be guided by the concept in regulatory investigations and enforcement proceedings in the future, whether these be against public sector controllers or private sector controllers. In other words, best practice will require a controller to consider whether it is processing protected personal data and to implement necessary controls if they are.

[1] Data Handling Procedures in Government: Final Report, June 2008.
[2] Data Handling Procedures in Government: Final Report, June 2008, page 17.

The main actors

2.33 Data protection laws focus on relationships between controllers, processors and data subjects. The data subject is the identifiable, living individual to whom the personal data that are being processed relate[1]. It is the data subject who is the beneficiary of the regulations and, as mentioned earlier, the data subject is given rights that they can enforce directly against the controller.

[1] See article 2(a) of the Directive and the Data Protection Act 1998, s 1(1).

DATA CONTROLLERS

2.34 If the data subject is the beneficiary of the regulations, it is the controller who carries the burdens. The Directive defines the controller as 'the natural or legal person, public authority, agency or any other body which alone or jointly with others determines the purposes and means of the processing of personal data; where the purposes and means of processing are determined by national or Community laws or regulations, the controller or the specific criteria for his

2.34 *Confidentiality, privacy and technology*

nomination may be designated by national or Community law'. The definition within the Data Protection Act 1998 is very similar, with the key difference being the substitution of the word 'manner' for 'means'[1]. As already indicated, this definition of controller includes individuals (natural persons) as well as organisations (legal persons).

[1] See the Data Protection Act 1998, s 1(1), which says that ' "data controller" means, subject to subsection (4), a person who (either alone or jointly or in common with other persons) determines the purposes for which and the manner in which any personal data are, or are to be, processed'.

DATA PROCESSORS

2.35 A data processor is a person or organisation that processes personal data on behalf of a data controller, giving as the distinguishing feature of the processor's character an obligation to act on the controller's instructions. In many respects the relationship between controller and processor is akin to that of principal and agent. The controller remains fully responsible for the processor's operations during the currency of their relationship.

Conducting due diligence

2.36 From the perspective of data security law the controller-processor relationship is very interesting. The security principle (the seventh data protection principle within the Data Protection Act 1998) requires relationships between controllers and processors to be controlled by contracts by which the processor agrees only to act on the controller's instructions. Prior to entering into the contract the controller must carry out appropriate due diligence, confirming for itself that the processor is an appropriate person or organisation to do business with. After the contract has been signed the controller continues to be under an obligation to monitor the processor's operations, to ensure that they remain fully compliant with the contract and the overriding objectives within the security principle.

REGULATORS

2.37 Member States are required to appoint independent authorities to monitor and supervise the application of the national provisions adopted to give effect to the Data Protection Directive[1]. These national supervisory authorities have primary responsibility for the enforcement of the law. In the UK the regulator is the Information Commissioner, whose office is based in Wilmslow, Cheshire. The Information Commissioner's general duties are described in the Data Protection Act 1998, s 51, the opening parts of which read as follows:

'(1) It shall be the duty of the Commissioner to promote the following of good practice by data controllers and, in particular, so to perform his functions under this Act as to promote the observance of the requirements of this Act by data controllers.

(2) The Commissioner shall arrange for the dissemination in such form and manner as he considers appropriate of such information as it may appear to him expedient to give to the public about the operation of this Act, about good practice, and about other matters within the scope of his functions under this Act, and may give advice to any person as to any of those matters.'

The Information Commissioner enjoys almost unparalled reach and influence, which includes a proven ability to influence the legislative agenda, as mentioned in Chapter 1. Further aspects of the Commissioner's powers are discussed in Chapter 6.

[1] See article 28 of the Data Protection Directive, which requires Member States to appoint a completely independent supervisory authority.

ARTICLE 29 WORKING PARTY

2.38 The national regulators meet regularly to discuss developments and to ensure the continued harmonisation of the law and regulatory responses. The main forum for these interactions is known as the Article 29 Working Party, after article 29 of the Data Protection Directive, which establishes this forum[1]. Each year the Article 29 Working Party publishes a work plan, which leads to the adoption of various working documents and opinions throughout the course of the year. These documents are one of the primary sources of data protection law, with some impacting directly on data security law and practice. Practitioners in the data security space would be well advised to keep abreast of developments within the Article 29 Working Party, as these are certain to inform regulatory attitudes and responses in the regulators' domestic jurisdictions.

[1] http://ec.europa.eu/justice_home/fsj/privacy/workinggroup/index_en.htm.

EUROPEAN COMMISSION

2.39 Last but not least, there is the European Commission. The Commission holds a series of critical law making powers. For example, it may make decisions about the adequacy of the laws within third countries[1], for the purposes of data exports out of Europe. The Commission is also empowered to issue proposals for Directives and in this context the Commission's current proposal for a Directive introducing breach notification laws for the electronic communications sector is necessary reading (the current proposals for breach notification are discussed at Chapter 7). The Commission may also issue 'Communications' on matters of importance. In the context of data security law the Commission's communication on privacy enhancing technologies (PETs) is another notable event. Finally, the Commission's representatives participate in the meetings of the Article 29 Working Party, giving the Commission even further influence over developments.

[1] See article 25.6 of the Data Protection Directive.

2.40   *Confidentiality, privacy and technology*

The regulatory mechanisms

2.40 There are four key regulatory mechanisms within the Data Protection Directive, namely the transparency provisions, the general rules on lawfulness and legitimacy, the data subject's right to object to processing and the enforcement mechanisms.

TRANSPARENCY – BEING OPEN ABOUT PROCESSING

2.41 The requirement that controllers should be transparent about their data processing operations is fundamental to the successful operation of the law. Without the appropriate degree of transparency data subjects will not be in a position to assess whether their fundamental rights are being affected. However, it should be noted that the requirement for transparency is not absolute, which reflects the formulation of the right to privacy within article 8 of the European Convention on Human Rights. Thus, some processing operations may be conducted without the knowledge of the data subject, as is often necessary for the purposes of law enforcement and national security.

These exemptions aside, the transparency mechanisms revolve around the supply of information about processing operations to the national regulators and the data subjects, with the principle being that this information should be provided before the commencement of processing. The obligation to supply 'prior' information is supplemented by the right of access to personal data, which the data subject enjoys; under this right the data subject is entitled to be told about the processing operations, their purpose and the controller's identity. Finally, as part of their supervision powers national regulators such as the Information Commissioner are generally entitled to request information from the controller about their processing operations.

Expanding the transparency obligations – breach notification and inspections

2.42 In the field of data security law there has been considerable activity directed towards the expansion of the transparency mechanisms. Breach notification is the best example of the injection of heightened transparency obligations into the regulatory framework. Another example is the 'access notice' procedure within the Coroners and Justice Bill, which will codify the Information Commissioner's right to carry out non-consensual inspections of public authorities, a power that was initially introduced by the Prime Minister shortly after the news of HMRC broke.

GENERAL RULES ON LAWFULNESS AND LEGITIMACY

2.43 The general rules on lawfulness and legitimacy set out the fundamental principles that need to be observed in order to ensure that fundamental rights are not infringed during the performance of processing operations. These rules are discussed below, within the section on the data protection principles.

RIGHT TO OBJECT

2.44 The right to object provides the data subject with grounds for preventing processing. For example, the data subject has the right to prevent processing for the purposes of direct marketing[1]. They can also prevent processing that is likely to cause substantial and unwarranted damage or distress[2]. The granting of these rights to the data subject effectively vests regulatory and enforcement functions with the data subject. Generally, the data subject can enforce the right to object before the courts.

[1] Data Protection Act 1998, s 11.
[2] Data Protection Act 1998, s 10.

ENFORCEMENT MECHANISMS

2.45 The enforcement mechanisms are the administrative powers that vest in the national regulator to bring about compliance with the legislation. These stem from article 28 of the Directive, which requires Member States to endow their regulators with investigative powers, effective powers of intervention, the power to engage in legal proceedings and the duty to hear claims of non-compliance and breach.

Enforcement is discussed in more detail at Chapter 6, but to summarise at the date of publication of this book the Information Commissioner's primary enforcement mechanism is the enforcement notice, which can be served to bring about the controller's compliance with the law. The enforcement notice procedure is supplemented by the information notice procedure. Finally, the Information Commissioner can assess a controller's compliance with the law.

In Chapter 1 the theme of the regulatory bear market was introduced, which is represented by the negative sentiment of the regulators; the Information Commissioner and the Financial Services Authority both consider that the state of data security practices is so poor in the UK that the application of tougher penalties are required. The Information Commissioner has also been very negative about the ability of the Data Protection Act 1998 to achieve compliance. This sentiment has impacted on the nature, quality and extent of enforcement action and in the case of the Data Protection Act 1998 it has contributed to an amendment that will give the Information Commissioner the additional power to fine organisations that are in serious non-compliance with the law. Similarly, there are proposals to amend the law to give the Information Commissioner the right to carry out inspections of public authorities without their consent. Thus, we are currently witnessing a significant evolution in the enforcement mechanisms.

The general rules on lawfulness and legitimacy and the data protection principles

2.46 The data protection principles have been a constant of data protection law ever since the Council of Europe took the first steps towards harmonisation of national laws, through the 1973 and 1974 resolutions and despite the

2.46 Confidentiality, privacy and technology

passage of time they have remained remarkably consistent over the years, both in terms of their content and effect. The data protection principles are found in the Data Protection Act 1998, Sch 1, Pt I. They provide as follows:

'1   Personal data shall be processed fairly and lawfully and, in particular, shall not be processed unless—
   (a)   at least one of the conditions in Schedule 2 is met, and
   (b)   in the case of sensitive personal data, at least one of the conditions in Schedule 3 is also met.
2   Personal data shall be obtained only for one or more specified and lawful purposes, and shall not be further processed in any manner incompatible with that purpose or those purposes.
3   Personal data shall be adequate, relevant and not excessive in relation to the purpose or purposes for which they are processed.
4   Personal data shall be accurate and, where necessary, kept up to date.
5   Personal data processed for any purpose or purposes shall not be kept for longer than is necessary for that purpose or those purposes.
6   Personal data shall be processed in accordance with the rights of data subjects under this Act.
7   Appropriate technical and organisational measures shall be taken against unauthorised or unlawful processing of personal data and against accidental loss or destruction of, or damage to, personal data.
8   Personal data shall not be transferred to a country or territory outside the European Economic Area unless that country or territory ensures an adequate level of protection for the rights and freedoms of data subjects in relation to the processing of personal data.'

Data Protection Act 1998, s 4 places the obligation on the controller to comply with the principles. Data processors, those who process personal data on behalf of controllers, are not regulated directly. Instead, the controller is responsible for ensuring that their processing remains within the boundaries of the law. As already indicated, the security principle, the seventh, contains specific provisions governing the controller-processor relationship.

As mentioned earlier, compliance with the seventh principle may be regarded as being a pre-requisite to compliance with the other principles.

The security principle – guarding against security breaches and data loss

2.47 The seventh data protection principle and its statutory interpretation[1], which transpose articles 16 and 17 of the Data Protection Directive, provide as follows:

'Appropriate technical and organisational measures shall be taken against unauthorised or unlawful processing of personal data and against accidental loss or destruction of, or damage to, personal data.
9   Having regard to the state of technological development and the cost of implementing any measures, the measures must ensure a level of security appropriate to—
   (a)   the harm that might result from such unauthorised or unlawful processing or accidental loss, destruction or damage as are mentioned in the seventh principle, and
   (b)   the nature of the data to be protected.

Confidentiality, privacy and technology **2.48**

10   The data controller must take reasonable steps to ensure the reliability of any employees of his who have access to the personal data.

11   Where processing of personal data is carried out by a data processor on behalf of a data controller, the data controller must in order to comply with the seventh principle—
  (a) choose a data processor providing sufficient guarantees in respect of the technical and organisational security measures governing the processing to be carried out, and
  (b) take reasonable steps to ensure compliance with those measures.

12   Where processing of personal data is carried out by a data processor on behalf of a data controller, the data controller is not to be regarded as complying with the seventh principle unless—
  (a) the processing is carried out under a contract—
    (i) which is made or evidenced in writing, and
    (ii) under which the data processor is to act only on instructions from the data controller, and
  (b) the contract requires the data processor to comply with obligations equivalent to those imposed on a data controller by the seventh principle.'

[1] Data Protection Act 1998, Sch 1, Pt II.

WHEN WILL A CONTROLLER BE IN BREACH OF THE SEVENTH PRINCIPLE?

2.48 The intention of the seventh data protection principle is that the controller will take appropriate technical and organisational measures to guard against security breaches and data losses. An interesting question arises from this; will a controller only be in breach of the seventh data protection principle if they suffer a security breach or data loss, or can the 'mere' failure to take appropriate technical and organisational measures be enough to constitute a breach? In other words does a security incident have to occur for the controller to be in breach?

Taking account of the utility of the seventh data protection principle and the ordinary meaning of its language, there seems little room to doubt the proposition that the seventh data protection principle does not require a security incident to occur (whether breach or data loss) for a breach of the principle to occur. The requirement to take appropriate measures is a substantive obligation in its own right, which is intended to help prevent security incidents occurring.

As far as the Information Commissioner's position is concerned, an indication was given in January 2007, when the Deputy Information Commissioner gave evidence to the House of Lords Science and Technology Committee, for the purposes of its inquiry into personal internet security[1]. The following passage is illuminating:

'Q367 Earl of Erroll: As this data should be kept in an encrypted form in the modern day and world on these databases, why do you not just pre-emptively issue your notifications to those companies which are not encrypting such sensitive data, and then you could act against them if they were in breach?

2.48   *Confidentiality, privacy and technology*

Mr Jones: Certainly we have not thought of that. I suspect it would be fairly hard to identify the large number of companies involved, but I think it is something which has not occurred to us.'

Again, taking things at face value, it seems to be clear from the Deputy Information Commissioner's evidence that the Information Commissioner's Office is of the opinion that the absence of appropriate technical and organisational measures constitutes a breach of the seventh principle in its own right, irrespective of whether a security incident occurs as a result of the absence of measures.

[1]   'Personal Internet Security', 5th Report of Session 2006–07, Volume II: Evidence, HL Paper 165-II, 10 August 2007: http://www.publications.parliament.uk/pa/ld200607/ldselect/ldsctech/165/165ii.pdf.

JUDGING THE APPROPRIATENESS OF THE MEASURES TAKEN

2.49   The requirement that technical and organisational security measures should be 'appropriate' poses its own special difficulties. Although most controllers will quickly work out who is responsible for judging appropriateness (the courts and regulator), there is very little clarity about the tests that will be applied to determine appropriateness. Even where there is relative clarity, such as in the area of encryption, there is still uncertainty about the outer boundaries. For example, while it is now relatively settled that personal data on moveable media should be encrypted, what is the regulator's position on, say, email encryption? The level of uncertainty in this area does not help the controller reach quick decisions on appropriateness.

APPROPRIATENESS AND INDUSTRY STANDARDS

2.50   So, to what extent will compliance with industry standards, such as the ISO 27000 series for information security management or PCI DSS, guarantee compliance with the seventh data protection principle?

In *Ward v The Ritz Hotel (London)*[1] the relevance of the defendants' failure to raise the height of a balustrade to that recommended by the British Standards Institute was considered. When the hotel was constructed in 1905 the balustrade had been approximately three feet and three and a half inches above the floor. In about 1976 the floor of the balcony had been resurfaced, raising the floor level by approximately four inches. This resulted in the balustrade being less than three feet above floor level. In 1976 the British Standards Institute had issued a recommended standard that stated the height of any balustrade should be a maximum of three feet and six inches.

The case came about when the plaintiff was severely injured when, as a result of a faint, he fell backwards over the low balustrade on the balcony. An expert for the defendant agreed that in the light of the British Standard he would not have allowed the defendants to raise the floor of the balcony without also raising the height of the balustrade. The defendant's expert was an architect, and his statement would suggest that standards are strictly adhered to within the industry and would not be departed from despite the fact that there was no statutory obligation to comply with them.

At first instance the trial judge held that although on the facts the plaintiff would not have fallen if the balustrade had been of the height required by the British Standard, the failure to observe the Standard did not necessarily constitute a breach of the defendant's duty of care owed to the plaintiff as their lawful visitor.

On appeal it was held that too little weight had been given to the British Standard. The view of the Court of Appeal was that such standards represent the consensus of professional opinion and practical experience as to sensible safety precautions. It should have been apparent to the defendant in 1976 that the floor resurfacing would result in the balustrade being significantly lowered, with the result that they knew or ought to have known that the result would plainly be in breach of the Standard. It was also foreseeable that a lawful visitor might stand in the position in which the plaintiff was and that if he fell he was likely to suffer severe injury, by reason of the drop.

In light of these holdings and the trial judge's finding that the plaintiff's fall would probably not have occurred if the balustrade had been raised to the recommended height, it was held by a majority decision of the Court of Appeal that the trial judge ought to have concluded that the defendant had not taken such care as in all the circumstances was reasonable to see that the plaintiff was reasonably safe in using the hotel for the purpose for which he was invited. The dissenting view of Lloyd LJ was that the trial judge was correct to observe that the Standard was no more than a recommendation and that it was for him to decide how much weight should be given to it in the particular circumstances of this case.

1   [1992] PIQR P315.

2.51 Despite the dissenting view of Lloyd LJ, this case highlights that failure to follow a British Standard can be used successfully as evidence of negligence in occupiers liability cases. There is no reason why this jurisprudence should not be extended to data security law, where it concerns compliance with industry standards, such as the ISO 27000 series.

Another case which examines the status given to British Standards by the courts is *Lips v Older*[1]. Here Older owned a house which was divided into a number of flats. The front door of the house was approached by a path flanked by two walls approximately two feet high. At one point the walls had been topped by railings but they were removed around 1940 during the Second World War. To the side of one wall there was a drop of nine feet down to a concrete floor in the basement area of the house. Lips rented the house from Older and returned home one day carrying a bag of heavy power tools. Lips was intoxicated, sat on the wall and fell the nine feet to the floor of the basement. He was seriously injured. The judge held that Older was in breach of the duty of care that he owed to Lips.

2.51 *Confidentiality, privacy and technology*

In coming to this conclusion on breach of the duty of care the court took account of the fact that there had never been a similar accident, despite many similar properties not having railings. However, relevant building regulations and British Standards required a low wall of this type to have a rail. Expert evidence from a surveyor stated that there was no breach of those regulations back in 1940, when the railings were taken down, but it was his expert opinion that any survey conducted upon an acquisition of the property would highlight the British Standards in relation to the wall requiring a railing.

The court in this case took account of the decision in *Ward v The Ritz Hotel (London)*[2] and concluded that whilst non-statutory standards do not necessarily define what is reasonably safe, they are relevant matters to be taken into account. Accordingly, the court concluded that Older was in breach of the duty of care owed to Lips because he should have erected the railing as a precaution, and had he done so the accident would have been prevented.

[1] [2004] EWHC 1686 (QB).
[2] [1992] PIQR P315.

2.52 Another case highlighting the weight attached to non-statutory codes of practice is *Froom v Butcher*[1]. This case discussed contributory negligence regarding the use of seat belts and was decided before Parliament had made the wearing of seat belts compulsory. The trial judge had held that the fact that there were differences of opinion among ordinary people as to the advisability of wearing seat belts meant that the plaintiff, who had not worn a seat belt, could not be held to have been guilty of contributory negligence. The Court of Appeal disagreed. Having reviewed the evidence and the guidance in the Highway Code ('fit seat belts in your car and make sure they are always used') Lord Denning said:

> 'I think the judges should say plainly that it is the sensible practice for all drivers and passengers in front seats to wear seat belts whenever and wherever going by car. It is a wise precaution which everyone should take.'

It followed that differences of view among ordinary people were not decisive. In fact, it appears to be the case that the guidance given by the Highway Code, was decisive. This case gives substantial weight to the proposition that non-statutory codes of practice can stand as evidence of negligence, whether contributory or not, regardless of the presence of legislation on the matter.

Finally, the position of government and the regulators should be noted. For example, the Data Handling Review recommends that central government departments should implement encryption to FIPS 140–2 level. The Information Commissioner has identified ISO 27001 in his guidance on the use of encryption[2]. The FSA, in its April 2008 report on data security[3], in the section on benchmarking, comments:

> 'There is an international quality standard for data security: the ISO 27001 Security Management Standard which was introduced in 2005. Some firms, particularly larger firms with dedicated information security officers, were aware of this code of practice and used it as a benchmark. However, it was interesting to observe that even some of the largest firms had not obtained certification to this standard.'

The combination of *Ward, Lips* and the official statements of the government and the regulators render it a racing certainty that the courts will treat non-compliance with mainstream standards, particularly the ISO 27000 series as evidence on non-compliance with the seventh data protection principle. Similarly, non-compliance with such standards is likely to be treated as evidence of negligence, in cases where a data controller is accused of not implementing sufficient security controls to protect confidential information.

1   [1976] QB 286, [1975] 3 All ER 520 at 525.
2   See 'Our approach to encryption': http://www.ico.gov.uk/about_us/news_and_views/current_topics/Our%20approach%20to%20encryption.aspx.
3   'Data Security in Financial Services – Firms' controls to prevent data loss by their employees and third-party suppliers': http://www.fsa.gov.uk/pubs/other/data_security.pdf.

Ensuring the reliability of employees

2.53 The data controller's obligation to take 'reasonable steps to ensure the reliability of any employees of his who have access to the personal data' often throws up acute challenges; a substantial proportion of security incidents are due to the failings of employees, yet employees enjoy a strong right of privacy within the workplace, as well as statutory protection from unfair dismissal and discriminatory and harassing behaviour. Thus, a properly motivated security minded data controller can find itself liable for a breach of an employee's workplace rights if it does not get the balance right.

PRIVACY WITHIN THE WORKPLACE

2.54 There is a long line of authority showing that employees enjoy a right of privacy (within the meaning of article 8 of the European Convention on Human Rights) within the workplace. Landmark cases include *Huvig v France*[1] (interception of business and personal telephone calls), *Niemietz v Germany*[2] (public authority searching a lawyer's office), *Halford v United Kingdom*[3] (monitoring of personal telephone calls made from office premises), and *Copland v UK*[4] (monitoring of employee's telephone, email and website use).

1   European Court of Human Rights, Application No. 11105/84, 24 April 1990.
2   (1992) 16 EHRR 97.
3   (1997) 24 EHRR 523, [1997] IRLR 471.
4   (2007) 45 EHRR 37.

Justifying interferences with worker privacy

2.55 As discussed earlier, in order to determine whether a person's privacy rights are engaged the issue is whether the person enjoys a reasonable expectation of privacy in the circumstances under review. As the above case law demonstrates, the answer as far as workers is concerned is yes, they do enjoy a reasonable expectation of privacy in the workplace. In order to determine whether there has been a breach of a person's privacy rights there

2.55 *Confidentiality, privacy and technology*

are three critical issues to be considered. First, is the interference with privacy in accordance with law? Second, is the interference necessary in a democratic society? Third, does the interference pursue a legitimate aim? These three issues are a distillation of the carve-out from privacy contained in article 8.2 of the European Convention on Human Rights.

MONITORING OF ELECTRONIC COMMUNICATIONS

2.56 The monitoring of employees' electronic communications can engage the anti-interception rules within the Regulation of Investigatory Powers Act 2000. These rules are discussed in more detail below, but at this juncture it is worth noting the Telecommunications (Lawful Business Practice) (Interception of Communications) Regulations 2000[1], which contain a comprehensive framework for the lawful interception of electronic communications for a variety of business purposes.

These regulations, which were made under RIPA 2000, s 4(2), allow for the monitoring of business communications, where the monitoring amounts to an interception of a communication during the course of its transmission by means of a telecommunication system. Section 4(2) provides:

> '(2) Subject to subsection (3), the Secretary of State may by regulations authorise any such conduct described in the regulations as appears to him to constitute a legitimate practice reasonably required for the purpose, in connection with the carrying on of any business, of monitoring or keeping a record of–
> (a) communications by means of which transactions are entered into in the course of that business; or
> (b) other communications relating to that business or taking place in the course of its being carried on.'

[1] SI 2000/2699.

2.57 For these purposes 'references to a business include references to activities of a government department, of any public authority or of any person or office holder on whom functions are conferred by or under any enactment'[1]. The grounds for which such monitoring is allowed are contained in reg 3, which provides:

> '3.— **Lawful interception of a communication**
>
> (1) For the purpose of section 1(5)(a) of the Act, conduct is authorised, subject to paragraphs (2) and (3) below, if it consists of interception of a communication, in the course of its transmission by means of a telecommunication system, which is effected by or with the express or implied consent of the system controller for the purpose of—
> (a) monitoring or keeping a record of communications—
>   (i) in order to—
>   (aa) establish the existence of facts, or
>   (bb) ascertain compliance with regulatory or self-regulatory practices or procedures which are—
>   applicable to the system controller in the carrying on of his business or

applicable to another person in the carrying on of his business where that person is supervised by the system controller in respect of those practices or procedures, or
- (cc) ascertain or demonstrate the standards which are achieved or ought to be achieved by persons using the system in the course of their duties, or
- (ii) in the interests of national security, or
- (iii) for the purpose of preventing or detecting crime, or
- (iv) for the purpose of investigating or detecting the unauthorised use of that or any other telecommunication system, or
- (v) where that is undertaken—
  - (aa) in order to secure, or
  - (bb) as an inherent part of,

the effective operation of the system (including any monitoring or keeping of a record which would be authorised by section 3(3) of the Act if the conditions in paragraphs (a) and (b) thereof were satisfied); or
- (b) monitoring communications for the purpose of determining whether they are communications relevant to the system controller's business which fall within regulation 2(b)(i) above; or
- (c) monitoring communications made to a confidential voice-telephony counselling or support service which is free of charge (other than the cost, if any, of making a telephone call) and operated in such a way that users may remain anonymous if they so choose.

(2) Conduct is authorised by paragraph (1) of this regulation only if—
- (a) the interception in question is effected solely for the purpose of monitoring or (where appropriate) keeping a record of communications relevant to the system controller's business;
- (b) the telecommunication system in question is provided for use wholly or partly in connection with that business;
- (c) the system controller has made all reasonable efforts to inform every person who may use the telecommunication system in question that communications transmitted by means thereof may be intercepted; and
- (d) in a case falling within—
  - (i) paragraph (1)(a)(ii) above, the person by or on whose behalf the interception is effected is a person specified in section 6(2)(a) to (i) of the Act;
  - (ii) paragraph (1)(b) above, the communication is one which is intended to be received (whether or not it has been actually received) by a person using the telecommunication system in question.

(3) Conduct falling within paragraph (1)(a)(i) above is authorised only to the extent that Article 5 of Directive 2002/58/EC of the European Parliament and of the Council of 12 July 2002 concerning the processing of personal data and the protection of privacy in the electronic communications sector so permits.'

1   SI 2000/2699, reg 2.

2.58 Critical components within this power of monitoring which appear within reg 3 are:
- The monitoring has to take place with the system controller's consent. The system controller is described as 'in relation to a particular

2.58 *Confidentiality, privacy and technology*

telecommunications system, a person with a right to control its operation or use'. The system controller must give their express or implied consent for the monitoring to be lawful.

- The monitoring should take place only in respect of communications relevant to the controller's business. The same rule applies for the keeping of records. A communication is relevant to a business only if (a) it is one that relates to a business transaction, or (b) it otherwise relates to the business or (c) it takes place in the course of carrying on the business.
- The system is provided for business use, whether wholly or in part. This covers private telecommunication systems as defined in RIPA 2000 as well apparatus contained outside of a private system, as long as the apparatus is provided for business use. The effect of this definition is to bring within regulation the commercial provision of communications monitoring services.
- The system controller must make all reasonable efforts to inform people affected by the monitoring that it is taking place. This imports a vital transparency requirement, to make the monitoring consistent with key principles of human rights and data protection law. It also acts to render cover monitoring lawful, but only if that is proportionate. The Information Commissioner's Employment Practices Code should be considered during the assessment of proportionality.

THE EMPLOYMENT PRACTICES CODE

2.59 The Information Commissioner's Employment Practices Code[1], made under the Data Protection Act 1998, s 51, is required reading for data controllers during the formulation of their systems and operations for compliance with the seventh data protection principle and the Data Protection Act 1998 generally. It claims that it will help to increase trust in the workplace, encourage good housekeeping, protect organisations from legal action, encourage workers to treat customers' personal data with respect, achieve compliance with other legal obligations (such as those found in the Human Rights Act 1998 and the Regulation of Investigatory Powers Act 2000), achieve global compliance and prevent the illicit use of information by workers.

The Code consists of four parts:

1   Recruitment and selection.
2   Employment records.
3   Monitoring at work.
4   Information about workers' health.

[1] http://www.ico.gov.uk/SearchResultAsHtml.aspx?cid=n6oc28uUpdAJ&page=http://www.ico.gov.uk/upload/documents/library/data_protection/detailed_specialist_guides/employment_practices_code.pdf&keywords=Employment%20Practices%20Code.

Information Commissioner's position on pre-employment vetting

2.60 As regards pre-employment vetting, the Code advises at part 1.6:

Confidentiality, privacy and technology **2.61**

'Only use vetting where there are particular and significant risks involved to the employer, clients, customers or others, and where there is no less intrusive and reasonably practicable alternative.

Only carry out pre-employment vetting on an applicant as at late a stage as is practicable in the recruitment process.

Make it clear early in the recruitment process that vetting will take place and how it will be conducted.

Only use vetting as a means of obtaining specific information, not as a means of general intelligence gathering. Ensure that the extent and nature of information sought is justified.

Only seek information from sources where it is likely that relevant information will be revealed. Only approach the applicant's family or close associates in exceptional cases.

Do not place reliance on information collected from possibly unreliable sources. Allow the applicant to make representations regarding information that will affect the decision to finally appoint.

Where information is collected about a person other than the applicant that affects the other person's privacy, ensure so far as practicable that the other person is made aware of this.

If it is necessary to secure the release of documents or information from a third party, obtain a signed consent from the applicant.'

Information Commissioner's position on employee monitoring

2.61 As regards employee monitoring, the Code advises controllers to carry out privacy impact assessments prior to the commencement of monitoring and warns them to be alert to any adverse impacts. Controllers are also advised to consider whether there are any alternatives to monitoring. In particular, it advises:

'Identify who within the organisation can authorise the monitoring of workers and ensure they are aware of the employer's responsibilities under the Act.

Before monitoring, identify clearly the purpose(s) behind the monitoring and the specific benefits it is likely to bring. Determine – preferably using an impact assessment – whether the likely benefits justify any adverse impact.

If monitoring is to be used to enforce the organisation's rules and standards make sure that the rules and standards are clearly set out in a policy which also refers to the nature and extent of any associated monitoring. Ensure workers are aware of the policy.

Tell workers what monitoring is taking place and why, and keep them aware of this, unless covert monitoring is justified.

If sensitive information is collected in the course of monitoring, ensure that a sensitive data condition is satisfied.

Keep to a minimum those who have access to personal information obtained through monitoring. Subject them to confidentiality and security requirements and ensure that they are properly trained where the nature of the information requires this.

2.61 Confidentiality, privacy and technology

Do not use personal information collected through monitoring for purposes other than those for which the monitoring was introduced unless: (a) it is clearly in the individual's interest to do so; or (b) it reveals activity that no employer could reasonably be expected to ignore.

If information gathered from monitoring might have an adverse impact on workers, present them with the information and allow them to make representations before taking action.

Ensure that the right of access of workers to information about them which is kept for, or obtained through, monitoring is not compromised. Monitoring systems must be capable of meeting this and other data protection requirements.

Do not monitor workers just because a customer for your products or services imposes a condition requiring you to do so, unless you can satisfy yourself that the condition is justified.

If you wish to monitor electronic communications, establish a policy on their use and communicate it to workers.

Ensure that where monitoring involves the interception of a communication it is not outlawed by the Regulation of Investigatory Powers Act 2000.

Consider – preferably using an impact assessment – whether any monitoring of electronic communications can be limited to that necessary to ensure the security of the system and whether it can be automated.

If telephone calls or voice-mails are, or are likely to be, monitored, consider – preferably using an impact assessment – whether the benefits justify the adverse impact. If so, inform workers about the nature and extent of such monitoring.

Ensure that those making calls to, or receiving calls from, workers are aware of any monitoring and the purpose behind it, unless this is obvious.

Ensure that workers are aware of the extent to which you receive information about the use of telephone lines in their homes, or mobile phones provided for their personal use, for which your business pays partly or fully. Do not make use of information about private calls for monitoring, unless they reveal activity that no employer could reasonably be expected to ignore.

If e-mails and/or internet access are, or are likely to be, monitored, consider, preferably using an impact assessment, whether the benefits justify the adverse impact. If so, inform workers about the nature and extent of all e-mail and internet access monitoring.

Wherever possible avoid opening e-mails, especially ones that clearly show they are private or personal.

Where practicable, and unless this is obvious, ensure that those sending e-mails to workers, as well as workers themselves, are aware of any monitoring and the purpose behind it.

If it is necessary to check the e-mail accounts of workers in their absence, make sure that they are aware that this will happen.

Inform workers of the extent to which information about their internet access and e-mails is retained in the system and for how long.

If video or audio monitoring is (or is likely) to be used, consider – preferably using an impact assessment – whether the benefits justify the adverse impact.

Confidentiality, privacy and technology 2.61

Give workers a clear notification that video or audio monitoring is being carried out and where and why it is being carried out.

Ensure that people other than workers, such as visitors or customers, who may inadvertently be caught by monitoring, are made aware of its operation and why it is being carried out.

Senior management should normally authorise any covert monitoring. They should satisfy themselves that there are grounds for suspecting criminal activity or equivalent malpractice and that notifying individuals about the monitoring would prejudice its prevention or detection.

Ensure that any covert monitoring is strictly targeted at obtaining evidence within a set timeframe and that the covert monitoring does not continue after the investigation is complete.

Do not use covert audio or video monitoring in areas which workers would genuinely and reasonably expect to be private.

If a private investigator is employed to collect information on workers covertly make sure there is a contract in place that requires the private investigator to only collect information in a way that satisfies the employer's obligations under the Act.

Ensure that information obtained through covert monitoring is used only for the prevention or detection of criminal activity or equivalent malpractice. Disregard and, where feasible, delete other information collected in the course of monitoring unless it reveals information that no employer could reasonably be expected to ignore.

If in-vehicle monitoring is or will be used, consider – preferably using an impact assessment – whether the benefits justify the adverse impact.

Set out a policy that states what private use can be made of vehicles provided by, or on behalf of, the employer, and any conditions attached to use.

Before undertaking any monitoring which uses information from third parties, ensure – preferably using an impact assessment – that the benefits justify the adverse impact.

Tell workers what information sources are to be used to carry out checks on them and why the checks are to be carried out.

Ensure that, if workers are monitored through the use of information held by a credit reference agency, the agency is aware of the use to which the information is put. Do not use a facility provided to conduct credit checks on customers to monitor or vet workers.

Take particular care with information about workers which you have as a result of a non-employment relationship with them.

Ensure that workers carrying out monitoring which involves information from third parties are properly trained. Put in place rules preventing the disclosure or inappropriate use of information obtained through such monitoring.

Do not retain all the information obtained through such monitoring. Simply record that a check has taken place and the result of this.'

2.62 *Confidentiality, privacy and technology*

FORCED SUBJECT ACCESS

2.62 Employers must avoid the possibility of being seen to require potential candidates for employment to use their rights of access to personal data[1] to obtain the disclosure of 'relevant records' from data controllers such as the police as part of the process of pre-employment vetting. Data Protection Act 1998, s 56 makes any such requirements a criminal offence:

> '56.— **Prohibition of requirement as to production of certain records**
> (1) A person must not, in connection with—
>   (a) the recruitment of another person as an employee,
>   (b) the continued employment of another person, or
>   (c) any contract for the provision of services to him by another person,
> require that other person or a third party to supply him with a relevant record or to produce a relevant record to him.
>
> ...
> (5) A person who contravenes subsection (1) or (2) is guilty of an offence.
> (6) In this section "a relevant record" means any record which—
>   (a) has been or is to be obtained by a data subject from any data controller specified in the first column of the Table below in the exercise of the right conferred by section 7, and
>   (b) contains information relating to any matter specified in relation to that data controller in the second column,
> and includes a copy of such a record or a part of such a record.'

The table referred to in subsection 6 covers criminal records relating to offences, convictions and cautions, which are held by the police, the Serious Organised Crime Agency and the Secretary of State. If a data controller wishes to gain access to this information it has two choices. First, it can ask the candidate for employment relevant questions, subject to the provisions of the Rehabilitation of Offenders Act 1974. Second, it can use the services of the Criminal Records Bureau.

[1] See the Data Protection Act 1998, s 7.

PROCEDURES FOR DISCIPLINING AND DISMISSING EMPLOYEES

2.63 Data controllers need to put in place clear and fair procedures for disciplining and dismissing employees for breaches of security policies and procedures. These procedures must be informed by employment law concerns as well as data security and privacy law concerns. Disciplinary procedures should be designed to be non-discriminatory and non-harassing, as well as being designed to avoid claims of constructive dismissal, unfair dismissal and wrongful dismissal.

In order to avoid problems with employment law it is vital that the controller's requirements and expectations for data security are clear and properly communicated to the employee. Wherever possible the controller should obtain written evidence that the employee has seen, read and understood their obligations[1].

Confidentiality, privacy and technology **2.65**

The final report of the Data Handling Review should also be considered, which provides that all government departments must 'amend HR processes where necessary to make clear that failing controls in handling personal data could amount to gross misconduct'[2].

[1] See, for example *British Telecommunications plc v Rodrigues* [1995] EAT (854/92).
[2] It also says that 'HR processes in Departments will be amended where necessary to make clear that failing to apply controls in handling sensitive data is a serious matter, and could amount to gross misconduct'.

BS 7858:2006 ON SECURITY SCREENING

2.64 Data controllers may be assisted in the development of employee screening programmes by BS 7858:2006, 'Security screening of individuals employed in a security environment – Code of practice', the scope of which is to give 'recommendation for the security screening of individuals to be employed in an environment where the security and safety of people, goods or property is a requirement of the employing organisation's operations and/or where such security screening is in the public interest'.

The Standard includes a series of pro forma documents that can be used for screening purposes.

PRACTICAL STEPS TO ENSURE RELIABILITY OF EMPLOYEES

2.65 The steps that a data controller can take to ensure the reliability of employees include:

1. The taking up of references on candidates for employment.
2. Obtaining verification of the candidate's complete employment and educational history.
3. Structured interviews of candidates.
4. Psychometric testing of candidates.
5. Medical testing of candidates, extending to a review of medical records and testing for substance use.
6. Background checks of candidates through the Criminal Records Bureau.
7. Credit reference agency checks on candidates.
8. Inspecting original qualification certificates.
9. Inspecting original documents that help to verify identity and address, such as passports, driving licences and utility bills.
10. Verifying any entitlements to work in the jurisdiction, such as visas and work permits.
11. Reviewing social networking sites for candidates' postings.
12. Obtaining the employee's contractual agreement, via the employment contract, to adhere to relevant policies and systems. If appropriate, statutory declarations can be sought.
13. Induction training on commencement of employment.
14. Periodic training and testing throughout the course of the employment.
15. Periodic medical checks and testing for substance use.

2.65 Confidentiality, privacy and technology

16   Physical checks of the employee on entry and departure from the workplace, including pat downs, bag searches, weight checking and scanning.
17   Limiting and controlling the employee's access rights and privileges to use computer systems and enter physical places.
18   Monitoring their electronic communications and use of computer systems, including home systems.
19   Installing CCTV in the workplace.
20   Covert monitoring and surveillance within the workplace and outside the workplace.

Some of these steps are highly intrusive and will require very compelling justifications in order to avoid an unjustifiable interference with privacy. However, if the circumstances justify it, all of these steps can be lawful as part of the requirement to ensure employee reliability.

Ensuring the reliability of data processors

2.66 The statutory interpretation to the seventh data protection principle[1] informs that compliance requires (a) the selection and monitoring of an appropriate data processor, with whom (b) a specified form of agreement with required content must be made.

[1]   Data Protection Act 1998, Sch 1, Pt II, paras 9–12.

THE AGREEMENT WITH A DATA PROCESSOR

2.67 Any processing of data by a third party must be carried out under a written contract[1] imposing obligations equivalent to the seventh data protection principle on the data processor, and permitting him or her to act only with instructions from the data controller[2]. Failure to comply with these requirements will automatically exclude the possibility of compliance with the principle by the controller.

[1]   Data Protection Act 1998, Sch 1, Pt II, para 12(a)(i).
[2]   Data Protection Act 1998, Sch 1, Pt II, para 12(a)(ii) and (b).

THE SELECTION OF A DATA PROCESSOR

2.68 In order to comply with the seventh principle, it is the responsibility of the data controller to choose a data processor providing sufficient guarantees[1] in respect of technical and organisational security measures. The controller must also take reasonable steps to ensure compliance with those measures[2].

The selection criteria appear to be divisible into three requirements:
1   The provision by the processor of technical and organisational security guarantees.
2   Which are sufficient.

3   With which the controller must take reasonable steps to ensure compliance.

The first of these requirements can presumably be fulfilled by effective contractual promises from the processor, but what form they must take to constitute guarantees is unclear. At law, a guarantee is an agreement to perform or procure performance of another party's contractual duties. To apply that meaning to the present scenario requires some imagination, as there is a conspicuous absence of a third party whose performance is to be guaranteed. The processor can guarantee its own performance, which it must presumably do by contractually binding itself to act in accordance with appropriate technical and security measures.

It seems rational to interpret the second requirement, for sufficiency, as a requirement that the guarantees, if fulfilled, would provide sufficient security to comply with the data protection principles, essentially contractually extending the controller's duties under the principles to the processor.

The third requirement is more difficult to interpret. Aside from obtaining effective contractual promises, there are a number of possible checks the data controller can carry out, ranging from simply checking that the processor has sufficient technical and organisational procedures in place to extensive micro-management of the processor, but there is no guidance on what level of activity will constitute reasonable steps and so avoid breaching the principle.

Robust indemnities given by the processor will create a strong and continuing incentive to ensure compliance, as they will, in effect, cause the controller's liability for the processor's breach to pass back to the processor. If the statutory penalties imposed on the controller are considered reasonable steps sufficient to ensure compliance with the statute, then perhaps contractually reflecting those penalties onto the processor should also be.

1   Data Protection Act 1998, Sch 1, Pt II, para 11(a).
2   Data Protection Act 1998, Sch 1, Pt II, para 11(b).

OSTENSIBLY COMPETENT INDEPENDENT CONTRACTORS

2.69 An area of law that deals with similar duties in respect of third parties, and the avoidance thereof, is the common law on liability for the torts of contractors, where the apparent suitability of a contractor is key to avoiding liability.

'It is trite law that an employer who employs an independent contractor is not vicariously responsible for the negligence of that contractor'[1], so a duty to take care in carrying out work may be discharged by employing a contractor to carry out the work, subject to the proviso that they are ostensibly competent[2]. The case law contains some direction on what constitutes sufficient evidence of competence to relieve an individual of liability.

2.69 *Confidentiality, privacy and technology*

In *Haseldine v Daw and Son*³, the Court of Appeal held that a landlord had discharged his duty of care to a visitor, who was injured when a lift fell from the second floor, by employing a reputable firm of engineers (whose negligence had caused the accident). In the comparable case of *Salsbury v Woodland*⁴ the same court ruled that the defendant had performed her duty to hire an ostensibly competent tree felling contractor by engaging a party she had witnessed carrying out similar work.

These and other similar examples demonstrate that the requirement for a contractor to be ostensibly competent is not particularly high. If these principles are applied to the statutory requirement to take reasonable steps to ensure that data processors comply with their data protection guarantees it seems to be enough that the processor is professionally employed and experienced in the relevant field. However, there is further authority limiting the extent of protection provided by a contractor's ostensible competence.

1   *Salsbury v Woodland* [1970] 1 QB 324, [1969] 3 All ER 863.
2   *Haseldine v C A Daw and Son Ltd* [1941] 2 KB 343, [1941] 3 All ER 156.
3   *Haseldine v C A Daw and Son Ltd* [1941] 2 KB 343, [1941] 3 All ER 156.
4   [1970] 1 QB 324.

THE RELEVANCE OF TECHNICAL KNOWLEDGE AND EXPERIENCE

2.70 The facts of *Green v Fibreglass Ltd*¹ are similar to the above examples, with a contractor's negligence causing severe injury to the claimant. Again it was held that the defendants could discharge their duty of care by employing reputable and apparently competent experts, but in this case the court placed considerable emphasis on the fact that the defendants had no technical knowledge or experience in the relevant field.

The line of cases supporting the existence of a requirement of technical ignorance and inexperience differ from the cases referred to above, in that the defendants were held to owe an indelegable duty to the claimants which could not be satisfactorily discharged by the employment of a contractor.

In *Woodward v Mayor of Hastings (Corpn)*² the defendant was held not to have discharged its responsibility by employing an ostensibly competent contractor to clean snow from a step, because 'the craft of the charwoman may have its mysteries, but there is no esoteric quality in the nature of the work which the cleaning of a snow-covered step demands'. In *Thomson v Cremin* it was considered relevant to a finding that the employment of a contractor had not discharged a duty that 'the work in question in that case does not seem to me to have called for any special technical knowledge or experience which the ordinary shipowner does not possess'.

Salmon J in *Green* interpreted these and other decisions³ as stating that, where a defendant's own knowledge and experience is sufficient for him to have performed his duty of care himself, the duty will be considered indelegable and not be discharged by employing the services of an ostensibly competent contractor. This interpretation is sustained by the comments of Scott LJ in

Haseldine, that the defendant 'having no technical skill ... cannot rely on his own judgment and the duty of care towards his invitees requires him to obtain and follow good technical advice'.

These examples aid in determining the extent to which the idea of performance by appointment of a contractor is applicable to the current question, that of the level of action required from data controllers to constitute reasonable steps to ensure processors' compliance with the guarantees required by the seventh principle.

If the analogy is to be fully applied, then the technical knowledge and experience of the data controller must be taken into account. This means that, on this interpretation, the seventh principle duty to take reasonable steps to ensure processor compliance will not be discharged solely by the selection of an ostensibly competent data processor, because a data controller will presumably have sufficient knowledge and experience in the field to be aware of any failure to comply.

1   [1958] 2 QB 245, [1958] 2 All ER 521.
2   [1945] KB 174, [1944] 2 All ER 565.
3   *Bloomstein v Railway Executive* [1952] 2 All ER 418, 96 Sol Jo 496; *Pickard v Smith* (1861) 10 CBNS 470, 142 ER 535; *Wilkinson v Rea Ltd* [1941] 1 KB 688, [1941] 2 All ER 50.

DISCHARGING THE DUTY VIA AN EXPERT

2.71 The Occupiers' Liability Act 1957 states[1] that where damage is due to the faulty execution of work by an independent contractor the occupier will not be liable 'if in all the circumstances he had ... taken such steps (if any) as he reasonably ought in order to satisfy himself that the contractor was competent and that the work had been properly done'.

This exclusion from liability is similar in effect to the duty currently under discussion; both centre on the reasonableness of the steps taken to monitor a contractor's compliance with the statutory duty of the employer.

The difference in the wording of the two statutes primarily appears to affect the timing of the effort required by the duty. The occupier's duty is to take reasonable steps to 'satisfy himself that the ... work had been properly done' whereas the data controller's duty is to 'take reasonable steps to ensure compliance'. The former is clearly phrased as to create a duty to check after the event. The latter does not specify time, so it is arguable that the duty could be performed by exertions in advance of the work being done. However, as the working relationship between a data controller and processor may last some time, and the practices and standards of processors may change over the life of the arrangement, it is likely that a preliminary check will not be sufficient to 'ensure compliance'.

In the case of *AMF International Ltd v Magnet Bowling Ltd*[2] Mocatta J directly considered the scope and application of this provision of the Occupiers' Liability Act 1957. He stated that the employment of a reputable,

2.71 *Confidentiality, privacy and technology*

competent contractor was not alone sufficient to discharge the duty; some further checking is required. However, this checking need not be carried out by the employer:

> 'In cases ... where it is reasonable for the [party burdened with the duty] to employ an independent contractor to perform technical work and he ought to see that the work has been properly done, then ... it [may be] reasonable ... to perform the latter duty through a professional man as an independent contractor, [and] he is not to be rendered liable because of the negligence by the latter.'

This interpretation allows that, where permitted delegation of a task is subject to a statutory duty, the delegation of the statutory requirement to ensure compliance is itself also delegable.

In the event, the court found against the defendant. Although it had appointed an expert independent contractor to oversee the building work, the duty to check the negligent work which caused the damage had not been effectively delegated to him.

The similarities between the two statutory duties suggest that an application of the logic of the decision in *AMF* to the Paragraph 11(b) duty to ensure compliance might be helpful.

As is the case with the *Green* contractor analogy above, this analogy also suggests that the appointment of a competent contractor will not alone constitute performance. It is more useful than the previous examples, however, as it answers in the positive as well as the negative, providing a specific method for compliance which is not simply direct oversight: the data controller can appoint an expert to ensure compliance with the processor's guarantees.

1   Occupiers' Liability Act 1957, s 2(4)(b).
2   [1968] 2 All ER 789, [1968] 1 WLR 1028.

WHAT IS AN EXPERT?

2.72 Mocatta J's reference to an architect as a 'properly qualified professional man' has no absolute analogy in the younger data security industry, but there are a number of qualifications available, for example the Information Systems Examination Board's Certificate in Information Security Management Principles offered by the British Standards Institution, and the various levels offered by the International Information Systems Security Certification Consortium.

The shorter OED definition of an expert makes reference to 'special skill, training ... knowledge' and 'experience'. In practice, it is likely that a properly qualified professional data security specialist would be an expert with experience, training and qualifications appropriate to the work they were carrying out.

It is likely that the properly qualified professional is permitted to perform a statutory duty not only due to their expertise; the professional standard also entails an ideal of impartiality and integrity. A role which exemplifies this standard is that of an expert witness. There are obvious divergences from the expert whose appointment discharges a statutory duty, but there are sufficient similarities to make the comparison worthwhile.

In the case of *The Ikarian Reefer*[1] Cresswell J provides an excellent summary of the duties and responsibilities of an expert witness in a civil case. It is made clear that the expert's evidence must be their own 'objective unbiased opinion', 'uninfluenced by the exigencies of litigation'. An expert 'should state the facts or assumption upon which his opinion is based', 'consider material facts which could detract from his opinion' and 'never assume the role of an advocate'. If the data upon which the expert's report is based is insufficient to the extent of preventing proper research, then 'this must be stated with an indication that the opinion is no more than a provisional one', and if the expert cannot vouch for the truth of anything contained in their report, a qualification to that effect must also be made.

[1] *The Ikarian Reefer* [1993] 2 Lloyd's Rep 68, [1993] FSR 563.

PROCESSOR AS AN EXPERT – DATA PROCESSOR SELF-MONITORING

2.73 Mocatta J's statement in *AMF* that the subject of the duty could avoid liability by '[causing the] work to be supervised by a properly qualified professional man' is not further clarified on the issue of the expert's independence from the contractor, as it was not an issue in the case.

If the important feature of this 'properly qualified professional man' (the appointment of whom excuses the subject of the statutory duty from checking the work himself under the Occupiers' Liability Act 1957 analogy) is the fact that they are a professional expert, rather than an independent third party, then a possibility with much commercial potential is available: the data processor itself could provide the expert knowledge to oversee its own technical and organisational security.

In the real world of data processing outsourcing, the data processor will frequently have more experience and knowledge than the controller, meaning that it will usually be in a better position than the controller to assess its practices. This approach obviously entails a problem – that it might be in the financial interests of a processor to give its security practices a clean bill of health when in fact they are inadequate.

To allow a professional expert whose position discharges a statutory duty to be in the employ of a party with an interest in the apparent discharge of that duty creates an uneasy state of potentially conflicting interests. Although (to continue the expert witness analogy) English law permits parties to a civil case to select their own experts, it should also be noted that the court provides a direct layer of security as the ultimate arbiter of the authority of the expert's testimony.

2.73   *Confidentiality, privacy and technology*

This inherent imbalance probably requires that, for the existence of a role of professional expert overseer within the processor organisation ever to be acceptable as discharging the controller's seventh principle duty to ensure compliance, the role should display a clear understanding of the importance of the professional standards of impartiality and integrity in the role's description and operation.

OUTSOURCING AND DATA PROCESSING SELF-MONITORING – THE DATA PROCESSOR AS EXPERT

2.74   The next step in continuing this line of argument is the suggestion that, instead of creating an internal role of professional expert, the data processor organisation itself fulfils this role. The professional requirements for experience and expertise can easily be mirrored as a group responsibility. Professional practice standards can be represented by the processor's information security policy and information security management system, and individual qualifications by organisational certifications, the obvious example being ISO/IEC 27001/2.

A purposive analysis of this solution to the duty will aid in evaluating the likelihood of judicial acceptance of the argument. The first, more straightforward, duty is to choose a data processor providing sufficient guarantees in respect of technical and organisational security measures. The second duty, which is currently under discussion, is to take reasonable steps to ensure compliance with those measures. If, as has been suggested, the data processor itself, by virtue of its expertise and qualifications, is permitted to perform the second duty on behalf of the controller, a question arises as to whether the line between the performance required by the duties becomes excessively blurred. It is, after all, the same expertise and qualifications which permit proper performance of the first duty, and to suggest that the guarantees provided in respect of data security themselves discharge the duty to ensure compliance with those same guarantees could be criticised as arguing the second duty entirely out of existence – the suggestion that the draftsman intended sufficient technical and organisational security measures to be capable of discharging the second duty begs the question of why the second duty to ensure compliance was created at all.

THE POSITION OF GOVERNMENT AND THE REGULATORS

2.75   Examining the documents produced by government departments, public authorities and the regulators will aid in assessing how they interpret the seventh principle responsibility on data controllers to ensure the compliance of data processors.

The Report on Data Handling Procedures in Government (the Data Handling Review)

2.76   Following high-profile data losses by government bodies, Data Handling Procedures in Government: Final Report was published by the Cabinet Office in June 2008.

This report sets out the government's policy on data handling and includes mandatory measures to be applied across government. It refers to the Data Protection Act 1998, and although it does not specifically contemplate the seventh data protection principle, it does consider the issue of applying the measures to third party data processors:

> 'The Government's guiding principle is that the protections outlined in this report, or their equivalent, should be in place and effective, no matter how information is held and processed for UK Government purposes. The same standards will be applied by contractors.'

At paragraph 3.5, the report clarifies how this is to be achieved:

> 'Contractors will, as part of their service provision, handle information belonging to the Department or to the public for whom the Department serves. Departments will build into new contracts the new requirements set out in this report.'

Paragraph 3.6 states that 'the Office of Government Commerce (OGC) is updating the security clauses within its model ICT contract for services, which Departments will use to provide assurance that any contractor will have processes in place which comply with the new cross-Government requirements'.

The tone of this report suggests that the government believes that its duty as a data controller to ensure the compliance with data protection rules of its data processors can be discharged by including data handling requirements in contracts. The report does mention that some departments are monitoring the performance of their data processors and that independent monitoring of compliance will be provided by the Information Commissioner and the National Audit Office, but it is not clearly stated whether this will include monitoring of third party data processors.

The OGC Model Terms

2.77 The OGC Model Terms for ICT Services Agreements include a series of detailed provisions for data security. Among other things they require the contractor to arrange regular auditing and testing of its security processes. Additionally, they provide that the contracting authority may, at any time and without notice, carry out tests itself, including penetration testing, to verify the contractor's compliance with its security plan.

The contractor's obligations to conduct audits etc lend support to the proposition that contractually requiring self-monitoring by the data processor may be sufficient to discharge the duty to ensure compliance. However, the right of the data controller to test and assess for itself the processor's systems for compliance with the data protection principles, as provided for in its security plan, implies that data processor self-monitoring may not be sufficient. Thus the Model Terms provide support for arguing for both greater or lesser supervision; the baseline position is that the data processor must

2.77 Confidentiality, privacy and technology

monitor its own compliance, but the controller is granted the rights to witness the testing and to conduct testing of its own.

On balance, it seems that the Model Terms do not support the proposition that self-monitoring by the processor will be sufficient. The permissions for the controller to monitor the processor's compliance are broad. The fact that monitoring by the controller is not made mandatory does not mean that the OGC envisages data controllers leaving assessment up to the processor; it merely reflects the commercial purpose of the Model Terms, which are designed (in part) to ensure that contractors are contractually bound to avoid causing authorities to be in breach of their duties. The Model Terms procure that authorities are equipped with the tools to achieve compliance with their statutory duties; it would be inappropriate for them to fully prescribe how the authority should achieve compliance, so the absence of a mandatory requirement for authority checking does not support the view that processor self-monitoring is sufficient.

Chapter 4 contains extracts from version 2.3 of the Model Terms, which was published in July 2009.

The Financial Services Authority: Data Security in Financial Services

2.78 The FSA data security report published in April 2008 sets out the findings of the FSA's review of firms' controls to prevent data loss by their employees and third-party suppliers. It found the data security practices of many firms to be inadequate. As to the extent the report can help with the present question, it quotes the seventh principle duty to ensure processor compliance, but does not explicitly clarify what the FSA understands to be the extent of the duty.

However, where the report criticises data controllers' relationships with third parties and highlights good practice, we can infer a framework of behaviour which the FSA considers suitable to discharge the seventh principle duty.

The FSA found that it was common throughout the financial services industry for firms to provide third parties access to customer data. The FSA was 'disappointed' to report that most firms 'were over-reliant on third parties to comply with contractual obligations', and that 'there was little evidence that firms either performed data security due diligence on third parties before agreeing a contract or that they exercised audit rights to ensure that third parties were meeting agreed standards throughout the contract term'. Specific factors that the FSA recommended should be monitored included which data processor individuals have access to data, how those individuals are vetted, whether data could be copied and methods of transmission and storage used by data processors.

In the section headed 'Managing third-party suppliers – examples of good practice' the FSA makes six recommendations for data controllers. These are: conducting due diligence of data security standards at third parties before

Confidentiality, privacy and technology **2.79**

contracts are agreed; conducting regular reviews of processors' data security systems; actively testing processors' staff vetting procedures; restricting access to the minimum necessary for specific tasks; subjecting processors to procedures for reporting data security breaches within an agreed timeframe; and ensuring security of data transfer to third parties.

The FSA also provide examples of poor practice, which include: failing to carry out due diligence of processor data security arrangements; not knowing exactly which staff have access to the data, or how they have been vetted (if at all); and failing to monitor third-party access to data.

Many of these examples of good and bad practice involve a degree of verification (or a failure to verify), with some being dependent on continued monitoring, suggesting that the FSA considers this to be a requirement for discharging the seventh principle duty. The idea of the self-monitoring processor is not directly considered, but the wording of the report indicates an assumption that the responsibility remains with the data controller.

The Information Commissioner's Office

2.79 The Information Commissioner's Office (ICO) has published responses, guidance and enforcement notices which provide some direction on its expectations for the relationship between data controllers and processors.

For example, on 3 November 2008 the ICO published its response to the Data Handling Review[1], the Poynter Report, the IPCC Report into HMRC and the Burton Report. The issue of data processor self-monitoring is not directly discussed in the response. The data controller's responsibility to ensure that a processor has 'suitable protections' in place is mentioned, but there is no direct reference to a continuing duty to monitor compliance.

On 21 February 2008 Skipton Financial Services signed an undertaking at the behest of the ICO, after an unencrypted laptop containing customer details was stolen. The undertaking included this paragraph:

> 'Risk assessments shall be carried out to confirm the adequacy and effectiveness of technical and organisational security measures governing any processing by those acting on the data controller's behalf prior to engaging any third party being appointed as a data processor.'

This suggests that a prior examination of data processor security measures will be required as a minimum, but the undertaking does not specifically mention continual monitoring. It does not specify the identity of the party that will do the assessments, leaving open the possibility of a third party expert monitor, and that of the self-monitoring expert.

The ICO's 'Data Protection Act Compliance Check Template'[2] is intended to investigate whether organisations' procedures 'comply with the data protection principles in Schedule 1 of the Data Protection Act'. It contains the following question on monitoring of data processors:

2.79 *Confidentiality, privacy and technology*

> 'Section 7.6: Choosing a Data Processor
>
> ...
>
> 4. Is there an on-going procedure for monitoring [the data processor's] data security measures?
>
> Yes No
>
> If yes, please describe. If no, please indicate why not'

This again demonstrates that the ICO considers ongoing monitoring of data processors a factor relevant to compliance with the seventh principle. However, the template does not ask whether the controller itself is actively involved with the monitoring, leaving the door open for a third party expert to fulfil the role. It does not strictly rule out the possibility of self-monitoring by the processor, as this could be described as 'an on-going procedure for monitoring'.

[1] 'Taking stock, taking action, The ICO position on the Government Data Handling Reviews': http://www.ico.gov.uk/upload/documents/library/data_protection/detailed_specialist_guides/ico%20position%20paper%20on%20data%20loss%20reports.pdf.

[2] See the Privacy Impact Assessment Handbook: http://www.ico.gov.uk/upload/documents/pia_handbook_html_v2/files/PIAhandbookV2.pdf.

2.80 The ICO has released its own legal guidance on the interpretation of the Data Protection Act 1998. The guidance on the part of the seventh principle under discussion here does not offer any clarification further than restating the guidance contained in the Data Protection Act 1998, Sch 1, Pt II, para 11. For further guidance the document suggests referring to BS 7799 and ISO/IEC Standard 17799.

BS 7799 was adopted as ISO/IEC 17799, 'Information technology – Security techniques – Code of practice for information security management' and renamed ISO/IEC 27002 in July 2007. It is the international standard for data security.

At 6.2.3 (Addressing security in third party agreements) the standard suggests terms to be considered for inclusion in agreements between data controllers and data processors to satisfy identified security requirements, which include:

> 'o)the right to audit responsibilities defined in the agreement, to have those audits carried out by a third party, and to enumerate the statutory rights of auditors.'

The same subsection recommends that, if information security management is outsourced, agreements should address how the third party will guarantee that adequate security is maintained.

In common with the OGC Model Terms and the FSA examples of good practice, the standard advises that the relationship between controller and processor should provide for continual monitoring, but, by omission, does not rule out the idea of a self-monitoring processor.

One part of the standard which comes close to commenting on the concept is at 15.3.1 (Information systems audit controls), which states that:

'The following guidelines should be observed:
i) the persons(s) carrying out the audit should be independent of the activities audited.'

This appears to be intended to apply to parties subject to a data protection duty themselves, rather than a duty to ensure the compliance of others, but it demonstrates that the principle of independence is taken into account in judging whether monitoring activities are carried out in accordance with good practice. This does not preclude acceptance of the self-monitoring processor, but it does strongly suggest that, as submitted above, the role of monitor within the processor organisation must clearly demonstrate impartiality and integrity in both description and operation if it is ever to be considered acceptable practice.

The tone of ICO guidance on the seventh principle indicates that processor self-monitoring is unlikely to be acceptable to the ICO as a method of discharging the controller's duty to ensure compliance.

2.81 A solution which is more likely to find acceptance is that of the independent third party monitor. As submitted above, there is legal precedent for the discharge via a third party expert of a duty to ensure the good performance of a contractor and with the elimination of independence as a serious hurdle, there are fewer arguments against this role.

An argument which could be raised against both of these solutions is that the drafting of the guidance to the seventh principle reflects the greater commercial power of the data controller, and is intended to ensure that the data controller cannot discharge the duty by any means other than direct monitoring of the processor.

However, if this is the intention, the drafting could certainly be clearer; the duty to 'take reasonable steps to ensure compliance' does not logically exclude the possibility of discharge by appointment of a third party expert, particularly (as noted above) as a similar duty[1] has been found to be discharged by a similar practice[2], nor does it preclude the possibility of self-monitoring.

Data processor self-monitoring has much to commend it from a commercial perspective, but it is susceptible to abuse and failure to a greater extent than other solutions. In order for processor self-monitoring to have any chance of being accepted in court, positions and procedures demonstrating a clear understanding of the rationale behind the seventh principle duties and the importance of independence will need to be established within processor organisations, and the procedures themselves should be subjected to scrutiny by controllers before contracting.

[1] Occupiers' Liability Act 1957, s 2(4)(b).
[2] *AMF International Ltd v Magnet Bowling Ltd* [1968] 2 All ER 789, [1968] 1 WLR 1028.

2.82   *Confidentiality, privacy and technology*

OFFSHORING AND TRANSBORDER DATA FLOWS – SENDING PERSONAL DATA OUT OF THE EEA

2.82 The European Commission has published model contractual clauses, which can be used by data controllers to legitimise the transfer of personal data to data processors situated in countries outside of the European Economic Area whose laws do not ensure adequate protection for personal data[1]. As recitals (11) and (12) point out:

> 'The standard contractual clauses should provide for the technical and organisational security measures ensuring a level of security appropriate to the risks represented by the processing and the nature of the data to be protected that a data processor established in a third country not providing adequate protection must apply. Parties should make provision in the contract for those technical and organisational measures which, having regard to applicable data protection law, the state of the art and the cost of their implementation, are necessary in order to protect personal data against accidental or unlawful destruction or accidental loss, alteration, unauthorised disclosure or access or any other unlawful forms of processing.
>
> In order to facilitate data flows from the Community, it is desirable that processors providing data processing services to several data controllers in the Community be allowed to apply the same technical and organisational security measures irrespective of the Member State from which the data transfer originates, in particular in those cases where the data importer receives data for further processing from different establishments of the data exporter in the Community, in which case the law of the designated Member State of establishment should apply.'

The description of the security measures that are to be adopted by the data processor are required to be inserted in Appendix 2 to the model clauses.

The Commission has also adopted model clauses for exports of personal data to data controllers situated outside the EEA[2] and it is likely that new model clauses will be adopted for the export of data from data processors to sub-processors situated outside the EEA[3].

[1]   Commission Decision of 27 December 2001 on standard contractual clauses for the transfer of personal data to processors established in third countries, under Directive 95/46/EC (2002/16/EC): http://eur-lex.europa.eu/LexUriServ/LexUriServ.do?uri=OJ:L:2002:006:0052:0062:EN:PDF.
[2]   Commission Decision of 15 June 2001 on standard contractual clauses for the transfer of personal data to third countries, under Directive 95/46/EC (2001/497/EC): http://eur-lex.europa.eu/LexUriServ/LexUriServ.do?uri=OJ:L:2001:181:0019:0031:EN:PDF.
      Commission Decision of 27 December 2004 amending Decision 2001/497/EC as regards the introduction of an alternative set of standard contractual clauses for the transfer of personal data to third countries (2004/915/EC): http://eur-lex.europa.eu/LexUriServ/LexUriServ.do?uri=OJ:L:2004:385:0074:0084:EN:PDF.
[3]   Opinion 3/2009 on the Draft Commission Decision on standard contractual clauses for the transfer of personal data to processors established in third countries, under Directive 95/46/EC: http://ec.europa.eu/justice_home/fsj/privacy/docs/wpdocs/2009/wp161_en.pdf.

PRACTICAL STEPS TO BE TAKEN TO ENSURE RELIABILITY OF DATA PROCESSORS

2.83 In conclusion, the data controller must implement practical measures to ensure that their relationships with data processors are and remain fully compliant with the seventh data protection principle. In summary, the following issues should be addressed by the controller:

1. *Pre-contractual due diligence.* Relevant enquiries should be raised about the processor's systems and operations for data security. In particular enquiries should be raised about policies, physical security, IT security, workers, risk assessments, incident prevention, incident detection, incident response, past security breaches, audit arrangements, notification under the Data Protection Act 1998, Pt III and any relevant prior dealings with government and regulators. In appropriate cases the controller should perform its own site visits and audits.

2. *Risk assessment.* In light of the pre-contractual due diligence the controller should perform a risk assessment, in order to arrive at an objectively supportable conclusion about the appropriateness of using the processor. If necessary this should be conducted in accordance with the Information Commissioner's Privacy Impact Assessment handbook.

3. *Contract formation.* The relationship with the controller should be governed by a written contract. Examples of suitable contractual terms can be found in the OGC Model Terms[1], although controllers should not fall into the trap of thinking that they are perfect or that they have covered all of the issues. However, at the very least they provide useful boilerplate clauses.

4. *Continual assessment.* The relationship with the processor should be subject to a process of continual assessment. This will include audits, penetration testing and interviews of key personnel, both announced and unannounced. The executive board of the data processor should be compelled to participate in interviews.

5. *Exit.* At the end of the relationship with the processor suitable mechanisms should be followed to ensure complete, verifiable cessation of processing. By way of reminder, the definition of processing is contained in the Data Protection Act 1998, s 1.

Of course, the controller must ensure that it retains a full written record of the measures that it has taken to ensure compliance.

[1] Copies can be obtained on the Partnerships UK website: http://www.partnershipsuk.org.uk/.

The state of technological development

2.84 The statutory interpretation accompanying the seventh data protection principle says that 'having regard to the state of technological development and the cost of implementing any measures, the measures must ensure a level of security appropriate' to the potential harm that might result from such theft, loss or damage, and the nature of the data protected. The Data Protection Act 1998 does not define 'the state of technological development' however.

The seventh data protection principle as espoused and explained in the Data Protection Act 1998 is derived from articles 16 and 17 of the Data Protection Directive. Article 17.1 contains the basis of the practical compromise between

2.84 *Confidentiality, privacy and technology*

cost, available technology, data protection and potential harm. Interestingly, the construction is slightly different: where the Data Protection Act 1998 requires regard for 'the state of technological development', the Directive provides for 'regard to the state of the art'.

It is unlikely that a court would interpret the wording of the Data Protection Act 1998 inconsistently with its interpretation of the wording of the Data Protection Directive[1]. Aside from the vertical direct effect of Directives in the courts of Member States, there is a general principle of statutory interpretation that municipal law should conform to international law[2], even where the international law is not expressly referred to in the Act[3]. Further, if the phrases are interpreted differently, and data protection law is administered in a manner inconsistent with the Data Protection Directive as a result, the European Commission may initiate proceedings in the European Court of Justice[4].

In natural use, the two phrases have very similar meanings, and so it is unlikely that a conflict will arise. An understanding of how 'the state of the art' is interpreted may help in ascertaining how the 'state of technological development' is likely to be interpreted.

[1] See, for example *Durant v Financial Services Authority* [2003] EWCA Civ 1746, [2004] FSR 573.
[2] 'Statutory Interpretation: A Code' Section 270, Francis Bennion, Butterworths 2002.
[3] *Salomon v Customs and Excise Comrs* [1967] 2 QB 116, [1966] 3 All ER 871.
[4] The European Commission has recently threatened such proceedings, due to the position taken in the UK on the Phorm case.

2.85 The 'state of the art' is defined by the Patents Act 1977, s 2, which, enacting article 54 of the European Patents Convention, states that:

'**2 Novelty**

...

(2) The state of the art in the case of an invention shall be taken to comprise all matter (whether a product, a process, information about either, or anything else) which has ... been made available to the public (whether in the United Kingdom or elsewhere) by written or oral description, by use or in any other way.'

This definition of 'state of the art' does not hold formidable weight, as the Patents Act 1977 is not dealing with the same issues as the Data Protection Directive. However it is still notable for its requirement that information be in the public domain.

The 'state of technological development' (and, by implication, the European Parliament's intention in using 'the state of the art') could, alternatively, be argued to be a very high standard, not containing a requirement of public availability, and might be interpreted in a very literal manner, as being the furthest limit of technological development. However, a construction without a requirement of public knowledge would be both unfair, as it would require data controllers to be aware of unpublished advances, and impracticable to enforce, as a court might be unable to determine a state of technological development which includes developments not in the public domain.

INDUSTRY PRACTICE – THE STATE OF TECHNOLOGY DEPLOYMENT

2.86 One way of measuring the state of technological development in the data security industry is to measure the state of technology deployment. This method suggests that a data controller should not be found to have breached the seventh principle if it has acted in accordance with industry practice, and, specifically, deployed technology which is in line with that used in similar circumstances by its contemporaries.

It can be argued that, as the statutory duty of the controller is worded specifically to take account of 'technological development' rather than 'technological deployment', this analogy is inappropriate. However, in many respects controllers do not act in a vacuum; the actions of contemporaries provide useful context for the evaluation of their practices. The practice of judicial benchmarking is well developed in the field of negligence law, where we may discover further direction.

The standard of care for negligence may be informed by 'ordinary and recognised practice'[1]. So 'where there is evidence that for a significant period of time a practice has been followed without untoward result, it will be regarded as a strong indication that to follow the practice is consistent with reasonable care'[2].

[1] *Wright v Cheshire CC* [1952] 2 All ER 789.
[2] 'Charlesworth and Percy on Negligence' Paragraph 6-37, Sweet and Maxwell 2006.

PROFESSIONAL NEGLIGENCE

2.87 The standard of care and skill required for a professional who has caused some harm to avoid being found guilty of negligence is espoused in the case of *Bolam v Friern Hospital Management Committee*[1]. The 'Bolam test', as it is known, requires that the professional acts with the standard of care and skill possessed by a professional of ordinary competence in the same field.

In the case of *Eckersley v Binnie*[2], Bingham LJ stated that the Bolam test required that a professional 'should not lag behind other ordinary assiduous and intelligent members of his profession in knowledge of new advances, discoveries and developments in his field'.

The Bolam test is a reference to the knowledge and practice of other members of the profession; for a professional to avoid breaching the standard of care and skill expected of them they must act in accordance with the accepted practices of their profession.

The data security profession has international standards, qualifications and guidelines, and the role of the data security officer is one which requires

2.87 *Confidentiality, privacy and technology*

special skill and training. This suggests that the Bolam test is suitable for measuring the standard of care and skill required for data security professionals.

This standard takes into account not only the spread of new methods, but also the availability of technology. In the case of *Whiteford v Hunter*[3] the House of Lords affirmed the Court of Appeal's decision that a London surgeon was not negligent in failing to use one of two specialist tools for a bladder examination, taking into account the fact that both instruments were difficult to obtain in England at the material time.

Continuing the analogy between the 'prevalent standards' defence to a claim of breach of duty and the meaning of 'regard to the state of technological development', the interesting factor in the case is that the House of Lords held that, although the technology was available, the fact that it was not easy to obtain was taken into account in whether the defendant had a duty to use it. If the analogy holds, this could suggest that 'the state of technological development' includes regard to the ease of obtaining technology, not simply whether a technology is publicly available[4].

It must be noted that the benchmarking of a defendant's actions against standard industry or professional practice is not a panacea; where general practice is below par it will be no defence to show that the defendant complied with it. In *Morris v West Hartlepool SN Co*[5], Lord Reid first quoted Lord Dunedin's statement of the law in *Morton v William Dixon Ltd*[6], that, to show negligent omission, it must be demonstrated either that the thing not done 'was a thing which was commonly done by other persons in like circumstances' or that 'it was a thing which was so obviously wanted that it would be folly in anyone to neglect to provide it', before adding his own conclusion, that evidence of general practice will hold little weight if it has not been followed sufficiently widely without mishap in similar circumstances.

[1] [1957] 2 All ER 118, [1957] 1 WLR 582.
[2] (1987) 18 Con LR 1.
[3] [1950] WN 553.
[4] See for example the TJ Hooper case, 60 F.2d 737 (1932), a decision of the US courts, which was concerned with the use of radio equipment on a tug boat. The tug boat lost its cargo in bad weather and the cargo owners argued that had the captain used radio to check the weather conditions he could have avoided the danger zone. The court found for the cargo owners despite the fact that the installation of radio equipment was not a standard practice. Prominent with the court's decision was the fact that the equipment was relatively cheap to install.
[5] [1956] AC 552, [1956] 1 All ER 385.
[6] 1909 SC 807.

2.88 Generally, the limit of benchmarking as establishing good practice is where standard practice is not good practice. The particular problem for any attempt to apply the process to the definition of 'regard to the state of technological development', is that, compared with older industries and professions, technological advances in the field of data protection occur more frequently, allowing less scope for a demonstration of widespread practice over time without mishap.

A further issue is that the Information Commissioner's Office has, in its enforcement actions, exhibited a belief that data controllers are remiss in their deployment of available technology as an industry, suggesting that conforming to general practice may not be accepted as evidence of conforming to good practice.

The example which first springs to mind is that of encryption. Encryption software is widely available, and has been for many years, but has arguably not yet become standard practice. Nearly half of enforcement notices published by the ICO in 2008 mentioned encryption of removable media or mobile computer equipment.

The comparative novelty of data security law, as mentioned above, is at the centre of the distinction between the rules relating to this industry and those permitting reference to common practice in defence of a negligence claim. The development of data security law is relatively new, as are the bodies and methods available for its enforcement, which arguably suggests that the very intention of the development is the changing of general practice, which is insufficient to meet acceptable standards.

This view is supported by the response from various state bodies to recent high-profile data security breaches. The Financial Services Authority and the Cabinet Office both released documents in 2008 requiring improvement in data security practices in the financial services industry and the public sector respectively – if general standards in data security merit the frequent attentions of the state and so many inches in newspaper columns, then perhaps they are not a sound basis for determining the application of laws passed to improve those practices.

WHOSE TECHNOLOGICAL DEVELOPMENT?

2.89 It is natural to focus on the technology available to the data controller in examining the state of technological development in determining sufficiency of technical measures, but the controller is not the only actor for whom the availability of technology is an issue.

Criminal organisations and malicious individuals with an interest in theft of or damage to private data exist and the level of technological development available to them should also be taken into account in determining appropriate technical security measures, as, apart from accidental loss, they constitute one of the main counterweights to successful data security practices.

PRIVACY ENHANCING TECHNOLOGIES (PETs)

2.90 There is now a growing expectation at European Commission level and within the national regulators for data protection that data controllers will install 'Privacy Enhancing Technologies' (PETs)[1].

2.90 Confidentiality, privacy and technology

PETs are discussed in more depth in Chapter 8, but at this juncture it is worth noting that in May 2007 the European Commission published a communication to the European Parliament and Council[2], calling for the promotion of privacy through the use of PET. The Information Commissioner has also issued a series of guidance papers supporting the use of PET by data controllers[3].

In Chapter 1 it was observed that encryption is now regarded as de facto PET, which is attributable in part to the restriction of breach notification laws to unencrypted data. Breach notification is discussed in detail in Chapter 7. Other evidence that the use of PET is now a legal expectation is found within the Information Commissioner's and FSA's enforcement cases, which are discussed in Chapter 6. The government's Data Handling Review and the Security Policy Framework also act to further embed PET within the legal framework for data security.

[1] See, for example 'Privacy-Enhancing Technologies – White Paper for Decision Makers', Ministry of the Interior and Kingdom Relations, the Netherlands, December 2004.
[2] Communication from the Commission to the European Parliament and the Council on Promoting Data Protection by Privacy Enhancing Technologies (PETs), Brussels, 2.5.2007, COM(2007) 228 final.
[3] See 'PETs – Your New Best Friends', 27 April 2006 and 'Data Protection Guidance Note: Privacy enhancing technologies (PETs)', 29 March 2007.

Remedies for breach of the security obligation

2.91 Article 23 of the Data Protection Directive gives data subjects a right to compensation if they suffer 'damage' as a result of a breach of the national legislation adopted to transpose the Directive:

> '1. Member States shall provide that any person who has suffered damage as a result of an unlawful processing operation or of any act incompatible with the national provisions adopted pursuant to this Directive is entitled to receive compensation from the controller for the damage suffered.
>
> 2. The controller may be exempted from this liability, in whole or in part, if he proves that he is not responsible for the event giving rise to the damage.'

The requirements of article 23 have been transposed by the Data Protection Act 1998, s 13, which provides:

> '**13.— Compensation for failure to comply with certain requirements**
> (1) An individual who suffers damage by reason of any contravention by a data controller of any of the requirements of this Act is entitled to compensation from the data controller for that damage.
> (2) An individual who suffers distress by reason of any contravention by a data controller of any of the requirements of this Act is entitled to compensation from the data controller for that distress if—
>   (a) the individual also suffers damage by reason of the contravention, or
>   (b) the contravention relates to the processing of personal data for the special purposes.
> (3) In proceedings brought against a person by virtue of this section it is a defence to prove that he had taken such care as in all the circumstances was reasonably required to comply with the requirement concerned.'

COMPENSATION FOR DAMAGE AND DISTRESS

2.92 Section 13 separates the concept of distress from damage, enabling compensation for distress to be recovered only if damage is also suffered, unless the processing is for the 'special purposes' (which are the purposes of journalism, artistic purposes and literary purposes[1]). This distinction does not arise within article 23, which talks only about damage. This implies that damage includes distress. It also implies that the Directive did not intend a distinction to be drawn between different kinds of damage.

[1] See the Data Protection Act 1998, s 3.

Johnson v MDU – a restricted meaning of damage

2.93 The importance of these points becomes clear when the leading case on the meaning of damage is considered, *Johnson v Medical Defence Union*[1], a decision of the Court of Appeal. The court held that for the purposes of s 13, 'there is no compelling reason to think that "damage" in the Directive has to go beyond its root meaning of pecuniary loss'. Leaving aside 'special purposes' cases, this means that a claimant will only be able to recover compensation for distress if they can prove that they have also suffered financial damage[2].

The approach to the meaning of damage preferred by the Court of Appeal does not fit well with the approach taken in the related area of negligence, where compensation, which is known as 'damages', is generally recoverable only if the claimant can prove physical damage, whether this be physical damage to the person or physical damage to a chattel[3]. In other words, the root meaning of damage in negligence cases is not pecuniary loss. Indeed, if only pecuniary loss is suffered (ie, pure economic loss) compensation (or 'damages') is generally only recoverable in negligence if the parties are in a close relationship, which might occur through an assumption of responsibility[4].

[1] [2007] EWCA Civ 262, [2007] 3 CMLR 181. See also *Quinton v Peirce* [2009] EWHC 912 (QB).
[2] See also the decision of Morland J in *Campbell v Mirror Group Newspapers* [2004] UKHL 22, [2004] 2 AC 457, who held that damage for the purposes of s 13 'means special or financial damages in contra-distinction to distress in the shape of injury to feelings'.
[3] The trial judge, Rimer J, identified pecuniary loss to include financial loss and physical damage.
[4] See the line of authority connecting cases such as *Hedley Byrne v Heller* [1964] AC 465, [1963] 2 All ER 575 and *Caparo Industries plc v Dickman* [1990] 2 AC 605, [1990] 1 All ER 568.

Problems with Johnson?

2.94 These points aside, there are other reasons to challenge the Court of Appeal's assertion that 'there is no compelling reason to think that "damage" in the Directive has to go beyond its root meaning of pecuniary loss'. Firstly, as already mentioned article 23 of the Directive does not make a distinction between damage and distress. Secondly, the Court of Appeal's approach might

2.94 *Confidentiality, privacy and technology*

have the effect of restricting the right to compensation to such an extent that compensation might never be recoverable, because it can be extremely difficult for potential claimants to prove that they have suffered pecuniary loss, even in the most outrageous cases of breach. In this sense the intention of article 23 might be emasculated by the Court of Appeal's approach. If this is the correct conclusion to draw, then the UK can be accused of failing to properly transpose article 23, exposing the country to the potential of a Francovich claim or infringement proceedings. Thirdly, this construction seems to ignore the true 'root' of data protection law, which is the European Convention on Human Rights. A breach of a fundamental right, like the right to privacy, is of itself such a serious issue that it can merit the award of compensation irrespective of any proof of pecuniary loss, in order to afford 'just satisfaction'[1]. In this sense a breach of fundamental rights can be treated as damage in its own right. Fourthly, awards of compensation also have a regulatory and deterrent effect, which can help to bring about compliance. Parliament has already accepted that due to the parlous state of data security in the UK the Information Commissioner should have a power to fine data controllers who breach the seventh data protection principle. Widening the application of s 13 to allow for the recovery of compensation for distress on a standalone basis could also help to improve data security in the same way as financial penalties, which could be said to be in the public interest. Fifthly, the Court of Appeal's approach encourages data subjects to incur low level pecuniary loss in order to overcome the barrier to distress compensation[2]. For example, following the notification of a security breach the individuals affected could subscribe to a low cost credit reporting service, which will provide a credit file watching service, a step designed to mitigate the risk of identify theft. While these may be low cost services when viewed on an individual basis, they can round up to truly massive sums of money in large-scale breach cases, such as HMRC, if everyone affected adopted the same behaviour. The effect of the Court of Appeal's judgment in *Johnson* is to encourage such behaviours, which has the potential of worsening the controller's position. Furthermore, if the pecuniary loss hurdle can be overcome through small and potentially unhelpful purchases, what utility is actually served by maintaining the pecuniary loss barrier to distress compensation?

The relationship between the Directive and the European Convention on Human Rights was examined before the Court of Appeal, as Buxton LJ's judgment reveals:

> 'Mr Johnson sought damages under three heads: pecuniary loss, incurred in achieving cover from another society, the MPS; damage for the distress caused to him by the removal of his cover with the MDU with no explanation given; and damage inflicted on his reputation by the removal of his MDU cover. Damages for distress are, by the plain terms of section 13(2)(a), only available if the claimant also suffers other "damage". Mr Howe argued that that limitation was inconsistent with the general rule of compensation for damage to be found in the Directive. The latter should be read in an autonomous Community sense, as requiring the provision of compensation for any sort of damage recognised in national law.
>
> While, like the Judge, I find this point not entirely straightforward, also like him I cannot accept it. In the absence of specific Community authority, none of which we were shown, I do not accept that the Directive has to be read so

widely. I bear in mind Mr Spearman's warning that the national laws of the member states differ in their approach to damages, and in particular in relation to compensation for injury to feelings or reputation. There is no compelling reason to think that "damage" in the Directive has to go beyond its root meaning of pecuniary loss. Nor do I accept Mr Howe's contention that the fact that the Directive envisages the protection of rights under article 8 of the European Convention (as to which, see §15 above) entails that compensation must be available in every case for loss of a type or category that would be covered by article 8: for example, damages for distress. If a party could establish that a breach of the requirements of the Directive had indeed led to a breach of his article 8 rights, then he could no doubt recover for that breach under the Directive, without necessarily pursuing the more tortuous path of recovery for a breach of article 8 as such. But that is not this case, since it is agreed that Mr Johnson can make no complaint under article 8: see §16 above. There is no reason to think that the Directive nonetheless requires Mr Johnson to be able to recover for a head of loss available under article 8 even if domestic law denies him that recovery.'

1   See, for example the Human Rights Act 1998, s 8(3)(b).
2   It should be noted that Mr Johnson was able to identify financial loss of £10.50. The trial judge, Rimer J, said that he would have awarded £5,000 distress compensation had causation been proved.

2.95 This part of Buxton LJ's judgment seems to accept that an article 8 claim can justify a standalone award of compensation for non-pecuniary loss, but it rejects the idea advanced earlier that a breach of the data protection principles will also constitute a breach of article 8. It is difficult to reconcile Buxton LJ's position with the position of Auld LJ in the earlier decision in *Durant v Financial Services Authority*, where Auld LJ held that for information to constitute personal data within the meaning of the Data Protection Act 1998, s 1 it must be 'information that affects his privacy', or, in other words it must be private in the sense understood by article 8. In *Durant* it seemed that Auld LJ was willing to accept a much closer connection between the Directive and the Convention than Buxton LJ was willing to accept in *Johnson*:

'It follows from what I have said that not all information retrieved from a computer search against an individual's name or unique identifier is personal data within the Act. Mere mention of the data subject in a document held by a data controller does not necessarily amount to his personal data. Whether it does so in any particular instance depends on where it falls in a continuum of relevance or proximity to the data subject as distinct, say, from transactions or matters in which he may have been involved to a greater or lesser degree. It seems to me that there are two notions that may be of assistance. The first is whether the information is biographical in a significant sense, that is, going beyond the recording of the putative data subject's involvement in a matter or an event that has no personal connotations, a life event in respect of which his privacy could not be said to be compromised. The second is one of focus. The information should have the putative data subject as its focus rather than some other person with whom he may have been involved or some transaction or event in which he may have figured or have had an interest, for example, as in this case, an investigation into some other person's or body's conduct that he may have instigated. In short, it is information that affects his privacy, whether in his personal or family life, business or professional capacity. A recent example is that considered by the European Court in Criminal Proceedings against Lindquist, Case C-101/01 (6th November 2003), in which the Court held, at para. 27, that "personal data" covered the name of a person or identification of him by some other means, for instance by giving his telephone number or information regarding his working conditions or hobbies.'

This apparent contradiction between the decisions in *Durant* and *Johnson* becomes even more puzzling when it is remembered that Buxton LJ gave the supporting judgment in *Durant*, where he said that he agreed 'with everything' said by Auld LJ. Buxton LJ then went on to say that:

'The guiding principle is that the Act, following Directive 95/46, gives rights to data subjects in order to protect their privacy. That is made plain in recitals (2), (7) and (11) to the Directive, and in particular by recital (10), which tells us that: "the object of the national laws on the processing of personal data is to protect fundamental rights and freedoms, notably the right to privacy, which is recognised both in Article 8 of the European Convention for the Protection of Human Rights and Fundamental Freedoms and in the general principle of Community law".'

The effect of the Court of Appeal's decision in *Durant* is that the Data Protection Directive is designed to protect privacy within the meaning of article 8 of the European Convention on Human Rights. On this basis it would seem to be logical to conclude that compensation for damage should be awarded on the same basis as under article 8 claims, without a requirement for proof of pecuniary loss. Such an approach would give effect to the intention of the Directive and would be more consistent with the judgment in *Durant*.

For a recent decision on the meaning of damage for the purpose of article 8 claims, see the decision of Mr Justice Eady in *Mosley v News Group Newspapers Ltd*[1], where the claimant was awarded £60,000 for non-pecuniary loss.

[1] [2008] EWHC 1777 (QB).

ARTICLE 29 WORKING PARTY'S VIEWS ON THE MEANING OF DAMAGE

2.96 It is worth noting the following opinion of the Article 29 Working Party, which has said:

'It should be borne in mind that "damage" in the sense of the Data Protection Directive includes not only physical damage and financial loss, but also any psychological or moral harm caused (known as "distress" under UK and US law).'[1]

Unfortunately, this opinion was not drawn to the Court of Appeal's attention in *Johnson*.

[1] 'Judging industry self-regulation: when does it make a meaningful contribution to the level of data protection in a third country?', Article 29 Working Party, 14 January 1998.

Consequences for controllers

2.97 So, what are the consequences for data controllers? For the time being at least the state of the law is that, special purposes cases aside, compensation will only be recoverable if pecuniary loss has been suffered. On first blush this should be a comfort for data controllers suffering a security breach. However, the comfort is limited, because it should be possible for data subjects to recover substantial compensation for distress when only nominal pecuniary loss has been suffered, which was the effect of Rimer J's judgment at first instance in *Johnson*. Rimer J effectively opened the floodgates to substantial distress compensation claims, which Buxton LJ failed to close. Buxton LJ said the following about Mr Johnson's claims:

> 'Mr Johnson originally claimed substantial amounts allegedly incurred in his attempt to obtain cover from the MPS. All of that case failed. However, at a late stage of the trial, and after Mr Johnson had left the witness box, a hotel bill was produced allegedly relating to the negotiations with the MPS. That bill showed items that, as the Judge found, were incurred by Mr Johnson for other purposes, but also included, apart from Mr Johnson's own bed and breakfast charges, a sum of £10.50 for an additional breakfast. After some lengthy consideration of the matter the Judge concluded, at his §230, that:
>
> "I am prepared to find, on the probabilities, that the £10.50 for the extra breakfast was referable to the meeting with the MPS representative. I have no reason not to accept Mr Johnson's evidence that such a meeting took place."
>
> No doubt the meeting took place, but the Judge had no evidence from Mr Johnson that it was over breakfast or that the extra breakfast that he paid for was eaten by the MPS representative; and much less that any purchase of breakfast was required of Mr Johnson as a step in the process of obtaining cover, a matter that I am certainly not prepared to assume. The Judge was not entitled to find that this, the only item of pecuniary damage that survived, was attributable to damage for which the MDU was responsible.
>
> Applying as I do the terms of section 13(2)(a), this claim fails in limine by reason of Mr Johnson's failure to prove damage in the terms of section 13(1). The Judge would have awarded £5,000 under this head if he had found the case proved. Mr Spearman criticised that amount, as plainly too high for the modest level of distress that the Judge had found, when compared with the standard measures for various kinds of personal damage. I agree with that criticism, but in view of the findings in the rest of this judgment it would be an undue use of judicial time to reason the matter out.'

Could 'claims farms' make business in data security breach litigation?

2.98 The critical point arising from the above passage is that Buxton LJ did not reject the idea that a claim for distress compensation could be built on a modest amount of pecuniary loss, £10.50. Furthermore, he did not provide any substantial reasoning for agreeing with the MDU's submission that £5,000 was 'plainly too high', nor did he provide any indication of what he considered to be a reasonable amount. However, these final points may not matter; for controllers what really matters is that a claim for distress

2.98 *Confidentiality, privacy and technology*

compensation can be built on very modest pecuniary loss. In other words, s 13 might contain a very low pecuniary loss barrier to the possibility of relatively substantial compensation for distress.

All it may take to make bulk litigation in the data security field a reality is an appreciation by claims farms of the true import of the Court of Appeal's decision in *Johnson* and the ease at which the pecuniary loss barrier to distress compensation can be overcome, perhaps through the funding of small purchases, such as credit file reporting.

Communications privacy

2.99 The providers of publicly available electronic communications services (telecommunications companies and internet service providers) are required to ensure the security of their services. Among other things, these security obligations should ensure the confidentiality of communications, in the sense that they should provide reasonable protection against unlawful surveillance and monitoring activities.

However, reflecting the carve-out from the right to privacy in article 8.2 of the European Convention on Human Rights and the public interest caveat within the duty of confidence, the protections against surveillance and monitoring are not absolute. The providers of publicly available electronic communications services are legally obliged to lower their security in order to permit surveillance and monitoring of communications if that is in the public interest. Thus, law enforcement agencies and intelligence agencies are entitled to bypass the service provider's security measures, thereby gaining a right of access to the very heart of communications systems. They can also be required to release traffic data for the purposes of civil proceedings, including in cases of alleged copyright infringement by file-sharers[1].

The malicious threats to data should also be kept in mind. These put communications and communications networks and services under constant attack.

In other words, there is no such thing as an absolutely secure electronic communication.

[1] See, for example, the decision of the European Court of Justice in *LSG-Gesellschaft zur Wahrnehmung von Leistungsschutzrechten GmbH v Tele2 Telecommunication* GmbH, C-557/07, 19 February 2009.

Regulators' obligation to ensure security

2.100 The provision of publicly available electronic communications networks and services is subject to a comprehensive legal framework consisting of five Directives. One of these Directives, the Electronic Communications Privacy Directive, which is discussed below, places specific security obligations on service providers, as previously mentioned.

Confidentiality, privacy and technology 2.102

In addition to the obligations placed on service providers, another one of the Directives, the Framework Directive[1], places an obligation on the national regulators for electronic communications, such as OFCOM in the UK, to ensure 'that the integrity and security of public communications networks are maintained'[2].

[1] Directive 2002/21/EC of the European Parliament and of the Council of 7 March 2002 on a common regulatory framework for electronic communications networks and services.
[2] Directive 2002/21/EC, article 8.4(f).

The Communications Directives of 1997, 2002 and 2006

2.101 In 1997 the European Community adopted a modified Data Protection Directive for the telecommunications sector[1], which applied to the provision of publicly available telecommunications networks and services. This Directive, which was sometimes known as the Telecommunications Privacy Directive, contained security and confidentiality provisions that echo those within articles 16 and 17 of the Data Protection Directive.

The Telecommunications Privacy Directive was repealed and replaced by Directive 2002/58/EC[2], which is sometimes called the Electronic Communications Privacy Directive. This contains similar security and confidentiality provisions.

Directive 2002/58/EC was itself amended by Directive 2006/24/EC[3], which is sometimes called the Communications Data Retention Directive, to require the compulsory retention of communications data by the providers of electronic communications services. This amending Directive also contains security provisions.

Since 2006 the 2002 Directive has been under further review and it is now subject to a variety of proposals for amendment, prominent within which are proposals for the introduction of a mandatory breach notification obligation. These proposals are discussed in Chapter 7.

[1] Directive 97/66/EC of the European Parliament and of the Council of 15 December 1997 concerning the processing of personal data and the protection of privacy in the telecommunications sector.
[2] Directive 2002/58/EC of the European Parliament and of the Council of 12 July 2002 concerning the processing of personal data and the protection of privacy in the electronic communications sector (Directive on privacy and electronic communications).
[3] Directive 2006/24/EC of the European Parliament and of the Council of 15 March 2006 on the retention of data generated or processed in connection with the provision of publicly available electronic communications services or of public communications networks and amending Directive 2002/58/EC.

THE REGIME FOR SECURITY AND CONFIDENTIALITY WITHIN THE
TELECOMMUNICATIONS PRIVACY DIRECTIVE

2.102 The security and confidentiality provisions in the 1997 Directive were as follows:

2.102   *Confidentiality, privacy and technology*

'Article 4 Security

1. The provider of a publicly available telecommunications service must take appropriate technical and organisational measures to safeguard security of its services, if necessary in conjunction with the provider of the public telecommunications network with respect to network security. Having regard to the state of the art and the cost of their implementation, these measures shall ensure a level of security appropriate to the risk presented.

2. In case of a particular risk of a breach of the security of the network, the provider of a publicly available telecommunications service must inform the subscribers concerning such risk and any possible remedies, including the costs involved.

Article 5 Confidentiality of the communications

1. Member States shall ensure via national regulations the confidentiality of communications by means of a public telecommunications network and publicly available telecommunications services. In particular, they shall prohibit listening, tapping, storage or other kinds of interception or surveillance of communications, by others than users, without the consent of the users concerned, except when legally authorised, in accordance with Article 14(1).

2. Paragraph 1 shall not affect any legally authorised recording of communications in the course of lawful business practice for the purpose of providing evidence of a commercial transaction or of any other business communication.'

THE REGIME FOR SECURITY AND CONFIDENTIALITY WITHIN THE ELECTRONIC COMMUNICATIONS PRIVACY DIRECTIVE

2.103   The security and confidentiality provisions in the 2002 Directive are as follows:

'Article 4

Security

1. The provider of a publicly available electronic communications service must take appropriate technical and organisational measures to safeguard security of its services, if necessary in conjunction with the provider of the public communications network with respect to network security. Having regard to the state of the art and the cost of their implementation, these measures shall ensure a level of security appropriate to the risk presented.

2. In case of a particular risk of a breach of the security of the network, the provider of a publicly available electronic communications service must inform the subscribers concerning such risk and, where the risk lies outside the scope of the measures to be taken by the service provider, of any possible remedies, including an indication of the likely costs involved.

Article 5

Confidentiality of the communications

1. Member States shall ensure the confidentiality of communications and the related traffic data by means of a public communications network and publicly available electronic communications services, through national legislation. In particular, they shall prohibit listening, tapping, storage or other kinds of interception or surveillance of communications and the related traffic data by

persons other than users, without the consent of the users concerned, except when legally authorised to do so in accordance with Article 15(1). This paragraph shall not prevent technical storage which is necessary for the conveyance of a communication without prejudice to the principle of confidentiality.

2. Paragraph 1 shall not affect any legally authorised recording of communications and the related traffic data when carried out in the course of lawful business practice for the purpose of providing evidence of a commercial transaction or of any other business communication.

3. Member States shall ensure that the use of electronic communications networks to store information or to gain access to information stored in the terminal equipment of a subscriber or user is only allowed on condition that the subscriber or user concerned is provided with clear and comprehensive information in accordance with Directive 95/46/EC, inter alia about the purposes of the processing, and is offered the right to refuse such processing by the data controller. This shall not prevent any technical storage or access for the sole purpose of carrying out or facilitating the transmission of a communication over an electronic communications network, or as strictly necessary in order to provide an information society service explicitly requested by the subscriber or user.'

THE REGIME FOR DATA PROTECTION AND DATA SECURITY WITHIN THE COMMUNICATIONS DATA RETENTION DIRECTIVE

2.104 The relevant provisions in the 2006 Directive are as follows:

'Article 7

Data protection and data security

Without prejudice to the provisions adopted pursuant to Directive 95/46/EC and Directive 2002/58/EC, each Member State shall ensure that providers of publicly available electronic communications services or of a public communications network respect, as a minimum, the following data security principles with respect to data retained in accordance with this Directive:

(a) the retained data shall be of the same quality and subject to the same security and protection as those data on the network;
(b) the data shall be subject to appropriate technical and organisational measures to protect the data against accidental or unlawful destruction, accidental loss or alteration, or unauthorised or unlawful storage, processing, access or disclosure;
(c) the data shall be subject to appropriate technical and organisational measures to ensure that they can be accessed by specially authorised personnel only;

and
(d) the data, except those that have been accessed and preserved, shall be destroyed at the end of the period of retention.'

KEY DIFFERENCES IN THE 1997 AND 2002 DIRECTIVES

2.105 The most obvious difference between the two Directives is the broader application of the 2002 Directive, which extends further than telecommunications, into the wider electronic communications sector, including the internet

2.105 Confidentiality, privacy and technology

sector, with the result that ISPs now carry clear obligations for security and confidentiality. Another obvious difference is the fact that article 5(3) of the 2002 Directive contains a qualified prohibition on the storage of (and access to) information within the subscriber or user's terminal equipment (which includes pcs and mobile phones).

There is a third critical distinction. Unlike the 1997 Directive, the 2002 Directive extends its confidentiality provisions at article 5(1) to traffic data; article 5(1) of the 1997 Directive refers only to 'the confidentiality of communications', whereas article 5(1) of the 2002 Directive refers to 'the confidentiality of communications and the related traffic data'.

Article 2 of the 2002 Directive defines 'traffic data' and 'communication' in the following manner:

> '(b) "traffic data" means any data processed for the purpose of the conveyance of a communication on an electronic communications network or for the billing thereof;
> ...
> (d) "communication" means any information exchanged or conveyed between a finite number of parties by means of a publicly available electronic communications service. This does not include any information conveyed as part of a broadcasting service to the public over an electronic communications network except to the extent that the information can be related to the identifiable subscriber or user receiving the information;'

This is clearly very significant; the 1997 Directive, like the 2002 Directive, regulated the processing of traffic data, but the European Commission decided to grant traffic data much greater protection under the 2002 Directive than that granted under the 1997 Directive. For the purposes of domestic law, the significance of this distinction is explained later.

THE EXCEPTIONS WITHIN THE REGIMES FOR CONFIDENTIALITY

2.106 The 1997 and 2002 Directives both contain carve-outs from the confidentiality obligations. Article 5(1) of the 1997 Directive referred to article 14(1), whereas the corresponding provision in the 2002 Directive refers to article 15(1). Article 15(1) provides as follows:

> '1. Member States may adopt legislative measures to restrict the scope of the rights and obligations provided for in Article 5, Article 6, Article 8(1), (2), (3) and (4), and Article 9 of this Directive when such restriction constitutes a necessary, appropriate and proportionate measure within a democratic society to safeguard national security (i.e. State security), defence, public security, and the prevention, investigation, detection and prosecution of criminal offences or of unauthorised use of the electronic communication system, as referred to in Article 13(1) of Directive 95/46/EC. To this end, Member States may, inter alia, adopt legislative measures providing for the retention of data for a limited period justified on the grounds laid down in this paragraph. All the measures referred to in this paragraph shall be in accordance with the general principles of Community law, including those referred to in Article 6(1) and (2) of the Treaty on European Union.'

As mentioned above, this carve-out corresponds with the carve-out from the right to privacy within article 8.2 of the European Convention on Human Rights[1] and it acts to 'lower' the service provider's security measures for the benefit of law enforcement and intelligence agencies.

The carve-outs in articles 5(2) of the Directives, which permit surveillance and monitoring for business purposes, do not act to lower security measures in the same way as article 5(1); the security implication is different, in the sense that the employee cannot keep their communications secure from inspection by their employers.

The security implication in article 5(3) of the 2002 Directive is different yet again. The starting point is that article 5(3) underlines the sanctity of the user's terminal equipment and information within. However, the service provider can overcome this if they operate transparently, or if storage/access is required from a technical perspective for the purposes of facilitating the transmission itself.

[1] The carve-out is contained in article 8.2.

The transposition of the 2002 Directive

2.107 The transposition of the 2002 Directive is represented by the Regulation of Investigatory Powers Act 2000, the Telecommunications (Lawful Business Practice) (Interception of Communications) Regulations 2000[1] and the Privacy and Electronic Communications (EC Directive) Regulations 2003[2].

It is immediately noticeable that two of the transposing instruments pre-date the 2002 Directive. The 2000 Act and Regulations actually gave effect to the 1997 Directive and they have not been updated to reflect the critical amendment within the 2002 Directive, which extended the article 5 protections to traffic data. In consequence of this a body of opinion has developed that questions the validity of the UK's transposition. In other words, it is considered that the UK might be in breach of its legal obligations.

[1] SI 2000/2699.
[2] SI 2003/2426.

REGULATION OF INVESTIGATORY POWERS ACT 2000

2.108 RIPA 2000 repealed and replaced the Interception of Communications Act 1985. Part of the explanation for the reform is that the UK needed to transpose the 1997 Directive and address the failings identified in the *Halford* case[1]. Thus RIPA 2000, Pt 1, Ch 1 deals with interception.

The rules on interception regulate interception by public authorities and interception by businesses (which includes public sector organisations), while recognising the principle of consent, which allows the parties to electronic communications, such as phone calls and emails, to waive their privacy rights

2.108 *Confidentiality, privacy and technology*

if they are minded to do so. It creates a series of criminal offences and a new tort, which contain deterrent effect. The law is also actively enforced[2].

In summary, RIPA 2000, s 1 makes it a criminal offence for a person to intentionally intercept communications in the course of their transmission by means of a public postal system, a public telecommunication system or a private telecommunication system without lawful authority. Section 1 also creates a tort of unlawful interception of communications transmitted by means of a private telecommunications system. The opening parts of s 1 read as follows:

> '**1.— Unlawful interception**
> (1) It shall be an offence for a person intentionally and without lawful authority to intercept, at any place in the United Kingdom, any communication in the course of its transmission by means of–
>   (a) a public postal service; or
>   (b) a public telecommunication system.
> (2) It shall be an offence for a person–
>   (a) intentionally and without lawful authority, and
>   (b) otherwise than in circumstances in which his conduct is excluded by subsection (6) from criminal liability under this subsection,
> to intercept, at any place in the United Kingdom, any communication in the course of its transmission by means of a private telecommunication system.
> (3) Any interception of a communication which is carried out at any place in the United Kingdom by, or with the express or implied consent of, a person having the right to control the operation or the use of a private telecommunication system shall be actionable at the suit or instance of the sender or recipient, or intended recipient, of the communication if it is without lawful authority and is either–
>   (a) an interception of that communication in the course of its transmission by means of that private system; or
>   (b) an interception of that communication in the course of its transmission, by means of a public telecommunication system, to or from apparatus comprised in that private telecommunication system.'

1   *Halford v United Kingdom* (1997) 24 EHRR 523, [1997] IRLR 471. The European Court of Human Rights found the UK to have violated article 8 of the Convention, because (1) the 1985 Act did not apply to interception of communications over private telecommunications systems and (2) it did not provide the subjects of interceptions with any effective legal remedies.
2   See, for example *R v Stanford* [2006] EWCA Crim 258, [2006] 1 WLR 1554.

The meaning of 'public telecommunication system'

2.109 The meaning of 'public telecommunication system' is defined in s 2(1), as follows:

> ' "public telecommunication system" means any such parts of a telecommunication system by means of which any public telecommunications service is provided as are located in the United Kingdom;'

'Telecommunication system' is defined as follows:

Confidentiality, privacy and technology 2.111

' "telecommunication system" means any system (including the apparatus comprised in it) which exists (whether wholly or partly in the United Kingdom or elsewhere) for the purpose of facilitating the transmission of communications by any means involving the use of electrical or electro-magnetic energy.'

A 'public telecommunications service' is defined as follows:

' "public telecommunications service" means any telecommunications service which is offered or provided to, or to a substantial section of, the public in any one or more parts of the United Kingdom;'

The meaning of 'private telecommunication system'

2.110 'Private telecommunication system' is defined as follows:

' "private telecommunication system" means any telecommunication system which, without itself being a public telecommunication system, is a system in relation to which the following conditions are satisfied—
(a) it is attached, directly or indirectly and whether or not for the purposes of the communication in question, to a public telecommunication system; and
(b) there is apparatus comprised in the system which is both located in the United Kingdom and used (with or without other apparatus) for making the attachment to the public telecommunication system;'

The meaning of 'communication'

2.111 The meaning of 'communication is defined in s 81(1):

' "communication" includes—
(a) (except in the definition of "postal service" in section 2(1)) anything transmitted by means of a postal service;
(b) anything comprising speech, music, sounds, visual images or data of any description; and
(c) signals serving either for the impartation of anything between persons, between a person and a thing or between things or for the actuation or control of any apparatus;'

For the purposes of communications by telecommunication systems it is clear that the definition incorporates 'traffic data', due to the definition contained in s 2(9). As can be seen, the words in s 81(1)(c) closely resemble the words in s 2(9)(c). Section 2(9) provides:

'(9) In this section "traffic data", in relation to any communication, means—
(a) any data identifying, or purporting to identify, any person, apparatus or location to or from which the communication is or may be transmitted,
(b) any data identifying or selecting, or purporting to identify or select, apparatus through which, or by means of which, the communication is or may be transmitted,
(c) any data comprising signals for the actuation of apparatus used for the purposes of a telecommunication system for effecting (in whole or in part) the transmission of any communication, and

2.111 *Confidentiality, privacy and technology*

    (d)   any data identifying the data or other data as data comprised in or attached to a particular communication, but that expression includes data identifying a computer file or computer program access to which is obtained, or which is run, by means of the communication to the extent only that the file or program is identified by reference to the apparatus in which it is stored.'

The meaning of 'interception'

2.112 The meaning of 'interception' is defined in s 2. As far as interceptions of communications transmitted by telecommunications systems are concerned, there are three key ingredients within an interception:

- There must be some kind of modification or interference with the system, or monitoring of transmissions.
- These activities must take place in respect of the contents of the communication while they are being transmitted by the system.
- These activities must make the contents of the communication available to a person other than the intended sender or recipient.

These key ingredients are contained in s 2(2), which provides:

'(2)   For the purposes of this Act, but subject to the following provisions of this section, a person intercepts a communication in the course of its transmission by means of a telecommunication system if, and only if, he–
    (a)   so modifies or interferes with the system, or its operation,
    (b)   so monitors transmissions made by means of the system, or
    (c)   so monitors transmissions made by wireless telegraphy to or from apparatus comprised in the system,
as to make some or all of the contents of the communication available, while being transmitted, to a person other than the sender or intended recipient of the communication.'

However, despite the definition of communication contained within s 81(1), which includes traffic data, s 2(5) goes on to exclude traffic data from the protections against interception, which is the point at which the protections in RIPA 2000 depart from the requirements of article 5(1) of the 2002 Directive:

'(5)   References in this Act to the interception of a communication in the course of its transmission by means of a postal service or telecommunication system do not include references to–
    (a)   any conduct that takes place in relation only to so much of the communication as consists in any traffic data comprised in or attached to a communication (whether by the sender or otherwise) for the purposes of any postal service or telecommunication system by means of which it is being or may be transmitted; or
    (b)   any such conduct, in connection with conduct falling within paragraph (a), as gives a person who is neither the sender nor the intended recipient only so much access to a communication as is necessary for the purpose of identifying traffic data so comprised or attached.'

The meaning of 'in the course of transmission'

2.113 Section 2(2) shows that the meaning of 'in the course of transmission' requires the intercepting activity (ie, the modification, interference or monitoring) to occur within the telecommunication system itself. This could be through the attachment or modification of physical devices within the system or through the use of physical devices that monitor the electrical or electromagnetic energy which telecommunications consist of[1].

If this requirement is applied to an ordinary telephone conversation, then it becomes clear that a transmission begins when the sound waves of the speaker's voice come into contact with the microphone receiver in the speaker's handset and ends when the sound waves depart from the speaker in the recipient's handset, because it is only between these two points that electrical or electro-magnetic energy are involved. This means that an interception will not occur if the ambient sounds of the speakers' voices are overhead or recorded by a third party as they travel to and from the handsets.

The meaning of 'in the course of transmission' has been considered in a number of cases. In *R v Hardy & Hardy*[2] the Court of Appeal was concerned with the secret recording of a telephone conversation by a police officer. The recording was done by way of a machine in the officer's possession. All the recording machine did was record the ambient sounds of the conversation (and, presumably, other ambient sounds in the environment). It was held by the Court of Appeal that this did not amount to interception, because the recording did not take place while the contents of the communication were in the course of transmission. The Court of Appeal reached the same conclusion in *R v E*[3], where the ambient sounds of a telephone conversation were monitored and recorded by a bug hidden in the defendant's car.

[1] See again the definition of telecommunication, which makes it clear that a transmission of a communication requires the means of electrical or electro-magnetic energy.
[2] [2002] EWCA Crim 3012, [2003] 1 Cr App Rep 494.
[3] [2004] EWCA Crim 1243, [2004] 1 WLR 3279.

In the course of transmission – stored emails and voicemail messages

2.114 Section 2(7) caters for the situation when emails, voicemail messages and other communications are stored within the telecommunication system pending their collection by the intended recipient:

> '(7) For the purposes of this section the times while a communication is being transmitted by means of a telecommunication system shall be taken to include any time when the system by means of which the communication is being, or has been, transmitted is used for storing it in a manner that enables the intended recipient to collect it or otherwise to have access to it.'

The effect of this section is to extend the duration of the transmission until the communication is finally collected by the intended recipient.

2.115 *Confidentiality, privacy and technology*

In the course of transmission – non-real time monitoring

2.115 Section 2(8) enables the interceptor to divert or record the transmission for later monitoring. Like s 2(7), this means that interceptions need not include a real time human component:

> '(8) For the purposes of this section the cases in which any contents of a communication are to be taken to be made available to a person while being transmitted shall include any case in which any of the contents of the communication, while being transmitted, are diverted or recorded so as to be available to a person subsequently.'

The meaning of 'lawful authority'

2.116 It is an essential ingredient of the offence of interception that it is done without lawful authority. The main kinds of lawful authority are:

- The interceptor has reasonable grounds for believing that the sender and intended recipient both consented to the interception (s 3(1)).
- The interceptor has the consent of one of the parties to the communication and 'surveillance by means of that interception has been authorised under Part II' of RIPA 2000[1] (s 3(2)).
- The interception is done by or on behalf of a provider of a telecommunications service in connection with the provision of the service or the enforcement of any enactments relating to the service (s 3(3)).
- The interception is of a transmission by means of wireless telegraphy and it is done with the authority of a designated person for purposes connected with the grant of a wireless telegraphy licence, or for preventing or detecting any interferences with wireless telegraphy or for the enforcement of licence rules or rules regulating the sale of apparatus (s 3(4) and (5)).
- The interception is of business communications, as set out in the Telecommunications (Lawful Business Practice) (Interception of Communications) Regulations 2000, SI 2000/2699 (s 4).
- The interception takes place pursuant to a warrant (s 5).

[1] RIPA 2000, Pt II is concerned with intrusive surveillance and directed surveillance, but it is only directed surveillance that is relevant to the lawful authority within s 3(2). Directed surveillance is surveillance that is not intrusive (ie, it does not take place in respect of residential premises or a private vehicle occupied by the subject of the investigation), that is conducted in respect of a specific investigation or operation, is likely to result in the obtaining of private information and is conducted pursuant to an authorisation for the purposes of national security, preventing or detecting crime, preventing disorder, the country's economic interest, public safety etc.

Exclusion of criminal liability – interception within private systems

2.117 The offence within s 1(2) applies 'otherwise than in circumstances in which [the interceptor's] conduct is excluded by subsection (6) from criminal liability'. Section 1(6) provides:

> '(6) The circumstances in which a person makes an interception of a communication in the course of its transmission by means of a private

telecommunication system are such that his conduct is excluded from criminal liability under subsection (2) if—
(a) he is a person with a right to control the operation or the use of the system; or
(b) he has the express or implied consent of such a person to make the interception.'

The effect of these subsections is to render any intentional interception that is conducted without lawful authority immune from the criminal process. This demonstrates the importance of the system controller's position.

The tort of unlawful interception

2.118 However, the system controller cannot avoid civil liability for intentional interceptions conducted without lawful authority, as s 1(3) provides:

'(3) Any interception of a communication which is carried out at any place in the United Kingdom by, or with the express or implied consent of, a person having the right to control the operation or the use of a private telecommunication system shall be actionable at the suit or instance of the sender or recipient, or intended recipient, of the communication if it is without lawful authority and is either—
(a) an interception of that communication in the course of its transmission by means of that private system; or
(b) an interception of that communication in the course of its transmission, by means of a public telecommunication system, to or from apparatus comprised in that private telecommunication system.'

Lowering the security barriers – interception of business communications

2.119 The Telecommunications (Lawful Business Practice) (Interception of Communications) Regulations 2000, SI 2000/2699 were discussed earlier in this chapter. These regulations apply only to the interception of communications in the course of transmission via business telecommunications systems. If the system controller complies with these regulations it will also be immune from civil liability under RIPA 2000, s 1(3).

Lowering the security barriers – facilities for interception

2.120 Law enforcement agencies gain cooperation with the actual carrying out of interception through regulations[1] made under RIPA 2000, s 12. The opening parts of s 12 provide:

'12.— **Maintenance of interception capability**
(1) The Secretary of State may by order provide for the imposition by him on persons who—
(a) are providing public postal services or public telecommunications services, or
(b) are proposing to do so,

2.120 *Confidentiality, privacy and technology*

of such obligations as it appears to him reasonable to impose for the purpose of securing that it is and remains practicable for requirements to provide assistance in relation to interception warrants to be imposed and complied with.

(2) The Secretary of State's power to impose the obligations provided for by an order under this section shall be exercisable by the giving, in accordance with the order, of a notice requiring the person who is to be subject to the obligations to take all such steps as may be specified or described in the notice.

(3) Subject to subsection (11), the only steps that may be specified or described in a notice given to a person under subsection (2) are steps appearing to the Secretary of State to be necessary for securing that that person has the practical capability of providing any assistance which he may be required to provide in relation to relevant interception warrants.'

[1] Regulation of Investigatory Powers (Maintenance of Interception Capability) Order 2002, SI 2002/1931.

2.121 The regulations do not apply to providers of public telecommunications services to less than 10,000 people, or to the providers of public telecommunications services relating to the provision of financial services. Where they do apply the service provider needs to comply with the requirements of part II of the schedule to the regulations, which provides:

'5. To provide a mechanism for implementing interceptions within one working day of the service provider being informed that the interception has been appropriately authorised.

6. To ensure the interception, in their entirety, of all communications and related communications data authorised by the interception warrant and to ensure their simultaneous (i.e. in near real time) transmission to a hand-over point within the service provider's network as agreed with the person on whose application the interception warrant was issued.

7. To ensure that the intercepted communication and the related communications data will be transmitted so that they can be unambiguously correlated.

8. To ensure that the hand-over interface complies with any requirements communicated by the Secretary of State to the service provider, which, where practicable and appropriate, will be in line with agreed industry standards (such as those of the European Telecommunications Standards Institute).

9. To ensure filtering to provide only the traffic data associated with the warranted telecommunications identifier, where reasonable.

10. To ensure that the person on whose application the interception warrant was issued is able to remove any electronic protection applied by the service provider to the intercepted communication and the related communications data.

11. To enable the simultaneous interception of the communications of up to 1 in 10,000 of the persons to whom the service provider provides the public telecommunications service, provided that those persons number more than 10,000.

12. To ensure that the reliability of the interception capability is at least equal to the reliability of the public telecommunications service carrying the communication which is being intercepted.

Confidentiality, privacy and technology 2.123

13. To ensure that the intercept capability may be audited so that it is possible to confirm that the intercepted communications and related communications data are from, or intended for the interception subject, or originate from or are intended for transmission to, the premises named in the interception warrant.

14. To comply with the obligations set out in paragraphs 5 to 13 above in such a manner that the chance of the interception subject or other unauthorised persons becoming aware of any interception is minimised.'

Lowering the security barriers – supplying decrypted information and encryption keys

2.122 With the growth in deployment of encryption technologies law enforcement agencies will regularly need to overcome the problem of encrypted communications. RIPA 2000, Pt III, which was discussed earlier in this chapter, provides a legal framework that can compel persons to deliver up unencrypted information and/or encryption keys.

PRIVACY AND ELECTRONIC COMMUNICATIONS (EC DIRECTIVE) REGULATIONS 2003

2.123 Regulations 5 and 6 of the 2003 regulations are the provisions that transpose articles 4 and 5 of the 2002 Directive. They provide as follows:

> 'Security of public electronic communications services
> 5. – (1) Subject to paragraph (2), a provider of a public electronic communications service ("the service provider") shall take appropriate technical and organisational measures to safeguard the security of that service.
> (2) If necessary, the measures required by paragraph (1) may be taken by the service provider in conjunction with the provider of the electronic communications network by means of which the service is provided, and that network provider shall comply with any reasonable requests made by the service provider for these purposes.
> (3) Where, notwithstanding the taking of measures as required by paragraph (1), there remains a significant risk to the security of the public electronic communications service, the service provider shall inform the subscribers concerned of–
> (a) the nature of that risk;
> (b) any appropriate measures that the subscriber may take to safeguard against that risk; and
> (c) the likely costs to the subscriber involved in the taking of such measures.
> (4) For the purposes of paragraph (1), a measure shall only be taken to be appropriate if, having regard to–
> (a) the state of technological developments, and
> (b) the cost of implementing it,
> it is proportionate to the risks against which it would safeguard.
> (5) Information provided for the purposes of paragraph (3) shall be provided to the subscriber free of any charge other than the cost to the subscriber of receiving or collecting the information.

2.123 *Confidentiality, privacy and technology*

Confidentiality of communications
6. – (1) Subject to paragraph (4), a person shall not use an electronic communications network to store information, or to gain access to information stored, in the terminal equipment of a subscriber or user unless the requirements of paragraph (2) are met.
(2) The requirements are that the subscriber or user of that terminal equipment–
  (a) is provided with clear and comprehensive information about the purposes of the storage of, or access to, that information; and
  (b) is given the opportunity to refuse the storage of or access to that information.
(3) Where an electronic communications network is used by the same person to store or access information in the terminal equipment of a subscriber or user on more than one occasion, it is sufficient for the purposes of this regulation that the requirements of paragraph (2) are met in respect of the initial use.
(4) Paragraph (1) shall not apply to the technical storage of, or access to, information–
  (a) for the sole purpose of carrying out or facilitating the transmission of a communication over an electronic communications network; or
  (b) where such storage or access is strictly necessary for the provision of an information society service requested by the subscriber or user.'

Computer Misuse Act 1990

2.124 The Computer Misuse Act 1990 is one of the core components of data security law, protecting computers and computer material from unauthorised access as well as other acts that can have a detrimental impact on the operation and use of computers and computer material. It specifically protects data held on computers, including computer programs, although, interestingly, the Act does not define the meaning of computer.

The territorial scope of the Act

2.125 The internet and electronic communications networks and infrastructures enable acts of computer misuse to be committed at a distance. Criminals do not need to be physically in contact with the computers that they are targeting. Instead they can act remotely, located in 'safe havens', seemingly out of the reach of the law of the country where the computers they are targeting are located. Of course, international cybercrime is difficult to detect and bring to justice and prosecutions are still rare. The *McKinnon*[1] case stands as a good example of the difficulties in this area.

The Computer Misuse Act 1990 seeks to cater for this contingency, by rendering it immaterial where the acts or events constituting computer misuse occurred[2]. Instead, the Act looks for a significant link with the jurisdiction. Section 4 provides as follows:

'4.— **Territorial scope of offences under sections 1 to 3**
(1)   Except as provided below in this section, it is immaterial for the purposes of any offence under section 1 or 3 above—
(a) whether any act or other event proof of which is required for conviction of the offence occurred in the home country concerned; or
(b) whether the accused was in the home country concerned at the time of any such act or event.
(2)   Subject to subsection (3) below, in the case of such an offence at least one significant link with domestic jurisdiction must exist in the circumstances of the case for the offence to be committed.
(3)   There is no need for any such link to exist for the commission of an offence under section 1 above to be established in proof of an allegation to that effect in proceedings for an offence under section 2 above.
(4)   Subject to section 8 below, where—
(a)   any such link does in fact exist in the case of an offence under section 1 above; and
(b)   commission of that offence is alleged in proceedings for an offence under section 2 above;
section 2 above shall apply as if anything the accused intended to do or facilitate in any place outside the home country concerned which would be an offence to which section 2 applies if it took place in the home country concerned were the offence in question.
(5)   This section is without prejudice to any jurisdiction exercisable by a court in Scotland apart from this section.
(6)   References in this Act to the home country concerned are references—
(a)   in the application of this Act to England and Wales, to England and Wales;
(b)   in the application of this Act to Scotland, to Scotland; and
(c)   in the application of this Act to Northern Ireland, to Northern Ireland.'

1   [2008] UKHL 59, [2008] 4 All ER 1012.
2   Computer Misuse Act 1990, s 9 renders British citizenship irrelevant.

2.126 The meaning of 'significant link' is found in s 5. In summary, there will be a significant link with the jurisdiction if either the computer or the criminal are in the jurisdiction. Section 5 says:

'5.— **Significant links with domestic jurisdiction**
(1)   The following provisions of this section apply for the interpretation of section 4 above.
(2)   In relation to an offence under section 1, either of the following is a significant link with domestic jurisdiction—
(a)   that the accused was in the home country concerned at the time when he did the act which caused the computer to perform the function; or
(b)   that any computer containing any program or data to which the accused by doing that act secured or intended to secure unauthorised access, or enabled or intended to enable unauthorised access to be secured, was in the home country concerned at that time.
(3)   In relation to an offence under section 3, either of the following is a significant link with domestic jurisdiction—
(a)   that the accused was in the home country concerned at the time when he did the unauthorised act (or caused it to be done) or

2.126 Confidentiality, privacy and technology

    (b)   that the unauthorised act was done in relation to a computer in the home country concerned.'

The consequences of these territorial provisions are very important. A hacker located abroad who targets a computer in the UK will be liable to criminal proceedings in this jurisdiction as will a hacker located in this jurisdiction who targets a computer situated overseas.

The international dimensions of computer misuse have been highlighted in a series of extradition cases. In *R v Governor of Brixton Prison and another, ex p Levin*[1] the United States government secured an order for Levin's extradition from the UK for hacking offences which diverted money from a US bank. Levin, a Russian national, used a computer in St Petersburg in Russia to commit the offence and was arrested while in the transfer lounge at Stanstead airport. In *Zezev v Governor of Brixton Prison*[2] the court ordered extradition to the United States in a case where the hackers, Zezev and Yarimaka, used computers in Kazakhstan to access the Bloomberg computer system in New York. In *McKinnon v Government of the USA*[3] the House of Lords authorised the claimant's extradition in respect of hacking offences that affected 97 US government computers.

[1] [1997] AC 741, [1997] 3 All ER 289.
[2] [2002] EWHC 589 (Admin), [2002] 2 Cr App Rep 515.
[3] [2008] UKHL 59, [2008] 4 All ER 1012.

Section 1 offence – unauthorised access to computer material

2.127 Computer Misuse Act 1990, s 1 contains the offence of unauthorised access to computer material. Unauthorised access offences can be tried in either the Magistrates' Court or in the Crown Court. Section 1 provides as follows:

'1.- Unauthorised access to computer material
(1)   A person is guilty of an offence if—
    (a)   he causes a computer to perform any function with intent to secure access to any program or data held in any computer or to enable any such access to be secured;
    (b)   the access he intends to secure or to enable to be secured, is unauthorised; and
    (c)   he knows at the time when he causes the computer to perform the function that that is the case.
(2)   The intent a person has to have to commit an offence under this section need not be directed at—
    (a)   any particular program or data;
    (b)   a program or data of any particular kind; or
    (c)   a program or data held in any particular computer.
(3)   A person guilty of an offence under this section shall be liable–
    (a)   on summary conviction in England and Wales, to imprisonment for a term not exceeding 12 months or to a fine not exceeding the statutory maximum or to both;
    (b)   on summary conviction in Scotland, to imprisonment for a term not exceeding six months or to a fine not exceeding the statutory maximum or to both;

(c) on conviction on indictment, to imprisonment for a term not exceeding two years or to a fine or to both.'

Section 1 aims to protect information contained in computers, whether this be data or computer programs. The actus reus of the offence is causing a computer to perform a function. The mens rea is the intent to secure access that is unauthorised. Breaking down s 1 into its constituent parts, a person will be convicted of a s 1 offence if:

- They cause a computer to perform a function.
- They have intent to secure access to programs or data within the computer.
- The access that is secured, or is intended to be secured, is unauthorised.
- They know that the access is unauthorised.

CAUSING A COMPUTER TO PERFORM A FUNCTION

2.128 The first requirement of causing a computer to perform a function captures a broad variety of activities, including merely turning a computer on. Such a function can be performed by the defendant personally (see, for example, *Attorney General's Reference (No 1 of 1991)*), or through third parties (as happened in the *Allison* case[1] and in *Ellis*), or remotely via the internet (see again the extradition cases mentioned earlier).

In *Attorney General's Reference (No 1 of 1991)*[2] the Court of Appeal considered the interesting question whether s 1(1)(a) requires two computers to be used. The essential facts of the case were that the defendant keyed in a discount code into a computerised shop till while the operator was not present, thereby gaining for himself a 70% discount. The point of law referred to the Court of Appeal by the Attorney General was 'in order for a person to commit an offence under section 1(1) of the Computer Misuse Act 1990 does the computer which the person causes to perform any function with the required intent have to be a different computer to the one into which he intends to secure unauthorised access to any program or data held there?' The Court of Appeal answered this question in the negative, holding that s 1(1)(a) should be given its ordinary meaning and that two computers are not necessary for an offence to be committed. Lord Taylor said:

> 'It is submitted by Mr. Moses that, for an offence to be committed under section 1(1) of the Act, there does not have to be use by the offender of one computer with intent to secure unauthorised access into another computer. The words used are not ambiguous. The vital phrase is "any computer" at the end of section 1(1)(a) and the Act has been drafted, it is submitted, so as to deal with someone who misuses a computer, whether he accesses it indirectly by using another computer, perhaps in other premises, or whether he accesses it directly, as happened in the present case. It may be that the major mischief at which the Act was directed was the mischief which has become endemic of persons using one computer to hack into another computer. But, submits Mr. Moses, the scope of the section is not confined to that form of access to any computer.

2.128 *Confidentiality, privacy and technology*

The ordinary canons of construction require this court to look at the words of the section and to give them their plain and natural meaning. Doing that, we look again at the relevant words. They are, "he causes a computer to perform any function with intent to secure access to any program or data held in any computer."

Mr. Lassman argued successfully before the judge, and sought to argue before this court, that that final phrase, "held in any computer," should really be read as "held in any other computer," or alternatively should be read as "held in any computer except the computer which has performed the function."

To read those words in that way, in our judgment, would be to give them a meaning quite different from their plain and natural meaning. It is a trite observation, when considering the construction of statutes, that one does not imply or introduce words which are not there when the plain and natural meaning is clear. In our judgment there are no grounds whatsoever for implying, or importing the word "other" between "any" and "computer," or excepting the computer which is actually used by the offender from the phrase "any computer" at the end of the subsection (1)(a).'

1   *R v Bow Street Metropolitan Stipendiary Magistrate, ex p United States Government* [2000] 2 AC 216, [1999] 4 All ER 1.
2   [1993] QB 94, [1992] 3 All ER 897.

SECURING ACCESS

2.129 Assistance with the meaning of securing access to programs or data is provided by s 17(2)–(4), which provides:

'(2) A person secures access to any program or data held in a computer if by causing a computer to perform any function he—
  (a) alters or erases the program or data;
  (b) copies or moves it to any storage medium other than that in which it is held or to a different location in the storage medium in which it is held;
  (c) uses it; or
  (d) has it output from the computer in which it is held (whether by having it displayed or in any other manner);
  and references to access to a program or data (and to an intent to secure such access or to enable such access to be secured) shall be read accordingly.
(3) For the purposes of subsection (2)(c) above a person uses a program if the function he causes the computer to perform—
  (a) causes the program to be executed; or
  (b) is itself a function of the program.
(4) For the purposes of subsection (2)(d) above—
  (a) a program is output if the instructions of which it consists are output; and
  (b) the form in which any such instructions or any other data is output (and in particular whether or not it represents a form in which, in the case of instructions, they are capable of being executed or, in the case of data, it is capable of being processed by a computer) is immaterial.'

The acts described at s 17(2) cover all of the permutations of access. There is nothing special about the kinds of access described, although proving some of them might require the assistance of forensic evidence, a point that was argued in *Ellis v DPP (No 1)*[1]. Ellis was a graduate of Newcastle University. He used a 'non-open access' computer (ie, a password controlled computer, which he knew he was not authorised to use) to browse some publicly available websites. The computer had been left logged-on and connected to the internet by a previous user. In interview under caution he admitted this use and was convicted in the Magistrates' Court. He appealed by way of case stated and in his skeleton argument he advanced the point that 'the programmes were already accessed and by his definition he browsed already activated sites'. Thus, he contended that his use did not fall within the definition of use in s 17(2)(c) and (3). He also submitted that 'it is incumbent on the prosecution to produce evidence of the programme and function present which is alleged to have been executed on the computer'. The Divisional Court had no difficulty dismissing the appeal. The Lord Chief Justice said that 'the statutory provisions are, as the magistrates indicate, sufficiently wide to cover the use which was made of the computers by the appellant'.

[1] [2001] EWHC Admin 362.

2.130 An interesting question is whether it is possible to cause a computer to perform a function without securing access. Taking s 17(2)–(4) at face value, particularly the definition of use within s 17(2)(c) and (3), it is very difficult to see how a person can fail to secure access if they cause a computer to perform a function. Merely turning a computer on, or pressing a key on the keyboard or moving the mouse, will always cause a 'program to be executed'. So, in many respects causing a computer to perform a function is synonymous with use of a computer. In the *Allison* case Lord Hobhouse touched upon a closely related issue, saying that s 1(1) 'creates an offence which can be committed as a result of having to secure unauthorised access without in fact actually succeeding in accessing any data'.

As regard intent, this is to be determined in accordance with the Criminal Justice Act 1967, s 8 which provides:

'A court or jury, in determining whether a person has committed an offence,—
(a) shall not be bound in law to infer that he intended or foresaw a result of his actions by reasons only of its being a natural and probable consequence of those actions; but
(b) shall decide whether he did intend or foresee that result by reference to all the evidence, drawing such inferences from the evidence as appear proper in the circumstances.'

In *Ellis* the court also held that intent could be inferred from the admitted facts.

UNAUTHORISED ACCESS

2.131 The meaning of 'unauthorised' is contained in s 17(5), which provides:

'(5) Access of any kind by any person to any program or data held in a computer is unauthorised if—

2.131 *Confidentiality, privacy and technology*

(a) he is not himself entitled to control access of the kind in question to the program or data; and
(b) he does not have consent to access by him of the kind in question to the program or data from any person who is so entitled
but this subsection is subject to section 10.'

The requirement that the access should be unauthorised has caused the courts difficulties on occasions. In the case of *DPP v Bignell*[1] the question considered was whether a police officer using the police national computer for a non-policing purpose committed unauthorised access. Bignell did not access the computer personally, but instead instructed the computer operators to do searches on cars that were owned by his ex-wife's new partner. The court described the operators as innocent agents. Bignell submitted that his use of the computer, 'even if it was found to be for private purposes, was not within the definition of "unauthorised access" provided by section 17(5) of the Act, because the access had been with authority even though that authority was used for an unauthorised purpose'. In other words Bignell was arguing that authority to access for one purpose gives authority to access for any purpose. Surprisingly, the Divisional Court accepted Bignell's argument.

The law was put back on track by the *Allison* case. Allison, who was based in London, worked in conspiracy with an employee at American Express based in Florida, Joan Ojomo, to gain access to confidential information within American Express' computer systems. The information was used to manufacture forged payments cards, which were used to withdraw money from cash machines. Allison was charged with conspiracy to commit two offences under the Computer Misuse Act 1990, s 2 and one offence under the previous version of s 3 (which was concerned with unauthorised modification to computer material). Lord Hobhouse summarised the facts as follows:

'Joan Ojomo was an employee of American Express. She was assigned to the credit section of the company's office in Plantation, Florida, as a credit analyst. In her daily work it was possible for her to access all customers' accounts but she was only authorised to access those accounts that were assigned to her. However she accessed various other accounts and files which had not been assigned to her and which she had not been given authority to work on. Having accessed those accounts and files without authority, she gave confidential information obtained from those accounts and files to, among others, Mr. Allison. The information she gave to him and to others was then used to encode other credit cards and supply P.I.N. numbers which could then be fraudulently used to obtain large sums of money from automatic teller machines.

The evidence concerning Joan Ojomo's authority to access the material data showed that she did not have authority to access the data she used for this purpose. At no time did she have any blanket authorisation to access any account or file not specifically assigned to her to work on. Any access by her to an account which she was not authorised to be working on would be considered a breach of company policy and ethics and would be considered an unauthorised access by the company. The computer records showed that she accessed 189 accounts that did not fall within the scope of her duties. Her accessing of these accounts was unauthorised.

Using these methods, she and her fellow conspirators defrauded American Express of approximately U.S.$1m. Mr. Allison was arrested with forged

American Express cards in his possession and was photographed using one such card to obtain money from an automatic teller machine in London.

The proposed charges against Mr. Allison therefore involved his alleged conspiracy with Joan Ojomo for her to secure unauthorised access to data on the American Express computer with the intent to commit the further offences of forging cards and stealing from that company. It is Joan Ojomo's alleged lack of authority which is an essential element in the offences charged.'

Lord Hobhouse had no difficulty accepting the argument that Ojomo's actions fell within the Computer Misuse Act 1990, s 1(1), in the sense that she committed unauthorised access. He said 'on the evidence before the magistrate, the conduct of Joan Ojomo came fairly and squarely within the provisions of section 1(1). She intentionally caused a computer to give her access to data which she knew she was not authorised to access'.

[1] [1998] 1 Cr App Rep 1, 161 JP 541.

2.132 As regards Allison, the Magistrates' Court declined to commit him for trial on the two charges under s 2, because of the ratio in Bignell. This decision was upheld by the Divisional Court on appeal. Lord Hobhouse observed:

'The reason why the magistrate did not commit Mr. Allison on charges 1 and 2 was that he felt constrained by the provisions of section 17 of the Act of 1990 and the interpretation put upon them by the Divisional Court in Director of Public Prosecutions v. Bignell [1998] Cr.App.R. 1; the Divisional Court also followed and applied Bignell's case.'

Lord Hobhouse then went on to analyse the effect of s 17:

'Section 17 is an interpretation section. Subsection (2) defines what is meant by access and securing access to any programme or data. It lists four ways in which this may occur or be achieved. Its purpose is clearly to give a specific meaning to the phrase "to secure access." Subsection (5) is to be read with subsection (2). It deals with the relationship between the widened definition of securing access and the scope of the authority which the relevant person may hold. That is why the subsection refers to "access of any kind" and "access of the kind in question." Authority to view data may not extend to authority to copy or alter that data. The refinement of the concept of access requires a refinement of the concept of authorisation. The authorisation must be authority to secure access of the kind in question. As part of this refinement, the subsection lays down two cumulative requirements of lack of authority. The first is the requirement that the relevant person be not the person entitled to control the relevant kind of access. The word "control" in this context clearly means authorise and forbid. If the relevant person is so entitled, then it would be unrealistic to treat his access as being unauthorised. The second is that the relevant person does not have the consent to secure the relevant kind of access from a person entitled to control, i.e. authorise, that access.

Subsection (5) therefore has a plain meaning subsidiary to the other provisions of the Act. It simply identifies the two ways in which authority may be acquired—by being oneself the person entitled to authorise and by being a person who has been authorised by a person entitled to authorise. It also makes clear that the authority must relate not simply to the data or programme but also to the actual kind of access secured. Similarly, it is plain that it is not using the word "control" in a physical sense of the ability to operate or manipulate the computer and that it is not derogating from the requirement that for access to be authorised it must be authorised to the relevant data or relevant programme or part of a programme. It does not introduce any concept that authority to access one piece of data should be treated as authority to access other pieces of data "of the same kind" notwithstanding that the relevant person did not in fact have authority to access that piece of data. Section 1 refers to the intent to secure unauthorised access to any programme or data. These plain words leave no room for any suggestion that the relevant person may say: "Yes, I know that I was not authorised to access that data but I was authorised to access other data of the same kind." '

The essence of s 17 is therefore quite straightforward. It requires the court to identify the actual access that was secured (or attempted), which should be measured against the authorisation that was given. If the access extends further than the authority it will be unauthorised for the purposes of the Act. In other words the Act is 'concerned with authority to access the actual data involved', as Lord Hobhouse put it. As far as gaining access through a third party is concerned, Lord Hobhouse continued by saying that 'the offence should cover a person who causes the computer to perform a function when he "should know that that access is unauthorised" '.

KNOWLEDGE THAT ACCESS IS UNAUTHORISED

2.133 The requirement of knowledge in s 1(1)(c) is a requirement for actual knowledge, although in the case of *Westminster City Council v Croyalgrange Ltd*[1] Lord Bridge said it is always open to the tribunal of fact 'to base a finding of knowledge on evidence that the defendant had deliberately shut his eyes to the obvious or refrained from inquiry because he suspected the truth but did not wish to have his suspicion confirmed'. In the *Allison* case Lord Hobhouse alluded to the difficulties within the knowledge component of the offence saying that 'an employee should only be guilty of an offence if his employer has clearly defined the limits of the employee's authority to access a program or data'.

[1] [1986] 2 All ER 353, [1986] 1 WLR 674.

Section 2 offence

2.134 Section 2 is concerned with the situation where the defendant commits an offence of unauthorised access under s 1 within the intention to commit, or facilitate the commission of, further offences for which the sentence is fixed in law, or where a sentence of five years' imprisonment can be imposed. Charges under s 2 are very rare, because the prosecution can decide to proceed with charges for the substantive offence, as happened in the case of *Re Holmes*[1]. Section 2 provides as follows:

'**2.—** **Unauthorised access with intent to commit or facilitate commission of further offences**
 (1) A person is guilty of an offence under this section if he commits an offence under section 1 above ("the unauthorised access offence") with intent—

(a) to commit an offence to which this section applies; or
(b) to facilitate the commission of such an offence (whether by himself or by any other person);
and the offence he intends to commit or facilitate is referred to below in this section as the further offence.
(2) This section applies to offences—
(a) for which the sentence is fixed by law; or
(b) for which a person of twenty-one years of age or over (not previously convicted) may be sentenced to imprisonment for a term of five years (or, in England and Wales, might be so sentenced but for the restrictions imposed by section 33 of the Magistrates' Courts Act 1980).[2]
(3) It is immaterial for the purposes of this section whether the further offence is to be committed on the same occasion as the unauthorised access offence or on any future occasion.
(4) A person may be guilty of an offence under this section even though the facts are such that the commission of the further offence is impossible.
(5) A person guilty of an offence under this section shall be liable—
(a) on summary conviction in England and Wales, to imprisonment for a term not exceeding 12 months or to a fine not exceeding the statutory maximum or to both;
(b) on summary conviction in Scotland, to imprisonment for a term not exceeding six months or to a fine not exceeding the statutory maximum or to both;
(c) on conviction on indictment, to imprisonment for a term not exceeding five years or to a fine or to both.'

[1] [2004] EWHC 2020 (Admin), [2005] 1 All ER 490.
[2] Computer Misuse Act 1990, s 2(2)(b) will be amended by the Criminal Justice and Court Services Act 2000 on a date to be appointed. See the Criminal Justice and Court Services Act 2000, Sch 7, Pt II, para 98.

Section 3 offence

2.135 The current version of s 3 was introduced into the Act by the Police and Justice Act 2006 and came into force on 1 October 2008. It provides as follows:

'**3 Unauthorised acts with intent to impair, or with recklessness as to impairing, operation of computer, etc**
(1) A person is guilty of an offence if–
(a) he does any unauthorised act in relation to a computer;
(b) at the time when he does the act he knows that it is unauthorised; and
(c) either subsection (2) or subsection (3) below applies.
(2) This subsection applies if the person intends by doing the act–
(a) to impair the operation of any computer;
(b) to prevent or hinder access to any program or data held in any computer;
(c) to impair the operation of any such program or the reliability of any such data; or
(d) to enable any of the things mentioned in paragraphs (a) to (c) above to be done.

2.135 *Confidentiality, privacy and technology*

(3) This subsection applies if the person is reckless as to whether the act will do any of the things mentioned in paragraphs (a) to (d) of subsection (2) above.

(4) The intention referred to in subsection (2) above, or the recklessness referred to in subsection (3) above, need not relate to–
  (a) any particular computer;
  (b) any particular program[1] or data; or
  (c) a program or data of any particular kind.

(5) In this section–
  (a) a reference to doing an act includes a reference to causing an act to be done;
  (b) "act" includes a series of acts;
  (c) a reference to impairing, preventing or hindering something includes a reference to doing so temporarily.

(6) A person guilty of an offence under this section shall be liable–
  (a) on summary conviction in England and Wales, to imprisonment for a term not exceeding 12 months or to a fine not exceeding the statutory maximum or to both;
  (b) on summary conviction in Scotland, to imprisonment for a term not exceeding six months or to a fine not exceeding the statutory maximum or to both;
  (c) on conviction on indictment, to imprisonment for a term not exceeding ten years or to a fine or to both.'

[1] The meaning of program is expanded upon by s 17(10), which says that 'references to a program include references to part of a program'.

2.136 The key ingredients of the s 3 offence are:

- The defendant commits an authorised act.
- In relation to a computer.
- Knowing that the act is unauthorised.
- With intent to achieve the impairment of any computer (or any of the other outcomes set out in subsection (2)), or if they are reckless as to whether these outcomes will occur.

The meaning of unauthorised is contained in s 17(8), which provides:

'(8) An act done in relation to a computer is unauthorised if the person doing the act (or causing it to be done)–
  (a) is not himself a person who has responsibility for the computer and is entitled to determine whether the act may be done; and
  (b) does not have consent to the act from any such person.

In this subsection "act" includes a series of acts.'

In *DPP v Lennon*[1] the meaning of unauthorised was examined. In this case the defendant mail bombed his former employer's email server, a denial of service attack, by sending 500,000 spam emails. In his defence he argued that his actions were not unauthorised, because the email server had been installed for the specific purpose of receiving emails. This argument was quickly rejected on appeal, where Jack J held:

'I agree, and it is not in dispute, that the owner of a computer which is able to receive emails is ordinarily to be taken as consenting to the sending of emails to the computer. His consent is to be implied from his conduct in relation to the computer. Some analogy can be drawn with consent by a householder to members of the public to walk up the path to his door when they have a legitimate reason for doing so, and also with the use of a private letter box. But that implied consent given by a computer owner is not without limit. The point can be illustrated by the same analogies. The householder does not consent to a burglar coming up his path. Nor does he consent to having his letter box choked with rubbish. That second example seems to me to be very much to the point here. I do not think that it is necessary for the decision in this case to try to define the limits of the consent which a computer owner impliedly gives to the sending of emails. It is enough to say that it plainly does not cover emails which are not sent for the purpose of communication with the owner, but are sent for the purpose of interrupting the proper operation and use of his system. That was the plain intent of Mr Lennon in using the Avalanche program. The difference can be demonstrated in this way. If Mr Lennon had telephoned Ms Rhodes and requested consent to send her an email raising a point about the termination of his employment, she would have been puzzled as to why he bothered to ask and said that of course he might. If he had asked if he might send the half million emails he did send, he would have got a quite different answer. In short the purpose of Mr Lennon in sending the half million emails was an unauthorised purpose and the use made of D&G's email facility was an unauthorised use.'

In the case of *Zezev v Governor of Brixton Prison*[2] the court considered the meaning of impairing reliability. Lord Woolf, the Lord Chief Justice, said:

'The question of the meaning of the words "reliability of such data" has in the first place to be considered against the language used by the draftsman in the section itself. If a computer is caused to record information which shows that it came from one person, when it in fact came from someone else, that manifestly affects its reliability. The information is undoubtedly data.'

[1] [2006] EWHC 1201 (Admin), 70 JP 523.
[2] [2002] EWHC 589 (Admin), [2002] 2 Cr App Rep 515.

PROGRAMS AND DATA STORED IN MOVEABLE MEDIA

2.137 The offence within s 3 will only apply to programs or data held in removable storage media while the media is actually contained inside a computer. Section 17(6) provides:

'(6) References to any program or data held in a computer include references to any program or data held in any removable storage medium which is for the time being in the computer; and a computer is to be regarded as containing any program or data held in any such medium.'

Overcoming security controls

2.138 Although the Computer Misuse Act 1990 is a cornerstone of data security law, it is of special interest that the Act does not actually require the defendant to overcome security controls in order to be guilty of an offence.

The Council of Europe's Cybercrime Convention[1] recognises that jurisdictions may wish to incorporate a need to overcome security controls within their domestic laws. Article 2 provides as follows:

2.138 *Confidentiality, privacy and technology*

'Article 2 – Illegal access

Each Party shall adopt such legislative and other measures as may be necessary to establish as criminal offences under its domestic law, when committed intentionally, the access to the whole or any part of a computer system without right. A Party may require that the offence be committed by infringing security measures, with the intent of obtaining computer data or other dishonest intent, or in relation to a computer system that is connected to another computer system.'

[1] Convention on Cybercrime, Budapest, 23 November 2001: http://conventions.coe.int/Treaty/EN/Treaties/Html/185.htm.

Electronic signatures

2.139 One of the core goals of the practice of data security is ensuring the confidentiality, integrity and availability of data and computer systems. Thus, the Cybercrime Convention groups together the offences of illegal access, illegal interception, data interference, system interference and misuse of devices in Title 1, which is called 'offences against the confidentiality, integrity and availability of computer data and systems'.

The legal framework for electronic signatures, represented by the Electronic Signatures Directive 1999[1] at EU level and the Electronic Signatures Regulations 2002[2] domestically, certainly contributes to the achievement of the aims of confidentiality and integrity of data, albeit the Directive has at its aim the promotion of ecommerce and the use of electronic communications:

'Electronic communication and commerce necessitate "electronic signatures" and related services allowing data authentication; divergent rules with respect to legal recognition of electronic signatures and the accreditation of certification-service providers in the Member States may create a significant barrier to the use of electronic communications and electronic commerce; on the other hand, a clear Community framework regarding the conditions applying to electronic signatures will strengthen confidence in, and general acceptance of, the new technologies; legislation in the Member States should not hinder the free movement of goods and services in the internal market;'[3]

The Directive also makes clear statements about the role of electronic signatures within data security practice, explaining that voluntary accreditation schemes for 'certification-service-providers' will enable them to 'further their services towards the levels of trust, security and quality demanded by the evolving market'[4] and that 'advanced electronic signatures based on qualified certificates aim at a higher level of security'[5].

[1] Directive 1999/93/EC of the European Parliament and of the Council of 13 December 1999 on a Community framework for electronic signatures.
[2] SI 2002/318.
[3] Directive 1999/93/EC, recital (4).
[4] Directive 1999/93/EC, recital (11).
[5] Directive 1999/93/EC, recital (20).

Types of electronic signatures

2.140 There are three types of electronic signatures identified by the Directive:

- *Electronic signatures*. These are defined in article 2(1) as 'data in electronic form which are attached to or logically associated with other electronic data and which serve as a method of authentication'. They do not involve any special security features, which limits their value for the purposes of data authentication.
- *Advanced electronic signatures*. These are defined in article 2(2) as electronic signatures that are 'uniquely linked to the signatory', 'capable of identifying the signatory', 'created using means that the signatory can maintain under his sole control' and are 'linked to the data to which it relates in such a manner that any subsequent change of the data is detectable'.
- *Advanced electronic signatures based on a 'qualified certificate'*. These are the most secure types of electronic signature and are accorded special legal effect.

Advanced electronic signatures

2.141 Advanced electronic signatures are generated by 'signature-creation devices'. A signature-creation device is defined in article 2(5) as 'configured software or hardware used to implement the signature-creation data'. Signature-creation data is defined in article 2(4) as 'unique data, such as codes or private cryptographic keys, which are used by the signatory to create an electronic signature'.

Advanced electronic signatures based on qualified certificates are created by 'secure-signature creation devices', which are defined in article 2(6) as 'a signature-creation device which meets the requirements laid down in Annex III'. A qualified certificate is defined in article 2(10) as a 'certificate which meets the requirements laid down in Annex I and is provided by a certification-service-provider who fulfils the requirements laid down in Annex II'. For these purposes a certificate is defined in article 2(9) as 'an electronic attestation which links signature-verification data to a person and confirms the identity of that person' and a certification-service-provider is defined in article 2(11) as 'an entity or a legal or natural person who issues certificates or provides other services related to electronic signatures'.

QUALIFIED CERTIFICATES – ANNEX I

2.142 Annex I contains the requirements for qualified certificates, providing that:

'Requirements for qualified certificates

Qualified certificates must contain:
(a) an indication that the certificate is issued as a qualified certificate;

2.142 *Confidentiality, privacy and technology*

- (b) the identification of the certification-service-provider and the State in which it is established;
- (c) the name of the signatory or a pseudonym, which shall be identified as such;
- (d) provision for a specific attribute of the signatory to be included if relevant, depending on the purpose for which the certificate is intended;
- (e) signature-verification data which correspond to signature-creation data under the control of the signatory;
- (f) an indication of the beginning and end of the period of validity of the certificate;
- (g) the identity code of the certificate;
- (h) the advanced electronic signature of the certification-service-provider issuing it;
- (i) limitations on the scope of use of the certificate, if applicable; and
- (j) limits on the value of transactions for which the certificate can be used, if applicable.'

CERTIFICATION-SERVICE-PROVIDERS – ANNEX II

2.143 Annex II contains the requirements for certification-service-providers who issue qualified certificates, providing that:

'**Requirements for certification-service-providers issuing qualified certificates**

Certification-service-providers must:
- (a) demonstrate the reliability necessary for providing certification services;
- (b) ensure the operation of a prompt and secure directory and a secure and immediate revocation service;
- (c) ensure that the date and time when a certificate is issued or revoked can be determined precisely;
- (d) verify, by appropriate means in accordance with national law, the identity and, if applicable, any specific attributes of the person to which a qualified certificate is issued;
- (e) employ personnel who possess the expert knowledge, experience, and qualifications necessary for the services provided, in particular competence at managerial level, expertise in electronic signature technology and familiarity with proper security procedures; they must also apply administrative and management procedures which are adequate and correspond to recognised standards;
- (f) use trustworthy systems and products which are protected against modification and ensure the technical and cryptographic security of the process supported by them;
- (g) take measures against forgery of certificates, and, in cases where the certification-service-provider generates signature-creation data, guarantee confidentiality during the process of generating such data;
- (h) maintain sufficient financial resources to operate in conformity with the requirements laid down in the Directive, in particular to bear the risk of liability for damages, for example, by obtaining appropriate insurance;
- (i) record all relevant information concerning a qualified certificate for an appropriate period of time, in particular for the purpose of providing evidence of certification for the purposes of legal proceedings. Such recording may be done electronically;
- (j) not store or copy signature-creation data of the person to whom the certification-service-provider provided key management services;

(k) before entering into a contractual relationship with a person seeking a certificate to support his electronic signature inform that person by a durable means of communication of the precise terms and conditions regarding the use of the certificate, including any limitations on its use, the existence of a voluntary accreditation scheme and procedures for complaints and dispute settlement. Such information, which may be transmitted electronically, must be in writing and in readily understandable language. Relevant parts of this information must also be made available on request to third-parties relying on the certificate;

(l) use trustworthy systems to store certificates in a verifiable form so that:
– only authorised persons can make entries and changes,
– information can be checked for authenticity,
– certificates are publicly available for retrieval in only those cases for which the certificate-holder's consent has been obtained, and
– any technical changes compromising these security requirements are apparent to the operator.'

SECURE-SIGNATURE CREATION DEVICES – ANNEX III

2.144 Annex III contains the requirements for secure-signature creation devices, providing that:

'Requirements for secure signature-creation devices

1. Secure signature-creation devices must, by appropriate technical and procedural means, ensure at the least that:
(a) the signature-creation-data used for signature generation can practically occur only once, and that their secrecy is reasonably assured;
(b) the signature-creation-data used for signature generation cannot, with reasonable assurance, be derived and the signature is protected against forgery using currently available technology;
(c) the signature-creation-data used for signature generation can be reliably protected by the legitimate signatory against the use of others.

2. Secure signature-creation devices must not alter the data to be signed or prevent such data from being presented to the signatory prior to the signature process.'

Legal effect of electronic signatures

2.145 The legal effect of electronic signatures is contained in article 5, which provides as follows:

'Article 5

Legal effects of electronic signatures

1. Member States shall ensure that advanced electronic signatures which are based on a qualified certificate and which are created by a secure-signature-creation device:
(a) satisfy the legal requirements of a signature in relation to data in electronic form in the same manner as a handwritten signature satisfies those requirements in relation to paper-based data; and
(b) are admissible as evidence in legal proceedings.

2.145 Confidentiality, privacy and technology

> 2. Member States shall ensure that an electronic signature is not denied legal effectiveness and admissibility as evidence in legal proceedings solely on the grounds that it is:
> – in electronic form, or
> – not based upon a qualified certificate, or
> – not based upon a qualified certificate issued by an accredited certification-service-provider, or
> – not created by a secure signature-creation device.'

The critical distinction between advanced electronic signatures based on qualified certificates and the other kinds is the guarantee that they have the same status in law as handwritten signatures on 'paper-based data'. Thus, where the law requires a physical signature on a paper document an advanced electronic signature based on a qualified certificate will have equivalent legal effect. The other forms of electronic signature, while having legal effect, do not have this status.

Accreditation and supervision

2.146 Article 3 of the Directive is concerned with market access, for example prohibiting Member States from making the provision of certification services subject to prior authorisation. It also contains rules on accreditation and supervision.

Article 3(2) says that 'Member States may introduce or maintain voluntary accreditation schemes aiming at enhanced levels of certification-service provision. All conditions related to such schemes must be objective, transparent, proportionate and non-discriminatory'. Voluntary accreditation is defined in article 2(13) as 'any permission, setting out rights and obligations specific to the provision of certification services, to be granted upon request by the certification-service-provider concerned, by the public or private body charged with the elaboration of, and supervision of compliance with, such rights and obligations, where the certification-service-provider is not entitled to exercise the rights stemming from the permission until it has received the decision by the body'.

Regarding supervision, article 3(3) says that 'each Member State shall ensure the establishment of an appropriate system that allows for supervision of certification-service-providers which are established on its territory and issue qualified certificates to the public'.

Liability for reliance upon a qualified certificate

2.147 The certificate accompanying an advanced electronic signature makes powerful representations to the recipient of the electronic communication or data; it tells the recipient that it can trust the integrity of the communication or data and that it has not been tampered with. In other words, the certificate makes representations about the security of the communication or data.

Article 6 of the Directive deals with the liability issues, providing as follows:

'Liability

1. As a minimum, Member States shall ensure that by issuing a certificate as a qualified certificate to the public or by guaranteeing such a certificate to the public a certification-service-provider is liable for damage caused to any entity or legal or natural person who reasonably relies on that certificate:
    (a) as regards the accuracy at the time of issuance of all information contained in the qualified certificate and as regards the fact that the certificate contains all the details prescribed for a qualified certificate;
    (b) for assurance that at the time of the issuance of the certificate, the signatory identified in the qualified certificate held the signature-creation data corresponding to the signature-verification data given or identified in the certificate;
    (c) for assurance that the signature-creation data and the signature-verification data can be used in a complementary manner in cases where the certification-service-provider generates them both;
    unless the certification-service-provider proves that he has not acted negligently.

2. As a minimum Member States shall ensure that a certification-service-provider who has issued a certificate as a qualified certificate to the public is liable for damage caused to any entity or legal or natural person who reasonably relies on the certificate for failure to register revocation of the certificate unless the certification-service-provider proves that he has not acted negligently.

3. Member States shall ensure that a certification-service-provider may indicate in a qualified certificate limitations on the use of that certificate provided that the limitations are recognisable to third parties. The certification-service-provider shall not be liable for damage arising from use of a qualified certificate which exceeds the limitations placed on it.

4. Member States shall ensure that a certification-service-provider may indicate in the qualified certificate a limit on the value of transactions for which the certificate can be used, provided that the limit is recognisable to third parties.

The certification-service-provider shall not be liable for damage resulting from this maximum limit being exceeded.

5. The provisions of paragraphs 1 to 4 shall be without prejudice to Council Directive 93/13/EEC of 5 April 1993 on unfair terms in consumer contracts.'

The transposition of the Directive

2.148 The Directive has been transposed by the Electronic Signatures Regulations 2002 and by ss 7 and 8 of the Electronic Communications Act 2000.

The regulations closely follow the scheme of the Directive. As far as supervision is concerned, regulation 3 places this duty on the Secretary of State, who is required to establish and maintain a register of certification-service-providers issuing qualified certificates who are established in the UK. As regards liability of certification-service-providers, regulation 4 reverses the burden of proof, saying that the 'certification-service-provider shall be so liable to the same extent notwithstanding that there is no proof that the

2.148 *Confidentiality, privacy and technology*

certification-service-provider was negligent, unless the certification-service-provider proves that he was not negligent'.

Section 7 of the Electronic Communications Act 2000 transposes the requirements of article 5(2) of the Directive, providing that an electronic signature accompanied by 'the certification by any person of such a signature' 'shall each be admissible in evidence in relation to any question as to the authenticity of the communication or data or as to the integrity of the communication or data'.

Section 8 gives effect to article 5(1), giving the Secretary of State the power to modify legislation 'for the purpose of authorising or facilitating the use of electronic communications or electronic storage'. Sections 7 and 8 provide as follows:

'7.— Electronic signatures and related certificates
(1) In any legal proceedings–
   (a) an electronic signature incorporated into or logically associated with a particular electronic communication or particular electronic data, and
   (b) the certification by any person of such a signature,
   shall each be admissible in evidence in relation to any question as to the authenticity of the communication or data or as to the integrity of the communication or data.
(2) For the purposes of this section an electronic signature is so much of anything in electronic form as–
   (a) is incorporated into or otherwise logically associated with any electronic communication or electronic data; and
   (b) purports to be so incorporated or associated for the purpose of being used in establishing the authenticity of the communication or data, the integrity of the communication or data, or both.
(3) For the purposes of this section an electronic signature incorporated into or associated with a particular electronic communication or particular electronic data is certified by any person if that person (whether before or after the making of the communication) has made a statement confirming that–
   (a) the signature,
   (b) a means of producing, communicating or verifying the signature, or
   (c) a procedure applied to the signature,
   is (either alone or in combination with other factors) a valid means of establishing the authenticity of the communication or data, the integrity of the communication or data, or both.

8.— Power to modify legislation
(1) Subject to subsection (3), the appropriate Minister may by order made by statutory instrument modify the provisions of–
   (a) any enactment or subordinate legislation, or
   (b) any scheme, licence, authorisation or approval issued, granted or given by or under any enactment or subordinate legislation,
   in such manner as he may think fit for the purpose of authorising or facilitating the use of electronic communications or electronic storage (instead of other forms of communication or storage) for any purpose mentioned in subsection (2).
(2) Those purposes are–

(a) the doing of anything which under any such provisions is required to be or may be done or evidenced in writing or otherwise using a document, notice or instrument;

(b) the doing of anything which under any such provisions is required to be or may be done by post or other specified means of delivery;

(c) the doing of anything which under any such provisions is required to be or may be authorised by a person's signature or seal, or is required to be delivered as a deed or witnessed;

(d) the making of any statement or declaration which under any such provisions is required to be made under oath or to be contained in a statutory declaration;

(e) the keeping, maintenance or preservation, for the purposes or in pursuance of any such provisions, of any account, record, notice, instrument or other document;

(f) the provision, production or publication under any such provisions of any information or other matter;

(g) the making of any payment that is required to be or may be made under any such provisions.

(3) The appropriate Minister shall not make an order under this section authorising the use of electronic communications or electronic storage for any purposes, unless he considers that the authorisation is such that the extent (if any) to which records of things done for that purpose will be available will be no less satisfactory in cases where use is made of electronic communications or electronic storage than in other cases.

(4) Without prejudice to the generality of subsection (1), the power to make an order under this section shall include power to make an order containing any of the following provisions–

(a) provision as to the electronic form to be taken by any electronic communications or electronic storage the use of which is authorised by an order under this section;

(b) provision imposing conditions subject to which the use of electronic communications or electronic storage is so authorised;

(c) provision, in relation to cases in which any such conditions are not satisfied, for treating anything for the purposes of which the use of such communications or storage is so authorised as not having been done;

(d) provision, in connection with anything so authorised, for a person to be able to refuse to accept receipt of something in electronic form except in such circumstances as may be specified in or determined under the order;

(e) provision, in connection with any use of electronic communications so authorised, for intermediaries to be used, or to be capable of being used, for the transmission of any data or for establishing the authenticity or integrity of any data;

(f) provision, in connection with any use of electronic storage so authorised, for persons satisfying such conditions as may be specified in or determined under the regulations to carry out functions in relation to the storage;

(g) provision, in relation to cases in which the use of electronic communications or electronic storage is so authorised, for the determination of any of the matters mentioned in subsection (5), or as to the manner in which they may be proved in legal proceedings;

(h) provision, in relation to cases in which fees or charges are or may be imposed in connection with anything for the purposes of which the use of electronic communications or electronic storage is so authorised, for different fees or charges to apply where use is made of such communications or storage;

(i) provision, in relation to any criminal or other liabilities that may arise (in respect of the making of false or misleading statements or otherwise) in connection with anything for the purposes of which the use of electronic communications or electronic storage is so authorised, for corresponding liabilities to arise in corresponding circumstances where use is made of such communications or storage;

(j) provision requiring persons to prepare and keep records in connection with any use of electronic communications or electronic storage which is so authorised;

(k) provision requiring the production of the contents of any records kept in accordance with an order under this section;

(l) provision for a requirement imposed by virtue of paragraph (j) or (k) to be enforceable at the suite or instance of such person as may be specified in or determined in accordance with the order;

(m) any such provision, in relation to electronic communications or electronic storage the use of which is authorised otherwise than by an order under this section, as corresponds to any provision falling within any of the preceding paragraphs that may be made where it is such an order that authorises the use of the communications or storage.

(5) The matters referred to in subsection (4)(g) are—
(a) whether a thing has been done using an electronic communication or electronic storage;
(b) the time at which, or date on which, a thing done using any such communication or storage was done;
(c) the place where a thing done using such communication or storage was done;
(d) the person by whom such a thing was done; and
(e) the contents, authenticity or integrity of any electronic data.

(6) An order under this section—
(a) shall not (subject to paragraph (b)) require the use of electronic communications or electronic storage for any purpose; but
(b) may make provision that a period of notice specified in the order must expire before effect is given to a variation or withdrawal of an election or other decision which—
(i) has been made for the purposes of such an order; and
(ii) is an election or decision to make use of electronic communications or electronic storage.

(7) The matters in relation to which provision may be made by an order under this section do not include any matter under the care and management of the Commissioners of Inland Revenue or any matter under the care and management of the Commissioners of Customs and Excise.

(8) In this section references to doing anything under the provisions of any enactment include references to doing it under the provisions of any subordinate legislation the power to make which is conferred by that enactment.'

Chapter 3
COMPANIES, CORPORATE GOVERNANCE AND FINANCIAL SERVICES

COMPANIES

3.1 Companies that are data controllers will have to comply with the security provisions in the Data Protection Act 1998 and with other relevant laws that are identified in Chapter 2. Additionally, companies legislation may impose security obligations on directors, as part of their general duties.

Directors' general duties are contained in Pt 10, Chapter 2 of the Companies Act 2006 (CA 2006) and they include a duty to promote the success of the company (s 172), a duty to exercise independent judgment (s 173) and a duty to exercise reasonable care and skill (s 174). The opening part of s 172 provides as follows:

'**172 Duty to promote the success of the company**
(1)   A director of a company must act in the way he considers, in good faith, would be most likely to promote the success of the company for the benefit of its members as a whole, and in doing so have regard (amongst other matters) to–
  (a)   the likely consequences of any decision in the long term,
  (b)   the interests of the company's employees,
  (c)   the need to foster the company's business relationships with suppliers, customers and others,
  (d)   the impact of the company's operations on the community and the environment,
  (e)   the desirability of the company maintaining a reputation for high standards of business conduct, and
  (f)   the need to act fairly as between members of the company.'

Section 173 merely requires the exercise of independent judgment, the requirement for which can be limited by 'an agreement duly entered into by the company that restricts the future exercise of discretion by its directors', or by the company's constitution (see s 173(2)).

Section 174 provides:

'**174 Duty to exercise reasonable care, skill and diligence**
(1)   A director of a company must exercise reasonable care, skill and diligence.

3.1   Companies, corporate governance and financial services

(2) This means the care, skill and diligence that would be exercised by a reasonably diligent person with–
  (a) the general knowledge, skill and experience that may reasonably be expected of a person carrying out the functions carried out by the director in relation to the company, and
  (b) the general knowledge, skill and experience that the director has.'

All of these provisions can be relevant to data security law, in the sense that they might require company directors to address security issues and implement controls. If these provisions do extend as far as data security, then company directors could be held personally liable for failures of security (see s 178).

3.2 Company law may also bite where a breach of security results in a failure of records keeping. CA 2006 is littered with records keeping obligations, including the one at s 386, which requires the keeping of 'adequate accounting records'. If these records are held purely electronically and they are corrupted or deleted, by malware for example, the company might be put in breach of the Act. In such circumstances the relevant officers of the company will be exposed to a risk of criminal proceedings, due to the provisions of s 387, which provide that:

'**387 Duty to keep accounting records: offence**
(1) If a company fails to comply with any provision of section 386 (duty to keep accounting records), an offence is committed by every officer of the company who is in default.
(2) It is a defence for a person charged with such an offence to show that he acted honestly and that in the circumstances in which the company's business was carried on the default was excusable.
(3) A person guilty of an offence under this section is liable–
  (a) on conviction on indictment, to imprisonment for a term not exceeding two years or a fine (or both);
  (b) on summary conviction–
    (i) in England and Wales, to imprisonment for a term not exceeding twelve months or to a fine not exceeding the statutory maximum (or both);
    (ii) in Scotland or Northern Ireland, to imprisonment for a term not exceeding six months, or to a fine not exceeding the statutory maximum (or both).'

Similarly, s 1138 makes it an offence to fail to guard against the falsification of electronic records, which naturally imposes data security obligations:

'**1138 Duty to take precautions against falsification**
(1) Where company records are kept otherwise than in bound books, adequate precautions must be taken–
  (a) to guard against falsification, and
  (b) to facilitate the discovery of falsification.
(2) If a company fails to comply with this section, an offence is committed by every officer of the company who is in default.'

Companies and transparency

3.3 CA 2006, s 1266 inserted ss 89A–G into the Financial Services and Markets Act 2000 (FSMA 2000). Section 89A allows the 'competent authority', which is the Financial Services Authority, to 'make rules for the purposes of the transparency obligations directive'.

Transparency Obligations Directive

3.4 The Transparency Obligations Directive[1] harmonises the reporting and disclosure rules for companies whose shares and debt securities are publicly traded, covering, in particular, financial reporting and the publication of half-yearly statements. These half-yearly statements should include 'an explanation of material events'[2], which could extend as far as requiring the reporting of very serious security breaches, particularly where they have had a significant financial impact.

Article 21 envisages that each Member State will create a publicly accessible central repository of information that has been disclosed. This system, which falls under the responsibility of Companies House in the UK, has to incorporate security controls:

> '2. The home Member State shall ensure that there is at least one officially appointed mechanism for the central storage of regulated information. These mechanisms should comply with minimum quality standards of security, certainty as to the information source, time recording and easy access by end users and shall be aligned with the filing procedure under Article 19(1).'

[1] Directive 2004/109/EC of the European Parliament and of the Council of 15 December 2004 on the harmonisation of transparency requirements in relation to information about issuers whose securities are admitted to trading on a regulated market and amending Directive 2001/34/EC.
[2] Directive 2004/109/EC, article 6(1).

3.5 A European Commission recommendation[1] has provided further insight into the expectations regarding these central repositories, particularly the linking together of all of the electronic versions created across Europe, including those built for compliance with the Prospectus Directive[2]. Chapter III of the recommendation contains the following provisions about security:

> '7. Security of communication
>
> 7.1. The storage mechanism should have in place sound security mechanisms designed to ensure the security of the means of communication used to link the issuer with the mechanism, and to provide certainty as to the source of the information being filed.
>
> 7.2. The storage mechanism should be, for security reasons, entitled to limit the means of communication to be used but it should be able, at least, to receive electronic filings through a system accessible to the issuer.
>
> In any event, the types of means of communication to be used should be easily accessible, commonly used and widely available at a low cost.

3.5 Companies, corporate governance and financial services

8. Integrity of stored regulated information

8.1. The storage mechanism should store the information in a secure electronic format and should have in place appropriate security mechanisms designed to minimise the risks of data corruption and unauthorised access.

8.2. The storage mechanism should ensure that the regulated information it holds as received from the issuer is complete and that the content of the regulated information is not editable while stored.

In case that the storage mechanism accepts the filing of information using means of communication other than electronic, the storage mechanism should ensure, when converting the documents into electronic documents, that the content of the information is complete and unedited as originally sent by the issuer the information.

8.3. Information that has been sent to the storage mechanism and displayed should not be taken out of the storage mechanism. If an addition or correction is necessary, then the correcting or additional piece of information should identify the item it modifies and should be identified as a correction or addendum.

9. Validation

9.1. The storage mechanism should be able to validate the information filed, meaning that the mechanism should enable an automatic inspection of the filed documents for technical adherence to standards required, completeness and accuracy of their formats.

9.2. The storage mechanism should have systems in place to detect interruptions of the electronic feed and to request the re-transmission of any data that it fails to receive from the sender.

10. Reliable access to services

10.1. The storage mechanism should have security systems in place so as to ensure that its services can be accessed by issuers and end users, without disruption, 24 hours a day and seven days a week.

Each storage mechanism should define its own requirements, based on the characteristics of its systems and the particular conditions in which it operates.

The capacity of the systems, namely, the capacity of its servers and the bandwidth available, should be sufficient to support the expected requests from issuers, as regards filing of information, and end users, as regards access to stored information.

10.2. The storage mechanism should be entitled to prevent access to its systems for brief periods when necessary in order to perform essential maintenance or in order to upgrade its services. Where possible, such interruptions should be announced in advance.

11. Acceptance of waivers and recovery

The storage mechanism should have an evaluation process for reviewing and accepting or denying waivers for late filings due to technical issues of the storage mechanism and non-standard submissions. The mechanism should also provide recovery tools that allow the issuer to use other mechanisms of filing in place of the prescribed one when this is out of order.

However, there should be an obligation on the issuer to re-file the information through the main mechanism when restored.

12. Back-up systems

12.1. The storage mechanism should be technologically independent and have sufficient back-up facilities in place in order to maintain and to re-establish its services in a reasonable timeframe.

12.2. The nature of these back-up systems will need to be evaluated by each storage mechanism taking into consideration the specific characteristics of the systems in place.'

1   Commission Recommendation of 11 October 2007 on the electronic network of officially appointed mechanisms for the central storage of regulated information referred to in Directive 2004/109/EC of the European Parliament and of the Council.
2   Directive 2003/71/EC.

UK transparency rules

3.6 The Financial Services Authority's rules on transparency are contained in the chapter of the FSA Handbook titled 'Disclosure Rules and Transparency Rules', or 'DTR' for short[1]. In addition to covering the Transparency Obligations Directive, the DTR covers the requirements of the Audit Directive[2], the Market Abuse Directive[3] and the Fourth Company Law Directive[4]. Despite the opportunities available to the FSA through the Transparency Obligations Directive, the DTR is silent on the issues of data security and security breaches. However, the DTR's corporate governance rules, which are discussed below, can certainly be interpreted to cover data security issues, particularly if there is a risk that a breach of security could affect the efficacy or reliability of the company's systems for financial reporting.

1   http://fsahandbook.info/FSA//handbook/DTR.pdf.
2   Directive 2006/43/EC of the European Parliament and of the Council of 17 May 2006 on statutory audits of annual accounts and consolidated accounts, amending Council Directives 78/660/EEC and 83/349/EEC and repealing Council Directive 84/253/EEC.
3   See paras 3.19–3.20.
4   Council Directive 78/660/EEC on the annual accounts of certain types of companies as amended by, amongst other instruments, Directive 2006/46/EC of the European Parliament and of the Council of 14 June 2006.

Companies and corporate governance

3.7 CA 2006, s 1269 inserted s 89O into the Financial Services and Markets Act 2000, the opening parts of which provide as follows:

'**89O Corporate governance rules**
(1)   The competent authority may make rules ("corporate governance rules")–
   (a)   for the purpose of implementing, enabling the implementation of or dealing with matters arising out of or related to, any Community obligation relating to the corporate governance of issuers who have requested or approved admission of their securities to trading on a regulated market;
   (b)   about corporate governance in relation to such issuers for the purpose of implementing, or dealing with matters arising out of or related to, any Community obligation.
(2)   "Corporate governance", in relation to an issuer, includes–

3.7 *Companies, corporate governance and financial services*

    (a)   the nature, constitution or functions of the organs of the issuer;
    (b)   the manner in which organs of the issuer conduct themselves;
    (c)   the requirements imposed on organs of the issuer;
    (d)   the relationship between the different organs of the issuer;
    (e)   the relationship between the organs of the issuer and the members of the issuer or holders of the issuer's securities.'

Again, the definition of corporate governance can extend to cover data security issues.

Audit Directive and Company Law Directives

3.8 The Audit Directive and the Fourth[1] and Seventh[2] Company Law Directives are among the principle sources of corporate governance laws within the EU. For example, article 41 of the Audit Directive requires 'public interest entities', which are listed companies, to appoint audit committees, whose role and function can be interpreted to cover systems for data security, as they are required to 'monitor the effectiveness of the company's internal control, internal audit where applicable, and risk management systems'.

[1] Council Directive 78/660/EEC on the annual accounts of certain types of companies as amended by, amongst other instruments, Directive 2006/46/EC of the European Parliament and of the Council of 14 June 2006.
[2] Seventh Council Directive 83/349/EEC of 13 June 1983 based on Article 54(3)(g) of the Treaty on consolidated accounts.

UK corporate governance rules

3.9 Returning to the FSA Handbook, section 7.1.3(2) of the DTR repeats the effect of article 41 of the Audit Directive, requiring the audit committee to 'monitor the effectiveness of the issuer's internal control, internal audit where applicable, and risk management systems'. DTR 7.2.1 requires issuers to 'include a corporate governance statement in its directors' report', which 'must contain a description of the main features of the issuer's internal control and risk management systems in relation to the financial reporting process'.

Corporate governance and the Financial Reporting Council

3.10 On a number of occasions the DTR confirms that compliance with the 'Combined Code on Corporate Governance' will constitute compliance with the DTR[1]. The Combined Code and its sister publication, the Turnbull Guidance, are published by the Financial Reporting Council (FRC)[2].

The FRC's website explains that:

    'The Combined Code on Corporate Governance sets out standards of good practice in relation to issues such as board composition and development, remuneration, accountability and audit and relations with shareholders.

    All companies incorporated in the UK and listed on the Main Market of the London Stock Exchange are required under the Listing Rules[3] to report on how they have applied the Combined Code in their annual report and accounts. Overseas companies listed on the Main Market are required to disclose the significant ways in which their corporate governance practices differ from those set out in the Code.

The Combined Code contains broad principles and more specific provisions. Listed companies are required to report on how they have applied the main principles of the Code, and either to confirm that they have complied with the Code's provisions or – where they have not – to provide an explanation.'

The latest version of the Combined Code[4] explains in its preamble that:

'1. Good corporate governance should contribute to better company performance by helping a board discharge its duties in the best interests of shareholders; if it is ignored, the consequence may well be vulnerability or poor performance. Good governance should facilitate efficient, effective and entrepreneurial management that can deliver shareholder value over the longer term. The Combined Code on Corporate Governance ("the Code") is published by the FRC to support these outcomes and promote confidence in corporate reporting and governance.

2. The Code is not a rigid set of rules. Rather, it is a guide to the components of good board practice distilled from consultation and widespread experience over many years. While it is expected that companies will comply wholly or substantially with its provisions, it is recognised that non-compliance may be justified in particular circumstances if good governance can be achieved by other means. A condition of non-compliance is that the reasons for it should be explained to shareholders, who may wish to discuss the position with the company and whose voting intentions may be influenced as a result. This "comply or explain" approach has been in operation since the Code's beginnings in 1992 and the flexibility it offers is valued by company boards and by investors in pursuing better corporate governance.'

Key provisions within the Combined Code that impact on data security are as follows:

'Every company should be headed by an effective board, which is collectively responsible for the success of the company.

The board should be supplied in a timely manner with information in a form and of a quality appropriate to enable it to discharge its duties. All directors should receive induction on joining the board and should regularly update and refresh their skills and knowledge.

The board should maintain a sound system of internal control to safeguard shareholders' investment and the company's assets. The board should, at least annually, conduct a review of the effectiveness of the group's system of internal controls and should report to shareholders that they have done so. The review should cover all material controls, including financial, operational and compliance controls and risk management systems.'

---

1   See DTR 7.1.7, 7.2.4 and 7.2.8.
2   http://www.frc.org.uk/.
3   The Listing Rules are contained in the FSA Handbook, within the chapter titled 'Listing, Prospectus and Disclosure', or 'LR' for short. LR 9.8.6(5) requires, for example, listed companies' financial reports to include 'a statement of how the listed company has applied the Main Principles set out in Section 1 of the Combined Code, in a manner that would enable shareholders to evaluate how the principles have been applied'. See also LR 9.8.6(6), 9.8.7, 9.8.10 and 15.6.6.

3.10 *Companies, corporate governance and financial services*

[4] http://www.frc.org.uk/documents/pagemanager/frc/Combined_Code_June_2008/
Combined%20Code%20Web%20Optimized%20June%202008(2).pdf.

3.11 The Turnbull Guidance[1] expands upon the Combined Code, focusing on companies' systems for control of risk. The opening parts of the guidance explain:

> '1. A company's system of internal control has a key role in the management of risks that are significant to the fulfilment of its business objectives. A sound system of internal control contributes to safeguarding the shareholders' investment and the company's assets.
>
> 2. Internal control (as referred to in paragraph 19) facilitates the effectiveness and efficiency of operations, helps ensure the reliability of internal and external reporting and assists compliance with laws and regulations.
>
> 3. Effective financial controls, including the maintenance of proper accounting records, are an important element of internal control. They help ensure that the company is not unnecessarily exposed to avoidable financial risks and that financial information used within the business and for publication is reliable. They also contribute to the safeguarding of assets, including the prevention and detection of fraud.
>
> 4. A company's objectives, its internal organisation and the environment in which it operates are continually evolving and, as a result, the risks it faces are continually changing. A sound system of internal control therefore depends on a thorough and regular evaluation of the nature and extent of the risks to which the company is exposed. Since profits are, in part, the reward for successful risk-taking in business, the purpose of internal control is to help manage and control risk appropriately rather than to eliminate it.'

The Guidance attempts to put the issue of risk management at the top of the corporate agenda. Among other things it reminds that:

- 'The board of directors is responsible for the company's system of internal control.'
- 'It is the role of management to implement board policies on risk and control', that 'all employees have some responsibility for internal control as part of their accountability for achieving objectives.'
- 'An internal control system encompasses the policies, processes, tasks, behaviours and other aspects of a company that ... facilitate its effective and efficient operation, ... help ensure the quality of internal and external reporting ... [and] help ensure compliance with applicable laws and regulations.'
- 'A company's system of internal control will reflect its control environment which encompasses its organisational structure ... control activities, information and communications processes and processes for monitoring the continuing effectiveness of the system of internal control.'
- 'The system of internal control should be embedded in the operations of the company and form part of its culture.'
- 'A sound system of internal control reduces, but cannot eliminate, the possibility of poor judgement in decision-making; human error; control

processes being deliberately circumvented by employees and others; management overriding controls; and the occurrence of unforeseeable circumstances.'
- 'Effective monitoring on a continuous basis is an essential component of a sound system of internal control.'
- 'The reports from management to the board should, in relation to the areas covered by them, provide a balanced assessment of the significant risks and the effectiveness of the system of internal control in managing those risks.'

[1] Internal Control, Revised Guidance for Directors on the Combined Code, Financial Reporting Council, October 2005: http://frc.org.uk/documents/pagemanager/frc/Revised%20Turnbull%20Guidance%20October%202005.pdf.

Corporate governance and SAS 70

3.12 The 'Statement on Auditing Standards No 70' (SAS 70) is an auditing methodology published by the American Institute of Certified Public Accountants that is used to audit the control objectives and control activities of service organisations. Service organisations are companies that provide outsourcing services, such as data processing or data storage, to businesses and other organisations. SAS 70 is generally considered to provide a useful methodology for determining the state of data security within service organisations.

FINANCIAL SERVICES

3.13 The financial services sector is subject to an additional layer of laws and rules that impact on data security. Key provisions are discussed below.

EU Directives

Capital Requirements Directive (CRD)

3.14 The 'Capital Requirements Directive', which actually consists of two Directives, namely the 'Banking Consolidation Directive'[1] and the 'Capital Adequacy Directive'[2], gives effect to the requirements of Basel II on capital measurement and standards[3]. Key components with the CRD include home country regulation and mutual recognition, rules governing the take up and pursuit of banking services, prudential supervision rules for banks, investment firms and credit institutions and methodologies for calculating risk. The CRD identifies three kinds of risk within banks, investment firms and credit institutions, namely credit risk, market risk and operational risk. In crude terms, the amount of capital that a regulated entity is required to hold is calculated by reference to its risk rating. In other words, the lower the risk the lower is the amount of capital that should be held and vice versa.

It is the provisions on operational risk that are most relevant within an analysis of data security law. The Banking Consolidation Directive defines

3.14 *Companies, corporate governance and financial services*

operational risk as 'the risk of loss resulting from inadequate or failed internal processes, people and systems or from external events, and includes legal risk'[4].

The relevance of operational risk is identified in article 102, which says that 'competent authorities shall require credit institutions to hold own funds against operational risk in accordance with the approaches set out in Articles 103, 104 and 105'.

In order to ensure that risk exposures are properly understood and addressed, article 22 sets out rules on corporate governance:

> '1. Home Member State competent authorities shall require that every credit institution have robust governance arrangements, which include a clear organisational structure with well defined, transparent and consistent lines of responsibility, effective processes to identify, manage, monitor and report the risks it is or might be exposed to, and adequate internal control mechanisms, including sound administrative and accounting procedures.
>
> 2. The arrangements, processes and mechanisms referred to in paragraph 1 shall be comprehensive and proportionate to the nature, scale and complexity of the credit institution's activities. The technical criteria laid down in Annex V shall be taken into account.'

Annex V on technical criteria concerning the organisation and treatment of risks says:

> '2. The management body described in Article 11 shall approve and periodically review the strategies and policies for taking up, managing, monitoring and mitigating the risks the credit institution is or might be exposed to, including those posed by the macroeconomic environment in which it operates in relation to the status of the business cycle.
>
> ...
>
> 12. Policies and processes to evaluate and manage the exposure to operational risk, including to low-frequency high severity events, shall be implemented. Without prejudice to the definition laid down in Article 4(22), credit institutions shall articulate what constitutes operational risk for the purposes of those policies and procedures.
>
> 13. Contingency and business continuity plans shall be in place to ensure a credit institution's ability to operate on an ongoing basis and limit losses in the event of severe business disruption.'

[1] Directive 2006/48/EC of the European Parliament and of the Council of 14 June 2006 relating to the taking up and pursuit of the business of credit institutions.
[2] Directive 2006/49/EC of the European Parliament and of the Council of 14 June 2006 on the capital adequacy of investment firms and credit institutions.
[3] Basel II: International Convergence of Capital Measurement and Capital Standards: a Revised Framework, June 2004, Basel Committee on Banking Supervision: http:www.bis.org/bcbs/index.htm.
[4] Directive 2006/48/EC, article 4(22).

3.15 The Banking Consolidation Directive provides banks with three methods for calculating risk, namely the basic indicator approach, the standardised approach and the advanced measurement approach. The final option, the advanced measurement approach, may be favoured as it can result in lower capital requirements than the others, but before a bank can take advantage of the advanced measurement approach it is required to satisfy the standards in Annex X Part 3, which contains detailed rules for the measurement and treatment of operation risk. For example, the opening parts of Annex X Part 3 provide as follows:

'1.1. Qualitative Standards

2. The credit institution's internal operational risk measurement system shall be closely integrated into its day-to-day risk management processes.

3. The credit institution must have an independent risk management function for operational risk.

4. There must be regular reporting of operational risk exposures and loss experience. The credit institution shall have procedures for taking appropriate corrective action.

5. The credit institution's risk management system must be well documented. The credit institution shall have routines in place for ensuring compliance and policies for the treatment of non-compliance.

6. The operational risk management processes and measurement systems shall be subject to regular reviews performed by internal and/or external auditors.

7. The validation of the operational risk measurement system by the competent authorities shall include the following elements:
(a) verifying that the internal validation processes are operating in a satisfactory manner;
(b) making sure that data flows and processes associated with the risk measurement system are transparent and accessible.'

Market in Financial Instruments Directive (MiFID) – including rules on outsourcing

3.16 MiFID consists of three instruments, namely two Directives, 2004/39/EC (the 'level 1 Directive')[1] and 2006/73/EC (the 'level 2 Directive')[2] and one regulation, (EC) No 1287/2006[3]. They apply to investment firms, regulated markets and certain credit institutions providing investment services and/or investment activities. They do not apply to insurance undertakings, collective investment undertakings or pension funds. The kinds of financial instruments that are regulated are transferable securities, money-market instruments, units in collective investment undertakings, various types of derivatives and financial contracts for differences. The kinds of activities that are regulated include the execution of client orders, portfolio management, investment advice, underwriting of financial instruments and the operation of multilateral trading facilities. Key elements within the regulatory regime are rules on home country regulation, best execution rules, pre and post trade transparency rules and client reporting rules. Within these rules are a plethora of obligations that concern or impact upon data security, including the issues within outsourcing, which are set out below.

Article 13 of the level 1 Directive, titled 'organisational requirements', provides:

3.16 Companies, corporate governance and financial services

'2. An investment firm shall establish adequate policies and procedures sufficient to ensure compliance of the firm including its managers, employees and tied agents with its obligations under the provisions of this Directive as well as appropriate rules governing personal transactions by such persons.

...

5. An investment firm shall ensure, when relying on a third party for the performance of operational functions which are critical for the provision of continuous and satisfactory service to clients and the performance of investment activities on a continuous and satisfactory basis, that it takes reasonable steps to avoid undue additional operational risk. Outsourcing of important operational functions may not be undertaken in such a way as to impair materially the quality of its internal control and the ability of the supervisor to monitor the firm's compliance with all obligations.

An investment firm shall have sound administrative and accounting procedures, internal control mechanisms, effective procedures for risk assessment, and effective control and safeguard arrangements for information processing systems.'

[1] Directive 2004/39/EC of the European Parliament and of the Council 21 April 2004 on markets in financial instruments amending Council Directives 85/611/EEC and 93/6/EEC and Directive 2000/12/EC of the European Parliament and of the Council and repealing Council Directive 93/22/EEC.
[2] Commission Directive 2006/73/EC of 10 August 2006 implementing Directive 2004/39/EC of the European Parliament and of the Council as regards organisational requirements and operating conditions for investment firms and defined terms for the purposes of that Directive.
[3] Commission Regulation (EC) No 1287/2006 of 10 August 2006 implementing Directive 2004/39/EC of the European Parliament and of the Council as regards recordkeeping obligations for investment firms, transaction reporting, market transparency, admission of financial instruments to trading, and defined terms for the purposes of that Directive.

3.17 Article 5 of the level 2 Directive, titled 'general organisational requirements', expands upon the requirements of article 13 of the level 1 Directive, providing that:

'2. Member States shall require investment firms to establish, implement and maintain systems and procedures that are adequate to safeguard the security, integrity and confidentiality of information, taking into account the nature of the information in question.'

Article 13 of the level 2 Directive, which also expands upon article 13 of the level 1 Directive, provides:

'1. For the purposes of the first subparagraph of Article 13(5) of Directive 2004/39/EC, an operational function shall be regarded as critical or important if a defect or failure in its performance would materially impair the continuing compliance of an investment firm with the conditions and obligations of its authorisation or its other obligations under Directive 2004/39/EC, or its financial performance, or the soundness or the continuity of its investment services and activities.

2. Without prejudice to the status of any other function, the following functions shall not be considered as critical or important for the purposes of paragraph 1:
(a)   the provision to the firm of advisory services, and other services which do not form part of the investment business of the firm, including the

provision of legal advice to the firm, the training of personnel of the firm, billing services and the security of the firm's premises and personnel;'

Article 14 of the level 2 Directive, which also expands upon article 13 of the level 1 Directive, provides further rules for outsourcing:

'1. Member States shall ensure that, when investment firms outsource critical or important operational functions or any investment services or activities, the firms remain fully responsible for discharging all of their obligations under Directive 2004/39/EC and comply, in particular, with the following conditions:
(a) the outsourcing must not result in the delegation by senior management of its responsibility;
(b) the relationship and obligations of the investment firm towards its clients under the terms of Directive 2004/39/EC must not be altered;
(c) the conditions with which the investment firm must comply in order to be authorised in accordance with Article 5 of Directive 2004/39/EC, and to remain so, must not be undermined;
(d) none of the other conditions subject to which the firm's authorisation was granted must be removed or modified.

2. Member States shall require investment firms to exercise due skill, care and diligence when entering into, managing or terminating any arrangement for the outsourcing to a service provider of critical or important operational functions or of any investment services or activities.

Investment firms shall in particular take the necessary steps to ensure that the following conditions are satisfied:
(a) the service provider must have the ability, capacity, and any authorisation required by law to perform the outsourced functions, services or activities reliably and professionally;
(b) the service provider must carry out the outsourced services effectively, and to this end the firm must establish methods for assessing the standard of performance of the service provider;
(c) the service provider must properly supervise the carrying out of the outsourced functions, and adequately manage the risks associated with the outsourcing;
(d) appropriate action must be taken if it appears that the service provider may not be carrying out the functions effectively and in compliance with applicable laws and regulatory requirements;
(e) the investment firm must retain the necessary expertise to supervise the outsourced functions effectively and manage the risks associated with the outsourcing and must supervise those functions and manage those risks;
(f) the service provider must disclose to the investment firm any development that may have a material impact on its ability to carry out the outsourced functions effectively and in compliance with applicable laws and regulatory requirements;
(g) the investment firm must be able to terminate the arrangement for outsourcing where necessary without detriment to the continuity and quality of its provision of services to clients;
(h) the service provider must cooperate with the competent authorities of the investment firm in connection with the outsourced activities;
(i) the investment firm, its auditors and the relevant competent authorities must have effective access to data related to the outsourced activities, as well as to the business premises of the service provider; and the competent authorities must be able to exercise those rights of access;

3.17 Companies, corporate governance and financial services

(j) the service provider must protect any confidential information relating to the investment firm and its clients;

(k) the investment firm and the service provider must establish, implement and maintain a contingency plan for disaster recovery and periodic testing of backup facilities, where that is necessary having regard to the function, service or activity that has been outsourced.

3. Member States shall require the respective rights and obligations of the investment firms and of the service provider to be clearly allocated and set out in a written agreement.

4. Member States shall provide that, where the investment firm and the service provider are members of the same group, the investment firm may, for the purposes of complying with this Article and Article 15, take into account the extent to which the firm controls the service provider or has the ability to influence its actions.

5. Member States shall require investment firms to make available on request to the competent authority all information necessary to enable the authority to supervise the compliance of the performance of the outsourced activities with the requirements of this Directive.'

Article 16 of the level 2 Directive, titled 'safeguarding of client financial instruments and funds', contains further relevant provisions. For example, article 16(1)(f) provides:

'(f) they must introduce adequate organisational arrangements to minimise the risk of the loss or diminution of client assets, or of rights in connection with those assets, as a result of misuse of the assets, fraud, poor administration, inadequate record-keeping or negligence.'

3.18 Article 12 of Commission Regulation (EC) No 1287/2006, which expands upon records keeping and anti money laundering rules in article 25(5) of the level 1 Directive provides:

'1. The reports of transactions in financial instruments shall be made in an electronic form except under exceptional circumstances, when they may be made in a medium which allows for the storing of the information in a way accessible for future reference by the competent authorities other than an electronic form, and the methods by which those reports are made shall satisfy the following conditions:

(a) they ensure the security and confidentiality of the data reported;

(b) they incorporate mechanisms for identifying and correcting errors in a transaction report;

(c) they incorporate mechanisms for authenticating the source of the transaction report;

(d) they include appropriate precautionary measures to enable the timely resumption of reporting in the case of system failure;'

Market Abuse Directive

3.19 The Market Abuse Directive consists of four Directives[1] and one regulation[2]. Directive 2003/6/EC, the framework Directive, observes that 'an integrated and efficient financial market requires market integrity. The smooth functioning of securities markets and public confidence in markets are prerequisites for economic growth and wealth. Market abuse harms the integrity of financial markets and public confidence in securities and derivatives'[3].

The framework Directive identifies two forms of market abuse, namely insider dealing and market manipulation. Both forms of illegal activity can build upon the misuse of computer systems and data; the Directive observes that 'new financial and technical developments enhance the incentives, means and opportunities for market abuse: through new products, new technologies, increasing cross-border activities and the Internet'[4]. As insider dealing and market manipulation are both activities born of misuse of information, it is vital that listed companies implement appropriate controls to keep relevant information safe from misuse. In other words, compliance with the Market Abuse Directive requires effective systems and operations for data security.

Articles 2 and 3 contain the prohibition against insider dealing, which takes the form of misuse of insider information, which is defined in article 1(1) as 'information of a precise nature which has not been made public, relating, directly or indirectly, to one or more issuers of financial instruments or to one or more financial instruments and which, if it were made public, would be likely to have a significant effect on the prices of those financial instruments or on the price of related derivative financial instruments'. Articles 2 and 3 provide that:

'Article 2

1. Member States shall prohibit any person referred to in the second subparagraph who possesses inside information from using that information by acquiring or disposing of, or by trying to acquire or dispose of, for his own account or for the account of a third party, either directly or indirectly, financial instruments to which that information relates.

The first subparagraph shall apply to any person who possesses that information:
(a) by virtue of his membership of the administrative, management or supervisory bodies of the issuer; or
(b) by virtue of his holding in the capital of the issuer; or
(c) by virtue of his having access to the information through the exercise of his employment, profession or duties; or
(d) by virtue of his criminal activities.

2. Where the person referred to in paragraph 1 is a legal person, the prohibition laid down in that paragraph shall also apply to the natural persons who take part in the decision to carry out the transaction for the account of the legal person concerned.

3. This Article shall not apply to transactions conducted in the discharge of an obligation that has become due to acquire or dispose of financial instruments where that obligation results from an agreement concluded before the person concerned possessed inside information.

Article 3

Member States shall prohibit any person subject to the prohibition laid down in Article 2 from:

3.19 Companies, corporate governance and financial services

(a) disclosing inside information to any other person unless such disclosure is made in the normal course of the exercise of his employment, profession or duties;
(b) recommending or inducing another person, on the basis of inside information, to acquire or dispose of financial instruments to which that information relates.'

[1] Directive 2003/6/EC of the European Parliament and of the Council of 28 January 2003 on insider dealing and market manipulation (market abuse); Commission Directive 2003/124/EC of 22 December 2003 implementing Directive 2003/6/EC of the European Parliament and of the Council as regards the definition and public disclosure of inside information and the definition of market manipulation; Commission Directive 2003/125/EC of 22 December 2003 implementing Directive 2003/6/EC of the European Parliament and of the Council as regards the fair presentation of investment recommendations and the disclosure of conflicts of interest; Commission Directive 2004/72/EC of 29 April 2004 implementing Directive 2003/6/EC of the European Parliament and of the Council as regards accepted market practices, the definition of inside information in relation to derivatives on commodities, the drawing up of lists of insiders, the notification of managers' transactions and the notification of suspicious transactions.
[2] Commission Regulation (EC) No 2273/2003 of 22 December 2003 implementing Directive 2003/6/EC of the European Parliament and of the Council as regards exemptions for buy-back programmes and stabilisation of financial instruments.
[3] Directive 2003/6/EC, recital (2).
[4] Directive 2003/6/EC, recital (10).

3.20 The prohibition against market manipulation is contained in article 5. Market manipulation is defined in article 1(2) as:

'2. "Market manipulation" shall mean:
(a) transactions or orders to trade:
— which give, or are likely to give, false or misleading signals as to the supply of, demand for or price of financial instruments, or
— which secure, by a person, or persons acting in collaboration, the price of one or several financial instruments at an abnormal or artificial level,
unless the person who entered into the transactions or issued the orders to trade establishes that his reasons for so doing are legitimate and that these transactions or orders to trade conform to accepted market practices on the regulated market concerned;
(b) transactions or orders to trade which employ fictitious devices or any other form of deception or contrivance;
(c) dissemination of information through the media, including the Internet, or by any other means, which gives, or is likely to give, false or misleading signals as to financial instruments, including the dissemination of rumours and false or misleading news, where the person who made the dissemination knew, or ought to have known, that the information was false or misleading. In respect of journalists when they act in their professional capacity such dissemination of information is to be assessed, without prejudice to Article 11, taking into account the rules governing their profession, unless those persons derive, directly or indirectly, an advantage or profits from the dissemination of the information in question.
In particular, the following instances are derived from the core definition given in points (a), (b) and (c) above:
— conduct by a person, or persons acting in collaboration, to secure a dominant position over the supply of or demand for a financial

instrument which has the effect of fixing, directly or indirectly, purchase or sale prices or creating other unfair trading conditions,
— the buying or selling of financial instruments at the close of the market with the effect of misleading investors acting on the basis of closing prices,
— taking advantage of occasional or regular access to the traditional or electronic media by voicing an opinion about a financial instrument (or indirectly about its issuer) while having previously taken positions on that financial instrument and profiting subsequently from the impact of the opinions voiced on the price of that instrument, without having simultaneously disclosed that conflict of interest to the public in a proper and effective way.

The definitions of market manipulation shall be adapted so as to ensure that new patterns of activity that in practice constitute market manipulation can be included.'

Prospectus Directive

3.21 The Prospectus Directive[1] harmonises the requirements 'for the drawing up, approval and distribution of the prospectus to be published when securities are offered to the public or admitted to trading on a regulated market situated or operating within a Member State'[2]. It requires the issuing of a prospectus whenever an offer of securities is made to the public and when securities are admitted to a regulated market for trading. Such prospectuses must 'contain all information which, according to the particular nature of the issuer and of the securities offered to the public or admitted to trading on a regulated market, is necessary to enable investors to make an informed assessment of the assets and liabilities, financial position, profit and losses, and prospects of the issuer and of any guarantor, and of the rights attaching to such securities'[3].

The Directive is supplemented by a regulation[4], which contains provisions requiring the security of electronic prospectuses:

'Where a prospectus is published in electronic form, additional safety measures compared to traditional means of publication, using best practices available, are necessary in order to maintain the integrity of the information, to avoid manipulation or modification from unauthorised persons, to avoid altering its comprehensibility and to escape from possible adverse consequences from different approaches on offer of securities to the public in third countries.'[5]

[1] Directive 2003/71/EC of the European Parliament and of the Council of 4 November 2003 on the prospectus to be published when securities are offered to the public or admitted to trading and amending Directive 2001/34/EC.
[2] Directive 2003/71/EC, article 1(1).
[3] Directive 2003/71/EC, article 5(1).
[4] Commission Regulation (EC) No 809/2004 of 29 April 2004 implementing Directive 2003/71/EC of the European Parliament and of the Council as regards information contained in prospectuses as well as the format, incorporation by reference and publication of such prospectuses and dissemination of advertisements.
[5] Commission Regulation (EC) No 809/2004, recital (31).

3.22 *Companies, corporate governance and financial services*

Money Laundering Directive

3.22 The third Money Laundering Directive[1] requires regulated entities[2] to keep customer due diligence records[3] for at least five years[4]. Regulated entities that report suspicious behaviour[5] to the authorities are also required to prevent disclosure through tipping off[6].

The database of customer due diligence records will constitute personal data within the meaning of the Data Protection Act 1998 and so will be subject to the security requirements within the seventh data protection principle. Irrespective of these obligations, the regulated entity is required to keep the database safe, so as to avoid accidental, negligent or deliberate deletion or alteration of records and tipping off.

[1] Directive 2005/60/EC of the European Parliament and of the Council of 26 October 2005 on the prevention of the use of the financial system for the purpose of money laundering and terrorist financing.
[2] See Directive 2005/60/EC, article 2, which says that the Directive applies to, among other things, credit institutions, financial institutions, external accountants and tax advisors, notaries and other independent legal professionals, trust or company service, real estate agents and casinos.
[3] See Directive 2005/60/EC, article 8 for the requirements.
[4] See Directive 2005/60/EC, article 30.
[5] See Directive 2005/60/EC, article 20.
[6] See Directive 2005/60/EC, article 28.

Payment Services Directive

3.23 The Payment Services Directive[1] provides the legal framework that underpins the creation of the Single European Payment Area[2] ('SEPA'). Its purpose is identified in article 1(2), which says:

> 'This Directive also lays down rules concerning transparency of conditions and information requirements for payment services, and the respective rights and obligations of payment service users and payment service providers in relation to the provision of payment services as a regular occupation or business activity.'

The Directive applies to the payment services listed in the Directive's annex, but it should also be noted that article 3, titled 'negative scope', provides a list of payment services that are excluded from regulation. The annex provides as follows:

> 'Payment Services (definition 3 in Article 4)
>
> 1. Services enabling cash to be placed on a payment account as well as all the operations required for operating a payment account.
>
> 2. Services enabling cash withdrawals from a payment account as well as all the operations required for operating a payment account.
>
> 3. Execution of payment transactions, including transfers of funds on a payment account with the user's payment service provider or with another payment service provider:
> — execution of direct debits, including one-off direct debits,

Financial services **3.24**

— execution of payment transactions through a payment card or a similar device,
— execution of credit transfers, including standing orders.

4. Execution of payment transactions where the funds are covered by a credit line for a payment service user:
— execution of direct debits, including one-off direct debits,
— execution of payment transactions through a payment card or a similar device,
— execution of credit transfers, including standing orders.

5. Issuing and/or acquiring of payment instruments.

6. Money remittance.

7. Execution of payment transactions where the consent of the payer to execute a payment transaction is given by means of any telecommunication, digital or IT device and the payment is made to the telecommunication, IT system or network operator, acting only as an intermediary between the payment service user and the supplier of the goods and services.'

1 Directive 2007/64/EC of the European Parliament and of the Council of 13 November 2007 on payment services in the internal market amending Directives 97/7/EC, 2002/65/EC, 2005/60/EC and 2006/48/EC and repealing Directive 97/5/EC Text with EEA relevance.
2 For further information about SEPA, visit http://www.ecb.eu/paym/sepa/html/index.en.html and http://www.europeanpaymentscouncil.eu/content.cfm?page=what_is_epc.

3.24 The need to maintain security in electronic systems for payment services will be obvious, but it is worth noting the following provisions nonetheless:

- Recital (32) provides that the provisions of the Directive are 'without prejudice to the payment service providers' responsibility for technical security of their own products'.
- Article 55(2) says that 'if agreed in the framework contract, the payment service provider may reserve the right to block the payment instrument for objectively justified reasons related to the security of the payment instrument'.
- Article 56(2) says that 'the payment service user shall, in particular, as soon as he receives a payment instrument, take all reasonable steps to keep its personalised security features safe'.
- Article 57(1)(a) says that the payment service provider is obliged 'to make sure that the personalised security features of the payment instrument are not accessible to parties other than the payment service user entitled to use the payment instrument'.
- Article 57(2) says that the payment service provider 'shall bear the risk of sending a payment instrument to the payer or of sending any personalised security features of it'.
- Article 61(1) says that the payer 'shall bear the losses relating to any unauthorised payment transactions, up to a maximum of EUR 150, resulting from the use of a lost or stolen payment instrument or, if the payer has failed to keep the personalised security features safe, from the misappropriation of a payment instrument'.

3.25 *Companies, corporate governance and financial services*

Electronic Money Directive

3.25 The Electronic Money Directive[1] regulates 'electronic money institutions', which are defined as 'an undertaking or any other legal person, other than a credit institution as defined in Article 1, point 1, first subparagraph (a) of Directive 2000/12/EC which issues means of payment in the form of electronic money'. Electronic money is defined as 'monetary value as represented by a claim on the issuer which is: (i) stored on an electronic device; (ii) issued on receipt of funds of an amount not less in value than the monetary value issued; (iii) accepted as means of payment by undertakings other than the issuer'.

Although the Directive does not say anything specific about data security, its rules about sound and prudent operations clearly include obligations for data security. Article 7 provides:

'Article 7

Sound and prudent operation

Electronic money institutions shall have sound and prudent management, administrative and accounting procedures and adequate internal control mechanisms. These should respond to the financial and non-financial risks to which the institution is exposed including technical and procedural risks as well as risks connected to its cooperation with any undertaking performing operational or other ancillary functions related to its business activities.'

[1] Directive 2000/46/EC of the European Parliament and of the Council of 18 September 2000 on the taking up, pursuit of and prudential supervision of the business of electronic money institutions.

Financial Services and Markets Act 2000

3.26 FSMA 2000, s 1 establishes the Financial Services Authority. The FSA, like the Information Commissioner, is very active in the field of data security; as mentioned in Chapter 1 it was the FSA's fine of Capita Financial Administrators in 2006 that provided the first concrete evidence of the creation of the regulatory bear market for data security. The FSA's 'general duties' are contained in FSMA 2000, s 2, which provides as follows:

'2.— **The Authority's general duties.**
(1) In discharging its general functions the Authority must, so far as is reasonably possible, act in a way–
    (a) which is compatible with the regulatory objectives; and
    (b) which the Authority considers most appropriate for the purpose of meeting those objectives.
(2) The regulatory objectives are–
    (a) market confidence;
    (b) public awareness;
    (c) the protection of consumers; and
    (d) the reduction of financial crime.
(3) In discharging its general functions the Authority must have regard to–
    (a) the need to use its resources in the most efficient and economic way;

	(b)	the responsibilities of those who manage the affairs of authorised persons;
	(c)	the principle that a burden or restriction which is imposed on a person, or on the carrying on of an activity, should be proportionate to the benefits, considered in general terms, which are expected to result from the imposition of that burden or restriction;
	(d)	the desirability of facilitating innovation in connection with regulated activities;
	(e)	the international character of financial services and markets and the desirability of maintaining the competitive position of the United Kingdom;
	(f)	the need to minimise the adverse effects on competition that may arise from anything done in the discharge of those functions;
	(g)	the desirability of facilitating competition between those who are subject to any form of regulation by the Authority.
(4)		The Authority's general functions are–
	(a)	its function of making rules under this Act (considered as a whole);
	(b)	its function of preparing and issuing codes under this Act (considered as a whole);
	(c)	its functions in relation to the giving of general guidance (considered as a whole); and
	(d)	its function of determining the general policy and principles by reference to which it performs particular functions.
(5)		"General guidance" has the meaning given in section 158(5).'

3.27 The regulation of data security could fit within any one of the four regulatory objectives, but the FSA has chosen the reduction of financial crime objective as the basis of its activities in this area. FSMA 2000, s 6 provides:

'**6.— The reduction of financial crime.**
(1)		The reduction of financial crime objective is: reducing the extent to which it is possible for a business carried on–
	(a)	by a regulated person, or
	(b)	in contravention of the general prohibition,
		to be used for a purpose connected with financial crime.
(2)		In considering that objective the Authority must, in particular, have regard to the desirability of–
	(a)	regulated persons being aware of the risk of their businesses being used in connection with the commission of financial crime;
	(b)	regulated persons taking appropriate measures (in relation to their administration and employment practices, the conduct of transactions by them and otherwise) to prevent financial crime, facilitate its detection and monitor its incidence;
	(c)	regulated persons devoting adequate resources to the matters mentioned in paragraph (b).
(3)		"Financial crime" includes any offence involving–
	(a)	fraud or dishonesty;
	(b)	misconduct in, or misuse of information relating to, a financial market; or
	(c)	handling the proceeds of crime.
(4)		"Offence" includes an act or omission which would be an offence if it had taken place in the United Kingdom.

3.27 Companies, corporate governance and financial services

(5) "Regulated person" means an authorised person, a recognised investment exchange or a recognised clearing house.'

The way in which s 6 is drafted is very interesting, containing provisions that echo the requirements within the seventh data protection principle of the Data Protection Act 1998. For example, the requirement that regulated persons take 'appropriate measures' to prevent financial crime (etc) is similar to the requirement for appropriate technical and organisational security measures which is imposed on data controllers by the seventh principle. The requirement that regulated persons take appropriate measures to facilitate the detection of financial crime and monitor its incidence also echo the requirements of the seventh principle as interpreted by the Information Commissioner[1]. The requirement that regulated persons devote adequate resources to the prevention of financial crime (etc) contains echoes of the requirement within the seventh principle that data controllers should have regard to cost when assessing the appropriateness of technological security measures. Collectively, these provisions also echo the requirements of standards for best practice, particularly the ISO 27000 series.

Of course, the principle difference between s 6 and the seventh data protection principle is the fact that s 6 does not specifically focus on security. The FSA is undoubtedly correct to interpret s 6 as requiring appropriate measures for data security however, as the 'terrors' that s 6 are addressing are often the result of data security breaches.

[1] See, for example, the Information Commissioner's guidance on the handling of security incidents, published in March 2008.

FSA Handbook

3.28 The FSA has expanded upon the requirements of the FSMA 2000 through its Handbook[1], which has been discussed above, in the context of corporate governance. The Handbook consists of a series of parts that address the full gamut of issues arising within the regulation of financial services. Each part of the Handbook consists of chapters. Additional parts and chapters that are relevant to data security are discussed below.

[1] The Handbook also expands upon matters arising under EU Directives.

High level standards – Principles for Business

3.29 The part of the Handbook titled 'Principles for Business' (or 'PRIN' for short) contains 'a general statement of the fundamental obligations of firms under the regulatory system'[1]. This general statement 'includes provisions which implement the Single Market Directives' and it derives its authority 'from the FSA's rule-making powers as set out in the [Financial Services and Markets] Act and reflect[s] the regulatory objectives'.

There are 11 principles for business[2]. The following ones are directly relevant to data security:

'1. Integrity: A firm must conduct its business with integrity.

2. Skill, care and diligence: A firm must conduct its business with due skill, care and diligence.

3. Management and control: A firm must take reasonable care to organise its affairs responsibly and effectively, with adequate risk management systems.

...

11. Relations with regulators: A firm must deal with its regulators in an open and cooperative way, and must disclose to the FSA appropriately anything relating to the firm of which the FSA would reasonably expect notice.'

The third principle for business has been cited by the FSA in all of its data security cases in which it imposed a fine (see the Capita Financial Administrators, Norwich Union Life, BNP Paribas Private Bank, Nationwide Building Society, Merchant Securities and HSBC cases[3]). The second principle was also cited in the Capita case.

[1] See chapter 2.1.1.
[2] See chapter 3 of the principles for business for an explanation of their scope.
[3] See Chapter 6 for further discussion.

3.30 The consequences of breaching the principles for business are explained in chapter 1.1.7. Breach will render a firm 'liable to disciplinary sanctions', although, reflecting the usual burden of proof, 'the onus will be on the FSA to show that a firm has been at fault in some way'. As regards breaches of the principles 1, 2 and 3, chapter 1.1.7 says:

'Under Principle 1 (Integrity), for example, the FSA would need to demonstrate a lack of integrity in the conduct of a firm's business. Under Principle 2 (Skill, care and diligence) a firm would be in breach if it was shown to have failed to act with due skill, care and diligence in the conduct of its business. Similarly, under Principle 3 (Management and control) a firm would not be in breach simply because it failed to control or prevent unforeseeable risks; but a breach would occur if the firm had failed to take reasonable care to organise and control its affairs responsibly or effectively.'

Chapter 1.1.8 then goes on to explain some of the wider consequences of breach:

'The Principles are also relevant to the FSA's powers of information-gathering, to vary a firm's Part IV permission, and of investigation and intervention, and provide a basis on 1.1.8 which the FSA may apply to a court for an injunction or restitution order or require a firm to make restitution. However, the Principles do not give rise to actions for damages by a private person.'

The requirements of principle 11 are expanded upon by schedule 2 to PRIN, which is titled 'notification requirements'. This states that firms are required to notify 'anything relating to the firm of which the FSA would reasonably expect notice'. The effect of this extends to the notification of security breaches. Breach notification is discussed in more depth in Chapter 7.

3.31 *Companies, corporate governance and financial services*

Senior Management Arrangements, Systems and Controls

3.31 The part of the Handbook titled 'Senior Management, Arrangements, Systems and Controls' ('SYSC') provides added detail about the requirements for data security in the financial services sector. Chapter 1, titled 'Application and purpose', identifies the purposes of SYSC at paragraph 1.2.1:

> '(1) to encourage firms' directors and senior managers to take appropriate practical responsibility for their firms' arrangements on matters likely to be of interest to the FSA because they impinge on the FSA's functions under the Act;
> (2) to increase certainty by amplifying Principle 3, under which a firm must take reasonable care to organise and control its affairs responsibly and effectively, with adequate risk management systems;
> (3) to encourage firms to vest responsibility for effective and responsible organisation in specific directors and senior managers; and
> (4) to create a common platform of organisational and systems and controls requirements for all firms.'

SYSC therefore puts the focus on the firm's management structures. Of course, the focus on management structures is a key part of data security best practice, as can be seen from the Data Handling Review and the ISO 27000 series. Thus, rules for data security should be found within SYSC.

SYSC 2.1.1 and 2.2.2 expand further on the core managerial goals, requiring the designation of roles and responsibilities:

> 'A firm must take reasonable care to maintain a clear and appropriate apportionment of significant responsibilities among its directors and senior managers in such a way that:
> (1) it is clear who has which of those responsibilities; and
> (2) the business and affairs of the firm can be adequately monitored and controlled by the directors, relevant senior managers and governing body of the firm.'

> 'A firm must appropriately allocate to one or more individuals, in accordance with SYSC 2.1.4 R, the functions of: 2.1.3:
> (1) dealing with the apportionment of responsibilities under SYSC 2.1.1 R; and
> (2) overseeing the establishment and maintenance of systems and controls under SYSC 3.1.1 R.'

As regards the standards that need to be met, these are described in 3.1.1 which says that 'a firm must take reasonable care to establish and maintain such systems and controls as are appropriate to its business'. This extends to the employment of personnel, with 3.1.2 saying that a firm 'must employ personnel with the skills, knowledge and expertise necessary for the discharge of the responsibilities allocated to them'. Of course, firms must be structured with reporting lines that are 'clear and appropriate'[1].

Connecting SYSC to PRIN, 3.2.6 requires appropriate controls to be implemented against the risk of financial crime; it will be recalled that the FSA has based its enforcement activity in the field of data security under the umbrella of financial crime. SYSC 3.2.6 says:

'A firm must take reasonable care to establish and maintain effective systems and controls for compliance with applicable requirements and standards 3.2.6 under the regulatory system and for countering the risk that the firm might be used to further financial crime.'

1   SYSC 3.2.3.

3.32 Other organisational issues to be addressed include:

- Compliance function: 3.2.7 says that 'depending on the nature, scale and complexity of its business, it may be appropriate for a firm to have a separate compliance function. The organisation and responsibilities of a compliance function should be documented. A compliance function should be staffed by an appropriate number of competent staff who are sufficiently independent to perform their duties objectively. It should be adequately resourced and should have unrestricted access to the firm's relevant records as well as ultimate recourse to its governing body'.
- Risk assessment: 3.2.10 says that 'depending on the nature, scale and complexity of its business, it may be appropriate for a firm to have a separate risk assessment function responsible for assessing the risks that the firm faces and advising the governing body and senior managers on them'.
- Management information: 3.2.11 says that 'a firm's arrangements should be such as to furnish its governing body with the information it needs to play its part in identifying, measuring, managing and controlling risks of regulatory concern. Three factors will be the relevance, reliability and timeliness of that information'.
- Employees and agents: 3.2.13 says that 'A firm's systems and controls should enable it to satisfy itself of the suitability of anyone who acts for it', which extends to 'assessing an individual's honesty, and competence', taking account of 'the level of responsibility that the individual will assume within the firm'.
- Audit committee: 3.2.15 says that 'depending on the nature, scale and complexity of its business, it may be appropriate for a firm to form an audit committee. An audit committee could typically examine management's process for ensuring the appropriateness and effectiveness of systems and controls, examine the arrangements made by management to ensure compliance with requirements and standards under the regulatory system, oversee the functioning of the internal audit function ... and provide an interface between management and the external auditors. It should have an appropriate number of non-executive directors and it should have formal terms of reference'.
- Internal audit: 3.2.16 says that 'depending on the nature, scale and complexity of its business, it may be appropriate for a firm to delegate much of the task of monitoring the appropriateness and effectiveness of its systems and controls to an internal audit function. An internal audit function should have clear responsibilities and reporting lines to an audit committee or appropriate senior manager, be adequately resourced and staffed by competent individuals, be independent of the day-to-day activities of the firm and have appropriate access to a firm's records'.

3.32 *Companies, corporate governance and financial services*

- Business strategy: 3.2.17 says that 'a firm should plan its business appropriately so that it is able to identify, measure, manage and control risks of regulatory concern. In some firms, depending on the nature, scale and complexity of their business, it may be appropriate to have business plans or strategy plans documented and updated on a regular basis to take account of changes in the business environment'.
- Business continuity: 3.2.19 says that 'a firm should have in place appropriate arrangements, having regard to the nature, scale and complexity of its business, to ensure that it can continue to function and meet its regulatory obligations in the event of an unforeseen interruption. These arrangements should be regularly updated and tested to ensure their effectiveness'.
- Records: 3.2.20 requires firms to 'take reasonable care to make and retain adequate records of matters and dealings (including accounting records) which are the subject of requirements and standards under the regulatory system'. 3.2.21 goes on to say that 'a firm should have appropriate systems and controls in place to fulfil the firm's regulatory and statutory obligations with respect to adequacy, access, periods of retention and security of records'.

Chapter 4 deals with general organisational requirements and contains some specific measures to implement MiFID, the Banking Consolidation Directive ('BCD') and the Capital Adequacy Directive. Notable rules are as follows:

- 4.1.1, which gives effect to provisions in article 22(1) of the BCD and article 13(5) of MiFID level 1 Directive says that 'a firm must have robust governance arrangements, which include a clear organisational structure with well defined, transparent and consistent lines of responsibility, effective processes to identify, manage, monitor and report the risks it is or might be exposed to, and internal control mechanisms, including sound administrative and accounting procedures and effective control and safeguard arrangements for information processing systems'.
- 4.1.5, which gives effect to provisions in article 5(2) of MiFID level 2 Directive says that 'a MiFID investment firm must establish, implement and maintain systems and procedures that are adequate to safeguard the security, integrity and confidentiality of information, taking into account the nature of the information in question'.
- 4.1.6, which gives effect to provisions in article 13(4) of MiFID level 1 Directive says that 'a common platform firm[1] must take reasonable steps to ensure continuity and regularity in the performance of its regulated activities. To this end the common platform firm must employ appropriate and proportionate systems, resources and procedures'.
- 4.1.7, which gives effect to provisions in Annex V of the BCD and article 5(3) of MiFID level 2 Directive says that 'a common platform firm must establish, implement and maintain an adequate business continuity policy aimed at ensuring, in the case of an interruption to its systems and procedures, that any losses are limited, the preservation of essential data and functions, and the maintenance of its regulated activities, or, where that is not possible, the timely recovery of such data and functions and the timely resumption of its regulated activities'.

Financial services **3.33**

[1] The Glossary to the FSA Handbook defines a common platform firm so as to include building societies, MiFID firms, certain firms regulated by the Capital Adequacy Directive and dormant account fund operators. The vast majority of firms regulated by the FSA will be common platform firms.

3.33 Chapter 8 deals with outsourcing, again giving effect to some of the requirements of MiFID. Notable rules are as follows:

- 8.1.1 says that a common platform firm must 'when relying on a third party for the performance of operational functions which are critical for the performance of regulated activities[1], listed activities or ancillary services (in this chapter "relevant services and activities") on a continuous and satisfactory basis, ensure that it takes reasonable steps to avoid undue additional operational risk' and must 'not undertake the outsourcing of important operational functions in such a way as to impair materially: (a) the quality of its internal control; and (b) the ability of the FSA to monitor the firm's compliance with all obligations under the regulatory system and, if different, of a competent authority to monitor the firm's compliance with all obligations under MiFID'.
- 8.1.6 says that 'If a firm outsources critical or important operational functions or any relevant services and activities, it remains fully responsible for discharging all of its obligations under the regulatory system and must comply, in particular, with the following conditions: (1) the outsourcing must not result in the delegation by senior personnel of their responsibility; (2) the relationship and obligations of the firm towards its clients under the regulatory system must not be altered; (3) the conditions with which the firm must comply in order to be authorised, and to remain so, must not be undermined; (4) none of the other conditions subject to which the firm's authorisation was granted must be removed or modified'.
- 8.1.7 says that 'a common platform firm must exercise due skill and care and diligence when entering into, managing or terminating any arrangement for the outsourcing to a service provider of critical or important operational functions or of any relevant services and activities'.
- 8.1.9 says that 'a common platform firm must ensure that the respective rights and obligations of the firm and of the service provider are clearly allocated and set out in a written agreement'.
- 8.2.1, which deals with the outsourcing of portfolio management for retail clients to a non-EEA State says that 'In addition to the requirements set out in the MiFID outsourcing rules, when a MiFID investment firm outsources the investment service of portfolio management to retail clients to a service provider located in a non-EEA state, it must ensure that the following conditions are satisfied: (a) the service provider must be authorised or registered in its home country to provide that service and must be subject to prudential supervision; (b) there must be an appropriate cooperation agreement between the FSA and the supervisor in the non-EEA state'.

Chapter 8 contains rules on operational risk for insurers. The following provisions are notable:

3.33 *Companies, corporate governance and financial services*

- 13.7.6 says that 'a firm should establish and maintain appropriate systems and controls for the management of its IT system risks, having regard to: (1) its organisation and reporting structure for technology operations (including the adequacy of senior management oversight); (2) the extent to which technology requirements are addressed in its business strategy; (3) the appropriateness of its systems acquisition, development and maintenance activities (including the allocation of responsibilities between IT development and operational areas, processes for embedding security requirements into systems); and (4) the appropriateness of its activities supporting the operation of IT systems (including the allocation of responsibilities between business and technology areas)'.
- 13.7.7 says that 'failures in processing information (whether physical, electronic or known by employees but not recorded) or of the security of the systems that maintain it can lead to significant operational losses. A firm should establish and maintain appropriate systems and controls to manage its information security risks. In doing so, a firm should have regard to: (1) confidentiality: information should be accessible only to persons or systems with appropriate authority, which may require firewalls within a system, as well as entry restrictions; (2) integrity: safeguarding the accuracy and completeness of information and its processing; (3) availability and authentication: ensuring that appropriately authorised persons or systems have access to the information when required and that their identity is verified; (4) non-repudiation and accountability: ensuring that the person or system that processed the information cannot deny their actions'.
- 13.7.8 says that 'a firm should ensure the adequacy of the systems and controls used to protect the processing and security of its information, and should have regard to established security standards such as ISO17799 (Information Security Management)'.

[1] 8.1.4 says that 'for the purposes of this chapter an operational function is regarded as critical or important if a defect or failure in its performance would materially impair the continuing compliance of a common platform firm with the conditions and obligations of its authorisation or its other obligations under the regulatory system, or its financial performance, or the soundness or the continuity of its relevant services and activities'.

Supervision

3.34 The part of the Handbook titled 'Supervision' ('SUP') explains how the FSA will supervise regulated firms. Chapter 15 deals with the disclosure of information by firms to the FSA. 15.2.1 explains:

'A firm is required to provide the FSA with a wide range of information to enable the FSA to meet its responsibilities for monitoring the firm's compliance with requirements imposed by or under the Act. Some of this information is provided through regular reports, including those set out in SUP 16 (Reporting requirements) and SUP 17 (Transaction reporting). In addition, other chapters in the Handbook set out specific notification and reporting requirements. Principle 11 includes a requirement for a firm to disclose to the FSA appropriately anything relating to the firm of which the FSA would reasonably expect notice.'

15.3.1 explains the FSA's expectations on notification:

> 'A firm must notify the FSA immediately it becomes aware, or has information which reasonably suggests, that any of the following has occurred, may have occurred or may occur in the foreseeable future:
> (1) the firm failing to satisfy one or more of the threshold conditions; or
> (2) any matter which could have a significant adverse impact on the firm's reputation; or
> (3) any matter which could affect the firm's ability to continue to provide adequate services to its customers and which could result in serious detriment to a customer of the firm; or
> (4) any matter in respect of the firm which could result in serious financial consequences to the financial system or to other firms.'

15.3.8 highlights that the FSA will expect the reporting of 'any significant failure in the firm's systems or controls, including those reported to the firm by the firm's auditor'. 15.3.2 explains that 'the circumstances which may give rise to any of the events in SUP 15.3.1 R are wide-ranging and the probability of any matter resulting in such an outcome, and the severity of the outcome, may be difficult to determine. However, the FSA expects firms to consider properly all potential consequences of events'. Clearly, the obligation to notify events will extend to serious data security breaches, as is explained in the FSA's report titled 'Data Security in Financial Services. Firm's controls to prevent data loss by their employees and third-party suppliers' (see the discussion in Chapter 7).

Other parts of the Handbook

3.35 See Chapter 6 for a discussion of other parts of the FSA Handbook, where they relate to regulatory investigations and enforcement action.

Payment Card Industry Data Security Standard (PCI DSS)

3.36 The Payment Card Industry's Data Security Standard is described as 'a set of comprehensive requirements for enhancing payment account data security'[1] that was 'developed by the founding payment brands of the PCI Security Standards Council, including American Express, Discover Financial Services, JCB International, MasterCard Worldwide and Visa Inc. Inc. International, to help facilitate the broad adoption of consistent data security measures on a global basis'[2].

The innovation within PCI DSS is the idea that card merchants and those that process card payments will agree under a contract with a payment card issuing company (an acquirer for Visa or Mastercard and American Express for its cards) to implement security measures to the specification set by the PCI[3]. In most cases the merchant or service provider will be required to undergo annual validation by a Qualified Security Assessor, although some smaller companies might be able to take advantage of self certification.

3.36 *Companies, corporate governance and financial services*

The contracts between the card companies and merchants/suppliers provide for sanctions in the event of non-compliance, which may be imposed in the form of fines, a requirement to undergo an audit or even loss of the right to process card payments[4]. Contracts will also impose obligations to ensure the compliance of third parties who are not in direct contractual relationships with a card company.

The specification covers 6 principles and 12 requirements, which are summarised in Table 3.1[5].

Table 3.1. Principles and requirements	
Principles	Requirements
Build and Maintain a Secure Network	1: Install and maintain a firewall configuration to protect cardholder data 2: Do not use vendor-supplied defaults for system passwords and other security parameters
Protect Cardholder Data	3: Protect stored cardholder data 4: Encrypt transmission of cardholder data across open, public networks
Maintain a Vulnerability Management Program	5: Use and regularly update anti-virus software 6: Develop and maintain secure systems and applications
Implement Strong Access Control Measures	7: Restrict access to cardholder data by business need-to-know 8: Assign a unique ID to each person with computer access 9: Restrict physical access to cardholder data
Regularly Monitor and Test Networks	10: Track and monitor all access to network resources and cardholder data 11: Regularly test security systems and processes
Maintain an Information Security Policy	12: Maintain a policy that addresses information security

---

[1] https://www.pcisecuritystandards.org/security_standards/pci_dss.shtml.
[2] https://www.pcisecuritystandards.org/security_standards/pci_dss.shtml.
[3] Version 2.1 of the specification can be obtained at https://www.pcisecuritystandards.org/security_standards/pci_dss_download.html.
[4] 'Visa drops Heartland, RBS WorldPay from PCI compliance list after breaches', Computerworld, 19 March 2009: http://www.computerworld.com/s/article/9129805/Visa_drops_Heartland_RBS_WorldPay_from_PCI_compliance_list_after_breaches.

⁵ For source information, see: https://www.pcisecuritystandards.org/security_standards/pci_dss.shtml.

3.37 The specification is intended to 'apply to all system components that are included in or connected to the cardholder data environment. The cardholder data environment is that part of the network that possesses cardholder data or sensitive authentication data, including network components, servers and applications'[1]. The specification also sets rules for the storage of card data. The primary account number, cardholder name, service code and expiration data may be stored. 'Sensitive authentication data', such as the full magnetic swipe data, the security code and PIN may not be stored. In other words, these sensitive data cannot be retained after they have been used for the purposes of the transactions.

The Payment Cards Industry has published two other security standards, namely the 'PIN Entry Device Security Requirements' (PCI PED) and the 'Payment Application Data Security Standard' (PA-DSS).

1 'Navigating PCI DSS – Understanding the Intent of the Requirements', Version 1.2, October 2008: https://www.pcisecuritystandards.org/pdfs/pci_dss_saq_navigating_dss.pdf.

Chapter 4

CONSIDERATIONS FOR THE PUBLIC SECTOR

THE INTENSITY OF REGULATION OF DATA SECURITY IN THE PUBLIC SECTOR

4.1 In the field of data security, the public sector is more intensely regulated than the private sector. There are many reasons for this.

There is obviously a political dynamic at play, which is accompanied by genuine public interest. This guarantees that data security is seen as a 'trust issue', feeding party political appetite and press and media scrutiny.

Another contributing factor is the sheer vastness of data processing within the public sector. This carries with it massive security risks and the inevitability of serious failures. These factors fuel and drive the others, keeping public sector data security constantly under the spotlight and within reach of the full bite of the law.

There is also the effect of the government's response to HMRC. This began with the announcement that the Information Commissioner would be given the right to carry out inspections of the public sector, a promise that found its way into the Coroners and Justice Bill. This constituted a significant power shift in the relationship between the Commissioner and the public sector, with the Commissioner being strengthened at the public sector's expense. Subsequently, the government mandated breach notification for the public sector, another transparency mechanism with the same consequences. In contrast, the private sector will not be brought within the scope of the new inspection regime until after a complex process of designation has been completed (see the discussion in Chapter 6) and will be much less affected by the government's ideas on breach notification, which in the absence of legislation are at their most powerful in the corridors of Whitehall, within government departments and within public authorities (see the discussion in Chapter 7).

The nature of the public sector's legal obligations for data security has also contributed to the intensity of regulation. The public sector was the original focus of human rights laws, a focus that looked directly at the horrors of war and the atrocities of the deviant State. For this reason the right to privacy

4.1 *Considerations for the public sector*

within article 8 of the European Convention on Human Rights, which is one of the core foundation stones of data security law, focuses on the activities of the State and its manifestations, public authorities. The Human Rights Act 1998, which incorporates the Convention into our domestic law, nails the ideals of human rights law to every part of the public sector in the UK and obliges the Information Commissioner to be very proactive when it comes to interpreting the public sector's legal obligations[1].

For these reasons (and many more) the laws discussed in Chapter 2 have added significance in the public sector. The materials discussed in this chapter amplify the detail of the law.

[1] This is because the Human Rights Act 1998, s 6 requires public authorities, including the Information Commissioner, to act compatibly with the European Convention on Human Rights.

TRANSFORMATIONAL GOVERNMENT – MORE TECHNOLOGY, MORE DATA PROCESSING AND MORE RISK

4.2 In November 2005 the Cabinet Office published 'Transformational Government – Enabled by Technology'[1]. This Report, which was commissioned by the Prime Minister, identified a strategy for more intensive use of technology within the delivery of public services. Of course, as just indicated, the increased adoption of technology leads to increased threats to the security of data, a phenomenon that the PET initiative seeks to address through the use of even more technology (see the discussion in Chapter 8). The Transformational Government agenda, which includes e-government initiatives, has major security implications.

It should be noted that Sir Edmund Burton's Report into the loss of MOD laptops, which is discussed later in this chapter, identified the Transformational Government agenda as one of the drivers towards increased data insecurity. The Data Handling Review identified the achievement of the transformational government agenda as being contingent upon public trust. HMRC and other high-profile public sector data security breaches and data losses act to fundamentally challenge the vision within the Report, which is described in the following terms:

> '4. Twenty First Century Government is enabled by technology – policy is inspired by it, business change is delivered by it, customer and corporate services are dependent on it, and democratic engagement is exploring it. Moreover modern governments with serious transformational intent see technology as a strategic asset and not just a tactical tool. Technology alone does not transform government, but government cannot transform to meet modern citizens' expectations without it.
>
> 5. So this strategy's vision is about better using technology to deliver public services and policy outcomes that have an impact on citizens' daily lives: through greater choice and personalisation, delivering better public services, such as health, education and pensions; benefiting communities by reducing

burdens on front line staff and giving them the tools to help break cycles of crime and deprivation; and improving the economy through better regulation and leaner government.'

[1] CM 6683: http://www.cabinetoffice.gov.uk/media/141734/transgov-strategy.pdf.

SECURITY CONSIDERATIONS WITHIN PUBLIC SECTOR RECORDS MANAGEMENT

4.3 The Transformational Government agenda compounds the already mighty problem of how to ensure the security of government systems and records. The State is by far the country's largest data controller, with all the apparatus and resources needed to continue to grow its processing operations.

Of course, all sophisticated data processing systems will require sophisticated systems for records management, to ensure that information assets are fairly and properly exploited. In response to these challenges standards for records management have developed, which are designed to address the actual, theoretical and legal challenges that records management professionals have to deal with on a daily basis. There is also a related body of legislative provisions, regulatory frameworks, official guidance and court cases that have to be considered during the design of records management systems.

The relevance of this discussion to data security law will be obvious; proper systems for records management need proper systems for security, to ensure that the record's character is protected from threats. The public sector's role as the nation's records-keeper magnifies the problem of data security.

Freedom of Information Act 2000

4.4 The Freedom of Information Act 2000 is the best example of legislation for records management in the public sector. The Act has introduced profound constitutional changes, albeit the MPs' expenses scandal has revealed that there are still deep pockets of resistance to what the Act is trying to achieve[1].

The Act requires public authorities to allow access to their records. This rule is subject to many broad qualifications, but case law is developing quickly in response to specific challenges.

Prominent within the Act's provisions is the Code of Practice on records management, which is required by s 46. The Code supplements many other codes and guidance for records management in the public sector. It says the following about security:

> '11 Security and access
>
> Authorities should ensure that records are stored securely and that access to them is controlled.
>
> 11.1 Authorities should ensure that their storage arrangements, handling procedures and arrangements for transmission of records reflect accepted

4.4 Considerations for the public sector

standards and good practice in information security. It is good practice to have an information security policy addressing these points.

11.2 Ease of internal access will depend on the nature and sensitivity of the records. Access restrictions should be applied when necessary to protect the information concerned and should be kept up to date. Particular care should be taken with personal information about living individuals in order to comply with the 7th data protection principle, which requires precautions against unauthorised or unlawful processing, damage, loss or destruction. Within central Government, particular care should be taken with information bearing a protective marking. Other information, such as information obtained on a confidential basis, may also require particular protection.

11.3 Transmission of records, especially outside the authority's premises, should require authorisation. The method of transmission should be subject to risk assessment before a decision is made.

11.4 External access should be provided in accordance with relevant legislation.

11.5 An audit trail should be kept of provision of access, especially to people outside the immediate work area.'

[1] See *Corporate Officer of the House of Commons v The Information Comr* [2008] EWHC 1084 (Admin), [2009] 3 All ER 403, the case about MPs expenses, which led, ultimately, to the downfall of the speaker of the House of Commons and various MPs.

Data Protection Act 1998

4.5 The Data Protection Act 1998 can also be regarded as being a records management law. A record by its very nature needs to be accurate, subject to deletion schedules and protected from corruption, degradation, loss and misuse, issues which are at the heart of the data protection principles. To be sure of achieving compliance with the data protection principles the data controller needs to implement a records management system. Again, the requirement for security is expressly stated within the Act, within the seventh data protection principle.

Codes of practice for records management

The National Archives

4.6 The National Archives publishes records management standards for the public sector. These standards address the need for security within properly functioning systems for records management. For example, 'Management, appraisal and preservation of electronic records. Vol 1: Principles'[1] says:

> '2.9 Unlike paper records, electronic records are susceptible to undetectable changes in content and format unless they are held securely and under defined and auditable procedures. To be acceptable as evidence, electronic records should be formally subject to well-defined and robust procedures which can be documented and to which adherence can be demonstrated. These procedures should be designed to ensure that electronic records are an authentic and accurate representation of the activity or transaction which took place and have been kept safe from alteration once declared as a record. Managers of electronic

record-keeping systems will require a framework of procedures which will give confidence in the security of the storage and access management processes, and which maintain a substantive audit trail of their handling.'

[1] http://collections.europarchive.org/tna/20080108103210/http://www.nationalarchives.gov.uk/documents/principles.pdf.

International standards

4.7 There are many international standards for record management, prominent within which is ISO 15489–1 'Information and Documentation – Records Management'. This is designed to ensure that 'appropriate attention and protection is given to all records, and that the evidence and information they contain can be retrieved more efficiently and effectively, using standard practices and procedures'. These standards apply to public and private sector organisations. Regarding storage, these standards say:

> 'Records should be stored on media that ensure their useability, reliability, authenticity and preservation for as long as they are needed.'

As regards electronic records these standards continue:

> 'Systems for electronic records should be designed so that records will remain accessible, authentic, reliable and useable through any kind of system change, for the entire period of their retention. This may include migration to different software, re-presentation in emulation formats or any other future ways of re-presenting records. Where such processes occur, evidence of these should be kept, along with details of any variation in records design and format.'

Regarding security, the following passage provides an interesting overview:

> 'Information security is key when discussing legal admissibility issues. The main discussion on this topic is likely to be the authenticity of the stored information. When the electronic information was captured by the storage system, was the process secure? Was the correct information captured, and was it complete and accurate? During storage, was the information changed in any way, either accidentally or maliciously? When responding to these questions, information security implementation and monitoring are key to demonstrating authenticity.'

PUBLIC AUTHORITIES WITH RESPONSIBILITY FOR ASPECTS OF DATA SECURITY

4.8 The following group of public authorities have responsibilities for developing thinking and rules on data security in the UK.

Central Sponsor for Information Assurance (CSIA)

4.9 On its website[1] the CSIA (now known as Information Security & Assurance (IS&A)) describes itself as 'a unit within the UK Government's Cabinet Office providing a central focus for Information Assurance (IA) activity across the UK'. Information Assurance is described as 'the confidence

4.9 Considerations for the public sector

that information systems will protect the information they carry and will function as they need to, when they need to, under the control of legitimate users'. One of the key functions of the CSIA is to set the National Information Assurance Strategy, which is discussed later in this chapter.

[1] http://www.cabinetoffice.gov.uk/csia.aspx.

The National Technical Authority for Information Assurance (CESG)

4.10 The CESG[1] website gives the following explanation of its role and purpose:

> 'CESG is the Information Assurance (IA) arm of GCHQ and we are based in Cheltenham, Gloucestershire, UK. We are the UK Government's National Technical Authority for IA, responsible for enabling secure and trusted knowledge sharing to help our customers achieve their business aims.
>
> There are five key principles, essential for safe electronic transactions:
> - Confidentiality – keeping information private
> - Integrity – ensuring information has not been tampered with
> - Authentication – confirming the identity of the individual who undertook the transaction
> - Non-repudiation – the individual who undertook the transaction cannot subsequently deny it
> - Availability – ensuring information is available when required
>
> Information Assurance is about meeting these requirements.'

The CESG provides a very specialised range of technical services to central government, the armed forces, the wider public sector and to parts of the private sector. It also runs a number of accreditation schemes, through which the private sector can offer its security products and services to the public sector. Many of these services are 'productised', with names such as CAPS, CLAS, CTAS, CCTM and Check, a selection of which are discussed below. The CESG also runs GovCERTUK.

[1] http://www.cesg.gov.uk/.

GovCERTUK

4.11 GovCERTUK[1] is an emergency response service for the public sector that gives 'technical support and advice during periods of electronic attack or other network security incidents'. This is a 24/7 service, which is provided by the 'Computer Emergency Response Team' (CERT). CERT has published 'Incident Response Guidelines' for the public sector[2]. The Cross Government Actions, discussed later in this chapter, require government departments to report network security incidents to CERT.

CERT classifies security incidents in four ways, namely critical, significant, minor and negligible impact. The Incident Response Guidelines provide the following explanations:

Public authorities with responsibility for aspects of data security 4.12

'Critical

These incidents will usually cause the degradation of vital service(s) for a large number of users, involve a serious breach of network security, affect mission-critical equipment or services, or damage public confidence in the government.

E.g. targeted attacks or loss of publicly available online service.

Significant

Less serious events are likely to impact a smaller group of users, disrupt non-essential services, breach network security policy, or affect the respect of government bodies and services.

E.g. website defacement or damaging unauthorised changes to a system.

Minor

Many types of incident can be capably handled by local IT support and security officers and do not require GovCertUK assistance, although GovCertUK should be notified of their occurrence. This aids the correlation of similar events, furthers the understanding of the IT security challenges facing government and may raise awareness of new attacks.

E.g. unsuccessful denial-of-service attack or the majority of network monitoring alerts.

Negligible impact

It is not necessary to report on incidents of limited impact or those affecting only a few users. This sort of event would include receipt of isolated spam or anti-virus alerts, minor computer hardware failure, loss of network connectivity to a peripheral device such as a printer, or loss of access to an external non-essential service. In general these would be considered to be part of normal IT support operations.

E.g. isolated anti-virus alert or spam email.'

[1] http://www.govcertuk.gov.uk/.
[2] http://www.govcertuk.gov.uk/pdfs/incident_response_guidelines_v1-1.pdf.

CAPS – accreditation of encryption products

4.12 CAPS is a service that can lead to the approval of private sector cryptographic products for sale to government and the private sector. The CESG website explains:

'CAPS was introduced to meet the increasing HMG demand for cryptographic products. It formalises and enhances the services that CESG has provided over a number of years and which have already provided a wide range of Commercial-Off-The-Shelf (COTS) products currently used by HMG. Products developed under CAPS can address all HMG cryptographic requirements.

CAPS enables products to be cryptographically verified by CESG to HMG cryptographic standards and formally approved for use by HMG and other appropriate organisations. For HMG customers, CAPS provides assured solutions: for CAPS vendors it provides enhanced opportunities to market their products to government.'

4.12 Considerations for the public sector

Clearly, the CAPS scheme has a role to play within the developing legal framework for Privacy Enhancing Technologies, albeit the accreditation of encryption products by the CESG does not remove the need for the regulators' accreditation.

CLAS

4.13 CLAS is a scheme that approves private sector consultants as suitable for working with the public sector on IA issues. The CESG's website explains:

> 'The Scheme aims to satisfy this demand [for consultancy expertise] by creating a pool of high quality consultants approved by CESG to provide Information Assurance advice to government departments and other organisations who provide vital services for the United Kingdom.
>
> CLAS consultants are approved to provide Information Assurance advice on systems processing protectively marked information up to, and including, SECRET. Potential customers of the CLAS Scheme should also note that if the information is not protectively marked then they do not need to specify membership of CLAS in their invitations to tender, and may be challenged if equally competent non-scheme members are prevented from bidding.'

CTAS

4.14 CTAS is another accreditation service, which is aimed at individual IT products used in the public sector right through to entire networks. The purpose is to evaluate the security of the product/network. The CESG website explains:

> 'CTAS is an independent, technical security evaluation of a system or product for a government department (or possibly a CNI) customer. CTAS is carried out by approved evaluation companies with support from CESG and results in advice on the extent to which technical risks have been addressed. CTAS is designed to meet the needs of HMG Infosec Standard 1(IS1) and equivalent documents like JSP440.
>
> Evaluations focus on the technical security of systems, COTS products and bespoke components within a system context. Procedures associated with technical security can also be included within scope but evaluations do not extend to an assessment of physical or personnel security. It does not deal with cryptography as this is covered by the CAPS scheme.'

Claims Tested Mark (CCTM)

4.15 The CCTM service is designed to test the claims made by the private sector about the security of their products and services, the purpose of which is to enable the public sector to know if 'a product or service does "what it says on the box"'[1]. The CESG maintains two registers of approved products and services, namely the 'Directory of Infosec Assured Products' and the 'Directory of CCTM Certified Products and Services'.

Again the CCTM service has an important role to play in the development of the PET initiative.

[1] http://www.cctmark.gov.uk/.

Centre for the Protection of National Infrastructure (CPNI)

4.16 The CPNI is 'the Government authority which provides protective security advice to businesses and organisations across the national infrastructure'[1].

[1] http://www.cpni.gov.uk/.

Office of Cyber Security (OCS) and Cyber Security Operations Centre (CSOC)

4.17 The OCS and the CSOC were established as part of the Cyber Security Strategy, which is discussed in the next section of this chapter.

MAJOR REPORTS AND POLICY STATEMENTS

4.18 In Chapter 6 the point is made that the public sector carries a huge responsibility for the regulation of its own practices for data security. This has been recognised by the government within the Data Handling Review, which acknowledges that data security has become a 'trust issue' for the public. In other words, failures of security in the public sector have massive scope for causing significant political damage to the government of the day.

Corresponding with this duty of regulation is the output of official reports and policy statements, which set both the detail and the tone for practices in the public sector. Not surprisingly, the public sector's output of official documents relevant to data security has increased substantially since the news broke of the loss of the HMRC data disks. The pace of output has been incredibly quick, like the pace of legislative reform up to January 2009, when the Coroners and Justice Bill was introduced in the House of Commons.

The reports and statements discussed below, which were mostly sponsored by the Cabinet Office, are primary resources for practitioners in public sector data security. Their legal effect is likely to be similar to rules of best practice, being relevant to the issue of negligence[1] and key concepts within the seventh data protection principle, the law of confidence and human rights law. If they generate any expectations concerning practices for data security within the minds of the general public, it might be possible to attach liability to the public sector under the principles of the law of legitimate expectation[2]. Data subjects may also litigate breaches of these expectations in compensation claims brought under the Data Protection Act 1998, s 13.

It will also be noted that there is a great degree of consistency in the messages delivered by these official documents. Collectively they knit together to

4.18 Considerations for the public sector

provide a comprehensive framework for the holistic management of data security in the public sector, with real consequences for the private sector too.

However, while it cannot be doubted that the output of official reports since HMRC has been prolific, it remains unclear whether this has been matched by real improvements on the ground. Indeed, the recent slew of reports brings with them a real sense of déjà vu, as if we have been here before. For example, later in this chapter data security issues within the NHS are discussed, which reveals the fact that the NHS was trying to tackle the same issues a decade ago. In the early years of the new millennium the 'Office of the e-Envoy', a long since defunct office within the Cabinet Office, addressed many of the issues that appear within the current crop of reports, in reports such as 'Security – e-Government Strategy Framework Policy and Guidelines', 2002. This begs the question does the publication of official reports actually make any difference on the ground?

The intensity of the focus on the publication of reports might attract the charge that the government is more concerned with outputs rather than outcomes. Indeed, within the community of data security professionals there is a real sense that things are actually getting worse on the ground, not better. This can be attributed to many different factors, including the growth in data processing associated with the Transformational Government agenda, which increases the risk of security failings occurring. The effect of the recession is also noted, as controllers scale back their security functions, head count and spending. Another issue is the skills-gap; not enough appropriately qualified professionals are coming through the ranks. Also, there is the problem of 'culture'; not enough attention is given to data security at board level, which means that controllers are falling further behind the threats and risks to their data as each day passes. This cultural failing is compounded by the cultural rift between the 'digital immigrant' and the 'digital native'; the 'Facebook Generation', those digital natives born after 1985, have a completely different attitude to data security-type issues, such as online privacy and the sharing of rights-protected information, to those persons who currently have their hands on the levers of power, whether in government or in companies; the Facebook Generation presents fundamental challenges, not necessarily malevolent, to current and future strategies for data security and, indeed, value-structures for data.

Thus, while the focus on reports is welcomed, because they have helped to draw attention to the fact that data security remains a significant problem in the public sector, it should not be pretended that they provide all of the answers. The fact remains that there is a very real disconnect between the abstract world of official reports and the real world of data security practice. In other words, the good work within the official reports needs to translate into concrete actions. There remains much room for improvement.

1   See the discussion of the principles in *Ward v The Ritz Hotel (London) Ltd* [1992] PIQR P315 and related cases in Chapter 2.
2   See *R v North and East Devon Health Authority, ex p Coughlan* [2001] QB 213, [2000] 3 All ER 850 and subsequent cases.

Consequences for the private sector

4.19 While not aimed directly at the private sector, it would still be highly risky for data controllers in the private sector to ignore the messages within these documents. They are likely to be very relevant within any determination of a private sector organisation's degree of compliance with data security law, whether in Data Protection Act 1998 cases, law of confidence cases, negligence cases or otherwise. This is because these documents make statements about best practice. In this context, it should be noted that the Information Commissioner has endorsed the Data Handling Review[1], helping to extend its reach from the public sector into the private sector. There is no logical reason to ignore the thrust of these documents during consideration of the private sector's degree of compliance with the law.

[1] 'Taking stock, taking action. The ICO position on the Government Data Handling Reviews', 3 November 2008: http://www.ico.gov.uk/upload/documents/library/data_protection/detailed_specialist_guides/ico%20position%20paper%20on%20data%20loss%20reports.pdf.

National Information Assurance Strategy, June 2007

4.20 In June 2007 the Central Sponsor for Information Assurance (the 'CSIA') published 'A National Information Assurance Strategy'[1], which updated an earlier work published in 2003. The CSIA explains on its website:

> 'The 2007 National Information Assurance Strategy outlines an approach for the UK in adopting information risk management by ensuring the right level of: professionalism, education and training; availability of IA products and services as well as compliance and adoption of standards. The Strategy aims to ensure that:
> - Government is better able to deliver public services through the appropriate use of ICT;
> - The UK's national security is strengthened by protecting information and ICT at risk of compromise;
> - The UK's economic and social well-being is enhanced as government, businesses and citizens realise the full benefits of ICT.'

It is clear from this explanation that the Strategy has a critical role to play within practices for data security within central government.

The foreword to the Strategy sums up perfectly the challenges that are addressed by Information Assurance:

> 'Information and communications technology is changing the way that the public, the private sector and the third sector deliver services, allowing Government, organisations and individuals to connect in more varied ways than ever before. The Transformational Government agenda is designed to take full advantage of this.
>
> Information is a valuable asset that must be safeguarded. In the case of information held by public authorities and businesses, especially personal information, people want to be certain that it is held securely, maintained accurately, available when necessary and used appropriately. Information

4.20 Considerations for the public sector

assurance (IA) is the term given to the management of risk to information. Effective IA ensures that the opportunities provided by new technology can be exploited to maximum benefit.

This National Information Assurance Strategy sets out a coherent approach to managing information risk by making it an integral and effective part of normal business process. Partnership between Government and industry is and will continue to be vital in delivering the clear and agreed standards and products and services that are necessary to effective IA. A Delivery Approach underpinning this Strategy will set out how the Government intends to develop this relationship further, build on existing good practice and drive the wider engagement to ensure that all organisations and individuals across the UK are able to make full use of the opportunities that technology offers us.'

[1] http://www.cabinetoffice.gov.uk/media/cabinetoffice/csia/assets/nia_strategy.pdf.

4.21 This passage makes three points. First, it recognises that information has value and that it should be treated as an asset. Second, it supports the idea that appropriate practices for data security can only be achieved if they are embedded within the business process, a message that is also communicated by ISO 27000. Third, it acknowledges the role played by the private sector in achieving government policy and the challenges this creates.

The Strategy proceeds on the basis that the achievement of the government's strategic aims (delivery of public services through the use of ICT, the strengthening of national security and the advancement of the country's economic and social well being) needs a proper assessment of the threat landscape, plus 'clear and effective information risk management by organisations', 'agreement upon and compliance with approved and appropriate IA standards' and 'the development and availability of appropriate IA Capabilities'. The Strategy then goes on to outline the CSIA's views on how these objectives can be achieved, giving more detailed insight into the context of IA, threats and vulnerabilities, the benefits of IA, IA capabilities, leadership and delivery models.

Connecting this document to the Data Protection Act 1998, many of the issues are evidentially significant within an assessment of a controller's compliance with its obligation to implement appropriate technical and organisational measures for data security, as required by the seventh data protection principle.

Data Handling Review, December 2007 to June 2008

4.22 On 21 November 2007, the day after the loss of the HMRC data disks was revealed, the Prime Minister announced that he had asked the Cabinet Secretary, Sir Gus O'Donnell, to head a review of the government's procedures for handling data.

It is worth noting that the Data Handling Review addressed all of the government's data handling, not just the processing of personal data within the meaning of the Data Protection Act 1998. This helps to demonstrate that

Major reports and policy statements **4.23**

data protection law is a subset of data security law, not the other way round. Data security is as much about non-personal data as it is about personal data.

Interim Report, December 2007

4.23 In December 2007 the Cabinet Office published 'Data Handling Procedures in Government: Interim Progress Report'[1]. It explains that the terms of reference of the Data Handling Review were to examine 'the procedures in Departments and agencies for the protection of data', 'their consistency with current Government-wide policies and standards', 'the arrangements for ensuring that procedures are being fully and properly implemented' and 'to make recommendations on improvements that should be made'. It then goes on to explain that improvements in data handling in government will be achieved in four ways:

- Through core measures to protect information.
- Through the development of a culture that 'properly values, protects and uses data'.
- With stronger accountability mechanisms.
- With stronger scrutiny of performance.

The Interim Report then provides an overview of the scheme for the protection of data by government, crediting the role played by the CSIA, its National Strategy for IA and the CESG.

The bulk of the report is made up of mini-reviews of the steps taken by government departments and agencies to review and improve their practices for data handling. This part is necessarily written at a high level, but key trends are detectable, such as the focus on policies and procedures and the use of portable storage media.

The final part of the Interim Report is titled 'next steps'. Key areas discussed include the role of security policies, managerial responsibility, transparency and accountability and law reform. As regards law reform, the Interim Report committed the government to new laws for inspections and sanctions and consideration of steps to implement the recommendations of the Data Sharing Review:

> '44. Legislative steps should be taken to enhance the ability of the Information Commissioner to provide external scrutiny of arrangements. The Government has already announced the powers to permit "spot checks" on central Government Departments, and should commit to extending this to the entire public sector, and consult early in the New Year on how this can best be achieved and funded. The review commissioned in October from Richard Thomas (the Information Commissioner) and Mark Walport of the Wellcome Trust will look at the issues around personal data in both the public and private sectors. The Government should consult quickly with those potentially affected on how the relevant recommendations can best be achieved.
>
> 45. Similarly, the Government should commit in principle to the introduction of new sanctions under the Data Protection Act for the most serious breaches of its principles. Such proposals will have to take account of the need not only to

4.23 *Considerations for the public sector*

provide high levels of data security, but also ensure that sensible data sharing practices can be conducted in an environment of legal certainty.'

The reference to the Data Sharing Review is illuminating, in that it reveals once again the influence of the Information Commissioner on the creation of policy for data security.

[1] http://www.cabinetoffice.gov.uk/media/65934/data_handling.pdf.

Cross Government Actions

4.24 The Interim Report was accompanied by the publication of 'Cross Government Actions: Mandatory Minimum Measures'[1], a document that sets out detailed 'process measures to ensure that Departments identify and manage their information risks' and 'specific minimum measures for the protection of personal data'. Again, this acts to emphasise that data protection law is a subset of data security law.

The process measures discuss the role of the Accounting Officer, the 'Statement of Internal Control', the use of information risk policies, the assessment of risks to the confidentiality, integrity and availability of data, the use of Privacy Impact Assessments within the Gateway Review process, the use of government contractual clauses for security, the application of controls across the supply chain, the role of Senior Information Risk Owners (SIROs)[2], the identification of information assets, the keeping of records of people involved in the handling of protected personal data, the need to review the public benefits of information use, the conduct of audits, the promotion of cultural change, incident response, breach notification and the publication of 'Information Charters'.

The minimum measures for the protection of personal data concern two categories of 'protected personal data'. Data falling into category A consist of identifying information (such as names, addresses, postcodes, email addresses, telephone numbers, driving licence numbers and dates of birth) when 'combined with' information the loss or release of which will be likely to cause harm or distress to the individuals concerned (such as sensitive personal data as defined in the Data Protection Act 1998, DNA or fingerprints, bank, financial or credit card details, mother's maiden name, National Insurance number, tax, benefit or pension records, health records, employment records, school attendance and records and material relating to social services including child protection and housing). Category B consists of 'any source of information about 1000 or more identifiable individuals, other than information sourced from the public domain', an approach to protection that echoes the Information Commissioner's 'rule of thumb' approach to breach notification[3].

The minimum measures for the protection of protected personal data include measures to prevent unauthorised access, measures to minimise authorised access, rules about the use of portable storage media and encryption, rules for the monitoring of individuals handling data, the forensic examination of IP

Major reports and policy statements **4.26**

logs, the engagement of independent experts for penetration testing, rules for the controlled disposal of data and equipment and rules for the safe provision and use of 'citizen-facing' systems (which captures the transformational government agenda and e-government initiatives).

1   http://www.cabinetoffice.gov.uk/media/cabinetoffice/csia/assets/dhr/cross_gov080625.pdf.
2   See also 'Mandatory Roles: AO, SIRO and IAO', Cabinet Office, 6 May 2008. This explains that the Accounting Officer 'has overall responsibility for ensuring that information risks are assessed and mitigated to an acceptable level. Information risks should be handled in a similar manner to other major risks such as financial, legal and reputational risks'. The SIRO is described as 'an executive familiar with information risks and leads the Department's response. The SIRO is the focus for the management of information risk at Board level'. Information Asset Owners are 'senior individuals involved in running the relevant business. Their role is to understand what information is held, what is added and what is removed, how information is moved and who has access and why. As a result they are able to understand and address risk to the information and ensure that information is fully used within the law for the public good and provide written input to the SIRO annually on the security and use of their asset'. See also the Burton Report, 'Report into the Loss of MOD Personal Data', April 2008, which explains the origins of the SIRO, which can be traced back to 2003.
3   See the discussion in Chapter 7.

4.25 The minimum measures on the use of portable media are very detailed. The presumption is that portable media will be used as a last resort and then only if encrypted to FIPS 140–2 level. The hierarchy for accessing data is described in the following passage:

> '13.1 the best option is to hold and access data on ICT systems on secure premises;
>
> 13.2 second best is secure remote access, so that data can be viewed or amended without being permanently stored on the remote computer. This is possible at PROTECT level over the internet using products meeting the FIPS 140–2 standard or equivalent, or using a smaller set of products at RESTRICTED level. The National Technical Authority for Information Assurance, CESG, provides advice on suitable products and how to use them;
>
> 13.3 third best is secured transfer of information to a remote computer on a secure site on which it will be permanently stored. Both the data at rest and the link should be protected at least to the FIPS 140–2 standard or equivalent, using approved products as above. Protectively marked information must not be stored on privately owned computers unless they are protected in this way;
>
> 13.4 in all cases, the remote computer should be password protected, configured so that its functionality is minimised to its intended business use only, and have up to date software patches and anti-virus software.'

The document also includes a table, known as the 'Suffolk Matrix', which describes the conditions for external access to government systems. For example, access to 'restricted' data is allowed from a government approved BlackBerry via the GSi network. Similarly, a government worker can use a government issued secure laptop in a wireless hotspot within an internet café to access 'NHS Confidential' data via the GSi network.

4.26 As regards encryption, the following passage should be noted:

4.26 *Considerations for the public sector*

> '14. Where it is not possible to avoid the use of removable media, all Departments should apply all of the following conditions:
>
> 14.1 the information transferred to the removable media should be the minimum necessary to achieve terms of the numbers of people covered by the information and the scope of information held. Where possible, only anonymised information should be held;
>
> 14.2 the removable media should be encrypted to a standard of at least FIPS 140-2 or equivalent in addition to being protected by a authentication mechanism, such as a password;
>
> 14.3 user rights to transfer data to removable media should be carefully considered and strictly limited to ensure that this is only provided where absolutely necessary for business purposes and subject to monitoring by managers and the Information Asset Owner; and
>
> 14.4 the individual responsible for the removable media should handle it – themselves or if they entrust it to others – as if it were the equivalent of a large amount of their own cash.'

The measures for the protection of personal data have now been subsumed within IA Standard No 6[1], which is the focus of mandatory requirement 14 within the HMG Security Policy Framework:

> 'Departments and Agencies must follow the minimum standards and procedures for handling and protecting citizen or personal data, as outlined in HMG IA Standard No.6 – Protecting Personal Data and Managing Information Risk.'

[1] See the explanation within the introduction to the HMG Security Policy Framework.

The political significance of the Data Handling Review and Interim Report

4.27 As soon as it was published it was quickly recognised that the Interim Report was a landmark event in the current cycle of development of the law. It also stood to re-emphasise the political damage caused by the loss of the HMRC data disks; it was published less than one month after the story broke, an incredibly short space of time for a government report of such range and magnitude, which encompassed every department and agency.

Clearly, it was incumbent upon the government to be seen to be dynamic in its response. If any further insight into the importance of data security at the end of 2007 is required, it need only be remembered that the Data Handling Review was headed-up by the country's most senior civil servant, who was working to the personal direction of the Prime Minister. In purely political terms it is clear that the loss of the HMRC data disks was of the highest priority to the government at the time.

Final Report, June 2008

4.28 In June 2008 the Cabinet Office published 'Data Handling Procedures in Government: Final Report'[1]. This document covers much of the same ground as the Interim Report, but with more detail about how compliance will be

Major reports and policy statements **4.29**

scrutinised and assessed. It also provided a timeline for the taking of corrective measures by government departments, plus an updated review of the actions that had already been taken.

As regards scrutiny by the way of audit, the following passage provides a succinct summary of the measures that were being put in place:

> 'Compliance will be assessed on an annual basis, and underpin the summary material in the Statement on Internal Control, and be the subject of peer review, through capability reviews and as requested by particular Departments. External scrutiny of performance and capability will be provided through:
> - National Audit Office scrutiny of the Statement on Internal Control, using their knowledge of the organisation in question;
> - spot checks by the Information Commissioner; and
> - targeted intervention by Departments and CESG, the National Technical Authority for Information Assurance in GCHQ, to assess counterparts' systems and protections.'

[1] http://www.cabinetoffice.gov.uk/media/65948/dhr080625.pdf.

4.29 The timeline within Annex II reads as follows:

'**Annex II: Timeline**

II.1. By end April 2008, all Departments had completed initial measures for the protection of personal data.

II.2. Departments will include summary material on information risk in their annual reporting, through the Management Commentary to their resource accounts for 2007/08, as those are issued.

II.3. Departments are currently:
- completing roll-out of new protection through their delivery chains, where they can require the use of particular measures;
- putting plans in place to encourage use of protective measures where they cannot require their use;
- completing initial changes to Departmental HR policies;
- putting in place cultural change plans;
- allocating responsibility to Information Asset Owners;
- formalising their information risk policy in light of the material in this report; and
- publishing their Information Charter.

II.4. From July 2008 onwards:
- new systems containing protected personal data will be accredited;
- new contracts will include standard contract clauses including new protection;
- Privacy Impact Assessments will be completed;
- greater access control will be introduced; and
- penetration testing will be in place.

II.5. By October 2008:
- Information Asset Owners will have their controls operating for their information assets; and
- mandatory training for data users and senior managers will have commenced, with its first cycle to have been completed within 12 months, so that the current population will have been covered in that time.

4.29 *Considerations for the public sector*

> II.6. During the 2008/09 reporting year, Departments will conduct their annual assessments, to inform their Accounting Officer's judgement in the Statement on Internal Control.
>
> II.7. Following the end of the 2008/09 reporting year, Cabinet Office will provide to Parliament material on information risk as a whole.'

National Security Strategy, March 2008

4.30 In March 2008 the Cabinet Office published 'The National Security Strategy of the United Kingdom – Security in an interdependent world'[1]. The report addresses the entire panoply of threats to the UK's security, such as terrorism, nuclear weapons, weapons of mass destruction, trans-national organised crime and global instability.

The purpose of the report is described in the following terms:

> 'The aim of this first National Security Strategy is to set out how we will address and manage this diverse though interconnected set of security challenges and underlying drivers, both immediately and in the longer term, to safeguard the nation, its citizens, our prosperity and our way of life.'

The relevance of the report to data security will be obvious, but to quote the report:

> 'We will need to safeguard the United Kingdom against the re-emergence of [State-led] threat[s], to defend the territory of the United Kingdom, its sea and air approaches, its information and communications systems and its other vital interests, including our Overseas Territories.'

The threat of cyber crime is discussed in some detail, with the report saying:

> 'In response to the technological challenges, we are committed to working with international, public, and private sector partners to ensure that our government systems and critical national infrastructure are adequately protected against cyber attack. We are also investing, through the interception modernisation programme, to update our intelligence and law-enforcement capability to meet the challenges of rapidly advancing communications technology. We are committed to maximising the opportunities and benefits of the internet, by protecting the freedom to develop and host new services, while also-reducing the scope for terrorists and criminals to exploit those opportunities and freedoms, and ensuring that the internet itself is resilient enough to withstand attacks and accidents. Finally, we support international efforts to monitor and protect the safety and security of new technology including the internet and communications networks, and the space assets that are increasingly important for communications. We will continue to explore how new confidence-building and arms control measures might contribute to international security in this area.'

[1] Cm 7291 http://interactive.cabinetoffice.gov.uk/documents/security/national_security_strategy.pdf.

Data Handling Review, June 2008

4.31 See above.

Coleman Report, June 2008

4.32 In June 2008 the Cabinet Office published the Coleman Report, 'Protecting Government Information – Independent Review of Government Information Assurance'[1]. The first version of the report was published in 2007[2].

The report, written by Mr Nick Coleman, identifies two key operational risks to information systems. The first arises from the nature of complex projects and difficulties with technology:

> 'There are the risks to implementation of programmes, many of which are well understood in departments – the vast scale of the projects' complexity, introduction of new technology and joining up with delivery partners to share information, services and systems.'

The second risk is described as creating a 'hostile environment for operational services'[3]. It includes fraud, espionage, cyber attack, insider threat and accidental damage and loss. In order to address these risks the Report made the following detailed recommendations:

> '1. The government creates a vision for Information Assurance and that this vision is incorporated into existing vision statements; laying out for citizens and other stakeholders what it considers are acceptable parameters for the sharing, management, and protection of information held and managed by government.
>
> The vision for Information Assurance is owned and agreed to by the whole of government and in doing so sets mandatory parameters for what can be shared, what cannot be shared; what needs to be protected and what does not. The vision covers the complexities of a shared services environment and the Global and European context and covers the availability and integrity of information as well privacy and data protection.
>
> 2. Create a new approach for reviewing and managing information risks across government. Enable new mechanisms to enhance the effectiveness of information risk management including a central facility for sharing risk information.
>
> Provide a central facility for sharing risk information and a central information risk register based on risks experienced by departments and their agencies. Have the centre invest in a core capability to understand the Information Assurance risks facing government. Ensure the level of information risk for critical assets is captured and addressed in departmental risk management processes.
>
> 3. Mandate board owners to report quarterly on information risks and performance backed up by an annual audit of department's capabilities. Within this, establish clear metrics for managing performance of suppliers.
>
> Require accountabilities be clearly set out in departments and programmes – as well as for shared services. Mandate board level owners in each department to report against standardised metrics. Have the Cabinet Office develop and issue these and within this, establish clear metrics for managing performance of suppliers.
>
> 4. Provide the Prime Minister with a summary of Information Assurance across government and associated spending required to deliver cross government security associated with Information Assurance.

4.32 Considerations for the public sector

Identify within this submission the budget required to develop cross government capabilities such as the Information Assurance Technical Programme. Establish a clear governance model for cross government Information Assurance.

5. Simplify the complexity twenty five plus working groups and structures in this area. Enable one central mechanism for developing coordinated joint working, for sharing best practice and establishing Information Assurance priorities across departments and agencies.

Set as a priority the re-use of assets and the development of common requirements across government in the area of Information Assurance. Enable mechanisms to share experiences and create common solutions across parties with similar interests and challenges. Enable the sharing of metrics and scorecards of departments and agencies to assist in procuring solutions and the development of shared services.

6. Create clear mandatory policy rules on security across government. Define minimum standards that departments sign up to. Enable independent monitoring for compliance.

Develop simple rules around Information Assurance. Have these rules defined for all aspects including people, processes and technology. Ensure policy is clear in regard to physical as well as electronic security and considers both national and international contexts. Make policy compliance a priority and ensure there are compliance tools available to departments and agencies. Include tools which can be deployed to check compliance at the user level. Ensure enforcement action is taken within three months where operations are identified to be non-compliant against policy.

7. Tackle identity management challenges through mandating the use of privacy impact assessments. Specify standards of protection for identity registration, management and use in government and the wider public sector.

Re-use, where possible, tried and tested common standards around identity. Revisit the mechanisms around obtaining consent from stakeholders when data or information is used for purposes other than its original intention.

8. Mandate professional certification for those working in Information Assurance in every government department across key defined roles. Ensure citizens, employees and other stakeholders are educated on Information Assurance and what is expected of them.

Define clear competencies and career paths for Information Assurance professionals. Establish mandatory professional certification for those working in Information Assurance in every government department and for contractors providing services to government. Provide appropriate remuneration for those achieving certification.

9. Measure security through audit and monitoring to a defined standard. Mandate the reporting of incidents to an independent organisation responsible for capturing incidents and ensuring investigations are conducted to a given standard and lessons are learned.

Establish testing and monitoring in all departments to a consistent standard as specified by National Technical Authority. Establish a body for departments and agencies to report breaches and task that authority with the responsibility to ensure investigations are carried out appropriately and lessons are learned.

Major reports and policy statements **4.33**

10. Have an independent oversight capability retained by government who can be called upon to give independent oversight and advice on Information Assurance to give stakeholders confidence. Provide this capability in addition to the formal regulatory roles that exist outside government.'

The government addressed these recommendations in the Final Report of the Data Handling Review, saying that it 'accepts the thrust of each of the key recommendations'. The government's response to each recommendation was that they were being addressed, or had been addressed. Examples are given for each recommendation. However, it is unclear if the improvements made by government satisfy the precise detail of the recommendations, not just the thrust. As an impartial, independent expert report, Coleman is likely to become a benchmark within assessment of the public sector's compliance with IA laws, as the Poynter and Burton Reports will become in their own areas.

1   http://www.cabinetoffice.gov.uk/media/cabinetoffice/csia/assets/dhr/ia_coleman080626.pdf.
2   http://www.cabinetoffice.gov.uk/media/cabinetoffice/csia/assets/coleman_review.pdf.
3   'There is also now a different class of risk: a hostile environment for operational services, where fraud and e-crime are on the agenda and increased threats of terrorism and espionage exist.' Coleman Report, page 12.

National Risk Register, November 2008

4.33 In November 2008 the Cabinet Office published the National Risk Register[1], which had been promised in the National Security Strategy. The introduction to the Register sets out its aims and objectives:

'1.1 The National Risk Register sets out "our assessment of the likelihood and potential impact of a range of different risks that may directly affect the UK" as promised in the National Security Strategy, published earlier this year. The publication of information on these risks, previously held confidentially within government, is intended to encourage public debate on security and help organisations, individuals, families and communities, who want to do so, to prepare for emergencies.

1.2 The Register provides an assessment of the most significant emergencies which the United Kingdom and its citizens could face over the next five years summarised into three categories: accidents, natural events (collectively known as hazards) and malicious attacks (known as threats).

1.3 Much of the information in risk registers is unsurprising, but emergency planners have found them useful because:
- they bring together a great deal of information about potential risks that is relevant and consistent;
- the different risks can be compared on a broadly like for like basis; and
- in an age when there appear to be so many possible kinds of emergency, they help in making decisions about which to plan for and what their consequences are likely to be.'

The Register points to all of the critical risks, such as major industrial accidents, pandemic influenza, coastal flooding, attacks on crowded places, severe weather, animal disease, attacks on critical infrastructure and electronic attacks.

4.33 *Considerations for the public sector*

[1] http://www.cabinetoffice.gov.uk/media/cabinetoffice/corp/assets/publications/reports/national_risk_register/national_risk_register.pdf.

4.34 The Register first addresses issues relevant to data security in its section titled 'malicious attacks', which focuses on covert intelligence gathering by foreign intelligence agencies, through the medium of the internet:

> '2.79 The Government's counter terrorism strategy, The National Security Strategy confirms the assessment in the 1998 Strategic Defence Review that, for the foreseeable future, no state or alliance will have both the intent and capability to threaten the UK militarily. The UK does, however, remain subject to high levels of covert non-military activity by foreign intelligence organisations. They are increasingly combining traditional intelligence methods with new and sophisticated technical attacks, for example attempting to penetrate computer networks through the internet.'

The section on the risk of electronic attacks provides as follows:

> '2.111 The risk and impact of electronic attacks on IT and communication systems varies greatly according to the particular sectors affected and the source of the threat. Electronic attacks have the potential to export, modify or delete information or cause systems to fail.
>
> 2.112 There is a known risk to commercially valuable and confidential information in some government and private sector systems from a range of well resourced and sophisticated attacks. Electronic attack may be used more widely by different groups or individuals with various motives.
>
> **Background**
>
> 2.113 IT systems in government departments and various organisations, including elements of the national infrastructure have been and continue to be attacked to obtain the sensitive information they hold. Some of these attacks are well planned and well executed.
>
> **Planning by Government and the Emergency Services**
>
> 2.114 IT systems are increasingly interconnected with each other and with the citizen using internet technologies. This provides huge benefit in terms of convenience, efficiency and cost saving but also requires that departments effectively manage the associated risks. CESG, the Information Assurance arm of GCHQ (Government Communications Headquarters), uses its expertise in this fast moving arena of internet security to provide help and support to government in dealing with these risks.
>
> The Centre for the Protection of National Infrastructure (CPNI) provides advice on protective security measures and direct technical support to organisations within the national infrastructure.
>
> 2.115 Business continuity plans in all critical national infrastructure sectors obviate the effects of any disruptions as far as possible (see sections on government planning for industrial accidents and attacks on critical infrastructure).'

HMG Security Policy Framework, December 2008

4.35 In December 2008 the Cabinet Office published the HMG Security Policy Framework, version 2 of which was published in May 2009[1]. The 'SPF', as it is known, consists of seven separate security policies. It replaces the Manual of Protective Security.

The foreword to the SPF, written by Sir Gus O'Donnell, who headed the Data Handling Review, explains its purpose and the issues that it addresses:

> 'Effective security is central to how we handle many of the challenges facing Government. It is vital for public confidence and for the efficient, effective and safe conduct of public business.
>
> Responsibility for security is delegated down from the Prime Minister and Cabinet to me, as Head of the Home Civil Service and chairman of the Official Committee on Security, and then to Heads of Department. Ultimately, however, security is the responsibility of everyone and our policies and processes will only work well if we all play our part.
>
> The new Security Policy Framework replaces the Manual of Protective Security and the Counter-Terrorist Protective Security Manual. It sets out universal mandatory standards, as well as offering guidance on risk management and defining new compliance and assurance arrangements. For the first time the framework allows for much of this material to be placed in the public domain, allowing greater access, increasing awareness, transparency and sharing good practice.
>
> The framework introduces changes in the way we do things, as part of our broader agenda to modernise and transform Government. Work to modernise security policy and processes will continue: to raise awareness, ensure that guidance is up to date, that policy reflects changes in threat and circumstance, and that Departments are supported from the centre.
>
> I am confident that this framework will enable Government to do its job better and I commend it to all in the public service.'

[1] http://www.cabinetoffice.gov.uk/media/207318/hmg_security_policy.pdf.

4.36 The following passage explains that the SPF consists of a hierarchy of four levels of minimum security requirements of increasing/decreasing levels of detail. It also identifies the five 'core security principles' and explains the fate of the Data Handling Review:

> 'The SPF has four tiers, or levels, each representing a key element (of increasing detail) within the Government's protective security system. First and foremost, is that security not only supports business goals, but must proactively be considered a business enabler, making government work better, safer and more confidently. Next are a set of five core security principles, highlighting accountability at senior levels, collective responsibility of all staff and contractors, and the need to employ trustworthy people. At the third tier is a series of concise key policy documents, which clearly identify (by highlighting in green boxed text), the minimum mandatory requirements. These standards include the new "Data Handling Procedures in Government" published by Cabinet Office in June 2008, which have now been formalised into a new Information Assurance

4.36 *Considerations for the public sector*

Standard (IA Standard no.6); 'Handling Personal Data and Managing Information Risk. It is important to stress here that these are the minimum requirements; it is expected that many Departments and Agencies will manage their specific security risks over and above these baseline measures, using sound risk management principles as outlined within the framework.'

The core security principles

4.37 The five core security principles are:

'1. Ultimate responsibility for HMG security policy lies with the Prime Minister and the Cabinet Office. Departments and Agencies, via their Permanent Secretaries and Chief Executives, must manage their security risks within the parameters set out in this framework, as endorsed by the Official Committee on Security (SO).

2. All HMG employees (including contractors) have a collective responsibility to ensure that government assets (information, property and staff) are protected in a proportionate manner from terrorist attack, and other illegal or malicious activity.

3. Departments and Agencies must be able to share information (including personal data) confidently knowing it is reliable, accessible and protected to agreed standards.

4. Departments and Agencies must employ staff (and contractors) in whom they can have confidence and whose identities are assured.

5. HMG business needs to be resilient in the face of major disruptive events, with plans in place to minimise damage and rapidly recover capabilities.'

These principles certainly identify the major issues within a programme for improvement of security and the maintenance of appropriate standards, but read in isolation of the other layers of the hierarchy they leave many issues unaddressed, such as the expectation that data will also be protected from accidental and negligent loss and damage. However, to illustrate the level of detail and prescriptiveness that is achieved, a sample of 'mandatory requirements' is set out below, with supporting discussion.

Access controls

4.38 SPF mandatory recommendation 38 provides that:

'All ICT systems must have suitable identification and authentication controls to manage the risk of unauthorised access, enable auditing and the correct management of user accounts.'

This should be considered in light of ISO 27001:2005, which contains detailed control objectives for access control at A.11. It should also be noted that in May 2007 the Information Commissioner's Office concluded enforcement action against Orange that arose from newly recruited employees being allowed to share user names and passwords. In November and December 2007 the ICO also concluded enforcement action against the Foreign and Commonwealth Office and the Department of Health, respectively. These

Major reports and policy statements **4.40**

cases arose from the failure of website access control mechanisms, which resulted in people being able to see others' personal data. See also the case against Talk Talk.

Access rights

4.39 SPF minimum requirement 16 says:

> 'Departments and Agencies must ensure that access to protectively marked assets is only granted on the basis of the "need to know" principle. All employees must be made fully aware of their personal responsibility in applying this principle.'

The following 'specific minimum measures to protect personal information', part of the Cross Government Actions, echo the SPF:

> '14.3 user rights to transfer data to removable media should be carefully considered and strictly limited to ensure that this is only provided where absolutely necessary for business purposes and subject to monitoring by managers and the Information Asset Owner; and
>
> 20. All Departments must plan their business taking into account the information risks involved in different business models as well as their benefits. Once a business model is adopted, Departments must explicitly define and document the access rights granted to protected personal data that users enjoy, and minimise access rights within the adopted model.'

Note also ISO 27001:2005 A.11.2.1., which requires that 'there shall be a formal user registration and de-registration procedure in place for granting and revoking access to all information systems and services'.

Accountability

4.40 The law is now structured around an expectation that the controller will define and maintain accountable management and operational structures[1]. In some areas this is supported by a requirement to appoint named officers, such as SIROs[2]. The following SPF mandatory requirements are relevant (3, 4 and 35 respectively):

> 'Departments must have a stated Board level representative responsible for security (e.g. Head of Department/Permanent Secretary). Departments must identify clearly where security responsibilities lie, including the relationship between the Department's main Board and the Boards of their Agencies or other bodies.'
>
> 'Departments and Agencies must have a designated Departmental Security Officer (DSO), with day-to-day responsibilities for all aspects of Protective Security (including physical, personnel and information security).'
>
> 'Departments and Agencies must have:
>
> a) A designated Senior Information Risk Owner (SIRO); a Board level individual responsible for managing departmental information risks, including

4.40 *Considerations for the public sector*

maintaining and reviewing an information risk register (the SIRO role may be combined with other security or information management board level roles).

b) A designated Information Technology Security Officer (ITSO); responsible for the security of information in electronic form.

c) A designated Communications Security Officer (ComSO) if cryptographic material is handled.

d) Information Asset Owners; senior named individuals responsible for each identified information asset.'

The Final Report of the Data Handling Review, identified stronger accountability as one of the main areas for improving data handling, saying:

'The onus has to remain on Departments to plan and secure their own information. This is because protection and use of data are part and parcel of their business, and they are best placed to understand requirements and manage risks. The best mechanism to ensure that this happens is the chain of command from the Accounting Officer, who is ultimately responsible for having the appropriate controls in place in their Department.

However, more can and should be done to increase accountability, in particular to standardise and enhance the processes by which Departments understand and manage their information risk, setting out the responsibilities for key individuals in doing so. Departments are required to establish:
- a process by which information assets are identified and allocated to a responsible owner; and
- an annual assessment process to support the Accounting Officer's judgment for the Statement in Internal Control.

Simplifier cross-Government structures will support this process, with Cabinet Office maintaining and updating the cross-Government requirements.'

[1] See, for example, The National Information Assurance Strategy, which requires there to be 'clear ownership of and accountability for the information risks within an organisation at board level' (at page 8).
[2] See, for example, The Coleman Report, 5.3 Governance and accountability, page 18.

4.41 Note also the following parts of the Cross Government Actions:

'5.1 name a board member as "Senior Information Risk Owner" (SIRO). The SIRO is an executive who is familiar with information risks and the organisation's response. The SIRO may also be the Chief Information Officer (CIO) if the latter is on the board. They own the information risk policy and risk assessment, act as an advocate for information risk on the board and in internal discussions, and provide written advice to the accounting officer on the content of their Statement of Internal Control relating to information risk;

5.2 identify their information assets, and name for each an "information asset owner". Asset owners must be senior individuals involved in running the relevant business. Their role is to understand what information is held, what is added and what is removed, how information is moved, and who has access and why. As a result they are able to understand and address risks to the information, and ensure that information is fully used within the law for the public good. They provide a written judgement of the security and use of their asset annually to support the audit process;'

In many EU jurisdictions there is a requirement to appoint a security officer and to set out the management structures and responsibilities in the security policy. In the UK the expectation now is that contracts of employment and other HR issues must be structured to ensure that serious transgressions are appropriately disciplined, extending to dismissal for gross misconduct. Standards for best practice, such as the ISO 27000 series, also address accountability[1]. ISO 27001:2005 A.8.2.3. requires there to be 'a formal disciplinary process for employees who have committed a security breach'. Implementing these controls will require expert advice on employment law principles.

[1] See section 5, titled 'management responsibility' within BS ISO/IEC 27001:2005.

Accreditation of technology

4.42 The need for the accreditation of technology is discussed in more detail in Chapter 8, in the context of PET. The need for accreditation is a long standing principle of data security law, with organisations like CESG providing substantial services in this area. SPF mandatory requirements 36 and 40 say:

> 'ICT systems that process protectively marked Government data must be accredited using HMG IA Standard No. 2 – Risk Management and Accreditation of Information Systems, and the accreditation status must be reviewed at least annually to judge whether material changes have occurred which could alter the original accreditation decision.'

> 'Departments and Agencies must comply with HMG IA Standard No.4 – Communications Security and Cryptography (parts 1–3) for the protection of protectively marked material. Paying particular attention to the circumstances when encryption is required, the requirement to only use CESG approved solutions, the control mechanisms for cryptographic items, and the requirement for specified levels of personnel security clearance for individuals handling cryptographic items.'

Audits

4.43 Systems and operations for data security should be subject to regular audits, as should the data that are being processed. The UK Information Commissioner has led the call for increased and more penetrating auditing (these are being introduced for the public sector in the Coroners and Justice Bill, which also contains a power to make audits of the private sector compulsory) and audit requirements have also been imposed by the Commissioner, as part of undertakings given by controllers in consideration of the cessation of enforcement action. For example, in January 2009 the Commissioner concluded enforcement action against the Home Office, through the obtaining of undertakings pursuant to which the Home Office promised to regularly inspect and audit the security of one of its data processors. SPF mandatory requirement 8 and 37 say:

> 'Departments and Agencies must comply with oversight arrangements including external audit/compliance arrangements as set out by Cabinet Office.'

4.43 Considerations for the public sector

> 'Departments and Agencies must have the ability to regularly audit information assets and ICT systems. This must include:
>
> a) Regular compliance checks carried out by the Accreditor, ITSO etc. (documented in the RMADS audit of the ICT system against configuration records).
>
> b) A forensic readiness policy that will maximise the ability to preserve and analyse data generated by an ICT system, that may be required for legal and management purposes.'

The Cross Government Actions provide:

> '7. All Departments must:
>
> 7.1 share and discuss the information risk assessment (see 4.2) with their audit committee and main board;
>
> 7.2 conduct at least an annual review of information risk for the SIRO to support their written advice to the Accounting Officer. That review must cover the effectiveness of the overarching policy. It must be informed by the written judgement of the Information Asset Owners, and chair of the audit committee; and
>
> 7.3 once the Statement on Internal Control has been completed, share the relevant material and the supporting annual assessment with Cabinet Office.'

See also ISO/IEC 27001:2005, section 6 which is titled 'Internal ISMS audits'.

Business continuity and disaster recovery

4.44 SPF mandatory requirement 49 says:

> 'Departments and Agencies must ensure that all locations where information and system assets (including cryptographic items) are kept must have appropriate Business Continuity and Disaster Recovery Plans.'

See also ISO 27001:2005 A.14.1. which requires controls to 'counteract interruptions to business activities and to protect critical business processes from the effects of major failures of information systems or disasters and to ensure their timely resumption'.

Contracts

4.45 The Data Protection Act 1998 contains an important example of the law's need for contractual control mechanisms; the interpretation to the seventh data protection principle clearly states that contracts are required for the appointment of data processors, which fixes a role for contracts within core principles for third party assurance. Contracts can also be used to legitimise data processing, including exports out of Europe. SPF mandatory requirement 43 says:

> 'Departments and Agencies must ensure that security requirements are specified in ICT contracts and all new ICT contracts handling personal data must adhere to the Office of Government Commerce (OGC) ICT model terms and conditions.'

Major reports and policy statements **4.46**

The Cross Government Actions deliver a similar message[1]:

> '4.5 use the security clauses from the Office of Government Commerce's model ICT contract for services, with any changes relevant to information risk being approved by the SIRO (defined below);'

ISO 27001:2005 envisages that the controller will enter into service delivery agreements with third party data processors and other relevant service providers (see A.10.2.1.).

The position taken by the SPF on the role of contracts also acts to re-emphasise that data protection law is a subset of data security law.

[1] See Procurement Policy Note, 'Data Handling Review, mandatory application of security provisions in contracts', Information Note 08/08, 1 July 2008 and Procurement Policy Note, 'Data Handling Review', Information Note 13/08, 26 November 2008, Office for Government Commerce. These introduced amendments to the OGC Model ICT Services Agreement.

Employee-worker due diligence

4.46 Very detailed guidance on pre-employment vetting and background checks is contained in SPF No. 3 Personnel Security. SPF mandatory requirement 23 says:

> 'Departments and Agencies must apply the requirements of the Baseline Personnel Security Standard (BPSS) to all HMG staff (including the armed forces), and contractors and temporary staff.'

SPF No. 3 goes on to explain at paragraph 4:

> 'The BPSS is the recognised standard for HMG pre-employment screening. It forms the foundation for National Security Vetting and seeks to address identity fraud, illegal working and deception generally. The BPSS comprises verification of four main elements: 1) identity; 2) employment history; 3) nationality and immigration status (including the right to work); and, if a formal NSV clearance is not required for the post, 4) unspent criminal records. In addition, prospective employees are required to account for any significant periods spent abroad. Satisfactory completion of the BPSS allows regular access to UK RESTRICTED and UK CONFIDENTIAL assets, and occasional access to UK SECRET assets, provided an individual has a "need to know".'

SPF 46 says:

> 'Departments and Agencies must ensure that ICT users with higher levels of privilege and/or potentially wide access (e.g. system administrators, architects, programmers etc.), or those with responsibility for ICT security, must be subject to evaluation for National Security clearances appropriate to the protective marking of the information processed.'

ISO 27001:2005 A.8.1.2. says that 'background verification checks on all candidates for employment, contractors, and third party users shall be carried out in accordance with relevant laws, regulations and ethics, and proportional to the business requirements, the classification of the information to be accessed, and the perceived risks'. It is also important to manage the

4.46 *Considerations for the public sector*

termination of employment properly, for example by including a process for return of assets and removal of access rights. See ISO 27001:2005 A.8. for relevant control objectives and controls.

Again, the implementation of security measures that impact on employees should take full account of employment law principles.

Encryption

4.47 The need for encryption is now fully embedded within the law. As previously explained, breach notification laws have been structured around the idea that it is only security incidents affecting unencrypted data that need to be reported. Both the Information Commissioner and the FSA have issued guidance on the need for encryption. They have both taken regulatory action for the absence of encryption[1]. SPF mandatory requirement 40 says:

> 'Departments and Agencies must comply with HMG IA Standard No.4 – Communications Security and Cryptography (parts 1–3) for the protection of protectively marked material. Paying particular attention to the circumstances when encryption is required, the requirement to only use CESG approved solutions, the control mechanisms for cryptographic items, and the requirement for specified levels of personnel security clearance for individuals handling cryptographic items.'

The Cross Government Actions say:

> '14.2 the removable media should be encrypted to a standard of at least FIPS 140-2 or equivalent in addition to being protected by a authentication mechanism, such as a password;'

ISO 27001:2005 A.12.3. deals with cryptographic controls, requiring a policy on the use of these controls and key management.

[1] See the case brought against Nationwide Building Society by the FSA (February 2009) and the cases brought by the Information Commissioner against Skipton Financial Services (February 2008), HMRC (July 2008), the Ministry of Defence (July 2008) and Virgin Media (September 2008).

Physical security

4.48 The SPF contains a number of mandatory requirements that deal with physical security. Requirement 47 says:

> 'Departments and Agencies must ensure that all locations where information and system assets (including cryptographic items) are kept must have an appropriate level of physical security as set out in this framework.'

SPF mandatory requirement 50 says:

> 'Departments and Agencies must adopt a "layered" approach to physical security, ensuring that their physical security policy incorporates identifiable elements of prevention, detection and response.'

Note also ISO 27001:2005 A.9. for control objectives and controls for physical and environmental security.

Security policy

4.49 A written, unified, single security policy is the holy grail of both the law and best practice for data security. This will address all of the issues and will be clear[1] and accessible. Fractured, highly distributed and unclear[2] policies will not achieve these requirements and have been strongly criticised in regulatory proceedings, such as in the Nationwide case[3], where the FSA said:

> 'Nationwide's information security procedures were contained in an unwieldy electronic format. The procedures were held on Nationwide's internal website; they were not housed in a single document. The procedures covered a very broad range of information handling issues. The policy document was not structured in a way which would have enabled staff to identify easily which part or parts of the procedure might be applicable to their particular role. In addition, there was no search facility within the procedures to assist with this.
>
> The policies contained inconsistencies and lacked any prioritisation; critical steps were given the same prominence as lesser issues. Within Nationwide's procedures, no clear distinction was made between mandatory requirements and guidance on best practice.'

SPF mandatory requirement 31 says:

> 'Departments and Agencies must have, as a component of their overarching security policy, an information security policy setting out how they, and their delivery partners (including offshore and nearshore (EU/EEA based) Managed Service Providers), comply with the minimum requirements set out in this policy and the wider framework.'

[1] SPF mandatory requirement 6.a. says that government departments must 'make their departmental security policy widely available internally and reference this in overall business plans'.
[2] The Coleman Report criticised the complexity and clarity of the government's policy for information assurance: 'Government wide policy around Information Assurance is complex and should be clearer', page 20. The lack of simple, clear guidelines is causing policy to be variable across departments and reduces the overall effectiveness of Information Assurance.
[3] http://www.fsa.gov.uk/pubs/final/nbs.pdf.

4.50 The Information Commissioner's position on security policies is stated in commentary on the Data Handling Review and the reviews into the HMRC and Ministry of Defence cases[1]. This commentary is aligned with the FSA's position, pointing out that security policy documents have to be accessible:

> 'Several reports highlighted that policy and procedure were quite often in place, but was rarely read and used appropriately by the majority of staff. This was down different factors, such as documents running to many hundreds of pages or specific policy documents have a limited circulation among staff.
>
> The ICO welcomes recommendations to simplify, shorten and make guidance more accessible across organisations, with structured hierarchies of guidance from short briefing documents for all staff to in-depth technical guidance for specialists. It is also useful to see recommendations that general policy guidance

4.50   *Considerations for the public sector*

should be translated in locally applicable procedures in each organisation and in some cases, in each line of business within an organisation.'

See also ISO/IEC 27001:2005, which says at section 5, titled 'security policy', that 'an information security policy document should be approved by management, and published and communicated to all employees and relevant external parties'.

[1] See 'Taking stock, taking action': http://www.ico.gov.uk/upload/documents/library/data_protection/detailed_specialist_guides/ico%20position%20paper%20on%20data%20loss%20reports.pdf.

Threat and vulnerability assessment

4.51 Data security law is intended to take a risk-based approach to regulation. For example, the seventh data protection principle requires controllers to implement technological measures for security that take account of the risk of harm that may be caused by a breach. Privacy Impact Assessments, which have been championed by the Information Commissioner and government, seek to put the process of risk assessments on a standardised footing.

The need for controllers to carry out risk assessments is so elementary that it forms part of every standard for best practice. For example, SPF mandatory requirement 32 requires 'annual technical risk assessments' for all ICT projects and programmes:

'Departments and Agencies must conduct an annual technical risk assessment (using HMG IA Standard No.1) for all HMG ICT Projects and Programmes and when there is a significant change in a risk component (Threat, Vulnerability, Impact etc.) to existing HMG ICT Systems in operation. The assessment and the risk management decisions made must be recorded in the Risk Management and Accreditation Documentation Set (RMADS), using HMG IA Standard No.2 – Risk Management and Accreditation of Information Systems.'

The corresponding provisions in the Cross Government Actions include:

'4.2 assess risks to the confidentiality, integrity and availability of information in their delivery chain at least quarterly, taking account of extant Government-wide guidance, and plan and implement proportionate responses, which must at least include implementation of the measures in Section II. At least once a year, the risk assessment must examine forthcoming potential changes in services, technology and threats;'

Another example within the Cross Government Actions is:

'18. All Departments whose delivery chain involves the handling of information relating to 100,000 or more identifiable individuals must engage independent experts to carry out penetration testing of their ICT systems and to make recommendations.'

Major reports and policy statements **4.53**

Third party assurance (use of data processors and outsourcing)

4.52 The need for data controllers to assess, vouch for and ensure the reliability of third parties was discussed earlier, in the context of controller-processor relationships under the Data Protection Act 1998. SPF mandatory requirement 2 says:

> 'Departments must ensure that their Agencies and main delivery partners are compliant with this framework, and must consider the extent to which those providing other goods and/or services to them, or carrying out functions on their behalf, are required to comply.'

SPF mandatory requirement 23 says:

> 'Departments and Agencies must apply the requirements of the Baseline Personnel Security Standard (BPSS) to all HMG staff (including the armed forces), and contractors and temporary staff.'

The Information Commissioner's case against the Home Office was essentially a third party assurance case, concerning as it did the loss of a memory stick by a government contractor.

Transparency

4.53 The main transparency issues in the field of data security are discussed in the context of breach notification, inspections and the established regime within the Data Protection Act 1998. SPF mandatory requirement 7 says:

> 'Departments must submit an annual security return to the Cabinet Office Security Policy Division, covering their Agencies and main delivery partners, and must include:
>
> a) Details of any changes to key individuals responsible for security matters (The appointment of a new DSO must be reported immediately).
>
> b) Significant departmental risks and mitigations that have implications for protective security.
>
> c) All significant security incidents (those involving serious criminal activity, damage to National Security, breaches of international security agreements, serious reputational damage, data losses or leaks) – individual breaches of this nature must also be reported immediately.
>
> d) Declaration of meeting all Mandatory Requirements (green boxes).
>
> e) Confirmation that any significant control weaknesses have been reflected in the Departmental Statement on Internal Control.'

The Cross Government Actions say:

> 'All Departments must:
>
> 10.1 publish an information charter setting out how they handle information and how members of the public can address any concerns that they have;
>
> 10.2 set out in the Departmental annual report summary material on information risk, covering the overall judgement in the Statement on Internal Control,

4.53 *Considerations for the public sector*

numbers of information risk incidents sufficiently significant for the Information Commissioner to be informed, the numbers of people potentially affected, and actions taken to contain the breach and prevent recurrence.'

Training and awareness

4.54 The need for data controllers to provide data security training and awareness programmes is addressed in many places within the SPF. Mandatory requirement 1 says:

'Departments and Agencies must ensure that all staff understand the relevant requirements and responsibilities placed upon them by the Security Policy Framework and that they are properly equipped to meet the mandatory security policies (green boxes) as set out in this framework.'

SPF mandatory requirement 9 says:

'Departments and Agencies must ensure that:

a) Board members responsible for security undergo security and risk management familiarisation upon appointment.

b) All DSOs are given a joint security briefing from Cabinet Office and the Centre for Protection of National Infrastructure (CPNI) on appointment, and have either attended the relevant training courses before, or at the earliest opportunity after appointment.

c) All Departmental Security Unit (DSU) staff possess competencies and training to the appropriate level, either by attending relevant internal departmental or external government training.

d) Security education and awareness must be built into all staff inductions, with regular familiarisation thereafter.

e) There are plans in place to foster a culture of proportionate protective security.

f) There is a clearly stated and available policy, and mechanisms in place, to allow for independent and anonymous reporting of security incidents.'

The Cross Government Actions say:

'19. All Departments must ensure that all data users must successfully undergo information risk awareness training on appointment and at least annually. In addition, all Information Asset Owners must pass information management training on appointment and at least annually, and accounting officers, SIROs, and members of the audit committee must pass strategic information risk management training at least annually.'

See also ISO 27000:1 paragraph 5.2.2. for provisions about training, awareness and competence, which says that 'the organisation shall ensure that all personnel who are assigned responsibilities defined in the ISMS are competent to perform the required tasks'.

The Information Commissioner's case against Brent PCT covered the issue of staff training.

Waste

4.55 The Information Commissioner's position on the disposal of confidential waste is unambiguously represented by the enforcement action taken against the banks, building societies and the Post Office in February 2007. See also the cases against Cash Generators, Phones 4U, NHS Lanarkshire and NHS Tayside.

SPF mandatory requirement 45 says:

> 'Departments and Agencies must ensure that all media used for storing or processing protectively marked or otherwise sensitive information must be disposed of or sanitised in accordance with HMG IA Standard No. 5 – Secure Sanitisation of Protectively Marked or Sensitive Information.'

ISO 27001:2005 A.9.2.6. identifies secure disposal or re-use of equipment to be a control objective, with the control being 'all items of equipment containing storage media shall be checked to ensure that any sensitive data and licensed software has been removed or securely overwritten prior to disposal'.

National Security Strategy Updated, June 2009

4.56 In June 2009 the Cabinet Office published 'The National Security Strategy of the United Kingdom: Update 2009 – Security for the Next Generation'[1]. This version of the Strategy is double the length of the original version.

The foreword to the Updated Strategy, written by the Prime Minister, provides the following insight into the concerns about cyber security:

> 'Our approach means we are responsive to new challenges like cyber security. Seizing the benefits of new technology is vital for our national prosperity. But hostile states, terrorists, and criminals can all potentially use cyber space to undermine our interests. This could be at the national level – for example through attacks on our essential infrastructure. But security threats in cyber space also threaten the interests of businesses and individuals. In the past, Governments thought about national security as being about protecting the state and its interests. This remains important, but the nature of the risks we face in today's world means our approach to national security must be focused just as much on protecting individual citizens and businesses. So today, alongside this strategy update, we are publishing the United Kingdom's first national strategy for cyber security, to help people make the most of the benefits of Digital Britain in a safe and secure way.'

The following passages on cyber security should also be noted:

> '46. Cyber space is the most important new domain in national security of recent years. Cyber space is increasingly vital for our prosperity and our way of life. There are tremendous commercial and other opportunities for the UK's business and people. But cyber space is also a domain in which hostile states, terrorists, and criminals can operate putting the interests of businesses and citizens at risk.

4.56 *Considerations for the public sector*

> 47. That is why, alongside Security for the Next Generation, the Government is publishing the first Cyber Security Strategy for the UK. This Strategy announces the establishment of an Office of Cyber Security to provide strategic leadership for, and coherence across, Government departments and agencies, a Cyber Security Operations Centre to coordinate incident response and monitor the health of cyber space, and a cross-Government programme working in partnership with business, international partners and the public on cyber security.
>
> 48. The new organisations will help citizens and businesses by providing assessments of risk, plugging skills gaps, and providing advice so that the UK can avail itself of the many opportunities in cyber space set out in the Government's Digital Britain strategy.'

[1] Cm 7590: http://www.cabinetoffice.gov.uk/media/216734/nss2009v2.pdf.

4.57 Chapter 7 of the Updated Report goes on to provide more detail about the government's approach to tackling the threats to cyber security. The following summary of the strategy should be noted:

> '7.44 In summary, the Government will:
> 1. establish a cross-government programme to address priority areas in pursuit of the UK's strategic cyber security objectives, including:
>   – providing additional funding for the development of innovative future technologies to protect UK networks;
>   – developing and promoting the growth of critical skills;
> 2. work closely with the wider public sector, industry, civil liberties groups, the public and with international partners;
> 3. set up an Office of Cyber Security (OCS) to provide strategic leadership for and coherence across Government;
> 4. create a Cyber Security Operations Centre (CSOC) to:
>   – actively monitor the health of cyber space and co-ordinate incident response;
>   – enable better understanding of attacks against UK networks and users;
>   – provide better advice and information about the risks to business and the public.'

Cyber Security Strategy, June 2009

4.58 In June 2009 the Cabinet Office published 'Cyber Security Strategy of the United Kingdom – safety, security and resilience in cyber space'[1]. The Executive Summary to the Strategy explains its context and purpose:

> 'Every day, millions of people across the United Kingdom rely on the services and information that make up cyber space: that is, all forms of networked, digital activities. They may be aware of this if surfing the web, shopping or social networking online, or they may be unaware of the networked activity underpinning the services they rely on, and of just how critically dependent the work of government, business and national infrastructure is on this new domain of human activity. Either way, the effective functioning of cyber space is of vital importance. As the Government's Digital Britain report says: "The Digital World is a reality in all of our lives". This document explains what the Government will be doing to ensure its safety, security and resilience and to exploit the opportunities it presents.'

The Strategy's 'vision' is explained as follows:

'Citizens, business and government can enjoy the full benefits of a safe, secure and resilient cyber space: working together, at home and overseas, to understand and address the risks, to reduce the benefits to criminals and terrorists, and to seize opportunities in cyber space to enhance the UK's overall security and resilience.'

In order to achieve this vision the Strategy makes a number of broad promises. It says that it will reduce the risk associated with the UK's 'use of cyber space', that it will exploit 'opportunities in cyber space' and that it will improve 'knowledge, capabilities and decision-making' in respect of the use of cyber space. It also promises that the government will establish 'a cross-government programme to address priority areas in pursuit of the UK's strategic cyber security objectives' and that the government will 'work closely with the wider public sector, industry, civil liberties groups, the public and international partners'. The establishment of the Office of Cyber Security (OCS) and the Cyber Security Operations Centre (CSOC) are also key components within the achievement of the vision.

The strategy provides the following definition of cyber space:

'Cyber space encompasses all forms of networked, digital activities; this includes the content of and actions conducted through digital networks.'

[1] Cm 7642: http://www.cabinetoffice.gov.uk/media/216620/css0906.pdf.

Digital Britain, June 2009

4.59 In June 2009 the Department for Culture, Media and Sport and the Department for Business Innovation and Skills jointly published 'Digital Britain: Final Report'[1]. The foreword to the report explains that it is geared towards helping the economy recover from the recession:

'Britain needs to plan for more than recovery from the global downturn. We face changes that are transforming the world in which our businesses and people operate. The move from analogue to digital technology is one of those revolutionary changes. It will define the competitiveness of our economy and change dramatically the way we lead our lives.

...

The Digital Britain Report does this. It offers a strategic view of the sector, backed by a programme of action:
(A) to complement and assist the private sector in delivering the effective modern communications infrastructure we need, built on new digital technologies;
(B) to enable Britain to be a global centre for the creative industries in the digital age, delivering an ever wider range of quality content, including public service content, within a clear and fair legal framework;
(C) to ensure that people have the capabilities and skills to flourish in the digital economy, and that all can participate in digital society; and
(D) for government to continue to modernise and improve its service to the taxpayer through digital procurement and the digital delivery of public services.'

4.59   *Considerations for the public sector*

1   Cm 7650: http://www.culture.gov.uk/images/publications/digitalbritain-finalreport-jun09.pdf.

4.60   Chapter 7 of the report is titled 'Digital Security and Safety'. It advocates a 'national approach to digital security' to ensure that 'the UK has a world class approach to digital security', which will deliver a range of benefits for the economy including 'a competitive edge in the global market place' for UK businesses, increasing use of internet services by consumers and expanded trust in e-government initiatives. In order to achieve these ambitions the report sets out strategies in three areas:

- High Level Cyber Security: by which we mean the approach to high level network security and to serious and organised crime and terrorism, often taking place at a supra-national level;
- Personal Digital and Data Security: by which we mean the approach to making consumers safer online in relation to online scams and rip-offs, identity and data privacy and personal network protection; and
- Content Safeguards: by which we mean protecting consumers from illegal content and protection of certain vulnerable groups from potentially harmful material, particularly children.'

High level cyber security is addressed by the Cyber Security Strategy. The strategy for personal digital and data security re-emphasises the trust issue and the need for education of the general public on security issues:

> '38. Getting to this level of confidence requires users to know enough about the dangers from hackers, viruses and fraudsters to take basic steps to protect their own data. Service providers must react quickly to instances of fraud and to patch vulnerabilities that are discovered. And suppliers must make their products more secure against digital threats. We will not succeed in our goals if consumers turn away from the online world through fear that they will be robbed or that their personal information will be exploited.
>
> 39. Giving users basic advice about avoiding known problems online must be a cornerstone of any approach to improving security. To that end, the Government has worked with the private sector to create GetSafeOnLine which offers advice in plain English on protecting your PC, avoiding online rip offs and taking care of your identity online. The GSOL initiative has reached maturity in terms of its ability to produce the right material for its audience, but lacks resources to deliver a greater impact.'

Other issues that are addressed in Chapter 7 are the security of home networks, the role of the OFT in enforcing security as part of consumer protection legislation, the Information Commissioner's initiatives, law reform, online content safeguards and children internet safety.

CIVIL SERVICE MANAGEMENT CODE

4.61   The Civil Service Management Code[1] is referred to in the Final Report of the Data Handling Review. Chapter 4.2, which is titled 'Conduct: Confidentiality and Official Information', will be relevant to the application of the Official Secrets Acts and any allegations of breach of duty by civil servants. It begins by explaining that government departments and agencies must remind civil servants of their legal obligations to respect the security and confidentiality of government data:

> 'Departments and agencies must remind staff on appointment, retirement or resignation that they are bound by the provisions of the criminal law, including the Official Secrets Acts, which protect certain categories of official information, and by their duty of confidentiality owed to the Crown as their former employer.'

[1] http://www.civilservice.gov.uk/about/work/codes/csmc/index.aspx.

CONTRACTING WITH THE PRIVATE SECTOR

4.62 The Data Handling Review and the HMG SPF both mandate the use of the model contractual terms published by the Office of Government Commerce for contracts with the private sector that impact on, or involve, the handling of government data[1]. In most cases these clauses should be followed to the letter, with any changes requiring high level approval on compelling grounds. The following provisions, which are contained in version 2.3 of the model terms (published in July 2009), are relevant to data security:

> **'Staffing Security**
>
> The Contractor shall comply with the Staff Vetting Procedures in respect of all Contractor Personnel employed or engaged in the provision of the Services. The Contractor confirms that all Contractor Personnel employed or engaged by the Contractor at the Effective Date were vetted and recruited on a basis that is equivalent to and no less strict than the Staff Vetting Procedures.
>
> The Contractor shall provide training on a continuing basis for all Contractor Personnel employed or engaged in the provision of the Services in compliance with the Security Policy and Security Plan.'
>
> **'41. PROTECTION OF PERSONAL DATA**
>
> 41.1 With respect to the parties' rights and obligations under this Agreement, the parties agree that the Authority is the Data Controller and that the Contractor is the Data Processor.
>
> 41.2 The Contractor shall:
>
> 41.2.1 Process the Personal Data only in accordance with instructions from the Authority (which may be specific instructions or instructions of a general nature as set out in this Agreement or as otherwise notified by the Authority to the Contractor during the Term);
>
> 41.2.2 Process the Personal Data only to the extent, and in such manner, as is necessary for the provision of the Services or as is required by Law or any Regulatory Body;
>
> 41.2.3 implement appropriate technical and organisational measures to protect the Personal Data against unauthorised or unlawful processing and against accidental loss, destruction, damage, alteration or disclosure. These measures shall be appropriate to the harm which might result from any unauthorised or unlawful Processing, accidental loss, destruction or damage to the Personal Data and having regard to the nature of the Personal Data which is to be protected;

4.62 Considerations for the public sector

41.2.4 take reasonable steps to ensure the reliability of any Contractor Personnel who have access to the Personal Data;

41.2.5 obtain prior written consent from the Authority in order to transfer the Personal Data to any Sub-contractors or Affiliates for the provision of the Services;

41.2.6 ensure that all Contractor Personnel required to access the Personal Data are informed of the confidential nature of the Personal Data and comply with the obligations set out in this clause 41;

41.2.7 ensure that none of Contractor Personnel publish, disclose or divulge any of the Personal Data to any third party unless directed in writing to do so by the Authority;

41.2.8 notify the Authority (within [five] Working Days) if it receives:

...

41.2.8.2 a complaint or request relating to the Authority's obligations under the Data Protection Legislation;

41.2.9 provide the Authority with full cooperation and assistance in relation to any complaint or request made, including by:

41.2.9.1 providing the Authority with full details of the complaint or request;

...

41.2.9.3 providing the Authority with any Personal Data it holds in relation to a Data Subject (within the timescales required by the Authority); and

41.2.9.4 providing the Authority with any information requested by the Authority;

41.2.10 permit the Authority or the Authority Representative (subject to reasonable and appropriate confidentiality undertakings), to inspect and audit, in accordance with clause 24 (Audits), the Contractor's data Processing activities (and/or those of its agents, subsidiaries and Sub-contractors) and comply with all reasonable requests or directions by the Authority to enable the Authority to verify and/or procure that the Contractor is in full compliance with its obligations under this Agreement;

41.2.11 provide a written description of the technical and organisational methods employed by the Contractor for processing Personal Data (within the timescales required by the Authority); and

41.2.12 [not Process or otherwise transfer any Personal Data outside the European Economic Area. If, after the Effective Date, the Contractor (or any Sub-contractor) wishes to Process and/or transfer any Personal Data outside the European Economic Area, the following provisions shall apply:

41.2.12.1 the Contractor shall submit a Change Request to the Authority which shall be dealt with in accordance with the Change Control Procedure and clauses 41.2.12.2 to 41.2.12.4 below;

41.2.12.2 the Contractor shall set out in its Change Request and/or Impact Assessment details of the following:
(a) the Personal Data which will be Processed and/or transferred outside the European Economic Area;
(b) the country or countries in which the Personal Data will be Processed and/or to which the Personal Data will be transferred outside the European Economic Area;

(c) any Sub-contractors or other third parties who will be Processing and/or transferring Personal Data outside the European Economic Area; and
(d) how the Contractor will ensure an adequate level of protection and adequate safeguards (in accordance with the Data Protection Legislation and in particular so as to ensure the Authority's compliance with the Data Protection Legislation) in respect of the Personal Data that will be Processed and/or transferred outside the European Economic Area;

41.2.12.3 in providing and evaluating the Change Request and Impact Assessment, the parties shall ensure that they have regard to and comply with then-current Authority, Government and Information Commissioner Office policies, procedures, guidance and codes of practice on, and any approvals processes in connection with, the Processing and/or transfers of Personal Data outside the European Economic Area and/or overseas generally; and

41.2.12.4 the Contractor shall comply with such other instructions and shall carry out such other actions as the Authority may notify in writing, including:
(a) incorporating standard and/or model clauses (which are approved by the European Commission as offering adequate safeguards under the Data Protection Legislation) in this Agreement or a separate data processing agreement between the parties; and
(b) procuring that any Sub-contractor or other third party who will be Processing and/or transferring the Personal Data outside the European Economic Area enters into a direct data processing agreement with the Authority on such terms as may be required by the Authority, which the Contractor acknowledges may include the incorporation of standard and/or model clauses (which are approved by the European Commission as offering adequate safeguards under the Data Protection Legislation).]

41.3 The Contractor shall comply at all times with the Data Protection Legislation and shall not perform its obligations under this Agreement in such a way as to cause the Authority to breach any of its applicable obligations under the Data Protection Legislation.'

'**48. SECURITY REQUIREMENTS**

48.1 The Contractor shall comply, and shall procure the compliance of the Contractor Personnel, with the Security Policy and the Security Plan and the Contractor shall ensure that the Security Plan produced by the Contractor fully complies with the Security Policy.

48.2 The Authority shall notify the Contractor of any changes or proposed changes to the Security Policy.

48.3 If the Contractor believes that a change or proposed change to the Security Policy will have a material and unavoidable cost implication to the Services it may submit a Change Request. In doing so, the Contractor must support its request by providing evidence of the cause of any increased costs and the steps that it has taken to mitigate those costs. Any change to the Charges shall then be agreed in accordance with the Change Control Procedure.

48.4 Until and/or unless a change to the Charges is agreed by the Authority pursuant to clause 48.3 the Contractor shall continue to perform the Services in accordance with its existing obligations.

Malicious Software
48.5 The Contractor shall, as an enduring obligation throughout the Term, use the latest versions of anti-virus definitions available [from an industry accepted anti-virus software vendor] to check for and delete Malicious Software from the ICT Environment.

4.62 Considerations for the public sector

> 48.6 Notwithstanding clause 48.5, if Malicious Software is found, the parties shall cooperate to reduce the effect of the Malicious Software and, particularly if Malicious Software causes loss of operational efficiency or loss or corruption of Authority Data, assist each other to mitigate any losses and to restore the Services to their desired operating efficiency.
>
> 48.7 Any cost arising out of the actions of the parties taken in compliance with the provisions of clause 48.6 shall be borne by the parties as follows:
>
> 48.7.1 by the Contractor where the Malicious Software originates from the Contractor Software, the Third Party Software supplied by the Contractor (except where the Authority has waived the obligation set out in Clause 48.5) or the Authority Data (whilst the Authority Data was under the control of the Contractor) unless the Contractor can demonstrate that such Malicious Software was present and not quarantined or otherwise identified by the Authority when provided to the Contractor; and
>
> 48.7.2 by the Authority if the Malicious Software originates from the Authority Software (in respect of which the Authority has waived its obligation set out in Clause 48.5) or the Authority Data (whilst the Authority Data was under the control of the Authority).'

[1] See also 'Procurement Policy Note: Data Handling Review', Information Note 13/08, 26 November 2008, Office of Government Commerce. See also 'Procurement Policy Note: Data Handling Review – mandatory application of security principles in contracts', Information Note 08/08, 1 July 2008, Office of Government Commerce.

4.63 Schedule 2.5 is titled 'security requirements and plan'. It contains a pro-forma security plan, which reads as follows:

> ' "Breach of Security" "in accordance with the Security requirements in Schedule 2.1 (Services Description) and the Security Policy, the occurrence of:
> (a) any unauthorised access to or use of the Services, the Authority Premises, the Sites, the Contractor System and/or any ICT, information or data (including the Confidential Information and the Authority Data) used by the Authority and/or the Contractor in connection with this Agreement; and/or
> (b) the loss and/or unauthorised disclosure of any information or data (including the Confidential Information and the Authority Data), including any copies of such information or data, used by the Authority and/or the Contractor in connection with this Agreement."
>
> "ISMS" The Information Security Management System as defined by ISO/IEC 27001. The scope of the ISMS will be as agreed by the parties and will directly reflect the scope of the Services.
>
> "Protectively Marked" shall have the meaning as set out in the Security Policy Framework.
>
> "Security Management Plan" the Contractor's security plan prepared pursuant to paragraph 9 of schedule 2.5 (Security Management Plan) and as attached as Appendix 2 to this schedule 2.5 (Security Management Plan);
>
> "Security Policy" the Authority's security policy as attached as Appendix 1 to this schedule 2.5 (Security Management Plan) as updated from time to time;
>
> "Security Policy Framework" means the Cabinet Office Security Policy Framework (available from the Cabinet Office Security Policy Division);

"Security Tests" shall have the meaning set out in paragraph 10.1 of schedule 2.5 (Security Management Plan);

"Statement of Applicability" shall have the meaning set out in ISO/IEC 27001 and as agreed by the parties during the procurement phase.

1. INTRODUCTION

1.1 This schedule covers:

1.1.1 principles of protective security to be applied in delivering the Services;

1.1.2 [wider aspects of security relating to the Service];

1.1.3 the development, implementation, operation, maintenance and continual improvement of an ISMS;

1.1.4 the creation and maintenance of the Security Management Plan;

1.1.5 audit and testing of ISMS compliance with the security requirements (as set out in Schedule 2.1 (Services Description));

1.1.6 conformance to ISO/IEC27001 (Information Security Requirements Specification) and ISO/IEC27002 (Information Security Code of Practice) and;

1.1.7 obligations in the event of actual, potential or attempted breaches of security.

2. PRINCIPLES OF SECURITY

2.1 The Contractor acknowledges that the Authority places great emphasis on the confidentiality, integrity and availability of information and consequently on the security provided by the ISMS.

2.2 The Contractor shall be responsible for the effective performance of the ISMS and shall at all times provide a level of security which:

2.2.1 is in accordance with Good Industry Practice, Law and this Agreement;

2.2.2 complies with the Security Policy;

2.2.3 [complies with at least the minimum set of security measures and standards as determined by the Security Policy Framework (Tiers 1–4) available from the Cabinet Office Security Policy Division (COSPD)];

2.2.4 meets any specific security threats to the ISMS; and

2.2.5 complies with ISO/IEC27001 and ISO/IEC27002 in accordance with paragraph 5 of this schedule;

2.2.6 complies with the security requirements as set out in Schedule 2.1 (Services Description);

2.2.7 complies with the Authority's ICT standards.

2.3 Subject to Clause 48.3, the references to standards, guidance and policies set out in paragraph 2.2 shall be deemed to be references to such items as developed and updated and to any successor to or replacement for such standards, guidance and policies, from time to time.

2.4 In the event of any inconsistency in the provisions of the above standards, guidance and policies, the Contractor should notify the Authority's Representative of such inconsistency immediately upon becoming aware of the same, and the Authority's Representative shall, as soon as practicable, advise the Contractor which provision the Contractor shall be required to comply with.

4.63 *Considerations for the public sector*

3. ISMS AND SECURITY MANAGEMENT PLAN

3.1 Introduction

3.1.1 The Contractor shall develop, implement, operate, maintain and continuously improve and maintain an ISMS which will, without prejudice to paragraph 2.2, be approved, by the Authority, tested in accordance with Schedule 6.2 (Testing Procedures), periodically updated and audited in accordance with ISO/IEC 27001.

3.1.2 The Contractor shall develop and maintain a Security Management Plan in accordance with this Schedule to apply during the Term.

3.1.3 The Contractor shall comply with its obligations set out in the Security Management Plan.

3.1.4 Both the ISMS and the Security Management Plan shall, unless otherwise specified by the Authority, aim to protect all aspects of the Services and all processes associated with the delivery of the Services, including the Authority Premises, the Sites, the Contractor System and any ICT, information and data (including the Authority Confidential Information and the Authority Data) to the extent used by the Authority or the Contractor in connection with this Agreement.

3.2 Development of the Security Management Plan

3.2.1 Within [20] Working Days after the Effective Date and in accordance with paragraph 3.4 (Amendment and Revision), the Contractor will prepare and deliver to the Authority for approval a fully complete and up to date Security Management Plan which will be based on the draft Security Management Plan set out in Appendix 2.

3.2.2 If the Security Management Plan, or any subsequent revision to it in accordance with paragraph 3.4 (Amendment and Revision), is approved by the Authority it will be adopted immediately and will replace the previous version of the Security Management Plan at Appendix 2. If the Security Management Plan is not approved by the Authority the Contractor shall amend it within [10] Working Days of a notice of non-approval from the Authority and re-submit to the Authority for approval.

The parties will use all reasonable endeavours to ensure that the approval process takes as little time as possible and in any event no longer than [15] Working Days (or such other period as the parties may agree in writing) from the date of its first submission to the Authority. If the Authority does not approve the Security Management Plan following its resubmission, the matter will be resolved in accordance with the Dispute Resolution Procedure. No approval to be given by the Authority pursuant to this paragraph 3.2.2 of this schedule may be unreasonably withheld or delayed. However any failure to approve the Security Management Plan on the grounds that it does not comply with the requirements set out in paragraph 3.3.4 shall be deemed to be reasonable.

3.3 Content of the Security Management Plan

3.3.1 The Security Management Plan will set out the security measures to be implemented and maintained by the Contractor in relation to all aspects of the Services and all processes associated with the delivery of the Services and shall at all times comply with and specify security measures and procedures which are sufficient to ensure that the Services comply with the provisions of this schedule (including the principles set out in paragraph 2.2).

3.3.2 The Security Management Plan (including the draft version) should also set out the plans for transiting all security arrangements and responsibilities from those in place at the Effective Date to those incorporated in the Contractor's ISMS at the date set out in the Schedule 6.1 (Implementation Plan) for the Contractor to meet the full obligations of the security requirements at Schedule 2.1.

3.3.3 The Security Management Plan will be structured in accordance with ISO/IEC27001 and ISO/IEC27002, cross-referencing if necessary to other schedules of this Agreement which cover specific areas included within that standard.

3.3.4 The Security Management Plan shall be written in plain English in language which is readily comprehensible to the staff of the Contractor and the Authority engaged in the Services and shall only reference documents which are in the possession of the Authority or whose location is otherwise specified in this schedule.

3.4 Amendment and Revision of the ISMS and Security Management Plan

3.4.1 The ISMS and Security Management Plan will be fully reviewed and updated by the Contractor annually, or from time to time to reflect:

3.4.1.1 emerging changes in Good Industry Practice;

3.4.1.2 any change or proposed change to the Contractor System, the Services and/or associated processes;

3.4.1.3 any new perceived or changed security threats;

3.4.1.4 any reasonable request by the Authority.

3.4.2 The Contractor will provide the Authority with the results of such reviews as soon as reasonably practicable after their completion and amend the ISMS and Security Management Plan at no additional cost to the Authority. The results of the review should include, without limitation:

3.4.2.1 Suggested improvements to the effectiveness of the ISMS;

3.4.2.2 Updates to the risk assessments;

3.4.2.3 Proposed modifications to the procedures and controls that effect information security to respond to events that may impact on the ISMS;

3.4.2.4 Suggested improvements in measuring the effectiveness of controls.

3.4.3 On receipt of the results of such reviews, the Authority will approve any amendments or revisions to the ISMS or Security Management Plan in accordance with the process set out at para 9.2.2.

3.4.4 Any change or amendment which the Contractor proposes to make to the ISMS or Security Management Plan (as a result of an Authority request or change to the schedule 2.1 (Service Description) or otherwise) shall be subject to the Change Control Procedure and shall not be implemented until approved in writing by the Authority.

4. TESTING

4.1 The Contractor shall conduct tests of the ISMS ("Security Tests") on an [annual] basis or as otherwise agreed by the parties. The date, timing, content and conduct of such Security Tests shall be agreed in advance with the Authority.

4.63 *Considerations for the public sector*

4.2 The Authority shall be entitled to send a representative to witness the conduct of the Security Tests. The Contractor shall provide the Authority with the results of such tests (in a form approved by the Authority in advance) as soon as practicable after completion of each Security Test.

4.3 Without prejudice to any other right of audit or access granted to the Authority pursuant to this Agreement, the Authority and/or its authorised representatives shall be entitled, at any time and without giving notice to the Contractor, to carry out such tests (including penetration tests) as it may deem necessary in relation to the ISMS and the Contractor's compliance with the ISMS and the Security Management Plan.

The Authority may notify the Contractor of the results of such tests after completion of each such test. Security Tests shall be designed and implemented so as to minimise the impact on the delivery of the Services. If such tests adversely affect the Contractor's ability to deliver the Services to the agreed Service Levels, the Contractor shall be granted relief against any resultant under-performance for the period of the tests.

4.4 Where any Security Test carried out pursuant to paragraphs 4.2 or 4.3 above reveals any actual or potential Breach of Security, the Contractor shall promptly notify the Authority of any changes to the ISMS and to the Security Management Plan (and the implementation thereof) which the Contractor proposes to make in order to correct such failure or weakness. Subject to the Authority's approval in accordance with paragraph 3.4.4, the Contractor shall implement such changes to the ISMS and the Security Management Plan in accordance with the timetable agreed with the Authority or, otherwise, as soon as reasonably possible. For the avoidance of doubt, where the change to the ISMS or Security Management Plan to address a non-compliance with the Security Policy or security requirements (as set out in Schedule 2.1), the change to the ISMS or Security Management Plan shall be at no cost to the Authority.

5. COMPLIANCE WITH ISO/IEC 27001

5.1 [The Contractor shall obtain independent certification of the ISMS to ISO/IEC 27001 within [12] months of the Effective Date and shall maintain such certification for the duration of the Agreement.]

5.2 [If certain parts of the ISMS do not conform to good industry practice, or controls as described in ISO/IEC 27002 are not consistent with the Security Policy, and, as a result, the Contractor reasonably believes that it is not compliant with ISO/IEC 27001, the Contractor shall promptly notify the Authority of this and the Authority in its absolute discretion may waive the requirement for certification in respect of the relevant parts.]

5.3 The Authority shall be entitled to carry out such regular security audits as may be required, and in accordance with Good Industry Practice, in order to ensure that the ISMS maintains compliance with the principles and practices of ISO 27001.

5.4 If, on the basis of evidence provided by such audits, it is the Authority's reasonable opinion that compliance with the principles and practices of ISO/IEC 27001 is not being achieved by the Contractor, then the Authority shall notify the Contractor of the same and give the Contractor a reasonable time (having regard to the extent and criticality of any non-compliance and any other relevant circumstances) to become compliant with the principles and practices of ISO/IEC 27001. If the Contractor does not become compliant within the required time then the Authority has the right to obtain an independent audit against these standards in whole or in part.

5.5 If, as a result of any such independent audit as described in paragraph 5.4 the Contractor is found to be non-compliant with the principles and practices of ISO/IEC 27001 then the Contractor shall, at its own expense, undertake those actions required in order to achieve the necessary compliance and shall reimburse in full the costs incurred by the Authority in obtaining such audit.

6. BREACH OF SECURITY

6.1 Either party shall notify the other in accordance with the agreed security incident management process as defined by the ISMS upon becoming aware of any Breach of Security or any potential or attempted Breach of Security.

6.2 Without prejudice to the security incident management process, upon becoming aware of any of the circumstances referred to in paragraph 6.1, the Contractor shall: 6.2.1 immediately take all reasonable steps necessary to:

6.2.1.1 remedy such breach or protect the integrity of the ISMS against any such potential or attempted breach or threat; and

6.2.1.2 prevent an equivalent breach in the future. Such steps shall include any action or changes reasonably required by the Authority. In the event that such action is taken in response to a breach that is determined by the Authority acting reasonably not to be covered by the obligations of the Contractor under this Agreement, then the Contractor shall be entitled to refer the matter to the Change Control Procedure; and

6.2.2 as soon as reasonably practicable provide to the Authority full details (using such reporting mechanism as defined by the ISMS) of the Breach of Security or the potential or attempted Breach of Security.'

DATA SECURITY IN THE NHS

4.64 The Information Commissioner has dedicated a significant amount of resource to dealing with data security issues within the NHS. In May 2009 the Assistant Information Commissioner said[1]:

> 'Medical history is very sensitive personal data, which is likely to cause harm or distress. The law dictates they must keep this information confidential, but the NHS is by far the biggest offender within the public sector.'

The duty of confidentiality and, consequentially, the requirement to keep information secure, goes to the heart of patient trust and is a cornerstone of the NHS. To borrow an anatomical metaphor, information is the 'lifeblood' of the NHS. It therefore causes great concern to learn that in the first four months of 2009 the NHS reported 140 data security breaches, involving the medical records of tens of thousands of individuals. This statistic is perhaps even more alarming given the sensitivity of the data and the ongoing programme of digitisation and modernisation of the health service's records and information systems.

1 'NHS "loses" thousands of medical records – Exclusive: Information watchdog orders overhaul after 140 security breaches in just four months', The Independent, 25 May 2009: http://www.independent.co.uk/news/uk/politics/nhs-loses-thousands-of-medical-records-1690398.html.

4.65 *Considerations for the public sector*

Information systems and technology within the NHS

4.65 Historically, the development and use of IT facilities was a low priority for the NHS. Progress was piecemeal, driven by technologically focused individuals rather than in pursuit of a national, coherent IT policy. However, in 1998 the focus finally shifted and the Department of Health recognised the importance of IT in healthcare. The resulting report, 'Information for health: an information strategy for the modern NHS 1998–2005', paved the way for the digital age, advocating 'lifelong electronic health records for every person in the country' and 'round-the-clock on-line access to patient records and information about best clinical practice, for all NHS clinicians'[1].

The National Programme for IT, launched in June 2002, arose from the 1998 plan and sought to develop a ten-year programme to transform the way the NHS uses, shares and handles information through the procurement, development and implementation of a modern, integrated and national IT system. As the National Audit Office concluded in June 2006:

> 'The Programme's scope, vision and complexity is wider and more extensive than any ongoing or planned healthcare IT programme in the world, and it represents the largest single IT investment in the UK to date. If successful, it will deliver important financial, patient safety and service benefits.'[2]

Central to the National Programme for IT is the creation of the NHS Care Records Service (NCRS), which will create two systems of Electronic Health Records (EHR):

- The Summary Care Record (SCR), which will be held nationally in a central database and will contain a summary of key health information such as details of allergies and current health problems, prescriptions and treatment plans.
- The Detailed Care Record (DCR), which will contain more comprehensive clinical information, including a copy of the GP's record and any notes or records made during any visit or course of treatment in any NHS department or related service. The DCR will be held locally in one of a number of regionalised databases.

NCRS will also include a 'Secondary Uses Service', which will consist of a database of data aggregated from the above systems for management, research and other 'secondary' purposes:

> 'DCR systems, which will allow local organisations to share detailed clinical information, are the "holy grail" for [the National Programme for IT]. Such systems can improve safety and efficiency, support key activities such as prescribing, and vastly increase the effectiveness of clinical communication.'[3]

---

[1] 'Information for health: an information strategy for the modern NHS 1998–2005', Frank Burns, September 1998: http://www.e-osiris.it/data/docs/uk005_info%20strat%201998-2005%20FIL315.pdf, at para 1.3.
[2] The Department of Health, The National Programme for IT in the NHS – National Audit Office Value for Money Report HC 1173 Session 2005–2006 – 16 June 2006, Executive Summary paragraph 4.
[3] The House of Commons Health Committee, The Electronic Patient Record, Sixth Report of Session 2006–7, Volume 1 (25 July 2007) HC-422-I, Summary.

4.66 The migration of paper records to an electronic system and the drive to create a seamless system accessible in any area of the country is consistent with the government's transformational agenda. Although the informational security challenges associated with a move from a paper based system are not confined to the NHS, the nature of the services provided by the organisation, its size and the type of information stored within it do create many peculiarities that exasperate the already complex task.

The information stored within a medical record is a complex mixture of interlinked numerical data (such as heart rate, blood pressure and test results), facts, opinions and observations from a wide range of sources and clinicians, covering numerous disciplines all of which must be retained for a variety of purposes. To separate such information into its constituent parts or to remove it from the contextual background would risk rendering it meaningless:

> 'The temporal and contextual properties of this varied information make health records unlike any other. Information that is hugely important in one context – such as automated blood pressure readings taken in hospital after heart surgery – may be of little significance to a GP during an appointment some weeks later, whereas a single routine reading can be highly significant years later in the event of unexplained heart failure.'[1]

[1] 'What's So Different About Electronic Patient Records?': http://www.bcs.org/server.php?show=ConWebDoc.2972, a report summarising the opinions voiced during a BCS Thought Leadership Debate on electronic medical records held on 16 May 2005 at the Institute of Directors, London.

Electronic records and data security

4.67 The potential benefits of an electronic record system are significant. The ability to store and share health data electronically can increase efficiency, reduce costs and assist doctors in diagnosis and treatment, particularly if a patient requires treatment away from their local NHS service. However, the introduction of EHRs creates a significant challenge to the security and confidentiality of the information contained within such records. The chosen model of storing the SCR centrally, with the functionality to allow the records to be accessed from anywhere in the country, by a wide range of different users, raises many operational concerns. Not only is the likelihood of a breach increased, but the large amount of centralised data increases the number of potential victims. 'In short, it provides both a bigger target and a larger number of points of attack than a series of smaller systems'[1].

Between April and July 2003, in the early stages of development of the National Programme for IT, the NHS Information Authority and the National Programme for IT, which later became Connecting for Health, commissioned research into the public's and patients' views, expectations and concerns in relation to the proposed electronic records system. Although, the overwhelming response was to welcome the changes, the vast majority of respondents expressed some degree of scepticism as to the security of an electronic system, despite acknowledging the vulnerabilities of the existing paper system[2].

4.67 Considerations for the public sector

Security policies and processes, such as smartcard activated and password protected user accounts, role-based access controls and audit systems, have been built into the system to protect the information. However, the size of the NHS, the disparate nature of the departments within it, the number of individuals that may require access to such records and the nature of busy hospital departments makes it difficult to predict, or even evaluate, the effectiveness of such controls. Despite this, BT, the supplier of the SCR system, is bullish about the technical security levels, claiming that it would be 'near impossible' to access the national system without the assistance of a registered user. However, this is precisely where the majority of the risk lies. A breach, if it were to occur, is most likely to be caused by a human element of the system, either through accidental or wilful misuse of the system, as it is the 'human factor which is not subject to system controls'[3].

[1] The UK Computing Research Council in their evidence to the House of Commons Health Committee in their Sixth Report of Session 2006–07 – The Electronic Patient Record HC422-I at paragraph 103.

[2] 'The public view of electronic health records', 7 October 2003, Summary of results – Qualitative research key findings and conclusions: http://www.dh.gov.uk/prod_consum_dh/groups/dh_digitalassets/@dh/@en/documents/digitalasset/dh_4055046.pdf.

[3] The Medical Protection Society in their written evidence to the House of Commons Health Committee in their Sixth Report of Session 2006–07 – The Electronic Patient Record HC422-I at paragraph 105.

4.68 Although the NHS has implemented operational security systems, and has made significant efforts to minimise the risk of operational security breaches in the new electronic system, an effective system also depends on an appropriate enforcement regime. It is therefore unfortunate that despite support from the Department of Health, the House of Commons Heath Committee and the ICO, the Government backed away from bringing into effect the amendment to the Data Protection Act 1998 that will allow for the imposition of custodial sentences for those people who unlawfully access personal information. It would be naïve to think that NHS staff are any less susceptible to corruption than certain members of the police force or staff at the DVLA and despite the Commissioner's best efforts the trade in personal data extracted from these databases continues. The electronic system will create detailed audit trails enabling access to the system to be monitored, but the sheer volume of records created may prohibit effective oversight of the system. 'If ... one has a system where it turns out that there are huge numbers of audit records being generated to the point where nobody is looking at them, that is a ... system that is not being properly designed.'[1]

In fact when questioned in 2003 the public's and patients' fears as to the security of their health information were directed more towards the routine sharing of data with organisations outside the Health Service, such as employers and insurance companies, rather than the illegal trade in personal data. Mr Harry Cayton, in his review of the NCRS, noted that:

> 'there is considerable pressure to obtain access to data on the NHS Care Records Service from other government departments, public services such as the police and immigration services and researchers. Clear ethical values and standard procedures consistently applied are essential if the right uses of the NHS Care Records Service are to be secured and maintained.'[2]

In a system that will create a single record, used and contributed to by numerous individuals, it is difficult to determine who will have ultimate control and ownership of it, with the result that lines of responsibility could become blurred and standards could start to slip. In order to maintain the public's confidence and trust in the electronic system it is essential that the NHS and the Department of Health maintain transparency over all aspects of information governance.

1 Professor Brian Randell, Professor of Computing Science, University of Newcastle, as quoted in the Health Committee's Sixth Report of Session at paragraph 110.
2 'Information governance in the Department of Health and the NHS', Harry Cayton, September 2006, Ref 3349 at para 1.7.

Codes of Practice, Procedures and Reviews – but is it an information policy?

4.69 Minimising the risk factors, whether technological or a human element, associated with an information system is at the heart of the seventh data protection principle. However, in order to reduce the risks created by the human factors of a system to an acceptable level a data controller must also implement an information system that includes effective policies and procedures, programmes of training and education, contractual controls and a means of deterrence. The NHS cannot be accused of failing to implement information governance policies, as there are numerous documents under a variety of titles. Therefore it must be questioned whether such policies, in fact, create a coherent information governance policy with effective data security provisions.

Information Security Management: NHS Code of Practice (ISM Code)

4.70 The ISM Code[1] states that its purpose is to 'identify and address security management in the processing and use of NHS information and is based on current legal requirements, relevant standards and professional best practice ... The Code provides a key component of Information Governance arrangements for the NHS'[2]. The ISM Code provides overarching, high level guidance rather than specific practical rules for ensuring informational security on a day-to-day basis. This identifies the following obligations for the NHS[3]:

- Identify threats to NHS data and to manage such risks through 'robust risk assessment and management arrangements'.
- Devise and implement 'a comprehensive, systematic and reliable programme for NHS information security management'.
- Ensure that the organisation's information systems are encompassed with the business continuity plans.
- Support all information governance arrangements with training and awareness programmes for all staff, audit provisions and reporting structures for both attainment levels and security breaches.

The ISM Code forms just part of the NHS 'Information Security Management Framework', with further detail being provided in the 'Information Governance Toolkit'[4]. The Toolkit forms the basis of the Information Security

4.70 *Considerations for the public sector*

Management System (ISMS), which is intended to measure compliance with the security standards and to contribute to the effectiveness of the information security system. The Toolkit establishes the minimum standards for information security, albeit the ISMS advocates a flexible and scalable approach to information security based on an organisation's specific information requirements and the principles of a Plan-Do-Check-Act model taken from ISO 27002.

The ISM Code also mandates that responsibility for information security is allocated appropriately within NHS organisations. Whilst responsibility ultimately rests with the Chief Executive, it also acknowledges that responsibility will be delegated to managers with operating responsibilities. Although this is unavoidable, it is essential that widely publicised chains of accountability are established and a single member of staff, with appropriate seniority and support at board level, is designated as the information security lead. The ISM Code also states that information security is the responsibility of every member of staff who works for, or under contract to, an NHS organisation and as such the contractual documents should reflect this.

1   Document Number 280361 (April 2007).
2   Document Number 280361 (April 2007) at paragraphs 1 and 3.
3   Document Number 280361 (April 2007) at paragraph 24.
4   https://www.igt.connectingforhealth.nhs.uk/.

Confidentiality – NHS Code of Practice

4.71 A governing principle of the NHS is that patient confidentiality is paramount. The duty of confidentiality, and the Code of Practice[1] which expounds it, is a key component of information governance. The Confidentiality Code of Practice sits alongside the other information policies and works in conjunction with them. The Code of Practice is intended to assist practitioners in making decisions as to when disclosures of patient-identifiable information are permissible and provides practical guidance on ways to ensure a confidential service.

However, there is an inherent tension between the duty of confidentiality and the requirements of the NHS to use a patient's information for purposes over and above direct clinical care, many of which are not immediately apparent to patients. Therefore, a body of law has built up which provides for the sharing of information for broader medical purposes (such as preventative medicine and health service management) where disclosure is in the public interest or is supported by the Health and Social Care Act 2001, s 60.

1   Document Number 33837 (November 2003).

Report on the Review of Patient-Identifiable Information

4.72 In 1997 the Caldicott Committee, chaired by Dame Fiona Caldicott, made a number of recommendations concerning the use and transfer of patient-identifiable information between NHS organisations and to bodies outside the NHS in the 'Report on the Review of Patient-Identifiable Information'. The report was commissioned following growing concerns over the sharing of patient-identifiable information within the NHS and to bodies outside the NHS. Its remit was to ensure that only the minimum necessary amount of patient-identifiable information is disclosed and that the disclosures occur for justified purposes.

The report recognises that the NHS poses particular challenges to the task of anonymising data. In the provision of healthcare and for some of the related services there is no acceptable error rate. Therefore it is difficult to envisage how a single item of information can ever be relied upon to identify an individual. Even the new NHS numbers must be used with a corroborating piece of data (for example a postcode or data of birth). However in these circumstances the Report states that the individual should only be identifiable, as distinguished from being identified. It concludes that 'outside the provision of care it should rarely be necessary for individuals to be identified.'[1] This, the report claims, 'is clearly a desirable goal ... [and] would represent substantial progress. This would remove the risk of immediate recognition of an individual patient by those staff handling the information who did not need to know the patient's identity'[2].

The Committee concluded that:

> 'whilst there was no significant evidence of use of patient-identifiable information, there was a general lack of awareness throughout the NHS at all levels of existing guidance on confidentiality and security, increasing the risk of error or misuse. Problems posed by poor access controls were identified. The Recommendations proposed in this Report are designed to focus attention on procedures and systems where we identified a weakness, and to propose solutions.'[3]

1 Department of Health, The Caldicott Committee, Report on the Review of Patient-Identifiable Information, December 1997 (11934 CA Q 1000 IP Dec 97 (CWP)) (The Caldicott Report) at paragraph 4.6.1.
2 The Caldicott Report at paragraph 4.6.4.
3 The Caldicott Report at paragraph 4.1.4.

4.73 The Report made 16 high level recommendations, which included:

- Every information flow of patient-identifiable information should be regularly reviewed and tested against the following principles, to ensure that such use of patient-identifiable information remains justifiable:
  Principle 1 – The use of confidentiality must be justifiable.
  Principle 2 – Confidential information may only be used when it is absolutely necessary.
  Principle 3 – Only the minimum amount of confidential information should be used.
  Principle 4 – Access to such confidential information should be on a need to know basis.
  Principle 5 – Anyone with access to such confidential information should be fully aware of and understand their responsibilities.
  Principle 6 – Legal obligations must be complied with.

4.73   *Considerations for the public sector*

- Increasing the awareness of existing policies and developing new clearer guidelines to ensure that the requirements of confidentiality and information security are known amongst all levels of NHS staff.
- The introduction of data guardians, which were christened the Caldicott Guardians, to ensure greater levels of accountability over data flows.
- Replacing patient-identifiable information with the NHS number, as soon as possible, where the patient needs to be distinguishable from other individuals but does not need to be identified. Databases used to store information should also be structured so that patient-identifiable information is separated from clinical information.
- Privacy Enhancing Technologies should be used whilst transferring particularly sensitive information to ensure its security.

The Caldicott Guardian Manual 2006

4.74 The Introduction to the Caldicott Guardian Manual[1] states that the 'recommendations of the Caldicott Committee defined the confidentiality agenda for NHS organisations for a number of years'[2]. The role of the Caldicott Guardian was central to the confidentiality and data assurance regimes; 'acting as the "conscience" of an organisation, the Guardian should actively support work to facilitate and enable information sharing and advise on options for lawful and ethical processing of information as required'[3]. The Guardian Manual seeks to provide further guidance as to the nature and scope of the role of a Caldicott Guardian defining the Guardian's responsibilities as:

- Strategy and Governance: the Caldicott Guardian should champion confidentiality issues at Board/management and team level, should sit on an organisation's Information Governance Board/Group and act as both the 'conscience' of the organisation and as an enabler for appropriate information sharing.
- Confidentiality and Data Protection expertise: the Caldicott Guardian should develop a knowledge of confidentiality and data protection matters, drawing upon support staff working within an organisation's Caldicott function but also on external sources of advice and guidance where available.
- Internal Information Processing: the Caldicott Guardian should ensure that confidentiality issues are appropriately reflected in organisational strategies, policies and working procedures for staff. The key areas of work that need to be addressed by the organisation's Caldicott function are detailed in the Information Governance Toolkit.
- Information Sharing: the Caldicott Guardian should oversee all arrangements, protocols and procedures where confidential patient information may be shared with external bodies both within, and outside, the NHS and CSSRs. This includes flows of information to and from partner agencies, sharing through the NHS Care Records Service (NHS CRS) and related IT systems, disclosure to research interests and disclosure to the police.[4]

[1]   Document Number 277311 (October 2006) (Caldicott Guardian Manual).
[2]   The Caldicott Guardian Manual 2006 at paragraph 1.2.

[3] The Caldicott Guardian Manual 2006 at paragraph 3.1.
[4] The Caldicott Guardian Manual 2006, Table 2: Key Caldicott Guardian Responsibilities.

Other policies and advice documents

4.75 The policies, reports and guidance notes listed above are just some of those that fall beneath the banner of information governance in the NHS. Despite the fact that Mr Cayton's review strongly recommended that such policy making should be centralised, the Guidance section of the Caldicott Guardian Manual lists the Department of Health, Connecting for Health, the Patient Advisory Group, the UK Caldicott Guardian Council and the Digital Information and Health Policy Branch as sources of general advice and support. In an organisation the size and scope of the NHS such fragmentation of policy can perhaps be expected, but whether it should be allowed to continue is another question.

INFORMATION GOVERNANCE IN THE DEPARTMENT OF HEALTH AND THE NHS

4.76 Mr Cayton's report, 'Information Governance in the Department of Health and the NHS'[1], was published in 2006, following a review commissioned by the Programme Board of the National Programme for IT following the creation of NCRS. The report's main conclusion was that information governance in the NHS lacked sufficient accountability:

> 'Clearly accountable bodies with clearly defined purposes do not always exist in the present arrangements around information governance. The coherence, clarity and consistency in the way information is governed within and between the various bodies involved in the development, delivery and monitoring of NHS care and services will need to be improved to support an electronic NHS.'[2]

It also concluded that information governance within the NHS was fragmented. Therefore, Mr Clayton's recommendations centre around ensuring that there is a single body responsible for policy and system development, that a line of accountability should be created stretching from the Caldicott Guardians up to the Chief Medical Officer and that a national Information Governance Board, with jurisdiction over all organisations providing services to the NHS and which have permitted access to NHS data, should be created to provide oversight, to develop and interpret best practice, to promote consistency, to arbitrate on the interpretation of policy and give advice and to build public confidence in the NCRS.'[3]

[1] Harry Cayton, September 2006, Ref 3349.
[2] Harry Cayton, September 2006, Ref 3349 at paragraph 1.1.
[3] Harry Cayton, September 2006, Ref 3349 at paragraph 3.4.

The Information Commissioner's position

4.77 Despite all of this work and investment NHS Trusts continue to come under fire for persistent security breaches. Between autumn 2008 and June

4.77 *Considerations for the public sector*

2009 the Information Commissioner took action against 17 NHS bodies for failing to comply with their obligations under the Data Protection Act 1998.

One type of breach that has concerned the Commissioner has been the failure to dispose of personal data securely, after unencrypted computers containing personal and medical details of 2,500 individuals were found beside a skip in the grounds of St Pancras Hospital London and confidential medical records were found in buildings of former hospital sites in Dundee and Carluke. Another area of focus has been the loss or theft of portable devices such as laptops or memory sticks.

Following the theft of two laptops and a desktop computer from hospitals operated by the North West London Hospitals NHS Trust the Commissioner stated that appropriate technical and organisation security measures include ensuring that 'personal details are properly protected by establishing physical safeguards, such as locking an office or ensuring a security swipe card system is working at all times'[1].

Such measures are surely common sense and undoubtedly represent the minimum security requirements rather than best practice. However, the number of thefts in recent months provides evidence that too many NHS bodies are failing to ensure the basic physical security of computers and laptops. In an organisation the size of the NHS, which by its nature has to be open to the public, safeguarding the physical security of its computers and laptops is always going to be a challenge. Although the law, and the Information Commissioner, is mindful of the criminal intent of a minority section of society, the repeated and continued enforcement action against NHS bodies leaves no doubt that in the Commissioner's opinion the NHS is not going far enough.

[1] Information Commissioner's Office Press Release 'ICO issues stark reminder to NHS bodies on patient records' dated 30 April 2009: http://www.ico.gov.uk/upload/documents/pressreleases/2009/nhs_trusts_undertakings_280409.pdf.

4.78 The Information Commissioner's Office has attributed the recent breaches to a 'Cavalier attitude' to personal data amongst NHS staff. However, it is worth questioning whether such a statement is in fact justified. It cannot be denied that many of the breaches have been caused by embarrassingly foolish lapses of security, but a cavalier attitude implies some degree of recklessness, which is a hefty charge to lay at the foot of NHS staff. In the busy environments of the NHS bodies it is not surprising to find that the staff's focus is on the treatment of patients, at the expense of data protection. It is noticeable that BT, in its evidence to the House of Commons Health Committee, stated that 'the nature of the environment in the NHS would make ensuring operational security difficult, for example because NHS buildings are freely accessible to the public and IT security is unlikely to be closely monitored in busy hospital departments'.[1]

Thus, as the House of Commons Health Committee's Sixth Report of Session 2006–7 explicitly acknowledged, there is an inevitable trade off between the security of an information system and its usability. However, it is vital for the security system to strike the right balance between the two otherwise users will simply find ways to work-around the measures.

An example of such behaviour was seen when staff in the A&E department of an acute trust in Warwickshire were authorised to share smartcards when accessing the trust's newly installed Patient Administrative System: '[T]here have been some graphic examples where perhaps security precautions have been circumvented by people logging on for a whole shift, using one card rather than their own cards. That must be stamped out; there cannot be any of that'[2]. Unfortunately this would seem to support the Commissioner's assertions that attitudes to security are cavalier. Until adequate training programmes are implemented and the security measures are improved so that they are not an obstacle to the treatment of patients, as the Health Committee concluded, 'security breaches are inevitable'[3].

1   BT's evidence to the House of Commons Health Committee in their Sixth Report of Session 2006–07 – The Electronic Patient Record HC422-I, at paragraph 105.
2   Jonathan Bamford, Assistant Information Commissioner's Office, as quoted in the Health Committee's Sixth Report of Session 2006-7, at paragraph 217.
3   Health Committee's Sixth Report of Session 2006–7, at paragraph 243.

The Google alternative

4.79 In July 2009 the Conservative Party revealed a different vision for the management of health records, which will rely upon private sector companies like Google[1]. The vision was not universally welcomed by Conservative MPs[2] however.

In August 2009 the Conservative Party followed-up with the publication of a report titled 'Independent Review of NHS and Social Care IT', which contained a more detailed insight into the alternatives to the government's Connecting for Health programme. Taking the news reports following publication of the report at face value it seemed that the Conservative's plans consisted merely of dismantling Labour's Central NHS IT infrastructure (Stephen O'Brien, Conservative health spokesman) and replacing it with a Google or Microsoft alternative, but, of course, the report covers much more ground than this.

The report's focus on Google and Microsoft is in relation to the alternatives to the government's HealthSpace programme. HealthSpace, which was introduced into the Connecting for Health programme in October 2005, is intended to give patients online access to their 'Summary Care Record', where they can also track basic health information, such as height, weight and blood pressure. It is still only in trial mode, being accessible by fewer than 35,000 patients.

The report does not green light the replacement of HealthSpace by Google Health or Microsoft HealthVault. In fact, the report was rather cold about Google Health. However, it did recognise that these systems could act as

4.79 *Considerations for the public sector*

replacements, provided that they are suitably adapted to fit the environment of the NHS. As far as the report's recommendations are concerned these were as follows:

> 'Further investigation is required into the use and role of personal health databases in the NHS such as HealthSpace, HealthVault, Google Health and any other commercial or NHS-funded solutions that may emerge. These products, if deployed, must prove their readiness for deployment in the NHS before they are considered.'

Assuming that the Conservative's investigations into the Google and Microsoft alternatives continue, what further work will need to be done to make this a reality?

In terms of data security there is no reason to think that Google or Microsoft are more exposed to data security breaches or data loss than the NHS. Indeed, if the Information Commissioner's recent run of enforcement action against the NHS is anything to go by, people might be forgiven for thinking that outsourcing to Google and Microsoft cannot come quickly enough. Thus, data security concerns are not in themselves barriers to the alternative vision.

A key area in which the Conservatives will need to improve performance if they form the next government is in the field of regulation. As has already been explained, since 2007, when the government announced that HM Revenue and Customs had lost the two data disks containing an entire copy of the child benefit database, there has been a considerable investment in improving the regulatory framework for data security in the public sector. This has been accompanied by massive progress in theories for best practice in data handling, as illustrated by the Data Handling Review and the development of HMG Security Policy Framework. Likewise, the work of the CESG has contributed significantly to the improvement of the regulatory framework for the public sector. The same is not the case for the private sector, where Google and Microsoft operate.

The best illustration of this point is found within the Coroners and Justice Bill, which was introduced in the House of Commons in January 2009. Among other things the Bill contains a power for the Information Commissioner to carry out compulsory inspections of government departments. The intention behind this power is to codify a non-statutory right of inspection that was gifted to the Information Commissioner by the Prime Minister immediately after HMRC.

From January 2009 to July 2009 the Information Commissioner and many Parliamentarians (among others) consistently argued the case for a comparable right of inspection for the private sector, but these calls were rejected. However, in July, during the Bill's committee reading in the House of Lords, the government made limited concessions that will allow the Secretary of State to designate categories of private sector data controllers as liable to inspections. This limited extension of the inspection power regime could result in a much-needed improvement to the regulatory framework for data security in the private sector.

Data security in the police service **4.81**

If the Conservatives form the next government they will need to designate controllers like Google and Microsoft for the purposes of the inspection regime. This will be essential if the public are to embrace private sector suppliers like Google and Microsoft within the NHS.

1   'Google or Microsoft could hold NHS patient records say Tories', The Times, 6 July 2009: http://www.timesonline.co.uk/tol/news/politics/article6644919.ece.
2   'David Davis: Google is the last company I would trust with my personal data', The Times, 27 July 2009: http://www.timesonline.co.uk/tol/news/politics/article6728408.ece.

DATA SECURITY IN THE POLICE SERVICE

ACPO/ACPOS Information Systems Community Security Policy

4.80 The ACPO/ACPOS Information Systems Community Security Policy[1] (CSP) sets the national strategy for IA within the police service. Its overall purpose is described as follows:

> '1. Provide appropriate and consistent protection for the information assets of member organisations.
>
> 2. Comply with statutory requirements and meet ACPO/ACPOS expectations of the Police Service to manage information securely.
>
> 3. Help assure Her Majesty's Government that Police Service elements of the Critical National Infrastructure (CNI) are appropriately protected.
>
> 4. Facilitate effective participation with Information Age Government (IAG) strategies.'

Forces are required to implement security policies that meet the requirements of the CSP. Their systems have to be audited on an annual basis and the results have to be supplied to the Police Information Assurance Board (PIAB), an ACPO committee. Forces' security policies that give effect to the requirements of the CSP are freely available[2].

1   http://www.cheshire.police.uk/uploads/acpo_community_security_policy.pdf.
2   See for example Hampshire Constabulary's policy, which is available at: http://www.hampshire.police.uk/NR/rdonlyres/4133EC94-20F1-4B9A-8F47-FB662EFB2E23/0/06100.pdf.

Code of Practice on the Management of Police Information

4.81 The Code of Practice on the Management of Police Information[1] (MOPI) was published by the National Centre for Policing Excellence on behalf of the Home Office in July 2005. The context and purpose of the MOPI are described as follows:

> '1.1 Purpose of the Code
>
> 1.1.1 Police forces have a duty to obtain and use a wide variety of information (including personal information), in order to discharge their responsibilities effectively. They need the support and cooperation of the public in doing so. The purpose of this Code and associated guidance is to assist the police to carry out that duty.

4.81 *Considerations for the public sector*

> 1.1.2 The responsibility for the management and use of information within the police service rests with the chief officer of the police force which owns the information.
>
> 1.1.3 Chief officers of police must therefore ensure that their forces adopt practices for the management of information that ensure such information is used effectively for police purposes and in compliance with the law.
>
> 1.1.4 The purpose of this Code is to ensure that there is broad consistency between forces in the way information is managed within the law, to ensure effective use of available information within and between individual police forces and other agencies, and to provide fair treatment to members of the public.
>
> 1.1.5 This Code sets out the principles governing the management of information (including personal information) which the police service may need to manage and use including:–
> a. procedures to be applied in obtaining and recording that information;
> b. procedures to ensure the accuracy of information managed by the police;
> c. procedures for reviewing the need to retain information and, where it is no longer needed, to destroy it;
> d. procedures governing authorised sharing of information within the police service and with other agencies; and
> e. measures to maintain consistent procedures for the management of information within all police forces so as to facilitate information sharing and the development of service-wide technological support for information management.
>
> 1.1.6 In doing so, it recognises that effective use of information for police purposes requires consistent procedures to be in place throughout the police service.
>
> 1.1.7 The procedures and equipment to give effect to the principles set out in this Code may change. This Code will therefore be supported by more detailed and extensive guidance that will define information management standards required within forces. That guidance may change from time to time, but must be framed in compliance with the principles established by this Code.'

[1] http://police.homeoffice.gov.uk/publications/operational-policing/CodeofPracticeFinal12073.pdf?view=Binary.

Statutory basis of the MOPI

4.82 The statutory basis of the MOPI is the Police Act 1997, ss 39 and 39A and the Police Act 2007, ss 28, 28A and 73. It is the job of HM Inspectors of Constabulary to monitor forces' compliance with the MOPI.

Information Management Strategy

4.83 The MOPI requires Chief Police Officers to 'establish and maintain within their forces an Information Management Strategy, under the direction of an officer of ACPO rank or equivalent, complying with guidance and standards to be issued under this Code unless that guidance is superseded by regulations made by the Secretary of State under section 53A of the Police

Data security in the police service **4.87**

Act 1996'. In order to ensure consistency of approach, the MOPI contemplates the publication of guidance, which 'may specify procedures to be adopted within police forces for the management of police information systems'.

Security

4.84 The MOPI says the following about security:

'3.4.1 Chief officers should ensure that arrangements within their forces for managing police information include procedures and technical measures to prevent unauthorised or accidental access to, amendment of, or loss of police information. Such procedures should comply with guidance issued under this Code unless superseded by regulations made by the Secretary of State under section 53 or section 53A of the Police Act 1996.'

Guidance on the MOPI

4.85 The National Centre for Policing Excellence published 'Guidance on the Management of Police Information'[1] in 2006. Referring to the requirement for an Information Management Strategy the Guidance says that it will set out 'what controls are applied to ensure the integrity and security of police information held by the force' and 'how the force will comply with national and local security policy and standards'. It reminds all staff coming into contact with police data that they have a responsibility to 'apply rules relating to information security'.

[1] http://police.homeoffice.gov.uk/publications/operational-policing/mopi_guidance.pdf?view=Binary.

PROCESSES FOR SHARING OF DATA

4.86 The processes that forces put in place for the sharing of data identify the following question and analysis for data security:

'How is the security of the information being shared ensured?

The [information sharing] agreement can be used to apply a protective marking to the information being shared in line with the GPMS, where applicable. There may also be a need to apply other safeguards to the processing of information that may affect its transit or storage at a partner's site.'

RELEVANCE OF ACPO/ACPOS COMMUNITY SECURITY POLICY

4.87 The CSP is referenced by the Guidance in the context of a discussion of the retention and disposal of police data. It reminds that 'a key point to consider' is that 'information that is to be retained must be managed in accordance with the ACPO/ACPOS (2002) Information Systems Community Security Policy'.

4.88 Considerations for the public sector

EMPLOYEES, CONTRACTORS, ACCESS RIGHTS AND SECURITY POLICIES

4.88 In the context of a discussion about the access and retrieval of records, the following guidance is given on the education of workers:

> 'Police information can only be accessed for authorised policing purposes, and force policy must ensure that only those staff who are vetted accordingly and who have a legitimate need to know are permitted to access protectively marked information.
>
> All employees, including contract staff, are personally responsible for ensuring that they have access to and fully understand and comply with all relevant force security policies and operating procedures. It is the supervisor's duty to ensure that all users of information systems are aware of these policies and procedures and adhere to them.'

SECURE DISPOSAL OF DATA

4.89 The section on the disposal of data also refers to the CSP and the Manual of Protective Security:

> 'The method of disposal for records of police information will depend on whether they carry a protective marking. The Cabinet Office (n.d.) Government Manual of Protective Security and the ACPO/ACPOS (2002) Information Systems Community Security Policy specify requirements for the handling and disposal of classified material. All forces must develop and implement a policy for disposing of records in accordance with these schemes.'

The Manual of Protective Security has been superseded by HMG Security Policy Framework.

NATIONAL POLICING IMPROVEMENT AGENCY

4.90 The National Policing Improvement Agency (NPIA)[1] is an executive agency of the Home Office, which is the successor organisation to the National Centre for Policing Excellence and the Police Information Technology Organisation. The NPIA has many roles, which are described in its 'Plan of Action', which is available on its website. These include responsibility for the building of the replacement for the Police National Computer, which is part of the 'IMPACT' programme. The NPIA's functions give it responsibility for data security in many fundamental areas of modern policing.

[1] http://www.npia.police.uk/.

MISUSE OF POLICE SYSTEMS AND DATA

4.91 Data security law has been shaped by a series of cases involving the misuse of the Police National Computer and other police systems. Prominent cases include *DPP v Bignell*[1] and *R v Rooney*[2].

[1] [1998] 1 Cr App Rep 1, 161 JP 541.
[2] [2006] EWCA Crim 1841.

DATA PROTECTION AT THE MINISTRY OF DEFENCE

4.92 In the febrile atmosphere following HMRC it was guaranteed that other stories of government data loss would hit the headlines. On 21 January 2008, only two months after HMRC, the government announced to the House of Commons that an unencrypted 'TAFMIS' MOD laptop containing records on approximately 600,000 Royal Navy recruits or potential recruits had been stolen from a Royal Navy recruiter's car. As with HMRC the government's reaction was swift and on 5 February 2008 the 'Burton Review Team' was assembled by the MOD, with the following terms of reference:

> 'To establish the exact circumstances and events that led to the loss by MOD of personal data; to examine the adequacy of the steps taken to prevent any recurrence, and of MOD policy, practice and management arrangements in respect of the protection of personal data more generally; to make recommendations; and to report to MOD's permanent secretary not later than 30 April 2008.'

The Review Team was headed by Sir Edmund Burton. Its report was delivered on 30 April 2008. The Burton Report's recommendations (51 in total) are a model of clarity that can work in the private sector as well as the public sector. They reinforce the messages delivered by the other reports discussed in this chapter, including the fact that information should be treated as an important asset. In purely military and defence terms, the importance of information is well understood; in crude terms information can sometimes mean the difference between life and death for members of the armed services. The Burton Report re-establishes in the mind of the reader the link between data security, data handling and serious real world consequences; it is these real world consequences, whether they be in the theatre of war or in civilian life, which are at the heart of the current cycle of development of the law.

Report into the Loss of MOD Personal Data, April 2008

4.93 The Burton Report[1] provides a very helpful overview of the cycle of development of data protection law at the MOD since 2001. For example, it reports that in 2001 Data Protection Officers were introduced at the MOD, including within the divisions of the army responsible for recruitment and other human resources issues. It also provides insight into the introduction of the SIRO role, the development of the National IA Strategy and the British Defence Doctrine. The Doctrine, which includes thinking on 'Network Enabled Capabilities' says that 'exploitation of information and its protection are, therefore, fundamental to the business of the Ministry of Defence, the Armed Forces and their commercial partners'.

[1] 'Report into the Loss of MOD Personal Data', Sir Edmund Burton, 30 April 2009: http://www.mod.uk/nr/rdonlyres/3e756d20-e762-4fc1-bab0-08c68fdc2383/0/burton_review_rpt20080430.pdf.

Transformational Government

4.94 The Report explains that part of the context to data security in the MOD is the Transformational Government agenda, which places emphasis on data sharing and the engagement of contractors from the private sector:

4.94 *Considerations for the public sector*

'One of the themes emerging from the Strategy for Transformational Government (2005) was the increased emphasis on sharing services, particularly in information and infrastructure. The Armed Forces have been early pioneers of this approach, through a range of Private Finance Initiative (PFI) and Public Private Partnership (PPP) contracts. In the operational arena, decades of experience of operations in coalitions and with allies, and in international collaborative programmes, have provided experience of the risks and benefits of sharing sensitive information.'

The Report then goes on to explain:

'The Strategy for Transformational Government acknowledged that "the Government's ambition for technology enabled change is challenging, but achievable, provided it is accompanied by a step-change in the professionalism with which it is delivered. This requires: coherent joined up leadership and governance; portfolio management of the technology programmes; development of IT professionalism and skills; strengthening of the controls and support to ensure reliable project delivery; improvements in supplier management; and a systematic focus on innovation." '

The Report gives the clear impression that the Transformational Government agenda has added to the information handling burden, which has been compounded by the introduction of the Freedom of Information Act 2000:

'34. Since 2000, Data Protection procedures within the Department have also struggled to keep up with the pace of these Government-driven changes and perceived priorities. It is understood that the Department's principal focus following the 1998 Data Protection Act concerned facilitating access requests. The proper management and security of data received less attention. For instance, the requirement of the Act to provide "adequate protection" was open to differing interpretations in the design of complex ICT systems. Additionally, the focus on the introduction of the Freedom of Information Act in 2005 exacerbated the tendency to focus on responses to information requests, rather than the proper management of information.'

The loss of the TAFMIS laptop

4.95 The theft of the laptop occurred on 9 January 2008. Ministers were informed that the laptop was unencrypted on 11 January. Five days later all TAFMIS laptops were recalled from the field. On 21 January the government announced both the loss and the appointment of the Burton Review Team. On the same day the MOD appointed a Head of Data Protection and Information Assurance and the Cabinet Office made a high level direction halting the movement of unencrypted laptops and other portable storage media.

The Executive Summary to the Report explains that the stolen laptop was part of a fleet of TAFMIS laptops that numbered 51 in total. Four of these laptops had been stolen from vehicles in the period since 2004 despite security instructions prohibiting their storage in unattended vehicles. However, there was no rule requiring their encryption:

'The stolen laptop, designated TAFMIS-R(H)SQL, was one of a small population of, currently, 512 laptops, which hold a large database incorporating over 600,000 personal records. Investigations revealed that a total of 4 of these

Data protection at the Ministry of Defence **4.96**

laptops have been stolen since 2004 (all from parked cars). Only the recent theft appears to have led to disciplinary proceedings. Although the security instructions for the safekeeping of laptops were clear in prohibiting them from being left in unattended vehicles, they did not dictate that the data must be encrypted.'

Unfortunately, there was no evidence that the use of these substantial databases had taken account of the data protection issues:

'8. However, there is no evidence to confirm that the data protection aspects arising from the RN/RAF requirement for a substantial database, available for use on a laptop, had been formally addressed, either by the service sponsors, or by the contractor.

9. It is likely that the Department was in breach of several principles set out in the Data Protection Act, as soon as the large TAFMIS recruit database was implemented and then made available on unencrypted laptops. However, the principles are not precise: they require judgment. The Department will, therefore, need to seek guidance on the exercise of that judgement from the Information Commissioner.

10. The evidence indicates that the overall management of the TAFMIS project lacked rigour. Consequently, it has proved impossible to trace records of requirements, approvals, decisions and actions at key stages. Both parties (ARTD and the prime contractor, Electronic Data Systems (EDS)) will wish to take appropriate action.'

Statistics about encryption

4.96 The Report reveals that the encryption problem at the MOD was acute, with a large number of the fleet being unprotected. However, there was a plan to tackle this:

'38. It will be useful here to give some overall statistics, which will set the context in which MOD handling of personal data and releasable media can be considered.

a. MOD holds some 60 million personal records in total (this includes duplicated records).

b. MOD owns an estimated 35,000 laptops, of which some 13,000 currently have full-disk encryption capability and 10,000 have a partial-disk encryption capability. The remaining 12,000 are unencrypted. It should be noted that MOD is currently in the process of ensuring that all but 2,000 of the entire laptop fleet will be equipped with full-disk encryption. (These remaining 2,000 laptops will be taken out of service).

c. Lost or stolen MOD-owned laptops numbered 130 in 2007. Out of a total laptop population of 35,000, this represents a loss rate of approximately 0.4%. A comparable figure for industry and the wider population is an annual loss/theft rate of between 1–2%.

d. 58 USBs/PDAs that contained MOD data have been recorded as lost or stolen in 2008 so far, set against figures of 78 in 2006, and 22 in 2007. However, there are no firm statistics on total MOD holdings of PDAs, USBs and other mobile data storage devices: the loss/theft rate cannot, therefore, be determined with accuracy.'

4.97 *Considerations for the public sector*

The TAFMIS system – rules for encryption broken

4.97 TAFMIS stands for 'Training Administration and Financial Management Information System'. The Report explains its context, purpose and background as follows:

> '2. The TAFMIS provides ICT support for the Army Recruiting and Training Division (ARTD) and for Training Development Teams within the Arms and Services Directorates. The system also supports the Adventurous Training Group in Germany, Regimental Headquarters and Royal Marines. It has also been extended to support recruiting functions of the Royal Navy and the Royal Air Force.
>
> 3. TAFMIS is deployed at some 300 locations throughout the UK mainland, Northern Ireland and at a few sites in Germany. There is a total population of 9967 terminals and 562 laptops supporting different versions of TAFMIS.
>
> 4. Recruiter laptops, which include R and R(H) variants, represent 418 of this fleet. TAFMIS-R devices are deployed in support of Army Recruiting and are allocated between Officer and Soldier recruiting. Officer recruiting involves a long timescale and therefore the system tends to contain more information about candidates. However, officer recruitment involves fewer people (c15,000 soldier records per year, c1,500 officer records). For both Officer and Soldier systems, users only download a small subset of information onto mobile devices at any time. Corps and Regimental HQs can also access officer recruiting data.
>
> 5. RN/RAF TAFMIS-R(H) laptops (also known as TRH) account for 138 of these. Some are used solely for Office Automation (OA) and have not had personal data records downloaded from the TRH database. 51 are used primarily for RN and RAF recruiting and have had SQL database installed: this database stores a complete copy of the main TRH database. There are also 300 PDAs, which can access, retrieve and, potentially, store TAFMIS data.'

4.98 The Report goes on to give a detailed chronological account of relevant issues within the development and use of the TAFMIS system. This reveals that in January 2003 it was ordered that all TAFMIS laptops should be encrypted:

> 'MOD issued directive Defence Council Instruction (DCI) General 23/03, all new laptops to be encrypted from April 2003. In-service laptops to be encrypted by January 2006.'

However, in April 2004 a decision was taken to allow the use of new laptops without encryption:

> 'Adjutant General Information Management Security Officer (AGIS SO2 Info Man Sy) confirms that ATRA could issue new laptops unencrypted, as long as encryption is installed before January 2006.'

In April 2006 the encryption programme suffered another setback, when the deadline for encryption of older laptops was extended by three years:

> 'JSP 440 extends encryption deadline to 1 January 2009 for laptops purchased before April 2003.'

This pattern of behaviour gives a flavour of the problem with the encryption programme for TAFMIS; deadlines were further extended; it was concluded that the programme was completed when it was not and the contractors from the private sector who where responsible for the encryption stopped reporting in. Along the way there were four thefts of TAFMIS laptops (in August 2004, December 2005, July 2006 and October 2006), three of which were thefts from vehicles. The laptop that was stolen in January 2008 was purchased in December 2002, meaning that it was in service in its unencrypted state for five full years. The Report said that 'the governance of the TAFMIS programme, which involves a major prime contractor and users from all three services, was unclear'. It delivered the following conclusion:

> 'From the original laptop encryption compliance date 1 January 2006 to 1 April 2006, the unencrypted TAFMIS laptops were in breach of MOD laptop encryption policy. This deadline was formally extended in April 2006 by JSP 440 Issue 3.5 to achieve laptop encryption by 1 January 2009.'

The effect of JSP 440 Issue 3.5 was to bind the Burton Review Team to the conclusion that the absence of encryption did not constitute a breach of any rules for encryption. However, the fact that the laptop was left in an unattended vehicle did constitute a clear breach of security:

> 'At the time the laptop was stolen on the night of 9/10 January 2008, although the user was in clear breach of physical security rules, it did not break any security rules relating to laptop encryption. However, there were two definite periods (from Jan 06 to Apr 06 and Sep 06 to Jul 07) when TAFMIS-R(H) laptops were being used in breach of MOD laptop encryption security policy. Indeed, the RN laptop stolen in October 2006, which contained the same dataset as that lost in January 2008, was in breach of the extant policy.'

Data protection – the failure to encrypt

4.99 The Report reveals that the stolen laptop might have contained somewhere in the region of 1,000,000 personnel records:

> 'The laptop stolen from Edgbaston in January 2008 was a TAFMIS-R(H) laptop using SQL, which contained the whole RN/RAF database, holding some 600,000 personal data records. Although the laptop held records relating to some 600,000 recruits or potential recruits, investigations by MOD DG Info staff, in conjunction with EDS, has indicated that the database includes personal details of some 400,000 additional individuals, who were either referees or parents of the recruits. Technically, therefore, the laptop held some 1,000,000 personal records. The reason for the large number of records is due to the original user requirement and design drawn up between RN, RAF and AFPAA. The TAFMIS-R(H) design synchronises the whole database from the main server to the laptop.'

However, despite the scale of data processing involved, the team responsible for TAFMIS did not appreciate the implications for data protection law and their obligations regarding the encryption of personal data:

> 'MOD issued instructions on Data Protection responsibilities in February 2001 and updated lists of MOD Data Protection Officers in July 2001 and periodically thereafter. However, the legal position of the TAFMIS-R(H) database does

4.99   *Considerations for the public sector*

not appear to have been questioned. There is no evidence that any of the key stakeholders (EDS, AFPAA, ATRA, ARTD, RN or RAF) raised concerns that the TAFMIS-R(H) design would breach data protection principles.'

For the purpose of data protection the Report identified two key areas for improvement. First, the MOD's rules for records retention need to be reviewed 'to remove potential ambiguities and ensure clarity where variations exist'. Second, improvements to the contracting process between the MOD and its suppliers need to be made, to detail 'responsibilities with reference to MOD's DPA record retention policy for personal data types'.

Data protection and management of data generally

4.100   The second part of the report takes a wider perspective than the first. Among other things it examines the wider context of technological change, the decline in security that accompanies increased data sharing between different organisations, the obligation to report security incidents, the need for regular audits, the need for regular data cleansing, the need to conduct risk-benefit analyses in respect of information held, the value of information as an asset within the British Defence Doctrine, the need to undertake privacy awareness training, the assessment of risk within OGC Gateway Reviews, the need to obtain the Information Commissioner's guidance on the status of the TAFMIS database, the need for data protection and privacy awareness training, the adoption of clear procedures for data sharing and the use of contracts, the need to reinforce the role of SIROs, the implementation of PET and the use of personal equipment on MOD business.

The recommendations

4.101   The Report made 51 recommendations, which provide a model for improvement for any organisation, whether or not it is part of the public sector:

'ANNEX A – SUMMARY OF RECOMMENDATIONS

1. PROCESSES

Recommendation 1: RN to undertake a review of their recruiter process and, in particular, the need to use mobile devices holding a complete copy of the recruiter database.

Recommendation 3: Supervising officers to be rigorous in enforcement of security instructions.

Recommendation 4: It has not been possible to locate evidence that would support formal disciplinary action. However, it is recommended that the senior leadership in ARTD and in EDS should review the project management processes and procedures, taking appropriate remedial action.

Recommendation 5: MOD to review DPA retention policy to remove potential ambiguities and ensure clarity where variations exist.

Data protection at the Ministry of Defence 4.101

Recommendation 6: Where MOD or an MOD contractor provides data management services, there should be an agreement between the relevant parties detailing responsibilities with reference to MOD's DPA record retention policy for personal data types.

Recommendation 7: Contractor to be tasked to cleanse TAFMIS data base as a matter of urgency.

Recommendation 8: MOD to show greater rigour in ensuring that system security procedures are enforced.

Recommendation 10: That all MOD organisations and business units report thefts and losses of removable media in strict accordance with JSP541.

Recommendation 11: MOD to review and adapt established staff procedures and processes, taking account of the opportunities and vulnerabilities implicit in new ICT.

Recommendation 12: MOD to carry out a full audit of its total personal data holdings, based on the work already completed as part of compliance with the Cabinet Office review.

Recommendation 13: MOD to introduce policy and procedures for both data cleansing and data governance, in order to ensure that boards understand the nature and scale of their data holdings and instigate appropriate audit and compliance measures.

Recommendation 14: MOD to carry out a risk-benefit analysis on the requirement to hold large amounts of personal data to meet Centre tasking.

Recommendation 15: That MOD identifies and facilitates the sharing of good practices.

Recommendation 16: A doctrine for Information Exploitation and Protection to be developed in order to set out the principles by which the UK's defence forces will deliver the Information capability underpinning British Defence Doctrine.

Recommendation 17: A coherent, Joint Service and Civil Service, awareness campaign to be launched to highlight the importance of information and data as a key operational and business asset, with appropriate attention devoted to exploitation and protection, within the law.

Recommendation 18: Information Risk to be addressed as a standing risk item on all Executive Boards and Audit Committees.

Recommendation 19: Mandated assurance processes analogous to those for Health and Safety to be introduced for Information Risk.

Recommendation 20: Information Risk to be formally assessed in Capability Reviews and in Office of Government Commerce (OGC) Gateway Reviews.

Recommendation 22: MOD to ensure that the governance processes for legacy programmes, and project approval and acceptance into service, take account both of the legal requirements of the Data Protection Act and of security accreditation.

Recommendation 25: That the Department supports initiatives making personal data accessible through secure links to central servers, on the basis that clear guidelines are in place for onward storage of this data, and the system itself is both secure and has adequate redundancy.

4.101 *Considerations for the public sector*

Recommendation 26: MOD to produce clear policy on sharing personal data with third parties, including changes to standard contractual clauses as required.

Recommendation 27: To instigate a full census of non-laptop removable media device holdings, in order to ensure that they are formally approved and accounted for on a routine basis.

Recommendation 28: MOD to implement guidelines on the storage of personal data on these devices, including the requirement for encryption, as necessary.

Recommendation 29: MOD to reiterate, or revise, Departmental guidance on the use of private mobile media devices to process MOD data.

Recommendation 32: MOD and TLBs to consider formalising a network of TLB CIOs and SIROs to provide coherent advice on the exploitation, security and assurance of information as a critical business asset.

Recommendation 33: MOD to determine the level of risk it is prepared to bear in the area of accreditation, and resource the accreditors accordingly.

Recommendation 34: MOD to appoint a professional head of accreditation with MOD.

Recommendation 39: Clear, brief guidance (ideally a 10 page limit) to be produced that is designed with the end user in mind. User feedback to inform future iterations.

Recommendation 40: Authoritative policy documents like JSP 440 to remain; but with "break-out" documents on e.g. the latest technological developments accompanying them.

Recommendation 45: Urgent arrangements to be made to ensure awareness across the Department of risks and mitigation procedures. Consideration to be given to adopting the RN "road show" approach.

Recommendation 51: Decisions on resourcing this initiative to be taken at Defence Board Level.

2. PEOPLE

Recommendation 2: MOD to ensure that all employees and contractors understand what key information and documents must be maintained as records, and to highlight consequences of failing to do so.

Recommendation 9: MOD to ensure that individual and corporate responsibilities under DPA 1998 are understood and complied with.

Recommendation 23: Detailed accountabilities for Data Protection across the Department to be clearly articulated.

Recommendation 30: MOD to define the full scope of responsibilities for the Departmental Chief Information Officer functions.

Recommendation 31: MOD to reinforce the authority of the MOD SIRO to act on behalf of the Defence Operating Board in respect of information risk.

Recommendation 38: MOD to review and formalise a coherent system of censure and punishment for those who lose or compromise personal data, where the level of punishment reflects the scale and seriousness of the loss; seeking to apply this equitably, regardless of whether the individual responsible is military or civilian, government employee or contractor.

Data protection at the Ministry of Defence 4.101

Recommendation 41: MOD to implement the principle of storing and handling only the minimum amount of personal data required to carry out core business.

Recommendation 42: MOD to implement a challenge process, both in terms of deciding whether personal data should be kept in the first place, and then on whether it should be accessed and downloaded on to removable media devices.

Recommendation 46: Arrangements to be made for senior leaders and managers to receive a comprehensive briefing on the current threat picture and for formal updates at appropriate intervals.

Recommendation 47: The current threat picture to be clearly and briefly set out to other relevant MOD staff, as a matter of urgency, with formal updates at appropriate intervals.

Recommendation 48: Security Doctrine and Operational Security work to be at the heart of the campaign for raising awareness of the importance of information and data to the Department and the significance of protection measures.

3. TRAINING AND EDUCATION

Recommendation 24: MOD to improve awareness and uptake of current Data Protection Act training.

Recommendation 35: Accreditors to receive appropriate training to enable them to address data protection issues.

Recommendation 37: System users to be made to prove, in quantifiable terms, their ability to handle personal data, prior to being given access to the relevant systems.

Recommendation 49: MOD to review all the current training on Data Protection and Information Management, and identify the uptake by the relevant post-holders, in order to determine future training needs.

Recommendation 50: Full use to be made of the Joint Training and Education institutions, such as the Defence Academy and proposed Defence Security School, in providing education and training in the effective exploitation and protection of information and data, including obligations under DPA 1998.

4. TECHNOLOGY

Recommendation 36: MOD to consider adopting appropriate technological solutions to achieve compliance with data protection regulations.

Recommendation 43: Urgent consideration to be given to procuring a simple, affordable solution to enable the safe, authorised, use of personal (privately owned) computers for limited Government tasks, on an individually licensed basis.

Recommendation 44: Urgent consideration to be given to offering free, safe, disposal of personal data devices.

5. OTHER

Recommendation 21: MOD to seek guidance from the Information Commissioner on the status of the TAFMIS database(s) as regards the Data Protection Act.'

4.102 *Considerations for the public sector*

Not everything is bad at the MOD

4.102 Despite the many failings discovered by The Burton Review Team it is important to acknowledge the fact that it also discovered important evidence of some good practices. In the section titled 'what does MOD do well' the following analysis is provided:

'WHAT DOES MOD DO WELL?

5. There are several areas in which the Department has already introduced good procedures, both before and after 9 January 2008.

a. MOD has been, consistently, one of the most proactive Departments in engaging with the cross-Government SIRO network. DSSO audits have revealed an upward trend in MOD data security over the past 5 years.

b. The Department has benefited from an experienced and authoritative SIRO, whose advice and support has been used by the Cabinet Office extensively since the launch of the initial National Information Assurance Strategy in 2003. His expertise has been applied to the evolution of the DII programme, which will replace a range of legacy systems across the Department.

c. Following the loss of HMRC data in November 2007, MOD anticipated the need to address any similar departmental risks and put in place work to address it. This has since dovetailed into the Department's response to the Cabinet Office review. The TAFMIS issues were not picked up on the first round of data collection in support of the Cabinet Office review. This was mainly because LAND would not have identified TAFMIS as a system with specific security concerns as, as far as they were concerned, it was fully accredited and compliant with policy. Moreover, the search was focussed at the time on areas of risk such as bulk data transfer. Whilst holding bulk data on a laptop resulted in the same risks as data transfer mechanism it was actually a feature of the design and again, was not declared.

d. Following the 9 January 2008 incident, the MOD HQ imposed a series of emergency measures. All laptops without full-disk encryption (for example, through the CESG-approved BeCrypt product) were recalled to secure MOD sites, and a large order was placed through the DG Info for commercial licences to install BeCrypt on as many laptops as possible. From the information gained in this review, it appears that all the departmental TLBs have fully complied with these directives. This prompt and effective response, and the efficiency of TLBs in implementing it, is to be commended. However, several stakeholders pointed out that this measure degraded their business capability significantly.

e. The VCDS is developing an action plan, which will produce a revised conceptual basis for security, an assessment of modern security vulnerabilities, and a Training Needs Analysis to help fill the security awareness gap. See paragraph 41 below for more details.

f. Data Protection. There are elements of good data protection practice within the Department. PJHQ provides data protection policy guidance, which enshrines the principle of only holding the minimum amount of data necessary. It also provides a checklist for data handling drawn from the eight principles of data protection within the DPA 1998. MOD HQ has recently moved to create a dedicated lead for compliance with information security and data protection enforcement (distinct from the predominantly Data Protection policy role of the MOD's Data Protection Officer). The 2008/9 editions of the Service Delivery

Agreements between MOD HQ and the Departmental TLBs will include an expanded section on data handling responsibilities.

g. Personnel Agencies. It was noted that those parts of MOD for which handling of large volumes of personal data is core business (for instance, SPVA and the Defence Vetting Agency (DVA)) have good security, data protection and information risk management procedures. These constitute good practice.

h. RN. HQ FLEET is implementing a roadshow to their sites on Data Protection, along similar lines to roadshows on raising Drug and Alcohol risk awareness.

i. HQ Land Forces. Other areas have also been proactive. HQ Land Forces have recently appointed a Chief Information Officer at Brigadier level, to ensure that "all Land Forces personnel using electronic data systems are briefed in succinct and clear terms on their responsibilities for Data Protection, and understand them". The Adjutant General has tasked the Army Inspectorate with auditing whether the Land Forces plans for better information risk management and data protection are carried through (similar to the function it performs for other issues e.g. implementation of the Blake reports).

j. RAF. The RAF has withdrawn laptops from users whose business no longer justifies the accompanying risk.

...

6. Maintenance of Momentum. The recent data losses have galvanised the Department and its constituent commands and business entities into action. The key now is to ensure that this activity is coherent and engages leaders and users at all levels.'

MOD Action Plan

4.103 In June 2008 the MOD published 'MOD Action Plan in Response to Burton Report'[1]. This contains a table setting out all 51 recommendations, the MOD's comments thereon and the tasks that had been allocated across 10 workstreams.

[1] http://www.mod.uk/NR/rdonlyres/F0437ECE-F5E6–4246-B4A8–8E63B789C915/0/burton _action_plan20080625.pdf.

Burton and the Information Commissioner

4.104 On 14 July 2008 the Information Commissioner served an enforcement notice on the Secretary of State for Defence[1], which relied on the findings within the Burton Report. The notice ordered as follows:

'The data controller, the Secretary of State for Defence, shall:

(1) Use his best endeavours to give effect to the Recommendations still to be implemented in Annex A of the Burton Report by 31st March 2009 in accordance with the data controller's Action Plan in response to the Burton Report (the "Action Plan"), and

4.104 *Considerations for the public sector*

(2) Provide the Commissioner with a copy of the 3 monthly progress report received by the Defence Operating Board who have oversight of the programme to implement the Recommendations in the Burton Report in accordance with the Action Plan.'

1   http://www.ico.gov.uk/upload/documents/library/data_protection/notices/mod_en_final.pdf.

Chapter 5

OFFICIAL SECRETS, REGULATORY AND PROFESSIONAL SECRECY

5.1 The need to retain secrecy in information has been enshrined within many statutes, which add detail to the law of confidence and, by extension, to data security law. In the public sector the most famous examples of legislation are the Official Secrets Acts. Some of the issues addressed by the Official Secrets Acts, for example spying, are relevant to the discussions within the National Security Strategy and the National Risk Register.

Distinct secrecy obligations are also imposed by statute on public authorities and on regulators. Furthermore, professional regulators invariably impose secrecy obligations on members of the professions. Some aspects of these laws are discussed in this chapter.

OFFICIAL SECRETS

5.2 The Official Secrets Acts (the OSA) are a series of legislative measures designed to protect official information. The Acts are renowned for dealing with spying and leaks of information by government officials, but they are generally relevant to data security, in the sense that they address key threats to systems and data. For example, the legislation was used against Richard Jackson[1], showing how the law can extend to ordinary acts of negligence by civil servants.

The OSA 1989 replaces OSA 1911, s 2. The remainder of the OSA 1911 (which itself was amended by the OSA 1920) is still in force.

[1] 'Whitehall official fined £2,500 for leaving secret al-Qaida files on train', The Guardian, 28 October 2008: http://www.guardian.co.uk/uk/2008/oct/28/terrorism-security-secret-documents1.

Official Secrets Act 1911

5.3 OSA 1911, s 1 contains the offence against spying. It protects sensitive buildings and spaces and information that can be directly or indirectly

5.3 Official secrets, regulatory and professional secrecy

relevant to the enemies of the State. The word 'enemy' does not mean necessarily someone with whom the country is at war, but also potential enemies.

Reading s 1 in the context of the National Security Strategy and National Risk Register, it is clear that the OSA 1911 still has an important role to play within data security law; the threats described in these reports certainly encompass the activities described in s 1. Section 1 says:

'Penalties for spying
(1) If any person for any purpose prejudicial to the safety or interests of the State—
 (a) approaches, inspects, passes over or is in the neighbourhood of, or enters any prohibited place within the meaning of this Act; or
 (b) makes any sketch, plan, model, or note which is calculated to be or might be or is intended to be directly or indirectly useful to an enemy; or
 (c) obtains, collects, records, or publishes, or communicates to any other person any secret official code word, or pass word, or any sketch, plan, model, article, or note, or other document or information which is calculated to be or might be or is intended to be directly or indirectly useful to an enemy;
 he shall be guilty of an offence.
(2) On a prosecution under this section, it shall not be necessary to show that the accused person was guilty of any particular act tending to show a purpose prejudicial to the safety or interests of the State, and, notwithstanding that no such act is proved against him, he may be convicted if, from the circumstances of the case, or his conduct, or his known character as proved, it appears that his purpose was a purpose prejudicial to the safety or interests of the State; and if any sketch, plan, model, article, note, document, or information relating to or used in any prohibited place within the meaning of this Act, or anything in such a place or any secret official code word or pass word, is made, obtained, collected, recorded, published, or communicated by any person other than a person acting under lawful authority, it shall be deemed to have been made, obtained, collected, recorded, published or communicated for a purpose prejudicial to the safety or interests of the State unless the contrary is proved.'

Official Secrets Act 1920

5.4 OSA 1920, s 1 prohibits making or using false documentation to gain entry to a prohibited place, or for any purpose prejudicial to State interests. It also prohibits any person from either retaining any official document for any purpose prejudicial to the safety or interests of the State, or passing on official information to another person without lawful authority. The offences in this Act are very specialised and for current purposes the key point to be borne in mind is that they address known threats to the security of systems and data. It is also worth noting that none of the Official Secrets Acts make the commission of offences conditional upon the offender overcoming security measures; this is also the approach of the Computer Misuse Act 1990.

Official Secrets Act 1989

5.5 OSA 1989, which came into force on 1 March 1990, was introduced to replace OSA 1911, s 2, which had been widely criticised for being unworkable.

Section 2 made it an offence for any civil servant having information in their possession by virtue of a contractual or employment relationship with the government to communicate it without authorisation to anyone else. This was subject to an exception for the public interest. One of the principal criticisms was that s 2 was too broadly drawn to be effective, capturing all government information and all civil servants.

Clive Ponting case, 1985

5.6 The Clive Ponting case[1] signalled the beginning of the end of OSA 1911, s 2. Ponting, a former assistant secretary at the Ministry of Defence (MOD), was acquitted by a jury of breaching s 2. He had been charged with leaking an MOD document relating to the Argentine cruiser, the General Belgrano, which the British Navy sank during the 1982 Falklands War, killing 360 people. The document indicated that, contrary to government claims, the Belgrano was sailing out of and away from the exclusion zone when it was attacked by British forces. The prosecution and defence both accepted that the person to whom Ponting leaked the document (an MP) was not authorised to receive it; the main issue was whether the MP was a person to whom it was Ponting's duty in the interest of the State to pass such information. Ponting argued that it was in the interests of the State for the information to be disclosed. He also argued that the government was using the legislation to avoid public embarrassment. The judge indicated that the jury should convict Ponting, but it acquitted him.

OSA 1989 takes a much narrower approach to protection than OSA 1920; it specifies categories of official information that are protected from disclosure, whereas OSA 1920 extended its reach to any information and to all civil servants. Thus, there is no longer a blanket ban on the disclosure of any information entrusted to government.

[1] [1985] Crim LR 318.

Information etc relating to national security and intelligence

COMPLETE BAN ON UNAUTHORISED DISCLOSURES BY THE SECURITY AND INTELLIGENCE SERVICES

5.7 OSA 1989, s 1(1) makes it an offence for a present or former member of the security and intelligence services (SIS), or someone who has been notified[1] that they are subject to the provisions of s 1(1), to disclose without lawful authority[2] any information, document or other article relating to security or

5.7 *Official secrets, regulatory and professional secrecy*

intelligence that is or has been in their possession by virtue of their position as a member of the SIS, or in the course of their work while the notification is or was in force.

Section 1(2) continues by saying that the offence includes 'making a statement which purports to be a disclosure of such information or is intended to be taken by those to whom it is addressed as being such a disclosure'. This covers any unauthorised disclosure and there is no need to prove that the disclosure was damaging. The reasoning for this was explained by Mr Justice Hooper in *R v Shayler*[3] where he stated that 'even the publication of untrue information is capable of causing damage' and 'the resultant loss of confidence in the Service on the part of the current and potential future agents would be just as real, because they would have no way of knowing that the allegation was in fact untrue'.

The offence 'focuses on the status of the individual who makes the disclosure, rather than on the nature of the information itself', as was explained in *Attorney General v Blake*[4]. Lord Nicholls said that 'it is of paramount importance that members of the service should have complete confidence in all their dealings with each other ... and that undermining the willingness of prospective informers to co-operate with the services, or undermining the morale and trust between members of the services when engaged on secret and dangerous operations, would jeopardise the effectiveness of the service'. Therefore an absolute ban on the unauthorised disclosure of any information by members of the SIS 'makes good sense'.

[1] See OSA 1989, s 1(6), which explains that notification shall be effected by a notice in writing served by a Minister or the Crown. A notice can only be served if the recipient's work is connected with the security and intelligence services. Section 1(7) states that a notice shall remain in force for five years, which can be extended. Section 1(8) is concerned with the revocation of notices.
[2] See OSA 1989, s 7, for the circumstances in which disclosures will be lawful.
[3] [2002] UKHL 11, [2003] 1 AC 247, [2002] 2 All ER 477.
[4] [2001] 1 AC 268.

HAS THERE BEEN A DISCLOSURE?

5.8 'Disclosure' is defined in OSA 1989, s 13(1) and includes 'parting with possession' of a document or article. This covers incidents where protected information ends up in the wrong hands, whether intentionally or not.

BANNING DAMAGING DISCLOSURES BY GOVERNMENT WORKERS AND CONTRACTORS

5.9 OSA 1989, s 1(3) also makes it an offence for a person who is or has been a Crown servant or government contractor to make a damaging disclosure without lawful authority. This covers unauthorised disclosures of any information, documents or other articles relating to security or intelligence which are or have been in their possession by virtue of their position or a notification as mentioned in s 1(1).

Official secrets **5.10**

Whether a disclosure is 'damaging' and therefore unlawful is relevant to all offences under the OSA 1989 except for s 1(1) and s 4. The definition of 'damaging' varies depending on the offence in question. In s 1(3), a disclosure is damaging if it either:

- Causes damage to the work of, or any part of, the security and intelligence services.
- Or is of information (or a document or other article) the nature of which is such that its unauthorised disclosure would be likely to cause such damage, or it falls within a class or description of information etc the unauthorised disclosure of which would be likely to have that effect.

Reference to a 'class or description' of information indicates that the security classifications given to documents may be relevant in deciding whether disclosure of that information would be likely to be damaging.

It is a defence to prove that at the time of the alleged offence the person charged did not know and had no reasonable cause to believe that the information etc in question related to security or intelligence or, in the case of an offence by a Crown servant or government contractor, that the disclosure would be damaging. Of course, the public interest can render a damaging disclosure lawful.

THE SHAYLER CASE

5.10 The Shayler case[1] was a landmark case that addressed the absence of a public interest defence within OSA 1989, s 1(1) and s 4 (which covers information obtained by interception) and whether its absence is compatible with article 10 of the European Convention on Human Rights (ECHR), which guarantees free speech.

Mr Shayler, a former member of the SIS, disclosed documents and other information to a national newspaper, which included information about the identities of British agents involved in a plot to assassinate Colonel Gadafy of Libya. Shayler argued that his disclosures were in the public interest. A preparatory hearing held that no public interest defence applied and that this was compatible with article 10. Shayler appealed unsuccessfully to the Court of Appeal and to the House of Lords. The Lords held that it was plain that in giving the sections their natural and ordinary meaning a defendant is not entitled to be acquitted 'if he showed that it was or that he believed that it was in the public or national interest to make the disclosure in question'. Lord Bingham confirmed that 'the sections leave no room for doubt'.

As regards article 10, the Lords reminded that a restriction on freedom of expression can only be lawful if it is prescribed by law, directed to one or more of the objectives specified in article 10(2) and is shown by the State to be necessary in a democratic society. Although Shayler's right to freedom of expression was restricted, it was held that the restriction for the purposes of maintaining secrecy of intelligence information satisfied these requirements. It was also pointed out that the ban on disclosure of security and intelligence

5.10 *Official secrets, regulatory and professional secrecy*

information by a former member of the SIS is not a complete one; they can make disclosures to the staff counsellor, the Attorney General, the DPP, the Commissioner of the Metropolitan Police and the Prime Minister and other ministers under OSA 1989, s 7(3)(a) and if effective action is not taken, they are entitled to seek authorisation to make a wider disclosure. If such a request for authorisation is refused they can then seek judicial review of that decision.

Shayler also ran a duress defence[2]. It was held that this did not apply. However in 2004 Katharine Gun, a GCHQ employee, was charged under OSA 1989, s 1, for her disclosure of the United States' request for the UK to spy on 'swing-states' in the United Nations during the run up to the Iraq war. Her defence was that she acted out of necessity, to prevent a war without a lawfully obtained UN resolution. The prosecution stated that although there was 'a clear prima facie breach of section 1 of the Official Secrets Act 1989' they could not pursue the case because they could not disprove her defence of necessity[3].

[1] *R v Shayler* [2002] UKHL 11, [2003] 1 AC 247, [2002] 2 All ER 477.
[2] See the Court of Appeal's analysis, *R v Shayler* [2001] EWCA Crim 1977, [2001] 1 WLR 2206.
[3] 'Statement on Katherine Gun', CPS Press Release 108/04, 26 February 2004: http://www.cps.gov.uk/news/press_releases/108_04/.

Information etc relating to the country's defence

5.11 OSA 1989, s 2 relates to defence information. A person who is or has been a Crown servant or government contractor is guilty of an offence if without lawful authority they make a damaging disclosure of any information, document or other article relating to defence which is or has been in their possession by virtue of their position. A disclosure is damaging if it:

- Damages the capability of the armed forces to carry out their tasks, or if it leads to loss of life or injury to service personnel, or serious damage to equipment or installations.
- Or endangers the national interests abroad, or it seriously obstructs the promotion or protection of those interests, or it endangers the safety of British citizens abroad.
- Or is of information etc the nature of which is such that its unauthorised disclosure would be likely to have any of those effects.

It is a defence for a person charged with an offence under this section to prove that at the time it was committed they did not know and had no reasonable cause to believe that the information etc related to defence, or that its disclosure would be damaging within the meaning of s 2.

In s 2(4) 'defence' means:

(a) the size, shape, organisation, logistics, order of battle, deployment, operations, state of readiness and training of the armed forces of the Crown;

(b) the weapons, stores or other equipment of those forces and the invention, development, production and operation of such equipment and research relating to it;
(c) defence policy and strategy and military planning and intelligence;
(d) plans and measures for the maintenance of essential supplies and services that are or would be needed in time of war.

Information etc relating to international relations

5.12 Under OSA 1989, s 3, a person who is or has been a Crown servant or government contractor is guilty of an offence if without lawful authority they make a damaging disclosure of (a) any information etc relating to international relations[1] or (b) any confidential information etc that was obtained from another State or international organisation, if that information is or has been in their possession by virtue of their position as a Crown servant or government contractor[2].

A disclosure is damaging if it (a) endangers the national interests abroad, or seriously obstructs the promotion or protection by the United Kingdom of those interests, or (b) it endangers the safety of British citizens abroad, or (c) it would be likely to have any of these effects.

The Pasquill case[3] considered the effect of s 3. Mr Pasquill was charged with disclosing confidential documents to a journalist that related to the government's attitude to 'extraordinary rendition' and the government's contact with extremist Islamic groups. The charges were dropped when evidence emerged at the last minute showing that senior Foreign Office civil servants disagreed over whether the disclosures were damaging to national security. The prosecutor told the court that 'the decision has been reached as a result of material provided by the Foreign and Commonwealth Office ... in the prosecution's assessment this evidence is capable of undermining evidence about the relevant damage caused'.

It is a defence for a person charged with an offence under s 3 to prove that at the time of the alleged offence they did not know, and had no reasonable cause to believe, that the information etc was such as is mentioned in subsections (1) or (2), or that its disclosure would be damaging.

[1] See OSA 1989, s 3(1).
[2] See OSA 1989, s 3(2).
[3] 'Official cleared in secrets case', BBC, 9 January 2008: http://news.bbc.co.uk/1/hi/uk/7178785.stm.

Information etc relating to crime

5.13 OSA 1989, s 4 makes it an offence for a Crown servant or government contractor to unlawfully disclose any information etc which is, or has been, in their possession by virtue of their position, the disclosure of which:

- Results in the commission of an offence.

5.13 *Official secrets, regulatory and professional secrecy*

- Facilitates an escape from legal custody or the doing of any other act prejudicial to the safekeeping of persons in legal custody.
- Impedes the prevention or detection of offences or the apprehension or prosecution of suspected offenders.
- Would be likely to have any of these effects.

SPECIAL INVESTIGATION POWERS UNDER STATUTORY WARRANT

5.14 OSA 1989, s 4 also applies to any information obtained pursuant to, or related to, the exercise of an interception warrant issued under the Regulation of Investigatory Powers Act 2000, s 5, or a warrant issued under the Security Service Act 1989, s 3, or one issued under the Intelligence Services Act 1994, s 5, or by an authorisation given under the Intelligence Services Act 1994, s 7.

As with offences under OSA 1989, s 1(1), a disclosure under s 4 does not have to be 'damaging'.

It is a defence for a person charged with an offence under s 4 to prove that they did not know, and had no reasonable cause to believe, that the disclosure would have any of the effects mentioned. It is also a defence to prove that at the time of the alleged offence they did not know, and had no reasonable cause to believe, that the information etc was one to which s 4 applies.

Information entrusted in confidence to other States or international organisations

5.15 OSA 1989, s 6(1) applies where any information relating to security, intelligence, defence or international relations that has been communicated in confidence by or on behalf of the UK to another State or international organisation, has come into a person's possession as a result of having been disclosed (whether to him or another) without the authority of the receiving State or organisation.

For the purposes of this section, 'security or intelligence', 'defence' and 'international relations' have the same meaning as in OSA 1989, ss 1, 2 and 3. Information etc is 'communicated in confidence' if it is communicated on terms requiring it to be held in confidence, or in circumstances in which the person communicating it could reasonably expect that it would be held in confidence[1].

It is an offence for the person in possession of the information etc to make a damaging disclosure of it, if they know, or have reasonable cause to believe, that it falls under the category of information to which s 6 applies, that it has come into their possession without authority and that its disclosure would be damaging[2].

Official secrets **5.16**

The question whether a disclosure is damaging shall be determined as it would be in relation to a disclosure of the information etc by a Crown servant in contravention of OSA 1989, ss 1, 2 and 3.

A person does not commit an offence if the information etc is disclosed by them with lawful authority, or if it has previously been made available to the public with the authority of the State or organisation concerned or, in the case of an organisation, of a member of it.

1   OSA 1989, s 6(5).
2   OSA 1989, s 6(2).

Information resulting from unauthorised disclosures or information entrusted in confidence

5.16 OSA 1989, s 5 applies to any information, document or article protected against disclosure under ss 1 to 4 that has come into the possession of any person as a result of having been:

(i)   Disclosed (whether to them or another) by a Crown servant or government contractor without lawful authority.
(ii) Entrusted to them by a Crown servant or government contractor on terms requiring it to be held in confidence or in circumstances in which the Crown servant or government contractor could reasonably expect that it would be so held.
(iii) Disclosed (whether to them or another) without lawful authority by a person to whom it was entrusted as mentioned in sub-paragraph (ii) above.

It is an offence for the person into whose possession the information etc has come to disclose it without lawful authority knowing, or while having reasonable cause to believe that it is protected against disclosure.

This section applies where a Crown servant or government contractor passes information to someone else without lawful authority. It does not matter whether the recipient received the information directly from that person or from a third party, creating a potentially endless line of people who could fall within the remit of the section.

The offence is qualified by s 5(3) which provides that the disclosure by the person in possession:

(a)   must be damaging (as defined in ss 1 to 4 respectively); and
(b)   made with the knowledge, or the reasonable belief that it would be damaging.

The question whether a disclosure is damaging shall be determined as it would be in relation to offences under ss 1, 2, or 3.

5.17 Official secrets, regulatory and professional secrecy

Returning and safeguarding of information

5.17 OSA 1989, s 8 is concerned with the return and safeguarding of information. It is broadly drawn, applying to situations where a person refuses to return official information, or where such information is disclosed unintentionally, through recklessness or negligence, as a result of a failure to take care of it. In other words s 8 covers security breaches. Section 8 provides:

'(1) Where a Crown servant or government contractor, by virtue of his position as such, has in his possession or under his control any document or other article which it would be an offence under any of the foregoing provisions of this Act for him to disclose without lawful authority he is guilty of an offence if—
    (a) being a Crown servant, he retains the document or article contrary to his official duty; or
    (b) being a government contractor, he fails to comply with an official direction for the return or disposal of the document or article,
or if he fails to take such care to prevent the unauthorised disclosure of the document or article as a person in his position may reasonably be expected to take.

(2) It is a defence for a Crown servant charged with an offence under subsection (1)(a) above to prove that at the time of the alleged offence he believed that he was acting in accordance with his official duty and had no reasonable cause to believe otherwise.

(3) In subsections (1) and (2) above references to a Crown servant include any person, not being a Crown servant or government contractor, in whose case a notification for the purposes of section 1(1) above is in force.

(4) Where a person has in his possession or under his control any document or other article which it would be an offence under section 5 above for him to disclose without lawful authority, he is guilty of an offence if—
    (a) he fails to comply with an official direction for its return or disposal; or
    (b) where he obtained it from a Crown servant or government contractor on terms requiring it to be held in confidence or in circumstances in which that servant or contractor could reasonably expect that it would be so held, he fails to take such care to prevent its unauthorised disclosure as a person in his position may reasonably be expected to take.

(5) Where a person has in his possession or under his control any document or other article which it would be an offence under section 6 above for him to disclose without lawful authority, he is guilty of an offence if he fails to comply with an official direction for its return or disposal.

(6) A person is guilty of an offence if he discloses any official information, document or other article which can be used for the purpose of obtaining access to any information, document or other article protected against disclosure by the foregoing provisions of this Act and the circumstances in which it is disclosed are such that it would be reasonable to expect that it might be used for that purpose without authority.

(7) For the purposes of subsection (6) above a person discloses information or a document or article which is official if—
    (a) he has or has had it in his possession by virtue of his position as a Crown servant or government contractor; or

(b) he knows or has reasonable cause to believe that a Crown servant or government contractor has or has had it in his possession by virtue of his position as such.
(8) Subsection (5) of section 5 above applies for the purposes of subsection (6) above as it applies for the purposes of that section.
(9) In this section "official direction" means a direction duly given by a Crown servant or government contractor or by or on behalf of a prescribed body or a body of a prescribed class.'

EXAMPLES OF OTHER PUBLIC SECTOR LAWS FOR SECRECY

5.18 As has been commented upon many times already, the State and its manifestations process more types and volumes of information than any other data controller, or any other sector. Consequently, the law has particularised specific obligations for confidentiality that are intended to prevent public sector workers from making unauthorised disclosures. These prohibitions protect a much wider range of data than the Official Secrets Acts.

Commissioners for Revenue and Customs Act 2005

5.19 A good example is contained in the Commissioners for Revenue and Customs Act 2005 (CRCA 2005), which imposes obligations of confidence on Revenue and Customs officers, prohibiting them from making unlawful disclosures of information received by HMRC in the performance of its duties. CRCA 2005, s 18 provides:

'**18. Confidentiality**
(1) Revenue and Customs officials may not disclose information which is held by the Revenue and Customs in connection with a function of the Revenue and Customs.
(2) But subsection (1) does not apply to a disclosure—
   (a) which—
      (i) is made for the purposes of a function of the Revenue and Customs, and
      (ii) does not contravene any restriction imposed by the Commissioners,
   (b) which is made in accordance with section 20 or 21,
   (c) which is made for the purposes of civil proceedings (whether or not within the United Kingdom) relating to a matter in respect of which the Revenue and Customs have functions,
   (d) which is made for the purposes of a criminal investigation or criminal proceedings (whether or not within the United Kingdom) relating to a matter in respect of which the Revenue and Customs have functions,
   (e) which is made in pursuance of an order of a court,
   (f) which is made to Her Majesty's Inspectors of Constabulary, the Scottish inspectors or the Northern Ireland inspectors for the purpose of an inspection by virtue of section 27,
   (g) which is made to the Independent Police Complaints Commission, or a person acting on its behalf, for the purpose of the exercise of a function by virtue of section 28, or

5.19 *Official secrets, regulatory and professional secrecy*

(h) which is made with the consent of each person to whom the information relates.
(3) Subsection (1) is subject to any other enactment permitting disclosure.
...'

CRCA 2005, s 19 contains the offence of wrongful disclosure, which provides as follows:

'**19. Wrongful disclosure**
(1) A person commits an offence if he contravenes section 18(1) or 20(9) by disclosing revenue and customs information relating to a person whose identity—
(a) is specified in the disclosure, or
(b) can be deduced from it.
(2) In subsection (1) "revenue and customs information relating to a person" means information about, acquired as a result of, or held in connection with the exercise of a function of the Revenue and Customs (within the meaning given by section 18(4)(c)) in respect of the person; but it does not include information about internal administrative arrangements of Her Majesty's Revenue and Customs (whether relating to Commissioners, officers or others).
(3) It is a defence for a person charged with an offence under this section of disclosing information to prove that he reasonably believed—
(a) that the disclosure was lawful, or
(b) that the information had already and lawfully been made available to the public.
...'

These provisions are actively enforced and there have been prosecutions for wrongful disclosure[1].

[1] http://www.ipcc.gov.uk/news/pr150908_hmrc.htm; http://www.ipcc.gov.uk/news/pr210808_hmrc_employee_pleads_guilty.htm.

Identity Cards Act 2006

5.20 The Identity Cards Act 2006 contains an important confidentiality provision at s 27, which operates in much the same way as the comparable scheme within CRCA 2005, s 18. The section, which is not yet in force[1], provides:

'**27 Unauthorised disclosure of information**
(1) A person is guilty of an offence if, without lawful authority–
(a) he provides any person with information that he is required to keep confidential; or
(b) he otherwise makes a disclosure of any such information.
(2) For the purposes of this section a person is required to keep information confidential if it is information that is or has become available to him by reason of his holding an office or employment the duties of which relate, in whole or in part, to–
(a) the establishment or maintenance of the Register;
(b) the issue, manufacture, modification, cancellation or surrender of ID cards; or
(c) the carrying out of the Commissioner's functions.

(3) For the purposes of this section information is provided or otherwise disclosed with lawful authority if, and only if the provision or other disclosure of the information–
   (a) is authorised by or under this Act or another enactment;
   (b) is in pursuance of an order or direction of a court or of a tribunal established by or under any enactment;
   (c) is in pursuance of a Community obligation; or
   (d) is for the purposes of the performance of the duties of an office or employment of the sort mentioned in subsection (2).
(4) It is a defence for a person charged with an offence under this section to show that, at the time of the alleged offence, he believed, on reasonable grounds, that he had lawful authority to provide the information or to make the other disclosure in question.
(5) A person guilty of an offence under this section shall be liable, on conviction on indictment, to imprisonment for a term not exceeding two years or to a fine, or to both.'

[1] See the Identity Cards Act 2006, s 44 for the rules on commencement.

PROFESSIONAL SECRECY LAWS FOR REGULATORS

5.21 Statutory regulators, such as the Information Commissioner and the Financial Services Authority, receive significant volumes of confidential information during the performance of their duties. Naturally, there are limitations on the use that can be made of this information.

Data Protection Act 1998

5.22 Data Protection Act 1998, s 59 imposes confidentiality obligations on the Information Commissioner and members of the Information Commissioner's Office, which is underpinned by an offence of unlawful disclosure:

'59.— **Confidentiality of information.**
(1) No person who is or has been the Commissioner, a member of the Commissioner's staff or an agent of the Commissioner shall disclose any information which—
   (a) has been obtained by, or furnished to, the Commissioner under or for the purposes of the information Acts,
   (b) relates to an identified or identifiable individual or business, and
   (c) is not at the time of the disclosure, and has not previously been, available to the public from other sources,
   unless the disclosure is made with lawful authority.
(2) For the purposes of subsection (1) a disclosure of information is made with lawful authority only if, and to the extent that—
   (a) the disclosure is made with the consent of the individual or of the person for the time being carrying on the business,
   (b) the information was provided for the purpose of its being made available to the public (in whatever manner) under any provision of the information Acts,
   (c) the disclosure is made for the purposes of, and is necessary for, the discharge of—
      (i) any functions under the information Acts, or
      (ii) any Community obligation,

5.22 Official secrets, regulatory and professional secrecy

    (d)   the disclosure is made for the purposes of any proceedings, whether criminal or civil and whether arising under, or by virtue of, the information Acts or otherwise, or

    (e)   having regard to the rights and freedoms or legitimate interests of any person, the disclosure is necessary in the public interest.

(3)   Any person who knowingly or recklessly discloses information in contravention of subsection (1) is guilty of an offence.'

Financial services

5.23 The FSA Handbook, SUP 2.2.4, imposes confidentiality obligations on the FSA:

'When the FSA obtains confidential information using the methods of information gathering described in SUP 2.3 or SUP 2.4, it is obliged under Part XXIII of the Act (Public Record, Disclosure of Information and Co-operation) to treat that information as confidential. The FSA will not disclose confidential information without lawful authority, for example if an exception applies under the Financial Services and Markets Act 2000 (Disclosure of Confidential Information) Regulations 2001 (SI 2001/2188) or with the consent of the person from whom that information was received and (if different) to whom the information relates.'

The rules in SUP are also intended to give effect to various confidentiality provisions within EU directives, some of which are discussed below.

Payment Services Directive

5.24 Article 22 of the Payment Services Directive[1] again imposes confidentiality provisions on the national regulators for financial services:

'Article 22

Professional secrecy

1. Member States shall ensure that all persons working or who have worked for the competent authorities, as well as experts acting on behalf of the competent authorities, are bound by the obligation of professional secrecy, without prejudice to cases covered by criminal law.

2. In the exchange of information in accordance with Article 24, professional secrecy shall be strictly applied to ensure the protection of individual and business rights.

3. Member States may apply this Article taking into account, mutatis mutandis, Articles 44 to 52 of Directive 2006/48/EC.'

[1] Directive 2007/64/EC.

Transparency Obligations Directive

5.25 Article 25 of the Transparency Obligations Directive[1] provides:

'Professional secrecy and cooperation between Member States

1. The obligation of professional secrecy shall apply to all persons who work or who have worked for the competent authority and for entities to which competent authorities may have delegated certain tasks. Information covered by professional secrecy may not be disclosed to any other person or authority except by virtue of the laws, regulations or administrative provisions of a Member State.

2. Competent authorities of the Member States shall cooperate with each other, whenever necessary, for the purpose of carrying out their duties and making use of their powers, whether set out in this Directive or in national law adopted pursuant to this Directive. Competent authorities shall render assistance to competent authorities of other Member States.

3. Paragraph 1 shall not prevent the competent authorities from exchanging confidential information. Information thus exchanged shall be covered by the obligation of professional secrecy to which the persons employed or formerly employed by the competent authorities receiving the information are subject.

4. Member States may conclude cooperation agreements providing for the exchange of information with the competent authorities or bodies of third countries enabled by their respective legislation to carry out any of the tasks assigned by this Directive to the competent authorities in accordance with Article 24. Such an exchange of information is subject to guarantees of professional secrecy at least equivalent to those referred to in this Article. Such exchange of information shall be intended for the performance of the supervisory task of the authorities or bodies mentioned. Where the information originates in another Member State, it may not be disclosed without the express agreement of the competent authorities which have disclosed it and, where appropriate, solely for the purposes for which those authorities gave their agreement.'

[1] Directive 2004/109/EC.

Market in Financial Instruments Directive

5.26 Article 54 of the Market in Financial Instruments Directive[1] (the level 1 Directive) provides:

'Professional secrecy

1. Member States shall ensure that competent authorities, all persons who work or who have worked for the competent authorities or entities to whom tasks are delegated pursuant to Article 48(2), as well as auditors and experts instructed by the competent authorities, are bound by the obligation of professional secrecy. No confidential information which they may receive in the course of their duties may be divulged to any person or authority whatsoever, save in summary or aggregate form such that individual investment firms, market operators, regulated markets or any other person cannot be identified, without prejudice to cases covered by criminal law or the other provisions of this Directive.

2. Where an investment firm, market operator or regulated market has been declared bankrupt or is being compulsorily wound up, confidential information which does not concern third parties may be divulged in civil or commercial proceedings if necessary for carrying out the proceeding.

5.26 *Official secrets, regulatory and professional secrecy*

> 3. Without prejudice to cases covered by criminal law, the competent authorities, bodies or natural or legal persons other than competent authorities which receive confidential information pursuant to this Directive may use it only in the performance of their duties and for the exercise of their functions, in the case of the competent authorities, within the scope of this Directive or, in the case of other authorities, bodies or natural or legal persons, for the purpose for which such information was provided to them and/or in the context of administrative or judicial proceedings specifically related to the exercise of those functions. However, where the competent authority or other authority, body or person communicating information consents thereto, the authority receiving the information may use it for other purposes.
>
> 4. Any confidential information received, exchanged or transmitted pursuant to this Directive shall be subject to the conditions of professional secrecy laid down in this Article. Nevertheless, this Article shall not prevent the competent authorities from exchanging or transmitting confidential information in accordance with this Directive and with other Directives applicable to investment firms, credit institutions, pension funds, UCITS, insurance and reinsurance intermediaries, insurance undertakings regulated markets or market operators or otherwise with the consent of the competent authority or other authority or body or natural or legal person that communicated the information.
>
> 5. This Article shall not prevent the competent authorities from exchanging or transmitting in accordance with national law, confidential information that has not been received from a competent authority of another Member State.'

[1] MiFID consists of Directive 2004/39/EC, Directive 2006/73/EC and Commission Regulation (EC) No 1287/2006.

Audit Directive

5.27 Article 36 of the Audit Directive[1] provides:

> '2. The obligation of professional secrecy shall apply to all persons who are employed or who have been employed by competent authorities. Information covered by professional secrecy may not be disclosed to any other person or authority except by virtue of the laws, regulations or administrative procedures of a Member State.
>
> 3. Paragraph 2 shall not prevent competent authorities from exchanging confidential information. Information thus exchanged shall be covered by the obligation of professional secrecy, to which persons employed or formerly employed by competent authorities are subject.'

[1] Directive 2006/43/EC.

Communications Act 2003

5.28 A further illustration is contained in the Communications Act 2003, s 393, which provides[1]:

> '**393. General restrictions on disclosure of information**
> (1) Subject to the following provisions of this section, information with respect to a particular business which has been obtained in exercise of a power conferred by—
> (a) this Act,

Professional secrecy rules for professionals 5.29

...
(c) the 1990 Act, or
(d) the 1996 Act,
is not, so long as that business continues to be carried on, to be disclosed without the consent of the person for the time being carrying on that business.

(2) Subsection (1) does not apply to any disclosure of information which is made—
  (a) for the purpose of facilitating the carrying out by OFCOM of any of their functions;
  (b) for the purpose of facilitating the carrying out by any relevant person of any relevant function;
  (c) for the purpose of facilitating the carrying out by the Comptroller and Auditor General of any of his functions;
  (d) for any of the purposes specified in section 17(2)(a) to (d) of the Anti-terrorism, Crime and Security Act 2001 (c. 24) (criminal proceedings and investigations);
  (e) for the purpose of any civil proceedings brought under or by virtue of this Act or any of the enactments or instruments mentioned in subsection (5); or
  (f) for the purpose of securing compliance with an international obligation of the United Kingdom.

...
(10) A person who discloses information in contravention of this section is guilty of an offence and shall be liable—
  (a) on summary conviction, to a fine not exceeding the statutory maximum;
  (b) on conviction on indictment, to imprisonment for a term not exceeding two years or to a fine, or to both.

...'

[1] See also Communications Act 2003 (Maximum Penalty and Disclosure of Information) Order 2005, SI 2005/3469.

PROFESSIONAL SECRECY RULES FOR PROFESSIONALS

5.29 The professions too are subject to overarching confidentiality provisions. For example, the Solicitors' Code of Conduct, published by the Solicitors Regulation Authority, says:

> '**4.01 Duty of confidentiality**
>
> You and your firm must keep the affairs of clients and former clients confidential except where disclosure is required or permitted by law or by your client (or former client).'[1]

The Barristers' Code of Conduct, published by the Bar Standards Board, says:

> '**Confidentiality**
>
> 702. Whether or not the relation of counsel and client continues a barrister must preserve the confidentiality of the lay client's affairs and must not without the prior consent of the lay client or as permitted by law lend or reveal the contents of the papers in any instructions to or communicate to any third person (other than another barrister, a pupil, in the case of a Registered European Lawyer, the person with whom he is acting in conjunction for the

5.29 *Official secrets, regulatory and professional secrecy*

purposes of paragraph 5(3) of the Registered European Lawyers Rules or any other person who needs to know it for the performance of their duties) information which has been entrusted to him in confidence or use such information to the lay client's detriment or to his own or another client's advantage.'[2]

The General Medical Council's guidance on 'Good Medical Practice' says:

'Confidentiality – paragraph 37

Patients have a right to expect that information about them will be held in confidence by their doctors. You must treat information about patients as confidential, including after a patient has died. If you are considering disclosing confidential information without a patient's consent, you must follow the guidance in *Confidentiality: Protecting and providing information*.'[3]

The Institute of Chartered Accountants of England and Wales' 'Members Handbook' says:

'Section 140 Confidentiality

The Principle of Confidentiality

140.0 The principle of confidentiality is not only to keep information confidential, but also to take all reasonable steps to preserve confidentiality. Whether information is confidential or not will depend on its nature. A safe and proper approach for professional accountants to adopt is to assume that all unpublished information about a client's or employer's affairs, however gained, is confidential. Professional accountants should be aware that some clients or employers may regard the mere fact of their relationship with a professional accountant as being confidential.

140.1 The principle of confidentiality imposes an obligation on professional accountants to refrain from:
(a) Disclosing outside the firm or employing organisation confidential information acquired as a result of professional and business relationships without proper and specific authority or unless there is a legal or professional right or duty to disclose; and
(b) Using confidential information acquired as a result of professional and business relationships to their personal advantage or the advantage of third parties.

Professional accountants in public practice must not disclose confidential information to a client even though the information is relevant to an engagement for, or would be beneficial to, that client.

Where professional accountants in public practice have confidential information which affects an assurance report, or other report which requires a professional accountant to state their opinion, the professional accountant cannot provide an opinion which they already know, from whatever source, to be untrue. If the professional accountant in public practice is to continue the engagement, the professional accountant must resolve this disparity. In order to do so, the professional accountant is entitled to apply normal procedures and to make such enquiries in order to enable the professional accountant to obtain that same information but from another source. Under no circumstances, however, should there be any disclosure of confidential information outside the firm.

140.2 A professional accountant should maintain confidentiality even in a social environment. The professional accountant should be alert to the possibility of inadvertent disclosure, particularly in circumstances involving long association with a business associate or a close or immediate family member.

140.3 A professional accountant should also maintain confidentiality of information disclosed by a prospective client or employer. This requirement extends not only to clients, past and present, but also to third parties from or about whom information has been received in confidence. The principle of confidentiality clearly does not prevent an employee from using the skills acquired while working with a former employer in undertaking a new role with a different organisation. Professional accountants should neither use nor appear to use special knowledge which could only have been acquired with access to confidential information. It is a matter of judgement as to the dividing line which separates experience gained, from special knowledge acquired.

140.4 A professional accountant should also consider the need to maintain confidentiality of information within the firm or employing organisation.

140.5 A professional accountant should take all reasonable steps to ensure that staff under the professional accountant's control and persons from whom advice and assistance is obtained respect the professional accountant's duty of confidentiality. Member firms should ensure that all who work on their behalf are trained in, and understand:
- The importance of confidentiality;
- The importance of identifying any conflicts of interest and confidentiality issues between clients, or between themselves or the firm and a client, in relation to a current or prospective engagement; and
- The procedures the firm has in place for the recognition and consideration of possible conflicts of interest and confidentiality issues.

140.6 The need to comply with the principle of confidentiality continues even after the end of relationships between a professional accountant and a client or employer. When a professional accountant changes employment or acquires a new client, the professional accountant is entitled to use prior experience. The professional accountant should not, however, use or disclose any confidential information either acquired or received as a result of a professional or business relationship.'[4]

The above passage should also be read in light of article 23 of the Audit Directive, which imposes confidentiality obligations on auditors:

'Article 23

Confidentiality and professional secrecy

1. Member States shall ensure that all information and documents to which a statutory auditor or audit firm has access when carrying out a statutory audit are protected by adequate rules on confidentiality and professional secrecy.'

[1] http://www.sra.org.uk/solicitors/code-of-conduct/214.article.
[2] http://www.barstandardsboard.rroom.net/standardsandguidance/codeofconduct/section1codeofconduct/partvii_conductofworkbypractisingbarristers/.
[3] http://www.gmc-uk.org/guidance/good_medical_practice/relationships_with_patients/confidentiality.asp.
[4] http://www.icaew.com/index.cfm/route/162804/icaew_ga/Members/Member_support/Professional_conduct/Members_handbook/3_2_Members_handbook_2009/pdf.

5.30 *Official secrets, regulatory and professional secrecy*

PRESS COMPLAINTS COMMISSION

5.30 The Press Complaints Commission's Code of Practice[1] is also worth considering, due to the focus that has been placed on the press by 'What price privacy?', the Clive Goodman case and the associated 'phone tapping' scandal, which came to light in summer 2009. As well as requiring the press to respect the right to privacy, it also places an obligation on the press to protect the confidentiality of their sources:

> **'14 Confidential sources**
>
> Journalists have a moral obligation to protect confidential sources of information.'

[1] http://www.pcc.org.uk/cop/practice.html.

Chapter 6
REGULATION AND ENFORCEMENT

LAW AS A RELAY RACE – THE CYCLE OF DEVELOPMENT

6.1 If we can imagine the cycle of development of regulatory law to be akin to a relay race, then, of course, the day-to-day actions of the regulators will provide one of the constituent legs. Parliament, or some other legislative body, will fire the starting pistol, through the passing of legislation. The regulators, who are in the blocks at the starting line, will be propelled by their statutory duties to move forward, pushing the development of law[1]. At some point in the development the baton will pass to the legal profession, who will advise regulated persons. Then, if a dispute occurs between the regulator and the regulated, the baton can pass to the courts (or tribunals), which will run the final leg to the finishing line, telling us what the law actually is, which can sometimes be very different to what we imagined it to be[2].

This law-as-relay-race metaphor for the cycle of legal development is particularly apt for data security law, as it is an area of the law that is built upon substantial legislative foundations, is one that is policed by activist regulators and is one where more and more disputes will arise. These dynamics mean that there is considerable momentum within the race to develop the law. The regulators in particular are running their leg at Olympic pace.

As submitted in Chapter 1 the regulators have run their leg of the race so as to create a regulatory bear market for data security. They have done this by taking a highly interventionalist approach, pursuing high-profile 'scalps' and, in the Information Commissioner's case, by highlighting perceived defects in the law, including a need for new powers and penalties. This bear market is epitomised by a loss of confidence, pessimism and negative sentiment.

[1] For example, see the Data Protection Act 1998, s 51, which sets out the general duties of the Information Commissioner. These include promoting the 'following of good practice by data controllers'.

[2] In the context of data security law, an excellent example of the courts arriving at an unexpected decision is provided by *Durant v Financial Services Authority* [2003] EWCA Civ 1746, [2004] FSR 573, a case that required a determination of the meaning of personal data. The Court of Appeal, in a leading judgment given by Auld LJ, unexpectedly introduced two previously unknown concepts into the law, focus and biographical significance, which may operate to greatly curtail the application of the Data Protection Act 1998.

6.2 *Regulation and enforcement*

WHO ARE THE REGULATORS?

6.2 This chapter focuses on the Information Commissioner and, to a lesser extent, the Financial Services Authority, who are the principle regulators for data security, in the sense that they both carry statutory duties to regulate in this area.

If the Commissioner and the Financial Services Authority are the principal regulators, then who are secondary ones? As far as statutory bodies are concerned, there are a number of other public authorities whose remit could extend to data security. It is possible that the OFT and OFCOM may eventually seek to cover more of the consumer interest and the network security interest respectively, but only time will tell.

Other regulators

6.3 Ideas about regulation encompass much more than statutory regulators. There is also a role for professional regulation and self-regulation. The professions, such as law, medicine and accountancy are all subject to forms of regulation that could easily cover data security issues, if they amounted to some form of professional misconduct.

The Press Complaints Commission's code could easily be applied to the activities of rogue journalists[1]. In the private investigations sector a new regulatory framework encompassing statutory licensing of private detectives under the Private Security Industry Act 2001 is already well advanced[2], in large part due to the Information Commissioner's efforts with 'What price privacy?'

[1] See the Press Complaints Commission Code of Practice, which is discussed in Chapter 5.
[2] For further information about the proposed licensing scheme for private investigators, see the Security Industry Authority's website: http://www.the-sia.org.uk/home/licensing/private_investigation/private_investigation.htm.

Self regulation and the contractual control mechanism

6.4 Ideas about self-regulation also encompass the idea that private law arrangements have a significant role to play. This is well illustrated by the Data Protection Act 1998, which requires data controllers to enter into contractual arrangements with data processors that contain and impose control mechanisms. It will also be recalled that the government has mandated the use of a new contractual framework for data security, to cover the supply of services by the private sector.

The contractual control mechanism in the Data Protection Act 1998 is, of course, statute-based, but the private sector has also adopted its own framework for contracting, indicating its popularity as a control mechanism. A good illustration of a widely adopted, non-statutory contractual framework is the Payment Card Industry Data Security Standard (PCI DSS), which is discussed in Chapter 3, in the context of financial services.

Data subjects as regulators

6.5 Data subjects also play a role in regulation, in a healthy self-interested way. They are given a number of important statutory rights that they can enforce directly against data controllers in court, albeit the courts have so far shown a deep reluctance to expand the law on data protection. In the field of data security, notable rights include the right to prevent processing that causes substantial and unwanted damage or distress and the right to compensation for damage caused by a contravention of the seventh data protection principle.

The State's obligation to regulate itself

6.6 Returning to the public sector, last but not least there is the State itself, which carries a huge responsibility to ensure that the law is upheld. In a democracy the State has to carry and deserve the public trust, hence why the public sector statements and reports that are discussed in Chapter 5 are so important within the interpretation and development of data security law.

Shoring up regulation

6.7 Collectively this multi-faceted regulatory framework should be enough to keep data security problems to a bare minimum, but it is clear from the current cycle of development of the law that the true situation is considerably different. In an attempt to shore up the edifice, the law has undergone rapid and radical reform, to improve the ability of the statutory regulators to do their jobs, albeit the government's recent reforms have not yet been brought into effect. This activity has been supported by a massive increase in the output of official guidance and rules for best practice.

GENERAL PRINCIPLES OF REGULATION – REGULATING THE REGULATORS

6.8 The Information Commissioner and the Financial Services Authority certainly deserve many plaudits for their recent approach to data security regulation. They have both raised public awareness of the importance of data security and they have contributed to the reform and development of the law. Of course, an important goal will be to ensure that the regulators exercise their powers both effectively and lawfully.

In recent years there has been an upheaval in the laws governing the regulators themselves. These laws apply to the Information Commissioner and the Financial Services Authority. It is critical for the lawful performance of their regulatory powers and duties that they meet the expectations of these overarching laws. If they fail to do so this can provide data controllers with a platform from which they may be able to challenge regulatory action.

6.9 Regulation and enforcement

Reports on better, more balanced regulation

Hampton Report

6.9 In March 2005 HM Treasury published the Hampton Report[1], which was commissioned by the Chancellor of the Exchequer. Its purpose was to 'consider the scope for reducing administrative burdens by promoting more efficient approaches to regulatory inspection and enforcement, without compromising regulatory standards or outcomes'.

The Report identified a number of failings in the regulatory system. Prominent within these is the failure of regulators to undertake proper risk assessments during the consideration of enforcement action. The Report said that 'this failure to use risk assessment comprehensively and consistently means that resources are not always targeted at the riskiest areas'[2]. Implicit within this observation is the proposition that regulators sometimes get things wrong.

Another key problem is the effectiveness of fines, which often fail to take into account the economic benefits of non-compliance that can sometimes accrue to those in default:

> 'Businesses and regulators have an interest in proper sanctions against illegal activity in order to prevent businesses operating outside the law from gaining a competitive advantage. At present, regulatory penalties do not take the economic value of a breach into consideration and it is quite often in a business's interest to pay the fine rather than comply. This is especially true where a business feels able to shrug off the reputational risk of prosecution. If businesses face no effective deterrent for illegal activity, some will be tempted to break the law, and regulators will need to inspect more businesses.'

This begs the question 'are financial penalties having the desired effect?' Obviously, until the amendments introduced by the Criminal Justice and Immigration Act 2008 are brought into effect the only regulator who is able to fine for data security breaches is the Financial Services Authority. Since the FSA's fine of Capita Financial Administrators in March 2006, the level of fines has been rising quickly, hitting over £3,000,000 in July 2009, when a group of HSBC companies were fined over £3,000,000 for various security problems[3].

£3,000,000 is a considerable sum of money in actual terms, but in relative terms it might not be enough to have an appreciable effect on improving practices for data security in the financial services sector. The great, unspoken 'elephant in the room' is the global banking crisis, which has fundamentally undermined confidence in the ability of regulation to impose control. The banking sector has been proved to be in a very special category of one, with privileges that are obvious to everyone through the process of bank bailouts and recapitalisation of the sector at taxpayers' expense. It is therefore hard to see how fines of this magnitude will encourage others in the sector to get their houses in order. Ultimately, most banks are beyond meaningful financial censure.

An alternative view is that fines have an effect on reputation, which might encourage consumers to vote with their feet. Connected to this is the theory that fines will also result in shareholder censure of the board. Thus, fines at the right level will result in consumers and shareholders applying regulatory control. However, due to the credit crunch consumers are not as free as they once were to move banks, a factor that builds upon the power of ubiquity, market share and customer apathy towards change. Whether shareholders have the ability, or willingness, to effect change remains to be seen.

1   'Reducing administrative burdens: effective inspection and enforcement', Philip Hampton, March 2005: http://www.berr.gov.uk/files/file22988.pdf.
2   The Hampton Report went on to say, at paragraph 2.22 that 'Unless risk assessment is carried through into resource allocations and regulatory practice, it is wasted effort. Risk assessment needs to be comprehensive, and inform all aspects of the regulatory lifecycle from the selection and development of appropriate regulatory and policy instruments through to the regulators work including data collection, inspection and prosecution. Regulators are still a long way from this comprehensive approach, though some are closer than others'.
3   'HSBC firms fined over £3m for information security failings': http://www.fsa.gov.uk/pages/Library/Communication/PR/2009/099.shtml.

Hampton's recommendations and principles of regulation

6.10 The Report made a series of key recommendations for the improvement of regulatory functions and identified a series of 'principles of regulation', which are to be obeyed by regulators during the performance of their duties. The recommendations were:

- '• entrenching the principle of risk assessment throughout the regulatory system, so that the burden of enforcement falls most on highest-risk businesses, and least on those with the best records of compliance;
- • in particular, ensuring that inspection activity is better focused, reduced where possible but, if necessary, enhanced where there is good cause; at present, not only are unnecessary inspections carried out but necessary inspections are not carried out;
- • making much more use of advice, again applying the principle of risk assessment;
- • substantially reducing the need for form filling – in practice, most businesses' most frequent and direct experience of regulatory enforcement – and other regulatory information requirements; and
- • applying tougher and more consistent penalties where these are deserved.'

The principles of regulation are:

- '• Regulators, and the regulatory system as a whole, should use comprehensive risk assessment to concentrate resources on the areas that need them most;
- • Regulators should be accountable for the efficiency and effectiveness of their activities, while remaining independent in the decisions they take;
- • All regulations should be written so that they are easily understood, easily implemented, and easily enforced, and all interested parties should be consulted when they are being drafted;
- • No inspection should take place without a reason;
- • Businesses should not have to give unnecessary information, nor give the same piece of information twice;

6.10 *Regulation and enforcement*

- The few businesses that persistently break regulations should be identified quickly, and face proportionate and meaningful sanctions;
- Regulators should provide authoritative, accessible advice easily and cheaply;
- When new policies are being developed, explicit consideration should be given to how they can be enforced using existing systems and data to minimise the administrative burden imposed;
- Regulators should be of the right size and scope, and no new regulator should be created where an existing one can do the work; and
- Regulators should recognise that a key element of their activity will be to allow, or even encourage, economic progress and only to intervene when there is a clear case for protection.'

Macrory Report

6.11 In November 2006 the Better Regulation Executive published the Macrory Report[1]. As explained in the foreword, this report was commissioned because 'the Minister wanted to ensure that regulatory sanctions were consistent with and appropriate for a risk based approach to regulation as set out in recommendation eight of the Hampton Review'. Noticeably, the foreword also said that 'a long term goal should be to change the culture of many of these regulators who will need to operate with greater transparency and accountability than is often the case now'.

[1] 'Regulatory Justice: Making Sanctions Effective', Professor Richard B Macrory, November 2006.

Designing sanctioning regimes – getting penalties right

6.12 Macrory observed that the onus is on the regulators to design appropriate sanctioning regimes. When doing so Macrory recommends that regulators should have regard to a series of penalties principles and other characteristics. These provide as follows:

'**Six Penalties Principles**

A sanction should:

1. Aim to change the behaviour of the offender;

2. Aim to eliminate any financial gain or benefit from non-compliance;

3. Be responsive and consider what is appropriate for the particular offender and regulatory issue, which can include punishment and the public stigma that should be associated with a criminal conviction;

4. Be proportionate to the nature of the offence and the harm caused;

5. Aim to restore the harm caused by regulatory non-compliance, where appropriate; and

6. Aim to deter future non-compliance.

General principles of regulation – regulating the regulators 6.14

Seven characteristics

Regulators should:

1. Publish an enforcement policy;

2. Measure outcomes not just outputs;

3. Justify their choice of enforcement actions year on year to stakeholders, Ministers and Parliament;

4. Follow-up enforcement actions where appropriate;

5. Enforce in a transparent manner;

6. Be transparent in the way in which they apply and determine administrative penalties; and

7. Avoid perverse incentives that might influence the choice of sanctioning response.'

Consequences of Hampton and Macrory

6.13 These reviews of regulatory law and practice have led directly to the 2006 and 2008 Acts discussed below. Another consequence is, of course, the exposing of the fallibility of regulators. The information in these reports can provide substantial assistance to data controllers that wish to resist or challenge regulatory action.

Legislative and Regulatory Reform Act 2006

6.14 The 2006 Act is intended to modernise regulation and promote the principles of regulation. For the purposes of modernisation s 1 allows government Ministers to make orders to remove 'any burden, or the overall burdens, resulting directly or indirectly for any person from any legislation'. The burdens to which s 1 is addressed are financial cost, administrative inconvenience, obstacles to efficiency, productivity or profitability and sanctions (criminal or otherwise) that affect the carrying on of any lawful activity[1].

The principles of regulation are set out in s 2(3). These say that 'regulatory activities should be carried out in a way which is transparent, accountable, proportionate and consistent' and 'regulatory activities should be targeted only at cases in which action is needed'.

Section 21 requires regulators to have regard to the regulatory principles, but this is not the only innovation in the Act; s 22 envisages that the Minister will issue a Code of Practice 'in relation to the exercise of regulatory functions' which the regulators must 'have regard to [when] determining any general policy or principles'. This means that the Code will apply to the creation of regulatory policies, but not to the performance of regulatory functions in individual cases. However, because the performance of regulatory functions should be compatible with regulatory policies, which in turn should be

6.14 *Regulation and enforcement*

compatible with the Code, it does follow that data controllers wishing to challenge enforcement action will also want to take account of the Code's provisions.

[1] Legislative and Regulatory Reform Act 2006, s 1(3).

Statutory Code of Practice for Regulators

6.15 On 17 December 2007[1] the government published the Statutory Code of Practice for Regulators. This is known as the 'Regulators' Compliance Code'. The Code came into force on 6 April 2008[2]. The ministerial foreword explains:

> 'The Regulators' Compliance Code is a central part of the Government's better regulation agenda. Its aim is to embed a risk-based, proportionate and targeted approach to regulatory inspection and enforcement among the regulators it applies to.
>
> Our expectation is that as regulators integrate the Code's standards into their regulatory culture and processes, they will become more efficient and effective in their work. They will be able to use their resources in a way that gets the most value out of the effort that they make, whilst delivering significant benefits to low risk and compliant businesses through better-focused inspection activity, increased use of advice for businesses, and lower compliance costs.
>
> ...
>
> I believe that the application of the Code can make a difference on the ground to the regulators, those they regulate, and society in general.'

The Code explicitly builds on one of the key messages within the Hampton Report: the approach to regulation and enforcement needs to improve. The general introduction within Part 1 of the Code goes on to identify its purpose:

> '1.1 Effective and well-targeted regulation is essential in promoting fairness and protection from harm. However, the Government believes that, in achieving these and other legitimate objectives, regulation and its enforcement should be proportionate and flexible enough to allow or even encourage economic progress.
>
> 1.2 This Code supports the Government's better regulation agenda and is based on the recommendations in the Hampton Report. Its purpose is to promote efficient and effective approaches to regulatory inspection and enforcement which improve regulatory outcomes without imposing unnecessary burdens on business, the Third Sector and other regulated entities.
>
> 1.3 The Code stresses the need for regulators to adopt a positive and proactive approach towards ensuring compliance by:
> - helping and encouraging regulated entities to understand and meet regulatory requirements more easily; and
> - responding proportionately to regulatory breaches.
>
> 1.4 The Code supports regulators' responsibility to deliver desirable regulatory outcomes. This includes having effective policies to deal proportionately with criminal behaviour which would have a damaging effect on legitimate businesses and desirable regulatory outcomes. The Code does not relieve regulated entities of their responsibility to comply with their obligations under the law.'

General principles of regulation – regulating the regulators 6.17

The tone of this passage is suggestive of another agenda, namely a desire to 'reign-in' the regulators; reminding regulators that they need to achieve 'desirable regulatory outcomes' makes it clear that some have not. The fact that the Code is used to remind regulators that they need to achieve these outcomes indicates that there are pockets of deep malaise within domestic regulation.

[1] http://www.berr.gov.uk/files/file45019.pdf.
[2] Legislative and Regulatory Reform Code of Practice (Appointed Day) Order 2007, SI 2007/3548.

6.16 Part 1 gives insight into the Code's 'purpose and scope', explaining the Code's key limitation, which is that it does not apply to the performance of regulatory functions in individual cases:

> '2.4 The duties to have regard to the Code under section 22(2) and (3) of the Act do not apply to the exercise by a regulator or its staff of any specified regulatory function in individual cases. This means, for example, that while an inspector or investigator should operate in accordance with a regulator's general policy or guidance on inspections, investigations and enforcement activities, the Code does not apply directly to the work of that inspector or investigator in carrying out any of these activities in individual cases.
>
> 2.5 The duty on a regulator to "have regard to" the Code means that the regulator must take into account the Code's provisions and give them due weight in developing their policies or principles or in setting standards or giving guidance.
>
> 2.6 The regulator is not bound to follow a provision of the Code if they properly conclude that the provision is either not relevant or is outweighed by another relevant consideration. They should ensure that any decision to depart from any provision of the Code is properly reasoned and based on material evidence. Where there are no such relevant considerations, regulators should follow the Code.'

Part 2 contains the 'specific obligations of the Code', which draw upon the Hampton Principles. However, Hampton's ten principles are reduced to seven obligations, under the headings 'economic progress', 'risk assessment', 'advice and guidance', 'inspections and other visits', 'information requirements', 'compliance and enforcement actions' and 'accountability'.

For current purposes it is worth considering the Code's provisions on 'inspections and other visits' and 'compliance and enforcement actions', due to the special place of these issues within the current cycle of development of the law; to recap, the Criminal Justice and Immigration Act 2008 has brought in monetary penalties, whereas the Coroners and Justice Bill contains a framework for inspections.

INSPECTIONS AND OTHER VISITS

6.17 The Code repeats the Hampton Principle, that 'no inspection should take place without a reason'. Key points to note are:

6.17 *Regulation and enforcement*

> '6.1 Regulators should ensure that inspections and other visits, such as compliance or advice visits, to regulated entities only occur in accordance with a risk assessment methodology (see paragraphs 4.2. and 4.3), except where visits are requested by regulated entities, or where a regulator acts on relevant intelligence.
>
> 6.2 Regulators should use only a small element of random inspection in their programme to test their risk methodologies or the effectiveness of their interventions.
>
> 6.3 Regulators should focus their greatest inspection effort on regulated entities where risk assessment shows that both:
> - a compliance breach or breaches would pose a serious risk to a regulatory outcome; and
> - there is high likelihood of non-compliance by regulated entities.
>
> 6.4 Where regulators visit or carry out inspections of regulated entities, they should give positive feedback to the regulated entities to encourage and reinforce good practices. Regulators should also share amongst regulated entities, and with other regulators, information about good practice.
>
> 6.5 Where two or more inspectors, whether from the same or different regulators, undertake planned inspections of the same regulated entity, regulators should have arrangements for collaboration to minimise burdens on the regulated entity, for example, through joint or coordinated inspections and data sharing.'

The inspection regime within the Coroners and Justice Bill[1], which is based around the service of 'assessment notices', may be interpreted to include a power for the Information Commissioner to carry out random inspections, but in general terms the Information Commissioner will be bound to follow risk assessment methodologies, to ensure that effort and resources are focused on the most serious cases. Naturally, controllers that are aggrieved by an inspection may wish to examine the Commissioner's risk assessment methodologies.

[1] See section 156 of the Bill as brought from the Commons, 26 March 2009: http://www.publications.parliament.uk/pa/ld200809/ldbills/033/2009033.pdf.

COMPLIANCE AND ENFORCEMENT ACTIONS

6.18 This part of the Code addresses the Hampton Principle that 'the few businesses that persistently break regulations should be identified quickly and face proportionate and meaningful sanctions':

> '8.1 Regulators should seek to reward those regulated entities that have consistently achieved good levels of compliance through positive incentives, such as lighter inspections and reporting requirements where risk assessment justifies this. Regulators should also take account of the circumstances of small regulated entities, including any difficulties they may have in achieving compliance.
>
> 8.2 When considering formal enforcement action, regulators should, where appropriate, discuss the circumstances with those suspected of a breach and take these into account when deciding on the best approach. This paragraph

General principles of regulation – regulating the regulators **6.19**

does not apply where immediate action is required to prevent or respond to a serious breach or where to do so is likely to defeat the purpose of the proposed enforcement action.

8.3 Regulators should ensure that their sanctions and penalties policies are consistent with the principles set out in the Macrory Review. This means that their sanctions and penalties policies should:
- aim to change the behaviour of the offender;
- aim to eliminate any financial gain or benefit from non-compliance;
- be responsive and consider what is appropriate for the particular offender and regulatory issue, which can include punishment and the public stigma that should be associated with a criminal conviction;
- be proportionate to the nature of the offence and the harm caused;
- aim to restore the harm caused by regulatory non-compliance, where appropriate; and
- aim to deter future non-compliance.

8.4 In accordance with the Macrory characteristics, regulators should also:
- publish an enforcement policy;
- measure outcomes not just outputs;
- justify their choice of enforcement actions year on year to interested parties;
- follow-up enforcement actions where appropriate;
- enforce in a transparent manner;
- be transparent in the way in which they apply and determine penalties; and
- avoid perverse incentives that might influence the choice of sanctioning response.

8.5 Regulators should ensure that clear reasons for any formal enforcement action are given to the person or entity against whom any enforcement action is being taken at the time the action is taken. These reasons should be confirmed in writing at the earliest opportunity. Complaints and relevant appeals procedures for redress should also be explained at the same time.

8.6 Regulators should enable inspectors and enforcement officers to interpret and apply relevant legal requirements and enforcement policies fairly and consistently between like-regulated entities in similar situations. Regulators should also ensure that their own inspectors and enforcement staff interpret and apply their legal requirements and enforcement policies consistently and fairly.'

Clearly, it will be incumbent on the regulators to review their enforcement policies in light of this passage; it may not be safe for them to assume that their pre-existing policies are Code-compliant.

Regulatory Enforcement and Sanctions Act 2008

6.19 One of the main purposes of this Act is to allow for the substitution of criminal prosecutions for regulatory offences with alternative remedies and sanctions, such as the imposition of 'fixed monetary penalties' (s 39), 'stop notices' (s 46) and 'enforcement undertakings' (s 50).

The monetary penalties regime introduced by the Criminal Justice and Immigration Act 2008 (CJIA 2008) should not be confused with the fixed monetary penalties regime described in s 39. The essential difference is that

6.19 *Regulation and enforcement*

the CJIA 2008's monetary penalties regime is intended to be a standalone administrative remedy, whereas fixed monetary penalties under the Regulatory Enforcement and Sanctions Act 2008 are intended to act as an alternative to criminal prosecutions. In other words, fixed monetary penalties can only be imposed under s 39 where the regulator 'is satisfied beyond reasonable doubt that the person has committed the relevant offence'[1]. In distinction monetary penalties under the CJIA 2008 regime are intended to deal with non-criminal contraventions of the Data Protection Act 1998.

The stop notices and enforcement undertakings alternatives to criminal prosecutions are also of interest in this field, because the Information Commissioner identified both as necessary reforms within 'The case for amending the Data Protection Act'. Two consequences flow. First, these powers, if they are to be introduced into the Data Protection Act 1998, will require orders to be made under the Regulatory Enforcement and Sanctions Act 2008. However, as there is still no primary criminal offence of failing to comply with the data protection principles, it is hard to see how these options could be introduced as alternatives to prosecutions, unless they are introduced as alternatives to prosecutions for non-compliance with enforcement notices under the Data Protection Act 1998, s 47. Second, the fact that the Act sets up the possibility of enforcement undertakings as an alternative to prosecutions places question marks over the Information Commissioner's current practice of taking undertakings as an alternative to the issuing of enforcement notices. The legal status of the Commissioner's practice is uncertain, but it would seem fair to conclude that the Commissioner cannot insist on the provision of undertakings and certainly cannot serve an enforcement notice if undertakings are refused. Indeed, the moment the Commissioner elects to offer undertakings is the moment when the enforcement notice procedure may be blocked as an option; in particular the controller might argue that the decision to serve an enforcement notice was not found on the nature of the alleged breach but, rather, on its refusal to give undertakings. An offer of undertakings signifies that the matter is not serious enough to justify an enforcement notice.

[1] Regulatory Enforcement and Sanctions Act 2008, s 39(2).

THE FOCUS OF THE INFORMATION COMMISSIONER AND THE FINANCIAL SERVICES AUTHORITY

6.20 As mentioned earlier, there is an overlap in the competencies of the Information Commissioner and the Financial Services Authority, with the result that they both have power to regulate data security breaches in the financial services sector. However, the regulators' powers are built upon very different foundations; the Information Commissioner is required to protect fundamental rights and freedoms whereas the Financial Services Authority is concerned with confidence in the financial system, public understanding of the financial system, consumer protection and preventing financial crime.

Information Commissioner's focus

6.21 The Data Protection Act 1998 does not specifically state that the Information Commissioner is required to protect fundamental rights and

The focus of the Information Commissioner and the FSA   6.22

freedoms, but that is the effect of the Data Protection Act 1998 when read in conjunction with the Data Protection Directive[1]. As can be seen from Table 6.1, article 1 of the Directive places an obligation on Member States to protect fundamental rights and freedoms, with article 28 saying that the provisions adopted by Member States for these purposes should be independently monitored. Under the Data Protection Act 1998, s 51, which gives effect to article 28, the Information Commissioner is charged with these monitoring obligations.

Table 6.1 – The foundations of the Information Commissioner's powers	
Data Protection Directive 1995	Data Protection Act 1998
Article 1 1. In accordance with this Directive, Member States shall protect the fundamental rights and freedoms of natural persons and in particular their right to privacy with respect to the processing of personal data.	
Article 28 1. Each Member State shall provide that one or more public authorities are responsible for monitoring the application within its territory of the provisions adopted by the Member States pursuant to this Directive. These authorities shall act with complete independence in exercising the functions entrusted to them. 2. Each Member State shall provide that the supervisory authorities are consulted when drawing up administrative measures or regulations relating to the protection of individuals' rights and freedoms with regard to the processing of personal data.	**Section 51** (1) It shall be the duty of the Commissioner to promote the following of good practice by data controllers and, in particular, so to perform his functions under this Act as to promote the observance of the requirements of this Act by data controllers. (2) The Commissioner shall arrange for the dissemination in such form and manner as he considers appropriate of such information as it may appear to him expedient to give to the public about the operation of this Act, about good practice, and about other matters within the scope of his functions under this Act, and may give advice to any person as to any of those matters.

[1]   Directive 95/46/EC.

FSA's focus

6.22   The Financial Services Authority is established by the Financial Services and Markets Act 2000 (FSMA 2000), s 1. Under FSMA 2000, s 2 the FSA is required to act compatibly with the 'regulatory objectives'. Section 2 provides:

6.22 *Regulation and enforcement*

'2 **The Authority's general duties**

(1) In discharging its general functions the Authority must, so far as is reasonably possible, act in a way–
    (a)   which is compatible with the regulatory objectives; and
    (b)   which the Authority considers most appropriate for the purpose of meeting those objectives.
(2)   The regulatory objectives are–
    (a)   market confidence;
    (b)   public awareness;
    (c)   the protection of consumers; and
    (d)   the reduction of financial crime.'

Who should regulate the financial services sector?

6.23 The differences in the focus of the Information Commissioner and the FSA are easy to work out. However, in practice it is very difficult to establish a bright line test that will help to determine which regulator should take precedence in the financial services sector.

The Nationwide Building Society provides a very good example of this problem. In early 2007 the Nationwide had the misfortune of suffering both Financial Services Authority and Information Commissioner regulatory action for security breaches. In the first case, which came to light in February 2007, the FSA fined the Nationwide £980,000 following the loss of an unencrypted laptop computer containing customer records[1]. The FSA considered that this gave rise to a risk of financial crime, the prevention of which is one of the regulatory objectives within FSMA 2000, s 2. In the second case, which came to light in March 2007, the Information Commissioner took action after discovering that customer data had been disposed of unsafely, as general refuse. The Nationwide provided written undertakings about future compliance with the Data Protection Act 1998[2]. The narrative within the undertakings explains that 'items of personal information were recovered from refuse bins used by the Oldham branch of Nationwide. This information included a personal financial review in respect of two individuals and a customer information document detailing the customer's name, addresses, dates of birth and telephone numbers'.

Having regard to the known facts, it would be fair to conclude that the Information Commissioner could have taken enforcement action in respect of the loss of the laptop and the Financial Services Authority could have taken action in respect of the disposal of customer information in the general refuse. In both of these cases the key area of overlap concerns the risk of financial crime, which has been cited in all of the FSA's security breach cases. Where such a risk affects individuals the Information Commissioner is always entitled to carry out an investigation, due to the construction of the enforcement regime within the Data Protection Act 1998 and if the risk is a real one the Commissioner can take enforcement action.

Presumably the Information Commissioner and the FSA liaised about jurisdiction, but from a purely presentational perspective, should it be concluded that the FSA deals with the more serious cases, while the Information Commissioner takes on a junior partner role? Or was there a greater likelihood of financial crime in the FSA's case? Whatever the basis of the carve-up of jurisdiction, the absence of a bright line test for determining which regulator should have carriage of a security breach in the financial services sector is very problematic for controllers and practitioners.

1   http://www.fsa.gov.uk/pubs/final/nbs.pdf.
2   http://www.ico.gov.uk/upload/documents/library/data_protection/notices/scan_nationwide.pdf.

THE CREATION OF THE REGULATORY BEAR MARKET

6.24 As explained earlier, the Information Commissioner and the Financial Services Authority have both contributed to the creation of a regulatory bear market. They are both highly pessimistic about the state of data security in regulated organisations and they have both accepted that there is a need for more interventionist regulatory strategies and the imposition of tougher penalties. The Information Commissioner also feels that the law is seriously defective. The evidence for this is found not only within their actions, but also within their public statements, which are explored here.

The FSA's public statements

6.25 The following reports and statements are notable within the creation of the regulatory bear market.

'Countering Financial Crime Risks in Information Security', November 2004

6.26 One of the first pieces of evidence of the emergence of the regulatory bear market is provided by the FSA's report 'Countering Financial Crime Risks in Information Security'[1]. This report, which was based on the findings of the FSA's Risk Review Department following visits to 18 regulated firms, holds a very special place in the FSA's view of data security, in the sense that it is cited or alluded to in the press releases that announced the fining of firms for security breaches[2]; clearly the FSA views security breaches occurring after November 2004 as being heightened in seriousness, because the report sounded a warning bell. The main conclusions section within the report's Executive Summary, contains much negative sentiment:

> '1.6 Our overall conclusion is that while crystallised losses are low, Information Security issues pose a material risk to our objective to reduce financial crime. Firms could be more active in managing Information Security risks rather than being reactive to events, to protect better their own assets and those of their customers from the risk of fraudulent activity.
>
> 1.7 We observed a heightened awareness of the financial crime risks arising from poor Information Security. However, we also learned of a number of serious incidents such as failed firewalls and virus infections, as well as other near misses caused by inadequate Information Security. While some larger firms

6.26 *Regulation and enforcement*

appear to have made progress, smaller and medium-size firms continue to carry more serious and substantial Information Security risks.

1.8 Many firms believe that their investment in Information Security is adequate, but they still experience Information Security breaches. Other firms appear to have increased spending on Information Security in response to a security breach, financial loss or a discovered vulnerability. We recognise that the level of Information Security investment should reflect the scale, nature and complexity of a firm. However, firms need to be alert to the Information Security risks they face and take risk-based, proportionate measures. Firms need to be aware of the ever-changing complexities of current Information Security threats and should review and prepare for them.

1.9 Most firms have had Information Security policies in place for many years, yet associated procedures and role responsibilities have not always been comprehensive. Firms' management have not always updated these policies to address the risks from new technologies, and control procedures may not be developed until firms' policies are updated.

1.10 The emergence of new threats to the industry has served to remind firms' management that they need to secure their assets and those of their customers from both internal and external threats.
- "Phishing" attacks aimed at identity theft are an increasing financial crime risk. Firms cannot afford to be complacent in their defence strategy to protect themselves and their customers from the threat of such fraudsters. Firms' education of consumers plays a role in prevention; and well defined Incident Management procedures contribute to addressing attacks efficiently.
- "Patch management" plays a significant role in addressing internet threats. Many smaller firms have yet to create an inventory of software versions; distribution of fixes was sometimes delayed through their inability to install patches automatically.
- The firms visited felt that outsourcing presented additional Information Security risks. The choice of function outsourced appeared to be critical – for example, outsourcing user administration made firms particularly vulnerable to financial crime risks. Although firms recognised the potential to save costs through outsourcing, their priority was to have direct control over critical processes.
- Few firms have created adequate reporting systems and automatic alerts on external threats using intrusion detection software because of a lack of technical expertise.

1.11 While new risks are emerging, we concluded that firms are still exposed to more traditional threats because information security frameworks, including risk management processes and practices, are not yet widely developed. Many firms have not invested sufficiently in controls – many "old" risks, such as legacy systems with poor security design, remain.
- In our review, some firms were unable to articulate how they identify and assess Information Security risks. Where risks are recognised, there are weaknesses in monitoring. For example, firms' internal monitoring of events remains patchy with inconsistent, non-independent checks over the use of privileged accounts.
- Staff can play an important role in controlling or mitigating Information Security risks. However, staff training often misses opportunities to promote a culture of Information Security. This exposes the firm to unnecessary risks and costs. Some education material lacks impact – although for a minimum cost, enhanced security focus and awareness

could effectively reduce exposure to viruses. For staff directly involved in Information Security controls, there are weaknesses in some cases. For example, firms lacking expertise to develop intrusion detection alerts and analytical reports, to deal with "phishing" and to carry out technical IT internal audit reviews.

- Deficiencies in user administration continue to present risks to the effective segregation of duties for both users and technicians. Central account management appeared to be more robust than distributed maintenance. Some firms have carried out identity management projects to improve user administration.

1.12 Various industry bodies and government agencies are working to reduce financial crime. However, there appears to be a degree of overlap and duplication of effort in terms of Information Security advice. Many small-to-medium size firms are unaware of the many industry and law enforcement programmes and initiatives designed to fight financial crime. These include issuing guidance on best practice and publicising existing guidance. Few firms have fostered relations with the relevant bodies that are able to provide technical assistance and standards guidance to firms.

1.13 Our supervisory approach has considered Information Security under the IT risk element of our risk assessment framework. This may not have encouraged supervisors to consider the financial crime risks associated with it. We will use the fraud awareness training programme to give supervisors more tools to consider related risks.'

[1] http://www.fsa.gov.uk/pubs/other/fcrime_sector.pdf.
[2] See Nationwide press release, February 2007: http://www.fsa.gov.uk/pages/Library/Communication/PR/2007/021.shtml; Norwich Union press release, December 2007: http://www.fsa.gov.uk/pages/Library/Communication/PR/2007/130.shtml; Merchant Securities press release, June 2008: http://www.fsa.gov.uk/pages/Library/Communication/PR/2008/058.shtml.

Financial Crime newsletter, October 2007

6.27 Issue 9[1] of the Financial Crime Sector's Financial Crime newsletter carried the following messages about data security within appointed representatives:

'The most common financial crime incident we have been dealing with this year is the compromise of customer data by firms holding large amounts of sensitive information. Worryingly, nearly all of these data compromises were because of carelessness, breaches of procedures or poor controls – they were not due to sophisticated hi-tech attacks by organised criminal gangs. Data compromises can affect a limited number of customers, but the sensitivity of the lost data puts those consumers at a very high risk of financial crime and identity fraud.

Information security risk cannot be mitigated by hi-tech means, such as encrypting laptops, alone – though these are of course important. Protecting customer data is just as much about good vetting practices and clear and appropriate policies and procedures communicated to staff in a sensible way.

Another cause for concern is the way we have seen many firms deal with data security incidents. The general trend we see is that they often appear more concerned about the possibility of adverse publicity and reputational damage to themselves than the risk to their customers of financial crime or identity fraud.'

[1] http://www.fsa.gov.uk/pubs/newsletters/fc_newsletter9.pdf.

6.28 *Regulation and enforcement*

'Data Security in Financial Services', April 2008

6.28 In April 2008 the FSA published a detailed report on data security, which presented dismal conclusions about the state of data security in the financial services sector[1]:

> 'This review and the incidents we have dealt with since the formation of our Financial Crime & Intelligence Division (FCID) at the beginning of 2007 has led us to conclude that poor data security is currently a serious, widespread and high-impact risk to our objective to reduce financial crime.
>
> Recent incidents of data loss have brought many firms to consider data security for the first time. Some progress has been made: firms in general are beginning to understand more about this risk and are becoming more assertive in their efforts to contain it.
>
> However, there exists a very wide variation between the good practice demonstrated by firms committed to ensuring data security, and the weaknesses seen in firms that are not taking adequate steps to treat fairly the customers whose data they hold.
>
> Overall, data security in financial services firms needs to be improved significantly. Many firms, particularly small firms, still need to make substantial progress to protect their customers from the risk of identity fraud and other financial crime.'

The report was launched at the FSA's annual conference on financial crime, by the FSA's Director of the FCID, who succinctly reinforced the negative view of data security in the sector:

> 'It is worrying that despite increased public awareness of the impact that identity theft can have on customers, many firms are still not taking this risk seriously. Customers have a right to be confident that firms are doing everything reasonably possible to keep their personal and financial details safe.
>
> Some firms have made progress by adopting good practice while others need to do more in this area to ensure that they are treating their customers fairly. Firms getting data security right is a key priority for the FSA and we expect the industry to raise its standards.
>
> This report provides a wealth of information including examples of good practice that could help firms benchmark their own systems and controls and make necessary improvements. We will follow up on this work with firms and will not hesitate to take action if future breaches are found.'[2]

[1] 'Data Security in Financial Services: Firms' controls to prevent data loss by their employees and third-party suppliers': http://www.fsa.gov.uk/pubs/other/data_security.pdf.
[2] 'Do more to protect customers' personal details, warns FSA': http://www.fsa.gov.uk/pages/Library/Communication/PR/2008/034.shtml.

'Review of financial crime controls in offshore centres', April 2009

6.29 In April 2009 the FSA published a short document titled 'Review of financial crime controls in offshore centres'[1]. The main findings of this document were:

'There are good data security controls but continued effort is needed to ensure those controls do not break down and that they remain valid and risk based.

High staff turnover presents a high financial crime risk, particularly around staff training. It is important that firms have in place appropriate vetting controls to fill gaps left by inadequate local electronic intelligence and search systems. Firms may want to consider using third-party recruitment specialists because of their local knowledge.

Local staff with financial crime responsibilities must be given proper financial crime training over and above their intimate knowledge of technical processes. Financial crime training in India needs to be better supported by financial crime teams in the UK.'

1   http://www.fsa.gov.uk/pages/About/What/financial_crime/library/reports/review_offshore.shtml.

The Information Commissioner's public statements

6.30 The Information Commissioner and the ICO have regularly expressed negative sentiment about the state of practices for data security within UK data controllers and the ability of the law to achieve controllers' compliance with the requirements of the data protection principles. Of course, it needs to be kept in mind that they have been engaged in a long-standing, highly political campaign for new powers, penalties and financial resources. However, even if this factor is stripped out, there is no denying the fact that recent events have acted to vindicate their position.

It should also be borne in mind that in June 2009 a new Information Commissioner, Charles Graham, was appointed, succeeding Richard Thomas. References to the Information Commissioner's position in this book are references to Mr Thomas's position.

The analysis in this chapter does not extend to breach notification, which is dealt with separately, in Chapter 7.

'What price privacy?', May 2006

6.31 This report[1] is discussed in Chapter 1, but to recap it has drawn attention to the 'unlawful trade in confidential personal information' and the need for the introduction of custodial penalties for those convicted of offences under the Data Protection Act 1998, s 55. Section 55 makes it a crime for a person to obtain, disclose or procure the disclosure of personal data without the consent of the data controller[2]. It is also an offence to sell personal data, or to offer to sell personal data, that have been unlawfully obtained[3]. However, despite the seriousness of these offences the Data Protection Act 1998 as originally enacted provided only for financial penalties on conviction. Furthermore, where fines have been imposed they have been derisory, which is one of the principal complaints of the Information Commissioner.

6.31   *Regulation and enforcement*

1   HC 1056, published 10 May 2006: http://www.ico.gov.uk/upload/documents/library/corporate/research_and_reports/what_price_privacy_low_resolution.pdf.
2   Data Protection Act 1998, s 55(1) and (3).
3   Data Protection Act 1998, s 55(3) and (4).

IMPRISONING THOSE WHO UNLAWFULLY OBTAIN PERSONAL DATA

6.32   In the foreword to the report the Information Commissioner explained that 'investigations by my officers and by the police have uncovered evidence of a pervasive and widespread "industry" devoted to the illegal buying and selling of such information'. This represents 'so serious a threat to individual privacy' that the Commissioner used special powers in the Data Protection Act 1998, s 52(2) for the very first time, to call upon Parliament to introduce custodial penalties for those convicted:

> 'The crime at present carries no custodial sentence. When cases involving the unlawful procurement or sale of confidential personal information come before the courts, convictions often bring no more than a derisory fine or a conditional discharge. Low penalties devalue the data protection offence in the public mind and mask the true seriousness of the crime, even within the judicial system. They likewise do little to deter those who seek to buy or supply confidential information that should rightly remain private. The remedy I am proposing is to introduce a custodial sentence of up to two years for persons convicted on indictment, and up to six months for summary convictions. The aim is not to send more people to prison but to discourage all who might be tempted to engage in this unlawful trade, whether as buyers or suppliers.'

'What price privacy?' was a damning indictment of the state of data security law in this highly specialised area. It marked the start of a repositioning of the Information Commissioner's strategy for data security, which moved from the 'carrot' approach of emphasising the upside of compliance to the 'stick' approach of punishing non-compliance. It also represented the beginning of a very successful period of Parliamentary and governmental lobbying, through which the Information Commissioner was able to reshape core legislation; the case for the introduction of custodial penalties received immediate political backing[1], triggering the Parliamentary process that led directly to the amendment of the Data Protection Act 1998 by the Criminal Justice and Immigration Act 2008.

1   'Increasing penalties for deliberate and wilful misuse of personal data', CP9/06, Department for Constitutional Affairs: http://www.dca.gov.uk/consult/misuse_data/consultation0906.pdf.

NEWS OF THE WORLD SCANDAL

6.33   In Chapter 1 the question was asked whether the Information Commissioner's focus on the unlawful trade in confidential data was 'worth it'.

If there are any remaining doubts about the value of the Information Commissioner's focus, these should have been finally extinguished by the news of the phone-tapping scandal, which broke in July 2009, when The Guardian newspaper reported systematic illegality by News of the World journalists[1]. At

The creation of the regulatory bear market **6.35**

first blush this seemed to be an old story[2], but the ensuing press, political and public outcry elevated the unlawful trade in personal data back to the top of the political agenda, thereby vindicating the Information Commissioner's focus on this subject matter[3].

[1] 'News of the World "bugging" claim', BBC, 8 July 2009: http://news.bbc.co.uk/1/hi/uk/8141300.stm.
[2] 'Pair jailed over royal phone taps', BBC, 26 January 2007: http://news.bbc.co.uk/1/hi/uk/6301243.stm.
[3] 'Andy Coulson faces questions over phone-hacking', The Guardian, http://www.guardian.co.uk/politics/blog/2009/jul/21/andy-coulson-news-of-the-world.

'Banks in unacceptable data protection breach', March 2007

6.34 In March 2007 the Information Commissioner's Office published a press release informing that it had taken regulatory action against 11 high street banks and building societies (and the Post Office), for various breaches of the seventh data protection principle[1]. The common theme within these cases was that customer personal data had been disposed of as ordinary refuse. The fact that enforcement action was taken on such a large scale against these high street stalwarts stands as evidence in its own right of the emergence of a regulatory bear market.

[1] http://www.ico.gov.uk/upload/documents/pressreleases/2007/banks_in_unacceptable_data_protection_breach.pdf.

INSPECTING CONTROLLERS THAT ARE PROVED TO BE IN BREACH (NOT RANDOM INSPECTIONS)

6.35 The press release contains other indicators of the emerging bear market, in that it also pointed to a belief at the Information Commissioner's Office that data controllers found in breach of the Data Protection Act 1998 should be opened up to inspection:

> 'The ICO believes that organisations in breach of the Data Protection Act security requirements should face a detailed inspection of their security procedures.'

Implicit within this statement seems to be a belief that defaulting organisations may not always be put on the correct path merely by the imposition of sanctions for breach; in some cases sanctions should be combined with closer scrutiny.

Interestingly, the focus at this time was the inspection of data controllers who are in contravention of the Data Protection Act 1998. This suggests that the Information Commissioner was not concerned with the possibility of random inspections.

6.36 Regulation and enforcement

Oral evidence to the House of Commons Home Affairs Committee inquiry into the Surveillance Society, May 2007

6.36 On 1 May 2007 the Information Commissioner, Deputy Information Commissioner and Assistant Information Commissioner all gave evidence to the House of Commons Home Affairs Committee inquiry into the Surveillance Society[1]. The Information Commissioner coined the phrase 'the Surveillance Society' during an interview with The Times in August 2004[2]. This clearly caught the imagination of Parliament, which launched two inquiries (these inquiries are considered below).

[1] See corrected transcript of oral evidence: http://www.publications.parliament.uk/pa/cm200607/cmselect/cmhaff/c508-i/c50802.htm.
[2] 'Beware rise of Big Brother state, warns data watchdog', The Times, 16 August 2004: http://www.timesonline.co.uk/tol/news/uk/article470264.ece.

CONTROLLERS ARE COMPLACENT, BUT ALSO HARD WORKING

6.37 The focus of the House of Commons inquiry was not data security per se, but the issue was addressed nevertheless, when the Information Commissioner gave this evidence in response to the question 'would it be helpful if [data controllers] had more liaison and more connection with the work you are doing?':

> 'Yes. I think there is a lot of complacency and a lot of people are very shocked when we reveal to them how their systems can be so easily breached. We work very closely with bodies like the DWP, British Telecom. We have arrangements in place. If they have suspicions, they come to us. My investigators are mostly ex-policemen and we go out and investigate. We have search warrant powers. We do cooperate, particularly with organisations with call centres because the telephone call centre can be a particularly vulnerable weak point, but there are other ways in which people are really quite shocked to find out how easily their systems have been breached. We do what we can but I think there is a lot of self-interest at work here because organisations do not want their security breached and they are working very hard themselves to prevent these problems.'

This evidence clearly expresses negative sentiment about the state of data security (the complacency point), but it is noteworthy that the Information Commissioner was also complimentary about the hard work that organisations were doing to prevent security breaches. This second piece of evidence is somewhat out of kilter with the general trend of the Information Commissioner's public statements on data security however.

CRIMINALISING CONTROLLERS FOR BAD SECURITY

6.38 Despite his positive sentiments, the Information Commissioner continued with his call for reform of the law. He repeated his call for new inspection powers and also called for the introduction of criminal penalties for controllers in serious breach of the law:

The creation of the regulatory bear market 6.39

'Now we have put out a lot of guidance notes, good practice notes – Do this, do that; do not do this, do not do that – in a wide range of areas, so we are getting a good feedback on that. More generally, we have already talked about strengthening our inspection powers. We would like to see a penalty associated with legislation. At the moment our only real stick is an enforcement notice which says "Do not do it again". ... We are exploring and we would like this Committee to explore the idea that for situations where there is a flagrant or a negligent or repeated disregard of the requirements of the law there should be some sort of penalty. This is not rocket science. It is the norm in other areas of regulatory life and we think it would serve as a very useful tool to concentrate minds to prevent the sort of problems you are talking about. I do not want to prosecute left, right and centre, but I would like there to be a deterrent and, in the extreme case, where there had been unacceptable disregard of the regulations, to be able to go to court and have a system of fines to sanction that behaviour.'

It is accepted that the Information Commissioner did not actually state that he was seeking new criminal penalties for controllers with poor security, but that was the effect of his evidence, due to the words that he used in the final sentence; a system of court imposed fines is a euphemism for penalties imposed on conviction of a criminal offence. Had the Information Commissioner had in mind administrative penalties, along the lines imposed by the Financial Services Authority on the Nationwide Building Society (or along the lines of the scheme introduced by the Criminal Justice and Immigration Act 2008), his choice of words would have been very different.

A SENSE OF EXASPERATION – GOVERNMENT NOT DELIVERING

6.39 As regards inspection powers, the Information Commissioner's evidence was pregnant with frustration, with the background being that he and the ICO had made many representations to government about amending the inspection regime in the Data Protection Act 1998 to allow for compulsory inspections, but with no success. The Information Commissioner said:

'I think this is where we move on to our inspection powers. The law says what I can do and what I cannot do and we take our obligations and our powers very seriously. The law at the moment says: "The Commissioner may with the consent of the data controller assess any processing of personal data for the following of good practice and shall inform the data controller of the results of his assessment." The key words there which we find very limiting are "with the consent of the data controller". This was a point I started making earlier. We are a regulatory body. We are unusual because we regulate government and other parts of the public sector. We are not completely unique in that. We certainly regulate the private sector as well. I have been a regulator in other environments. I find it very bizarre, frankly, that we have to have the consent of the organisations we are regulating in order to find out what is happening in practice. This case has been put to the Home Office, the Lord Chancellor's Department, the Department for Constitutional Affairs, the Ministry of Justice. We have been putting this case on a regular basis, where they smile and say, "We will do what we can" but we have not yet had a firm commitment that they will change the law. There is some pressure now from the European Commission to change it as well. I hope this Committee will understand that whatever protocols or codes of practice, data protection principles, whatever

6.39 *Regulation and enforcement*

> people tell us about what they are doing, sometimes it is what is happening in practice that we need to go in and investigate – not necessarily in a threatening way. We often will go in and carry out an audit to help people get it right, but, to know the regulator can step in has a very sharp deterrent and therapeutic effect upon organisations. To know that they can turn me down and say No and my inspectors and my investigators and my auditors cannot go in now, or not until they have put things right in 12 months time, does have an unfortunate effect on the dynamic of us as regulators. We have come to this Committee with one or two specific proposals. We are recycling something we have said to the Government in the past but we hope you understand why we attach weight and importance to it.'

PRIVACY IMPACT ASSESSMENTS – MAKING THEM COMPULSORY FOR THE PUBLIC SECTOR

6.40 The Information Commissioner also promoted the use of Privacy Impact Assessments, which provide a methodology for data protection risk assessments. In identifying a possible case for the introduction of a mandatory scheme for the public sector, the Commissioner explained as follows:

> 'Could I break it down into two sections, first of all, just to share with the Committee what we mean by privacy impact assessments and then discuss whether it should be mandatory or not. My colleagues will amplify my remarks, I am sure. It is a methodology which is quite widely used in other parts of the world which is still not familiar in this country. We are looking at something entirely new. Essentially a privacy impact assessment is an attempt by the organisation which is going to be collecting information in new or enlarged ways to record what they are going to do, why they are going to do it, how they are going to do it, to identify the various risks associated and to spell out publicly how they are going to mitigate those various risks. It is a discipline. It is a sort of risk management or risk assessment programme. It has caught on in other parts of the world. In the United States now it has been mandatory under the E.Government Act of 2002. I have here, and I would be happy to send a copy, "The privacy impact assessment" – the official guidance from the Department of Homeland Security. In the United States this is mandatory but they embrace this approach with a very constructive positive spirit and it seems to be beneficial. Here is the DHS charged with safeguarding the security of the American people. They are taking it seriously. We have talked to a number of government departments and they all say "It sounds a good idea, but we are not really quite sure what it would involve". There is no hostility to the idea. Later this year we are going to be producing a great deal more guidance for a UK environment as to how it might work and what the benefits would be. We are expecting a fairly warm reception to what they have to say. I think people do genuinely want to find out how it would work. We all want to avoid unnecessary bureaucracy. We are keen to spell out this will not be a bureaucratic intervention. The second part is whether it should be mandatory. My answer is that if public sector bodies, particularly central government, refuse or are reluctant to go down this road, then I think the case for a mandatory requirement to carry out a privacy assessment becomes very much stronger. It will only work if it is done in a positive spirit and you explore that first.'

Written evidence to the House of Lords Constitution Committee inquiry into the Surveillance Society, June 2007

THE THRIVING BLACK MARKET FOR PERSONAL DATA – 'WHAT PRICE PRIVACY?' REVISITED

6.41 On 7 June 2007 the ICO submitted written evidence to the House of Lords Constitution Committee inquiry into the Surveillance Society[1]. On the issue of data security and referring back to the themes of 'What price privacy?' it warned that:

> 'Breaches of security can have even more significant consequences. There is a thriving black market in personal details and there are frequent reports of the most personal of details being inadvertently revealed in security lapses. Both these can have serious consequences for individuals putting them at risk of identity fraud.'

[1] 'Inquiry into "The Impact of Surveillance and Data Collection upon the Privacy of Citizens and their Relationship with the State" – Evidence Submitted by the Information Commissioner', 7 June 2007. This evidence also addressed the unlawful trade in personal data, Privacy Enhancing Technologies and Privacy Impact Assessments: http://www.ico.gov.uk/upload/documents/library/corporate/detailed_specialist_guides/holconstitutioncommitteeicofinal.pdf.

INSPECTION POWERS AND CRIMINALISING CONTROLLERS WITH BAD SECURITY

6.42 The ICO used this opportunity to repeat the call for increased inspection powers and 'effective penalties for serious disregard for the requirements of the data protection principles'. It said:

> 'The Commissioner has a power to conduct audit and inspections to ensure compliance but this is fettered by a requirement to have the consent of the data controller concerned. This limits proactive oversight and the deterrent effect of possible inspection in areas where there may be real risks to compliance. There are also limitations to the sanctions that may be imposed where data protection principles are breached. Whilst the Commissioner has the power to issue enforcement notices, these are remedial in effect and do not impose any element of punishment for wrong doing. Such an approach may be appropriate for isolated contraventions of the law or where there is a genuine misunderstanding but a more effective sanction is needed where there are flagrant far reaching breaches of the law. This is particularly true where significant security breaches occur because of the negligence or recklessness of the data controller. Improvements to the Commissioner's powers to undertake proactive audits and the introduction of a penalty for flagrant breaches of the Data Protection Act would send a strong signal that compliance with the law is not just for the virtuous but needs to be taken seriously by all.'

Again, as with the Information Commissioner's oral evidence to the House of Commons Home Affairs Committee in May 2007, the ICO was careful not to actually say that it was seeking the introduction of a new criminal offence for bad security, but that is the effect of this evidence.

6.43   *Regulation and enforcement*

Privacy Enhancing Technologies – expanding the technological control mechanism

6.43 The ICO also reminded of its interest in Privacy Enhancing Technologies (PETs) saying that 'the Commissioner is also concerned that best use is made of what may be described as "privacy enhancing technologies". This involves using technology itself to minimise data collection and provide intrinsic safeguards'. While the ICO's focus at this time was 'identity management and the opportunities technologies provide to minimise the identifying particulars', the ICO's PETs agenda subsequently became more geared towards security, as is demonstrated by the ICO paper 'Our approach to encryption', which is discussed later.

PETs are discussed in more detail in Chapter 8. For current purposes, it should be noted that one of the innovative steps within the PETs initiative is the expansion of the role played by technology within data protection compliance generally.

Privacy Impact Assessments

6.44 Finally, the ICO referred once again to Privacy Impact Assessments, saying:

> 'One of the most significant new initiatives is based on privacy impact assessments. Privacy impact assessments are commonly used in other countries, most notably Australia, Canada, New Zealand and the USA. In the USA, the E-Government Act 2002 requires that a privacy impact assessment is undertaken and published before the government develops a new information system or initiates a new collection of personally identifiable information. Such impact assessments are based on assessing a proposed development by gauging the likely privacy impact on those whose data may be collected and identifying more privacy friendly ways for the same objectives to be achieved. One of the significant benefits of the assessment process is that this takes place during the development of proposals when there is still an opportunity to influence the proposal. Furthermore it can be undertaken by a third party thereby providing a degree of external validation.'

As regards the ICO's purpose in focusing on Privacy Impact Assessments, the evidence said:

> 'The aim of the ICO's work on privacy impact assessments is to provide a practical tool that can be used to help shape developments. There is a danger that a privacy impact assessment might be viewed as a further, unwelcome bureaucratic procedure. This would be a mistake. The privacy impact assessment is an aid to designing and implementing privacy friendly ways of working. They help inspire public's confidence in how their information will be handled.'

'CEOs urged to raise their game following unacceptable privacy breaches', July 2007

6.45 The extent of the ICO's negative sentiment was further revealed by a press release published in July 2007[1], which announced the launch of the Commissioner's annual report to Parliament[2]:

The creation of the regulatory bear market **6.46**

> 'The Information Commissioner is today calling on UK chief executives to take the security of employees' and customers' personal information more seriously. His call follows a number of unacceptable security breaches over the last year, involving leading names such as Orange and several high street banks.
>
> Speaking at the launch of his annual report in London, Richard Thomas, the Information Commissioner, will say: "Over the last year we have seen far too many careless and inexcusable breaches of people's personal information. The roll call of banks, retailers, government departments, public bodies and other organisations which have admitted serious security lapses is frankly horrifying."
>
> "How can laptops holding details of customer accounts be used away from the office without strong encryption? How can millions of store cards fall into the wrong hands? How can online recruitment allow applicants to see each others' forms? How can any bank chief executive face customers and shareholders and admit that loan rejections, health insurance applications, credit cards and bank statements can be found, unsecured in non-confidential waste bags?"
>
> The Information Commissioner will add: "Business and public sector leaders must take their data protection obligations more seriously. The majority of organisations process personal information appropriately – but privacy must be given more priority in every UK boardroom. Organisations that fail to process personal information in line with the Principles of the Data Protection Act not only risk enforcement action by the ICO, they also risk losing the trust of their customers." '

The language used in the press release is not only powerful, but highly emotive and ordinary readers would be forgiven for thinking that the state of data security in the UK in July 2007 was truly abysmal, which presumably was the intention. The poor state of data security was also underscored by the repetition of the message delivered in the March 2007 press release, which called for new inspection powers:

> 'To ensure personal information stays private, the Information Commissioner has called for stronger audit and inspection powers for his Office. Currently the ICO can only audit organisations' information handling practices with their consent. The Commissioner wants the right to inspect and audit practices where poor practice is suspected.'

[1] http://www.ico.gov.uk/upload/documents/pressreleases/2007/annual_report_press_releases_110707004.pdf.
[2] http://www.ico.gov.uk/upload/documents/library/corporate/detailed_specialist_guides/annual_report_2007.pdf.

Warnings about identity theft

6.46 In 2007 warnings about the risks of 'identity theft' started to feature with increasing regularity within the ICO's public statements, which contributed to the impression of a country under siege. In addition to its written evidence to the House of Lords Constitution Committee inquiry into the Surveillance Society, a press release issued in August 2007 warned university students to take precautions to protect themselves from identity theft[1], with the Deputy Information Commissioner saying 'almost every day we give out our personal details which can leave us open to identity theft'. In November

6.46 *Regulation and enforcement*

2007 the ICO issued a further warning, in a press release informing about the taking of undertakings from the Foreign and Commonwealth Office[2]. On this occasion the Assistant Information Commissioner observed that 'if organisations fail to take this responsibility seriously, they not only leave individuals vulnerable to identity theft but risk losing individuals' confidence and trust'.

[1] 'ICO warns students to protect personal information', 17 August 2007: http://www.ico.gov.uk/upload/documents/pressreleases/2007/students_back_to_uni_0807_final.pdf.
[2] 'Foreign Office in breach of Data Protection Act', 13 November 2007: http://www.ico.gov.uk/upload/documents/pressreleases/2007/fco_undertaking_131107.pdf. The FCO's undertakings can be found at: http://www.ico.gov.uk/upload/documents/library/data_protection/notices/foreign%20_commonwealth_office.pdf.

Written evidence to the House of Commons Home Affairs Committee inquiry into the Surveillance Society, November 2007

6.47 On 9 November 2007 the ICO submitted additional written evidence to the Home Affairs Committee inquiry into the Surveillance Society, which covered a variety of data security issues, including breach notification, Privacy Impact Assessments, data sharing, CCTV, criminal offences for reckless non-compliance with the data protection principles and inspections powers[1].

[1] 'Home Affairs Committee Inquiry into "The Surveillance Society?" Additional Evidence Submitted by the Information Commissioner', 9 November 2007: http://www.ico.gov.uk/upload/documents/library/corporate/detailed_specialist_guides/hacssadditionalevidenceicofinal.pdf.

CRIMINALISING CONTROLLERS FOR BAD SECURITY, BUT CUSTODIAL PENALTIES RULED OUT

6.48 On the matter of criminal offences the ICO said:

'25. The Commissioner would like to see the creation of a criminal offence of knowingly or recklessly failing to comply with the data protection principles so as to create a substantial risk that damage or distress will be caused to any person. He is also seeking a power to inspect personal data to assess whether or not it is being processed in compliance with the Data Protection Act. He believes that the introduction of such penalties and powers would significantly increase the ability of his office to fulfil its commitment to strengthen public confidence in data protection and to take a risk-based approach to regulation.

26. The penalty would be linked to a failure, knowingly or recklessly to discharge the duty imposed on data controllers under section 4(4) of the Data Protection Act which states that "… it shall be the duty of a data controller to comply with the data protection principles in relation to all personal data with respect to which he is the data controller." The Commissioner is suggesting an unlimited fine for such offences, not a custodial sentence and a defence that the data controller concerned exercised "all due diligence".'

INSPECTION POWERS

6.49 On the matter of inspection powers the ICO said:

'In terms of powers of inspection, the Commissioner would like to see a broadening of section 54A of the Data Protection Act which relates to the inspection of overseas information systems in which the UK participates such as Europol. He is suggesting that this inspection power should apply to any information system in which personal data are recorded falling within his jurisdiction.'

PRIVACY IMPACT ASSESSMENTS

6.50 On the matter of Privacy Impact Assessments the ICO focused on the benefits of making them a compulsory process for data protection within the public sector, as part of the OGC Gateway Review process, saying:

'As a similarly useful measure, the Commissioner would welcome a commitment to use privacy impact assessments as part of the OGC Gateway Review Process, thus embedding data protection and wider privacy considerations into the process of setting up any new and substantial government IT system. Not only would this help to ensure that adequate and relevant consideration is given to privacy from the outset, it would also help achieve compliance with the data protection legislation and would go some way towards fostering public trust in the use of their personal information. This approach has been adopted in other jurisdictions overseas and the Commissioner feels there is much merit in adopting a similar approach in the UK.'

Oral evidence to the House of Lords Constitution Committee inquiry into the Surveillance Society, November 2007

6.51 On 14 November 2007 the Information Commissioner, the Deputy Information Commissioner and the Assistant Information Commission all gave evidence to the House of Lords Constitution Committee inquiry into the Surveillance Society[1]. During the course of their evidence they again discussed their ideas on the introduction of new criminal penalties, inspections, financial penalties, encryption, Privacy Enhancing Technologies and Privacy Impact Assessments.

[1] http://www.publications.parliament.uk/pa/ld200708/ldselect/ldconst/999/const141107_ev1.pdf.

CRIMINALISING CONTROLLERS FOR BAD SECURITY

6.52 On the issue of criminal penalties, the Deputy Information Commissioner said, referring to the example of the loss of an unencrypted laptop computer, that:

'We have submitted a draft proposal to the Ministry of Justice. This is in two areas. One is to introduce a criminal offence for those who, broadly, knowingly and recklessly flout the data protection principles with a serious consequence. So say the doctor, the hospital that leaves the laptop in the back of the car with the patients' records on, it is hard to say that that is anything other than gross negligence. At the moment our power would only be to issue a notice to say

6.52 *Regulation and enforcement*

that that should not happen again and if it happened again then there would be a criminal offence committed. That blatant breach of fundamental obligations should attract a criminal penalty.'

FINANCIAL PENALTIES FOR NON-CRIMINAL CONTRAVENTIONS RULED OUT?

6.53 On the issue of financial penalties for non-criminal contraventions of the Data Protection Act 1998, the Deputy Information Commissioner might have intended to rule out the idea that the ICO should be given powers to fine failing data controllers. Comparing the ICO's powers to the FSA's, he said:

> 'You can contrast it with the approach to security and the sort of information taken in the financial services sector, where the Financial Services Authority imposed the penalty and it was close on £1m on Nationwide, in similar circumstances – and I have to say not just because they had a laptop stolen but because that was illustrative of a lack of proper procedures. We are not seeking those sorts of powers but it is an anomaly that in financial services financial information, because of the risks to the market you can, as a business, face that sort of penalty, whereas if you fall outside those regulatory frameworks then all you fall back on is general data protection regulation where there is no penalty.'

There is an ambiguity in this passage. As well as being interpreted to mean that the Information Commissioner was not seeking the right to fine controllers, it could be interpreted to mean that the Commissioner was not seeking a power to fine at the level of the FSA. However, the Criminal Justice and Immigration Act 2008 has made this issue irrelevant.

INSPECTION POWERS

6.54 The Deputy Information Commissioner then turned to inspections, saying:

> 'The other area is a power to inspect. At the moment we can inspect the processing of personal data by organisations, public and private, but only with their consent – in only some very limited areas to do with European systems, Europol and so on, do we have a right to go in and say that we have come to make some checks. We are, as far as we can see, almost unique as a regulator in having a set of responsibilities to oversee and not then having a power to inspect that they are being put into practice. We think it will concentrate minds. We would concentrate any inspection power where the greatest risk applies, and we would not be able to inspect thousands and thousands of organisations, but it would help, we believe, to deliver data protection compliance and to get business – public and private sector – to take data protection seriously.'

The Deputy Information Commissioner's ideas here seem to be fully aligned with the intention of the Data Protection Directive, which requires an effective monitoring regime. However, it should also be remembered that the Data Protection Act 1998 has always contained an inspection regime, albeit one that relies upon the issuing of a judicial search warrant. The search warrant regime is discussed in more detail later in this chapter.

PRIVACY ENHANCING TECHNOLOGIES

6.55 The issue of PETs was addressed by the Assistant Information Commissioner, who specifically identified encryption as being a key PET. He said:

> 'We are very keen in the data protection community – and I think this is something which is gaining credence more widely – to deploy things which we call privacy enhancing technologies. The people who come up with all these technologies are clever people and they can think of more privacy friendly ways to actually process people's personal information, and we have seen that, as the Commissioner referred to with the Council for Science and Technology report. Also, the Royal Academy of Engineers did a report on a surveillance society and they used a phrase there about how engineers should exploit engineering ingenuity to protect personal privacy. It is an idea that we could actually use technology in a way which provides some sorts of safeguards. To use an example in Europe, in Austria they have an e-government programme there which involves government departments sharing information between each other, but they do it on a basis of certain computer algorithms, which means that the government departments cannot see all the data that is held by the other department, they can only unlock what they need to in a particular transaction, and that is basically on the basis of an encryption key. That happens to be held by the Austrian Data Protection Commissioner in that country as a trusted third party to make sure it is used properly. There is an example of the big scale privacy enhancing approach. It can be done in a much smaller way – just putting encryption on a laptop is a way of providing some element of privacy protection there which is relatively simple and cost effective to do. We would hope that anybody who is developing technology and policy application should do it on the basis that they ask the people who are going to provide the technology to look at privacy friendly ways of using that technology.'

PRIVACY IMPACT ASSESSMENTS FOR THE PUBLIC SECTOR AND PERHAPS FOR THE PRIVATE SECTOR

6.56 However, the dominant issue within the evidence was the use of Privacy Impact Assessments, which the Assistant Information Commissioner identified as being a suitable risk assessment tool for the public sector and possibly for large corporations:

> 'the vision is based on other jurisdictions where it tends to be public authorities who are actually engaging in the use of information that applies to lots of people, used for potentially sensitive purposes like health. Obvious examples that we have touched on this morning in terms of public policy initiatives would be ones like ID cards, would be ones like in England, Connecting for Health and the wider use of patients' information beyond their own surgeries. We would have issues to do with road user charging. Those would be ones where you would use the privacy impact assessment. We do not think this is a tool for use with a small businessman. We think this is dealt with at public policy level in many ways. Of course, a major corporation such as a major supermarket with a loyalty scheme may want to think about a privacy impact assessment with something like that, and a credit reference agency might; but the corner shop, we do not think it is right for that.'

6.57   *Regulation and enforcement*

'Confidential details lost by Revenue and Customs', November 2007

6.57   In November 2007 the ICO issued a press release about the loss of the HMRC data disks[1], which described the incident as an alarm bell for all organisations:

> 'This is an extremely serious and disturbing security breach. This is not the first time that we have been made aware of breaches at the HM Revenue and Customs – we are already investigating two other breaches. Incidents like these illustrate that any system is only as good as its weakest link. The alarm bells must now ring in every organisation about the risks of not protecting people's personal information properly. As I highlighted earlier this year (in my annual report), it is imperative that organisations earn public trust and confidence by addressing security and other data protection safeguards with the utmost vigour.'

In many respects HMRC acted to vindicate the general impression that had been created by the Information Commissioner over the course of 2007, that there was something seriously wrong with the state of practice for data security in the UK[2]. It also gave the ICO the moral high ground in its call for new powers and penalties. It also acted as an impetus to more frequent use of formal enforcement powers, thereby further embedding the regulatory bear market.

[1]   http://www.ico.gov.uk/upload/documents/pressreleases/2007/personal_details_lost_by_hmrc_201107003.pdf.
[2]   The House of Commons Justice Committee in their report 'Protection of Private Data' treated HMRC as a vindication of the ICO's public position on data security, saying 'we are extremely concerned to hear from the Information Commissioner that there are more cases involving the loss of personal data which have not yet fully come to light. The warning which he issued in the summer about the dangers of mishandling personal data and the extensive security lapses in a wide range of organisations has been proved correct'.

'Our approach to encryption', November 2007

6.58   In November 2007 the ICO published its formal statement on the use of encryption, in a short document titled 'Our approach to encryption'[1]. The version of this document updated on 23 December 2008 reads as follows:

> 'There have been a number of reports recently of laptop computers, containing personal information which have been stolen from vehicles, dwellings or left in inappropriate places without being protected adequately. The Information Commissioner has formed the view that in future, where such losses occur and where encryption software has not been used to protect the data, enforcement action will be pursued.
>
> The ICO recommends that portable and mobile devices including magnetic media, used to store and transmit personal information, the loss of which could cause damage or distress to individuals, should be protected using approved encryption software which is designed to guard against the compromise of information.
>
> Personal information, which is stored, transmitted or processed in information, communication and technical infrastructures, should also be managed and protected in accordance with the organisation's security policy and using best

The creation of the regulatory bear market **6.60**

practice methodologies such as using the International Standard 27001. Further information can be found at 27001-online.com.

There are a number of different commercial options available to protect stored information on mobile and static devices and in transmission, such as across the internet.

Encryption software uses a complex series of embedded mathematical algorithms to protect and encrypt information. This process hides the data and prevents any inadvertent access or unauthorised disclosure of information. Since encryption standards are always evolving, it is recommended that data controllers ensure that any solution which is implemented, meets the current standard such as the recommended FIPS 140-2 (cryptographic modules, software and hardware) and FIPS – 197.'

[1] http://www.ico.gov.uk/about_us/news_and_views/current_topics/Our%20approach%20to%20encryption.aspx.

A MORE PRESCRIPTIVE APPROACH TO REGULATORY GUIDANCE ACCEPTED

6.59 'Our approach to encryption' represented a critical moment in the current cycle of development of data security law. Among other things, it represents a more prescriptive approach to the issuing of regulatory guidance on the requirements of the Data Protection Act 1998 and a much stricter approach to enforcement. The document also acts to embed the ideas within Privacy Enhancing Technologies within the enforcement of the law, thereby rendering the absence of PETs an aggravating feature within the assessment of harm.

LEGAL STATUS OF THE GUIDANCE

6.60 Dealing first with the document's legal status, this appears to be found in the Data Protection Act 1998, s 51, which identifies the general duties of the Information Commissioner. In particular, s 51(2) gives the Information Commissioner the right and obligation to issue information about 'good practice'. So, the document establishes that the Information Commissioner considers encryption to be a requirement of good practice. This is a reasonable position for the law to take and is consistent with one of the key theories within breach notification laws, that the obligation to give notification of a security breach arises only where the incident affects unencrypted data. The document also serves another purpose; it identifies the ICO's enforcement policy, which is now required by the Regulators' Compliance Code[1] made under the Legislative and Regulatory Reform Act 2006, s 22[2].

[1] 'Regulators' Compliance Code. Statutory Code of Practice for Regulators', 17 December 2007: http://www.berr.gov.uk/files/file45019.pdf.
[2] Legislative and Regulatory Reform Act 2006, s 21(2) identifies principles that all regulators must abide by. These are (a) regulatory activities should be carried out in a way which is transparent, accountable, proportionate and consistent and (b) regulatory activities should be targeted only at cases in which action is needed.

6.61   *Regulation and enforcement*

UNANSWERED QUESTIONS

6.61 A striking feature of the document is that it addresses only the question of encryption as it relates to movable devices and media, leaving over ambiguities about the Information Commissioner's position on other encryption issues, such as the encryption of email and other electronic communications and the encryption of non-portable devices. It seems to be reasonable to say that while the current state of law has encryption as a de facto obligatory PET, the outer parameters of the obligation to encrypt are still unclear.

The document also leaves many other interesting questions about the trajectory of the law unanswered. PETs are discussed in more detailed in Chapter 8, but for now it may be worthwhile remembering that a significant element within the current thinking about PETs is the issue of accreditation and the role that national regulators have to play in identifying or validating products and services in the PETs marketplace. The overall trajectory of the law seems to point towards a time when the regulators will start to prescribe other technologies, which will provide suppliers with opportunities for commercial exploitation.

AN UNLAWFUL ENFORCEMENT POLICY?

6.62 The very strict line taken by the ICO shines the spotlight on its lawfulness. The document includes a statement about the ICO's enforcement policy, saying that the ICO will take enforcement action after the occurrence of the prohibited event (loss of unencrypted portable devices). This could constitute an unlawful fetter on the discretionary nature of the enforcement power within the Data Protection Act 1998, s 40. To summarise, s 40 says that the Information Commissioner 'may' serve enforcement notices, not 'will'.

The ICO has pointed out in the past that the document does not actually say that an 'enforcement notice' will be served after the occurrence of the prohibited event, meaning that the discretionary nature of s 40 is not offended. That is one interpretation, but it does not provide a compelling reason not to treat the words 'enforcement action' to include the service of an enforcement notice; enforcement action is represented by the service of an enforcement notice after all. Furthermore, it is important not to forget the document's position within the cycle of development of data security law. It was published very shortly after HMRC, which gave the ICO a never-to-be-repeated opportunity to accelerate law reform. It served the ICO's purpose to sound tough on enforcement, indicating that it intended for the document to be read literally. However, if we assume for the time being that the policy statement does not act as an unlawful fetter of discretion, the document still causes legal difficulties, because of the uncertainties surrounding the extent of the obligation to encrypt and the circumstances in which enforcement action will be taken. So, if the ICO's real intention was to say that the loss of unencrypted portable devices may result in enforcement action, the document's failure to spell out the boundaries may become highly relevant in cases where the controller wishes to consider disputing the Commissioner's decision to take enforcement action based on the absence of encryption.

Oral evidence to the House of Commons Justice Committee, December 2007

6.63 On 4 December 2007 the Information Commissioner and the Deputy Information Commissioner both gave evidence to the House of Commons Justice Committee, which was carrying out an inquiry into the protection of private data. This inquiry was a direct response to the loss of the HMRC data disks. The Justice Committee's report was published on 3 January 2008[1].

During the course of this evidence the Information Commissioner once again explained his position on inspections, criminal offences, breach notification, PETs and encryption.

[1] 'Protection of Private Data', House of Commons Justice Committee, First Report of Session 2007–08, 3 January 2008, HC 154: http://www.publications.parliament.uk/pa/cm 200708/cmselect/cmjust/154/154.pdf.

CRIMINALISING CONTROLLERS FOR BAD SECURITY – KNOWING AND RECKLESS NON-COMPLIANCE

6.64 On the issue of criminal offences the Information Commissioner provided a detailed explanation of how the offence would operate in the event of knowing or reckless breaches of the security principle. He also identified the parameters of the defences:

'In the area of new criminal sanctions, what we have put forward in some detail is the need for a new criminal offence which is linked to the existing duty under the Act. Already the Act says: "It shall be the duty of a data controller to comply with the data protection principles in relation to all personal data with respect to which he is data controller." That is already, and has been for many years, a legal duty. That is section 4 of the Data Protection Act. What we are now suggesting is that there should be a new criminal offence linked to that duty, but limited to breaches that are avoidable, those that give rise to a serious data protection risk, and those where a criminal state of mind exists. We have elaborated on this in saying that the offence should be created where a data controller knowingly or recklessly fails to discharge the duty imposed by section 4, and where that failure results in a substantial risk that any person will suffer damage or distress. We then go on to say it should be a defence that the data controller exercised all due diligence to comply with the section. So I hope you will see we are trying to take a balanced approach. We are not just creating criminal offences for the sake of it, we recognise the regulatory burdens which can be excessive, we are looking for a targeted new criminal sanction to serve the prophylactic effect that you already have described, and to, if you like, raise the profile of the importance of complying with these principles, but also to give us a real power to take punitive action in those cases where that is merited.'

6.65   *Regulation and enforcement*

ENCRYPTION – A MORE PRESCRIPTIVE APPROACH TO REGULATORY GUIDANCE REJECTED

6.65 The Deputy Information Commissioner gave interesting evidence on the issue of encryption, in which he gave reasons for rejecting a more prescriptive approach to regulatory guidance. Prominent within his argument was a concern that strong encryption will be cracked eventually:

> 'Encryption is, as you know, technology for scrambling data so it cannot be readily accessed, but the techniques for that change all the time. I will not go into the technicalities of 128-bit encryption, but what, if you like, today is entirely secure, in three years' time will be fairly easily broken into, and the technology will have moved on. So to write that and the proper standards into the legislation is extremely difficult. I think we do largely take the right approach by setting out the general principle in the legislation of appropriate security, and then through guidance, and through, I think, businesses, whether it is Government or others, taking responsibility.'

'The Case for Amending the Data Protection Act', December 2007

6.66 On 21 December 2007 the ICO published a document containing very detailed proposals for the amendment of the Data Protection Act 1998[1]. This was preceded by a draft version that was sent to the Ministry of Justice in September or October 2007[2].

These proposals, which built upon the earlier work discussed above, included a proposal for a new criminal offence of knowing or reckless non-compliance with the data protection principles, a proposal for new inspection powers, a proposal for a power to require a report from a skilled person, a proposal for enhanced enforcement powers, a proposal for statutory undertakings and a proposal for an enhanced information notice power. If implemented in full they would constitute a radical repositioning of data protection law, immediately elevating the UK's legal regime to one of the toughest in the world. Moreover, as regards the creation of the regulatory bear market the reasonable reader would be entitled to conclude having read the proposals that the state of data security in the UK must be truly awful; why else would the regulator make such radical proposals for wholesale reform?

In justifying these proposals the ICO compared its powers with those of other regulators, saying 'they would help put the Information Commissioner's Office (ICO) on a comparable footing to other UK regulators and to other EU data protection authorities'. This reveals a touch of 'regulatory envy', albeit the ICO was careful to state that it 'is not seeking powers comparable to those available to the FSA'. In justifying the proposals the ICO observed:

> 'There is though a shortfall in the sanctions available to the Information Commissioner and the means of enforcing those sanctions swiftly and effectively. There is no effective punishment or deterrent available for those who knowingly or recklessly disregard the requirements of data protection law in a way that causes a significant risk of harm whether directly to individuals or indirectly by undermining respect for the law.'

[1] 'Data Protection Powers and Penalties. The Case for Amending the Data Protection Act 1998', V.1.0, 21 December 2007: http://www.ico.gov.uk/upload/documents/library/corporate/detailed_specialist_guides/data_protection_powers_penalties_v1_dec07.pdf.
[2] See evidence of Richard Thomas to the House of Commons Justice Committee on 4 December 2007 in response to question 20: http://www.publications.parliament.uk/pa/cm200708/cmselect/cmjust/154/154.pdf.

CRIMINALISING CONTROLLERS FOR BAD SECURITY – KNOWING OR RECKLESS NON-COMPLIANCE

6.67 The proposal for the new criminal offence was the most radical proposal within a very long shopping list, further underpinning the creation of the regulatory bear market; clearly the regulator's sentiment about the state of data security at this stage was very negative. The ICO's suggested formulation for the new offence was:

> '1. A data controller who, knowingly or recklessly, fails to discharge the duty imposed by section 4(4)[1] is guilty of an offence where that failure results in a substantial risk that any person will suffer damage or distress.
>
> 2. It is a defence for a data controller charged with an offence under subsection (1) to prove that he exercised all due diligence to comply with the section 4(4) duty.'

The ICO stressed again that it was not seeking a custodial penalty for this offence, differentiating its position on section 55 offences within 'What price privacy?'. Yet, astutely, the ICO made it clear that it would be content to accept enhanced civil penalties as an alternative to a new criminal offence:

> 'For the avoidance of doubt the Commissioner wants to make clear that he is not seeking a custodial sentence for any new offence. The possibility of an unlimited fine is the appropriate penalty. He is also open to the possibility that sanctions other than the power to bring a prosecution in the criminal courts might be appropriate. A civil penalty regime is one possibility and might have the advantage over a criminal penalty of being equally applicable to the Crown. The powers of the Financial Services Authority as set out in the Financial Services and Markets Act 2000 could provide a useful model to work from in the context of civil penalties. The Regulatory Enforcement and Sanctions Bill is also relevant. The intention of the Bill is to make available to designated regulators an "extended sanctioning toolkit". This "toolkit" includes fixed monetary penalties that can be imposed as an alternative to criminal prosecution where criminal offences exist. The Commissioner expressed reservations about the value of the "extended sanctioning toolkit" in the context of the criminal offences for which he can currently prosecute. Nevertheless he can see that were an offence to be introduced of the type suggested above the proposed "toolkit" could well provide added flexibility by enabling him not just to prosecute but to select the most appropriate and effective response to any particular instance of non compliance.'

Parliament did not accept the ICO's case for the introduction of a new criminal offence; instead it chose to take the monetary penalties route within the Criminal Justice and Immigration Act 2008.

[1] Data Protection Act 1998, s 4(4) places an obligation on data controllers to comply with the data protection principles. This means that the Commissioner was proposing the introduction of criminal penalties for non-compliance with the data protection principles.

6.68   *Regulation and enforcement*

NEW INSPECTION POWERS – COMPULSORY INSPECTIONS, BUT ON NOTICE

6.68 The ICO's case for new inspection powers, which has been partially accepted by government (see the Coroners and Justice Bill), amplified the case made out in their written evidence to the House of Commons Home Affairs Committee and House of Lords Constitution Committee inquiries into the Surveillance Society and, again, the ICO supported its case by contrasting its powers with those of other regulators:

> 'A wider ability to inspect the processing of personal data is important to the Commissioner. As explained in more detail below it is usual in any regulatory regime that those subject to regulation can be subject to inspection by the regulator. This provides an important incentive to regulated organisations to comply with the law. It also provides reassurance to the public that the regulation is effective in protecting their interest. Furthermore it gives the regulator opportunities to gain an insight into the practices adopted in the regulated sector.'

The innovative step within the proposal was the removal of the need to obtain the data controller's consent to an inspection, which apart from the cases governed by the Data Protection Act 1998, ss 50[1] and 54A[2], is always required. However, echoing the approach taken by s 54A, the ICO proposed that any new inspection power should be based around the giving of notice, except for cases of urgency. Of course, advocates of enhanced inspection powers may call into question the wisdom of basing the power on the giving of notice, as this could enable the controller to hide or destroy evidence. The ICO's suggested draft was:

> '1. The Commissioner may inspect any personal data recorded in any information system which he has reason to believe is used or intended to be used for the processing of personal data.
>
> 2. The power conferred by subsection (1) is exercisable only for the purpose of assessing whether or not any processing of the data has been or is being carried out in compliance with this Act.
>
> 3. The power includes power to inspect, operate and test equipment which is used for the processing of personal data and power to examine policies, procedures and records relating to the processing of personal data.
>
> 4. Before exercising the power, the Commissioner must give notice in writing of his intention to do so to the data controller.
>
> 5. Subsection (4) does not apply if the Commissioner considers that the case is one of urgency.
>
> 6. Any person who–
> (a)   intentionally obstructs a person exercising the power conferred by subsection (1), or
> (b)   fails without reasonable excuse to give any person exercising the power any assistance he may reasonably require, is guilty of an offence.'

Interestingly, the ICO was careful to emphasise that they would not abuse their powers of inspection, which indicates that they recognised that their proposals might be controversial, being met with pockets of resistance. They said that they 'would use any new power responsibly' and that they would 'give an assurance that any new powers will be used in accordance with good regulatory practice'.

In supporting the call for new inspection powers the ICO also called into question the UK's compliance with the Data Protection Directive. As already explained, article 28 of the Directive requires Member States to appoint at least one independent supervisory authority to monitor the application of the provisions adopted to implement the Directive. The ICO pointed out that the introduction of new inspection powers would eliminate any doubts about the state of the UK's compliance with the Directive:

> 'It is also well known that the European Commission has been examining the compatibility of UK legislation with the requirements of Directive 95/46/EC. One area that the Commission has particularly focussed on is the powers of the Information Commissioner. Whilst the Commissioner would not claim that there is an incontestable case that the Directive requires him to have a compulsory inspection power the Directive does require that each supervisory authority has "investigative powers such as powers of access to data forming the subject matter of processing operations and power to collect all the information necessary for the performance of its supervisory duties". Extending the Commissioner's powers would place beyond doubt the question of whether the UK has properly implemented this aspect of the EU Directive.'

[1] Data Protection Act 1998, s 50 refers to Sch 9, which is titled 'Powers of Entry and Inspection'. Section 50 gives a judge the power to issue a warrant allowing the ICO to enter and inspect premises where there are reasonable grounds for suspecting that a controller has contravened or is contravening any of the data protection principles or that an offence under the Act has been or is being committed.

[2] Data Protection Act 1998, s 54A gives the ICO the power to inspect any personal data recorded in the Schengen information system, the Europol information system or the Customs information system. This power is exercisable on notice, unless the case is one of urgency.

REPORT OF A SKILLED PERSON

6.69 The essence of this proposal is that a data controller should be required to commission a report by an independent expert for onward supply to the ICO. In other words this proposal would require the controller to obtain, pay for and disclose evidence that could be used against it in regulatory proceedings. If implemented this would radically empower the ICO at the controller's expense, but at the date of publication of this book the government has not given any reason to think that it is inclined to accept it.

It might be fair to classify this proposal as highly optimistic, yet the ICO was able to identify a similar regime within the Financial Services and Markets Act 2000. The ICO said:

> 'Coupled with a new inspection power is the proposal that the Information Commissioner should have a power to require a data controller to provide him with a report by a skilled person. This is based on the power given to the Financial Services Authority in section 166 of the Financial Services and Markets Act 2000. It would be used, in particular, where there are grounds to believe that there has been or could be a significant breach of the Act's

6.69 Regulation and enforcement

requirements and technical expertise is needed to determine whether this is the case and if so what remedial action might be appropriate. This is most likely to arise in the context of security breaches.

An example is the recent breach of security on a visa application website operated by the Foreign and Commonwealth Office (FCO). Given the technical nature of the security breach the FCO commissioned their own expert report and agreed to provide the ICO with a copy. They have subsequently provided the Information Commissioner with a formal undertaking based on the recommendations in the report. Although the FCO voluntarily commissioned an expert report there is no guarantee that another data controller would do so in similar circumstances in the future. Whilst the ICO could, if it is given the inspection powers referred to above, commission its own expert report there is a strong argument that the obligation to do so and the costs involved should fall on the data controller concerned.'

ENHANCED ENFORCEMENT POWERS

6.70 The proposal for enhanced enforcement powers consisted of three parts. First, the ICO was seeking a power to obtain injunctive relief. Second, it was seeking a power to obtain statutory undertakings. Third, it was seeking an extension of the enforcement notice power within s 40, to cover cases where a breach of the data protection principles is likely to occur. These powers were sought because 'the ICO's experience of exercising the enforcement powers in the Act has led the Information Commissioner to conclude that they are cumbersome and ineffective in addressing the most serious cases of deliberate and persistent misconduct'.

The ICO justified this proposal by reference to its power to serve an enforcement notice. It was the ICO's opinion that the construction of the Data Protection Act 1998, s 40 combined with the right to appeal an enforcement notice (see Data Protection Act 1998, s 48) did not allow it to deal properly with urgent issues:

'At present, following service of an enforcement notice (under section 40 of the Act) to address a breach of principle, that notice can be appealed to the Information Tribunal and pending the determination of that appeal the effect of the notice is suspended (see section 40(7) of the Act). It can take many months for an appeal to be heard and a determined data controller can deliberately delay progress.

Section 40(8) of the Act makes specific provision for an urgency statement to be endorsed on the notice where the Commissioner adjudges there to be "special circumstances". The inclusion of such statement can be appealed to the Information Tribunal (see section 48(3)). Only once any such appeal is determined (and only then if the appeal is dismissed) will the inclusion of an urgency statement have the effect of requiring compliance with the notice pending any substantive appeal against the notice. Any notice including an urgency statement does not have to be complied with during the seven day period after service within which the data controller can appeal against the inclusion of the statement. As such, the Commissioner does not have an effective injunctive power to stop immediately the most serious breaches – including breaches which, if the new offence suggested earlier becomes law, would be criminal breaches.

The creation of the regulatory bear market **6.72**

To address this the Commissioner seeks such injunctive powers, either by way of an adaptation of the provisions of section 40, or by way of additional powers. In either case it is suggested that such powers might be modelled on the Part 8 Enterprise Act powers which provide for enforcement orders and interim enforcement orders. The Information Commissioner recognises that the scope of the Enterprise Act does not extend beyond the business community whereas any new enforcement powers would need to be exercisable against all data controllers. The Commissioner also recognises that the procedure would need to be more streamlined than that under the Enterprise Act 2002 in that it should not include prior reference to another enforcement body (such as the OFT in the Enterprise Act). Any such prior approval, other than through the Courts, would compromise the Commissioner's independence as the UK supervisory authority for data protection.'

STATUTORY UNDERTAKINGS – REGULARISING CURRENT PRACTICE

6.71 The intention behind the proposal for statutory undertakings was to put the Commissioner's practice of taking informal undertakings from controllers as an alternative to the service of enforcement notices on a statutory footing[1]. The ICO explained:

'In addition, the Commissioner would welcome the specific inclusion of undertakings (as provided for in the Enterprise Act enforcement regime) as a regulatory outcome in connection with the exercise of enforcement powers. This route is already pursued on a non-statutory basis in the exercise of the Commissioner's existing enforcement powers. In this context it is relevant to refer again to the Commissioner's response to the Regulatory and Enforcement Sanctions Bill consultation. His response to the proposal contained in clause 34 of that draft legislation, for the availability of "enforcement undertakings" to designated regulators (including the Commissioner) is relevant in this context. He recognised that such provisions would merely place on a statutory footing a regulatory tool that the ICO has used to date quite effectively on a non-statutory basis. The proposals in that Bill for an extended sanctioning toolkit to be available to designated regulators were built on the premise that the additional sanctions available would all be alternatives to prosecution for criminal offences but some provisions, including enforcement undertakings, could have a role in their own right.'

[1] 'A Strategy for Data Protection Regulatory Action', November 2005, explains the role of undertakings in the context of negotiated settlements saying that negotiation is 'not a formal regulatory power but a form of Regulatory Action that will be used widely in order to bring about compliance with the Act and related laws. Negotiated resolution can be backed by a formal undertaking given by an organisation to the Commissioner': http://www.ico.gov.uk/upload/documents/library/data_protection/detailed_specialist_guides/data_protection_regulatory_action_strategy.pdf. See also the ICO's enforcement pages for copies of non-statutory undertakings: http://www.ico.gov.uk/what_we_cover/data_protection/enforcement.aspx.

ANTICIPATORY ENFORCEMENT NOTICES – PREVENTING THE CONSEQUENCES OF BAD SECURITY

6.72 As regards the proposal to extend the scope of the Data Protection Act 1998, s 40, the ICO also pointed out that it wished to be able to serve enforcement notices before any actual contraventions occur. It said:

6.72 *Regulation and enforcement*

'There is a further weakness in the Commissioner's enforcement powers that needs to be addressed. This is that enforcement notices can only be served if the Commissioner is satisfied that a data controller "has contravened or is contravening" any of the data protection principles. There are occasions when the Commissioner becomes aware that a data controller is likely to contravene the data protection principles but has not yet done so. This can occur where a data controller seeks advice from the ICO on a proposal for processing personal data but then declines to follow the advice given. There is an unnecessary and avoidable risk created for individuals by preventing the Information Commissioner from intervening until a breach and any associated damage or distress to individuals, has actually occurred. This risk could be removed by extending the basis on which an enforcement notice can be served to include circumstances where the Commissioner is satisfied that a data controller "is likely to contravene" any of the data protection principles.'

ENHANCED INFORMATION NOTICES

6.73 The ICO's power to serve an information notice is contained in the Data Protection Act 1998, s 43. This confines the ICO's right to serve a notice only on data controllers. The ICO saw this as an encumbrance on effective regulation, which it sought to remove by extending the range of recipients to any person:

'Currently the Commissioner's information notice power under the DPA only enables him to require information from the data controller. He has some information gathering powers under the Regulation of Investigating Powers Act but these can only be used in the investigation of criminal offences. There are circumstances where he needs to obtain information from someone other than the data controller in order to investigate non-criminal data protection breaches. This happens most commonly in relation to PECR breaches, where it may be necessary to identify who the subscriber to a particular phone or fax number is, or who is "behind" an e-mail address or website. Typically it is the provider of the relevant telecommunications service who holds this information. Without the necessary information it can prove impossible either to identify the sender of an offending message or to tie an offending message evidentially to a particular sender.

This defect in the information notice power could be rectified by changing references to "the data controller" to "any person" in section 43 of the Act.'

Foreword to FSA report, April 2008

6.74 The FSA invited the Information Commissioner to provide a foreword to its April 2008 report 'Data Security in Financial Services'. The Commissioner, who was obviously disheartened by the FSA's findings, said:

'I welcome this report on the protection of customer data within the financial services industry. It includes examples of good practice by some financial institutions which others could usefully learn from. However, I am disappointed – but not altogether surprised – that the FSA has found that financial services firms, in general, could significantly improve their controls to prevent data loss or theft.

> The blunt truth is that all organisations need to take the protection of customer data with the utmost seriousness. I have made clear publicly on several occasions over the past year that organisations holding individuals' data must in particular take steps to ensure that it is adequately protected from loss or theft. There have been several high profile incidents of data loss in public and private sectors during that time which have highlighted that some organisations could do much better. The coverage of these incidents has also raised public awareness of how lost or stolen data can be used for crimes like identity fraud. Getting data protection wrong can bring commercial, reputational, regulatory and legal penalties. Getting it right brings rewards in terms of customer trust and confidence.
>
> The financial services industry needs to pay close attention to what its regulator is saying here. But this report is also relevant to organisations outside the financial services industry which hold data about private individuals. All organisations handling individuals' data, in both the public and private sectors, could benefit from the good practice advice it contains.'

RSA conference speech, October 2008

6.75 On 29 October 2008 the Information Commissioner gave a keynote speech on data security breaches at the RSA Conference Europe[1]. He described 2008 as 'the year of data breaches and data loss' and gave some 'serious and worrying' statistics:

> 'I can reveal today that the number of data breaches reported to my office has soared to 277 since November 2007. There have been 28 breaches by central government; 75 within the NHS and other health bodies; with 80 reported in the private sector. We are currently investigating 30 of the most serious cases. We have already taken enforcement action against HMRC, the Ministry of Defence, the Department of Health, the Foreign and Commonwealth Office, Virgin Media Ltd, Skipton Financial Services, Carphone Warehouse, Talk Talk, and Orange Personal Communications Services Ltd.'

[1] 'Speech to RSA Conference Europe on data breaches, Richard Thomas, Information Commissioner – 29 October 2008': http://www.ico.gov.uk/upload/documents/pressreleases/2008/rsa_speech_oct08_final.pdf.

THE TRUST ISSUE

6.76 The Commissioner continued by identifying the trust issue within data security:

> 'As government, public, private and third sectors harness new technology to collect vast amounts of personal information, the risks of information being abused increases. It is time for the penny to drop. The more databases that are set up and the more information exchanged from one placed to another, the greater the risk of things going wrong. The more you centralise data collection, the greater the risk of multiple records going missing or wrong decisions about real people being made. The more you lose the trust and confidence of customers and the public, the more your prosperity and standing will suffer. Put simply, holding huge collections of personal data brings significant risks.'

6.77 *Regulation and enforcement*

PRACTICES ARE NOT IMPROVING

6.77 The Commissioner also expressed the view that despite the high publicity surrounding security breaches and the high-profile enforcement action that had been taken, practices for data security were not improving at the desired rate:

> 'It is therefore alarming that – despite high profile data losses, the threat of enforcement action, a plethora of reports on data handling and clear ICO guidance – the flow of data breaches and sloppy information handling continues. ... There must be a wake-up call each time there are headlines about unencrypted laptops which have gone missing, health or financial records found in the streets or memory sticks or hard drives which cannot be accounted for. But are there still too many people asleep at the helm?'

PRACTICAL GUIDANCE FOR IMPROVEMENT

6.78 The Commissioner then went on to give some guidance on the practical steps that controllers can take to improve their performance:

> 'There is no single magic bullet, but there will always be three key elements:
> - Clear thinking and paperwork – Ensuring the right policies, procedures, contracts, compliance arrangements etc.
> - Getting the technology right – Awareness of the power of technology, the risks of ever-cheaper storage and mobile data and looking to use technology to minimise risks – "Privacy by Design".
> - Focussing on people and behaviour – Recognising that the challenge is cultural and psychological – and must be led from the top – with the right approaches to awareness programmes training, managements, and supervision.'

MANAGEMENT RESPONSIBILITY

6.79 The Commissioner then addressed the issue of managerial responsibility and accountability:

> 'Those at the top of organisations – chief executives, permanent secretaries and so on – must be certain that the right framework is in place to address the risks of personal information and must be certain that responsibilities are clear. There must be complete clarity on who, inside each organisation, has responsibility for safeguarding each set of personal data. This is equally important where data is shared, sometimes amongst several sources, and where processing is outsourced to contractors. Given the levels of risk, there is also a role here – as we elaborated in the Thomas/Walport Report on Data Sharing – for reassurance to be provided through Audit Committees and Statements of Internal Control in annual reports. This should be enlightened self-interest and bodies such as the CBI can help to ensure adequate controls and disclosures. But the Financial Reporting Council and others will need to intervene if high-level accountability is not achieved in practice.'

THE INFORMATION COMMISSIONER'S ROLE

6.80 The Commissioner then went on to explain the role played by him and his office and their recent activities, identifying that regulation was moving away from the light touch approach:

> 'There is also an important role for my Office as the regulatory body, with a role to educate, scrutinise and police. As approaches to regulation become less light-touch, the law plays an increasingly important symbolic and substantive role in showing that data protection must be taken seriously. I have already mentioned that we have taken enforcement action in suitable cases, but the current law has limited impact.'

LAW REFORM AND IMPROVEMENTS TO REGULATORY POWERS

6.81 As regards law reform and the need for new powers and penalties, the Commissioner said:

> 'We (and many others) have long argued that our powers, sanctions and resources – fixed in another era – are now wholly inadequate. The ICO has made clear for some time that a stronger approach is required to help prevent unacceptable information handling. At last there is movement. Earlier this year Parliament decided that the ICO should have the power to impose substantial penalties for deliberate or reckless breaches. I understand that the government is working to ensure this measure is implemented as soon as possible. The threat and reality of substantial penalties will concentrate minds and act as a real deterrent. The notification fee for the largest organisations needs to be increased to give the ICO the resources we need to do our job properly. We are also looking forward to new powers to undertake inspections and audits of data controllers.'

'Taking stock, taking action', November 2008

6.82 On 3 November 2008[1] the ICO published a position paper in response to the Data Handling Review, the Poynter Report, the IPCC report on the HMRC data loss and the Burton Report on the loss of the MOD laptops. As explained in the introduction, 'the publication of these reports represents the culmination of the unprecedented examination of information sharing and data protection issues that has occurred over the last twelve months'.

[1] 'Taking stock, taking action – The ICO position on the Government Data Handling Reviews': http://www.ico.gov.uk/upload/documents/library/data_protection/detailed_specialist_guides/ico%20position%20paper%20on%20data%20loss%20reports.pdf.

INFORMATION GOVERNANCE

6.83 The first part of the paper, titled 'information governance', commented upon the improvements identified in the reports that are designed to remedy the 'shortfalls in corporate accountability and the governance of information'. The improvements include the creation of a board level role in larger organisations to deal with risk, the appointment of a senior executive to

6.83 Regulation and enforcement

oversee information security, the adoption of information risk policies, the identification of information assets, the implementation of formalised processes for information assurance and so on. In respect of these initiatives, the paper said:

> 'The ICO welcomes these themes. Not only do they make for sound business practice in the management of information assets, they also go a long way to ensuring compliance with the seventh and other data protection principles. Sound information governance structures are vital to ensure that the protection of personal information is given proper attention at all levels of the organisation. While the reports focussed on the handling of personal information in large government departments, the common themes that they present are undoubtedly relevant to other large organisations. The thinking behind these themes, if not all the detail presented in the reports, should be considered by any organisation that processes large amounts of personal information or personal information of a particularly private or sensitive nature. Sound information governance should take account of governance of the process, technology and people in an organisation.'

However, the paper was also clear in its view that despite all of this activity, improvements in practice still have a long way to go:

> 'While we recognise that much work has been done in improving information governance over the last year and are realistic in recognising that one can never completely eliminate the risk of data loss, the fact that the ICO continues to receive significant numbers of notifications of information losses indicates that both the public and private sector have to continue to improve in this area.'

POLICIES AND PROCEDURES

6.84 This part of the paper opened with a reference to the 'Cross Government Actions: Mandatory Minimum Measures' for better data handling, which were published with the interim report of the Data Handling Review. The ICO welcomed the introduction of specific measures for 'more proactive incident management', 'clearer and more robust storage, retention and deletion policies', 'internal data handling and sharing procedures', 'definitive external disclosure and sharing procedures', 'the development of a new protective marking for personal information in Central Government' and other improvements. It also endorsed the introduction of the new protective marking scheme for the government's personal data:

> 'The ICO welcomes the development of a new protective marking for personal information in Central Government. The "PROTECT – PERSONAL DATA" marking, with the related guidelines for handling such information, will provide clear and easy to follow procedures when using, storing and disclosing the personal data. It will also ensure that personal information which falls within the definition of the protected marking will be treated with the same degree of sensitivity as other "PROTECT" marked information across government. The level of protection required for this information is spelt out in direct and understandable terms in the Cabinet Office's document Cross Government Actions: Mandatory Minimum Measures. Other personal information will still be considered "personal data" and will require a basic level of security and protection in order to meet the requirements of the Data Protection Act 1998.'

The creation of the regulatory bear market **6.85**

It concluded by addressing Privacy Impact Assessments:

'One of the key recommendations that appeared across the various reports was greater use of Privacy Impact Assessment (PIA). PIA is a process by which the privacy risks inherent in the use, sharing or disclosure of personal information can be addressed at the design stage of a project and solutions found. Issues such as proportionality and necessity can be adequately addressed during the PIA process and this can inform decision making in relation to the use of personal information. A PIA is a transparent, consultative process which relies not only on robust internal analysis of risks and liabilities from an information assurance perspective, but also on wider privacy concerns raised by stakeholders such as the citizen, private sector partners or other bodies and agencies to whom information is disclosed or from whom it is received.'

TECHNOLOGY

6.85 This part of the paper encourages the adoption of PETs, while reminding of the fact that technology is not a silver bullet; PETs need to be installed within a generally compliant environment, which will be one with appropriate policies and procedures for data handling:

'Technology is constantly changing and the means and methods that we use today to protect information may be obsolete by tomorrow. Use of security technologies should always be proportionate to the nature of the information being protected. However, better use of technology alone will not be enough to make the transfer or use of personal information secure. For this reason the ICO welcomes the recommendation that the use of technology should be underpinned by clear and accessible guidance and policy on its use.

The ICO supports recommendations on making personal information accessible through secure links to central servers, as this is generally a more secure way to transfer information than through removable media. Transfers should only occur on the basis that satisfactory arrangements are in place for storage of the transferred information, and the system for transfer itself is both secure and has adequate recovery processes in place should it be compromised.

The ICO also welcomes recommendations to:
- audit the use of all removable media devices;
- make access control consistent across all systems;
- ensure that all non-laptop removable media are formally approved and accounted for on a regular basis;
- to adopt appropriate technological solutions in accordance with the seventh data protection principle;
- ensure that the technology supports audit trails of the use of personal information and the secure but easy interrogation and monitoring of these audit trails;
- issue clear guidance to staff on the use of private mobile devices to process an organisation's information assets;
- examine the practicality of limited use of privately owned personal computers for limited organisational tasks; and
- offer free, safe disposal for technology which is used to process personal data.'

6.86 *Regulation and enforcement*

TRAINING AND AWARENESS

6.86 This part gave hearty endorsement to the fact that 'all five reports have recognised as vital to the protection of personal information ... staff training and awareness'. It then went on to identify some key steps for controllers:

'The ICO welcomes recommendations that take a strategic approach to staff training and awareness, in particular recommendations to:
- closely align training, human resources and communications functions within organisations to ensure that process and procedures are embedded in staff behaviours;
- ensure that staff at all levels understand their responsibilities and apply their learning in day-to-day activities;
- ensure senior staff are regularly briefed on information security risks and vulnerabilities;
- provide regular refresher training to staff;
- ensure that training and awareness are seen in the context of the life cycle of employment, not merely as part of an induction process or a one-off training event;
- make poor information handling a competency or disciplinary issue;
- treat information security as a key staff competency;
- develop clear, brief guidance that is easily accessible to staff;
- provide shorter, more accessible versions of policies and procedures to staff;
- make staff aware of risks and vulnerabilities specific to the processes they are undertaking and provide training to mitigate and avoid these;
- make staff aware of the key information assets they use and the records and audit trails that must be kept; and
- provide specific training on the Data Protection Act 1998.'

The paper concluded this part by drawing attention to the importance of training and awareness within data security:

'The importance of staff training cannot be overstated in increasing information security. As the Data Sharing Review reported, most breaches of information security occur as a result of human error. Effective staff training and awareness of information security and wider data protection issues will not only address the risks of breaches, but also equip staff to be better able to identify risks and vulnerabilities themselves and escalate concerns where necessary.'

CULTURE CHANGE

6.87 This part addressed the need for data controllers to embrace cultural change within their organisations, reminding them also of the fact that the culture of contractors and consultants is also critical:

'The need for culture change is strong. Since the reports were published there have been more examples of personal information being treated in an almost cavalier way. Part of this culture change can be adopting the information charter, but this needs to be accompanied by a meaningful commitment by senior management to data protection. And this commitment needs to permeate not just the culture of the organisation, but the culture of contractors and consultants with whom personal data is shared.'

Memorandum on the Coroners and Justice Bill, January 2009

6.88 On 30 January 2009[1] the Information Commissioner submitted a memorandum on the Coroners and Justice Bill, setting out its position on data sharing, assessment notices and information notices. It was positive about the Bill, saying that 'there is much to be welcomed in the data protection clauses', but cautioned that it needed to be further improved.

The memorandum expresses four broad concerns about the assessment notice power as then proposed. First, it was unclear how far the power extended into the public sector. Second, it did not extend into the private sector. Third, no sanction for breach was prescribed. Fourth, the requirement for the Information Commissioner to seek the Secretary of State's approval to a code of practice on assessment notice could undermine the Commissioner's independence. The following comments in particular are worth noting:

> '2.5 We have no desire to undertake heavy handed or widespread inspections. We only take action where we identify a specific risk to individuals, for example by analysing the tens of thousands of complaints that we receive each year – most of which are about private sector organisations. We are strongly of the view that if individuals are to be protected properly, we must be able to serve assessment notices on all data controllers – including private sector, public sector and third sector organisations.
>
> 2.6 It is also very worrying that the Bill does not provide for any sanction if an assessment notice isn't complied with, but does provide for a formal right of appeal against a notice. In order to make our power of inspection effective, and to ensure the credibility of the inspection process, even if it is limited to public bodies, there must be a sanction where an organisation fails to comply with an assessment notice. One approach would be to introduce a clause similar to s.54 of the Freedom of Information Act 2000. This treats failures by public authorities to comply with our FOI notices as a contempt of court.
>
> 2.7 The Bill provides for a code of practice concerning assessment notices. Whilst this is welcome, we cannot see the justification for needing the Secretary of State's approval for issuing the code. This could call our independence into question and could undermine the code's credibility.'

As regards information notices, the message delivered was that the Information Commissioner requires the power to serve them on any person, not just data controllers:

> '5.1 Currently we can only serve an information notice on "the data controller". The data controller is the organisation with legal responsibility for processing personal data. The nature of modern business means that it is not always easy to determine who this is. In complex outsourcing arrangements it can be unclear who, if anyone, is ultimately in control of a data processing operation. We need to be able to serve notices on anyone who may hold relevant information, sometimes to identify who the responsible data controller is and sometimes to collect evidence of breaches.'

[1] http://www.ico.gov.uk/Home/about_us/news_and_views/current_topics/cj_bill.aspx.

6.89 *Regulation and enforcement*

Additional commentary on the Coroners and Justice Bill, February 2009

6.89 On 13 February 2009[1] the Information Commissioner published a clause-by-clause commentary on the Coroners and Justice Bill as it then stood. The core messages delivered were the same as those delivered in January, but with added detail.

In particular, it is worth noting the Commissioner's comments on the clause that would require his office to make a determination of whether a contravention of the Data Protection Act 1998 had actually occurred. The Commissioner was opposed to this formulation, because, for example, it would make the assessment notice process unnecessarily confrontational:

> 'The requirement that an assessment report contains a determination as to whether a data controller has complied or is complying with the data protection principles is impractical and likely to make the assessment process unnecessarily confrontational. Where the Commissioner makes an assessment under s.42 of the Data Protection Act 1998 (DPA), the determination is not an absolute one: it is whether it is likely or unlikely that the Act is being complied with.'

The Commissioner's concern here is very curious. It is difficult to see why a requirement to determine whether a breach had occurred is more confrontational than a requirement to assess whether a breach is likely, particularly as the process leading to these outcomes will be the same, as will be the consequences. The Commissioner's distinction here is splitting hairs; by its very nature an inspections procedure is confrontational and it is hard to see how controllers will feel more comforted by the fact that they are 'merely' being assessed for a likelihood of breach rather than actual breach. Indeed, many controllers when they think about it might actually prefer the proposed formulation to the Commissioner's alternative, because it protects their interests, placing distinct legal and evidential obligations on the Commissioner, which will require great care and skill to be discharged properly. 'Merely' assessing a likelihood of breach leaves controllers who have not actually breached the law fully exposed to the law's consequences.

Another notable part of this document is the submission on inspections powers under the Data Protection Act 1998, s 50, the use of which are contingent upon the prior obtaining of a judicial warrant; under the Data Protection Act 1998 as originally enacted, a judge can only issue a warrant if they are persuaded that a breach of the Act has occurred, or is occurring. The Commissioner considered that approach to be sub-optimal; instead he preferred a system that would allow warrants to be issued on an anticipatory basis:

> 'The Information Commissioner should be able to obtain a warrant for entry and inspection where he has reason to believe that the data controller is likely to contravene any of the data protection principles. The Commissioner should have the power to intervene where there is a significant risk, and not only once a breach has taken place.'

[1] http://www.ico.gov.uk/upload/documents/library/data_protection/detailed_specialist_guides/ico_commentary_170209.pdf.

Response to Joint Committee on Human Rights, February 2009

6.90 On 27 February 2009[1] the Information Commissioner responded to a letter from Mr Andrew Dismore MP (Chair, Joint Committee on Human Rights), which invited his comments on a series of questions concerning the Coroners and Justice Bill. In his introductory comments the Commissioner made clear once again his view that the Bill was sub-optimal. He also lamented Parliament's failure to bring into effect the monetary penalties regime introduced by the Criminal Justice and Immigration Bill:

> 'As it stands, we regret that the Bill will not give us powers to ensure that all those processing personal information do so in compliance with the principles of data protection. In particular, we must be able to serve an Assessment Notice on any data controller and there must be meaningful sanctions for ignoring a Notice. We received welcome new powers in the Criminal Justice and Immigration Act 2008 to levy fines on data controllers for deliberately or recklessly breaching the data protection principles. However it is important that the Government brings these powers into force as soon as possible.'

Most of Mr Dismore's questions were addressed towards the Bill's information sharing provisions, but they did give the Commissioner a further opportunity to spell out his views of the deficiencies within the assessment notice procedure as then formulated, ie, that it excluded the private sector (and 'third sector') from its scope and it did not provide any sanctions for breach.

[1] http://www.ico.gov.uk/upload/documents/library/data_protection/detailed_specialist_guides/jchr_memorandum_letter_270209.pdf.

Response to House of Lords Constitution Committee inquiry into the Surveillance Society, April 2009

6.91 On 15 April 2009[1] the Information Commissioner's Office published its response to the House of Lords Constitution Committee inquiry into the Surveillance Society.

For current purposes the point that is worth considering is the Commissioner's first substantive point, which is that he was frustrated with government, pointing out that the ICO is consulted too late in the formulation of policy:

> 'In our evidence to the Constitution Committee, we made the point that we are regularly frustrated that policy developments in Central Government can often proceed a long way before we are called upon to express a view. For the ICO to be effective in improving practice in handling personal information, it is vital that organisations approach us early enough in the process of policy and project design. Our views can then be considered when there is still opportunity for change and adequate safeguards can be built in without the additional expense of trying to include them at a later date.'

The frustration that is expressed here echoes the frustration that was expressed in the run up to HMRC and in its immediate aftermath.

[1] http://www.ico.gov.uk/upload/documents/library/data_protection/detailed_specialist_guides/ico_response_to_hol_constitution_committee.pdf.

6.92   *Regulation and enforcement*

Commentary on the Coroners and Justice Bill, May 2009

6.92 On 12 May 2009 the ICO published commentary[1] on Part 8 of the Coroners and Justice Bill, for the purposes of its second reading in the House of Lords[2]. The ICO used this opportunity to restate their case about the need for greater powers and penalties, reminding that 'the loss of large amounts of data by HMRC and other public and private organisations has left very few in doubt about the need for strong and effective safeguards'.

Once again, the ICO identified three concerns within the Bill. To recap, it limited the assessment notice procedure to the public sector. Second, it did not provide for a sanction for non-compliance with an assessment notice. Third, it did not provide any significant enhancements to the information notice power in the Data Protection Act 1998, s 43.

The submissions on sanctions for non-compliance with an assessment notice are very clear and compelling:

> 'It seems very strange, however, that clause 156 of the Bill provides for a right of appeal against an Assessment Notice, but no sanction or other procedure where there is failure to comply. The organisations whose activities are least likely to comply with the data protection principles are the ones that are most likely to refuse an inspection. Clause 156 speaks of "requirements" in an Assessment Notice. But the Commissioner would be powerless when a Notice is ignored or there is otherwise a failure to comply with a so-called requirement. Any regulatory body must be able to take meaningful steps where a statutory requirement is ignored. Otherwise, the Commissioner's authority and credibility are damaged and the signal is sent that that the law need not be taken seriously.
>
> More specifically, the lack of any sanction matters for two reasons:
> - There is no pressure (neither incentive, nor deterrent) for a data controller to comply with a requirement of an Assessment Notice when it is served.
> - There is no consequence for a data controller who in fact refuses or fails to comply.
>
> The situation is therefore little improved from section 51(7) of the current Data Protection Act, which only provides for a good practice assessment where the data controller consents.'

[1] 'Coroners and Justice Bill Part 8 – Data Protection, Commentary from the Information Commissioner's Office, House of Lords 2nd Reading: 18 May 2009': http://www.ico.gov.uk/upload/documents/library/data_protection/detailed_specialist_guides/cj_bill_lords_2nd_reading_v2%200.pdf.

[2] At the second reading the government's spokesperson maintained its position. The government's spokesperson, Lord Bach, said 'I assure the House that we are not unsympathetic to the arguments that have been put forward. I make a couple of observations. On the scope of the assessment notice regime, there is already a power to apply the regime to private and third sector organisations exercising functions of a public nature. I accept there is not a neat dividing line between the public, private and third sectors and that we need to promote compliance with data protection principles across all sectors. The question for the House is whether that existing power goes far enough, or whether certain parts of the private sector should be subject to assessment notices—perhaps those that process particularly sensitive information or very high volumes of data. On enforcement for non-compliance, it is important to put on record that the Information Commissioner already has a number of separate enforcement tools available to him, including issuing an information or enforcement notice or applying for a search warrant

The creation of the regulatory bear market **6.94**

under Schedule 9 to the Data Protection Act. But I acknowledge the argument that a failure by a data controller to comply with an assessment notice should have direct consequences. All regulatory systems need to be proportionate and targeted. I look forward to debating whether Part 8 of the Bill as drafted gets the balance right'. Speaking out against the government position and in support of the ICO's position Lord Goodlad referred to two reports of the House of Lords Constitution Committee, the first on the Bill, published on 14 May 2009 and the second on the Surveillance Society, published in February 2009. See Hansard: http://www.publications.parliament.uk/pa/ld200809/ldhansrd/text/90518-0002.htm#0905182000422.

WHAT SANCTIONS SHOULD BE APPLIED?

6.93 The submissions offered the Commissioner's views on the sanctions that could be applied for non-compliance. One option would be to criminalise non-compliance. The other would be to treat it as a contempt of court. The third option would be to treat non-compliance as a ground upon which the Commissioner could apply for a search warrant under the Data Protection Act 1998, s 50:

'The main options appear to be:
- Criminal offence for a data controller who fails to comply with a valid Assessment Notice requirement (modelled on section 47 of the Data Protection Act which provides for failure to comply with an Information or Enforcement Notice served by the Commissioner.)
- Contempt of Court (the sanction for non-compliance with a Decision by the Commissioner under the Freedom of Information Act).
- Providing that non-compliance should be an additional ground on which the Commissioner can apply to a judge for a search warrant under Schedule 9 of the Act.'

INFORMATION NOTICES

6.94 The ICO also repeated its argument that the information notice procedure should be expanded to cover people other than data controllers, such as data processors:

'The current provisions of the DPA only allow the Commissioner to serve an Information Notice on the data controller. The ICO needs to be able to serve a notice on data controllers and others involved in an enterprise, such as data processors. This would allow us to:
- make the initial identification of the data controller, assisting our investigation of cases where a number of organisations are involved in a complex data processing operation
- obtain relevant information from another data controller, for example information about an organisation involved in a "scam" from the telecommunications company that provides its telephone line
- obtain further information where a security breach by a data processor may be causing problems for a number of data controllers that it provides services for, whose identity we may not know and who may themselves be unaware of the problem.

As it stands, Schedule 18 will not offer significant practical advantage in carrying out the ICO's regulatory activity. Schedule 18 should be amended to allow the Commissioner to serve an Information Notice on anyone who may hold relevant information.'

6.95 *Regulation and enforcement*

Memorandum on the Coroners and Justice Bill, July 2009

6.95 On 31 July 2009 the Information Commissioner published a memorandum on the Bill, following government amendments introduced in the House of Lords[1]. This document is significant in two respects. First, it is signed by the new Information Commissioner, Charles Graham, representing his first substantial public foray into the area of law reform and the continuance of his predecessor's policy. Second, it finally expresses happiness with the content of the proposed regime for inspections.

The July 2009 amendments to the Bill are discussed later in this chapter.

[1] http://www.ico.gov.uk/upload/documents/library/data_protection/detailed_specialist_guides/ico_commentary_on_lords_govt_amendment_130709.pdf.

Impact of regulators' statements and interventions – consequences for regulation

6.96 Aside from the legislative reforms, the regulators' statements and interventions inform controllers about current regulatory strategies and priorities, which in turn should inform them of the 'behaviours' that they should adopt to remain on the right side of the law. So, for example, the Information Commissioner's expectations about PETs, Privacy Impact Assessments, breach notification etc should lead controllers very quickly to an understanding of the steps that they need to take to meet the regulators' expectations.

REGULATION AND ENFORCEMENT UNDER THE DATA PROTECTION ACT 1998

6.97 In the area of financial services the Information Commissioner and the Financial Services Authority both have competence to regulate security incidents, but for all other sectors the principal regulator is the Information Commissioner. This section analyses the Information Commissioner's and data subjects' powers to enforce the Data Protection Act 1998.

The Information Commissioner's regulatory and enforcement strategy

6.98 The Information Commissioner is obliged to be transparent about his regulatory strategy and to this end the ICO has published a series of documents that are intended to achieve this goal. In the field of data security law prominent documents include 'Our approach to encryption', the guidance on PETs, the guidance on PIA and the guidance on the handling of security breaches and breach notification. In addition to these documents controllers should consider 'A strategy for data protection regulatory action', November 2005 (version 1.1)[1] and 'A Data Protection Strategy for the Information Commissioner's Office', March 2008[2].

[1] http://www.ico.gov.uk/upload/documents/library/data_protection/detailed_specialist_guides/data_protection_regulatory_action_strategy.pdf.

Regulation and enforcement under the Data Protection Act 1998 **6.100**

2   http://www.ico.gov.uk/upload/documents/library/data_protection/detailed_specialist_guides/ico_dps_final.pdf.

The scheme within the Data Protection Act 1998

6.99 The regulatory and enforcement regime within the Data Protection Act 1998 is intended to give effect to the requirements of articles 22, 23, 24 and 28 of the Data Protection Directive. In broad terms these prescribe a regulatory and enforcement regime with the following characteristics.

- There shall be an independent regulator.
- The regulator shall have sufficient powers to properly regulate and enforce the law.
- The regulator shall have the power to impose administrative penalties.
- Very serious cases of non-compliance shall be met with criminal penalties.
- Data subjects and others affected by data processing should have the ability to take complaints to the regulator and to enforce their rights in the courts.

The Data Protection Act 1998 certainly addresses these requirements, but perhaps not to the required level. Parliament has reacted positively to many of the Commissioner's complaints about the adequacy of the regime, introducing legislation for gaol sentences, financial penalties and non-consensual inspections.

As regards the distinct issue of enforcement, in summary the provisions of the Data Protection Act 1998 can be enforced in the following ways:

- The Information Commissioner can serve enforcement notices under s 40 of the Act, or information notices under ss 43 or 44.
- The Commissioner can bring criminal proceedings for specialised offences, such as the unlawful obtaining of personal data in breach of s 55.
- The Commissioner can carry out inspections pursuant to judicial search warrants issued under Sch 9.
- The data subject can make a request for an assessment of a controller's degree of compliance with the Act, under s 42. A request for an assessment can trigger the use of any of the Commissioner's enforcement powers.
- The data subject can enforce their rights before the courts, utilising remedies under ss 10 and 13.

6.100 Due to the amendments contained within the Criminal Justice and Immigration Act 2008 and the Coroners and Justice Bill, the Information Commissioner can expect the following additional powers:

- The power to impose monetary penalties under the Data Protection Act 1998, s 55A (inserted by CJIA 2008, s 144).
- The power to serve an assessment notice, assuming that the Coroners and Justice Bill receives Royal Assent.

6.100 *Regulation and enforcement*

Furthermore, the Commissioner can expect that the Secretary of State will eventually take advantage of CJIA 2008, s 77, to bring in custodial penalties for persons convicted of offences under s 55.

All of the enforcement mechanisms discussed here are relevant to security breaches and data loss. The information notice power and the inspection powers can be used by the Commissioner to establish key facts about security incidents and the controller's systems for security. The enforcement notice power can be used to force improvements to systems and, in very serious cases, to prevent the processing of personal data that are particularly at risk. The monetary penalty notice power can be used to punish controllers who suffer security breaches or data loss. The power to prosecute controllers who habitually fail to achieve the right level of security and the power to prosecute those who threaten the security of data ensure the application of the criminal law in the most serious cases. The powers that are available to data subjects also have a considerable role to play in enforcement of the seventh data protection principle.

The Coroners and Justice Bill

6.101 In the Queen's Speech in December 2008 the government announced that it would introduce the Coroners and Justice Bill, through which the Information Commissioner would be given a formal power to carry out inspections of the public sector without first having to obtain a warrant. This 'assessment notice' procedure is intended to put on a statutory footing the Commissioner's right to 'spot check' the public sector, which was granted by the Prime Minister when the loss of the HMRC data disks was announced. In addition to introducing assessment notices the Coroners and Justice Bill contains amendments to the Data Protection Act 1998, ss 43 and 44, to Sch 9 and to the monetary penalties regime introduced by the CJIA 2008.

The Bill was introduced in the House of Commons in January 2009[1]. On 21 July 2009 the relevant parts of the Bill received a line-by-line reading in the House of Lords committee stage. The provisions of the Coroners and Justice Bill discussed here are those within the formulation published on 22 July 2009[2]. This version of the Bill has met with a favourable response from the Information Commissioner[3].

[1] http://www.publications.parliament.uk/pa/cm200809/cmbills/009/2009009.pdf.
[2] http://www.publications.parliament.uk/pa/ld200809/ldbills/069/2009069.pdf.
[3] See the memorandum dated 31 July 2009.

Enforcement notices

6.102 The Information Commissioner has frequently poured scorn on the effectiveness of the enforcement notice procedure in the Data Protection Act 1998, s 40. The principal charge levied against s 40 is that it does not

Regulation and enforcement under the Data Protection Act 1998 **6.103**

provide effective punishment or deterrent. For example, in 'The case for amending the Data Protection Act'[1] the Information Commissioner's Office argued that:

> 'There is though a shortfall in the sanctions available to the Information Commissioner and the means of enforcing those sanctions swiftly and effectively. There is no effective punishment or deterrent available for those who knowingly or recklessly disregard the requirements of data protection law in a way that causes a significant risk of harm whether directly to individuals or indirectly by undermining respect for the law.'

In casting the spotlight on the inadequacies of enforcement notices in s 40 the Information Commissioner invites questions about the residual utility of s 40. As explained in 'The case for amending the Data Protection Act', it is clear that enforcement notices still have an important role to play:

> 'These enforcement powers are, and will continue to be, an important regulatory tool for the Commissioner. Where an organisation has acted responsibly but has misunderstood or misapplied the Act, where it has taken a considered but different view of the requirements of the Act from that taken by the Commissioner or where the consequences of a breach are less serious an order requiring future compliance is an appropriate and proportionate sanction.'

1 'Data Protection Powers and Penalties. The Case for Amending the Data Protection Act 1998', Information Commissioner's Office, V.1.0, 21 December 2007: http://www.ico.gov.uk/upload/documents/library/corporate/detailed_specialist_guides/data_protection_powers_penalties_v1_dec07.pdf.

The statutory purpose of enforcement notices

6.103 Taking 'The case for amending the Data Protection Act' at face value it would seem to be clear that the ICO does not see enforcement notices as containing either sufficient deterrent effect or any sanctions for non-compliance. This begs the question what is the residual purpose of enforcement notices? In order to answer this question it is worth considering the operative parts of s 40:

> '(1) If the Commissioner is satisfied that a data controller has contravened or is contravening any of the data protection principles, the Commissioner may serve him with a notice (in this Act referred to as "an enforcement notice") requiring him, for complying with the principle or principles in question, to do either or both of the following —
>   (a) to take within such time as may be specified in the notice, or to refrain from taking after such time as may be so specified, such steps as are so specified, or
>   (b) to refrain from processing any personal data, or any personal data of a description specified in the notice, or to refrain from processing them for a purpose so specified or in a manner so specified, after such time as may be so specified.
> (2) In deciding whether to serve an enforcement notice, the Commissioner shall consider whether the contravention has caused or is likely to cause any person damage or distress.'

Section 40(1) prescribes the core circumstances in which the Information Commissioner can serve an enforcement notice. The Commissioner needs to

6.103 *Regulation and enforcement*

be satisfied that there has been a contravention of the data protection principles. For the purposes of data security law this means that the Commissioner will have to be satisfied that the controller is guilty of failing to take appropriate technical and organisational measures to keep personal data safe and secure. If the Commissioner is satisfied that there has been a breach he may then serve an enforcement notice. The notice will prescribe the steps to be taken by the controller, which can include ordering the cessation of processing, or the implementation of specific technological controls, such as encryption, or the imposition of process and procedural controls. They can also be structured to achieve periodic reporting.

The remaining parts of s 40(1) identify the statutory purpose; the Information Commissioner may serve an enforcement notice if one is required 'for complying with the principle or principles in question'. In other words the statutory purpose is achieving compliance. The Information Commissioner's Office seems to accept this[1], saying in 'The case for amending the Data Protection Act' that:

> 'The sanctions currently available to the Information Commissioner under the DPA are primarily concerned with bringing an organisation's future conduct into compliance with the Act.'

[1] See also 'Notification of Data Security Breaches to the Information Commissioner's Office', 27 March 2008, where it is said 'It should be noted that the Information Commissioner does not have the power to impose a fine or other penalty as punishment for a breach. Our powers only extend to imposing obligations as to future conduct': http://www.ico.gov.uk/upload/documents/library/data_protection/practical_application/breach_reporting.pdf.

6.104 This approach to construction does have some interesting effects and poses some problems. For example, if the statutory purpose is achieving compliance, what is the effect where the controller agrees to take all the steps required of them by the ICO? Is the Commissioner then prevented from serving an enforcement notice, perhaps on the grounds that the statutory purpose, achieving compliance, has already been satisfied, or can an enforcement notice still be served, to achieve another purpose, such as a deterrent?

From the information that is available it is possible to detect the ICO's likely position. In its regulatory guidance on breach notification published in March 2008[1] it identified circumstances in which enforcement action will be pursued following the report of a security incident. Three circumstances were envisaged; the controller might refuse to take the required steps, the controller's ability or intention to comply is doubted or there is a need to re-assure the public. The guidance says:

> 'However the Commissioner will not normally take regulatory action unless a data controller declines to take any recommended action, he has other reasons to doubt future compliance or there is a need to provide reassurance to the public. Such a need is most likely to arise where the circumstances of the breach are already in the public domain.'

There seems to be no ambiguity in the opinion expressed in this passage; the statutory purpose extends to giving re-assurance to the public. It remains to be seen whether this is a correct interpretation of the purpose of s 40, but it is probably fair to conclude that the purpose of enforcement notices is likely to extend past the narrow boundaries of achieving compliance. While there cannot be any dispute with the ICO's view that enforcement notices themselves do not impose sanctions, it has to be acknowledged that they do provide a clear pathway to serious, criminal sanctions and that they can often cause the controller to suffer serious and immediate disruption and direct financial consequences. As such they have deterrent effect, as described earlier. Thus the statutory purpose may extend to providing deterrence, a construction that is also supported by the Legislative and Regulatory Reform Act 2006.

[1] 'Notification of Data Security Breaches to the Information Commissioner's Office', 27 March 2008: http://www.ico.gov.uk/upload/documents/library/data_protection/practical_application/breach_reporting.pdf.

How serious does a breach of the seventh data protection principle have to be to justify an enforcement notice?

6.105 When Parliament passed the Data Protection Act 1998 its intention was to reserve the use of enforcement notices to the most serious cases of non-criminal non-compliance.

The Information Commissioner's campaign for new powers and penalties necessarily requires an adjustment of thinking about the relative seriousness of a breach required to justify the service of an enforcement notice. Clearly, once financial penalties and inspection powers are brought into effect they will overtake the enforcement notice in terms of seriousness. The implication for the enforcement notice is that it is being downgraded in terms of importance.

This deflation in the value of the enforcement notice might result in enforcement notices being served with increasing frequency. While reasonable increases in the use of enforcement notices are to be expected, the Information Commissioner will need to be very careful to get the balance right. A particular consideration is the fact that despite all of the criticisms that can be levied at enforcement notices, sometimes the consequences of serving an enforcement notice can be extremely serious, in two respects. As stated earlier, they can result in considerable disruption to the controller and associated costs and they can expose the controller and its senior personnel to the risk of criminal proceedings.

Obstacles to the service of enforcement notices

6.106 Section 40 sets up a series of hurdles for the Information Commissioner, which are as follows:

- The Commissioner must be satisfied that there has been a breach of the principles.
- The Commissioner must be satisfied that the steps that are required by the enforcement notice are reasonably required to achieve compliance.

6.106   *Regulation and enforcement*

- The Commissioner must consider the likelihood of damage or distress.

HAS THERE BEEN A CONTRAVENTION OF THE PRINCIPLES?

6.107   The requirement that the Information Commissioner should be satisfied that there has been a contravention of the data protection principles imports a requirement that the Commissioner should be objectively satisfied. In all cases the Information Commissioner will need to conduct a proper investigation into the question of breach, although it may be permissible for the Commissioner to 'adopt' investigations conducted by others, as happened in the HMRC case. In the HMRC case the Information Commissioner awaited the outcome of the Poynter and IPCC investigations before taking the decision to serve an enforcement notice. The enforcement notice that was served in July 2008 made it abundantly clear that it adopted the findings and recommendations of Poynter[1]:

> 'Having considered the report referred to in paragraph 4 above together with the IPCC report, the Commissioner is satisfied that the data controller has contravened the Third Data Protection Principle in that the personal data processed on the missing compact discs were excessive for the purpose for which they were processed. Moreover, the Commissioner is also satisfied that the data controller has contravened the Seventh Data Protection Principle in that he failed to take appropriate measures to ensure the security of its data.'

The circumstances in which it is legitimate for the Information Commissioner to 'adopt' investigations carried out by third parties are probably limited. In the HMRC case the Poynter report was an official report that was commissioned by the government, with terms of reference that are relevant to an investigation for the purposes of the Data Protection Act 1998, s 40. Poynter was also a properly funded enquiry, with access to all of the evidence. Against this background it is hard to criticise the Commissioner's adoption of the Poynter report. However, it would be wrong to think that the Commissioner can routinely delegate his investigations to third parties. If he were to do that as a matter of course controllers would be able to mount substantial challenges to decisions to serve enforcement notices, including on public law grounds.

[1]   http://www.ico.gov.uk/upload/documents/library/data_protection/notices/hmrc_en_final.pdf.

DOES THE ENFORCEMENT NOTICE ADDRESS THE CONTRAVENTION?

6.108   The Information Commissioner also needs to be satisfied that the steps ordered by the enforcement notice arise directly from the contravention which they are designed to cure. Suppose, for example, that the contravention took the form of the absence of a controller-processor contract, which is required by the statutory interpretation to the seventh data protection principle. An enforcement notice that required the controller to ensure that relevant contracts are used in these relationships will arise directly from the breach. However, a requirement that the controller should also implement a privacy awareness campaign might not. The Information Commissioner therefore needs to be careful in the choice and selection of steps. Likewise, when defending enforcement action controllers may choose to focus on the degree of relevance of the steps required to the contravention that is alleged to have occurred.

THE LIKELIHOOD OF DAMAGE OR DISTRESS

6.109 Finally, the Information Commissioner needs to consider the likelihood of damage or distress being caused by the contravention. This obligation is very interesting, because, as already discussed, the seventh data protection principle can be breached through the 'mere' failure to take appropriate technical and organisational measures; the suffering of damage or distress is not a factor in assessing whether a breach of the seventh data protection principle has actually occurred, which begs the question 'what is the relevance of damage and distress within enforcement proceedings?'

If a contravention of the seventh data protection principle also causes damage or distress, this will be an aggravating feature that will have to be factored into a determination of the relative seriousness of the contravention under examination. It should follow that where damage or distress is suffered as a result of the contravention, the Commissioner will be on stronger ground. However, the absence of damage or distress does not act as a barrier to the service of an enforcement notice. It would be perfectly legitimate for the Commissioner to serve an enforcement notice where the absence of appropriate technical and organisational measures is in itself a serious contravention. Conversely, the absence of damage or distress might act to tip the balance against the service of an enforcement notice.

Damage and distress are synonyms for 'harm' and in this sense damage and distress is always a relevant consideration within an assessment of whether a controller has complied with the seventh data protection principle or has contravened it. In broad terms, the purpose of the seventh data protection principle is to prevent harm occurring. In a narrow sense harm is also a consideration within a determination of the appropriateness of technological security measures.

An interesting question is what is meant by the word 'damage' within s 40(2). The answer might be found in the Data Protection Act, 1998, s 13, which creates a right to compensation for damage and distress. Section 13 provides as follows:

'(1) An individual who suffers damage by reason of any contravention by a data controller of any of the requirements of this Act is entitled to compensation from the data controller for that damage.
(2) An individual who suffers distress by reason of any contravention by a data controller of any of the requirements of this Act is entitled to compensation from the data controller for that distress if—
    (a) the individual also suffers damage by reason of the contravention, or

6.109 *Regulation and enforcement*

        (b)   the contravention relates to the processing of personal data for the special purposes.

(3)   In proceedings brought against a person by virtue of this section it is a defence to prove that he had taken such care as in all the circumstances was reasonably required to comply with the requirement concerned.'

6.110 The meaning of damage for the purposes of s 13 was analysed by the Court of Appeal in the case of *Johnson v Medical Defence Union*[1]. In this case, which concerned the cancellation of a medical practitioner's professional liability insurance, Buxton LJ held that 'there is no compelling reason to think that "damage" in the Directive has to go beyond its root meaning of pecuniary loss'. In other words, damage means financial loss and to adopt the words of Buxton LJ there is no compelling reason to say that damage for the purposes of s 40(2) should be interpreted differently.

This places the Information Commissioner in a difficult position, because if a decision to serve an enforcement notice is taken on the basis that the contravention of the seventh data protection principle has caused, or is likely to cause damage, it will be incumbent on him to prove the occurrence of pecuniary loss, or the likelihood of pecuniary loss, in the event of a challenge to the service of the enforcement notice being mounted by the controller. If such a challenge is mounted and the Commissioner is unable to substantiate his conclusion with evidence of the fact of, or likelihood of, pecuniary loss, the enforcement notice will be vulnerable to cancellation on an appeal to the Information Tribunal.

The Information Commissioner's position is not helped by the fact that the consideration of damage is a mandatory requirement within s 40. This means that the Commissioner is bound to reach a conclusion on whether the evidence substantiates the occurrence of pecuniary damage or the likelihood of pecuniary damage. If the conclusion is negative that might militate against the service of an enforcement notice, as already stated.

The next consideration is distress, which is also a mandatory consideration under s 40(2), but before turning to the analysis it is worth remembering that the concepts of damage and distress are not co-joined, unlike the position within s 13. This means that the suffering of 'mere' distress in the absence of damage is a relevant feature within the Information Commissioner's decision-making process. In this sense distress can also be considered to be an aggravating feature; it can be part and parcel of harm.

[1] *Johnson v Medical Defence Union* [2007] EWCA Civ 262, [2007] 3 CMLR 181.

6.111 An important question is how much distress needs to be suffered to turn a borderline case into one deserving of an enforcement notice? Another important question is how much stock does the Information Commissioner place by distress? Similarly, is there a de minimis principle in operation, which requires distress over a certain level to be suffered before it becomes a material consideration?

Regulation and enforcement under the Data Protection Act 1998 **6.112**

These questions remain unanswered, but the Information Commissioner's position on distress is revealed by the enforcement notice served on Camden Primary Care Trust in February 2009[1]. In this document the Information Commissioner said that the likelihood of distress was self evident:

> 'The Commissioner considered, as he is required to do under Section 40(2) of the Act when deciding whether to serve an Enforcement Notice, whether any contravention has caused or is likely to cause any person damage or distress. The Commissioner took the view that the likelihood of distress is self-evident. The 2,500 or so individuals whose sensitive personal data has been lost are likely to have suffered worry and anxiety on account of the risk that their data will come into the possession of unauthorised individuals. Whilst there is no evidence that damage has been caused there was a significant risk that it could have been.'

It is also worth considering the enforcement notice served on HMRC in July 2008, in which the Information Commissioner took exactly the same position on distress being self evident[2], or the enforcement notice served on the Ministry of Defence[3]. However, in the Marks and Spencer enforcement notice the Information Commissioner took a different line, saying that he 'takes the view that damage or distress is likely as a result of personal data getting into the hands of unauthorised persons'[4].

[1] http://www.ico.gov.uk/upload/documents/library/data_protection/notices/camden_pct_final_en.pdf.
[2] http://www.ico.gov.uk/upload/documents/library/data_protection/notices/hmrc_en_final.pdf.
[3] http://www.ico.gov.uk/upload/documents/library/data_protection/notices/mod_en_final.pdf.
[4] http://www.ico.gov.uk/upload/documents/library/data_protection/notices/m_and_s_sanitiseden.pdf.

The discretionary component

6.112 The enforcement notice procedure is a discretionary remedy, so even where there is a contravention of the seventh data protection principle coupled with damage and distress the Information Commissioner is not obliged to serve one. This means that the Information Commissioner must exercise his discretion properly, in accordance with applicable principles of public and administrative law and regulatory law. For example, the Commissioner must not act in a discriminatory fashion, or pursue an illegitimate purpose.

There are many ways to challenge the exercise of a discretionary power, but one foreseeable challenge arises from the wording of 'Our approach to encryption'[1], which says that 'enforcement action will be pursued' in the event of the loss of unencrypted portable devices containing personal data. As discussed earlier, controllers may wish to challenge enforcement action based on the absence of encryption on the grounds that the Information Commissioner has fettered his discretion through this policy, by turning a discretionary power into a mandatory obligation.

[1] http://www.ico.gov.uk/about_us/news_and_views/current_topics/Our%20approach%20to%20encryption.aspx.

6.113 *Regulation and enforcement*

Form and content of enforcement notices

6.113 The Data Protection Act 1998 does not prescribe a form for enforcement notices, but it is clear from the enforcement action taken by the Information Commissioner that the ICO uses a standard template. The Act does prescribe content however, providing at s 40 that:

> '(6) An enforcement notice must contain—
> (a) a statement of the data protection principle or principles which the Commissioner is satisfied have been or are being contravened and his reasons for reaching that conclusion, and
> (b) particulars of the rights of appeal conferred by section 48.'

Additional content is also prescribed for cases of urgency, where the Information Commissioner considers that the enforcement notice needs to be complied with quickly. Section 40 continues:

> '(8) If by reason of special circumstances the Commissioner considers that an enforcement notice should be complied with as a matter of urgency he may include in the notice a statement to that effect and a statement of his reasons for reaching that conclusion; and in that event subsection (7) shall not apply but the notice must not require the provisions of the notice to be complied with before the end of the period of seven days beginning with the day on which the notice is served.'

Period of time allowed for compliance

6.114 The time for compliance with an enforcement notice is 28 days, unless the case is one of urgency, or the ICO specifies a longer period. This 28-day period constitutes the period of time for appealing enforcement notices and is calculated from the date that the enforcement was served on or given to the controller[1]. Section 40(7) says:

> '(7) Subject to subsection (8), an enforcement notice must not require any of the provisions of the notice to be complied with before the end of the period within which an appeal can be brought against the notice and, if such an appeal is brought, the notice need not be complied with pending the determination or withdrawal of the appeal.'

[1] Information Tribunal (Enforcement Appeals) Rules 2005, SI 2005/14.

Cancellation and variation of an enforcement notice

6.115 Naturally, the Data Protection Act 1998 gives the Information Commissioner the power to cancel or vary an enforcement notice. This power is contained in s 41. Enforcement notices can be cancelled or varied on two grounds.

First, under s 41(1) the Commissioner may cancel or vary an enforcement notice on the grounds that it 'need not be complied with in order to ensure compliance with the data protection principle or principles to which it relates'. As well as emphasising the point that the statutory purpose of enforcement notices is to achieve the controller's compliance with the principles, the way in which s 41(1) is constructed makes it implicitly clear that it applies to situations where the Commissioner has served an enforcement notice in error. Thus, where a controller is aggrieved by the service of an enforcement notice, on the grounds that it should not have been issued, achieving cancellation under s 41(1) would be the preferred route.

The second ground for cancellation or variation is contained in s 41(2). This ground gives the controller the right to apply to the Commissioner for cancellation or variation due to a change in circumstances; the change in circumstances is one that should result in 'all or any of the provisions of that notice [not needing to] be complied with in order to ensure compliance with the data protection principles or principles to which that notice relates'. Comparing this power to the first one, the key distinction seems to lie in the fact that s 41(2) proceeds on the basis that the enforcement notice was correct when originally served.

Appealing the service of an enforcement notice

6.116 Data Protection Act 1998, s 48 gives the controller the right to appeal an enforcement notice or the refusal of the Commissioner to cancel or vary it following a request under s 41(2). Appeals lie to the Information Tribunal and the time period for appealing is 28 days[1].

Section 49 sets out two grounds for appeals. The first ground within s 49(1) is that the notice is 'not in accordance with the law'. The second ground, within s 49(2), is that the Information Commissioner exercised his discretion incorrectly.

The first ground will obviously cover situations where the controller says that it has not contravened the data protection principles. However, the reference to 'the law' within s 49(1) is not limited to the Data Protection Act 1998. This means that the controller could appeal under s 49(1) if the Commissioner breaches principles of regulatory law or public law, by acting ultra vires. It would also cover the situation where the notice does not serve the statutory purpose (achieving compliance), but some other purpose (such as example-making).

The second ground points to the need for proportionality in the Commissioner's decision and decision-making process, as well as covering a failure to take account of all of the considerations within an assessment of a contravention and the service of an enforcement notice. So, if, for example, the Commissioner failed to consider the likelihood of damage or distress, that would leave the enforcement notice vulnerable to challenge. Another example of a wrong exercise of discretion would be where the controller agrees to take all of the steps required of them and the Commissioner has no objective grounds to doubt the controller's intentions.

6.116 *Regulation and enforcement*

The Commissioner will also be very vulnerable to challenge in cases where the enforcement notice concerns encryption, because of the inherent fetter placed on the discretion by 'Our approach to encryption'. Similarly, in cases where the Commissioner is willing to take undertakings a subsequent decision to serve an enforcement notice will render the notice very vulnerable to challenge.

In January 2010 the appeals process will change as responsibility for the Information Tribunal is transferred to the General Regulatory Chamber of the new, unified tribunal service. This will introduce a two-tier scheme for appeals, with simpler cases being heard by the First Tier Tribunal and more complex cases being heard by the Upper Chamber.

[1] Information Tribunal (Enforcement Appeals) Rules 2005, SI 2005/14.

POWERS OF THE INFORMATION TRIBUNAL

6.117 Data Protection Act 1998, s 49 sets out the Information Tribunal's powers on appeal. It has the power to 'review any determination of fact' on which an enforcement notice is based. The practical effect of this requirement is that the Information Commissioner's decision-making process and evidence relied upon will be subjected to scrutiny. This also gives the controller the right to cross examine the Commissioner's officers and inspect their documents.

The Tribunal's powers are considerable. It can cancel the enforcement notice, vary it or replace it with a completely different notice. If the appeal is rejected the enforcement notice will stand.

APPEALS FROM THE INFORMATION TRIBUNAL

6.118 If the controller is dissatisfied with the Tribunal's decision it can appeal to the High Court. The appeals process will change in 2010 when the Information Tribunal is transferred to the General Regulatory Chamber; appeals from First-Tier decisions will lie to the Upper Chamber and appeals from the Upper Chamber will lie to the Court of Appeal.

Criminal offence of breaching an enforcement notice

6.119 If the controller decides not to appeal the notice it will crystallise 28 days after service, meaning that the controller should comply with its provisions. Under the Data Protection Act 1998, s 47, failure to comply with an enforcement notice is a criminal offence, although this is subject to a due diligence defence:

'(1) A person who fails to comply with an enforcement notice, an information notice or a special information notice is guilty of an offence.
(2) A person who, in purported compliance with an information notice or a special information notice–

Regulation and enforcement under the Data Protection Act 1998 6.121

> (a) makes a statement which he knows to be false in a material respect, or
> (b) recklessly makes a statement which is false in a material respect, is guilty of an offence.
> (3) It is a defence for a person charged with an offence under subsection (1) to prove that he exercised all due diligence to comply with the notice in question.'

The fact that non-compliance is a crime is a very significant feature and is one that should concentrate the minds of controllers.

The penalties on conviction are prescribed by s 61. Upon conviction in the Magistrates' Court the defendant can be fined a maximum of £5,000. In the Crown Court the fines are unlimited.

Criminal liability of directors and other officers

6.120 These provisions should also be read in light of s 61 of the Act, which allows criminal proceedings to be brought against directors, managers and others personally, provided that their culpability can be proved. Section 61 provides:

> '(1) Where an offence under this Act has been committed by a body corporate and is proved to have been committed with the consent or connivance of or to be attributable to any neglect on the part of any director, manager, secretary or similar officer of the body corporate or any person who was purporting to act in any such capacity, he as well as the body corporate shall be guilty of that offence and be liable to be proceeded against and punished accordingly.
> (2) Where the affairs of a body corporate are managed by its members subsection (1) shall apply in relation to the acts and defaults of a member in connection with his functions of management as if he were a director of the body corporate.
> (3) Where an offence under this Act has been committed by a Scottish partnership and the contravention in question is proved to have occurred with the consent or connivance of, or to be attributable to any neglect on the part of, a partner, he as well as the partnership shall be guilty of that offence and shall be liable to be proceeded against and punished accordingly.'

Information notices

6.121 As can be seen from the earlier analysis in this chapter, the Information Commissioner's power to serve information notices has been under intense review. For example, in 'The case for amending the Data Protection Act' the Commissioner explained that he would like to see the introduction of an 'enhanced information notice' power, which would give him the power to serve an information notice on any person, not just the data controller. Thus, under the Commissioner's preferred scheme data processors would be obliged to comply with information notices.

6.121 *Regulation and enforcement*

At 21 July 2009, when the Coroners and Justice Bill was discussed in committee in the House of Lords, the Commissioner's case on enhanced information notices had not been accepted by government. However, the Coroners and Justice Bill does contain a series of provisions that will amend the information notice power. These amendments are discussed here.

The power to serve information notices

6.122 The Information Commissioner's power to serve information notices is contained in the Data Protection Act 1998, ss 43 and 44. As with enforcement notices, the Commissioner's power to serve information notices is a discretionary one.

Section 43 is concerned with information notices while s 44 is concerned with 'special information notices'. The distinction between the two kinds of notice lies in the fact that special information notices are concerned with processing for 'the special purposes', which are identified in s 3 of the Act as being processing for the purposes of journalism, for artistic purposes or literary purposes. So, if the Commissioner were minded to serve an information notice on a newspaper he would serve a special information notice.

This section examines information notices. The provisions on special information notices are very similar.

When can an information notice be served?

6.123 Section 43(1) allows the Commissioner to serve an information notice on a data controller following the receipt of a request for an assessment under s 42 of the Act, or when he reasonably requires information for the purposes of determining whether the controller has complied, or is complying, with the data protection principles. Even in its original state this is a wide and expansive power, which the Commissioner can use to obtain evidence that can provide the foundations for other enforcement action, such as the service of an enforcement notice.

What obligations are imposed on a data controller?

6.124 Section 43(1) as originally enacted requires the controller to furnish the Commissioner with 'such information relating to the request or to compliance with the principles as is so specified'. The amendments within the Coroners and Justice Bill contain a subtle expansion of the meaning of 'specified information' to include information that is described in the information notice and information that falls 'within a category which is specified, or described, in the information notice'[1]. The practical significance of this proposed amendment remains to be seen, although it seems to allow the Commissioner to be more general in his expression of the information that he requires.

Regulation and enforcement under the Data Protection Act 1998 **6.125**

As with search warrants under the Data Protection Act 1998, Sch 9, the information notice procedure does not bite on information that is protected by legal professional privilege[2]. The Act also contains important provisions to secure the privilege from self-incrimination. Section 43(8) says that the controller is not obliged to furnish the Commissioner with evidence that would expose it to criminal proceedings for an offence other than an offence under the Data Protection Act 1998. However, the privilege from self-incrimination does not extend to evidence of offences under the Data Protection Act 1998. The Coroners and Justice Bill contains amendments that will limit the scope of the privilege from self-incrimination, with the result that the controller will also be obliged to furnish information that could expose it to criminal proceedings for offences of perjury and similar offences relating to the making of false statements[3].

1   Coroners and Justice Bill, Sch 19, Pt 3, para 7, which will insert s 43(1A) into the Data Protection Act 1998.
2   Data Protection Act 1998, s 43(6).
3   Coroners and Justice Bill, Sch 19, Pt 4, para 9, which will insert s 43(8A) into the Data Protection Act 1998.

How and when should the information be furnished?

6.125 Section 43(1) as originally enacted requires the controller to furnish the specified information 'in such form as may be so specified'. It also prescribes that the information should be furnished 'within such time as is specified in the notice'.

The amendments within the Coroners and Justice Bill are again very subtle, yet very significant, in that they will require the information notice to also specify the 'time and place' at which the information must be furnished[1]. Taking the amendment at face value, this will allow the Commissioner to specify that the data controller should attend the Commissioner's offices in Wilmslow, Cheshire to deliver the information. It could also be interpreted to allow the Commissioner to specify that the information should be delivered to the Commissioner's officers at the controller's premises.

The fact that the Commissioner may specify the 'form' of the information implies that the Commissioner may request the controller to deliver the information orally, a construction that is supported by the amendments within the Coroners and Justice Bill[2]. Combining this with the amendment that allows the Commissioner to specify the place at which the information should be supplied, it seems to be possible to construe the amendments within the Coroners and Justice Bill to effectively permit the Commissioner to interview the data controller at its premises as part of the information notice procedure.

1   Coroners and Justice Bill, Sch 19, Pt 3, para 7, which will insert s 43(1B) into the Data Protection Act 1998.
2   Coroners and Justice Bill, Sch 19, Pt 4, para 9, which will insert s 43(8C) into the Data Protection Act 1998.

6.126 *Regulation and enforcement*

Time for compliance

6.126 The effect of s 43(4) as originally enacted is that the time period for compliance with an information notice is no less than 28 days from the date of service, although s 43(4) allows for this period to be truncated to seven days in cases of urgency. The Coroners and Justice Bill contains some contextual amendments, but the period of time for compliance is not changed.

Appealing the service of an information notice

6.127 The rules on appeals are the same as for appeals from enforcement notices.

Criminal offences

6.128 Section 47(1) also makes it an offence for a controller to fail to comply with an information notice. As with enforcement notices, the due diligence offence applies.

Section 47(2) also makes it an offence for a person knowingly or recklessly to make a statement that is false in a material respect.

Inspections

6.129 The importance of inspection powers within successful schemes for regulation is abundantly clear. In a general sense, this has been emphasised by Hampton, Macrory and the new legislation for regulation, discussed earlier. In a specific sense, this has been repeatedly emphasised by the Information Commissioner, by many Parliamentarians and by others on regular occasions during the recent cycle of development of the law. The earlier analysis of the Information Commissioner's public statements reveals just how prominent the debate about inspection powers has been.

Search warrants (the original inspection regime)

6.130 The Coroners and Justice Bill does not represent the first steps towards an inspection regime for data protection; the Data Protection Act 1998 has always contained an inspection regime. This is found in Sch 9 of the Act, which has effect by virtue of s 50.

In broad terms Sch 9 allows the Information Commissioner to apply to a judge for a warrant to enter and inspect premises, to test systems and to gather evidence. The Commissioner has to persuade the judge, or a magistrate[1], that there are reasonable grounds for suspecting that a breach of the Act, or an offence under the Act, has been committed (or is being committed)[2] and that evidence of this will be found on the premises named in the warrant[3]. The

Regulation and enforcement under the Data Protection Act 1998 6.132

Coroners and Justice Bill contains amendments that will also allow the court to issue a warrant where it is satisfied that the controller has failed to comply with an assessment notice; this is discussed again below.

The Commissioner's evidence must be given on oath[4] and in most cases the data controller has the right to speak at the hearing.

Even if the Commissioner is able to overcome all of the obstacles set out in Sch 9, the court is not obliged to issue a warrant. The court is required to look at the overall circumstances of the case and it always retains the discretion to reject an application for a warrant.

1   Data Protection Act 1998, Sch 9, para 1(1).
2   Data Protection Act 1998, Sch 9, para 1(1).
3   Data Protection Act 1998, Sch 9, para 1(1).
4   Data Protection Act 1998, Sch 9, para 1(1).

Time for compliance

GIVING NOTICE OF THE WISH TO GAIN ACCESS

6.131 Before applying for a warrant the Commissioner must consider whether he should give the data controller notice of his wish to gain access[1]. The default position under Sch 9 is that the Commissioner must give seven days' written notice, unless the case is urgent or the giving of notice would defeat the purpose of entry (perhaps through the controller destroying evidence)[2]. It should also be noted that the Coroners and Justice Bill contains amendments that will disapply the seven days' notice requirement where an assessment notice has been served.

Where the facts of the case demand the giving of notice, it is the controller's reasons for refusing access that must be considered by the court[3]; this places a duty on the Commissioner to be frank with the court about the controller's reasons as well as his own. This duty obviously increases in cases where the controller is not in attendance, or is not represented.

1   Data Protection Act 1998, Sch 9, para 2.
2   Data Protection Act 1998, Sch 9, para 2.
3   Data Protection Act 1998, Sch 9, para 2.

GIVING NOTICE OF THE INTENTION TO APPLY FOR WARRANT

6.132 Of course, in most cases the Commissioner is also obliged to give the controller notice of his intention to apply for a warrant, because the controller has the right to be heard at court[1]. Again, the court will only waive this requirement in cases of urgency, or if the giving of notice would defeat the purpose of the warrant.

1   Data Protection Act 1998, Sch 9, para 2.

6.133 *Regulation and enforcement*

CONTROLLING THE USE OF THE INSPECTION POWER THROUGH THE NOTICE REQUIREMENTS

6.133 Just as the Act leaves the final decision on the issue of warrants to the discretion of the court, these control mechanisms are designed to limit the use of inspection powers to the most serious cases. Implicit within this formulation of the rules is the recognition of the fact that warrants for entry into premises should not be issued without very good reason.

POWERS GRANTED BY WARRANT

6.134 If the court is persuaded that a warrant should be issued, this gives the Commissioner's officers the power to force entry to the premises in question if necessary[1], although entry should be sought only at a reasonable hour, unless that would defeat its purpose[2]. Once on the premises the Commissioner's officers can then 'inspect, examine, operate and test any equipment found there which is used or is intended to be used for the processing of personal data' and can 'inspect and seize any documents, or other material found there' that may provide evidence of the contravention or offence[3]. Materials that are protected by legal professional privilege are exempt from inspection and seizure[4]. There is also an exemption for national security[5].

[1] Data Protection Act 1998, Sch 9, para 4.
[2] Data Protection Act 1998, Sch 9, para 5.
[3] Data Protection Act 1998, Sch 9, para 1(3).
[4] Data Protection Act 1998, Sch 9, para 9.
[5] Data Protection Act 1998, Sch 9, para 8.

FORMALITIES

6.135 The Commissioner's officers need to comply with certain other formalities, such as providing a copy of the warrant[1] when it is executed and giving a receipt for materials that are seized, if the controller asks for one[2].

[1] Data Protection Act 1998, Sch 9, para 6.
[2] Data Protection Act 1998, Sch 9, para 7.

CRIMINAL OFFENCES OF OBSTRUCTION AND FAILING TO PROVIDE ASSISTANCE

6.136 It is a criminal offence for any person to obstruct the Information Commissioner's officers in the execution of a warrant, or to fail to provide them with reasonable assistance[1]. The offence of failing to provide reasonable assistance is conditional upon the person not having a reasonable excuse.

[1] Data Protection Act 1998, Sch 9, para 12.

AMENDMENTS MADE BY THE CORONERS AND JUSTICE BILL

6.137 As mentioned, the Coroners and Justice Bill contains amendments to Sch 9. These are intended to align the powers granted by a warrant with the powers within the assessment notice procedure. In addition to the amendments already mentioned, others will expand the powers so as 'to require any person on the premises to provide an explanation of any document or other material found on the premises' and 'to require any person on the premises to provide such other information as may reasonably be required for the purpose of determining whether the data controller has contravened, or is contravening, the data protection principles'[1].

[1] Coroners and Justice Bill, Sch 19, Pt 6, para 13.

Assessment notices (the new regime)

6.138 The first version of the Coroners and Justice Bill was widely criticised for not extending the assessment notice procedure to the private sector and for not containing an appropriate sanctioning regime to cater for situations where a public sector data controller refuses to comply with an assessment notice. The Information Commissioner's criticisms are detailed earlier in this chapter.

However, on 21 July 2009 the government introduced amendments that are intended to expand the scope of the assessment notice regime to the private sector. As already indicated, these amendments met with a favourable response from the Information Commissioner[1]. The Bill inserts a new s 41A into the Data Protection Act 1998, which reads as follows:

'41A Assessment notices
- (1) The Commissioner may serve a data controller within subsection (2) with a notice (in this Act referred to as an "assessment notice") for the purpose of enabling the Commissioner to determine whether the data controller has complied or is complying with the data protection principles.
- (2) A data controller is within this subsection if the data controller is—
  - (a) a government department,
  - (b) a public authority designated for the purposes of this section by an order made by the Secretary of State, or
  - (c) a person of a description designated for the purposes of this section by such an order.
- (3) An assessment notice is a notice which requires the data controller to do all or any of the following—
  - (a) permit the Commissioner to enter any specified premises;
  - (b) direct the Commissioner to any documents on the premises that are of a specified description;
  - (c) assist the Commissioner to view any information of a specified description that is capable of being viewed using equipment on the premises;
  - (d) comply with any request from the Commissioner for—
    - (i) a copy of any of the documents to which the Commissioner is directed;
    - (ii) a copy (in such form as may be requested) of any of the information which the Commissioner is assisted to view;
  - (e) direct the Commissioner to any equipment or other material on the premises which is of a specified description;

6.138 *Regulation and enforcement*

    (f) permit the Commissioner to inspect or examine any of the documents, information, equipment or material to which the Commissioner is directed or which the Commissioner is assisted to view;
    (g) permit the Commissioner to observe the processing of any personal data that takes place on the premises;
    (h) make available for interview by the Commissioner a specified number of persons of a specified description who process personal data on behalf of the data controller (or such number as are willing to be interviewed).
 (4) In subsection (3) references to the Commissioner include references to the Commissioner's officers and staff.
 (5) An assessment notice must, in relation to each requirement imposed by the notice, specify—
    (a) the time at which the requirement is to be complied with, or
    (b) the period during which the requirement is to be complied with.
 (6) An assessment notice must also contain particulars of the rights of appeal conferred by section 48.
 (7) The Commissioner may cancel an assessment notice by written notice to the data controller on whom it was served.
 (8) Where a public authority has been designated by an order under subsection (2)(b) the Secretary of State must reconsider, at intervals of no greater than 5 years, whether it continues to be appropriate for the authority to be designated.
 (9) The Secretary of State may not make an order under subsection (2)(c) which designates a description of persons unless—
    (a) the Commissioner has made a recommendation that the description be designated, and
    (b) the Secretary of State has consulted—
      (i) such persons as appear to the Secretary of State to represent the interests of those that meet the description;
      (ii) such other persons as the Secretary of State considers appropriate.
 (10) The Secretary of State may not make an order under subsection (2)(c), and the Commissioner may not make a recommendation under subsection (9)(a), unless the Secretary of State or (as the case may be) the Commissioner is satisfied that it is necessary for the description of persons in question to be designated having regard to—
    (a) the nature and quantity of data under the control of such persons, and
    (b) any damage or distress which may be caused by a contravention by such persons of the data protection principles.
 (11) Where a description of persons has been designated by an order under subsection (2)(c) the Secretary of State must reconsider, at intervals of no greater than 5 years, whether it continues to be necessary for the description to be designated having regard to the matters mentioned in subsection (10).
 (12) In this section—
   "public authority" includes any body, office-holder or other person in respect of which—
    (a) an order may be made under section 4 or 5 of the Freedom of Information Act 2000, or
    (b) an order may be made under section 4 or 5 of the Freedom of Information (Scotland) Act 2002;

"specified" means specified in an assessment notice.'

[1] See the memorandum dated 31 July 2009.

WHAT IS AN ASSESSMENT NOTICE?

6.139 The purpose of an assessment notice is set out in s 41A(1) of the Coroners and Justice Bill; it is intended to enable the Information Commissioner to enter premises to assess whether a data controller has complied, or is complying, with the data protection principles.

At the heart of the assessment notice process is a requirement that the controller shall allow the Commissioner access to its premises, so that his officers can (1) inspect and examine documents, information, equipment or other materials, (2) observe processing operations and (3) interview people. In other words the assessment notice procedure gives the Commissioner the power to enter premises after a request for entry has been made; it is not equivalent to a 'dawn raid' power.

The powers granted by the assessment notice procedure extend beyond those within Sch 9 as originally enacted, in two ways. First, Sch 9 does not allow the Commissioner to inspect data processing operations. Second, Sch 9 does not allow the Commissioner to interview people. In this sense the assessment notice procedure can be considered to be innovative. However, as discussed above the Coroners and Justice Bill will make amendments to Sch 9, to bring it into alignment with the assessment notice power.

WHO CAN BE SERVED WITH AN ASSESSMENT NOTICE?

6.140 Section 41A(2) identifies the data controllers who are subject to the enforcement notice procedure. These are (1) government departments, (2) designated public authorities and (3) other designated persons.

The reference to other designated persons at s 41A(2)(c) is the provision that can bring the private sector within the scope of assessment notices. During the House of Lords committee reading on 21 July 2009 the government's spokesperson, Lord Bach, explained the government's reasoning:

'During the debates in the other place, we listened to the arguments about the blurred distinction between the public and private sectors and the need to extend assessment notices to all data collectors, and we are grateful for the conversations that have been had since then. In response, we explained that, as the Bill stands, it is possible in certain circumstances to include some private or third-sector data controllers within the scope of assessment notices. This designation would be by order made by the Secretary of State when a person exercises public functions or provides, under a contract with a public authority, a service the provision of which is a function of the public authority.

However, we have listened to the arguments made in favour of further extending the scope of assessment notices to the private sector. We recognise that there are genuine concerns about the private sector's handling of personal

6.140 Regulation and enforcement

> data—indeed, the noble Baroness, Lady Miller, referred to them—and that there are certain categories of private-sector data controller whose circumstances merit the application of assessment notices.
>
> Government Amendments 198A, 199A and 199C address those scenarios. We remain unpersuaded that the assessment notice regime should apply automatically to all data controllers. Such an approach would be a little excessive and impose disproportionate burdens on business. Instead, our amendments enable the Secretary of State to designate by order certain descriptions of private-sector data controller as liable for assessment notices.'

If this represents the final scheme for the assessment notice power it will follow that only government departments will be affected when the Coroners and Justice Act achieves Royal Assent.

DESIGNATING PRIVATE SECTOR DATA CONTROLLERS

6.141 The process by which private sector data controllers can become designated for the purposes of s 41A(2)(c) is contained in s 41A(9). It should be noted that the designation power is not intended to apply to individual data controllers by name. Rather, it is intended to apply to categories of data controllers. For example, this means that the government could not designate a particular law firm. Instead, if the Information Commissioner and the government wish to bring a law firm into scope they will have to identify the solicitors' profession as a whole. This intention is not crystal clear on the wording of s 41A(2)(c), but Lord Bach's speech leaves no doubt about the government's intentions:

> 'This amendment does not provide for the designation of a particular data controller but for a description of a data controller. This means that the designation would not single out or list individual data controllers but would provide a description of a class of data controller—for example, credit reference agencies, which have been referred to in the debate—as liable to assessment notices.'

The starting point in the process leading to designation is that the Information Commissioner must make 'a recommendation' for designation, which again illustrates the Commissioner's critical role in the development of the law.

Once a recommendation has been made the Secretary of State must open a process of consultation. This must cover those who represent the interests of the class of data controllers under designation and 'such other persons as the Secretary of State considers appropriate'. This approach to consultation means that the government can avoid a full public consultation, which may help to shorten the process leading to designation. This might be helpful if an emergency situation arises.

6.142 In order to ensure that any designations are proportionate, s 41A(10) includes an important control mechanism. This makes the issuing of recommendations and orders for designation conditional upon the Commissioner and the government both considering the nature of the data that are under the

Regulation and enforcement under the Data Protection Act 1998 **6.144**

control of the controllers who are under examination and the nature and extent of the damage and distress which may be caused if the controllers were to contravene the Data Protection Act.

If an order for designation is made, the government must keep it under review. Section 41A(11) sets a long stop, five-year period for the carrying out of reviews.

Lord Bach summarised the process in this manner:

> 'The amendments provide the Secretary of State with the power to make an order following a recommendation from the Information Commissioner. Where the Secretary of State was minded to accept such a recommendation, we would be able to proceed to make an order, which would be subject to the affirmative procedure, only following consultation with the affected sectors. Such consultations would be accompanied by a full impact assessment. The Secretary of State and the Information Commissioner will have to be satisfied that designation is necessary, taking into account the nature and quantity of data under the control of such persons and the damage or distress that may be caused by a contravention by such persons of the data protection principles.'

In distinction, the process for the designation of public authorities for the purposes of s 41A(2)(c) is the making of an order by the Secretary of State. The Information Commissioner is not given a formal role in the process, although it is anticipated that he will continue to exert influence over government.

MATERIALS THAT ARE EXEMPT FROM THE ASSESSMENT NOTICE PROCEDURE

6.143 As with the Data Protection Act 1998, Sch 9, the regime within the Coroners and Justice Bill contains an exemption for materials that are legally privileged[1]. The judiciary, bodies dealing with national security matters and the Office for Standards in Education, Children's Services and Skills will be exempt from assessment notices[2].

1 Coroners and Justice Bill, s 41B(3).
2 Coroners and Justice Bill, s 41B(5).

TIME PERIOD FOR COMPLIANCE WITH ASSESSMENT NOTICES

6.144 Section 41A(5) specifies the time period for compliance with an assessment notice, but this should be read in accordance with s 41B, which provides as follows:

'**41B Assessment notices: limitations**
(1) A time specified in an assessment notice under section 41A(5) in relation to a requirement must not fall, and a period so specified must not begin, before the end of the period within which an appeal can be brought against the notice, and if such an appeal is brought the requirement need not be complied with pending the determination or withdrawal of the appeal.

6.144 *Regulation and enforcement*

>   (2)   If by reason of special circumstances the Commissioner considers that it is necessary for the data controller to comply with a requirement in an assessment notice as a matter of urgency, the Commissioner may include in the notice a statement to that effect and a statement of the reasons for that conclusion; and in that event subsection (1) applies in relation to the requirement as if for the words from "within" to the end there were substituted "of 7 days beginning with the day on which the notice is served".'

The pattern here is the same as for enforcement notices. The starting point is that assessment notices must not take effect until at least 28 days after service, because that is the time period for bringing an appeal. However, this period can be truncated in urgent cases. It should be noted that Part 2 of Schedule 19 to the Bill contains consequential amendments to the Data Protection Act 1998, s 48, to bring assessment notices within the appeal procedure. The right to appeal should be explained in the assessment notice.

SANCTIONS FOR NON-COMPLIANCE WITH AN ASSESSMENT NOTICE

6.145 The sanction for non-compliance with an assessment notice is described in Part 6 of Schedule 19 to the Bill. In summary, this will amend the Data Protection Act 1998, Sch 9 to allow the court to issue a warrant on the grounds of the person's refusal to comply with the assessment notice. The Information Commissioner's alternatives (making non-compliance a criminal offence or a contempt of court) were specifically rejected by the government during the House of Lords committee stage. Lord Bach explained as follows:

> 'I turn now to sanctions for non-compliance with an assessment notice. Again, we have listened to the representations in the other place on this issue. The case for some express sanction in the event of non-compliance is reinforced now that private-sector data controllers can be brought within the scope of assessment notices. Our Amendments 206ZA to 206ZD would introduce changes to Schedule 18 to provide the Information Commissioner with the power to apply for a warrant under Schedule 9 to the Data Protection Act where a data controller had failed to comply with a requirement imposed by an assessment notice. As now, the Information Commissioner's office would need to satisfy the judge that there were sufficient grounds for the issue of a warrant to search the data controller's premises.

> We have taken a different approach to enforcement from that taken in Amendments 195, 200, 201, 203, and 204, tabled by my noble friend Lord Dubs and the noble Baroness, Lady Miller. The key difficulty with treating the failure to comply with an assessment notice as a contempt of court or as an offence is that ultimately it does not provide the Information Commissioner with access to the premises in question, which is exactly what a warrant does; it provides the Information Commissioner with access. The former Information Commissioner agreed with us that this would not provide him with the access he believed was required.'

The final part of this extract of Lord Bach's explanation makes it clear that the purpose of an assessment notice is to facilitate the Information Commissioner's access to premises, hence why ultimately they dovetail with the warrant regime in the Data Protection Act 1998, Sch 9.

Use of material obtained by an assessment notice

6.146 Part 5 of Schedule 19 of the Bill amends the Data Protection Act 1998, s 55A, the monetary penalties regime that was introduced by the Criminal Justice and Immigration Act 2008, through the insertion of a new s 55A(3A):

> '(3A) The Commissioner may not be satisfied as mentioned in subsection (1) by virtue of any matter which comes to the Commissioner's attention as a result of anything done in pursuance of—
> (a) an assessment notice;
> (b) an assessment under section 51(7).'

The effect of this amendment is to prevent the Commissioner from using materials obtained by an assessment notice to provide the basis of a monetary penalty. In other words, data controllers who are in receipt of an assessment notice can use that opportunity to gain an effective amnesty from the monetary penalties regime. Lord Bach described this as 'a strong incentive for data controllers to consent to a good practice assessment'.

However, assessment notices still contain peril for controllers, as nothing will prevent the Commissioner from relying upon the materials obtained by an assessment notice to support the service of an enforcement notice under the Data Protection Act 1998, s 40. In the context of the exemption from the monetary penalties regime Lord Bach explained:

> 'This exemption will not—I emphasise, not—provide immunity to data controllers from all enforcement action in relation to breaches that might be discovered during a good practice assessment or an assessment notice. The commissioner will still be able to issue an enforcement notice under Section 40 of the Data Protection Act to compel the data controller to comply with their data protection obligations if he discovers a breach of the data protection principles during any of these assessments.'

Code of practice for assessment notices

6.147 Section 41C will require the Information Commissioner to issue a code of practice on the use of assessment notices. The effect of this code of practice will be to describe the Commissioner's policy on assessment notices, which will provide data controllers with a yardstick to measure the lawfulness of an assessment notice in any given case. The requirement for a code of practice represents a significant improvement on the enforcement notice procedure, which does not contain equivalent provisions:

> '41C Code of practice about assessment notices
> (1) The Commissioner must prepare and issue a code of practice as to the manner in which the Commissioner's functions under and in connection with section 41A are to be exercised.
> (2) The code must in particular—
>   (a) specify factors to be considered in determining whether to serve an assessment notice on a data controller;
>   (b) specify descriptions of documents and information that—
>   (i) are not to be examined or inspected in pursuance of an assessment notice, or

6.147 *Regulation and enforcement*

    (ii) are to be so examined or inspected only by persons of a description specified in the code;
  (c) deal with the nature of inspections and examinations carried out in pursuance of an assessment notice;
  (d) deal with the nature of interviews carried out in pursuance of an assessment notice;
  (e) deal with the preparation, issuing and publication by the Commissioner of assessment reports in respect of data controllers that have been served with assessment notices.
(3) The provisions of the code made by virtue of subsection (2)(b) must, in particular, include provisions that relate to—
  (a) documents and information concerning an individual's physical or mental health;
  (b) documents and information concerning the provision of social care for an individual.
(4) An assessment report is a report which contains—
  (a) a determination as to whether a data controller has complied or is complying with the data protection principles,
  (b) recommendations as to any steps which the data controller ought to take, or refrain from taking, to ensure compliance with any of those principles, and
  (c) such other matters as are specified in the code.
(5) The Commissioner may alter or replace the code.
(6) If the code is altered or replaced, the Commissioner must issue the altered or replacement code.
(7) The Commissioner may not issue the code (or an altered or replacement code) without the approval of the Secretary of State.
(8) The Commissioner must arrange for the publication of the code (and any altered or replacement code) issued under this section in such form and manner as the Commissioner considers appropriate.
(9) In this section "social care" has the same meaning as in Part 1 of the Health and Social Care Act 2008 (see section 9(3) of that Act).'

6.148 An indication of the likely contents of a code of practice is provided by the Information Commissioner's memorandum on the government amendments published on 31 July 2009. This provides a summary of how the process will work:

'- The ICO decides to carry out an assessment where it appears that there is a particular risk to individuals or suspicion of non-compliance, e.g. where a large number of sensitive records are held, or where a series of complaints have been received. This risk-based approach is in line with the principles of regulatory good practice.
- An assessment of a larger organisation typically involves three or four ICO auditors visiting for three or four days and interviewing 12–30 staff. We usually focus on a particular aspect of an organisation's activity, e.g. its security procedures, leaving other parts unaffected. Most assessments involve larger organisations. Where smaller organisations are involved, the scale of the operation (and hence the burden) is considerably reduced.
- After an assessment, an organisation found lacking receives good practice recommendations. Our constructive feedback helps organisations to improve standards and, in most cases, reduces the likelihood of more formal action in the future. Only where there is evidence of a

serious contravention, and the organisation fails to respond appropriately, will we issue an enforcement notice.
- We work with organisations in a spirit of co-operation including agreeing the time, place and scope of any assessment. We intend to continue on this basis. However, there must be a fall-back position in which we can carry out checks on organisations whose activities pose a particular risk to individuals, but who will not co-operate with us voluntarily.
- We already have a formal agreement with the Government on detailed arrangements for "spot-checks" on Government departments. This makes clear what departments can reasonably expect and provide safeguards. The proposed statutory code of practice will provide a similar level of transparency and safeguards for all organisations subject to assessment notices.
- The number of assessments undertaken is primarily dependent on the ICO's resources and will not change significantly as a result of strengthening of our powers. However, new powers will make our assessments more effective, through better targeting and less time wasted negotiating entry. They will also help us to target areas of risk, leaving the majority of low-risk organisations alone. For many organisations, the existence of the powers would be a powerful spur to compliance, whether or not they need to be deployed.'

Assessment notices – a distinction without a difference?

6.149 While it is fair to say that the assessment notice procedure contains some innovations, does it constitute a truly significant development in the law?

Detractors of the regime can point to the fact that it ultimately requires a judicial warrant for the Information Commissioner to secure entry to premises when the controller is resistant to an assessment notice, which has always been the case under the Data Protection Act 1998, Sch 9. Therefore, it would be a fair criticism to say that the amendments do not give the Commissioner anything new.

Likewise, it would be fair to observe that the Commissioner has always been able to use the materials gathered by an inspection to support the service of an enforcement notice. In that sense too the amendments do not give the Commissioner anything new.

In support of the assessment notice procedure it might be argued that the amendments are truly significant because of the effect that they will have on perceptions. Controllers will be cognisant of the fact that the assessment notice procedure will make the issuing of judicial warrants more likely and in an objective sense they would be wise to treat inspections as forming part of the reality of day-to-day regulatory practice, which, currently, is not the case. Perhaps the biggest incentive to agreeing to inspections is the amnesty from the monetary penalty regime. For many data controllers, particularly those operating in sensitive areas, the amnesty may be very attractive.

6.150   *Regulation and enforcement*

6.150   To a very large extent the 'success' of the amendments will be measured against the extent to which the Commissioner manages to gain entry without having to resort to a warrant. If data controllers routinely respond positively to the service of assessment notices, by letting the Commissioner in and complying with recommendations for improvements, the regime will be regarded as being a success. If this is taken as the measure of success, then there is a precedent that gives great cause for optimism; this is the way that data controllers have responded to the Commissioner's willingness to take undertakings in lieu of the service of an enforcement notice.

Of course, it is still fair to observe that the Information Commissioner has got significantly less than was argued for; an assessment notice procedure backed up with a new criminal offence was the Commissioner's preference after all. Yet, the Commissioner's comments on the amendments made in July 2009 are very positive. Taking the 31 July memorandum at face value, it would seem that the Commissioner is satisfied with the outcome:

> 'The Information Commissioner is content that the Government amendments will open the way to a more effective data protection inspection regime, providing better protections for individuals against organisations whose activities pose a particular risk, and improving public trust and confidence in the processing of personal data.'

On balance the Commissioner's sense of satisfaction seems to be justified, particularly given the role that he has to play in designating private sector data controllers. The process described in s 41A(5) puts the Commissioner in the driving seat in a wholly unprecedented way and while it would be possible for the government to drag its heels following a recommendation from the Commissioner, the highly activist stance adopted by the Commissioner since 2006 indicates that the Commissioner will protest in a very public fashion if that were to occur. The Commissioner's July 2009 memorandum points very clearly to this likelihood:

> 'If the necessary improvements to the ICO's inspection powers are to be achieved, the process for designating a "description of the persons" subject to the assessment notice power must be effective. We recognise that those likely to be affected by any designation should be consulted, but the new inspection regime will not get off the ground if the designation process is overly bureaucratic or time-consuming, or if the Information Commissioner's initial recommendation is not given due weight.'

Monetary penalties (fining data controllers)

6.151   Section 144 of the Criminal Justice and Immigration Act 2008 inserted ss 55A–E into the Data Protection Act 1998, to give the Information Commissioner the power to impose monetary penalties on data controllers who are in serious contravention of the data protection principles. The introduction of the monetary penalties regime is one of the most important post-HMRC innovations and it is to the credit of government and Parliament that it took only six months from the announcement of the loss of the disks for this landmark reform to be introduced. However, it is very unfortunate that the initial momentum has not been maintained. As will be seen, the monetary penalties regime needs regulations to be brought into effect.

It should also be noted that the Coroners and Justice Bill contains an amendment to the monetary penalties regime, which will prevent the Commissioner from relying upon materials gathered during an assessment notice to support the imposition of a monetary penalty.

The power to impose a monetary penalty

6.152 Before the Information Commissioner can impose a monetary penalty he has to be objectively satisfied that the controller is in serious contravention of the data protection principles and that substantial damage or distress is likely to be caused as a result of the contravention. These are clearly higher hurdles than within the enforcement notice regime.

In addition the Commissioner has to be objectively satisfied that the controller had the requisite level of knowledge. Where the contravention is deliberate, the issues should be relatively straightforward. However, in the majority of cases the contravention will not be deliberate. In these cases the Commissioner also has to be objectively satisfied that the controller knew, or ought to have known, that (1) there was a risk that the contravention would occur, (2) it would be likely to cause substantial damage or distress and (3) it failed to take reasonable steps to prevent the contravention occurring. These requirements place a very high evidential burden on the Commissioner.

These initial considerations are set out in the opening parts of the Data Protection Act 1998, s 55A, which provides as follows:

'**55A Power of Commissioner to impose monetary penalty**
(1) The Commissioner may serve a data controller with a monetary penalty notice if the Commissioner is satisfied that—
    (a) there has been a serious contravention of section 4(4) by the data controller,
    (b) the contravention was of a kind likely to cause substantial damage or substantial distress, and
    (c) subsection (2) or (3) applies.
(2) This subsection applies if the contravention was deliberate.
(3) This subsection applies if the data controller—
    (a) knew or ought to have known—
        (i) that there was a risk that the contravention would occur, and
        (ii) that such a contravention would be of a kind likely to cause substantial damage or substantial distress, but
    (b) failed to take reasonable steps to prevent the contravention.'

The amount of the fine

6.153 Section 55A continues by saying that the amount of the fine must be specified in the notice itself. It cannot exceed the 'prescribed amount' however:

6.153 *Regulation and enforcement*

'55A Power of Commissioner to impose monetary penalty

…

(4) A monetary penalty notice is a notice requiring the data controller to pay to the Commissioner a monetary penalty of an amount determined by the Commissioner and specified in the notice.

(5) The amount determined by the Commissioner must not exceed the prescribed amount.

(6) The monetary penalty must be paid to the Commissioner within the period specified in the notice.

(7) The notice must contain such information as may be prescribed.

(8) Any sum received by the Commissioner by virtue of this section must be paid into the Consolidated Fund.

(9) In this section—
"data controller" does not include the Crown Estate Commissioners or a person who is a data controller by virtue of section 63(3);
"prescribed" means prescribed by regulations made by the Secretary of State.'

As can be seen from the final part of s 55A, the prescribed amount means the amount prescribed by regulations made by the Secretary of State. Unfortunately regulations were not made in time for the publication of this book.

Procedural rights

6.154 The monetary penalty regime contains two important safeguards against abuse. First, prior to imposing a penalty the Information Commissioner must serve a notice of intent, which should contain information that will be prescribed by the regulations. The data controller then has the right to make written representations in response. Second, the controller can appeal the imposition of a penalty. These requirements are contained in the Data Protection Act 1998, s 55B, which provides as follows:

'55B Monetary penalty notices: procedural rights

(1) Before serving a monetary penalty notice, the Commissioner must serve the data controller with a notice of intent.

(2) A notice of intent is a notice that the Commissioner proposes to serve a monetary penalty notice.

(3) A notice of intent must—
　(a) inform the data controller that he may make written representations in relation to the Commissioner's proposal within a period specified in the notice, and
　(b) contain such other information as may be prescribed.

(4) The Commissioner may not serve a monetary penalty notice until the time within which the data controller may make representations has expired.

(5) A person on whom a monetary penalty notice is served may appeal to the Tribunal against—
　(a) the issue of the monetary penalty notice;
　(b) the amount of the penalty specified in the notice.

(6) In this section, "prescribed" means prescribed by regulations made by the Secretary of State.'

Guidance about monetary penalty notices

6.155 Section 55C places an obligation on the Information Commissioner to publish guidance on the circumstances in which he will impose a penalty and how he will determine the amount of the penalty. This requirement reflects the principles discussed in Hampton, Macrory and the related legislation.

The Commissioner is not given carte blanche in the issuing of guidance however. Instead, government and Parliament retain final oversight. Section 55C provides as follows:

'**55C Guidance about monetary penalty notices**
(1) The Commissioner must prepare and issue guidance on how he proposes to exercise his functions under sections 55A and 55B.
(2) The guidance must, in particular, deal with—
  (a) the circumstances in which he would consider it appropriate to issue a monetary penalty notice, and
  (b) how he will determine the amount of the penalty.
(3) The Commissioner may alter or replace the guidance.
(4) If the guidance is altered or replaced, the Commissioner must issue the altered or replacement guidance.
(5) The Commissioner may not issue guidance under this section without the approval of the Secretary of State.
(6) The Commissioner must lay any guidance issued under this section before each House of Parliament.
(7) The Commissioner must arrange for the publication of any guidance issued under this section in such form and manner as he considers appropriate.
(8) In subsections (5) to (7), "guidance" includes altered or replacement guidance.'

Enforcement of monetary penalty notices

6.156 The Information Commissioner will need to obtain a court order to enforce a monetary penalty notice:

'**55D Monetary penalty notices: enforcement**
(1) This section applies in relation to any penalty payable to the Commissioner by virtue of section 55A.
(2) In England and Wales, the penalty is recoverable—
  (a) if a county court so orders, as if it were payable under an order of that court;
  (b) if the High Court so orders, as if it were payable under an order of that court.
(3) In Scotland, the penalty may be enforced in the same manner as an extract registered decree arbitral bearing a warrant for execution issued by the sheriff court of any sheriffdom in Scotland.
(4) In Northern Ireland, the penalty is recoverable—
  (a) if a county court so orders, as if it were payable under an order of that court;
  (b) if the High Court so orders, as if it were payable under an order of that court.'

6.157 *Regulation and enforcement*

Miscellany

6.157 Section 55E contains a series of supplemental provisions concerning monetary penalty notices and notices of intent. These envisage that the Secretary of State may make exemptions from the regime for the special purposes (processing for journalism etc) as well as rules about cancellation and variation of notices and appeals.

> **'55E Notices under sections 55A and 55B: supplemental**
> (1) The Secretary of State may by order make further provision in connection with monetary penalty notices and notices of intent.
> (2) An order under this section may in particular—
>   (a) provide that a monetary penalty notice may not be served on a data controller with respect to the processing of personal data for the special purposes except in circumstances specified in the order;
>   (b) make provision for the cancellation or variation of monetary penalty notices;
>   (c) confer rights of appeal to the Tribunal against decisions of the Commissioner in relation to the cancellation or variation of such notices;
>   (d) make provision for the proceedings of the Tribunal in respect of appeals under section 55B(5) or appeals made by virtue of paragraph (c);
>   (e) make provision for the determination of such appeals;
>   (f) confer rights of appeal against any decision of the Tribunal in relation to monetary penalty notices or their cancellation or variation.
> (3) An order under this section may apply any provision of this Act with such modifications as may be specified in the order.
> (4) An order under this section may amend this Act.'

Assessment notices and monetary penalties

6.158 The Coroners and Justice Bill contains amendments to the Data Protection Act 1998, s 55A, to prevent the Information Commissioner from relying upon information obtained through an assessment notice to support the imposition of a monetary penalty:

> '(3A) The Commissioner may not be satisfied as mentioned in subsection (1) by virtue of any matter which comes to the Commissioner's attention as a result of anything done in pursuance of—
>   (a) an assessment notice;
>   (b) an assessment under section 51(7).'[1]

As observed by Lord Bach, this exemption may incentivise controllers to cooperate with assessment notices.

[1] Coroners and Justice Bill, Sch 19, Pt 5, para 12.

Criminal proceedings against those who threaten the security of personal data

6.159 In Chapter 1 the Information Commissioner's special report to Parliament, 'What price privacy?' is discussed. To recap, this drew attention to the trade in unlawfully obtained personal data, which is an offence under the Data Protection Act 1998, s 55.

As a direct result of the Commissioner's interventions the Criminal Justice and Immigration Act 2008 has amended the Data Protection Act 1998 to give the Secretary of State the power to introduce custodial penalties for those convicted.

Regulation and enforcement by the data subject

6.160 The data subject plays a critical role within the regulation and enforcement of the law, which is based on enlightened self-interest; who else is more incentivised to ensure that data are kept safe and secure than the person who will be most affected by a security breach or data loss?

Requests for assessments

6.161 The main route by which a data subject can play a role in regulation is the 'request for assessment' route, which is contained in the Data Protection Act 1998, s 42. Section 42 provides that if a person believes that they are, or are likely to be, affected by data processing they can make a request to the Information Commissioner for an assessment of 'whether it is likely or unlikely that the processing has been or is being carried out in compliance with the provisions of [the DPA]'.

It is the Commissioner's practice to treat any complaint about data processing as requests for assessments, irrespective of whether the complainant refers to s 42 or not. Upon receipt of a request for an assessment the Commissioner 'shall make an assessment in such manner as appears to him to be appropriate'. Once the assessment has been carried out, the Commissioner will inform the complainant of his conclusions.

There are many reasons why it is fair to conclude that the s 42 procedure is the main route by which a data subject can play a role in regulation. First and foremost, it removes the financial and resources burdens of enforcement from the data subject, placing them on the Information Commissioner, who in most cases is in the best position to regulate the Data Protection Act 1998. Second, s 42 is one of the key processes by which enforcement action is triggered; a request for an assessment can trigger the service of an information notice, an enforcement notice, an application for a search warrant and, when the new powers are in force, an assessment notice or a monetary penalty. Requests for assessments are one of the foundation stones underpinning the regulatory framework.

6.162   *Regulation and enforcement*

Proceedings for the cessation of processing

6.162 Data Protection Act 1998, s 10 contains a power that has great potential for regulation of data security law. It gives individuals the right to request the cessation of processing that is likely to cause substantial and unwarranted damage or distress.

The significance of this power to data security law lies in the fact that the Information Commissioner regularly states in enforcement notices based on breaches of the seventh data protection principle that the suffering of distress is likely. Thus, if a security breach is likely to cause distress for the purpose of enforcement notices, distress should also be likely for the purposes of s 10, if the Commissioner's logical pathway is followed.

If the individual wishes to take advantage of this right they must serve a notice on the data controller specifying their request and their reasons. This puts the controller under an obligation to serve a counter notice in response, setting out their intentions. If the individual is unhappy with the controller's response they then have the right to apply to the court for an order to enforce their request.

This right to object is subject to some important limitations however; it will not apply where the individual gave their consent to the processing, or where the processing is necessary for the performance of a contract or where the processing is necessary in order to protect the data subject's vital interests. This means that the right to object is likely to be of most relevance to security breaches and data loss occurring in the public sector.

Compensation claims

6.163 Data subjects who suffer damage and distress as a result of contraventions of the data protection principles can bring claims for compensation under the Data Protection Act 1998, s 13. Compensation claims are discussed in more detail in Chapter 2.

Subject access requests

6.164 The data subject's right of access to information about data processing is contained in the Data Protection Act 1998, s 7. This gives the data subject the right to key information about the controller's identity and their data processing operations. The right of access has the same utility for data subjects as information notices and assessment notices have for the Information Commissioner; it opens the controller up to scrutiny. The data subject can use s 7 to establish whether the controller has suffered a security breach, or lost data, information that can support requests under ss 10 and 42 and compensation claims under s 13.

Responding to and challenging regulatory action

6.165 The point was made in Chapter 1 that the regulators are bound to make mistakes during the course of regulatory action. This is an inevitable fact of life, which becomes increasingly more likely as the volume of regulatory action increases. Therefore data controllers need to implement strategies for coping with the Information Commissioner.

The 'lens of litigation'

6.166 Data controllers and their advisors who are inexperienced in defending data protection regulatory actions generally fail to appreciate the truly contentious nature of this area of the law. Of course, this does not mean that controllers should take a provocative, argumentative or unproductive stance; rather they should deal with the regulator politely, but always cognisant of the fact that everything done or said should be viewed through the 'lens of litigation'. In other words, everything that the Information Commissioner and the controller do and say have legal consequences. For example, poor quality investigations by the Information Commissioner can be as relevant to the final outcome of any legal proceedings as poor quality data handling by the controller. This is because we have an adversarial legal system; if a case comes before the Information Tribunal or the court, both parties will be on trial.

Viewing interactions with the Information Commissioner through the lens of litigation puts an entirely different gloss on them. The controller starts to appreciate and understand the limitations of the Commissioner's powers and the obstacles that the Commissioner must pass to ensure that his actions are lawful in the fullest sense of the word, which means lawful per the Data Protection Act 1998, lawful per principles of regulatory law, lawful per principles of public law and lawful per principles of human rights law. A controller with this perspective can implement strategies for taking control of the regulatory proceedings and can set up the situation for its victory and the Commissioner's loss.

Understanding the full legal landscape

6.167 The lens of litigation therefore tells the data controller that data security law requires an understanding of the full legal landscape. If the controller merely gears itself up to address the narrow issues within the seventh data protection principle and its statutory interpretation, it will significantly restrict its room for manoeuvre. Furthermore, such a data controller can create significantly more problems for itself downstream. This point is illustrated in the section immediately below, which discusses the litigation issues relating to undertakings.

6.168 Regulation and enforcement

The giving of undertakings – is this wise?

6.168 The point was made earlier in this chapter that the Information Commissioner regularly accepts undertakings about compliance from data controllers in consideration of not serving enforcement notices. The Commissioner's preference for undertakings will be obvious from a cursory glance of the enforcement cases discussed in Appendix A; the number of undertakings given far outstrips the number of enforcement notices served. The use of undertakings is not actually part of the statutory enforcement regime for data protection however. It will also be recalled that the government has not accepted the Commissioner's case for the reform of the law by the way of introduction of a formal undertakings regime in the Data Protection Act 1998[1].

For data controllers the upside of undertakings compared to enforcement notices seems to be apparent; if enforcement notices give the controller two bites at the cherry, then undertakings gives them three bites, in the sense that the route to criminal prosecutions under the Data Protection Act 1998, s 47 requires a breach of an enforcement notice to occur. Thus, a breach of undertakings can only lead to criminal proceedings if the Commissioner then serves an enforcement notice, which is itself breached. From this perspective the advantage of giving undertakings is obvious.

However, if the controller digs a little deeper, the counter arguments against undertakings also become apparent. The primary problem with undertakings is their informal nature. As they exist outside of the statutory enforcement regime the controller does not have the benefit of the statutory protections that apply with enforcement notices. For example, none of the substantive obstacles or constraints within the Data Protection Act 1998, s 40 apply and nor does the appeal route to the Information Tribunal. Consequently, the potential for abuse of undertakings is considerably greater than with enforcement notices. They can be used in a much broader range of circumstances than enforcement notices and they can be used to achieve a broader range of outcomes. In other words undertakings can be used to extract more from the controller than the law allows.

The controller should also focus on the fact that breach of undertakings can lead to the service of an enforcement notice. So, if the undertakings themselves have a broader utility than could have been achieved directly through the service of an enforcement notice, it can follow that an enforcement notice based on a breach of undertakings can also have broader utility than in a case where undertakings were not given. Ultimately this contagion can affect the final stage of enforcement, namely criminal prosecutions under the Data Protection Act 1998, s 47.

[1] See 'The case for amending the Data Protection Act', which is discussed earlier in this chapter.

6.169 Focusing further on criminal prosecutions under s 47, the controller would be wise to consider the appearance that is given when undertakings are breached. From the perspective of the judge and jury (in Crown Court trials) and the perspective of the magistrates (in summary trials), a breach of a promise can appear more serious than the breach of an order. Where the controller is alleged to have breached undertakings it cannot avoid cross examination on the fact that it was cognisant that it was making a solemn promise and that it was cognisant of the consequences of breach. Thus, it can be argued that enforcement action based on breach of undertakings is more serious than enforcement action that does not have this component.

So, why are data controllers giving undertakings so freely in data security cases? Perhaps some of them fail to see the full consequences. Perhaps they misunderstand the full range of consequences. Perhaps they are just being complacent, thinking that having three bites of the cherry is so much more to their advantage than two. Perhaps they are just badly advised. Of course, it is easy to see why the extra bite can be appealing, but if the full consequences are not appreciated the controller could be guilty of short-termism.

Similarly, when considering undertakings the controller should remain fully vigilant of the realities of the regulatory bear market and the trajectory of the law. Undertakings are not only relevant to the issue of enforcement notices and subsequent criminal proceedings, but they will also be relevant to financial penalties and inspections. Indeed, as far as monetary penalties are concerned, they can provide the Information Commissioner with the very evidence he needs to establish the requirements that the breach should be knowing or reckless; a promise of compliance volunteered and freely given is bound to be of relevance in this area, perhaps even more so than an enforcement notice.

6.170 Next, the consequences of undertakings for other areas of the law need to be considered. Undertakings should be construed as amounting to an admission of breach. An enforcement notice does not have that status; it represents the Commissioner's opinion that the controller has breached the law. The significance of an admission of breach when compared to the significance of an opinion of breach will be obvious in data subject litigation for example. Of course, it may be argued that the failure to appeal an enforcement notice constitutes the controller's acceptance of the correctness of the Commissioner's opinion. That is one construction that would be open, but it is not the only one. For example, the controller might not appeal an enforcement notice because of concerns about costs, or because it is occupied with more pressing issues. These possibilities do not seem to be available with undertakings.

Finally, undertakings may be relevant to the issue of personal criminal liability of directors, managers, secretaries and other officials employed by the data controller under the Data Protection Act 1998, s 61, as they may constitute admissions of personal negligence. Of course, the wording of the undertakings is critical and so the controller must be alert to this possibility.

In conclusion, it is easy to see the attractions in undertakings compared to enforcement notices; the additional bite at the cherry is undoubtedly significant, but this does not mean that undertakings are the softer opinion. They

6.170   *Regulation and enforcement*

may entail consequences for the controller that it may not have appreciated. If a controller later comes to regret giving undertakings, feeling that they might have been abused, its only remedy will be judicial review proceedings.

Litigation strategies and posture

6.171 The wise data controller will always develop a litigation strategy and posture as part of its core strategies for data security. This will inform and guide incident response strategies, including the identity of the personnel who will be involved in incident response, and dealings with the Information Commissioner. An appropriate litigation strategy is one that focuses on the bigger picture, not just the temporary issues of individual cases. It will appreciate the fact that the outcomes of individual cases can be directly relevant to the outcome of subsequent cases. It will also appreciate the duty of care that is owed by the data controller to its directors, secretaries, managers and other officers and it will make provisions to address conflicts of interest that arise from time to time. It will also take full account of the entirety of the law, including corporate governance requirements, not just the internal issues within the Data Protection Act 1998. It will also take account of all jurisdictional issues and the relevance of the outcomes of foreign proceedings.

Enforcement action taken by the Information Commissioner

Enforcement notices and undertakings

6.172 Appendix A contains a summary of enforcement action taken by the Information Commissioner in 2007, 2008 and 2009, for breaches of the seventh data protection principle.

A review of the cases reveals several trends in the Commissioner's enforcement strategy. A clear trend is that the Commissioner focuses for a time on a particular industry, for example the financial services sector or NHS Trusts, or a specific type of security breach, such as improper disposal of personal data, or the loss of unencrypted data stored on portable media or devices. There has also been a focus on security breaches at call centres and failures of website security. This approach is consistent with the Commissioner's 2005 enforcement strategy, which was referenced earlier in this chapter[1], which says that the Commissioner will take a selective, risk-based approach to enforcement.

The 2005 strategy reveals that regulatory action will be focused on cases where there is a risk of 'significant actual or potential detriment caused by non-compliance with the data protection principles or other relevant legal requirements'. This policy is evidenced by the actions taken against the banks and financial institutions (including Barclays, NatWest, Royal Bank of Scotland and HBOS) at the beginning of 2007, for their failure to dispose of personal data, including names of banking customers, debit card numbers, various application forms and transaction histories, securely. Although in each individual case the numbers of affected individuals was not particularly large, the nature of the data resulted in there being a significant actual or potential risk of serious harm.

The 2005 strategy lists the specific criteria that will be used to determine whether regulatory action will be taken, the form of any action and how far it will be pursued. Two such considerations are that action will be justified where the organisation and its practices are 'representative of a particular sector or activity to the extent that the case for action is supported by the need to set an example' and where it is likely that a 'breach will recur if action is not taken'. When viewed against this criteria it is clear to see that the Commissioner's decision to pursue action against so many organisations in a similar sector was driven by the desire to set an example and to highlight that the practice of improperly disposing of data, despite being commonplace within the industry, was unacceptable.

However, the 2005 strategy and the cases discussed in Appendix A point to other drivers for enforcement action, as there is an obvious correlation between issues that attract the public's and media's attention and the Commissioner's subsequent actions. The strategy is unequivocal on this point, and clearly states that an initial driver for enforcement action will be 'issues of general public concern (including those raised in the media)'. Therefore, it is not surprising to see that following HMRC's highly publicised loss of the two unencrypted disks the Commissioner's enforcement action has been substantially concerned with organisations that suffered security breaches of this nature.

1   'A strategy for data protection regulatory action'.

6.173 The Commissioner's enforcement action in relation to lost or stolen data on unencrypted laptops and portable media dominated his attention throughout 2008. However, even in relation to this specific problem trends can be seen, as the public sector seems to have borne the brunt of the regulatory action. Regulatory action against the Ministry of Defence, in relation to the theft of an unencrypted laptop, was taken at the same time as the Commissioner was pursuing action against HMRC, whilst NHS Trusts were the main focus for the remainder of 2008 and into 2009. This too is consistent with the Commissioner's regulatory strategy which states that:

> 'in selecting areas for attention we will bear in mind the extent to which market forces can themselves act as a regulator. Thus the public sector, particularly where processing is hidden from view and where the risks of a "surveillance society" may be greater, might well receive more attention from us than the private sector.'

Mobile telecommunication providers are one area of the private sector that feature several times within the cases. This may be due to the fact that they are consumer-facing, rendering it highly likely that the Commissioner will receive complaints about their handling of data. Although complaints about a data controller's actions is just one way regulatory action may be initiated, the Commissioner has identified this as a key driver for such action.

6.173 *Regulation and enforcement*

The Commissioner's highly targeted selective strategy is not misguided. In resisting a scatter-gun approach to enforcement action the Commissioner is sending clear messages as to the types of behaviour that will not be tolerated. Furthermore, numerous actions against one particular sector, or in relation to a particular breach, has the effect of reinforcing the message. However, the extent to which the Commissioner's action is resulting in improving practices for data security is very much open to doubt, a point that can be illustrated by reference to the encryption example.

When HMRC lost the two disks, encryption technologies were used by relatively few organisations. However, within 12 to 18 months of the breach occurring encryption of laptops and portable devices has become a standard security requirement as far as the law is concerned. Yet despite the intensity of the media coverage generated by the loss of unencrypted devices (and the intensity of the enforcement action) encryption is still used by relatively few organisations. In this sense enforcement action may not be having an impact.

Enforcement by way of criminal prosecution and applications for search warrants

6.174 The Information Commissioner's annual reports to Parliament[1] contain the best source materials for information about enforcement by way of criminal prosecution and applications for search warrants. The 2008–2009 report[2] reveals that there were only two criminal prosecutions in the period 1 April 2008 to 31 March 2009 for offences under the Data Protection Act 1998, s 55. It seems that there were no prosecutions under s 47 (breach of an enforcement notice or information notice) and no applications for search warrants under Sch 9. Table 6.2 provides an overview of the key statistics extracted from the annual reports.

Table 6.2. Enforcement by way of prosecutions and applications for search warrants – statistics extracted from the Commissioner's annual reports			
Year	DPA 1998, s 55	DPA 1998, s 47	DPA 1998, Sch 9
2009	2	0	15 (warrants applied for)
2008[3]	3	1	0
2007[4]	3	1	7 (warrants applied for)
2006[5]	6	0	12 (warrants applied for)
2005[6]	9	0	0
2004[7]	8	0	0

2003[8]	unclear	unclear	5 (warrants obtained)
2002[9]	unclear	unclear	3 (warrants obtained)
2001[10]	unclear	unclear	9 (warrants obtained)
2000[11]	Report not available		11 (warrants obtained)[12]
1999[13]	Report not available		10 (warrants obtained)[14]

[1] http://www.ico.gov.uk/about_us/what_we_do/corporate_information/annual_reports.aspx.
[2] http://www.ico.gov.uk/upload/documents/library/corporate/detailed_specialist_guides/annual_report_2009.pdf.
[3] http://www.ico.gov.uk/upload/documents/library/corporate/detailed_specialist_guides/annual_report_2007_08.pdf.
[4] http://www.ico.gov.uk/upload/documents/library/corporate/detailed_specialist_guides/annual_report_2007.pdf.
[5] http://www.ico.gov.uk/upload/documents/library/corporate/detailed_specialist_guides/Annual_Report_2006.pdf.
[6] http://www.ico.gov.uk/upload/documents/library/corporate/detailed_specialist_guides/Annual_Report_2005.pdf.
[7] http://www.ico.gov.uk/upload/documents/library/corporate/detailed_specialist_guides/Annual_Report_2004.pdf.
[8] http://www.ico.gov.uk/upload/documents/library/corporate/detailed_specialist_guides/Annual_Report_2003.pdf.
[9] http://www.ico.gov.uk/upload/documents/library/corporate/detailed_specialist_guides/Annual_Report_2002.pdf.
[10] http://www.ico.gov.uk/upload/documents/library/corporate/detailed_specialist_guides/Annual_Report_2001.pdf.
[11] No report available.
[12] See 2003 report.
[13] No report available.
[14] See 2003 report.

How effective is the Commissioner's enforcement strategy for data security?

6.175 If the success of the Information Commissioner's enforcement strategy is to be judged by reference to the number of enforcement notices issued and undertakings obtained, then it might be fair to conclude that it has been very successful. However, this is not necessarily the measure of success; counting the number of enforcement notices and undertakings is merely an exercise in measuring outputs, not outcomes, which offends the second of Macrory's seven characteristics of effective regulation. As Macrory observed 'most regulators are able to comment on their outputs such as numbers of prosecutions or number of Statutory Notices imposed, but are unable to draw any conclusions on what impact this has on overall compliance'[1].

Of course, measuring outcomes can be very difficult as Macrory accepts, but this does not detract from the fact that the Commissioner's approach, at least as revealed in the annual reports, might be Macrory-deficient:

6.175 Regulation and enforcement

'Regulatory outputs are quantitative measures such as the number of prosecutions, or the number of Statutory Notices imposed by a regulator, whereas a regulatory outcome seeks to measure what impact regulatory outputs may have had. Measuring outcomes will enable regulators and the public to know what impact the enforcement actions are having, whether these have improved compliance, or remedied the harm caused by regulatory non-compliance, and whether there needs to be any modification to the balance between different types of enforcement actions to get better results. I acknowledge this may not be an easy exercise and there may be difficulties in determining these measures, but I maintain that regulators and government departments should make every effort to identify and measure regulatory outcomes.'[2]

Macrory does provide some assistance with the identification of methodologies for assessing outcomes:

'Appropriate outcome measures will vary in different areas of regulatory activity, but are essentially concerned with the expected consequences and goals of the regulator's enforcement activity rather than an account of the amount and type of enforcement activity it undertakes. In some cases, the regulatory requirements themselves may clearly identify a policy goal. In other cases, it may be appropriate to formulate an outcome that can be measured, such as the quantifiable reduction of pollution incidents or reduction in deaths and serious injuries. Evaluating the extent to which non-compliant businesses become compliant could also form an outcome measure. Determining the appropriate outcome measures and the methodology by which they should be measured are challenging tasks. However, it is only by measuring outcomes that regulators, the regulated community, and the public will begin to know what impact enforcement actions are having on regulatory outcomes and whether these have improved compliance. It will also highlight for the regulator if there needs to be any modification to its choice of enforcement actions in order to better meet regulatory objectives.

During the course of the review, it became apparent how little information is available on the effectiveness of sanctioning regimes. If Government accepts my recommendation, I would suggest that sponsoring departments and/or regulators use the opportunity of introducing new sanctioning tools to study and develop information, including commissioning independent research, relating to the sanctions and their effectiveness especially during the transition period. This will be very helpful to many within the regulatory sector.

Alongside providing the regulatory community with greater information, a focus on outcomes will also ensure that industry is better served. Regulators will need to demonstrate that their enforcement actions are having a measured impact. Simply publishing the number of enforcement actions, will no longer suffice as a demonstration of the effectiveness of a regulator in meeting its regulatory objectives. Business should be reassured because the regulator will need to go one step further in supporting its enforcement strategy. It will, for example, need to demonstrate that imposing administrative sanctions is improving regulatory outcomes compared with sanctioning by criminal prosecutions alone.

I do recognise that regulation is not an exact science and that regulatory outcomes are not the only measure of a regulator's success. Nonetheless I believe that measuring outcomes has been a neglected area of reporting within the regulatory community that is essential to the credible functioning of a modern regulatory system and I would like to see regulators strive towards achieving this.

Regulation and enforcement under FSMA 2000 **6.177**

Regulators and sponsoring departments should in their annual reports:
- Summarise the relevant regulatory output measures for the relevant period;
- Summarise the relevant regulatory outcome measures during the relevant period; and
- Comment on the relationship between the outcomes and the outputs.'[3]

[1] 'Regulatory Justice: Making Sanctions Effective', Professor Richard B Macrory, November 2006, para 1.34.
[2] 'Regulatory Justice: Making Sanctions Effective', Professor Richard B Macrory, November 2006, para 2.12.
[3] 'Regulatory Justice: Making Sanctions Effective', Professor Richard B Macrory, November 2006, paras 5.20–5.24.

6.176 If the Commissioner's 2009 annual report is measured against Macrory's formulations for the measurement of outcomes, then despite the fact that it uses the term 'outcome' on five occasions it is still impossible to tell what impact his enforcement strategy is actually having. In blunt terms, it is impossible to tell if the Commissioner's strategy is actually leading to an improvement in practices for data security or not.

Of course, a major contributing factor for the failure to measure outcomes might be the fact that the Commissioner does not have an adequate sanctioning toolkit, as he has consistently argued in recent years. Connected to this is the issue of resources and whether the Commissioner has enough money and people to do the right kind of work on the measurement of outcomes. Some of these problems are being addressed; the introduction of the assessment notice power and the anticipated increase in the fee for notification[1] should help to improve the Commissioner's position.

However, counterbalancing these points is the suspicion that the Commissioner might not be using his current powers effectively. The fact that there are so few prosecutions under s 47 is not only an indicator of improvements within the controller organisations that have received enforcement notices; it is also an indicator that the Commissioner is not effectively following-up after the service of enforcement notices. In a purely statistical sense it is very curious that none of the recent enforcement notices or undertakings for breach of the seventh data protection principle have resulted in criminal proceedings under s 47. If the Commissioner is not following-up, then the efficacy of the Commissioner's enforcement strategy is placed in doubt, leading to the suspicion that the introduction of monetary penalties and assessment notices will be merely window dressing.

[1] For further information about the changes to the notification fee structure see: http://www.ico.gov.uk/what_we_cover/data_protection/notification/fees_consultation.aspx.

REGULATION AND ENFORCEMENT UNDER THE FINANCIAL SERVICES AND MARKETS ACT 2000

6.177 Chapter 3 contains an overview of how data security law operates in the area of financial services. To recap, for the purposes of the Financial Services and Markets Act 2000 data security is regarded as a financial crime

6.177 *Regulation and enforcement*

issue; the reduction of financial crime is one of the FSA's regulatory objectives (see FSMA 2000, s 2(2)(d)). The FSA handbook contains a series of provisions that expand upon the obligation placed on financial services businesses to ensure data security.

The FSA's Financial Crime Sector Team

6.178 The FSA has established nine sector teams that are charged with the responsibility of regulating critical areas of compliance. The Financial Crime Sector Team[1] is responsible for the reduction of financial crime regulatory objective within FSMA 2000, s 2(2)(d). Thus the regulation of data security sits within the Financial Crime Sector Team's area of responsibility. The data security components in this area are immediately apparent from this passage on the Financial Crime Sector Team's web pages:

> 'In pursuing our financial crime objective, our main focus is on firms' risk management, systems and controls.'

The Financial Crime Sector Team publishes a quarterly newsletter[2], which provides further insight into the FSA's expectations for data security, albeit these newsletters are careful to warn that their contents are 'not FSA guidance'. For example, the January 2009[3] newsletter provides the following thoughts about the data security issues involved in customer communications:

> 'Think about when you send out communications, such as promotional offers and annual statements to your customers. Do you take appropriate steps to reduce the risk of your customers becoming victims of identity fraud and other crimes? Our research indicates that the answer may well be "no".'

[1] http://www.fsa.gov.uk/Pages/About/Teams/Crime/index.shtml.
[2] http://www.fsa.gov.uk/pages/About/What/financial_crime/library/index.shtml.
[3] http://www.fsa.gov.uk/pubs/newsletters/fc_newsletter12.pdf.

The scheme under the Financial Services and Markets Act 2000

6.179 A useful starting point for understanding the scope of the FSA's enforcement powers is the Information Commissioner's document 'The case for amending the Data Protection Act'. This document explains that the FSA's powers include the withdrawal of authorisations[1], disciplinary powers against authorised firms and approved persons[2], financial penalties, the right to apply for injunctions[3], restitution orders[4], the power to carry out investigations[5], the power to order a report from a skilled person[6] and various criminal offences, which include non-cooperation with investigations.

[1] Financial Services and Markets Act 2000, s 33. See also s 54.
[2] Financial Services and Markets Act 2000, s 66.
[3] Financial Services and Markets Act 2000, s 380.
[4] Financial Services and Markets Act 2000, s 382.
[5] Financial Services and Markets Act 2000, Pt XI.
[6] Financial Services and Markets Act 2000, s 166.

General rule making power and the FSA handbook

6.180 FSMA 2000, s 138 contains the FSA's general rule making power. The rules made pursuant to this power (and other rule making powers within FSMA 2000, Pt X) are contained in 'instruments'[1] published by the FSA, which are contained within the FSA handbook, which also contains supporting guidance[2]. A breach of the rules causing damage is actionable at the suit of the individual concerned, as a breach of statutory duty[3]. Thus, individuals suffering loss as a result of a failure of security within a financial services company will be able to sue for breach of statutory duty.

[1] Financial Services and Markets Act 2000, s 153.
[2] Financial Services and Markets Act 2000, s 157.
[3] Financial Services and Markets Act 2000, s 150.

Investigations

6.181 The FSA's power to investigate regulated businesses and persons is contained in FSMA 2000, Pt XI. The general power to gather information is expansively drawn and provides as follows:

'165.— **Authority's power to require information.**
(1) The Authority may, by notice in writing given to an authorised person, require him–
  (a) to provide specified information or information of a specified description; or
  (b) to produce specified documents or documents of a specified description.
(2) The information or documents must be provided or produced–
  (a) before the end of such reasonable period as may be specified; and
  (b) at such place as may be specified.
(3) An officer who has written authorisation from the Authority to do so may require an authorised person without delay–
  (a) to provide the officer with specified information or information of a specified description; or
  (b) to produce to him specified documents or documents of a specified description.
(4) This section applies only to information and documents reasonably required in connection with the exercise by the Authority of functions conferred on it by or under this Act.
(5) The Authority may require any information provided under this section to be provided in such form as it may reasonably require.
(6) The Authority may require–
  (a) any information provided, whether in a document or otherwise, to be verified in such manner, or
  (b) any document produced to be authenticated in such manner, as it may reasonably require.
(7) The powers conferred by subsections (1) and (3) may also be exercised to impose requirements on–
  (a) a person who is connected with an authorised person;
  (b) an operator, trustee or depositary of a scheme recognised under section 270 or 272 who is not an authorised person;
  (c) a recognised investment exchange or recognised clearing house.

6.181 Regulation and enforcement

(8) "Authorised person" includes a person who was at any time an authorised person but who has ceased to be an authorised person.
(9) "Officer" means an officer of the Authority and includes a member of the Authority's staff or an agent of the Authority.
(10) "Specified" means –
 (a) in subsections (1) and (2), specified in the notice; and
 (b) in subsection (3), specified in the authorisation.
(11) For the purposes of this section, a person is connected with an authorised person ("A") if he is or has at any relevant time been–
 (a) a member of A's group;
 (b) a controller of A;
 (c) any other member of a partnership of which A is a member; or
 (d) in relation to A, a person mentioned in Part I of Schedule 15.'

The powers in s 165 are broadly comparable with the information notice power within the Data Protection Act 1998. The major difference between the two regimes lies in the fact that the FSA can require the supply of information from a wider class of persons than the Information Commissioner, such as persons connected to an authorised person. The more expansive nature of s 165 is comparable with the 'enhanced information notice' power that the Information Commissioner argued for in 'The case for amending the Data Protection Act'.

6.182 The FSA's power to require a report from a skilled person is contained in FSMA 2000, s 166. As discussed earlier, the Information Commissioner argued for a comparable power in 'The case for amending the Data Protection Act', but without success. Section 166 provides as follows:

'**166.— Reports by skilled persons.**
(1) The Authority may, by notice in writing given to a person to whom subsection (2) applies, require him to provide the Authority with a report on any matter about which the Authority has required or could require the provision of information or production of documents under section 165.
(2) This subsection applies to–
 (a) an authorised person ("A"),
 (b) any other member of A's group,
 (c) a partnership of which A is a member, or
 (d) a person who has at any relevant time been a person falling within paragraph (a), (b) or (c), who is, or was at the relevant time, carrying on a business.
(3) The Authority may require the report to be in such form as may be specified in the notice.
(4) The person appointed to make a report required by subsection (1) must be a person–
 (a) nominated or approved by the Authority; and
 (b) appearing to the Authority to have the skills necessary to make a report on the matter concerned.
(5) It is the duty of any person who is providing (or who at any time has provided) services to a person to whom subsection (2) applies in relation to a matter on which a report is required under subsection (1) to give a person appointed to provide such a report all such assistance as the appointed person may reasonably require.

(6) The obligation imposed by subsection (5) is enforceable, on the application of the Authority, by an injunction or, in Scotland, by an order for specific performance under section 45 of the Court of Session Act 1988.'

Sections 170 to 176 concern the actual conduct of investigations. The FSA's investigator has the power to require the person under investigation (or a person connected to a person under investigation) to attend for interview[1] and to produce relevant documents[2]. Where documents are in the possession of third parties, the investigator can require the third party to produce them[3]. A lawyer can also be compelled to reveal the name of their client[4]. Under s 176 a magistrate can issue a search warrant, which has similar effect to search warrants issued under the Data Protection Act 1998, Sch 9.

Section 177 makes it an offence for a person to fail to cooperate within an investigation. As with the Data Protection Act 1998, s 61, section 177 pierces the corporate veil, exposing directors and similar persons to prosecution. The maximum penalty on conviction is two years' imprisonment, coupled with an unlimited fine.

[1] Financial Services and Markets Act 2000, s 171.
[2] Financial Services and Markets Act 2000, s 171.
[3] Financial Services and Markets Act 2000, s 175.
[4] Financial Services and Markets Act 2000, s 175.

Disciplinary measures

6.183 FSMA 2000, Pt XIV deals with disciplinary measures. The FSA has two broad powers under Part XIV. Under s 205 it may publicly censure an authorised person if it considers that the 'authorised person has contravened a requirement imposed on him by or under [the Act or MiFID]'. The censure takes the form of a public statement published on the FSA's website and supported by a press release. Under s 206 the FSA can levy a financial penalty. However, before these sanctions can be imposed the FSA must give the person a warning notice under s 207.

In order to ensure proportionality and fairness, s 210 requires the FSA to publish a 'statement of policy' concerning the imposition and amount of financial penalties. The requirements within the Data Protection Act 1998, s 55C mirror the requirements of s 210.

Decision Procedure and Penalties Manual (DEPP)

6.184 The Decision Procedure and Penalties Manual (DEPP) sets out the FSA's decision-making procedure for the giving of statutory notices, its policy on the imposition and amount of fines and its policy on the conduct of interviews by investigators.

6.185 *Regulation and enforcement*

Policy on financial penalties

6.185 Chapter 6 sets out the FSA's position on financial penalties and public censure. When deciding whether to take action the FSA will have regard to six criteria namely:

- The nature, seriousness and impact of the suspected breach.
- The conduct of the person after the breach.
- The person's previous disciplinary record and compliance history.
- The guidance published by the FSA.
- Action taken by the FSA in other cases.
- Action taken by other domestic and international regulators.

As action for data security breaches will be based around the principles for business, which are always cited in the FSA's final notices in these cases, DEPP recognises that the FSA carries the burden of proving that the principles have been breached:

> 'In determining whether a Principle has been breached, it is necessary to look to the standard of conduct required by the Principle in question at the time. Under each of the Principles, the onus will be on the FSA to show that a firm has been at fault in some way.'[1]

[1] DEPP 6.2.15.

OVERLAP WITH OTHER REGULATORS

6.186 DEPP provides some insight into how the FSA will tackle the jurisdictional point that arises in data security cases; as mentioned earlier in this chapter both the FSA and the Information Commissioner have jurisdiction to regulate security breaches occurring in the financial services sector.

> 'Some types of breach may potentially result not only in action by the FSA, but also action by other domestic or overseas regulatory authorities or enforcement agencies.
>
> When deciding how to proceed in such cases, the FSA will examine the circumstances of the case, and consider, in the light of the relevant investigation, disciplinary and enforcement powers, whether it is appropriate for the FSA or another authority to take action to address the breach. The FSA will have regard to all the circumstances of the case including whether the other authority has adequate powers to address the breach in question.'[1]

[1] DEPP 6.2.19 et seq.

PUBLIC CENSURE OR FINANCIAL PENALTY?

6.187 DEPP 6.4 identifies the factors that the FSA will take account of when deciding to fine instead of following the route of public censure. The non-exhaustive list of indicative factors is as follows:

'(1) whether or not deterrence may be effectively achieved by issuing a public censure;

(2) if the person has made a profit or avoided a loss as a result of the breach, this may be a factor in favour of a financial penalty, on the basis that a person should not be permitted to benefit from its breach;

(3) if the breach is more serious in nature or degree, this may be a factor in favour of a financial penalty, on the basis that the sanction should reflect the seriousness of the breach; other things being equal, the more serious the breach, the more likely the FSA is to impose a financial penalty;

(4) if the person has brought the breach to the attention of the FSA, this may be a factor in favour of a public censure, depending upon the nature and seriousness of the breach;

(5) if the person has admitted the breach and provides full and immediate co-operation to the FSA, and takes steps to ensure that those who have suffered loss due to the breach are fully compensated for those losses, this may be a factor in favour of a public censure, rather than a financial penalty, depending upon the nature and seriousness of the breach;

(6) if the person has a poor disciplinary record or compliance history (for example, where the FSA has previously brought disciplinary action resulting in adverse findings in relation to the same or similar behaviour), this may be a factor in favour of a financial penalty, on the basis that it may be particularly important to deter future cases;

(7) the FSA's approach in similar previous cases: the FSA will seek to achieve a consistent approach to its decisions on whether to impose a financial penalty or issue a public censure; and

(8) the impact on the person concerned. In exceptional circumstances, if the person has inadequate means (excluding any manipulation or attempted manipulation of their assets) to pay the level of financial penalty which their breach would otherwise attract, this may be a factor in favour of a lower level of penalty or a public statement. However, it would only be in an exceptional case that the FSA would be prepared to agree to issue a public censure rather than impose a financial penalty if a financial penalty would otherwise be the appropriate sanction. Examples of such exceptional cases could include where there is:

(a) verifiable evidence that a person would suffer serious financial hardship if the FSA imposed a financial penalty;

(b) verifiable evidence that the person would be unable to meet other regulatory requirements, particularly financial resource requirements, if the FSA imposed a financial penalty at an appropriate level; or

(c) in Part VI cases in which the FSA may impose a financial penalty, where there is the likelihood of a severe adverse impact on a person's shareholders or a consequential impact on market confidence or market stability if a financial penalty was imposed. However, this does not exclude the imposition of a financial penalty even though this may have an impact on a person's shareholders.'

DETERMINING THE SIZE OF THE FINANCIAL PENALTY

6.188 DEPP 6.5 emphasises that the FSA does not have a tariff of financial penalties. Instead, it will look at all of the circumstances of the case in order to arrive at a proportionate penalty. The factors that it considers when determining the size of the penalty include:

- The need for deterrence.

6.188 *Regulation and enforcement*

- The nature, seriousness and impact of the breach.
- The extent to which the breach is deliberate or reckless.
- Whether the person to be fined is an individual.
- The size, financial resources and other circumstances of the person to be fined.
- The amount of benefit gained or loss avoided.
- The difficulty of detecting the breach.
- The conduct following the breach.
- The disciplinary record and compliance record of the person to be fined.
- Action taken by other domestic and international regulators.
- FSA guidance and other published materials.

On the final point, it should be noted that the FSA always cites its own reports and speeches in the final notices imposing fines for security breaches. DEPP 6.5.2 says:

> '(a) A person does not commit a breach by not following FSA guidance or other published examples of compliant behaviour. However, where a breach has otherwise been established, the fact that guidance or other published materials had raised relevant concerns may inform the seriousness with which the breach is to be regarded by the FSA when determining the level of penalty.
> (b) The FSA will consider the nature and accessibility of the guidance or other published materials when deciding whether they are relevant to the level of penalty and, if they are, what weight to give them in relation to other relevant factors.'

DISCOUNT FOR EARLY SETTLEMENT

6.189 DEPP 6.7 sets out the FSA's policy on discounting of fines for early settlement. This explains that there are four stages to an investigation and that the discounts for early settlement are 30% at stage 1, 20% at stage 2 and 10% at stage 3. There is no discount for settlements at stage 4. The stages are as follows:

> '(1) The FSA has identified four stages of an action for these purposes:
>   (a) the period from commencement of an investigation until the FSA has:
>   (i) a sufficient understanding of the nature and gravity of the breach to make a reasonable assessment of the appropriate penalty; and
>   (ii) communicated that assessment to the person concerned and allowed a reasonable opportunity to reach agreement as to the amount of the penalty ("stage 1");
>   (b) the period from the end of stage 1 until the expiry of the period for making written representations or, if sooner, the date on which the written representations are sent in response to the giving of a warning notice ("stage 2");
>   (c) the period from the end of stage 2 until the giving of a decision notice ("stage 3");
>   (d) the period after the end of stage 3, including proceedings before the Tribunal and any subsequent appeals ("stage 4").'

CP09/19: Enforcement financial penalties

6.190 Since March 2006 the FSA has been increasing the size of its fines for security failings, which exceeded £3,000,000 in July 2009, when a group of HSBC companies were fined for a variety of security breaches. The largest fine before that was £1.26m (Norwich Union) and before then £980,000 (Nationwide). The trajectory of fines will continue to be upwards.

The FSA's plans in this area are fully revealed by a consultation paper published in July 2009, 'CP09/19: Enforcement financial penalties'[1], which explains at paragraph 2.9:

> 'To achieve credible deterrence, wrongdoers must not only realise that they face a real and tangible risk of being held to account, but must also expect a significant penalty. We believe that our penalties need to be increased.'

The FSA's rationale is that financial penalties need to increase in order to achieve three objectives, namely disgorgement, discipline and deterrence. The idea within the disgorgement objective is that firms should not benefit financially from non-compliance with the rules. The idea within the discipline objective is that firms should be suitably punished for their wrongdoing. The idea with the deterrence objective is that fines should be set at the right level to discourage others from adopting similar behaviours to those of the defaulting firm. Paragraph 2.10 set out the FSA's thinking:

> 'Our proposals are based on a framework that will be applied in all cases, against both firms and individuals. The framework is broad enough to apply to the range of cases we have, while being sufficiently flexible to reflect the circumstances of a particular case. This framework comprises five steps, based on the following three objectives:
> - Disgorgement – a person should not benefit from any breach;
> - Discipline – a firm or individual should be penalised for wrongdoing; and
> - Deterrence – the financial penalty should be sufficient to deter the person who committed the breach from committing further breaches and also deter other persons from committing similar breaches.'

In order to achieve these objectives the Consultation Paper proposed a series of amendments to the Decision Procedure and Penalties Manual (DEPP) and the Enforcement Guide (EG).

[1] http://www.fsa.gov.uk/pubs/cp/cp09_19.pdf.

Enforcement action taken by the FSA

6.191 An analysis of the FSA's enforcement action for data security breaches is contained in Appendix A.

6.192 *Regulation and enforcement*

THE TRAJECTORY OF THE LAW – CARROTS, STICKS AND MORE DISPUTES

6.192 In conclusion, one inevitable consequence of the regulatory bear market will be greater instances of conflict between the regulators and the regulated, which will lead inevitably to a growth in data security litigation. The 'carrot' approach to regulation in this area, which is based on education, advice and incentives, is being displaced by the 'stick' approach, whereby the regulated are forced into compliance through direct application of enforcement and supervisory powers. The regulators' focus on more interventionist strategies and tougher penalties amounts to a tactic acceptance that the 'carrot' approach to regulation is not working, or has not worked as well as it might. Unless the regulators adopt the position that the mere threat of harsher regulation has already caused a sea-change in attitudes towards data security within regulated organisations and big improvements – and there is no evidence to suggest that this is or will be the regulators' position – they will be forced to follow through more often with the 'stick' approach, until the sea-change finally occurs. Indeed, having emphasised the need for harsher regulation, it would be bizarre for the regulators not to follow through with the stick, as that would attract a charge that they have been alarmist and opportunistic. To a large extent the regulators' credibility now rests on them taking strong action. If they fail to do so having created such a commotion they will be feared by no one and respected by few.

However, this cannot be a one way street; eventually the regulated community will react, if they perceive their treatment to be unfair, and this means disputes and litigation. This is the current trajectory of the law.

Chapter 7

BREACH NOTIFICATION

7.1 Should data controllers be under a legal obligation to notify security breaches or the loss of data to the authorities or to people affected? This is one of the most interesting, but contentious, issues within data security law, where the law is moving very quickly, with many proposals for change. In Chapter 1 the opinion was advanced that breach notification will be one of the main drivers towards better practice in the handling of data security.

In the United States there has already been a plethora of legislation mandating the reporting of security incidents to regulators and people affected, but in Europe the framework for new legislation is still hotly debated; the European Commission, Parliament and Council have all made competing proposals for amendments to the Electronic Communications Privacy Directive[1], which vary in scope and effect. However, it seems certain that legislation will be introduced requiring providers of publicly available electronic communications services to give notice of serious security breaches to those affected and to the national regulators.

In the UK the Information Commissioner, the government and the Financial Services Authority have also revealed their hands, stating that they expect controllers to make notifications, a position supported by best practice standards.

[1] Directive 2002/58/EC.

7.2 Thus, the trajectory of the law is obvious; a requirement to notify security breaches is becoming part of the law. However, the parameters of the obligation are unclear. This area of the law currently presents more unanswered questions than it does clarity, which causes many problems in practice. Interesting questions include:

- Is breach notification part of data protection law, in the sense that the obligation to notify security breaches applies only to incidents affecting individuals, or is it of wider application, applying also to information about companies and other organisations?
- When does the obligation to notify apply? Does the obligation arise immediately upon the occurrence of a security breach, or does there

7.2 Breach notification

need to be data loss, or does there need to be data loss causing harm? If harm is the operative feature triggering the obligation to notify, what kind of harm is required and how is harm assessed and quantified?
- To whom should notifications be given? Should the data subjects be notified, or should notifications be given to an official body, or, indeed, to both?
- What purposes does notification serve? Is it intended to mitigate harm, or does it serve some other purpose?
- Is breach notification a worthwhile discipline? Does it actually serve the intended purposes (whatever they may be), or can it be counter productive to those purposes?
- Is breach notification an absolute obligation, or is it discretionary?

Supporters of breach notification legislation regard it as among the most powerful drivers towards compliance, because it has a series of significant, distinct benefits. First, breach notification is seen as the last line of defence in data security practice, as it acts as an 'early warning system' for the victims, enabling them to take action that may reduce harm. The mitigation of harm is one of the overriding considerations during the handling of security breaches, meaning that breach notification plays a critical role within best practice. Second, it improves the knowledge of the regulators, which can lead to enforcement action. Third, it has a deterrent effect. It is believed that there is a significant name and shame component within breach notification, which may incentivise some organisations towards compliance.

BREACH NOTIFICATION AND THE DATA PROTECTION ACT 1998

7.3 The Data Protection Act 1998 does not contain any provisions that expressly state that data controllers must notify data security breaches. However, there are a number of provisions within the Act that are suggestive of the existence of such an obligation. Collectively these provisions constitute the Act's transparency mechanisms. The requirement for transparency within data processing operations has been a constant since the first iterations of data protection law in the early 1970s, albeit there are exemptions to this obligation, such as where transparency could somehow prejudice the core processing purpose[1].

Specifically the transparency provisions within the Data Protection Act 1998 are:
- The fair processing requirements within the first and second data protection principles.
- The registration and notification regime within Pt III.
- The right of subject access within Pt II.
- The information notice and enforcement regimes within Pt V.

[1] For instance, where data processing is undertaken for the purposes of law enforcement, say the apprehension of criminals, it is easy to understand that there will be a need for secrecy (see, for example, the Data Protection Act 1998, s 29, which contains exemptions from the fair processing requirements and subject access so as to avoid prejudicing law enforcement). In the context of data security, the need for secrecy in law enforcement was

dramatically played out in the Bob Quick case, April 2009. Mr Quick, who was the Assistant Commissioner of the Metropolitan Police in charge of counter-terrorism, was forced to resign after he was photographed entering Downing Street holding a briefing paper about a major terrorism operation the contents of which were visible on the resulting photographs. See 'Police chief quits over blunder', BBC, 9 April 2009: http://news.bbc.co.uk/1/hi/uk/7991307.stm.

The Quick case had interesting parallels with the Richard Jackson case; in October 2008 Mr Jackson was fined £2,500 by the City of Westminster Magistrates for an offence under the Official Secrets Act 1989, after he left a top secret file on a train. See 'Official fined over missing files', BBC, 28 October 2008: http://news.bbc.co.uk/1/hi/uk/7695095.stm.

Fair processing (transparency)

7.4 The fair processing requirements within the Data Protection Act 1998 require data controllers to provide data subjects with information about their processing operations. The information that has to be provided includes the identity of the controller (and their nominated representative, if they have one), the purpose for which the data are to be processed and 'any further information which is necessary, having regard to the specific circumstances in which the data are or are to be processed, to enable the processing in respect of the data subject to be fair'[1].

[1] Data Protection Act 1998, Sch 1, Pt II, para 2(3).

Breach notification as part of fair processing

7.5 It can be argued that the notification of security breaches and/or data loss to the data subject is the kind of information that can fall within the category of 'any further information which is necessary ... to enable the processing in respect of the data subject to be fair', because these are factors that may influence the data subject in their dealings with the data controller, particularly in cases that rely upon the data subject's consent, or willingness to enter into contract, as the ground for legitimacy[1]. However, the argument starts to fall down when the continuum of data processing is considered; in cases where the personal data are collected direct from the data subject the fair processing requirements apply at or about the point of collection, while security breaches and/or data loss will occur after the point of collection. Therefore, the fair processing requirements seem to operate at the wrong point in time as far as security breaches and/or data loss are concerned.

Yet on closer analysis the argument can be re-inflated, because not all personal data are collected directly from the data subject; in many cases there is an intervening person, a 'middle man', from whom the controller collects the data[2], a situation that the Act recognises. In these cases the information has to be provided at 'the relevant time or as soon as practicable after that time'. The Data Protection Act 1998 defines the relevant time as follows:

'(a) the time when the data controller first processes the data, or
(b) in a case where at that time disclosure to a third party within a reasonable period is envisaged—
    (i) if the data are in fact disclosed to such a person within that period, the time when the data are first disclosed,

7.5 Breach notification

(ii) if within that period the data controller becomes, or ought to become, aware that the data are unlikely to be disclosed to such a person within that period, the time when the data controller does become, or ought to become, so aware, or

(iii) in any other case, the end of that period.'[3]

[1] The requirement that data processing should be legitimate is contained within the first data protection principle, where it refers to Schedules 2 and 3.
[2] Or, of course, personal data can be collected from a source on the internet, from a newspaper or magazine, a database etc.
[3] Data Protection Act 1998, Sch 1, Pt II, para 2(2).

7.6 The first limb of the definition – 'the time when the data controller first processes the data' – can set up an interesting scenario. Suppose that the data controller procures a database of sensitive personal data from a third party and very shortly after it is received they suffer a serious security breach, caused by a hacker. If the controller has not supplied the fair processing information at the time of the breach, why should the obligation to supply 'any further information which is necessary ... to enable the processing in respect of the data subject to be fair' not be interpreted to include a requirement to give the data subject notice of the security breach? Surely fairness will require this.

If the Data Protection Act 1998 is interpreted purposively, then there seems to be no rational basis to say that this fair processing requirement can never extend to breach notification, but it would seem to be only in the minority of cases that the Act will work in this way, due to the relative position of security breaches in the continuum of processing compared to the position when most fair processing information is supplied.

Registration and notification (transparency)

7.7 The registration and notification regime might also extend to a requirement to give the Information Commissioner notice of a security breach and/or data loss, with, perhaps, greater frequency than the previous example, due to the fact that the notification regime contains a requirement for updating of notifications where the processing purpose changes.

The starting point is the Data Protection Act 1998, s 17, which prohibits data processing 'unless an entry in respect of the data controller is included in the register maintained by the [Information] Commissioner'. Data controllers satisfy their obligation to register/notify through the supply of 'registrable particulars', which include 'a description of the purpose or purposes for which the data are being or are to be processed'[1]. The controller must also provide a 'general description of measures to be taken for the purpose of complying with the seventh data protection principle'[2]. Controllers are also required to keep their registration/notification up to date, due to the duty to notify changes[3]. Failure to comply with these requirements is an offence[4].

The duty to keep registrations/notifications up to date is expanded by regulations[5] and it extends to notifying the Commissioner of any respect in which their registration particulars or description of security measures 'becomes inaccurate or incomplete'. This is the provision that could trigger an obligation to notify the Commissioner of security breaches and/or data loss.

1   Data Protection Act 1998, s 16(1).
2   Data Protection Act 1998, s 18(2).
3   Data Protection Act 1998, s 20.
4   Data Protection Act 1998, s 21.
5   Data Protection (Notification and Notification Fees) Regulations 2000, SI 2000/188. See reg 12.

Breach notification as part of registration/notification

7.8 The argument turns on the meaning of the processing purpose, which has to be notified as part of the registrable particulars; a security breach and/or data loss can trigger a new processing purpose, in the sense that personal data might be processed as part of the investigation of a serious incident, perhaps in order to determine the cause of the breach, or perhaps the extent of the breach. Suppose, for instance, that personal data are attacked by malware, causing alterations to the data. The diligent controller may then inspect or investigate the data, to determine whether there has been any damage, perhaps through alteration, amendment or deletion. In these circumstances the processing purpose might be said to have changed, giving rise to an obligation to notify the Commissioner. Of course, it might be argued that the duty to notify changes does not extend to transitory or temporary purposes, but only to permanent changes, but even if that is so, it is possible to imagine scenarios where the controller is put to long-term investigations, perhaps where the incident is concerned with prolonged and repeated attacks on the data, as might happen with denial of service attacks. Again, if the Act is interpreted purposively, it would seem to be impossible to rule out the possibility that the notification/registration applies so as to require the notification of security breaches and/or data loss to the Commissioner; the purpose of registration/notification is not confined to merely tax-raising[1], but serves a substantive purpose, being intended to give the regulator and the public a mechanism through which they can form their own views on the extent, quality and lawfulness of data processing. Sometimes the consequences of a security breach are so dramatic that they alter the fundamentals of the processing purpose to such an extent that it becomes a new purpose requiring notification.

1   The process of registration/notification attracts a fee. See also 'The Information Commissioner's inspection powers and funding arrangements under the Data Protection Act 1998', Ministry of Justice, CP(L) 15/08, 16 July 2008: http://www.justice.gov.uk/consultations/docs/cp1508.pdf.

Subject access (transparency)

7.9 The subject access regime may work in a similar manner. Data Protection Act 1998, s 7 creates the right of access by which data subjects can obtain information about a controller's processing operations. As with the previous

7.9 Breach notification

transparency mechanisms, subject access extends to the supply of a 'description of – the purposes for which [the personal data] are being or are to be processed'[1].

[1] Data Protection Act 1998, s 7(1)(b).

Breach notification as part of subject access

7.10 As with the registration/notification example, the consequences of a security breach and/or data loss might include the creation of a new processing purpose, with the result that the subject access request may impose an obligation on the controller to reveal that processing is being undertaken for the purpose of, say, investigating a security breach.

Information notices (transparency)

7.11 However, it is the information notice procedure within the Data Protection Act 1998 that provides the best support for the argument that it already contains provisions that are indicative of the existence of a breach notification obligation. Section 43 says:

'(1) If the Commissioner—
    (a) has received a request under section 42 in respect of any processing of personal data, or
    (b) reasonably requires any information for the purpose of determining whether the data controller has complied or is complying with the data protection principles,
he may serve the data controller with a notice (in this Act referred to as "an information notice") requiring the data controller, within such time as is specified in the notice, to furnish the Commissioner, in such form as may be so specified, with such information relating to the request or to compliance with the principles as is so specified.'

Breach notification as part of information notices

7.12 It is apparent from s 43 that the use of the information notice procedure can be triggered in two ways. The first, which arises under s 42, is where the Commissioner receives a complaint from a person about the lawfulness of a controller's operations. If such a complaint is received the Commissioner may use the information notice procedure as an investigatory tool, to ask the controller questions about a security breach. The second is where the Commissioner acts on his own volition, perhaps after reading about an incident in a newspaper. Due to the generality of ss 42 and 43, it is clear that the Commissioner can use the information notice procedure to investigate issues within the seventh data protection principle, enabling him to ask the controller to confirm whether they have suffered a security breach and/or data loss. Failure to comply with an information notice is an offence under s 47, as is providing false information either knowingly or recklessly.

Human rights issues

7.13 Of course, the Human Rights Act 1998 demands that the Data Protection Act 1998 must be interpreted so as to give effect to the right to privacy within article 8 of the European Convention on Human Rights and it is perhaps this convergence of laws that provides the best support for an argument that breach notification is already a component of the data protection regime. There are two limbs to this argument. First, if the Data Protection Act 1998 is to be read compatibly with article 8 it would amount to an unacceptable lacunae to leave personal data unprotected and the controller effectively unregulated when those data are at their greatest peril, which is after a security breach and/or data loss; the data protection regime should not avoid transparency at the moment of greatest risk. Thus, the transparency mechanisms could be extended by the Human Rights Act 1998 to require breach notification. Second, the way in which article 8 has been accorded respect under domestic law, through the extension of the law of confidence[1], sets up a mechanism for breach notification. At its most simplest, the law of confidence has always recognised forms of injunctive relief and interim orders that require a defendant to a breach of confidence claim to provide accounts of their behaviour. As breach notification is akin to holding a controller to account, it is likely to be the case that a breach of privacy case brought under the law of confidence will eventually result in the court ordering a controller to provide an account of their state of compliance with the seventh data protection principle. That would appear to be only a matter of time[2].

Of course, breach notification rules can be introduced into the law by the Commissioner, which is how the law is currently developing in the UK. There are two reasons for this. First, the Commissioner is a public body and so is required by the Human Rights Act 1998 to give effect to article 8 during the performance of his duties. Thus, the Commissioner has grounds to introduce breach notification into the law for these purposes. Second, the Commissioner carries an obligation to 'promote the following of good practice by data controllers', which is contained in the Data Protection Act 1998, s 51. He is also under a duty to 'perform his duties under this Act as to promote the observance of the requirements of this Act by data controllers'. Against this background it can be said that the introduction of regulatory guidance setting out the circumstances in which a controller will be expected to notify security breaches and/or data loss operates to satisfy the Commissioner's duties under both Acts. For example, the Commissioner might argue that regulatory guidance requiring breach notification encourages controllers to improve their systems and operations because it has a deterrent effect against poor practices.

[1] See the discussion in Chapter 2.
[2] See the discussion of *L v Finland* Application No 20511/03, 17 July 2008 in Chapter 2.

7.14 Breach notification

THE INFORMATION COMMISSIONER'S POSITION ON BREACH NOTIFICATION

7.14 The Information Commissioner's interest in the subject of breach notification can be traced back to mid 2007, before the loss of the HMRC data disks. Key events in the development of the Commissioner's position on breach notification are:

- Evidence given to the House of Lords Science and Technology Committee in August 2007[1].
- Written evidence given to the Home Affairs Select Committee on the 'Surveillance Society' in November 2007[2].
- Evidence given to the House of Commons Justice Committee in December 2007[3].
- Two guidance documents published in March 2008[4].
- The 'Data Sharing Review', published in July 2008[5].
- Speech at the RSA Conference in October 2008[6].
- Response to the 'Data Handling Review', published in November 2008[7].

[1] 'Personal Internet Security', House of Lords Science and Technology Committee, 5th Report of Session 2006–07, 10 August 2007, HL Paper 165–1.
[2] 'Home Affairs Committee Inquiry into "The Surveillance Society?" Additional Evidence Submitted by the Information Commissioner', 9 November 2007.
[3] 'Protection of Private Data', House of Commons Justice Committee, First Report of Session 2007–08, 3 January 2008, HC 154.
[4] 'Guidance on data security breach management', 27 March 2008 and 'Notification of Security Breaches to the Information Commissioner's Office', 27 March 2008.
[5] 'Data Sharing Review Report', Thomas & Walport, 11 July 2008.
[6] 'Speech to RSA Conference Europe on Data Breaches', 29 October 2008.
[7] 'Taking stock, taking action. The ICO position on the Government Data Handling Reviews', 3 November 2008.

The House of Lords report on 'Personal Internet Security', August 2007

7.15 A notable feature of this report is that it contains one of the earliest public statements from the Information Commissioner's Office on breach notification. In response to a question from Lord Patel[1], the Deputy Information Commissioner, Mr Jones, said:

> 'to follow on from the previous point, we are certainly not opposed in principle to the idea of breach notification. We do think it is quite important that thought would have to be given to getting the thresholds right. We fully understand the name and shame element. Where I think we have some concerns is, what do you tell individuals they can do to mitigate the risk? If it is a very serious case where numbers have been lost, and I understand that what banks will traditionally do is actually withdraw those cards and re-issue. So we think there are some detailed points to address about what constitutes a significant enough security breach to inform the public and then what do you tell them that enables them to do something useful about it?'

[1] See questions 362 and 363, page 134, Volume II.

Rejection of blanket obligation

7.16 Mr Jones' evidence encompassed themes that repeat through the Commissioner's later public statements on breach notification. It is clear that he had already decided that a blanket breach notification rule was not required, as he identified the need for a seriousness threshold within whatever system is established. It is also interesting that the Deputy Commissioner was considering a system that would only involve notification to the people affected; there is no mention of a reciprocal obligation to notify the Information Commissioner's Office. It also touched upon the practical issue of the actual content of reports of serious incidents.

Since then the law and expectations have developed far enough to say that, at the very least, breach notification is now a requirement of best practice, which will be considered during the regulation of data protection and certainly in litigation in appropriate cases. However, the law's development is still facing a difficult future, in particular with the question who should be responsible for setting rules? Should it be Parliament, or government or the regulators? While government is clearly supportive of breach notification philosophies it has ruled out legislation, preferring to leave the detail to the Information Commissioner. Indeed, the government has declined two opportunities for legislation amending the Data Protection Act 1998[1].

[1] See the Criminal Justice and Immigration Act 2008 and Coroners and Justice Bill.

Written evidence to the House of Commons Home Affairs Committee inquiry into the Surveillance Society, November 2007

7.17 The Information Commissioner gave oral evidence to the Home Affairs Committee on 1 May 2007. This was followed-up with written additional evidence on 9 November 2007[1], which said the following about breach notification:

> 'Allied to the call for a penalty to be introduced for breaches of the data protection principles, the Commissioner believes that consideration should be given to security breach notification obligations in the UK. These are used in other jurisdictions and involve the organisation which is the subject of a breach being obliged to tell those individuals affected by it such as those whose personal information is involved, as well as, in some cases, the regulator. Such obligatory notifications could, if applied sensibly, not only provide protection for individuals but would also help the Information Commissioner to take appropriate action where necessary.'[2]

This evidence is firm about the need for a breach notification regime to encompass both notifications to individuals affected and to the Commissioner, but it is thin on detail. An important omission concerns the seriousness of the incident giving rise to a requirement to notify. However, it does ally itself to 'the call for a penalty' for a criminal offence of 'recklessly failing to comply with the data protection principles so as to create a substantial risk that damage or distress will be caused to any person'[3], indicating a high threshold to the reporting obligation. The Commissioner's position on the need for legislation is not stated.

7.17 Breach notification

1 Additional evidence Submitted by the Information Officer: http://www.ico.gov.uk/upload/documents/library/corporate/detailed_specialist_guides/hacssadditionalevidenceicofinal.pdf.
2 Additional evidence Submitted by the Information Officer, paragraph 28.
3 Additional evidence Submitted by the Information Officer, paragraph 29.

The House of Commons report on 'Protection of Private Data', January 2008

7.18 The House of Commons Justice Committee was convened to examine the issues arising from the HMRC data loss. The Committee, which took evidence from the Information Commissioner and Deputy Commissioner on 4 December 2007, identified breach reporting as a possible change that could be made to the Data Protection Act 1998. In his evidence to the Committee the Information Commissioner said:

> 'We are not alone in this country in encountering security breaches. There have been a number of incidents, particularly in the United States, and a number of laws have been enacted in I think now the majority of the states requiring some sort of breach notification. Most of the American laws require notification to the individuals concerned. As we said to the House of Lords Select Committee on surveillance issues, we think that prima facie, there is a good case for introducing a breach notification law into this country. I think it is for debate still as to whom you notify, whether it is the individuals who have been affected or the Commissioner responsible for regulation of the market. Our instincts are that it would be wise to include provision for notification both to the individuals and to ourselves, but only on what I might call a discriminatory approach – only in those situations where there has been a substantial risk of damage or distress, because we have to be careful not to get bogged down with trivia.'

When asked by the Committee to describe the circumstances where breach notification would be beneficial the Commissioner said:

> 'Certainly any significant case having a substantial risk of damage or distress. You started by asking whether it would have made a particular difference in this situation. At one level, no, because we were told about it once the politicians knew about it, and as I have explained earlier, they came to see us almost straight away, so we had no complaint on that. But I think it might have made a difference if people were aware that there had to be a notice given to those affected. I think that will serve a very valuable deterrent purpose, and make both organisations, the system, and the individuals, the top, the middle, and the junior, take these matters that much more seriously.'

Developments in the Commissioner's thinking

7.19 This evidence revealed new thinking. For example, the Commissioner seemed to indicate that he saw a need for legislation, while he modified his position on reporting to the individuals affected, identifying a two-tier system (the discriminatory approach) with individuals being notified only in significant cases, which would be when there is a substantial risk of damage or distress.

The Information Commissioner's guidance, March 2008

7.20 In March 2008 the Information Commissioner published two documents on data security breaches. The first document is about the handling of security breaches[1]. The second is about the notification of security breaches to the Commissioner[2]. Both documents reject the idea that breach notification is a legal requirement. The first document says 'at present, there is no law expressly requiring you to notify a breach' and the second says 'there is no legal obligation on data controllers to report breaches of security which result in loss, release or corruption of personal data'. However, it is unknown whether the Commissioner attributed this to the absence of an express provision within the Data Protection Act 1998, or whether he received advice on the totality of the law. Be that as it may, the first document invites controllers to consider whether they should notify people affected by a security breach, while the second says that the Commissioner 'believes serious breaches should be brought to the attention of his Office'. The reason for the Commissioner's belief is itself not expressly stated, but it is very hard to reconcile it with his opinion that there is no legal obligation to report. Yet the second document immediately goes on to say 'the nature of the breach or loss can then be considered together with whether the data controller is properly meeting his responsibilities under the DPA'. So, it would seem that the Commissioner's belief is founded in a need to assess the controller's degree of compliance with the Act, which is very similar to the utility of the assessment procedure and information notice procedure.

[1] 'Guidance on data security breach management', 27 March 2008.
[2] 'Notification of Security Breaches to the Information Commissioner's Office', 27 March 2008.

'Guidance on data security breach management'

7.21 Dealing with the first document, while recognising that notifying individuals and organisations 'can be an important element in [the controller's] breach management strategy', it cautions against purposeless notifications, saying:

> 'informing people about a breach is not an end in itself. Notification should have a clear purpose, whether this is to enable individuals who may have been affected to take steps to protect themselves or to allow the appropriate regulatory bodies to perform their functions, provide advice and deal with complaints.'

INITIAL CONSIDERATIONS

7.22 It then continues by providing an indicative list of issues for the controller to consider when making a decision on notification, namely:

- Are there any sector-specific rules that may require the controller to make notifications?
- Can notification help the controller meet its security obligations under the seventh data protection principle?

7.22 *Breach notification*

- Can notification help to mitigate harm?
- Do the circumstances of the incident require the controller to inform the Information Commissioner? It says that this will be the case 'if a large number of people are affected, or there are very serious consequences'.
- How can notification be made appropriate for the individuals concerned? The document gives as examples the special interests of children and vulnerable adults.
- Is there a danger of over notifying? The document says that 'not every incident will warrant notification and notifying a whole 2 million strong customer base of an issue affecting only 2,000 customers may well cause disproportionate enquiries and work'.

REPORTING TO OTHER THIRD PARTIES

7.23 The document advises controllers to consider whether they should also inform the media, police, insurers, professional bodies, banks, credit card companies and trade unions.

CONTENT OF REPORTS

7.24 As regards the content and manner of notifications to the individuals affected, the document says that they 'should at the very least include a description of how and when the breach occurred and what data was involved'. They should 'include details of what you have already done to respond to the risks posed by the breach'. They should also 'give specific and clear advice on the steps [the individuals] can take to protect themselves and what [the controller is] willing to do to help them' and contact information such as helpline telephone numbers and website pages.

'Notification of Security Breaches to the Information Commissioner's Office'

7.25 Turning to the Commissioner's second document, this is concerned with the reporting of serious breaches to the Commissioner only, not breaches per se. Naturally, this focuses attention on the meaning of serious. On this point the document says that 'serious breaches are not defined', but it continues by providing assistance on the meaning of serious, pointing to three considerations:

- The potential harm to data subjects.
- The volume of personal data lost/released/corrupted.
- The sensitivity of the data lost/released/unlawfully corrupted[1].

The document says that the potential harm to individuals is the 'overriding consideration in deciding whether a breach of data security should be reported', with the extent of harm being 'dependant on both the volume of personal data involved and the sensitivity of the data'. As regards the meaning of harm, the document observes that this can include distress, which accords

The Information Commissioner's position on breach notification **7.28**

with how the Data Protection Act 1998 approaches the circumstances in which enforcement notices can be served².

1   Presumably the inclusion/omission of the word 'unlawfully' before 'corrupted' is a drafting error.
2   Data Protection Act 1998, s 40(2). This says that 'in deciding whether to serve an enforcement notice, the Commissioner shall consider whether the contravention has caused or is likely to cause any person damage or distress'. Furthermore, the Data Protection Act 1998, s 13, which describes the circumstances in which a data subject may recover compensation from a data controller, permits the recovery of damages for distress. Moreover, the statutory interpretation to the seventh data protection principle requires controllers to have regard to 'the harm that might result from such unauthorised or unlawful processing or accidental loss, destruction or damage as are mentioned in the seventh principle'; see the Data Protection Act 1998, Sch 1, Pt II, para 9.

THE PRESUMPTION TO REPORT

7.26 The document says that there is a 'presumption to report' where the breach causes significant actual or potential harm. So, it must follow that where there is not significant actual or potential harm the presumption is displaced. In cases where there is no evidence of actual harm – which will be in the majority of cases – data controllers will wish to focus on the meaning of 'potential harm', asking themselves what degree of likelihood is required for harm to be a potential.

CAUSING HARM

7.27 In cases where the harm might take the form of damage to the data subject rather than distress, the focus might well be the potential for pecuniary loss, to give effect to the leading judgment on the meaning of damage for the purposes of the Data Protection Act 1998, s 13, *Johnson v Medical Defence Union*¹. However, while there is undoubtedly a risk that pecuniary loss will follow a data loss, this result is not axiomatic. Furthermore, the strength of the underlying evidence of pecuniary loss is unclear, which has allowed somewhat nebulous ideas about consequences, such as the exposure to identify theft, to emerge to the forefront of data security law. Some data controllers will wish to challenge conventional thinking on the causation of damage during their deliberations on whether the incident has the potential to cause harm. Similarly, it might not always be the case that serious incidents have the potential to cause distress; perhaps the constituent body of data subjects affected will not be predisposed easily to distress.

1   [2007] EWCA Civ 262, [2007] CMLR 181. See the discussion in Chapter 2.

EXAMPLES OF INCIDENTS CAUSING HARM

7.28 The document does provide a useful insight into the Commissioner's opinion about the kind of incidents that have the potential to cause harm, giving two examples:

7.28 Breach notification

- Exposure to identity theft through the release of non-public identifiers, such as passport numbers.
- Information about the private aspects of a person's life becoming known to others, such as financial circumstances.

The problem with these examples is that the Commissioner does not explain how the release of passport numbers or information about a person's financial circumstances can cause harm, or whether the harm is likely to fall within the damage category or the distress category, or, indeed, both.

Indeed, the passport numbers example is one that is worthy of further scrutiny, because it seems to have become established thinking that the release of passport numbers is a major problem, yet the thinking behind this is unclear. However, when the 'keep your documents safe' page of the UK Identity Theft website[1] is considered it becomes clear that the identity theft issue within passports is the loss of the document itself, rather than the release of the passport number. In other words, the value of passports to criminals lies in gaining possession of the physical item. This is the impression that is also given by the Identity and Passport Service (IPS) website, which includes a function for the reporting of lost or stolen passports[2], but not for the reporting or release of the passport number. Indeed, the author's own inquiries of the IPS in the context of actual cases have revealed that they do not consider the release of passport numbers to be troubling.

[1] http://www.identitytheft.org.uk/keep-your-documents-safe.asp.
[2] https://passports.ips.gov.uk/lsrr1a/index.aspx?c=1.

THE POTENTIAL FOR SIGNIFICANT HARM

7.29 Of course, the Commissioner does stress in the first section of the document, under the subheading 'the potential harm to data subjects', that the presumption to report applies only where there is a potential for significant harm. The use of the word 'significant' is significant in itself; its use is deliberate and it acts to provide a very strong indication that there is a high threshold to the reporting obligation.

However, the second section of the document, under the subheading 'the volume of personal data lost/released/corrupted', immediately injects confusion, because it says that the presumption to report in cases where large volumes of personal data are concerned arises where there is a 'real risk of individuals suffering some harm'. The use of the words 'some harm' has a very different meaning to 'significant harm', rendering the document open to criticism for loose drafting.

RULE OF THUMB APPROACH – VOLUME OF DATA AFFECTED

7.30 This point aside, the document goes on to observe that 'it is difficult to be precise what constitutes a large volume of personal data', so it advises that 'every case must be considered on its own merits'. During these assessments

The Information Commissioner's position on breach notification **7.31**

controllers are advised to adopt a 'rule of thumb' approach, which says that 'any collection containing information about 1,000 or more individuals' will constitute a 'large volume of personal data'.

EXAMPLES OF INCIDENTS THAT SHOULD BE REPORTED

7.31 The document provides examples of the volumes of data involved in cases where the Commissioner would expect reporting to his office:

- The theft/loss of unencrypted portable storage media (laptop etc) holding names, addresses, dates of birth and national insurance numbers of 1,000 individuals; the Commissioner would expect this incident to be reported, presumably on the grounds that there would be potential for significant harm to the individuals concerned.
- The theft/loss of a marketing list of 500 names and addresses or other contact details where there is no particular sensitivity of the product being marketed; the Commissioner would not expect this incident to be reported, presumably on the grounds that there would not be potential for significant harm to the individuals concerned.

In the first example, the theft/loss of the portable storage media, it is quite easy to see why the Commissioner feels that the incident falls on the reporting side of the rule of thumb, but his position on the second example is less easy to understand. Both examples are concerned with theft or loss, so if the marketing list was actually stolen, rather than just being lost, it is foreseeable that some of the individuals may suffer distress, perhaps even significant distress once they start to focus on precisely why thieves were targeting their data. So what is the difference in the two examples that the Commissioner considers to be relevant for the purposes of breach notification? For example, does he foresee a potential for significant damage in the first example, whereas the second example was only likely to cause some non-significant distress? Or is the first example about potential significant damage and/or distress, while the second involves no potential for damage and/or distress? Or are both examples about distress, with only the first involving a potential for significant distress? There are other permutations of possibility, but the point is hopefully well illustrated.

The Commissioner concludes his section about volume with a paragraph that effectively hedges everything:

> 'However it may be appropriate to report much lower volumes in some circumstances where the risk is particularly high perhaps because of the circumstances of the loss or the extent of information about each individual. If the data controller is unsure whether to report or not, then the presumption should be to report.'

The final piece of advice, that there should be a presumption to report in cases of confusion, is one that is likely to be rejected by many data controllers, particularly where the consequences of reporting are considered, as they are later.

7.32 Breach notification

THE SENSITIVITY OF THE DATA AFFECTED – ANOTHER THRESHOLD
TO REPORTING

7.32 The third section of the document, under the subheading 'the sensitivity of the data lost/released/unlawfully corrupted', injects more confusion; the previous two sections identified two different thresholds to reporting – (1) significant actual harm or significant potential harm and (2) a real risk of some harm – and the third section introduces another, namely 'a significant risk of individuals suffering substantial harm'. This third threshold to reporting seems to focus on cases involving very small volumes of data, saying that where there is an incident involving the risk of personal data being released that could cause a significant risk of substantial harm there should be a presumption to report.

The document says that this presumption is most likely to apply where the data are sensitive within the meaning of the Data Protection Act 1998, s 2 and where the data are 'particularly sensitive' the loss (etc) of as few as 10 records could trigger the obligation to report.

As with the other sections, the document provides some examples:

- A manual, paper-based filing system, or unencrypted digital media, holding the personal data relating to 50 named individuals and their financial records; the Commissioner would expect this to be reported.
- A manual, paper-based filing system, or unencrypted digital media, holding the trade union subscription records relating to 50 individuals where there were 'no special circumstances surrounding the loss'; the Commissioner would not expect this to be reported.

The Commissioner's analysis within these examples does not withstand close scrutiny. The first and most obvious point of concern is the fact that financial records do not fall within the categories of sensitive personal data identified in the Data Protection Act 1998, s 2. However, information about trade union membership does. Quite why the Commissioner's examples prefer protection for non-sensitive personal data is impossible to understand. Second, the concept of 'particularly sensitive' personal data is novel and undefined. Does this relate to the type of data, in the sense that some categories of sensitive personal data are to be accorded more protection than others – which was not the intention of Parliament – or does this relate to the content of the information? For example, is a detailed set of GP records particularly sensitive when compared with a list maintained for equal opportunities purposes? Furthermore, how does the Commissioner's position on trade union membership lists alter in light of the Consulting Association[1] case? Third, where the examples refer to manual, paper-based filing systems, is this to mean just 'relevant filing systems'[2] or does it extend to any paper-based filing system irrespective of its structure? Fourth, what is meant by the phrase 'no special circumstances surrounding the loss' within the second example? Does it refer, for example, to the manner of the loss (etc), perhaps indicating that loss through theft is worse than loss through negligence and, if so, why?

[1] See the Consulting Association enforcement notice: http://www.ico.gov.uk/upload/documents/library/data_protection/notices/tca_enforcement_notice.pdf.
[2] See the discussion in Chapter 2.

INFORMATION TO BE REPORTED

7.33 The next section of the document deals with the information that is to be reported. This consists of:

- The type of information affected and the number of records.
- The circumstances of the loss/release/corruption.
- Action taken to minimise/mitigate the effect on the individuals involved, including whether they have been informed.
- Details of how the breach is being investigated.
- Whether any other regulatory body has been informed and their response.
- Remedial action taken to prevent future incidents.
- Any other information that the controller feels may assist the Commissioner in making an assessment.

CONSEQUENCES OF REPORTING

7.34 The document continues by describing the action that the Commissioner may take after being notified of the incident, pointing out that the 'nature and seriousness of the breach and the adequacy of any remedial action will be assessed' before a 'course of action [is] determined'.

The courses of action that the Commissioner may take are set out in the section of the document titled 'What will the Information Commissioner's Office do when a breach is reported?' The options identified are:

- The Commissioner may 'record the breach and take no further action'.
- The Commissioner may investigate the circumstances of the breach and any remedial action, leading to (1) no further action, (2) a requirement on the controller to undertake a course of action to prevent further breaches or (3) formal enforcement action.

The reference to 'formal enforcement action' means the service of an enforcement notice under the Data Protection Act 1998, s 40, but the taking of undertakings should be considered to be 'informal' enforcement action, as the Act does not actually contain a power for the Commissioner to require undertakings. This is obviously a lacunae within the Act, which the Commissioner identified in his December 2007 paper 'Our Case for Amending the Data Protection Act', where he submitted that he would:

> 'welcome the specific inclusion of undertakings (as provided for in the Enterprise Act enforcement regime) as a regulatory outcome in connection with the exercise of enforcement powers. This route is already pursued on a non-statutory basis in the exercise of the Commissioner's existing enforcement powers.'

7.35 Breach notification

FORMAL AND INFORMAL ACTION

7.35 The Commissioner expanded his thinking on formal/informal enforcement action in the final section of the document, titled 'will a reported breach be made public?', the thrust of which is that he will publicise a security breach if he takes either formal action (ie, if he serves an enforcement notice) or informal action (ie, if he takes undertakings), unless there are exceptional reasons for not doing so. However, the document fails to provide any insight into the Commissioner's thinking on what may or may not amount to exceptional reasons for not publicising the breach, which, from the controller's perspective at least, is unsatisfactory.

So, in what circumstances will the Commissioner take formal/informal enforcement action (or 'regulatory action' as the document prefers) after receiving notice of a security breach? The document identifies three situations:

- The controller 'declines to take any recommended action'.
- The Commissioner 'has other reasons to doubt future compliance'.
- There is a 'need to reassure the public'. The Commissioner says that such a need 'is most likely to arise where the circumstances of the breach are already in the public domain'.

INCENTIVISING NON-REPORTING?

7.36 These permutations have interesting, although perhaps unintended, consequences for data controllers, in that they might actually discourage them from adopting the 'good behaviour' of notifying the individuals affected. At the very least, they may cause some controllers to think twice about notifying individuals.

Imagine a case where the controller acts in an exemplary fashion and notifies the incident to the data subjects affected, per the 'guidance on data security breach management'. If one of those persons leaks the story to the press the circumstances of the breach will enter the public domain, which triggers the need to reassure the public according to the Commissioner's position. Thus, regulatory action might follow despite the fact that the controller accepts all the Commissioner's recommendations and there is no reason to doubt future compliance. In that sense the document might discourage the controller from notifying the individuals affected.

The Thomas-Walport Data Sharing Review, July 2008

7.37 On 25 October 2007 the Prime Minister, Gordon Brown, announced that he had asked the Information Commissioner and Mark Walport to undertake a review of the framework for the use of personal data in the public and private sectors. The resulting report, published in July 2008, is known as 'The Data Sharing Review'[1]. The Review covers much ground, including the

The Information Commissioner's position on breach notification 7.39

topic of breach notification. As such, it is an important document within a discussion of breach notification within the context of the Data Protection Act 1998.

1   'Data Sharing Review Report', Thomas & Walport, 11 July 2008.

Yet another formulation

7.38 Recommendation 11 of the Review says as follows:

> 'We believe that as a matter of good practice, organisations should notify the Information Commissioner when a significant data breach occurs. We do not propose this as a mandatory requirement, but in cases involving the likelihood of substantial damage or distress, we recommend the Commissioner should take into account any failure to notify when deciding what, if any, penalties to set for a data breach. Updated guidance should make this clear.'[1]

The recommendation introduces a fourth formulation for breach notification, namely a likelihood of substantial damage or distress, enveloping the March 2008 documents in a cloak of further confusion. Furthermore, the reference to the need for updated guidance renders the status of the March 2008 documents ambiguous. As regards the utility of this recommendation, this is set out in the second paragraph of the recommendation, namely:

> 'This should encourage good practice while leaving the initial decisions to the relevant data controller. It recognises that each breach carries different levels of risk and, consequently, requires a different response.'[2]

As regards the recipients of notifications, the Review makes it clear that reporting to the individuals affected is part of the process, saying 'where individuals face a real risk, for example of identity theft or fraud, it will usually be necessary to notify them directly so that they can take mitigating action'[3]. This is expanded upon for 'cases of imminent and serious risk to an individual', where it is recommended that 'the organisation should inform the individual at the same time as – or even before – it notifies the ICO'[4].

1   'Data Sharing Review Report', Thomas & Walport, 11 July 2008, paragraph 8.59.
2   'Data Sharing Review Report', Thomas & Walport, 11 July 2008, paragraph 8.60.
3   'Data Sharing Review Report', Thomas & Walport, 11 July 2008, paragraph 8.55.
4   'Data Sharing Review Report', Thomas & Walport, 11 July 2008, paragraph 8.56.

Legislation rejected

7.39 However, the Review rejected the idea that legislation should be introduced mandating the reporting of 'all serious security breaches' to the Information Commissioner. The reasoning for this is:

> 'Laws requiring the notification of data breaches have become commonplace in some other countries, including the United States and Japan. However, we do not favour placing an explicit statutory duty on organisations to report all breaches. Not only would this add a significant extra burden for organisations but more worryingly, it could produce "breach fatigue" among the wider public if it were to result in frequent and unnecessary notifications of minor incidents.

7.39 Breach notification

> This carries the very real danger that people will ultimately ignore notifications when there is, in fact, significant risk of harm.'[1]

While the phenomena of breach fatigue is well recognised[2], it is difficult to understand the Review's logic against legislation; it is submitted that if breach fatigue is to occur, this will happen irrespective of whether the obligation is codified in statute or contained within regulatory guidance. Furthermore, if the formulations for breach notification that were discussed earlier can be categorised as requiring the reporting of 'all serious security breaches', as they seem to do, it would appear to be the case that the Information Commissioner has already created a system which the Review says will lead to breach fatigue. Of course, it might be argued that the phrase 'serious security breach' means something less serious than a breach involving a 'significant risk of harm' (or any of the other formulations), but if this is the point at the heart of the Review's argument, then it only acts to further demonstrate the need for clarity of language, which can be provided by the Parliamentary drafting office.

Indeed, it is the absence of clarity within the March 2008 documents and the Data Sharing Review that can provide perhaps the best support to the argument for legislation, as controllers will then be concerned with only one formulation for the reporting obligation[3].

[1] 'Data Sharing Review Report', Thomas & Walport, 11 July 2008, paragraph 8.58.
[2] See 'Personal Internet Security', House of Lords Science and Technology Committee, 5th Report of Session 2006–07, 10 August 2007, HL Paper 165–1, at paragraph 5.36, which refers to the evidence of Mr Bruce Schneier. The report says 'Bruce Schneier suggested to us that while the laws had done "a lot of good", they might also have "outlived their usefulness". The key to the value of data security breach notification, in his view, was the "public shaming" of offenders. But this relied on publicity, and the publicity was attenuated over time—"it is no longer news when someone's innovation is stolen. It happens too often". A related risk was that individuals would be overwhelmed by breach notifications, and, lacking the information to enable them to assess the actual risks, would quickly lose interest'.
[3] See 'Personal Internet Security', House of Lords Science and Technology Committee, 5th Report of Session 2006–07, 10 August 2007, HL Paper 165–1, at paragraph 5.35, which refers to the evidence of Dr Chris Hoofnagle. The report says 'Dr Chris Hoofnagle, a lawyer working at the CITRIS research institute, told us, different definitions of what constituted a security breach, and differences in requirements as far as demonstrating potential harm, and in reporting requirements, to some extent undermined their effectiveness, as well as the reliability of the data generated'.

RSA Conference Europe

7.40 On 29 October 2008 the Information Commissioner addressed the RSA Conference Europe, one of the leading conferences on data security and related technologies. Describing information as a 'toxic liability' the Commissioner addressed the issue of breach notification in these terms:

> 'It is unfortunate that it has taken calamity to convince the government that we need stronger powers, resources and sanctions, but we must also take care not to overreact. We do not need laws for their own sake or ill-considered laws. I am very sceptical about the value or viability of laws requiring individuals to be notified when there is a breach. When personal information has been lost,

The Information Commissioner's position on breach notification 7.42

stolen or otherwise compromised, the immediate priority is to manage the security breach and take all necessary steps to reduce the risks to individuals and to the integrity of the organisation's operations. As a matter of good practice, the ICO should be contacted immediately when any significant breach is discovered and, with the benefit of risk assessments applying to the particular situation, we can ensure that individuals who are affected are being told where that is necessary or genuinely useful. But I do not favour placing a statutory duty on organisations to notify people directly whenever a breach occurs and I am doubtful that a satisfactory law could satisfactorily distinguish in advance between situations where notification is needed and those where it is not. Each breach carries different levels of risk and, consequently, requires a different response. Unless written and interpreted with very great care, a mandatory notification requirement would add a significant extra burden for organisations and, more worryingly, could produce "breach fatigue" if it were to result in frequent and unnecessary notifications of minor incidents. This carries the very real danger that people will ultimately ignore notifications when there is, in fact, significant risk of harm. Notifying people, when there is often not much they can do about the situation wrongly shifts responsibility from the organisation to the individual and diverts attention and resources away from prevention. Put simply, where the risks posed by security breaches are serious, a notification requirement would be too timid. If they are not, it would be excessive.'

Dramatic language and rhetoric

7.41 The Commissioner's speech contains dramatic language and rhetoric; it cautions against overreacting, yet contains emotive language, such as 'toxic liability', 'the year of data breaches', 'serious and worrying' and 'calamity'. In this sense it provides a perfect snapshot of the regulatory mood and the developing regulatory bear market.

Legislation rejected once again

7.42 The message that was delivered was clear; the Information Commissioner was opposed to legislation requiring notification of security breaches to individuals, because that would be a distraction in the immediate aftermath of an incident and because it would be difficult to draft appropriate legislation. Instead, he was supporting a non-statutory approach, where notifications to his office are part of best practice.

It is easy to agree with many of the Commissioner's messages. It is right that breach notification should not become an unnecessary distraction in the immediate aftermath of an incident. It is probably also correct that a blanket breach notification requirement that ignores the seriousness of the incident will be counter-productive, perhaps leading to 'breach fatigue'. It is also correct to say that we do not need laws for their own sake or ones that are ill-considered. However, these points do not necessarily provide a concrete argument against legislation, or concrete support for the scheme described.

A key point within the speech was that legislation should not distinguish in advance between situations where notification is needed and those where it is

7.42 Breach notification

not. Again, this is correct. However, it would be wrong to say that suitable legislation would be too difficult to draft properly. Legislation could set the broad parameters of the obligation, leaving day-to-day enforcement to the Commissioner, supervised by the Information Tribunal and the courts, a framework that is already one of the hallmarks of the Data Protection Act 1998.

Criticism of the Commissioner's scheme

7.43 It also needs to be asked whether the Commissioner's alternative to legislation is to be preferred. In a narrow sense the answer would be yes, if the legislation was to require blanket notifications etc, of the kind that the Commissioner cautioned against. Properly debated legislation would have an immediate advantage over the alternative, because it would clearly identify the seriousness threshold triggering an obligation to notify, whereas the Commissioner has offered at least four different formulations for the threshold. Legislation would also clarify the nature of the penalty for non-compliance. The alternative leaves this to the vagaries of 'best practice', pointing out that non-reporting can be an aggravating feature within enforcement proceedings; in an objective sense it is currently impossible to be sure of the regulatory consequences of non-reporting. This is particularly troubling in light of the associated vagaries concerning the scope of the monetary penalty notices regime established by the Criminal Justice and Immigration Act 2008.

Another area within Mr Thomas' scheme that is not as clear cut as it may seem is the Commissioner's actual role in the breach notification process. An issue that needs to be confronted is that earlier guidance and enforcement actions have given some controllers reason to be hesitant in their dealings with the Commissioner, which can ultimately lead to a decision against notification being taken. In other words, there is a 'trust' issue involved in the relationship between regulator and regulated. Many controllers are confused about fines, enforcement action and the Commissioner's objectives.

There are many issues within an appropriate breach notification regime that may be better to leave to Parliament. Of course, any legislation for breach notification should be aligned to the objectives of the Data Protection Act 1998, as interpreted by the Human Rights Act 1998, which will require an appropriate seriousness threshold to their application. Appropriate legislation could be drafted.

Furthermore, we should not forget the legislative proposals for the introduction of breach notification in the electronic communications sector. The current proposals tackle the substantive questions raised by the Commissioner and they will eventually lead to new UK regulations for breach notification in the sector. That experience will capably inform the Parliamentary drafting office of the parameters for wider legislation.

The Information Commissioner's position on breach notification **7.45**

Data Handling Review – taking stock, taking action

7.44 In this document the Information Commissioner gave his response to the government's Data Handling Review[1] and the Poynter, IPCC and Burton reports. The introductory parts of this document say:

> 'In light of the importance of the issues that have been raised in the various reports, the Information Commissioner considers it appropriate to put on record his position on some of their recommendations, and provide some further information on action the ICO intends to take as a result of their findings.'

As regards breach notification, the document said:

> 'We note the fact that none of the reports recommended that notification to the Information Commissioner of information security breaches should be set on a statutory basis. Since the HMRC loss of personal information, the ICO has had voluntary notification of over 270 information security breaches from other organisations on a "confessional" basis[2]. As part of this the ICO has developed some guidelines for organisations on when a security breach should be notified and what information about the breach needs to be provided to the ICO. This has been working well in practice.
>
> The ICO can see the potential benefit of some limited form of formal, statutory notification of information security breaches, whether to the individuals affected, the ICO or both. This has been introduced in a number of jurisdictions around the world, most notably in the USA. In some cases, it appears to have been successful as a driver for encouraging good practice. In others, an initial glut of public breach notifications has led to "breach fatigue". We have doubts as to whether it would be possible to frame legislation that strikes the right balance. It is therefore important that before any new legislation is brought forward that the practicality and long term effect of such a requirement is fully explored. We also agree with the findings of the Data Sharing Review, which states a failure to notify security breaches should be a factor which is taken into account should a monetary penalty be considered under section 55A of the Data Protection Act 1998.
>
> It is worth noting that breach notification is being considered as part of the review of Directive 2002/58/EC (the EU Directive on privacy and electronic communications).'

[1] 'Data Handling Procedures in Government: Interim Progress Report', Cabinet Office, December 2007; see paragraph 14.
[2] More firms 'admit disc failings', BBC, 4 December 2007: http://news.bbc.co.uk/1/hi/uk_politics/7127951.stm.

A shift in position on legislation

7.45 This document seems to indicate a different position to the Commissioner's speech to the RSA Conference, as it acknowledges the 'potential benefit' of a limited statutory regime for requiring breach notifications to the Information Commissioner and individuals affected; legislation was clearly rejected by Mr Thomas at the RSA Conference. However, the document does persist with an earlier theme, that it would be difficult to frame legislation that would strike the right balance.

7.46 *Breach notification*

THE GOVERNMENT'S POSITION ON BREACH NOTIFICATION

The House of Lords report on 'Personal Internet Security', August 2007

7.46 The first big test of the government's position on breach notification occurred prior to the loss of the child benefit data disks by HMRC, when the House of Lords Science and Technology Committee embarked on an inquiry into 'Personal Internet Security'[1]. The scope of the resulting report is described as follows:

> 'The title of this Report is Personal Internet Security – we have considered primarily issues pertaining to individual experiences of the Internet. We have not generally considered business security issues, except insofar as these affect the security of the data of individual customers. Thus we have made recommendations around the theft of personal data but not around industrial espionage. Nor have we considered matters of business continuity, risks to services, or possible failure of the critical national infrastructure as a result of the Internet ceasing to operate for an extended period. These are all important issues – but outside the scope of this Report.'[2]

The Report covered many different aspects of security on the internet, including breach notification. It made the following recommendation:

> 'We further believe that a data security breach notification law would be among the most important advances that the United Kingdom could make in promoting personal Internet security. We recommend that the Government, without waiting for action at European Commission level, accept the principle of such a law, and begin consultation on its scope as a matter of urgency.'[3]

The recommendation continued:

> 'We recommend that a data security breach notification law should incorporate the following key elements:
> - Workable definitions of data security breaches, covering both a threshold for the sensitivity of the data lost, and criteria for the accessibility of that data;
> - A mandatory and uniform central reporting system;
> - Clear rules on form and content of notification letters, which must state clearly the nature of the breach and provide advice on the steps that individuals should take to deal with it.'

[1] 'Personal Internet Security', House of Lords Science and Technology Committee, 5th Report of Session 2006–07, 10 August 2007, HL Paper 165-1.
[2] 'Personal Internet Security', House of Lords Science and Technology Committee, 5th Report of Session 2006–07, 10 August 2007, HL Paper 165-1, paragraph 1.8.
[3] 'Personal Internet Security', House of Lords Science and Technology Committee, 5th Report of Session 2006–07, 10 August 2007, HL Paper 165-1, paragraph 5.55. See also, paragraph 8.18.

Online banking fraud

7.47 The Science and Technology Committee entered into an examination of breach notification laws in the context of online banking fraud, observing that 'a more fundamental change, raising the profile of online security across the board, is required'[1]. It saw as a 'key issue' within the raising of the profile of

The government's position on breach notification 7.48

online security the fact that 'businesses are not currently required to report or publicise breaches'. In this context the Committee was struck by evidence from the Foundation for Information Policy Research[2], which submitted:

'A company whose systems have been compromised has every incentive to keep quiet about it, and will probably receive legal advice against notifying affected individuals ... Thus security breaches affecting the individual are typically detected when the individual complains of fraud. Such complaints are often met with hostility or denial by financial institutions, or with a demand that the customer explain how the dispute might have arisen.'[3]

The Committee considered this 'state of affairs [to be] self-defeating'; referencing the TKMaxx data security breach[4], the Committee considered that the absence of a breach notification law in the UK deprived TKMaxx's UK customers of an opportunity to 'examine credit card and bank statements more closely, so identifying minor frauds or thefts they would otherwise have missed'. Furthermore, 'the fact of disclosure would have given them evidence to support a prima facie case that they had been victims of fraud'[5].

The Committee identified other negative consequences flowing from the absence of a breach reporting law:

- It leads to a 'vicious circle of under-reporting' of security breaches[6].
- It is a key reason why there are no 'really dependable statistics' regarding the incidence of online fraud[7].
- It deprives companies of an incentive to 'prioritise data security at the highest level'; reporting can lead to 'public embarrassment and loss of share value'[8].
- It reduces the reporting of serious incidents to law enforcement agencies, which was noted as being a 'beneficial side-effect' of US breach notifications[9].

[1] 'Personal Internet Security', House of Lords Science and Technology Committee, 5th Report of Session 2006–07, 10 August 2007, HL Paper 165-1, paragraph 5.29.
[2] http://www.fipr.org.
[3] 'Personal Internet Security', House of Lords Science and Technology Committee, 5th Report of Session 2006–07, 10 August 2007, HL Paper 165-1, paragraph 5.29.
[4] 'Hackers target TK Maxx customers', BBC, 30 March 2007: http://news.bbc.co.uk/1/hi/business/6508983.stm.
[5] 'Personal Internet Security', House of Lords Science and Technology Committee, 5th Report of Session 2006–07, 10 August 2007, HL Paper 165-1, paragraph 5.30.
[6] 'Personal Internet Security', House of Lords Science and Technology Committee, 5th Report of Session 2006–07, 10 August 2007, HL Paper 165-1, paragraph 5.31.
[7] 'Personal Internet Security', House of Lords Science and Technology Committee, 5th Report of Session 2006–07, 10 August 2007, HL Paper 165-1, paragraph 5.31.
[8] 'Personal Internet Security', House of Lords Science and Technology Committee, 5th Report of Session 2006–07, 10 August 2007, HL Paper 165-1, paragraph 5.32. This conclusion builds upon the US experience following the introduction of the first breach notification law in California in 2003.
[9] 'Personal Internet Security', House of Lords Science and Technology Committee, 5th Report of Session 2006–07, 10 August 2007, HL Paper 165-1, paragraph 5.33.

Government rejects legislation

7.48 The government's position on breach notification, which was given by Margaret Hodge, was described as being 'lukewarm'. The following passages are very illuminating of the government's position and reasoning and the Committee's reaction to them:

7.48 Breach notification

'Margaret Hodge described security breach notification as "an enticing bit of legislation", but then focused on "the difficulty of framing that intent in a practical way because you would have to decide what breaches would you report precisely, what is the trigger for a report, those sorts of issues, and you do not want to end up in a situation where people either become really blasé about it because they get so many reports of breaches or they become so scared that they do not take advantage of the new information communication technology ... The devil is in the detail".

We fully acknowledge the Minister's points—it is essential, in particular, that any obligation to disclose security breaches should set a sensible threshold in terms of the potential risk to those affected. For instance, if a laptop is lost, but the data are securely encrypted, or if the laptop was contained in the boot of a car that has driven off a bridge into a deep river, the risk of data breach may be minimal. The detail must be got right. But we believe that the United Kingdom is now ideally placed to learn from the successes and failures of the many state laws in force in the United States and get this detail right, establishing a workable and effective legislative framework.

However, we find it alarming that the Minister appeared to regard with equanimity a situation in which security breaches were so common that if companies were to be obliged to inform individuals of security breaches affecting their personal data, these individuals would respond either with bored indifference or fear. In the Foreword to his latest Annual Report, the Information Commissioner noted that "The roll call of banks, retailers, government departments, public bodies and other organisations which have admitted serious security lapses is frankly horrifying". The evidence heard in this inquiry fully bears out this description. The sheer volume of breaches must not be used as an excuse for inaction.'

Why the government rejected legislation

7.49 Thus, there were three components to the government's resistance to breach notification laws:

- It would be difficult to draft legislation of sufficient precision.
- Breach notification might cause people to become blasé about data security, through enurement.
- Breach notification might scare people from adopting new technologies.

The government's formal response to the Report was published in October 2007[1], the month before the news of the HMRC data loss broke. Although couched in diplomatic language, the government firmly rejected the proposal for the introduction of breach notification legislation, although it did encourage the reporting of security breaches to the Information Commissioner:

'The Government provided evidence to the Committee that recognised that the move towards breach notification laws in other jurisdictions was an interesting development. We are, however, clearly not so convinced as the Committee that this would immediately lead to an improvement in performance by business in regard to protecting personal information and we do not see that it would have any significant impact on other elements of personal internet safety. The experience in the United States has yet to be fully analysed but there is a strong body of opinion that doubts whether there has been significant differences to corporate behaviour and may, in fact, have desensitised consumers to security

The government's position on breach notification **7.51**

issues and undermined confidence in the internet as a business medium. It has to be remembered that the US does not have the same legal framework in respect of privacy and the state laws on data breach have been an attempt to provide market incentives as an alternative to imposing such a framework. We will continue to observe the US experience and consider whether we need to find more formal ways of ensuring that companies do – as a matter of routine – contact the Office of the Information Commissioner when problems arise. This enables a proportionate response to be taken and ICO acknowledge that there are occasions when notifying consumers of a breach of security might not be appropriate. Such discussions also enable a discussion to take place about precautions taken and how they might be improved.

We agree with the Committee's conclusions that there appears no obvious justification to apply such requirements to the communications providers in isolation.'

[1] 'The Government Reply to the Fifth Report from the House of Lords Science and Technology Committee, Session 2006–07, HL Paper 165', October 2007, Cm 7234.

The House of Commons report on 'Protection of Private Data', January 2008

7.50 This report[1] is discussed earlier in this chapter. While the Justice Committee recognised that breach notification could be a change to the law, it did not go as far as making a recommendation that the law should be amended. The report was discussed within the final report of the Data Handling Review.

[1] 'Protection of Private Data', House of Commons Justice Committee, First Report of Session 2007–08, 3 January 2008, HC 154: http://www.publications.parliament.uk/pa/cm200708/cmselect/cmjust/154/154.pdf.

The Coleman Report on 'Protecting Government Information', June 2008

7.51 The Coleman Report[1] was commissioned by the Cabinet Office by way of a review of all elements of 'Information Assurance' within government, namely data protection, the availability of information and the integrity of information. For these purposes 'Information Assurance' is defined by the government as being 'the confidence that information systems will protect the information they handle and will function as they need to, under the control of legitimate users'[2].

The report made ten recommendations to improve the government's Information Assurance, the ninth of which is:

'Measure security through audit and monitoring to a defined standard. Mandate the reporting of incidents to an independent organisation responsible for capturing incidents and ensuring investigations are conducted to a given standard and lessons are learned.'

[1] 'Protecting Government Information. Independent Review of Government Information Assurance', Nick Coleman, June 2008. Referred to as 'the Coleman Report'.
[2] The Coleman Report, page 6.

7.52   Breach notification

The 'Data Handing Review', December 2007 to June 2008

7.52   The 'Data Handling Review' was the Prime Minister's official response to HMRC. This Cabinet Office project, headed by Sir Gus O'Donnell, commenced work in November 2007, following an announcement by the Prime Minister that he had 'asked the Cabinet Secretary, with the advice of security experts, to work with Departments to ensure that all Departments and all agencies check their procedures for the storage and use of data'[1].

[1]   'Data Handling Procedures in Government: Interim Progress Report', Cabinet Office, December 2007, paragraph 1.

Breach reporting made mandatory

7.53   The mandating of breach reporting requirements for central government departments and agencies was one of the first fruits of the Review. The 'Interim Progress Report' says the following:

'The focus in these early stages has been on policy and procedure, but has involved Departments identifying specific instances of potential data compromise. As part of good practice, Departments should routinely notify the Information Commissioner of any significant instances of potential data loss and this process will continue as the work progresses.'[1]

The Interim Progress Report was accompanied by a document titled 'Cross Government Actions: Mandatory Minimum Measures', which also contained guidance on breach notification:

'All Departments must:

9.1 have a policy for reporting, managing and recovering from information risk incidents, including losses of protected personal data and ICT security incidents, defining responsibilities, and make staff aware of the policy; and

9.2 report security incidents to HMG's incident management schemes (GovCERTUK for network security incidents and CINRAS for incidents involving cryptographic items). Significant actual or potential losses of personal data should be shared with the Information Commissioner and the Cabinet Office.'

This guidance required departments to have arrangements in place by 1 April 2008 to meet the reporting requirements in paragraph 9.2.

[1]   'Data Handling Procedures in Government: Interim Progress Report', Cabinet Office, December 2007, paragraph 14. This concluded by saying that 'the Information Commissioner has indicated that on the basis of the information he has received so far, none of the instances appear to present a substantial risk to large numbers of individuals'.

Final report repeats the obligation to report

7.54   The Final Report of the Data Handling Review[1] was published in June 2008. In addition to requiring the reporting of incidents to the Information Commissioner, it required incidents to form part of departmental reporting:

The government's position on breach notification 7.55

'In order to strike the appropriate balance the Government has committed to report on information breaches in summary form in Departments' annual reporting. The first such material will be included in annual reporting for 2007/08. There are two exceptions to this: when the interests of those affected are best served through public announcement, or when issues are so serious that Ministers judge that their immediate accountability to Parliament overrides other considerations.'[2]

The Final Report also provided the government's response to the House of Commons Justice Committee and the Coleman Report, as well as an additional response to the Science and Technology Committee. In response to the Justice Committee it said that the government would consider the wider legal framework in light of the conclusions of the Data Sharing Review[3]. In response to the Coleman Report, it said 'reporting of incidents will take place to the Information Commissioner, who will take enforcement action where justified and appropriate'[4].

[1] 'Data Handling Procedures in Government: Final Report', Cabinet Office, June 2008.
[2] 'Data Handling Procedures in Government: Final Report', Cabinet Office, June 2008, paragraph 2.41.
[3] 'Data Handling Procedures in Government: Final Report', Cabinet Office, June 2008, page 38.
[4] 'Data Handling Procedures in Government: Final Report', Cabinet Office, June 2008, page 40.

7.55 The government's response to the Thomas-Walport Data Sharing Review was provided by the Ministry of Justice[1], in November 2008. To recap, the eleventh recommendation of the Review was that 'organisations should notify the Information Commissioner when a significant data breach occurs'. The Ministry of Justice responded:

'We agree with this recommendation. As a matter of good practice any significant data breach should be brought to the attention of the ICO and that organisation should work with the ICO to ensure that remedial action is taken.

Following the publication of the DHR it is mandatory for Government departments to share details of significant actual or potential losses of personal data with the ICO. The ICO has already produced guidance for data controllers on when data breaches should be notified as a matter of good practice. The government is committed to the safe and secure handling of personal information and takes the loss of that information very seriously. We will give a mandate to the ICO to publish guidance for organisations on when to notify breaches of the data protection principles. The ICO will take into account the failure of an organisation to notify any breaches of the data protection principles when considering enforcement action.

In the Fourth Report of the House of Lord's Science and Technology Committee the Government provided evidence to the Committee that recognised that the move towards breach notification legislation in other jurisdictions is an interesting development.

After considering the analysis of the experience of the United States in the area of data breach notification legislation the Government is not intending to implement similar legislation to that in operation in the US. By implementing the US system of mandatory breach notifications, we risk facing the same problems and mistakes that have occurred from the US experience. The recent

7.55 Breach notification

paper by the Centre for Information Policy Leadership – "Information Security Breaches – Thinking Back and Looking Ahead" – warns that the US approach to breach notification contributes little toward the security of personal data, with the framework being of "diminishing utility over time".

The Government is therefore committed to developing an approach that tackles the problems encountered in the US and is more suitable for the needs of robust data protection in the UK.'

[1] 'Response to the Data Sharing Review Report', Ministry of Justice, 24 November 2008.

HMG Security Policy Framework

7.56 In December 2008 the Cabinet Office published the HMG Security Policy Framework, which replaced the Manual of Protective Security and the Counter-Terrorist Protective Security Manual and which incorporated the Data Handling Review[1]. The SPF contains 70 'mandatory requirements', of which numbers 7 and 44 are the most pertinent from the perspective of breach reporting. Recommendation 7 says that 'departments must submit an annual security return to the Cabinet Office Security Policy Division, covering their Agencies and main delivery partners' which 'must include' 'all significant security incidents (those involving serious criminal activity, damage to National Security, breaches of international security agreements, serious reputational damage, data losses or leaks) – individual breaches of this nature must also be reported immediately'. Recommendation 44 says:

'Departments and Agencies must have clear policies and processes for reporting, managing and resolving ICT security incidents. All security incidents must be reported to:
a) Appropriate departmental security authorities.
b) HMG incident management bodies: GovCERT for network incidents and CINRAS for communications security (involving cryptographic items).
c) The Information Commissioner's Office and the Cabinet Office Central Sponsor for Information Assurance for significant actual or possible losses of personal data.'

[1] The introduction to the Security Policy Framework explains at page 7 that the standards within the Data Handling Review 'have now been formalised into a new Information Assurance Standard (IA Standard no.6); "Handling Personal Data and Managing Information Risk" '.

THE EU'S POSITION ON BREACH NOTIFICATION

7.57 It is not only the UK that has struggled to arrive at a consensus point on breach notification; the European Community has experienced its own problems, in the context of the amendment of Directive 2002/58/EC[1]. There is however one key differentiator between the UK position and the EU position; the EU has no choice but to go down the route of legislation.

Directive 2002/58/EC regulates the processing of personal data in the context of the provision of publicly available electronic communications networks and services and is part of a wider framework of Directives governing this space. It replaced an earlier Directive[2] that applied only to the telecommunications sector and was itself amended in 2006, to require the retention of communications data by telecommunications companies and ISPs, for law enforcement purposes. Directive 2002/58/EC covers issues as diverse as the provision of telephone directories, itemised billing, calling line identification, the use of location data and direct marketing, as well as the confidentiality and security of electronic communications.

Since 2006 the Directive has been under review[3], a process that has resulted in the publication of a series of very contentious proposals for breach notification[4].

Article 4 of Directive 2002/58/EC currently provides the following provisions on data security:

'Article 4

Security

1. The provider of a publicly available electronic communications service must take appropriate technical and organisational measures to safeguard security of its services, if necessary in conjunction with the provider of the public communications network with respect to network security. Having regard to the state of the art and the cost of their implementation, these measures shall ensure a level of security appropriate to the risk presented.

2. In case of a particular risk of a breach of the security of the network, the provider of a publicly available electronic communications service must inform the subscribers concerning such risk and, where the risk lies outside the scope of the measures to be taken by the service provider, of any possible remedies, including an indication of the likely costs involved.'

[1] Directive 2002/58/EC of the European Parliament and of the Council of 12 July 2002 concerning the processing of personal data and the protection of privacy in the electronic communications sector (Directive on privacy and electronic communications): http://eur-lex.europa.eu/pri/en/oj/dat/2002/l_201/l_20120020731en00370047.pdf.
[2] See the discussion in Chapter 2.
[3] See page 3 of 'Communication from the Commission to the European Parliament, the Council, the European Economic and Social Committee and the Committee of the Regions, Report on the outcome of the Review of the EU regulatory framework for electronic communications networks and services in accordance with Directive 2002/21/EC and Summary of the 2007 Reform Proposals', COM(2007) 696 final, 13 November 2007. 'In 2006 and 2007, the Commission has reviewed the functioning of the EU framework against its main objectives, which are to promote competition, to consolidate the internal market and to promote the interests of the citizen. In the light of technological and market developments, especially improved competition in some areas, but also continued dominance by one or a few operators on a number of key markets as well as a continued lack of a single market for electronic communications and increasing divergence of regulatory approaches in the enlarged EU, a substantial reform of the regulatory framework is considered necessary by the Commission.'
[4] The review generated three proposals; a 'Better Regulation Directive', a 'Citizens' Rights Directive' and a Regulation setting up a regulatory body. The proposals on breach notification form part of the 'Citizens' Rights Directive'.

European Commission's proposal, November 2007

7.58 On 13 November 2007 the European Commission published proposals for the amendment of Directive 2002/58/EC[1]. These proposals included

7.58 Breach notification

amendments that would insert a breach notification obligation into the Directive, which had the central aim of 'enhancing the protection of individuals' privacy and personal data in the electronic communications sector, in particular through strengthened security-related provisions and improved enforcement mechanisms'[2]. Within the 'general context' part of the Proposal the wider background is explained:

> 'As part of the renewed Lisbon strategy for growth and jobs, the Commission proposed in June 2005 a new strategy – the i2010 Initiative: A European Information Society for growth and employment – laying down broad policy orientation to promote an open and competitive digital economy. The creation of a Single European Information Space, which is one of the main pillars of the i2010 Initiative, includes the reform of the regulatory framework as one of its key challenges, with a particular emphasis on security and the protection of privacy and personal data.'

The first proposed change was to the title of article 4, from 'security' to 'security of processing', but it is not clear how significant this change actually is. The substantive changes were the introduction of two new paragraphs into article 4, which prescribe the scope of the proposed breach notification obligation:

> '3. In case of a breach of security leading to the accidental or unlawful destruction, loss, alteration, unauthorised disclosure of or access to personal data transmitted, stored or otherwise processed in connection with the provision of publicly available communications services in the Community, the provider of publicly available electronic communications services shall, without undue delay, notify the subscriber concerned and the national regulatory authority of such a breach. The notification to the subscriber shall at least describe the nature of the breach and recommend measures to mitigate its possible negative effects. The notification to the national regulatory authority shall, in addition, describe the consequences of and the measures taken by the provider to address the breach.
>
> 4. In order to ensure consistency in implementation of the measures referred to in paragraphs 1, 2 and 3, the Commission may, following consultation with the European Electronic Communications Market Authority (hereinafter referred to as "the Authority"), and the European Data Protection Supervisor, adopt technical implementing measures concerning inter alia the circumstances, format and procedures applicable to information and notification requirements referred to in this Article.
>
> Those measures designed to amend non-essential elements of this Directive by supplementing it shall be adopted in accordance with the regulatory procedure with scrutiny referred to in Article 14a (2). On imperative grounds of urgency, the Commission may use the urgency procedure referred to in Article 14a (3).'

[1] Proposal for a Directive of the European Parliament and of the Council amending Directive 2002/22/EC on universal service and users' rights relating to electronic communications networks, Directive 2002/58/EC concerning the processing of personal data and the protection of privacy in the electronic communications sector and Regulation (EC) No 2006/2004 on consumer protection cooperation, COM(2007) 698 final, 13 November 2007. This is known as the Citizens' Rights Directive.

[2] Proposal for a Directive of the European Parliament and of the Council amending Directive 2002/22/EC on universal service and users' rights relating to electronic communications networks, Directive 2002/58/EC concerning the processing of personal data and the

protection of privacy in the electronic communications sector and Regulation (EC) No 2006/2004 on consumer protection cooperation, COM(2007) 698 final, 13 November 2007, page 3.

Seriousness threshold to reporting not included

7.59 The first notable feature within the Commission's formulation is that it expects notification to be given to both the national regulators and subscribers in all cases of breach of security, regardless of the issue of harm; the only trigger to the obligation being the occurrence of a security breach that leads to 'the accidental or unlawful destruction, loss, alteration, unauthorised disclosure of or access to personal data'. This absence of a seriousness threshold to reporting immediately distinguishes the Commission's position from that of the Information Commissioner, who has rejected the idea of compulsory notifications to subscribers in all cases.

Objectives of reporting

7.60 The proposals also recognise that the information to be provided to the subscribers and national regulators will be different. This is because notification to the subscribers and regulators serves different purposes, a view shared by the Information Commissioner, in the sense that the focus of notifications to subscribers is the mitigation of harm, while notifications to the regulators are intended to assist them in their regulation of the incident, helping particularly with their assessment of the seriousness of the situation and the need for regulatory action.

Technical implementing measures

7.61 The second amendment is also very significant, in that it gives the European Commission a broad power to take decisions[1] on 'technical implementing measures' required for the purposes of security and breach notification, which indicates very strongly that the Commission will be proactive in taking an interventionalist, prescriptive approach on these issues, perhaps after consulting with the European Electronic Communications Market Authority[2] and the European Data Protection Supervisor.

[1] The European Commission's power to take decisions in the field of data protection is mature and well established. For example, decisions have been taken on adequacy of countries and systems for the purposes of international transfers of personal data. Transfer of data to countries that are non-adequate, as viewed from the European Commission's perspective, involve additional security obligations.
[2] See Proposal for a Regulation of the European Parliament and of the Council of 13 November 2007 establishing the European Electronic Communications Market Authority, COM(2007) 699 final: http://eur-lex.europa.eu/smartapi/cgi/sga_doc?smartapi! celexplus!prod!DocNumber&lg=en&type_doc=COMfinal&an_doc=2007&nu_doc=699.

7.62 *Breach notification*

European Economic and Social Committee (EESC) opinion, May 2008

7.62 The EESC's opinion provided no dissent on the issue of breach notification, merely noting that 'steps will also be taken to ensure that end-users are notified about breaches of security resulting in their personal data being lost or otherwise compromised, and are informed about precautions that they may take in order to minimise the resulting damage'.

Committee of the Regions opinion, June 2008

7.63 The Committee of the Region's opinion was as favourable as the EESC's, saying within its Political Recommendations that it 'appreciates the Commission's efforts to improve consumer protection and user rights, in particular, by giving consumers more information about prices and supply conditions, by improving data protection and security'. As regards the proposed amendments to article 4 of Directive 2002/58/EC, it said that it:

> 'appreciates the proposals which seek to enhance the protection of individuals' privacy and personal data in the electronic communications sector, in particular through strengthened security-related provisions and improved enforcement mechanisms.'

European Parliament debate and amendments, September 2008

7.64 In September 2008 the European Parliament made radical amendments to the Commission's proposals, which, if implemented, would have the effect of considerably widening the scope of Directive 2002/58/EC. They were also much more prescriptive of the technical and organisational measures for security and provided greater detail of the scope of the breach notification obligation.

Widening the scope of reporting – regulating anyone with an internet presence

7.65 The widening of the scope of Directive 2002/58/EC was firstly[1] represented by a proposed amendment to article 1(1), which identified a new fundamental right, namely 'the right to confidentiality and security of information technology systems' and secondly by an amendment to article 3, to apply the Directive to a sweeping, new range of services, covering any website and extranet[2].

The increased prescriptive approach is seen particularly well in the proposal for article 4. Firstly, the Parliament proposed a new paragraph 1[3], which departed radically from the original, unamended version, in that it removed all references to the state of the art, cost and risk in the context of the obligation to take appropriate technical and organisational measures to safeguard the

The EU's position on breach notification 7.66

security of service, it was prescriptive of some security measures, it introduced an obligation to 'stress test' systems and it provided new powers to national regulators, including a right of audit:

> '1a. Without prejudice to the provisions of Directive 95/46/EC and Directive 2006/24/EC of the European Parliament and of the Council of 15 March 2006 on the retention of data generated or processed in connection with the provision of publicly available electronic communications services or of public communications networks, these measures shall include:
>
> – appropriate technical and organisational measures to ensure that personal data can be accessed only by authorised personnel for legally authorised purposes and to protect personal data stored or transmitted against accidental or unlawful destruction, accidental loss or alteration and unauthorised or unlawful storage, processing, access or disclosure;
>
> – appropriate technical and organisational measures to protect the network and services against accidental, unlawful or unauthorised usage or interference with or hindering of their functioning or availability;
>
> – a security policy with respect to the processing of personal data;
>
> – a process for identifying and assessing reasonably foreseeable vulnerabilities in the systems maintained by the provider of electronic communications services, which shall include regular monitoring for security breaches; and
>
> – a process for taking preventive, corrective and mitigating action against any vulnerabilities discovered in the process described under the fourth indent and a process for taking preventive, corrective and mitigating action against security incidents that can lead to a security breach.
>
> 1b. National regulatory authorities shall be able to audit the measures taken by providers of publicly available electronic communication services and information society services and to issue recommendations about best practices and performance indicators concerning the level of security which these measures should achieve.'

[1] See amendment 119.
[2] See amendment 121, which reads 'this Directive shall apply to the processing of personal data in connection with the provision of publicly available electronic communications services in public communications networks in the Community, including public communications networks supporting data collection and identification devices. This Directive shall apply to the processing of personal data in connection with the provision of publicly available electronic communications services in public and private communications networks and publicly accessible private networks in the Community, including public and private communications networks and publicly accessible private networks supporting data collection and identification devices'. The original, unamended version provides '1. This Directive shall apply to the processing of personal data in connection with the provision of publicly available electronic communications services in public communications networks in the Community. 2. Articles 8, 10 and 11 shall apply to subscriber lines connected to digital exchanges and, where technically possible and if it does not require a disproportionate economic effort, to subscriber lines connected to analogue exchanges. 3. Cases where it would be technically impossible or require a disproportionate economic effort to fulfil the requirements of Articles 8, 10 and 11 shall be notified to the Commission by the Member States'.
[3] See amendment 122.

7.66 Secondly, the Parliament provided a considerably changed version of the new article 4.3. In particular, it extended the breach notification obligation to any undertaking with an internet presence and extended its benefit from

7.66 *Breach notification*

subscribers to users. However, the obligation to notify individuals was left to the determination of the 'competent authority', albeit the obligation would not apply in cases where the service provider/data controller had implemented 'technological protection measures [that] render the data unintelligible to any person who is not authorized to access [them]', whereas the Commission's proposal required breach notification to subscribers and regulators in all cases:

> '3. In case of a breach of security leading to the accidental or unlawful destruction, loss, alteration, unauthorised disclosure of or access to personal data transmitted, stored or otherwise processed in connection with the provision of publicly available communications services in the Community, the provider of publicly available electronic communications services, as well as any undertaking operating on the internet and providing services to consumers, which is the data controller and the provider of information society services shall, without undue delay, notify the national regulatory authority or the competent authority according to the individual law of the Member State of such a breach. The notification to the competent authority shall at least describe the nature of the breach and recommend measures to mitigate its possible negative effects. The notification to the competent authority shall, in addition, describe the consequences of and the measures taken by the provider to address the breach.
>
> The provider of publicly available electronic communications services, as well as any undertaking operating on the Internet and providing services to consumers, which is the data controller and the provider of information society services, shall notify their users beforehand to avoid imminent and direct danger to the rights and interests of consumers.
>
> Notification of a security breach to a subscriber or individual shall not be required if the provider has demonstrated to the competent authority that it has implemented appropriate technological protection measures, and those measures were applied to the data concerned by the security breach. Such technological protection measures shall render the data unintelligible to any person who is not authorized to access the data.[1]
>
> 3a. The competent authority shall consider and determine the seriousness of the breach. If the breach is deemed to be serious, the competent authority shall require the provider of publicly available electronic communications services and the provider of information society services to give an appropriate notification without undue delay to the persons affected by the breach. The notification shall contain the elements described in paragraph 3.
>
> The notification of a serious breach may be postponed in cases where the notification may hinder the progress of a criminal investigation related to the serious breach.
>
> Providers shall annually notify affected users of all breaches of security that have led to the accidental or unlawful destruction, loss or alteration or the unauthorised disclosure of or access to personal data transmitted, stored or otherwise processed in connection with the provision of publicly available communications services in the Community.
>
> National regulatory authorities shall also monitor whether companies have complied with their notification obligations under this Article and impose appropriate sanctions, including publication, as appropriate, in the event of a failure to do so.[2]

3b. The seriousness of a breach requiring notification to subscribers shall be determined according to the circumstances of the breach, such as the risk to the personal data affected by the breach, the type of data affected by the breach, the number of subscribers involved, and the immediate or potential impact of the breach on the provision of services.'[3]

[1] See amendment 187/rev and 184.
[2] See amendment 124.
[3] See amendment 125.

7.67 Thirdly, it proposed a considerably enhanced version of the new article 4.4, making it compulsory for the Commissioner to consult with the EDPS, ENISA, not EECMA, and all other relevant stakeholders:

'4. In order to ensure consistency in implementation of the measures referred to in paragraphs 1 to 3b, the Commission shall, following consultation with the European Data Protection Supervisor, relevant stakeholders and ENISA, recommend technical implementing measures concerning inter alia the measures set out in paragraph 1a and the circumstances, format and procedures applicable to information and notification requirements referred to in paragraphs 3a and 3b.

The Commission shall involve all relevant stakeholders, particularly in order to be informed of the best available technical and economic methods for improving the implementation of this Directive.'[1]

[1] See amendment 127.

European Commission's amended proposal, November 2008

7.68 The Commission's response to the Parliament's radical amendments is contained in an amended proposal published on 6 November 2008. This partially accepted amendments 122, 127 and 187/rev, but rejected the remainder of the Parliament's amendments. The partially accepted amendments led to new proposals for article 4.1, 4.3 and 4.4. As amended article 4.1 provided:

'1a. Without prejudice to the provisions of Directive 95/46/EC these measures shall at least:

– ensure that personal data can be accessed only by authorised personnel for legally authorised purposes;

– protect personal data stored or transmitted against accidental or unlawful destruction, accidental loss or alteration, or unauthorised or unlawful storage, processing, access or disclosure; and

– implement a security policy with respect to the processing of personal data;

1b. National regulatory authorities shall be able to audit the measures taken by providers of publicly available electronic communication services and to issue recommendations about best practices concerning the level of security which these measures should achieve.'

7.69 The amended article 4.3 provided:

7.69 Breach notification

> '3. In the case of a personal data breach of security leading to the accidental or unlawful destruction, loss, alteration, unauthorised disclosure of or access to personal data transmitted, stored or otherwise processed in connection with the provision of publicly available communications services in the Community, the provider of publicly available electronic communications services shall, without undue delay, notify the national regulatory authority and the subscriber or individual concerned of such a breach, subject to paragraphs 3a and 3b below. The notification to the subscriber or individual concerned shall at least describe the nature of the breach and the contact points where more information can be obtained, and shall recommend measures to mitigate its possible negative effects of the personal data breach. The notification to the authority shall, in addition, describe the consequences of the personal data breach and the measures proposed or taken by the provider to address the breach.
>
> 3a. Notification of a personal data breach to a subscriber or individual concerned shall not be required if the provider has demonstrated to the satisfaction of the competent authority that no harm is reasonably likely to occur as a result of the personal data breach.
>
> 3b. Notification of a security personal data breach to a subscriber or individual concerned shall not be required if the provider has demonstrated to the satisfaction of the competent authority that it has implemented appropriate technological protection measures, and those measures were applied to the data concerned by the security breach. Such technological protection measures shall render the data unintelligible to any person who is not authorised to access the data.
>
> 3c. Member States shall ensure that the competent national authority is able to set detailed rules and, where necessary, issue instructions concerning the circumstances when the notification of personal data breaches by the provider of a publicly available electronic communications service is required, in compliance with paragraphs 3a and 3b, the format applicable to such notification, as well as the manner in which the notification is made. Competent national authorities shall also monitor whether companies have complied with their notification obligations under this Article and impose appropriate sanctions and remedies, including publication, as appropriate, in the event of a failure to do so.'

Personal data breaches

7.70 To support these amendments, the Commission formulated a definition of 'personal data breach', which it intended to have been inserted into Directive 2002/58/EC at article 2(i):

> ' "Personal data breach" means a breach of security leading to the accidental or unlawful destruction, loss, alteration, unauthorised disclosure of or access to personal data transmitted, stored or otherwise processed in connection with the provision of publicly available electronic communications services in the Community.'

The new proposals for article 4.3 represented a considerable shift in the Commission's position[1]; it moved very close to the Parliament's position, away from a 'blanket' obligation to notify individuals to one restricted to cases where there is a 'reasonable likelihood of harm', which was a considerable improvement on the meaning of seriousness. However, there was still a massive gulf between the two positions, due to the rejection of the proposal to extend the scope of the obligation to anyone with a publicly accessible website or extranet.

The amendment to article 4.4 returned the matter of consultation to a discretionary consideration, and substituted ENISA with the Article 29 Working Party.

> 'In order to ensure consistency in implementation of the measures referred to in paragraphs 1 to 3d, the Commission may, following consultation with the European Data Protection Supervisor, the Working Party on the Protection of Individuals with regard to the Processing of Personal Data established by Article 29 of Directive 95/46/EC, adopt technical implementing measures concerning inter alia the circumstances, format and procedures applicable to information and notification requirements referred to in paragraphs 3a and to 3d.
>
> The Commission shall involve all relevant stakeholders, particularly in order to be informed of the best available technical and economic methods for improving the implementation of this Directive.'

[1] Which the Commissioner justified by saying 'the amendment proposes an alternative solution for the mandatory notification of security breaches involving personal data, taking into account the concerns about possible "notification fatigue" (i.e. the need to avoid notification in cases of minor importance or where appropriate technology measures are in place), while ensuring the harmonisation of implementing measures at EU level'. See page 2 of the Commission's amended proposal.

Article 29 Working Party opinion, February 2009

7.71 On 10 February the Article 29 Working Party provided its opinion on the competing proposals[1], coming out fully in support of breach notification. However, like the Information Commissioner, it included a seriousness threshold to breach reporting, distinguishing it from the Commission's original approach:

> 'The Working Party fully supports the proposed strengthening of Article 4 of the ePrivacy Directive by requiring providers of publicly available communication services to notify security breaches. Breach notifications may become an important tool for Data Protection Authorities to increase focus and effectiveness when enforcing the obligation of service providers to take appropriate security measures.
>
> In general, the Working Party recommends the following approach to the issue of personal data breach notifications:
>
> – the competent national regulatory authority is informed whenever there is a risk of adverse effects to individuals' privacy and data protection;
>
> – it is essential that affected users are informed immediately by the service providers in those cases where the security breach is likely to lead to adverse effects to individuals' privacy and data protection, notwithstanding the possibility for the competent national regulatory authority to disclose publicly information about the breach and to force the service provider to disclose information about the breach;
>
> – each service provider should maintain records of all personal data breaches.'

7.71 Breach notification

[1] These included the Council's first political agreement on 27 November 2008. See the Draft Minutes of the 2907th meeting of the Council of the European Union (Transport, Telecommunications and Energy), 16396/2008.

Agreeing with the Parliament – expanding the scope to those with an internet presence

7.72 The Article 29 Working Party also shared the Parliament's position on extending the scope of the obligation to providers of Information Society Services, thereby capturing everyone with a publicly available internet presence, because of the 'ever increasing role these services play in the daily lives of European citizens'. The Working Party's commitment to the expansion of the Directive's scope is clearly indicated by its comment that it 'deeply regrets that this proposal was not backed by the Commission and the Council', recalling that 'some provisions of the ePrivacy Directive already apply beyond the strict scope of electronic communication services'.

Seriousness threshold

7.73 The Working Party's position on a 'seriousness threshold' to reporting is similar to the Information Commissioner's, in that it leaves the initial assessment of seriousness to the service provider, requiring them to notify the regulator when 'there is a risk of adverse effects' and to 'determine if notification to subscribers or individuals is required'. Such a need will be required if the security breach[1] 'may lead to adverse effects to individual's privacy and data protection'. Following notification the regulator will be in a 'position to exercise supervision over the process of notification to individuals', which may include publicising of the breach and '[forcing] the service provider to disclose information about the breach'.

[1] The Working Party said that it 'welcomes the introduction of a new definition of "personal data breach" in Article 2, as proposed in the Commission's Comments'. 'The Commission's Comments' means their comments on amendments 187/rev and 184 at the Parliament's amendments, contained in the Commission's amended proposal for a Directive amending Directive 2002/58/EC.

Harmonising the format of reports

7.74 The Working Party also touched upon some practical issues flowing from the introduction of a breach notification law, pointing out a need for harmonisation of the form and process of notification in order to help with the handling of increased volumes of notifications:

> 'The format of the notification should be harmonised on a European level and should include objective and clear criteria that assist in assessing the impact of the adverse effects caused by the breach. In addition, the competent national regulatory authority should check if the assessment of the breach was correctly carried out by the service provider, and if appropriate measures were taken following the personal data breach.'

Tougher sanctions

7.75 Finally, echoing the Information Commissioner's calls for tougher sanctions the Working Party said that the need for financial penalties to deter non-compliance was essential:

> 'Finally, to prevent the concealing of breaches it is essential that the Directive provides the competent national regulatory authority with the power to impose punitive financial sanctions (penalties) in cases where a service provider fails to report or incorrectly reports the personal data breaches to the individuals and or the NRA.'

Council's Common Position, February 2009

Rejection of the Parliament's approach

7.76 The Council adopted its Common Position on 16 February 2009, which, while generally in line with the European Parliament's overall position on amendments of the various communications directives, rejected the Parliament's approach on breach notification. In its Statement of Reasons[1] it said:

> 'The Council examined in detail the question of notification of breaches of security. It opted for an approach enabling the provider of an electronic communication service accessible to the public to assess the seriousness of the breach and the need to notify the NRA and/or the subscriber concerned, contrary to the European Parliament which would not like to leave such assessment entirely up to the discretion of the provider and would prefer to make notification to the NRA compulsory in all cases together with publication of the breaches committed. To ensure an appropriate level of harmonisation, the Council is making it compulsory for Member States to see that the NRAs are able to issue detailed rules concerning the circumstances, format and procedures applicable to the information and notification requirements relating to breaches of personal data.'

[1] Statement of the Council's Reason: Common position adopted by the Council on 16 February 2009 with a view to the adoption of a Directive of the European Parliament and of the Council amending Directive 2002/22/EC on universal service and users' rights relating to electronic communications networks, Directive 2002/58/EC concerning the processing of personal data and the protection of privacy in the electronic communications sectors and Regulation (EC) No 2006/2004 on consumer protection cooperation, 16497/1/0, page 5.

The Council's position

7.77 The Council's Common Position provides its own version of the Amending Directive. Breach notification is addressed at recital 47, which says:

> 'A breach of security resulting in the loss or compromising of personal data of an individual subscriber may, if not addressed in an adequate and timely manner, result in substantial economic loss and social harm, including identity fraud. Therefore, as soon as the provider of publicly available electronic communications service becomes aware that such a breach has occurred, it should assess the risks associated with it, e.g. by establishing the type of data affected by the breach (including their sensitivity, context and the security

7.77 Breach notification

measures in place), the cause and extent of the breach, the number of subscribers affected and the possible harm for subscribers as a result of the breach (e.g. identity theft, financial loss, loss of business or employment opportunities or physical harm). The subscribers concerned by security incidents that could result in a serious risk to their privacy (e.g. identity theft or fraud, physical harm, significant humiliation or damage to reputation) should be notified without delay in order to allow them to take the necessary precautions. The notification should include information about measures taken by the provider to address the breach, as well as recommendations for the users affected. Notification of a security breach to a subscriber should not be required if the provider has demonstrated to the competent authority that it has implemented appropriate technological protection measures, and that those measures were applied to the data concerned by the security breach. Such technological protection measures should render the data unintelligible to any person who is not authorised to access it.'

Recital 51 says:

'In setting detailed rules concerning the format and procedures applicable to the notification of personal data breaches, due consideration should be given to the circumstances of the breach, including whether or not personal data had been protected by encryption or other means effectively limiting the likelihood of identity fraud or other forms of misuse. Moreover, such rules and procedures should take into account the legitimate interests of law enforcement authorities in cases where early disclosure could unnecessarily hamper the investigation of the circumstances of a breach.'

Personal data breaches

7.78 The first amendment relevant to breach notification is the insertion of a new paragraph (h) into article 2, which sets out the definition of personal data breach:

' "personal data breach" means a breach of security leading to the accidental or unlawful destruction, loss, alteration, unauthorised disclosure of, or access to, personal data transmitted, stored or otherwise processed in connection with the provision of a publicly available electronic communications service in the Community.'

Expansion of the obligation – data collection

7.79 The second amendment of relevance is a new article 3, which extends the scope of the services concerned:

'This Directive shall apply to the processing of personal data in connection with the provision of publicly available electronic communications services in public communications networks in the Community, including public communications networks supporting data collection and identification devices.'

Amended article 4

7.80 The third amendment of relevance is the insertion of new paragraphs 3, 4 and 5 within article 4, which is renamed 'security of processing':

'3. In the case of a personal data breach, the provider of publicly available electronic communications services shall assess the scope of the personal data breach, evaluate its seriousness and consider whether it is necessary to notify the personal data breach to the competent national authority and subscriber concerned, taking into account the relevant rules set by the competent national authority in accordance with paragraph 4.

When the personal data breach represents a serious risk for the subscriber's privacy, the provider of publicly available electronic communications services shall notify the competent national authority and the subscriber of the breach without undue delay.

The notification to the subscriber shall at least describe the nature of the personal data breach and the contact points where more information can be obtained, and shall recommend measures to mitigate the possible negative effects of the personal data breach. The notification to the competent national authority shall, in addition, describe the consequences of, and the measures proposed or taken by the provider to address, the personal data breach.

4. Member States shall ensure that the competent national authority is able to set detailed rules and, where necessary, issue instructions concerning the circumstances in which notification of personal data breaches by providers of a publicly available electronic communications service is necessary, the format applicable to such notification and the manner in which the notification is to be made.

5. In order to ensure consistency in implementation of the measures referred to in paragraphs 1 to 4 the Commission may, following consultation with the European Network and Information Security Agency (ENISA), the Article 29 Working Party and the European Data Protection Supervisor, adopt recommendations concerning, inter alia, the circumstances, format and procedures applicable to the information and notification requirements referred to in this Article.'

Rejection of blanket obligation – service provider to assess seriousness

7.81 The Council clearly rejected 'blanket' notifications, leaving it to the service provider to assess whether the scope and seriousness of the personal data breach necessitates notification to the competent national authority and the subscriber. However, where the personal data breach represents 'serious risk to subscriber's privacy' the obligation is to notify the competent national authority and the subscriber 'without undue delay'.

Enhanced role for national regulators

7.82 There is also an enhanced role for the competent national authorities, who may set detailed rules on breach notification, including rules about the format for giving notification; the intention is that the rules should be considered by the service provider during their assessment of scope and seriousness. Likewise, the Commission is given a modified power to issue recommendations (not decisions) on breach notification and may consult with ENISA, EDPS and the Article 29 Working Party.

7.82 Breach notification

The Council's amendments represent a much slimmed-down regime for breach notification when compared to the proposals advanced by the European Parliament and the Article 29 Working Party. They are also less radical than the original proposals of the Commission. However, they do chime well with the Information Commissioner's position in his March 2008 guidance, in that they leave it to the service provider to make the initial assessment about breach notification.

Commission Communication, February 2009

7.83 On 17 February the Commission published a Communication to the European Parliament, about the Council common position. This Communication noted that 'the Council's position departs substantially from those of the Commission and the European Parliament', while accepting that the divergences on the proposed Citizens' Rights Directive 'are not of the same magnitude as those relating to the proposed Better Regulation Directive and the proposed Regulation setting up a regulatory body'.

The conciliatory language adopted by the Commission cannot disguise the fundamental difference of opinion however. The Council's position, which puts the controller in charge of the decision-making process on breach notification, cannot be reconciled with the Commission's amended proposal, requiring breach notification in all cases to the national regulators.

European Parliament debate and vote, May 2009

7.84 On 6 May 2009 the European Parliament voted to support the Commission's amended proposals, to the delight of the Telecommunications Commissioner, Viviane Reding, who was quick to point out that this put the ball back in the Council's court:

> 'I welcome the European Parliament's strong endorsement of the reform of the EU telecoms rules. All three reports on the reform[1] have been voted today by the Parliament with overwhelming majorities: 565 votes in favour of the establishment of the new European Telecoms Body BEREC, 493 votes in favour of the new Directives on e-Privacy and Universal Service and 605 votes in favour of a modern set of rules for ensuring efficient management of radio spectrum and helping to remove regulatory obstacles and inconsistencies in the single telecoms market. The Parliament also voted with 578 votes for the reform of the GSM Directive, which would allow industry savings of up to €1.6 billion.
>
> Now the ball is in the court of the Council of Telecoms Ministers to decide whether or not to accept this package of reforms.'[2]

[1] Draft Recommendation for Second Reading on the Council common position for adopting a directive of the European Parliament and of the Council on amending Directive 2002/22/EC on universal service and users' rights relating to electronic communications networks, Directive 2002/58/EC concerning the processing of personal data and the protection of privacy in the electronic communications sector and Regulation (EC) No 2006/2004 on cooperation between national authorities for the enforcement of

The EU's position on breach notification 7.85

consumer protection laws (16497/1/2008 – C6–0068/2009 – 2007/0248(COD)), Committee on the Internal Market and Consumer Protection, Rapporteur: Malcolm Harbour: http://www.europarl.europa.eu/sides/getDoc.do?pubRef=-//EP//NONSGML+COMPARL+PE-421.119+02+DOC+PDF+V0//EN&language=EN.

2 'European Parliament Approves EU Telecoms Reform but Adds 1 Amendment: Commission Reaction', Memo 09/219, 6 May 2009: http://europa.eu/rapid/pressReleasesAction.do?reference=MEMO/09/219&format=HTML&aged=0&language=EN&guiLanguage=en.

Parliament's new resolution

7.85 The European Parliament Resolution[1], which was accepted by the Commission in July 2009[2], provides for the following formulation:

'1a. Without prejudice to Directive 95/46/EC, the measures referred to in paragraph 1 shall at least:
- ensure that personal data can be accessed only by authorised personnel for legally authorised purposes;
- protect personal data stored or transmitted against accidental or unlawful destruction, accidental loss or alteration, and unauthorised or unlawful storage, processing, access or disclosure; and
- ensure the implementation of a security policy with respect to the processing of personal data.

Relevant national authorities shall be able to audit the measures taken by providers of publicly available electronic communication services and to issue recommendations about best practices concerning the level of security which those measures should achieve.

3. In the case of a personal data breach, the provider of publicly available electronic communications services shall, without undue delay, notify the personal data breach to the competent national authority.

When the personal data breach is likely to adversely affect the personal data and privacy of a subscriber or an individual, the provider shall also notify the subscriber or individual of the breach without undue delay.

Notification of a personal data breach to a subscriber or individual concerned shall not be required if the provider has demonstrated to the satisfaction of the competent authority that it has implemented appropriate technological protection measures, and those measures were applied to the data concerned by the security breach. Such technological protection measures shall render the data unintelligible to any person who is not authorized to access the data.

Without prejudice to the provider's obligation to notify subscribers and individuals concerned, if the provider has not already notified the subscriber or individual of the personal data breach, the competent national authority, having considered the likely adverse effects of the breach, may require it to do so.

The notification to the subscriber or individual shall at least describe the nature of the personal data breach and the contact points where more information can be obtained, and shall recommend measures to mitigate the possible adverse effects of the personal data breach. The notification to the competent national authority shall, in addition, describe the consequences of, and the measures proposed or taken by the provider to address, the personal data breach.

4. Subject to any technical implementing measures adopted under paragraph 5, the competent national authorities may adopt guidelines and, where necessary,

7.85 *Breach notification*

issue instructions concerning the circumstances in which notification by providers of personal data breaches is required, the format of such notification and the manner in which the notification is to be made. They shall also be able to audit whether providers have complied with their notification obligations under this paragraph and impose appropriate sanctions in the event of a failure to do so.

Providers shall maintain an inventory of personal data breaches, comprising the facts surrounding such breaches, their effects and the remedial action taken, sufficient for the purpose of enabling the competent national authorities to verify compliance with the provisions of paragraph 3. The inventory shall only include the information necessary for this purpose.

5. In order to ensure consistency in implementation of the measures referred to in paragraphs 2, 3 and 4, the Commission may, following consultation with the European Network and Information Security Agency (ENISA), the Working Party on the Protection of Individuals with regard to the Processing of Personal Data established by Article 29 of Directive 95/46/EC and the European Data Protection Supervisor, adopt technical implementing measures concerning the circumstances, format and procedures applicable to the information and notification requirements referred to in this Article. The Commission shall involve all relevant stakeholders in order particularly to be informed of the best available technical and economic means of implementation of this Article.

Those measures, designed to amend non-essential elements of this Directive by supplementing it, shall be adopted in accordance with the regulatory procedure with scrutiny referred to in Article 14a(2).'

[1] European Parliament legislative resolution of 6 May 2009 on the common position adopted by the Council with a view to the adoption of a directive of the European Parliament and of the Council amending Directive 2002/22/EC on universal service and users' rights relating to electronic communications networks, Directive 2002/58/EC concerning the processing of personal data and the protection of privacy in the electronic communications sector and Regulation (EC) No 2006/2004 on cooperation between national authorities responsible for the enforcement of consumer protection laws (16497/1/2008 – C6-0068/2009 – 2007/0248(COD)): http://www.europarl.europa.eu/sides/getDoc.do?type=TA&language=EN&reference=P6-TA-2009-0360.

[2] Opinion of the Commission of 29 July 2009 pursuant to Article 251(2), third subparagraph, point (c) of the EC Treaty, on the European Parliament's amendments to the Council's Common Position regarding the Proposal for a Directive of the European Parliament and of the Council amending Directives 2002/22/EC on universal service and users' rights relating to electronic communications networks and services and 2002/58/EC concerning the processing of personal data and the protection of privacy in the electronic communications sector and Regulation (EC) No 2006/2004 on cooperation between national authorities responsible for the enforcement of consumer protection laws, COM(2009) 421 final: http://eur-lex.europa.eu/LexUriServ/LexUriServ.do?uri=COM:2009:0421:FIN:EN:PDF.

Composite view of the EU proposals for breach notification

7.86 Table 7.1 contains a composite view of the various EU proposals for breach notification.

Table 7.1 EU proposals for breach notification

	Commission's original proposals	Parliament	Commission's amended proposals	Article 29 Working Party	Council
1. To whom does breach notification obligation apply?	Provider of publicly available electronic communications services.	Provider of publicly available electronic communications services and any undertaking operating on the internet and providing services to consumers.	Provider of publicly available electronic communications services.	Provider of publicly available electronic communications services and providers of Information Society Services.	Provider of publicly available electronic communications services.
2. When would the obligation to notify apply?	In all cases where security breach leads to destruction, loss, alteration or disclosure of personal data.	In all cases where security breach leads to destruction, loss, alteration or disclosure of personal data.	1. In all cases of 'personal data loss' that leads to destruction, loss, alteration or disclosure of personal data (regulator to be notified). 2. As above, in serious cases, where there is a reasonable likelihood of harm (subscriber or individual concerned to be notified).	1. In all security breach cases where there is a risk of adverse effect to individuals' privacy and data protection (regulator to be notified). 2. In all security breach cases that are likely to lead to adverse effect to individuals' privacy and data protection (affected users to be notified).	1. In cases of 'personal data breach', where scope and seriousness necessitates notification (regulator and subscriber to be notified). 2. In cases of personal data breach that represent a serious risk to subscribers' privacy (regulator and subscriber to be notified).
3. Who should be notified?	Subscriber and national regulatory authority.	National regulatory authority or competent authority, subscribers and individuals, persons affected and affected users.	Subscriber, individual concerned and NRA.	Competent national regulatory authority and affected users.	Competent national authority and subscribers.

7.86 Breach notification

4. When should notification take place?	Notification must be given without undue delay.	1. Users should be notified first, to avoid imminent and direct danger to the rights and interests of consumers. 2. The NRA or competent authority should be notified without undue delay. 3. In serious cases the persons affected by the breach should be notified, if the NRA or competent authority so directs after assessing seriousness. 4. However, notification to subscribers and individuals is not required if provider has implemented technical measures to make data unintelligible.	Notification must be given without undue delay.	If affected users need to be notified, that should take place immediately.	1. Following an assessment of the scope and seriousness of the breach, in accordance with detailed rules set by the competent national authority. 2. Without undue delay if breach represents a serious risk to subscribers' privacy.
5. Is there a 'seriousness threshold' to notification?	No	No for notifications to NRA or competent authority. Yes, in other cases.	No for notifications to NRA or competent authority. Yes, in other cases.	Yes, for notifications to competent national regulatory authority and for notifications to affected users.	Yes, in all cases. The assessment of seriousness is made by the service provider.

The Privacy Laws and Business survey of European regulators

7.87 In May 2009 data protection training and consultancy firm, Privacy Law and Business[1], published a 130-page report on the attitudes of EU data protection regulators towards breach notification. The report, titled 'Data Breach Notification Laws in Europe', represents the most thorough analysis of regulatory attitudes that is available. To quote from the report's abstract, it addresses the following issues across 21 European jurisdictions:

- Current data breach laws.
- Demand for data breach laws.
- Impact of US breach notification laws in Europe.
- Purpose and scope of new data breach provisions.
- Regulatory options for implementing breach notification.
- Advantages and disadvantages for national authorities, data subjects and companies.

The report includes a detailed analysis of the survey results, together with dedicated country reports. It draws many interesting conclusions, although, not surprisingly it observes that there are no distinct legislative obligations for breach notification within the national transpositions of the Data Protection Directive[2].

A distinct trend within the evidence highlighted in the report is that there is conditional support for new legislation on breach notification:

> 'The majority of DPAs which do not consider their country to have sufficient legislation in place already consider that some form of data breach provisions would be a good idea. This view is conditional on the data breach provisions being well drafted and that they offer clear advice and guidance to those affected before and after the breach occurs.'

This conditional support is also counterbalanced by a view that breach notification is already covered in data protection and other legislation. The conclusion says:

> 'The authorities' attitude towards a specific data breach law is, in the main, that it is not necessary. Currently, data breaches are covered by data protection laws, criminal and civil codes and additional E-communications legislation.'

Interestingly, the conclusion reveals a strong sense of regulatory complacency, in that there appears to be a regulatory consensus that data security is not a problem in mainline Europe.

> 'However, for the majority of countries surveyed, data breaches are not seen as a problem. Whilst the concept is well understood, the reality is that data breaches are not visibly occurring throughout the rest of the European Economic Area on the same scale as they are in the UK.'

[1] http://www.privacylaws.com/.
[2] Directive 95/46/EC.

7.88 The feeling that data security is mainly a US-UK problem is one that is commonly held by European regulators and is one that the author has

7.88 Breach notification

encountered many times in private practice. However, anecdotal evidence obtained by the author from security professionals working in multi-nationals show that their concerns are universal and not restricted to the US or the UK. Furthermore, stronger rules for employee privacy within continental Europe cause manifest problems within the carrying out of risk assessments, which might be masking some of the problems.

Opinions were divided on the actual giving of notice of security breaches, as reflected in the following part of the conclusion:

> 'How, when and who should companies or public sector organizations notify appears to be a common question amongst the authorities. Whilst a number of authorities thought that data subjects have a right to know when their personal data is lost, not all were convinced that notification of all types of breaches would be entirely beneficial for those affected.'

The absence of a consensus on the scope of the obligation is not surprising. This is a common problem, which has emerged in the Information Commissioner's efforts to define scope and throughout the review of Directive 2002/58/EC. However, there does seem to be broad support for the idea that breach notification should be subject to a seriousness threshold, which reflects the analysis earlier in this chapter.

Opinions on criminal penalties are also split. The conclusion reports:

> 'The national DPAs are, however, divided in their views on whether sanctions should be enforced upon those that "lose" data. Some believe it is the only way for a law to be effective. Others are of the opinion that introducing a criminal offence would not, in fact, help the data subject and in turn negate what any data breach law should be setting out to achieve. In some cases of data loss or theft due to a mistake, it would be difficult to prove a criminal intention.'

The conclusion also identifies uncertainties in the thinking on civil remedies. In this context it is particularly notable that there was a view that breach notification should concentrate on changing the behaviour of the data controller, rather than on compensating the individuals affected:

> 'Although, data subjects can seek a remedy from the civil courts, the question still remains as to whether this is the most beneficial approach in dealing with the issue itself. For example, if medical records are lost or stolen, and the patients' medical privacy is endangered, it is difficult to put a financial value on this loss of privacy. In such cases, is compensation an adequate response? Whilst data subjects can be recompensed, it would be preferable to alter the behaviour of companies and public sector data controllers and processors.'

THE FINANCIAL SERVICES AUTHORITY'S POSITION ON BREACH NOTIFICATION

7.89 The FSA position on breach notification also differs from the approach of the ICO. In April 2008 the FSA issued a detailed report on data security, which set out the FSA's position that customers have a right to know of any losses of their data, even where there is no evidence of theft or fraud[1]. The report said:

'When customer data is lost, consumers that are affected have a right to know the enhanced personal risk they face so they can take adequate precautions. Even if there is no evidence of theft or fraud, it is good practice for firms to inform affected customers of a data loss in writing, unless the data is encrypted or there is law enforcement or regulatory advice to the contrary. Firms should consider telling affected consumers exactly what data has been lost, give them an assessment of the risk and give advice and assistance to consumers at a heightened risk of identity fraud.

Our experience of dealing with cases of data loss shows firms are still learning to communicate appropriately with customers affected by data loss. A financial adviser did the right thing by writing to a group of customers whose account-opening forms had accidentally been thrown away by cleaners. But the letter acknowledged the risk without helping customers take precautions against identity fraud. It said: "We wish to apologise for this most unfortunate incident, and also to let you know that the cleaning company stated that it was a genuine mistake and that the account opening information was destroyed at the compressing plant. We understand that this event will be of considerable concern to you, as it is to us. We hope that by notifying you of this matter, you will have the opportunity to take whatever remedial steps you consider appropriate."

It would have been better practice for the firm to assess the risk itself, rather than quoting the cleaners' assertion that the documents were destroyed. In addition, the firm could have suggested measures that their customers could take to protect themselves against identity fraud.

In a significant number of cases of data loss brought to our attention, firms have failed to consider the wider risks of identity fraud arising from data loss. Indeed, many firms appear more concerned about adverse media coverage than in being open and transparent with their customers about the risks they face. However, some firms are beginning to take a more responsible approach by writing to their customers to explain the circumstances, give advice and some are even offering to pay for precautions such as credit record checks and CIFAS Protective Registration.'

The FSA's formulation for the reporting obligation applies it to the loss of customer data only. The seriousness threshold preferred by the FSA is 'enhanced personal risk'.

[1] 'Data Security in Financial Services. Firms' controls to prevent data loss by their employees and third-party suppliers', FSA Financial Crime and Intelligence Division, April 2008: http://www.fsa.gov.uk/pubs/other/data_security.pdf.

BREACH NOTIFICATION IN THE UNITED STATES

7.90 Data Protection in the United States developed differently from the European Union. Unlike the EU the US, while having legislated on the topic of data security, has never proclaimed that protection of personal information is a fundamental right, or a constitutional right (the US equivalent to declaring a right fundamental). The reasons for this are varied; however, it is certainly not because the US is immune from the threat of compromised personal data. Indeed, since January 2005, over 245,201,693 records containing sensitive[1] personal information have been compromised in the US[2]. The more likely reason is the way privacy law is viewed in the US; privacy law in the US is

7.90 *Breach notification*

generally concerned with upholding individual privacy rights against the government[3]. At its core, the American right to privacy maintains the same form that it did in the eighteenth century; it is the right to freedom from intrusions by the state, especially in one's own home. Regarding private actors, the information privacy philosophy of the US is most often characterised as a market-based or largely laissez-faire type of approach. Privacy rights are almost property-like, in that they are alienable, tradable, and waivable. The most important thing from the US perspective is to protect the individual from state intrusion into the choices they make regarding their personal information. Preserving both individual autonomy and commercial flexibility has traditionally been paramount, and industry has historically been trusted to police itself, particularly where such self-policing would support continued growth and development of the internet. As a result, it has been left primarily to the states to respond to its constituents' concerns regarding data security.

[1] Albeit not in the sense of 'sensitive personal data' within the meaning of the Data Protection Act 1998.
[2] Privacy Rights Clearing House, A Chronology of Data Breaches, available at: http://www.privacyrights.org/ar/ChronDataBreaches.htm#CP.
[3] Horace E. Anderson, Jr. The Privacy Gambit: Toward a Game Theoretic Approach to International Data Protection, 9 Vand. J. Ent. & Tech. L. 7, 17.

Breach notification rules at State level

7.91 Breach notification laws were first enacted in the State of California in 2003. As at 16 December 2008 44 States, together with the District of Columbia, Puerto Rico and the Virgin Islands, had enacted breach notification laws[1].

[1] http://www.ncsl.org/programs/lis/cip/priv/breachlaws.htm. For links to other websites providing lists of US breach notification laws, see http://www.privacyrights.org/ar/ChronDataBreaches.htm. See also http://datalossdb.org/us_states.

Harm threshold to reporting

7.92 The variations between each state's laws are small, but prove significant for an entity conducting business, or with customers in multiple states. In general, all states require that if a data controller suffers a security breach that is likely to cause harm to its residents, it must disclose the breach to those directly impacted. Some states require notice only if personal data have been compromised, while others require disclosure for all security breaches[1]. However, even in those states that require disclosure only if personal data is compromised, there is at minimum a requirement of a good faith investigation[2].

[1] Compare Iowa Code § 715C.1 with Alaska Stat. § 45.48.010.
[2] For example, Alaska Stat. § 45.48.010.

Rules for data processors

7.93 States also proscribe rules for third party information holders. For all states, there is no direct disclosure requirement for third parties who sustain a security breach. Instead, the third party must inform the original data collector who is then responsible for complying with the state's disclosure requirements. However, third parties are required to cooperate in the original data collector's investigation of the breach. This is true with the exception of Florida who instead looks to the contract between the parties to determine which party is responsible for providing notice[1]. If there is no agreement between the parties, the original data collector is responsible for providing notice.

[1] Fla. Stat. § 817–56819(2)(a).

Personal information

7.94 In general, states define 'personal information' as including an individual's first name or first initial and their last name in combination with one or more of the following data elements: (1) social security number; (2) driver's license or state identification card number; or (3) bank account number, credit card or debit card number along with the access code for these accounts. Alternately, some state laws use a less restrictive definition stating that any of the above data elements alone is considered personal information[1].

[1] See Ga. Code §§ 10-1-910, 911.

Form and content of reports

7.95 The time frame and form of the notice also differs between the states. For example, in Illinois notification to consumers may be either through written or electronic means, while in Arizona, disclosure of a breach may also be done via telephone[1]. Each state does, however, allow for alternative methods of contact if the company can prove hardship. Specifically, the company must show that the cost to provide notice exceeds a statutorily defined amount, impacts a particular amount of customers, or it is without sufficient contact information. In those situations, the company may fulfil its notification requirement by doing all of the following: (1) electronic mail notice to its customers; (2) conspicuous posting of the notice on the company's website if one is maintained; and (3) notification to a major statewide media company.

[1] 815 ILCS 530/1 et seq.; Ariz. Rev. Stat. § 44–7501.

Policies

7.96 Interestingly, an entity is deemed to have complied with the state's disclosure requirements if it has established a notification policy within its information security policy that is consistent with state requirements, and it is followed when there is a breach. Therefore, state laws may be viewed as a 'default' security protection policy in those cases where a company fails to implement one. Additionally, a company's notification duty is satisfied if it complies with its primary Federal regulation. This portion of the statute

7.96 *Breach notification*

allows for Federal preemption of state laws despite no overarching constitutionally protected right to data protection. However, Federal law will only preempt where state laws are inconsistent with its directive[1]. If, however, a state's laws provide more protection than its Federal counterpart, then it is not considered inconsistent with Federal law and will stand. This is the situation that arises with current data protection laws in the US.

[1] Ethan Preston & Paul Turner, The Global Rise of a Duty to Disclose Information Security Breaches, 22 J. Marshall J. Computer & Info. L. 457, 477 (2004).

Other laws

7.97 Federal data protection laws have developed in a piecemeal manner that varies from industry to industry. The following Federal acts concern themselves with the protection of privacy and data protection within particular sectors: (1) Fair Credit Reporting Act 1970; (2) Financial Services Modernization Act 1999 (Gramm-Leach-Bliley Act ('GLB')); (3) Health Insurance Portability and Accountability Act 1996 ('HIPPA'); (4) Children's Online Privacy Protection Act 1998 ('COPPA'); (5) Telemarketing and Consumer Fraud and Abuse Prevention Act 2003; and (7) Controlling the Assault of Non Solicited Pornography and Marketing Act 2003 ('CAN SPAM'). None of these acts, however, provide overarching protection for consumers. Instead they are sector specific laws designed to address specific types and uses of personal information. Unless a piece of personal information fits within one of the above types, it is likely not covered by any specific Federal statute.

FTC initiatives for breach notification

7.98 Some protection has been provided by the role played by the Federal Trade Commission ('FTC') in protecting consumers against unfair trade practices. The FTC Act authorises the FTC to pursue complaints of 'unfair or deceptive acts or practices in or affecting commerce', including deceptive practices relating to the collection and use of personal data[1]. The FTC has successfully litigated actions against US companies claiming that the disparity between their announced privacy policies and their actual policies were an unfair or deceptive practice affecting commerce[2]. While this theory has been successful in cases dealing with a failure to protect sensitive customer data, it has not been used in regards to breach notification.

[1] 15 U.S.C. §§ 41–58.
[2] Ethan Preston & Paul Turner, The Global Rise of a Duty to Disclose Information Security Breaches, 22 J. Marshall J. Computer & Info. L. 457, 477 (2004) at 479; see also Federal Trade Commission, Mortgage Company Settles Data Security Charges, available at: http://www1.ftc.gov/opa/2008/11/pcl.shtm.

Red Flag Rules

7.99 There are other mechanisms on the horizon that will facilitate data protection at the Federal level. Red Flag Rules are regulations issued by the

FTC, Federal bank regulatory agencies, and the National Credit Union Administration, pursuant to the Fair and Accurate Credit Transactions Act 2003, s 114 ('FACTA')[1].

[1] 'Fighting Fraud with the Red Flag Rule, A How-To Guide for Business', March 2000: http://www.ftc.gov/redflagsrule.

WARNING SIGNS

7.100 Under the Red Flag Rules, financial institutions and creditors must develop a written programme that identifies and detects the relevant warning signs – or 'red flags' – of identity theft[1]. These may include, for example, unusual account activity, fraud alerts on a consumer report, or attempted use of suspicious account application documents. The programme must also describe appropriate responses that would prevent and mitigate the crime and detail a plan to update the program. The mitigation element lends itself towards a requirement of breach notification. If an individual is notified of a breach, they are better able to prevent identity theft.

[1] Federal Trade Commission, FTC Business Alert, available at: http://www.ftc.gov/bcp/edu/pubs/business/alerts/alt050.shtm.

MANAGEMENT RESPONSIBILITY

7.101 The rules require that the programme must be managed by the Board of Directors or senior employees of the financial institution or creditor, include appropriate staff training, and provide for oversight of any service providers. These requirements make data security the responsibility of everyone in the organisation and not just the IT department. Indeed, in combination with the new requirements for directors and officers under the Sarbanes-Oxley Act 2002, directors may be held personally liable for not fulfilling their duties under this Act[1]. Additionally, the rules are applicable to broadly defined financial institutions and creditors.

[1] See 18 U.S.C. § 1350.

FINANCIAL INSTITUTIONS

7.102 Financial institution is defined by FACTA, s 111 to include all banks, savings and loan associations, credit unions, and any other person that holds a consumer transaction account as defined by the Federal Reserve Act, s 19(b)[1]. Creditors are defined within the rules as any entity that regularly extends, renews, or continues credit; any entity that regularly arranges for the extension, renewal, or continuation of credit; or any assignee of an original creditor who is involved in the decision to extend, renew, or continue credit. Credit is defined as a right granted to defer payment for any purchase. Therefore, any person that provides a product or service for which the consumer pays after delivery is a creditor. For example, a furniture store offering its customers the opportunity to purchase furniture and not pay for 12 months would be an entity defined as a creditor under the rules and thus be

7.102 Breach notification

responsible for creating and implementing a program that will protect its customer's data from theft. The laws were originally supposed to go into force on 1 November 2008 but this was delayed until 1 August 2009[2].

[1] Federal Trade Commission, available at: http://www.ftc.gov/bcp/edu/pubs/business/alerts/alt050.shtm.
[2] http://www.ftc.gov/opa/2009/04/redflagsrule.shtm.

Breach notification for electronic health information

7.103 Another initiative of the FTC is a proposal for a breach notification rule for electronic health information, which was announced in April 2009[1]. In compliance with the American Recovery and Reinvestment Act 2009 (the 'Act'), the FTC has issued a formal notice seeking public comment on a proposed interim rule relating to security breaches of consumers' electronic health records. The consultation was open for responses until 1 June 2009, with the final interim rule being issued in August 2009.

[1] http://www.ftc.gov/opa/2009/04/healthbreach.shtm. See also http://www.ftc.gov/os/2009/04/R911002healthbreach.pdf for the text of the Federal Register Notice.

AIMS AND OBJECTIVES

7.104 One of the aims of the Act is to advance the use of information technology within the healthcare industry, whilst increasing the security and privacy protections for health information, which responds to the increased number of web-based services which collect and process consumers' health information. In order to fully realise the benefits of such services, consumers must be able to trust that their sensitive information will remain secure and confidential. Examples of these services include electronic, personal stores for users' medical information, online applications which allow users to upload information in order to manage their medications, or services that use information from a health record to monitor a user's physical health, or their compliance with an exercise or dietary regime. Interestingly the definition of 'personal health record (PHR) related entity' can encompass a business not engaged in the healthcare industry which advertises its products or services on a website of a vendor of personal health records.

The Act requires the Department of Health and Human Services (HHS), in consultation with the FTC, to study the potential privacy, security and breach notification requirements for vendors of personal health records and related entities. A report on their findings and any recommendations is to be submitted to Congress within 12 months of enactment of the Act (February 2010). The proposed interim rule, to be enforced by the FTC, will apply until Congress implements any recommendations contained in the report.

THE OBLIGATION TO REPORT

7.105 The proposed rule requires vendors of personal health records and entities offering related services to notify consumers, the media and the FTC if they suffer a security breach in relation to personal health information from which an individual may be identified. The rule stipulates the timing, method and content of the notice. The rule is very far reaching for the following reasons:

- The definition of personal health record is widely drawn and includes information that relates to 'the health or condition' of the consumer, including, without limitation, an unsecured customer list of a vendor of personal health records directed at cancer patients, even if no specific health information is contained in that list.
- The rule imposes obligations on third party service providers that provide services in connection with the offering or maintenance of a personal health record, including without limitation billing or data storage services, and which processes unsecured personal health information in connection with the service. In the event of a breach, the third party service provider must notify the vendor, which in turn must notify the consumers.

Furthermore, entities that collect and process unsecured PHR identifiable health information are required to maintain reasonable security standards, including breach detection measures that should assist them in discovering breaches in a timely manner. Failure to do so will constitute a breach of the rule.

Other initiatives and Federal rules

7.106 Also on the horizon are Regulations S-P, rules promulgated by the SEC that implement the Gramm-Leach-Bliley Act, s 30(a) requiring companies to safeguard and protect customers' information[1]. These regulations apply to brokers, dealers, registered investment advisors, and investment companies and would require that security programs include procedures for responding to security breaches. Such procedures would necessarily include notice to affected individuals as well as notice to the commission or designated examining authorities.

Aware of the need for a Federal breach notification, both the 109th and 110th Congress considered such legislation[2]. However, because the discussion on data security and data breach notification legislation has become significantly more politicised, analysts believe it is unlikely that a Federal data security or data breach notification law will be enacted any time soon. Until then, the US will continue to rely on the multitude of state laws and Federal law in the area of data protection.

[1] The Securities and Exchange Commission, available at: http://www.sec.gov/rules/proposed/2008/34-57427.pdf.
[2] Bruce Johnson & Kaustuv Das, Data Breach Notice Legislation: New Technologies and New Privacy Duties?, 865 PLI/Pat 203, 233 (2006).

7.107 *Breach notification*

Breach notification in California

7.107 Returning to the California law, the core obligation in California is contained at section 1798.29 of the Civil Code:

'(a) Any agency that owns or licenses computerized data that includes personal information shall disclose any breach of the security of the system following discovery or notification of the breach in the security of the data to any resident of California whose unencrypted personal information was, or is reasonably believed to have been, acquired by an unauthorized person. The disclosure shall be made in the most expedient time possible and without unreasonable delay, consistent with the legitimate needs of law enforcement, as provided in subdivision (c), or any measures necessary to determine the scope of the breach and restore the reasonable integrity of the data system.

(b) Any agency that maintains computerized data that includes personal information that the agency does not own shall notify the owner or licensee of the information of any breach of the security of the data immediately following discovery, if the personal information was, or is reasonably believed to have been, acquired by an unauthorized person.

(c) The notification required by this section may be delayed if a law enforcement agency determines that the notification will impede a criminal investigation. The notification required by this section shall be made after the law enforcement agency determines that it will not compromise the investigation.

(d) For purposes of this section, "breach of the security of the system" means unauthorized acquisition of computerized data that compromises the security, confidentiality, or integrity of personal information maintained by the agency. Good faith acquisition of personal information by an employee or agent of the agency for the purposes of the agency is not a breach of the security of the system, provided that the personal information is not used or subject to further unauthorized disclosure.

(e) For purposes of this section, "personal information" means an individual's first name or first initial and last name in combination with any one or more of the following data elements, when either the name or the data elements are not encrypted:

(1) Social security number.

(2) Driver's license number or California Identification Card number.

(3) Account number, credit or debit card number, in combination with any required security code, access code, or password that would permit access to an individual's financial account.

(4) Medical information.

(5) Health insurance information.

(f) (1) For purposes of this section, "personal information" does not include publicly available information that is lawfully made available to the general public from federal, state, or local government records.

(2) For purposes of this section, "medical information" means any information regarding an individual's medical history, mental or physical condition, or medical treatment or diagnosis by a health care professional.

(3) For purposes of this section, "health insurance information" means an individual's health insurance policy number or subscriber identification number,

any unique identifier used by a health insurer to identify the individual, or any information in an individual's application and claims history, including any appeals records.

(g) For purposes of this section, "notice" may be provided by one of the following methods:

(1) Written notice.

(2) Electronic notice, if the notice provided is consistent with the provisions regarding electronic records and signatures set forth in Section 7001 of Title 15 of the United States Code.

(3) Substitute notice, if the agency demonstrates that the cost of providing notice would exceed two hundred fifty thousand dollars ($250,000), or that the affected class of subject persons to be notified exceeds 500,000, or the agency does not have sufficient contact information. Substitute notice shall consist of all of the following:

(A) E-mail notice when the agency has an e-mail address for the subject persons.

(B) Conspicuous posting of the notice on the agency's Web site page, if the agency maintains one.

(C) Notification to major statewide media.

(h) Notwithstanding subdivision (g), an agency that maintains its own notification procedures as part of an information security policy for the treatment of personal information and is otherwise consistent with the timing requirements of this part shall be deemed to be in compliance with the notification requirements of this section if it notifies subject persons in accordance with its policies in the event of a breach of security of the system.'

Computerised data containing personal information

7.108 The Californian law regulates those owning or licensing computerised data containing personal information, which is very similar to the position within the Information Commissioner's scheme for breach notifications and the various EU proposals for the amendment of Directive 2002/58/EC, albeit they focus on control over personal data, rather than ownership or licensing.

Encryption

7.109 However, there is a marked difference in the application of the breach notification obligation in California, as it only operates where a breach of a security system leads, or may lead, to the acquisition of unencrypted personal information by an unauthorised person; while the Information Commissioner and most parts of the EU both recognise that the loss of encrypted personal data should not be reported[1], the UK and EU schemes will have wider application than the Californian scheme, because they concern a wider variety of security breaches, not just acquisition by an unauthorised person. Furthermore, the meaning of personal data is wider than the meaning of personal information.

7.109 Breach notification

In some respects it would be fair to say that the Californian definition of personal information is similar to the intention within the meaning of sensitive personal data within the Data Protection Act 1998, in that they both recognise that some kinds of data need greater protection than others, but the Californian focus on first names, initials and second names within the meaning of personal information is a substantial limiting factor when compared with the UK and EU position, which will require breach notification even where a person's name is not involved.

[1] For example, see recital 51 of the Council's version of the proposed Citizens' Rights Directive within its common positions.

Seriousness threshold

7.110 The Californian scheme also bypasses the 'seriousness threshold' issue, which is such a large part of the UK and later EU schemes, but this is a consequence of the prescriptive language used in California; in many ways the issue of seriousness is assumed within the Californian scheme, due to its narrower focus on unauthorised acquisition and the narrower meaning of personal information; when personal information of the kind described in the Californian scheme are acquired by an unauthorised person that will be of a magnitude of seriousness to pass the threshold to notification in the UK and EU. Furthermore, as the US does not have EU-style 'omnibus' data protection legislation California does not have to focus on seriousness in order to show the dividing line between what kind of breaches are – or are not – within the scope of breach reporting; in the absence of legislation nothing is in scope.

Guidance issued by the California Office of Privacy Protection

7.111 The COPP issued guidance on the California law in October 2003[1], which ties the need for breach notification[2] to identity theft:

> 'Identity theft has been called the crime of the 21st century, favored, according to law enforcement, for its low risks and high rewards. Not only do identity theft victims have to spend money out of pocket to clear up their records, but they also must devote their time – up to hundreds of hours in some cases – to doing so. In the meantime, victims may be unjustly harassed by debt collectors, denied credit or employment opportunities; they may lose their cars or their homes, or be repeatedly arrested for crimes they did not commit.'[3]

[1] 'Recommended Practices on Notice of Security Breach Involving Personal Information', California Office of Privacy Protection, October 2003 (revised April 2006, February 2007).

[2] Identity theft is also the reason stated for an information security program: 'Implementing an effective information security program is essential for an organization to fulfill its responsibilities towards the individuals who entrust it with their personal information. It is the best way to reduce the risk of exposing individuals to the possibility of identity theft. It is also the best way to reduce the risk of an information security breach and the resultant cost to an organization's reputation and finances'.

[3] 'Recommended Practices on Notice of Security Breach Involving Personal Information', California Office of Privacy Protection, October 2003 (revised April 2006, February 2007), page 5.

EARLY WARNING SYSTEM

7.112 It says that the aim of breach notification is to give 'early warning' of security breaches to those affected, so that they can take steps to mitigate harm:

> 'One of the most significant privacy laws in recent years is the California law intended to give individuals early warning when their personal information has fallen into the hands of an unauthorized person, so that they can take steps to protect themselves against identity theft or to mitigate the crime's impact.'

SUCCESSES

7.113 In operation the law had two other important consequences. First, there was increased public awareness of the issue of information security, due to the news stories that had been generated. Second, it had 'improved privacy and security practices in many organizations'. The success of the law in operation is also indicated by the fact that 'notifying affected individuals in such cases has become a fairly standard practice', as well as the fact that the California approach had been adopted in the majority of States. Thus, it would seem that the law had been an operational and political success[1].

1 The California law will forever be associated with Arnold Schwarzenegger, the Governor of California, who has signed the guidance. In political terms the law has clearly been extremely successful, as it has been copied by nearly all of the States and has been proposed at Federal level.

BREACH NOTIFICATION UNDER THE ISO 27000 SERIES

7.114 Breach notification forms part of best practice under both ISO 27001 and ISO 27002. Both standards cover incident reporting, in the sense that they require internal reporting of incidents, as part of the controller's incident response strategies. ISO 27001 covers incident reporting at A.13.1 and 2. A.15 also requires the controller's compliance with its legal obligations, which directly incorporates the prevailing legal landscape for breach notification. ISO 27002 deals with incident reporting at section 13 and compliance at section 15. The implementation guidance within ISO 27002, at 13.2.1 says that 'in addition to normal contingency plans ... the procedures [for incident response] should also cover ... communication with those affected by or involved with recovery from the incident' and 'reporting the action to the appropriate authority'.

Chapter 8

PRIVACY ENHANCING TECHNOLOGIES (PETs)

DATA PROTECTION LAW – REACTING TO TECHNOLOGICAL THREATS

8.1 The European data protection regime was born of concerns about the implications for privacy resulting from the use of new technologies. In the late 1960s it was thought that these developments, including the increased use of computers, posed new and significant threats to personal data, which the right to privacy in article 8 of the European Convention on Human Rights might not have catered for.

It is easy for us, spoilt by the availability of technology, its relative ease of use and low cost, to lose sight of the extent and speed of technological development over the past 50 years. By the mid-1960s computer use within the private sector was becoming widespread, but when compared to today the penetration rate was actually very small and the technology was a long way from being user-friendly. Nor had it made the leap to consumer products and services in any meaningful sense. However, it was becoming very clear how things would develop; computers would become more powerful, they would achieve greater penetration into the private sector and they would be adopted by consumers, resulting in greater quantities of personal information being processed in increasingly invasive ways. That caused European lawmakers great concern, hence why they set about building the new legal regime for data protection, which regulates the processing of personal data.

The first lawmakers for data protection clearly had their eyes on the future, but they were not sages or soothsayers; although it is fair to say that in relative terms the technologies of 50 years ago were quite primitive when compared to today's, they were far from prehistoric; the 1950s and 1960s saw marvellous technical achievements, with the biggest of them all, the NASA Apollo series, never having been matched; therefore it was entirely predictable that the lawmakers of those days would turn their attentions to data processing, because those days marked the beginning of the information revolution, a fact that they were aware of and which it would have been impossible for them to ignore.

8.1   Privacy Enhancing Technologies (PETs)

The lawmakers of the 1960s were also much closer to the philosophies underpinning human rights law than we are now. The Council of Europe, which is famously responsible for both the European Convention on Human Rights and the Data Protection Convention, was one of Europe's first major efforts to put in place systems to prevent a recurrence of the horrors of the Nazi regime and the wartime atrocities. There is a direct connection between the right to privacy within article 8 of the European Convention on Human Rights and the genocide that was committed by the Nazis. The early years of the new data protection regime were clearly backwards looking as well as forward looking.

8.2 The theoretical concepts tying data protection to the right to privacy are quite easy to grasp. One of the ideas behind the right to privacy is that human beings (and therefore society as a whole) need privacy in order to be able to fully exercise and enjoy our moral autonomy. This is represented in part by the freedom to make substantive decisions about the way we live our lives, free from interference by others and the core manifestation of society, 'the State'. The Nazi regime represented every possible perversion of these ideas and millions of innocent people were condemned to death, sometimes because of the substantive choices they had made about the way they wanted to live their lives.

However, evil's ability to do harm is partly affected by the information it possesses and has access to. The Nazis therefore built a terror network that provided the infrastructure for the flow of information from the villages, town and cities to the very heart of its leadership. In enacting the right to privacy the Council of Europe was trying to protect substantive and informational privacy. It also recognised that within the right to privacy informational privacy is often an essential pre-requisite to the enjoyment of substantive privacy. Thus, privacy law should regulate the processing of personal data, which has been achieved through data protection law, which expands article 8 for the computer and internet age.

The introduction to the 1973 Council of Europe resolution[1] explained:

> '1. It is generally recognised that the development of modern science and technology, which enable man to attain an advanced standard of living, brings in its wake certain dangers threatening the rights of individuals.
>
> This is the case, for instance, with the utilisation of new techniques for surveillance or observation of persons and for compiling and processing data pertaining to them.
>
> 2. A survey, conducted in 1968–70 by the Committee of Experts on Human Rights of the Council of Europe, on the legislation of the member States with regard to human rights and modern scientific and technological developments has shown that the existing law does not provide sufficient protection for the citizen against intrusions on privacy by technical devices. Generally, the existing laws touch upon the protection of privacy only from a limited point of view, such as secrecy of correspondence and telecommunications, inviolability of the domicile etc. Moreover, the ramifications of the concept of privacy have never been established.

It is also doubtful whether the European Convention on Human Rights, of which Article 8(1) guarantees to everyone "the right to respect for his private and family life, his home and his correspondence", offers satisfactory safeguards against technological intrusions into privacy. The Committee of Experts on Human Rights has noted, for example, that the Convention takes into account only interferences with private life by public authorities, not by private parties.

3. A particular new source of possible intrusion into privacy has been created by the rapid growth and popularisation of computer technology. The purposes which computers are increasingly serving in the public and private sectors are by themselves not basically different from those served by more traditional forms of data storage and processing.

What is setting computers apart from the traditional means of data storage and processing is the extraordinary ease with which they have overcome at a stroke a whole series of problems raised by the management of information: the great volume of data, the techniques for their storage and retrieval, their transmission over large distances, their correct interpretation and, finally, the speed with which all these operations can be performed.

Thus, computers permit the building up in the form of "data banks", of data collections or integrated networks of data collections. These "data banks" are capable of providing instantly and over large distances massive information on individuals.

While few would deny the great advantages offered by the application of electronic data processing techniques, there is a growing concern among the public about the possibility of improper use being made of sensitive personal information stored electronically.

It is, for example, much more difficult for an individual to take steps to protect his personal interests vis-à-vis a computerised information system than it is with regard to a traditional data register. Moreover, data concerning him, which are by themselves inoffensive, may be correlated in such a way that their availability becomes a threat to his private interests.'

[1] Resolution (73) 22 on the protection of the privacy of individuals vis-à-vis electronic data banks in the private sector, adopted by the Committee of Ministers on 26 September 1973 at the 224th meeting of the Ministers' Deputies. See the discussion in Chapter 2.

CONTROL MECHANISMS WITHIN DATA PROTECTION LAW

8.3 As part of the reaction to these new threats the law has placed obligations on data controllers to implement technologies to guard against security breaches. As explained in Chapter 2, these obligations are contained in articles 16 and 17 of the Data Protection Directive[1], the requirements of which have been transposed by the seventh data protection principle in the Data Protection Act 1998 (see also the Table in Appendix B, which contains the national transpositions for most countries in Europe). In other words the European approach has been to require data controllers to use technology to defend against the threats of technology. Thus, from the privacy perspective technology can be regarded as both the disease and the cure.

8.3 Privacy Enhancing Technologies (PETs)

Of course, the law has implemented other control mechanisms, which collectively aim at ensuring that personal data are processed fully in accordance with the data protection principles. Prominent within these other control mechanisms are the geographical control mechanism and the contractual control mechanism.

[1] Directive 95/46/EC.

The geographical control mechanism

8.4 The central idea within the geographical control mechanism is that only Europe provides a safe environment for the processing of personal data[1]. Countries outside Europe are not considered to provide adequate protections for personal data until proved otherwise[2]. In other words, Europe views its laws as being superior to those of third countries.

While this superior attitude now seems anachronistic, vestiges of it still remain[3]. However, a more modern, alternative view is that the geographical control mechanism is no longer as effective as it once was, or, at least, it is no longer as effective as far as data security is concerned.

The central problem within the geographical control mechanism is its simplicity, which borders on naivety. It requires data controllers in Europe to view the world as being carved up into 'good' and 'bad' territories; this can encourage complacency in the good areas and one dimensional solutions to the problems in the bad areas. The truth is that (1) Europe is at least as likely to suffer serious security breaches as non-European countries and (2) the routes by which a data controller can overcome the embargo on data transfers out of Europe[4] do not provide any actual guarantees that personal data will be kept safe.

[1] Data Protection Directive, article 25.
[2] Data Protection Directive, article 26.
[3] See, for example, the conclusion of the Privacy Laws and Business report on regulatory attitudes to breach notification in Europe, particularly the finding that most data protection regulators did not see data breaches as a problem, which is discussed in Chapter 7.
[4] These include the data subject's consent, the European Commission's decisions on the adequacy of the laws of third countries, the Commission's endorsement of the US Safe Harbor scheme, the Commission's model contractual clauses and Binding Corporate Rules.

The contractual control mechanism

8.5 The contractual control mechanism consists of requirements for contracts in the strict sense understood by law, as well as contracts in a colloquial, non-legal sense. Thus, the seventh data protection principle requires contracts to be created for the purposes of compliance with the rules on outsourcing and the use of data processors (ie, formal contracts in the strict legal sense), while the first data protection principle legitimates processing done with the data subject's consent[1], which falls short of a requirement for formal contracts but which nonetheless echoes one of the basic ideas within formal contract-making, that the parties must consent to enter into legal relationships.

The value of the contractual control mechanism is also being doubted, particularly as a result of high-profile data security breaches involving data processors, who, as said, must be engaged on contracts; these cases demonstrate beyond doubt that contracts can provide only limited protection against security breaches. Similarly, where the legal basis of processing is found in the principle of non-contractual consent, there must be doubts about the quality of the protections afforded to the data subject. For example, if it is not possible for the data controller to provide sufficient information about security so as to enable the data subject to make a truly informed choice about the giving of consent to processing[2], the controller will be automatically in breach of the fair processing requirements within the Data Protection Act 1998, which require the supply of any information that is required to make the processing fair[3]. Likewise, if the controller fails without justification to report a serious security incident to the data subject, this could have the effect of undermining the consensual basis of the processing going forward.

[1] The data subject's consent can legitimise most aspects of data processing, including the transfer of personal data out of Europe. Of course, contracts in the formal sense of the word can provide legitimacy for data processing.
[2] The supply of this kind of information is already a specific requirement within Directive 2002/58/EC (see article 4(2)). For the meaning of consent see the Data Protection Directive, article 2(h) which defines the data subject's consent as 'any freely given specific and informed indication of his wishes by which the data subject signifies his agreement to personal data relating to him being processed'. See also recitals (30), (33), (58) and (70).
[3] Data Protection Act 1998, Sch 1, Pt II, para 2(3)(d).

Refocusing on the technological control mechanism

8.6 In recent years the role of the technological control mechanism within compliance has been reassessed. This has given rise to the PETs initiative. This is due, in part, to doubts about the value of the geographical and contractual control mechanisms and their ability to keep data safe. As a result PETs are now taking on more of the compliance burden.

In other words the technological control mechanism is currently in the ascendancy. This is not to say that technology provides all of the answers to the current threat landscape; technology is not a silver bullet. Rather, it is now considered that technology has a much greater role to play in compliance. As such it can be concluded that best practice for data security requires an understanding of PETs and their role within the legal framework; the use of PETs is already an established requirement within best practice standards such as the ISO 27000 series, albeit impliedly or inferentially so.

Furthermore, regulators are also regulating for PETs, through the issuing of guidance on the use of technology and through the use of their enforcement powers. Likewise, lawmakers and opinion formers are re-examining how policy and law should be shaped around PETs.

8.6 *Privacy Enhancing Technologies (PETs)*

Nor should we forget the activities of the big IT companies, who develop and market PET; as well as making PET widely available, some of them, like RSA, the Security Division of EMC, and Symantec are actively investing in educational programmes, which provide consumers and end users of PETs with insight into how the law operates in this field and how their technologies can help to achieve compliance.

EXAMPLES OF PETs

8.7 One of the major problems within the PETs initiative is the absence of an official, or approved, list of available PETs. This must disadvantage the data controller and other consumers and end users of PETs. How does the law expect them to sort the wheat from the chaff? How can they feel comfortable that the law will regard them as having installed the right technologies?

Some of these issues are discussed in Chapter 2, but what is different within the PETs initiative when compared with the standard obligations for technology in the seventh data protection principle, is that the lawmakers consider that there are already technologies out there, on the market, that are privacy enhancing in the general sense of the word. This is the factor that distinguishes these technologies from the narrow confines of security within the seventh data protection principle. However, it is submitted that the lawmakers need to show more leadership on PETs, which will extend to making available a list of approved technologies from which the data controller can make its selections. Presently, controllers are caught in a most invidious position; they are being told to install PETs, yet they are not being given sufficient official guidance on what technologies are considered to be deserving of that title.

Despite the lack of leadership at the lawmakers' end, it is still possible to provide an indicative list of the kinds of technologies that are likely to be regarded as privacy enhancing and therefore deserving of the PETs appellation. Examples of PETs are encryption technologies, digital signatures, authentication technologies (such as two factor authentication), biometrics, data loss prevention technologies, IP log management technologies, perimeter security technologies (such as email screening, firewalls and anti-virus), content addressable storage technologies, records management and archiving technologies and personal internet security technologies.

Encryption

8.8 Encryption is a good example of a PET, because the use of encryption is now widely regarded as being part of best practice for the protection of certain kinds of data, particularly 'sensitive' data[1] that are in motion or that are stored in portable media. It also works well as an example because it has been embraced by the regulators within their official guidance and in their enforcement activities, by the government within official reports and at the EU[2]. There are also many clear statements to the effect that adopting encryption will be treated as a 'good behaviour' by the regulators. For

Examples of PETs 8.9

example, the Information Commissioner has said that the loss of an encrypted laptop does not need to be reported under breach notification rules[3], which echoes the Californian approach on breach notification[4]. Furthermore, in the Commissioner's guidance on encryption[5], the following PETs-related messages were delivered:

> 'There have been a number of reports recently of laptop computers, containing personal information which have been stolen from vehicles, dwellings or left in inappropriate places without being protected adequately. The Information Commissioner has formed the view that in future, where such losses occur and where encryption software has not been used to protect the data, enforcement action will be pursued.
>
> The ICO recommends that portable and mobile devices including magnetic media, used to store and transmit personal information, the loss of which could cause damage or distress to individuals, should be protected using approved encryption software which is designed to guard against the compromise of information.
>
> Personal information, which is stored, transmitted or processed in information, communication and technical infrastructures, should also be managed and protected in accordance with the organisation's security policy and using best practice methodologies such as using the International Standard 27001. Further information can be found at 27001-online.com.
>
> There are a number of different commercial options available to protect stored information on mobile and static devices and in transmission, such as across the internet.
>
> Encryption software uses a complex series of embedded mathematical algorithms to protect and encrypt information. This process hides the data and prevents any inadvertent access or unauthorised disclosure of information. Since encryption standards are always evolving, it is recommended that data controllers ensure that any solution which is implemented, meets the current standard such as the recommended FIPS 140–2 (cryptographic modules, software and hardware) and FIPS – 197.'

[1] The Data Protection Act 1998 regulates the processing of personal data and sensitive personal data, but there are some concerns about the adequacy of these definitions. For example, financial information is not a category of sensitive personal data, which might be considered to be a serious omission, particularly when the issue of harm is factored in; most people would regard financial information as being sensitive. This problem was encountered during the Data Handling Review, which has adopted a third category of personal data called 'Protected Personal Data'.

[2] See for example, the proposed Directive of the European Parliament and Council amending Directive 2002/58/EC, 16497/1/08, 16 February 2009, at recital (51), which says 'in setting detailed rules concerning the format and procedures applicable to the notification of personal data breaches, due consideration should be given to the circumstances of the breach, including whether or not personal data had been protected by encryption or other means effectively limiting the likelihood of identity fraud or other forms of misuse'.

[3] 'Notification of Data Security Breaches to the Information Commissioner's Office', 27 March 2008: http://www.ico.gov.uk/upload/documents/library/data_protection/practical_application/breach_reporting.pdf.

[4] See the discussion in Chapter 1 and Chapter 7.

[5] 'Our approach to encryption', updated 23 December 2008: http://www.ico.gov.uk/about_us/news_and_views/current_topics/Our%20approach%20to%20encryption.aspx.

8.9 These factors operating in conjunction with the press and media interest in data security have contributed to a high level of public awareness of the

8.9 Privacy Enhancing Technologies (PETs)

need for encryption and almost universal support for what encryption seeks to achieve. There is also a broad consensus on encryption being a mandatory requirement in some situations. Against this background it is not surprising that the loss of unencrypted laptops has now become an archetypal taboo.

However, in the UK encryption's elevation to the level of best practice is a relatively recent occurrence, arguably as recent as 2007 or 2008[1]. For example, a cursory examination of the Burton Report[2] into Ministry of Defence security incidents reveals that encryption was not fully deployed for MOD laptops, despite official guidance. The Data Handling Review and the Information Commissioner's recent enforcement activities have also acted to underline the extent to which encryption has not been deployed in the UK.

Yet encryption has moved from the periphery of data security law to its very centre. The fact that it has done this so quickly stands to illustrate that PETs is a very dynamic and fast moving subject. This carries with it a number of noteworthy consequences for controllers, practitioners, regulators and the courts. Included within these are:

1 There is a need to actively track and monitor the state of technological development. The seventh data protection principle has always required organisations to keep abreast of the changes in technological development, but the realities and consequences of this obligation are only now starting to be fully appreciated, which is attributable in part to the movement in attitudes to encryption. Other technologies could quickly emerge as de facto PETs, but this might not be appreciated by the controller that fails to put in place systems for tracking and monitoring developments.
2 Likewise, systems and operations should be kept under constant review. PETs will continue to take on more of the compliance burden, which will have a direct impact on the expectations of best practice. Controllers should review their systems and operations in order to determine whether there is an enhanced role for PETs within their organisations.
3 There will continue to be a high level of confusion about core issues, such as definitions and classifications[3], particularly if the PETs initiative does not receive the political and regulatory investment that it deserves. As argued later, the PETs initiative needs a scheme of accreditation if it is to achieve its full potential, an outcome that undoubtedly needs governments, the EU and the regulators to take on more of the leadership.

For these reasons and despite all of the legal, political and regulatory activity, there is still a lack of clarity about the scope of PETs, even in the field of encryption, particularly email encryption.

[1] In the sense that some of the best indicators of current practices, such as the government, financial services sector and the Information Commissioner's public statements and enforcement actions were not pursuing a highly visible strategy for encryption. Of course, encryption was installed by many data controllers prior to 2007, but the point is they were still in a small minority.
[2] 'Report into the Loss of MOD Personal Data', Sir Edmund Burton: http://www.mod.uk/nr/rdonlyres/3e756d20-e762–4fc1-bab0–08c68fdc2383/0/burton_review_rpt20080430.pdf.
[3] Such as the criteria for breach notification.

DEFINITIONS OF PETs AND SCOPE OF THE INITIATIVE

8.10 People who are new to the PETs initiative can be discouraged from engaging properly when they learn that there is still confusion about the core issues. This could cause some people to think that PETs is not a serious or mainstream initiative. While understandable, this would be a mistake, particularly in light of the trajectory of the law, which is discussed in Chapter 1, and the likelihood of more disputes and litigation about data security law and practice. The role played by technology within data protection compliance will only increase; it is predictable that future legal action will focus on the extent to which the controller has implemented a plan or strategy for PETs.

Of course, it is very unhelpful that definitions have yet to be agreed, that regulatory guidance is still slim and there are no court cases to speak of. Yet despite this vagueness it is still possible to identify some core legal obligations for PETs, both within legislation and within the work of the regulators, as already mentioned. To repeat, the seventh data protection principle within the Data Protection Act 1998 requires data controllers to have regard to the state of technological development and both the Information Commissioner and the Financial Services Authority have taken enforcement action against companies and organisations that have failed to implement encryption; this constitutes a clear legal trend enabling the conclusion to be made that the PETs initiative is here to stay.

PETs for compliance with the data protection principles generally

8.11 As already indicated, the PETs initiative is not just about data security and the seventh data protection principle. Rather, it is about the role of technology within compliance generally. One of the results of the PETs initiative is the expansion of the compliance role of technology beyond the security principle to all of the data protection principles. Thus, data controllers should be considering how technology can help them comply with the purpose limitation principle (the second data protection principle), the adequacy principle (the third principle), the accuracy principle (the fourth principle) and so on. Indeed, it is impossible to identify a data protection principle that could not benefit from the application of PETs. For example, data loss protection technologies have a role to play in enforcing the geographical control mechanism, because they can be configured to prevent the movement of data from endpoints on the computer network and the transmission of data by electronic communication.

This point is further illustrated by the subject access procedure within the Data Protection Act 1998, s 7, breach of which is covered by the sixth data protection principle. In order for a controller to feel confident about complying with an access request within the 40 days allowed they may wish to consider installing archiving technologies for unstructured data, like email. An adequate data archiving system will classify data as it enters the archive and will allow full content searches of the archive and the subsequent production of data in native file format, with added functionality to preserve the integrity

8.11 *Privacy Enhancing Technologies (PETs)*

of records and their redaction. The archiving system will also enforce access rights and produce an audit trail of activity. All of this is very positive from the perspective of compliance with access requests. As such it is easy to see how an archive can be regarded as privacy enhancing as far as subject access and the sixth data protection principle are concerned. Of course, they also help achieve compliance with the security principle.

Thus, it can be said that it is inherent within the meaning of PETs that the technology under consideration should make an appreciable contribution to an organisation's compliance with key privacy laws, such as the generality of the data protection principles as already discussed, or the right to privacy within the Human Rights Act 1998, or more specialised laws, such as the Regulation of Investigatory Powers Act 2000. Technology that can tick a series of compliance functions will be a serious candidate for PETs accreditation, if such a scheme were to be adopted.

PETs – your new best friends, April 2006

8.12 This expansive nature of the PETs initiative is borne out by the Information Commissioner's amusingly titled press release on PETs, published in April 2006[1]. This announced the publication of a technical guidance note[2], which is discussed in the next section. The press release explains:

> 'PETs have traditionally been considered to be software and other systems which allow individuals to withhold their true identity when using electronic operating systems, such as anonymous web browsers, specialist email services, and digital cash. However, the ICO considers them to include any technology which exists to protect or enhance an individual's privacy. So a system that allowed a doctor to see all the details of a medical record but only allowed the receptionist to see the contact and administrative information would be using a privacy enhancing approach.'

This passage confirms the point that PETs are about more than the security principle. It gives helpful encouragement to data controllers and IT companies that the law currently has an open mind about the kinds of technology that can qualify as PETs. It also points to the belief that leadership has to be shown by the users and the vendors of PETs, who are not excluded from the process that will lead eventually to the completion of the initiative by the introduction of a scheme of accreditation. In other words, there is opportunity for the users and vendors to have their own voices heard. For example, there is no reason why the IT industry as a whole could not sponsor, or help to develop, a scheme of voluntary accreditation, as has happened to a limited extent with the EuroPriSe initiative.

The press release then goes on to give some examples of the kinds of technologies that the Information Commissioner considers to be privacy enhancing:

- '• Encrypted biometric access systems that allow the use of a fingerprint to authenticate an individual's identity without retaining the actual fingerprint;

- Secure online access for individuals to their own personal data to check its accuracy and make amendments;
- Software that allows browsers to automatically detect the privacy policy of websites and compares it to the preferences expressed by the user and alerting the user to any clashes; and
- "Sticky" electronic privacy policies that are attached to the information itself preventing it being used in any way that is not compatible with that policy.'

This is a revealing list. Not surprisingly, it talks about encryption, but its reference to fingerprint biometrics is controversial as a privacy-friendly control mechanism. At first blush the idea of a non-retained fingerprint biometric process seems to be privacy-friendly, particularly as the initially invasive use of the fingerprint is counterbalanced by the rule against its retention. This process leads to the outcome of secure, verification of identity.

1 'PETs – Your New Best Friends', 27 April 2006.
2 'Data Protection Technical Guidance Note: Privacy enhancing technologies (PETs)', V1.0, 11 April 2006: http://www.ico.gov.uk/upload/documents/library/data_protection/detailed_specialist_guides/privacy_enhancing_technologies.pdf.

8.13 The idea becomes controversial however when questions are asked about how the process will work in practice. Firstly, what does the threat landscape look like for this kind of process? It is likely to be very complex, containing very acute threats to security. Secondly, who is going to run the scheme? The consequences for privacy will be different in the public and private sectors. In the public sector there will be Surveillance Society and function-creep concerns. In the private sector there will commercial concerns. Thirdly, what is the extent of the data processing? Is it actually possible to build a system that does not require the retention of the fingerprint somewhere in the process? This may demonstrate that there is a need to be very cautious about claims that a particular technology is privacy enhancing and may act to provide further support to the proposition that PETs needs a scheme of accreditation to work properly.

A common manifestation of the Information Commissioner's second example is online banking, where the customer is put in control of key account information. However, the ability for people to go online to make amendments to data is still very limited. The vast majority of personal data are not subject to such a process of data subject control.

The third example given by the Information Commissioner is interesting, in that it proposes the use of PETs to enforce the contractual control mechanism, through the matching of website privacy policies to user preferences, which, presumably would be set in the user's internet browser, like security settings for cookies and parental controls.

The attributes of the fourth example are found in some data loss prevention technologies, which can be configured so as to enforce policy at the individual file level.

8.14 *Privacy Enhancing Technologies (PETs)*

Data protection guidance note, March 2007

8.14 In March 2007 the Information Commissioner' Officer published version 2 of its guidance note on PETs[1] (the first version was the one launched by the April 2006 press release). In the passage titled 'what are privacy enhancing technologies?' the following guidance is given about their nature and role:

> 'Technology can assist companies' compliance with the principles that protect individuals' privacy and can go further to empower individuals, giving them easier access to and control over information about them and allowing them to decide how and when it will be disclosed to and used by third parties.
>
> The best protection for individuals is that their personal information is only collected where this is essential. Privacy enhancing technologies have traditionally been limited to "pseudonymisation tools". These are software and systems that allow individuals to withhold their true identity from those operating electronic systems or providing services through them, and only reveal it when absolutely necessary. These technologies help to minimise the information collected about individuals and include anonymous web browsers, specialist email services, and digital cash.
>
> Federated identity management systems potentially allow individuals to access the services of organisations without having to provide information to them. They involve one trusted organisation verifying the identity of an individual and then vouching for them using an electronic token that also specifies their particular entitlements. This allows the individual to access the services provided by third parties using the token without having to disclose their identity or other information necessary to prove their entitlement.
>
> The Information Commissioner considers that privacy enhancing technologies are not limited to tools that provide a degree of anonymity for individuals but they are also any technology that exists to protect or enhance an individual's privacy, including facilitating individuals' access to their rights under the Data Protection Act 1998.'

This part of the guidance pays particular attention to identity management tools. Again, the ideas within pseudonymisation and federated identity management are privacy enhancing, but on closer inspection a raft of problems are revealed, as happens when the fingerprint biometric example is examined. Leaving aside questions about security, scaleability and so on, it is difficult to see how the withholding of identity from a data controller can work in many commercial settings. For example, anti money laundering rules require positive customer due diligence procedures, which would be defeated by pseudonymisation and federated identity management. International travel is another problematic area. These systems will also require a huge amount of technical coordination, the setting of formal technical standards for interoperability and, of course, a scheme of accreditation if they are to be accepted as being PETs.

[1] 'Data Protection Guidance Note: Privacy enhancing technologies (PETs)', V2.0, 29 March 2007: http://www.ico.gov.uk/upload/documents/library/data_protection/detailed_specialist_guides/privacy_enhancing_technologies_v2.pdf.

8.15 The guidance then goes on to repeat the examples of PETs set out in the April 2006 press release, after which it highlights some of the benefits of their use:

Definitions of PETs and scope of the initiative **8.16**

'They can save you money. The cost of including privacy at the system design stage is much less than the cost of having to amend a finished system to make sure it complies with legal requirements and respects individuals' privacy.

They help to reduce risks. Privacy controls that are incorporated into electronic information systems to supplement organisational procedures help to provide additional safeguards which better protect individuals' information from human error.

They help to build trust. The use of privacy enhancing technology in systems helps to signal the integrity and intention of organisations regarding the information that they hold, and encourages trust in those organisations by citizens and customers.'

These benefits (costs saving, reduction of risk and building trust) are part of conventional thinking on PETs and are only controversial to the extent that the evidential basis behind them is unclear. Despite this, it is probably fair to say that these benefits are real, albeit they are not quantified.

The guidance concludes with the topic of 'design philosophy', saying:

'A system designer who starts from the position of trying to protect individuals' privacy by creating or implementing privacy enhancing technologies might ask the following questions as an essential part of the task.
- Do I need to collect any personal data at all?
- If so, what is the minimum needed?
- Who will have access to which data?
- How can accesses be controlled to allow only those which are for the purposes stated when the data was collected, and then only by those employees and processes that have an essential need?
- Can individuals make total or partial use of the system anonymously?
- How can I help individuals to exercise their rights securely?'

This 'design philosophy' idea was expanded upon by the Information Commissioner's report titled 'Privacy by Design', which is discussed later, and the initiative for 'Privacy Impact Assessments'.

'White Paper for Decision-Makers'

8.16 In December 2004 the Dutch Ministry of Interior and Kingdom Relations published its 'White Paper for Decision-Makers', a very substantial report about PETs[1]. The management summary begins by explaining the high level benefits of PETs:

'PET enables processes that would otherwise be impossible;

Privacy controls incorporated in information systems can be more effective and efficient than organisational procedures and manual actions. Processes can therefore be optimised by the application of PET;

Utilisation of PET signals trustworthiness, and creates public confidence in the processing of their personal data in government information systems;

The costs associated with the application of PET technology in information systems can be minimised when privacy aspects are already taken into account

8.16 Privacy Enhancing Technologies (PETs)

during the design phase of the system. Both the quantitative and the qualitative benefits of PET are considerable, for the organisations involved, for the public and for society in general.'

This report reveals that there is a 'PET staircase', with each step representing greater privacy enhancing attributes. It starts with 'general PET controls', which leads on to 'data separation', then 'Privacy Management Systems' and, finally, 'anonymisation'. It recognises that what is appropriate will depend upon the circumstances, saying that 'suitability of the different PET options primarily depends on the characteristics of the information system, the required level of protection and the sensitivity of the personal data concerned'.

[1] http://www.dutchdpa.nl/downloads_overig/PET_whitebook.pdf.

8.17 It is clear that the report influenced the Information Commissioner's guidance. The following paragraphs provide a more detailed analysis of the access control and identity management tools described by the Commissioner:

> 'Encryption and logical access security controls are two familiar and widely used basic PET options. In the context of logical access controls, adequate management of uniquely identifying personal data and the corresponding authorisation data are particularly important.
>
> An important PET technique concerns the separation of data in several domains. One domain contains the identifying personal data and another the other personal data. As a result, for example financial, legal or medical information is then contained in one or more domains – separate from the domain containing information on the person's identity. The data contained in each separate domain is not sensitive as it cannot be attributed to a single natural person. In this PET option, software is used to ensure that only authorised system users are able to link data from the different information domains. A different form of data separation is the introduction of a system function that only verifies the information detail that is stored in the database, but does not release the information. For example, the function only responds positively or negatively to a prompt.'

The report also supports the Information Commissioner's design philosophies. The following passage is notable:

> 'With PET the safeguards for data protection are embedded in the system design, and therefore the requirements for organisational safeguards and accountability are easier to fulfil. PET has to claim its place in the product lifecycle management of information systems. This implies that, in addition to the design and implementation, attention should also be focused on privacy-related aspects, such as privacy governance, risk analysis, testing and maintaining PET controls.'

The report provides plenty of help with developing the business and legal case for PETs and provides a number of helpful examples of the options that are available. Case studies of successful PETs installations are provided, as are a series of network diagrams.

EU position on PETs

8.18 In May 2007 the European Commission published its PETs Communication[1]. This report, which was addressed to the European Parliament and Council, contains a strategy for the promotion of data protection through PETs. The introduction gives a reminder of one of the key ideas within PETs, that if technology is the disease it can also be the cure, explaining that PETs 'would facilitate ensuring that breaches of the data protection rules and violations of individual's rights are ... technically more difficult'.

As regards the issue of leadership, the Communication quickly identifies a widened scope of responsibility, which extends beyond the data controller to cover the IT industry and important players within it, such as systems integrators and similar. This, of course, is consistent with one of the major planks of thinking on best practice, which says that everyone playing a part in data processing carries personal responsibility for security. The Communication says:

> 'Whilst strictly speaking data controllers bear the legal responsibility for complying with data protection rules, others also bear some responsibility for data protection from a societal and ethical point of view. These involve those who design technical specifications and those who actually build or implement applications or operating systems.'

[1] Communication from the Commission to the European Parliament and the Council on Promoting Data Protection by Privacy Enhancing Technologies (PETs), Brussels, 2.5.2007 COM(2007) 228 final: http://eur-lex.europa.eu/LexUriServ/LexUriServ.do?uri=COM: 2007: 0228: FIN:EN:PDF.

Further clarification of the risks to personal data and the core philosophies of data protection

8.19 The introduction to the Communication also includes a reminder of the fact that the threat landscape is ever changing and the fact that data protection law needs to evolve to ensure its own adequacy and relevancy. Echoing the points made at the beginning of this chapter, it says:

> 'The intensive and sustained development of information and communication technologies (ICT) is constantly offering new services which improve people's life. To a large extent, the raw material for interactions in cyberspace is the personal data of individuals moving around in it when they purchase goods and services, establish or maintain contact with others or communicate their ideas on the world wide web. Alongside the benefits brought about by these developments, new risks also arise for the individual, such as identity theft, discriminatory profiling, continuous surveillance or fraud.
>
> The Charter of Fundamental Rights of the European Union recognises in Article 8 the right to the protection of personal data. This fundamental right is set forth in a European legal framework on the protection of personal data consisting in particular of the Data Protection Directive 95/46/EC and the ePrivacy Directive 2002/58/EC as well as the Data Protection Regulation (EC) 45/2001 relating to processing by Community institution and bodies. This legislation lays down several substantive provisions imposing obligations on data controllers and recognizing rights of data subjects. It also prescribes

8.19 *Privacy Enhancing Technologies (PETs)*

sanctions and appropriate remedies in cases of breach and establishes enforcement mechanisms to make them effective.

However, this system may prove insufficient when personal data is disseminated worldwide through ICT networks and the processing of data crosses several jurisdictions, often outside the EU. In such situations the current rules may be considered to apply and to provide a clear legal response. Furthermore, a competent authority to enforce the rules may also be identified. However, considerable practical obstacles may exist as a result of difficulties with the technology used involving data processing by different actors in different locations and there may be hurdles intrinsic to the enforcement of national administrative and court rulings in another jurisdiction, especially in non-EU countries.'

It is also noticeable that the final part of this passage refers to the difficulties of regulating beyond the boundaries of the EU. This is obviously relevant to the earlier discussion about the geographical control mechanism and the ascendancy of the technological control mechanism. From this part of the Communication we gather that the European Commission is willing to look seriously at the flaws in the regulatory framework.

The Commission's definition of PETs

8.20 The Communication tackles the issue of definitions, in the following passage:

'There are a number of definitions of PETs used by the academic community and by pilot projects on this matter. For instance, according to the EC-funded PISA project, PET stands for a coherent system of ICT measures that protects privacy by eliminating or reducing personal data or by preventing unnecessary and/or undesired processing of personal data, all without losing the functionality of the information system. The use of PETs can help to design information and communication systems and services in a way that minimises the collection and use of personal data and facilitate compliance with data protection rules. The Commission in its First Report on the implementation of the Data Protection Directive considers that "... the use of appropriate technological measures is an essential complement to legal means and should be an integral part in any efforts to achieve a sufficient level of privacy protection ...". The use of PETs should result in making breaches of certain data protection rules more difficult and/or helping to detect them.

In the dynamic landscape of ICT, the effectiveness of different PETs to ensure the protection of privacy, including aspects of compliance with data protection law, is varied and changes over time. Their typology is also varied. They can be stand-alone tools requiring positive action by consumers (who must purchase and install them in their PCs) or be built into the very architecture of information systems. Several examples of PETs can be mentioned here:
- Automatic anonymisation of data, after a certain lapse of time, supports the principle that processed data should be kept in a form which permits identification of data subjects for no longer than necessary for the purposes for which the data were originally collected.
- Encryption tools, preventing hacking when information is transmitted over the Internet, supports the data controller's obligation to take appropriate measures to protect personal data against unlawful processing.

- Cookie-cutters, that block cookies placed on the user's PC to make it perform certain instructions without the user being aware of them, enhance compliance with the principle that data must be processed fairly and lawfully, and that the data subject must be informed about the processing going on.
- The Platform for Privacy Preferences (P3P), allowing internet users to analyze the privacy policies of websites and compare them with the user's preferences as to the information they wish to release, helps to ensure that data subjects' consent to processing of their data is an informed one.'

Again, this passage emphasises that the role of PETs within compliance goes beyond security, to all of the data protection principles. It also repeats the point that PETs are seen as the technological cure to the technological disease. The examples of PETs that are given clearly dovetail with those given by the Information Commissioner and the Dutch report. However, the Communication later goes on to caution, quite properly, that technology does not provide a silver bullet solution to all of the terrors:

'The Commission is aware of the fact that technology – although having a crucial role in privacy protection – is not sufficient in itself to secure privacy. PETs need to be applied according to a regulatory framework of enforceable data protection rules providing a number of negotiable levels of privacy protection for all individuals. The use of PETs does not mean that operators can be discharged of certain of their legal obligations (e.g. granting individual users a right of access to their data).'

The Commission's objectives

8.21 The Communication sets out the Commission's three key objectives. These are to support the development of PET, to support the use of available PETs by data controllers and to encourage consumers to use PETs. In achievement of these objectives, specific action points are set out. The objectives and their related action points are contained in Table 8.1.

Table 8.1 European Commission's objectives and action points	
1 Support the development of PETs.	(a) Identifying the need and technological requirements of PETs. (b) Developing PETs.
2 Support the use of available PETs by data controllers.	(a) Promoting the use of PETs by industry. (b) Ensuring respect for appropriate standards in the protection of personal data through PETs. This covers (i) standardisation and (ii) coordination of national technical rules on security measures for data processing. (c) Promoting the use of PETs by public authorities.
3 Encourage consumers to use PETs.	(a) Raising awareness of consumers. (b) Facilitating consumers' informed choice: Privacy Seals.

8.22 Privacy Enhancing Technologies (PETs)

Supporting the development of PETs

8.22 The Commission's analysis for the purposes of the first objective begins by making a serious point about how PETs are developed, namely that technological solutions are developed in response to the threat landscape. It says:

> 'PETs are heavily dependent on the evolution of ICT. Once the dangers posed by technological developments are detected, the appropriate requirements for a technological solution must be identified.'

In order to accelerate the development of PETs, the Commission commits itself to supporting a stakeholder forum which will have the task of assessing the threat landscape, the risks and the required responses[1]. This work will then inform the actual development of PETs by the industry[2]. The Commission also commits itself to investing EU money into research and supporting projects[3], but it calls on national regulators, like the Information Commissioner, and the private sector to contribute[4].

[1] 'The Commission will encourage various stakeholder groups to come together and debate PETs ... These stakeholders should regularly look into the evolution of technology, detect the dangers it poses to fundamental rights and data protection, and outline the technical requirements of a PETs response ...'
[2] 'As the need for and technological requirements of PETs are identified, concrete action has to be taken to arrive at an end-product ready to use ...'
[3] '... the Commission intends to support other RTD projects and large-scale pilot demonstrations to develop and stimulate the uptake of PETs. The aim is to provide the foundation for user-empowering privacy protection services reconciling legal and technical differences across Europe through public-private partnerships ...'
[4] 'The Commission also calls on national authorities and on the private sector to invest in the development of PETs.'

Supporting the use of available PETs by data controllers

8.23 The analysis recognises that nothing concrete can be achieved without the IT industry[1]. Thus, the Commission plans to hold seminars with industry representatives, to analyse how they can contribute[2]. However, the Commission is clearly sceptical about the idea of industry self-regulation[3], particularly in technical standards, pointing clearly to a preference for open standards against proprietary ones[4]. Thus, it explains that it may involve both European and international standards making bodies[5], who will be required to ensure that the standards reflect the requirements of privacy law and the data protection principles[6].

It also makes comments on the issue of leadership, observing that the national regulators, such as the Information Commissioner, have a powerful ability to influence the development of PETs in their own jurisdictions[7]. The Commission wants to tap and maximise that potential, which, if it is to be achieved, requires coordination, by the Article 29 Working Party[8].

Finally, the Commission calls on national governments to implement PETs strategies, particularly in the field of e-government[9], and commits itself to the use of PETs[10].

Definitions of PETs and scope of the initiative **8.24**

1. 'The Commission believes that all those involved in processing of personal data would benefit from a wider use of PETs. The ICT industry, as the primary developer and provider of PETs, has a particularly important role to play with respect to the promotion of PETs.'
2. 'The Commission calls on all data controllers to more widely and intensely incorporate and apply PETs in their processes. For that purpose, the Commission will organise seminars with key actors of the ICT industry, and in particular PETs developers, with the aim of analyzing their possible contribution to promoting the use of PETs among data controllers.'
3. 'While wide-reaching promotional activity requires the active involvement of the ICT industry, as the PETs producer, respect for appropriate standards requires action beyond self regulation or the goodwill of the actors involved.'
4. 'The Commission will assess the need to develop standards regarding the lawful processing of personal data with PETs through appropriate impact assessments.'
5. 'The Commission may invite the European Standardisation Organisations (CEN, CENELEC, ETSI) to assess specific European needs, and to subsequently bring them to the international level by means of applying the current agreements between European and international standardisation organisations.'
6. 'The Commission will consider the need for respect of data protection rules to be taken into account in standardisation activities.'
7. 'National legislation adopted pursuant to the Data Protection Directive gives national data protection authorities certain influence in determining precise technical requirements such as providing guidance for controllers, examining the systems put in place or issuing technical instructions.'
8. 'The Commission thus calls on the Article 29 Working Party to continue its work in the field by including in its programme a permanent activity of analyzing the needs for incorporating PETs in data processing operations as an effective means of ensuring respect for data protection rules.'
9. 'The Commission calls upon governments to ensure that data protection safeguards are embedded in eGovernment applications, including through the widest possible use of PETs in their design and implementation.'
10. 'The Commission itself will ensure that it complies with the requirements of Regulation (EC) 45/2001 in particular through a wider use of PETs in the implementation of ICT applications involving the processing of personal data. At the same time, the Commission calls on other EU institutions to do the same.'

Encouraging consumers to use PETs

8.24 The analysis reminds the reader that the goal of the PETs initiative is consumer protection[1]. It therefore recommends that the national regulators should take responsibility for awareness-raising campaigns within their jurisdiction[2], supported by consumer associations[3]. In order to give consumers confidence in the technologies they are purchasing, it postulates the introduction of a 'privacy seal'[4], which will be awarded to deserving technologies. However, it wants the number of these seals to be kept to a minimum[5] and suggests that the seal could be incorporated into a general security certification[6].

1. 'Consumers will remain the most concerned party in ensuring personal information is properly used, that data protection rules are properly enacted, and that PETs are an efficient means to guarantee them.'
2. 'A consistent strategy should be adopted to raise consumer awareness of the risks involved in processing their data and of the solutions that PETs may provide as a complement to the existing systems of remedies contained in data protection legislation. The Commission intends to launch a series of EU-wide awareness-raising activities on PETs. The main responsibility for conducting this activity falls within the realm of national data protection authorities which already have relevant experience in this area.'

8.24 *Privacy Enhancing Technologies (PETs)*

³ '... consumer associations and other players such as the Consumer Centres Network (ECC-Net), in its role as an EU-wide network to advise citizens on their rights as consumers, could become partners in the quest to educate consumers.'
⁴ '... the Commission intends to investigate the feasibility of an EU-wide system of privacy seals ...'
⁵ 'The number of privacy seal systems should be kept to a minimum. In fact, a proliferation of seals may create more confusion to the consumer and undermine their trust in all seals.'
⁶ 'Therefore, an assessment should be made about whether and to what extent it would be appropriate to integrate a European privacy seal in a more general security certification scheme.'

The economic benefits of PETs – promoting the EU IT industry

8.25 Of course, the PETs initiative is about much more than privacy. It is also about money, or, more accurately, the growth of the IT industry in Europe and the market for technologies. If PETs take off, the revenues will be considerable, a point not lost on the Commission, which noted:

> 'Increased use of PETs and increased use of e-services which incorporate PETs will in turn mean economic reward to the industries using them, and may result in a snowball effect, encouraging other companies to pay greater attention to respecting the data protection rules.'

Follow-up

8.26 For a detailed account of the follow-up work undertaken on PETs, see the 'Privacy Protection and Electronic Identity Management' section within the ICT pages on the Cordis website[1]. The ICT Work Programme 2009–10[2], which supports the 7th Framework Programme for EU funded research-related project[3] also contains core information. Relevant EU funded projects to consider include PRIMELIFE ('Privacy and identity management in Europe for life')[4] and PICOS ('Privacy and Identity Management for Community Services')[5]. See also the 'Critical Infrastructure Protection' pages on Cordis[6] and ENISA ('European Network and Information Security Agency')[7].

[1] http://cordis.europa.eu/fp7/ict/security/eid-management_en.html.
[2] 'ICT – Information and Communication Technologies'. A Theme for research and development under the specific programme 'Cooperation' implementing the Seventh Framework Programme (2007–2013) of the European Community for research, technological development and demonstration activities: ftp://ftp.cordis.europa.eu/pub/fp7/ict/docs/ict-wp-2009–10_en.pdf.
[3] http://cordis.europa.eu/fp7/home_en.html.
[4] http://cordis.europa.eu/fetch?CALLER=FP7_PROJ_EN&ACTION=D&DOC=2&CAT=PROJ&QUERY=01226a04e1f7:3cf8:6a30e81a&RCN=85453.
[5] http://www.picos-project.eu/.
[6] http://cordis.europa.eu/fp7/ict/critinfpro/home_en.html.
[7] http://www.enisa.europa.eu/.

Legal effect

8.27 The Communication as a legal instrument falls far short of a proposal for the amendment of the Data Protection Directive. Yet this does not undermine the place of PETs within the legal regime. The endorsement of the concepts at national regulatory level creates at the very least an expectation that controllers will take account of the PETs initiative during the design of their systems. In other words, the Communication puts the controller on enhanced notice of the trajectory of the law. Over time, if the law continues its current trajectory, the status of PETs will continue to be enhanced and the details of the law's expectations will become clearer.

FUNCTIONALITY AND ACCREDITATION

8.28 In order to be successful as an initiative there is a need for a scheme of accreditation, to enable makers of PETs to get official recognition for their products. A scheme of accreditation would also have various consumer protection benefits and would provide a useful framework for the regulation of the IT sector. Both of these points are made in the European Commission's Communication.

As the Communication demonstrates, there are many arguments that can be marshalled in support of a scheme of independent accreditation, one that is separate from the control of the IT industry. For example, individual consumers who are not technology-savvy may have more confidence in their purchasing decisions if the scheme of accreditation is truly independent of the vendors. Accreditation may even help to counter the problem of mis-selling of technologies. There is also the position of data controllers; they deserve more clarity in the regulatory framework and a proper steer from the regulators about the kinds of technologies that they should be installing. However, at this time there is a massive void in the official information that can help inform purchasing decisions. This may stifle the take up and use of PETs and the growth of the PETs marketplace in Europe.

The scheme that the Commission identifies, which is based around the setting of technical standards and the involvement of European and international standards-making bodies, should satisfy all of the requirements of independence, but this does not necessarily mean that it is the best way forward. Considerable drawbacks include the fact that it will take years to establish, it may not gain the buy-in of the IT industry and it may be too complex to run. Furthermore, it does not deal with the fact that there are already many technologies on the market that have earned the right to be called privacy enhancing.

One alternative would be to extend the role of the national regulators. As explained in the Communication, their role within any scheme of accreditation will be significant, but they could actually take on a bigger role than the one identified by the Commission. Perhaps the national regulators, properly coordinated by the Article 29 Working Party, could hold the power of accreditation.

This would probably speed up the process towards accreditation, but the obvious problem is that the regulators may not have the skills, resources, or the appetite to take on this role. There is also a philosophical concern about

8.28 Privacy Enhancing Technologies (PETs)

the efficacy of a system of regulation that endorses products and services supplied mainly by the private sector[1]. In this sense any reluctance on the part of the regulators to take on the role of the accreditation body will be understandable.

[1] There are many examples of public sector endorsement of private sector suppliers, to undermine the philosophical difficulties. For example, the public sector procurement process puts private sector bidders in direct competition, leaving it to the public sector purchaser to select the winner.

8.29 There is another alternative. The accreditation scheme could be built around expert opinions on the functionality of the product under review. This is precisely the scheme within the EuroPriSe programme[1]:

> 'EuroPriSe is a European project funded by the European Commission with 1.2 Mio. Euro under the eTEN programme. The consortium of nine European partners is led by the Independent Centre for Privacy Protection Schleswig-Holstein (Unabhängiges Landeszentrum für Datenschutz, ULD).
>
> EuroPriSe introduced a European Privacy Seal for IT-products and IT-based services that have proven privacy compliance in a two-step certification procedure: firstly an evaluation by specialized experts and secondly a check of the evaluation report by an independent certification body.
>
> The project offered pilot certification according to the European Privacy Seal procedure in Germany, Austria, United Kingdom, Slovakia, Spain, Sweden and in further EU countries on request.
>
> Technical and legal IT-experts were trained in two workshops to evaluate IT products and IT-based services according to the European Privacy Seal Criteria.
>
> The project started in June 2007. The first Experts were trained in November 2007. Pilot Trials started in February 2008. The project ended in February 2009 with a successfull market validation and six successfull pilot certifications. EuroPriSe is now permanently established at ULD.'

EuroPriSe avoids the issue of technical standards, by focusing instead on functionality. Those applying for a Privacy Seal need to show how their product or services meet the EuroPriSe criteria[2]. Their applications are then reviewed by two registered experts and then passed over to EuroPriSe, which checks the experts' evaluation and then awards the seal if everything is in order.

The EuroPriSe project, while funded by the EU, is actually the brainchild of the data protection authority for Schleswig-Holstein, which may remove doubts about the capacity of the national regulators to run a scheme of functional accreditation.

[1] https://www.european-privacy-seal.eu/.
[2] EuroPriSe Criteria, Version 1.0: https://www.european-privacy-seal.eu/criteria/EuroPriSe%20Criteria%20Catalogue%20public%20version%201.0.pdf.

'PRIVACY BY DESIGN'

8.30 The Information Commissioner's report on 'Privacy by Design'[1], which was commissioned to 'try to identify why more has not been done to design in

'Privacy by Design' 8.30

privacy protections from first principles and what needs to be done to rectify the situation', provides further support for the role of PETs within compliance for data protection and data security. It recognises, however, that there has been some reluctance within data controllers to embrace PETs. One of the reasons why is identified in the following passage:

> 'PETs have yet to find widespread adoption in "real world" environments because organisations and vendors are fearful of committing to specific PETs in case these quickly prove to be obsolete as technologies develop. Web 2.0, cloud computing and service oriented architecture developments will most likely add further complexity to this problem.'

Taking the report's findings at face value, it agrees with the need for a scheme of accreditation, but it does not commit itself to the model proposed by the European Commission:

> 'Once practical PETs are available, there will be a need for an independent but trusted body – such as a regulator or trade association – which is able to test and accredit PETs-enabled products to confirm the level of protection offered and certify them accordingly. This is not dissimilar to the CAPS-approved function currently provided by CESG.'

As regards the short to medium term future of PETs, the report does not make for optimistic reading. The general reluctance of controllers to adopt PETs means that 'vendors are not under pressure to deliver PETs in their products'. That must be correct, but only to a certain extent. For example, in the field of data loss prevention the market demand has started to appear, leading the major IT security companies to invest heavily. Of course, the overall demand for PETs is still patchy, as the report refers. However, the problems with demand may also be associated by a lack of awareness, rather than a lack of demand, another point recognised by the report, which places the onus on the regulators and the IT industry to raise awareness.

[1] 'Privacy by Design', November 2008: http://www.ico.gov.uk/upload/documents/pdb_report_html/privacy_by_design_report_v2.pdf.

Appendix A
FSA AND ICO ENFORCEMENT ACTION

FSA CASES

FSA v Capita Financial Administrators Limited ('CFA')	
Date of Decision Notice	15 March 2006
Overview	The FSA reported on a number of internal actual or attempted frauds, including:
	– an incident in which a client's name and address were changed and units were sold without client instructions;
	– data relating to five other clients was subject to unauthorised change and fraudulent requests for payments were made (but avoided); and
	– data relating to five other clients was subject to unauthorised change and fraudulent requests for payments were made (but avoided); and
	– the fraudulent processing of instructions in respect of 20 clients totalling £416,321.
Decision	The FSA found that weaknesses in CFA's systems and controls contributed to the frauds. The FSA also found that there were insufficient controls to ensure that changes to client data and instructions for payments were genuine, or that payments were only made to genuine customers.
	The FSA stated that the discovery of the frauds by CFA's customers and not by the company itself amounted to a serious failing, and noted that the cumulative impact of these failings constituted a significant risk to the FSA's objective of reducing financial crime.

FSA and ICO enforcement action

	The FSA found there to be breaches of Principles 2 and 3 of the FSA's Principles for Businesses, and breaches of SYSC 3.2.6R. The FSA found there to be breaches of Principles 2 and 3 of the FSA's Principles for Businesses, and breaches of SYSC 3.2.6R. A financial penalty of £300,000 was imposed on CFA.
Key words	Personal data; Financial data; Data security; Internal fraud; Identity theft; Financial penalty
Website link	http://www.fsa.gov.uk/pubs/final/capita.pdf

FSA v Nationwide Building Society ('Nationwide')	
Date of Final Notice	14 February 2007
Overview	In this case the FSA investigated the theft of a laptop computer containing confidential customer information from a Nationwide employee's house. The data and computer could have been used to further financial crime. Nationwide reported the laptop loss to the police, Information Commissioner and the FSA.
Decision	The FSA found Nationwide to have breached Principle 3 of its Principles for Business by failing to take reasonable care to organise its affairs responsibly and effectively, with adequate risk management systems. In particular the FSA noted that: – the company failed to sufficiently assess the risks to security of customer information; – the information security procedures in place failed to adequately and effectively manage the risks faced; – the company failed to implement appropriate training and monitoring to ensure that information security procedures were understood by staff; – Nationwide failed to implement adequate controls to mitigate information security risks, to ensure that employees adhered to procedures and to ensure that it provided an appropriate level of information security; and – the company failed to implement appropriate procedures to deal with the loss of customer information and as a result did not respond in a timely manner to establish the risks of financial crime arising from the theft of the company's computer. A financial penalty of £1.4 million was imposed upon the company. This penalty was subsequently reduced to £980,000 due to the willingness of Nationwide to settle at an early stage of the FSA's investigation.
Key words	Personal data; Financial data; Laptop; Data security; Staff training; Financial penalty
Website link	http://www.fsa.gov.uk/pubs/final/nbs.pdf

FSA and ICO enforcement action

FSA v BNP Paribas Private Bank ('BNPP')	
Date of Decision Notice	3 May 2007
Overview	Between February 2002 and March 2005 a serious fraudulent transaction was entered into by a senior BNPP employee. The transactions amounted to a loss of £1.4 million, and included the dishonest debiting of client accounts without authority, forgery of client instructions and signatures and false requests for changes of correspondence addresses.
Decision	The FSA found that BNPP failed to take reasonable care to organise and control its affairs responsibly and effectively with adequate risk management systems and that BNPP did not take reasonable care to ensure it had effective systems and controls in place to manage fraud risks. The FSA also held that BNPP was in breach of Principle 3 of the FSA's Principles of Business. The FSA consider the company's failings as serious on the grounds that: – they facilitated actual and significant fraud; – the fraud was not discovered for a significant period of time; – the failure of systems and controls continued over a significant period of time; – certain failings were identified as needing remedial action, but this remediation was not undertaken in a timely manner; and – BNPP failed to enhance its procedures despite highlighted regulatory and industry awareness of fraud and risk during the period in which the frauds occurred. The FSA stated that the cumulative impact of these failings presented to its objective of reducing financial crime. As a result of the FSA's findings a financial penalty of £350,000 was imposed on BNPP.
Key words	Personal data; Financial data; Data security; Fraud; Identity theft; Financial penalty
Website link	http://www.fsa.gov.uk/pubs/final/bnpp_10may07.pdf

FSA v Norwich Union Life ('Norwich Union')	
Date of Decision Notice	10 December 2007
Overview	Fraudsters used publicly available information (including names, addresses and dates of birth) to impersonate customers in telephone calls to seek confidential information about those customers and/or to change customer records. Norwich Union was then instructed by the fraudsters to surrender the proceeds of policies held by the impersonated customers to bank accounts held by the criminals. Over 632 policies were targeted and 74 fraudulent surrenders amounting to around £3.3 million were made.

		The information disclosed by Norwich Union includes sensitive financial and personal information and confidential information regarding policies was disclosed to fraudsters in almost all of the 632 cases.
Decision		The FSA found that Norwich Union lacked effective systems and controls to protect customers' confidential information and to manage its financial crime risks. The company was also found to be in breach of Principle 3 of the FSA's Principles for Business. The FSA also found those failings particularly important as Norwich Union: – is one of the UK's largest life insurance businesses; – was aware that fraud and identity theft were increasing problems in the industry; and – on discovering the frauds it took action to identify, inform and protect all current and former directors of the company and the new Aviva Group who were policyholders, but it was held by the FSA that the cumulative impact of these failings constituted a significant risk to its objective of reducing financial crime. A financial penalty of £1.26 million was imposed on Norwich Union.
Key words		Personal data; Financial data; Data security; Fraud; Identity theft; Financial penalty
Website link		http://www.fsa.gov.uk/pubs/final/Norwich_Union_Life.pdf

FSA v Merchant Securities Group Ltd ('Merchant Securities')	
Date of Decision Notice	12 June 2008
Overview	In this case the FSA found no evidence of actual compromise of customer information, but held that lack of adequate risk management systems could result in actual data compromise and customer detriment. The failures on the part of Merchant Securities included: – the exposure of customers to the risk of impersonation as a result of the procedures in place for their identification when obtaining telephone instructions; – the reliance placed by advisors on the recognition of customers' voices; – the inclusion of customer account numbers in written communications that were interceptable; – the absence of an adequate procedure for the secure storage of back-up tapes. Instead tapes containing unencrypted personal client information were stored overnight in a bag at the home of a member of staff; and – the absence of adequate procedure for controlling and monitoring the use of instant messaging and web-based email. The monitoring undertaken by the company was ad hoc and focused on productivity.

FSA and ICO enforcement action

Decision	The FSA found that Merchant Securities failed to take reasonable care to organise and control its affairs responsibly and effectively. It did not have in place adequate risk management systems, and had not established or maintained effective controls for countering the risk that customer information may be compromised by theft, loss or unauthorised alteration. The FSA considered the company's actions to be a breach of Principle 3 of its Principles for Business. The failures increased the risk of exposure to financial crime and the failings occurred in a period of heightened public awareness of information security during which the FSA had published a number of Final Notices regarding regulatory actions. It was found that Merchant Securities should have been aware of the ways in which business practices can place customer information at risk and that its own failings could have resulted in actual data compromise and customer detriment. Merchant Securities received a financial penalty of £77,000.
Key words	Financial data; Data security; Phone identification procedures; Absence of fraud or compromise; Data security risk; Financial penalty
Website link	http://www.fsa.gov.uk/pubs/final/merchant_13jun08.pdf

FSA v HSBC Actuaries and Consultants Limited ('HSBC Actuaries')	
Date of Decision Notice	17 July 2009
Overview	In this case the FSA found that HSBC Actuaries failed to take reasonable care to establish and maintain effective systems and controls to manage the risks relating to data security, which culminated in the loss in ordinary post of an unencrypted floppy disk containing the names, addresses, dates of birth and National Insurance numbers of 1,917 members of a pension scheme administered by HSBC Actuaries. The failures on the part of HSBC Actuaries included to ensure that: – customer data sent to third parties via portable media was secure in the event data was lost or intercepted; – customer data kept in its offices was secure from the risk of internal fraud or theft; – customer data received from third parties on portable electronic media was properly recorded upon receipt.
Decision	The FSA found that HSBC Actuaries failed to undertake an adequate assessment of the risks relating to data security, failed to assess whether its existing controls effectively managed those risks and failed to implement effective procedures, guidance, training and monitoring to address those risks. The FSA considered the company's actions to be a breach of Principle 3 of its Principles for Businesses. In particular, the weak data security controls resulted in staff practices that placed customer data at risk, including:

FSA and ICO enforcement action

	– sending unencrypted electronic media containing customer data to third parties through the post; and – not verifying the receipt of customer data sent to the firm by third parties. The failures had the potential to expose those customers to the risk of identity theft and financial loss and occurred during a period of heightened awareness of financial crime and a FSA campaign about such financial crime, including the threat of fraud and identity theft. It was found that HSBC Actuaries was already aware of the risks of fraud and identity theft in the financial services industry but failed to take sufficient steps within the relevant period and failed to respond to problems identified in June 2007 from this data loss incident – which occurred in April 2007. HSBC Actuaries received a financial penalty of £875,000.
Key words	Financial data; Personal data; Data security; Portable electronic media; Data encryption; Staff practices; Data security Risk; Financial penalty
Website link	http://www.fsa.gov.uk/pubs/final/hsbc_actuaris0709.pdf

FSA v HSBC Insurance Brokers Limited ('HSBC Insurance')	
Date of Decision Notice	17 July 2009
Overview	In this case the FSA found that HSBC Insurance failed to take reasonable care to establish and maintain effective systems and controls to manage the risks relating to data security, particularly those relating to the threat that confidential customer data may be lost or stolen. Although HSBC Insurance did not actually lose any customer data, the failings were such to merit a significant financial penalty. The failures on the part of HSBC Insurance included to ensure that: – customer data sent to third parties via portable media was secure in the event that data was lost or stolen; – customer data sent to third parties in hard copy form was sent securely; – customer data kept in offices was secure at all times from the risk of internal fraud or theft; and – an appropriate due diligence process was followed prior to contracting services to third parties, particularly waste disposal firms.
Decision	The FSA found that HSBC Insurance, which had over 65,000 customers (most of whom were companies in the UK), failed to undertake an adequate assessment of the risks relating to data security, and whether its existing controls were adequate to manage those risks, and failed to implement adequate and effective procedures, guidance, training and monitoring to address those risks. The FSA considered the company's actions to be a breach of Principle 3 of its Principles for Businesses.

FSA and ICO enforcement action

		The failures had the potential to expose individuals to the risk of identity theft and financial loss and represented a wider material risk to the FSA objective of reducing financial crime. In particular, the confidential customer data held by HSBC Insurance, not only included financial data, but also physical or mental health data and applicable criminal offences data, including data relating to alleged offences. It was found that HSBC Insurance were already aware that data security, fraud and identity theft were increasing problems for the financial services industry, but failed to take sufficient steps within the relevant period to ensure that business data security procedures were adequate. HSBC Insurance received a financial penalty of £700,000.
Key words		Financial Data; Personal data; Sensitive personal data; Data security; Portable electronic media; Data encryption; Staff practices; Data security Risk; Financial penalty
Website link		http://www.fsa.gov.uk/pubs/final/hsbc_ins0709.pdf

FSA v 'HSBC Life (UK) Limited ('HSBC Life')	
Date of Decision Notice	17 July 2009
Overview	In this case the FSA found that HSBC Life failed to take reasonable care to establish and maintain effective systems and controls to manage the risks relating to data security, specifically the risk that confidential customer data may be lost or stolen. This failure culminated in February 2008 in the loss by HSBC Life's finance department of an unencrypted CD containing confidential data of 180,000 policy holders sent through the post to a third party by unrecorded delivery, with its loss not formally escalated within HSBC Life until over one month after the date of the incident. The failures on the part of HSBC Life included to ensure that: – customer data sent to third parties on portable electronic media was secure in the event that the data was lost or intercepted; and – customer data kept in its offices was at all times secure from the risk of internal fraud or theft.
Decision	The FSA found that HSBC Life, which had over 740,000 individual and corporate customers, failed to undertake an adequate assessment of the risks relating to data security, and in particular whether existing controls were adequate to manage those risks, and failed to implement adequate and effective procedures, guidance, training and monitoring to address those risks. In particular the FSA found that the weak controls resulted in practices that placed customer data at risk of loss or theft in that: – HSBC Life routinely sent unencrypted CDs to third parties by unrecorded delivery; and

FSA and ICO enforcement action

	– notwithstanding that access to the firm's offices was securely restricted, confidential customer data was routinely kept in unlocked cabinets – including electronic copies of over 740,000 'live' policies and over 1 million 'non-live' (inactive or matured) policies. The FSA considered the company's actions to be a breach of Principle 3 of its Principles for Businesses. The failures had the potential to expose these individual and corporate customers to the risk of identity theft and financial loss. Further, HSBC Life was aware that data security and the associated risks of fraud and identity theft were increasing problems in the financial services industry but failed to take sufficient steps to ensure its data security procedures were adequate. HSBC Life received a financial penalty of £1.61 million.
Key words	Financial Data; Personal data; Medical data; Data security; Portable electronic media; Data encryption; Staff practices; Data security Risk; Financial penalty
Website link	http://www.fsa.gov.uk/pubs/final/hsbc_inuk0907.pdf

ICO CASES

ICO v HBOS	
Date of undertaking	1 February 2007
Overview	The UK's ICO received complaints over HBOS plc's processing of personal data, particularly that valuable personal financial information was recovered from refuse bins at certain bank branches. The personal information included 'paying in' envelopes that disclosed the names of customers, debit card numbers and papers enclosing a customer's PIN. The ICO considered the data controller's compliance with the provisions of the Data Protection Act, particularly the seventh data protection principle of Schedule 1 Part 1 of the Act, which requires appropriate data security provisions to be in place to protect personal data ('the Seventh Principle').
Decision	Although no Enforcement Notice was issued, HBOS gave a formal undertaking which required the data controller to ensure that personal data is processed in accordance with the Seventh Principle, including that: – procedures are in place for handling/disposal of confidential data; and – adequate and relevant training is given to all employees.
Key words	Data security; Data disposal; Financial data
Website link	http://www.ico.gov.uk/upload/documents/library/data_protection/notices/scan_hbos.pdf

ICO v Barclays Bank plc	
Date of undertaking	2 February 2007
Overview	The ICO received a complaint regarding Barclays' processing of personal data as personal information was recovered from refuse bins outside the Park Gate and Bristol branches. The data included cut up debit/visa cards and a deposit envelope. The ICO considered compliance with the Act, in particular with the Seventh Principle.
Decision	No Enforcement Notice was issued but instead an undertaking was given by Barclays to comply with the Seventh Principle, including that it will use reasonable endeavours to ensure that: – all procedures are updated and strictly adhered to, in particular for the handling and disposal by the bank's branches of confidential waste; – adequate and relevant data protection training is given to employees who may have access to the bank branches' confidential waste;

FSA and ICO enforcement action

	– arrangements with third parties and sub-contractors shall require them to comply with the bank's data protection procedures governing the handling and disposal of confidential waste and that such parties' staff are aware of the procedures; and – a new process is implemented for the disposal of plastic cards including the secure transport of such cards from branches to the bank's contractor's premises for secure destruction.
Key words	Financial data; Data security; Data disposal; Plastic card disposal; Staff training; Contractor and sub-contractor training
Website link	http://www.ico.gov.uk/upload/documents/library/data_protection/notices/scan_barclays.pdf

ICO v Clydesdale Bank plc ('Clydesdale')	
Date of undertaking	5 February 2007
Overview	The ICO received a complaint relating to Clydesdale's processing of personal data in particular items that were recovered from refuse bins outside the Glasgow (Giffnock) branch. The data included a telephone banking form detailing customers' names and contact details, six cash deposit bags showing customers' names and account numbers, 22 computerised printouts showing details of direct debits and bank giro credits to customer accounts. The ICO considered compliance with the Act in particular the Seventh Principle.
Decision	No Enforcement Notice was issued but instead an undertaking was given by Clydesdale stating that: – systems and procedures regarding the confidential disposal of waste containing personal data will be implemented within the branch network. These will include enhanced procedures for the disposal of redundant plastic cards, plastic deposit envelopes and digital media and the secure destruction of paper waste; and – adequate and relevant data protection training, including on the Seventh Principle, will be given to all employees on an ongoing basis, and any amendments to the bank's business processes shall not be restricted provided that it remains compliant with the Seventh Principle.
Key words	Financial data; Data security; Data disposal; Plastic card, plastic deposit envelopes and digital media disposal; Staff training
Website link	http://www.ico.gov.uk/upload/documents/library/data_protection/notices/scan_clydesdale.pdf

FSA and ICO enforcement action

ICO v Scarborough Building Society	
Date of undertaking	9 February 2007
Overview	The ICO received a complaint regarding the processing of personal data by the data controller, particularly that items of personal financial information were recovered from refuse bins outside a local branch of the data controller. The personal information was contained in a variety of items including a customer's mortgage application, personal bank statements and account details. The ICO considered data controller's compliance with the data protection principles, particularly the Seventh Principle.
Decision	No Enforcement Notice was issued but instead a formal undertaking was given requiring that all future processing be carried out in accordance with the Seventh Principle, including that: – appropriate procedures are in place for handling and disposal of confidential waste; and – appropriate training is given to staff in handling and disposal of confidential waste.
Key words	Financial data; Data security; Data disposal; Staff training
Website link	http://www.ico.gov.uk/upload/documents/library/data_protection/notices/scan_scarborough.pdf

ICO v The Co-operative Bank plc ('CB')	
Date of undertaking	14 February 2007
Overview	The ICO received a complaint relating to CB's processing of personal data and in particular that items containing personal information were found in a refuse bin outside its Watford branch. The data found included a letter from a customer and a computer printout relating to another customer showing their names, addresses and account numbers. A motor insurance quote showing details of the vehicle and its owner was also found. The ICO considered the data controller's compliance with the Act and in particular the Seventh Principle.
Decision	No Enforcement Notice was issued but instead an undertaking was given by CB that it would comply with the Seventh Principle and in particular that: – all data protection procedures would be updated and strictly adhered to and that it would implement procedures for the handling and proper disposal of personal data; and – adequate and relevant data protection training is given to all employees including sub-contractors who may have responsibility for confidential waste disposal.

FSA and ICO enforcement action

Key words	Financial data; Data security; Data disposal; Staff training; Sub-contractor training
Website link	http://www.ico.gov.uk/upload/documents/library/data_protection/notices/scan_coop.pdf

ICO v Alliance & Leicester plc	
Date of undertaking	15 February 2007
Overview	The ICO received a complaint relating to Alliance & Leicester's processing of personal data. Personal data was recovered from refuse bins outside the Nottingham Branch. This personal data included an account application form, a life assurance letter in the name of a customer and a credit card application form containing the personal details of the applicant. The ICO considered compliance with the Act and in particular the Seventh Principle.
Decision	Alliance & Leicester gave an undertaking that it shall ensure that personal data is processed in accordance with the Seventh Principle and that it has in place the correct procedures for the handling and disposal of confidential waste. In particular, the bank shall ensure that its data protection procedures including the Confidential Waste Policy are strictly adhered to. Alliance & Leicester confirmed that its employees had been reminded of their obligations relating to the processing of personal information and all other aspects of customer confidentiality.
Key words	Financial data; Data security; Data disposal; Staff briefing
Website link	http://www.ico.gov.uk/upload/documents/library/data_protection/notices/scan_alliance.pdf

ICO v Nationwide Building Society' ('Nationwide') case	
Date of undertaking	20 February 2007
Overview	The ICO received a complaint regarding data processing procedures. A personal financial review and a customer information document containing personal information were recovered from refuse bins outside a branch.
Decision	No Enforcement Notice was issued but instead a formal undertaking was given requiring Nationwide to ensure that personal data is processed in accordance with the Seventh Principle, including that: – all data protection procedures are reviewed and updated; – a review programme to monitor waste disposal and handling procedures is implemented; – adequate and relevant staff training programmes are to be put in place; and

FSA and ICO enforcement action

	– a review of contracts with Nationwide's waste disposal companies is carried out.
Key words	Financial data; Data security; Data disposal; Staff training
Website link	http://www.ico.gov.uk/upload/documents/library/data_protection/notices/scan_nationwide.pdf

ICO v HFC Bank Limited ('HFC')	
Date of undertaking	21 February 2007
Overview	The ICO received a complaint regarding HFC's processing of personal data following the recovery of personal data from refuse bins outside the Newport branch. The data included a loan application form, collections history printouts in relation to a customer and other miscellaneous papers. The ICO considered the data controller's compliance with the Act and in particular the Seventh Principle.
Decision	No Enforcement Notice was issued but instead an undertaking was given by HFC that they will comply with the Seventh Data Protection Principle, in particular that: – data protection procedures are updated and strictly adhered to in particular in respect of the handling and disposal of confidential waste; – adequate and relevant training is given to all employees with an emphasis on the disposal of confidential waste; and – staff are required to complete an online data protection refresher course and test on a regular basis and at least once every two years.
Key words	Financial data; Data security; Data disposal; Staff training
Website link	http://www.ico.gov.uk/upload/documents/library/data_protection/notices/scan_hfc.pdf

ICO v National Westminster Bank ('NatWest')	
Date of undertaking	23 February 2007
Overview	The ICO received complaints in relation to the processing of personal data following the recovery of personal data from refuse bins outside NatWest branches in Manchester and Southampton. The personal data included customer insurance application forms, account transaction details, details of products sold at a customer meeting, list of a customer's standing orders and direct debits and a customer's email address and the related account holder's name and account details.
Decision	An undertaking was given by NatWest to ensure that personal data is processed in accordance with the Seventh Principle, including that:

FSA and ICO enforcement action

	– the data controller's data protection procedures are regularly reviewed to ensure that proper procedures are in place for the handling and proper disposal of personal data; and – appropriate data protection training is given to staff to ensure the proper disposal of personal data.
Key words	Financial data; Data security; Data disposal; Staff training
Website link	http://www.ico.gov.uk/upload/documents/library/data_protection/notices/scan_natwest.pdf

ICO v Royal Bank of Scotland	
Date of undertaking	23 February 2007
Overview	The ICO received complaints regarding the processing of personal data following the recovery of documents from refuse bins outside bank branches. The personal data recovered included documents relating to individual bank accounts, computerised printouts, application forms and a letter to a customer. The ICO considered the data controller's compliance with the provisions of the Data Protection Act, particularly the Seventh Principle.
Decision	The ICO issued a formal undertaking requiring the data controller to ensure that personal data is processed in accordance with the Seventh Principle, including that: – appropriate procedures are in place for the handling and disposal of personal and confidential data; and – appropriate training is given to employees regarding the secure disposal of personal data.
Key words	Data security; Data disposal; Financial data
Website link	http://www.ico.gov.uk/upload/documents/library/data_protection/notices/scan_royal_bank.pdf

ICO v Post Office Limited	
Date of undertaking	26 February 2007
Overview	The ICO received a complaint regarding the Post Office's processing of personal data following the recovery of personal data from refuse bins at several branches. The lost data included 65 E1–11 application forms, 158 receipts showing signatures of the payees and full details of Switch/Maestro cards, 12 travel insurance application forms, eight daily passport schedules detailing names and telephone numbers and a money transfer form showing the names, addresses and telephone numbers of seven customers. The ICO considered compliance with the Act and in particular the Seventh Principle.

FSA and ICO enforcement action

Decision	No Enforcement Notice was issued but instead an undertaking was given by the Post Office that it will comply with the Seventh Principle and in particular will:

– review and where necessary update all data protection procedures to ensure the correct procedures are in place for the handling and disposal of personal data and that action is taken in response to failures which result in breach of the Seventh Principle;

– give adequate and relevant data protection training to relevant employees. In the case of its agents, the data controller will update the Operations Manual to contain clear instructions on the secure destruction of personal data; and

– remind all staff of their obligations in relation to the personal data that they process on behalf of the data controller. |
| Key words | Financial data; Medical data; Name and contact details data; Data security; Data disposal; Staff training and briefing; Agent training |
| Website link | http://www.ico.gov.uk/upload/documents/library/data_protection/notices/scan_post_office.pdf |

ICO v Dipesh Ltd (trading as Cash Generator)	
Date of undertaking	23 April 2007
Overview	The ICO received a complaint against Cash Generator after personal data was found in a rubbish bin outside their premises in Nuneaton.
The data included correspondence showing customer names and addresses.
The ICO considered compliance with the Act and in particular the Seventh Principle.
Decision	No Enforcement Notice was issued but instead an undertaking was given by Cash Generators that it would comply with the Seventh Principle and in particular that:
– all paper waste would be treated as confidential and that a shredder be installed so papers could be shredded before being disposed of; and
– that adequate and relevant data protection training be given to all employees who may have responsibility for confidential waste disposal.
Key words	Name and contact details data; Data security; Data disposal; Staff training
Website link	http://www.ico.gov.uk/upload/documents/library/data_protection/notices/dipesh_limited_undertaking.pdf

FSA and ICO enforcement action

ICO v Phones 4U Limited	
Date of undertaking	17 May 2007
Overview	The ICO received complaints regarding Phones 4U following the recovery of personal data from rubbish bins outside two of their premises. The data included customers' names, addresses and bank account details. The ICO considered compliance with the Act and in particular the Seventh Principle.
Decision	No Enforcement Notice was issued but instead an undertaking was given by Phones 4U that it would comply with the Seventh Principle and in particular that: – all paperwork containing customer personal data shall be treated as confidential and shredded before disposal; and – regular, adequate and relevant data protection training shall be given to all employees who may have responsibility for confidential waste disposal.
Key words	Personal data; Financial data; Data security; Data disposal; Staff training
Website link	http://www.ico.gov.uk/upload/documents/library/data_protection/notices/phones4u_undertaking.pdf

ICO v Orange Personal Communications Services Limited ('Orange')	
Date of undertaking	23 May 2007
Overview	The ICO received a complaint relating to Orange's processing of personal data. In this instance newly recruited employees were allowed to share user names and passwords to access company computer systems holding personal data of customers. The ICO considered compliance with the Act and in particular the Seventh Principle.
Decision	The ICO did not issue an Enforcement Notice but instead an undertaking was given by Orange that it would comply with the Seventh Principle and in particular that it would not allow the sharing of user names and passwords by Customer Service Representatives in any circumstances.
Key words	Access to passwords and user names; Data security; Data access
Website link	http://www.ico.gov.uk/upload/documents/library/data_protection/notices/orange_undertaking.pdf

FSA and ICO enforcement action

ICO v The Foreign & Commonwealth Office ('the FCO')	
Date of undertaking	13 November 2007
Overview	UKvisas (the joint Home Office and FCO Directorate responsible for processing visa applications) informed the ICO of a security breach of a third party contractor's online visa application facility. The breach resulted in the ability of applicants to view the personal data of others. The ICO considered compliance with the Act and in particular the Seventh Principle. An investigation was conducted by Ms Linda Costelloe Baker at the direction of the FCO, the report of which was forwarded to the ICO.
Decision	No Enforcement Notice was issued but instead an undertaking was given by the FCO to comply with the Seventh Principle in particular: – not to re-open the VFS online application websites and to replace them with the 'visa4UK' website as the only online application system used by UKvisas; – for UKvisas to undertake a strategic review of data processing to strengthen management processes, including a detailed audit of the data processor's data security procedures; – to regularly monitor the 'visa4UK' website to ensure that effective protection against unauthorised access are operating correctly; and – to give adequate and relevant data protection training to all UKvisas staff on an ongoing basis.
Key words	Data security; Data access; Website; Data processor/third party contractor; Staff training
Website link	http://www.ico.gov.uk/upload/documents/library/data_protection/notices/foreign%20_commonwealth_office.pdf

ICO v Department of Health ('the DoH')	
Date of undertaking	11 December 2007
Overview	The ICO received a complaint in relation to the DoH's processing of personal data. In this incident it was found that the personal details of junior doctors held on the Medical Training Application Service ('MTAS') website were readily available to any person accessing the website. The ICO considered compliance with the Act and in particular the Seventh Principle.
Decision	No Enforcement Notice was issued but instead the DoH gave an undertaking to comply with the Seventh Principle and in particular that:

	– personal data, which if disclosed could cause damage or distress and which is held on any website (by a data controller or a data processor), must be encrypted to effectively protect such data from unauthorised access; – instructions and advice as to the use of passwords and PIN numbers must be given to those entitled to access the site; – adequate and relevant data protection training is to be given to appropriate staff on an ongoing basis; – adequate and effective contract management is to be implemented to ensure that technical and organisational security measures governing any processing by those acting on DoH's behalf are being complied with; – regular 'penetration and vulnerability' tests for developing applications and systems are to be implemented to minimise unauthorised access; – regular monitoring of the new MMC Applications website is conducted during future rounds of applications to ensure that systems for effective protection against unauthorised access are operating correctly; and – such other security measures as are deemed appropriate by the data controller to protect against unauthorised and unlawful processing, accidental loss, destruction and/or damage of personal data are implemented.
Key words	Data security; Data access; Website; PIN and passwords; Encryption; Third Party Contracts management; Testing and monitoring; Data processor; Staff training
Website link	http://www.ico.gov.uk/upload/documents/library/data_protection/notices/department_of_health2001.pdf

ICO v The Carphone Warehouse Limited ('CPW')	
Date of Enforcement Notice	9 January 2008
Overview	The ICO received several complaints from members of the public relating to the following incidents: – a subject access request with which the company failed to comply despite cashing cheques. The company also made unreasonable requests for further information; – accuracy and fairness in relation to the use of incorrect name, address and bank details obtained from old contract or purchase data and the refusal of the company to amend inaccurate records without permission of account holder; – security issues, specifically in relation to customers' access to the confidential personal data of other customers when using online accounts and in some instances the emailing of such data to other customers; and

FSA and ICO enforcement action

	– the disclosure of inaccurate data to credit reference or debt collection agencies, and the failure of the company to amend any of the data unless instructed by the Commissioner. The ICO considered the data controller's compliance with the Act.
Decision	The ICO found that CPW failed to comply with subject access requests, unfairly and unlawfully processed data, failed to take appropriate technical and organisational measures to ensure there was no unauthorised or unlawful processing and processed inaccurate and/or out-of-date data. The ICO issued an Enforcement Notice stating that CPW must ensure that: – all subject access requests are dealt with in compliance with the provisions contained in Section 7 of the Act; – the procedures and staff training for loading of new customer account details are appropriately modified or corrected to ensure the new customer details are not incorrectly matched to the details of existing or previous customers; – appropriate procedures and systems are introduced to ensure that when inaccuracies are brought to the data controller's attention they can be corrected within a maximum of 21 days; – appropriate technical measures are introduced to ensure that: – online customers cannot view other customers' account details and personal data in error; and – no personal data is sent to the email address of anyone other than the data subject themselves; and – appropriate procedures are implemented to ensure that when complaints regarding the insecurity of CPW email systems or its website are brought to the attention of the data controller, they are urgently investigated and any breach is immediately contained.
Key words	Subject access request; Data accuracy and fair process; Data security; Data access; Disclosure of inaccurate data; Email; Website; Records; Complaint procedure; Staff training
Website link	http://www.ico.gov.uk/upload/documents/library/data_protection/notices/carphone_warehouse_en.pdf

ICO v Talk Talk Telecom Ltd ('Talk Talk')	
Date of Enforcement Notice	9 January 2008
Overview	The ICO received several complaints from members of the public regarding: – Talk Talk's failure to comply with a subject access request, despite having cashed cheques and made unreasonable requests for further information; – the Company's use of incorrect name, address and bank details obtained from old contract/purchase data and their refusal to amend inaccurate records without the permission of account holder;

	– customers' ability to access the confidential personal data of other customers when using online accounts, and the emailing of such data to other customers; and
	– the holding by the company of inaccurate data, its disclosure to credit reference or debt collection agencies, and the failure to amend this data unless instructed by the Commissioner.
	The ICO considered the date controller's compliance with the Act.
Decision	The ICO considered that Talk Talk failed to comply with subject access requests, unfairly and unlawfully processed data, failed to take appropriate technical and organisational measures to ensure there was no unauthorised or unlawful processing, and processed inaccurate and/or out-of-date data.
	The ICO issued an Enforcement Notice stating that Talk Talk must ensure:
	(1) all subject access requests are dealt with in compliance with the provisions contained in Section 7 of the Act;
	(2) the procedures for and staff training relating to the loading of new customer account details are appropriately modified or corrected to guarantee that new customer details are not incorrectly matched to details of existing or previous customers;
	– the introducing of appropriate procedures and systems to enable the correction of inaccuracies brought to the data controller's attention within a maximum of 21 days; and
	(3) appropriate technical measures are introduced to guarantee that:
	– online customers cannot view other customers' account details and other personal data in error; and
	– no personal data is sent to the email address of anyone other than the data subject themselves.
	In addition Talk Talk were obliged to introduce appropriate procedures to ensure complaints regarding the security of the company's email system or website brought to the attention of the data controller were urgently investigated, and any breach is immediately contained.
Key words	Subject access request; Data accuracy and fair process; Data security; Data access; Disclosure of inaccurate data; Email; Website; Records; Complaint procedure; Staff training
Website link	http://www.ico.gov.uk/upload/documents/library/data_protection/notices/talk_talk_telecom_en.pdf

FSA and ICO enforcement action

ICO v Marks & Spencer ('M&S')	
Date of Enforcement Notice	23 January 2008
Overview	The ICO considered a report into the theft of an unencrypted laptop computer holding personal data of 26,000 members of the M&S Pension Scheme. The laptop was stolen from the home of an employee of an independent contractor engaged to prepare personal pension change statements for members of the scheme. The ICO considered the data controller's compliance with the Act.
Decision	The ICO considered that the personal data on the laptop should have been encrypted and that in failing to take appropriate measures to ensure the security of the data, the data controller's processing contravened the Seventh Principle. M&S was prepared to give undertakings if they were not made public, a position which was not acceptable to the Information Commissioner. The ICO issued an Enforcement Notice requiring M&S to ensure that personal data is processed in accordance with the Seventh Principle and in particular to ensure that the process of laptop hard drive encryption was completed by 1 April 2008. M&S issued appeal proceedings resulting in the cancellation of the Enforcement Notice on 14 July 2008.
Key words	Data security; Data access; Laptop; Encryption; Theft; Contractor/Data processor
Website link	http://www.ico.gov.uk/upload/documents/library/data_protection/notices/m_and_s_sanitiseden.pdf

ICO v Skipton Financial Services Ltd ('Skipton')	
Date of undertaking	20 February 2008
Overview	The ICO received a report regarding the theft of a laptop computer from a contractor (the data processor) engaged by Skipton to provide professional consultancy services in relation to a software development project. The laptop contained personal data relating to a large number of Skipton's customers and was not encrypted. The ICO considered the data controller's compliance with the Act and in particular with the Seventh Principle.
Decision	No Enforcement Notice was issued but instead an undertaking was given by Skipton to comply with the Seventh Principle and in particular that: – personal data which if disclosed could cause damage or distress, if held on a laptop, must be suitably encrypted to prevent unauthorised access (whether the personal data) is held on the computer's hard drive or in any other storage device;

483

FSA and ICO enforcement action

	– risk assessments must be carried out to confirm the adequacy and effectiveness of technical and organisational security measures governing any processing by those acting on behalf of the data controller prior to engaging any third party as data processor; and – other security measures must be implemented as deemed appropriate to ensure the protection of personal data against unauthorised and unlawful processing, accidental loss, destruction and damage.
Key words	Data security; Data access; Laptop; Encryption; Theft; Contractor/Data processor
Website link	http://www.ico.gov.uk/upload/documents/library/data_protection/notices/skipton_final_undertaking.pdf

ICO v Shirley (Warwickshire) Royal British Legion Club Ltd ('the British Legion')	
Date of undertaking/ Enforcement Notice	20 March 2008
Overview	The ICO received a complaint that the British Legion had breached the Seventh Principle.
Decision	Although the ICO concluded that the British Legion was in breach, no Enforcement Notice was issued. Instead an undertaking was given by the British Legion to process data in accordance with the Seventh Principle.
Key words	Seventh principle; Data security
Website link	http://www.ico.gov.uk/upload/documents/library/data_protection/notices/undertaking_royal_british_legion_club2.pdf

ICO v Her Majesty's Revenue and Customs ('HMRC')	
Date of Enforcement Notice	14 July 2008
Overview	The ICO was informed of the loss of two compact discs holding the personal data of up to 25 million individuals. Included on the discs was an 'excessive amount' of confidential personal data on Child Benefit recipients. Both compact discs were sent by the Child Benefit Office in Washington Tyne and Wear to the National Audit Office via the internal post system of the data controller (operated by a courier company). The package containing the discs was not recorded or registered and the discs were lost. The Chancellor of the Exchequer subsequently commissioned an independent report to establish the circumstances of the loss (the 'Poynter Report').

FSA and ICO enforcement action

	The Poynter Report contained 45 recommendations and was reviewed by the ICO together with a report of the Independent Police Complaints Commission. The ICO considered the data controller's compliance with the Act.
Decision	The ICO found that HMRC had contravened the Third and Seventh Principles and issued an Enforcement Notice requiring HMRC to: – use its best endeavours to give effect to the 45 recommendations of the Poynter Report within 36 months of the date of the report; and – provide a progress report to the ICO through its Data Security Programme after 12, 24, and 36 months following 31 July 2008 on the implementation of the recommendations.
Keywords	Data adequacy; Data security; Discs; Internal post system; Poynter Report; Reporting; Encryption
Website link	http://www.ico.gov.uk/upload/documents/library/data_protection/notices/hmrc_en_final.pdf

ICO v Secretary of State for Defence	
Date of Enforcement Notice	14 July 2008
Overview	The ICO received a report regarding the theft from a car of a Royal Navy recruiter's unencrypted laptop computer holding personal data. The report also referred to smaller scale losses of personal data as a result of the theft of laptops. Included on the recruiter's laptop was an 'excessive amount' of personal data relating to approximately 600,000 recruits or potential recruits, and 400,000 individuals being referees or parents of the recruits. The data controller commissioned a report on the circumstances of the loss. The resultant 'Report into the Loss of MoD Personal Data' (30 April 2008) by Sir Burton ('the Burton Report') contained 51 recommendations. The ICO considered the data controller's compliance with the Act.
Decision	The ICO was satisfied that the MoD contravened the Third and Seventh Principles. An Enforcement Notice was issued stating that the MoD shall: – use its best endeavours to give effect to the 51 recommendations of the Burton Report by 31 March 2009 in accordance with the data controller's Action Plan (in response to the Burton Report); and – provide a copy of the three monthly report received by the Defence Operating Board overseeing the implementation of the recommendations in accordance with the Action Plan.

FSA and ICO enforcement action

Key words	Data adequacy; Data security; Laptop; Encryption; Theft; Burton Report; Reporting
Website link	http://www.ico.gov.uk/upload/documents/library/data_protection/notices/mod_en_final.pdf

ICO v Virgin Media Ltd ('Virgin Media')	
Date	30 September 2008 (date of press release)
Overview	The ICO received a report regarding the loss of a compact disc passed to Virgin Media by Carphone Warehouse ('CPW'), their data processor. CPW was engaged by Virgin Media to collect the personal data of individuals interested in opening a Virgin Media account within its CPW stores. The disc contained personal data relating to 3,383 customers and was not encrypted. The ICO considered the data controller's compliance with the Act and in particular the Seventh Principle.
Decision	The ICO issued an Enforcement Notice requiring Virgin Media to ensure that personal data be processed in accordance with the Seventh Principle and in particular that: – portable and mobile devices (including magnetic media used to store and transmit data), the loss of which could cause damage or distress to individuals, must be encrypted using encryption software meeting the current standard or equivalent; – contracts with data processors must specifically require that such portable and mobile devices must be encrypted using encryption software meeting the current standard or equivalent; and – Virgin Media must implement any other security measures appropriate to ensure that personal data is protected against unauthorised and unlawful processing, accidental loss, destruction and/or damage.
Keywords	Data security; Laptop; Portable and mobile devices; Encryption; Loss; Contractor/Data processor
Website link	http://www.ico.gov.uk/upload/documents/library/data_protection/notices/virgin_media_undertaking_redacted.pdf

ICO v NHS Lanarkshire	
Date	26 November 2008 (date of press release)
Overview	The ICO was informed that personal data had been found by members of the public in buildings on the site of the former Law Hospital in Lanarkshire. An investigation and report were commissioned by NHS Lanarkshire.

FSA and ICO enforcement action

	Lanarkshire NHS subsequently implemented a number of Quality Improvement recommendations made by NHS Quality Improvement regarding disused buildings, the disposal of patient information, the application of new national protocols for NHS site decommissioning and staff training and guidance. The ICO considered the data controller's compliance with the Act and in particular the Fifth and Seventh Principle.
Decision	The ICO did not issue an Enforcement Notice but instead an undertaking was given by NHS Lanarkshire that it shall ensure personal data is processed in accordance with the Fifth and Seventh Principles.
Keywords	Data security; Data disposal; Hospital decommissioning; Sensitive data
Website link	http://www.ico.gov.uk/upload/documents/library/data_protection/notices/nhs_lanarkshire_undertaking.pdf

ICO v NHS Tayside	
Date	26 November 2008 (date of press release)
Overview	The ICO was informed that personal data had been found by members of the public in buildings on the site of the former Strathmartine Hospital in Tayside. An investigation and report were commissioned by NHS Tayside. NHS Quality Improvement Scotland issued recommendations regarding disused buildings, the disposal of patient information and the application of new national protocols for NHS site decommissioning and staff training and guidance. The ICO considered the data controller's compliance with the Act in particular the Fifth and Seventh Principle.
Decision	No Enforcement Notice was issued by the ICO, but instead an undertaking was given by NHS Tayside that it shall ensure that personal data is processed in accordance with the Fifth and Seventh Principles.
Keywords	Data security; Data disposal; Hospital decommissioning; Sensitive data
Website link	http://www.ico.gov.uk/upload/documents/library/data_protection/notices/nhs_tayside_undertaking.pdf

ICO v Hampshire Partnership NHS Trust ('the Trust')	
Date	20 January 2009 (date reported on ICO website)
Overview	The ICO was informed by the Trust that 1,161 Trust payslips containing employee personal data had been lost. The Trust produced a report into the incident and made various recommendations. The ICO considered both the report and the Trust's compliance with the Seventh Principle.

Decision	No Enforcement Notice was issued but instead an undertaking was given stating that the Trust shall ensure that personal data is processed in accordance with the Seventh Principle and that: – the transporting of all types of personal data should be risk-assessed and, where appropriate, the tracking of personal data by signed hand-over should be implemented each time custody of the data is transferred; – a review of all internal post procedures should be conducted; – data flow mapping of payslips should be reviewed at all stages; and – on an ongoing basis, adequate and relevant data protection training, including training on the Seventh Principle, should be provided to all employees.
Keywords	Data security; Payslips; Data transporting; Staff training; Risk assessment; Procedure reviews
Website link	http://www.ico.gov.uk/upload/documents/library/data_protection/notices/hampshire_partnership_nhs_trust_undertaking.pdf

ICO v Southampton City Primary Care Trust ('the Trust')	
Date of undertaking/ Enforcement Date	20 January 2009 (date reported on ICO website)
Overview	The Trust informed the ICO of a breach of data security following the loss of 168 Trust payslips containing employee personal data. The ICO noted that the Trust had produced a report into the incident and that various recommendations had been made.
Decision	No Enforcement Notice was issued but instead an undertaking was given that the Trust shall ensure that personal data is processed in accordance with the Seventh Principle and that: – the transportation of all types of personal data should be risk-assessed and, where appropriate, the tracking of personal data by signed hand-over should be implemented each time custody of that data is transferred; – a review of all internal post procedures, rooms, safe haven areas, containers and sacks should be conducted for security purposes; – data flow mapping of payslips should be reviewed at all stages to ensure adequate security is in place; and – adequate and relevant training on an ongoing basis is given to all employees, including training on the Seventh Principle.
Key words	Data security; Payslips; Data transportation; Data flow mapping; Data security policy; Staff training
Website link	http://www.ico.gov.uk/upload/documents/library/data_protection/notices/southampton_city_pct_undertaking.pdf

FSA and ICO enforcement action

ICO v Secretary of State for the Home Department	
Date	22 January 2009 (date reported on ICO website)
Overview	The ICO was informed of the loss of an unencrypted memory stick under the control of PA Consulting Group which was contracted to the Secretary of State for the Home Department. The memory stick is thought to have held sensitive personal data relating to prisoners and offenders. Two reports were produced, one from the Secretary of State for the Home Department's Security Unit (29 August 2008) and an external report by Dr Stephen Hickey into the Secretary of State for the Home Department's response to the data loss. The ICO considered both reports and the Secretary of State for the Home Department's compliance with the Seventh Principle.
Decision	The ICO considered the remedial action taken by the Secretary of State for the Home Department was such that no Enforcement Notice was required. Instead an undertaking was given by the Permanent Secretary of the Home Department stating that: – personal data will be processed in accordance with the Seventh Principle; – where the processing of personal data is carried out by a data processor on behalf of the data controller, the data controller shall take reasonable steps to ensure compliance with the guarantees made by the data processor in respect of technical and security measures; and – the data controller shall carry out and document regular inspections and audits of the security of the data processor's facilities.
Key words	Data security; Sensitive personal data; Memory stick; Data loss; Data contractor/processor
Website link	http://www.ico.gov.uk/upload/documents/library/data_protection/notices/home_office_undertaking.pdf

ICO v Abertawe Bro Morgannwg University NHS Trust ('the Trust')	
Date	22 January 2009 (date reported on ICO website)
Overview	The ICO received a report regarding the theft of a laptop computer from an unlocked office. The laptop contained unencrypted personal and some health data ('sensitive' personal data) relating to approximately 5,000 patients.
Decision	No Enforcement Notice was issued but instead the Trust gave an undertaking to ensure that personal data is processed in accordance with the Seventh Principle and that: – portable and mobile devices, including laptops, are encrypted using software which meets current standards or equivalent; and – other security measures deemed appropriate by the Trust shall be implemented to ensure that personal data is protected against unauthorised/unlawful processing, accidental loss, destruction and/or damage.

FSA and ICO enforcement action

Key words	Data security; Laptop computer; Health data; Data encryption; Portable devices; Security measures
Website link	http://www.ico.gov.uk/upload/documents/library/data_protection/notices/abm_swansea_undertaking.pdf

ICO v Tees, Esk and Wear Valleys NHS Foundation Trust ('the Trust')	
Date	22 January 2009 (date reported on ICO website)
Overview	The Trust reported to the ICO that an unencrypted memory stick holding personal and sensitive personal data relating to patients and Trust staff had been lost. The memory stick was found by a member of the public who passed it to the press.
Decision	No Enforcement Notice was issued. However, an undertaking was given by the Trust that it shall ensure personal data is processed in accordance with the Seventh Principle and that: – only memory sticks with an appropriate encryption standard are used by Trust staff and external contractors, and that sufficient guidance on their use is given; – adequate encryption policy and procedures are in place to ensure that Trust staff and external contractors are made aware of the policy and procedures and adhere to them; – sufficient checks are made to ensure external contractors are aware of the Trust's information governance and data security issues; – Trust protocol on the use of mobile storage devices is such as to prevent the recurrence of similar incidents; and – adequate, relevant and ongoing data protection training is provided to Trust employees, including training on the Seventh Principle.
Key words	Data security; Data stick; Sensitive personal data; Health data; Security policy; Staff training
Website link	http://www.ico.gov.uk/upload/documents/library/data_protection/notices/tees_esk_and_wear_valleys_nhs_trust_undertaking.pdf

ICO v Brent Teaching Primary Care Trust ('BTPCT')	
Date	5 February 2009 (date reported on ICO website)
Overview	The ICO was provided with a report from BTPCT regarding the theft of two laptop computers. The laptops were left on a desk in a locked office with no further security measures in place. This was contrary to BTPCT's security policy. The laptops contained unencrypted personal data relating to 380 patients, including health data on the patients ('sensitive' personal data).
Decision	The ICO did not issue an Enforcement Notice. An undertaking was instead given that BTPCT would ensure personal data is processed in accordance with the Seventh Principle and:

FSA and ICO enforcement action

	– that portable and mobile devices/storage media are encrypted using encryption software which meets the current standards or equivalent; – all reasonable measures shall be taken to ensure the physical security of equipment used to process personal data, whether the equipment is on the BTPCT's own premises or the premises of another organisation; – that all staff are adequately trained on the BTPCT's information security policies; and – to implement other security measures it deems appropriate to ensure personal data is protected against unauthorised and unlawful processing, accidental loss, destruction and/or damage.
Key words	Data security; Laptop computer; Health data; Portable devices; Data encryption; Physical security; Staff training
Website link	http://www.ico.gov.uk/upload/documents/library/data_protection/notices/brent_pct_undertaking.pdf

ICO v Hastings and Rother Primary Care Trust ('the Trust')	
Date	13 February 2009 (date reported on ICO website)
Overview	The ICO received a report regarding the theft of a desktop computer by a thief who entered the building via temporary scaffolding. Personal and some health data relating to patients ('sensitive' personal data) was contained on the computer. The Trust did not own the building from which the computer was stolen and had raised concerns over its security. However, the Trust did not take its own measures to safeguard the personal data it held at these premises.
Decision	No Enforcement Notice was issued but instead an undertaking was given that the Trust shall ensure personal data is processed in accordance with the Seventh Principle and that: – all reasonable measures to ensure the physical security of its own equipment used to process personal data shall be taken ' whether that equipment is on the Trust's own premises or on the premises of another organisation; – the Trust shall ensure its policies on the storage of personal data are clear and that staff are adequately trained on how to fulfil their obligations under these policies; and – the Trust shall implement other security measures it deems appropriate to ensure personal data is protected against unauthorised/unlawful processing, accidental loss, destruction or damage.
Key words	Data security; Desktop computer theft; Health data; Security policy; Data storage; Staff training
Website link	http://www.ico.gov.uk/upload/documents/library/data_protection/notices/hastings_and_rother_undertaking_redacted.pdf

FSA and ICO enforcement action

ICO v Camden Primary Care Trust ('the Trust')	
Date of Enforcement Notice	25 February 2009
Overview	The ICO was informed of the loss of redundant personal computers holding sensitive personal data (including names, addresses and medical diagnoses) relating to over 2,500 individuals. The computers had been left near a skip for a period of 13 days before the Trust had discovered they had been removed without its authority. The Trust conducted a report into the incident and made the following recommendations: – the implementation of a communication campaign to all staff informing them of the policies and procedures surrounding the disposal of redundant IT equipment; – the expedition of the encryption of all USB sticks, laptops and desktop computers; – the implementation of a robust asset and recommissioning register for all IT equipment; – to implement a robust decommissioning register; and – the establishment of a Data Security Action Group to oversee the urgent implementation of recommendations. The ICO considered the recommendations, the Trust's compliance with the Seventh Principle, paragraph 9, Part II of Schedule 1 of the Data Protection Act and the effect of Article 8 of the Human Rights Act.
Decision	The ICO issued an Enforcement Notice stating that the Trust shall, within 35 days of the date of the Enforcement Notice, take the following steps: – ensure that any personal data is expunged from computer equipment as soon as it has been decommissioned, for example by the removal and destruction of hard drives; – give effect to the recommendations of the Trust's report, to be implemented by 31 December 2009 at the latest; and – provide the ICO, by 31 March 2009, with a progress report through its Data Security Action Group programme, documenting in detail the implementation of the recommendations of the report.
Key words	Data security; Desktop computer; Health data; Staff training; Security policy
Website link	http://www.ico.gov.uk/upload/documents/library/data_protection/notices/camden_pct_final_en.pdf

ICO v 2gether NHS Foundation Trust ('the Trust')	
Date	24 March 2009 (date reported on ICO website)
Overview	The ICO was provided with a report from Ms Susan O'Connell, acting on behalf of the Trust, regarding the theft of four desktop computers, one laptop computer and one memory stick.

FSA and ICO enforcement action

	The desktop computers, laptop computer and memory stick were stolen from a locked room. The laptop and memory stick held information relating to 56 Trust patients including their names, contact details, dates of birth, GPs, referral dates and form, interventions and technical occupational therapy data and data relating to the physical and mental health of the patients. The data was not encrypted and the portable devices were not locked away out of sight, contrary to Trust policy.
Decision	The ICO did not issue an Enforcement Notice instead the Trust gave an undertaking to ensure that personal data is processed in accordance with the Seventh Principle and that: – portable and mobile devices are encrypted using encryption software which meets the current standard or equivalent, particularly where the data potentially lost could cause damage or distress to individuals; – the physical security measures and procedures in place are adequate to prevent the theft of computers or that such computers are encrypted using encryption software which meets the current standard or equivalent; – a clear policy covering the storage and use of personal data is implemented and adhered to; – staff are aware of the data controller's policy for the storage and use of personal data and are appropriately trained on how to follow that policy; and – the data controller shall implement such other security measures it deems appropriate to ensure personal data is protected against unauthorised and unlawful processing, accidental loss, destruction and/or damage.
Key words	Data security; Laptop; Desktop; Data stick; Health data; Sensitive data; Data encryption; Physical security; Security policy; Staff training
Website link	http://www.ico.gov.uk/upload/documents/library/data_protection/notices/2gether_nhs_undertaking.pdf

ICO v Stockport NHS Foundation Trust ('the Trust')	
Date	25 March 2009 (date reported on ICO website)
Overview	The ICO was provided with a report from Dr Chris Burke, acting on behalf of the Trust, regarding the theft of a laptop computer which held personal data relating to 1,588 patients, including data concerning their physical or mental health ('sensitive' personal data). The laptop was stolen from a locked room and was password protected but not encrypted. Due to refurbishment work the laptop was not locked in a cabinet as usual, but stored in a covered box under a desk. The laptop was installed by a private company before the Trust's Network facility was available and did not appear to have been registered with the Trust's IT department.

Decision	No Enforcement Notice was issued but instead an undertaking was given by the Trust to ensure that personal data is processed in accordance with the Seventh Principle and that: – portable and mobile devices are encrypted using encryption software which meets the current standard or equivalent, particularly where lost data could cause damage or distress to individuals; – all computers and portable devices used by the data controller to process personal data are registered with the IT department; – staff are aware of the data controller's policy on the storage and use of personal data and are trained on how to follow that policy; – adequate alternative data security arrangements are implemented when normal working practices cannot be followed; and – the data controller shall implement such other security measures it deems appropriate to ensure personal data is protected against unauthorised and unlawful process, accidental loss, destruction and/or damage.
Key words	Data security; Laptop; Sensitive data; Health data; Encryption; Device registration; Data security policy; Staff training
Website link	http://www.ico.gov.uk/upload/documents/library/data_protection/notices/stockport_nhs_undertaking.pdf

ICO v The British Council ('the Council')	
Date	17 April 2009 (date reported on ICO website)
Overview	The ICO was provided with a report from a party acting on behalf of the British Council regarding the loss of an unencrypted computer data storage disc containing the personal data of some 2,000 Council staff. The disc included data relating to trade union membership ('sensitive' personal data) and bank account details. The data was allegedly lost in transit by a courier service employed by the Council and was not in the possession of Council staff when lost. The Council did not take its own measures to safeguard the personal data held on the disc and failed to ensure that the data was protected by the Government minimum standard of encryption. The ICO considered the fact that the missing personal data related to trade union membership and bank account details could result in significant distress being caused to the individuals concerned.
Decision	The ICO did not issue an Enforcement Notice but instead an undertaking was given by the Council that it would ensure that personal data is processed in accordance with the Seventh Principle and that: – it shall take all reasonable measures to ensure the physical security of personal data being processed in furtherance of its duties, whether the data is physically in its possession, or held by an authorised data processor acting on its behalf.

FSA and ICO enforcement action

	– portable and mobile devices containing personal data, the loss of which could cause damage or distress to individuals, are encrypted using software which meets the current standard or equivalent; – it shall ensure that its policies on the transfer/sharing of personal data by means of a portable device are clear and comply with Government standards, and that staff are adequately trained on how to fulfil their obligations under them; and – it shall implement such other security measures it deems appropriate to ensure that personal data is protected against unauthorised and unlawful processing, accidental loss, destruction and/or damage.
Key words	Data security; Data storage disc; Sensitive data; Courier; Data encryption; Physical security; Portable device; Security policy; Staff training
Website link	http://www.ico.gov.uk/upload/documents/library/data_protection/notices/bc_undertaking.pdf

ICO v The University of Manchester ('the University')	
Date	21 April 2009 (date reported on ICO website)
Overview	The ICO was provided with a report from a party acting on behalf of the University regarding the accidental publication of a computerised spreadsheet containing the personal data of some 1,755 students, including information relating to the disabilities of some students ('sensitive' personal data). The information was published when a member of the University staff accidentally sent it as an email attachment to some 469 students. The information was originally provided to the University staff member by a colleague in response to a request for certain student email addresses. Instead of providing only email addresses, an extract of the full student personal data was provided, despite the fact that the staff member had no business need to acquire the full information. The provision of the information was due to a fault in the relevant University internal procedure. The University failed to ensure compliance with procedures and training to prevent the inappropriate internal transfer and publication of information. The ICO considered that the publication of sensitive personal data relating to disability could result in significant distress being caused to the individuals concerned.
Decision	Instead of the issue of an Enforcement Notice the University undertook to ensure that personal data is processed in accordance with the Seventh Principle and that: – it shall take all reasonable measures to guarantee the physical security of personal data processed in furtherance of the University's duties; – that policies on the transfer, sharing and publication of personal data are clear, and that staff are adequately trained on their obligations under such policies;

	– it shall implement such other security measures it deems appropriate to ensure personal data is protected against unauthorised and unlawful processing, accidental loss, destruction or damage.
Key words	Data security; Computer spreadsheet; Sensitive data; Email attachment; Staff training
Website link	http://www.ico.gov.uk/upload/documents/library/data_protection/notices/machester_uni_undertaking.pdf

ICO v Leasowes Community College ('the College')	
Date	30 April 2009 (date reported on ICO website)
Overview	The ICO was provided with a report from an individual acting on behalf of Dudley Metropolitan Borough Council regarding the loss and subsequent recovery of a memory stick containing the personal and 'sensitive' personal data of 1,500 pupils who attended the College. The lost data included names, contact details, school identifiers, free meal entitlements and English as a second language and ethnicity information. The memory stick was found by a member of the public, who, after opening it, handed it to the police. The memory stick was found to be of a poor quality, unencrypted and used by the College Data Manager in breach of College Policy. The device did not appear to have been missed by the College, nor did the College have adequate relevant training or staff training in place.
Decision	No Enforcement Notice was issued but instead an undertaking was given that the College shall ensure personal data is processed in accordance with the Seventh Principle and that: – portable and mobile devices containing personal data, the loss of which could cause damage or distress to individuals, are encrypted using software which meets the current standard or equivalent; – staff are aware of the College's policy for the storage and use of personal data, and are appropriately trained on how to follow that policy; and – the College shall implement such other security measures it deems appropriate to ensure that personal data is protected against unauthorised and unlawful processing, accidental loss, destruction and/or damage.
Key words	Data security; USB memory stick; Sensitive data; Education data; Security policy; Data encryption; Staff training
Website link	http://www.ico.gov.uk/upload/documents/library/data_protection/notices/leasowes_undertaking.pdf

FSA and ICO enforcement action

ICO v Doncaster Primary Care Trust ('the Trust')	
Date	30 April 2009 (date reported on ICO website)
Overview	The ICO was provided with a report from the Trust regarding the unauthorised removal of an obsolete out of hours GP service voice recording server that held personal data, including information relating to the physical and mental health of individuals ('sensitive' personal data).
	The server, which held some 220,000 clinical voice records, was replaced by an external engineer. The obsolete server was not missed until the replacement server failed. By this time the obsolete server had been out of the Trust's control for almost three weeks, during which time it was booted up twice.
	Although the server records were not accessed, the ICO considered that some of the data involved related to the sensitive personal data of individuals.
Decision	No Enforcement Notice was issued. Instead the Trust gave an undertaking to comply with the Seventh Principle and to ensure that:
	– portable and mobile devices are encrypted using encryption software which meets the current standard or equivalent;
	– physical security measures and procedures are adequate to prevent the unauthorised removal or theft of computer equipment, or that such equipment is encrypted using software that meets the current standard or equivalent; and
	– such other security measures to ensure personal data is protected against unauthorised and unlawful processing, accidental loss, destruction and or damage to personal data are implemented.
Key words	Data security; Data server; Voice records; Sensitive data; Data encryption; Security procedures
Website link	http://www.ico.gov.uk/upload/documents/library/data_protection/notices/doncaster_pct_undertaking.pdf

ICO v Cambridge University Hospitals NHS Foundation Trust ('the Trust')	
Date of undertaking	3 April 2009
Overview	The ICO was provided with a report from a party acting on behalf of the Trust regarding the loss of an unencrypted memory stick containing the personal data of some 741 Trust patients. The memory stick, which was privately owned, contained medical treatment data ('sensitive' personal data) and was left unattended in a car by a Trust employee. A car-wash attendant accessed the device and established its ownership.
	The data had been downloaded on to the memory stick without the knowledge of the Trust.

497

FSA and ICO enforcement action

	It was found that the Trust did not ensure sufficient security measures to prevent the unauthorised transfer of data on to a non-Trust owned unencrypted memory stick, and that the Trust failed to ensure that the data was protected by the Government minimum standard of encryption. The ICO considered that the loss of 'sensitive' personal data could cause significant distress to the individuals concerned.
Decision	Although no Enforcement Notice was issued, the Trust gave an undertaking that it would ensure that personal data is processed in accordance with the Seventh Principle and that: – the Trust shall take all reasonable measures to ensure the physical security of the personal data being processed; – portable and mobile devices are encrypted using encryption software which meets the current standard or equivalent; – the Trust shall implement other security measures, as appropriate, to ensure that personal data is protected against unauthorised and unlawful process, accidental loss, destruction and/or damage; – physical security measures are adequate to prevent unauthorised access to personal data; and – staff are aware of and appropriately trained in the Trust's policy regarding the storage and use of personal data.
Key words	Data security; USB memory stick; Sensitive data; Security procedures; Data encryption; Staff training
Website link	http://www.ico.gov.uk/upload/documents/library/data_protection/notices/cambridge_university_hospitals_nhs_ft_undertaking.pdf

ICO v Central Lancashire Primary Care Trust ('the Trust')	
Date	30 April 2009 (date reported on ICO website)
Overview	The ICO received a report from a party acting on behalf of the Trust regarding the loss of an encrypted memory stick containing the personal and 'sensitive' personal medic's data of some 6,360 inmates/patients at HMP Preston. The memory stick, which was lost by a staff member, had a 'Post-it' sticker attached with the applicable password. The Trust did not have sufficient security measures in place, including the use of a container to house the stick during transport. The ICO found data including sensitive personal data which could cause distress to the individuals concerned, and that the data had been retained for longer than necessary. There was no business need to retain data relating to records from 2000.
Decision	The Trust gave formal undertakings requiring the Trust to ensure personal data are processed in accordance with the Seventh Principle and to: – take all reasonable measures to ensure the physical security of personal data being processed;

FSA and ICO enforcement action

	– encrypted portable and mobile devices using software which meets the current standard or equivalent and applicable passwords will not be written down; – implement such other security measures, as appropriate, to ensure that personal data is protected against unauthorised and unlawful processing, accidental loss, destruction and/or damage; – delete data once it is no longer necessary to retain it; and – ensure staff are aware of the policy for storage and use of personal data and are trained on how to follow that policy.
Key words	Data security; USB memory stick; Sensitive data; Data retention; Security measures; Software security; Staff training
Website link	http://www.ico.gov.uk/upload/documents/library/data_protection/notices/central_lancs_pct_undertaking.pdf

ICO v The North West London Hospitals NHS Trust ('the Trust')	
Date	30 April 2009 (date reported on ICO website)
Overview	The ICO received two reports regarding the theft of two laptop computers, and in a separate incident, the theft of a desktop computer, each holding the personal data (including 'sensitive' personal data) of patients. The laptops held information relating to 181 patients, including names, dates of birth, NHS/hospital numbers and hearing test results. There was no indication of forced entry to offices in which the computers were kept. The lost data was password protected but not encrypted. The stolen desktop computer held password protected but unencrypted information relating to 180 patients, also including names, hospital numbers, dates of birth and some clinical follow-up information. The swipe card security system for the building had been disabled for maintenance at the time of the theft. The ICO considered that some of the data stolen was 'sensitive' personal data.
Decision	In the absence of an Enforcement Notice the Trust gave an undertaking to ensure that personal data is processed in accordance with the Seventh Data Protection Principle and that: – portable devices are encrypted using software which meets the current standard or equivalent; – physical security measures and procedures are adequate to prevent the theft of computers that contain personal data or ensure that such computers are encrypted using software which meets the current standard or equivalent; – a clear policy covering the storage and use of personal data is implemented; – staff are aware of the Trust's policy for the storage and use of personal data and are appropriately trained on how to follow it; and – other security measures, as appropriate, to ensure that personal data is protected against unauthorised and unlawful process, accidental loss, destruction and/or damage be implemented.

FSA and ICO enforcement action

Key words	Data security; Laptop computer; Desktop computer; Sensitive data; Password protection; Data encryption; Security policy; Staff training
Website link	http://www.ico.gov.uk/upload/documents/library/data_protection/notices/nwlht_undertaking.pdf

ICO v Hull & East Yorkshire Hospitals NHS Trust ('the Trust')	
Date	30 April 2009 (date reported on ICO website)
Overview	The ICO received a report from the Trust's Information Governance Manager setting out two separate incidents involving the loss of personal data (including 'sensitive' personal data) of some 2,300 patients. In the first incident, a desktop computer containing personal data of about 300 patients was lost during the refurbishment of an office. The second incident concerned the theft from a locked office of a disused laptop containing personal data of 2,000 cancer patients originating from pre-January 2007. Both devices were unencrypted. Although the Trust had data security policies in place, they were not followed.
Decision	The Trust undertook to ensure that personal data be processed in accordance with the Fifth and Seventh Data Protection Principles and that: – personal data held on a device by the Trust or by a data processor acting on behalf of the Trust be suitably encrypted according to Department of Health guidance so as to protect against unauthorised access; – personal data is not held on any media for longer than is required for the purpose for which it was originally stored and that when it is no longer needed the data is securely erased; – through appropriate training all staff, including contract or temporary staff, are made fully aware of internal policies and procedures relating to data and IT security and the requirements of the Data Protection Act; – adequate security measures are in place to control access to buildings and offices; and – such other security measures as it deemed appropriate to ensure personal data are protected against unauthorised or unlawful processing, accidental loss, destruction and/or damage are implemented.
Key words	Data security; Desktop computer; Laptop computer; Sensitive data; Data retention; Data encryption; Security policy; Data processor; Data erasure; Staff training
Website link	http://www.ico.gov.uk/upload/documents/library/data_protection/notices/hull_ey_undertaking.pdf

FSA and ICO enforcement action

ICO v Leicester City Council	
Date	12 May 2009 (date reported on ICO website)
Overview	The ICO received a notification of a security breach from the data controller, concerning the loss of an unencrypted USB memory stick from a Council-run nursery containing personal data of about 80 children. Some of the data was sensitive data.
	The controller discovered that contrary to its policies and procedures, and without management knowledge, temporary staff were storing personal data on the memory stick in question.
Decision	Leicester City Council undertook to comply with the Seventh Data Protection Principle and in particular to:
	– use its best endeavours to ensure that any data held on any portable media is encrypted;
	– improve its induction and training courses for all staff, including temporary staff, to emphasise the importance of data security, and the need to comply with the Controller's policies and shall periodically review and refresh such training as necessary.
Key words	Data security; Sensitive data; Loss; Encryption; Mobile devices
Website link	www.ico.gov.uk/upload/documents/library/data–protection/notices/leicester_city_council_final_undertaking.pdf

ICO v The Highland Council	
Date	2 June 2009 (date reported on ICO website)
Overview	The ICO received a report of the theft of two laptop computers from the data controller's premises. Although the laptops were stored within a locked office, no additional security measures were in place. The laptops contained personal data relating to some 1,400 individuals, including medical information. The laptops were password protected, but not encrypted.
Decision	The data controller undertook to comply with the Seventh Data Protection Principle and in particular to: – ensure portable and mobile devices and other portable media are encrypted by no later than 30 September 2009 using appropriate encryption software; – ensure adequate physical security measures and procedures are in place to prevent the theft of such devices; and – ensure other appropriate security measures, to ensure that personal data is protected, are put in place.
Key words	Date Security; Theft; Physical security; Sensitive personal data; Encryption
Website link	http://www.ico.gov.uk/upload/documents/library/data_protection/notices/highland_council_undertaking.pdf

FSA and ICO enforcement action

ICO v Salford Royal NHS Foundation Trust ('The Trust')	
Date	4 June 2009 (date reported on ICO website)
Overview	The ICO received a notification from the data controller's Information Governance Manager concerning the theft on an unencrypted desktop computer from a locked office in the neurosciences department. The computer contained personal data, some of it sensitive, relating to about 3,500 patients. The computer was password protected, but the files holding the data had no further protection. There was a delay of over one month in reporting the theft.
Decision	The Trust undertook to comply with the Seventh Data Protection Principle and in particular to: – restrict access to areas where personal data is stored through the use of appropriate security measures; – ensure that all personal data is stored on secure network servers so that it is not stored on the hard drives of desktop computers; – physically secure all desktop computers and laptops located on the wards to prevent easy removal; – suitably encrypt all personal data which is required to be stored or transmitted on portable devices; – ensure that data is not retained for longer than necessary and to securely dispose of such data when it is no longer required; – enforce the use of strong passwords on all computer terminals; and – implement an appropriate training programme on induction and to refresh such training at appropriate intervals.
Key words	Data security; Sensitive data; Theft; Encryption; Physical security
Website link	http://www.ico.gov.uk/upload/documents/library/data_protection/notices/salford_royal_undertaking.pdf

ICO v Amicus Legal Ltd	
Date	9 June 2009 (date reported on ICO website)
Overview	The ICO received a notification of a security breach from the data controller, concerning the theft of an unencrypted laptop computer containing the personal data of 100,000 of its customers. The laptop was privately owned by a contracted consultant and was stolen from a locked hotel room by a member of the hotel staff. The data controller failed to ensure that sufficient security measures were in place to prevent personal data being downloaded to a privately owned unencrypted laptop. Some of the personal data related to the legal advice and so could result in significant distress to the individuals concerned.
Decision	The data controller undertook to comply with the Seventh Data Protection Principle and in particular to: – take reasonable measures to ensure the physical security of all personal data processed in furtherance of the company's business;

	– encrypt all portable devices used to process personal data, particularly if the loss of such data could cause distress to individuals. Such encryption software should meet the current standards or equivalent;
	– implement physical security measures to prevent unauthorised access to personal data; and
	– ensure all staff, including contractors, are aware of the controller's processes and security policies and have received adequate training on the same.
Key words	Data security; Legal advice; Personal data which could cause significant distress; Theft; Contractors; Encryption
Website link	http://www.ico.gov.uk/upload/documents/library/data_protection/notices/amicus_undertaking.pdf

ICO v Manchester City Council	
Date	16 June 2009 (date reported on ICO website)
Overview	The ICO received a notification of a security breach from the data controller, concerning the theft of two laptop computers from the internal audit department that, in breach of the data controller's policies and procedures, were not encrypted, password protected or secured to an immovable object. One of the laptops contained personal data relating to 1,754 staff employed in local schools.
Decision	The data controller undertook to comply with the Seventh Data Protection Principle and in particular to:
– use best endeavours to ensure that all personal data stored on a laptop computer or other portable media are encrypted;
– use best endeavours to ensure that all laptop computers are secured to desks when in use in its offices, and stored securely in locked cabinets when the offices are unattended;
– ensure that wherever possible data is not downloaded to mobile devices for audit purposes or that only such data as is absolutely necessary to perform the audit is downloaded and only then if the data is securely encrypted;
– implement improved (and regular) data protection and IT security training for all staff. Staff's knowledge should also be tested to identify training needs.
Key words	Data security; Theft; Physical security; Training; Encryption
Website link	http://www.ico.gov.uk/upload/documents/library/data_protection/notices/mcr_city_council_undertaking.pdf

ICO v Jubilee Managing Agency Ltd	
Date	7 July 2009 (date reported on ICO website)
Overview	The ICO received a notification of a security breach from the data controller, concerning the loss of an unencrypted disc containing the personal data belonging to 2,100 policy holders. The data included financial information and in some cases related to policies that had expired or been cancelled or to policy holders that had since died, or changed their details. Following the security breach the data controller conducted a full investigation into the breach and commissioned an independent third party to audit its security arrangements.
Decision	The data controller undertook to comply with the Seventh Data Protection Principle and in particular to: – ensure that all personal data stored on removable media, whether by the data controller or by a processor, are encrypted; – implement suitable written policies to govern staff's day-to-day operations and which provide for risk assessments and compliance monitoring; – data is not retained for any longer than is necessary and that it is securely deleted when it is no longer required; – implement mandatory, improved and regular data protection training for all staff; – ensure that all data processors comply with the Seventh Principle.
Key words	Loss of portable media; Written policies; Training; Encryption
Website link	http://www.ico.gov.uk/upload/documents/library/data_protection/notices/jubilee_undertaking.pdf

ICO v Neath Port Talbot County Borough Council	
Date	23 July 2009 (date reported on ICO website)
Overview	The ICO received a report from the data controller regarding the loss of an unencrypted USB memory stick that held the personal data of children looked after by the data controller – comprising the data of 65 children that was not password protected.
Decision	The data controller undertook to comply with the Seventh Data Protection Principle and in particular to: – ensure portable and mobile devices, including laptops and other portable media are appropriately encrypted; – ensure staff are aware of the data controller's policy for the storage and use of personal data and are trained on how to follow that policy; – ensure the policy covering the storage and use of personal data is actively followed by staff; and – ensure the implementation of such other security measures it deems appropriate to ensure that personal data is protected against unauthorised and unlawful process, accidental loss, destruction and/or damage.

FSA and ICO enforcement action

Key words	Date Security; Theft; Portable media; Physical security; Sensitive personal data; Encryption; Training
Website link	http://www.ico.gov.uk/upload/documents/library/data_protection/notices/neath_council_undertaking.pdf

ICO v London Clubs International Limited	
Date	28 July 2009 (date reported on ICO website)
Overview	The ICO received a report of an incident in which a laptop computer was stolen from the data controller's premises, containing the personal data of approximately 26,000 individuals. The laptop was password protected but not encrypted.
Decision	The data controller undertook to comply with the Seventh Data Protection Principle and in particular to: – ensure portable and mobile devices, including laptops and other portable media are appropriately encrypted; and – the data controller shall implement such other security measures it deems appropriate to ensure that personal data is protected against unauthorised and unlawful process, accidental loss, destruction and/or damage.
Key words	Date Security; Theft; Portable media; Physical security; Encryption
Website link	http://www.ico.gov.uk/upload/documents/library/data_protection/notices/london_clubs_international_undertaking.pdf

ICO v NHS Lothian	
Date	28 July 2009 (date reported on ICO website)
Overview	The ICO received two reports from the data controller, regarding the temporary loss of a document wallet, left in a shop, containing 25 paper files containing personal data of home-based patients and the loss of a USB memory stick containing personal data of 137 patients – the latter USB stick was the personal property of an employee and should not therefore have been used to store NHS data – the memory stick was also not encrypted to ensure an adequate level of security.
Decision	The data controller undertook to comply with the Seventh Data Protection Principle and in particular to: – ensure that portable and mobile devices, including memory sticks and other portable media are appropriately encrypted; – ensure that network systems are introduced to prevent the use of unauthorised or personal memory devices or computer systems to download personal data; – ensure the physical security of any paper files containing personal data, whether those files are on the data controller's own premises or in transit to other locations; – ensure all staff are adequately trained on the data controller's information security policies; and

	– the data controller shall implement such other security measures it deems appropriate to ensure that personal data is protected against unauthorised and unlawful process, accidental loss, destruction and/or damage.
Key words	Date Security; Theft; Portable media; Physical security; Encryption; Health data; Paper files; Training
Website link	http://www.ico.gov.uk/upload/documents/library/data_protection/notices/nhs_lothian_undertaking.pdf

Appendix B

TRANSPOSITION OF ARTICLES 16 AND 17 OF THE DATA PROTECTION DIRECTIVE

Article 16:

Confidentiality of processing

Any person acting under the authority of the controller or of the processor, including the processor himself, who has access to personal data must not process them except on instructions from the controller, unless he is required to do so by law

Article 17:

Security of processing

1. Member States shall provide that the controller must implement appropriate technical and organisational measures to protect personal data against accidental or unlawful destruction or accidental loss, alteration, unauthorised disclosure or access, in particular where the processing involves the transmission of data over a network, and against all other unlawful forms of processing.

Having regard to the state of the art and the cost of their implementation, such measures shall ensure a level of security appropriate to the risks represented by the processing and the nature of the data to be protected.

2. The Member States shall provide that the controller must, where processing is carried out on his behalf, choose a processor providing sufficient guarantees in respect of the technical security measures and organisational measures governing the processing to be carried out, and must ensure compliance with those measures.

3. The carrying out of processing by way of a processor must be governed by a contract or legal act binding the processor to the controller and stipulating in particular that:

– the processor shall act only on instructions from the controller,

– the obligations set out in paragraph 1, as defined by the law of the Member States in which the processor is established, shall also be incumbent on the processor.

4. For the purposes of keeping proofs, the parts of the contract or the legal act relating to data protection and the requirements relating to the measures referred to in paragraph 1 shall be in writing or in another equivalent form.

Transposition of Articles 16 and 17 of the Data Protection Directive

Juris-diction	Relevant provision transposing Articles 16 and 17
Austria	*Federal Act concerning the Protection of Personal Data (Datenschutzgesetz 2000)* Section 11 Paragraph 1 Irrespective of contractual obligations, all processors have the following obligations when using data for a controller: (1) to use data only according to the instructions of the controller; in particular, the transmission of the data used is prohibited unless so instructed by the controller; (2) to take all required safety measures pursuant to section 14; in particular to employ only operatives who have committed themselves to confidentiality vis-à-vis the processor or are under a statutory obligation of confidentiality; (3) to enlist another processor only with the permission of the controller and therefore to inform the controller of this intended enlistment of another processor in such a timely fashion that the controller has the possibility to object; (4) – insofar as this is possible given the nature of the service processing – to create in agreement with the controller the necessary technical and organisational requirements for the fulfilment of the controller's obligation to grant the right of information, rectification and erasure; (5) to hand over to the controller after the end of the service processing all results of processing and documentation containing data or to keep or destroy them on his request; (6) to make available to the controller all information necessary to control the compliance with the obligations according to sub-paras. 1 to 5. Paragraph 2 Agreements between the controller and the processor concerning the details of the obligations according to para. 1 shall be laid down in writing to perpetuate the evidence. Section 14 Paragraph 1 Measures to ensure data security shall be taken by all organisational units of a controller or processor that use data. Depending on the kind of data used as well as the extent and purpose of the use and considering the state of technical possibilities and economic justifiability it shall be ensured that the data are protected against accidental or intentional destruction or loss, that they are properly used and are not accessible to unauthorised persons. Paragraph 2 In particular, the following measures are to be taken insofar as this is necessary with regard to the last sentence of para. 1:

Transposition of Articles 16 and 17 of the Data Protection Directive

Juris-diction	Relevant provision transposing Articles 16 and 17
	1. The distribution of functions between the organisational units as well as the operatives regarding the use of data shall be laid down expressly, 2. The use of data must be tied to valid orders of the authorised organisational units or operatives, 3. every operative is to be instructed about his duties according to this Federal Act and the internal data protection regulations, including data security regulations, 4. The right of access to the premises of the data controller or processor is to be regulated, 5. The right of access to data and programs is to be regulated as well as the protection of storage media against access and use by unauthorised persons, 6. The right to operate the data processing equipment is to be laid down and every device is to be secured against unauthorised operation by taking precautions for the machines and programs used, 7. Logs shall be kept in order that the processing steps that were actually performed, in particular modifications, consultations and transmissions can be traced to the extent necessary with regard to their permissibility, 8. A documentation shall be kept on the measures taken pursuant to sub-paras. 1 to 7 to facilitate control and conservation of evidence. These measures must, taking into account the technological state of the art and the cost incurred in their execution, safeguard a level of data protection appropriate with regard to the risks arising from the use and the type of data to be protected. Paragraph 3 Unregistered transmissions from data applications subject to an obligation to grant information pursuant to sect. 26 shall be logged in such a manner that the right of information can be granted to the subject pursuant to sect. 26. Transmissions provided for in the standard ordinance (sect. 17 para. 2 lit. 6) and the model ordinance (sect. 19 para. 2) do not require logging. Paragraph 4 Logs and documentation data may not be used for purposes that are incompatible with the purpose of the collection – viz., monitoring the legitimacy of the use of the logged and documented data files. In particular, any further use for the purpose of supervising the data subjects whose data is contained in the logged data files, as well as for the purpose of monitoring the persons who have accessed the logged data files, or for any purpose other than checking access rights shall be considered incompatible, unless the data is used is for the purpose of preventing or prosecuting a crime according to sect. 278a StGB (criminal organisation) or a crime punishable with a maximum sentence of more than five years' imprisonment.

Transposition of Articles 16 and 17 of the Data Protection Directive

Juris-diction	Relevant provision transposing Articles 16 and 17
	Paragraph 5 Unless expressly provided for otherwise by law, logs and documentation data shall be kept for three years. Deviations from this rule shall be permitted to the same extent that the logged or documented data files may legitimately be erased earlier or kept longer. Paragraph 6 Data security regulations are to be issued and kept available in such a manner that the operatives can inform themselves about the regulations to which they are subject at any time. Section 15 Confidentiality of Data Paragraph 1 Controllers, processors and their operatives – these being the employees and persons comparable to employees – shall keep data from uses of data confidential that have been entrusted or made accessible to them solely for professional reasons, without prejudice to other professional obligations of confidentiality, unless a legitimate reason exists for the transmission of the entrusted or accessed data (confidentiality of data). Paragraph 2 Operatives shall transmit data only if expressly ordered to do so by their employer. Controllers and processors shall oblige their operatives by contract, insofar as they are not already obliged by law, to transmit data from uses of data only if so ordered and to adhere to the confidentiality of data even after the end of their professional relationship with the controller or processor. Paragraph 3 Controllers and processors may only issue orders for the transmission of data if this is permitted pursuant to the provisions of this Federal Act. They shall inform the operatives affected by these orders about the transmission orders in force and about the consequences of a violation of data confidentiality. Paragraph 4 Without prejudice to the constitutional right to issue instructions, a refusal to follow an order to transmit data on the grounds that it violates the provisions of this Federal Act shall not be to the operatives detriment.
Belgium	*Belgian Law of 8 December 1992 on Privacy in relation to the Processing of Personal Data as modified by the law of 11 December 1998 implementing Directive 95/46/EC and the law of 26 February 2003* Article 16 Paragraph 1 If the processing is consigned to a processor, the controller or his representative in Belgium, if such is the case, shall:

Transposition of Articles 16 and 17 of the Data Protection Directive

Juris-diction	Relevant provision transposing Articles 16 and 17
	(1) choose a processor providing sufficient guarantees in respect of the technical and organisational measures governing the processing to be carried out; (2) supervise the compliance with these measures, in particular by laying them down in contractual stipulations; (3) lay down in the contract the responsibility of the processor in respect to the controller; (4) agree with the processor that the processor only acts on behalf of the controller and that the processor is bound by the same obligations as by which the controller is bound pursuant to paragraph 3; (5) lay down in writing or on electronic carrier the elements of the contract with regard to the protection of data and the requirements with regard to the measures referred to in paragraph 3. Paragraph 2 The controller or, if such is the case, his representative in Belgium, shall: (1) watch carefully that the data are updated, that inaccurate, incomplete and irrelevant data, as well as data that have been obtained or further processed in violation of the Articles 4–8, are corrected or erased; (2) take care that the access to the data and possibilities of processing for the persons who are acting under his authority, are limited to what is necessary for the fulfilment of their duties or for the requirements of the service; (3) notify all persons acting under his authority about the provisions of this law and its implementing decrees, as well as about all relevant provisions in respect of the protection of the privacy with regard to the processing of personal data; (4) ascertain that the programmes for the automatic processing of personal data are in accordance with the statements in the notification referred to in Article 17 and that no unlawful use is made thereof. Paragraph 3 Any person acting under the authority of the controller or of the processor, as well as the processor himself having access to the personal data, may only process them on the instructions of the controller, except for the case of an obligation imposed by or by virtue of a law, decree or ordinance. Paragraph 4 In order to guarantee the security of personal data the controller or, if such is the case, his representative in Belgium, as well as the processor shall take the appropriate technical and organisational measures that are necessary for the protection of personal data against accidental or unauthorised destruction, accidental loss, as well as against alteration of, access to and any other unauthorised processing of personal data.

Transposition of Articles 16 and 17 of the Data Protection Directive

Juris-diction	Relevant provision transposing Articles 16 and 17
	There measures shall ensure an appropriate level of security taking into account the state of the art in this field and the cost of implementing the measures on the one hand, and the nature of the data to be protected and the potential risks on the other hand. On the advice of the Commission for the protection of privacy the King may promulgate appropriate standards in the matter of informatics security for all or certain categories of processing.
Bulgaria	*Law for the protection of Personal Data (2001)* Article 23 Paragraph 1 The personal data administrator must implement appropriate technical and organisational measures to protect the data against accidental or unlawful destruction, or against accidental loss, unauthorised access, alteration or dissemination, and against other unlawful forms of processing. Paragraph 2 The administrator shall implement special protection measures where processing involves the transmission of data over an electronic network. Paragraph 3 Measures referred to in paragraph (1) and paragraph (2) shall take into account state-of-the-art technology and ensure a level of security corresponding to the risks involved in processing, and the nature of the data to be protected. Paragraph 4 The measures referred to in paragraph (1) and paragraph (2) shall be determined in an instruction issued by the personal data administrator. Paragraph 5 The Commission shall specify the minimum level of technical and organisational measures, as well as the admissible type of protection in a regulation. Such regulation shall be published in the State Gazette. Article 24 Paragraph 1 Administrators may process data on their own or through assignment to data processors. When this is needed for organisational reasons, the processing may be assigned to more than one data processor with a view, inter alia, to deliminate their specific tasks. Paragraph 2 Where the data processing is not performed by the administrator, the latter shall designate the data processor and provide sufficient data protection guarantees.

Juris-diction	Relevant provision transposing Articles 16 and 17
	Paragraph 3 (repealed)
Paragraph 4
The relationship between the administrator and the personal data processor must be governed by a piece of legislation, a written contract or another act of the administrator defining the scope of duties assigned by the administrator to the data processor.
Paragraph 5
The administrator shall be jointly and severally liable for any damages caused to any third party resulting from any action or failure to act on behalf of the data processor.
Paragraph 6
The personal data processor or any person acting under the guidance of the administrator or of the processor who has access to personal data may process them only on instructions from the administrator, unless otherwise provided for by law.
Article 25
Paragraph 1
Upon the achievement of the purpose of personal data processing, the personal data administrator must:
(1) either destroy the data, or
(2) having given prior notification to the Commission, transfer them to another administrator provided that such transfer is provided for in a law and the purposes of processing are identical.
Paragraph 2
Upon the achievement of the intended purposes of personal data processing, the personal data administrator shall store data only in the cases laid down by law.
Paragraph 3
In cases where, having achieved the purpose of personal data processing, the administrator wishes to store the personal data processed as anonymous data for historical, statistical or research purposes, it must inform the Commission thereof.
Paragraph 4
The Commission for Personal Data Protection may prohibit the storage of data for the purposes under Paragraph 3 if the administrator has failed to provide sufficient protection of the anonymous storage of the data processed.
Paragraph 5
The decision of the Commission under Paragraph 4 shall be subject to appeal before the Supreme Administrative Court. Where the Supreme Administrative Court fails to grant an appeal against the decision of the Commission, the personal data administrator shall destroy the data.

Transposition of Articles 16 and 17 of the Data Protection Directive

Juris-diction	Relevant provision transposing Articles 16 and 17
Cyprus	*The Processing of Personal Data (Protection of Individuals) Law (138/2001)* Section 10 Subsection 1 The processing of data is confidential. It shall be carried out only by persons acting under the instructions from the controller. Subsection 2 For carrying out the processing, the controller must select persons who possess appropriate qualifications and who provide sufficient guarantees as regards technical knowledge and personal integrity for the observance of confidentiality. Subsection 3 The controller must take the appropriate organizational and technical measures for the security of data and their protection against accidental or unlawful destruction, accidental loss, alteration, unauthorised dissemination or access and any other form of unlawful processing. Such measures shall ensure a level of security which is appropriate to the risks involved in the processing and the nature of the data processed. The Commissioner gives, from time to time, directions with regard to the degree of security of the data and to the measures of protection required to be taken for every category of data, taking also into account technological developments. Subsection 4 If processing is performed by the processor, the assignment for the processing must be made in writing. The assignment must provide that the processor shall perform the processing only upon instructions from the controller and that the remaining obligations set out in this section shall also lie on the processor.
Czech Republic	*Personal Data Protection Act 101 of April 4, 2000 on the Protection of Personal Data and on Amendment to Some Acts* Article 6 Where authorization does not follow from a legal regulation, the controller must conclude with the processor an agreement on personal data processing. The agreement must be made in writing. In particular, the agreement shall explicitly stipulate the scope, purpose and period of time for which it is concluded and must contain guarantees by the processor related to technical and organisational securing of the protection of personal data. Article 13 (1) The controller and the processor shall be obliged to adopt measures preventing unauthorised or accidental access to personal data, their alteration, destruction or loss, unauthorised transmission, other unauthorised processing, as well as other misuse of personal data. This obligation shall remain valid after terminating personal data processing.

Transposition of Articles 16 and 17 of the Data Protection Directive

Juris-diction	Relevant provision transposing Articles 16 and 17
	(2) The controller or the processor shall be obliged to develop and to document the technical-organisational measures adopted and implemented to ensure the personal data protection in accordance with the law and other legal regulations. (3) In the framework of measures pursuant to paragraph (1), the controller or the processor perform a risk assessment concerning (a) the carrying out of instructions for personal data processing by persons who have immediate access to the personal data, (b) prevention of unauthorized persons' access to personal data and means for their processing, (c) prevention of unauthorized reading, creating, copying, transferring, modifying or deleting of records containing personal data, and (d) measures enabling to determine and verify to whom the personal data were transferred. (4) In the area of automatic processing of personal data, the controller or processor shall, in the framework of measures under paragraph 1, be obliged to (a) ensure that the systems for automatic processing of personal data are used only by authorized persons, (b) ensure that the natural persons authorized to use systems for automatic processing of personal data have access only to the personal data corresponding to their authorization, and this on the basis of specific user authorizations established exclusively for these persons, (c) make electronic records enabling to identify and verify when, by whom and for what reason the personal data were recorded or otherwise processed, and (d) prevent any unauthorized access to data carriers.
Denmark	*Act on Processing of Personal Data (Act No. 429 of 31 May 2000)* Title IV Security, Chapter 11 Section 41 Subsection 1 Individuals, companies etc. performing work for the controller or the processor and who have access to data may process these only on instructions from the controller unless otherwise provided by law or regulations. Subsection 2 The instruction mentioned in subsection (1) may not restrict journalistic freedom or impede the production of an artistic or literary product. Subsection 3 The controller shall implement appropriate technical and organizational security measures to protect data against accidental or unlawful destruction, loss or alteration and against unauthorized disclosure, abuse or other processing in violation of the provisions laid down in this Act. The same shall apply to processors.

Transposition of Articles 16 and 17 of the Data Protection Directive

Juris-diction	Relevant provision transposing Articles 16 and 17
	Subsection 4 As regards data which are processed for the public administration and which are of special interest to foreign powers, measures shall be taken to ensure that they can be disposed of or destroyed in the event of war or similar conditions. Subsection 5 The Minister of Justice may lay down more detailed rules concerning the security measures mentioned in subsection (3). Section 42 Subsection 1 Where a controller leaves the processing of data to a processor, the controller shall make sure that the processor is in a position to implement the technical and organizational security measures mentioned in section 41 (3) to (5), and shall ensure compliance with those measures. Subsection 2 The carrying out of processing by way of a processor must be governed by a written contract between the parties. This contract must stipulate that the processor shall act only on instructions from the controller and that the rules laid down in section 41 (3) to (5) shall also apply to processing by way of a processor. If the processor is established in a different Member State, the contract must stipulate that the provisions on security measures laid down by the law in the Member State in which the processor is established shall also be incumbent on the processor.
Estonia	*Personal Data Protection Act (12 February 2003)* Section 18 Personal data processing requirements In the processing of personal data, chief processors and authorised processors are required to: (1) promptly erase or block personal data unnecessary for the given purposes unless otherwise prescribed by law; (2) ensure that personal data are correct and, if necessary for the given purposes, up to date; (3) block incomplete and inaccurate personal data and immediately take the necessary measures for the amendment or rectification of the data; (4) store inaccurate data with a notation concerning their period of use together with accurate data; (5) block personal data which are contested on the basis of accuracy until the accuracy of the data is verified or the accurate data are determined.

Transposition of Articles 16 and 17 of the Data Protection Directive

Juris-diction	Relevant provision transposing Articles 16 and 17
	Section 19 Organisational, physical and IT security measures to protect personal data Subsection 1 In order to protect personal data, chief processors and authorised processors are required to take organisational, physical and IT security measures: (1) as regards the integrity of the data, against accidental or intentional unauthorised alteration of data; (2) as regards the availability of the data, against accidental loss and intentional destruction and against prevention of access to the data for entitled persons; (3) as regards the confidentiality of the data, against unauthorised processing. Subsection 2 In the processing of personal data, chief processors and authorised processors are required to: (1) prevent the access of unauthorised persons to equipment used for processing personal data; (2) avoid unauthorised reading, copying and alteration in the data processing system and unauthorised removal of data media; (3) prevent the unauthorised recording, alteration or erasure of personal data and ensure that it be subsequently possible to determine when, by whom and which personal data were recorded, altered or erased; (4) ensure that every user of a data processing system only has access to personal data permitted to be processed by him or her and to the data processing permitted for him or her; (5) ensure the existence of information on the transmission of personal data regarding when, to whom and which personal data were transmitted and the unaltered storage of such data; (6) ensure that unauthorised reading, copying, alteration or erasure of personal data is not carried out in the transmission of the personal data by data communication equipment and in the transportation of data media; (7) organise the work of enterprises, agencies and associations in a manner that allows compliance with data protection requirements. Subsection 3 Chief processors and authorised processors are required to maintain records on the devices and software which are under the supervision thereof and used in the processing of personal data and they shall document the following information: (1) the name, type and location of the device and the name of the manufacturer of the device; (2) the name and version and the name and details of the manufacturer of the software and the location of the documents of the software.

Transposition of Articles 16 and 17 of the Data Protection Directive

Juris-diction	Relevant provision transposing Articles 16 and 17
Finland	*Personal Data Act (523/1999)* Chapter 7 – Data Security and storage of personal data Section 32 – Data Security Paragraph 1 The controller shall carry out the technical and organisational measures necessary for securing personal data against unauthorised access, against accidental or unlawful destruction, manipulation, disclosure and transfer and against other unlawful processing. The techniques available, the associated costs, the quality, quantity and age of the data, as well as the significance of the processing to the protection of privacy shall be taken into account when carrying out the measures. Paragraph 2 Anyone who as an independent trader or business operates on the behalf of the controller shall, before starting the processing of data, provide the controller with appropriate commitments and other adequate guarantees of the security of the data as provided in paragraph (1). Section 33 – Secrecy obligation Anyone who has gained knowledge of the characteristics, personal circumstances or economic situation of another person while carrying out measures relating to data processing shall not disclose the data to a third person against the provisions of this Act. Section 34 – Destruction of a personal data file If a personal data file is no longer necessary for the operations of the controller, it shall be destroyed, unless specific provisions have been issued by an Act or by lower-level regulation on the continued storage of the data contained therein or the file is transferred to be archived in accordance with section 35.
France	*Act No 78–17 on Data Processing, Data Files and Individual Liberties (6 January 1978) (Amended by Act of 6 August 2004)* Article 34 Paragraph 1 The data controller shall take all useful precautions, with regard to the nature of the data and the risks of the processing, to preserve the security of the data and, in particular, prevent their alteration and damage, or access by non-authorised third parties. Paragraph 2 Decrees taken upon an opinion of the 'Commission nationale de l'informatique et des libertés' may determine the technical requirements that the processing mentioned in sub-section (2) [processing necessary for the protection of human life with the impossibility of obtaining consent] and sub-section (6) [processing necessary to medicine and administration of care] of Section II of Article 8 should meet.

Transposition of Articles 16 and 17 of the Data Protection Directive

Juris-diction	Relevant provision transposing Articles 16 and 17
Germany	*Federal Data Protection Act (15 November 2006)* Section 5 – Confidentiality Persons employed in data processing shall not collect, process or use personal data without authorisation (confidentiality). On taking up their duties such persons, in so far as they work for private bodies, shall be required to give an undertaking to maintain such confidentiality. This undertaking shall continue to be valid after termination of their activity. Section 9 – Technical and Organisational Measures Public and private bodies processing personal data either on their own behalf or on behalf of others shall take the technical and organisational measures necessary to ensure the implementation of the provisions of this Act, in particular the requirements set out in the annex to this Act. Measures shall be required only if the effort involved is reasonable in relation to the desired level of protection. Annex 9 Where personal data are processed or used automatically, the internal organisation of authorities or enterprises is to be arranged in such a way that it meets the specific requirements of data protection. In particular, measures suited to the type of personal data or data categories to be protected shall be taken: (1) to prevent unauthorised persons from gaining access to data processing systems with which personal data are processed or used (access control) (2) to prevent data processing systems from being used without authorisation (access control) (3) to ensure that persons entitled to use a data processing system have access only to the data to which they have a right of access, and that personal data cannot be read, copied, modified or removed without authorisation in the course of processing or use and after storage (access control) (4) to ensure that personal data cannot be read, copied, modified or removed without authorisation during electronic transmission or transport, and that it is possible to check and establish to which bodies the transfer of personal data by means of data transmission facilities is envisaged (transmission control) (5) to ensure that it is possible to check and establish whether and by whom personal data have been input into data processing systems, modified or removed (input control) (6) to ensure that, in the case of commissioned processing of personal data, the data are processed strictly in accordance with the instructions of the principal (job control) (7) to ensure that personal data are protected from accidental destruction or loss (availability control) (8) to ensure that data collected for different purposes can be processed separately.

Transposition of Articles 16 and 17 of the Data Protection Directive

Juris-diction	Relevant provision transposing Articles 16 and 17
Greece	*Law 2472/1997 on the Protection of Individuals with regard to the Processing of Personal Data* Article 10(3) 3. The Controller must implement appropriate organisational and technical measures to secure data and protect them against accidental or unlawful destruction, accidental loss, alteration, unauthorised disclosure or access as well as any other form of unlawful processing. Such measures must ensure a level of security appropriate to the risks presented by processing and the nature of the data subject to processing. Without prejudice to other provisions, the Authority shall offer instructions and issue regulations in accordance with article 19 paragraph 1 k involving the level of security of data and of the computer and information infrastructure, the security measures that are required for each category and processing of data as well as the use of technology for the strengthening of privacy.
Hungary	*Act LXIII of 1992 on the Protection of Personal Data and Public Access to Data of Public Interest* Article 10 – Data Security Paragraph 1 The data controller and, within its scope of activities the technical data processor, shall ensure data security and shall take all technical and organisational measures and elaborate the rules of procedure necessary to enforce compliance with this Act and other rules pertaining to data protection and confidentiality. Paragraph 2 Data shall be protected in particular against unauthorised access, alteration, transfer, making public, deletion or destruction, as well as against accidental destruction or damage. If personal data are transferred via a network or other information technology equipment, the data controller, technical data processor and the operator of the telecommunications or information technology equipment shall take special protective measures to ensure the technical protection of personal data.
Ireland	*Consolidated version of Data Protection Acts 1988 and 2003* Section 2 Subsection 1 A data controller shall, as respects personal data kept by him or her, comply with the following provisions: ... (d) appropriate security measures shall be taken against unauthorised access to, or unauthorised alteration, disclosure or destruction of, the data, in particular where the processing involves the transmission of data over a network, and against all other unlawful forms of processing.

Transposition of Articles 16 and 17 of the Data Protection Directive

Juris-diction	Relevant provision transposing Articles 16 and 17
	Subsection 2 A data processor shall, as respects personal data processed by him, comply with paragraph (d) of subsection (1) of this section. Section 2C Subsection 1 In determining appropriate security measures for the purposes of section 2(1)(d) of this Act, in particular (but without prejudice to the generality of that provision), where the processing involves the transmission of data over a network, a data controller– (a) may have regard to the state of technological development and the cost of implementing the measures, and (b) shall ensure that the measures provide a level of security appropriate to– (i) the harm that might result from unauthorised or unlawful processing, accidental or unlawful destruction or accidental loss of, or damage to, the data concerned, and (ii) the nature of the data concerned. Subsection 2 A data controller or data processor shall take all reasonable steps to ensure that– (a) persons employed by him or her, and (b) other persons at the place of work concerned, are aware of and comply with the relevant security measures aforesaid. Subsection 3 Where processing of personal data is carried out by a data processor on behalf of a data controller, the data controller shall: (a) ensure that the processing is carried out in pursuance of a contract in writing or in another equivalent form between the data controller and the data processor and that the contract provides that the data processor carries out the processing only on and subject to the instructions of the data controller and that the data processor complies with obligations equivalent to those imposed on the data controller by section 2(1)(d) of this Act, (b) ensure that the data processor provides sufficient guarantees in respect of the technical security measures, and organisational measures, governing the processing, and (c) take reasonable steps to ensure compliance with those measures.
Italy	*Personal Data Protection Code Legislative Decree no. 196 of 30 June 2003* Section 31 Personal data undergoing processing shall be kept and controlled, also in consideration of technological innovations, of their nature and the specific features of the processing, in such a way as to minimise, by means of suitable preventative security measures, the risk of their destruction or loss, whether by accident or not, of

Transposition of Articles 16 and 17 of the Data Protection Directive

Juris-diction	Relevant provision transposing Articles 16 and 17
	unauthorized access to the data or of processing operations that are either unlawful or inconsistent with the purposes for which the data have been collected. Section 32 Paragraph 1 The provider of a publicly available electronic communications service shall take suitable technical and organisational measures under Section 31 that are adequate in the light of the existing risk, in order to safeguard security of its services and integrity of traffic data, location data and electronic communications against any form of unauthorised utilisation or access. Paragraph 2 Whenever security of service or personal data makes it necessary to also take measures applying to the network, the provider of a publicly available electronic communications service shall take those measures jointly with the provider of the public communications network. Failing an agreement between said providers, the dispute shall be settled, at the instance of either provider, by the Authority for Communications Safeguards in pursuance of the arrangements set out in the legislation in force. Paragraph 3 In case of a particular risk of a breach of network security, the provider of a publicly available electronic communications service shall inform subscribers and, if possible, users concerning said risk and, when the risk lies outside the scope of the measures to be taken by said provider pursuant to paragraphs 1 and 2, of all the possible remedies including an indication of the likely costs involved. This information shall be also provided to the Garante and the Authority for Communications Safeguards. Section 33 Within the framework of the more general security requirements referred to in Section 31, or else provided for by specific regulations, data controllers shall be required in any case to adopt the minimum security measures pursuant either to this Chapter or to Section 58(3) in order to ensure a minimum level of personal data protection. Section 34 Paragraph 1 Processing personal data by electronic means shall only be allowed if the minimum security measures referred to below are adopted in accordance with the arrangements laid down in the technical specifications as per Annex B: a) computerised authentication, b) implementation of authentication credentials management procedures, c) use of an authorisation system,

Juris-diction	Relevant provision transposing Articles 16 and 17
	d) regular update of the specifications concerning scope of the processing operations that may be performed by the individual entities in charge of managing and/or maintenancing electronic means,

e) protection of electronic means and data against unlawful data processing operations, unauthorised access and specific software,

f) implementation of procedures for safekeeping backup copies and restoring data and system availability,

g) keeping an up-to-date security policy document,

h) implementation of encryption techniques or identification codes for specific processing operations performed by health care bodies in respect of data disclosing health and sex life.

Section 35

Paragraph 1

Processing personal data without electronic means shall only be allowed if the minimum security measures referred to below are adopted in accordance with the arrangements laid down in the technical specifications as per Annex B:

a) regular update of the specifications concerning scope of the processing operations that may be performed by the individual entities in charge of the processing and/or by the individual organisational departments,

b) implementing procedures such as to ensure safekeeping of records and documents committed to the entities in charge of the processing for the latter to discharge the relevant tasks,

c) implementing procedures to keep certain records in restricted-access filing systems and regulating access mechanisms with a view to enabling identification of the entities in charge of the processing.

Section 36

Paragraph 1

The technical specifications as per Annex B concerning the minimum measures referred to in this Chapter shall be regularly updated by a decree of the Minister of Justice issued in agreement with the Minister for Innovation and Technologies and the Minister for De-Regulation by having regard to both technical developments and the experience gathered in this sector.

Annex B

PROCESSING BY ELECTRONIC MEANS

The following technical arrangements to be implemented by the data controller, data processor – if nominated – and person(s) in charge of the processing whenever data are processed by electronic means: |

Juris- diction	Relevant provision transposing Articles 16 and 17
	Computerised Authentication System 1. Persons in charge of the processing shall be allowed to process personal data by electronic means if they are provided with authentication credentials such as to successfully complete an authentication procedure relating either to a specific processing operation or to a set of processing operations. 2. Authentication credentials shall consist in an ID code for the person in charge of the processing as associated with a secret password that shall only be known to the latter person; alternatively, they shall consist in an authentication device that shall be used and held exclusively by the person in charge of the processing and may be associated with either an ID code or a password, or else in a biometric feature that relates to the person in charge of the processing and may be associated with either an ID code or a password. 3. One or more authentication credentials shall be assigned to or associated with each person in charge of the processing. 4. The instructions provided to the persons in charge of the processing shall lay down the obligation to take such precautions as may be necessary to ensure that the confidential component(s) in the credentials are kept secret and that the devices used and held exclusively by persons in charge of the processing are kept with due care. 5. Where provided for by the relevant authentication system, a password shall consist of at least eight characters; if this is not allowed by the electronic equipment, a password shall consist of the maximum permitted number of characters. It shall not contain any item that can be easily related to the person in charge of the processing and shall be modified by the latter when it is first used as well as at least every six months thereafter. If sensitive or judicial data are processed, the password shall be modified at least every three months. 6. An ID code, if used, may not be assigned to another person in charge of the processing even at a different time. 7. Authentication credentials shall be de-activated if they have not been used for at least six months, except for those that have been authorised exclusively for technical management purposes. 8. Authentication credentials shall be also de-activated if the person in charge of the processing is disqualified from accessing personal data. 9. The persons in charge of the processing shall be instructed to the effect that electronic equipment should not be left unattended and made accessible during processing sessions.

Transposition of Articles 16 and 17 of the Data Protection Directive

Juris-diction	Relevant provision transposing Articles 16 and 17
	10. Where data and electronic equipment may only be accessed by using the confidential component(s) of the authentication credential, appropriate instructions shall be given in advance, in writing, to clearly specify the mechanisms by which the data controller can ensure that data or electronic equipment are available in case the person in charge of the processing is either absent or unavailable for a long time and it is indispensable to carry out certain activities without further delay exclusively for purposes related to system operationality and security. In this case, copies of the credentials shall be kept in such a way as to ensure their confidentiality by specifying, in writing, the entities in charge of keeping such credentials. Said entities shall have to inform the person in charge of the processing, without delay, as to the activities carried out. 11. The provisions concerning the authentication system referred to above as well as those concerning the authorisation system shall not apply to the processing of personal data that are intended for dissemination. Authorisation System 12. Where authorisation profiles with different scope have been set out for the persons in charge of the processing, an authorisation system shall be used. 13. Authorisation profiles for each person or homogeneous set of persons in charge of the processing shall be set out and configured prior to start of the processing in such a way as to only enable access to the data that are necessary to perform processing operations. 14. It shall be regularly verified, at least at yearly intervals, that the prerequisites for retaining the relevant authorisation profiles still apply. Other Security Measures 15. Within the framework of the regular update – to be performed at least at yearly intervals – of the specifications concerning the scope of the processing operations that are entrusted to the individual persons in charge of the processing as well as to the technicians responsible for management and/or maintenance of electronic equipment, the list of the persons in charge of the processing may also be drawn up by homogeneous categories of task and corresponding authorisation profile. 16. Personal data shall be protected against the risk of intrusion and the effects of programmes as per Section 615-quinquies of the Criminal Code by implementing suitable electronic means to be updated at least every six months. 17. The regular update of computer programmes as aimed at preventing vulnerability and removing flaws of electronic means shall be carried out at least annually. If sensitive or judicial data are processed, such update shall be carried out at least every six months.

Transposition of Articles 16 and 17 of the Data Protection Directive

Juris-diction	Relevant provision transposing Articles 16 and 17
	18. Organisational and technical instructions shall be issued such as to require at least weekly data back-ups. Security Policy Document 19. By 31 March of each year, the controller of processing operations concerning sensitive and/or judicial data shall draw up, also by the agency of the data processor, if nominated, a security policy document containing appropriate information with regard to: 19.1 the list of processing operations concerning personal data, 19.2 the distribution of tasks and responsibilities among the departments/divisions in charge of processing data, 19.3 an analysis of the risks applying to the data, 19.4 the measures to be taken in order to ensure data integrity and availability as well as protection of areas and premises insofar as they are relevant for the purpose of keeping and accessing such data, 19.5 a description of the criteria and mechanisms to restore data availability following destruction and/or damage as per point 23 below, 19.6 a schedule of training activities concerning the persons in charge of the processing with a view to informing them on the risks applying to the data, the measures that are available to prevent harmful events, the most important features of personal data protection legislation in connection with the relevant activities, the resulting liability and the arrangements to get updated information on the minimum security measures adopted by the data controller. Said training activities shall be planned as of the start of the employment relationship as well as in connection with changes in the task(s) discharged and/or the implementation of new, significant means that are relevant to the processing of personal data, 19.7 a description of the criteria to be implemented in order to ensure adoption of the minimum security measures whenever processing operations concerning personal data are externalised in accordance with the Code, 19.8 as for the personal data disclosing health and sex life referred to under point 24, the specification of the criteria to be implemented in order to either encrypt such data or keep them separate from other personal data concerning the same data subject. Additional Measures Applying to Processing of Sensitive or Judicial Data 20. Sensitive or judicial data shall be protected against unauthorised access as per Section 615-ter of the Criminal Code by implementing suitable electronic means. 21. Organisational and technical instructions shall be issued with regard to keeping and using the removable media on which the data are stored in order to prevent unauthorised access and processing.

Transposition of Articles 16 and 17 of the Data Protection Directive

Juris-diction	Relevant provision transposing Articles 16 and 17
	22. The removable media containing sensitive or judicial data shall be destroyed or made unusable if they are not used; alternatively, they may be re-used by other persons in charge of the processing, who are not authorised to process the same data, if the information previously contained in them is not intelligible and cannot be re-constructed by any technical means. 23. If either the data or electronic means have been damaged, suitable measures shall be adopted to ensure that data access is restored within a specific deadline, which must be compatible with data subjects' rights and not in excess of seven days. 24. Health care bodies and professionals shall process data disclosing health and sex life as contained in lists, registers or data banks in accordance with the mechanisms referred to in Section 22(6) of the Code also in order to ensure that said data are processed separately from the other personal data allowing data subjects to be identified directly. Data concerning genetic identity shall only be processed in protected premises that may only be accessed by such persons in charge of the processing and entities as have been specifically authorised to access them. Containers equipped with locks or equivalent devices shall have to be used in order to remove the data outside the premises reserved for their processing; the data shall have to be encrypted for the purpose of electronically transferring them. Safeguards and Protections 25. Where a data controller adopts minimum security measures by committing the relevant tasks to external entities, prior to implementing such measures he or she shall require the installing technician(s) to supply a written description of the activities performed by which it is certified that they are compliant with the provisions set out in these technical specifications. 26. The circumstance that the security policy document has been drawn up and/or updated shall be referred to in the management report that the data controller may be required to submit together with the relevant balance sheet. *PROCESSING WITHOUT ELECTRONIC MEANS* The following technical arrangements to be implemented by the data controller, data processor – if nominated – and person(s) in charge of the processing whenever data are processed without electronic means: 27. The persons in charge of the processing shall be instructed in writing with regard to controlling and keeping, throughout the steps required to perform processing operations, records and documents containing personal data. Within the framework of the regular update – to be performed at least at yearly intervals – of the

Transposition of Articles 16 and 17 of the Data Protection Directive

Juris-diction	Relevant provision transposing Articles 16 and 17
	specifications concerning the scope of the processing operations that are entrusted to the individual persons in charge of the processing, the list of the persons in charge of the processing may also be drawn up by homogeneous categories of task and corresponding authorisation profile. 28. If records and documents containing sensitive or judicial personal data are entrusted to the persons in charge of the processing for the latter to discharge the relevant tasks, said records and documents shall be kept and controlled by the persons in charge of the processing until they are returned so as to prevent unauthorised entities from accessing them; they shall be returned once the relevant tasks have been discharged. 29. Access to archives containing sensitive or judicial data shall be controlled. The persons authorised to access said archives for whatever purpose after closing time shall be identified and registered. If an archive is not equipped with electronic devices for access control or is not placed under the surveillance of security staff, the persons accessing said archive shall have to be authorised in advance.
Latvia	*Personal Data Protection Law as amended December 2006* Section 14 Paragraph 1 A system administrator may entrust personal data processing to a personal data processor provided a written contract is entered into between them. Paragraph 2 A personal data processor may process personal data entrusted to him or her only within the amount determined in the contract and in conformity with the purposes provided for therein and in accordance with the instructions of the system administrator if they are not in conflict with regulatory enactments. Paragraph 3 Prior to commencing personal data processing, a personal data processor shall perform safety measures determined by the system administrator for the protection of the system in accordance with the requirements of this Law. Section 25 Paragraph 1 A system administrator and personal data processor have a duty to use the necessary technical and organisational measures in order to protect personal data and to prevent their illegal processing. Paragraph 2 A system administrator shall control the form of personal data entered in the personal data processing system and the time of recording and is responsible for the actions of persons who carry out personal data processing.

Transposition of Articles 16 and 17 of the Data Protection Directive

Juris-diction	Relevant provision transposing Articles 16 and 17
	Section 26 Paragraph 1 The mandatory technical and organisational requirements for the protection of personal data processing systems shall be determined by the Cabinet. Paragraph 2 Every year State and local government institutions shall submit to the Data State Inspectorate a personal data processing system internal audit findings (also a system risk analysis) and a report regarding measures performed in the field of information security. Paragraph 3 The Data State Inspectorate in accrediting a person who wishes to perform systems audits in State and local government personal data processing systems shall perform the following in relation to external systems auditors: 1) initial accreditation; 2) repeated accreditation; 3) accreditation for the renewal of activities; 4) extension of the time period of the accreditation; and 5) issuing of duplicates of accreditation certificates. Paragraph 4 For the performance of each of the activities referred to in Paragraph three of this Section, a State fee shall be paid according to the procedures and in the amount specified by the Cabinet. Section 27 Paragraph 1 Natural persons involved in personal data processing shall make a commitment in writing to preserve and not, in an unlawful manner, disclose personal data. Such persons have a duty not to disclose the personal data even after termination of legal employment or other contractually specified relations. Paragraph 2 A system administrator is obliged to record the persons referred to in Paragraph one of this Section. Paragraph 3 When processing personal data, a processor of the personal data shall comply with the instructions of the system administrator.
Lithuania	*Law on Legal Protection of Personal Data* Article 24 Paragraph 1 The data controller and data processor must implement appropriate organizational and technical measures intended for the protection of personal data against any accidental or unlawful destruction, alteration, disclosure as well as against any other unlawful processing. These measures must ensure a level of security

Transposition of Articles 16 and 17 of the Data Protection Directive

Juris-diction	Relevant provision transposing Articles 16 and 17
	appropriate to the nature of the data to be protected and the risks represented by the processing and must be specified in a written document or its equivalent (data processing regulations approved by the data controller, a contract concluded by the data controller and the data processor etc).
	Paragraph 2
	The data controller shall himself process personal data and/or shall authorize the data processor to do so. If the data controller authorizes the data processor to process personal data, he must choose a processor providing guarantees in respect of adequate technical and organizational data protection measures and ensuring compliance with those measures.
	Paragraph 3
	When authorizing the data processor to process personal data, the data controller shall stipulate that personal data must be processed only on instructions from the data controller.
	Paragraph 4
	The relations between the data controller and the data processor who is not the data controller shall be regulated by a written contract except where such relations are provided for by laws or other legal acts.
	Paragraph 5
	The employees of the data controller, the data processor and their representatives who are processing personal data must keep confidentiality of personal data if these personal data are not intended for public disclosure. This obligation shall continue after leaving the public service, transfer to another position or upon termination of employment or contractual relations.
Luxem-bourg	*Data Protection Act (2 August 2002 as amended)* Article 22. Security of processing operations (Law of 27 July 2007) (1) The controller must implement all appropriate technical and organisational measures to ensure the protection of the data he processes against accidental or unlawful destruction or accidental loss, falsification, unauthorised dissemination or access, in particular where the processing involves the transmission of data over a network, and against all other unlawful forms of processing. "A description of these measures and of any subsequent major change must be communicated to the Commission Nationale at its request, within fifteen days." (2) If the processing is carried out on behalf of the controller, the latter must choose a processor that provides sufficient guarantees as regards the technical and organisational security measures pertaining to the processing to be carried out. It is up to the controller as well as the processor to ensure that the said measures are respected.

Transposition of Articles 16 and 17 of the Data Protection Directive

Juris-diction	Relevant provision transposing Articles 16 and 17
	(3) Any processing carried out on another's behalf must be governed by a written contract or legal instrument binding the processor to the controller and providing in particular that: (a) the processor will act only on instructions from the controller, and (b) the obligations referred to in this Article will be also incumbent on the latter. Article 23. Special security measures Depending on the risk of the breach of privacy, as well as the state of the art and the costs associated with their implementation, the measures referred to in Article 22, paragraph (1) must: (a) prevent any unauthorised person from accessing the facilities used for data processing (monitoring of entry to facilities); (b) prevent data media from being read, copied, amended or moved by any authorised persons (monitoring of media); (c) prevent the unauthorised introduction of any data into the information system, as well as any unauthorised knowledge, amendment or deletion of the recorded data (monitoring of memory); (d) prevent data processing systems from being used by unauthorised person using data transmission facilities (monitoring of usage); (e) guarantee that authorised persons when using an automated data processing system may access only data that are within their competence (monitoring of access); (f) guarantee the checking and recording of the identity of third parties to whom the data can be transmitted by transmission facilities (monitoring of transmission); (g) guarantee that the identity of the persons having had access to the information system and the data introduced into the system can be checked and recorded ex post facto at any time and by any person (monitoring of introduction); (h) prevent data from being read, copied, amended or deleted in an unauthorised manner when data are disclosed and data media transported (monitoring of transport); (i) safeguard data by creating backup copies (monitoring of availability).
Malta	*Data Protection Act* Article 25 Paragraph 1 Any person acting under the authority of the controller or of the processor, including the processor himself, who has access to personal data may only process personal data in accordance with instructions from the controller unless the person is otherwise required to do so by law.

Transposition of Articles 16 and 17 of the Data Protection Directive

Juris-diction	Relevant provision transposing Articles 16 and 17
	Paragraph 2 The carrying out of processing by way of a processor is to be governed by a contract or other legally binding instrument in a written or in an equivalent form binding the processor to the controller and stipulating in particular that the processor: (a) shall act only on instructions from the controller; (b) shall take those measures referred to in article 26(1). Article 26 Paragraph 1 The controller shall implement appropriate technical and organisational measures to protect the personal data that is processed against accidental destruction or loss or unlawful forms of processing thereby providing an adequate level of security that gives regard to the: (a) technical possibilities available; (b) cost of implementing the security measures; (c) special risks that exist in the processing of personal data; (d) sensitivity of the personal data being processed. Paragraph 2 If the controller engages a processor, the controller shall ensure that the processor: (a) can implement the security measures that must be taken; (b) actually takes the measures so identified by the controller.
The Netherlands	*Personal Data Protection Act of 6 July 2000, containing rules regarding the protection of personal data (Dutch Personal Data Protection Act) as amended* Article 13 The responsible party shall implement appropriate technical and organizational measures to secure personal data against loss or against any form of unlawful processing. These measures shall guarantee an appropriate level of security, taking into account the state of the art and the costs of implementation, and having regard to the risks associated with the processing and the nature of the data to be protected. These measures shall also aim at preventing unnecessary collection and further processing of personal data. Article 14 Paragraph 1 Where responsible parties have personal data processed for the purposes by a processor, these responsible parties shall make sure that the processor provides adequate guarantees concerning the technical and organizational security measures for the processing to be carried out. The responsible parties shall make sure that these measures are complied with.

Transposition of Articles 16 and 17 of the Data Protection Directive

Juris-diction	Relevant provision transposing Articles 16 and 17
	Paragraph 2 The carrying out of processing by a processor shall be governed by an agreement or another legal act whereby an obligation is created between the processor and the responsible party. Paragraph 3 The responsible party shall make sure that the processor: (a) processes the personal data in accordance with Article 12(l) and (b) complies with the obligations incumbent upon the responsible party under Article 13. Paragraph 4 Where the processor is established in another country of the European Union, the responsible party shall make sure that the processor complies with the laws of that other country, notwithstanding the provisions of (3)(b). Paragraph 5 With a view to the keeping of proof, the parties of the agreement or legal act relating to personal data protection and the security measures referred to in Article 13, shall be set down in writing or in another equivalent form.
Poland	*Act of 29 August 1997 on the Protection of Personal Data* Article 31 Paragraph 1 The controller may authorise another subject to carry out the processing of personal data pursuant to a contract concluded in writing. Paragraph 2 The subject, referred to in paragraph 1 above, may process the data solely within the scope and for the purpose determined in the contract. Paragraph 3 The subject, referred to in paragraph 1, prior to processing the data shall be obliged to provide security measures protecting the data filing system, as defined in Article 36 – 39, and to meet the requirements specified in the provisions referred to in Article 39a. With regard to the observance of these provisions the data subject shall bear the liability as the controller. Paragraph 4 In cases referred to in paragraphs 1 to 3, the liability for compliance with the provisions hereof shall remain with the controller, whereas the contracting party shall not be exempted from the liability in case the data are processed in a way incompatible with the contract. Paragraph 5 The provisions of Articles 14 – 19 shall apply respectively to supervision over ensuring the compliance of data processing conducted by the subject referred to in paragraph 1 with the provisions on the protection of personal data.

533

Transposition of Articles 16 and 17 of the Data Protection Directive

Juris-diction	Relevant provision transposing Articles 16 and 17
	Article 36 Paragraph 1 The controller shall be obliged to implement technical and organisational measures to protect the personal data being processed, appropriate to the risks and category of data being protected, and in particular to protect data against their unauthorised disclosure, takeover by an unauthorised person, processing with the violation of the Act, any change, loss, damage or destruction. Paragraph 2 The controller shall keep the documentation describing the way of data processing and measures referred to in paragraph 1. Paragraph 3 The controller shall appoint an administrator of information security who supervises the compliance with security principles referred to in paragraph 1, unless the controller performs these activities by himself.
Portugal	*Data Protection Act (26 October 1998 no. 67)* Article 14 – Security of processing Paragraph 1 The controller must implement appropriate technical and organisational measures to protect personal data against accidental or unlawful destruction or accidental loss, alteration, unauthorised disclosure or access, in particular where the processing involves the transmission of data over a network, and against all other unlawful forms of processing. Having regard to the state of the art and the cost of their implementation, such measures shall ensure a level of security appropriate to the risks represented by the processing and the nature of the data to be protected. Paragraph 2 Where processing is carried out on his behalf the controller must choose a processor providing sufficient guarantees in respect of the technical security measures and organisational measures governing the processing to be carried out, and must ensure compliance with those measures. Paragraph 3 The carrying out of processing by way of a processor must be governed by a contract or legal act binding the processor to the controller and stipulating in particular that the processor shall act only on instructions from the controller and that the obligations referred to in 1 shall also be incumbent on the processor. Paragraph 4 Proof of the will to negotiate, the contract or the legal act relating to data protection and the requirements relating to the measures referred to in 1 shall be in writing in a supporting document legally certified as affording proof.

Transposition of Articles 16 and 17 of the Data Protection Directive

Juris-diction	Relevant provision transposing Articles 16 and 17
	Article 15 – Special security measures Paragraph 1 The controllers of the data referred to in Articles 7 (2) and Article 8 shall take appropriate measures to: a) prevent unauthorised persons from entering the premises used for processing such data (control of entry to the premises); b) prevent data media from being read, copied, altered or removed by unauthorised persons (control of data media); c) prevent unauthorised input and unauthorised obtaining of knowledge, alteration or elimination of personal data input (control of input); d) prevent automatic data processing systems from being used by unauthorised persons by means of data transmission premises (control of use); e) guarantee that authorised persons may only access data covered by the authorisation (control of access); f) guarantee the checking of the bodies to whom personal data may be transmitted by means of data transmission premises (control of transmission); g) guarantee that it is possible to check a posteriori, in a period appropriate to the nature of the processing, the establishment in the regulations applicable to each sector of which personal data are input, when and by whom (control of input); h) in transmitting personal data and in transporting the respective media, prevent unauthorised reading, copying, alteration or elimination of data (control of transport). Paragraph 2 Taking account of the nature of the bodies responsible for processing and the type of premises in which it is carried out, the CNPD may waive the existence of certain security measures, subject to guaranteeing respect for the fundamental rights, freedoms and guarantees of the data subjects. Paragraph 3 The systems must guarantee logical separation between data relating to health and sex life, including genetic data, and other personal data. Paragraph 4 Where circulation over a network of the data referred to in articles 7 and 8 may jeopardise the fundamental rights, freedoms and guarantees of their data subjects the CNPD may determine that transmission must be encoded. Article 16 – Processing by a processor Any person acting under the authority of the controller or the processor, including the processor himself, who has access to personal data must not process them except on instructions from the controller, unless he is required to do so by law.

Transposition of Articles 16 and 17 of the Data Protection Directive

Juris-diction	Relevant provision transposing Articles 16 and 17
	Article 17 – Professional secrecy Paragraph 1 Controllers and persons who obtain knowledge of the personal data processed in carrying out their functions shall be bound by professional secrecy, even after their functions have ended. Paragraph 2 Members of the CNPD shall be subject to the same obligation, even after their mandate has ended. Paragraph 3 The provision in the previous numbers shall not exclude the duty to supply the obligatory information according to the law, except when it is contained in filing systems organised for statistical purposes. Paragraph 4 Officers, agents or staff who act as consultants for the CNPD or its members shall be subject to the same obligation of professional secrecy.
Romania	*Law no. 677/2001 for the Protection of Persons concerning the Processing of Personal Data and Free Circulation of Such Data* Article 19: Confidentiality of Data Processing Any person who acts under the authority of the data controller or of the data processor, including the data processor, who has access to personal data, may process them only in accordance with the data controller's specific instructions, except when the above-mentioned person's actions are based on a legal obligation. Article 20: Security of Data Processing (1) It is the data controller's obligation to apply the adequate technical and organizational measures in order to protect the data against accidental or unlawful destruction, loss, alteration, disclosure or unauthorized access, notably if the respective processing involves the data's transmission within a network, as well as against any other form of illegal processing. (2) These measures shall ensure, depending on the state of the art techniques employed and the costs, adequate security against processing risks as well as observing the nature of the data that must be protected. The minimum security requirements shall be issued by the supervisory authority and shall be periodically updated, according to the technological progress and the accumulated experience. (3) When appointing a data processor, the data controller has the obligation to assign a person who presents sufficient guarantees regarding technical security and the organizational measures concerning the data to be processed, as well as the obligation to ensure that the assigned person complies with these measures.

Transposition of Articles 16 and 17 of the Data Protection Directive

Juris-diction	Relevant provision transposing Articles 16 and 17
	(4) The supervisory authority may decide, in individual cases, that the data controller should adopt additional security measures, except such measures that regard the guaranteed security of telecommunication services. (5) Data processing performed by an appointed data processor shall be initiated following a written contract which should necessarily contain the following: a) the processor's obligation to act strictly in accordance with the instructions received from the data controller; b) the fact that accomplishing the obligations set out in paragraph (1) also applies to the data processor.
Slovak Republic	*Act on Protection of Personal Data as amended (3 July 2002 no. 428)* Section 15 Paragraph 1 The controller and the processor shall be responsible for security of personal data by protecting them against accidental or unlawful damage or destruction, accidental loss, alteration, unauthorized access and making available, as well as against any other unauthorized forms of processing. For this purpose he shall take due technical, organisational and personal measures adequate to the manner of processing, while he shall take into account above all (a) the existing technical means, (b) the extent of possible risk that could violate security or functionality of the filing system, (c) confidentiality and importance of the processed personal data. Paragraph 2 The controller and the processor shall take the measures under Paragraph 1 in the form of a security project of the filing system (hereinafter the "Security Project") and they shall provide its development if (a) special categories of personal data under Section 8 are processed in the filing system and the filing system is interconnected with a publicly accessible computer network or it is operated in a computer network interconnected with a publicly accessible computer network, (b) special categories of personal data under Section 8 are processed in the filing system; in such case the controller and the processor shall only document the taken technical, organisational and personal measures in the extent stipulated by Section 16 Paragraph 3 subparagraph (c) and paragraph 6, or (c) the filing system is used for safeguarding the public interest under Section 2 Paragraph 1; the provision of Section 16 shall not apply to development of the Security Project only provided that an obligation to elaborate a Security Project pursuant to a special Act [Act no. 215/2004 Coll] simultaneously applies to the respective case.

Transposition of Articles 16 and 17 of the Data Protection Directive

Juris-diction	Relevant provision transposing Articles 16 and 17
	Paragraph 3 Upon request of the Office the controller and the processor shall prove the extent and contents of the taken technical, organisational and personal measures under Paragraph 1 or 2. Paragraph 4 If the subject of the inspection is constituted by the filing systems under Paragraph 2, the Office shall be entitled to request the controller or the processor for submittal or an evaluation report on the outcome of an audit of the filing system's security (hereinafter the 'evaluation report'), provided that there are serious doubts about its security or about practical implementation of the measures referred to in the Security Project. The controller or the processor shall submit the evaluation report, not older than two years, to the Office without undue delay, otherwise he shall provide performance of an audit of the filing system's security at his own expense and submit an evaluation report within three months from the day of the obligation's imposition. Paragraph 5 The audit of the filing system's security may only be performed by an external, professionally qualified legal or natural person, who did not participate in development of the Security Project of the respective filing system and there are no doubts about its impartiality. Section 16 Security Project Paragraph 1 The Security Project shall define the extent and manner of the technical, organisational and personal measure necessary for elimination and minimizing of the threats and risks affecting the filing system from the viewpoint of impairing its security, reliability and functionality. Paragraph 2 The Security Project shall be developed in accordance with the basic rules of filing system's security, the issued security standards, legal regulations and international treaties binding for the Slovak Republic. Paragraph 3 The Security Project shall include above all a) a security policy, b) analysis of the filing system's security, c) security directives. Paragraph 4 The security policy shall specify the basic security objectives that must be achieved for protection of the filing system against violation of its security and it shall contain above all a) specification of the basic security objectives and the minimum required security measures,

Juris-diction	Relevant provision transposing Articles 16 and 17
	b) specification of the technical, organisational and personal measures for ensuring protection of personal data in the filing system and the manner of their use, c) definition of the filing system's environment and its relation to the possible security violation, d) definition of the limits determining residual risks. Paragraph 5 Analysis of the filing system's security shall mean a detailed analysis of the state of the filing system's security containing above all a) qualitative risk analysis, within which the threats affecting individual items of the filing system capable of violating its security or functionality are identified; the result of the qualitative risk analysis shall be a list of threats that could endanger confidentiality, integrity and availability of the processed personal data, while it shall also state the extent of the possible risk, proposals of the measures eliminating or minimizing the affect of the risk and a list of the remaining risks, b) use of security standards and determination of other methods and means of the protection of personal data; evaluation of conformity of the proposed security measures with the applied security standards, methods and means shall constitute a part of the analysis of the filing system's security. Paragraph 6 Security directives shall specify and apply the conclusions resulting from the Security Project to the concrete conditions of the operated filing system and they shall include above all a) description of the technical, organisational and personal measures defined in the Security Project and their use in concrete conditions, b) the scope of powers and description of the permitted activities of individual entitled persons, the manner of the identification and authentication in accessing the filing system, c) the scope of liability of entitled persons and of the personal data protection official (Section 19), d) the manner, form and periodicity of performance of the inspection activities focused on observation of the filing system's security, e) procedures during breakdowns, failures and other extraordinary situations including preventive measures for restricting the occurrence of extraordinary situations and possibilities of an effective restoration of the state before the breakdown. Section 17 The controller or the processor shall be obliged to advise the entitled persons on the rights and obligations stipulated by this Act and on the liability for their breach. The controller or the processor shall advise on the above before giving the first instruction to the entitled person to perform any processing operation with the personal data. The entitled person shall confirm the advice by his signature; the controller or the processor shall make a written record of the advice.

Transposition of Articles 16 and 17 of the Data Protection Directive

Juris-diction	Relevant provision transposing Articles 16 and 17
	Section 18 Paragraph 1 The controller and the processor shall be obliged to maintain secrecy about the personal data which they process. The obligation to maintain secrecy also applies after termination of the processing. The obligation to maintain secrecy shall not apply to them if pursuant to a special Act it is necessary for fulfilment of the tasks of the law enforcement agencies; this shall not affect provisions of special Acts.[1] Paragraph 2 The entitled person shall be obliged to maintain secrecy about the personal data which he comes across; he must not use them even for his personal needs and he must not make them public, provide them or make them available to anybody without consent of the controller. Paragraph 3 The obligation to maintain secrecy under Paragraph 2 shall also apply to other natural persons, who come across the personal data at the controller's or processor's place within the framework of their activities (e.g. maintenance and service of the technical means). Paragraph 4 The obligation to maintain secrecy under Paragraph 2 shall also apply after termination of the function of the entitled person or after termination of his employment relationship or similar labour relation, as well as the civil service employment relationship or the relation under Paragraph 3. Paragraph 5 Paragraphs 1 to 4 and the obligation to maintain secrecy imposed on controllers, processors and entitled persons pursuant to special regulations shall not apply in respect of the Office in the course of fulfilment of its task (Sections 38 to 44).[2]

[1] E.g. Section 40 of the Act of the National Council of the Slovak Republic No. 566/1992 Coll. on National Bank of Slovakia, as amended by the Act No. 149/2001 Coll.

[2] E.g. Section 6 Paragraph 1 of the Act No. 150/2001 Coll. on Tax Authorities and on Changing and Amending of the Act No. 440/2000 Coll. on Reports of Financial Control, Section 14 of the Act No. 330/2000 Coll. on Security Exchange, Section 134 of the Act No. 566/2001 Coll. on Securities and Investment Services and on Changing and Amending of Some Acts (Securities Act), Sections 91 to 93 of the Act No. 483/2001 Coll. on Banks and on Changing and Amending of Some Acts, Section 24 of the Act No. 24/1991 Coll. on Insurance Business, as amended, Section 81 e) and Section 240 Paragraph 5 of the Act No. 311/2001 Coll. Labour Code, Section 53 Paragraph 1 Subparagraph e) of the Act No. 312/2001 Coll. on Civil Service and on Changing and Amending of Some Acts, Section 9 Paragraph 2 Subparagraph b) of the Act No. 313/2001 Coll. on Public Service, Section 8 of the Act No. 367/2000 Coll., Section 80 of the Act of the National Council of the Slovak Republic No. 171/1993., as amended, Section 15 Paragraphs 2 and 3 of the Act of the National Council of the Slovak Republic No. 38/1993 Coll. on Organisation of the Constitutional Court of the Slovak Republic, on Proceedings before It and on Status of Its Judges.

Transposition of Articles 16 and 17 of the Data Protection Directive

Juris-diction	Relevant provision transposing Articles 16 and 17
Slovenia	*Personal Data Protection Act 2004* Article 24 Paragraph 1 Security of personal data comprises organisational, technical and logical-technical procedures and measures to protect personal data, and to prevent accidental or deliberate unauthorised destruction, modification or loss of data, and unauthorised processing of such data: (1) by processing premises, equipment and systems software, including input-output units; (2) by protecting software applications used to process personal data; (3) by preventing unauthorised access to personal data during transmission thereof, including transmission via telecommunications means and networks; (4) by ensuring effective methods of blocking, destruction, deletion or anonymisation of personal data; (5) by enabling subsequent determination of when individual personal data were entered into a filing system, used or otherwise processed, and who did so, for the period covered by statutory protection of the rights of an individual due to unauthorised supply or processing of personal data. Paragraph 2 In cases of processing of personal data accessible over telecommunications means or network, the hardware, systems software and software applications must ensure that the processing of personal data in filing systems is within the limits of authorisations of the data recipient. Paragraph 3 The procedures and measures to protect personal data must be adequate in view of the risk posed by processing and the nature of the specific personal data being processed. Paragraph 4 Functionaries, employees and other individuals performing work or tasks at persons that process personal data shall be bound to protect the secrecy of personal data with which they become familiar in performing their functions, work and tasks. The duty to protect the secrecy of personal data shall also be binding on them after termination of their function, work or tasks, or the performance of contractual processing services. Article 25 Paragraph 1 Data controllers and data processors shall be bound to ensure the protection of personal data in the manner set out in Article 24 of this Act.

Transposition of Articles 16 and 17 of the Data Protection Directive

Juris-diction	Relevant provision transposing Articles 16 and 17
	Paragraph 2 Data controllers shall prescribe in their internal acts the procedures and measures for security of personal data and shall define the persons responsible for individual filing systems and the persons who, due to the nature of their work, shall process individual personal data.
Spain	*Organic Law 15/1999 of 13 December on the Protection of Personal Data* Article 9 Paragraph 1 The controller or, where applicable, the processor shall adopt the technical and organisational measures necessary to ensure the security of the personal data and prevent their alteration, loss, unauthorised processing or access, having regard to the state of the art, the nature of the data stored and the risks to which they are exposed by virtue of human action or the physical or natural environment. Paragraph 2 No personal data shall be recorded in files which do not meet the conditions laid down by rules regarding their integrity and security, as well as the rules governing the processing centres, premises, equipment, systems and programs. Paragraph 3 Rules shall be laid down governing the requirements and conditions to be met by the files and the persons involved in the data processing referred to in Article 7 of this Law. Royal Decree 1720/2007 of 21 December which approves the regulation implementing Organic Law 15/1999 of 13 December on the Protection of Personal Data *Title VIII: Regarding security measures in the processing of personal data* CHAPTER I: GENERAL PROVISIONS Article 79 Data controllers and data processors shall implement the security measures pursuant to the provisions of this Title, whatever may be the system of processing. Article 80 There are three levels of applicable security measures for files and processing: basic, medium and high. Article 81 1. All files or processing of personal data shall adopt the basic-level security measures. 2. The following files or processing of personal data shall also implement medium-level security measures, in addition to the basic-level security measures: a) Those relating to criminal or administrative offences;

Transposition of Articles 16 and 17 of the Data Protection Directive

Juris-diction	Relevant provision transposing Articles 16 and 17
	b) Those whose operation is subject to Article 29 of Organic Law 15/1999, of 13 December;
	c) Those controlled by the tax administrations and relating to the exercise of the powers of taxation;
	d) Those controlled by financial institutions for purposes related to the provision of financial services;
	e) Those controlled by the Management Agencies and Common Services of the Social Security and relating to the exercise of their powers. Similarly, those controlled by the Mutual Funds for accidents at work and occupational illness associated with the Social Security;
	f) Those containing a set of personal data that provide a definition of the characteristics or identity of citizens and which permit the evaluation of specific aspects of their identity or behaviour.
	3. The following files or processing of personal data shall also implement high-level security measures, in addition to the basic- and medium-level measures:
	a) Those referring to data on ideology, trade union membership, religion, beliefs, racial origin, health or sex life;
	b) Those containing or referring to data collected for security forces without the consent of the data subjects;
	c) Those concerning data arising from acts of gender-based violence.
	4. As well as the basic- and medium-level security measures, the high-level security measure contained in Article 103 hereof shall be applied to files controlled by operators providing electronic communications services to the public or that exploit public electronic communications networks with regard to traffic and location data.
	5. The implementation of basic-level security measure shall be sufficient for files or processing or data on ideology, trade union membership, religion, beliefs, racial origin, health or sex life if:
	a) The data are used for the sole purpose of carrying out a monetary transfer to organisations to which the data subjects are associated or are members of;
	b) Regarding non-automated files or processing that incidentally contain such data that have no relation with its purpose.
	6. Basic-level security measures may also be implemented in the files or processing that contain data relating to health, referring exclusively to the degree of disability or the simple declaration of the condition of disability of the data subject, for the purpose of fulfilling public duties.
	7. The measures included in each of the aforesaid levels are the minimum that can be applied, without prejudice to the current specific regulations or legal provisions that may be applicable in each case or those adopted on the initiative of the data controller.

Transposition of Articles 16 and 17 of the Data Protection Directive

Juris-diction	Relevant provision transposing Articles 16 and 17
	8. For the purposes of facilitating compliance with the provisions herein, when an information system has files or processing that, depending on their specific purpose or use, or on the nature of the data they contain, require the application of a level of security measures different to that of the main system, they may be separated from the latter, with the relevant level of security measures being applicable in each case and whenever the relevant data and users with access to them can be delimited, and this is recorded in the security document. Article 82 1. When the data controller provides access to the data, to the supports that contain them or to the resources of the information system that processes them, for a data processor providing his services on the premises of the data controller this shall be recorded in the security document of the latter. The staff of the data processor shall commit themselves to the fulfilment of the security measures set out therein. 2. If the service is provided by the data processor on his own premises, outside those of the data controller, he shall draw up a security document under the terms required by Article 88 hereof or complete that already drafted, if appropriate, identifying the fling system or processing and the data controller and including the security measures that are to be implemented in relation to such processing. 3. In any case, access to the data by the data processor shall be subject to the security measures set out herein. Article 83 The data controller shall adopt the adequate measures to limit access of staff to personal data, to the supports that contain them or to the resources of the information system, for the execution of tasks that do not involve the processing of personal data. With regard to external personnel, the service provision contract shall expressly record the prohibition of access to the personal data and the obligation of confidentiality regarding the data that personnel may become aware of due to provision of the service. Article 84 The authorisations in this Title that are attributed to the data controller may be delegated to the persons designated for this purpose. The security document shall record the persons able to grant such authorisations as well as those who are delegated. Under no circumstances shall such delegation imply a delegation of the liability corresponding to the data controller. Article 85 The applicable security measures for the access to personal data through communications networks, whether public or not, shall guarantee a level of security equivalent to that applicable to local access, pursuant to the criteria established in Article 80.

Transposition of Articles 16 and 17 of the Data Protection Directive

Juris-diction	Relevant provision transposing Articles 16 and 17
	Article 86 1. When the personal data are stored in portable devices or are processed outside the premises of the data controller or the data processor, the data controller shall necessarily give his prior authorisation, and in any case shall guarantee the level of security relevant to the type of file processed. 2. The authorisation to which the previous paragraph refers shall be recorded in the security document and may be established for a user or for a user profile and shall set out the duration of its validity. Article 87 1. Temporary filing systems or copies of documents that have been created exclusively for the execution of temporary or auxiliary tasks shall comply with the relevant level of security pursuant to the criteria established in Article 81. 2. All temporary filing systems or working copies thus created shall be erased or destroyed once they are no longer necessary for the purposes for which they were created. CHAPTER II: SECURITY DOCUMENT Article 88 1. The data controller shall draw up a security document including the technical and organisational measures according to current legislation on security that shall be binding on the personnel with access to the information systems. 2. The security document shall be of general application to all the filing systems or processing, or individual for each filing system or processing. Different security documents may be drawn up grouping filing systems or processing according to the processing system used for their organisation, or bearing in mind the organisational criteria of the data controller. In any case, it shall be considered an internal document of the organisation. 3. The document shall contain, at least, the following aspects: a) Scope of application of the document with detailed specifications of the protected resources; b) Measures, regulations, protocols for action, rules and standards aimed at guaranteeing the level of security required herein; c) Tasks and obligations of the staff in relation to the processing of personal data included in the filing system; d) Structure of the filing systems with personal data and description of the information systems that process them; e) Procedure of notification, management and response to incidents; f) The procedures for making backup copies and recovery of the data in the automated filing systems or processing; g) The measures that shall necessarily be adopted for the transport of the supports or documents, as well as for their destruction, or if appropriate, their re-use.

Transposition of Articles 16 and 17 of the Data Protection Directive

Juris- diction	Relevant provision transposing Articles 16 and 17
	4. In the event of the medium- or high-level security measures provided in this Title being applicable to the filing systems, the security document shall also contain: a) The identification of the data controller(s); b) The monitoring that shall be carried out from time to time to verify fulfilment of that provided therein. 5. In the event of data processing by third parties, the security document shall contain the identification of the files or processing that have been commissioned with express reference to the contract or document regulating the conditions of the commission, as well as the identification of the data controller and the duration of validity of the commission. 6. In those cases where the personal data of a filing system or processing are included and processed exclusively in the systems of the data processor, the data controller shall record this in the security document. When this affects part or all of the filing systems or processing of the data controller, he shall delegate the security document to the data processor, with the exception of that relating to the data contained in his own resources. This fact shall be expressly indicated in the contract executed under Article 12 of Organic Law 15/1999, of 13 December, specifying the affected files or processing. In this case, reference shall be made to the security document of the data processor for the purpose of fulfilment of that provided herein. 7. The security document shall be kept up-to-date at all times and shall be reviewed whenever any material changes are made to the information system, the processing system used, its organisation, the contents of the information included in the filing systems or processing or, if appropriate, as a result of the periodic monitoring. In any case, a change shall be deemed material when it may have repercussions on the fulfilment of the implemented security measures. 8. The content of the security document shall be adapted, at all times, to the current provisions of the security of personal data. CHAPTER III: SECURITY MEASURES APPLICABLE TO AUTOMATED FILING SYSTEMS AND PROCESSING Section One: Basic-level security measures Article 89 1. The functions and obligations of each of the users or profiles of users with access to the personal data and to the information systems shall be clearly defined and documented in the security document. The monitoring functions or authorisations delegated by the data controller of the filing system or processing shall also be defined.

Transposition of Articles 16 and 17 of the Data Protection Directive

Juris-diction	Relevant provision transposing Articles 16 and 17
	2. The data controller shall adopt the necessary measures so that the staff members understand the security regulations that affect the performance of their functions as well as the consequences that may arise in the event of non-performance. Article 90 There shall be a procedure for notification and management of incidents that affect personal data and a register established for recording the type of incident, the moment it occurred, or if appropriate, was detected, the person making the notification, to whom it was communicated, the effect arising from it and the corrective measures applied. Article 91 1. The users shall only have access to those resources required for the performance of their functions. 2. The data controller shall ensure there is an updated list of users and user profiles, and the authorised accesses for each one. 3. The data controller shall establish mechanisms to avoid a user being able to access resources with rights other than those authorised. 4. Only staff members authorised in the security document shall grant, alter or annul the access authorised to resources, pursuant to the criteria established by the data controller. 5. Should personnel not pertaining to the data controller have access to the resources they shall be subject to the same security conditions and obligations as the internal personnel. Article 92 1. The supports and documents containing personal data shall permit identification of the type of information they contain, allow an inventory to be taken and shall only be accessible by the personnel authorised in the security document. An exception to these obligations shall be made when the physical characteristics of the support makes their fulfilment impossible, a record justifying this fact being made in the security document. 2. The departure of supports and documents containing personal data, including those comprising and/or attached to e-mails, outside the premises under the control of the data controller shall be authorised by the data controller or be duly authorised in the security document. 3. Measures aimed at avoiding the theft, loss or unauthorised access to the information during transport shall be taken in the transfer of documentation. 4. Any document or support containing personal data that is to be discarded shall always be erased or destroyed, by taking measures aimed at avoiding access to the information contained therein or its later recovery.

Transposition of Articles 16 and 17 of the Data Protection Directive

Juris- diction	Relevant provision transposing Articles 16 and 17
	5. The identification of the supports containing personal data that the organisation deems particularly sensitive may be made using logical labelling systems permitting authorised users of such supports and documents to identify their content, and making identification difficult for anyone else not so authorised. Article 93 1. The data controller shall take the measures that guarantee the correct identification and authentication of the users. 2. The data controller shall establish a mechanism that permits the unequivocal and personalised identification of any user who tries to access the information system and the verification of his authorisation. 3. When the authentication mechanism is based on the existence of passwords there shall be a procedure of disclosure, distribution and storage guaranteeing their confidentiality and integrity. 4. The security document shall establish the frequency, which under no circumstances shall be less than yearly, with which the passwords shall be changed. Whilst in force, passwords shall be stored in an unintelligible way. Article 94 1. Protocols for action shall be established for making weekly backup copies, at least, unless data have been updated during that time. 2. Similarly, procedures for the recovery of data shall be established to guarantee at all times their reconstruction to the original state at the moment the loss or destruction occurred. Manual recording of the data shall only be done when the loss or destruction affects partially automated filing systems or processing, and whenever the existence of documentation allows for the objective to be met to which the previous paragraph refers; a justified record of this fact being made in the security document. 3. The data controller shall ensure verification every six months of the correct definition, operation and application of the procedures for making backup copies and for the recovery of data. 4. The tests prior to the implementation or amendment of the information systems the process filing systems with personal data shall not be done with real data, unless the relevant level of security for the processing is ensured and it is recorded in the security document. If tests are to be done with real data, a backup copy shall be made first. Section Two: Medium-level security measures Article 95 The security document shall appoint one or several security officers commissioned with co-ordinating and monitoring the measures defined therein. This appointment may be general for all the filing systems or processing of personal data or specific depending on the information systems used, which shall be clearly recorded in the security document.

Transposition of Articles 16 and 17 of the Data Protection Directive

Juris-diction	Relevant provision transposing Articles 16 and 17
	Under no circumstances shall this designation imply an exemption of the liability corresponding to the data controller or data processor pursuant to this Regulation. Article 96 1. At the medium and higher levels the information systems and processing and data storage installations shall be subject, at least every two years, to an internal or external audit that verifies compliance with this Title. In extraordinary circumstances the audit shall be done whenever substantial amendments to the information system are made that may have repercussions in the fulfilment of the implemented security measures for the purpose of verifying their adaptation, adjustment and efficiency. This audit starts the calculation of the aforesaid two years. 2. The audit report shall report on the adaptation of the measures and monitoring to the Law and its regulations, identifying deficiencies and proposing the necessary corrective or complementary measures. It shall also include the data, facts and observations on which the reports are based and recommendations proposed. 3. The audit reports shall be analysed by the competent security officer, who shall inform the data controller of the conclusions so he may take the adequate corrective measures and they shall be made available to the Spanish Data Protection Agency or, if appropriate, the supervisory authorities of the Autonomous Communities. Article 97 1. A registration system for the entry of supports shall be established permitting, directly or indirectly, the type of document or support to be known, as well as the date and time, the issuer, the number of documents or supports included in the despatch, the type of information they contain, the method of despatch and the person responsible for receipt, who shall be duly authorised. 2. Similarly, a registration system for the departure of supports shall be provided permitting, directly or indirectly, the type of document or support to be known, as well as the date and time, the recipient, the number of documents or supports included in the despatch, the type of information they contain, the method of despatch and the person responsible for delivery, who shall be duly authorised. Article 98 The data controller shall establish a mechanism to limit the possibility of repeated attempts of unauthorised access to the information systems. Article 99 Only the personnel authorised in the security document shall have access to the places housing the physical equipment that supports the information systems.

Transposition of Articles 16 and 17 of the Data Protection Directive

Juris-diction	Relevant provision transposing Articles 16 and 17
	Article 100 1. The register regulated in Article 90 shall also provide the procedures for the recovery of data, indicating the person who executed the process, the data restored and, if appropriate, which data have had to be manually recorded in the recovery process. 2. Authorisation of the data controller shall be necessary for the execution of the data recovery procedures. Section Three: High-level security measures Article 101 1. The identification of the supports shall be done using logical labelling systems allowing users with authorised access to such supports and documents to identify their contents, and making identification difficult for everyone else. 2. The distribution of supports containing personal data shall be done encoding such data or using another mechanism that guarantees that such information is not accessible or manipulated during transport. Similarly, the data contained in portable devices shall be encoded when they are outside the installations of the data controller. 3. The processing of personal data in portable devices that do not permit encoding shall be avoided. Should it be strictly necessary it shall be recorded with the justification in the security document and measures shall be taken bearing in mind the risks of processing in unprotected environments. Article 102 A backup copy of the data and of their recovery procedures shall be kept in a different place to that housing the computer equipment that processes them, which shall in any case comply with the security measures required herein, or use elements that guarantee the integrity and recovery of the information, so that their recovery is possible. Article 103 1. For each attempt at access at least the following shall be stored: identification of the user, the date and time it was done, the filing system accessed, the type of access and whether it has been authorised or denied. 2. Should access be authorised, it shall be necessary to store the information allowing the accessed register to be identified. 3. The mechanisms that permit the register of accesses shall be under the direct control of the competent security officer and shall not permit their deactivation or manipulation. 4. The minimum period for storing the registered data shall be two years. 5. The security officer shall review the registered monitoring information at least once a month and shall draft a report of the revisions and the problems detected.

Transposition of Articles 16 and 17 of the Data Protection Directive

Juris-diction	Relevant provision transposing Articles 16 and 17
	6. The registration of accesses defined herein shall not be necessary when the following circumstances concur: a) The data controller is a natural person; b) The data controller guarantees that only he has access and processes the personal data. The concurrence of these aforesaid circumstances shall be expressly recorded in the security document. Article 104 When, pursuant to Article 81.3, the high-level security measures must be implemented, the transfer of personal data through public or wireless electronic communications networks shall be done encoding such data or using any other mechanism that guarantees the information shall not be intelligible or manipulated by third parties. CHAPTER IV: SECURITY MEASURES APPLICABLE TO NON-AUTOMATED FILING SYSTEMS AND PROCESSING Article 105 1. In addition to the provisions of this Chapter, the provisions of Chapters I and II of this Title shall be applicable to non-automated files relating to: a) Scope b) Levels of security c) The data processor d) Provisions of services without access to personal data e) Delegation of authorisations f) Working procedure outside the premises of the data controller or data processor g) Working copies of documents h) The security document. 2. The provisions established in section one of Chapter III of this Title shall also be applicable relating to: a) Functions and obligations of staff members b) Register of incidents c) Control of access d) Management of supports. Article 106 The filing of supports or documents shall be done pursuant to the criteria set out in the respective legislation. Such criteria shall guarantee the correct storage of the documents, the location and consultation of the information and allow the exercise of the rights of objection to the processing, access, rectification and erasure. Should there not be any applicable regulation, the data controller shall establish the criteria and protocols for action that must be followed for the filing.

Transposition of Articles 16 and 17 of the Data Protection Directive

Juris-diction	Relevant provision transposing Articles 16 and 17
	Article 107 The storage devices for the documents containing personal data shall have mechanisms that hinder opening. When their physical characteristics do not permit such a measure, the data controller shall adopt the measures that prevent access by unauthorised persons. Article 108 Whilst the documentation containing personal data is not filed in the storage devices established above, due to undergoing revision or processing, whether before or after their filing, the person who is responsible for them shall ensure their safekeeping and prevent at all times their access by unauthorised persons. Section Two: Medium-level security measures Article 109 One or several security officers shall be designated under the terms and with the functions set out in Article 95 hereof. Article 110 The filing systems comprising this section shall be subject to an internal or external audit, at least every two years, which verifies compliance with this Title. Section Three: High-level security measures Article 111 1. The cupboards, filing cabinets or other elements for storing non-automated files with personal data shall be in areas to which access is protected by entrance doors with locks or another equivalent device. Such areas shall remain closed when access to the documents included in the filing system is not required. 2. If, bearing in mind the characteristics of the premises available to the data controller, it is not possible to comply with that provided above, the data controller shall adopt alternative measures that, duly justified, shall be included in the security document. Article 112 1. The generation of copies or the reproduction of the documents shall only be done under the control of the personnel authorised in the security document. 2. Copies or reproductions to be discarded shall be destroyed to avoid access to the information contained therein or its later recovery. Article 113 1. Access to the documentation shall be exclusively limited to the authorised personnel. 2. Mechanisms shall be established to permit identification of access to documents that may be used by multiple users.

Transposition of Articles 16 and 17 of the Data Protection Directive

Juris-diction	Relevant provision transposing Articles 16 and 17
	3. The access of persons not included above shall be adequately registered pursuant to the procedure established for this purpose in the security document. Article 114 Whenever there is a physical transfer of the documentation contained in a filing system, measures shall be adopted aimed at preventing access or manipulation of the information being transferred.
Sweden	*Personal Data Act 204/1998* Section 30 A personal data assistant and a person or those persons who work under the assistant's or the controller of personal data's direction may only process personal data in accordance with instructions from the controller of personal data. There shall be a written contract on the processing by the personal data assistant of personal data on behalf of the controller of personal data. It shall be specifically stipulated in the contract that the personal data assistant may only process personal data in accordance with instructions from the controller of personal data and that the personal data assistant is liable to take those measures referred to in Section 31, first paragraph. If there are special provisions in a statute or other enactment concerning processing of personal data in public operations as regards matters referred to in the first paragraph, these shall apply instead of that stated in the first paragraph. Section 31 The controller of personal data shall implement appropriate technical and organisational measures to protect the personal data that is processed. The measures shall provide a level of security that is appropriate having regard to: (a) the technical possibilities available; (b) what it would cost to implement the measures; (c) the special risks that exist with processing of personal data; and (d) how sensitive the personal data processed really is. If the controller of the personal data engages a personal data assistant, the controller of personal data shall ensure for him/herself that the personal data assistant can implement the security measures that must be taken and ensure that the personal data assistant actually takes the measures. Section 32 The supervisory authority may in an individual case decide on which security measures the controller of personal data shall implement in accordance with Section 31.

Transposition of Articles 16 and 17 of the Data Protection Directive

Juris-diction	Relevant provision transposing Articles 16 and 17
UK	*Data Protection Act 1998* Schedule 1, Part I, Condition 7 Appropriate technical and organisational measures shall be taken against unauthorised or unlawful processing of personal data and against accidental loss or destruction of, or damage to, personal data. Schedule 1, Part II, The Seventh Principle Paragraph 9 Having regard to the state of technological development and the cost of implementing any measures, the measures must ensure a level of security appropriate to– (a) the harm that might result from such unauthorised or unlawful processing or accidental loss, destruction or damage as are mentioned in the seventh principle, and (b) the nature of the data to be protected. Paragraph 10 The data controller shall take reasonable steps to ensure the reliability of any employees of his who have access to the personal data. Paragraph 11 Where processing of personal data is carried out by a data processor on behalf of a data controller, the data controller must in order to comply with the seventh principle– (a) choose a data processor providing sufficient guarantees in respect of the technical and organisational security measures governing the processing to be carried out, and (b) take reasonable steps to ensure compliance with those measures. Paragraph 12 Where processing of personal data is carried out by a data processor on behalf of a data controller, the data controller is not to be regarded as complying with the seventh principle unless– (a) the processing is carried out under a contract– (i) which is made or evidenced in writing, and (ii) under which the data processor is to act only on instructions from the data controller, and (b) the contract requires the data processor to comply with obligations equivalent to those imposed on a data controller by the seventh principle.

Appendix C
PRECEDENTS

1 EXAMPLE CHECKLIST FOR HANDLING A DATA SECURITY BREACH (NON-EXHAUSTIVE)

An incident management policy governing how the data controller will react to and handle a data security breach is just part of the suite of measures that an organisation needs to implement in order to fulfil their obligations under data security law. This document contains a non-exhaustive list of considerations for the incident response team.

1. Preliminary considerations – data audit and planning

1.1 Assessment of the data held by the organisation ('data mapping')
The controller will be ill equipped to cope with a security incident if it does not understand the data held by it and its flows around the organisation and to third parties. The incident response team should ask itself whether it fully understands these issues. Typical issues to be addressed include:
 (a) What information are you holding?
  For example, personal data, sensitive personal data, organisation or financial information, confidential information.
 (b) How valuable, sensitive, or confidential are the data?
 (c) If the information are personal data, who does it belong to (for example, employees, customers, clients or suppliers)?
 (d) What are the possible effects for the individuals (and corporate data subjects) and the organisation if a security breach was to occur?
  - Is there a risk that personal data could be used in identity fraud?
  - Could a breach result in harm or distress to individuals (including physical safety, financial loss, invasion of privacy or aspects of an individual's financial, private or family life)?
  - Is there a risk of damage to the controller's reputation, or the trust which individuals (and corporate data subjects) place in the organisation?
  - Is there a public interest element or a risk that the breach will attract media interest?
  - What are the possible financial consequences for the organisation of dealing with an incident?
 (e) Where and how are the data held? For example, are they spread throughout the organisation (very likely) or contained in one location

555

Precedents

          (unlikely)? Do third parties hold copies of, or have access to, the data? Are the data held electronically or manually?

    (f)   How are the data processed and for what purposes? What elements of processing are electronic and what are manual?

1.2   Potential threats to security

Data security breach can arise in a number of ways. Considering how the organisation may be exposed to such risks can focus its mind to the potential threats. Whilst considering these risks it is important to consider any third party processors engaged on the organisation's behalf. Even if a contractor is responsible for the breach it is often the data controller who will suffer the adverse consequences of the breach. Threats to consider include:

(a)   Loss or theft of data or equipment on which data is stored;
(b)   Software or hardware failure;
(c)   Breaches of security procedures – building's physical security, access controls and passwords, encryption policies;
(d)   Threat from employees or contractors – human error or intentional breach;
(e)   'Acts of God', such as fire or flood;
(f)   Hacking offences; and
(g)   Blagging offences.

What is the controller's risk profile/appetite? Do the controls adopted when measured against the known threats accord with the risk profile/appetite?

1.3   Assign responsibility for data protection and security

Although the appointment of an individual (or a team) that is responsible for data protection and security is not a strict legal requirement, it is highly advisable that individuals/persons are appointed, due to best practice considerations and regulatory guidance. Furthermore, allocating responsibility and assembling a team in advance of any security breach will allow the organisation to effectively manage its response and to act quickly should a breach occur.

A comprehensive incident management policy will involve input from a number of areas of the organisation including IT, HR, legal, security/facilities department and any external parties that hold or have access to data. Therefore, their involvement in this initial planning stage will be essential. The team must be trained so that they fully understand the planned approach to dealing with a breach no matter what the circumstances. Once the organisation has undergone an audit of its data flows and the areas of risk, the incident management policy can be tested against various 'what if' scenarios.

The incident response team is likely to be made up of representatives from a number of departments including IT, legal, public relations (PR), security commercial and compliance. The team must also include at least one member of senior management with the authority to take and act on decisions.

The team must have sufficient budget and resources to act quickly and effectively.

2.   Initial response – damage limitation – recovery of the data and containing the risk

2.1   Investigate the facts

This is likely to be a priority in the immediate aftermath of the breach. There will be some interplay with the organisation's disaster recovery policies, which may be implemented alongside the data security breach policy.

(a)   What is the nature and cause of the breach?
(b)   Who is the data controller (remember there may be more than one data controller, in which case all may be liable for the breach)?

(c)   Is the data backed up and can any of the lost data be recovered?
(d)   Which parts of the organisation should be made aware of the breach, so that the risks may be contained? Have staff with customer facing roles been trained to recognise situations where stolen data may be used?
- Do any third parties need to be notified in order to contain the risk or limit potential harm (the section on notification)?

2.2 Mitigate the breach
This is identified by the government's, FSA's and ICO's guidance as an essential part in an organisation's response to a breach. Action must be taken to stop the security breach from continuing or recurring and to mitigate the harm that may result from the breach.

2.3 Risk assessment
An assessment of the risks posed by the loss of data will inform and dictate the next stage of the organisation's response. The risks involved will be determined by type of breach i.e. corruption of data caused by a computer virus will carry different risks to those associated with theft of a laptop or loss of data to a hacker.
Questions (a)–(d) in part 1.1 will need to be readdressed in relation to the specific data involved in the breach, as well as the following considerations:
(a)   If the data have been lost or stolen were there any technological security measures (e.g. encryption, password protections) in place to protect the data? What was the target of the theft, was it the data or the hardware on which the data is stored?
(b)   How much data are involved? If it is personal data, will a large number of individuals be affected?

3.   Notification

3.1 Sector specific regulators
There may be sector specific obligations requiring an organisation to notify a particular regulator, for example the Financial Services Authority (FSA) in the case of regulated organisations.

3.2 The Information Commissioner's Office (ICO)
There is no strict legal obligation to notify the ICO, however, the Commissioner believes that 'serious breaches' involving personal data should be brought to his attention.
A serious breach is one where there is a risk of significant actual or potential harm, including distress, to the data subjects affected by the breach. This will be the case where:
- Large volumes of personal data are involved (about 1,000 individuals); or
- Where the breach involves sensitive information, such as medical or financial information or unencrypted personal data. In such cases the duty to notify may be triggered if as few as 10 individuals are affected.

It is also worth noting that it is better for the ICO to be informed about the breach from the organisation itself rather than the press, an affected individual or another regulator.
The decision whether or not to report may also be a commercial one that involves balancing various risks, such as the threat of regulatory action (which may be made worse if the breach is not reported), the damage to PR and customer confidence. In deciding whether or not to report the breach it is often

Precedents

helpful to look at the organisation's relationship with the ICO in an attempt to determine how they would view the breach.

Content – When determining whether to take action against an organisation, the ICO will look to the nature of the breach and whether the data controller is meeting its obligations under the DPA. Therefore the notification to the ICO should contain details of the:

- Circumstances of the breach including the volume and type of data affected;
- Remedial steps that the organisation has taken to minimise the risks involved (including details of any security measures in place at the time of the breach and whether the breach has been investigated); and
- Remedial steps taken to prevent the occurrence of future breaches.

The ICO also needs to be informed whether the media has been contacted as this is likely to increase the number of enquiries received by its office.

Note that similar principles apply for the FSA.

3.3 The media

The ICO believes that it is the duty of the data controller to inform the media of any breach, and may recommend that the media is notified if there are public interest arguments involved, or if it is in the interests of the affected individuals. It is worth noting that it is the ICO's policy to notify the media of any enforcement action taken, unless there are exceptional reasons not to do so.

3.4 Individuals

If personal data were involved the organisation should consider whether it is appropriate to inform the affected individuals. When deciding the best means of communicating a breach the organisation should consider:

- How many individuals have been affected;
- Whether the individuals are identifiable and can be personally contacted;
- The urgency of the situation.

Content – The notification should contain:

- A description of the breach, including how and when it occurred;
- Details of the information that has been affected;
- Details of the steps taken to minimise the risks;
- Clear and tailored advice as to how the individuals may protect themselves;
- Contact information (e.g. helpline number or webpage address) so that the organisation may provide further information or answer specific queries.

3.5 Insurers and other organisations that may be able to assist in containing or mitigating the harm

- Insurers – There may be a requirement in the insurance policy document that notification of potential claims;
- Police;
- Banks, building societies and credit card companies.

4. Evaluation and review – restorative actions and remedial measures

Following a breach it is important that the organisation considers whether the appropriate systems, policies and procedures were in place and whether improvements to those procedures would prevent such a breach from recurring. The obligations under the DPA are continual, therefore the organisation must continue to reassess its exposure to risks and whether the risks can be minimised.

Precedents

Furthermore if the ICO investigates the breach the Commissioner will be particularly interested in the actions the organisation has taken to review its systems and implement any improvements.

4.1 Contractual review

If there is a possibility that the breach was caused by a third party, the organisation should consider whether it has any redress against that party under a relevant contract. In reviewing the contract, the following are just some points that the organisation should consider:

- Whether any specific data protection or security obligations have been breached, for example an explicit duty not to transfer data on memory sticks, an obligation to only use a trackable, secure postal service or an obligation to implement appropriate technological and organisation measures to protect the data;
- Whether the organisation has a claim for breach or a more general obligation has been breached, for example a duty to exercise all reasonable care and skill or a duty to keep all information confidential;
- Whether there are any limitations or exclusions on the third party's liability, which would restrict the amount of damages the organisation could claim for and/or limit the circumstances in which the organisation could make a claim against the third party;
- Whether the breach gives rise to a right to terminate the contract. The right to terminate may be an express right or if the breach was sufficiently serious, so that it impacts on the parties' ability to continue to perform their obligations under the contract, the breach may be said to have been a 'repudiatory breach', allowing the parties to terminate.

It is worth remembering that if the third party was also a data controller in respect of the data involved in the breach the parties may be jointly liable.

4.2 Employees

A security breach may give rise to disciplinary proceedings against one or more employees within an organisation. However, before initiating such action the organisation should consider whether the employees have received thorough training and whether the security policies and procedures were sufficiently clear to enable employees to follow such policies and implement the security practices on a day-to-day basis.

Precedents

2 EXAMPLE INCIDENT RESPONSE CHECKLIST FOR HANDLING LOSS OF UNENCRYPTED LAPTOP COMPUTER (SHORT FORM, NON-EXHAUSTIVE)

Introduction

The loss of a laptop, whether through theft or negligence, causes serious problems for organisations without a response strategy. This ten-point guide is designed to focus the organisation's mind on the key issues to be considered after the theft of a laptop.

1. Secure scene of crime

The crime scene will contain important evidence, perhaps fingerprints or DNA data. It is important that you do not compromise the crime scene.

Thus, if the theft takes place on business premises consider limiting access to it. All non-essential staff may need to be excluded. Similarly, if the theft takes place offsite, try to identify the sources of important evidence; perhaps there is a CCTV system in the locality, which might have captured important footage.

2. Establish nature of the data and of the security measures on the laptop

If the laptop contained sensitive data but no security measures were in place, you have a serious case. You cannot plan properly without this information. Key questions are: was data stored locally on the laptop?; was data encrypted at rest?; was the computer password protected?; does the data include client data?; could any of the data be used for identity theft purposes?

3. If stolen from premises, establish window of opportunity and suspects

Theft from your organisation's premises might indicate an insider operation. You need to be realistic about this, because an insider job makes the case even more serious.

4. Inform key senior personnel within the organisation

An incident of laptop theft is likely to require rapid decision-taking. People with the authority to take decisions need to be informed as soon as possible. You will need to take quick decisions about the instruction of legal and other experts and take decisions on other matters identified within this strategy.

5. Inform police

In most cases the police should be informed, but there will be situations where this might not be the correct decision. Furthermore, there is evidence to suggest leakage of data from the police to the press and media, which might be a factor for you to consider if you are aiming for secrecy and confidentiality. Of course, informing the police is often a vital component within insurance claims, so make sure that your decision takes this into account.

6. Establish whether internal investigators should be instructed

Complementary to informing the police – or as an alternative – is the use of private sector agencies. Consider whether there is a role for private investigators. When considering this point be realistic in your expectations of what the police can or will do; many people are disappointed by the police reaction, so if a strong and sustained reaction is required you might need to use the private sector.

7. Establish your reporting obligations

You need to determine quickly whether you need to inform third parties, including regulators, data subjects, clients, insurers etc.

8. Establish internal communications strategy, including confidentiality

You need to reach a decision quickly on your communications strategy; are you aiming for secrecy or will you 'go public'? Your communications strategy must focus on internal issues; what will you tell staff etc? Remember, when determining your communications strategy you should always be realistic about the possibility of leakage.

9. Establish media strategy

If your case 'goes public' the media could be very interested. You need to appreciate that there is a massive public interest in data theft; these stories sell newspapers. Negative publicity brings with it the risk of reputational damage, so make sure you are prepared for handling the media.

10. Establish new systems

A laptop theft indicates a failure of systems. These failures need to be addressed. Broadly speaking, a data theft can arise from failures in physical systems (for example, as simple as not locking the door), failures of people (malevolence or negligence) and failure in technology (for example, not having suitable encryption). You should fix these.

Precedents

3 EXAMPLE BREACH NOTIFICATION LETTER TO INFORMATION COMMISSIONER

Information Commissioner's Office
Wycliffe House,
Water Lane,
Wilmslow,
Cheshire
SK9 5AF

Dear Sir/Madam

Notification of security breach

We are writing to advise you of the [*loss/corruption/release*] of [*Insert details in general terms of the type of information and number of records (e.g. payslips for 200 of our employees/an unencrypted laptop containing the personal information of our employees and customers/membership/application details, including name, address, date of birth etc)*].

Following the [*loss/corruption/release*] we immediately carried out an investigation into the circumstances surrounding the [*loss/corruption/release*]. By way of explanation, [*Insert a short paragraph setting out the details of the circumstances of the loss/release/corruption. If it involved a third party contractor include details of the role they provided and how they were involved in the breach. If relevant, include any details of how the breach is being investigated*].

Prior to making this notification we have [*state what action has been taken to minimise/mitigate the effect on individuals involved and whether any other regulatory body or the police have been informed and their response. If you have sought legal advice or consulted any ICO guidance notes you may provide details*]. Please note that we are writing to the individuals concerned to inform them that we have discovered a security breach.

We take our responsibilities as a data controller extremely seriously, therefore in order to help minimise the risks of such an incident recurring in the future we have [*Include short details of any remedial action taken to prevent future occurrence e.g. implementing a new data security policy, introducing compulsory training for all staff, reviewing your contractual arrangements with third parties, encrypting all laptops and removable media*].

[*Any other information you feel may assist the ICO in making an assessment of the loss should also be included*]

Please do not hesitate to contact us if you have any questions or require further information.

Yours faithfully

Precedents

4 EXAMPLE BREACH NOTIFICATION LETTER TO DATA SUBJECT

Drafting note: Please consider the intended audience of this letter. The language and tone adopted should be appropriate for the recipient. Therefore if the security breach impacted vulnerable adults the style of this letter should be varied accordingly.

Dear [ ],

I am writing to you because of a recent security incident at [*insert name of organisation*].

[*Describe what happened in general terms. Include sufficient details of the loss/release/corruption so that individuals understand the risks involved (e.g. if the data was in soft copy, was it protected by any technological security measures? If a laptop was stolen was it stolen for the hardware rather than the data? Consider whether it is necessary to provide details of why the data was stored on the lost/damaged/stolen hardware, why the breach occurred or why the third party had access to the information, if this is not immediately obvious.*]

We are aware that the [*laptop/disc/memory stick/files/documents*] contained your personal data, consisting of your [*insert details of the personal data involved (e.g. name, telephone number, employee number, credit card details, passport number etc)*].

[*State what action has been taken to minimise/mitigate the effect on the individuals involved and whether any other regulatory body or the police have been informed and their response*]

We have taken advice about this matter and [*while we consider that it should not have any adverse consequences for you/include a brief assessment of the perceived risks to individuals*], if you are concerned about the risk of 'Identity Theft', we recommend that you contact your [*bank/credit card provider/DVLA/other relevant institution*] to notify them that your account may have been compromised. [In order to assist you we have [*provide details of any relevant helplines or websites that you have set up/actions you have taken in conjunction with banks, the UK Identity and Passport Service etc to combat the risks of identity fraud or to provide guidance to those affected individuals*].

If you have any questions that you would like to raise with us, please contact us on [*insert contact details*].

Yours [ ]

Precedents

5 EXAMPLE DATA PROTECTION CLAUSES FOR EMPLOYMENT CONTRACT

Drafting note: Under the Seventh Data Protection Principle a controller must have appropriate organisational security measures to safeguard personal data from accidental loss and unauthorised or unlawful processing. Paragraph 10 in Part 2 of Schedule 1 of the 1998 Act further describes this principle as requiring controllers to take reasonable steps to ensure the reliability of any employees who have access to the personal data.

As a minimum, controllers must have provisions in the employment contract to govern employees' use of personal data.

[ ]   Data Protection

[ ].1   You confirm that You have read and understood the Company's [data protection policy and the information and communications systems security policy], copies of which are [available on the intranet/contained in the Staff Handbook/ annexed to this Employment Contract]. The Company may make changes to these policies at any time. You will be notified of any changes in writing.

[ ].2   The Company's telecommunications, computer equipment and associated internet and email services are provided solely to enable the Company to carry out its business. You shall comply with the data protection and information systems security policies at all times when handling personal data or using these services in the course of Your employment. [The Company may require you to attend training and/or refresher courses on Your data protection and security obligations, at its discretion. Attendance at these courses is compulsory and forms part of Your duties as an employee.]

[ ].3   Breaching the provisions of the data protection or information security systems policies and/or misusing the Company's telecommunications, computer equipment and associated internet and email services including but not limited to 'surfing' or downloading/transmitting offensive or illegal material on the internet may be treated as a disciplinary matter and, in serious cases, may be treated as gross misconduct leading to a summary dismissal.

[ ].4   You shall keep confidential any personal information that You receive and process on behalf of the Company.

Precedents

6 EXAMPLE INFORMATION AND COMMUNICATIONS SYSTEMS SECURITY POLICY (SHORT FORM, NON-EXHAUSTIVE)

Drafting note: Under the Seventh Data Protection Principle a controller must take appropriate technical and organisational measures to safeguard personal data. One aspect of this obligation is producing policies and guidance on the use of IT and communications systems. Depending on the size of the controller, the complexity of the operations and the reasons for processing personal data, a security policy may be produced as a standalone document or may be incorporated into a wider data protection policy.

In determining what measures are appropriate a controller must consider the state of technological development at the time and the cost of implementing any measures. The measures implemented must reflect the nature and sensitivity of the data being processed and the harm that may result from a security breach. It is worth noting that management and organisational measures are as important as technical ones therefore it is essential that policies and systems are supported by a thorough training programme with clear lines of accountability for data protection and security.

This precedent is for guidance only. It should be tailored to suit the needs of the business by inserting specific provisions applicable to the controller's security systems. The policy may also contain details of the controller's policy on the use of the internet and email systems and the controller's policy of monitoring employees' communications.

1. Introduction

1.1   The Company's information and communications systems and equipment are provided to promote business efficiency and effective working practices within the organisation. This policy deals with the use (and misuse) of computer equipment, email, internet connections, telephones, Blackberries, personal digital assistants (PDAs), voicemail, fax machines, copiers, scanners, CCTV and electronic key fobs and cards belonging to the Company.

1.2   Under the Data Protection Act 1998 (the 'DPA'), the Company must ensure that appropriate security measures are used to protect personal data (i.e. information which relates to an identified or identifiable living individual for example names, addresses, emails, employee numbers, National Insurance numbers and health data) against unlawful or unauthorised processing and against the accidental loss of, or damage to, personal data. This includes putting in place procedures and technologies to maintain the security of any personal data and ensuring that all workers with access to such data comply with such policies.

1.3   The Company has a duty to ensure the:
- **Confidentiality of the data**, meaning that only people who are authorised to use the data can access it; and
- **Integrity of the data**, meaning that personal data should be accurate and suitable for the purpose for which it is processed,

whilst limiting access to the data so that only authorised workers have access to the data and only for authorised purposes. Personal data should therefore only be stored on the Company's central computer system and not on individual PCs.

1.4   Although the DPA only applies to personal data, its principles are equally applicable to all confidential or sensitive information. Therefore this policy

Precedents

applies to all confidential information, which includes personal data, as described above, as well as business critical or sensitive information (for example [the details of high-profile or confidential projects or contracts, trade secrets, sensitive financial information and/or information which would impact the price of the company's shares or have a public relations impact]).

1.5 In accordance with the terms of the Contract of Employment, workers have an obligation to comply with the requirements of the DPA and this policy at all times when handling and sharing confidential information.

1.6 Further information regarding the DPA is available [on the intranet/in the Employee Handbook]. If any worker is in any doubt about the requirements or the application of the DPA, they should consult [the data protection officer/the data protection compliance manager/a data guardian].

1.7 Aside from the DPA the Company is also required to comply with the Regulation of Investigatory Powers Act 2000, the Telecommunications (Lawful Business Practice) (Interception of Communications) Regulations 2000 and the Human Rights Act 1998.

2. Worker Responsibilities

2.1 This policy applies to any person working for the company including officers, directors, employees (whether part-time, permanent or temporary), contractors, advisers, trainees, seconded employees and agency staff (collectively known as 'Workers') and to third parties who have access to the Company's communication and IT systems.

2.2 All users of the information and communications systems have a responsibility to maintain the security of both the systems themselves and of the confidential information the Company holds (whether electronically or in hard copy form and whether contained in emails, contracts, employee absence, performance and personal records, customer databases etc).

2.3 Failure to adhere to the policy may constitute misconduct and lead to appropriate disciplinary action under the Company's disciplinary procedures.

3. Mandatory Rules
All workers must comply with the following rules:

3.1 Passwords

3.1.1 Workers are responsible for the security of the equipment allocated to or used by them, and must not allow it to be used by anyone other than in accordance with this policy. The use of passwords is an integral part of the security regime of the Company's IT system. Passwords are unique to each worker and should not be written down, shared or disclosed to any other worker, or to anyone outside the Company, save for:
(a) if there is a genuine business need in which case workers should seek permission from a [member of the IT team/Head of IT]; or
(b) to a member of the IT team for the purpose of IT support.

3.1.2 Workers are required to change their password [regularly/every [thirty] days] to ensure the confidentiality and security of the IT system. Passwords may be changed at any time and workers must change their password if they believe somebody, without authorisation, has become aware of their password. [*Insert details of how workers can change their password or direct them to the appropriate guidance*]

3.1.3 Workers should choose a password that is not obvious. Workers should avoid words or combinations which are easy to guess including real words, names, anniversary dates, car registrations, place of birth, and telephone numbers. Acronyms, mnemonics, random letters are recommended.

3.1.4 On the termination of employment, for whatever reason, workers' user accounts will be cancelled and their rights of access to the IT system removed.

3.2 Physical Security

3.2.1 Workers are responsible for the security of the equipment and their user account. Therefore, when away from their desk for any extended period of time, workers should log-off or lock their PC. This is particularly important if you are working on personal or sensitive information. Workers should log-off and shut down their computers at the end of each day.

3.2.2 Workers should ensure that individual monitors do not show confidential information to passers-by.

3.2.3 Workers should not leave documents containing confidential information on printers or fax machines. Fax transmissions are not a secure medium. Sensitive material should not be sent in this manner. Where it is absolutely necessary to transmit sensitive information by fax, use a fax cover sheet, ensure that the recipient number is correct and has been correctly entered and, after sending the fax, check the transmission report to ensure that delivery has been successful.

3.2.4 The Company has deployed entry controls to restrict the physical movement of persons within the premises. Entry passes must be worn at all times and any stranger seen in an entry-controlled area should be reported.

3.2.5 Workers should ensure that offices, desks and cupboards are kept locked if they hold confidential information of any kind.

3.2.6 Workers should use secure methods of disposal of any media containing confidential information. Paper documents should be shredded and obsolete floppy disks, CD-ROMs, memory sticks, mobile phones, Blackberries, laptops and hard drives should be physically destroyed in accordance with the Company's policies.

3.3 System Security

3.3.1 Workers should not delete, destroy or modify existing systems, programs, information or data which could have the effect of harming the business or exposing it to risk.

3.3.2 Workers should not download or install software including programs, photographs, games, music or video files from external sources without authorisation from [the IT department **OR** [POSITION]]. If in doubt, workers should seek advice from the IT department.

Precedents

3.3.3 No device or equipment including USB or MP3 devices, telephones or PDAs should be attached to our systems without the prior approval of the IT department.

3.3.4 The company scans all emails sent and received by the system for viruses. Workers should exercise caution when opening emails from unknown external sources or where, for any reason, an email appears suspicious. The IT department should be informed immediately if a suspected virus is received. The Company reserves the right to block access to email attachments for the purpose of effective use of the system and for compliance with this policy. The Company also reserves the right not to transmit any email message.

3.4 Transferring Data

3.4.1 Workers must obtain permission from a senior manager before using any portable media to store or transfer confidential information. If any confidential information is stored and transported on CDs/DVDs, diskettes or memory sticks then such information must be encrypted and fully password protected.

3.4.2 A security breach resulting in the loss of information can be seriously damaging to the subject(s) of the information and/or to the Company's reputation. Any loss of information must be reported immediately to a relevant manager, the Data Protection Officer and to the Head of IT.

3.4.3 If confidential information has to be sent to another organisation, it is the responsibility of the worker who is sending the information, in consultation with their manager, to ensure that:
(a) any disclosures or exchanges of information are made in accordance with the provisions of the DPA, the common law duty of confidentiality and any other applicable regulations, protocols or agreements including the Company's own policies and procedures; and
(b) all necessary security measures are implemented to protect the information whilst it is in transit, for example password protection and encryption if the data is electronic and/or the use of a secure method of transfer (such as a secure trackable delivery service) appropriate to the sensitivity of the data.

3.5 Information Security outside the Office

3.5.1 Workers should take special care to minimise the risk of theft, loss or damage to documents, confidential information, telecommunications or computer equipment. When transferring such items between the office and other locations workers should observe basic safety and security rules such as keeping items out of sight and not leaving them unattended at any time.

3.5.2 Workers should not use computer equipment or read documents containing confidential information in a public place, such as on a train or in the offices of another organisation, unless privacy is guaranteed.

3.5.3 Documents and information should not be removed from the Company's premises unless absolutely necessary. If documents are taken off the premises they should be stored in a secure fashion, preferably in a locked draw or filing cabinet.

3.6 Email use

[*Drafting note: The Company's restrictions on email use and monitoring policy may be set out here*].

3.6.1 External email is an insecure method of communication. Content from external systems may be easily copied, forwarded or archived. Confidential information should not be sent by email unless it is sufficiently protected. Workers should consider whether technological measures, such as password protection [and/or encryption technologies] should be used to protect particularly sensitive information or large volumes of personal information. [*Drafting note: If the business does not have the technological facilities to offer such protection consider whether other methods of data transfer such as hand delivery or a secure, trackable courier or postal service should be used*].

3.6.2 In accordance with the Company's [data retention policy], workers are responsible for the deletion of old emails, bearing in mind the Company's data protection obligations and permitted storage levels, [audit trail, evidence and legal discovery issues].

Precedents

7 EXAMPLE OF SEVENTH DATA PROTECTION PRINCIPLE CLAUSES FOR DATA PROCESSOR CONTRACT (SHORT FORM, NON-EXHAUSTIVE)

Drafting note: The following terms should be included in the definitions section of the Agreement:

'Customer Personal Data' means any personal data processed by the Supplier as a result of, or in connection with, the provision of the Services.

The terms 'data processor', 'personal data' and 'processing' will have the meaning given to them by the Data Protection Act 1998.

[ ]   **Data Protection**

[ ].1   With respect to the Customer Personal Data, the Customer appoints the Supplier as data processor. The Supplier will not assume any responsibility for determining the purposes for which and the manner in which the Customer Personal Data is processed.

[ ].2   The Supplier will and will procure that all Sub-contractors will:
  (a)   Process the Customer Personal Data only in accordance with instructions from the Customer (which may be specific instructions or instructions of a general nature as set out in this Agreement or as otherwise notified by the Customer to the Supplier during the Term) and keep a record of all processing of personal data carried out on behalf of the Customer;
  (b)   unless otherwise requested by the Customer, process the Customer Personal Data only to the extent, and in such manner, as is necessary for the provision of the Services;
  (c)   implement, keep under review and update when necessary appropriate technical and organisational measures to protect the Customer Personal Data against unauthorised or unlawful processing and against accidental loss, destruction, damage, alteration or disclosure; and
  (d)   notify the Customer of any unauthorised or unlawful processing or any accidental loss, destruction, damage, alteration or disclosure of the Customer Personal Data as soon as it becomes aware and keep the Customer informed of any related developments.

[ ].3   The Supplier and all Sub-contractors will not:
  (a)   process the Customer Personal Data for their own purposes;
  (b)   include the Customer Personal Data in any product or service offered by the Supplier to third parties;
  (c)   carry out any further research, analysis or profiling activity which involves the use of any element of the Customer Personal Data (including in aggregate form) or any information derived from any processing of such Customer Personal Data outside the scope of the Services; and
  (d)   pass files containing the Customer Personal Data to any third party for further processing by that third party or its agents.

[ ].4   The Supplier acknowledges:
  (a)   that the Customer is relying upon the Supplier's skill and knowledge in order to assess what is 'appropriate' to protect the Customer Personal Data against unauthorised or unlawful processing and against accidental loss, destruction, damage, alteration or disclosure; and

(b) that the technical and organisational measures shall be appropriate to the harm which might result from any unauthorised or unlawful processing and accidental loss, destruction or damage to the Customer Personal Data and having regard to the nature of the Customer Personal Data which is to be protected.

[ ].5 When implementing, reviewing and updating technical and organisational measures, the Supplier will have regard to:
(a) the sensitive nature of the personal data contained within the Customer Personal Data and the substantial harm which would result from unauthorised or unlawful processing or accidental loss or destruction of or damage to such personal data; and
(b) the state of technological development and the cost of implementing such measures.

[ ].6 The Supplier will ensure:
(a) the reliability of any employees and Sub-contractor personnel who have access to the Customer Personal Data;
(b) that all employees and Sub-contractor personnel involved in the processing of the Customer Personal Data have undergone adequate training in the care, protection and handling of personal data; and
(c) that all such employees and Sub-contractor personnel perform their duties strictly in compliance with the provisions of clause [CONFIDENTIALITY] by treating such Customer Personal Data as Confidential Information.

[ ].7 The Supplier will within [ ] working days inform the Customer if it receives:
(a) a request from a data subject concerning any information that may be contained in the Customer Personal Data; or
(b) a complaint, communication or request relating to the Customer's obligations under the Data Protection Act (including requests from the Information Commissioner).

[ ].8 Upon reasonable request of the Customer, the Supplier agrees to submit its data processing facilities, data files and documentation needed for processing the Customer Personal Data (and/or those of its agents, Affiliates and Sub-contractors) to reviewing, auditing and/or certifying by the Customer (or any independent or impartial inspection agents or auditors, selected by the Customer and not reasonably objected to by the Supplier) to ascertain compliance with the warranties and undertakings in this Agreement, with reasonable notice and during regular business hours.

[ ].9 The requirement of the Customer under clause [8] to give notice will not apply if the Customer believes that the Supplier is in breach of any of its obligations under this Agreement [or the Data Protection Act].

[ ].10 The Supplier will not process or permit the processing of Customer Personal Data outside the European Economic Area other than with the prior written consent of the Customer and, where such consent is granted, undertakes to enter into a suitable agreement with the Customer and/or any relevant parties and/or adopt any necessary measures in order to ensure an adequate level of protection with respect to the privacy rights of individuals.

[ ].11 The Supplier will at its own expense assist the Customer to comply with any obligations under the Data Protection Act and any other applicable data

Precedents

protection legislation and will not perform its obligations under this Agreement in such a way as to cause the Customer to breach any of its obligations under the Data Protection Act or any other applicable data protection legislation.

Precedents

8 EXAMPLE OF PRE-CONTRACTUAL DUE DILIGENCE FOR ENGAGEMENT OF DATA PROCESSOR (SHORT FORM, NON-EXHAUSTIVE)

Drafting note: The seventh data protection principle requires a data controller to appoint data processors, who provide sufficient guarantees in respect of the technical and organisational security measures governing the processing to be carried out and who take reasonable steps to ensure compliance with those measures. This is particularly important because under the Data Protection Act 1998 the liability for breaches of the Act or for security breaches remains with the data controller.

It is therefore advisable for businesses to:

(a)   include appropriate data protection and data security provisions in the contract (see third party supply contracts);

(b)   conduct a thorough due diligence into any proposed suppliers to ensure that they have adequate organisational and technical security measures in place; and

(c)   conduct regular audits of all third party suppliers throughout the life of the contracts.

This questionnaire can be used for pre contract due diligence investigations and audits throughout the contract life.

Please address the following questions as comprehensively as possible so that we can carry out an assessment of the data processing practices of your business.

1. POINTS OF COLLECTION OF DATA

In connection with the [proposed] contract:

1.2   Describe all instances where personal data about individuals is collected by you directly from those individuals (This may include registration forms and telephone helplines);

1.3   Describe all instances where personal data about individuals is <u>received from third parties</u> (This may include corporate clients that provide access to information about their employees);

1.4   [Is data about users of the website [*www.insertdetails.com*] <u>automatically</u> collected via 'cookies' or by any other means?]

2. DATA PROCESSING ACTIVITIES

In connection with the [proposed] contract:

2.1   Is 'sensitive personal data' collected or used you? (Sensitive personal data includes information relating to racial or ethnic origin, political opinions, religious or other beliefs, trade union membership, health, sex life and criminal convictions)

2.2   Have you nominated a representative for the purposes of dealing with data protection enquiries or concerns from individuals?

Precedents

2.3 Describe the purposes for which personal data is used by you.

2.4 Are individuals contacted by CLIENT for marketing purposes?
If so, please describe the ways in which individuals may be contacted for this purpose (e.g. direct mailings, telephone, fax, e-mail).

2.5 Describe all potential recipients of personal data collected or held by you.

2.6 What are the likely uses of the data made by those recipients?

2.7 Describe how data is stored on your systems.

2.8 How is data transferred:
    a.   internally within your organisation, e.g. by email, internal post, royal mail (recorded delivery or standard post)?
    b.   to external parties?

3. DATA QUALITY

In connection with the [proposed] contract:

3.1 Describe any procedures currently in place to ensure that all personal data is accurate and up to date (This may include writing to individuals to request confirmation as to the accuracy of the data held about them).

3.2 For how long is personal data usually kept by you?

3.3 Is there any policy regarding the periodic destruction or deletion of obsolete data?

If so, please provide details.

4. DEALING WITH INDIVIDUALS' RIGHTS

In connection with the [proposed] contract:

4.1 Describe any procedures currently in place to deal with requests by individuals to be supplied with information about the data held about them (This may include the use of checklists or standard letters dealing with 'access requests').

4.2 Do you market to individuals? If so:
    a.   Do you give individuals the opportunity to opt-out from marketing-related communications?
    b.   What steps are taken if an individual objects to receiving marketing-related information?

5. SECURITY MEASURES

In connection with the [proposed] contract:

5.1 What security measures do you have in place to ensure the confidentiality of personal data?

5.2 In particular, please indicate whether you have adopted any of the following:

a. Information security policy;
b. Physical security measures;
c. Controls on access to information;
d. Controls on the use of portable media, or a policy to encrypt all laptops and such media;
e. Business continuity plan;
f. Internal training programme on security systems and procedures;
g. Procedures to investigate breaches of security when they occur;
h. British Standard on Information Security Management BS7799.

6. INTERNATIONAL DIMENSION

In connection with the [proposed] contract:

6.1 Do you share personal data with organisations outside the UK?
   a. If so, indicate which of those organisations are part of your Group of companies and which ones are not.
   b. In the case of those organisations that are part of your Group of companies, is there any internal policy governing the use of personal data?
   If so, please provide details.
   c. In the case of those organisations that are not part of your Group of companies, is there a written contract governing the relationship between such organisations and CLIENT?
   If so, please provide details.

6.2 Does any third party process personal data on behalf of you from outside the UK?
   a. If so, is there a written contract governing that relationship?
   If so, please provide details.

Appendix D
CORE RESOURCES

DATA PROTECTION ACT 1998 (AS AMENDED)

DATA PROTECTION ACT 1998

1998 CHAPTER 29

An Act to make new provision for the regulation of the processing of information relating to individuals, including the obtaining, holding, use or disclosure of such information.

[16th July 1998]

BE IT ENACTED by the Queen's most Excellent Majesty, by and with the advice and consent of the Lords Spiritual and Temporal, and Commons, in this present Parliament assembled, and by the authority of the same, as follows:—

PART I
PRELIMINARY

1 Basic interpretative provisions

(1) In this Act, unless the context otherwise requires—

'data' means information which—
- (a) is being processed by means of equipment operating automatically in response to instructions given for that purpose,
- (b) is recorded with the intention that it should be processed by means of such equipment,
- (c) is recorded as part of a relevant filing system or with the intention that it should form part of a relevant filing system, …
- (d) does not fall within paragraph (a), (b) or (c) but forms part of an accessible record as defined by section 68; [or
- (e) is recorded information held by a public authority and does not fall within any of paragraphs (a) to (d);]

Core resources

> 'data controller' means, subject to subsection (4), a person who (either alone or jointly or in common with other persons) determines the purposes for which and the manner in which any personal data are, or are to be, processed;
> 'data processor', in relation to personal data, means any person (other than an employee of the data controller) who processes the data on behalf of the data controller;
> 'data subject' means an individual who is the subject of personal data;
> 'personal data' means data which relate to a living individual who can be identified—
> > (a) from those data, or
> > (b) from those data and other information which is in the possession of, or is likely to come into the possession of, the data controller,
>
> and includes any expression of opinion about the individual and any indication of the intentions of the data controller or any other person in respect of the individual;
> 'processing', in relation to information or data, means obtaining, recording or holding the information or data or carrying out any operation or set of operations on the information or data, including—
> > (a) organisation, adaptation or alteration of the information or data,
> > (b) retrieval, consultation or use of the information or data,
> > (c) disclosure of the information or data by transmission, dissemination or otherwise making available, or
> > (d) alignment, combination, blocking, erasure or destruction of the information or data;
>
> ['public authority' means a public authority as defined by the Freedom of Information Act 2000 or a Scottish public authority as defined by the Freedom of Information (Scotland) Act 2002;]
> 'relevant filing system' means any set of information relating to individuals to the extent that, although the information is not processed by means of equipment operating automatically in response to instructions given for that purpose, the set is structured, either by reference to individuals or by reference to criteria relating to individuals, in such a way that specific information relating to a particular individual is readily accessible.

(2) In this Act, unless the context otherwise requires—

(a) 'obtaining' or 'recording', in relation to personal data, includes obtaining or recording the information to be contained in the data, and
(b) 'using' or 'disclosing', in relation to personal data, includes using or disclosing the information contained in the data.

(3) In determining for the purposes of this Act whether any information is recorded with the intention—

(a) that it should be processed by means of equipment operating automatically in response to instructions given for that purpose, or
(b) that it should form part of a relevant filing system,

it is immaterial that it is intended to be so processed or to form part of such a system only after being transferred to a country or territory outside the European Economic Area.

(4) Where personal data are processed only for purposes for which they are required by or under any enactment to be processed, the person on whom the obligation to process the data is imposed by or under that enactment is for the purposes of this Act the data controller.

[(5) In paragraph (e) of the definition of 'data' in subsection (1), the reference to information 'held' by a public authority shall be construed in accordance with

Data Protection Act 1998

section 3(2) of the Freedom of Information Act 2000 [or section 3(2), (4) and (5) of the Freedom of Information (Scotland) Act 2002].

(6) Where

    [(a)] section 7 of the Freedom of Information Act 2000 prevents Parts I to V of that Act [or

    (b) section 7(1) of the Freedom of Information (Scotland) Act 2002 prevents that Act,]

from applying to certain information held by a public authority, that information is not to be treated for the purposes of paragraph (e) of the definition of 'data' in subsection (1) as held by a public authority.]

NOTES

Initial Commencement

Royal Assent
Royal Assent: 16 July 1998: see s 75(2)(a).

Amendment

Sub-s (1): in definition 'data' word omitted at the end of para (c) repealed by the Freedom of Information Act 2000, ss 68(1), (2), 86, Sch 8, Pt III.
Date in force: 1 January 2005: see SI 2004/1909, art 2(1), (2)(f), (3).

Sub-s (1): in definition 'data' para (e) and the word 'or' immediately preceding it inserted by the Freedom of Information Act 2000, s 68(1), (2)(a).
Date in force: 1 January 2005: see SI 2004/1909, art 2(1), (2)(f), (3).

Sub-s (1): definition 'public authority' (inserted by the Freedom of Information Act 2000, s 68(1), (2)(b)) substituted by SI 2004/3089, art 2(1), (2)(a).
Date in force: 1 January 2005: see SI 2004/3089, art 1.

Sub-ss (5), (6): inserted by the Freedom of Information Act 2000, s 68(1), (3).
Date in force: 1 January 2005: see SI 2004/1909, art 2(1), (2)(f), (3).

Sub-s (5): words 'or section 3(2), (4) and (5) of the Freedom of Information (Scotland) Act 2002' in square brackets inserted by SI 2004/3089, art 2(1), (2)(b).
Date in force: 1 January 2005: see SI 2004/3089, art 1.

Sub-s (6): para (a) numbered as such by SI 2004/3089, art 2(1), (2)(c).
Date in force: 1 January 2005: see SI 2004/3089, art 1.

Sub-s (6): para (b) and word 'or' immediately preceding it inserted by SI 2004/3089, art 2(1), (2)(c).
Date in force: 1 January 2005: see SI 2004/3089, art 1.

2   Sensitive personal data

In this Act 'sensitive personal data' means personal data consisting of information as to—

    (a) the racial or ethnic origin of the data subject,
    (b) his political opinions,
    (c) his religious beliefs or other beliefs of a similar nature,
    (d) whether he is a member of a trade union (within the meaning of the Trade Union and Labour Relations (Consolidation) Act 1992,
    (e) his physical or mental health or condition,
    (f) his sexual life,

Core resources

    (g) the commission or alleged commission by him of any offence, or
    (h) any proceedings for any offence committed or alleged to have been committed by him, the disposal of such proceedings or the sentence of any court in such proceedings.

NOTES

Initial Commencement

Royal Assent
Royal Assent: 16 July 1998: see s 75(2)(a).

3   The special purposes

In this Act 'the special purposes' means any one or more of the following—

    (a) the purposes of journalism,
    (b) artistic purposes, and
    (c) literary purposes.

NOTES

Initial Commencement

Royal Assent
Royal Assent: 16 July 1998: see s 75(2)(a).

4   The data protection principles

(1) References in this Act to the data protection principles are to the principles set out in Part I of Schedule 1.

(2) Those principles are to be interpreted in accordance with Part II of Schedule 1.

(3) Schedule 2 (which applies to all personal data) and Schedule 3 (which applies only to sensitive personal data) set out conditions applying for the purposes of the first principle; and Schedule 4 sets out cases in which the eighth principle does not apply.

(4) Subject to section 27(1), it shall be the duty of a data controller to comply with the data protection principles in relation to all personal data with respect to which he is the data controller.

NOTES

Initial Commencement

Royal Assent
Royal Assent (so far as is necessary for bringing into force those provisions of Schs 1–4 which confer power to make subordinate legislation): 16 July 1998: see s 75(2)(i).

To be appointed
To be appointed (for remaining purposes): see s 75(3).

Appointment

Appointment (for remaining purposes): 1 March 2000: see SI 2000/183, art 2(1).

Data Protection Act 1998

5 Application of Act

(1) Except as otherwise provided by or under section 54, this Act applies to a data controller in respect of any data only if—

    (a) the data controller is established in the United Kingdom and the data are processed in the context of that establishment, or

    (b) the data controller is established neither in the United Kingdom nor in any other EEA State but uses equipment in the United Kingdom for processing the data otherwise than for the purposes of transit through the United Kingdom.

(2) A data controller falling within subsection (1)(b) must nominate for the purposes of this Act a representative established in the United Kingdom.

(3) For the purposes of subsections (1) and (2), each of the following is to be treated as established in the United Kingdom—

    (a) an individual who is ordinarily resident in the United Kingdom,

    (b) a body incorporated under the law of, or of any part of, the United Kingdom,

    (c) a partnership or other unincorporated association formed under the law of any part of the United Kingdom, and

    (d) any person who does not fall within paragraph (a), (b) or (c) but maintains in the United Kingdom—

        (i) an office, branch or agency through which he carries on any activity, or

        (ii) a regular practice;

and the reference to establishment in any other EEA State has a corresponding meaning.

NOTES

Initial Commencement

To be appointed
To be appointed: see s 75(3).

Appointment

Appointment: 1 March 2000: see SI 2000/183, art 2(1).

6 The Commissioner and the Tribunal

[(1) For the purposes of this Act and of the Freedom of Information Act 2000 there shall be an officer known as the Information Commissioner (in this Act referred to as 'the Commissioner').]

(2) The Commissioner shall be appointed by Her Majesty by Letters Patent.

[(3) For the purposes of this Act and of the Freedom of Information Act 2000 there shall be a tribunal known as the Information Tribunal (in this Act referred to as 'the Tribunal').]

(4) The Tribunal shall consist of—

    (a) a chairman appointed by the Lord Chancellor after consultation with the [Secretary of State],

    (b) such number of deputy chairmen so appointed as the Lord Chancellor may determine, and

    (c) such number of other members appointed by the [Secretary of State] as he may determine.

Core resources

(5) The members of the Tribunal appointed under subsection (4)(a) and (b) shall be—

- [(a) persons who satisfy the judicial-appointment eligibility condition on a 5-year basis,]
- (b) advocates or solicitors in Scotland of at least [5] years' standing, or
- (c) members of the bar of Northern Ireland or *solicitors of the Supreme Court of Northern Ireland* [solicitors of the Court of Judicature of Northern Ireland] of at least [5] years' standing.

(6) The members of the Tribunal appointed under subsection (4)(c) shall be—

- (a) persons to represent the interests of data subjects,
- [(aa) persons to represent the interests of those who make requests for information under the Freedom of Information Act 2000,]
- (b) persons to represent the interests of data controllers [and
- (bb) persons to represent the interests of public authorities].

(7) Schedule 5 has effect in relation to the Commissioner and the Tribunal.

NOTES

Initial Commencement

Royal Assent
Sub-s (7): Royal Assent (so far as is necessary for bringing into force those provisions of Sch 5 which confer power to make subordinate legislation): 16 July 1998: see s 75(2)(i).

To be appointed
Sub-ss (1)–(6): To be appointed: see s 75(3).
Sub-s (7): To be appointed (for remaining purposes): see s 75(3).

Appointment

Sub-ss (1)–(6): Appointment: 1 March 2000: see SI 2000/183, art 2(1).
Sub-s (7): Appointment (for remaining purposes): 1 March 2000: see SI 2000/183, art 2(1).

Amendment

Sub-s (1): substituted by the Freedom of Information Act 2000, s 18(4), Sch 2, Pt I, para 13(1), (2).
Date in force: 30 January 2001: see the Freedom of Information Act 2000, s 87(2)(c).

Sub-s (3): substituted by the Freedom of Information Act 2000, s 18(4), Sch 2, Pt I, para 13(1), (3).
Date in force: 14 May 2001: see SI 2001/1637, art 2(b).

Sub-s (4): in para (a) words 'Secretary of State' in square brackets substituted by virtue of SI 1999/678, art 2(1), Schedule.
Date in force: 19 May 1999: see SI 1999/678, art 1.

Sub-s (4): in para (c) words 'Secretary of State' in square brackets substituted by SI 2003/1887, art 9, Sch 2, para 9(1)(a).
Date in force: 19 August 2003: see SI 2003/1887, art 1(2).

Sub-s (5): para (a) substituted by the Tribunals, Courts and Enforcement Act 2007, s 50, Sch 10, Pt 1, para 30(1), (2).
Date in force: 21 July 2008: see SI 2008/1653, art 2(d); for transitional provisions see arts 3, 4 thereof.

Data Protection Act 1998

Sub-s (5): in para (b) reference to '5' in square brackets substituted by the Tribunals, Courts and Enforcement Act 2007, s 50, Sch 10, Pt 1, para 30(1), (3).
Date in force: 21 July 2008: see SI 2008/1653, art 2(d); for transitional provisions see arts 3, 4 thereof.

Sub-s (5): in para (c) words 'solicitors of the Supreme Court of Northern Ireland' in italics repealed and subsequent words in square brackets substituted by the Constitutional Reform Act 2005, s 59(5), Sch 11, Pt 3, para 5.
Date in force: to be appointed: see the Constitutional Reform Act 2005, s 148(1).

Sub-s (5): in para (c) reference to '5' in square brackets substituted by the Tribunals, Courts and Enforcement Act 2007, s 50, Sch 10, Pt 1, para 30(1), (3).
Date in force: 21 July 2008: see SI 2008/1653, art 2(d); for transitional provisions see arts 3, 4 thereof.

Sub-s (6): para (aa) substituted, for the word 'and' at the end of para (a), by the Freedom of Information Act 2000, s 18(4), Sch 2, Pt II, para 16(a).
Date in force: 14 May 2001: see SI 2001/1637, art 2(b).

Sub-s (6): para (bb) and the word 'and' immediately preceding it inserted by the Freedom of Information Act 2000, s 18(4), Sch 2, Pt II, para 16(b).
Date in force: 14 May 2001: see SI 2001/1637, art 2(b).

Transfer of Functions

The Secretary of State: functions of the Secretary of State under sub-s (4)(a) and (b) are transferred, in so far as they are exercisable in or as regards Scotland, to the Scottish Ministers, by the Scotland Act 1998 (Transfer of Functions to the Scottish Ministers etc) Order 1999, SI 1999/1750, art 2, Sch 1.

PART II
RIGHTS OF DATA SUBJECTS AND OTHERS

7 Right of access to personal data

(1) Subject to the following provisions of this section and to [sections 8, 9 and 9A], an individual is entitled—
- (a) to be informed by any data controller whether personal data of which that individual is the data subject are being processed by or on behalf of that data controller,
- (b) if that is the case, to be given by the data controller a description of—
  - (i) the personal data of which that individual is the data subject,
  - (ii) the purposes for which they are being or are to be processed, and
  - (iii) the recipients or classes of recipients to whom they are or may be disclosed,
- (c) to have communicated to him in an intelligible form—
  - (i) the information constituting any personal data of which that individual is the data subject, and
  - (ii) any information available to the data controller as to the source of those data, and
- (d) where the processing by automatic means of personal data of which that individual is the data subject for the purpose of evaluating matters relating to him such as, for example, his performance at work, his creditworthiness, his reliability or his conduct, has constituted or is likely to constitute the sole basis for any decision significantly affecting him, to be informed by the data controller of the logic involved in that decision-taking.

(2) A data controller is not obliged to supply any information under subsection (1) unless he has received—

    (a) a request in writing, and
    (b) except in prescribed cases, such fee (not exceeding the prescribed maximum) as he may require.

[(3) Where a data controller—

    (a) reasonably requires further information in order to satisfy himself as to the identity of the person making a request under this section and to locate the information which that person seeks, and
    (b) has informed him of that requirement,

the data controller is not obliged to comply with the request unless he is supplied with that further information.]

(4) Where a data controller cannot comply with the request without disclosing information relating to another individual who can be identified from that information, he is not obliged to comply with the request unless—

    (a) the other individual has consented to the disclosure of the information to the person making the request, or
    (b) it is reasonable in all the circumstances to comply with the request without the consent of the other individual.

(5) In subsection (4) the reference to information relating to another individual includes a reference to information identifying that individual as the source of the information sought by the request; and that subsection is not to be construed as excusing a data controller from communicating so much of the information sought by the request as can be communicated without disclosing the identity of the other individual concerned, whether by the omission of names or other identifying particulars or otherwise.

(6) In determining for the purposes of subsection (4)(b) whether it is reasonable in all the circumstances to comply with the request without the consent of the other individual concerned, regard shall be had, in particular, to—

    (a) any duty of confidentiality owed to the other individual,
    (b) any steps taken by the data controller with a view to seeking the consent of the other individual,
    (c) whether the other individual is capable of giving consent, and
    (d) any express refusal of consent by the other individual.

(7) An individual making a request under this section may, in such cases as may be prescribed, specify that his request is limited to personal data of any prescribed description.

(8) Subject to subsection (4), a data controller shall comply with a request under this section promptly and in any event before the end of the prescribed period beginning with the relevant day.

(9) If a court is satisfied on the application of any person who has made a request under the foregoing provisions of this section that the data controller in question has failed to comply with the request in contravention of those provisions, the court may order him to comply with the request.

(10) In this section—

    'prescribed' means prescribed by the [Secretary of State] by regulations;
    'the prescribed maximum' means such amount as may be prescribed;
    'the prescribed period' means forty days or such other period as may be prescribed;

'the relevant day', in relation to a request under this section, means the day on which the data controller receives the request or, if later, the first day on which the data controller has both the required fee and the information referred to in subsection (3).

(11) Different amounts or periods may be prescribed under this section in relation to different cases.

NOTES

Initial Commencement

Royal Assent
Sub-ss (7), (10): Royal Assent (so far as conferring power to make subordinate legislation): 16 July 1998: see s 75(2)(i).
Sub-s (11): Royal Assent: 16 July 1998: see s 75(2)(i).

To be appointed
Sub-ss (1)–(6), (8), (9): To be appointed: see s 75(3).
Sub-ss (7), (10): To be appointed (for remaining purposes): see s 75(3).

Appointment

Sub-ss (1)–(6), (8), (9): Appointment: 1 March 2000: see SI 2000/183, art 2(1).
Sub-ss (7), (10): Appointment (for remaining purposes): 1 March 2000: see SI 2000/183, art 2(1).

Amendment

Sub-s (1): words 'sections 8, 9 and 9A' in square brackets substituted by the Freedom of Information Act 2000, s 69(1).
Date in force: 1 January 2005: see SI 2004/1909, art 2(1), (2)(f), (3).

Sub-s (3): substituted by the Freedom of Information Act 2000, s 73, Sch 6, para 1.
Date in force: 14 May 2001: see SI 2001/1637, art 2(d).

Sub-s (10): in definition 'prescribed' words 'Secretary of State' in square brackets substituted by SI 2003/1887, art 9, Sch 2, para 9(1)(a).
Date in force: 19 August 2003: see SI 2003/1887, art 1(2).

Modification

Modified, in relation to data controllers who are not health professionals, by the Data Protection (Subject Access Modification) (Health) Order 2000, SI 2000/413, arts 6, 7(3).

Modified, in relation to certain data, by the Data Protection (Subject Access Modification) (Health) Order 2000, SI 2000/413, art 8.

Modified, in relation to the Principal Reporter, by the Data Protection (Subject Access Modification) (Education) Order 2000, SI 2000/414, art 6.

Modified, in relation to certain data, by the Data Protection (Subject Access Modification) (Education) Order 2000, SI 2000/414, art 7.

Modified, in relation to the Principal Reporter, by the Data Protection (Subject Access Modification) (Social Work) Order 2000, SI 2000/415, art 6.

Core resources

Modified, in relation to certain data, by the Data Protection (Subject Access Modification) (Social Work) Order 2000, SI 2000/415, art 7 (as amended by the Data Protection (Subject Access Modification) (Social Work) (Amendment) Order 2005, SI 2005/467, art 4).

Subordinate Legislation

Data Protection (Subject Access) (Fees and Miscellaneous Provisions) Regulations 2000, SI 2000/191 (made under sub-ss (2), (7), (8), (11)).

Data Protection (Subject Access) (Fees and Miscellaneous Provisions) (Amendment) Regulations 2001, SI 2001/3223 (made under sub-ss (2), (11)).

8   Provisions supplementary to section 7

(1) The [Secretary of State] may by regulations provide that, in such cases as may be prescribed, a request for information under any provision of subsection (1) of section 7 is to be treated as extending also to information under other provisions of that subsection.

(2) The obligation imposed by section 7(1)(c)(i) must be complied with by supplying the data subject with a copy of the information in permanent form unless—

(a) the supply of such a copy is not possible or would involve disproportionate effort, or
(b) the data subject agrees otherwise;

and where any of the information referred to in section 7(1)(c)(i) is expressed in terms which are not intelligible without explanation the copy must be accompanied by an explanation of those terms.

(3) Where a data controller has previously complied with a request made under section 7 by an individual, the data controller is not obliged to comply with a subsequent identical or similar request under that section by that individual unless a reasonable interval has elapsed between compliance with the previous request and the making of the current request.

(4) In determining for the purposes of subsection (3) whether requests under section 7 are made at reasonable intervals, regard shall be had to the nature of the data, the purpose for which the data are processed and the frequency with which the data are altered.

(5) Section 7(1)(d) is not to be regarded as requiring the provision of information as to the logic involved in any decision-taking if, and to the extent that, the information constitutes a trade secret.

(6) The information to be supplied pursuant to a request under section 7 must be supplied by reference to the data in question at the time when the request is received, except that it may take account of any amendment or deletion made between that time and the time when the information is supplied, being an amendment or deletion that would have been made regardless of the receipt of the request.

(7) For the purposes of section 7(4) and (5) another individual can be identified from the information being disclosed if he can be identified from that information, or from that and any other information which, in the reasonable belief of the data controller, is likely to be in, or to come into, the possession of the data subject making the request.

NOTES

Initial Commencement

Royal Assent
Sub-s (1): Royal Assent: 16 July 1998: see s 75(2)(i).

To be appointed
Sub-ss (2)–(7): To be appointed: see s 75(3).

Appointment

Sub-ss (2)–(7): Appointment: 1 March 2000: see SI 2000/183, art 2(1).

Amendment

Sub-s (1): words 'Secretary of State' in square brackets substituted by SI 2003/1887, art 9, Sch 2, para 9(1)(a).
Date in force: 19 August 2003: see SI 2003/1887, art 1(2).

Subordinate Legislation

Data Protection (Subject Access) (Fees and Miscellaneous Provisions) Regulations 2000, SI 2000/191 (made under sub-s (1)).

9 Application of section 7 where data controller is credit reference agency

(1) Where the data controller is a credit reference agency, section 7 has effect subject to the provisions of this section.

(2) An individual making a request under section 7 may limit his request to personal data relevant to his financial standing, and shall be taken to have so limited his request unless the request shows a contrary intention.

(3) Where the data controller receives a request under section 7 in a case where personal data of which the individual making the request is the data subject are being processed by or on behalf of the data controller, the obligation to supply information under that section includes an obligation to give the individual making the request a statement, in such form as may be prescribed by the [Secretary of State] by regulations, of the individual's rights—

  (a) under section 159 of the Consumer Credit Act 1974 , and
  (b) to the extent required by the prescribed form, under this Act.

NOTES

Initial Commencement

Royal Assent
Sub-s (3): Royal Assent (so far as conferring power to make subordinate legislation): 16 July 1998: see s 75(2)(i).

To be appointed
Sub-ss (1), (2): To be appointed: see s 75(3).
Sub-s (3): To be appointed (for remaining purposes): see s 75(3).

Core resources

Appointment

Sub-ss (1), (2): Appointment: 1 March 2000: see SI 2000/183, art 2(1).
Sub-s (3): Appointment (for remaining purposes): 1 March 2000: see SI 2000/183, art 2(1).

Amendment

Sub-s (3): words 'Secretary of State' in square brackets substituted by SI 2003/1887, art 9, Sch 2, para 9(1)(a).
Date in force: 19 August 2003: see SI 2003/1887, art 1(2).

[9A Unstructured personal data held by public authorities]

[(1) In this section 'unstructured personal data' means any personal data falling within paragraph (e) of the definition of 'data' in section 1(1), other than information which is recorded as part of, or with the intention that it should form part of, any set of information relating to individuals to the extent that the set is structured by reference to individuals or by reference to criteria relating to individuals.

(2) A public authority is not obliged to comply with subsection (1) of section 7 in relation to any unstructured personal data unless the request under that section contains a description of the data.

(3) Even if the data are described by the data subject in his request, a public authority is not obliged to comply with subsection (1) of section 7 in relation to unstructured personal data if the authority estimates that the cost of complying with the request so far as relating to those data would exceed the appropriate limit.

(4) Subsection (3) does not exempt the public authority from its obligation to comply with paragraph (a) of section 7(1) in relation to the unstructured personal data unless the estimated cost of complying with that paragraph alone in relation to those data would exceed the appropriate limit.

(5) In subsections (3) and (4) 'the appropriate limit' means such amount as may be prescribed by the [Secretary of State] by regulations, and different amounts may be prescribed in relation to different cases.

(6) Any estimate for the purposes of this section must be made in accordance with regulations under section 12(5) of the Freedom of Information Act 2000.]

NOTES

Amendment

Inserted by the Freedom of Information Act 2000, s 69(2).
Date in force (in so far as this section confers powers to make regulations): 30 November 2000: see the Freedom of Information Act 2000, s 87(1)(m).
Date in force (for remaining purposes): 1 January 2005: see SI 2004/1909, art 2(1), (2)(f), (3).

Sub-s (5): words 'Secretary of State' in square brackets substituted by SI 2003/1887, art 9, Sch 2, para 9(1)(a).
Date in force: 19 August 2003: see SI 2003/1887, art 1(2).

Subordinate Legislation

Freedom of Information and Data Protection (Appropriate Limit and Fees) Regulations 2004, SI 2004/3244 (made under sub-s (5)).

10 Right to prevent processing likely to cause damage or distress

(1) Subject to subsection (2), an individual is entitled at any time by notice in writing to a data controller to require the data controller at the end of such period as is reasonable in the circumstances to cease, or not to begin, processing, or processing for a specified purpose or in a specified manner, any personal data in respect of which he is the data subject, on the ground that, for specified reasons—

   (a) the processing of those data or their processing for that purpose or in that manner is causing or is likely to cause substantial damage or substantial distress to him or to another, and
   (b) that damage or distress is or would be unwarranted.

(2) Subsection (1) does not apply—

   (a) in a case where any of the conditions in paragraphs 1 to 4 of Schedule 2 is met, or
   (b) in such other cases as may be prescribed by the [Secretary of State] by order.

(3) The data controller must within twenty-one days of receiving a notice under subsection (1) ('the data subject notice') give the individual who gave it a written notice—

   (a) stating that he has complied or intends to comply with the data subject notice, or
   (b) stating his reasons for regarding the data subject notice as to any extent unjustified and the extent (if any) to which he has complied or intends to comply with it.

(4) If a court is satisfied, on the application of any person who has given a notice under subsection (1) which appears to the court to be justified (or to be justified to any extent), that the data controller in question has failed to comply with the notice, the court may order him to take such steps for complying with the notice (or for complying with it to that extent) as the court thinks fit.

(5) The failure by a data subject to exercise the right conferred by subsection (1) or section 11(1) does not affect any other right conferred on him by this Part.

NOTES

Initial Commencement

Royal Assent
Sub-s (2): Royal Assent (so far as conferring power to make subordinate legislation): 16 July 1998: see s 75(2)(i).

To be appointed
Sub-ss (1), (3)–(5): To be appointed: see s 75(3).
Sub-s (2): To be appointed (for remaining purposes): see s 75(3).

Appointment

Sub-ss (1), (3)–(5): Appointment: 1 March 2000: see SI 2000/183, art 2(1).
Sub-s (2): Appointment (for remaining purposes): 1 March 2000: see SI 2000/183, art 2(1).

Amendment

Sub-s (2): in para (b) words 'Secretary of State' in square brackets substituted by SI 2003/1887, art 9, Sch 2, para 9(1)(a).
Date in force: 19 August 2003: see SI 2003/1887, art 1(2).

Core resources

11 Right to prevent processing for purposes of direct marketing

(1) An individual is entitled at any time by notice in writing to a data controller to require the data controller at the end of such period as is reasonable in the circumstances to cease, or not to begin, processing for the purposes of direct marketing personal data in respect of which he is the data subject.

(2) If the court is satisfied, on the application of any person who has given a notice under subsection (1), that the data controller has failed to comply with the notice, the court may order him to take such steps for complying with the notice as the court thinks fit.

[(2A) This section shall not apply in relation to the processing of such data as are mentioned in paragraph (1) of regulation 8 of the Telecommunications (Data Protection and Privacy) Regulations 1999 (processing of telecommunications billing data for certain marketing purposes) for the purposes mentioned in paragraph (2) of that regulation.]

(3) In this section 'direct marketing' means the communication (by whatever means) of any advertising or marketing material which is directed to particular individuals.

NOTES

Initial Commencement

To be appointed
To be appointed: see s 75(3).

Appointment

Appointment: 1 March 2000: see SI 2000/183, art 2(1).

Amendment

Sub-s (2A): inserted by SI 1999/2093, reg 3(3), Sch 1, Pt II, para 3.
Date in force: 1 March 2000: see SI 1999/2093, reg 1(2)(b).

12 Rights in relation to automated decision-taking

(1) An individual is entitled at any time, by notice in writing to any data controller, to require the data controller to ensure that no decision taken by or on behalf of the data controller which significantly affects that individual is based solely on the processing by automatic means of personal data in respect of which that individual is the data subject for the purpose of evaluating matters relating to him such as, for example, his performance at work, his creditworthiness, his reliability or his conduct.

(2) Where, in a case where no notice under subsection (1) has effect, a decision which significantly affects an individual is based solely on such processing as is mentioned in subsection (1)—

    (a) the data controller must as soon as reasonably practicable notify the individual that the decision was taken on that basis, and
    (b) the individual is entitled, within twenty-one days of receiving that notification from the data controller, by notice in writing to require the data controller to reconsider the decision or to take a new decision otherwise than on that basis.

(3) The data controller must, within twenty-one days of receiving a notice under subsection (2)(b) ('the data subject notice') give the individual a written notice specifying the steps that he intends to take to comply with the data subject notice.

Data Protection Act 1998

(4) A notice under subsection (1) does not have effect in relation to an exempt decision; and nothing in subsection (2) applies to an exempt decision.

(5) In subsection (4) 'exempt decision' means any decision—

  (a) in respect of which the condition in subsection (6) and the condition in subsection (7) are met, or
  (b) which is made in such other circumstances as may be prescribed by the [Secretary of State] by order.

(6) The condition in this subsection is that the decision—

  (a) is taken in the course of steps taken—
   (i) for the purpose of considering whether to enter into a contract with the data subject,
   (ii) with a view to entering into such a contract, or
   (iii) in the course of performing such a contract, or
  (b) is authorised or required by or under any enactment.

(7) The condition in this subsection is that either—

  (a) the effect of the decision is to grant a request of the data subject, or
  (b) steps have been taken to safeguard the legitimate interests of the data subject (for example, by allowing him to make representations).

(8) If a court is satisfied on the application of a data subject that a person taking a decision in respect of him ('the responsible person') has failed to comply with subsection (1) or (2)(b), the court may order the responsible person to reconsider the decision, or to take a new decision which is not based solely on such processing as is mentioned in subsection (1).

(9) An order under subsection (8) shall not affect the rights of any person other than the data subject and the responsible person.

NOTES

Initial Commencement

Royal Assent
Sub-s (5): Royal Assent (so far as conferring power to make subordinate legislation): 16 July 1998: see s 75(2)(i).

To be appointed
Sub-s (5): To be appointed (for remaining purposes): see s 75(3).
Sub-ss (1)–(4), (6)–(9): To be appointed: see s 75(3).

Appointment

Sub-ss (1)–(4), (6)–(9): Appointment: 1 March 2000: see SI 2000/183, art 2(1).
Sub-s (5): Appointment (for remaining purposes): 1 March 2000: see SI 2000/183, art 2(1).

Amendment

Sub-s (5): in para (b) words 'Secretary of State' in square brackets substituted by SI 2003/1887, art 9, Sch 2, para 9(1)(a).
Date in force: 19 August 2003: see SI 2003/1887, art 1(2).

Core resources

13   Compensation for failure to comply with certain requirements

(1) An individual who suffers damage by reason of any contravention by a data controller of any of the requirements of this Act is entitled to compensation from the data controller for that damage.

(2) An individual who suffers distress by reason of any contravention by a data controller of any of the requirements of this Act is entitled to compensation from the data controller for that distress if—

   (a) the individual also suffers damage by reason of the contravention, or
   (b) the contravention relates to the processing of personal data for the special purposes.

(3) In proceedings brought against a person by virtue of this section it is a defence to prove that he had taken such care as in all the circumstances was reasonably required to comply with the requirement concerned.

NOTES

Initial Commencement

To be appointed
To be appointed: see s 75(3).

Appointment

Appointment: 1 March 2000: see SI 2000/183, art 2(1).

14   Rectification, blocking, erasure and destruction

(1) If a court is satisfied on the application of a data subject that personal data of which the applicant is the subject are inaccurate, the court may order the data controller to rectify, block, erase or destroy those data and any other personal data in respect of which he is the data controller and which contain an expression of opinion which appears to the court to be based on the inaccurate data.

(2) Subsection (1) applies whether or not the data accurately record information received or obtained by the data controller from the data subject or a third party but where the data accurately record such information, then—

   (a) if the requirements mentioned in paragraph 7 of Part II of Schedule 1 have been complied with, the court may, instead of making an order under subsection (1), make an order requiring the data to be supplemented by such statement of the true facts relating to the matters dealt with by the data as the court may approve, and
   (b) if all or any of those requirements have not been complied with, the court may, instead of making an order under that subsection, make such order as it thinks fit for securing compliance with those requirements with or without a further order requiring the data to be supplemented by such a statement as is mentioned in paragraph (a).

(3) Where the court

   (a) makes an order under subsection (1), or
   (b) is satisfied on the application of a data subject that personal data of which he was the data subject and which have been rectified, blocked, erased or destroyed were inaccurate,

it may, where it considers it reasonably practicable, order the data controller to notify third parties to whom the data have been disclosed of the rectification, blocking, erasure or destruction.

(4) If a court is satisfied on the application of a data subject—

(a) that he has suffered damage by reason of any contravention by a data controller of any of the requirements of this Act in respect of any personal data, in circumstances entitling him to compensation under section 13, and

(b) that there is a substantial risk of further contravention in respect of those data in such circumstances,

the court may order the rectification, blocking, erasure or destruction of any of those data.

(5) Where the court makes an order under subsection (4) it may, where it considers it reasonably practicable, order the data controller to notify third parties to whom the data have been disclosed of the rectification, blocking, erasure or destruction.

(6) In determining whether it is reasonably practicable to require such notification as is mentioned in subsection (3) or (5) the court shall have regard, in particular, to the number of persons who would have to be notified.

NOTES

Initial Commencement

To be appointed
To be appointed: see s 75(3).

Appointment

Appointment: 1 March 2000: see SI 2000/183, art 2(1).

15 Jurisdiction and procedure

(1) The jurisdiction conferred by sections 7 to 14 is exercisable by the High Court or a county court or, in Scotland, by the Court of Session or the sheriff.

(2) For the purpose of determining any question whether an applicant under subsection (9) of section 7 is entitled to the information which he seeks (including any question whether any relevant data are exempt from that section by virtue of Part IV) a court may require the information constituting any data processed by or on behalf of the data controller and any information as to the logic involved in any decision-taking as mentioned in section 7(1)(d) to be made available for its own inspection but shall not, pending the determination of that question in the applicant's favour, require the information sought by the applicant to be disclosed to him or his representatives whether by discovery (or, in Scotland, recovery) or otherwise.

NOTES

Initial Commencement

To be appointed
To be appointed: see s 75(3).

Appointment

Appointment: 1 March 2000: see SI 2000/183, art 2(1).

Core resources

PART III
NOTIFICATION BY DATA CONTROLLERS

16   Preliminary

(1) In this Part 'the registrable particulars', in relation to a data controller, means—

- (a) his name and address,
- (b) if he has nominated a representative for the purposes of this Act, the name and address of the representative,
- (c) a description of the personal data being or to be processed by or on behalf of the data controller and of the category or categories of data subject to which they relate,
- (d) a description of the purpose or purposes for which the data are being or are to be processed,
- (e) a description of any recipient or recipients to whom the data controller intends or may wish to disclose the data,
- (f) the names, or a description of, any countries or territories outside the European Economic Area to which the data controller directly or indirectly transfers, or intends or may wish directly or indirectly to transfer, the data,
- [(ff) where the data controller is a public authority, a statement of that fact,] and
- (g) in any case where—
    - (i) personal data are being, or are intended to be, processed in circumstances in which the prohibition in subsection (1) of section 17 is excluded by subsection (2) or (3) of that section, and
    - (ii) the notification does not extend to those data,

a statement of that fact.

(2) In this Part—

'fees regulations' means regulations made by the [Secretary of State] under section 18(5) or 19(4) or (7);

'notification regulations' means regulations made by the [Secretary of State] under the other provisions of this Part;

'prescribed', except where used in relation to fees regulations, means prescribed by notification regulations.

(3) For the purposes of this Part, so far as it relates to the addresses of data controllers—

- (a) the address of a registered company is that of its registered office, and
- (b) the address of a person (other than a registered company) carrying on a business is that of his principal place of business in the United Kingdom.

NOTES

Initial Commencement

To be appointed
To be appointed: see s 75(3).

Appointment

Appointment: 1 March 2000: see SI 2000/183, art 2(1).

Amendment

Sub-s (1): para (ff) inserted by the Freedom of Information Act 2000, s 71.
Date in force: 1 January 2005: see SI 2004/1909, art 2(1), (2)(f), (3).

Data Protection Act 1998

Sub-s (2): in definitions 'fees regulations', 'notification regulations' words 'Secretary of State' in square brackets substituted by SI 2003/1887, art 9, Sch 2, para 9(1)(a).
Date in force: 19 August 2003: see SI 2003/1887, art 1(2).

17 Prohibition on processing without registration

(1) Subject to the following provisions of this section, personal data must not be processed unless an entry in respect of the data controller is included in the register maintained by the Commissioner under section 19 (or is treated by notification regulations made by virtue of section 19(3) as being so included).

(2) Except where the processing is assessable processing for the purposes of section 22, subsection (1) does not apply in relation to personal data consisting of information which falls neither within paragraph (a) of the definition of 'data' in section 1(1) nor within paragraph (b) of that definition.

(3) If it appears to the [Secretary of State] that processing of a particular description is unlikely to prejudice the rights and freedoms of data subjects, notification regulations may provide that, in such cases as may be prescribed, subsection (1) is not to apply in relation to processing of that description.

(4) Subsection (1) does not apply in relation to any processing whose sole purpose is the maintenance of a public register.

NOTES

Initial Commencement

Royal Assent
Sub-s (3): Royal Assent (so far as conferring power to make subordinate legislation): 16 July 1998: see s 75(2)(i).

To be appointed
Sub-ss (1), (2), (4): To be appointed: see s 75(3).
Sub-s (3): To be appointed (for remaining purposes): see s 75(3).

Appointment

Sub-ss (1), (2), (4): Appointment: 1 March 2000: see SI 2000/183, art 2(1).
Sub-s (3): Appointment (for remaining purposes): 1 March 2000: see SI 2000/183, art 2(1).

Amendment

Sub-s (3): words 'Secretary of State' in square brackets substituted by SI 2003/1887, art 9, Sch 2, para 9(1)(a).
Date in force: 19 August 2003: see SI 2003/1887, art 1(2).

Subordinate Legislation

Data Protection (Notification and Notification Fees) Regulations 2000, SI 2000/188 (made under sub-s (3)).

Data Protection (Notification and Notification Fees) (Amendment) Regulations 2009, SI 2009/1677 (made under sub-s (3)).

18 Notification by data controllers

(1) Any data controller who wishes to be included in the register maintained under section 19 shall give a notification to the Commissioner under this section.

Core resources

(2) A notification under this section must specify in accordance with notification regulations—
  (a) the registrable particulars, and
  (b) a general description of measures to be taken for the purpose of complying with the seventh data protection principle.

(3) Notification regulations made by virtue of subsection (2) may provide for the determination by the Commissioner, in accordance with any requirements of the regulations, of the form in which the registrable particulars and the description mentioned in subsection (2)(b) are to be specified, including in particular the detail required for the purposes of section 16(1)(c), (d), (e) and (f) and subsection (2)(b).

(4) Notification regulations may make provision as to the giving of notification—
  (a) by partnerships, or
  (b) in other cases where two or more persons are the data controllers in respect of any personal data.

(5) The notification must be accompanied by such fee as may be prescribed by fees regulations.

(6) Notification regulations may provide for any fee paid under subsection (5) or section 19(4) to be refunded in prescribed circumstances.

NOTES

Initial Commencement

Royal Assent
Sub-ss (2), (5): Royal Assent (so far as conferring power to make subordinate legislation): 16 July 1998: see s 75(2)(i).
Sub-ss (3), (4), (6): Royal Assent: 16 July 1998: see s 75(2)(i).

To be appointed
Sub-s (1): To be appointed: see s 75(3).
Sub-ss (2), (5): To be appointed (for remaining purposes): see s 75(3).

Appointment

Sub-s (1): Appointment: 1 March 2000: see SI 2000/183, art 2(1).
Sub-ss (2), (5): Appointment (for remaining purposes): 1 March 2000: see SI 2000/183, art 2(1).

Subordinate Legislation

Data Protection (Notification and Notification Fees) Regulations 2000, SI 2000/188 (made under sub-ss (2), (4), (5)).

Data Protection (Notification and Notification Fees) (Amendment) Regulations 2009, SI 2009/1677 (made under sub-s (5)).

19   Register of notifications

(1) The Commissioner shall—
  (a) maintain a register of persons who have given notification under section 18, and
  (b) make an entry in the register in pursuance of each notification received by him under that section from a person in respect of whom no entry as data controller was for the time being included in the register.

Data Protection Act 1998

(2) Each entry in the register shall consist of—

(a) the registrable particulars notified under section 18 or, as the case requires, those particulars as amended in pursuance of section 20(4), and

(b) such other information as the Commissioner may be authorised or required by notification regulations to include in the register.

(3) Notification regulations may make provision as to the time as from which any entry in respect of a data controller is to be treated for the purposes of section 17 as having been made in the register.

(4) No entry shall be retained in the register for more than the relevant time except on payment of such fee as may be prescribed by fees regulations.

(5) In subsection (4) 'the relevant time' means twelve months or such other period as may be prescribed by notification regulations; and different periods may be prescribed in relation to different cases.

(6) The Commissioner—

(a) shall provide facilities for making the information contained in the entries in the register available for inspection (in visible and legible form) by members of the public at all reasonable hours and free of charge, and

(b) may provide such other facilities for making the information contained in those entries available to the public free of charge as he considers appropriate.

(7) The Commissioner shall, on payment of such fee, if any, as may be prescribed by fees regulations, supply any member of the public with a duly certified copy in writing of the particulars contained in any entry made in the register.

NOTES

Initial Commencement

Royal Assent
Royal Assent (so far as conferring power to make subordinate legislation): 16 July 1998: see s 75(2)(i).

To be appointed
To be appointed (for remaining purposes): see s 75(3).

Appointment

Appointment (for remaining purposes): 1 March 2000: see SI 2000/183, art 2(1).

Subordinate Legislation

Data Protection (Fees under section 19(7)) Regulations 2000, SI 2000/187 (made under sub-s (7)).

Data Protection (Notification and Notification Fees) Regulations 2000, SI 2000/188 (made under sub-ss (2), (3), (4), (5)).

Data Protection (Notification and Notification Fees) (Amendment) Regulations 2001, SI 2001/3214 (made under sub-s (5)).

Data Protection (Notification and Notification Fees) (Amendment) Regulations 2009, SI 2009/1677 (made under sub-s (4)).

Core resources

20 Duty to notify changes

(1) For the purpose specified in subsection (2), notification regulations shall include provision imposing on every person in respect of whom an entry as a data controller is for the time being included in the register maintained under section 19 a duty to notify to the Commissioner, in such circumstances and at such time or times and in such form as may be prescribed, such matters relating to the registrable particulars and measures taken as mentioned in section 18(2)(b) as may be prescribed.

(2) The purpose referred to in subsection (1) is that of ensuring, so far as practicable, that at any time—

    (a) the entries in the register maintained under section 19 contain current names and addresses and describe the current practice or intentions of the data controller with respect to the processing of personal data, and

    (b) the Commissioner is provided with a general description of measures currently being taken as mentioned in section 18(2)(b).

(3) Subsection (3) of section 18 has effect in relation to notification regulations made by virtue of subsection (1) as it has effect in relation to notification regulations made by virtue of subsection (2) of that section.

(4) On receiving any notification under notification regulations made by virtue of subsection (1), the Commissioner shall make such amendments of the relevant entry in the register maintained under section 19 as are necessary to take account of the notification.

NOTES

Initial Commencement

Royal Assent
Sub-s (1): Royal Assent: 16 July 1998: see s 75(2)(i).

To be appointed
Sub-ss (2)–(4): To be appointed: see s 75(3).

Appointment

Sub-ss (2)–(4): Appointment: 1 March 2000: see SI 2000/183, art 2(1).

Subordinate Legislation

Data Protection (Notification and Notification Fees) Regulations 2000, SI 2000/188 (made under sub-s (1)).

21 Offences

(1) If section 17(1) is contravened, the data controller is guilty of an offence.

(2) Any person who fails to comply with the duty imposed by notification regulations made by virtue of section 20(1) is guilty of an offence.

(3) It shall be a defence for a person charged with an offence under subsection (2) to show that he exercised all due diligence to comply with the duty.

NOTES

Initial Commencement

To be appointed
To be appointed: see s 75(3).

Appointment

Appointment: 1 March 2000: see SI 2000/183, art 2(1).

22 Preliminary assessment by Commissioner

(1) In this section 'assessable processing' means processing which is of a description specified in an order made by the [Secretary of State] as appearing to him to be particularly likely—

    (a) to cause substantial damage or substantial distress to data subjects, or
    (b) otherwise significantly to prejudice the rights and freedoms of data subjects.

(2) On receiving notification from any data controller under section 18 or under notification regulations made by virtue of section 20 the Commissioner shall consider—

    (a) whether any of the processing to which the notification relates is assessable processing, and
    (b) if so, whether the assessable processing is likely to comply with the provisions of this Act.

(3) Subject to subsection (4), the Commissioner shall, within the period of twenty-eight days beginning with the day on which he receives a notification which relates to assessable processing, give a notice to the data controller stating the extent to which the Commissioner is of the opinion that the processing is likely or unlikely to comply with the provisions of this Act.

(4) Before the end of the period referred to in subsection (3) the Commissioner may, by reason of special circumstances, extend that period on one occasion only by notice to the data controller by such further period not exceeding fourteen days as the Commissioner may specify in the notice.

(5) No assessable processing in respect of which a notification has been given the Commissioner as mentioned in subsection (2) shall be carried on unless either—

    (a) the period of twenty-eight days beginning with the day on which the notification is received by the Commissioner (or, in a case falling within subsection (4), that period as extended under that subsection) has elapsed, or
    (b) before the end of that period (or that period as so extended) the data controller has received a notice from the Commissioner under subsection (3) in respect of the processing.

(6) Where subsection (5) is contravened, the data controller is guilty of an offence.

(7) The [Secretary of State] may by order amend subsections (3), (4) and (5) by substituting for the number of days for the time being specified there a different number specified in the order.

NOTES

Initial Commencement

Royal Assent
Sub-ss (1), (7): Royal Assent: 16 July 1998: see s 75(2)(i).

Core resources

To be appointed
Sub-ss (2)–(6): To be appointed: see s 75(3).

Appointment

Sub-ss (2)–(6): Appointment: 1 March 2000: see SI 2000/183, art 2(1).

Amendment

Sub-s (1): words 'Secretary of State' in square brackets substituted by SI 2003/1887, art 9, Sch 2, para 9(1)(a).
Date in force: 19 August 2003: see SI 2003/1887, art 1(2).

Sub-s (7): words 'Secretary of State' in square brackets substituted by SI 2003/1887, art 9, Sch 2, para 9(1)(a).
Date in force: 19 August 2003: see SI 2003/1887, art 1(2).

23   Power to make provision for appointment of data protection supervisors

(1) The [Secretary of State] may by order—

- (a) make provision under which a data controller may appoint a person to act as a data protection supervisor responsible in particular for monitoring in an independent manner the data controller's compliance with the provisions of this Act, and
- (b) provide that, in relation to any data controller who has appointed a data protection supervisor in accordance with the provisions of the order and who complies with such conditions as may be specified in the order, the provisions of this Part are to have effect subject to such exemptions or other modifications as may be specified in the order.

(2) An order under this section may—

- (a) impose duties on data protection supervisors in relation to the Commissioner, and
- (b) confer functions on the Commissioner in relation to data protection supervisors.

NOTES

Initial Commencement

Royal Assent
Royal Assent: 16 July 1998: see s 75(2)(i).

Amendment

Sub-s (1): words 'Secretary of State' in square brackets substituted by SI 2003/1887, art 9, Sch 2, para 9(1)(a).
Date in force: 19 August 2003: see SI 2003/1887, art 1(2).

24   Duty of certain data controllers to make certain information available

(1) Subject to subsection (3), where personal data are processed in a case where—

- (a) by virtue of subsection (2) or (3) of section 17, subsection (1) of that section does not apply to the processing, and
- (b) the data controller has not notified the relevant particulars in respect of that processing under section 18,

the data controller must, within twenty-one days of receiving a written request from any person, make the relevant particulars available to that person in writing free of charge.

(2) In this section 'the relevant particulars' means the particulars referred to in paragraphs (a) to (f) of section 16(1).

(3) This section has effect subject to any exemption conferred for the purposes of this section by notification regulations.

(4) Any data controller who fails to comply with the duty imposed by subsection (1) is guilty of an offence.

(5) It shall be a defence for a person charged with an offence under subsection (4) to show that he exercised all due diligence to comply with the duty.

NOTES

Initial Commencement

Royal Assent
Sub-s (3): Royal Assent: 16 July 1998: see s 75(2)(i).

To be appointed
Sub-ss (1), (2), (4), (5): To be appointed: see s 75(3).

Appointment

Sub-ss (1), (2), (4), (5): Appointment: 1 March 2000: see SI 2000/183, art 2(1).

25 Functions of Commissioner in relation to making of notification regulations

(1) As soon as practicable after the passing of this Act, the Commissioner shall submit to the Secretary of State proposals as to the provisions to be included in the first notification regulations.

(2) The Commissioner shall keep under review the working of notification regulations and may from time to time submit to the [Secretary of State] proposals as to amendments to be made to the regulations.

(3) The [Secretary of State] may from time to time require the Commissioner to consider any matter relating to notification regulations and to submit to him proposals as to amendments to be made to the regulations in connection with that matter.

(4) Before making any notification regulations, the [Secretary of State] shall—

(a) consider any proposals made to him by the Commissioner under [subsection (2) or (3)], and
(b) consult the Commissioner.

NOTES

Initial Commencement

Royal Assent
Sub-ss (1), (4): Royal Assent: 16 July 1998: see s 75(2)(b).

To be appointed
Sub-ss (2), (3): To be appointed: see s 75(3).

Core resources

Appointment

Sub-ss (2), (3): Appointment: 1 March 2000: see SI 2000/183, art 2(1).

Amendment

Sub-s (2): words 'Secretary of State' in square brackets substituted by SI 2003/1887, art 9, Sch 2, para 9(1)(a).
Date in force: 19 August 2003: see SI 2003/1887, art 1(2).

Sub-s (3): words 'Secretary of State' in square brackets substituted by SI 2003/1887, art 9, Sch 2, para 9(1)(a).
Date in force: 19 August 2003: see SI 2003/1887, art 1(2).

Sub-s (4): words 'Secretary of State' in square brackets substituted by SI 2003/1887, art 9, Sch 2, para 9(1)(a).
Date in force: 19 August 2003: see SI 2003/1887, art 1(2).

Sub-s (4): in para (a) words 'subsection (2) or (3)' in square brackets substituted by SI 2001/3500, art 8, Sch 2, Pt I, para 6(2).
Date in force: 26 November 2001: see SI 2001/3500, art 1(2).

26   Fees regulations

(1) Fees regulations prescribing fees for the purposes of any provision of this Part may provide for different fees to be payable in different cases.

(2) In making any fees regulations, the [Secretary of State] shall have regard to the desirability of securing that the fees payable to the Commissioner are sufficient to offset—

   (a)   the expenses incurred by the Commissioner and the Tribunal in discharging their functions [under this Act] and any expenses of the Secretary of State in respect of the Commissioner or the Tribunal [so far as attributable to their functions under this Act], and
   (b)   to the extent that the [Secretary of State] considers appropriate—
      (i)   any deficit previously incurred (whether before or after the passing of this Act) in respect of the expenses mentioned in paragraph (a), and
      (ii) expenses incurred or to be incurred by the [Secretary of State] in respect of the inclusion of any officers or staff of the Commissioner in any scheme under section 1 of the Superannuation Act 1972.

NOTES

Initial Commencement

Royal Assent
Royal Assent: 16 July 1998: see s 75(2)(c).

Amendment

Sub-s (2): words 'Secretary of State' in square brackets in each place they occur substituted by SI 2003/1887, art 9, Sch 2, para 9(1)(a).
Date in force: 19 August 2003: see SI 2003/1887, art 1(2).

Sub-s (2): in para (a) words 'under this Act' and 'so far as attributable to their functions under this Act' in square brackets inserted by the Freedom of Information Act 2000, s 18(4), Sch 2, Pt II, para 17.
Date in force: 30 November 2000: see the Freedom of Information Act 2000, s 87(1)(i).

Subordinate Legislation

Data Protection (Notification and Notification Fees) Regulations 2000, SI 2000/188 (made under sub-s (1)).

Data Protection (Notification and Notification Fees) (Amendment) Regulations 2009, SI 2009/1677 (made under sub-s (1)).

PART IV
EXEMPTIONS

27 Preliminary

(1) References in any of the data protection principles or any provision of Parts II and III to personal data or to the processing of personal data do not include references to data or processing which by virtue of this Part are exempt from that principle or other provision.

(2) In this Part 'the subject information provisions' means—

(a) the first data protection principle to the extent to which it requires compliance with paragraph 2 of Part II of Schedule 1, and
(b) section 7.

(3) In this Part 'the non-disclosure provisions' means the provisions specified in subsection (4) to the extent to which they are inconsistent with the disclosure in question.

(4) The provisions referred to in subsection (3) are—

(a) the first data protection principle, except to the extent to which it requires compliance with the conditions in Schedules 2 and 3,
(b) the second, third, fourth and fifth data protection principles, and
(c) sections 10 and 14(1) to (3).

(5) Except as provided by this Part, the subject information provisions shall have effect notwithstanding any enactment or rule of law prohibiting or restricting the disclosure, or authorising the withholding, of information.

NOTES

Initial Commencement

To be appointed
To be appointed: see s 75(3).

Appointment

Appointment: 1 March 2000: see SI 2000/183, art 2(1).

28 National security

(1) Personal data are exempt from any of the provisions of—

(a) the data protection principles,
(b) Parts II, III and V, and
(c) [sections 54A and] 55,

if the exemption from that provision is required for the purpose of safeguarding national security.

Core resources

(2) Subject to subsection (4), a certificate signed by a Minister of the Crown certifying that exemption from all or any of the provisions mentioned in subsection (1) is or at any time was required for the purpose there mentioned in respect of any personal data shall be conclusive evidence of that fact.

(3) A certificate under subsection (2) may identify the personal data to which it applies by means of a general description and may be expressed to have prospective effect.

(4) Any person directly affected by the issuing of a certificate under subsection (2) may appeal to the Tribunal against the certificate.

(5) If on an appeal under subsection (4), the Tribunal finds that, applying the principles applied by the court on an application for judicial review, the Minister did not have reasonable grounds for issuing the certificate, the Tribunal may allow the appeal and quash the certificate.

(6) Where in any proceedings under or by virtue of this Act it is claimed by a data controller that a certificate under subsection (2) which identifies the personal data to which it applies by means of a general description applies to any personal data, any other party to the proceedings may appeal to the Tribunal on the ground that the certificate does not apply to the personal data in question and, subject to any determination under subsection (7), the certificate shall be conclusively presumed so to apply.

(7) On any appeal under subsection (6), the Tribunal may determine that the certificate does not so apply.

(8) A document purporting to be a certificate under subsection (2) shall be received in evidence and deemed to be such a certificate unless the contrary is proved.

(9) A document which purports to be certified by or on behalf of a Minister of the Crown as a true copy of a certificate issued by that Minister under subsection (2) shall in any legal proceedings be evidence (or, in Scotland, sufficient evidence) of that certificate.

(10) The power conferred by subsection (2) on a Minister of the Crown shall not be exercisable except by a Minister who is a member of the Cabinet or by the Attorney General or the [Advocate General for Scotland].

(11) No power conferred by any provision of Part V may be exercised in relation to personal data which by virtue of this section are exempt from that provision.

(12) Schedule 6 shall have effect in relation to appeals under subsection (4) or (6) and the proceedings of the Tribunal in respect of any such appeal.

NOTES

Initial Commencement

Royal Assent
Sub-s (12): Royal Assent (so far as is necessary for bringing into force those provisions of Sch 6 which confer power to make subordinate legislation): 16 July 1998: see s 75(2)(i).

To be appointed
Sub-ss (1)–(11): To be appointed: see s 75(3).
Sub-s (12): To be appointed (for remaining purposes): see s 75(3).

Data Protection Act 1998

Appointment

Sub-ss (1)–(11): Appointment: 1 March 2000: see SI 2000/183, art 2(1).
Sub-s (12): Appointment (for remaining purposes): 1 March 2000: see SI 2000/183, art 2(1).

Amendment

Sub-s (1): in para (c) words 'sections 54A and' in square brackets substituted by the Crime (International Co-operation) Act 2003, s 91(1), Sch 5, paras 68, 69.
Date in force: 26 April 2004: see SI 2004/786, art 3(1), (2).

Sub-s (10): words 'Advocate General for Scotland' in square brackets substituted by virtue of SI 1999/679, art 2, Schedule.
Date in force: 20 May 1999: see SI 1999/679, art 1(2).

29 Crime and taxation

(1) Personal data processed for any of the following purposes—

    (a) the prevention or detection of crime,
    (b) the apprehension or prosecution of offenders, or
    (c) the assessment or collection of any tax or duty or of any imposition of a similar nature,

are exempt from the first data protection principle (except to the extent to which it requires compliance with the conditions in Schedules 2 and 3) and section 7 in any case to the extent to which the application of those provisions to the data would be likely to prejudice any of the matters mentioned in this subsection.

(2) Personal data which—

    (a) are processed for the purpose of discharging statutory functions, and
    (b) consist of information obtained for such a purpose from a person who had it in his possession for any of the purposes mentioned in subsection (1),

are exempt from the subject information provisions to the same extent as personal data processed for any of the purposes mentioned in that subsection.

(3) Personal data are exempt from the non-disclosure provisions in any case in which—

    (a) the disclosure is for any of the purposes mentioned in subsection (1), and
    (b) the application of those provisions in relation to the disclosure would be likely to prejudice any of the matters mentioned in that subsection.

(4) Personal data in respect of which the data controller is a relevant authority and which—

    (a) consist of a classification applied to the data subject as part of a system of risk assessment which is operated by that authority for either of the following purposes—
        (i) the assessment or collection of any tax or duty or any imposition of a similar nature, or
        (ii) the prevention or detection of crime, or apprehension or prosecution of offenders, where the offence concerned involves any unlawful claim for any payment out of, or any unlawful application of, public funds, and
    (b) are processed for either of those purposes,

are exempt from section 7 to the extent to which the exemption is required in the interests of the operation of the system.

(5) In subsection (4)—

Core resources

'public funds' includes funds provided by any Community institution;
'relevant authority' means—
   (a) a government department,
   (b) a local authority, or
   (c) any other authority administering housing benefit or council tax benefit.

NOTES

Initial Commencement

To be appointed
To be appointed: see s 75(3).

Appointment

Appointment: 1 March 2000: see SI 2000/183, art 2(1).

30   Health, education and social work

(1) The [Secretary of State] may by order exempt from the subject information provisions, or modify those provisions in relation to, personal data consisting of information as to the physical or mental health or condition of the data subject.

(2) The [Secretary of State] may by order exempt from the subject information provisions, or modify those provisions in relation to—
   (a) personal data in respect of which the data controller is the proprietor of, or a teacher at, a school, and which consist of information relating to persons who are or have been pupils at the school, or
   (b) personal data in respect of which the data controller is an education authority in Scotland, and which consist of information relating to persons who are receiving, or have received, further education provided by the authority.

(3) The [Secretary of State] may by order exempt from the subject information provisions, or modify those provisions in relation to, personal data of such other descriptions as may be specified in the order, being information—
   (a) processed by government departments or local authorities or by voluntary organisations or other bodies designated by or under the order, and
   (b) appearing to him to be processed in the course of, or for the purposes of, carrying out social work in relation to the data subject or other individuals;

but the [Secretary of State] shall not under this subsection confer any exemption or make any modification except so far as he considers that the application to the data of those provisions (or of those provisions without modification) would be likely to prejudice the carrying out of social work.

(4) An order under this section may make different provision in relation to data consisting of information of different descriptions.

(5) In this section—
   'education authority' and 'further education' have the same meaning as in the Education (Scotland) Act 1980 ('the 1980 Act'), and
   'proprietor'—
      (a) in relation to a school in England or Wales, has the same meaning as in the Education Act 1996,
      (b) in relation to a school in Scotland, means—
         (i) ...

Data Protection Act 1998

      (ii) in the case of an independent school, the proprietor within the meaning of the 1980 Act,
      (iii) in the case of a grant-aided school, the managers within the meaning of the 1980 Act, and
      (iv) in the case of a public school, the education authority within the meaning of the 1980 Act, and
  (c) in relation to a school in Northern Ireland, has the same meaning as in the Education and Libraries (Northern Ireland) Order 1986 and includes, in the case of a controlled school, the Board of Governors of the school.

NOTES

Initial Commencement

Royal Assent
Royal Assent: 16 July 1998: see s 75(2)(i).

Amendment

Sub-s (1): words 'Secretary of State' in square brackets substituted by SI 2003/1887, art 9, Sch 2, para 9(1)(a).
Date in force: 19 August 2003: see SI 2003/1887, art 1(2).

Sub-s (2): words 'Secretary of State' in square brackets substituted by SI 2003/1887, art 9, Sch 2, para 9(1)(a).
Date in force: 19 August 2003: see SI 2003/1887, art 1(2).

Sub-s (3): words 'Secretary of State' in square brackets in both places they occur substituted by SI 2003/1887, art 9, Sch 2, para 9(1)(a).
Date in force: 19 August 2003: see SI 2003/1887, art 1(2).

Sub-s (5): in definition 'proprietor' para (b)(i) repealed by the Standards in Scotland's Schools etc Act 2000, s 60(2), Sch 3.
Date in force: 31 December 2004: see SSI 2004/528, art 2(b).

Transfer of Functions

Transfer of functions to and from the National Assembly for Wales: the National Assembly for Wales (Transfer of Functions) Order 1999, SI 1999/672, art 2(a), Sch 1 provided that, subject to art 2(b) to (f), all functions of a Minister of the Crown under this section were, in so far as exercisable in relation to Wales, transferred to the National Assembly for Wales. As a consequence of the amendment of Sch 1 to the 1999 Order by the National Assembly for Wales (Transfer of Functions) Order 2000, SI 2000/253, art 4, Sch 3(g), the functions transferred to the Assembly by the 1999 Order ceased to be exercisable by the Assembly and instead (by virtue of art 5 of the 2000 Order) became exercisable by the Minister of the Crown by whom they were exercisable, in relation to Wales, immediately before 1 July 1999.

Subordinate Legislation

Data Protection (Subject Access Modification) (Health) Order 2000, SI 2000/413 (made under sub-ss (1), (4)).

Data Protection (Subject Access Modification) (Education) Order 2000, SI 2000/414 (made under sub-ss (2), (4)).

Data Protection (Subject Access Modification) (Social Work) Order 2000, SI 2000/415 (made under sub-ss (3), (4)).

Core resources

Data Protection (Subject Access Modification) (Social Work) (Amendment) Order 2005, SI 2005/467 (made under sub-ss (3), (4)).

31   Regulatory activity

(1) Personal data processed for the purposes of discharging functions to which this subsection applies are exempt from the subject information provisions in any case to the extent to which the application of those provisions to the data would be likely to prejudice the proper discharge of those functions.

(2) Subsection (1) applies to any relevant function which is designed—
- (a) for protecting members of the public against—
  - (i) financial loss due to dishonesty, malpractice or other seriously improper conduct by, or the unfitness or incompetence of, persons concerned in the provision of banking, insurance, investment or other financial services or in the management of bodies corporate,
  - (ii) financial loss due to the conduct of discharged or undischarged bankrupts, or
  - (iii) dishonesty, malpractice or other seriously improper conduct by, or the unfitness or incompetence of, persons authorised to carry on any profession or other activity,
- (b) for protecting charities [or community interest companies] against misconduct or mismanagement (whether by trustees[, directors] or other persons) in their administration,
- (c) for protecting the property of charities [or community interest companies] from loss or misapplication,
- (d) for the recovery of the property of charities [or community interest companies],
- (e) for securing the health, safety and welfare of persons at work, or
- (f) for protecting persons other than persons at work against risk to health or safety arising out of or in connection with the actions of persons at work.

(3) In subsection (2) 'relevant function' means—
- (a) any function conferred on any person by or under any enactment,
- (b) any function of the Crown, a Minister of the Crown or a government department, or
- (c) any other function which is of a public nature and is exercised in the public interest.

(4) Personal data processed for the purpose of discharging any function which—
- (a) is conferred by or under any enactment on—
  - (i) the Parliamentary Commissioner for Administration,
  - (ii) the Commission for Local Administration in England [...] ...,
  - (iii) the Health Service Commissioner for England [...] ...,
  - [(iv) the Public Services Ombudsman for Wales,]
  - (v) the Assembly Ombudsman for Northern Ireland, ...
  - (vi) the Northern Ireland Commissioner for Complaints, [or]
  - [(vii) the Scottish Public Services Ombudsman, and]
- (b) is designed for protecting members of the public against—
  - (i) maladministration by public bodies,
  - (ii) failures in services provided by public bodies, or
  - (iii) a failure of a public body to provide a service which it was a function of the body to provide,

are exempt from the subject information provisions in any case to the extent to which the application of those provisions to the data would be likely to prejudice the proper discharge of that function.

Data Protection Act 1998

[(4A) Personal data processed for the purpose of discharging any function which is conferred by or under Part XVI of the Financial Services and Markets Act 2000 on the body established by the Financial Services Authority for the purposes of that Part are exempt from the subject information provisions in any case to the extent to which the application of those provisions to the data would be likely to prejudice the proper discharge of the function.]

[(4B) Personal data processed for the purposes of discharging any function of the Legal Services Board are exempt from the subject information provisions in any case to the extent to which the application of those provisions to the data would be likely to prejudice the proper discharge of the function.]

[(4C) Personal data processed for the purposes of the function of considering a complaint under the scheme established under Part 6 of the Legal Services Act 2007 (legal complaints) are exempt from the subject information provisions in any case to the extent to which the application of those provisions to the data would be likely to prejudice the proper discharge of the function.]

(5) Personal data processed for the purpose of discharging any function which—

    (a) is conferred by or under any enactment on [the Office of Fair Trading], and
    (b) is designed—
        (i) for protecting members of the public against conduct which may adversely affect their interests by persons carrying on a business,
        (ii) for regulating agreements or conduct which have as their object or effect the prevention, restriction or distortion of competition in connection with any commercial activity, or
        (iii) for regulating conduct on the part of one or more undertakings which amounts to the abuse of a dominant position in a market,

are exempt from the subject information provisions in any case to the extent to which the application of those provisions to the data would be likely to prejudice the proper discharge of that function.

[(5A) Personal data processed by a CPC enforcer for the purpose of discharging any function conferred on such a body by or under the CPC Regulation are exempt from the subject information provisions in any case to the extent to which the application of those provisions to the data would be likely to prejudice the proper discharge of that function.

(5B) In subsection (5A)—

    (a) 'CPC enforcer' has the meaning given to it in section 213(5A) of the Enterprise Act 2002 but does not include the Office of Fair Trading;
    (b) 'CPC Regulation' has the meaning given to it in section 235A of that Act.]

[(6) Personal data processed for the purpose of the function of considering a complaint under [section 14 of the NHS Redress Act 2006,] section 113(1) or (2) or 114(1) or (3) of the Health and Social Care (Community Health and Standards) Act 2003, or section 24D, 26... or 26ZB of the Children Act 1989, are exempt from the subject information provisions in any case to the extent to which the application of those provisions to the data would be likely to prejudice the proper discharge of that function.]

[(7) Personal data processed for the purpose of discharging any function which is conferred by or under Part 3 of the Local Government Act 2000 on—

    (a) the monitoring officer of a relevant authority,
    (b) an ethical standards officer, or
    (c) the Public Services Ombudsman for Wales,

Core resources

are exempt from the subject information provisions in any case to the extent to which the application of those provisions to the data would be likely to prejudice the proper discharge of that function.

(8) In subsection (7)—

    (a) 'relevant authority' has the meaning given by section 49(6) of the Local Government Act 2000, and

    (b) any reference to the monitoring officer of a relevant authority, or to an ethical standards officer, has the same meaning as in Part 3 of that Act.]

NOTES

Initial Commencement

To be appointed
To be appointed: see s 75(3).

Appointment

Appointment: 1 March 2000: see SI 2000/183, art 2(1).

Amendment

Sub-s (2): in paras (b)–(d) words 'or community interest companies' in square brackets inserted by the Companies (Audit, Investigations and Community Enterprise) Act 2004, s 59(3)(a).
Date in force: 1 July 2005: see SI 2004/3322, art 2(3), Sch 3.

Sub-s (2): in para (b) word ', directors' in square brackets inserted by the Companies (Audit, Investigations and Community Enterprise) Act 2004, s 59(3)(b).
Date in force: 1 July 2005: see SI 2004/3322, art 2(3), Sch 3.

Sub-s (4): in para (a)(ii) first word omitted inserted by SI 2004/1823, art 19(a)(i).
Date in force: 14 July 2004: see SI 2004/1823, art 1.

Sub-s (4): in para (a)(ii) first words omitted repealed by the Public Services Ombudsman (Wales) Act 2005, s 39, Sch 6, para 60(a), Sch 7.
Date in force: 1 April 2006: see SI 2005/2800, art 5(1); for further effect in relation to complaints made or referred to the Ombudsman about a matter relating to events that occurred before or after 1 April 2006, and in relation to estimates for income and expenses in relation to the financial year ending 31 March 2007, see arts 6, 7 thereof.

Sub-s (4): in para (a)(ii) final words omitted repealed by SI 2004/1823, art 19(a)(ii).
Date in force: 14 July 2004: see SI 2004/1823, art 1.

Sub-s (4): in para (a)(iii) first word omitted inserted by SI 2004/1823, art 19(b)(i).
Date in force: 14 July 2004: see SI 2004/1823, art 1.

Sub-s (4): in sub-para (a)(iii) first words omitted repealed by the Public Services Ombudsman (Wales) Act 2005, s 39, Sch 6, para 60(b), Sch 7.
Date in force: 1 April 2006: see SI 2005/2800, art 5(1); for further effect in relation to complaints made or referred to the Ombudsman about a matter relating to events that occurred before or after 1 April 2006, and in relation to estimates for income and expenses in relation to the financial year ending 31 March 2007, see arts 6, 7 thereof.

Sub-s (4): in para (a)(iii) final words omitted repealed by SI 2004/1823, art 19(b)(ii).
Date in force: 14 July 2004: see SI 2004/1823, art 1.

Sub-s (4): sub-para (a)(iv) substituted by the Public Services Ombudsman (Wales) Act 2005, s 39(1), Sch 6, para 60(c).

Date in force: 1 April 2006: see SI 2005/2800, art 5(1); for further effect in relation to complaints made or referred to the Ombudsman about a matter relating to events that occurred before or after 1 April 2006, and in relation to estimates for income and expenses in relation to the financial year ending 31 March 2007, see arts 6, 7 thereof.

Sub-s (4): in para (v) word omitted repealed by SI 2004/1823, art 19(c).
Date in force: 14 July 2004: see SI 2004/1823, art 1.

Sub-s (4): in para (a)(vi) word 'or' in square brackets substituted by SI 2004/1823, art 19(d).
Date in force: 14 July 2004: see SI 2004/1823, art 1.

Sub-s (4): para (a)(vii) inserted by SI 2004/1823, art 19(e).
Date in force: 14 July 2004: see SI 2004/1823, art 1.

Sub-s (4A): inserted by the Financial Services and Markets Act 2000, s 233.
Date in force: 1 December 2001: see SI 2001/3538, art 2(1).

Sub-s (4B): inserted by the Legal Services Act 2007, s 170.
Date in force: to be appointed: see the Legal Services Act 2007, s 211(2).

Sub-s (4C): inserted by the Legal Services Act 2007, s 153.
Date in force: to be appointed: see the Legal Services Act 2007, s 211(2).

Sub-s (5): in para (a) words 'the Office of Fair Trading' in square brackets substituted by the Enterprise Act 2002, s 278(1), Sch 25, para 37.
Date in force: 1 April 2003: see SI 2003/766, art 2, Schedule; for transitional and transitory provisions and savings see the Enterprise Act 2002, s 276, Sch 24, paras 2–6.

Sub-ss (5A), (5B): inserted by SI 2006/3363, reg 29.
Date in force: 8 January 2007: see SI 2006/3363, reg 1(2).

Sub-s (6): inserted by the Health and Social Care (Community Health and Standards) Act 2003, s 119.
Date in force: 1 June 2004: see SI 2004/759, art 8.

Sub-s (6): words 'section 14 of the NHS Redress Act 2006,' in square brackets inserted by the NHS Redress Act 2006, s 14(10).
Date in force: to be appointed: see the NHS Redress Act 2006, s 19(4).

Sub-s (6): reference omitted repealed by the Education and Inspections Act 2006, ss 157, 184, Sch 14, para 32, Sch 18, Pt 5.
Date in force: 1 April 2007: see SI 2007/935, art 5(gg), (ii).

Sub-ss (7), (8): inserted by the Local Government and Public Involvement in Health Act 2007, s 200.
Date in force: 1 April 2008: see SI 2008/172, art 4(k).

32 Journalism, literature and art

(1) Personal data which are processed only for the special purposes are exempt from any provision to which this subsection relates if—

    (a) the processing is undertaken with a view to the publication by any person of any journalistic, literary or artistic material,

    (b) the data controller reasonably believes that, having regard in particular to the special importance of the public interest in freedom of expression, publication would be in the public interest, and

    (c) the data controller reasonably believes that, in all the circumstances, compliance with that provision is incompatible with the special purposes.

(2) Subsection (1) relates to the provisions of—

Core resources

    (a) the data protection principles except the seventh data protection principle,
    (b) section 7,
    (c) section 10,
    (d) section 12, and
    (e) section 14(1) to (3).

(3) In considering for the purposes of subsection (1)(b) whether the belief of a data controller that publication would be in the public interest was or is a reasonable one, regard may be had to his compliance with any code of practice which—

    (a) is relevant to the publication in question, and
    (b) is designated by the [Secretary of State] by order for the purposes of this subsection.

(4) Where at any time ('the relevant time') in any proceedings against a data controller under section 7(9), 10(4), 12(8) or 14 or by virtue of section 13 the data controller claims, or it appears to the court, that any personal data to which the proceedings relate are being processed—

    (a) only for the special purposes, and
    (b) with a view to the publication by any person of any journalistic, literary or artistic material which, at the time twenty-four hours immediately before the relevant time, had not previously been published by the data controller,

the court shall stay the proceedings until either of the conditions in subsection (5) is met.

(5) Those conditions are—

    (a) that a determination of the Commissioner under section 45 with respect to the data in question takes effect, or
    (b) in a case where the proceedings were stayed on the making of a claim, that the claim is withdrawn.

(6) For the purposes of this Act 'publish', in relation to journalistic, literary or artistic material, means make available to the public or any section of the public.

NOTES

Initial Commencement

Royal Assent
Sub-s (3): Royal Assent (so far as conferring power to make subordinate legislation): 16 July 1998: see s 75(2)(i).

To be appointed
Sub-s (3): To be appointed (for remaining purposes): see s 75(3).
Sub-ss (1), (2), (4)–(6): To be appointed: see s 75(3).

Appointment

Sub-ss (1), (2), (4)–(6): Appointment: 1 March 2000: see SI 2000/183, art 2(1).
Sub-s (3): Appointment (for remaining purposes): 1 March 2000: see SI 2000/183, art 2(1).

Amendment

Sub-s (3): in para (b) words 'Secretary of State' in square brackets substituted by SI 2003/1887, art 9, Sch 2, para 9(1)(a).
Date in force: 19 August 2003: see SI 2003/1887, art 1(2).

Subordinate Legislation

Data Protection (Designated Codes of Practice) (No 2) Order 2000, SI 2000/1864 (made under sub-s (3)).

33 Research, history and statistics

(1) In this section—

'research purposes' includes statistical or historical purposes;
'the relevant conditions', in relation to any processing of personal data, means the conditions—
  (a) that the data are not processed to support measures or decisions with respect to particular individuals, and
  (b) that the data are not processed in such a way that substantial damage or substantial distress is, or is likely to be, caused to any data subject.

(2) For the purposes of the second data protection principle, the further processing of personal data only for research purposes in compliance with the relevant conditions is not to be regarded as incompatible with the purposes for which they were obtained.

(3) Personal data which are processed only for research purposes in compliance with the relevant conditions may, notwithstanding the fifth data protection principle, be kept indefinitely.

(4) Personal data which are processed only for research purposes are exempt from section 7 if—
  (a) they are processed in compliance with the relevant conditions, and
  (b) the results of the research or any resulting statistics are not made available in a form which identifies data subjects or any of them.

(5) For the purposes of subsections (2) to (4) personal data are not to be treated as processed otherwise than for research purposes merely because the data are disclosed—
  (a) to any person, for research purposes only,
  (b) to the data subject or a person acting on his behalf,
  (c) at the request, or with the consent, of the data subject or a person acting on his behalf, or
  (d) in circumstances in which the person making the disclosure has reasonable grounds for believing that the disclosure falls within paragraph (a), (b) or (c).

NOTES

Initial Commencement

To be appointed
To be appointed: see s 75(3).

Appointment

Appointment: 1 March 2000: see SI 2000/183, art 2(1).

[33A Manual data held by public authorities]

[(1) Personal data falling within paragraph (e) of the definition of 'data' in section 1(1) are exempt from—
  (a) the first, second, third, fifth, seventh and eighth data protection principles,
  (b) the sixth data protection principle except so far as it relates to the rights conferred on data subjects by sections 7 and 14,

Core resources

(c) sections 10 to 12,
(d) section 13, except so far as it relates to damage caused by a contravention of section 7 or of the fourth data protection principle and to any distress which is also suffered by reason of that contravention,
(e) Part III, and
(f) section 55.

(2) Personal data which fall within paragraph (e) of the definition of 'data' in section 1(1) and relate to appointments or removals, pay, discipline, superannuation or other personnel matters, in relation to—

(a) service in any of the armed forces of the Crown,
(b) service in any office or employment under the Crown or under any public authority, or
(c) service in any office or employment, or under any contract for services, in respect of which power to take action, or to determine or approve the action taken, in such matters is vested in Her Majesty, any Minister of the Crown, the National Assembly for Wales, any Northern Ireland Minister (within the meaning of the Freedom of Information Act 2000) or any public authority,

are also exempt from the remaining data protection principles and the remaining provisions of Part II.]

NOTES

Amendment

Inserted by the Freedom of Information Act 2000, s 70(1).
Date in force: 1 January 2005: see SI 2004/1909, art 2(1), (2)(f), (3).

See Further

See further, immediately after the 2007 election, any reference in sub-s (2) above to employment by or under the Crown, or a person in service of the Crown, shall be treated as including employment as a member of staff of the National Assembly for Wales Commission or (as the case may be) a person so employed: the National Assembly for Wales Commission (Crown Status) Order 2007, SI 2007/1118, art 5(1), (3), (4)(a) and the Government of Wales Act 2006, s 161(1).

34 Information available to the public by or under enactment

Personal data are exempt from—

(a) the subject information provisions,
(b) the fourth data protection principle and section 14(1) to (3), and
(c) the non-disclosure provisions,

if the data consist of information which the data controller is obliged by or under any enactment [other than an enactment contained in the Freedom of Information Act 2000] to make available to the public, whether by publishing it, by making it available for inspection, or otherwise and whether gratuitously or on payment of a fee.

NOTES

Initial Commencement

To be appointed
To be appointed: see s 75(3).

Data Protection Act 1998

Appointment

Appointment: 1 March 2000: see SI 2000/183, art 2(1).

Amendment

Words 'other than an enactment contained in the Freedom of Information Act 2000' in square brackets inserted by the Freedom of Information Act 2000, s 72.
Date in force: 30 November 2002: see SI 2002/2812, art 2(k).

35 Disclosures required by law or made in connection with legal proceedings etc

(1) Personal data are exempt from the non-disclosure provisions where the disclosure is required by or under any enactment, by any rule of law or by the order of a court.

(2) Personal data are exempt from the non-disclosure provisions where the disclosure is necessary—

   (a) for the purpose of, or in connection with, any legal proceedings (including prospective legal proceedings), or
   (b) for the purpose of obtaining legal advice,

or is otherwise necessary for the purposes of establishing, exercising or defending legal rights.

NOTES

Initial Commencement

To be appointed
To be appointed: see s 75(3).

Appointment

Appointment: 1 March 2000: see SI 2000/183, art 2(1).

[35A Parliamentary privilege]

[Personal data are exempt from—

   (a) the first data protection principle, except to the extent to which it requires compliance with the conditions in Schedules 2 and 3,
   (b) the second, third, fourth and fifth data protection principles,
   (c) section 7, and
   (d) sections 10 and 14(1) to (3),

if the exemption is required for the purpose of avoiding an infringement of the privileges of either House of Parliament.]

NOTES

Amendment

Inserted by the Freedom of Information Act 2000, s 73, Sch 6, para 2.
Date in force: 1 January 2005: see SI 2004/1909, art 2(1), (2)(f), (3).

Core resources

36 Domestic purposes

Personal data processed by an individual only for the purposes of that individual's personal, family or household affairs (including recreational purposes) are exempt from the data protection principles and the provisions of Parts II and III.

NOTES

Initial Commencement

To be appointed
To be appointed: see s 75(3).

Appointment

Appointment: 1 March 2000: see SI 2000/183, art 2(1).

37 Miscellaneous exemptions

Schedule 7 (which confers further miscellaneous exemptions) has effect.

NOTES

Initial Commencement

Royal Assent
Royal Assent (so far as is necessary for bringing into force those provisions of Sch 7 which confer power to make subordinate legislation): 16 July 1998: see s 75(2)(i).

To be appointed
To be appointed (for remaining purposes): see s 75(3).

Appointment

Appointment (for remaining purposes): 1 March 2000: see SI 2000/183, art 2(1).

38 Powers to make further exemptions by order

(1) The [Secretary of State] may by order exempt from the subject information provisions personal data consisting of information the disclosure of which is prohibited or restricted by or under any enactment if and to the extent that he considers it necessary for the safeguarding of the interests of the data subject or the rights and freedoms of any other individual that the prohibition or restriction ought to prevail over those provisions.

(2) The [Secretary of State] may by order exempt from the non-disclosure provisions any disclosures of personal data made in circumstances specified in the order, if he considers the exemption is necessary for the safeguarding of the interests of the data subject or the rights and freedoms of any other individual.

NOTES

Initial Commencement

Royal Assent
Royal Assent: 16 July 1998: see s 75(2)(i).

Amendment

Sub-s (1): words 'Secretary of State' in italics repealed and subsequent words in square brackets substituted by SI 2003/1887, art 9, Sch 2, para 9(1)(a).
Date in force: 19 August 2003: see SI 2003/1887, art 1(2).

Sub-s (2): words 'Secretary of State' in square brackets substituted by SI 2003/1887, art 9, Sch 2, para 9(1)(a).
Date in force: 19 August 2003: see SI 2003/1887, art 1(2).

Subordinate Legislation

Data Protection (Miscellaneous Subject Access Exemptions) Order 2000, SI 2000/419 (made under sub-s (1)).

Data Protection (Miscellaneous Subject Access Exemptions) (Amendment) Order 2000, SI 2000/1865 (made under sub-s (1)).

39 Transitional relief

Schedule 8 (which confers transitional exemptions) has effect.

NOTES

Initial Commencement

To be appointed
To be appointed: see s 75(3).

Appointment

Appointment: 1 March 2000: see SI 2000/183, art 2(1).

PART V
ENFORCEMENT

40 Enforcement notices

(1) If the Commissioner is satisfied that a data controller has contravened or is contravening any of the data protection principles, the Commissioner may serve him with a notice (in this Act referred to as 'an enforcement notice') requiring him, for complying with the principle or principles in question, to do either or both of the following—

 (a) to take within such time as may be specified in the notice, or to refrain from taking after such time as may be so specified, such steps as are so specified, or

 (b) to refrain from processing any personal data, or any personal data of a description specified in the notice, or to refrain from processing them for a purpose so specified or in a manner so specified, after such time as may be so specified.

(2) In deciding whether to serve an enforcement notice, the Commissioner shall consider whether the contravention has caused or is likely to cause any person damage or distress.

(3) An enforcement notice in respect of a contravention of the fourth data protection principle which requires the data controller to rectify, block, erase or destroy any inaccurate data may also require the data controller to rectify, block, erase or destroy

any other data held by him and containing an expression of opinion which appears to the Commissioner to be based on the inaccurate data.

(4) An enforcement notice in respect of a contravention of the fourth data protection principle, in the case of data which accurately record information received or obtained by the data controller from the data subject or a third party, may require the data controller either—

(a) to rectify, block, erase or destroy any inaccurate data and any other data held by him and containing an expression of opinion as mentioned in subsection (3), or
(b) to take such steps as are specified in the notice for securing compliance with the requirements specified in paragraph 7 of Part II of Schedule 1 and, if the Commissioner thinks fit, for supplementing the data with such statement of the true facts relating to the matters dealt with by the data as the Commissioner may approve.

(5) Where—

(a) an enforcement notice requires the data controller to rectify, block, erase or destroy any personal data, or
(b) the Commissioner is satisfied that personal data which have been rectified, blocked, erased or destroyed had been processed in contravention of any of the data protection principles,

an enforcement notice may, if reasonably practicable, require the data controller to notify third parties to whom the data have been disclosed of the rectification, blocking, erasure or destruction; and in determining whether it is reasonably practicable to require such notification regard shall be had, in particular, to the number of persons who would have to be notified.

(6) An enforcement notice must contain—

(a) a statement of the data protection principle or principles which the Commissioner is satisfied have been or are being contravened and his reasons for reaching that conclusion, and
(b) particulars of the rights of appeal conferred by section 48.

(7) Subject to subsection (8), an enforcement notice must not require any of the provisions of the notice to be complied with before the end of the period within which an appeal can be brought against the notice and, if such an appeal is brought, the notice need not be complied with pending the determination or withdrawal of the appeal.

(8) If by reason of special circumstances the Commissioner considers that an enforcement notice should be complied with as a matter of urgency he may include in the notice a statement to that effect and a statement of his reasons for reaching that conclusion; and in that event subsection (7) shall not apply but the notice must not require the provisions of the notice to be complied with before the end of the period of seven days beginning with the day on which the notice is served.

(9) Notification regulations (as defined by section 16(2)) may make provision as to the effect of the service of an enforcement notice on any entry in the register maintained under section 19 which relates to the person on whom the notice is served.

(10) This section has effect subject to section 46(1).

NOTES

Initial Commencement

Royal Assent
Sub-s (9): Royal Assent: 16 July 1998: see s 75(2)(i).

To be appointed
Sub-ss (1)–(8), (10): To be appointed: see s 75(3).

Appointment

Sub-ss (1)–(8), (10): Appointment: 1 March 2000: see SI 2000/183, art 2(1).

41 Cancellation of an enforcement notice

(1) If the Commissioner considers that all or any of the provisions of an enforcement notice need not be complied with in order to ensure compliance with the data protection principle or principles to which it relates, he may cancel or vary the notice by written notice to the person on whom it was served.

(2) A person on whom an enforcement notice has been served may, at any time after the expiry of the period during which an appeal can be brought against that notice, apply in writing to the Commissioner for the cancellation or variation of that notice on the ground that, by reason of a change of circumstances, all or any of the provisions of that notice need not be complied with in order to ensure compliance with the data protection principle or principles to which that notice relates.

NOTES

Initial Commencement

To be appointed
To be appointed: see s 75(3).

Appointment

Appointment: 1 March 2000: see SI 2000/183, art 2(1).

42 Request for assessment

(1) A request may be made to the Commissioner by or on behalf of any person who is, or believes himself to be, directly affected by any processing of personal data for an assessment as to whether it is likely or unlikely that the processing has been or is being carried out in compliance with the provisions of this Act.

(2) On receiving a request under this section, the Commissioner shall make an assessment in such manner as appears to him to be appropriate, unless he has not been supplied with such information as he may reasonably require in order to—

    (a) satisfy himself as to the identity of the person making the request, and
    (b) enable him to identify the processing in question.

(3) The matters to which the Commissioner may have regard in determining in what manner it is appropriate to make an assessment include—

    (a) the extent to which the request appears to him to raise a matter of substance,
    (b) any undue delay in making the request, and
    (c) whether or not the person making the request is entitled to make an application under section 7 in respect of the personal data in question.

Core resources

(4) Where the Commissioner has received a request under this section he shall notify the person who made the request—
- (a) whether he has made an assessment as a result of the request, and
- (b) to the extent that he considers appropriate, having regard in particular to any exemption from section 7 applying in relation to the personal data concerned, of any view formed or action taken as a result of the request.

NOTES

Initial Commencement

To be appointed
To be appointed: see s 75(3).

Appointment

Appointment: 1 March 2000: see SI 2000/183, art 2(1).

43 Information notices

(1) If the Commissioner—
- (a) has received a request under section 42 in respect of any processing of personal data, or
- (b) reasonably requires any information for the purpose of determining whether the data controller has complied or is complying with the data protection principles,

he may serve the data controller with a notice (in this Act referred to as 'an information notice') requiring the data controller, within such time as is specified in the notice, to furnish the Commissioner, in such form as may be so specified, with such information relating to the request or to compliance with the principles as is so specified.

(2) An information notice must contain—
- (a) in a case falling within subsection (1)(a), a statement that the Commissioner has received a request under section 42 in relation to the specified processing, or
- (b) in a case falling within subsection (1)(b), a statement that the Commissioner regards the specified information as relevant for the purpose of determining whether the data controller has complied, or is complying, with the data protection principles and his reasons for regarding it as relevant for that purpose.

(3) An information notice must also contain particulars of the rights of appeal conferred by section 48.

(4) Subject to subsection (5), the time specified in an information notice shall not expire before the end of the period within which an appeal can be brought against the notice and, if such an appeal is brought, the information need not be furnished pending the determination or withdrawal of the appeal.

(5) If by reason of special circumstances the Commissioner considers that the information is required as a matter of urgency, he may include in the notice a statement to that effect and a statement of his reasons for reaching that conclusion; and in that event subsection (4) shall not apply, but the notice shall not require the information to be furnished before the end of the period of seven days beginning with the day on which the notice is served.

(6) A person shall not be required by virtue of this section to furnish the Commissioner with any information in respect of—
  (a) any communication between a professional legal adviser and his client in connection with the giving of legal advice to the client with respect to his obligations, liabilities or rights under this Act, or
  (b) any communication between a professional legal adviser and his client, or between such an adviser or his client and any other person, made in connection with or in contemplation of proceedings under or arising out of this Act (including proceedings before the Tribunal) and for the purposes of such proceedings.

(7) In subsection (6) references to the client of a professional legal adviser include references to any person representing such a client.

(8) A person shall not be required by virtue of this section to furnish the Commissioner with any information if the furnishing of that information would, by revealing evidence of the commission of any offence other than an offence under this Act, expose him to proceedings for that offence.

(9) The Commissioner may cancel an information notice by written notice to the person on whom it was served.

(10) This section has effect subject to section 46(3).

NOTES

Initial Commencement

To be appointed
To be appointed: see s 75(3).

Appointment

Appointment: 1 March 2000: see SI 2000/183, art 2(1).

44 Special information notices

If the Commissioner—
  (a) has received a request under section 42 in respect of any processing of personal data, or
  (b) has reasonable grounds for suspecting that, in a case in which proceedings have been stayed under section 32, the personal data to which the proceedings relate—
    (i) are not being processed only for the special purposes, or
    (ii) are not being processed with a view to the publication by any person of any journalistic, literary or artistic material which has not previously been published by the data controller,

he may serve the data controller with a notice (in this Act referred to as a 'special information notice') requiring the data controller, within such time as is specified in the notice, to furnish the Commissioner, in such form as may be so specified, with such information as is so specified for the purpose specified in subsection (2).

(2) That purpose is the purpose of ascertaining—
  (a) whether the personal data are being processed only for the special purposes, or

Core resources

    (b)   whether they are being processed with a view to the publication by any person of any journalistic, literary or artistic material which has not previously been published by the data controller.

(3)   A special information notice must contain—

    (a)   in a case falling within paragraph (a) of subsection (1), a statement that the Commissioner has received a request under section 42 in relation to the specified processing, or

    (b)   in a case falling within paragraph (b) of that subsection, a statement of the Commissioner's grounds for suspecting that the personal data are not being processed as mentioned in that paragraph.

(4)   A special information notice must also contain particulars of the rights of appeal conferred by section 48.

(5)   Subject to subsection (6), the time specified in a special information notice shall not expire before the end of the period within which an appeal can be brought against the notice and, if such an appeal is brought, the information need not be furnished pending the determination or withdrawal of the appeal.

(6)   If by reason of special circumstances the Commissioner considers that the information is required as a matter of urgency, he may include in the notice a statement to that effect and a statement of his reasons for reaching that conclusion; and in that event subsection (5) shall not apply, but the notice shall not require the information to be furnished before the end of the period of seven days beginning with the day on which the notice is served.

(7)   A person shall not be required by virtue of this section to furnish the Commissioner with any information in respect of—

    (a)   any communication between a professional legal adviser and his client in connection with the giving of legal advice to the client with respect to his obligations, liabilities or rights under this Act, or

    (b)   any communication between a professional legal adviser and his client, or between such an adviser or his client and any other person, made in connection with or in contemplation of proceedings under or arising out of this Act (including proceedings before the Tribunal) and for the purposes of such proceedings.

(8)   In subsection (7) references to the client of a professional legal adviser include references to any person representing such a client.

(9)   A person shall not be required by virtue of this section to furnish the Commissioner with any information if the furnishing of that information would, by revealing evidence of the commission of any offence other than an offence under this Act, expose him to proceedings for that offence.

(10)   The Commissioner may cancel a special information notice by written notice to the person on whom it was served.

NOTES

Initial Commencement

To be appointed
To be appointed: see s 75(3).

Data Protection Act 1998

Appointment

Appointment: 1 March 2000: see SI 2000/183, art 2(1).

45 Determination by Commissioner as to the special purposes

(1) Where at any time it appears to the Commissioner (whether as a result of the service of a special information notice or otherwise) that any personal data—

   (a) are not being processed only for the special purposes, or
   (b) are not being processed with a view to the publication by any person of any journalistic, literary or artistic material which has not previously been published by the data controller,

he may make a determination in writing to that effect.

(2) Notice of the determination shall be given to the data controller; and the notice must contain particulars of the right of appeal conferred by section 48.

(3) A determination under subsection (1) shall not take effect until the end of the period within which an appeal can be brought and, where an appeal is brought, shall not take effect pending the determination or withdrawal of the appeal.

NOTES

Initial Commencement

To be appointed
To be appointed: see s 75(3).

Appointment

Appointment: 1 March 2000: see SI 2000/183, art 2(1).

46 Restriction on enforcement in case of processing for the special purposes

(1) The Commissioner may not at any time serve an enforcement notice on a data controller with respect to the processing of personal data for the special purposes unless—

   (a) a determination under section 45(1) with respect to those data has taken effect, and
   (b) the court has granted leave for the notice to be served.

(2) The court shall not grant leave for the purposes of subsection (1)(b) unless it is satisfied—

   (a) that the Commissioner has reason to suspect a contravention of the data protection principles which is of substantial public importance, and
   (b) except where the case is one of urgency, that the data controller has been given notice, in accordance with rules of court, of the application for leave.

(3) The Commissioner may not serve an information notice on a data controller with respect to the processing of personal data for the special purposes unless a determination under section 45(1) with respect to those data has taken effect.

NOTES

Initial Commencement

To be appointed
To be appointed: see s 75(3).

Core resources

Appointment

Appointment: 1 March 2000: see SI 2000/183, art 2(1).

47   Failure to comply with notice

(1)   A person who fails to comply with an enforcement notice, an information notice or a special information notice is guilty of an offence.

(2)   A person who, in purported compliance with an information notice or a special information notice—

   (a)   makes a statement which he knows to be false in a material respect, or
   (b)   recklessly makes a statement which is false in a material respect,

is guilty of an offence.

(3)   It is a defence for a person charged with an offence under subsection (1) to prove that he exercised all due diligence to comply with the notice in question.

NOTES

Initial Commencement

To be appointed
To be appointed: see s 75(3).

Appointment

Appointment: 1 March 2000: see SI 2000/183, art 2(1).

48   Rights of appeal

(1)   A person on whom an enforcement notice, an information notice or a special information notice has been served may appeal to the Tribunal against the notice.

(2)   A person on whom an enforcement notice has been served may appeal to the Tribunal against the refusal of an application under section 41(2) for cancellation or variation of the notice.

(3)   Where an enforcement notice, an information notice or a special information notice contains a statement by the Commissioner in accordance with section 40(8), 43(5) or 44(6) then, whether or not the person appeals against the notice, he may appeal against—

   (a)   the Commissioner's decision to include the statement in the notice, or
   (b)   the effect of the inclusion of the statement as respects any part of the notice.

(4)   A data controller in respect of whom a determination has been made under section 45 may appeal to the Tribunal against the determination.

(5)   Schedule 6 has effect in relation to appeals under this section and the proceedings of the Tribunal in respect of any such appeal.

NOTES

Initial Commencement

Royal Assent
Sub-s (5): Royal Assent (so far as is necessary for bringing into force those provisions of Sch 6 which confer power to make subordinate legislation): 16 July 1998: see s 75(2)(i).

Data Protection Act 1998

To be appointed
Sub-ss (1)–(4): To be appointed: see s 75(3).
Sub-s (5): To be appointed (for remaining purposes): see s 75(3).

Appointment

Sub-ss (1)–(4): Appointment: 1 March 2000: see SI 2000/183, art 2(1).
Sub-s (5): Appointment (for remaining purposes): 1 March 2000: see SI 2000/183, art 2(1).

49   Determination of appeals

(1) If on an appeal under section 48(1) the Tribunal considers—

   (a) that the notice against which the appeal is brought is not in accordance with the law, or
   (b) to the extent that the notice involved an exercise of discretion by the Commissioner, that he ought to have exercised his discretion differently,

the Tribunal shall allow the appeal or substitute such other notice or decision as could have been served or made by the Commissioner; and in any other case the Tribunal shall dismiss the appeal.

(2) On such an appeal, the Tribunal may review any determination of fact on which the notice in question was based.

(3) If on an appeal under section 48(2) the Tribunal considers that the enforcement notice ought to be cancelled or varied by reason of a change in circumstances, the Tribunal shall cancel or vary the notice.

(4) On an appeal under subsection (3) of section 48 the Tribunal may direct—

   (a) that the notice in question shall have effect as if it did not contain any such statement as is mentioned in that subsection, or
   (b) that the inclusion of the statement shall not have effect in relation to any part of the notice,

and may make such modifications in the notice as may be required for giving effect to the direction.

(5) On an appeal under section 48(4), the Tribunal may cancel the determination of the Commissioner.

(6) Any party to an appeal to the Tribunal under section 48 may appeal from the decision of the Tribunal on a point of law to the appropriate court; and that court shall be—

   (a) the High Court of Justice in England if the address of the person who was the appellant before the Tribunal is in England or Wales,
   (b) the Court of Session if that address is in Scotland, and
   (c) the High Court of Justice in Northern Ireland if that address is in Northern Ireland.

(7) For the purposes of subsection (6)—

   (a) the address of a registered company is that of its registered office, and
   (b) the address of a person (other than a registered company) carrying on a business is that of his principal place of business in the United Kingdom.

Core resources

NOTES

Initial Commencement

To be appointed
To be appointed: see s 75(3).

Appointment

Appointment: 1 March 2000: see SI 2000/183, art 2(1).

50   Powers of entry and inspection

Schedule 9 (powers of entry and inspection) has effect.

NOTES

Initial Commencement

To be appointed
To be appointed: see s 75(3).

Appointment

Appointment: 1 March 2000: see SI 2000/183, art 2(1).

PART VI
MISCELLANEOUS AND GENERAL

Functions of Commissioner

51   General duties of Commissioner

(1) It shall be the duty of the Commissioner to promote the following of good practice by data controllers and, in particular, so to perform his functions under this Act as to promote the observance of the requirements of this Act by data controllers.

(2) The Commissioner shall arrange for the dissemination in such form and manner as he considers appropriate of such information as it may appear to him expedient to give to the public about the operation of this Act, about good practice, and about other matters within the scope of his functions under this Act, and may give advice to any person as to any of those matters.

(3) Where—
   (a) the [Secretary of State] so directs by order, or
   (b) the Commissioner considers it appropriate to do so,

the Commissioner shall, after such consultation with trade associations, data subjects or persons representing data subjects as appears to him to be appropriate, prepare and disseminate to such persons as he considers appropriate codes of practice for guidance as to good practice.

(4) The Commissioner shall also—
   (a) where he considers it appropriate to do so, encourage trade associations to prepare, and to disseminate to their members, such codes of practice, and
   (b) where any trade association submits a code of practice to him for his consideration, consider the code and, after such consultation with data

Data Protection Act 1998

subjects or persons representing data subjects as appears to him to be appropriate, notify the trade association whether in his opinion the code promotes the following of good practice.

(5) An order under subsection (3) shall describe the personal data or processing to which the code of practice is to relate, and may also describe the persons or classes of persons to whom it is to relate.

(6) The Commissioner shall arrange for the dissemination in such form and manner as he considers appropriate of—

- (a) any Community finding as defined by paragraph 15(2) of Part II of Schedule 1,
- (b) any decision of the European Commission, under the procedure provided for in Article 31(2) of the Data Protection Directive, which is made for the purposes of Article 26(3) or (4) of the Directive, and
- (c) such other information as it may appear to him to be expedient to give to data controllers in relation to any personal data about the protection of the rights and freedoms of data subjects in relation to the processing of personal data in countries and territories outside the European Economic Area.

(7) The Commissioner may, with the consent of the data controller, assess any processing of personal data for the following of good practice and shall inform the data controller of the results of the assessment.

(8) The Commissioner may charge such sums as he may with the consent of the [Secretary of State] determine for any services provided by the Commissioner by virtue of this Part.

(9) In this section—

'good practice' means such practice in the processing of personal data as appears to the Commissioner to be desirable having regard to the interests of data subjects and others, and includes (but is not limited to) compliance with the requirements of this Act;
'trade association' includes any body representing data controllers.

NOTES

Initial Commencement

Royal Assent
Sub-s (3): Royal Assent (so far as conferring power to make subordinate legislation): 16 July 1998: see s 75(2)(i).
Sub-s (5): Royal Assent: 16 July 1998: see s 75(2)(i).

To be appointed
Sub-ss (1), (2), (4), (6)–(9): To be appointed: see s 75(3).
Sub-s (3): To be appointed (for remaining purposes): see s 75(3).

Appointment

Sub-ss (1), (2), (4), (6)–(9): Appointment: 1 March 2000: see SI 2000/183, art 2(1).
Sub-s (3): Appointment (for remaining purposes): 1 March 2000: see SI 2000/183, art 2(1).

Amendment

Sub-s (3): in para (a) words 'Secretary of State' in square brackets substituted by SI 2003/1887, art 9, Sch 2, para 9(1)(a).
Date in force: 19 August 2003: see SI 2003/1887, art 1(2).

Core resources

Sub-s (8): words 'Secretary of State' in square brackets substituted by SI 2003/1887, art 9, Sch 2, para 9(1)(a).
Date in force: 19 August 2003: see SI 2003/1887, art 1(2).

52 Reports and codes of practice to be laid before Parliament

(1) The Commissioner shall lay annually before each House of Parliament a general report on the exercise of his functions under this Act.

(2) The Commissioner may from time to time lay before each House of Parliament such other reports with respect to those functions as he thinks fit.

(3) The Commissioner shall lay before each House of Parliament any code of practice prepared under section 51(3) for complying with a direction of the [Secretary of State], unless the code is included in any report laid under subsection (1) or (2).

NOTES

Initial Commencement

To be appointed
To be appointed: see s 75(3).

Appointment

Appointment: 1 March 2000: see SI 2000/183, art 2(1).

Amendment

Sub-s (3): words 'Secretary of State' in square brackets substituted by SI 2003/1887, art 9, Sch 2, para 9(1)(a).
Date in force: 19 August 2003: see SI 2003/1887, art 1(2).

53 Assistance by Commissioner in cases involving processing for the special purposes

(1) An individual who is an actual or prospective party to any proceedings under section 7(9), 10(4), 12(8) or 14 or by virtue of section 13 which relate to personal data processed for the special purposes may apply to the Commissioner for assistance in relation to those proceedings.

(2) The Commissioner shall, as soon as reasonably practicable after receiving an application under subsection (1), consider it and decide whether and to what extent to grant it, but he shall not grant the application unless, in his opinion, the case involves a matter of substantial public importance.

(3) If the Commissioner decides to provide assistance, he shall, as soon as reasonably practicable after making the decision, notify the applicant, stating the extent of the assistance to be provided.

(4) If the Commissioner decides not to provide assistance, he shall, as soon as reasonably practicable after making the decision, notify the applicant of his decision and, if he thinks fit, the reasons for it.

(5) In this section—
  (a) references to 'proceedings' include references to prospective proceedings, and
  (b) 'applicant', in relation to assistance under this section, means an individual who applies for assistance.

(6) Schedule 10 has effect for supplementing this section.

Data Protection Act 1998

NOTES

Initial Commencement

To be appointed
To be appointed: see s 75(3).

Appointment

Appointment: 1 March 2000: see SI 2000/183, art 2(1).

54   International co-operation

(1) The Commissioner—

(a) shall continue to be the designated authority in the United Kingdom for the purposes of Article 13 of the Convention, and
(b) shall be the supervisory authority in the United Kingdom for the purposes of the Data Protection Directive.

(2) The [Secretary of State] may by order make provision as to the functions to be discharged by the Commissioner as the designated authority in the United Kingdom for the purposes of Article 13 of the Convention.

(3) The [Secretary of State] may by order make provision as to co-operation by the Commissioner with the European Commission and with supervisory authorities in other EEA States in connection with the performance of their respective duties and, in particular, as to—

(a) the exchange of information with supervisory authorities in other EEA States or with the European Commission, and
(b) the exercise within the United Kingdom at the request of a supervisory authority in another EEA State, in cases excluded by section 5 from the application of the other provisions of this Act, of functions of the Commissioner specified in the order.

(4) The Commissioner shall also carry out any data protection functions which the [Secretary of State] may by order direct him to carry out for the purpose of enabling Her Majesty's Government in the United Kingdom to give effect to any international obligations of the United Kingdom.

(5) The Commissioner shall, if so directed by the [Secretary of State], provide any authority exercising data protection functions under the law of a colony specified in the direction with such assistance in connection with the discharge of those functions as the [Secretary of State] may direct or approve, on such terms (including terms as to payment) as the [Secretary of State] may direct or approve.

(6) Where the European Commission makes a decision for the purposes of Article 26(3) or (4) of the Data Protection Directive under the procedure provided for in Article 31(2) of the Directive, the Commissioner shall comply with that decision in exercising his functions under paragraph 9 of Schedule 4 or, as the case may be, paragraph 8 of that Schedule.

(7) The Commissioner shall inform the European Commission and the supervisory authorities in other EEA States—

(a) of any approvals granted for the purposes of paragraph 8 of Schedule 4, and
(b) of any authorisations granted for the purposes of paragraph 9 of that Schedule.

(8) In this section—

Core resources

> 'the Convention' means the Convention for the Protection of Individuals with regard to Automatic Processing of Personal Data which was opened for signature on 28th January 1981;
> 'data protection functions' means functions relating to the protection of individuals with respect to the processing of personal information.

NOTES

Initial Commencement

Royal Assent
Sub-ss (2)–(5): Royal Assent: 16 July 1998: see s 75(2)(i).

To be appointed
Sub-ss (1), (6)–(8): To be appointed: see s 75(3).

Appointment

Sub-ss (1), (6)–(8): Appointment: 1 March 2000: see SI 2000/183, art 2(1).

Amendment

Sub-s (2): words 'Secretary of State' in square brackets substituted by SI 2003/1887, art 9, Sch 2, para 9(1)(a).
Date in force: 19 August 2003: see SI 2003/1887, art 1(2).

Sub-s (3): words 'Secretary of State' in square brackets substituted by SI 2003/1887, art 9, Sch 2, para 9(1)(a).
Date in force: 19 August 2003: see SI 2003/1887, art 1(2).

Sub-s (4): words 'Secretary of State' in square brackets substituted by SI 2003/1887, art 9, Sch 2, para 9(1)(a).
Date in force: 19 August 2003: see SI 2003/1887, art 1(2).

Sub-s (5): words 'Secretary of State' in square brackets in each place they occur substituted by SI 2003/1887, art 9, Sch 2, para 9(1)(a).
Date in force: 19 August 2003: see SI 2003/1887, art 1(2).

Subordinate Legislation

Data Protection (Functions of Designated Authority) Order 2000, SI 2000/186 (made under sub-s (2)).

Data Protection (International Co-operation) Order 2000, SI 2000/190 (made under sub-s (3)).

[54A Inspection of overseas information systems]

[(1) The Commissioner may inspect any personal data recorded in—

(a) the Schengen information system,
(b) the Europol information system,
(c) the Customs information system.

(2) The power conferred by subsection (1) is exercisable only for the purpose of assessing whether or not any processing of the data has been or is being carried out in compliance with this Act.

(3) The power includes power to inspect, operate and test equipment which is used for the processing of personal data.

Data Protection Act 1998

(4) Before exercising the power, the Commissioner must give notice in writing of his intention to do so to the data controller.

(5) But subsection (4) does not apply if the Commissioner considers that the case is one of urgency.

(6) Any person who—
- (a) intentionally obstructs a person exercising the power conferred by subsection (1), or
- (b) fails without reasonable excuse to give any person exercising the power any assistance he may reasonably require,

is guilty of an offence.

(7) In this section—

'the Customs information system' means the information system established under Chapter II of the Convention on the Use of Information Technology for Customs Purposes,

'the Europol information system' means the information system established under Title II of the Convention on the Establishment of a European Police Office,

'the Schengen information system' means the information system established under Title IV of the Convention implementing the Schengen Agreement of 14th June 1985, or any system established in its place in pursuance of any Community obligation.]

NOTES

Amendment

Inserted by the Crime (International Co-operation) Act 2003, s 81.
Date in force: 26 April 2004: see SI 2004/786, art 3(1), (2).

Unlawful obtaining etc of personal data

55   Unlawful obtaining etc of personal data

(1) A person must not knowingly or recklessly, without the consent of the data controller—
- (a) obtain or disclose personal data or the information contained in personal data, or
- (b) procure the disclosure to another person of the information contained in personal data.

(2) Subsection (1) does not apply to a person who shows—
- (a) that the obtaining, disclosing or procuring—
  - (i) was necessary for the purpose of preventing or detecting crime, or
  - (ii) was required or authorised by or under any enactment, by any rule of law or by the order of a court,
- (b) that he acted in the reasonable belief that he had in law the right to obtain or disclose the data or information or, as the case may be, to procure the disclosure of the information to the other person,
- (c) that he acted in the reasonable belief that he would have had the consent of the data controller if the data controller had known of the obtaining, disclosing or procuring and the circumstances of it,
- [(ca) that he acted—
  - (i) for the special purposes,

Core resources

> > (ii) with a view to the publication by any person of any journalistic, literary or artistic material, and
> >
> > (iii) in the reasonable belief that in the particular circumstances the obtaining, disclosing or procuring was justified as being in the public interest,]
> >
> > or
>
> (d) that in the particular circumstances the obtaining, disclosing or procuring was justified as being in the public interest.

(3) A person who contravenes subsection (1) is guilty of an offence.

(4) A person who sells personal data is guilty of an offence if he has obtained the data in contravention of subsection (1).

(5) A person who offers to sell personal data is guilty of an offence if—

> (a) he has obtained the data in contravention of subsection (1), or
> (b) he subsequently obtains the data in contravention of that subsection.

(6) For the purposes of subsection (5), an advertisement indicating that personal data are or may be for sale is an offer to sell the data.

(7) Section 1(2) does not apply for the purposes of this section; and for the purposes of subsections (4) to (6), 'personal data' includes information extracted from personal data.

(8) References in this section to personal data do not include references to personal data which by virtue of section 28 [or 33A] are exempt from this section.

NOTES

Initial Commencement

To be appointed
To be appointed: see s 75(3).

Appointment

Appointment: 1 March 2000: see SI 2000/183, art 2(1).

Amendment

Sub-s (2): para (ca) inserted by the Criminal Justice and Immigration Act 2008, s 78; for transitional provisions and savings see s 148(2), Sch 27, Pt 5, para 28 thereto.
Date in force: to be appointed: see the Criminal Justice and Immigration Act 2008, s 153(7).

Sub-s (8): words 'or 33A' in square brackets inserted by the Freedom of Information Act 2000, s 70(2).
Date in force: 1 January 2005: see SI 2004/1909, art 2(1), (2)(f), (3).

[Monetary penalties]

NOTES

Amendment

Inserted by the Criminal Justice and Immigration Act 2008, s 144(1).
Date in force: to be appointed: see the Criminal Justice and Immigration Act 2008, s 153(7).

Data Protection Act 1998

[55A Power of Commissioner to impose monetary penalty]

[(1) The Commissioner may serve a data controller with a monetary penalty notice if the Commissioner is satisfied that—

 (a) there has been a serious contravention of section 4(4) by the data controller,
 (b) the contravention was of a kind likely to cause substantial damage or substantial distress, and
 (c) subsection (2) or (3) applies.

(2) This subsection applies if the contravention was deliberate.

(3) This subsection applies if the data controller—

 (a) knew or ought to have known—
  (i) that there was a risk that the contravention would occur, and
  (ii) that such a contravention would be of a kind likely to cause substantial damage or substantial distress, but
 (b) failed to take reasonable steps to prevent the contravention.

(4) A monetary penalty notice is a notice requiring the data controller to pay to the Commissioner a monetary penalty of an amount determined by the Commissioner and specified in the notice.

(5) The amount determined by the Commissioner must not exceed the prescribed amount.

(6) The monetary penalty must be paid to the Commissioner within the period specified in the notice.

(7) The notice must contain such information as may be prescribed.

(8) Any sum received by the Commissioner by virtue of this section must be paid into the Consolidated Fund.

(9) In this section—

 'data controller' does not include the Crown Estate Commissioners or a person who is a data controller by virtue of section 63(3);
 'prescribed' means prescribed by regulations made by the Secretary of State.]

NOTES

Amendment

Inserted by the Criminal Justice and Immigration Act 2008, s 144(1).
Date in force: to be appointed: see the Criminal Justice and Immigration Act 2008, s 153(7).

[55B Monetary penalty notices: procedural rights]

[(1) Before serving a monetary penalty notice, the Commissioner must serve the data controller with a notice of intent.

(2) A notice of intent is a notice that the Commissioner proposes to serve a monetary penalty notice.

(3) A notice of intent must—

 (a) inform the data controller that he may make written representations in relation to the Commissioner's proposal within a period specified in the notice, and
 (b) contain such other information as may be prescribed.

Core resources

(4) The Commissioner may not serve a monetary penalty notice until the time within which the data controller may make representations has expired.

(5) A person on whom a monetary penalty notice is served may appeal to the Tribunal against—

(a) the issue of the monetary penalty notice;
(b) the amount of the penalty specified in the notice.

(6) In this section, 'prescribed' means prescribed by regulations made by the Secretary of State.]

NOTES

Amendment

Inserted by the Criminal Justice and Immigration Act 2008, s 144(1).
Date in force: to be appointed: see the Criminal Justice and Immigration Act 2008, s 153(7).

[55C Guidance about monetary penalty notices]

[(1) The Commissioner must prepare and issue guidance on how he proposes to exercise his functions under sections 55A and 55B.

(2) The guidance must, in particular, deal with—

(a) the circumstances in which he would consider it appropriate to issue a monetary penalty notice, and
(b) how he will determine the amount of the penalty.

(3) The Commissioner may alter or replace the guidance.

(4) If the guidance is altered or replaced, the Commissioner must issue the altered or replacement guidance.

(5) The Commissioner may not issue guidance under this section without the approval of the Secretary of State.

(6) The Commissioner must lay any guidance issued under this section before each House of Parliament.

(7) The Commissioner must arrange for the publication of any guidance issued under this section in such form and manner as he considers appropriate.

(8) In subsections (5) to (7), 'guidance' includes altered or replacement guidance.]

NOTES

Amendment

Inserted by the Criminal Justice and Immigration Act 2008, s 144(1).
Date in force: to be appointed: see the Criminal Justice and Immigration Act 2008, s 153(7).

[55D Monetary penalty notices: enforcement]

[(1) This section applies in relation to any penalty payable to the Commissioner by virtue of section 55A.

(2) In England and Wales, the penalty is recoverable—

Data Protection Act 1998

(a) if a county court so orders, as if it were payable under an order of that court;
(b) if the High Court so orders, as if it were payable under an order of that court.

(3) In Scotland, the penalty may be enforced in the same manner as an extract registered decree arbitral bearing a warrant for execution issued by the sheriff court of any sheriffdom in Scotland.

(4) In Northern Ireland, the penalty is recoverable—

(a) if a county court so orders, as if it were payable under an order of that court;
(b) if the High Court so orders, as if it were payable under an order of that court.]

NOTES

Amendment

Inserted by the Criminal Justice and Immigration Act 2008, s 144(1).
Date in force: to be appointed: see the Criminal Justice and Immigration Act 2008, s 153(7).

[55E   Notices under sections 55A and 55B: supplemental]

[(1) The Secretary of State may by order make further provision in connection with monetary penalty notices and notices of intent.

(2) An order under this section may in particular—

(a) provide that a monetary penalty notice may not be served on a data controller with respect to the processing of personal data for the special purposes except in circumstances specified in the order;
(b) make provision for the cancellation or variation of monetary penalty notices;
(c) confer rights of appeal to the Tribunal against decisions of the Commissioner in relation to the cancellation or variation of such notices;
(d) make provision for the proceedings of the Tribunal in respect of appeals under section 55B(5) or appeals made by virtue of paragraph (c);
(e) make provision for the determination of such appeals;
(f) confer rights of appeal against any decision of the Tribunal in relation to monetary penalty notices or their cancellation or variation.

(3) An order under this section may apply any provision of this Act with such modifications as may be specified in the order.

(4) An order under this section may amend this Act.]

NOTES

Amendment

Inserted by the Criminal Justice and Immigration Act 2008, s 144(1).
Date in force: to be appointed: see the Criminal Justice and Immigration Act 2008, s 153(7).

Records obtained under data subject's right of access

56   Prohibition of requirement as to production of certain records

(1) A person must not, in connection with—

(a) the recruitment of another person as an employee,

Core resources

    (b) the continued employment of another person, or
    (c) any contract for the provision of services to him by another person,

require that other person or a third party to supply him with a relevant record or to produce a relevant record to him.

(2) A person concerned with the provision (for payment or not) of goods, facilities or services to the public or a section of the public must not, as a condition of providing or offering to provide any goods, facilities or services to another person, require that other person or a third party to supply him with a relevant record or to produce a relevant record to him.

(3) Subsections (1) and (2) do not apply to a person who shows—

    (a) that the imposition of the requirement was required or authorised by or under any enactment, by any rule of law or by the order of a court, or
    (b) that in the particular circumstances the imposition of the requirement was justified as being in the public interest.

(4) Having regard to the provisions of Part V of the Police Act 1997 (certificates of criminal records etc), the imposition of the requirement referred to in subsection (1) or (2) is not to be regarded as being justified as being in the public interest on the ground that it would assist in the prevention or detection of crime.

(5) A person who contravenes subsection (1) or (2) is guilty of an offence.

(6) In this section 'a relevant record' means any record which—

    (a) has been or is to be obtained by a data subject from any data controller specified in the first column of the Table below in the exercise of the right conferred by section 7, and
    (b) contains information relating to any matter specified in relation to that data controller in the second column,

and includes a copy of such a record or a part of such a record.

Data controller	*Subject-matter*
1 Any of the following persons— (a) a chief officer of police of a police force in England and Wales. (b) a chief constable of a police force in Scotland. (c) the [Chief Constable of the Police Service of Northern Ireland]. [(d) the Director General of the Serious Organised Crime Agency.]	(a) Convictions. (b) Cautions.
2 The Secretary of State.	(a) Convictions. (b) Cautions. (c) His functions under [section 92 of the Powers of Criminal Courts (Sentencing) Act 2000], section 205(2) or 208 of the Criminal Procedure (Scotland) Act 1995 or section 73 of the Children and Young Persons Act (Northern Ireland) 1968 in relation to any person sentenced to detention.

Data Protection Act 1998

	(d) His functions under the Prison Act 1952, the Prisons (Scotland) Act 1989 or the Prison Act (Northern Ireland) 1953 in relation to any person imprisoned or detained.
	(e) His functions under the Social Security Contributions and Benefits Act 1992, the Social Security Administration Act 1992 or the Jobseekers Act 1995.
	(f) His functions under Part V of the Police Act 1997.
	[(g) His functions under the Safeguarding Vulnerable Groups Act 2006 [or the Safeguarding Vulnerable Groups (Northern Ireland) Order 2007]].
3 The Department of Health and Social Services for Northern Ireland.	Its functions under the Social Security Contributions and Benefits (Northern Ireland) Act 1992, the Social Security Administration (Northern Ireland) Act 1992 or the Jobseekers (Northern Ireland) Order 1995.
[4 The Independent Barring Board.	Its functions under the Safeguarding Vulnerable Groups Act 2006 [or the Safeguarding Vulnerable Groups (Northern Ireland) Order 2007]].

[(6A) A record is not a relevant record to the extent that it relates, or is to relate, only to personal data falling within paragraph (e) of the definition of 'data' in section 1(1).]

(7) In the Table in subsection (6)—

'caution' means a caution given to any person in England and Wales or Northern Ireland in respect of an offence which, at the time when the caution is given, is admitted;
'conviction' has the same meaning as in the Rehabilitation of Offenders Act 1974 or the Rehabilitation of Offenders (Northern Ireland) Order 1978.

(8) The [Secretary of State] may by order amend—

(a) the Table in subsection (6), and
(b) subsection (7).

(9) For the purposes of this section a record which states that a data controller is not processing any personal data relating to a particular matter shall be taken to be a record containing information relating to that matter.

(10) In this section 'employee' means an individual who—

(a) works under a contract of employment, as defined by section 230(2) of the Employment Rights Act 1996, or
(b) holds any office,

whether or not he is entitled to remuneration; and 'employment' shall be construed accordingly.

NOTES

Initial Commencement

Royal Assent
Royal Assent (so far as conferring power to make subordinate legislation): 16 July 1998: see s 75(2)(i).

Core resources

To be appointed
To be appointed (for remaining purposes): see s 75(3), (4).

Appointment

Sub-s (6): Appointment (for certain purposes): 7 July 2008: see SI 2008/1592, art 2.

Amendment

Sub-s (6): Table: in entry numbered 1(c) words 'Chief Constable of the Police Service of Northern Ireland' in square brackets substituted by the Police (Northern Ireland) Act 2000, s 78(2)(a).
Date in force: 4 November 2001: see the Police (Northern Ireland) Act 2000 (Commencement No 3 and Transitional Provisions) Order 2001, SR 2001/396, art 2, Schedule.

Sub-s (6): Table: entry numbered 1(d) substituted, for entries 1(d), (e) as originally enacted, by the Serious Organised Crime and Police Act 2005, Sch 4, para 112.
Date in force: 1 April 2006: see SI 2006/378, art 4(1), Schedule, para 10.

Sub-s (6): Table: in entry numbered 2 column 2, para (c) words 'section 92 of the Powers of Criminal Courts (Sentencing) Act 2000' in square brackets substituted by the Powers of Criminal Courts (Sentencing) Act 2000, s 165(1), Sch 9, para 191.
Date in force: 25 August 2000: see the Powers of Criminal Courts (Sentencing) Act 2000, s 168(1).

Sub-s (6): Table: in entry numbered 2 in column 2 para (g) inserted by the Safeguarding Vulnerable Groups Act 2006, s 63(1), Sch 9, Pt 2, para 15(1), (2)(a).
Date in force: 19 May 2008: see SI 2008/1320, art 3.

Sub-s (6): Table: in entry numbered 2 in column 2 para (g) words 'or the Safeguarding Vulnerable Groups (Northern Ireland) Order 2007' in square brackets inserted by the Safeguarding Vulnerable Groups (Northern Ireland) Order 2007, SI 2007/1351, art 60(1), Sch 7, para 4(1).
Date in force: to be appointed: see the Safeguarding Vulnerable Groups (Northern Ireland) Order 2007, SI 2007/1351, art 1(3).

Sub-s (6): Table: entry numbered 4 inserted by the Safeguarding Vulnerable Groups Act 2006, s 63(1), Sch 9, Pt 2, para 15(1), (2)(b).
Date in force: 19 May 2008: see SI 2008/1320, art 3.

Sub-s (6): Table: in entry numbered 4 in column 2 words 'or the Safeguarding Vulnerable Groups (Northern Ireland) 2007' in square brackets inserted by the Safeguarding Vulnerable Groups (Northern Ireland) Order 2007, SI 2007/1351, art 60(1), Sch 7, para 4(1).
Date in force: to be appointed: see the Safeguarding Vulnerable Groups (Northern Ireland) Order 2007, SI 2007/1351, art 1(3).

Sub-s (6A): inserted by the Freedom of Information Act 2000, s 68(4).
Date in force: 1 January 2005: see SI 2004/1909, art 2(1), (2)(f), (3).

Sub-s (8): words 'Secretary of State' in square brackets substituted by SI 2003/1887, art 9, Sch 2, para 9(1)(a).
Date in force: 19 August 2003: see SI 2003/1887, art 1(2).

57 Avoidance of certain contractual terms relating to health records

(1) Any term or condition of a contract is void in so far as it purports to require an individual—

Data Protection Act 1998

    (a) to supply any other person with a record to which this section applies, or with a copy of such a record or a part of such a record, or

    (b) to produce to any other person such a record, copy or part.

(2) This section applies to any record which—

    (a) has been or is to be obtained by a data subject in the exercise of the right conferred by section 7, and

    (b) consists of the information contained in any health record as defined by section 68(2).

NOTES

Initial Commencement

To be appointed
To be appointed: see s 75(3).

Appointment

Appointment: 1 March 2000: see SI 2000/183, art 2(1).

Information provided to Commissioner or Tribunal

58   Disclosure of information

No enactment or rule of law prohibiting or restricting the disclosure of information shall preclude a person from furnishing the Commissioner or the Tribunal with any information necessary for the discharge of their functions under this Act [or the Freedom of Information Act 2000].

NOTES

Initial Commencement

To be appointed
To be appointed: see s 75(3).

Appointment

Appointment: 1 March 2000: see SI 2000/183, art 2(1).

Amendment

Words 'or the Freedom of Information Act 2000' in square brackets inserted by the Freedom of Information Act 2000, s 18(4), Sch 2, Pt II, para 18.
Date in force: 30 November 2000: see the Freedom of Information Act 2000, s 87(1)(*i*).

59   Confidentiality of information

(1) No person who is or has been the Commissioner, a member of the Commissioner's staff or an agent of the Commissioner shall disclose any information which—

    (a) has been obtained by, or furnished to, the Commissioner under or for the purposes of [the information Acts],

    (b) relates to an identified or identifiable individual or business, and

Core resources

    (c) is not at the time of the disclosure, and has not previously been, available to the public from other sources,

unless the disclosure is made with lawful authority.

(2) For the purposes of subsection (1) a disclosure of information is made with lawful authority only if, and to the extent that—

    (a) the disclosure is made with the consent of the individual or of the person for the time being carrying on the business,
    (b) the information was provided for the purpose of its being made available to the public (in whatever manner) under any provision of [the information Acts],
    (c) the disclosure is made for the purposes of, and is necessary for, the discharge of—
        (i) any functions under [the information Acts], or
        (ii) any Community obligation,
    (d) the disclosure is made for the purposes of any proceedings, whether criminal or civil and whether arising under, or by virtue of, [the information Acts] or otherwise, or
    (e) having regard to the rights and freedoms or legitimate interests of any person, the disclosure is necessary in the public interest.

(3) Any person who knowingly or recklessly discloses information in contravention of subsection (1) is guilty of an offence.

[(4) In this section 'the information Acts' means this Act and the Freedom of Information Act 2000.]

NOTES

Initial Commencement

To be appointed
To be appointed: see s 75(3).

Appointment

Appointment: 1 March 2000: see SI 2000/183, art 2(1).

Amendment

Sub-s (1): in para (a) words 'the information Acts' in square brackets substituted by the Freedom of Information Act 2000, s 18(4), Sch 2, Pt II, para 19(1), (2).
Date in force: 30 November 2000: see the Freedom of Information Act 2000, s 87(1)(i).

Sub-s (2): words 'the information Acts' in square brackets in each place they occur substituted by the Freedom of Information Act 2000, s 18(4), Sch 2, Pt II, para 19(1), (2).
Date in force: 30 November 2000: see the Freedom of Information Act 2000, s 87(1)(i).

Sub-s (4): inserted by the Freedom of Information Act 2000, s 18(4), Sch 2, Pt II, para 19(1), (3).
Date in force: 30 November 2000: see the Freedom of Information Act 2000, s 87(1)(i).

Data Protection Act 1998

See Further

See further, in relation to the extension of disclosure powers under sub-s (1) above: the Anti-terrorism, Crime and Security Act 2001, s 17, Sch 4, Pt 1, para 42.

General provisions relating to offences

60 Prosecutions and penalties

(1) No proceedings for an offence under this Act shall be instituted—

(a) in England or Wales, except by the Commissioner or by or with the consent of the Director of Public Prosecutions;
(b) in Northern Ireland, except by the Commissioner or by or with the consent of the Director of Public Prosecutions for Northern Ireland.

(2) A person guilty of an offence under any provision of this Act other than [section 54A and] paragraph 12 of Schedule 9 is liable—

(a) on summary conviction, to a fine not exceeding the statutory maximum, or
(b) on conviction on indictment, to a fine.

(3) A person guilty of an offence under [section 54A and] paragraph 12 of Schedule 9 is liable on summary conviction to a fine not exceeding level 5 on the standard scale.

(4) Subject to subsection (5), the court by or before which a person is convicted of—

(a) an offence under section 21(1), 22(6), 55 or 56,
(b) an offence under section 21(2) relating to processing which is assessable processing for the purposes of section 22, or
(c) an offence under section 47(1) relating to an enforcement notice,

may order any document or other material used in connection with the processing of personal data and appearing to the court to be connected with the commission of the offence to be forfeited, destroyed or erased.

(5) The court shall not make an order under subsection (4) in relation to any material where a person (other than the offender) claiming to be the owner of or otherwise interested in the material applies to be heard by the court, unless an opportunity is given to him to show cause why the order should not be made.

NOTES

Initial Commencement

To be appointed
To be appointed: see s 75(3).

Appointment

Appointment: 1 March 2000: see SI 2000/183, art 2(1).

Amendment

Sub-s (2): words 'section 54A and' in square brackets inserted by the Crime (International Co-operation) Act 2003, s 91(1), Sch 5, paras 68, 70.
Date in force: 26 April 2004: see SI 2004/786, art 3(1), (2).

Sub-s (3): words 'section 54A and' in square brackets inserted by the Crime (International Co-operation) Act 2003, s 91(1), Sch 5, paras 68, 70.
Date in force: 26 April 2004: see SI 2004/786, art 3(1), (2).

Core resources

61   Liability of directors etc

(1)   Where an offence under this Act has been committed by a body corporate and is proved to have been committed with the consent or connivance of or to be attributable to any neglect on the part of any director, manager, secretary or similar officer of the body corporate or any person who was purporting to act in any such capacity, he as well as the body corporate shall be guilty of that offence and be liable to be proceeded against and punished accordingly.

(2)   Where the affairs of a body corporate are managed by its members subsection (1) shall apply in relation to the acts and defaults of a member in connection with his functions of management as if he were a director of the body corporate.

(3)   Where an offence under this Act has been committed by a Scottish partnership and the contravention in question is proved to have occurred with the consent or connivance of, or to be attributable to any neglect on the part of, a partner, he as well as the partnership shall be guilty of that offence and shall be liable to be proceeded against and punished accordingly.

NOTES

Initial Commencement

To be appointed
To be appointed: see s 75(3).

Appointment

Appointment: 1 March 2000: see SI 2000/183, art 2(1).

Amendments of Consumer Credit Act 1974

62   Amendments of Consumer Credit Act 1974

(1)   In section 158 of the Consumer Credit Act 1974 (duty of agency to disclose filed information)—

- (a)   in subsection (1)—
    - (i)   in paragraph (a) for 'individual' there is substituted 'partnership or other unincorporated body of persons not consisting entirely of bodies corporate', and
    - (ii)   for 'him' there is substituted 'it',
- (b)   in subsection (2), for 'his' there is substituted 'the consumer's', and
- (c)   in subsection (3), for 'him' there is substituted 'the consumer'.

(2)   In section 159 of that Act (correction of wrong information) for subsection (1) there is substituted—

'(1)   Any individual (the 'objector') given—

- (a)   information under section 7 of the Data Protection Act 1998 by a credit reference agency, or
- (b)   information under section 158,

who considers that an entry in his file is incorrect, and that if it is not corrected he is likely to be prejudiced, may give notice to the agency requiring it either to remove the entry from the file or amend it.'.

(3)   In subsections (2) to (6) of that subsection—

- (a)   for 'consumer', wherever occurring, there is substituted 'objector', and

(b) for 'Director', wherever occurring, there is substituted 'the relevant authority'.

(4) After subsection (6) of that section there is inserted—

'(7) The Data Protection Commissioner may vary or revoke any order made by him under this section.

(8) In this section 'the relevant authority' means—

   (a) where the objector is a partnership or other unincorporated body of persons, the Director, and
   (b) in any other case, the Data Protection Commissioner.'.

(5) In section 160 of that Act (alternative procedure for business consumers)—

   (a) in subsection (4)—
      (i) for 'him' there is substituted 'to the consumer', and
      (ii) in paragraphs (a) and (b) for 'he' there is substituted 'the consumer' and for 'his' there is substituted 'the consumer's', and
   (b) after subsection (6) there is inserted—

'(7) In this section 'consumer' has the same meaning as in section 158.'.

NOTES

Initial Commencement

To be appointed
To be appointed: see s 75(3).

Appointment

Appointment: 1 March 2000: see SI 2000/183, art 2.

General

63 Application to Crown

(1) This Act binds the Crown.

(2) For the purposes of this Act each government department shall be treated as a person separate from any other government department.

(3) Where the purposes for which and the manner in which any personal data are, or are to be, processed are determined by any person acting on behalf of the Royal Household, the Duchy of Lancaster or the Duchy of Cornwall, the data controller in respect of those data for the purposes of this Act shall be—

   (a) in relation to the Royal Household, the Keeper of the Privy Purse,
   (b) in relation to the Duchy of Lancaster, such person as the Chancellor of the Duchy appoints, and
   (c) in relation to the Duchy of Cornwall, such person as the Duke of Cornwall, or the possessor for the time being of the Duchy of Cornwall, appoints.

(4) Different persons may be appointed under subsection (3)(b) or (c) for different purposes.

(5) Neither a government department nor a person who is a data controller by virtue of subsection (3) shall be liable to prosecution under this Act, but [sections 54A and] 55 and paragraph 12 of Schedule 9 shall apply to a person in the service of the Crown as they apply to any other person.

Core resources

NOTES

Initial Commencement

To be appointed
To be appointed: see s 75(3).

Appointment

Appointment: 1 March 2000: see SI 2000/183, art 2(1).

Amendment

Sub-s (5): words 'sections 54A and' in square brackets substituted by the Crime (International Co-operation) Act 2003, s 91(1), Sch 5, paras 68, 71.
Date in force: 26 April 2004: see SI 2004/786, art 3(1), (2).

See Further

See further, immediately after the 2007 election, the National Assembly for Wales Commission shall be treated as a government department for the purposes of sub-ss (2), (5) above and any reference to a person in service of the Crown, shall be treated as including a person employed as a member of staff of the National Assembly for Wales Commission: the National Assembly for Wales Commission (Crown Status) Order 2007, SI 2007/1118, art 5(1), (2)(a), (3), (4)(b) and the Government of Wales Act 2006, s 161(1).

[63A Application to Parliament]

[(1) Subject to the following provisions of this section and to section 35A, this Act applies to the processing of personal data by or on behalf of either House of Parliament as it applies to the processing of personal data by other persons

(2) Where the purposes for which and the manner in which any personal data are, or are to be, processed are determined by or on behalf of the House of Commons, the data controller in respect of those data for the purposes of this Act shall be the Corporate Officer of that House.

(3) Where the purposes for which and the manner in which any personal data are, or are to be, processed are determined by or on behalf of the House of Lords, the data controller in respect of those data for the purposes of this Act shall be the Corporate Officer of that House.

(4) Nothing in subsection (2) or (3) is to be taken to render the Corporate Officer of the House of Commons or the Corporate Officer of the House of Lords liable to prosecution under this Act, but section 55 and paragraph 12 of Schedule 9 shall apply to a person acting on behalf of either House as they apply to any other person.]

NOTES

Amendment

Inserted by the Freedom of Information Act 2000, s 73, Sch 6, para 3.
Date in force: 1 January 2005: see SI 2004/1909, art 2(1), (2)(f), (3).

64 Transmission of notices etc by electronic or other means

(1) This section applies to

    (a) a notice or request under any provision of Part II,

(b) a notice under subsection (1) of section 24 or particulars made available under that subsection, or
(c) an application under section 41(2),

but does not apply to anything which is required to be served in accordance with rules of court.

(2) The requirement that any notice, request, particulars or application to which this section applies should be in writing is satisfied where the text of the notice, request, particulars or application—

(a) is transmitted by electronic means,
(b) is received in legible form, and
(c) is capable of being used for subsequent reference.

(3) The [Secretary of State] may by regulations provide that any requirement that any notice, request, particulars or application to which this section applies should be in writing is not to apply in such circumstances as may be prescribed by the regulations.

NOTES

Initial Commencement

Royal Assent
Sub-s (3): Royal Assent: 16 July 1998: see s 75(2)(i).

To be appointed
Sub-ss (1), (2): To be appointed: see s 75(3).

Appointment

Sub-ss (1), (2): Appointment: 1 March 2000: see SI 2000/183, art 2(1).

Amendment

Sub-s (3): words 'Secretary of State' in square brackets substituted by SI 2003/1887, art 9, Sch 2, para 9(1)(a).
Date in force: 19 August 2003: see SI 2003/1887, art 1(2).

65 Service of notices by Commissioner

(1) Any notice authorised or required by this Act to be served on or given to any person by the Commissioner may—

(a) if that person is an individual, be served on him—
 (i) by delivering it to him, or
 (ii) by sending it to him by post addressed to him at his usual or last-known place of residence or business, or
 (iii) by leaving it for him at that place;
(b) if that person is a body corporate or unincorporate, be served on that body—
 (i) by sending it by post to the proper officer of the body at its principal office, or
 (ii) by addressing it to the proper officer of the body and leaving it at that office;
(c) if that person is a partnership in Scotland, be served on that partnership—
 (i) by sending it by post to the principal office of the partnership, or
 (ii) by addressing it to that partnership and leaving it at that office.

Core resources

(2) In subsection (1)(b) 'principal office', in relation to a registered company, means its registered office and 'proper officer', in relation to any body, means the secretary or other executive officer charged with the conduct of its general affairs.

(3) This section is without prejudice to any other lawful method of serving or giving a notice.

NOTES

Initial Commencement

To be appointed
To be appointed: see s 75(3).

Appointment

Appointment: 1 March 2000: see SI 2000/183, art 2(1).

66 Exercise of rights in Scotland by children

(1) Where a question falls to be determined in Scotland as to the legal capacity of a person under the age of sixteen years to exercise any right conferred by any provision of this Act, that person shall be taken to have that capacity where he has a general understanding of what it means to exercise that right.

(2) Without prejudice to the generality of subsection (1), a person of twelve years of age or more shall be presumed to be of sufficient age and maturity to have such understanding as is mentioned in that subsection.

NOTES

Initial Commencement

To be appointed
To be appointed: see s 75(3).

Appointment

Appointment: 1 March 2000: see SI 2000/183, art 2(1).

67 Orders, regulations and rules

(1) Any power conferred by this Act on the [Secretary of State] to make an order, regulations or rules shall be exercisable by statutory instrument.

(2) Any order, regulations or rules made by the [Secretary of State] under this Act may—
   (a) make different provision for different cases, and
   (b) make such supplemental, incidental, consequential or transitional provision or savings as the [Secretary of State] considers appropriate;

and nothing in section 7(11), 19(5), 26(1) or 30(4) limits the generality of paragraph (a).

(3) Before making—
   (a) an order under any provision of this Act other than section 75(3),
   (b) any regulations under this Act other than notification regulations (as defined by section 16(2)),

Data Protection Act 1998

the [Secretary of State] shall consult the Commissioner.

(4) A statutory instrument containing (whether alone or with other provisions) an order under—

section 10(2)(b),
section 12(5)(b),
section 22(1),
section 30,
section 32(3),
section 38,
[section 55E(1),]
section 56(8),
paragraph 10 of Schedule 3, or
paragraph 4 of Schedule 7,

shall not be made unless a draft of the instrument has been laid before and approved by a resolution of each House of Parliament.

(5) A statutory instrument which contains (whether alone or with other provisions)—

(a) an order under—
section 22(7),
section 23,
section 51(3),
section 54(2), (3) or (4),
paragraph 3, 4 or 14 of Part II of Schedule 1,
paragraph 6 of Schedule 2,
paragraph 2, 7 or 9 of Schedule 3,
paragraph 4 of Schedule 4,
paragraph 6 of Schedule 7,
(b) regulations under section 7 which—
(i) prescribe cases for the purposes of subsection (2)(b),
(ii) are made by virtue of subsection (7), or
(iii) relate to the definition of 'the prescribed period',
(c) regulations under section 8(1) [, 9(3) or 9A(5)],
[(ca) regulations under section 55A(5) or (7) or 55B(3)(b),]
(d) regulations under section 64,
(e) notification regulations (as defined by section 16(2)), or
(f) rules under paragraph 7 of Schedule 6,

and which is not subject to the requirement in subsection (4) that a draft of the instrument be laid before and approved by a resolution of each House of Parliament, shall be subject to annulment in pursuance of a resolution of either House of Parliament.

(6) A statutory instrument which contains only—

(a) regulations prescribing fees for the purposes of any provision of this Act, or
(b) regulations under section 7 prescribing fees for the purposes of any other enactment,

shall be laid before Parliament after being made.

NOTES

Initial Commencement

Royal Assent
Royal Assent: 16 July 1998: see s 75(2)(d).

Core resources

Amendment

Sub-s (1): words 'Secretary of State' in square brackets substituted by SI 2003/1887, art 9, Sch 2, para 9(1)(a).
Date in force: 19 August 2003: see SI 2003/1887, art 1(2).

Sub-s (2): words 'Secretary of State' in square brackets in both places they occur substituted by SI 2003/1887, art 9, Sch 2, para 9(1)(a).
Date in force: 19 August 2003: see SI 2003/1887, art 1(2).

Sub-s (3): words 'Secretary of State' in square brackets substituted by SI 2003/1887, art 9, Sch 2, para 9(1)(a).
Date in force: 19 August 2003: see SI 2003/1887, art 1(2).

Sub-s (4): words 'section 55E(1)' in square brackets inserted by the Criminal Justice and Immigration Act 2008, s 144(2)(a).
Date in force: to be appointed: see the Criminal Justice and Immigration Act 2008, s 153(7).

Sub-s (5): in para (c) words ', 9(3) or 9A(5)' in square brackets substituted by the Freedom of Information Act 2000, s 69(3).
Date in force: 1 January 2005: see SI 2004/1909, art 2(1), (2)(f), (3).

Sub-s (5): para (ca) inserted by the Criminal Justice and Immigration Act 2008, s 144(2)(b).
Date in force: to be appointed: see the Criminal Justice and Immigration Act 2008, s 153(7).

68 Meaning of 'accessible record'

(1) In this Act 'accessible record' means—

    (a) a health record as defined by subsection (2),
    (b) an educational record as defined by Schedule 11, or
    (c) an accessible public record as defined by Schedule 12.

(2) In subsection (1)(a) 'health record' means any record which—

    (a) consists of information relating to the physical or mental health or condition of an individual, and
    (b) has been made by or on behalf of a health professional in connection with the care of that individual.

NOTES

Initial Commencement

Royal Assent
Royal Assent: 16 July 1998: see s 75(2)(d).

69 Meaning of 'health professional'

(1) In this Act 'health professional' means any of the following—

    (a) a registered medical practitioner,
    (b) a registered dentist as defined by section 53(1) of the Dentists Act 1984,
    [(c) a registered dispensing optician or a registered optometrist within the meaning of the Opticians Act 1989,]

Data Protection Act 1998

(d) [a registered pharmacist or registered pharmacy technician within the meaning of the Pharmacists and Pharmacy Technicians Order 2007] or a registered person as defined by Article 2(2) of the Pharmacy (Northern Ireland) Order 1976,
[(e) a registered nurse or midwife,]
(f) a registered osteopath as defined by section 41 of the Osteopaths Act 1993,
(g) a registered chiropractor as defined by section 43 of the Chiropractors Act 1994,
(h) any person who is registered as a member of a profession to which [the Health Professions Order 2001] for the time being extends,
(i) a ... [child psychotherapist],
(j) ... and
(k) a scientist employed by such a body as head of a department.

(2) In subsection (1)(a) 'registered medical practitioner' includes any person who is provisionally registered under section 15 or 21 of the Medical Act 1983 and is engaged in such employment as is mentioned in subsection (3) of that section.

(3) In subsection (1) 'health service body' means—

(a) a [Strategic Health Authority] [established under section 13 of the National Health Service Act 2006],
(b) a Special Health Authority established under [section 28 of that Act, or section 22 of the National Health Service (Wales) Act 2006],
[(bb) a Primary Care Trust established under [section 18 of the National Health Service Act 2006],]
[(bbb) Local Health Board established under [section 11 of the National Health Service (Wales) Act 2006],]
(c) a Health Board within the meaning of the National Health Service (Scotland) Act 1978,
(d) a Special Health Board within the meaning of that Act,
(e) the managers of a State Hospital provided under section 102 of that Act,
(f) a National Health Service trust first established under section 5 of the National Health Service and Community Care Act 1990[, section 25 of the National Health Service Act 2006, section 18 of the National Health Service (Wales) Act 2006] or section 12A of the National Health Service (Scotland) Act 1978,
[(fa) an NHS foundation trust;]
(g) a Health and Social Services Board established under Article 16 of the Health and Personal Social Services (Northern Ireland) Order 1972,
(h) a special health and social services agency established under the Health and Personal Social Services (Special Agencies) (Northern Ireland) Order 1990, or
(i) a Health and Social Services trust established under Article 10 of the Health and Personal Social Services (Northern Ireland) Order 1991.

NOTES

Initial Commencement

Royal Assent
Royal Assent: 16 July 1998: see s 75(2)(d).

Amendment

Sub-s (1): para (c) substituted by SI 2005/848, art 28, Sch 1, Pt 2, para 12.
Date in force: 30 June 2005: see SI 2005/848, art 1(4)–(6) and the London Gazette, 3 June 2005; for transitional provisions see SI 2005/848, art 29(1), Sch 2.

Core resources

Sub-s (1): in para (d) words from 'a registered pharmacist' to 'Pharmacists and Pharmacy Technicians Order 2007' in square brackets substituted by SI 2007/289, art 67, Sch 1, Pt 1, para 7.
Date in force: 30 March 2007: see SI 2007/289, art 1(2)(c), (3) and the London, Edinburgh and Belfast Gazettes, 23 March 2007; for transitional provisions see SI 2007/289, art 68(1), Sch 2.

Sub-s (1): para (e) substituted by SI 2002/253, art 54(3), Sch 5, para 14.
Date in force: 1 August 2004: see the London Gazette, 21 July 2004; for transitional provisions see SI 2002/253, Sch 2.

Sub-s (1): in para (h) words 'the Health Professions Order 2001' in square brackets substituted by SI 2002/254, art 48(3), Sch 4, para 7; for transitional provisions see Sch 2 thereto.
Date in force: 1 April 2002: see SI 2002/254, art 1(2), (3), and the London Gazette, 25 March 2002.

Sub-s (1): in para (i) words omitted repealed by SI 2009/1182, art 4(2), Sch 5, Pt 1, para 4.
Date in force: 1 July 2009: see SI 2009/1357, art 2(1)(d).

Sub-s (1): in para (i) words 'child psychotherapist' in square brackets substituted by virtue of SI 2003/1590, art 3, Schedule, Pt 1, para 1(a).
Date in force: 9 July 2003: see SI 2003/1590, art 1.

Sub-s (1): para (j) repealed by SI 2003/1590, art 3, Schedule, Pt 1, para 1(b).
Date in force: 9 July 2003: see SI 2003/1590, art 1.

Sub-s (3): in para (a) words 'Strategic Health Authority' in square brackets inserted by SI 2002/2469, reg 4, Sch 1, Pt 1, para 24.
Date in force: 1 October 2002: see SI 2002/2469, reg 1.

Sub-s (3): in para (a) words 'established under section 13 of the National Health Service Act 2006' in square brackets substituted by the National Health Service (Consequential Provisions) Act 2006, s 2, Sch 1, paras 190, 191(a).
Date in force: 1 March 2007: see the National Health Service (Consequential Provisions) Act 2006, s 8(2).

Sub-s (3): in para (b) words from 'section 28 of' to 'National Health Service (Wales) Act 2006' in square brackets substituted by the National Health Service (Consequential Provisions) Act 2006, s 2, Sch 1, paras 190, 191(b).
Date in force: 1 March 2007: see the National Health Service (Consequential Provisions) Act 2006, s 8(2).

Sub-s (3): para (bb) inserted by SI 2000/90, art 3(1), Sch 1, para 33.
Date in force: 8 February 2000: see SI 2000/90, art 1.

Sub-s (3): in para (bb) words 'section 18 of the National Health Service Act 2006' in square brackets substituted by the National Health Service (Consequential Provisions) Act 2006, s 2, Sch 1, paras 190, 191(c).
Date in force: 1 March 2007: see the National Health Service (Consequential Provisions) Act 2006, s 8(2).

Sub-s (3): para (bbb) inserted by the National Health Service Reform and Health Care Professions Act 2002, s 6(2), Sch 5, para 41.
Date in force: 10 October 2002: see SI 2002/2532, art 2, Schedule. See also SI 2006/1407, arts 1(1), 2, Sch 1, Pt 2, para 12(c).

Sub-s (3): in para (bbb) words 'section 11 of the National Health Service (Wales) Act 2006' in square brackets substituted by the National Health Service (Consequential

Provisions) Act 2006, s 2, Sch 1, paras 190, 191(d).
Date in force: 1 March 2007: see the National Health Service (Consequential Provisions) Act 2006, s 8(2).

Sub-s (3): in para (f) words from ', section 25 of' to 'National Health Service (Wales) Act 2006' in square brackets inserted by the National Health Service (Consequential Provisions) Act 2006, s 2, Sch 1, paras 190, 191(e).
Date in force: 1 March 2007: see the National Health Service (Consequential Provisions) Act 2006, s 8(2).

Sub-s (3): para (fa) inserted by the Health and Social Care (Community Health and Standards) Act 2003, s 34, Sch 4, paras 106, 107.
Date in force: 1 April 2004: see SI 2004/759, art 2.

70   Supplementary definitions

(1) In this Act, unless the context otherwise requires—

'business' includes any trade or profession;
'the Commissioner' means [the Information Commissioner];
'credit reference agency' has the same meaning as in the Consumer Credit Act 1974;
'the Data Protection Directive' means Directive 95/46/EC on the protection of individuals with regard to the processing of personal data and on the free movement of such data;
'EEA State' means a State which is a contracting party to the Agreement on the European Economic Area signed at Oporto on 2nd May 1992 as adjusted by the Protocol signed at Brussels on 17th March 1993;
'enactment' includes an enactment passed after this Act [and any enactment comprised in, or in any instrument made under, an Act of the Scottish Parliament];
'government department' includes a Northern Ireland department and any body or authority exercising statutory functions on behalf of the Crown;
'Minister of the Crown' has the same meaning as in the Ministers of the Crown Act 1975;
'public register' means any register which pursuant to a requirement imposed—
  (a) by or under any enactment, or
  (b) in pursuance of any international agreement,
is open to public inspection or open to inspection by any person having a legitimate interest;
'pupil'—
  (a) in relation to a school in England and Wales, means a registered pupil within the meaning of the Education Act 1996,
  (b) in relation to a school in Scotland, means a pupil within the meaning of the Education (Scotland) Act 1980, and
  (c) in relation to a school in Northern Ireland, means a registered pupil within the meaning of the Education and Libraries (Northern Ireland) Order 1986;
'recipient', in relation to any personal data, means any person to whom the data are disclosed, including any person (such as an employee or agent of the data controller, a data processor or an employee or agent of a data processor) to whom they are disclosed in the course of processing the data for the data controller, but does not include any person to whom disclosure is or may be made as a result of, or with a view to, a particular inquiry by or on behalf of that person made in the exercise of any power conferred by law;
'registered company' means a company registered under the enactments relating to companies for the time being in force in the United Kingdom;

Core resources

'school'—
  (a) in relation to England and Wales, has the same meaning as in the Education Act 1996,
  (b) in relation to Scotland, has the same meaning as in the Education (Scotland) Act 1980, and
  (c) in relation to Northern Ireland, has the same meaning as in the Education and Libraries (Northern Ireland) Order 1986;

'teacher' includes—
  (a) in Great Britain, head teacher, and
  (b) in Northern Ireland, the principal of a school;

'third party', in relation to personal data, means any person other than—
  (a) the data subject,
  (b) the data controller, or
  (c) any data processor or other person authorised to process data for the data controller or processor;

'the Tribunal' means [the Information Tribunal].

(2) For the purposes of this Act data are inaccurate if they are incorrect or misleading as to any matter of fact.

NOTES

Initial Commencement

Royal Assent
Royal Assent: 16 July 1998: see s 75(2)(d).

Amendment

Sub-s (1): in definition 'the Commissioner' words 'the Information Commissioner' in square brackets substituted by the Freedom of Information Act 2000, s 18(4), Sch 2, Pt I, para 14(a).
Date in force: 30 January 2001: see the Freedom of Information Act 2000, s 87(2)(c).

Sub-s (1): in definition 'enactment' words from 'and any enactment' to 'the Scottish Parliament' in square brackets inserted by SI 1999/1820, art 4, Sch 2, Pt I, para 133.
Date in force: 1 July 1999: see SI 1999/1820, art 1(2).

Sub-s (1): in definition 'the Tribunal' words 'the Information Tribunal' in square brackets substituted by the Freedom of Information Act 2000, s 18(4), Sch 2, Pt I, para 14(b).
Date in force: 14 May 2001: see SI 2001/1637, art 2(b).

71 Index of defined expressions

The following Table shows provisions defining or otherwise explaining expressions used in this Act (other than provisions defining or explaining an expression only used in the same section or Schedule)—

accessible record	section 68
address (in Part III)	section 16(3)
business	section 70(1)
the Commissioner	section 70(1)
credit reference agency	section 70(1)
data	section 1(1)
data controller	sections 1(1) and (4) and 63(3)
data processor	section 1(1)

the Data Protection Directive	section 70(1)
data protection principles	section 4 and Schedule 1
data subject	section 1(1)
disclosing (of personal data)	section 1(2)(b)
EEA State	section 70(1)
enactment	section 70(1)
enforcement notice	section 40(1)
fees regulations (in Part III)	section 16(2)
government department	section 70(1)
health professional	section 69
inaccurate (in relation to data)	section 70(2)
information notice	section 43(1)
Minister of the Crown	section 70(1)
the non-disclosure provisions (in Part IV)	section 27(3)
notification regulations (in Part III)	section 16(2)
obtaining (of personal data)	section 1(2)(a)
personal data	section 1(1)
prescribed (in Part III)	section 16(2)
processing (of information or data)	section 1(1) and paragraph 5 of Schedule 8
[public authority	section 1(1)]
public register	section 70(1)
publish (in relation to journalistic, literary or artistic material)	section 32(6)
pupil (in relation to a school)	section 70(1)
recipient (in relation to personal data)	section 70(1)
recording (of personal data)	section 1(2)(a)
registered company	section 70(1)
registrable particulars (in Part III)	section 16(1)
relevant filing system	section 1(1)
school	section 70(1)
sensitive personal data	section 2
special information notice	section 44(1)
the special purposes	section 3
the subject information provisions (in Part IV)	section 27(2)
teacher	section 70(1)
third party (in relation to processing of personal data)	section 70(1)
the Tribunal	section 70(1)
using (of personal data)	section 1(2)(b).

NOTES

Initial Commencement

Royal Assent
Royal Assent: 16 July 1998: see s 75(2)(d).

Amendment

Table: entry 'public authority' inserted by the Freedom of Information Act 2000, s 68(5).
Date in force: 1 January 2005: see SI 2004/1909, art 2(1), (2)(f), (3).

Core resources

72   Modifications of Act

During the period beginning with the commencement of this section and ending with 23rd October 2007, the provisions of this Act shall have effect subject to the modifications set out in Schedule 13.

NOTES

Initial Commencement

To be appointed
To be appointed: see s 75(3).

Appointment

Appointment: 1 March 2000: see SI 2000/183, art 2(1).

73   Transitional provisions and savings

Schedule 14 (which contains transitional provisions and savings) has effect.

NOTES

Initial Commencement

Royal Assent
Royal Assent (so far as is necessary for bringing into force those provisions of Sch 14 which confer power to make subordinate legislation): 16 July 1998: see s 75(b)(i).

To be appointed
To be appointed (for remaining purposes): see s 75(3).

Appointment

Appointment (for remaining purposes): 1 March 2000: see SI 2000/183, art 2(1).

74   Minor and consequential amendments and repeals and revocations

(1)   Schedule 15 (which contains minor and consequential amendments) has effect.

(2)   The enactments and instruments specified in Schedule 16 are repealed or revoked to the extent specified.

NOTES

Initial Commencement

To be appointed
To be appointed: see s 75(3).

Appointment

Appointment: 1 March 2000: see SI 2000/183, art 2(1).

75 Short title, commencement and extent

(1) This Act may be cited as the Data Protection Act 1998.

(2) The following provisions of this Act—

 (a) sections 1 to 3,
 (b) section 25(1) and (4),
 (c) section 26,
 (d) sections 67 to 71,
 (e) this section,
 (f) paragraph 17 of Schedule 5,
 (g) Schedule 11,
 (h) Schedule 12, and
 (i) so much of any other provision of this Act as confers any power to make subordinate legislation,

shall come into force on the day on which this Act is passed.

(3) The remaining provisions of this Act shall come into force on such day as the [Secretary of State] may by order appoint; and different days may be appointed for different purposes.

(4) The day appointed under subsection (3) for the coming into force of section 56 must not be earlier than the first day on which sections 112, 113 and 115 of the Police Act 1997 (which provide for the issue by the Secretary of State of criminal conviction certificates, criminal record certificates and enhanced criminal record certificates) are all in force.

[(4A) Subsection (4) does not apply to section 56 so far as that section relates to a record containing information relating to—

 (a) the Secretary of State's functions under the Safeguarding Vulnerable Groups Act 2006 [or the Safeguarding Vulnerable Groups (Northern Ireland) Order 2007], or
 (b) the Independent Barring Board's functions under that Act [or that Order].]

(5) Subject to subsection (6), this Act extends to Northern Ireland.

(6) Any amendment, repeal or revocation made by Schedule 15 or 16 has the same extent as that of the enactment or instrument to which it relates.

NOTES

Initial Commencement

Royal Assent
Royal Assent: 16 July 1998: see sub-s (2)(e) above.

Amendment

Sub-s (3): words 'Secretary of State' in square brackets substituted by SI 2003/1887, art 9, Sch 2, para 9(1)(a).
Date in force: 19 August 2003: see SI 2003/1887, art 1(2).

Sub-s (4A): inserted by the Safeguarding Vulnerable Groups Act 2006, s 63(1), Sch 9, Pt 2, para 15(1), (3).
Date in force: 19 May 2008: see SI 2008/1320, art 3.

Sub-s (4A): in para (a) words 'or the Safeguarding of Vulnerable Groups (Northern Ireland) Order 2007' in square brackets inserted by the Safeguarding Vulnerable

Core resources

Groups (Northern Ireland) Order 2007, SI 2007/1351, art 60(1), Sch 7, para 4(2)(a).
Date in force: to be appointed: see the Safeguarding Vulnerable Groups (Northern Ireland) Order 2007, SI 2007/1351, art 1(3).

Sub-s (4A): in para (b) words 'or that Order' in square brackets inserted by the Safeguarding Vulnerable Groups (Northern Ireland) Order 2007, SI 2007/1351, art 60(1), Sch 7, para 4(2)(b).
Date in force: to be appointed: see the Safeguarding Vulnerable Groups (Northern Ireland) Order 2007, SI 2007/1351, art 1(3).

Subordinate Legislation

Data Protection Act 1998 (Commencement) Order 2000, SI 2000/183 (made under sub-s (3)).

Data Protection Act 1998 (Commencement No 2) Order 2008, SI 2008/1592 (made under sub-s (3)).

SCHEDULE 1
THE DATA PROTECTION PRINCIPLES

Section 4(1) and (2)

PART I
THE PRINCIPLES

1   Personal data shall be processed fairly and lawfully and, in particular, shall not be processed unless—

(a)   at least one of the conditions in Schedule 2 is met, and
(b)   in the case of sensitive personal data, at least one of the conditions in Schedule 3 is also met.

2   Personal data shall be obtained only for one or more specified and lawful purposes, and shall not be further processed in any manner incompatible with that purpose or those purposes.

3   Personal data shall be adequate, relevant and not excessive in relation to the purpose or purposes for which they are processed.

4   Personal data shall be accurate and, where necessary, kept up to date.

5   Personal data processed for any purpose or purposes shall not be kept for longer than is necessary for that purpose or those purposes.

6   Personal data shall be processed in accordance with the rights of data subjects under this Act.

7   Appropriate technical and organisational measures shall be taken against unauthorised or unlawful processing of personal data and against accidental loss or destruction of, or damage to, personal data.

8   Personal data shall not be transferred to a country or territory outside the European Economic Area unless that country or territory ensures an adequate level of protection for the rights and freedoms of data subjects in relation to the processing of personal data.

Data Protection Act 1998

NOTES

Initial Commencement

To be appointed
To be appointed: see s 75(3).

Appointment

Appointment: 1 March 2000: see SI 2000/183, art 2(1).

PART II
INTERPRETATION OF THE PRINCIPLES IN PART I

The first principle

1 (1) In determining for the purposes of the first principle whether personal data are processed fairly, regard is to be had to the method by which they are obtained, including in particular whether any person from whom they are obtained is deceived or misled as to the purpose or purposes for which they are to be processed.

(2) Subject to paragraph 2, for the purposes of the first principle data are to be treated as obtained fairly if they consist of information obtained from a person who—

- (a) is authorised by or under any enactment to supply it, or
- (b) is required to supply it by or under any enactment or by any convention or other instrument imposing an international obligation on the United Kingdom.

2 (1) Subject to paragraph 3, for the purposes of the first principle personal data are not to be treated as processed fairly unless—

- (a) in the case of data obtained from the data subject, the data controller ensures so far as practicable that the data subject has, is provided with, or has made readily available to him, the information specified in sub-paragraph (3), and
- (b) in any other case, the data controller ensures so far as practicable that, before the relevant time or as soon as practicable after that time, the data subject has, is provided with, or has made readily available to him, the information specified in sub-paragraph (3).

(2) In sub-paragraph (1)(b) 'the relevant time' means—

- (a) the time when the data controller first processes the data, or
- (b) in a case where at that time disclosure to a third party within a reasonable period is envisaged—
  - (i) if the data are in fact disclosed to such a person within that period, the time when the data are first disclosed,
  - (ii) if within that period the data controller becomes, or ought to become, aware that the data are unlikely to be disclosed to such a person within that period, the time when the data controller does become, or ought to become, so aware, or
  - (iii) in any other case, the end of that period.

(3) The information referred to in sub-paragraph (1) is as follows, namely—

- (a) the identity of the data controller,
- (b) if he has nominated a representative for the purposes of this Act, the identity of that representative,
- (c) the purpose or purposes for which the data are intended to be processed, and

Core resources

(d) any further information which is necessary, having regard to the specific circumstances in which the data are or are to be processed, to enable processing in respect of the data subject to be fair.

3 (1) Paragraph 2(1)(b) does not apply where either of the primary conditions in sub-paragraph (2), together with such further conditions as may be prescribed by the [Secretary of State] by order, are met.

(2) The primary conditions referred to in sub-paragraph (1) are—

(a) that the provision of that information would involve a disproportionate effort, or
(b) that the recording of the information to be contained in the data by, or the disclosure of the data by, the data controller is necessary for compliance with any legal obligation to which the data controller is subject, other than an obligation imposed by contract.

4 (1) Personal data which contain a general identifier falling within a description prescribed by the [Secretary of State] by order are not to be treated as processed fairly and lawfully unless they are processed in compliance with any conditions so prescribed in relation to general identifiers of that description.

(2) In sub-paragraph (1) 'a general identifier' means any identifier (such as, for example, a number or code used for identification purposes) which—

(a) relates to an individual, and
(b) forms part of a set of similar identifiers which is of general application.

The second principle

5 The purpose or purposes for which personal data are obtained may in particular be specified—

(a) in a notice given for the purposes of paragraph 2 by the data controller to the data subject, or
(b) in a notification given to the Commissioner under Part III of this Act.

6 In determining whether any disclosure of personal data is compatible with the purpose or purposes for which the data were obtained, regard is to be had to the purpose or purposes for which the personal data are intended to be processed by any person to whom they are disclosed.

The fourth principle

7 The fourth principle is not to be regarded as being contravened by reason of any inaccuracy in personal data which accurately record information obtained by the data controller from the data subject or a third party in a case where—

(a) having regard to the purpose or purposes for which the data were obtained and further processed, the data controller has taken reasonable steps to ensure the accuracy of the data, and
(b) if the data subject has notified the data controller of the data subject's view that the data are inaccurate, the data indicate that fact.

The sixth principle

8 A person is to be regarded as contravening the sixth principle if, but only if—

(a) he contravenes section 7 by failing to supply information in accordance with that section,

Data Protection Act 1998

    (b) he contravenes section 10 by failing to comply with a notice given under subsection (1) of that section to the extent that the notice is justified or by failing to give a notice under subsection (3) of that section,

    (c) he contravenes section 11 by failing to comply with a notice given under subsection (1) of that section, or

    (d) he contravenes section 12 by failing to comply with a notice given under subsection (1) or (2)(b) of that section or by failing to give a notification under subsection (2)(a) of that section or a notice under subsection (3) of that section.

The seventh principle

9   Having regard to the state of technological development and the cost of implementing any measures, the measures must ensure a level of security appropriate to—

    (a) the harm that might result from such unauthorised or unlawful processing or accidental loss, destruction or damage as are mentioned in the seventh principle, and

    (b) the nature of the data to be protected.

10   The data controller must take reasonable steps to ensure the reliability of any employees of his who have access to the personal data.

11   Where processing of personal data is carried out by a data processor on behalf of a data controller, the data controller must in order to comply with the seventh principle—

    (a) choose a data processor providing sufficient guarantees in respect of the technical and organisational security measures governing the processing to be carried out, and

    (b) take reasonable steps to ensure compliance with those measures.

12   Where processing of personal data is carried out by a data processor on behalf of a data controller, the data controller is not to be regarded as complying with the seventh principle unless—

    (a) the processing is carried out under a contract—
        (i) which is made or evidenced in writing, and
        (ii) under which the data processor is to act only on instructions from the data controller, and

    (b) the contract requires the data processor to comply with obligations equivalent to those imposed on a data controller by the seventh principle.

The eighth principle

13   An adequate level of protection is one which is adequate in all the circumstances of the case, having regard in particular to—

    (a) the nature of the personal data,
    (b) the country or territory of origin of the information contained in the data,
    (c) the country or territory of final destination of that information,
    (d) the purposes for which and period during which the data are intended to be processed,
    (e) the law in force in the country or territory in question,
    (f) the international obligations of that country or territory,
    (g) any relevant codes of conduct or other rules which are enforceable in that country or territory (whether generally or by arrangement in particular cases), and
    (h) any security measures taken in respect of the data in that country or territory.

Core resources

14 The eighth principle does not apply to a transfer falling within any paragraph of Schedule 4, except in such circumstances and to such extent as the [Secretary of State] may by order provide.

15 (1) Where—

(a) in any proceedings under this Act any question arises as to whether the requirement of the eighth principle as to an adequate level of protection is met in relation to the transfer of any personal data to a country or territory outside the European Economic Area, and

(b) a Community finding has been made in relation to transfers of the kind in question,

that question is to be determined in accordance with that finding.

(2) In sub-paragraph (1) 'Community finding' means a finding of the European Commission, under the procedure provided for in Article 31(2) of the Data Protection Directive, that a country or territory outside the European Economic Area does, or does not, ensure an adequate level of protection within the meaning of Article 25(2) of the Directive.

NOTES

Initial Commencement

Royal Assent
Paras 3, 4, 14: Royal Assent (so far as conferring power to make subordinate legislation): 16 July 1998: see s 75(2)(i).

To be appointed
Paras 1, 2, 5–13, 15: To be appointed: see s 75(3).
Paras 3, 4, 14: To be appointed (for remaining purposes): see s 75(3).

Appointment

Paras 1, 2, 5–13, 15: Appointment: 1 March 2000: see SI 2000/183, art 2(1).
Paras 3, 4, 14: Appointment (for remaining purposes): 1 March 2000: see SI 2000/183, art 2(1).

Amendment

Para 3: in sub-para (1) words 'Secretary of State' in square brackets substituted by SI 2003/1887, art 9, Sch 2, para 9(1)(b).
Date in force: 19 August 2003: see SI 2003/1887, art 1(2).

Para 4: in sub-para (1) words 'Secretary of State' in square brackets substituted by SI 2003/1887, art 9, Sch 2, para 9(1)(b).
Date in force: 19 August 2003: see SI 2003/1887, art 1(2).

Para 14: words 'Secretary of State' in square brackets substituted by SI 2003/1887, art 9, Sch 2, para 9(1)(b).
Date in force: 19 August 2003: see SI 2003/1887, art 1(2).

Subordinate Legislation

Data Protection (Conditions under Paragraph 3 of Part II of Schedule 1) Order 2000, SI 2000/185 (made under para 3(1)).

Data Protection Act 1998

SCHEDULE 2
CONDITIONS RELEVANT FOR PURPOSES OF THE FIRST PRINCIPLE: PROCESSING OF ANY PERSONAL DATA

Section 4(3)

1   The data subject has given his consent to the processing.

2   The processing is necessary—
   (a) for the performance of a contract to which the data subject is a party, or
   (b) for the taking of steps at the request of the data subject with a view to entering into a contract.

3   The processing is necessary for compliance with any legal obligation to which the data controller is subject, other than an obligation imposed by contract.

4   The processing is necessary in order to protect the vital interests of the data subject.

5   The processing is necessary—
   (a) for the administration of justice,
   [(aa) for the exercise of any functions of either House of Parliament,]
   (b) for the exercise of any functions conferred on any person by or under any enactment,
   (c) for the exercise of any functions of the Crown, a Minister of the Crown or a government department, or
   (d) for the exercise of any other functions of a public nature exercised in the public interest by any person.

6   (1) The processing is necessary for the purposes of legitimate interests pursued by the data controller or by the third party or parties to whom the data are disclosed, except where the processing is unwarranted in any particular case by reason of prejudice to the rights and freedoms or legitimate interests of the data subject.

(2) The [Secretary of State] may by order specify particular circumstances in which this condition is, or is not, to be taken to be satisfied.

NOTES

Initial Commencement

Royal Assent
Para 6: Royal Assent (so far as conferring power to make subordinate legislation): 16 July 1998: see s 75(2)(i).

To be appointed
Paras 1–5: To be appointed: see s 75(3).
Para 6: To be appointed (for remaining purposes): see s 75(3).

Appointment

Para 1–5: Appointment: 1 March 2000: see SI 2000/183, art 2(1).
Para 6: Appointment (for remaining purposes): 1 March 2000: see SI 2000/183, art 2(1).

Amendment

Para 5: sub-para (aa) inserted by the Freedom of Information Act 2000, s 73, Sch 6, para 4.
Date in force: 1 January 2005: see SI 2004/1909, art 2(1), (2)(f), (3).

Core resources

Para 6: in sub-para (2) words 'Secretary of State' in square brackets substituted by SI 2003/1887, art 9, Sch 2, para 9(1)(b).
Date in force: 19 August 2003: see SI 2003/1887, art 1(2).

See Further

See further, immediately after the 2007 election, the National Assembly for Wales Commission shall be treated as a government department for the purposes of para 5 above: the National Assembly for Wales Commission (Crown Status) Order 2007, SI 2007/1118, art 5(1), (2)(b) and the Government of Wales Act 2006, s 161(1).

SCHEDULE 3
CONDITIONS RELEVANT FOR PURPOSES OF THE FIRST PRINCIPLE: PROCESSING OF SENSITIVE PERSONAL DATA

Section 4(3)

1 The data subject has given his explicit consent to the processing of the personal data.

2 (1) The processing is necessary for the purposes of exercising or performing any right or obligation which is conferred or imposed by law on the data controller in connection with employment.

(2) The [Secretary of State] may by order—

(a) exclude the application of sub-paragraph (1) in such cases as may be specified, or
(b) provide that, in such cases as may be specified, the condition in subparagraph (1) is not to be regarded as satisfied unless such further conditions as may be specified in the order are also satisfied.

3 The processing is necessary—

(a) in order to protect the vital interests of the data subject or another person, in a case where—
    (i) consent cannot be given by or on behalf of the data subject, or
    (ii) the data controller cannot reasonably be expected to obtain the consent of the data subject, or
(b) in order to protect the vital interests of another person, in a case where consent by or on behalf of the data subject has been unreasonably withheld.

4 The processing—

(a) is carried out in the course of its legitimate activities by any body or association which—
    (i) is not established or conducted for profit, and
    (ii) exists for political, philosophical religious or trade-union purposes,
(b) is carried out with appropriate safeguards for the rights and freedoms of data subjects,
(c) relates only to individuals who either are members of the body or association or have regular contact with it in connection with its purposes, and
(d) does not involve disclosure of the personal data to a third party without the consent of the data subject.

5 The information contained in the personal data has been made public as a result of steps deliberately taken by the data subject.

6 The processing—

(a) is necessary for the purpose of, or in connection with, any legal proceedings (including prospective legal proceedings),

Data Protection Act 1998

(b) is necessary for the purpose of obtaining legal advice, or
(c) is otherwise necessary for the purposes of establishing, exercising or defending legal rights.

7 (1) The processing is necessary—
  (a) for the administration of justice,
  [(aa) for the exercise of any functions of either House of Parliament,]
  (b) for the exercise of any functions conferred on any person by or under an enactment, or
  (c) for the exercise of any functions of the Crown, a Minister of the Crown or a government department.

(2) The [Secretary of State] may by order—
  (a) exclude the application of sub-paragraph (1) in such cases as may be specified, or
  (b) provide that, in such cases as may be specified, the condition in subparagraph (1) is not to be regarded as satisfied unless such further conditions as may be specified in the order are also satisfied.

[7A (1) The processing—
  (a) is either—
    (i) the disclosure of sensitive personal data by a person as a member of an anti-fraud organisation or otherwise in accordance with any arrangements made by such an organisation; or
    (ii) any other processing by that person or another person of sensitive personal data so disclosed; and
  (b) is necessary for the purposes of preventing fraud or a particular kind of fraud.

(2) In this paragraph 'an anti-fraud organisation' means any unincorporated association, body corporate or other person which enables or facilitates any sharing of information to prevent fraud or a particular kind of fraud or which has any of these functions as its purpose or one of its purposes.]

8 (1) The processing is necessary for medical purposes and is undertaken by—
  (a) a health professional, or
  (b) a person who in the circumstances owes a duty of confidentiality which is equivalent to that which would arise if that person were a health professional.

(2) In this paragraph 'medical purposes' includes the purposes of preventative medicine, medical diagnosis, medical research, the provision of care and treatment and the management of healthcare services.

9 (1) The processing—
  (a) is of sensitive personal data consisting of information as to racial or ethnic origin,
  (b) is necessary for the purpose of identifying or keeping under review the existence or absence of equality of opportunity or treatment between persons of different racial or ethnic origins, with a view to enabling such equality to be promoted or maintained, and
  (c) is carried out with appropriate safeguards for the rights and freedoms of data subjects.

(2) The [Secretary of State] may by order specify circumstances in which processing falling within sub-paragraph (1)(a) and (b) is, or is not, to be taken for the purposes of sub-paragraph (1)(c) to be carried out with appropriate safeguards for the rights and freedoms of data subjects.

Core resources

10   The personal data are processed in circumstances specified in an order made by the [Secretary of State] for the purposes of this paragraph.

NOTES

Initial Commencement

Royal Assent
Paras 2, 7, 9, 10: Royal Assent (so far as conferring power to make subordinate legislation): 16 July 1998: see s 75(2)(i).

To be appointed
Paras 1, 3–6, 8: To be appointed: see s 75(3).
Paras 2, 7, 9, 10: To be appointed (for remaining purposes): see s 75(3).

Appointment

Paras 1, 3–6, 8: Appointment: 1 March 2000: see SI 2000/183, art 2(1).
Paras 2, 7, 9, 10: Appointment (for remaining purposes): 1 March 2000: see SI 2000/183, art 2(1).

Amendment

Para 2: in sub-para (2) words 'Secretary of State' in square brackets substituted by SI 2003/1887, art 9, Sch 2, para 9(1)(b).
Date in force: 19 August 2003: see SI 2003/1887, art 1(2).

Para 7: sub-para (1)(aa) inserted by the Freedom of Information Act 2000, s 73, Sch 6, para 5.
Date in force: 1 January 2005: see SI 2004/1909, art 2(1), (2)(f), (3).

Para 7: in sub-para (2) words 'Secretary of State' in square brackets substituted by SI 2003/1887, art 9, Sch 2, para 9(1)(b).
Date in force: 19 August 2003: see SI 2003/1887, art 1(2).

Para 7A: inserted by the Serious Crime Act 2007, s 72.
Date in force: 1 October 2008: see SI 2008/2504, art 2(e).

Para 9: in sub-para (2) words 'Secretary of State' in square brackets substituted by SI 2003/1887, art 9, Sch 2, para 9(1)(b).
Date in force: 19 August 2003: see SI 2003/1887, art 1(2).

Para 10: words 'Secretary of State' in square brackets substituted by SI 2003/1887, art 9, Sch 2, para 9(1)(b).
Date in force: 19 August 2003: see SI 2003/1887, art 1(2).

See Further

See further, immediately after the 2007 election, the National Assembly for Wales Commission shall be treated as a government department for the purposes of para 7 above: the National Assembly for Wales Commission (Crown Status) Order 2007, SI 2007/1118, art 5(1), (2)(c) and the Government of Wales Act 2006, s 161(1).

Subordinate Legislation

Data Protection (Processing of Sensitive Personal Data) Order 2000, SI 2000/417 (made under para 10).

Data Protection (Processing of Sensitive Personal Data) (Elected Representatives) Order 2002, SI 2002/2905 (made under para 10).

Data Protection Act 1998

Data Protection (Processing of Sensitive Personal Data) Order 2006, SI 2006/2068 (made under para 10).

Data Protection (Processing of Sensitive Personal Data) Order 2009, SI 2009/1811 (made under para 10).

SCHEDULE 4
CASES WHERE THE EIGHTH PRINCIPLE DOES NOT APPLY

Section 4(3)

1   The data subject has given his consent to the transfer.

2   The transfer is necessary—
    (a) for the performance of a contract between the data subject and the data controller, or
    (b) for the taking of steps at the request of the data subject with a view to his entering into a contract with the data controller.

3   The transfer is necessary—
    (a) for the conclusion of a contract between the data controller and a person other than the data subject which—
        (i) is entered into at the request of the data subject, or
        (ii) is in the interests of the data subject, or
    (b) for the performance of such a contract.

4   (1) The transfer is necessary for reasons of substantial public interest.

(2) The [Secretary of State] may by order specify—
    (a) circumstances in which a transfer is to be taken for the purposes of subparagraph (1) to be necessary for reasons of substantial public interest, and
    (b) circumstances in which a transfer which is not required by or under an enactment is not to be taken for the purpose of sub-paragraph (1) to be necessary for reasons of substantial public interest.

5   The transfer—
    (a) is necessary for the purpose of, or in connection with, any legal proceedings (including prospective legal proceedings),
    (b) is necessary for the purpose of obtaining legal advice, or
    (c) is otherwise necessary for the purposes of establishing, exercising or defending legal rights.

6   The transfer is necessary in order to protect the vital interests of the data subject.

7   The transfer is of part of the personal data on a public register and any conditions subject to which the register is open to inspection are complied with by any person to whom the data are or may be disclosed after the transfer.

8   The transfer is made on terms which are of a kind approved by the Commissioner as ensuring adequate safeguards for the rights and freedoms of data subjects.

9   The transfer has been authorised by the Commissioner as being made in such a manner as to ensure adequate safeguards for the rights and freedoms of data subjects.

Core resources

NOTES

Initial Commencement

Royal Assent
Para 4: Royal Assent (so far as conferring power to make subordinate legislation): 16 July 1998: see s 75(2)(i).

To be appointed
Paras 1–3, 5–9: To be appointed: see s 75(3).
Para 4: To be appointed (for remaining purposes): see s 75(3).

Appointment

Paras 1–3, 5–9: Appointment: 1 March 2000: see SI 2000/183, art 2(1).
Para 4: Appointment (for remaining purposes): 1 March 2000: see SI 2000/183, art 2(1).

Amendment

Para 4: in sub-para (2) words 'Secretary of State' in square brackets substituted by SI 2003/1887, art 9, Sch 2, para 9(1)(b).
Date in force: 19 August 2003: see SI 2003/1887, art 1(2).

SCHEDULE 5
[THE INFORMATION COMMISSIONER] AND [THE INFORMATION TRIBUNAL]

NOTES

Amendment

Words 'The Information Commissioner' in square brackets substituted by virtue of the Freedom of Information Act 2000, s 18(4), Sch 2, Pt I, para 1(1).
Date in force: 30 January 2001: see the Freedom of Information Act 2000, s 87(2)(c).

Words 'the Information Tribunal' in square brackets substituted by virtue of the Freedom of Information Act 2000, s 18(4), Sch 2, Pt I, para 1(2).
Date in force: 14 May 2001: see SI 2001/1637, art 2(b).

Section 6(7)

PART I
THE COMMISSIONER

Status and capacity

1 (1) The corporation sole by the name of the Data Protection Registrar established by the Data Protection Act 1984 shall continue in existence by the name of the [Information Commissioner].

(2) The Commissioner and his officers and staff are not to be regarded as servants or agents of the Crown.

Tenure of office

2 (1) Subject to the provisions of this paragraph, the Commissioner shall hold office for such term not exceeding five years as may be determined at the time of his appointment.

(2) The Commissioner may be relieved of his office by Her Majesty at his own request.

(3) The Commissioner may be removed from office by Her Majesty in pursuance of an Address from both Houses of Parliament.

(4) The Commissioner shall in any case vacate his office—

(a) on completing the year of service in which he attains the age of sixty-five years, or
(b) if earlier, on completing his fifteenth year of service.

(5) Subject to sub-paragraph (4), a person who ceases to be Commissioner on the expiration of his term of office shall be eligible for re-appointment, but a person may not be re-appointed for a third or subsequent term as Commissioner unless, by reason of special circumstances, the person's re-appointment for such a term is desirable in the public interest.

Salary etc

3 (1) There shall be paid—
   (a) to the Commissioner such salary, and
   (b) to or in respect of the Commissioner such pension,

as may be specified by a resolution of the House of Commons.

(2) A resolution for the purposes of this paragraph may—

(a) specify the salary or pension,
(b) provide that the salary or pension is to be the same as, or calculated on the same basis as, that payable to, or to or in respect of, a person employed in a specified office under, or in a specified capacity in the service of, the Crown, or
(c) specify the salary or pension and provide for it to be increased by reference to such variables as may be specified in the resolution.

(3) A resolution for the purposes of this paragraph may take effect from the date on which it is passed or from any earlier or later date specified in the resolution.

(4) A resolution for the purposes of this paragraph may make different provision in relation to the pension payable to or in respect of different holders of the office of Commissioner.

(5) Any salary or pension payable under this paragraph shall be charged on and issued out of the Consolidated Fund.

(6) In this paragraph 'pension' includes an allowance or gratuity and any reference to the payment of a pension includes a reference to the making of payments towards the provision of a pension.

Officers and staff

4 (1) The Commissioner—
   (a) shall appoint a deputy commissioner [or two deputy commissioners], and
   (b) may appoint such number of other officers and staff as he may determine.

[(1A) The Commissioner shall, when appointing any second deputy commissioner, specify which of the Commissioner's functions are to be performed, in the circumstances referred to in paragraph 5(1), by each of the deputy commissioners.]

(2) The remuneration and other conditions of service of the persons appointed under this paragraph shall be determined by the Commissioner.

Core resources

(3) The Commissioner may pay such pensions, allowances or gratuities to or in respect of the persons appointed under this paragraph, or make such payments towards the provision of such pensions, allowances or gratuities, as he may determine.

(4) The references in sub-paragraph (3) to pensions, allowances or gratuities to or in respect of the persons appointed under this paragraph include references to pensions, allowances or gratuities by way of compensation to or in respect of any of those persons who suffer loss of office or employment.

(5) Any determination under sub-paragraph (1)(b), (2) or (3) shall require the approval of the [Secretary of State].

(6) The Employers' Liability (Compulsory Insurance) Act 1969 shall not require insurance to be effected by the Commissioner.

5 (1) The deputy commissioner [or deputy commissioners] shall perform the functions conferred by this Act [or the Freedom of Information Act 2000] on the Commissioner during any vacancy in that office or at any time when the Commissioner is for any reason unable to act.

(2) Without prejudice to sub-paragraph (1), any functions of the Commissioner under this Act [or the Freedom of Information Act 2000] may, to the extent authorised by him, be performed by any of his officers or staff.

Authentication of seal of the Commissioner

6 The application of the seal of the Commissioner shall be authenticated by his signature or by the signature of some other person authorised for the purpose.

Presumption of authenticity of documents issued by the Commissioner

7 Any document purporting to be an instrument issued by the Commissioner and to be duly executed under the Commissioner's seal or to be signed by or on behalf of the Commissioner shall be received in evidence and shall be deemed to be such an instrument unless the contrary is shown.

Money

8 The [Secretary of State] may make payments to the Commissioner out of money provided by Parliament.

9 (1) All fees and other sums received by the Commissioner in the exercise of his functions under this Act[, under section 159 of the Consumer Credit Act 1974 or under the Freedom of Information Act 2000] shall be paid by him to the [Secretary of State].

(2) Sub-paragraph (1) shall not apply where the [Secretary of State], with the consent of the Treasury, otherwise directs.

(3) Any sums received by the [Secretary of State] under sub-paragraph (1) shall be paid into the Consolidated Fund.

Accounts

10 (1) It shall be the duty of the Commissioner—
   (a) to keep proper accounts and other records in relation to the accounts,
   (b) to prepare in respect of each financial year a statement of account in such form as the [Secretary of State] may direct, and

(c) to send copies of that statement to the Comptroller and Auditor General on or before 31st August next following the end of the year to which the statement relates or on or before such earlier date after the end of that year as the Treasury may direct.

(2) The Comptroller and Auditor General shall examine and certify any statement sent to him under this paragraph and lay copies of it together with his report thereon before each House of Parliament.

(3) In this paragraph 'financial year' means a period of twelve months beginning with 1st April.

Application of Part I in Scotland

11 Paragraphs 1(1), 6 and 7 do not extend to Scotland.

NOTES

Initial Commencement

Royal Assent
Royal Assent: 16 July 1998 (so far as conferring power to make subordinate legislation): see s 75(2)(i).

Appointment

Appointment (for remaining purposes): 1 March 2000: see SI 2000/183, art 2(1).

Amendment

Para 1: in sub-para (1) words 'Information Commissioner' in square brackets substituted by the Freedom of Information Act 2000, s 18(4), Sch 2, Pt I, para 15(1), (2).
Date in force: 30 January 2001: see the Freedom of Information Act 2000, s 87(2)(c).

Para 4: in sub-para (1)(a) words 'or two deputy commissioners' in square brackets inserted by the Freedom of Information Act 2000, s 18(4), Sch 2, Pt II, para 20(1), (2).
Date in force: 30 November 2000: see the Freedom of Information Act 2000, s 87(1)(i).

Para 4: sub-para (1A) inserted by the Freedom of Information Act 2000, s 18(4), Sch 2, Pt II, para 20(1), (3).
Date in force: 30 November 2000: see the Freedom of Information Act 2000, s 87(1)(i).

Para 4: in sub-para (5) words 'Secretary of State' in square brackets substituted by SI 2003/1887, art 9, Sch 2, para 9(1)(c).
Date in force: 19 August 2003: see SI 2003/1887, art 1(2).

Para 5: in sub-para (1) words 'or deputy commissioners' and 'or the Freedom of Information Act 2000' in square brackets inserted by the Freedom of Information Act 2000, s 18(4), Sch 2, Pt II, para 21(1), (2).
Date in force: 30 November 2000: see the Freedom of Information Act 2000, s 87(1)(i).

Para 5: in sub-para (2) words 'or the Freedom of Information Act 2000' in square brackets inserted by the Freedom of Information Act 2000, s 18(4), Sch 2, Pt II, para 21(1), (3).
Date in force: 30 November 2000: see the Freedom of Information Act 2000, s 87(1)(i).

Core resources

Para 8: words 'Secretary of State' in square brackets substituted by SI 2003/1887, art 9, Sch 2, para 9(1)(c).
Date in force: 19 August 2003: see SI 2003/1887, art 1(2).

Para 9: in sub-para (1) words from ', under section 159' to 'Freedom of Information Act 2000' in square brackets substituted by the Freedom of Information Act 2000, s 18(4), Sch 2, Pt II, para 22.
Date in force: 30 November 2000: see the Freedom of Information Act 2000, s 87(1)(i).

Para 9: in sub-para (1) words 'Secretary of State' in square brackets substituted by SI 2003/1887, art 9, Sch 2, para 9(1)(c).
Date in force: 19 August 2003: see SI 2003/1887, art 1(2).

Para 9: in sub-para (2) words 'Secretary of State' in square brackets substituted by SI 2003/1887, art 9, Sch 2, para 9(1)(c).
Date in force: 19 August 2003: see SI 2003/1887, art 1(2).

Para 9: in sub-para (3) words 'Secretary of State' in square brackets substituted by SI 2003/1887, art 9, Sch 2, para 9(1)(c).
Date in force: 19 August 2003: see SI 2003/1887, art 1(2).

Para 10: in sub-para (1)(b) words 'Secretary of State' in square brackets substituted by SI 2003/1887, art 9, Sch 2, para 9(1)(c).
Date in force: 19 August 2003: see SI 2003/1887, art 1(2).

PART II
THE TRIBUNAL

Tenure of office

12 (1) Subject to the following provisions of this paragraph, a member of the Tribunal shall hold and vacate his office in accordance with the terms of his appointment and shall, on ceasing to hold office, be eligible for re-appointment.

(2) Any member of the Tribunal may at any time resign his office by notice in writing to the Lord Chancellor ... [(in the case of the chairman or a deputy chairman) or to the Secretary of State (in the case of any other member)].

(3) A person who is the chairman or deputy chairman of the Tribunal shall vacate his office on the day on which he attains the age of seventy years; but this sub-paragraph is subject to section 26(4) to (6) of the Judicial Pensions and Retirement Act 1993 (power to authorise continuance in office up to the age of seventy-five years).

Salary etc

13 The [Secretary of State] shall pay to the members of the Tribunal out of money provided by Parliament such remuneration and allowances as he may determine.

Officers and staff

14 The [Secretary of State] may provide the Tribunal with such officers and staff as he thinks necessary for the proper discharge of its functions.

Expenses

15 Such expenses of the Tribunal as the [Secretary of State] may determine shall be defrayed by the [Secretary of State] out of money provided by Parliament.

NOTES

Initial Commencement

Royal Assent
Royal Assent: 16 July 1998 (so far as conferring power to make subordinate legislation): see s 75(2)(i).

Appointment

Appointment (for remaining purposes): 1 March 2000: see SI 2000/183, art 2(1).

Amendment

Para 12: in sub-para (2) words omitted repealed by SI 2001/3500, art 8, Sch 2, Pt I, para 6(3).
Date in force: 26 November 2001: see SI 2001/3500, art 1(2).

Para 12: in sub-para (2) words '(in the case of the chairman or a deputy chairman) or to the Secretary of State (in the case of any other member)' in square brackets inserted by SI 2003/1887, art 9, Sch 2, para 9(2).
Date in force: 19 August 2003: see SI 2003/1887, art 1(2).

Para 13: words 'Secretary of State' in square brackets substituted by SI 2003/1887, art 9, Sch 2, para 9(1)(c).
Date in force: 19 August 2003: see SI 2003/1887, art 1(2).

Para 14: words 'Secretary of State' in square brackets substituted by SI 2003/1887, art 9, Sch 2, para 9(1)(c).
Date in force: 19 August 2003: see SI 2003/1887, art 1(2).

Para 15: words 'Secretary of State' in square brackets in both places they occur substituted by SI 2003/1887, art 9, Sch 2, para 9(1)(c).
Date in force: 19 August 2003: see SI 2003/1887, art 1(2).

PART III
...

NOTES

Amendment

Repealed by the Freedom of Information Act 2000, ss 18(4), 86, Sch 2, Pt I, para 15(1), (3), Sch 8, Pt II.
Date in force: 14 May 2001: see SI 2001/1637, art 2(b).

...

NOTES

Amendment

Repealed by the Freedom of Information Act 2000, ss 18(4), 86, Sch 2, Pt I, para 15(1), (3), Sch 8, Pt II.
Date in force: 14 May 2001: see SI 2001/1637, art 2(b).

Core resources

SCHEDULE 6
APPEAL PROCEEDINGS

Sections 28(12), 48(5)

Hearing of appeals

1   For the purpose of hearing and determining appeals or any matter preliminary or incidental to an appeal the Tribunal shall sit at such times and in such places as the chairman or a deputy chairman may direct and may sit in two or more divisions.

Constitution of Tribunal in national security cases

2   (1)   The Lord Chancellor shall from time to time designate, from among the chairman and deputy chairmen appointed by him under section 6(4)(a) and (b), those persons who are to be capable of hearing appeals under section 28(4) or (6) [or under section 60(1) or (4) of the Freedom of Information Act 2000].

(2)   A designation under sub-paragraph (1) may at any time be revoked by the Lord Chancellor.

[(3)   The Lord Chancellor may make, or revoke, a designation under this paragraph only with the concurrence of all of the following—

(a)   the Lord Chief Justice;
(b)   the Lord President of the Court of Session;
(c)   the Lord Chief Justice of Northern Ireland.

(4)   The Lord Chief Justice of England and Wales may nominate a judicial office holder (as defined in section 109(4) of the Constitutional Reform Act 2005) to exercise his functions under sub-paragraph (3) so far as they relate to a designation under this paragraph.

(5)   The Lord President of the Court of Session may nominate a judge of the Court of Session who is a member of the First or Second Division of the Inner House of that Court to exercise his functions under sub-paragraph (3) so far as they relate to a designation under this paragraph.

(6)   The Lord Chief Justice of Northern Ireland may nominate any of the following to exercise his functions under sub-paragraph (3) so far as they relate to a designation under this paragraph—

(a)   the holder of one of the offices listed in Schedule 1 to the Justice (Northern Ireland) Act 2002;
(b)   a Lord Justice of Appeal (as defined in section 88 of that Act).]

[3   [(1)]   The Tribunal shall be duly constituted—

(a)   for an appeal under section 28(4) or (6) in any case where the application of paragraph 6(1) is excluded by rules under paragraph 7, or
(b)   for an appeal under section 60(1) or (4) of the Freedom of Information Act 2000,

if it consists of three of the persons designated under paragraph 2(1), of whom one shall be designated by the Lord Chancellor to preside.

[(2)   The Lord Chancellor may designate a person to preside under this paragraph only with the concurrence of all of the following—

(a)   the Lord Chief Justice of England and Wales;
(b)   the Lord President of the Court of Session;
(c)   the Lord Chief Justice of Northern Ireland.

Data Protection Act 1998

(3) The Lord Chief Justice of England and Wales may nominate a judicial office holder (as defined in section 109(4) of the Constitutional Reform Act 2005) to exercise his functions under this paragraph.

(4) The Lord President of the Court of Session may nominate a judge of the Court of Session who is a member of the First or Second Division of the Inner House of that Court to exercise his functions under this paragraph.

(5) The Lord Chief Justice of Northern Ireland may nominate any of the following to exercise his functions under this paragraph—

   (a) the holder of one of the offices listed in Schedule 1 to the Justice (Northern Ireland) Act 2002;
   (b) a Lord Justice of Appeal (as defined in section 88 of that Act).]]

Constitution of Tribunal in other cases

4 (1) Subject to any rules made under paragraph 7, the Tribunal shall be duly constituted for an appeal under section 48(1), (2) or (4) if it consists of—

   (a) the chairman or a deputy chairman (who shall preside), and
   (b) an equal number of the members appointed respectively in accordance with paragraphs (a) and (b) of section 6(6).

[(1A) Subject to any rules made under paragraph 7, the Tribunal shall be duly constituted for an appeal under section 57(1) or (2) of the Freedom of Information Act 2000 if it consists of—

   (a) the chairman or a deputy chairman (who shall preside), and
   (b) an equal number of the members appointed respectively in accordance with paragraphs (aa) and (bb) of section 6(6).]

(2) The members who are to constitute the Tribunal in accordance with subparagraph (1) [or (1A)] shall be nominated by the chairman or, if he is for any reason unable to act, by a deputy chairman.

Determination of questions by full Tribunal

5 The determination of any question before the Tribunal when constituted in accordance with paragraph 3 or 4 shall be according to the opinion of the majority of the members hearing the appeal.

Ex parte proceedings

6 (1) Subject to any rules made under paragraph 7, the jurisdiction of the Tribunal in respect of an appeal under section 28(4) or (6) shall be exercised ex parte by one or more persons designated under paragraph 2(1).

(2) Subject to any rules made under paragraph 7, the jurisdiction of the Tribunal in respect of an appeal under section 48(3) shall be exercised ex parte by the chairman or a deputy chairman sitting alone.

Rules of procedure

7 (1) The [Secretary of State] may make rules for [regulating—

   (a) the exercise of the rights of appeal conferred—
      (i) by sections 28(4) and (6) and 48, and
      (ii) by sections 57(1) and (2) and section 60(1) and (4) of the Freedom of Information Act 2000, and
   (b) the practice and procedure of the Tribunal].

Core resources

(2) Rules under this paragraph may in particular make provision—

    (a) with respect to the period within which an appeal can be brought and the burden of proof on an appeal,

    [(aa) for the joinder of any other person as a party to any proceedings on an appeal under the Freedom of Information Act 2000,

    (ab) for the hearing of an appeal under this Act with an appeal under the Freedom of Information Act 2000,]

    (b) for the summoning (or, in Scotland, citation) of witnesses and the administration of oaths,

    (c) for securing the production of documents and material used for the processing of personal data,

    (d) for the inspection, examination, operation and testing of any equipment or material used in connection with the processing of personal data,

    (e) for the hearing of an appeal wholly or partly in camera,

    (f) for hearing an appeal in the absence of the appellant or for determining an appeal without a hearing,

    (g) for enabling an appeal under section 48(1) against an information notice to be determined by the chairman or a deputy chairman,

    (h) for enabling any matter preliminary or incidental to an appeal to be dealt with by the chairman or a deputy chairman,

    (i) for the awarding of costs or, in Scotland, expenses,

    (j) for the publication of reports of the Tribunal's decisions, and

    (k) for conferring on the Tribunal such ancillary powers as the [Secretary of State] thinks necessary for the proper discharge of its functions.

(3) In making rules under this paragraph which relate to appeals under section 28(4) or (6) the [Secretary of State] shall have regard, in particular, to the need to secure that information is not disclosed contrary to the public interest.

Obstruction etc

8 (1) If any person is guilty of any act or omission in relation to proceedings before the Tribunal which, if those proceedings were proceedings before a court having power to commit for contempt, would constitute contempt of court, the Tribunal may certify the offence to the High Court or, in Scotland, the Court of Session.

(2) Where an offence is so certified, the court may inquire into the matter and, after hearing any witness who may be produced against or on behalf of the person charged with the offence, and after hearing any statement that may be offered in defence, deal with him in any manner in which it could deal with him if he had committed the like offence in relation to the court.

NOTES

Initial Commencement

Royal Assent
Royal Assent (so far as conferring power to make subordinate legislation): 16 July 1998: see s 75(2)(i).

To be appointed
To be appointed (for remaining purposes): see s 75(3).

Appointment

Appointment (for remaining purposes): 1 March 2000: see SI 2000/183, art 2(1).

Data Protection Act 1998

Amendment

Para 2: in sub-para (1) words 'or under section 60(1) or (4) of the Freedom of Information Act 2000' in square brackets inserted by the Freedom of Information Act 2000, s 61(1), Sch 4, para 1.
Date in force: 14 May 2001: see SI 2001/1637, art 2(c).

Para 2: sub-paras (3)–(6) inserted by the Constitutional Reform Act 2005, s 15(1), Sch 4, Pt 1, para 275(1), (2).
Date in force: 3 April 2006: see SI 2006/1014, art 2(a), Sch 1, paras 10, 11(v).

Para 3: substituted by the Freedom of Information Act 2000, s 61(1), Sch 4, para 2.
Date in force: 1 January 2005: see SI 2004/1909, art 2(1), (2)(d), (3).

Para 3: sub-para (1) numbered as such by the Constitutional Reform Act 2005, s 15(1), Sch 4, Pt 1, para 275(1), (3)(a).
Date in force: 3 April 2006: see SI 2006/1014, art 2(a), Sch 1, paras 10, 11(v).

Para 3: sub-paras (2)–(5) inserted by the Constitutional Reform Act 2005, s 15(1), Sch 4, Pt 1, para 275(1), (3)(b).
Date in force: 3 April 2006: see SI 2006/1014, art 2(a), Sch 1, paras 10, 11(v).

Para 4: sub-para (1A) inserted by the Freedom of Information Act 2000, s 61(1), Sch 4, para 3(1), (2).
Date in force: 30 November 2002: see SI 2002/2812, art 2(i).

Para 4: in sub-para (2) words 'or (1A)' in square brackets inserted by the Freedom of Information Act 2000, s 61(1), Sch 4, para 3(1), (3).
Date in force: 30 November 2002: see SI 2002/2812, art 2(i).

Para 7: in sub-para (1) words 'Secretary of State' in square brackets substituted by SI 2003/1887, art 9, Sch 2, para 9(1)(d).
Date in force: 19 August 2003: see SI 2003/1887, art 1(2).

Para 7: words in square brackets from 'regulating—' to the end of para (b) substituted by the Freedom of Information Act 2000, 61(1), Sch 4, para 4(1), (2).
Date in force: 14 May 2001: see SI 2001/1637, art 2(c).

Para 7: sub-para (2)(aa), (ab) inserted by the Freedom of Information Act 2000, s 61(1), Sch 4, para 4(1), (3).
Date in force: 14 May 2001: see SI 2001/1637, art 2(c).

Para 7: in sub-para (2)(k) words 'Secretary of State' in square brackets substituted by SI 2003/1887, art 9, Sch 2, para 9(1)(d).
Date in force: 19 August 2003: see SI 2003/1887, art 1(2).

Para 7: in sub-para (3) words 'Secretary of State' in square brackets substituted by SI 2003/1887, art 9, Sch 2, para 9(1)(d).
Date in force: 19 August 2003: see SI 2003/1887, art 1(2).

Subordinate Legislation

Data Protection Tribunal (National Security Appeals) (Telecommunications) Rules 2000, SI 2000/731 (made under para 7).

Information Tribunal (National Security Appeals) Rules 2005, SI 2005/13 (made under para 7).

Information Tribunal (Enforcement Appeals) Rules 2005, SI 2005/14 (made under para 7).

Information Tribunal (Enforcement Appeals) (Amendment) Rules 2005, SI 2005/450 (made under para 7).

SCHEDULE 7
MISCELLANEOUS EXEMPTIONS

Section 37

Confidential references given by the data controller

1 Personal data are exempt from section 7 if they consist of a reference given or to be given in confidence by the data controller for the purposes of—

   (a) the education, training or employment, or prospective education, training or employment, of the data subject,
   (b) the appointment, or prospective appointment, of the data subject to any office, or
   (c) the provision, or prospective provision, by the data subject of any service.

Armed forces

2 Personal data are exempt from the subject information provisions in any case to the extent to which the application of those provisions would be likely to prejudice the combat effectiveness of any of the armed forces of the Crown.

Judicial appointments and honours

3 Personal data processed for the purposes of—

   (a) assessing any person's suitability for judicial office or the office of Queen's Counsel, or
   (b) the conferring by the Crown of any honour [or dignity],

are exempt from the subject information provisions.

Crown employment and Crown or Ministerial appointments

4 [(1)] The [Secretary of State] may by order exempt from the subject information provisions personal data processed for the purposes of assessing any person's suitability for—

   (a) employment by or under the Crown, or
   (b) any office to which appointments are made by Her Majesty, by a Minister of the Crown or by a [Northern Ireland authority].

[(2) In this paragraph 'Northern Ireland authority' means the First Minister, the deputy First Minister, a Northern Ireland Minister or a Northern Ireland department.]

Management forecasts etc

5 Personal data processed for the purposes of management forecasting or management planning to assist the data controller in the conduct of any business or other activity are exempt from the subject information provisions in any case to the extent to which the application of those provisions would be likely to prejudice the conduct of that business or other activity.

Corporate finance

6 (1) Where personal data are processed for the purposes of, or in connection with, a corporate finance service provided by a relevant person—

   (a) the data are exempt from the subject information provisions in any case to the extent to which either—

(i) the application of those provisions to the data could affect the price of any instrument which is already in existence or is to be or may be created, or

(ii) the data controller reasonably believes that the application of those provisions to the data could affect the price of any such instrument, and

(b) to the extent that the data are not exempt from the subject information provisions by virtue of paragraph (a), they are exempt from those provisions if the exemption is required for the purpose of safeguarding an important economic or financial interest of the United Kingdom.

(2) For the purposes of sub-paragraph (1)(b) the [Secretary of State] may by order specify—

(a) matters to be taken into account in determining whether exemption from the subject information provisions is required for the purpose of safeguarding an important economic or financial interest of the United Kingdom, or

(b) circumstances in which exemption from those provisions is, or is not, to be taken to be required for that purpose.

(3) In this paragraph—

'corporate finance service' means a service consisting in—

(a) underwriting in respect of issues of, or the placing of issues of, any instrument,

(b) advice to undertakings on capital structure, industrial strategy and related matters and advice and service relating to mergers and the purchase of undertakings, or

(c) services relating to such underwriting as is mentioned in paragraph (a);

'instrument' means any instrument listed in [section C of Annex I to Directive 2004/39/EC of the European Parliament and of the Council of 21 April 2004 on markets in financial instruments]…;

'price' includes value;

'relevant person' means—

[(a) any person who, by reason of any permission he has under Part IV of the Financial Services and Markets Act 2000, is able to carry on a corporate finance service without contravening the general prohibition, within the meaning of section 19 of that Act,

(b) an EEA firm of the kind mentioned in paragraph 5(a) or (b) of Schedule 3 to that Act which has qualified for authorisation under paragraph 12 of that Schedule, and may lawfully carry on a corporate finance service,

(c) any person who is exempt from the general prohibition in respect of any corporate finance service—

(i) as a result of an exemption order made under section 38(1) of that Act, or

(ii) by reason of section 39(1) of that Act (appointed representatives),

(cc) any person, not falling within paragraph (a), (b) or (c) who may lawfully carry on a corporate finance service without contravening the general prohibition,]

(d) any person who, in the course of his employment, provides to his employer a service falling within paragraph (b) or (c) of the definition of 'corporate finance service', or

(e) any partner who provides to other partners in the partnership a service falling within either of those paragraphs.

Negotiations

7 Personal data which consist of records of the intentions of the data controller in relation to any negotiations with the data subject are exempt from the subject

information provisions in any case to the extent to which the application of those provisions would be likely to prejudice those negotiations.

Examination marks

8 (1) Section 7 shall have effect subject to the provisions of sub-paragraphs (2) to (4) in the case of personal data consisting of marks or other information processed by a data controller—

    (a) for the purpose of determining the results of an academic, professional or other examination or of enabling the results of any such examination to be determined, or

    (b) in consequence of the determination of any such results.

(2) Where the relevant day falls before the day on which the results of the examination are announced, the period mentioned in section 7(8) shall be extended until—

    (a) the end of five months beginning with the relevant day, or

    (b) the end of forty days beginning with the date of the announcement,

whichever is the earlier.

(3) Where by virtue of sub-paragraph (2) a period longer than the prescribed period elapses after the relevant day before the request is complied with, the information to be supplied pursuant to the request shall be supplied both by reference to the data in question at the time when the request is received and (if different) by reference to the data as from time to time held in the period beginning when the request is received and ending when it is complied with.

(4) For the purposes of this paragraph the results of an examination shall be treated as announced when they are first published or (if not published) when they are first made available or communicated to the candidate in question.

(5) In this paragraph—

    'examination' includes any process for determining the knowledge, intelligence, skill or ability of a candidate by reference to his performance in any test, work or other activity;

    'the prescribed period' means forty days or such other period as is for the time being prescribed under section 7 in relation to the personal data in question;

    'relevant day' has the same meaning as in section 7.

Examination scripts etc

9 (1) Personal data consisting of information recorded by candidates during an academic, professional or other examination are exempt from section 7.

(2) In this paragraph 'examination' has the same meaning as in paragraph 8.

Legal professional privilege

10 Personal data are exempt from the subject information provisions if the data consist of information in respect of which a claim to legal professional privilege [or, in Scotland, to confidentiality of communications] could be maintained in legal proceedings.

Self-incrimination

11 (1) A person need not comply with any request or order under section 7 to the extent that compliance would, by revealing evidence of the commission of any offence other than an offence under this Act, expose him to proceedings for that offence.

(2) Information disclosed by any person in compliance with any request or order under section 7 shall not be admissible against him in proceedings for an offence under this Act.

NOTES

Initial Commencement

Royal Assent
Para 4: Royal Assent: 16 July 1998: see s 75(2)(i).
Para 6: Royal Assent (so far as conferring power to make subordinate legislation): 16 July 1998: see s 75(2)(i).

To be appointed
Paras 1–3, 5, 7–11: To be appointed: see s 75(3).
Para 6: To be appointed (for remaining purposes): see s 75(3).

Appointment

Paras 1–3, 5, 7–11: Appointment: 1 March 2000: see SI 2000/183, art 2(1).
Para 6: Appointment (for remaining purposes): 1 March 2000: see SI 2000/183, art 2(1).

Amendment

Para 3: in sub-para (b) words 'or dignity' inserted by the Freedom of Information Act 2000, s 73, Sch 6, para 6.
Date in force: 14 May 2001: see SI 2001/1637, art 2(d).

Para 4: sub-para (1) numbered as such by the Northern Ireland Act 1998, s 99, Sch 13, para 21(2).
Date in force: 2 December 1999: see SI 1999/3209, art 2, Schedule.

Para 4: in sub-para (1) words 'Secretary of State' in square brackets substituted by SI 2003/1887, art 9, Sch 2, para 9(1)(e).
Date in force: 19 August 2003: see SI 2003/1887, art 1(2).

Para 4: in sub-para (1)(b) words 'Northern Ireland authority' in square brackets substituted by the Northern Ireland Act 1998, s 99, Sch 13, para 21(1).
Date in force: 2 December 1999: see SI 1999/3209, art 2, Schedule.

Para 4: sub-para (2) inserted by the Northern Ireland Act 1998, s 99, Sch 13, para 21(2).
Date in force: 2 December 1999: see SI 1999/3209, art 2, Schedule.

Para 6: in sub-para (2) words 'Secretary of State' in square brackets substituted by SI 2003/1887, art 9, Sch 2, para 9(1)(e).
Date in force: 19 August 2003: see SI 2003/1887, art 1(2).

Para 6: in sub-para (3) in definition 'instrument' words from 'section C of' to 'in financial instruments' in square brackets substituted by SI 2007/126, reg 3(6), Sch 6, Pt 1, para 12.
Date in force (for certain purposes): 1 April 2007: see SI 2007/126, reg 1(2).
Date in force (for remaining purposes): 1 November 2007: see SI 2007/126, reg 1(2).

Para 6: in sub-para (3) in definition 'instrument' words omitted repealed by SI 2002/1555, art 25(1), (2).
Date in force: 3 July 2002: see SI 2002/1555, art 1.

Core resources

Para 6: in sub-para (3) in definition 'relevant person' paras (a)–(c), (cc) substituted, for paras (a)–(c) as originally enacted, by SI 2002/1555, art 25(1), (3).
Date in force: 3 July 2002: see SI 2002/1555, art 1.

Para 10: words 'or, in Scotland, to confidentiality of communications' in square brackets substituted by the Freedom of Information Act 2000, s 73, Sch 6, para 7.
Date in force: 14 May 2001: see SI 2001/1637, art 2(d).

See Further

See further, immediately after the 2007 election, any reference in para 4 above to employment by or under the Crown shall be treated as including employment as a member of staff of the National Assembly for Wales Commission: the National Assembly for Wales Commission (Crown Status) Order 2007, SI 2007/1118, art 5(1), (3), (4)(c) and the Government of Wales Act 2006, s 161(1).

Subordinate Legislation

Data Protection (Corporate Finance Exemption) Order 2000, SI 2000/184 (made under para 6(2)).

Data Protection (Crown Appointments) Order 2000, SI 2000/416 (made under para 4).

SCHEDULE 8
Transitional Relief

Section 39

PART I
INTERPRETATION OF SCHEDULE

1 (1) For the purposes of this Schedule, personal data are 'eligible data' at any time if, and to the extent that, they are at that time subject to processing which was already under way immediately before 24th October 1998.

(2) In this Schedule—

    'eligible automated data' means eligible data which fall within paragraph (a) or (b) of the definition of 'data' in section 1(1);
    'eligible manual data' means eligible data which are not eligible automated data;
    'the first transitional period' means the period beginning with the commencement of this Schedule and ending with 23rd October 2001;
    'the second transitional period' means the period beginning with 24th October 2001 and ending with 23rd October 2007.

NOTES

Initial Commencement

To be appointed
To be appointed: see s 75(3).

Appointment

Appointment: 1 March 2000: see SI 2000/183, art 2(1).

Data Protection Act 1998

PART II
EXEMPTIONS AVAILABLE BEFORE 24TH OCTOBER 2001

Manual data

2 (1) Eligible manual data, other than data forming part of an accessible record, are exempt from the data protection principles and Parts II and III of this Act during the first transitional period.

(2) This paragraph does not apply to eligible manual data to which paragraph 4 applies.

3 (1) This paragraph applies to—
   (a) eligible manual data forming part of an accessible record, and
   (b) personal data which fall within paragraph (d) of the definition of 'data' in section 1(1) but which, because they are not subject to processing which was already under way immediately before 24th October 1998, are not eligible data for the purposes of this Schedule.

(2) During the first transitional period, data to which this paragraph applies are exempt from—
   (a) the data protection principles, except the sixth principle so far as relating to sections 7 and 12A,
   (b) Part II of this Act, except—
      (i) section 7 (as it has effect subject to section 8) and section 12A, and
      (ii) section 15 so far as relating to those sections, and
   (c) Part III of this Act.

4 (1) This paragraph applies to eligible manual data which consist of information relevant to the financial standing of the data subject and in respect of which the data controller is a credit reference agency.

(2) During the first transitional period, data to which this paragraph applies are exempt from—
   (a) the data protection principles, except the sixth principle so far as relating to sections 7 and 12A,
   (b) Part II of this Act, except—
      (i) section 7 (as it has effect subject to sections 8 and 9) and section 12A, and
      (ii) section 15 so far as relating to those sections, and
   (c) Part III of this Act.

Processing otherwise than by reference to the data subject

5 During the first transitional period, for the purposes of this Act (apart from paragraph 1), eligible automated data are not to be regarded as being 'processed' unless the processing is by reference to the data subject.

Payrolls and accounts

6 (1) Subject to sub-paragraph (2), eligible automated data processed by a data controller for one or more of the following purposes—
   (a) calculating amounts payable by way of remuneration or pensions in respect of service in any employment or office or making payments of, or of sums deducted from, such remuneration or pensions, or
   (b) keeping accounts relating to any business or other activity carried on by the data controller or keeping records of purchases, sales or other transactions for

681

Core resources

   the purpose of ensuring that the requisite payments are made by or to him in respect of those transactions or for the purpose of making financial or management forecasts to assist him in the conduct of any such business or activity,

are exempt from the data protection principles and Parts II and III of this Act during the first transitional period.

(2) It shall be a condition of the exemption of any eligible automated data under this paragraph that the data are not processed for any other purpose, but the exemption is not lost by any processing of the eligible data for any other purpose if the data controller shows that he had taken such care to prevent it as in all the circumstances was reasonably required.

(3) Data processed only for one or more of the purposes mentioned in subparagraph (1)(a) may be disclosed—

 (a) to any person, other than the data controller, by whom the remuneration or pensions in question are payable,
 (b) for the purpose of obtaining actuarial advice,
 (c) for the purpose of giving information as to the persons in any employment or office for use in medical research into the health of, or injuries suffered by, persons engaged in particular occupations or working in particular places or areas,
 (d) if the data subject (or a person acting on his behalf) has requested or consented to the disclosure of the data either generally or in the circumstances in which the disclosure in question is made, or
 (e) if the person making the disclosure has reasonable grounds for believing that the disclosure falls within paragraph (d).

(4) Data processed for any of the purposes mentioned in sub-paragraph (1) may be disclosed—

 (a) for the purpose of audit or where the disclosure is for the purpose only of giving information about the data controller's financial affairs, or
 (b) in any case in which disclosure would be permitted by any other provision of this Part of this Act if sub-paragraph (2) were included among the non-disclosure provisions.

(5) In this paragraph 'remuneration' includes remuneration in kind and 'pensions' includes gratuities or similar benefits.

Unincorporated members' clubs and mailing lists

7 Eligible automated data processed by an unincorporated members' club and relating only to the members of the club are exempt from the data protection principles and Parts II and III of this Act during the first transitional period.

8 Eligible automated data processed by a data controller only for the purposes of distributing, or recording the distribution of, articles or information to the data subjects and consisting only of their names, addresses or other particulars necessary for effecting the distribution, are exempt from the data protection principles and Parts II and III of this Act during the first transitional period.

9 Neither paragraph 7 nor paragraph 8 applies to personal data relating to any data subject unless he has been asked by the club or data controller whether he objects to the data relating to him being processed as mentioned in that paragraph and has not objected.

10 It shall be a condition of the exemption of any data under paragraph 7 that the data are not disclosed except as permitted by paragraph 11 and of the exemption

under paragraph 8 that the data are not processed for any purpose other than that mentioned in that paragraph or as permitted by paragraph 11, but—

(a) the exemption under paragraph 7 shall not be lost by any disclosure in breach of that condition, and
(b) the exemption under paragraph 8 shall not be lost by any processing in breach of that condition,

if the data controller shows that he had taken such care to prevent it as in all the circumstances was reasonably required.

11 Data to which paragraph 10 applies may be disclosed—

(a) if the data subject (or a person acting on his behalf) has requested or consented to the disclosure of the data either generally or in the circumstances in which the disclosure in question is made,
(b) if the person making the disclosure has reasonable grounds for believing that the disclosure falls within paragraph (a), or
(c) in any case in which disclosure would be permitted by any other provision of this Part of this Act if paragraph 10 were included among the non-disclosure provisions.

Back-up data

12 Eligible automated data which are processed only for the purpose of replacing other data in the event of the latter being lost, destroyed or impaired are exempt from section 7 during the first transitional period.

Exemption of all eligible automated data from certain requirements

13 (1) During the first transitional period, eligible automated data are exempt from the following provisions—

(a) the first data protection principle to the extent to which it requires compliance with—
 (i) paragraph 2 of Part II of Schedule 1,
 (ii) the conditions in Schedule 2, and
 (iii) the conditions in Schedule 3,
(b) the seventh data protection principle to the extent to which it requires compliance with paragraph 12 of Part II of Schedule 1;
(c) the eighth data protection principle,
(d) in section 7(1), paragraphs (b), (c)(ii) and (d),
(e) sections 10 and 11,
(f) section 12, and
(g) section 13, except so far as relating to—
 (i) any contravention of the fourth data protection principle,
 (ii) any disclosure without the consent of the data controller,
 (iii) loss or destruction of data without the consent of the data controller, or
 (iv) processing for the special purposes.

(2) The specific exemptions conferred by sub-paragraph (1)(a), (c) and (e) do not limit the data controller's general duty under the first data protection principle to ensure that processing is fair.

NOTES

Initial Commencement

To be appointed
To be appointed: see s 75(3).

Core resources

Appointment

Appointment: 1 March 2000: see SI 2000/183, art 2(1).

PART III
EXEMPTIONS AVAILABLE AFTER 23RD OCTOBER 2001 BUT BEFORE 24TH OCTOBER 2007

14 (1) This paragraph applies to—

(a) eligible manual data which were held immediately before 24th October 1998, and
(b) personal data which fall within paragraph (d) of the definition of 'data' in section 1(1) but do not fall within paragraph (a) of this subparagraph,

but does not apply to eligible manual data to which the exemption in paragraph 16 applies.

(2) During the second transitional period, data to which this paragraph applies are exempt from the following provisions—

(a) the first data protection principle except to the extent to which it requires compliance with paragraph 2 of Part II of Schedule 1,
(b) the second, third, fourth and fifth data protection principles, and
(c) section 14(1) to (3).

[**14A** (1) This paragraph applies to personal data which fall within paragraph (e) of the definition of 'data' in section 1(1) and do not fall within paragraph 14(1)(a), but does not apply to eligible manual data to which the exemption in paragraph 16 applies

(2) During the second transitional period, data to which this paragraph applies are exempt from—

(a) the fourth data protection principle, and
(b) section 14(1) to (3).]

NOTES

Initial Commencement

To be appointed
To be appointed: see s 75(3).

Appointment

Appointment: 1 March 2000: see SI 2000/183, art 2(1).

Amendment

Para 14A: inserted by the Freedom of Information Act 2000, s 70(3).
Date in force: 1 January 2005: see SI 2004/1909, art 2(1), (2)(f), (3).

PART IV
EXEMPTIONS AFTER 23RD OCTOBER 2001 FOR HISTORICAL RESEARCH

15 In this Part of this Schedule 'the relevant conditions' has the same meaning as in section 33.

16 (1) Eligible manual data which are processed only for the purpose of historical research in compliance with the relevant conditions are exempt from the provisions specified in sub-paragraph (2) after 23rd October 2001.

(2) The provisions referred to in sub-paragraph (1) are—

(a) the first data protection principle except in so far as it requires compliance with paragraph 2 of Part II of Schedule 1,
(b) the second, third, fourth and fifth data protection principles, and
(c) section 14(1) to (3).

17 (1) After 23rd October 2001 eligible automated data which are processed only for the purpose of historical research in compliance with the relevant conditions are exempt from the first data protection principle to the extent to which it requires compliance with the conditions in Schedules 2 and 3.

(2) Eligible automated data which are processed—

(a) only for the purpose of historical research,
(b) in compliance with the relevant conditions, and
(c) otherwise than by reference to the data subject,

are also exempt from the provisions referred to in sub-paragraph (3) after 23rd October 2001.

(3) The provisions referred to in sub-paragraph (2) are—

(a) the first data protection principle except in so far as it requires compliance with paragraph 2 of Part II of Schedule 1,
(b) the second, third, fourth and fifth data protection principles, and
(c) section 14(1) to (3).

18 For the purposes of this Part of this Schedule personal data are not to be treated as processed otherwise than for the purpose of historical research merely because the data are disclosed—

(a) to any person, for the purpose of historical research only,
(b) to the data subject or a person acting on his behalf,
(c) at the request, or with the consent, of the data subject or a person acting on his behalf, or
(d) in circumstances in which the person making the disclosure has reasonable grounds for believing that the disclosure falls within paragraph (a), (b) or (c).

NOTES

Initial Commencement

To be appointed
To be appointed: see s 75(3).

Appointment

Appointment: 1 March 2000: see SI 2000/183, art 2(1).

PART V
EXEMPTION FROM SECTION 22

19 Processing which was already under way immediately before 24th October 1998 is not assessable processing for the purposes of section 22.

Core resources

NOTES

Initial Commencement

To be appointed
To be appointed: see s 75(3).

Appointment

Appointment: 1 March 2000: see SI 2000/183, art 2(1).

SCHEDULE 9
POWERS OF ENTRY AND INSPECTION

Section 50

Issue of warrants

1 (1) If a circuit judge [or a District Judge (Magistrates' Courts)] is satisfied by information on oath supplied by the Commissioner that there are reasonable grounds for suspecting—

   (a) that a data controller has contravened or is contravening any of the data protection principles, or
   (b) that an offence under this Act has been or is being committed,

and that evidence of the contravention or of the commission of the offence is to be found on any premises specified in the information, he may, subject to subparagraph (2) and paragraph 2, grant a warrant to the Commissioner.

(2) A judge shall not issue a warrant under this Schedule in respect of any personal data processed for the special purposes unless a determination by the Commissioner under section 45 with respect to those data has taken effect.

(3) A warrant issued under sub-paragraph (1) shall authorise the Commissioner or any of his officers or staff at any time within seven days of the date of the warrant to enter the premises, to search them, to inspect, examine, operate and test any equipment found there which is used or intended to be used for the processing of personal data and to inspect and seize any documents or other material found there which may be such evidence as is mentioned in that sub-paragraph.

2 (1) A judge shall not issue a warrant under this Schedule unless he is satisfied—

   (a) that the Commissioner has given seven days' notice in writing to the occupier of the premises in question demanding access to the premises, and
   (b) that either—
       (i) access was demanded at a reasonable hour and was unreasonably refused, or
       (ii) although entry to the premises was granted, the occupier unreasonably refused to comply with a request by the Commissioner or any of the Commissioner's officers or staff to permit the Commissioner or the officer or member of staff to do any of the things referred to in paragraph 1(3), and
   (c) that the occupier, has, after the refusal, been notified by the Commissioner of the application for the warrant and has had an opportunity of being heard by the judge on the question whether or not it should be issued.

(2) Sub-paragraph (1) shall not apply if the judge is satisfied that the case is one of urgency or that compliance with those provisions would defeat the object of the entry.

Data Protection Act 1998

3   A judge who issues a warrant under this Schedule shall also issue two copies of it and certify them clearly as copies.

Execution of warrants

4   A person executing a warrant issued under this Schedule may use such reasonable force as may be necessary.

5   A warrant issued under this Schedule shall be executed at a reasonable hour unless it appears to the person executing it that there are grounds for suspecting that the evidence in question would not be found if it were so executed.

6   If the person who occupies the premises in respect of which a warrant is issued under this Schedule is present when the warrant is executed, he shall be shown the warrant and supplied with a copy of it; and if that person is not present a copy of the warrant shall be left in a prominent place on the premises.

7   (1)   A person seizing anything in pursuance of a warrant under this Schedule shall give a receipt for it if asked to do so.

(2)   Anything so seized may be retained for so long as is necessary in all the circumstances but the person in occupation of the premises in question shall be given a copy of anything that is seized if he so requests and the person executing the warrant considers that it can be done without undue delay.

Matters exempt from inspection and seizure

8   The powers of inspection and seizure conferred by a warrant issued under this Schedule shall not be exercisable in respect of personal data which by virtue of section 28 are exempt from any of the provisions of this Act.

9   (1)   Subject to the provisions of this paragraph, the powers of inspection and seizure conferred by a warrant issued under this Schedule shall not be exercisable in respect of—

   (a)   any communication between a professional legal adviser and his client in connection with the giving of legal advice to the client with respect to his obligations, liabilities or rights under this Act, or
   (b)   any communication between a professional legal adviser and his client, or between such an adviser or his client and any other person, made in connection with or in contemplation of proceedings under or arising out of this Act (including proceedings before the Tribunal) and for the purposes of such proceedings.

(2)   Sub-paragraph (1) applies also to—

   (a)   any copy or other record of any such communication as is there mentioned, and
   (b)   any document or article enclosed with or referred to in any such communication if made in connection with the giving of any advice or, as the case may be, in connection with or in contemplation of and for the purposes of such proceedings as are there mentioned.

(3)   This paragraph does not apply to anything in the possession of any person other than the professional legal adviser or his client or to anything held with the intention of furthering a criminal purpose.

(4)   In this paragraph references to the client of a professional legal adviser include references to any person representing such a client.

10   If the person in occupation of any premises in respect of which a warrant is issued under this Schedule objects to the inspection or seizure under the warrant of any

Core resources

material on the grounds that it consists partly of matters in respect of which those powers are not exercisable, he shall, if the person executing the warrant so requests, furnish that person with a copy of so much of the material as is not exempt from those powers.

Return of warrants

11 A warrant issued under this Schedule shall be returned to the court from which it was issued—

(a) after being executed, or
(b) if not executed within the time authorised for its execution;

and the person by whom any such warrant is executed shall make an endorsement on it stating what powers have been exercised by him under the warrant.

Offences

12 Any person who—

(a) intentionally obstructs a person in the execution of a warrant issued under this Schedule, or
(b) fails without reasonable excuse to give any person executing such a warrant such assistance as he may reasonably require for the execution of the warrant,

is guilty of an offence.

Vessels, vehicles etc

13 In this Schedule 'premises' includes any vessel, vehicle, aircraft or hovercraft, and references to the occupier of any premises include references to the person in charge of any vessel, vehicle, aircraft or hovercraft.

Scotland and Northern Ireland

14 In the application of this Schedule to Scotland—

(a) for any reference to a circuit judge there is substituted a reference to the sheriff,
(b) for any reference to information on oath there is substituted a reference to evidence on oath, and
(c) for the reference to the court from which the warrant was issued there is substituted a reference to the sheriff clerk.

15 In the application of this Schedule to Northern Ireland—

(a) for any reference to a circuit judge there is substituted a reference to a county court judge, and
(b) for any reference to information on oath there is substituted a reference to a complaint on oath.

NOTES

Initial Commencement

To be appointed
To be appointed: see s 75(3).

Appointment

Appointment: 1 March 2000: see SI 2000/183, art 2(1).

Data Protection Act 1998

Amendment

Para 1: in sub-para (1) words 'or a District Judge (Magistrates' Courts)' in square brackets inserted by the Courts Act 2003, s 65, Sch 4, para 8.
Date in force: to be appointed: see the Courts Act 2003, s 110(1).

See Further

See further, in relation to additional powers of seizure from premises: the Criminal Justice and Police Act 2001, s 50, Sch 1, Pt 1, para 65.

SCHEDULE 10
FURTHER PROVISIONS RELATING TO ASSISTANCE UNDER SECTION 53

Section 53(6)

1   In this Schedule 'applicant' and 'proceedings' have the same meaning as in section 53.

2   The assistance provided under section 53 may include the making of arrangements for, or for the Commissioner to bear the costs of—

  (a) the giving of advice or assistance by a solicitor or counsel, and
  (b) the representation of the applicant, or the provision to him of such assistance as is usually given by a solicitor or counsel—
    (i) in steps preliminary or incidental to the proceedings, or
    (ii) in arriving at or giving effect to a compromise to avoid or bring an end to the proceedings.

3   Where assistance is provided with respect to the conduct of proceedings—

  (a) it shall include an agreement by the Commissioner to indemnify the applicant (subject only to any exceptions specified in the notification) in respect of any liability to pay costs or expenses arising by virtue of any judgment or order of the court in the proceedings,
  (b) it may include an agreement by the Commissioner to indemnify the applicant in respect of any liability to pay costs or expenses arising by virtue of any compromise or settlement arrived at in order to avoid the proceedings or bring the proceedings to an end, and
  (c) it may include an agreement by the Commissioner to indemnify the applicant in respect of any liability to pay damages pursuant to an undertaking given on the grant of interlocutory relief (in Scotland, an interim order) to the applicant.

4   Where the Commissioner provides assistance in relation to any proceedings, he shall do so on such terms, or make such other arrangements, as will secure that a person against whom the proceedings have been or are commenced is informed that assistance has been or is being provided by the Commissioner in relation to them.

5   In England and Wales or Northern Ireland, the recovery of expenses incurred by the Commissioner in providing an applicant with assistance (as taxed or assessed in such manner as may be prescribed by rules of court) shall constitute a first charge for the benefit of the Commissioner—

  (a) on any costs which, by virtue of any judgment or order of the court, are payable to the applicant by any other person in respect of the matter in connection with which the assistance is provided, and
  (b) on any sum payable to the applicant under a compromise or settlement arrived at in connection with that matter to avoid or bring to an end any proceedings.

Core resources

6   In Scotland, the recovery of such expenses (as taxed or assessed in such manner as may be prescribed by rules of court) shall be paid to the Commissioner, in priority to other debts—

(a) out of any expenses which, by virtue of any judgment or order of the court, are payable to the applicant by any other person in respect of the matter in connection with which the assistance is provided, and
(b) out of any sum payable to the applicant under a compromise or settlement arrived at in connection with that matter to avoid or bring to an end any proceedings.

NOTES

Initial Commencement

To be appointed
To be appointed: see s 75(3).

Appointment

Appointment: 1 March 2000: see SI 2000/183, art 2(1).

SCHEDULE 11
EDUCATIONAL RECORDS

Section 68(1)(b)

Meaning of 'educational record'

1   For the purposes of section 68 'educational record' means any record to which paragraph 2, 5 or 7 applies.

England and Wales

2   This paragraph applies to any record of information which—

(a) is processed by or on behalf of the governing body of, or a teacher at, any school in England and Wales specified in paragraph 3,
(b) relates to any person who is or has been a pupil at the school, and
(c) originated from or was supplied by or on behalf of any of the persons specified in paragraph 4,

other than information which is processed by a teacher solely for the teacher's own use.

3   The schools referred to in paragraph 2(a) are—

(a) a school maintained by a local education authority, and
(b) a special school, as defined by section 6(2) of the Education Act 1996, which is not so maintained.

4   The persons referred to in paragraph 2(c) are—

(a) an employee of the local education authority which maintains the school,
(b) in the case of—
    (i) a voluntary aided, foundation or foundation special school (within the meaning of the School Standards and Framework Act 1998), or
    (ii) a special school which is not maintained by a local education authority,
a teacher or other employee at the school (including an educational psychologist engaged by the governing body under a contract for services),
(c) the pupil to whom the record relates, and

(d) a parent, as defined by section 576(1) of the Education Act 1996, of that pupil.

Scotland

5   This paragraph applies to any record of information which is processed—
   (a) by an education authority in Scotland, and
   (b) for the purpose of the relevant function of the authority,

other than information which is processed by a teacher solely for the teacher's own use.

6   For the purposes of paragraph 5—
   (a) 'education authority' means an education authority within the meaning of the Education (Scotland) Act 1980 ('the 1980 Act') ...,
   (b) 'the relevant function' means, in relation to each of those authorities, their function under section 1 of the 1980 Act and section 7(1) of the 1989 Act, and
   (c) information processed by an education authority is processed for the purpose of the relevant function of the authority if the processing relates to the discharge of that function in respect of a person—
      (i) who is or has been a pupil in a school provided by the authority, or
      (ii) who receives, or has received, further education (within the meaning of the 1980 Act) so provided.

Northern Ireland

7 (1) This paragraph applies to any record of information which—
   (a) is processed by or on behalf of the Board of Governors of, or a teacher at, any grant-aided school in Northern Ireland,
   (b) relates to any person who is or has been a pupil at the school, and
   (c) originated from or was supplied by or on behalf of any of the persons specified in paragraph 8,

other than information which is processed by a teacher solely for the teacher's own use.

(2) In sub-paragraph (1) 'grant-aided school' has the same meaning as in the Education and Libraries (Northern Ireland) Order 1986.

8   The persons referred to in paragraph 7(1) are—
   (a) a teacher at the school,
   (b) an employee of an education and library board, other than such a teacher,
   (c) the pupil to whom the record relates, and
   (d) a parent (as defined by Article 2(2) of the Education and Libraries (Northern Ireland) Order 1986) of that pupil.

England and Wales: transitory provisions

9 (1) Until the appointed day within the meaning of section 20 of the School Standards and Framework Act 1998, this Schedule shall have effect subject to the following modifications.

(2) Paragraph 3 shall have effect as if for paragraph (b) and the 'and' immediately preceding it there were substituted—

   '(aa) a grant-maintained school, as defined by section 183(1) of the Education Act 1996,
   (ab) a grant-maintained special school, as defined by section 337(4) of that Act, and

Core resources

(b) a special school, as defined by section 6(2) of that Act, which is neither a maintained special school, as defined by section 337(3) of that Act, nor a grant-maintained special school.'.

(3) Paragraph 4(b)(i) shall have effect as if for the words from 'foundation', in the first place where it occurs, to '1998)' there were substituted 'or grant-maintained school'.

NOTES

Initial Commencement

Royal Assent
Royal Assent: 16 July 1998: see s 75(2)(g).

Amendment

Para 6: in sub-para (a) words omitted repealed by the Standards in Scotland's Schools etc Act 2000, s 60(2), Sch 3.
Date in force: 31 December 2004: see SSI 2004/528, art 2(b).

SCHEDULE 12
ACCESSIBLE PUBLIC RECORDS

Section 68(1)(c)

Meaning of 'accessible public record'

1   For the purposes of section 68 'accessible public record' means any record which is kept by an authority specified—

(a) as respects England and Wales, in the Table in paragraph 2,
(b) as respects Scotland, in the Table in paragraph 4, or
(c) as respects Northern Ireland, in the Table in paragraph 6,

and is a record of information of a description specified in that Table in relation to that authority.

Housing and social services records: England and Wales

2   The following is the Table referred to in paragraph 1(a).

The authorities	*The accessible information*
Housing Act local authority.	Information held for the purpose of any of the authority's tenancies.
Local social services authority.	Information held for any purpose of the authority's social services functions.

3   (1) The following provisions apply for the interpretation of the Table in paragraph 2.

(2) Any authority which, by virtue of section 4(e) of the Housing Act 1985, is a local authority for the purpose of any provision of that Act is a 'Housing Act local authority' for the purposes of this Schedule, and so is any housing action trust established under Part III of the Housing Act 1988.

(3) Information contained in records kept by a Housing Act local authority is 'held for the purpose of any of the authority's tenancies' if it is held for any purpose of the relationship of landlord and tenant of a dwelling which subsists, has subsisted or may

Data Protection Act 1998

subsist between the authority and any individual who is, has been or, as the case may be, has applied to be, a tenant of the authority.

(4) Any authority which, by virtue of section 1 or 12 of the Local Authority Social Services Act 1970, is or is treated as a local authority for the purposes of that Act is a 'local social services authority' for the purposes of this Schedule; and information contained in records kept by such an authority is 'held for any purpose of the authority's social services functions' if it is held for the purpose of any past, current or proposed exercise of such a function in any case.

(5) Any expression used in paragraph 2 or this paragraph and in Part II of the Housing Act 1985 or the Local Authority Social Services Act 1970 has the same meaning as in that Act.

Housing and social services records: Scotland

4   The following is the Table referred to in paragraph 1(b).

The authorities	*The accessible information*
Local authority.	Information held for any purpose of any of the body's tenancies.
Scottish Homes.	
Social work authority.	Information held for any purpose of the authority's functions under the Social Work (Scotland) Act 1968 and the enactments referred to in section 5(1B) of that Act.

5 (1) The following provisions apply for the interpretation of the Table in paragraph 4.

(2) 'Local authority' means—

  (a) a council constituted under section 2 of the Local Government etc (Scotland) Act 1994,
  (b) a joint board or joint committee of two or more of those councils, or
  (c) any trust under the control of such a council.

(3) Information contained in records kept by a local authority *or Scottish Homes* is held for the purpose of any of their tenancies if it is held for any purpose of the relationship of landlord and tenant of a dwelling-house which subsists, has subsisted or may subsist between the authority *or, as the case may be, Scottish Homes* and any individual who is, has been or, as the case may be, has applied to be a tenant of theirs.

(4) 'Social work authority' means a local authority for the purposes of the Social Work (Scotland) Act 1968; and information contained in records kept by such an authority is held for any purpose of their functions if it is held for the purpose of any past, current or proposed exercise of such a function in any case.

Housing and social services records: Northern Ireland

6   The following is the Table referred to in paragraph 1(c).

The authorities	*The accessible information*
The Northern Ireland Housing Executive.	Information held for the purpose of any of the Executive's tenancies.

Core resources

A Health and Social Services Board.	Information held for the purpose of any past, current or proposed exercise by the Board of any function exercisable, by virtue of directions under Article 17(1) of the Health and Personal Social Services (Northern Ireland) Order 1972, by the Board on behalf of the Department of Health and Social Services with respect to the administration of personal social services under— (a) the Children and Young Persons Act (Northern Ireland) 1968; (b) the Health and Personal Social Services (Northern Ireland) Order 1972; (c) Article 47 of the Matrimonial Causes (Northern Ireland) Order 1978; (d) Article 11 of the Domestic Proceedings (Northern Ireland) Order 1980; (e) the Adoption (Northern Ireland) Order 1987; or (f) the Children (Northern Ireland) Order 1995.
An HSS trust.	Information held for the purpose of any past, current or proposed exercise by the trust of any function exercisable, by virtue of an authorisation under Article 3(1) of the Health and Personal Social Services (Northern Ireland) Order 1994, by the trust on behalf of a Health and Social Services Board with respect to the administration of personal social services under any statutory provision mentioned in the last preceding entry.

7 (1) This paragraph applies for the interpretation of the Table in paragraph 6.

(2) Information contained in records kept by the Northern Ireland Housing Executive is 'held for the purpose of any of the Executive's tenancies' if it is held for any purpose of the relationship of landlord and tenant of a dwelling which subsists, has subsisted or may subsist between the Executive and any individual who is, has been or, as the case may be, has applied to be, a tenant of the Executive.

NOTES

Initial Commencement

Royal Assent
Royal Assent: 16 July 1998: see s 75(2)(h).

Amendment

Para 4: entry 'Scottish Homes' repealed by the Housing (Scotland) Act 2001, s 112, Sch 10, para 26(a).
Date in force: to be appointed: see the Housing (Scotland) Act 2001, s 113(1).

Para 5: in sub-para (3) words 'or Scottish Homes' and 'or, as the case may be, Scottish Homes' in italics repealed by the Housing (Scotland) Act 2001, s 112, Sch 10, para 26(b).
Date in force: to be appointed: see the Housing (Scotland) Act 2001, s 113(1).

Data Protection Act 1998

SCHEDULE 13
MODIFICATIONS OF ACT HAVING EFFECT BEFORE 24TH OCTOBER 2007

Section 72

1   After section 12 there is inserted—

'**12A   Rights of data subjects in relation to exempt manual data**

(1)   A data subject is entitled at any time by notice in writing—

(a) to require the data controller to rectify, block, erase or destroy exempt manual data which are inaccurate or incomplete, or
(b) to require the data controller to cease holding exempt manual data in a way incompatible with the legitimate purposes pursued by the data controller.

(2)   A notice under subsection (1)(a) or (b) must state the data subject's reasons for believing that the data are inaccurate or incomplete or, as the case may be, his reasons for believing that they are held in a way incompatible with the legitimate purposes pursued by the data controller.

(3)   If the court is satisfied, on the application of any person who has given a notice under subsection (1) which appears to the court to be justified (or to be justified to any extent) that the data controller in question has failed to comply with the notice, the court may order him to take such steps for complying with the notice (or for complying with it to that extent) as the court thinks fit.

(4)   In this section 'exempt manual data' means—

(a) in relation to the first transitional period, as defined by paragraph 1(2) of Schedule 8, data to which paragraph 3 or 4 of that Schedule applies, and
(b) in relation to the second transitional period, as so defined, data to which paragraph 14 [or 14A] of that Schedule applies.

(5)   For the purposes of this section personal data are incomplete if, and only if, the data, although not inaccurate, are such that their incompleteness would constitute a contravention of the third or fourth data protection principles, if those principles applied to the data.'.

2   In section 32—

(a) in subsection (2) after 'section 12' there is inserted—
'(dd) section 12A,', and
(b) in subsection (4) after '12(8)' there is inserted ', 12A(3)'.

3   In section 34 for 'section 14(1) to (3)' there is substituted 'sections 12A and 14(1) to (3).'

4   In section 53(1) after '12(8)' there is inserted ', 12A(3)'.

5   In paragraph 8 of Part II of Schedule 1, the word 'or' at the end of paragraph (c) is omitted and after paragraph (d) there is inserted

'or
(e) he contravenes section 12A by failing to comply with a notice given under subsection (1) of that section to the extent that the notice is justified.'.

NOTES

Initial Commencement

To be appointed
To be appointed: see s 75(3).

Core resources

Appointment

Appointment: 1 March 2000: see SI 2000/183, art 2(1).

Amendment

Para 1: in section 12A(4)(b), as set out, words 'or 14A' in square brackets inserted by the Freedom of Information Act 2000, s 70(4).
Date in force: 1 January 2005: see SI 2004/1909, art 2(1), (2)(f), (3).

SCHEDULE 14
Transitional Provisions and Savings

Section 73

Interpretation

1   In this Schedule—

'the 1984 Act' means the Data Protection Act 1984;
'the old principles' means the data protection principles within the meaning of the 1984 Act;
'the new principles' means the data protection principles within the meaning of this Act.

Effect of registration under Part II of 1984 Act

2   (1) Subject to sub-paragraphs (4) and (5) any person who, immediately before the commencement of Part III of this Act—

(a)   is registered as a data user under Part II of the 1984 Act, or
(b)   is treated by virtue of section 7(6) of the 1984 Act as so registered,

is exempt from section 17(1) of this Act until the end of the registration period ...

(2) In sub-paragraph (1) 'the registration period', in relation to a person, means—

(a)   where there is a single entry in respect of that person as a data user, the period at the end of which, if section 8 of the 1984 Act had remained in force, that entry would have fallen to be removed unless renewed, and
(b)   where there are two or more entries in respect of that person as a data user, the period at the end of which, if that section had remained in force, the last of those entries to expire would have fallen to be removed unless renewed.

(3) Any application for registration as a data user under Part II of the 1984 Act which is received by the Commissioner before the commencement of Part III of this Act (including any appeal against a refusal of registration) shall be determined in accordance with the old principles and the provisions of the 1984 Act.

(4) If a person falling within paragraph (b) of sub-paragraph (1) receives a notification under section 7(1) of the 1984 Act of the refusal of his application, sub-paragraph (1) shall cease to apply to him—

(a)   if no appeal is brought, at the end of the period within which an appeal can be brought against the refusal, or
(b)   on the withdrawal or dismissal of the appeal.

(5) If a data controller gives a notification under section 18(1) at a time when he is exempt from section 17(1) by virtue of sub-paragraph (1), he shall cease to be so exempt.

(6) The Commissioner shall include in the register maintained under section 19 an entry in respect of each person who is exempt from section 17(1) by virtue of

Data Protection Act 1998

sub-paragraph (1); and each entry shall consist of the particulars which, immediately before the commencement of Part III of this Act, were included (or treated as included) in respect of that person in the register maintained under section 4 of the 1984 Act.

(7) Notification regulations under Part III of this Act may make provision modifying the duty referred to in section 20(1) in its application to any person in respect of whom an entry in the register maintained under section 19 has been made under sub-paragraph (6).

(8) Notification regulations under Part III of this Act may make further transitional provision in connection with the substitution of Part III of this Act for Part II of the 1984 Act (registration), including provision modifying the application of provisions of Part III in transitional cases.

Rights of data subjects

3 (1) The repeal of section 21 of the 1984 Act (right of access to personal data) does not affect the application of that section in any case in which the request (together with the information referred to in paragraph (a) of subsection (4) of that section and, in a case where it is required, the consent referred to in paragraph (b) of that subsection) was received before the day on which the repeal comes into force.

(2) Sub-paragraph (1) does not apply where the request is made by reference to this Act.

(3) Any fee paid for the purposes of section 21 of the 1984 Act before the commencement of section 7 in a case not falling within sub-paragraph (1) shall be taken to have been paid for the purposes of section 7.

4 The repeal of section 22 of the 1984 Act (compensation for inaccuracy) and the repeal of section 23 of that Act (compensation for loss or unauthorised disclosure) do not affect the application of those sections in relation to damage or distress suffered at any time by reason of anything done or omitted to be done before the commencement of the repeals.

5 The repeal of section 24 of the 1984 Act (rectification and erasure) does not affect any case in which the application to the court was made before the day on which the repeal comes into force.

6 Subsection (3)(b) of section 14 does not apply where the rectification, blocking, erasure or destruction occurred before the commencement of that section.

Enforcement and transfer prohibition notices served under Part V of 1984 Act

7 (1) If, immediately before the commencement of section 40—

(a) an enforcement notice under section 10 of the 1984 Act has effect, and
(b) either the time for appealing against the notice has expired or any appeal has been determined,

then, after that commencement, to the extent mentioned in sub-paragraph (3), the notice shall have effect for the purposes of sections 41 and 47 as if it were an enforcement notice under section 40.

(2) Where an enforcement notice has been served under section 10 of the 1984 Act before the commencement of section 40 and immediately before that commencement either—

(a) the time for appealing against the notice has not expired, or
(b) an appeal has not been determined,

Core resources

the appeal shall be determined in accordance with the provisions of the 1984 Act and the old principles and, unless the notice is quashed on appeal, to the extent mentioned in sub-paragraph (3) the notice shall have effect for the purposes of sections 41 and 47 as if it were an enforcement notice under section 40.

(3) An enforcement notice under section 10 of the 1984 Act has the effect described in sub-paragraph (1) or (2) only to the extent that the steps specified in the notice for complying with the old principle or principles in question are steps which the data controller could be required by an enforcement notice under section 40 to take for complying with the new principles or any of them.

8 (1) If, immediately before the commencement of section 40—
- (a) a transfer prohibition notice under section 12 of the 1984 Act has effect, and
- (b) either the time for appealing against the notice has expired or any appeal has been determined,

then, on and after that commencement, to the extent specified in sub-paragraph (3), the notice shall have effect for the purposes of sections 41 and 47 as if it were an enforcement notice under section 40.

(2) Where a transfer prohibition notice has been served under section 12 of the 1984 Act and immediately before the commencement of section 40 either—
- (a) the time for appealing against the notice has not expired, or
- (b) an appeal has not been determined,

the appeal shall be determined in accordance with the provisions of the 1984 Act and the old principles and, unless the notice is quashed on appeal, to the extent mentioned in sub-paragraph (3) the notice shall have effect for the purposes of sections 41 and 47 as if it were an enforcement notice under section 40.

(3) A transfer prohibition notice under section 12 of the 1984 Act has the effect described in sub-paragraph (1) or (2) only to the extent that the prohibition imposed by the notice is one which could be imposed by an enforcement notice under section 40 for complying with the new principles or any of them.

Notices under new law relating to matters in relation to which 1984 Act had effect

9 The Commissioner may serve an enforcement notice under section 40 on or after the day on which that section comes into force if he is satisfied that, before that day, the data controller contravened the old principles by reason of any act or omission which would also have constituted a contravention of the new principles if they had applied before that day.

10 Subsection (5)(b) of section 40 does not apply where the rectification, blocking, erasure or destruction occurred before the commencement of that section.

11 The Commissioner may serve an information notice under section 43 on or after the day on which that section comes into force if he has reasonable grounds for suspecting that, before that day, the data controller contravened the old principles by reason of any act or omission which would also have constituted a contravention of the new principles if they had applied before that day.

12 Where by virtue of paragraph 11 an information notice is served on the basis of anything done or omitted to be done before the day on which section 43 comes into force, subsection (2)(b) of that section shall have effect as if the reference to the data controller having complied, or complying, with the new principles were a reference to the data controller having contravened the old principles by reason of any such act or omission as is mentioned in paragraph 11.

Data Protection Act 1998

Self-incrimination, etc

13 (1) In section 43(8), section 44(9) and paragraph 11 of Schedule 7, any reference to an offence under this Act includes a reference to an offence under the 1984 Act.

(2) In section 34(9) of the 1984 Act, any reference to an offence under that Act includes a reference to an offence under this Act.

Warrants issued under 1984 Act

14 The repeal of Schedule 4 to the 1984 Act does not affect the application of that Schedule in any case where a warrant was issued under that Schedule before the commencement of the repeal.

Complaints under section 36(2) of 1984 Act and requests for assessment under section 42

15 The repeal of section 36(2) of the 1984 Act does not affect the application of that provision in any case where the complaint was received by the Commissioner before the commencement of the repeal.

16 In dealing with a complaint under section 36(2) of the 1984 Act or a request for an assessment under section 42 of this Act, the Commissioner shall have regard to the provisions from time to time applicable to the processing, and accordingly—

(a) in section 36(2) of the 1984 Act, the reference to the old principles and the provisions of that Act includes, in relation to any time when the new principles and the provisions of this Act have effect, those principles and provisions, and

(b) in section 42 of this Act, the reference to the provisions of this Act includes, in relation to any time when the old principles and the provisions of the 1984 Act had effect, those principles and provisions.

Applications under Access to Health Records Act 1990 or corresponding Northern Ireland legislation

17 (1) The repeal of any provision of the Access to Health Records Act 1990 does not affect—

(a) the application of section 3 or 6 of that Act in any case in which the application under that section was received before the day on which the repeal comes into force, or

(b) the application of section 8 of that Act in any case in which the application to the court was made before the day on which the repeal comes into force.

(2) Sub-paragraph (1)(a) does not apply in relation to an application for access to information which was made by reference to this Act.

18 (1) The revocation of any provision of the Access to Health Records (Northern Ireland) Order 1993 does not affect—

(a) the application of Article 5 or 8 of that Order in any case in which the application under that Article was received before the day on which the repeal comes into force, or

(b) the application of Article 10 of that Order in any case in which the application to the court was made before the day on which the repeal comes into force.

(2) Sub-paragraph (1)(a) does not apply in relation to an application for access to information which was made by reference to this Act.

Core resources

Applications under regulations under Access to Personal Files Act 1987 or corresponding Northern Ireland legislation

19 (1) The repeal of the personal files enactments does not affect the application of regulations under those enactments in relation to—

(a) any request for information,
(b) any application for rectification or erasure, or
(c) any application for review of a decision,

which was made before the day on which the repeal comes into force.

(2) Sub-paragraph (1)(a) does not apply in relation to a request for information which was made by reference to this Act.

(3) In sub-paragraph (1) 'the personal files enactments' means—

(a) in relation to Great Britain, the Access to Personal Files Act 1987, and
(b) in relation to Northern Ireland, Part II of the Access to Personal Files and Medical Reports (Northern Ireland) Order 1991.

Applications under section 158 of Consumer Credit Act 1974

20 Section 62 does not affect the application of section 158 of the Consumer Credit Act 1974 in any case where the request was received before the commencement of section 62, unless the request is made by reference to this Act.

NOTES

Initial Commencement

Royal Assent
Royal Assent (so far as conferring power to make subordinate legislation): 16 July 1998: see s 75(2)(i).

To be appointed
To be appointed (for remaining purposes): see s 75(3).

Appointment

Appointment (for remaining purposes): 1 March 2000: see SI 2000/183, art 2(1).

Amendment

Para 2: in sub-para (1) words omitted repealed by the Freedom of Information Act 2000, ss 73, 86, Sch 6, para 8, Sch 8, Pt I.
Date in force: 30 November 2000: see the Freedom of Information Act 2000, s 87(1)(k).

Modification

The Northern Ireland Act 1998 makes new provision for the government of Northern Ireland for the purpose of implementing the Belfast Agreement (the agreement reached at multi-party talks on Northern Ireland and set out in Command Paper 3883). As a consequence of that Act, any reference in this Schedule to the Parliament of Northern Ireland or the Assembly established under the Northern Ireland Assembly Act 1973, s 1, certain office-holders and Ministers, and any legislative act and certain financial dealings thereof, shall, for the period specified, be construed in accordance with Sch 12, paras 1–11 to the 1998 Act.

Data Protection Act 1998

Subordinate Legislation

Data Protection (Notification and Notification Fees) Regulations 2000, SI 2000/188 (made under para 2(7), (8)).

Data Protection (Notification and Notification Fees) (Amendment) Regulations 2001, SI 2001/3214 (made under para 2(8)).

SCHEDULE 15
MINOR AND CONSEQUENTIAL AMENDMENTS

Section 74(1)

...

1 (1) ...
(2) ...
(3) ...

...

2 ...
3 ...

...

4 ...

...

5 (1) ...
(2) ...

...

6 (1) ...
(2) ...

Representation of the People Act 1983 (c 2)

7 In Schedule 2 of the Representation of the People Act 1983 (provisions which may be included in regulations as to registration etc), in paragraph 11A(2)—

(a) for 'data user' there is substituted 'data controller', and
(b) for 'the Data Protection Act 1984' there is substituted 'the Data Protection Act 1998'.

Access to Medical Reports Act 1988 (c 28)

8 In section 2(1) of the Access to Medical Reports Act 1988 (interpretation), in the definition of 'health professional', for 'the Data Protection (Subject Access Modification) Order 1987' there is substituted 'the Data Protection Act 1998'.

...

9 ...

Core resources

Education (Student Loans) Act 1990 (c 6)

10 Schedule 2 to the Education (Student Loans) Act 1990 (loans for students) so far as that Schedule continues in force shall have effect as if the reference in paragraph 4(2) to the Data Protection Act 1984 were a reference to this Act.

Access to Health Records Act 1990 (c 23)

11 For section 2 of the Access to Health Records Act 1990 there is substituted—

'Health professionals.   2 In this Act 'health professional' has the same meaning as in the Data Protection Act 1998.'

12 In section 3(4) of that Act (cases where fee may be required) in paragraph (a), for 'the maximum prescribed under section 21 of the Data Protection Act 1984' there is substituted 'such maximum as may be prescribed for the purposes of this section by regulations under section 7 of the Data Protection Act 1998'.

13 In section 5(3) of that Act (cases where right of access may be partially excluded) for the words from the beginning to 'record' in the first place where it occurs there is substituted 'Access shall not be given under section 3(2) to any part of a health record'.

Access to Personal Files and Medical Reports (Northern Ireland) Order 1991 (1991/1707 (NI 14))

14 In Article 4 of the Access to Personal Files and Medical Reports (Northern Ireland) Order 1991 (obligation to give access), in paragraph (2) (exclusion of information to which individual entitled under section 21 of the Data Protection Act 1984) for 'section 21 of the Data Protection Act 1984' there is substituted 'section 7 of the Data Protection Act 1998'.

15 In Article 6(1) of that Order (interpretation), in the definition of 'health professional', for 'the Data Protection (Subject Access Modification) (Health) Order 1987' there is substituted 'the Data Protection Act 1998'.

Tribunals and Inquiries Act 1992 (c 53)

16 In Part 1 of Schedule 1 to the Tribunals and Inquiries Act 1992 (tribunals under direct supervision of Council on Tribunals), for paragraph 14 there is substituted—

'Data protection   14
(a) The Data Protection Commissioner appointed under section 6 of the Data Protection Act 1998;
(b) the Data Protection Tribunal constituted under that section, in respect of its jurisdiction under section 48 of that Act.'

Access to Health Records (Northern Ireland) Order 1993 (1993/1250 (NI 4))

17 For paragraphs (1) and (2) of Article 4 of the Access to Health Records (Northern Ireland) Order 1993 there is substituted—

'(1) In this Order 'health professional' has the same meaning as in the Data Protection Act 1998.'.

18 In Article 5(4) of that Order (cases where fee may be required) in subparagraph (a), for 'the maximum prescribed under section 21 of the Data Protection Act 1984' there is substituted 'such maximum as may be prescribed for the purposes of this Article by regulations under section 7 of the Data Protection Act 1998'.

19 In Article 7 of that Order (cases where right of access may be partially excluded) for the words from the beginning to 'record' in the first place where it occurs there is substituted 'Access shall not be given under Article 5(2) to any part of a health record'.

NOTES

Initial Commencement

To be appointed
To be appointed: see s 75(3).

Appointment

Appointment: 1 March 2000: see SI 2000/183, art 2(1).

Amendment

Para 1: sub-para (1) repealed by the Freedom of Information Act 2000, s 86, Sch 8, Pt II.
Date in force: 30 January 2001: see the Freedom of Information Act 2000, s 87(2)(d).

Para 1: sub-paras (2), (3) repealed by the Freedom of Information Act 2000, s 86, Sch 8, Pt III.
Date in force: 30 November 2005: see the Freedom of Information Act 2000, s 87(3).

Paras 2, 4: repealed by the Freedom of Information Act 2000, s 86, Sch 8, Pt II.
Date in force: 30 January 2001: see the Freedom of Information Act 2000, s 87(2)(d).

Para 3: repealed by the Freedom of Information Act 2000, s 86, Sch 8, Pt III.
Date in force: 30 November 2005: see the Freedom of Information Act 2000, s 87(3).

Para 5: sub-para (1) repealed by the Freedom of Information Act 2000, s 86, Sch 8, Pt III.
Date in force: 30 November 2005: see the Freedom of Information Act 2000, s 87(3).

Para 5: sub-para (2) repealed by the Freedom of Information Act 2000, s 86, Sch 8, Pt II.
Date in force: 30 January 2001: see the Freedom of Information Act 2000, s 87(2)(d).

Para 6: sub-para (1) repealed by the Freedom of Information Act 2000, s 86, Sch 8, Pt III.
Date in force: 30 November 2005: see the Freedom of Information Act 2000, s 87(3).

Para 6: sub-para (2) repealed by the Freedom of Information Act 2000, s 86, Sch 8, Pt II.
Date in force: 30 January 2001: see the Freedom of Information Act 2000, s 87(2)(d).

Para 9: repealed by the Violent Crime Reduction Act 2006, s 65, Sch 5.
Date in force: 6 April 2007: see SI 2007/858, art 2(m), (n)(vii).

SCHEDULE 16
Repeals and Revocations

Section 74(2)

PART I
REPEALS

Chapter	Short title	Extent of repeal
1984 c 35.	The Data Protection Act 1984.	The whole Act.
1986 c 60.	The Financial Services Act 1986.	Section 190.
1987 c 37.	The Access to Personal Files Act 1987.	The whole Act.
1988 c 40.	The Education Reform Act 1988.	Section 223.
1988 c 50.	The Housing Act 1988.	In Schedule 17, paragraph 80.
1990 c 23.	The Access to Health Records Act 1990.	In section 1(1), the words from 'but does not' to the end. In section 3, subsection (1)(a) to (e) and, in subsection (6)(a), the words 'in the case of an application made otherwise than by the patient'. Section 4(1) and (2). In section 5(1)(a)(i), the words 'of the patient or' and the word 'other'. In section 10, in subsection (2) the words 'or orders' and in subsection (3) the words 'or an order under section 2(3) above'. In section 11, the definitions of 'child' and 'parental responsibility'.
1990 c 37.	The Human Fertilisation and Embryology Act 1990.	Section 33(8).
1990 c 41.	The Courts and Legal Services Act 1990.	In Schedule 10, paragraph 58.
1992 c 13.	The Further and Higher Education Act 1992.	Section 86.
1992 c 37.	The Further and Higher Education (Scotland) Act 1992.	Section 59.
1993 c 8.	The Judicial Pensions and Retirement Act 1993.	In Schedule 6, paragraph 50.
1993 c 10.	The Charities Act 1993.	Section 12.
1993 c 21.	The Osteopaths Act 1993.	Section 38.
1994 c 17.	The Chiropractors Act 1994.	Section 38.
1994 c 19.	The Local Government (Wales) Act 1994.	In Schedule 13, paragraph 30.

1994 c 33.	The Criminal Justice and Public Order Act 1994.	Section 161.
1994 c 39.	The Local Government etc (Scotland) Act 1994.	In Schedule 13, paragraph 154.

NOTES

Initial Commencement

To be appointed
To be appointed: see s 75(3).

Appointment

Appointment: 1 March 2000: see SI 2000/183, art 2(1).

PART II
REVOCATIONS

Number	Title	Extent of revocation
SI 1991/1142.	The Data Protection Registration Fee Order 1991.	The Whole Order.
SI 1991/1707 (NI 14).	The Access to Personal Files and Medical Reports (Northern Ireland) Order 1991.	Part II.
SI 1992/3218.	The Banking Co-ordination (Second Council Directive) Regulations 1992.	The Schedule. In Schedule 10, paragraphs 15 and 40.
SI 1993/1250 (NI 4).	The Access to Health Records (Northern Ireland) Order 1993.	In Article 2(2), the definitions of 'child' and 'parental responsibility'. In Article 3(1), the words from 'but does not include' to the end. In Article 5, paragraph (1)(a) to (d) and, in paragraph (6)(a), the words 'in the case of an application made otherwise than by the patient'. Article 6(1) and (2). In Article 7(1)(a)(i), the words 'of the patient or' and the word 'other'.
SI 1994/429 (NI 2).	The Health and Personal Social Services (Northern Ireland) Order 1994.	In Schedule 1, the entries relating to the Access to Personal Files and Medical Reports (Northern Ireland) Order 1991.
SI 1994/1696.	The Insurance Companies (Third Insurance Directives) Regulations 1994.	In Schedule 8, paragraph 8.

Core resources

SI 1995/755 (NI 2).	The Children (Northern Ireland) Order 1995.	In Schedule 9, paragraphs 177 and 191.
SI 1995/3275.	The Investment Services Regulations 1995.	In Schedule 10, paragraphs 3 and 15.
SI 1996/2827.	The Open-Ended Investment Companies (Investment Companies with Variable Capital) Regulations 1996.	In Schedule 8, paragraphs 3 and 26.

NOTES

Initial Commencement

To be appointed
To be appointed: see s 75(3).

Appointment

Appointment: 1 March 2000: see SI 2000/183, art 2(1)

REGULATION OF INVESTIGATORY POWERS ACT 2000

2000 CHAPTER 23

An Act to make provision for and about the interception of communications, the acquisition and disclosure of data relating to communications, the carrying out of surveillance, the use of covert human intelligence sources and the acquisition of the means by which electronic data protected by encryption or passwords may be decrypted or accessed; to provide for Commissioners and a tribunal with functions and jurisdiction in relation to those matters, to entries on and interferences with property or with wireless telegraphy and to the carrying out of their functions by the Security Service, the Secret Intelligence Service and the Government Communications Headquarters; and for connected purposes.

[28th July 2000]

BE IT ENACTED by the Queen's most Excellent Majesty, by and with the advice and consent of the Lords Spiritual and Temporal, and Commons, in this present Parliament assembled, and by the authority of the same, as follows:—

PART I
COMMUNICATIONS

Chapter I
Interception

Unlawful and authorised interception

1   Unlawful interception

(1) It shall be an offence for a person intentionally and without lawful authority to intercept, at any place in the United Kingdom, any communication in the course of its transmission by means of—

(a)   a public postal service; or
(b)   a public telecommunication system.

(2) It shall be an offence for a person—

(a)   intentionally and without lawful authority, and
(b)   otherwise than in circumstances in which his conduct is excluded by subsection (6) from criminal liability under this subsection,

to intercept, at any place in the United Kingdom, any communication in the course of its transmission by means of a private telecommunication system.

(3) Any interception of a communication which is carried out at any place in the United Kingdom by, or with the express or implied consent of, a person having the right to control the operation or the use of a private telecommunication system shall be

Core resources

actionable at the suit or instance of the sender or recipient, or intended recipient, of the communication if it is without lawful authority and is either—

- (a) an interception of that communication in the course of its transmission by means of that private system; or
- (b) an interception of that communication in the course of its transmission, by means of a public telecommunication system, to or from apparatus comprised in that private telecommunication system.

(4) Where the United Kingdom is a party to an international agreement which—

- (a) relates to the provision of mutual assistance in connection with, or in the form of, the interception of communications,
- (b) requires the issue of a warrant, order or equivalent instrument in cases in which assistance is given, and
- (c) is designated for the purposes of this subsection by an order made by the Secretary of State,

it shall be the duty of the Secretary of State to secure that no request for assistance in accordance with the agreement is made on behalf of a person in the United Kingdom to the competent authorities of a country or territory outside the United Kingdom except with lawful authority.

(5) Conduct has lawful authority for the purposes of this section if, and only if—

- (a) it is authorised by or under section 3 or 4;
- (b) it takes place in accordance with a warrant under section 5 ('an interception warrant'); or
- (c) it is in exercise, in relation to any stored communication, of any statutory power that is exercised (apart from this section) for the purpose of obtaining information or of taking possession of any document or other property;

and conduct (whether or not prohibited by this section) which has lawful authority for the purposes of this section by virtue of paragraph (a) or (b) shall also be taken to be lawful for all other purposes.

(6) The circumstances in which a person makes an interception of a communication in the course of its transmission by means of a private telecommunication system are such that his conduct is excluded from criminal liability under subsection (2) if—

- (a) he is a person with a right to control the operation or the use of the system; or
- (b) he has the express or implied consent of such a person to make the interception.

(7) A person who is guilty of an offence under subsection (1) or (2) shall be liable—

- (a) on conviction on indictment, to imprisonment for a term not exceeding two years or to a fine, or to both;
- (b) on summary conviction, to a fine not exceeding the statutory maximum.

(8) No proceedings for any offence which is an offence by virtue of this section shall be instituted—

- (a) in England and Wales, except by or with the consent of the Director of Public Prosecutions;
- (b) in Northern Ireland, except by or with the consent of the Director of Public Prosecutions for Northern Ireland.

NOTES

Initial Commencement

To be appointed
To be appointed: see s 83(2).

Appointment

Sub-ss (1), (2), (4)–(8): Appointment: 2 October 2000: see SI 2000/2543, art 3.
Sub-s (3): Appointment: 24 October 2000: see SI 2000/2543, art 4.

Subordinate Legislation

Regulation of Investigatory Powers (Designation of an International Agreement) Order 2004, SI 2004/158 (made under sub-s (4)(c)).

2 Meaning and location of 'interception' etc

(1) In this Act—
'postal service' means any service which—
  (a) consists in the following, or in any one or more of them, namely, the collection, sorting, conveyance, distribution and delivery (whether in the United Kingdom or elsewhere) of postal items; and
  (b) is offered or provided as a service the main purpose of which, or one of the main purposes of which, is to make available, or to facilitate, a means of transmission from place to place of postal items containing communications;
'private telecommunication system' means any telecommunication system which, without itself being a public telecommunication system, is a system in relation to which the following conditions are satisfied—
  (a) it is attached, directly or indirectly and whether or not for the purposes of the communication in question, to a public telecommunication system; and
  (b) there is apparatus comprised in the system which is both located in the United Kingdom and used (with or without other apparatus) for making the attachment to the public telecommunication system;
'public postal service' means any postal service which is offered or provided to, or to a substantial section of, the public in any one or more parts of the United Kingdom;
'public telecommunications service' means any telecommunications service which is offered or provided to, or to a substantial section of, the public in any one or more parts of the United Kingdom;
'public telecommunication system' means any such parts of a telecommunication system by means of which any public telecommunications service is provided as are located in the United Kingdom;
'telecommunications service' means any service that consists in the provision of access to, and of facilities for making use of, any telecommunication system (whether or not one provided by the person providing the service); and
'telecommunication system' means any system (including the apparatus comprised in it) which exists (whether wholly or partly in the United Kingdom or elsewhere) for the purpose of facilitating the transmission of communications by any means involving the use of electrical or electro-magnetic energy.

(2) For the purposes of this Act, but subject to the following provisions of this section, a person intercepts a communication in the course of its transmission by means of a telecommunication system if, and only if, he—

Core resources

    (a) so modifies or interferes with the system, or its operation,
    (b) so monitors transmissions made by means of the system, or
    (c) so monitors transmissions made by wireless telegraphy to or from apparatus comprised in the system,

as to make some or all of the contents of the communication available, while being transmitted, to a person other than the sender or intended recipient of the communication.

(3) References in this Act to the interception of a communication do not include references to the interception of any communication broadcast for general reception.

(4) For the purposes of this Act the interception of a communication takes place in the United Kingdom if, and only if, the modification, interference or monitoring or, in the case of a postal item, the interception is effected by conduct within the United Kingdom and the communication is either—

    (a) intercepted in the course of its transmission by means of a public postal service or public telecommunication system; or
    (b) intercepted in the course of its transmission by means of a private telecommunication system in a case in which the sender or intended recipient of the communication is in the United Kingdom.

(5) References in this Act to the interception of a communication in the course of its transmission by means of a postal service or telecommunication system do not include references to—

    (a) any conduct that takes place in relation only to so much of the communication as consists in any traffic data comprised in or attached to a communication (whether by the sender or otherwise) for the purposes of any postal service or telecommunication system by means of which it is being or may be transmitted; or
    (b) any such conduct, in connection with conduct falling within paragraph (a), as gives a person who is neither the sender nor the intended recipient only so much access to a communication as is necessary for the purpose of identifying traffic data so comprised or attached.

(6) For the purposes of this section references to the modification of a telecommunication system include references to the attachment of any apparatus to, or other modification of or interference with—

    (a) any part of the system; or
    (b) any wireless telegraphy apparatus used for making transmissions to or from apparatus comprised in the system.

(7) For the purposes of this section the times while a communication is being transmitted by means of a telecommunication system shall be taken to include any time when the system by means of which the communication is being, or has been, transmitted is used for storing it in a manner that enables the intended recipient to collect it or otherwise to have access to it.

(8) For the purposes of this section the cases in which any contents of a communication are to be taken to be made available to a person while being transmitted shall include any case in which any of the contents of the communication, while being transmitted, are diverted or recorded so as to be available to a person subsequently.

(9) In this section 'traffic data', in relation to any communication, means—

    (a) any data identifying, or purporting to identify, any person, apparatus or location to or from which the communication is or may be transmitted,

Regulation of Investigatory Powers Act 2000

  (b) any data identifying or selecting, or purporting to identify or select, apparatus through which, or by means of which, the communication is or may be transmitted,
  (c) any data comprising signals for the actuation of apparatus used for the purposes of a telecommunication system for effecting (in whole or in part) the transmission of any communication, and
  (d) any data identifying the data or other data as data comprised in or attached to a particular communication,

but that expression includes data identifying a computer file or computer program access to which is obtained, or which is run, by means of the communication to the extent only that the file or program is identified by reference to the apparatus in which it is stored.

(10) In this section—
  (a) references, in relation to traffic data comprising signals for the actuation of apparatus, to a telecommunication system by means of which a communication is being or may be transmitted include references to any telecommunication system in which that apparatus is comprised; and
  (b) references to traffic data being attached to a communication include references to the data and the communication being logically associated with each other;

and in this section 'data', in relation to a postal item, means anything written on the outside of the item.

(11) In this section 'postal item' means any letter, postcard or other such thing in writing as may be used by the sender for imparting information to the recipient, or any packet or parcel.

NOTES

Initial Commencement

To be appointed
To be appointed: see s 83(2).

Appointment

Appointment: 2 October 2000: see SI 2000/2543, art 3.

3   Lawful interception without an interception warrant

(1) Conduct by any person consisting in the interception of a communication is authorised by this section if the communication is one which, or which that person has reasonable grounds for believing, is both—
  (a) a communication sent by a person who has consented to the interception; and
  (b) a communication the intended recipient of which has so consented.

(2) Conduct by any person consisting in the interception of a communication is authorised by this section if—
  (a) the communication is one sent by, or intended for, a person who has consented to the interception; and
  (b) surveillance by means of that interception has been authorised under Part II.

(3) Conduct consisting in the interception of a communication is authorised by this section if—

Core resources

(a) it is conduct by or on behalf of a person who provides a postal service or a telecommunications service; and

(b) it takes place for purposes connected with the provision or operation of that service or with the enforcement, in relation to that service, of any enactment relating to the use of postal services or telecommunications services.

(4) Conduct by any person consisting in the interception of a communication in the course of its transmission by means of wireless telegraphy is authorised by this section if it takes place—

(a) with the authority of a designated person under [section 48 of the Wireless Telegraphy Act 2006 (interception and disclosure of wireless telegraphy messages)]; and

(b) for purposes connected with anything falling within subsection (5).

(5) Each of the following falls within this subsection—

[(a) the grant of wireless telegraphy licences under the Wireless Telegraphy Act 2006;]

(b) the prevention or detection of anything which constitutes interference with wireless telegraphy; and

(c) the enforcement of[—
  (i) any provision of Part 2 (other than Chapter 2 and sections 27 to 31) or Part 3 of that Act, or
  (ii) any enactment not falling within sub-paragraph (i),]
that relates to such interference.

NOTES

Initial Commencement

To be appointed
To be appointed: see s 83(2).

Appointment

Appointment: 2 October 2000: see SI 2000/2543, art 3.

Amendment

Sub-s (4): in para (a) words from 'section 48 of' to 'wireless telegraphy messages)' in square brackets substituted by the Wireless Telegraphy Act 2006, s 123, Sch 7, paras 21, 22(1), (2).
Date in force: 8 February 2007: see the Wireless Telegraphy Act 2006, s 126(2).
Sub-s (5): para (a) substituted by the Wireless Telegraphy Act 2006, s 123, Sch 7, paras 21, 22(1), (3)(a).
Date in force: 8 February 2007: see the Wireless Telegraphy Act 2006, s 126(2).
Sub-s (5): para (c)(i), (ii) substituted by the Wireless Telegraphy Act 2006, s 123, Sch 7, paras 21, 22(1), (3)(b).
Date in force: 8 February 2007: see the Wireless Telegraphy Act 2006, s 126(2).

4 Power to provide for lawful interception

(1) Conduct by any person ('the interceptor') consisting in the interception of a communication in the course of its transmission by means of a telecommunication system is authorised by this section if—

Regulation of Investigatory Powers Act 2000

(a) the interception is carried out for the purpose of obtaining information about the communications of a person who, or who the interceptor has reasonable grounds for believing, is in a country or territory outside the United Kingdom;

(b) the interception relates to the use of a telecommunications service provided to persons in that country or territory which is either—
   (i) a public telecommunications service; or
   (ii) a telecommunications service that would be a public telecommunications service if the persons to whom it is offered or provided were members of the public in a part of the United Kingdom;

(c) the person who provides that service (whether the interceptor or another person) is required by the law of that country or territory to carry out, secure or facilitate the interception in question;

(d) the situation is one in relation to which such further conditions as may be prescribed by regulations made by the Secretary of State are required to be satisfied before conduct may be treated as authorised by virtue of this subsection; and

(e) the conditions so prescribed are satisfied in relation to that situation.

(2) Subject to subsection (3), the Secretary of State may by regulations authorise any such conduct described in the regulations as appears to him to constitute a legitimate practice reasonably required for the purpose, in connection with the carrying on of any business, of monitoring or keeping a record of—

(a) communications by means of which transactions are entered into in the course of that business; or

(b) other communications relating to that business or taking place in the course of its being carried on.

(3) Nothing in any regulations under subsection (2) shall authorise the interception of any communication except in the course of its transmission using apparatus or services provided by or to the person carrying on the business for use wholly or partly in connection with that business.

(4) Conduct taking place in a prison is authorised by this section if it is conduct in exercise of any power conferred by or under any rules made under section 47 of the Prison Act 1952, section 39 of the Prisons (Scotland) Act 1989 or section 13 of the Prison Act (Northern Ireland) 1953 (prison rules).

(5) Conduct taking place in any hospital premises where high security psychiatric services are provided is authorised by this section if it is conduct in pursuance of, and in accordance with, any direction given under [section 8 of the National Health Service Act 2006, or section 19 or 23 of the National Health Service (Wales) Act 2006] (directions as to the carrying out of their functions by health bodies) to the body providing those services at those premises.

(6) Conduct taking place in a state hospital is authorised by this section if it is conduct in pursuance of, and in accordance with, any direction given to the State Hospitals Board for Scotland under section 2(5) of the National Health Service (Scotland) Act 1978 (regulations and directions as to the exercise of their functions by health boards) as applied by Article 5(1) of and the Schedule to The State Hospitals Board for Scotland Order 1995 (which applies certain provisions of that Act of 1978 to the State Hospitals Board).

(7) In this section references to a business include references to any activities of a government department, of any public authority or of any person or office holder on whom functions are conferred by or under any enactment.

(8) In this section—

Core resources

      'government department' includes any part of the Scottish Administration, a Northern Ireland department and [the Welsh Assembly Government];
      'high security psychiatric services' has the same meaning as in [section 4 of the National Health Service Act 2006];
      'hospital premises' has the same meaning as in section 4(3) of that Act; and
      'state hospital' has the same meaning as in the National Health Service (Scotland) Act 1978.

(9) In this section 'prison' means—

(a) any prison, young offender institution, young offenders centre or remand centre which is under the general superintendence of, or is provided by, the Secretary of State under the Prison Act 1952 or the Prison Act (Northern Ireland) 1953, or
(b) any prison, young offenders institution or remand centre which is under the general superintendence of the Scottish Ministers under the Prisons (Scotland) Act 1989,

and includes any contracted out prison, within the meaning of Part IV of the Criminal Justice Act 1991 or section 106(4) of the Criminal Justice and Public Order Act 1994, and any legalised police cells within the meaning of section 14 of the Prisons (Scotland) Act 1989.

NOTES

Initial Commencement

To be appointed
To be appointed: see s 83(2).

Appointment

Appointment: 2 October 2000: see SI 2000/2543, art 3.

Amendment

Sub-s (5): words from 'section 8 of' to 'National Health Service (Wales) Act 2006' in square brackets substituted by the National Health Service (Consequential Provisions) Act 2006, s 2, Sch 1, paras 207, 208(a).
Date in force: 1 March 2007: see the National Health Service (Consequential Provisions) Act 2006, s 8(2).

Sub-s (8): in definition 'government department' words 'the Welsh Assembly Government' in square brackets substituted by SI 2007/1388, art 3, Sch 1, paras 76(1), (2).
Date in force: this amendment came into force on 25 May 2007 being the date on which the initial period ended (following the appointment of the First Minister): see SI 2007/1388, art 1(2) and the Government of Wales Act 2006, ss 46, 161(5).

Sub-s (8): in definition 'high security psychiatric services' words 'section 4 of the National Health Service Act 2006' in square brackets substituted by the National Health Service (Consequential Provisions) Act 2006, s 2, Sch 1, paras 207, 208(b).
Date in force: 1 March 2007: see the National Health Service (Consequential Provisions) Act 2006, s 8(2).

Subordinate Legislation

Telecommunications (Lawful Business Practice) (Interception of Communications) Regulations 2000, SI 2000/2699 (made under sub-s (2)).

Regulation of Investigatory Powers (Conditions for the Lawful Interception of Persons outside the United Kingdom) Regulations 2004, SI 2004/157 (made under sub-s (1)(d)).

5   Interception with a warrant

(1) Subject to the following provisions of this Chapter, the Secretary of State may issue a warrant authorising or requiring the person to whom it is addressed, by any such conduct as may be described in the warrant, to secure any one or more of the following—

(a) the interception in the course of their transmission by means of a postal service or telecommunication system of the communications described in the warrant;

(b) the making, in accordance with an international mutual assistance agreement, of a request for the provision of such assistance in connection with, or in the form of, an interception of communications as may be so described;

(c) the provision, in accordance with an international mutual assistance agreement, to the competent authorities of a country or territory outside the United Kingdom of any such assistance in connection with, or in the form of, an interception of communications as may be so described;

(d) the disclosure, in such manner as may be so described, of intercepted material obtained by any interception authorised or required by the warrant, and of related communications data.

(2) The Secretary of State shall not issue an interception warrant unless he believes—

(a) that the warrant is necessary on grounds falling within subsection (3); and

(b) that the conduct authorised by the warrant is proportionate to what is sought to be achieved by that conduct.

(3) Subject to the following provisions of this section, a warrant is necessary on grounds falling within this subsection if it is necessary—

(a) in the interests of national security;

(b) for the purpose of preventing or detecting serious crime;

(c) for the purpose of safeguarding the economic well-being of the United Kingdom; or

(d) for the purpose, in circumstances appearing to the Secretary of State to be equivalent to those in which he would issue a warrant by virtue of paragraph (b), of giving effect to the provisions of any international mutual assistance agreement.

(4) The matters to be taken into account in considering whether the requirements of subsection (2) are satisfied in the case of any warrant shall include whether the information which it is thought necessary to obtain under the warrant could reasonably be obtained by other means.

(5) A warrant shall not be considered necessary on the ground falling within subsection (3)(c) unless the information which it is thought necessary to obtain is information relating to the acts or intentions of persons outside the British Islands.

(6) The conduct authorised by an interception warrant shall be taken to include—

(a) all such conduct (including the interception of communications not identified by the warrant) as it is necessary to undertake in order to do what is expressly authorised or required by the warrant;

(b) conduct for obtaining related communications data; and

(c) conduct by any person which is conduct in pursuance of a requirement imposed by or on behalf of the person to whom the warrant is addressed to be provided with assistance with giving effect to the warrant.

Core resources

NOTES

Initial Commencement

To be appointed
To be appointed: see s 83(2).

Appointment

Appointment: 2 October 2000: see SI 2000/2543, art 3.

Transfer of Functions

Functions under this section: certain functions under this section are transferred, in so far as they are exercisable in or as regards Scotland, to the Scottish Ministers, by the Scotland Act 1998 (Transfer of Functions to the Scottish Ministers etc) (No 2) Order 2000, SI 2000/3253, arts 2, 3, Sch 1, para 2 (as amended by SI 2003/2617, art 4(a)), Sch 2.

Functions under this section: certain functions under this section are transferred, in so far as they are exercisable in or as regards Scotland, to the Scottish Ministers, by the Scotland Act 1998 (Transfer of Functions to the Scottish Ministers etc) (No 2) Order 2003, SI 2003/2617, arts 2, 3, Sch 1, para 1, Sch 2.

Functions under this section: certain functions under this section are transferred, in so far as they are exercisable in or as regards Scotland, to the Scottish Ministers, by the Scotland Act 1998 (Transfer of Functions to the Scottish Ministers etc) Order 2007, SI 2007/2915, arts 2, 3, Sch 1, Sch 2; for transitional and savings provisions see art 6 thereof.

Interception warrants

6   Application for issue of an interception warrant

(1) An interception warrant shall not be issued except on an application made by or on behalf of a person specified in subsection (2).

(2) Those persons are—
    (a) the Director-General of the Security Service;
    (b) the Chief of the Secret Intelligence Service;
    (c) the Director of GCHQ;
    (d) the Director General of the [Serious Organised Crime Agency];
    [(da) the Director General of the Scottish Crime and Drug Enforcement Agency;]
    (e) the Commissioner of Police of the Metropolis;
    (f) the [Chief Constable of the Police Service of Northern Ireland];
    (g) the chief constable of any police force maintained under or by virtue of section 1 of the Police (Scotland) Act 1967;
    (h) [the Commissioners for Her Majesty's Revenue and Customs];
    (i) the Chief of Defence Intelligence;
    (j) a person who, for the purposes of any international mutual assistance agreement, is the competent authority of a country or territory outside the United Kingdom.

(3) An application for the issue of an interception warrant shall not be made on behalf of a person specified in [paragraph (a), (b), (c), (e), (f), (g), (h), (i) or (j) of] subsection (2) except by a person holding office under the Crown.

Regulation of Investigatory Powers Act 2000

NOTES

Initial Commencement

To be appointed
To be appointed: see s 83(2).

Appointment

Appointment: 2 October 2000: see SI 2000/2543, art 3.

Amendment

Sub-s (2): in para (d) words 'Serious Organised Crime Agency' in square brackets substituted by the Serious Organised Crime and Police Act 2005, s 59, Sch 4, paras 131, 132(1), (2).
Date in force: 1 April 2006: see SI 2006/378, art 4(1), Schedule, para 10; for transitional provisions see art 4(4), (8) thereof.

Sub-s (2): para (da) inserted by SI 2007/1098, art 6, Schedule, Pt 1, para 4(1), (2).
Date in force: 1 April 2007: see SI 2007/1098, art 1(3).

Sub-s (2): in para (f) words 'Chief Constable of the Police Service of Northern Ireland' in square brackets substituted by the Police (Northern Ireland) Act 2000, s 78(2)(a).
Date in force: 4 November 2001: see the Police (Northern Ireland) Act 2000 (Commencement No 3 and Transitional Provisions) Order 2001, SR 2001/396, art 2, Schedule.

Sub-s (2): in para (h) words 'the Commissioners for Her Majesty's Revenue and Customs' in square brackets substituted by the Serious Crime Act 2007, s 88, Sch 12, paras 5, 6.
Date in force: 15 February 2008: see SI 2008/219, art 2(b).

Sub-s (3): words 'paragraph (a), (b), (c), (e), (f), (g), (h), (i) or (j) of' in square brackets inserted by virtue of the Serious Organised Crime and Police Act 2005, s 59, Sch 4, paras 131, 132(1), (3).
Date in force: 1 April 2006: see SI 2006/378, art 4(1), Schedule, para 10; for transitional provisions see art 4(4), (8) thereof.

7 Issue of warrants

(1) An interception warrant shall not be issued except—

   (a) under the hand of the Secretary of State [or, in the case of a warrant issued by the Scottish Ministers (by virtue of provision made under section 63 of the Scotland Act 1998), a member of the Scottish Executive]; or

   (b) in a case falling within subsection (2)[(a) or (b)], under the hand of a senior official[; or

   (c) in a case falling within subsection (2)(aa), under the hand of a member of the staff of the Scottish Administration who is a member of the Senior Civil Service and who is designated by the Scottish Ministers as a person under whose hand a warrant may be issued in such a case].

(2) Those cases are—

   (a) an urgent case in which the Secretary of State has himself expressly authorised the issue of the warrant in that case; and

   [(aa) an urgent case in which the Scottish Ministers have themselves (by virtue of provision made under section 63 of the Scotland Act 1998) expressly authorised the use of the warrant in that case and a statement of that fact is endorsed on the warrant; and]

Core resources

(b) a case in which the warrant is for the purposes of a request for assistance made under an international mutual assistance agreement by the competent authorities of a country or territory outside the United Kingdom and either—
   (i) it appears that the interception subject is outside the United Kingdom; or
   (ii) the interception to which the warrant relates is to take place in relation only to premises outside the United Kingdom.

(3) An interception warrant—
   (a) must be addressed to the person falling within section 6(2) by whom, or on whose behalf, the application for the warrant was made; and
   (b) in the case of a warrant issued under the hand of a senior official, must contain, according to whatever is applicable—
      (i) one of the statements set out in subsection (4); and
      (ii) if it contains the statement set out in subsection (4)(b), one of the statements set out in subsection (5).

(4) The statements referred to in subsection (3)(b)(i) are—
   (a) a statement that the case is an urgent case in which the Secretary of State has himself expressly authorised the issue of the warrant;
   (b) a statement that the warrant is issued for the purposes of a request for assistance made under an international mutual assistance agreement by the competent authorities of a country or territory outside the United Kingdom.

(5) The statements referred to in subsection (3)(b)(ii) are—
   (a) a statement that the interception subject appears to be outside the United Kingdom;
   (b) a statement that the interception to which the warrant relates is to take place in relation only to premises outside the United Kingdom.

NOTES

Initial Commencement

To be appointed
To be appointed: see s 83(2).

Appointment

Appointment: 2 October 2000: see SI 2000/2543, art 3.

Amendment

Sub-s (1): in para (a) words from 'or, in the case' to 'the Scottish Executive' in square brackets inserted by SI 2000/3253, art 4(1), Sch 3, Pt II, paras 3, 4(a).
Date in force: 15 December 2000: see SI 2000/3253, art 1(1).

Sub-s (1): in para (b) words '(a) or (b)' in square brackets inserted by SI 2000/3253, art 4(1), Sch 3, Pt II, paras 3, 4(b).
Date in force: 15 December 2000: see SI 2000/3253, art 1(1).

Sub-s (1): para (c) and word '; or' immediately preceding it inserted by SI 2000/3253, art 4(1), Sch 3, Pt II, paras 3, 4(c).
Date in force: 15 December 2000: see SI 2000/3253, art 1(1).

Sub-s (2): para (aa) inserted by SI 2000/3253, art 4(1), Sch 3, Pt II, paras 3, 4(d).
Date in force: 15 December 2000: see SI 2000/3253, art 1(1).

8 Contents of warrants

(1) An interception warrant must name or describe either—
- (a) one person as the interception subject; or
- (b) a single set of premises as the premises in relation to which the interception to which the warrant relates is to take place.

(2) The provisions of an interception warrant describing communications the interception of which is authorised or required by the warrant must comprise one or more schedules setting out the addresses, numbers, apparatus or other factors, or combination of factors, that are to be used for identifying the communications that may be or are to be intercepted.

(3) Any factor or combination of factors set out in accordance with subsection (2) must be one that identifies communications which are likely to be or to include—
- (a) communications from, or intended for, the person named or described in the warrant in accordance with subsection (1); or
- (b) communications originating on, or intended for transmission to, the premises so named or described.

(4) Subsections (1) and (2) shall not apply to an interception warrant if—
- (a) the description of communications to which the warrant relates confines the conduct authorised or required by the warrant to conduct falling within subsection (5); and
- (b) at the time of the issue of the warrant, a certificate applicable to the warrant has been issued by the Secretary of State certifying—
    - (i) the descriptions of intercepted material the examination of which he considers necessary; and
    - (ii) that he considers the examination of material of those descriptions necessary as mentioned in section 5(3)(a), (b) or (c).

(5) Conduct falls within this subsection if it consists in—
- (a) the interception of external communications in the course of their transmission by means of a telecommunication system; and
- (b) any conduct authorised in relation to any such interception by section 5(6).

(6) A certificate for the purposes of subsection (4) shall not be issued except under the hand of the Secretary of State.

NOTES

Initial Commencement

To be appointed
To be appointed: see s 83(2).

Appointment

Appointment: 2 October 2000: see SI 2000/2543, art 3.

9 Duration, cancellation and renewal of warrants

(1) An interception warrant—
- (a) shall cease to have effect at the end of the relevant period; but
- (b) may be renewed, at any time before the end of that period, by an instrument under the hand of the Secretary of State [or, in the case of a warrant issued by

the Scottish Ministers (by virtue of provision made under section 63 of the Scotland Act 1998), a member of the Scottish Executive] or, in a case falling within section 7(2)(b), under the hand of a senior official.

(2) An interception warrant shall not be renewed under subsection (1) unless the Secretary of State believes that the warrant continues to be necessary on grounds falling within section 5(3).

(3) The Secretary of State shall cancel an interception warrant if he is satisfied that the warrant is no longer necessary on grounds falling within section 5(3).

(4) The Secretary of State shall cancel an interception warrant if, at any time before the end of the relevant period, he is satisfied in a case in which—

(a) the warrant is one which was issued containing the statement set out in section 7(5)(a) or has been renewed by an instrument containing the statement set out in subsection (5)(b)(i) of this section, and
(b) the latest renewal (if any) of the warrant is not a renewal by an instrument under the hand of the Secretary of State,

that the person named or described in the warrant as the interception subject is in the United Kingdom.

(5) An instrument under the hand of a senior official that renews an interception warrant must contain—

(a) a statement that the renewal is for the purposes of a request for assistance made under an international mutual assistance agreement by the competent authorities of a country or territory outside the United Kingdom; and
(b) whichever of the following statements is applicable—
   (i) a statement that the interception subject appears to be outside the United Kingdom;
   (ii) a statement that the interception to which the warrant relates is to take place in relation only to premises outside the United Kingdom.

(6) In this section 'the relevant period'—

(a) in relation to an unrenewed warrant issued in a case falling within section 7(2)(a) under the hand of a senior official, means the period ending with the fifth working day following the day of the warrant's issue;
[(ab) in relation to an unrenewed warrant which is endorsed under the hand of the Secretary of State with a statement that the issue of the warrant is believed to be necessary on grounds falling within section 5(3)(a) or (c), means the period of six months beginning with the day of the warrant's issue;]
(b) in relation to a renewed warrant the latest renewal of which was by an instrument endorsed under the hand of the Secretary of State with a statement that the renewal is believed to be necessary on grounds falling within section 5(3)(a) or (c), means the period of six months beginning with the day of the warrant's renewal; and
(c) in all other cases, means the period of three months beginning with the day of the warrant's issue or, in the case of a warrant that has been renewed, of its latest renewal.

NOTES

Initial Commencement

To be appointed
To be appointed: see s 83(2).

Appointment

Appointment: 2 October 2000: see SI 2000/2543, art 3.

Amendment

Sub-s (1): in para (b) words from 'or, in the case' to 'the Scottish Executive' in square brackets inserted by SI 2000/3253, art 4(1), Sch 3, Pt II, paras 3, 5.
Date in force: 15 December 2000: see SI 2000/3253, art 1(1).

Sub-s (6): para (ab) inserted by the Terrorism Act 2006, s 32(1), (2).
Date in force: 13 April 2006: see SI 2006/1013, art 2(1), (2)(b).

Transfer of Functions

Functions under this section: certain functions under sub-ss (1)(b), (3) are transferred, in so far as they are exercisable in or as regards Scotland, to the Scottish Ministers, by the Scotland Act 1998 (Transfer of Functions to the Scottish Ministers etc) (No 2) Order 2000, SI 2000/3253, arts 2, 3, Sch 1, para 3 (as amended by SI 2003/2617, art 4(b)), Sch 2.

Functions under this section: certain functions under sub-ss (1)(b), (3) are transferred, in so far as they are exercisable in or as regards Scotland, to the Scottish Ministers, by the Scotland Act 1998 (Transfer of Functions to the Scottish Ministers etc) (No 2) Order 2003, SI 2003/2617, arts 2, 3, Sch 1, para 2, Sch 2.

Functions under this section: certain functions under sub-ss (1)(b), (3) are transferred, in so far as they are exercisable in or as regards Scotland, to the Scottish Ministers, by the Scotland Act 1998 (Transfer of Functions to the Scottish Ministers etc) Order 2007, SI 2007/2915, arts 2, 3, Sch 1, Sch 2; for transitional and savings provisions see art 6 thereof.

10 Modification of warrants and certificates

(1) The Secretary of State may at any time—

(a) modify the provisions of an interception warrant; or
(b) modify a section 8(4) certificate so as to include in the certified material any material the examination of which he considers to be necessary as mentioned in section 5(3)(a), (b) or (c).

(2) If at any time the Secretary of State considers that any factor set out in a schedule to an interception warrant is no longer relevant for identifying communications which, in the case of that warrant, are likely to be or to include communications falling within section 8(3)(a) or (b), it shall be his duty to modify the warrant by the deletion of that factor.

(3) If at any time the Secretary of State considers that the material certified by a section 8(4) certificate includes any material the examination of which is no longer necessary as mentioned in any of paragraphs (a) to (c) of section 5(3), he shall modify the certificate so as to exclude that material from the certified material.

(4) Subject to subsections (5) to (8), a warrant or certificate shall not be modified under this section except by an instrument under the hand of the Secretary of State or of a senior official.

[(4A) Subject to subsections (5A), (6) and (8), a warrant issued by the Scottish Ministers (by virtue of provision made under section 63 of the Scotland Act 1998) shall not be modified under this section except by an instrument under the hand of a member of the Scottish Executive or a member of the staff of the Scottish Administration who is a member of the Senior Civil Service and is designated by the Scottish

Core resources

Ministers as a person under whose hand an instrument may be issued in such a case (in this section referred to as 'a designated official')]

(5) Unscheduled parts of an interception warrant shall not be modified under the hand of a senior official except in an urgent case in which—

(a) the Secretary of State has himself expressly authorised the modification; and
(b) a statement of that fact is endorsed on the modifying instrument.

[(5A) Unscheduled parts of an interception warrant issued by the Scottish Ministers shall not be modified under the hand of a designated official except in an urgent case in which—

(a) they have themselves (by virtue of provision made under section 63 of the Scotland Act 1998) expressly authorised the modification; and
(b) a statement of that fact is endorsed on the modifying instrument.]

[(6) Subsection (4) authorises the modification of the scheduled parts of an interception warrant under the hand of a senior official who is either—

(a) the person to whom the warrant is addressed, or
(b) a person holding a position subordinate to that person,

only if the applicable condition specified in subsection (6A) is satisfied and a statement that the condition is satisfied is endorsed on the modifying instrument.

(6A) The applicable condition is—

(a) in the case of an unrenewed warrant, that the warrant is endorsed with a statement that the issue of the warrant is believed to be necessary in the interests of national security; and
(b) in the case of a renewed warrant, that the instrument by which it was last renewed is endorsed with a statement that the renewal is believed to be necessary in the interests of national security.]

(7) A section 8(4) certificate shall not be modified under the hand of a senior official except in an urgent case in which—

(a) the official in question holds a position in respect of which he is expressly authorised by provisions contained in the certificate to modify the certificate on the Secretary of State's behalf; or
(b) the Secretary of State has himself expressly authorised the modification and a statement of that fact is endorsed on the modifying instrument.

(8) Where modifications in accordance with this subsection are expressly authorised by provision contained in the warrant, the scheduled parts of an interception warrant may, in an urgent case, be modified by an instrument under the hand of—

(a) the person to whom the warrant is addressed; or
(b) a person holding any such position subordinate to that person as may be identified in the provisions of the warrant.

(9) Where—

(a) a warrant or certificate is modified by an instrument under the hand of a person other than the Secretary of State [or, as the case may be, the Scottish Ministers (by virtue of provision made under section 63 of the Scotland Act 1998)], and
(b) a statement for the purposes of subsection (5)(b)[, (5A)(b)][, (6)] or (7)(b) is endorsed on the instrument, or the modification is made under subsection (8),

that modification shall cease to have effect at the end of the fifth working day following the day of the instrument's issue.

(10) For the purposes of this section—
  (a) the scheduled parts of an interception warrant are any provisions of the warrant that are contained in a schedule of identifying factors comprised in the warrant for the purposes of section 8(2); and
  (b) the modifications that are modifications of the scheduled parts of an interception warrant include the insertion of an additional such schedule in the warrant;

and references in this section to unscheduled parts of an interception warrant, and to their modification, shall be construed accordingly.

NOTES

Initial Commencement

To be appointed
To be appointed: see s 83(2).

Appointment

Appointment: 2 October 2000: see SI 2000/2543, art 3.

Amendment

Sub-s (4A): inserted by SI 2000/3253, art 4(1), Sch 3, Pt II, paras 3, 6(a).
Date in force: 15 December 2000: see SI 2000/3253, art 1(1).

Sub-s (5A): inserted by SI 2000/3253, art 4(1), Sch 3, Pt II, paras 3, 6(b).
Date in force: 15 December 2000: see SI 2000/3253, art 1(1).

Sub-ss (6), (6A): substituted, for sub-s (6) as originally enacted, by the Terrorism Act 2006, s 32(1), (3).
Date in force: 13 April 2006: see SI 2006/1013, art 2(1), (2)(b).

Sub-s (9): in para (a) words from 'or, as the case' to 'the Scotland Act 1998)' in square brackets inserted by SI 2000/3253, art 4(1), Sch 3, Pt II, paras 3, 6(d)(i).
Date in force: 15 December 2000: see SI 2000/3253, art 1(1).

Sub-s (9): in para (b) words ', (5A)(b)' in square brackets inserted by SI 2000/3253, art 4(1), Sch 3, Pt II, paras 3, 6(d)(ii).
Date in force: 15 December 2000: see SI 2000/3253, art 1(1).

Sub-s (9): in para (b) reference to ', (6)' in square brackets inserted by the Terrorism Act 2006, s 32(1), (4).
Date in force: 13 April 2006: see SI 2006/1013, art 2(1), (2)(b).

Transfer of Functions

Functions under this section: certain functions under sub-ss (1)(a), (2) are transferred, in so far as they are exercisable in or as regards Scotland, to the Scottish Ministers, by the Scotland Act 1998 (Transfer of Functions to the Scottish Ministers etc) (No 2) Order 2000, SI 2000/3253, arts 2, 3, Sch 1, para 3 (as amended by SI 2003/2617, art 4(b)), Sch 2.

Functions under this section: certain functions under sub-ss (1)(a), (2) are transferred, in so far as they are exercisable in or as regards Scotland, to the Scottish Ministers, by the Scotland Act 1998 (Transfer of Functions to the Scottish Ministers etc) (No 2) Order 2003, SI 2003/2617, arts 2, 3, Sch 1, para 2, Sch 2.

Core resources

Functions under this section: certain functions under sub-ss (1)(a), (2) are transferred, in so far as they are exercisable in or as regards Scotland, to the Scottish Ministers, by the Scotland Act 1998 (Transfer of Functions to the Scottish Ministers etc) Order 2007, SI 2007/2915, arts 2, 3, Sch 1, Sch 2; for transitional and savings provisions see art 6 thereof.

11   Implementation of warrants

(1)   Effect may be given to an interception warrant either—

(a)   by the person to whom it is addressed; or
(b)   by that person acting through, or together with, such other persons as he may require (whether under subsection (2) or otherwise) to provide him with assistance with giving effect to the warrant.

(2)   For the purpose of requiring any person to provide assistance in relation to an interception warrant the person to whom it is addressed may—

(a)   serve a copy of the warrant on such persons as he considers may be able to provide such assistance; or
(b)   make arrangements under which a copy of it is to be or may be so served.

(3)   The copy of an interception warrant that is served on any person under subsection (2) may, to the extent authorised—

(a)   by the person to whom the warrant is addressed, or
(b)   by the arrangements made by him for the purposes of that subsection,

omit any one or more of the schedules to the warrant.

(4)   Where a copy of an interception warrant has been served by or on behalf of the person to whom it is addressed on—

(a)   a person who provides a postal service,
(b)   a person who provides a public telecommunications service, or
(c)   a person not falling within paragraph (b) who has control of the whole or any part of a telecommunication system located wholly or partly in the United Kingdom,

it shall (subject to subsection (5)) be the duty of that person to take all such steps for giving effect to the warrant as are notified to him by or on behalf of the person to whom the warrant is addressed.

(5)   A person who is under a duty by virtue of subsection (4) to take steps for giving effect to a warrant shall not be required to take any steps which it is not reasonably practicable for him to take.

(6)   For the purposes of subsection (5) the steps which it is reasonably practicable for a person to take in a case in which obligations have been imposed on him by or under section 12 shall include every step which it would have been reasonably practicable for him to take had he complied with all the obligations so imposed on him.

(7)   A person who knowingly fails to comply with his duty under subsection (4) shall be guilty of an offence and liable—

(a)   on conviction on indictment, to imprisonment for a term not exceeding two years or to a fine, or to both;
(b)   on summary conviction, to imprisonment for a term not exceeding six months or to a fine not exceeding the statutory maximum, or to both.

(8)   A person's duty under subsection (4) to take steps for giving effect to a warrant shall be enforceable by civil proceedings by the Secretary of State for an injunction, or

for specific performance of a statutory duty under section 45 of the Court of Session Act 1988, or for any other appropriate relief.

(9) For the purposes of this Act the provision of assistance with giving effect to an interception warrant includes any disclosure to the person to whom the warrant is addressed, or to persons acting on his behalf, of intercepted material obtained by any interception authorised or required by the warrant, and of any related communications data.

NOTES

Initial Commencement

To be appointed
To be appointed: see s 83(2).

Appointment

Appointment: 2 October 2000: see SI 2000/2543, art 3.

Interception capability and costs

12 Maintenance of interception capability

(1) The Secretary of State may by order provide for the imposition by him on persons who—

(a) are providing public postal services or public telecommunications services, or
(b) are proposing to do so,

of such obligations as it appears to him reasonable to impose for the purpose of securing that it is and remains practicable for requirements to provide assistance in relation to interception warrants to be imposed and complied with.

(2) The Secretary of State's power to impose the obligations provided for by an order under this section shall be exercisable by the giving, in accordance with the order, of a notice requiring the person who is to be subject to the obligations to take all such steps as may be specified or described in the notice.

(3) Subject to subsection (11), the only steps that may be specified or described in a notice given to a person under subsection (2) are steps appearing to the Secretary of State to be necessary for securing that that person has the practical capability of providing any assistance which he may be required to provide in relation to relevant interception warrants.

(4) A person shall not be liable to have an obligation imposed on him in accordance with an order under this section by reason only that he provides, or is proposing to provide, to members of the public a telecommunications service the provision of which is or, as the case may be, will be no more than—

(a) the means by which he provides a service which is not a telecommunications service; or
(b) necessarily incidental to the provision by him of a service which is not a telecommunications service.

(5) Where a notice is given to any person under subsection (2) and otherwise than by virtue of subsection (6)(c), that person may, before the end of such period as may be specified in an order under this section, refer the notice to the Technical Advisory Board.

Core resources

(6) Where a notice given to any person under subsection (2) is referred to the Technical Advisory Board under subsection (5)—

- (a) there shall be no requirement for that person to comply, except in pursuance of a notice under paragraph (c)(ii), with any obligations imposed by the notice;
- (b) the Board shall consider the technical requirements and the financial consequences, for the person making the reference, of the notice referred to them and shall report their conclusions on those matters to that person and to the Secretary of State; and
- (c) the Secretary of State, after considering any report of the Board relating to the notice, may either—
  - (i) withdraw the notice; or
  - (ii) give a further notice under subsection (2) confirming its effect, with or without modifications.

(7) It shall be the duty of a person to whom a notice is given under subsection (2) to comply with the notice; and that duty shall be enforceable by civil proceedings by the Secretary of State for an injunction, or for specific performance of a statutory duty under section 45 of the Court of Session Act 1988, or for any other appropriate relief.

(8) A notice for the purposes of subsection (2) must specify such period as appears to the Secretary of State to be reasonable as the period within which the steps specified or described in the notice are to be taken.

(9) Before making an order under this section the Secretary of State shall consult with—

- (a) such persons appearing to him to be likely to be subject to the obligations for which it provides,
- (b) the Technical Advisory Board,
- (c) such persons representing persons falling within paragraph (a), and
- (d) such persons with statutory functions in relation to persons falling within that paragraph,

as he considers appropriate.

(10) The Secretary of State shall not make an order under this section unless a draft of the order has been laid before Parliament and approved by a resolution of each House.

(11) For the purposes of this section the question whether a person has the practical capability of providing assistance in relation to relevant interception warrants shall include the question whether all such arrangements have been made as the Secretary of State considers necessary—

- (a) with respect to the disclosure of intercepted material;
- (b) for the purpose of ensuring that security and confidentiality are maintained in relation to, and to matters connected with, the provision of any such assistance; and
- (c) for the purpose of facilitating the carrying out of any functions in relation to this Chapter of the Interception of Communications Commissioner;

but before determining for the purposes of the making of any order, or the imposition of any obligation, under this section what arrangements he considers necessary for the purpose mentioned in paragraph (c) the Secretary of State shall consult that Commissioner.

(12) In this section 'relevant interception warrant'—

(a) in relation to a person providing a public postal service, means an interception warrant relating to the interception of communications in the course of their transmission by means of that service; and
(b) in relation to a person providing a public telecommunications service, means an interception warrant relating to the interception of communications in the course of their transmission by means of a telecommunication system used for the purposes of that service.

NOTES

Initial Commencement

To be appointed
To be appointed: see s 83(2).

Appointment

Appointment: 2 October 2000: see SI 2000/2543, art 3.

Subordinate Legislation

Regulation of Investigatory Powers (Maintenance of Interception Capability) Order 2002, SI 2002/1931 (made under sub-ss (1), (2), (5)).

13 Technical Advisory Board

(1) There shall be a Technical Advisory Board consisting of such number of persons appointed by the Secretary of State as he may by order provide.

(2) The order providing for the membership of the Technical Advisory Board must also make provision which is calculated to ensure—
 (a) that the membership of the Technical Advisory Board includes persons likely effectively to represent the interests of the persons on whom obligations may be imposed under section 12;
 (b) that the membership of the Board includes persons likely effectively to represent the interests of the persons by or on whose behalf applications for interception warrants may be made;
 (c) that such other persons (if any) as the Secretary of State thinks fit may be appointed to be members of the Board; and
 (d) that the Board is so constituted as to produce a balance between the representation of the interests mentioned in paragraph (a) and the representation of those mentioned in paragraph (b).

(3) The Secretary of State shall not make an order under this section unless a draft of the order has been laid before Parliament and approved by a resolution of each House.

NOTES

Initial Commencement

To be appointed
To be appointed: see s 83(2).

Appointment

Appointment: 2 October 2000: see SI 2000/2543, art 3.

Core resources

Subordinate Legislation

Regulation of Investigatory Powers (Technical Advisory Board) Order 2001, SI 2001/3734 (made under sub-ss (1), (2)).

14   Grants for interception costs

(1)   It shall be the duty of the Secretary of State to ensure that such arrangements are in force as are necessary for securing that a person who provides—

  (a)   a postal service, or
  (b)   a telecommunications service,

receives such contribution as is, in the circumstances of that person's case, a fair contribution towards the costs incurred, or likely to be incurred, by that person in consequence of the matters mentioned in subsection (2).

(2)   Those matters are—

  (a)   in relation to a person providing a postal service, the issue of interception warrants relating to communications transmitted by means of that postal service;
  (b)   in relation to a person providing a telecommunications service, the issue of interception warrants relating to communications transmitted by means of a telecommunication system used for the purposes of that service;
  (c)   in relation to each description of person, the imposition on that person of obligations provided for by an order under section 12.

(3)   For the purpose of complying with his duty under this section, the Secretary of State may make arrangements for payments to be made out of money provided by Parliament.

NOTES

Initial Commencement

To be appointed
To be appointed: see s 83(2).

Appointment

Appointment: 2 October 2000: see SI 2000/2543, art 3.

Restrictions on use of intercepted material etc

15   General safeguards

(1)   Subject to subsection (6), it shall be the duty of the Secretary of State to ensure, in relation to all interception warrants, that such arrangements are in force as he considers necessary for securing—

  (a)   that the requirements of subsections (2) and (3) are satisfied in relation to the intercepted material and any related communications data; and
  (b)   in the case of warrants in relation to which there are section 8(4) certificates, that the requirements of section 16 are also satisfied.

(2)   The requirements of this subsection are satisfied in relation to the intercepted material and any related communications data if each of the following—

  (a)   the number of persons to whom any of the material or data is disclosed or otherwise made available,

(b) the extent to which any of the material or data is disclosed or otherwise made available,
(c) the extent to which any of the material or data is copied, and
(d) the number of copies that are made,

is limited to the minimum that is necessary for the authorised purposes.

(3) The requirements of this subsection are satisfied in relation to the intercepted material and any related communications data if each copy made of any of the material or data (if not destroyed earlier) is destroyed as soon as there are no longer any grounds for retaining it as necessary for any of the authorised purposes.

(4) For the purposes of this section something is necessary for the authorised purposes if, and only if—

(a) it continues to be, or is likely to become, necessary as mentioned in section 5(3);
(b) it is necessary for facilitating the carrying out of any of the functions under this Chapter of the Secretary of State;
(c) it is necessary for facilitating the carrying out of any functions in relation to this Part of the Interception of Communications Commissioner or of the Tribunal;
(d) it is necessary to ensure that a person conducting a criminal prosecution has the information he needs to determine what is required of him by his duty to secure the fairness of the prosecution; or
(e) it is necessary for the performance of any duty imposed on any person by the Public Records Act 1958 or the Public Records Act (Northern Ireland) 1923.

(5) The arrangements for the time being in force under this section for securing that the requirements of subsection (2) are satisfied in relation to the intercepted material or any related communications data must include such arrangements as the Secretary of State considers necessary for securing that every copy of the material or data that is made is stored, for so long as it is retained, in a secure manner.

(6) Arrangements in relation to interception warrants which are made for the purposes of subsection (1)—

(a) shall not be required to secure that the requirements of subsections (2) and (3) are satisfied in so far as they relate to any of the intercepted material or related communications data, or any copy of any such material or data, possession of which has been surrendered to any authorities of a country or territory outside the United Kingdom; but
(b) shall be required to secure, in the case of every such warrant, that possession of the intercepted material and data and of copies of the material or data is surrendered to authorities of a country or territory outside the United Kingdom only if the requirements of subsection (7) are satisfied.

(7) The requirements of this subsection are satisfied in the case of a warrant if it appears to the Secretary of State—

(a) that requirements corresponding to those of subsections (2) and (3) will apply, to such extent (if any) as the Secretary of State thinks fit, in relation to any of the intercepted material or related communications data possession of which, or of any copy of which, is surrendered to the authorities in question; and
(b) that restrictions are in force which would prevent, to such extent (if any) as the Secretary of State thinks fit, the doing of anything in, for the purposes of or in connection with any proceedings outside the United Kingdom which would result in such a disclosure as, by virtue of section 17, could not be made in the United Kingdom.

Core resources

(8) In this section 'copy', in relation to intercepted material or related communications data, means any of the following (whether or not in documentary form)—

(a) any copy, extract or summary of the material or data which identifies itself as the product of an interception, and

(b) any record referring to an interception which is a record of the identities of the persons to or by whom the intercepted material was sent, or to whom the communications data relates,

and 'copied' shall be construed accordingly.

NOTES

Initial Commencement

To be appointed
To be appointed: see s 83(2).

Appointment

Appointment: 2 October 2000: see SI 2000/2543, art 3.

Transfer of Functions

Functions under this section: certain functions under sub-s (1) are transferred, in so far as they are exercisable in or as regards Scotland, to the Scottish Ministers, by the Scotland Act 1998 (Transfer of Functions to the Scottish Ministers etc) (No 2) Order 2000, SI 2000/3253, arts 2, 3, Sch 1, para 3 (as amended by SI 2003/2617, art 4(b)), Sch 2.

Functions under this section: certain functions under sub-s (1) are transferred, in so far as they are exercisable in or as regards Scotland, to the Scottish Ministers, by the Scotland Act 1998 (Transfer of Functions to the Scottish Ministers etc) (No 2) Order 2003, SI 2003/2617, arts 2, 3, Sch 1, para 2, Sch 2.

Functions under this section: certain functions under sub-s (1) are transferred, in so far as they are exercisable in or as regards Scotland, to the Scottish Ministers, by the Scotland Act 1998 (Transfer of Functions to the Scottish Ministers etc) Order 2007, SI 2007/2915, arts 2, 3, Sch 1, Sch 2; for transitional and savings provisions see art 6 thereof.

16 Extra safeguards in the case of certificated warrants

(1) For the purposes of section 15 the requirements of this section, in the case of a warrant in relation to which there is a section 8(4) certificate, are that the intercepted material is read, looked at or listened to by the persons to whom it becomes available by virtue of the warrant to the extent only that it—

(a) has been certified as material the examination of which is necessary as mentioned in section 5(3)(a), (b) or (c); and

(b) falls within subsection (2).

(2) Subject to subsections (3) and (4), intercepted material falls within this subsection so far only as it is selected to be read, looked at or listened to otherwise than according to a factor which—

(a) is referable to an individual who is known to be for the time being in the British Islands; and

(b) has as its purpose, or one of its purposes, the identification of material contained in communications sent by him, or intended for him.

(3) Intercepted material falls within subsection (2), notwithstanding that it is selected by reference to any such factor as is mentioned in paragraph (a) and (b) of that subsection, if—
- (a) it is certified by the Secretary of State for the purposes of section 8(4) that the examination of material selected according to factors referable to the individual in question is necessary as mentioned in subsection 5(3)(a), (b) or (c); and
- (b) the material relates only to communications sent during [a period specified in the certificate that is no longer than the permitted maximum].

[(3A) In subsection (3)(b) 'the permitted maximum' means—
- (a) in the case of material the examination of which is certified for the purposes of section 8(4) as necessary in the interests of national security, six months; and
- (b) in any other case, three months.]

(4) Intercepted material also falls within subsection (2), notwithstanding that it is selected by reference to any such factor as is mentioned in paragraph (a) and (b) of that subsection, if—
- (a) the person to whom the warrant is addressed believes, on reasonable grounds, that the circumstances are such that the material would fall within that subsection; or
- (b) the conditions set out in subsection (5) below are satisfied in relation to the selection of the material.

(5) Those conditions are satisfied in relation to the selection of intercepted material if—
- (a) it has appeared to the person to whom the warrant is addressed that there has been such a relevant change of circumstances as, but for subsection (4)(b), would prevent the intercepted material from falling within subsection (2);
- (b) since it first so appeared, a written authorisation to read, look at or listen to the material has been given by a senior official; and
- (c) the selection is made before the end of [the permitted period].

[(5A) In subsection (5)(c) 'the permitted period' means—
- (a) in the case of material the examination of which is certified for the purposes of section 8(4) as necessary in the interests of national security, the period ending with the end of the fifth working day after it first appeared as mentioned in subsection (5)(a) to the person to whom the warrant is addressed; and
- (b) in any other case, the period ending with the end of the first working day after it first so appeared to that person.]

(6) References in this section to its appearing that there has been a relevant change of circumstances are references to its appearing either—
- (a) that the individual in question has entered the British Islands; or
- (b) that a belief by the person to whom the warrant is addressed in the individual's presence outside the British Islands was in fact mistaken.

NOTES

Initial Commencement

To be appointed
To be appointed: see s 83(2).

Core resources

Appointment

Appointment: 2 October 2000: see SI 2000/2543, art 3.

Amendment

Sub-s (3): in para (b) words 'a period specified in the certificate that is no longer than the permitted maximum' in square brackets substituted by the Terrorism Act 2006, s 32(1), (5)(a).
Date in force: 13 April 2006: see SI 2006/1013, art 2(1), (2)(b).

Sub-s (3A): inserted by the Terrorism Act 2006, s 32(1), (6).
Date in force: 13 April 2006: see SI 2006/1013, art 2(1), (2)(b).

Sub-s (5): in para (c) words 'the permitted period' in square brackets substituted by the Terrorism Act 2006, s 32(1), (5)(b).
Date in force: 13 April 2006: see SI 2006/1013, art 2(1), (2)(b).

Sub-s (5A): inserted by the Terrorism Act 2006, s 32(1), (7).
Date in force: 13 April 2006: see SI 2006/1013, art 2(1), (2)(b).

17 Exclusion of matters from legal proceedings

(1) Subject to section 18, no evidence shall be adduced, question asked, assertion or disclosure made or other thing done in, for the purposes of or in connection with any legal proceedings [or Inquiries Act proceedings] which (in any manner)—

  (a) discloses, in circumstances from which its origin in anything falling within subsection (2) may be inferred, any of the contents of an intercepted communication or any related communications data; or
  (b) tends (apart from any such disclosure) to suggest that anything falling within subsection (2) has or may have occurred or be going to occur.

(2) The following fall within this subsection—

  (a) conduct by a person falling within subsection (3) that was or would be an offence under section 1(1) or (2) of this Act or under section 1 of the Interception of Communications Act 1985;
  (b) a breach by the Secretary of State of his duty under section 1(4) of this Act;
  (c) the issue of an interception warrant or of a warrant under the Interception of Communications Act 1985;
  (d) the making of an application by any person for an interception warrant, or for a warrant under that Act;
  (e) the imposition of any requirement on any person to provide assistance with giving effect to an interception warrant.

(3) The persons referred to in subsection (2)(a) are—

  (a) any person to whom a warrant under this Chapter may be addressed;
  (b) any person holding office under the Crown;
  [(c) any member of the staff of the Serious Organised Crime Agency;]
  [(ca) any member of the Scottish Crime and Drug Enforcement Agency;]
  (e) any person employed by or for the purposes of a police force;
  (f) any person providing a postal service or employed for the purposes of any business of providing such a service; and
  (g) any person providing a public telecommunications service or employed for the purposes of any business of providing such a service.

(4) [In this section—

  'Inquiries Act proceedings' means proceedings of an inquiry under the Inquiries Act 2005;

'intercepted communications' means] any communication intercepted in the course of its transmission by means of a postal service or telecommunication system.

NOTES

Initial Commencement

To be appointed
To be appointed: see s 83(2).

Appointment

Appointment: 2 October 2000: see SI 2000/2543, art 3.

Amendment

Sub-s (1): words 'or Inquiries Act proceedings' in square brackets inserted by the Inquiries Act 2005, s 48(1), Sch 2, Pt 1, para 20(1), (2).
Date in force: 7 June 2005: see SI 2005/1432, art 2.

Sub-s (3): para (c) substituted, for paras (c), (d) as originally enacted, by the Serious Organised Crime and Police Act 2005, s 59, Sch 4, paras 131, 133.
Date in force: 1 April 2006: see SI 2006/378, art 4(1), Schedule, para 10; for transitional provisions see art 4(4), (8) thereof.

Sub-s (3): para (ca) inserted by SI 2007/1098, art 6, Schedule, Pt 1, para 4(1), (3).
Date in force: 1 April 2007: see SI 2007/1098, art 1(3).

Sub-s (4): words from 'In this section—' to "intercepted communications' means' in square brackets substituted by the Inquiries Act 2005, s 48(1), Sch 2, Pt 1, para 20(1), (3).
Date in force: 7 June 2005: see SI 2005/1432, art 2.

18 Exceptions to section 17

(1) Section 17(1) shall not apply in relation to—

- (a) any proceedings for a relevant offence;
- (b) any civil proceedings under section 11(8);
- (c) any proceedings before the Tribunal;
- (d) any proceedings on an appeal or review for which provision is made by an order under section 67(8);
- [(da) any control order proceedings (within the meaning of the Prevention of Terrorism Act 2005) or any proceedings arising out of such proceedings;]
- [(db) any financial restrictions proceedings as defined in section 65 of the Counter-Terrorism Act 2008, or any proceedings arising out of such proceedings;]
- (e) any proceedings before the Special Immigration Appeals Commission or any proceedings arising out of proceedings before that Commission; or
- (f) any proceedings before the Proscribed Organisations Appeal Commission or any proceedings arising out of proceedings before that Commission.

(2) Subsection (1) shall not, by virtue of [paragraphs (da) to (f)], authorise the disclosure of anything—

[(za) in the case of any proceedings falling within paragraph (da) to—
  (i) a person who, within the meaning of the Schedule to the Prevention of Terrorism Act 2005, is or was a relevant party to the control order proceedings; or

(ii) any person who for the purposes of any proceedings so falling (but otherwise than by virtue of an appointment under paragraph 7 of that Schedule) represents a person falling within sub-paragraph (i);]
[(zb) in the case of proceedings falling within paragraph (db), to—
(i) a person, other than the Treasury, who is or was a party to the proceedings, or
(ii) any person who for the purposes of the proceedings (but otherwise than by virtue of appointment as a special advocate) represents a person falling within sub-paragraph (i);]
(a) in the case of any proceedings falling within paragraph (e), to—
(i) the appellant to the Special Immigration Appeals Commission; or
(ii) any person who for the purposes of any proceedings so falling (but otherwise than by virtue of an appointment under section 6 of the Special Immigration Appeals Commission Act 1997) represents that appellant;
or
(b) in the case of proceedings falling within paragraph (f), to—
(i) the applicant to the Proscribed Organisations Appeal Commission;
(ii) the organisation concerned (if different);
(iii) any person designated under paragraph 6 of Schedule 3 to the Terrorism Act 2000 to conduct proceedings so falling on behalf of that organisation; or
(iv) any person who for the purposes of any proceedings so falling (but otherwise than by virtue of an appointment under paragraph 7 of that Schedule) represents that applicant or that organisation.

(3) Section 17(1) shall not prohibit anything done in, for the purposes of, or in connection with, so much of any legal proceedings as relates to the fairness or unfairness of a dismissal on the grounds of any conduct constituting an offence under section 1(1) or (2), 11(7) or 19 of this Act, or section 1 of the Interception of Communications Act 1985.

(4) Section 17(1)(a) shall not prohibit the disclosure of any of the contents of a communication if the interception of that communication was lawful by virtue of section 1(5)(c), 3 or 4.

(5) Where any disclosure is proposed to be or has been made on the grounds that it is authorised by subsection (4), section 17(1) shall not prohibit the doing of anything in, or for the purposes of, so much of any ... proceedings as relates to the question whether that disclosure is or was so authorised.

(6) Section 17(1)(b) shall not prohibit the doing of anything that discloses any conduct of a person for which he has been convicted of an offence under section 1(1) or (2), 11(7) or 19 of this Act, or section 1 of the Interception of Communications Act 1985.

(7) Nothing in section 17(1) shall prohibit any such disclosure of any information that continues to be available for disclosure as is confined to—

(a) a disclosure to a person conducting a criminal prosecution for the purpose only of enabling that person to determine what is required of him by his duty to secure the fairness of the prosecution; ...
(b) a disclosure to a relevant judge in a case in which that judge has ordered the disclosure to be made to him alone[; or]
[(c) a disclosure to the panel of an inquiry held under the Inquiries Act 2005 or to a person appointed as counsel to such an inquiry where, in the course of the inquiry, the panel has ordered the disclosure to be made to the panel alone or (as the case may be) to the panel and the person appointed as counsel to the inquiry].

Regulation of Investigatory Powers Act 2000

(8) A relevant judge shall not order a disclosure under subsection (7)(b) except where he is satisfied that the exceptional circumstances of the case make the disclosure essential in the interests of justice.

[(8A) The panel of an inquiry shall not order a disclosure under subsection (7)(c) except where it is satisfied that the exceptional circumstances of the case make the disclosure essential to enable the inquiry to fulfil its terms of reference.]

(9) Subject to subsection (10), where in any criminal proceedings—

(a) a relevant judge does order a disclosure under subsection (7)(b), and
(b) in consequence of that disclosure he is of the opinion that there are exceptional circumstances requiring him to do so,

he may direct the person conducting the prosecution to make for the purposes of the proceedings any such admission of fact as that judge thinks essential in the interests of justice.

(10) Nothing in any direction under subsection (9) shall authorise or require anything to be done in contravention of section 17(1).

(11) In this section 'a relevant judge' means—

(a) any judge of the High Court or of the Crown Court or any Circuit judge;
(b) any judge of the High Court of Justiciary or any sheriff;
(c) in relation to a court-martial, the judge advocate appointed in relation to that court-martial under section 84B of the Army Act 1955, section 84B of the Air Force Act 1955 or section 53B of the Naval Discipline Act 1957; or
[(c) in relation to proceedings before the Court Martial, the judge advocate for those proceedings; or]
(d) any person holding any such judicial office as entitles him to exercise the jurisdiction of a judge falling within paragraph (a) or (b).

(12) In this section 'relevant offence' means—

(a) an offence under any provision of this Act;
(b) an offence under section 1 of the Interception of Communications Act 1985;
(c) an offence under [section 47 or 48 of the Wireless Telegraphy Act 2006];
(d) an offence under ... [section 83 or 84 of the Postal Services Act 2000];
(e) ...
(f) an offence under section 4 of the Official Secrets Act 1989 relating to any such information, document or article as is mentioned in subsection (3)(a) of that section;
(g) an offence under section 1 or 2 of the Official Secrets Act 1911 relating to any sketch, plan, model, article, note, document or information which incorporates or relates to the contents of any intercepted communication or any related communications data or tends to suggest as mentioned in section 17(1)(b) of this Act;
(h) perjury committed in the course of any proceedings mentioned in subsection (1) or (3) of this section;
(i) attempting or conspiring to commit, or aiding, abetting, counselling or procuring the commission of, an offence falling within any of the preceding paragraphs; and
(j) contempt of court committed in the course of, or in relation to, any proceedings mentioned in subsection (1) or (3) of this section.

(13) In subsection (12) 'intercepted communication' has the same meaning as in section 17.

Core resources

NOTES

Initial Commencement

To be appointed
To be appointed: see s 83(2).

Appointment

Appointment: 2 October 2000: see SI 2000/2543, art 3.

Amendment

Sub-s (1): para (da) inserted by the Prevention of Terrorism Act 2005, s 11(5), Schedule, para 9(1), (2).
Date in force: this amendment came into force on 11 March 2005 (date of Royal Assent of the Prevention of Terrorism Act 2005) in the absence of any specific commencement provision.

Sub-s (1): para (db) inserted by the Counter-Terrorism Act 2008, s 69(1), (2).
Date in force: 27 November 2008: see the Counter-Terrorism Act 2008, s 100(2).

Sub-s (2): words 'paragraph (da) to (f)' in square brackets substituted by the Prevention of Terrorism Act 2005, s 11(5), Schedule, para 9(1), (3).
Date in force: this amendment came into force on 11 March 2005 (date of Royal Assent of the Prevention of Terrorism Act 2005) in the absence of any specific commencement provision.

Sub-s (2): para (za) inserted by the Prevention of Terrorism Act 2005, s 11(5), Schedule, para 9(1), (4).
Date in force: this amendment came into force on 11 March 2005 (date of Royal Assent of the Prevention of Terrorism Act 2005) in the absence of any specific commencement provision.

Sub-s (2): para (zb) inserted by the Counter-Terrorism Act 2008, s 69(1), (3).
Date in force: 27 November 2008: see the Counter-Terrorism Act 2008, s 100(2).

Sub-s (5): word omitted repealed by the Inquiries Act 2005, ss 48(1), 49(2), Sch 2, Pt 1, para 21(1), (2), Sch 3.
Date in force: 7 June 2005: see SI 2005/1432, art 2.

Sub-s (7): in para (a) word omitted repealed by the Inquiries Act 2005, s 49(2), Sch 3.
Date in force: 7 June 2005: see SI 2005/1432, art 2; for transitional provisions and savings see the Inquiries Act 2005, ss 44(5).

Sub-s (7): para (c) and word '; or' immediately preceding it inserted by the Inquiries Act 2005, s 48(1), Sch 2, Pt 1, para 21(1), (3).
Date in force: 7 June 2005: see SI 2005/1432, art 2.

Sub-s (7): para (c) substituted by the Counter-Terrorism Act 2008, s 74(1).
Date in force: 16 February 2009: see SI 2009/58, art 2(b); for effect in relation to inquiries under the Inquiries Act 2005 see the Counter-Terrorism Act 2008 s 28, s 74(2).

Sub-s (8A): inserted by the Inquiries Act 2005, s 48(1), Sch 2, Pt 1, para 21(1), (4).
Date in force: 7 June 2005: see SI 2005/1432, art 2.

Sub-s (11): para (c) substituted by the Armed Forces Act 2006, s 378(1), Sch 16, para 169.
Date in force (for certain purposes): 28 March 2009: see SI 2009/812, art 3(a), (b).
Date in force (for remaining purposes): to be appointed: see the Armed Forces Act 2006, s 383(2).

Regulation of Investigatory Powers Act 2000

Sub-s (12): in para (c) words 'section 47 or 48 of the Wireless Telegraphy Act 2006' in square brackets substituted by the Wireless Telegraphy Act 2006, s 123, Sch 7, paras 21, 23.
Date in force: 8 February 2007: see the Wireless Telegraphy Act 2006, s 126(2).

Sub-s (12): in para (d) words omitted repealed by SI 2001/1149, art 3(2), Sch 2.
Date in force: 26 March 2001: see SI 2001/1149, art 1(2).

Sub-s (12): in para (d) words 'section 83 or 84 of the Postal Services Act 2000' in square brackets substituted by SI 2001/1149, art 3(1), Sch 1, para 135(1), (2).
Date in force: 26 March 2001: see SI 2001/1149, art 1(2).

Sub-s (12): para (e) repealed by the Communications Act 2003, s 406(7), Sch 19(1).
Date in force (for the purpose only of enabling the networks and services functions and the spectrum functions to be carried out by the Director General of Telecommunications and the Secretary of State respectively, during the transitional period (as provided for by the Communications Act 2003, s 408(6)): 25 July 2003–29 December 2003: see SI 2003/1900, arts 2(1), 3(1), Sch 1 and the Communications Act 2003, ss 406(6), 408, Sch 18, para 2.
Date in force (for the purpose of conferring the networks and services functions and the spectrum functions on OFCOM): 29 December 2003: by virtue of SI 2003/3142, art 3(2).

19 Offence for unauthorised disclosures

(1) Where an interception warrant has been issued or renewed, it shall be the duty of every person falling within subsection (2) to keep secret all the matters mentioned in subsection (3).

(2) The persons falling within this subsection are—

 (a) the persons specified in section 6(2);
 (b) every person holding office under the Crown;
 [(c) every member of the staff of the Serious Organised Crime Agency;]
 [(ca) every member of the Scottish Crime and Drug Enforcement Agency;]
 (e) every person employed by or for the purposes of a police force;
 (f) persons providing postal services or employed for the purposes of any business of providing such a service;
 (g) persons providing public telecommunications services or employed for the purposes of any business of providing such a service;
 (h) persons having control of the whole or any part of a telecommunication system located wholly or partly in the United Kingdom.

(3) Those matters are—

 (a) the existence and contents of the warrant and of any section 8(4) certificate in relation to the warrant;
 (b) the details of the issue of the warrant and of any renewal or modification of the warrant or of any such certificate;
 (c) the existence and contents of any requirement to provide assistance with giving effect to the warrant;
 (d) the steps taken in pursuance of the warrant or of any such requirement; and
 (e) everything in the intercepted material, together with any related communications data.

(4) A person who makes a disclosure to another of anything that he is required to keep secret under this section shall be guilty of an offence and liable—

 (a) on conviction on indictment, to imprisonment for a term not exceeding five years or to a fine, or to both;

Core resources

    (b)   on summary conviction, to imprisonment for a term not exceeding six months or to a fine not exceeding the statutory maximum, or to both.

(5) In proceedings against any person for an offence under this section in respect of any disclosure, it shall be a defence for that person to show that he could not reasonably have been expected, after first becoming aware of the matter disclosed, to take steps to prevent the disclosure.

(6) In proceedings against any person for an offence under this section in respect of any disclosure, it shall be a defence for that person to show that—

    (a)   the disclosure was made by or to a professional legal adviser in connection with the giving, by the adviser to any client of his, of advice about the effect of provisions of this Chapter; and
    (b)   the person to whom or, as the case may be, by whom it was made was the client or a representative of the client.

(7) In proceedings against any person for an offence under this section in respect of any disclosure, it shall be a defence for that person to show that the disclosure was made by a legal adviser—

    (a)   in contemplation of, or in connection with, any legal proceedings; and
    (b)   for the purposes of those proceedings.

(8) Neither subsection (6) nor subsection (7) applies in the case of a disclosure made with a view to furthering any criminal purpose.

(9) In proceedings against any person for an offence under this section in respect of any disclosure, it shall be a defence for that person to show that the disclosure was confined to a disclosure made to the Interception of Communications Commissioner or authorised—

    (a)   by that Commissioner;
    (b)   by the warrant or the person to whom the warrant is or was addressed;
    (c)   by the terms of the requirement to provide assistance; or
    (d)   by section 11(9).

NOTES

Initial Commencement

To be appointed
To be appointed: see s 83(2).

Appointment

Appointment: 2 October 2000: see SI 2000/2543, art 3.

Amendment

Sub-s (2): para (c) substituted, for paras (c), (d) as originally enacted, by the Serious Organised Crime and Police Act 2005, s 59, Sch 4, paras 131, 134.
Date in force: 1 April 2006: see SI 2006/378, art 4(1), Schedule, para 10; for transitional provisions see art 4(4), (8) thereof.

Sub-s (2): para (ca) inserted by SI 2007/1098, art 6, Schedule, Pt 1, para 4(1), (4).
Date in force: 1 April 2007: see SI 2007/1098, art 1(3).

Interpretation of Chapter I

20 Interpretation of Chapter I

In this Chapter—

'certified', in relation to a section 8(4) certificate, means of a description certified by the certificate as a description of material the examination of which the Secretary of State considers necessary;

'external communication' means a communication sent or received outside the British Islands;

'intercepted material', in relation to an interception warrant, means the contents of any communications intercepted by an interception to which the warrant relates;

'the interception subject', in relation to an interception warrant, means the person about whose communications information is sought by the interception to which the warrant relates;

'international mutual assistance agreement' means an international agreement designated for the purposes of section 1(4);

'related communications data', in relation to a communication intercepted in the course of its transmission by means of a postal service or telecommunication system, means so much of any communications data (within the meaning of Chapter II of this Part) as—
   (a) is obtained by, or in connection with, the interception; and
   (b) relates to the communication or to the sender or recipient, or intended recipient, of the communication;

'section 8(4) certificate' means any certificate issued for the purposes of section 8(4).

NOTES

Initial Commencement

To be appointed
To be appointed: see s 83(2).

Appointment

Appointment: 2 October 2000: see SI 2000/2543, art 3.

COMPUTER MISUSE ACT 1990

1990 CHAPTER 18

An Act to make provision for securing computer material against unauthorised access or modification; and for connected purposes

[29th June 1990]

BE IT ENACTED by the Queen's most Excellent Majesty, by and with the advice and consent of the Lords Spiritual and Temporal, and Commons, in this present Parliament assembled, and by the authority of the same, as follows:—

Computer Misuse Offences

1 Unauthorised access to computer material

(1) A person is guilty of an offence if—

   (a) he causes a computer to perform any function with intent to secure access to any program or data held in any computer[, or to enable any such access to be secured];

   (b) the access he intends to secure[, or to enable to be secured,] is unauthorised; and

   (c) he knows at the time when he causes the computer to perform the function that that is the case.

(2) The intent a person has to have to commit an offence under this section need not be directed at—

   (a) any particular program or data;

   (b) a program or data of any particular kind; or

   (c) a program or data held in any particular computer.

[(3) A person guilty of an offence under this section shall be liable—

   (a) on summary conviction in England and Wales, to imprisonment for a term not exceeding 12 months or to a fine not exceeding the statutory maximum or to both;

   (b) on summary conviction in Scotland, to imprisonment for a term not exceeding six months or to a fine not exceeding the statutory maximum or to both;

   (c) on conviction on indictment, to imprisonment for a term not exceeding two years or to a fine or to both.]

NOTES

Initial Commencement

Specified date
Specified date: 29 August 1990: see s 18(2).

Core resources

Amendment

Sub-s (1): in para (a) words ', or to enable any such access to be secured' in square brackets inserted by the Police and Justice Act 2006, s 35(1), (2)(a).
Date in force (in relation to Scotland): 1 October 2007: see SSI 2007/434, art 2(a).
Date in force (in relation to England, Wales and Northern Ireland): 1 October 2008: see SI 2008/2503, art 2(a); for transitional provisions see the Police and Justice Act 2006, s 38(1)(a).

Sub-s (1): in para (b) words ', or to enable to be secured,' in square brackets inserted by the Police and Justice Act 2006, s 35(1), (2)(b).
Date in force (in relation to Scotland): 1 October 2007: see SSI 2007/434, art 2(a).
Date in force (in relation to England, Wales and Northern Ireland): 1 October 2008: see SI 2008/2503, art 2(a); for transitional provisions see the Police and Justice Act 2006, s 38(1)(a).

Sub-s (3): substituted by the Police and Justice Act 2006, s 35(1), (3).
Date in force (in relation to Scotland): 1 October 2007: see SSI 2007/434, art 2(a).
Date in force (in relation to England, Wales and Northern Ireland): 1 October 2008: see SI 2008/2503, art 2(a); for transitional provisions see the Police and Justice Act 2006, s 38(2)(a), (6)(a), (7)(a).

2   Unauthorised access with intent to commit or facilitate commission of further offences

(1) A person is guilty of an offence under this section if he commits an offence under section 1 above ('the unauthorised access offence') with intent—

(a) to commit an offence to which this section applies; or
(b) to facilitate the commission of such an offence (whether by himself or by any other person);

and the offence he intends to commit or facilitate is referred to below in this section as the further offence.

(2) This section applies to offences—

(a) for which the sentence is fixed by law; or
(b) for which a person *of twenty-one years of age or over (not previously convicted)* [who has attained the age of twenty-one years (eighteen in relation to England and Wales) and has no previous convictions] may be sentenced to imprisonment for a term of five years (or, in England and Wales, might be so sentenced but for the restrictions imposed by section 33 of the Magistrates' Courts Act 1980).

(3) It is immaterial for the purposes of this section whether the further offence is to be committed on the same occasion as the unauthorised access offence or on any future occasion.

(4) A person may be guilty of an offence under this section even though the facts are such that the commission of the further offence is impossible.

[(5) A person guilty of an offence under this section shall be liable—

(a) on summary conviction in England and Wales, to imprisonment for a term not exceeding 12 months or to a fine not exceeding the statutory maximum or to both;
(b) on summary conviction in Scotland, to imprisonment for a term not exceeding six months or to a fine not exceeding the statutory maximum or to both;
(c) on conviction on indictment, to imprisonment for a term not exceeding five years or to a fine or to both.]

Computer Misuse Act 1990

NOTES

Initial Commencement

Specified date
Specified date: 29 August 1990: see s 18(2).

Amendment

Sub-s (2): in para (b) words 'of twenty-one years of age or over (not previously convicted)' in italics repealed and subsequent words in square brackets substituted by the Criminal Justice and Court Services Act 2000, s 74, Sch 7, Pt II, para 98.
Date in force: to be appointed: see the Criminal Justice and Court Services Act 2000, s 80(1).

Sub-s (5): substituted by the Police and Justice Act 2006, s 52, Sch 14, para 17.
Date in force (in relation to Scotland): 1 October 2007: see SSI 2007/434, art 2(b), (c).
Date in force (in relation to England, Wales and Northern Ireland): 1 October 2008: see SI 2008/2503, art 2(a)–(c); for transitional provisions and savings see the Police and Justice Act 2006, s 38(6)(b), (7)(b).

[3 Unauthorised acts with intent to impair, or with recklessness as to impairing, operation of computer, etc]

[(1) A person is guilty of an offence if—

  (a) he does any unauthorised act in relation to a computer;
  (b) at the time when he does the act he knows that it is unauthorised; and
  (c) either subsection (2) or subsection (3) below applies.

(2) This subsection applies if the person intends by doing the act—

  (a) to impair the operation of any computer;
  (b) to prevent or hinder access to any program or data held in any computer; [or]
  (c) to impair the operation of any such program or the reliability of any such data; ...
  (d) ...

(3) This subsection applies if the person is reckless as to whether the act will do any of the things mentioned in paragraphs (a) [to (c)] of subsection (2) above.

(4) The intention referred to in subsection (2) above, or the recklessness referred to in subsection (3) above, need not relate to—

  (a) any particular computer;
  (b) any particular program or data; or
  (c) a program or data of any particular kind.

(5) In this section—

  (a) a reference to doing an act includes a reference to causing an act to be done;
  (b) 'act' includes a series of acts;
  (c) a reference to impairing, preventing or hindering something includes a reference to doing so temporarily.

(6) A person guilty of an offence under this section shall be liable—

  (a) on summary conviction in England and Wales, to imprisonment for a term not exceeding 12 months or to a fine not exceeding the statutory maximum or to both;
  (b) on summary conviction in Scotland, to imprisonment for a term not exceeding six months or to a fine not exceeding the statutory maximum or to both;

Core resources

(c) on conviction on indictment, to imprisonment for a term not exceeding ten years or to a fine or to both.]

NOTES

Amendment

Substituted by the Police and Justice Act 2006, s 36.
Date in force (in relation to Scotland): 1 October 2007: see SSI 2007/434, art 2(a).
Date in force (in relation to England, Wales and Northern Ireland): 1 October 2008: see SI 2008/2503, art 2(a); for transitional provisions and savings see the Police and Justice Act 2006, s 38(3), (4), (6)(c), (7)(c).

Sub-s (2): in para (b) word 'or' in square brackets inserted by virtue of the Serious Crime Act 2007, s 61(1), (3)(a)(i).
Date in force: 1 October 2008: see SI 2008/2504, art 2(a).

Sub-s (2): para (d) and word omitted immediately preceding it repealed by virtue of the Serious Crime Act 2007, ss 61(1), (3)(a)(ii), 92, Sch 14.
Date in force: 1 October 2008: see SI 2008/2504, art 2(a), (i)(viii).

Sub-s (3): words 'to (c)' in square brackets substituted by virtue of the Serious Crime Act 2007, s 61(1), (3)(b).
Date in force: 1 October 2008: see SI 2008/2504, art 2(a).

[3A **Making, supplying or obtaining articles for use in offence under section 1 or 3**]

[(1) A person is guilty of an offence if he makes, adapts, supplies or offers to supply any article intending it to be used to commit, or to assist in the commission of, an offence under section 1 or 3.

(2) A person is guilty of an offence if he supplies or offers to supply any article believing that it is likely to be used to commit, or to assist in the commission of, an offence under section 1 or 3.

(3) A person is guilty of an offence if he obtains any article with a view to its being supplied for use to commit, or to assist in the commission of, an offence under section 1 or 3.

(4) In this section 'article' includes any program or data held in electronic form.

(5) A person guilty of an offence under this section shall be liable—

(a) on summary conviction in England and Wales, to imprisonment for a term not exceeding 12 months or to a fine not exceeding the statutory maximum or to both;
(b) on summary conviction in Scotland, to imprisonment for a term not exceeding six months or to a fine not exceeding the statutory maximum or to both;
(c) on conviction on indictment, to imprisonment for a term not exceeding two years or to a fine or to both.]

NOTES

Amendment

Inserted by the Police and Justice Act 2006, s 37.
Date in force (in relation to Scotland): 1 October 2007: see SSI 2007/434, art 2(a).

Computer Misuse Act 1990

Date in force (in relation to England, Wales and Northern Ireland): 1 October 2008: see SI 2008/2503, art 2(a); for transitional provisions see the Police and Justice Act 2006, s 38(5), (6)(d), (7)(d).

Jurisdiction

4   Territorial scope of [offences under sections 1 to 3]

(1) Except as provided below in this section, it is immaterial for the purposes of any offence under section 1 or 3 above—

   (a) whether any act or other event proof of which is required for conviction of the offence occurred in the home country concerned; or
   (b) whether the accused was in the home country concerned at the time of any such act or event.

(2) Subject to subsection (3) below, in the case of such an offence at least one significant link with domestic jurisdiction must exist in the circumstances of the case for the offence to be committed.

(3) There is no need for any such link to exist for the commission of an offence under section 1 above to be established in proof of an allegation to that effect in proceedings for an offence under section 2 above.

(4) Subject to section 8 below, where—

   (a) any such link does in fact exist in the case of an offence under section 1 above; and
   (b) commission of that offence is alleged in proceedings for an offence under section 2 above;

section 2 above shall apply as if anything the accused intended to do or facilitate in any place outside the home country concerned which would be an offence to which section 2 applies if it took place in the home country concerned were the offence in question.

(5) This section is without prejudice to any jurisdiction exercisable by a court in Scotland apart from this section.

(6) References in this Act to the home country concerned are references—

   (a) in the application of this Act to England and Wales, to England and Wales;
   (b) in the application of this Act to Scotland, to Scotland; and
   (c) in the application of this Act to Northern Ireland, to Northern Ireland.

NOTES

Initial Commencement

Specified date
Specified date: 29 August 1990: see s 18(2).

Amendment

Section heading: words 'offences under sections 1 to 3' in square brackets substituted by the Police and Justice Act 2006, s 52, Sch 14, para 18.
Date in force (in relation to Scotland): 1 October 2007: see SSI 2007/434, art 2(b), (c).
Date in force (in relation to England, Wales and Northern Ireland): 1 October 2008: see SI 2008/2503, art 2(a)–(c).

Core resources

5 Significant links with domestic jurisdiction

(1) The following provisions of this section apply for the interpretation of section 4 above.

(2) In relation to an offence under section 1, either of the following is a significant link with domestic jurisdiction—

(a) that the accused was in the home country concerned at the time when he did the act which caused the computer to perform the function; or

[(b) that any computer containing any program or data to which the accused by doing that act secured or intended to secure unauthorised access, or enabled or intended to enable unauthorised access to be secured, was in the home country concerned at that time].

(3) In relation to an offence under section 3, either of the following is a significant link with domestic jurisdiction—

(a) that the accused was in the home country concerned at the time when [he did the unauthorised act (or caused it to be done)]; or

[(b) that the unauthorised act was done in relation to a computer in the home country concerned].

NOTES

Initial Commencement

Specified date
Specified date: 29 August 1990: see s 18(2).

Amendment

Sub-s (2): para (b) substituted by the Police and Justice Act 2006, s 52, Sch 14, para 19(1), (2).
Date in force (in relation to Scotland): 1 October 2007: see SSI 2007/434, art 2(b), (c).
Date in force (in relation to England, Wales and Northern Ireland): 1 October 2008: see SI 2008/2503, art 2(a)–(c); for transitional provisions and savings see the Police and Justice Act 2006, s 38(1)(b).

Sub-s (3): in para (a) words 'he did the unauthorised act (or caused it to be done)' in square brackets substituted by the Police and Justice Act 2006, s 52, Sch 14, para 19(1), (3)(a).
Date in force (in relation to Scotland): 1 October 2007: see SSI 2007/434, art 2(b), (c).
Date in force (in relation to England, Wales and Northern Ireland): 1 October 2008: see SI 2008/2503, art 2(a)–(c); for transitional provisions and savings see the Police and Justice Act 2006, s 38(4)(b).

Sub-s (3): para (b) substituted by the Police and Justice Act 2006, s 52, Sch 14, para 19(1), (3)(b).
Date in force (in relation to Scotland): 1 October 2007: see SSI 2007/434, art 2(b), (c).
Date in force (in relation to England, Wales and Northern Ireland): 1 October 2008: see SI 2008/2503, art 2(a)–(c); for transitional provisions and savings see the Police and Justice Act 2006, s 38(4)(b).

6 Territorial scope of inchoate offences related to [offences under sections 1 to 3]

(1) On a charge of conspiracy to commit an [offence under section 1, 2 or 3 above] the following questions are immaterial to the accused's guilt—

(a) the question where any person became a party to the conspiracy; and

(b) the question whether any act, omission or other event occurred in the home country concerned.

(2) On a charge of attempting to commit an offence under section 3 above the following questions are immaterial to the accused's guilt—

(a) the question where the attempt was made; and
(b) the question whether it had an effect in the home country concerned.

(3) ...

(4) This section does not extend to Scotland.

NOTES

Initial Commencement

Specified date
Specified date: 29 August 1990: see s 18(2).

Extent

This section does not extend to Scotland: see sub-s (4) above.

Amendment

Section heading: words 'offences under sections 1 to 3' in square brackets substituted by the Police and Justice Act 2006, s 52, Sch 14, para 20(a).
Date in force: 1 October 2008: see SI 2008/2503, art 2(b), (c).

Sub-s (1): words 'offence under section 1, 2 or 3 above' in square brackets substituted by the Police and Justice Act 2006, s 52, Sch 14, para 20(b).
Date in force: 1 October 2008: see SI 2008/2503, art 2(b), (c).

Sub-s (3): repealed by the Serious Crime Act 2007, ss 63(2), 92, Sch 6, Pt 2, paras 59(1), (2), Sch 14.
Date in force: 1 October 2008: see SI 2008/2504, art 2(a), (i)(vi).

7 Territorial scope of inchoate offences related to offences under external law corresponding to [offences under sections 1 to 3]

(1)–(3) ...

(4) ...

NOTES

Initial Commencement

Specified date
Specified date: 29 August 1990: see s 18(2).

Amendment

Section heading: words 'offences under sections 1 to 3' in square brackets substituted by the Police and Justice Act 2006, s 52, Sch 14, para 21(a).
Date in force: 1 October 2008: see SI 2008/2503, art 2(b), (c).

Core resources

Sub-ss (1), (2): repealed by the Criminal Justice (Terrorism and Conspiracy) Act 1998, s 9(2), Sch 2, Pt II.
Date in force: 4 September 1998: (no specific commencement provision).

Sub-s (3): amends the Criminal Attempts Act 1981, s 1.
Sub-s (4): repealed by the Serious Crime Act 2007, ss 63(2), 92, Sch 6, Pt 2, paras 59(1), (3), Sch 14.
Date in force: 1 October 2008: see SI 2008/2504, art 2(a), (i)(vi).

8 Relevance of external law

(1) A person is guilty of an offence triable by virtue of section 4(4) above only if what he intended to do or facilitate would involve the commission of an offence under the law in force where the whole or any part of it was intended to take place.

(2) ...

(3) A person is guilty of an offence triable by virtue of section 1(1A) of the Criminal Attempts Act 1981 ... only if what he had in view would involve the commission of an offence under the law in force where the whole or any part of it was intended to take place.

(4) Conduct punishable under the law in force in any place is an offence under that law for the purposes of this section, however it is described in that law.

(5) Subject to subsection (7) below, a condition specified in [subsection (1) or (3)] above shall be taken to be satisfied unless not later than rules of court may provide the defence serve on the prosecution a notice—

(a) stating that, on the facts as alleged with respect to the relevant conduct, the condition is not in their opinion satisfied;
(b) showing their grounds for that opinion; and
(c) requiring the prosecution to show that it is satisfied.

(6) In subsection (5) above 'the relevant conduct' means—

(a) where the condition in subsection (1) above is in question, what the accused intended to do or facilitate;
(b) ...
(c) where the condition in subsection (3) above is in question, what the accused had in view.

(7) The court, if it thinks fit, may permit the defence to require the prosecution to show that the condition is satisfied without the prior service of a notice under subsection (5) above.

(8) If by virtue of subsection (7) above a court of solemn jurisdiction in Scotland permits the defence to require the prosecution to show that the condition is satisfied, it shall be competent for the prosecution for that purpose to examine any witness or to put in evidence any production not included in the lists lodged by it.

(9) In the Crown Court the question whether the condition is satisfied shall be decided by the judge alone.

(10) In the High Court of Justiciary and in the sheriff court the question whether the condition is satisfied shall be decided by the judge or, as the case may be, the sheriff alone.

Computer Misuse Act 1990

NOTES

Initial Commencement

Specified date
Specified date: 29 August 1990: see s 18(2).

Amendment

Sub-s (2): repealed by the Criminal Justice (Terrorism and Conspiracy) Act 1998, s 9(1), (2), Sch 1, para 6(1)(a), Sch 2, Pt II.
Date in force: 4 September 1998: (no specific commencement provision).

Sub-s (3): words omitted repealed by the Serious Crime Act 2007, ss 63(2), 92, Sch 6, Pt 2, paras 59(1), (4), Sch 14.
Date in force: 1 October 2008: see SI 2008/2504, art 2(a), (i)(vi).

Sub-s (5): words 'subsection (1) or (3)' in square brackets substituted by the Criminal Justice (Terrorism and Conspiracy) Act 1998, s 9(1), Sch 1, para 6(1)(b).
Date in force: 4 September 1998: (no specific commencement provision).

Sub-s (6): para (b) repealed by the Criminal Justice (Terrorism and Conspiracy) Act 1998, s 9(1), (2), Sch 1, para 6(1)(c), Sch 2, Pt II.
Date in force: 4 September 1998: (no specific commencement provision).

9 British citizenship immaterial

(1) In any proceedings brought in England and Wales in respect of any offence to which this section applies it is immaterial to guilt whether or not the accused was a British citizen at the time of any act, omission or other event proof of which is required for conviction of the offence.

(2) This section applies to the following offences—

    (a) any [offence under section 1, 2 or 3 above];
    (b) ...
    (c) any attempt to commit an offence under section 3 above; and
    (d) ...

NOTES

Initial Commencement

Specified date
Specified date: 29 August 1990: see s 18(2).

Amendment

Sub-s (2): in para (a) words 'offence under section 1, 2 or 3 above' in square brackets substituted by the Police and Justice Act 2006, s 52, Sch 14, para 22.
Date in force: 1 October 2008: see SI 2008/2503, art 2(b), (c).

Sub-s (2): para (b) repealed by the Criminal Justice (Terrorism and Conspiracy) Act 1998, s 9(1), (2), Sch 1, para 6(2), Sch 2, Pt II.
Date in force: 4 September 1998: (no specific commencement provision).

Sub-s (2): para (d) repealed by the Serious Crime Act 2007, ss 63(2), 92, Sch 6, Pt 2, paras 59(1), (5), Sch 14.
Date in force: 1 October 2008: see SI 2008/2504, art 2(a), (i)(vi).

Core resources

Miscellaneous and General

10   Saving for certain law enforcement powers

Section 1(1) above has effect without prejudice to the operation—

(a) in England and Wales of any enactment relating to powers of inspection, search or seizure; and
(b) in Scotland of any enactment or rule of law relating to powers of examination, search or seizure

[and nothing designed to indicate a withholding of consent to access to any program or data from persons as enforcement officers shall have effect to make access unauthorised for the purposes of the said section 1(1).

In this section 'enforcement officer' means a constable or other person charged with the duty of investigating offences; and withholding consent from a person 'as' an enforcement officer of any description includes the operation, by the person entitled to control access, of rules whereby enforcement officers of that description are, as such, disqualified from membership of a class of persons who are authorised to have access.]

NOTES

Initial Commencement

Specified date
Specified date: 29 August 1990: see s 18(2).

Amendment

Words in square brackets inserted by the Criminal Justice and Public Order Act 1994, s 162(1).

11   …

…

NOTES

Amendment

Repealed by the Police and Justice Act 2006, s 52, Sch 14, para 23, Sch 15, Pt 4.
Date in force: 1 October 2008: see SI 2008/2503, art 2(a)–(c), (d)(i); for savings see the Police and Justice Act 2006, s 38(2)(b).

12   …

…

NOTES

Amendment

Repealed by the Police and Justice Act 2006, s 52, Sch 14, para 24, Sch 15, Pt 4.
Date in force: 1 October 2008: see SI 2008/2503, art 2(a)–(c), (d)(i); for savings see the Police and Justice Act 2006, s 38(2)(b).

13 Proceedings in Scotland

(1) A sheriff shall have jurisdiction in respect of an offence under section 1 or 2 above if—

(a) the accused was in the sheriffdom at the time when he did the act which caused the computer to perform the function; or

[(b) any computer containing any program or data to which the accused by doing that act secured or intended to secure unauthorised access, or enabled or intended to enable unauthorised access to be secured, was in the sheriffdom at that time].

(2) A sheriff shall have jurisdiction in respect of an offence under section 3 above if—

(a) the accused was in the sheriffdom at the time when [he did the unauthorised act (or caused it to be done)]; or

[(b) the unauthorised act was done in relation to a computer in the sheriffdom].

(3) ...

(4) ...

(5) ...

(6) ...

(7) ...

(8) In proceedings in which a person is charged with an offence under section 2 or 3 above and is found not guilty or is acquitted of that charge, he may be found guilty of an offence under section 1 above if on the facts shown he could have been found guilty of that offence in proceedings for that offence ...

(9) Subsection (8) above shall apply whether or not an offence under section 1 above has been libelled in the complaint or indictment.

(10) A person found guilty of an offence under section 1 above by virtue of subsection (8) above shall be liable, in respect of that offence, only to the penalties set out in section 1.

(11) This section extends to Scotland only.

NOTES

Initial Commencement

Specified date
Specified date: 29 August 1990: see s 18(2).

Amendment

Sub-s (1): para (b) substituted by the Police and Justice Act 2006, s 52, Sch 14, para 25(1), (2).
Date in force: 1 October 2007: see SSI 2007/434, art 2(b), (c); for transitional provisions and savings see the Police and Justice Act 2006, s 38(1)(b).

Sub-s (2): in para (a) words 'he did the unauthorised act (or caused it to be done)' in square brackets substituted by the Police and Justice Act 2006, s 52, Sch 14, para 25(1), (3)(a).
Date in force: 1 October 2007: see SSI 2007/434, art 2(b), (c); for transitional provisions and savings see the Police and Justice Act 2006, s 38(4)(b).

Core resources

Sub-s (2): para (b) substituted by the Police and Justice Act 2006, s 52, Sch 14, para 25(1), (3)(b).
Date in force: 1 October 2007: see SSI 2007/434, art 2(b), (c); for transitional provisions and savings see the Police and Justice Act 2006, s 38(4)(b).

Sub-ss (3)–(7): repealed by the Police and Justice Act 2006, s 52, Sch 14, para 25(1), (4), Sch 15, Pt 4.
Date in force: 1 October 2007: see SSI 2007/434, art 2(b), (c), (d)(i); for transitional provisions and savings see the Police and Justice Act 2006, s 38(2)(b), (4)(b).

Sub-s (8): words omitted repealed by the Police and Justice Act 2006, s 52, Sch 14, para 25(1), (5), Sch 15, Pt 4.
Date in force: 1 October 2007: see SSI 2007/434, art 2(b), (c), (d)(i); for transitional provisions and savings see the Police and Justice Act 2006, s 38(2)(b), (4)(b).

14 ...

...

NOTES

Amendment

Repealed by the Police and Justice Act 2006, s 52, Sch 14, para 26, Sch 15, Pt 4.
Date in force: 1 October 2008: see SI 2008/2503, art 2(a)–(c), (d)(i); for savings see the Police and Justice Act 2006, s 38(2)(b).

15 ...

...

NOTES

Amendment

Repealed by the Extradition Act 2003, ss 219(1), 220, Sch 3, paras 1, 7, Sch 4.
Date in force: 1 January 2004 (except in relation to any request for extradition, whether made under the Extradition Act 1989 or the Backing of Warrants (Republic of Ireland) Act 1965 or otherwise, which is received by the relevant authority in the United Kingdom and an extradition made from or to the United Kingdom on or before 31 December 2003): see SI 2003/3103, arts 2–4 (as amended by SI 2003/3312, art 2).

16 Application to Northern Ireland

(1) The following provisions of this section have effect for applying this Act in relation to Northern Ireland with the modifications there mentioned.

[(1A) In section 1(3)(a)—

  (a) the reference to England and Wales shall be read as a reference to Northern Ireland; and
  (b) the reference to 12 months shall be read as a reference to six months.]

(2) In section 2(2)(b)—

  (a) the reference to England and Wales shall be read as a reference to Northern Ireland; and

Computer Misuse Act 1990

(b) the reference to section 33 of the Magistrates' Courts Act 1980 shall be read as a reference to Article 46(4) of the Magistrates' Courts (Northern Ireland) Order 1981.

[(2A) In section 2(5)(a)—
  (a) the reference to England and Wales shall be read as a reference to Northern Ireland; and
  (b) the reference to 12 months shall be read as a reference to six months.]

(3) ...

[(3A) In section 3(6)(a)—
  (a) the reference to England and Wales shall be read as a reference to Northern Ireland; and
  (b) the reference to 12 months shall be read as a reference to six months.]

[(3B) In section 3A(5)(a)—
  (a) the reference to England and Wales shall be read as a reference to Northern Ireland; and
  (b) the reference to 12 months shall be read as a reference to six months.]

(4) [Subsection (7) below shall apply in substitution for subsection (3) of section 7]; ...

(5) ...

(6) ...

(7) The following paragraphs shall be inserted after Article 3(1) of that Order—

'(1A) Subject to section 8 of the Computer Misuse Act 1990 (relevance of external law), if this paragraph applies to an act, what the person doing it had in view shall be treated as an offence to which this Article applies.

(1B) Paragraph (1A) above applies to an act if—
  (a) it is done in Northern Ireland; and
  (b) it would fall within paragraph (1) as more than merely preparatory to the commission of an offence under section 3 of the Computer Misuse Act 1990 but for the fact that the offence, if completed, would not be an offence triable in Northern Ireland.'.

(8) In section 8—
  (a) ...
  (b) the reference in subsection (3) to section 1(1A) of the Criminal Attempts Act 1981 shall be read as a reference to Article 3(1A) of that Order.

(9) The references in sections 9(1) and 10 to England and Wales shall be read as references to Northern Ireland.

(10) ...

(11) ...

(12) ...

NOTES

Initial Commencement

Specified date
Specified date: 29 August 1990: see s 18(2).

Core resources

Amendment

Sub-s (1A): inserted by the Police and Justice Act 2006, s 52, Sch 14, para 27(1), (2).
Date in force: 1 October 2008: see SI 2008/2503, art 2(a)–(c); for transitional provisions see the Police and Justice Act 2006, s 38(2)(b).

Sub-s (2A): inserted by the Police and Justice Act 2006, s 52, Sch 14, para 27(1), (3).
Date in force: 1 October 2008: see SI 2008/2503, art 2(b), (c).

Sub-s (3): repealed by the Police and Justice Act 2006, s 52, Sch 14, para 27(1), (4), Sch 15, Pt 4.
Date in force: 1 October 2008: see SI 2008/2503, art 2(a)–(c), (d)(i); for savings see the Police and Justice Act 2006, s 38(4)(b).

Sub-s (3A): inserted by the Police and Justice Act 2006, s 52, Sch 14, para 27(1), (5).
Date in force: 1 October 2008: see SI 2008/2503, art 2(a)–(c); for transitional provisions see the Police and Justice Act 2006, s 38(4)(b).

Sub-s (3B): inserted by the Police and Justice Act 2006, s 52, Sch 14, para 27(1), (6).
Date in force: 1 October 2008: see SI 2008/2503, art 2(b), (c).

Sub-s (4): words 'Subsection (7) below shall apply in substitution for subsection (3) of section 7' in square brackets substituted by the Criminal Justice (Terrorism and Conspiracy) Act 1998, s 9(1), Sch 1, para 6(3)(a).
Date in force: 4 September 1998: (no specific commencement provision).

Sub-s (4): words omitted repealed by the Serious Crime Act 2007, ss 63(2), 92, Sch 6, Pt 2, paras 59(1), (6), Sch 14.
Date in force: 1 October 2008: see SI 2008/2504, art 2(a), (i)(vi).

Sub-ss (5), (6): repealed by the Criminal Justice (Terrorism and Conspiracy) Act 1998, s 9(1), (2), Sch 1, para 6(3)(b), Sch 2, Pt II.
Date in force: 4 September 1998: (no specific commencement provision).

Sub-s (8): para (a) repealed by the Criminal Justice (Terrorism and Conspiracy) Act 1998, s 9(1), (2), Sch 1, para 6(3)(b), Sch 2, Pt II.
Date in force: 4 September 1998: (no specific commencement provision).

Sub-ss (10)–(12): repealed by the Police and Justice Act 2006, s 52, Sch 14, para 27(1), (7), Sch 15, Pt 4.
Date in force: 1 October 2008: see SI 2008/2503, art 2(a)–(c), (d)(i); for savings see the Police and Justice Act 2006, s 38(2)(b).

[16A Northern Ireland: search warrants for offences under section 1]

[(1) Where a county court judge is satisfied by information on oath given by a constable that there are reasonable grounds for believing—

(a) that an offence under section 1 above has been or is about to be committed in any premises, and
(b) that evidence that such an offence has been or is about to be committed is in those premises,

he may issue a warrant authorising a constable to enter and search the premises, using such reasonable force as is necessary.

(2) The power conferred by subsection (1) above does not extend to authorising a search for material of the kinds mentioned in Article 11(2) of the Police and Criminal Evidence (Northern Ireland) Order 1989 (privileged, excluded and special procedure material).

(3) A warrant under this section—

(a) may authorise persons to accompany any constable executing the warrant; and
(b) remains in force for twenty-eight days from the date of its issue.

(4) In exercising a warrant issued under this section a constable may seize an article if he reasonably believes that it is evidence that an offence under section 1 above has been or is about to be committed.

(5) In this section 'premises' includes land, buildings, movable structures, vehicles, vessels, aircraft and hovercraft.

(6) This section extends only to Northern Ireland.]

NOTES

Amendment

Inserted by the Police and Justice Act 2006, s 52, Sch 14, para 28.
Date in force: 1 October 2008: see SI 2008/2503, arts 2(a), 3; for transitional provisions see the Police and Justice Act 2006, s 38(2)(b).

17   Interpretation

(1) The following provisions of this section apply for the interpretation of this Act.

(2) A person secures access to any program or data held in a computer if by causing a computer to perform any function he—

(a) alters or erases the program or data;
(b) copies or moves it to any storage medium other than that in which it is held or to a different location in the storage medium in which it is held;
(c) uses it; or
(d) has it output from the computer in which it is held (whether by having it displayed or in any other manner);

and references to access to a program or data (and to an intent to secure such access [or to enable such access to be secured]) shall be read accordingly.

(3) For the purposes of subsection (2)(c) above a person uses a program if the function he causes the computer to perform—

(a) causes the program to be executed; or
(b) is itself a function of the program.

(4) For the purposes of subsection (2)(d) above—

(a) a program is output if the instructions of which it consists are output; and
(b) the form in which any such instructions or any other data is output (and in particular whether or not it represents a form in which, in the case of instructions, they are capable of being executed or, in the case of data, it is capable of being processed by a computer) is immaterial.

(5) Access of any kind by any person to any program or data held in a computer is unauthorised if—

(a) he is not himself entitled to control access of the kind in question to the program or data; and
(b) he does not have consent to access by him of the kind in question to the program or data from any person who is so entitled

[but this subsection is subject to section 10].

Core resources

(6) References to any program or data held in a computer include references to any program or data held in any removable storage medium which is for the time being in the computer; and a computer is to be regarded as containing any program or data held in any such medium.

(7) ...

[(8) An act done in relation to a computer is unauthorised if the person doing the act (or causing it to be done)—

(a) is not himself a person who has responsibility for the computer and is entitled to determine whether the act may be done; and
(b) does not have consent to the act from any such person.

In this subsection 'act' includes a series of acts.]

(9) References to the home country concerned shall be read in accordance with section 4(6) above.

(10) References to a program include references to part of a program.

NOTES

Initial Commencement

Specified date
Specified date: 29 August 1990: see s 18(2).

Amendment

Sub-s (2): words 'or to enable such access to be secured' in square brackets inserted by the Police and Justice Act 2006, s 52, Sch 14, para 29(1), (2).
Date in force (in relation to Scotland): 1 October 2007: see SSI 2007/434, art 2(b), (c).
Date in force (in relation to England, Wales and Northern Ireland): 1 October 2008: see SI 2008/2503, art 2(a)–(c); for transitional provisions see the Police and Justice Act 2006, s 38(1)(b).

Sub-s (5): words 'but this subsection is subject to section 10' in square brackets inserted by the Criminal Justice and Public Order Act 1994, s 162(2).
Sub-s (7): repealed by the Police and Justice Act 2006, s 52, Sch 14, para 29(1), (3), Sch 15, Pt 4.
Date in force (in relation to Scotland): 1 October 2007: see SSI 2007/434, art 2(b), (c), (d)(i).
Date in force (in relation to England, Wales and Northern Ireland): 1 October 2008: see SI 2008/2503, art 2(a)–(c), (d)(i); for savings see the Police and Justice Act 2006, s 38(4)(b).

Sub-s (8): substituted by the Police and Justice Act 2006, s 52, Sch 14, para 29(1), (4).
Date in force (in relation to Scotland): 1 October 2007: see SSI 2007/434, art 2(b), (c).
Date in force (in relation to England, Wales and Northern Ireland): 1 October 2008: see SI 2008/2503, art 2(a)–(c); for transitional provisions see the Police and Justice Act 2006, s 38(4)(b).

18 Citation, commencement etc

(1) This Act may be cited as the Computer Misuse Act 1990.

(2) This Act shall come into force at the end of the period of two months beginning with the day on which it is passed.

(3) An offence is not committed under this Act unless every act or other event proof of which is required for conviction of the offence takes place after this Act comes into force.

NOTES

Initial Commencement

Specified date
Specified date: 29 August 1990: see sub-s (2) above.

OFFICIAL SECRETS ACT 1989

1989 CHAPTER 6

An Act to replace section 2 of the Official Secrets Act 1911 by provisions protecting more limited classes of official information

[11th May 1989]

BE IT ENACTED by the Queen's most Excellent Majesty, by and with the advice and consent of the Lords Spiritual and Temporal, and Commons, in this present Parliament assembled, and by the authority of the same, as follows:-

1 Security and intelligence

(1) A person who is or has been—
   (a) a member of the security and intelligence services; or
   (b) a person notified that he is subject to the provisions of this subsection,

is guilty of an offence if without lawful authority he discloses any information, document or other article relating to security or intelligence which is or has been in his possession by virtue of his position as a member of any of those services or in the course of his work while the notification is or was in force.

(2) The reference in subsection (1) above to disclosing information relating to security or intelligence includes a reference to making any statement which purports to be a disclosure of such information or is intended to be taken by those to whom it is addressed as being such a disclosure.

(3) A person who is or has been a Crown servant or government contractor is guilty of an offence if without lawful authority he makes a damaging disclosure of any information, document or other article relating to security or intelligence which is or has been in his possession by virtue of his position as such but otherwise than as mentioned in subsection (1) above.

(4) For the purposes of subsection (3) above a disclosure is damaging if—
   (a) it causes damage to the work of, or of any part of, the security and intelligence services; or
   (b) it is of information or a document or other article which is such that its unauthorised disclosure would be likely to cause such damage or which falls within a class or description of information, documents or articles the unauthorised disclosure of which would be likely to have that effect.

(5) It is a defence for a person charged with an offence under this section to prove that at the time of the alleged offence he did not know, and had no reasonable cause to believe, that the information, document or article in question related to security or intelligence or, in the case of an offence under subsection (3), that the disclosure would be damaging within the meaning of that subsection.

(6) Notification that a person is subject to subsection (1) above shall be effected by a notice in writing served on him by a Minister of the Crown; and such a notice may be

Core resources

served if, in the Minister's opinion, the work undertaken by the person in question is or includes work connected with the security and intelligence services and its nature is such that the interests of national security require that he should be subject to the provisions of that subsection.

(7) Subject to subsection (8) below, a notification for the purposes of subsection (1) above shall be in force for the period of five years beginning with the day on which it is served but may be renewed by further notices under subsection (6) above for periods of five years at a time.

(8) A notification for the purposes of subsection (1) above may at any time be revoked by a further notice in writing served by the Minister on the person concerned; and the Minister shall serve such a further notice as soon as, in his opinion, the work undertaken by that person ceases to be such as is mentioned in subsection (6) above.

(9) In this section 'security or intelligence' means the work of, or in support of, the security and intelligence services or any part of them, and references to information relating to security or intelligence include references to information held or transmitted by those services or by persons in support of, or of any part of, them.

NOTES

Initial Commencement

To be appointed
To be appointed: see s 16(6).

Appointment

Appointment: 1 March 1990: see SI 1990/199, art 2.

2 Defence

(1) A person who is or has been a Crown servant or government contractor is guilty of an offence if without lawful authority he makes a damaging disclosure of any information, document or other article relating to defence which is or has been in his possession by virtue of his position as such.

(2) For the purposes of subsection (1) above a disclosure is damaging if—

 (a) it damages the capability of, or of any part of, the armed forces of the Crown to carry out their tasks or leads to loss of life or injury to members of those forces or serious damage to the equipment or installations of those forces; or
 (b) otherwise than as mentioned in paragraph (a) above, it endangers the interests of the United Kingdom abroad, seriously obstructs the promotion or protection by the United Kingdom of those interests or endangers the safety of British citizens abroad; or
 (c) it is of information or of a document or article which is such that its unauthorised disclosure would be likely to have any of those effects.

(3) It is a defence for a person charged with an offence under this section to prove that at the time of the alleged offence he did not know, and had no reasonable cause to believe, that the information, document or article in question related to defence or that its disclosure would be damaging within the meaning of subsection (1) above.

(4) In this section 'defence' means—

 (a) the size, shape, organisation, logistics, order of battle, deployment, operations, state of readiness and training of the armed forces of the Crown;

(b) the weapons, stores or other equipment of those forces and the invention, development, production and operation of such equipment and research relating to it;
(c) defence policy and strategy and military planning and intelligence;
(d) plans and measures for the maintenance of essential supplies and services that are or would be needed in time of war.

NOTES

Initial Commencement

To be appointed
To be appointed: see s 16(6).

Appointment

Appointment: 1 March 1990: see SI 1990/199, art 2.

3 International relations

(1) A person who is or has been a Crown servant or government contractor is guilty of an offence if without lawful authority he makes a damaging disclosure of—

(a) any information, document or other article relating to international relations; or
(b) any confidential information, document or other article which was obtained from a State other than the United Kingdom or an international organisation,

being information or a document or article which is or has been in his possession by virtue of his position as a Crown servant or government contractor.

(2) For the purposes of subsection (1) above a disclosure is damaging if—

(a) it endangers the interests of the United Kingdom abroad, seriously obstructs the promotion or protection by the United Kingdom of those interests or endangers the safety of British citizens abroad; or
(b) it is of information or of a document or article which is such that its unauthorised disclosure would be likely to have any of those effects.

(3) In the case of information or a document or article within subsection (1)(b) above—

(a) the fact that it is confidential, or
(b) its nature or contents,

may be sufficient to establish for the purposes of subsection (2)(b) above that the information, document or article is such that its unauthorised disclosure would be likely to have any of the effects there mentioned.

(4) It is a defence for a person charged with an offence under this section to prove that at the time of the alleged offence he did not know, and had no reasonable cause to believe, that the information, document or article in question was such as is mentioned in subsection (1) above or that its disclosure would be damaging within the meaning of that subsection.

(5) In this section 'international relations' means the relations between States, between international organisations or between one or more States and one or more such organisations and includes any matter relating to a State other than the United Kingdom or to an international organisation which is capable of affecting the relations of the United Kingdom with another State or with an international organisation.

Core resources

(6) For the purposes of this section any information, document or article obtained from a State or organisation is confidential at any time while the terms on which it was obtained require it to be held in confidence or while the circumstances in which it was obtained make it reasonable for the State or organisation to expect that it would be so held.

NOTES

Initial Commencement

To be appointed
To be appointed: see s 16(6).

Appointment

Appointment: 1 March 1990: see SI 1990/199, art 2.

4   Crime and special investigation powers

(1) A person who is or has been a Crown servant or government contractor is guilty of an offence if without lawful authority he discloses any information, document or other article to which this section applies and which is or has been in his possession by virtue of his position as such.

(2) This section applies to any information, document or other article—

   (a) the disclosure of which—
      (i) results in the commission of an offence; or
      (ii) facilitates an escape from legal custody or the doing of any other act prejudicial to the safekeeping of persons in legal custody; or
      (iii) impedes the prevention or detection of offences or the apprehension or prosecution of suspected offenders; or
   (b) which is such that its unauthorised disclosure would be likely to have any of those effects.

(3) This section also applies to—

   (a) any information obtained by reason of the interception of any communication in obedience to a warrant issued under section 2 of the Interception of Communications Act 1985 [or under the authority of an interception warrant under section 5 of the Regulation of Investigatory Powers Act 2000], any information relating to the obtaining of information by reason of any such interception and any document or other article which is or has been used or held for use in, or has been obtained by reason of, any such interception; and
   (b) any information obtained by reason of action authorised by a warrant issued under section 3 of the Security Service Act 1989 [or under section 5 of the Intelligence Services Act 1994 or by an authorisation given under section 7 of that Act], any information relating to the obtaining of information by reason of any such action and any document or other article which is or has been used or held for use in, or has been obtained by reason of, any such action.

(4) It is a defence for a person charged with an offence under this section in respect of a disclosure falling within subsection (2)(a) above to prove that at the time of the alleged offence he did not know, and had no reasonable cause to believe, that the disclosure would have any of the effects there mentioned.

(5) It is a defence for a person charged with an offence under this section in respect of any other disclosure to prove that at the time of the alleged offence he did not know,

and had no reasonable cause to believe, that the information, document or article in question was information or a document or article to which this section applies.

(6) In this section 'legal custody' includes detention in pursuance of any enactment or any instrument made under an enactment.

NOTES

Initial Commencement

To be appointed
To be appointed: see s 16(6).

Appointment

Appointment: 1 March 1990: see SI 1990/199, art 2.

Amendment

Sub-s (3): in para (a) words from 'or under the authority' to 'Investigatory Powers Act 2000' in square brackets inserted by the Regulation of Investigatory Powers Act 2000, s 82(1), Sch 4, para 5.
Date in force: 2 October 2000: see SI 2000/2543, art 3.

Sub-s (3): in para (b) words in square brackets inserted by the Intelligence Services Act 1994, s 11(2), Sch 4, para 4.

5   Information resulting from unauthorised disclosures or entrusted in confidence

(1) Subsection (2) below applies where—
- (a) any information, document or other article protected against disclosure by the foregoing provisions of this Act has come into a person's possession as a result of having been—
    - (i) disclosed (whether to him or another) by a Crown servant or government contractor without lawful authority; or
    - (ii) entrusted to him by a Crown servant or government contractor on terms requiring it to be held in confidence or in circumstances in which the Crown servant or government contractor could reasonably expect that it would be so held; or
    - (iii) disclosed (whether to him or another) without lawful authority by a person to whom it was entrusted as mentioned in sub-paragraph (ii) above; and
- (b) the disclosure without lawful authority of the information, document or article by the person into whose possession it has come is not an offence under any of those provisions.

(2) Subject to subsections (3) and (4) below, the person into whose possession the information, document or article has come is guilty of an offence if he discloses it without lawful authority knowing, or having reasonable cause to believe, that it is protected against disclosure by the foregoing provisions of this Act and that it has come into his possession as mentioned in subsection (1) above.

(3) In the case of information or a document or article protected against disclosure by sections 1 to 3 above, a person does not commit an offence under subsection (2) above unless—
- (a) the disclosure by him is damaging; and

Core resources

    (b)   he makes it knowing, or having reasonable cause to believe, that it would be damaging;

and the question whether a disclosure is damaging shall be determined for the purposes of this subsection as it would be in relation to a disclosure of that information, document or article by a Crown servant in contravention of section 1(3), 2(1) or 3(1) above.

(4) A person does not commit an offence under subsection (2) above in respect of information or a document or other article which has come into his possession as a result of having been disclosed—

    (a)   as mentioned in subsection (1)(a)(i) above by a government contractor; or
    (b)   as mentioned in subsection (1)(a)(iii) above,

unless that disclosure was by a British citizen or took place in the United Kingdom, in any of the Channel Islands or in the Isle of Man or a colony.

(5) For the purposes of this section information or a document or article is protected against disclosure by the foregoing provisions of this Act if—

    (a)   it relates to security or intelligence, defence or international relations within the meaning of section 1, 2 or 3 above or is such as is mentioned in section 3(1)(b) above; or
    (b)   it is information or a document or article to which section 4 above applies;

and information or a document or article is protected against disclosure by sections 1 to 3 above if it falls within paragraph (a) above.

(6) A person is guilty of an offence if without lawful authority he discloses any information, document or other article which he knows, or has reasonable cause to believe, to have come into his possession as a result of a contravention of section 1 of the Official Secrets Act 1911.

NOTES

Initial Commencement

To be appointed
To be appointed: see s 16(6).

Appointment

Appointment: 1 March 1990: see SI 1990/199, art 2.

6   Information entrusted in confidence to other States or international organisations

(1) This section applies where—

    (a)   any information, document or other article which—
        (i)   relates to security or intelligence, defence or international relations; and
        (ii)   has been communicated in confidence by or on behalf of the United Kingdom to another State or to an international organisation,
has come into a person's possession as a result of having been disclosed (whether to him or another) without the authority of that State or organisation or, in the case of an organisation, of a member of it; and
    (b)   the disclosure without lawful authority of the information, document or article by the person into whose possession it has come is not an offence under any of the foregoing provisions of this Act.

(2) Subject to subsection (3) below, the person into whose possession the information, document or article has come is guilty of an offence if he makes a damaging disclosure of it knowing, or having reasonable cause to believe, that it is such as is mentioned in subsection (1) above, that it has come into his possession as there mentioned and that its disclosure would be damaging.

(3) A person does not commit an offence under subsection (2) above if the information, document or article is disclosed by him with lawful authority or has previously been made available to the public with the authority of the State or organisation concerned or, in the case of an organisation, of a member of it.

(4) For the purposes of this section 'security or intelligence', 'defence' and 'international relations' have the same meaning as in sections 1, 2 and 3 above and the question whether a disclosure is damaging shall be determined as it would be in relation to a disclosure of the information, document or article in question by a Crown servant in contravention of section 1(3), 2(1) and 3(1) above.

(5) For the purposes of this section information or a document or article is communicated in confidence if it is communicated on terms requiring it to be held in confidence or in circumstances in which the person communicating it could reasonably expect that it would be so held.

NOTES

Initial Commencement

To be appointed
To be appointed: see s 16(6).

Appointment

Appointment: 1 March 1990: see SI 1990/199, art 2.

7   Authorised disclosures

(1) For the purposes of this Act a disclosure by—
  (a) a Crown servant; or
  (b) a person, not being a Crown servant or government contractor, in whose case a notification for the purposes of section 1(1) above is in force,

is made with lawful authority if, and only if, it is made in accordance with his official duty.

(2) For the purposes of this Act a disclosure by a government contractor is made with lawful authority if, and only if, it is made—
  (a) in accordance with an official authorisation; or
  (b) for the purposes of the functions by virtue of which he is a government contractor and without contravening an official restriction.

(3) For the purposes of this Act a disclosure made by any other person is made with lawful authority if, and only if, it is made—
  (a) to a Crown servant for the purposes of his functions as such; or
  (b) in accordance with an official authorisation.

(4) It is a defence for a person charged with an offence under any of the foregoing provisions of this Act to prove that at the time of the alleged offence he believed that he had lawful authority to make the disclosure in question and had no reasonable cause to believe otherwise.

Core resources

(5) In this section 'official authorisation' and 'official restriction' mean, subject to subsection (6) below, an authorisation or restriction duly given or imposed by a Crown servant or government contractor or by or on behalf of a prescribed body or a body of a prescribed class.

(6) In relation to section 6 above 'official authorisation' includes an authorisation duly given by or on behalf of the State or organisation concerned or, in the case of an organisation, a member of it.

NOTES

Initial Commencement

To be appointed
To be appointed: see s 16(6).

Appointment

Appointment: 1 March 1990: see SI 1990/199, art 2.

Transfer of Functions

Functions under this section: functions under sub-s (5) are transferred, in so far as they are exercisable in or as regards Scotland, to the Scottish Ministers, by the Scotland Act 1998 (Transfer of Functions to the Scottish Ministers etc) Order 1999, SI 1999/1750, art 2, Sch 1.

Subordinate Legislation

Official Secrets Act 1989 (Prescription) Order 1990, SI 1990/200 (made under sub-s (5)).

Official Secrets Act 1989 (Prescription) (Amendment) Order 2003, SI 2003/1918 (made under sub-s (5)).

8 Safeguarding of information

(1) Where a Crown servant or government contractor, by virtue of his position as such, has in his possession or under his control any document or other article which it would be an offence under any of the foregoing provisions of this Act for him to disclose without lawful authority he is guilty of an offence if—

(a) being a Crown servant, he retains the document or article contrary to his official duty; or
(b) being a government contractor, he fails to comply with an official direction for the return or disposal of the document or article,

or if he fails to take such care to prevent the unauthorised disclosure of the document or article as a person in his position may reasonably be expected to take.

(2) It is a defence for a Crown servant charged with an offence under subsection (1)(a) above to prove that at the time of the alleged offence he believed that he was acting in accordance with his official duty and had no reasonable cause to believe otherwise.

(3) In subsections (1) and (2) above references to a Crown servant include any person, not being a Crown servant or government contractor, in whose case a notification for the purposes of section 1(1) above is in force.

(4) Where a person has in his possession or under his control any document or other article which it would be an offence under section 5 above for him to disclose without lawful authority, he is guilty of an offence if—

    (a) he fails to comply with an official direction for its return or disposal; or

    (b) where he obtained it from a Crown servant or government contractor on terms requiring it to be held in confidence or in circumstances in which that servant or contractor could reasonably expect that it would be so held, he fails to take such care to prevent its unauthorised disclosure as a person in his position may reasonably be expected to take.

(5) Where a person has in his possession or under his control any document or other article which it would be an offence under section 6 above for him to disclose without lawful authority, he is guilty of an offence if he fails to comply with an official direction for its return or disposal.

(6) A person is guilty of an offence if he discloses any official information, document or other article which can be used for the purpose of obtaining access to any information, document or other article protected against disclosure by the foregoing provisions of this Act and the circumstances in which it is disclosed are such that it would be reasonable to expect that it might be used for that purpose without authority.

(7) For the purposes of subsection (6) above a person discloses information or a document or article which is official if—

    (a) he has or has had it in his possession by virtue of his position as a Crown servant or government contractor; or

    (b) he knows or has reasonable cause to believe that a Crown servant or government contractor has or has had it in his possession by virtue of his position as such.

(8) Subsection (5) of section 5 above applies for the purposes of subsection (6) above as it applies for the purposes of that section.

(9) In this section 'official direction' means a direction duly given by a Crown servant or government contractor or by or on behalf of a prescribed body or a body of a prescribed class.

NOTES

Initial Commencement

To be appointed
To be appointed: see s 16(6).

Appointment

Appointment: 1 March 1990: see SI 1990/199, art 2.

Transfer of Functions

Functions under this section: functions under sub-s (9) are transferred, in so far as they are exercisable in or as regards Scotland, to the Scottish Ministers, by the Scotland Act 1998 (Transfer of Functions to the Scottish Ministers etc) Order 1999, SI 1999/1750, art 2, Sch 1.

Subordinate Legislation

Official Secrets Act 1989 (Prescription) Order 1990, SI 1990/200 (made under sub-s (9)).

Core resources

Official Secrets Act 1989 (Prescription) (Amendment) Order 2003, SI 2003/1918 (made under sub-s (9)).

9 Prosecutions

(1) Subject to subsection (2) below, no prosecution for an offence under this Act shall be instituted in England and Wales or in Northern Ireland except by or with the consent of the Attorney General or, as the case may be, the *Attorney General for Northern Ireland* [Advocate General for Northern Ireland].

(2) Subsection (1) above does not apply to an offence in respect of any such information, document or article as is mentioned in section 4(2) above but no prosecution for such an offence shall be instituted in England and Wales or in Northern Ireland except by or with the consent of the Director of Public Prosecutions or, as the case may be, the Director of Public Prosecutions for Northern Ireland.

NOTES

Initial Commencement

To be appointed
To be appointed: see s 16(6).

Appointment

Appointment: 1 March 1990: see SI 1990/199, art 2.

Amendment

Sub-s (1): words 'Attorney General for Northern Ireland' in italics repealed and subsequent words in square brackets substituted by the Justice (Northern Ireland) Act 2002, s 28(2), Sch 7, para 32.
Date in force: to be appointed: see the Justice (Northern Ireland) Act 2002, s 87(1).

10 Penalties

(1) A person guilty of an offence under any provision of this Act other than section 8(1), (4) or (5) shall be liable—

   (a) on conviction on indictment, to imprisonment for a term not exceeding two years or a fine or both;
   (b) on summary conviction, to imprisonment for a term not exceeding six months or a fine not exceeding the statutory maximum or both.

(2) A person guilty of an offence under section 8(1), (4) or (5) above shall be liable on summary conviction to imprisonment for a term not exceeding *three months* [51 weeks] or a fine not exceeding level 5 on the standard scale or both.

NOTES

Initial Commencement

To be appointed
To be appointed: see s 16(6).

Appointment

Appointment: 1 March 1990: see SI 1990/199, art 2.

Amendment

Sub-s (2): words 'three months' in italics repealed and subsequent words in square brackets substituted by the Criminal Justice Act 2003, s 280(2), (3), Sch 26, para 39.
Date in force: to be appointed: see the Criminal Justice Act 2003, s 336(3).

11 Arrest, search and trial

(1) ...

(2) Offences under any provision of this Act other than section 8(1), (4) or (5) and attempts to commit them shall be arrestable offences within the meaning of section 2 of the Criminal Law Act (Northern Ireland) 1967.

(3) Section 9(1) of the Official Secrets Act 1911 (search warrants) shall have effect as if references to offences under that Act included references to offences under any provision of this Act other than section 8(1), (4) or (5); and the following provisions of the Police and Criminal Evidence Act 1984, that is to say—

- (a) section 9(2) (which excludes items subject to legal privilege and certain other material from powers of search conferred by previous enactments); and
- (b) paragraph 3(b) of Schedule 1 (which prescribes access conditions for the special procedure laid down in that Schedule),

shall apply to section 9(1) of the said Act of 1911 as extended by this subsection as they apply to that section as originally enacted.

(4) Section 8(4) of the Official Secrets Act 1920 (exclusion of public from hearing on grounds of national safety) shall have effect as if references to offences under that Act included references to offences under any provision of this Act other than section 8(1), (4) or (5).

(5) Proceedings for an offence under this Act may be taken in any place in the United Kingdom.

NOTES

Initial Commencement

To be appointed
To be appointed: see s 16(6).

Appointment

Appointment: 1 March 1990: see SI 1990/199, art 2.

Amendment

Sub-s (1): repealed by the Police Reform Act 2002, s 107(2), Sch 8.
Date in force: 1 October 2002: see SI 2002/2306, art 2(g)(i), (iii)(b).

12 'Crown servant' and 'government contractor'

(1) In this Act 'Crown servant' means—
- (a) a Minister of the Crown;
- [(aa) a member of the Scottish Executive or a junior Scottish Minister;]
- [(ab) the First Minister for Wales, a Welsh Minister appointed under section 48 of the Government of Wales Act 2006, the Counsel General to the Welsh Assembly Government or a Deputy Welsh Minister;]
- (b) ...

Core resources

    (c) any person employed in the civil service of the Crown, including Her Majesty's Diplomatic Service, Her Majesty's Overseas Civil Service, the civil service of Northern Ireland and the Northern Ireland Court Service;

    (d) any member of the naval, military or air forces of the Crown, including any person employed by an association established for the purposes of [Part XI of the Reserve Forces Act 1996];

    (e) any constable and any other person employed or appointed in or for the purposes of any police force [(including the Police Service of Northern Ireland and the Police Service of Northern Ireland Reserve)] [or of the Serious Organised Crime Agency];

    (f) any person who is a member or employee of a prescribed body or a body of a prescribed class and either is prescribed for the purposes of this paragraph or belongs to a prescribed class of members or employees of any such body;

    (g) any person who is the holder of a prescribed office or who is an employee of such a holder and either is prescribed for the purposes of this paragraph or belongs to a prescribed class of such employees.

(2) In this Act 'government contractor' means, subject to subsection (3) below, any person who is not a Crown servant but who provides, or is employed in the provision of, goods or services—

    (a) for the purposes of any Minister or person mentioned in paragraph (a)[, (ab)] or (b) of subsection (1) above, [of any office-holder in the Scottish Administration,] of any of the services, forces or bodies mentioned in that subsection or of the holder of any office prescribed under that subsection;

[(aa) ...] or

    (b) under any agreement or arrangement certified by the Secretary of State as being one to which the government of a State other than the United Kingdom or an international organisation is a party or which is subordinate to, or made for the purposes of implementing, any such agreement or arrangement.

(3) Where an employee or class of employees of any body, or of any holder of an office, is prescribed by an order made for the purposes of subsection (1) above—

    (a) any employee of that body, or of the holder of that office, who is not prescribed or is not within the prescribed class; and

    (b) any person who does not provide, or is not employed in the provision of, goods or services for the purposes of the performance of those functions of the body or the holder of the office in connection with which the employee or prescribed class of employees is engaged,

shall not be a government contractor for the purposes of this Act.

[(4) In this section 'office-holder in the Scottish Administration' has the same meaning as in section 126(7)(a) of the Scotland Act 1998.]

[(4A) In this section the reference to a police force includes a reference to the Civil Nuclear Constabulary.]

[(5) This Act shall apply to the following as it applies to persons falling within the definition of Crown servant—

    (a) the First Minister and deputy First Minister in Northern Ireland; and

    (b) Northern Ireland Ministers and junior Ministers.]

NOTES

Initial Commencement

To be appointed
To be appointed: see s 16(6).

Appointment

Appointment: 1 March 1990: see SI 1990/199, art 2.

Amendment

Sub-s (1): para (aa) inserted by the Scotland Act 1998, s 125, Sch 8, para 26(2).
Date in force: 6 May 1999: see SI 1998/3178, art 2(2), Sch 3.

Sub-s (1): para (ab) inserted by the Government of Wales Act 2006, s 160(1), Sch 10, para 34(a).
Date in force: this amendment came into force on 25 May 2007 being the date on which the initial period ended (following the appointment of the First Minister): see the Government of Wales Act 2006, ss 46, 161(4), (5).

Sub-s (1): para (b) repealed by the Northern Ireland Act 1998, ss 99, 100(2), Sch 13, para 9(1), (2), Sch 15.
Date in force: 2 December 1999: see SI 1999/3209, art 2, Schedule.

Sub-s (1): in para (d) words 'Part XI of the Reserve Forces Act 1996' in square brackets substituted by the Reserve Forces Act 1996, s 131(1), Sch 10, para 22.

Sub-s (1): in para (e) words from '(including the Police' to 'Northern Ireland Reserve)' in square brackets substituted by the Police (Northern Ireland) Act 2000, s 78(1), Sch 6, para 9.
Date in force: 4 November 2001: see the Police (Northern Ireland) Act 2000 (Commencement No 3 and Transitional Provisions) Order 2001, SR 2001/396, art 2, Schedule.

Sub-s (1): in para (e) words 'or of the Serious Organised Crime Agency' in square brackets substituted (for words as inserted by the Police Act 1997, s 134(1), Sch 9, para 62) by the Serious Organised Crime and Police Act 2005, s 59, Sch 4, para 58.
Date in force: 1 April 2006: see SI 2006/378, art 4(1), Schedule, para 10.

Sub-s (2): in para (a) reference to ', (ab)' in square brackets inserted by the Government of Wales Act 2006, s 160(1), Sch 10, para 34(b).
Date in force: this amendment came into force on 25 May 2007 being the date on which the initial period ended (following the appointment of the First Minister): see the Government of Wales Act 2006, ss 46, 161(4), (5).

Sub-s (2): in para (a) words 'of any office-holder in the Scottish Administration,' in square brackets inserted by the Scotland Act 1998, s 125, Sch 8, para 26(3).
Date in force: 6 May 1999: see SI 1998/3178, art 2(2), Sch 3.

Sub-s (2): para (aa) inserted by the Government of Wales Act 1998, s 125, Sch 12, para 30.
Date in force: 1 April 1999: see SI 1999/782, art 2.

Sub-s (2): para (aa) repealed by the Government of Wales Act 2006, ss 160(1), 163, Sch 10, para 34(b), Sch 12.
Date in force: this repeal came into force on 25 May 2007 being the date on which the initial period ended (following the appointment of the First Minister): see the Government of Wales Act 2006, ss 46, 161(4), (5).

Sub-s (4): inserted by the Scotland Act 1998, s 125, Sch 8, para 26(4).
Date in force: 6 May 1999: see SI 1998/3178, art 2(2), Sch 3.

Sub-s (4A): inserted by the Energy Act 2004, s 69(1), Sch 14, para 6.
Date in force: 1 March 2005: see SI 2005/442, art 2(1), Sch 1.

Sub-s (5): inserted by the Northern Ireland Act 1998, s 99, Sch 13, para 9(1), (3).
Date in force: 2 December 1999: see SI 1999/3209, art 2, Schedule.

Core resources

Transfer of Functions

Functions of the Secretary of State, so far as exercisable in relation to Wales, transferred to the National Assembly for Wales, by the National Assembly for Wales (Transfer of Functions) Order 1999, SI 1999/672, art 2, Sch 1.

Functions under this section: functions under this section are transferred, in so far as they are exercisable in or as regards Scotland, to the Scottish Ministers, by the Scotland Act 1998 (Transfer of Functions to the Scottish Ministers etc) Order 1999, SI 1999/1750, art 2, Sch 1.

Subordinate Legislation

Official Secrets Act 1989 (Prescription) Order 1990, SI 1990/200.

Official Secrets Act 1989 (Prescription) (Amendment) Order 1993, SI 1993/847 (made under sub-s (1)(f)).

Official Secrets Act 1989 (Prescription) (Amendment) Order 2003, SI 2003/1918 (made under sub-s (1)(f)).

Official Secrets Act 1989 (Prescription) (Amendment) Order 2007, SI 2007/2148 (made under sub-s (1)(f)).

13 Other interpretation provisions

(1) In this Act—

'disclose' and disclosure', in relation to a document or other article, include parting with possession of it;
'international organisation' means, subject to subsections (2) and (3) below, an organisation of which only States are members and includes a reference to any organ of such an organisation;
'prescribed' means prescribed by an order made by the Secretary of State;
'State' includes the government of a State and any organ of its government and references to a State other than the United Kingdom include references to any territory outside the United Kingdom.

(2) In section 12(2)(b) above the reference to an international organisation includes a reference to any such organisation whether or not one of which only States are members and includes a commercial organisation.

(3) In determining for the purposes of subsection (1) above whether only States are members of an organisation, any member which is itself an organisation of which only States are members, or which is an organ of such an organisation, shall be treated as a State.

NOTES

Initial Commencement

To be appointed
To be appointed: see s 16(6).

Appointment

Appointment: 1 March 1990: see SI 1990/199, art 2.

Transfer of Functions

Functions of the Secretary of State, so far as exercisable in relation to Wales, transferred to the National Assembly for Wales, by the National Assembly for Wales (Transfer of Functions) Order 1999, SI 1999/672, art 2, Sch 1.

14 Orders

(1) Any power of the Secretary of State under this Act to make orders shall be exercisable by statutory instrument.

(2) No order shall be made by him for the purposes of section 7(5), 8(9) or 12 above unless a draft of it has been laid before, and approved by a resolution of, each House of Parliament.

(3) If, apart from the provisions of this subsection, the draft of an order under any of the provisions mentioned in subsection (2) above would be treated for the purposes of the Standing Orders of either House of Parliament as a hybrid instrument it shall proceed in that House as if it were not such an instrument.

NOTES

Initial Commencement

To be appointed
To be appointed: see s 16(6).

Appointment

Appointment: 1 March 1990: see SI 1990/199, art 2.

15 Acts done abroad and extent

(1) Any act—
   (a) done by a British citizen or Crown servant; or
   (b) done by any person in any of the Channel Islands or the Isle of Man or any colony,

shall, if it would be an offence by that person under any provision of this Act other than section 8(1), (4) or (5) when done by him in the United Kingdom, be an offence under that provision.

(2) This Act extends to Northern Ireland.

(3) Her Majesty may by Order in Council provide that any provision of this Act shall extend, with such exceptions, adaptations and modifications as may be specified in the Order, to any of the Channel Islands or the Isle of Man or any colony.

NOTES

Initial Commencement

To be appointed
To be appointed: see s 16(6).

Appointment

Appointment: 1 March 1990: see SI 1990/199, art 2.

Core resources

16 Short title, citation, consequential amendments, repeals, revocation and commencement

(1) This Act may be cited as the Official Secrets Act 1989.

(2) This Act and the Official Secrets Acts 1911 to 1939 may be cited together as the Official Secrets Acts 1911 to 1989.

(3) Schedule 1 to this Act shall have effect for making amendments consequential on the provisions of this Act.

(4) The enactments and Order mentioned in Schedule 2 to this Act are hereby repealed or revoked to the extent specified in the third column of that Schedule.

(5) Subject to any Order under subsection (3) of section 15 above the repeals in the Official Secrets Act 1911 and the Official Secrets Act 1920 do not extend to any of the territories mentioned in that subsection.

(6) This Act shall come into force on such day as the Secretary of State may by order appoint.

NOTES

Initial Commencement

To be appointed
To be appointed: see sub-s (6) above.

Appointment

Appointment: 1 March 1990: see SI 1990/199, art 2.

Subordinate Legislation

Official Secrets Act 1989 (Commencement) Order 1990, SI 1990/199 (made under sub-s (6)).

SCHEDULE 1
CONSEQUENTIAL AMENDMENTS

Section 16(3)

1 < ... >

2 ...

3 ...

4 Any provision in a public service pension scheme (within the meaning of the [Pension Schemes Act 1993] or the [Pension Schemes (Northern Ireland) Act 1993]) which has effect in relation to conviction of an offence under the Official Secrets Acts 1911 to 1939 shall be construed as if the reference to such an offence included a reference to an offence under this Act.

NOTES

Initial Commencement

To be appointed
To be appointed: see s 16(6).

Official Secrets Act 1989

Appointment

Appointment: 1 March 1990: see SI 1990/199, art 2.

Amendment

Para 1: contains amendments only.

Para 1: repealed in part by the Pension Schemes Act 1993, s 188, Sch 5, Pt I.

Para 1: repealed in part by the Pension Schemes (Northern Ireland) Act 1993, s 189, Sch 4, Pt I.

Para 1: repealed in part by the Health Service Commissioners Act 1993, s 20, Sch 3.

Para 1: repealed in part by SI 1996/1297, art 23(3), Sch 5.

Para 1: repealed in part by SI 1996/1298, art 21(2), Sch 6.

Para 1: repealed in part by the Scottish Public Services Ombudsman Act 2002, s 25(1), Sch 6, para 12.
Date in force: 23 October 2002: see SSI 2002/467, art 2.

Para 2: repealed by the Northern Ireland (Emergency Provisions) Act 1991, s 70(4), Sch 8.

Para 3: repealed by the Regulation of Investigatory Powers Act 2000, s 82(2), Sch 5.
Date in force: 2 October 2000: see SI 2000/2543, art 3.

Para 4: first words in square brackets substituted by the Pension Schemes Act 1993, s 190, Sch 8, para 21; final words in square brackets substituted by the Pension Schemes (Northern Ireland) Act 1993, s 184, Sch 7.

SCHEDULE 2
REPEALS AND REVOCATION

Section 16(4)

Chapter	Short title	Extent of repeal
1911 c 28	The Official Secrets Act 1911.	Section 2. In section 12, in the paragraph beginning 'Expressions referring', the words 'or receiving' (in both places where they occur) and 'or received'.
1920 c 75.	The Official Secrets Act 1920.	Section 9(1). In Schedule 1, the amendments of section 2 of the Official Secrets Act 1911.
1946 c 27.	The Bank of England Act 1946.	Section 4(4) and (5).
1954 c 32.	The Atomic Energy Authority Act 1954.	In Schedule 3, the words from 'For the purposes of section 2 of the Official Secrets Act 1911' to 'shall be deemed to be a contract with Her Majesty'.
1965 c 57.	The Nuclear Installations Act 1965.	In Schedule 1, paragraph 2.
1967 c 13.	The Parliamentary Commissioner Act 1967.	Section 11(1).

Core resources

1969 c 48.	The Post Office Act 1969.	In Schedule 4, in paragraph 21(1), the words from the beginning to 'Her Majesty; and'.
1969 c 10 (NI).	The Parliamentary Commissioner Act (Northern Ireland) 1969.	Section 11(1).
1969 c 25 (NI).	The Commissioner for Complaints Act (Northern Ireland) 1969.	Section 12(1).
1970 c 46.	The Radiological Protection Act 1970.	Sections 2(8) and 4(7).
1971 c 11.	The Atomic Energy Authority Act 1971.	In section 19(1) the words '2 and'. In the Schedule, paragraph 2.
1977 c 49.	The National Health Service Act 1977.	In Schedule 13, paragraph 15.
1982 c 16.	The Civil Aviation Act 1982.	Section 18(1).
1983 c 44.	The National Audit Act 1983.	In section 3(5) the words 'Except for the purposes of section 2 of the Official Secrets Act 1911 (wrongful communication of information)'.
1984 c 12.	The Telecommunications Act 1984.	In Schedule 4, paragraph 12(1).
1984 c 35.	The Data Protection Act 1984.	Section 17(2) and (3). In Schedule 2, in paragraph 1(2) the words 'Except as provided in section 17(2) of this Act'.
1985 c 56.	The Interception of Communications Act 1985.	In section 9(4)(b) the words 'or 2'.

Number	Title	Extent of revocation
SI 1987/460 (NI 5).	The Audit (Northern Ireland) Order 1987.	In Schedule 1, in paragraph 3(3) the words 'Except for the purposes of section 2 of the Official Secrets Act 1911 (wrongful communication of information)'.

NOTES

Initial Commencement

To be appointed
To be appointed: see s 16(6).

Appointment

Appointment: 1 March 1990: see SI 1990/199, art 2.

COMMUNICATION FROM THE COMMISSION TO THE EUROPEAN PARLIAMENT AND THE COUNCIL ON PROMOTING DATA PROTECTION BY PRIVACY ENHANCING TECHNOLOGIES (PETS) – BRUSSELS, 2.5.2007, COM(2007) 228 FINAL

COMMISSION OF THE EUROPEAN COMMUNITIES

Brussels, 2.5.2007
COM(2007) 228 final

COMMUNICATION FROM THE COMMISSION TO THE EUROPEAN PARLIAMENT AND THE COUNCIL

on Promoting Data Protection by Privacy Enhancing Technologies (PETs)

Core resources

COMMUNICATION FROM THE COMMISSION TO THE EUROPEAN PARLIAMENT AND THE COUNCIL

on Promoting Data Protection by Privacy Enhancing Technologies (PETs)

(Text with EEA relevance)

1. INTRODUCTION

The intensive and sustained development of information and communication technologies (ICT) is constantly offering new services which improve people's life. To a large extent, the raw material for interactions in cyberspace is the personal data of individuals moving around in it when they purchase goods and services, establish or maintain contact with others or communicate their ideas on the world wide web. Alongside the benefits brought about by these developments, new risks also arise for the individual, such as identity theft, discriminatory profiling, continuous surveillance or fraud.

The Charter of Fundamental Rights of the European Union recognises in Article 8 the right to the protection of personal data. This fundamental right is set forth in a European legal framework on the protection of personal data consisting in particular of the Data Protection Directive 95/46/EC[1] and the ePrivacy Directive 2002/58/EC[2] as well as the Data Protection Regulation (EC) 45/2001[3] relating to processing by Community institution and bodies. This legislation lays down several substantive provisions imposing obligations on data controllers and recognizing rights of data subjects. It also prescribes sanctions and appropriate remedies in cases of breach and establishes enforcement mechanisms to make them effective.

However, this system may prove insufficient when personal data is disseminated worldwide through ICT networks and the processing of data crosses several jurisdictions, often outside the EU. In such situations the current rules may be considered to apply and to provide a clear legal response. Furthermore, a competent authority to enforce the rules may also be identified. However, considerable practical obstacles may exist as a result of difficulties with the technology used involving data processing by different actors in different locations and there may be hurdles intrinsic to the enforcement of national administrative and court rulings in another jurisdiction, especially in non-EU countries.

Whilst strictly speaking data controllers bear the legal responsibility for complying with data protection rules, others also bear some responsibility for data protection from a societal and

---

[1] Directive 95/46/EC of the European Parliament and of the Council of 24 October 1995 on the protection of individuals with regard to the processing of personal data and on the free movement of such data, OJ L 281, 23.11.1995, p. 31.
[2] Directive 2002/58/EC of the European Parliament and of the Council of 12 July 2002 concerning the processing of personal data and the protection of privacy in the electronic communications sector (Directive on privacy and electronic communications), OJ L 201, 31.07.2002, p. 37.
[3] Regulation (EC) 45/2001 of the European Parliament and of the Council of 18 December 2000 on the protection of individuals with regard to the processing of personal data by the Community institutions and bodies and on the free movement of such data, OJ L 8, 12.1.2001, p. 1-22.

ethical point of view. These involve those who design technical specifications and those who actually build or implement applications or operating systems.

Article 17 of the Data Protection Directive lays down the data controller's obligation to implement appropriate technical and organisational measures and to ensure a level of security appropriate to the nature of the data and the risks of processing it. The use of technology to support the respect for legislation, in particular the data protection rules, is already envisaged to some extent in the ePrivacy Directive[4].

A further step to pursue the aim of the legal framework, whose objective is to minimise the processing of personal data and using anonymous or pseudonymous data where possible, could be supported by measures called Privacy Enhancing Technologies or PETs - that would facilitate ensuring that breaches of the data protection rules and violations of individual's rights are not only something forbidden and subject to sanctions, but technically more difficult.

The purpose of this Communication, which follows from the First Report on the implementation of the Data Protection Directive[5], is to consider the benefits of PETs, lay down the Commission's objectives in this field to promote these technologies, and set out clear actions to achieve this goal by supporting the development of PETs and their use by data controllers and consumers.

2. WHAT ARE PETS?

There are a number of definitions of PETs used by the academic community and by pilot projects on this matter. For instance, according to the EC-funded PISA project, PET stands for a coherent system of ICT measures that protects privacy by eliminating or reducing personal data or by preventing unnecessary and/or undesired processing of personal data, all without losing the functionality of the information system. The use of PETs can help to design information and communication systems and services in a way that minimises the collection and use of personal data and facilitate compliance with data protection rules. The Commission in its First Report on the implementation of the Data Protection Directive considers that "...*the use of appropriate technological measures is an essential complement to legal means and should be an integral part in any efforts to achieve a sufficient level of privacy protection...*". The use of PETs should result in making breaches of certain data protection rules more difficult and/or helping to detect them.

In the dynamic landscape of ICT, the effectiveness of different PETs to ensure the protection of privacy, including aspects of compliance with data protection law, is varied and changes over time. Their typology is also varied. They can be stand-alone tools requiring positive action by consumers (who must purchase and install them in their PCs) or be built into the very architecture of information systems. Several examples of PETs can be mentioned here:

- Automatic anonymisation of data, after a certain lapse of time, supports the principle that processed data should be kept in a form which permits identification of data subjects for no longer than necessary for the purposes for which the data were originally collected.

---

[4] Recital 46 and Article 14(3) of Directive 2002/58/EC
[5] COM (2003) 265(01), 15.5.2003, see
http://eurlex.europa.eu/LexUriServ/site/en/com/2003/com2003_0265en01.pdf

Core resources

- Encryption tools, preventing hacking when information is transmitted over the Internet, supports the data controller's obligation to take appropriate measures to protect personal data against unlawful processing.

- Cookie-cutters, that block cookies placed on the user's PC to make it perform certain instructions without the user being aware of them, enhance compliance with the principle that data must be processed fairly and lawfully, and that the data subject must be informed about the processing going on.

- The Platform for Privacy Preferences (P3P), allowing internet users to analyze the privacy policies of websites and compare them with the user's preferences as to the information they wish to release, helps to ensure that data subjects' consent to processing of their data is an informed one.

3. THE COMMISSION SUPPORTS PETs

The Commission considers that PETs should be developed and more widely used, in particular where personal data is processed through ICT networks. The Commission considers that wider use of PETs would improve the protection of privacy as well as help fulfil data protection rules. The use of PETs would be complementary to the existing legal framework and enforcement mechanisms.

In its Communication on a strategy for a secure Information Society, COM(2006) 251 of 31 May 2006, the Commission invited in particular the private sector to *"stimulate the deployment of security-enhancing products, processes and services to prevent and fight ID theft and other privacy-intrusive attacks"*. Furthermore, in the Commission's Roadmap for a pan-European eIDM Framework by 2010[6] one of the key principles governing electronic identity management is that *"the system must be secure, implement the necessary safeguards to protect the user's privacy, and allow its usage to be aligned with local interest and sensitivities"*.

The intervention of different actors in data processing and the existence of different national jurisdictions involved could make enforcement of the legal framework difficult. On the other hand, PETs could ensure that certain breaches of data protection rules, resulting in invasions of fundamental rights including privacy, could be avoided because they would become technologically more difficult to carry out. The Commission is aware of the fact that technology – although having a crucial role in privacy protection – is not sufficient in itself to secure privacy. PETs need to be applied according to a regulatory framework of enforceable data protection rules providing a number of negotiable levels of privacy protection for all individuals. The use of PETs does not mean that operators can be discharged of certain of their legal obligations (e.g. granting individual users a right of access to their data).

Important public interests could also be better served. The data protection legal framework provides for restrictions to the general principles and interference in the rights of individuals for important public interests such as public security, the fight against crime or public health. The conditions for such restrictions are laid down in Article 13 of the Data Protection Directive and Article 15 of the ePrivacy Directive. They are substantially similar to those set

---

[6] http://ec.europa.eu/information_society/activities/egovernment_research/doc/eidm_roadmap_paper.pdf

by Article 8 of the European Convention on Human Rights (ECHR), namely that such interference is done in accordance with the law and is proportionate and necessary in a democratic society for a legitimate public purpose[7]. The use of PETs should not prevent law enforcement agencies or other competent authorities from intervening in the lawful exercise of their functions for an important public interest, e.g. fighting cybercrime, combating terrorism or preventing the spread of contagious diseases. The responsible authorities should be in a position to access personal data where necessary to achieve those purposes and in accordance with the procedures, conditions and safeguards laid down by the law.

Better respect of data protection rules would also have a positive impact on consumer trust, in particular in cyberspace. A number of promising and value-added services that rely on transfers of personal data across IT-Networks, such as e-learning, e-government, e-health, e-banking, e-commerce or "intelligent car" systems would certainly benefit. People could be sure that the data they are providing to identify themselves, receive services or make payments will only be used for legitimate purposes and that their participation in the digital community is not done at the expense of sacrificing their rights.

4. WORK DONE AND THE WAY FORWARD

To pursue the objective of enhancing the level of privacy and data protection in the Community by, among others, promoting the development and the use of PETs, the Commission intends to conduct the following activities, involving a vast array of actors, including its own services, national authorities, industry and consumers.

In these discussions attention will be given to the specific situation of small and medium-sized enterprises (SMEs) and the possibilities or incentives for their use of PETs. The Commission should also, among other issues, consider trust and awareness - issues which are of particular importance to SMEs.

4.1. First objective: to support the development of PETs

If PETs are to be widely used, there needs to be further design, development and manufacturing of PETs. Whilst these activities are already done to a certain degree by the public and private sector the Commission considers that these activities should be stepped up. With this aim in mind, the need for PETs and their technological requirements should be identified and RTD activities should develop the tools.

4.1.1. Action 1.1.: Identifying the need and technological requirements of PETs

PETs are heavily dependent on the evolution of ICT. Once the dangers posed by technological developments are detected, the appropriate requirements for a technological solution must be identified.

The Commission will encourage various stakeholder groups to come together and debate PETs. These groups will include in particular representatives from the ICT sector, PETs developers, data protection authorities, law enforcement bodies, technology partners including experts from relevant fields, such as eHealth or information security, consumers and civil

---

[7] European Court of Justice, judgment of 20.5.2003, Joined cases C-465/00, C-138/01 and C-139/01 "Österreichischer Rundfunk and Others" ("Rechnungshof") ECR [2003] I-04989, paragraphs 71 and 72.

Core resources

rights associations. These stakeholders should regularly look into the evolution of technology, detect the dangers it poses to fundamental rights and data protection, and outline the technical requirements of a PETs response. .This may include fine-tuning the technological measures in accordance with the different risks and the different data at stake and taking into account the need to safeguard public interests, such as public security.

4.1.2. Action 1.2.: Developing PETs

As the need for and technological requirements of PETs are identified, concrete action has to be taken to arrive at an end-product ready to use.

The Commission has already addressed the need for PETs. Under the auspices of the 6th Framework Programme it sponsors the PRIME[8] project tackling issues of digital identity management and privacy in the information society. The OPEN-TC[9] project will allow privacy protection based on open trusted computing and the DISCREET[10] project develops middleware to enforce privacy in advanced network services. In the future, under the 7th Framework Programme, the Commission intends to support other RTD projects and large-scale pilot demonstrations to develop and stimulate the uptake of PETs. The aim is to provide the foundation for user-empowering privacy protection services reconciling legal and technical differences across Europe through public-private partnerships.

The Commission also calls on national authorities and on the private sector to invest in the development of PETs. Such investment is key to placing European industry ahead in a sector that will grow as these technologies become increasingly required by technological standards and by consumers more aware of the need to protect their rights in cyberspace.

4.2. Second objective: to support the use of available PETs by data controllers

PETs will only be truly beneficial if they are effectively incorporated into and used by technical equipment and software tools that carry out processing of personal data. The participation of the industry that manufactures such equipment and of data controllers who avail themselves of it to carry out data processing activities is therefore paramount.

4.2.1. Action 2.1.: Promoting the use of PETs by industry

The Commission believes that all those involved in processing of personal data would benefit from a wider use of PETs. The ICT industry, as the primary developer and provider of PETs, has a particularly important role to play with respect to the promotion of PETs. The Commission calls on all data controllers to more widely and intensely incorporate and apply PETs in their processes. For that purpose, the Commission will organise seminars with key actors of the ICT industry, and in particular PETs developers, with the aim of analyzing their possible contribution to promoting the use of PETs among data controllers.

The Commission will also conduct a study on the economic benefits of PETs and disseminate its results in order to encourage enterprises, in particular SMEs, to use them.

---

[8] https://www.prime-project.eu/
[9] http://www.opentc.net/
[10] http://www.ist-discreet.org/

4.2.2. Action 2.2.: Ensuring respect for appropriate standards in the protection of personal data through PETs

While wide-reaching promotional activity requires the active involvement of the ICT industry, as the PETs producer, respect for appropriate standards requires action beyond self-regulation or the goodwill of the actors involved. The Commission will assess the need to develop standards regarding the lawful processing of personal data with PETs through appropriate impact assessments. On the basis of the outcome of such assessments, two sorts of instruments might be considered:

- *Action 2.2.a) Standardisation*

The Commission will consider the need for respect of data protection rules to be taken into account in standardisation activities. The Commission will endeavour to take account of the input of the multi-stakeholder debate on PETs in preparing the corresponding Commission actions and the work of the European standardisation bodies. This will be paramount, in particular, where the debate identifies appropriate data protection standards requiring the incorporation and use of certain PETs.

The Commission may invite the European Standardisation Organisations (CEN, CENELEC, ETSI) to assess specific European needs, and to subsequently bring them to the international level by means of applying the current agreements between European and international standardisation organisations. Where appropriate, the ESOs should establish a specific standardisation work programme covering European needs and thus complementing the on-going work at international level.

- *Action 2.2.b) Coordination of national technical rules on security measures for data processing*

National legislation adopted pursuant to the Data Protection Directive[11] gives national data protection authorities certain influence in determining precise technical requirements such as providing guidance for controllers, examining the systems put in place or issuing technical instructions. National data protection authorities could also require the incorporation and use of certain PETs where the processing of personal data involved makes them necessary. The Commission considers that this is an area where coordination of national practice could contribute positively to promoting the use of PETs. In particular the Article 29 Working Party[12] could contribute in its role of considering the uniform application of national measures adopted under the Directive. The Commission thus calls on the Article 29 Working Party to continue its work in the field by including in its programme a permanent activity of analysing the needs for incorporating PETs in data processing operations as an effective means of ensuring respect for data protection rules. This work should then produce guidelines for data protection authorities to implement at national level through coordinated adoption of the appropriate instruments.

---

[11] e.g. Article 17
[12] Working Party on the Protection of Individuals with regard to the Processing of Personal Data set up by Article 29 of Directive 95/46/EC.

Core resources

4.2.3. Action 2.3.: Promoting the use of PETs by public authorities

A consistent number of processing operations involving personal data are conducted by public authorities in the exercise of their competences, both at national and at Community level. Public bodies are themselves bound to respect fundamental rights, including the right to protect personal data, and ensure respect by others, and should therefore set a clear example.

As regards national authorities, the Commission notes the proliferation of eGoverment applications as a tool for enhancing effectiveness of public service. As stated in the *Commission's Communication on the Role of eGoverment for Europe's Future*[13], the use of PETs in eGovernment is necessary to provide trust and confidence to ensure its success. The Commission calls upon governments to ensure that data protection safeguards are embedded in eGovernment applications, including through the widest possible use of PETs in their design and implementation.

As for Community institutions and bodies, the Commission itself will ensure that it complies with the requirements of Regulation (EC) 45/2001 in particular through a wider use of PETs in the implementation of ICT applications involving the processing of personal data. At the same time, the Commission calls on other EU institutions to do the same. The European Data Protection Supervisor could contribute with his advice to Community institutions and bodies on drawing up internal rules relating to the processing of personal data. When selecting new ICT applications for its own use, or when developing existing applications, the Commission will consider the possibility of introducing privacy enhancing technologies. The importance of PETs will be reflected in the Commissions' overall IT governance strategy. The Commission will also continue to raise awareness in its own staff. However, the implementation of PETs in the Commissions' ICT applications depends on the availability of the corresponding products and will have to be evaluated on a case by case basis, in line with the application's development cycle.

4.3. Third objective: to encourage consumers to use PETs

Consumers will remain the most concerned party in ensuring personal information is properly used, that data protection rules are properly enacted, and that PETs are an efficient means to guarantee them.

Consumers should therefore be made fully aware of the advantages that the use of PETs may bring to diminish the risks posed by operations involving processing of their personal data. They should also be placed in a position where they may exercise an informed choice when purchasing IT equipment and software, or using e-services. This should reflect their awareness of the risks involved, in particular whether PETs offer appropriate protection. Simple and understandable information about possible technological tools to protect privacy must thus be provided to the user. Increased use of PETs and increased use of e-services which incorporate PETs will in turn mean economic reward to the industries using them, and may result in a snowball effect, encouraging other companies to pay greater attention to respecting the data protection rules. In order to achieve this, a series of steps should be taken.

---

[13] COM (2003) 567 final, 26.9.2003.

4.3.1. Action 3.1.: Raising awareness of consumers

A consistent strategy should be adopted to raise consumer awareness of the risks involved in processing their data and of the solutions that PETs may provide as a complement to the existing systems of remedies contained in data protection legislation. The Commission intends to launch a series of EU-wide awareness-raising activities on PETs.

The main responsibility for conducting this activity falls within the realm of national data protection authorities which already have relevant experience in this area. The Commission calls on them to increase their awareness-raising activities to include information on PETs through all possible means within their reach. The Commission also urges the Article 29 Working Party to coordinate national practice in a coherent work plan for awareness-raising on PETs and to serve as a meeting point for the sharing of good practice already in place at national level. In particular, consumer associations and other players such as the Consumer Centres Network (ECC-Net), in its role as an EU-wide network to advise citizens on their rights as consumers, could become partners in the quest to educate consumers.

4.3.2. Action 3.2.: Facilitating consumers' informed choice: Privacy Seals

The take-up and use of PETs could be encouraged if the presence of these technologies in a certain product and its basic features are easily recognizable. For that purpose, the Commission intends to investigate the feasibility of an EU-wide system of privacy seals, which would also include an economic and societal impact analysis. The purpose of such privacy seals would be to ensure consumers can easily identify a certain product as ensuring or enhancing data protection rules in the processing of data, in particular by incorporating appropriate PETs.

In order for privacy seals to achieve their purpose, the Commission considers that the following principles should be respected:

– The number of privacy seal systems should be kept to a minimum. In fact, a proliferation of seals may create more confusion to the consumer and undermine their trust in all seals. Therefore, an assessment should be made about whether and to what extent it would be appropriate to integrate a European privacy seal in a more general security certification scheme[14].

– Privacy seals should only be awarded for a product's compliance with a set of standards corresponding to data protection rules. The standards should be as uniform as possible throughout the EU.

– Public authorities, in particular national data protection authorities, should play an important role in the system through their involvement in the definition of relevant standards and procedures as well as in monitoring the functioning of the seal system.

With this in mind, and taking account of previous experience concerning seal programmes in other areas (e.g. environment, agriculture, security certification for products and services), the

---

[14] In its Communication of 31 May 2006 on a Strategy for a secure Information Society "Dialogue, partnership and empowerment"(COM (2006) 251 final), the Commission has already invited the private sector to "work towards affordable security certification schemes for products, processes and services that will address EU-specific needs (in particular with respect to privacy)".

Core resources

Commission will conduct a dialogue with all the stakeholders concerned, including national data protection authorities, industrial and consumer associations and standardisation bodies.

HMG SECURITY POLICY FRAMEWORK, VERSION 2.0, MAY 2009

CabinetOffice

v.2.0
May 09

HMG Security Policy Framework

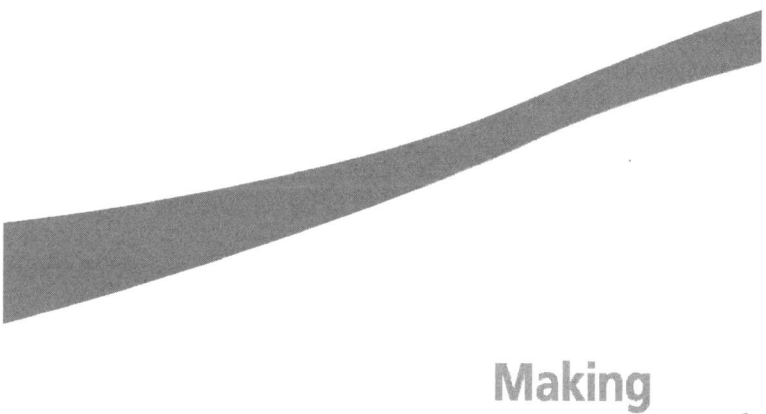

Making **government** work better

© Crown copyright. Reproduced by permission of Her Majesty's Stationery Office. Published by LexisNexis 2009.

Core resources

HMG Security Policy Framework		v.2.0
		May 09

# Contents					Page

Foreword by Sir Gus O' Donnell	5
Introduction to the Security Policy Framework	7 - 8
Overarching Security Policy Statement	9
Core Security Principles	9
Security Policy No. 1: Governance, Risk Management and Compliance	10-16
Security Policy No. 2: Protective Marking and Asset Control	17 -28
Security Policy No. 3: Personnel Security	29-34
Security Policy No. 4: Information Security and Assurance	35-43
Security Policy No. 5: Physical Security	44-50
Security Policy No. 6: Counter-Terrorism	51-56
Security Policy No. 7: Business Continuity	57-59
Version History	60
Contact Details	60

HMG Security Policy Framework

Foreword by Sir Gus O'Donnell

Effective security is central to how we handle many of the challenges facing Government. It is vital for public confidence and for the efficient, effective and safe conduct of public business.

Responsibility for security is delegated down from the Prime Minister and Cabinet to me, as Head of the Home Civil Service and chairman of the Official Committee on Security, and then to Heads of Department. Ultimately, however, security is the responsibility of everyone and our policies and processes will only work well if we all play our part.

The new Security Policy Framework replaces the Manual of Protective Security and the Counter-Terrorist Protective Security Manual. It sets out universal mandatory standards, as well as offering guidance on risk management and defining new compliance and assurance arrangements. For the first time the framework allows for much of this material to be placed in the public domain, allowing greater access, increasing awareness, transparency and sharing good practice.

The framework introduces changes in the way we do things, as part of our broader agenda to modernise and transform Government. Work to modernise security policy and processes will continue: to raise awareness, ensure that guidance is up to date, that policy reflects changes in threat and circumstance, and that Departments are supported from the centre.

I am confident that this framework will enable Government to do its job better and I commend it to all in the public service.

Gus O'Donnell

Core resources

HMG Security Policy Framework

v.2.0
May 09

Introduction

The Security Policy Framework (SPF) represents a new and innovative approach to protective security and risk management in government. The SPF has a solid policy basis, taking and adapting much of the Manual of Protective Security (MPS) and the Counter-Terrorist Protective Security Manual (CTPSM).

Whilst much of the existing policy within those manuals has found its way into the new framework, it must be noted that the SPF represents a new approach. It is vital that organisations understand that the SPF cannot simply be applied as their own departmental security policy, but that it must be used, adapted and applied in framing departmental security policies to meet the specific business needs of the organisation and its delivery partners.

In general terms the framework is aimed primarily at Government Departments and Agencies in supporting its protective security and counter-terrorism responsibilities; however, it does have wider application. The commercial sector plays an increasingly intimate role within the UK government matrix, as well as making up the core sectors within the Critical National Infrastructure (energy, water, agriculture, etc). Similarly, organisations such as the National Health Service, Police forces and local Government all handle government assets on a regular basis.

It should be noted for contractual purposes that any general reference to MPS or CTPSM should now be considered as the SPF. As there have been no fundamental changes in policy it is felt that there should be no requirement to re-negotiate existing contracts on this basis

The SPF has four tiers, or levels, each representing a key element (of increasing detail) within the Government's protective security system. First and foremost, is that security not only supports business goals, but must proactively be considered a business enabler, making government work better, safer and more confidently. Next are a set of five core security principles, highlighting accountability at senior levels, collective responsibility of all staff and contractors, and the need to employ trustworthy people. At the third tier is a series of concise key policy documents, which clearly identify (by highlighting in green boxed text), the minimum mandatory requirements. These standards include the new 'Data Handling Procedures in Government' published by Cabinet Office in June 2008, which have now been formalised into a new Information Assurance Standard (IA Standard no.6); 'Handling Personal Data and Managing Information Risk. It is important to stress here that these are the minimum requirements; it is expected that many Departments and Agencies will manage their specific security risks over and above these baseline measures, using sound risk management principles as outlined within the framework.

These higher levels, particularly tier three, provide the fundamentals of security policy and represent the essence of the framework. They have been made publicly available (http://www.cabinetoffice.gov.uk/spf) representing our commitment to transparency and openness, but also and perhaps more importantly, to support a cultural shift required to ensure that security and risk management are given sufficient prominence in all areas and at all levels of business across Government.

The tier four level of the framework is aimed primarily at the security practitioner; containing an assortment of detailed technical standards, supplementary policy and guidance, as well as references to other security and risk management websites and organisations. Much of this material is protected and will only be made available to those who have a legitimate 'need to know' through secure web access. However, where there is universally applicability, added value, and no increase in vulnerability, material has been made publicly accessible at this level. Tier 4 provides the tools to support the core policy and principles, the material will be fluid, being up dated regularly to meet specific vulnerabilities and adapted to the changing threat picture.

To this extent the principles, core values and minimum requirements expressed within the SPF are highly and widely applicable.

Compliance arrangements and assurance mechanisms are based around three elements: self assessment, central reporting and internal audit. Departments and Agencies will continue to decide on their own arrangements for assuring themselves of their security standards and the SPF provides guidance on this; however, Departments will also be required, in the form of an annual security assessment, to report to Cabinet Office on compliance with the minimum mandatory requirements. Further assurance is provided by internal audit committee's recognition of the SPF, and that the policies therein can inform internal audit assessment programmes. It must be noted that any weakness or non-compliance will need to be addressed in the Departmental Statement of Internal Control; a publicly available document.

The information collected by the Cabinet Office annual security assessment, will, along with other data, be used to inform an annual Security report to the Official Committee on Security, (SO) chaired by the Cabinet Secretary.

This has been a truly collective and co-ordinated exercise, drawing on technical policy and operational experts from across the security community. Particular thanks must go to the Centre for Protection of National Infrastructure (CPNI), based within the Security Service and the National Technical Authority for Information Assurance (CESG) based within the Government Communication Headquarters, who have provided expertise and support to the Cabinet Office's Security Policy Division.

Core resources

HMG Security Policy Framework

v.2.0
May 09

Overarching Security Statement

Protective Security, including physical, personnel and information security, is an essential enabler to making government work better. Security risks must be managed effectively, collectively and proportionately, to achieve a secure and confident working environment.

Core Security Principles

1. Ultimate responsibility for HMG security policy lies with the Prime Minister and the Cabinet Office. Departments and Agencies, via their Permanent Secretaries and Chief Executives, must manage their security risks within the parameters set out in this framework, as endorsed by the Official Committee on Security (SO).

2. All HMG employees (including contractors) have a collective responsibility to ensure that government assets (information, property and staff) are protected in a proportionate manner from terrorist attack, and other illegal or malicious activity.

3. Departments and Agencies must be able to share information (including personal data) confidently knowing it is reliable, accessible and protected to agreed standards.

4. Departments and Agencies must employ staff (and contractors) in whom they can have confidence and whose identities are assured.

5. HMG business needs to be resilient in the face of major disruptive events, with plans in place to minimise damage and rapidly recover capabilities.

Security Policy No.1: Governance, Risk Management and Compliance

1. This is the first of seven Security Policies within the HMG Security Policy Framework (SPF); outlining the mandatory security requirements and management arrangements to which all Departments and Agencies (defined as including all bodies directly responsible to them) **must** adhere.

Governance

2. Governance arrangements for security rely on the partnership between the centre of Government, Departments and Agencies, their delivery partners, individuals working in the security community, and ultimately all staff employed on behalf of HMG. The role of Cabinet Office at the centre of Government is to provide leadership and co-ordination of shared risks (such as asset control and vetting) by setting policy and overseeing regulation. Departments are responsible for the protection and utilisation of their assets – information, personnel and physical – as appropriate to their business needs and circumstance. Departments are best placed to assess the risks they face, and must develop their own security policies in line with this framework. It is for the Centre to set minimum measures, providing an agreed level of protection and assurance across Government.

3. The Security Policy Framework (SPF) outlines mandatory security policy requirements that all Departments and Agencies must meet. This framework should also be extended, where necessary, to any organisations working on behalf of, or handling HMG assets, such as Non-Departmental Public Bodies (NDPBs), contractors, Emergency Services, devolved administrations, Local Authorities, or any regular suppliers of goods and / or services. In areas where statutory security requirements apply (e.g. air safety, nuclear security) this framework must be applied in line with those requirements. Departmental Security Officers (DSOs) (in consultation with the Senior Information Risk Owner (SIRO) as necessary) will need to determine where and what level of compliance is required of their delivery partners, and where equivalent

Core resources

security policies are acceptable. This policy is supplemented by detailed advice and guidance which the DSO can distribute on a 'need to know' basis.

> **MANDATORY REQUIREMENT 1**
> Departments and Agencies must ensure that all staff understand the relevant requirements and responsibilities placed upon them by the Security Policy Framework and that they are properly equipped to meet the mandatory security policies (green boxes) as set out in this framework.
>
> Where Departments, Agencies and their contractors are subject to statutory security requirements, such requirements shall take precedence. The requirements set by security regulators and actions carried out by them will be consistent with this framework.

> **MANDATORY REQUIREMENT 2**
> Departments must ensure that their Agencies and main delivery partners are compliant with this framework, and must consider the extent to which those providing other goods and / or services to them, or carrying out functions on their behalf, are required to comply.

Cabinet Office leadership

4. The Official Committee on Security (SO) is responsible for formulating security policy and coordinating its application across government. SO is also the National Security Authority for dealing with international organisations such as NATO and the EU. Cabinet Office Security Policy Division (COSPD) provides the secretariat for SO and is responsible for developing and communicating this framework, ensuring compliance with the minimum requirements, supporting Departments and preparing an annual report to SO on the state of security across Government. COSPD works closely with the security and intelligence community in developing and reviewing security policy.

Roles, accountability and responsibilities

5. Whilst security is a collective responsibility for all staff and contractors, ultimate responsibility for security rests with Ministers, Permanent Secretaries, and / or other Accounting Officers and their respective Management Boards which must include a Senior Information Risk Owner (SIRO). Cabinet Office will write to newly appointed Heads of Department setting out their responsibilities with regard to security – the Head of Department/Permanent Secretary is ultimately accountable for security within their Department. The Prime Minister and the Cabinet Secretary have ultimate responsibility for ensuring overall coherence of security across Government, and that security objectives are met.

> **MANDATORY REQUIREMENT 3**
> Departments must have a stated Board level representative responsible for security (e.g. Head of Department/Permanent Secretary). Departments must identify clearly where security responsibilities lie, including the relationship between the Department's main Board and the Boards of their Agencies or other bodies.

> **MANDATORY REQUIREMENT 4**
> Departments and Agencies must have a designated Departmental Security Officer (DSO), with day-to-day responsibilities for all aspects of Protective Security (including physical, personnel and information security).

6. In addition to the mandatory roles above, and those outlined within Security Policy No. 4: Information Security and Assurance (see MR 35); organisations need to consider appropriate roles within their security/business machinery. For example larger bodies may consider appointing Deputies and / or creating other specific security roles (e.g. Personnel Security Officer), whilst smaller bodies may combine roles. Agencies may wish to consider their parent departmental DSO as their designated DSO. The Head of Department/Permanent Secretary has

overall responsibility for security and it is for them to determine appropriate security structures within their organisation and any Agencies for which they are responsible.

Risk management

7. Departments need to 1) identify their assets and those responsible for them, 2) understand the vulnerability and likelihood of attack from various threats, 3) value them in terms of the impact from loss or failure of confidentiality, integrity and availability, and 4) assign a proportionate level of protection to mitigate, and / or recover from, the potential loss or failure of those assets. Departments should see this as a continuous cycle of assessing and re-evaluating risk.

Departments should use the HM Treasury Orange Book on Risk Management for a broad approach to principles and concepts, however, within the disciplines of Information Assurance and Counter-Terrorism Protective Security there are detailed methods of risk assessment that must be adopted (see Security Policy No. 4 – Information Security and Assurance and Security Policy No. 6 – Counter-Terrorism for these areas).

> **MANDATORY REQUIREMENT 5**
> **Departments and Agencies must adopt a risk management approach (including a detailed risk register) to cover all areas of protective security across their organisation.**

Assurance

8. Self-assessment, central reporting, audit and review, must combine together to provide for a robust level of assurance across Government, as well as assisting the centre in developing and refining policy.

Self assessment

> **MANDATORY REQUIREMENT 6**
>
> Departments and Agencies must:
>
> a) Make their departmental security policy widely available internally and reference this in overall business plans.
>
> b) Have a system of assurance of compliance with security policy, and produce an annual report to their Head of Department / Management Board on the state of all aspects of protective security.

9. Departments should include details of any agencies or other bodies that report to them directly in the annual report to their Head of Department.

Central reporting

> **MANDATORY REQUIREMENT 7**
>
> Departments must submit an annual security return to the Cabinet Office Security Policy Division, covering their Agencies and main delivery partners, and must include:
>
> a) Details of any changes to key individuals responsible for security matters (The appointment of a new DSO must be reported immediately).
>
> b) Significant departmental risks and mitigations that have implications for protective security.
>
> c) All significant security incidents (those involving serious criminal activity, damage to National Security, breaches of international security agreements, serious reputational damage, data losses or leaks) – individual breaches of this nature must also be reported immediately.
>
> d) Declaration of meeting all Mandatory Requirements (green boxes).
>
> e) Confirmation that any significant control weaknesses have been reflected in the Departmental Statement on Internal Control.

Core resources

HMG Security Policy Framework

v.2.0
May 09

Audit and review

10. Departments will be responsible for carrying out internal reviews of security arrangements as they judge to be necessary. The Cabinet Office, in consultation with Departments and the Official Committee on Security, will review compliance as appropriate on the basis of the minimum mandatory requirements (green boxes) and annual security returns.

> **MANDATORY REQUIREMENT 8**
> Departments and Agencies must comply with oversight arrangements including external audit / compliance arrangements as set out by Cabinet Office.

Culture, training and professionalism

11. Fostering a professional culture and developing a positive attitude toward security is critical to the successful delivery of this framework. Security must be seen as an integral part of and a key enabler to, effective departmental business. Cabinet Office, in conjunction with professional bodies such as the Centre for Protection of National Infrastructure (CPNI) and CESG, the National Technical Authority for Information Assurance, maintain a programme of familiarisation, training and re-fresher courses appropriate for security personnel, including an induction visit to all new DSOs. Departments and Agencies must ensure that regular refresher training, awareness programmes and security briefings are provided to <u>all</u> staff. These should cover individual security responsibilities, as defined by the Civil Service Code, including the reporting of security incidents and criminal behaviour and / or any knowledge of leaking. In addition to line management reporting, all staff must also have recourse to consult with, or report anonymously to a welfare officer or independent arbiter.

> **MANDATORY REQUIREMENT 9**
> Departments and Agencies must ensure that:
> a) Board members responsible for security undergo security and risk management

familiarisation upon appointment.

b) All DSOs are given a joint security briefing from Cabinet Office and the Centre for Protection of National Infrastructure (CPNI) on appointment, and have either attended the relevant training courses before, or at the earliest opportunity after appointment.

c) All Departmental Security Unit (DSU) staff possess competencies and training to the appropriate level, either by attending relevant internal departmental or external government training.

d) Security education and awareness must be built into all staff inductions, with regular familiarisation thereafter.

e) There are plans in place to foster a culture of proportionate protective security.

f) There is a clearly stated and available policy, and mechanisms in place, to allow for independent and anonymous reporting of security incidents.

International security agreements

12. HMG is party to a range of multilateral and bilateral international agreements governing the use, handling and protection of classified material. Departments and Agencies engaged in sensitive work with international organisations, or those that handle protectively marked information on their behalf, must ensure that their internal procedures are compliant with the relevant international obligation. Detailed requirements may vary across organisations (e.g. NATO, EU etc.).

MANDATORY REQUIREMENT 10

Departments and Agencies must ensure that they adhere to any UK obligations in multilateral or bilateral international agreements.

Core resources

HMG Security Policy Framework v.2.0
May 09

Security Policy No.2: Protective Marking and Asset Control

1. This is the second of seven Security Policies within the HMG Security Policy Framework (SPF); outlining the mandatory security requirements and management arrangements to which all Departments and Agencies (defined as including all bodies directly responsible to them) **must** adhere.

Introduction

2. The Protective Marking System (often referred to as the Government Protective Marking System/Scheme or GPMS) is the Government's administrative system to ensure that access to information and other assets is correctly managed and safeguarded to an agreed and proportionate level throughout their lifecycle, including creation, storage, transmission and destruction. The system is designed to support HMG business, and meet the requirements of relevant legislation, international standards and international agreements.

> **MANDATORY REQUIREMENT 11**
> Departments and Agencies must apply the Protective Marking System and the necessary controls and technical measures as outlined in this framework.

Legal requirements

3. The Official Secrets Acts 1911 to 1989 (OSAs), and the Data Protection Act 1998 (DPA) impose statutory obligations regarding the protection and handling of official information and of personal data respectively. In contrast, the Freedom of Information Act 2000 (FOIA) establishes a statutory regime for the release of information held by public authorities to any person requesting it. Both FOIA and DPA are subject to a number of important exemptions, which apply for example, to material which may prejudice law enforcement or damage national security if disclosed. All staff who handle government material must have an understanding of this

legislation and how it specifically relates to their role. The Protective Marking System is an administrative system designed to protect information (and other assets) from accidental or deliberate compromise, which may lead to damage, and/or be a criminal offence, and must therefore be viewed against the legal background.

> **MANDATORY REQUIREMENT 12**
> Departments and Agencies must provide all staff with guidance on the Official Secrets Acts, Data Protection Act and Freedom of Information Act. Staff handling protectively marked information must be given guidance on how this legislation relates to their role.

Official Secrets Acts

4. Sections 1 to 6 of the Official Secrets Act 1989 (OSA 1989) contain a range of offences concerning damaging disclosures of information, documents or other articles. These criminal prohibitions are aimed primarily at those in Government service, although they are equally applicable to anyone else in receipt of official information (whether or not as a result of an unauthorised disclosure). The OSA 1989 makes no reference to the Protective Marking System, but does specify the categories of interests to which damage must, or must potentially, be caused by the unauthorised disclosure. These are: 1) Security and intelligence; 2) Defence; 3) International relations; 4) Foreign confidences; 5) Crime; 6) Special investigation powers.

5. Members of the security and intelligence services, by virtue of Section 1(1) of the OSA 1989, are subject to an absolute prohibition against unauthorised disclosure of information, or other assets relating to security or intelligence regardless of whether or not it is a damaging disclosure. Similarly, any persons who are 'notified' under Section 1(1) of the OSA (because, for example, they have regular access to information relating to security or intelligence) are subject to the same prohibition. It should also be noted that it is an offence to disclose information or assets which it would be reasonable to expect might be used to obtain access to information protected under the Act (e.g. access codes, passwords, keys, etc).

Core resources

HMG Security Policy Framework

v.2.0
May 09

MANDATORY REQUIREMENT 13

Departments and Agencies must ensure that those who are notifiable under Section 1(1) of the Official Secrets Act 1989 are notified in writing. Any organisation responsible for notified employees or individuals must:

a) Renew notices every five years.

b) Keep under review the need for continuing notification of individual posts.

c) Maintain and keep under review the number of notifiable posts.

Data Protection Act 1998 (DPA)

6. Compliance with data protection legislation requires appropriate management structure and control. Proper application of the Protective Marking System will also ensure that protectively marked personal information is appropriately safeguarded and that requirements of the DPA are met. Section 7 of the DPA entitles an individual to be informed whether their personal data is being processed by the data controller, and to be given access to that personal data (a subject access request). This right is subject to exemptions for specified categories of information as defined by the Act. Whilst the DPA makes no reference to the Protective Marking System, protective markings may be a helpful indicator that an exemption applies. The presence, or absence, of a protective marking is not in itself a deciding factor as to whether or not information should be released in response to a subject access request, but it may nevertheless provide some initial guidance as to whether and which exemption applies.

MANDATORY REQUIREMENT 14

Departments and Agencies must follow the minimum standards and procedures for handling and protecting citizen or personal data, as outlined in HMG IA Standard No.6 - Protecting Personal Data and Managing Information Risk.

Freedom of Information Act

7. The Freedom of Information Act 2000 (FOIA) gives any person the right to request and be provided with information held by public authorities, although exemptions apply to specific information as defined by the Act. Whilst FOIA makes no reference to the Protective Marking System, protective markings may be a helpful indicator that an exemption applies. However, the presence, or absence, of a protective marking is not the deciding factor as to whether information should be released or not under FOIA. It should also be noted that the protective marking may no longer be current, and, while it reflects the highest classification of the information contained in a document, the file may also contain information that is not sensitive and may be subject to disclosure in a redacted form.

8. Under FOIA the holder of the information is responsible for answering a request for information; however, if the holder is proposing to disclose protectively marked information, the originator, or specified owner of the information must be consulted before disclosure. When a classified document has been released under FOIA it should be marked accordingly, for example, 'Released under FOIA in full on [date]'.

9. Foreign FOI legislation, where it exists, can differ from the UK; therefore the 'UK' prefix must be used when sending protectively marked material abroad. The onus is on those sending the material to seek to ensure that any UK protectively marked material is not subject to release under foreign FOI legislation unless by prior agreement.

10. Departments must consult the Ministry of Justice FOI Clearing House (clearinghouse@justice.gsi.gov.uk; 020 3334 3891) for guidance about any FOI requests that concern information supplied by or relating to bodies dealing with security matters (section 23), National Security (section 24), or any other triggers for automatic referral. This includes any requests concerning protectively marked information originating from an overseas government or international organisation (or commercial entity).

Core resources

HMG Security Policy Framework

v.2.0
May 09

Where possible, the originator or specific UK departmental owner must also be consulted when considering the request.

> **MANDATORY REQUIREMENT 15**
> Departments and Agencies must ensure that any protectively marked material that is to be released under the Freedom of Information Act is de-classified first and is marked as such. The originator, or specified owner, must be consulted before protectively marked material can be de-classified.

The 'need to know' principle

11. The effective use (including the sharing and protection) of information is a key priority for Government. Access to sensitive information or assets will be required for the efficient management of HMG business. However, access must only be granted to those who have a business need and the appropriate personnel security control (BPSS or National Security Vetting). This 'need to know' principle is fundamental to the security of all protectively marked Government assets – casual access to protectively marked assets is never acceptable. If there is any doubt about giving access to sensitive assets individuals should consult their managers or security staff before doing so.

> **MANDATORY REQUIREMENT 16**
> Departments and Agencies must ensure that access to protectively marked assets is only granted on the basis of the 'need to know' principle. All employees must be made fully aware of their personal responsibility in applying this principle.

International security standards

12. The Government Protective Marking System is designed to meet the principles of the international standard on Information Security Management Systems (ISO/IEC 27000 series). This standard represents good practice to which this framework is aligned. More details are to be

found in Security Policy No.4 - Information Security and Assurance and a copy of ISO/IEC (270001) is reproduced as a supplement to this framework.

International security agreements

13. HMG is party to a range of multilateral and bilateral international agreements governing the use, handling and protection of material. It should be noted that the PROTECT marking is a non-National Security marking and is not covered by international agreements.

> **MANDATORY REQUIREMENT 17**
>
> Departments and Agencies must ensure they adhere to any UK obligations in regard to international markings, as set out in this framework and governed by multilateral and bilateral international security agreements.

Material originating outside of HMG

14. Outside HMG there is no agreed UK system for marking sensitive material, although terms such as PRIVATE and CONFIDENTIAL are in common use, particularly in relation to personal information. Any material originating outside of government, that is not covered by a recognisable protective marking, international agreement, contract or other arrangements, but is marked in such a way to indicate sensitivity, must when handled by HMG, be protected to at least the level offered by the PROTECT marking, and a higher marking should be considered.

> **MANDATORY REQUIREMENT 18**
>
> Departments and Agencies must ensure that non-HMG material which is marked to indicate sensitivity is handled at the equivalent level within the Protective Marking System, or where there is no equivalence, to the level offered by PROTECT as a minimum.

The Government Protective Marking System

15. The Protective Marking System comprises five markings. In descending order of sensitivity

Core resources

HMG Security Policy Framework
v.2.0
May 09

they are: **TOP SECRET, SECRET, CONFIDENTIAL, RESTRICTED and PROTECT.** Unmarked material is considered 'unclassified'. The term 'UNCLASSIFIED' or 'NON' or 'NOT PROTECTIVELY MARKED' may be used to indicate positively that a protective marking is not needed. These markings can be applied to any government assets, although they are most commonly applied to information held electronically or in paper documents. The methodology used to assess these principles within information systems is expressed in Business Impact levels.

Universal controls

16. There are a number of specified technical controls for each level of protective marking. The controls below apply to all protectively marked information.

> **MANDATORY REQUIREMENT 19**
>
> Departments and Agencies must apply the following baseline controls to all protectively marked material:
>
> a) Access is granted on a genuine 'need to know' basis.
>
> b) Assets must be clearly and conspicuously marked. Where this is not practical (for example the asset is a building, computer etc) staff must still have the appropriate personnel security control and be made aware of the protection and controls required.
>
> c) Only the originator or designated owner can protectively mark an asset. Any change to the protective marking requires the originator or designated owner's permission. If they cannot be traced, a marking may be changed, but only by consensus with other key recipients.
>
> d) Assets sent overseas (including to UK posts) must be protected as indicated by the originator's marking and in accordance with any international agreement. Particular care must be taken to protect assets from foreign Freedom of Information legislation by use of national prefixes and caveats or special handling instructions.
>
> e) No official record, held on any media, can be destroyed unless it has been formally

reviewed for historical interest under the provisions of the Public Records Act.

f) A file, or group of protectively marked documents or assets, must carry the protective marking of the highest marked document or asset contained within it (e.g. a file containing CONFIDENTIAL and RESTRICTED material must be marked CONFIDENTIAL).

Applying the correct protective marking

17. The originator or nominated owner of information, or an asset, is responsible for applying the correct protective marking. When protectively marking a document, it is recommended that a damage or 'harm test' is conducted to consider the likely impact if the asset were to be compromised and to help determine the correct level of marking required. The 'harm test' should be done by assessing the asset against the criteria for each protective marking.

18. If applied correctly, the Protective Marking System will ensure that only genuinely sensitive material is safeguarded. The following points should be considered when applying a protective marking:

- Applying too high a protective marking can inhibit access, lead to unnecessary and expensive protective controls, and impair the efficiency of an organisation's business.
- Applying too low a protective marking may lead to damaging consequences and compromise of the asset.
- The compromise of aggregated or accumulated information of the same protective marking is likely to have a higher impact (particularly in relation to personal data). Generally this will not result in a higher protective marking but may require additional handling arrangements. However, if the accumulation of that data results in a more sensitive asset being created, then a higher protective marking should be considered.
- The sensitivity of an asset may change over time and it may be necessary to reclassify assets. If a document is being de-classified or the marking changed, the file should also be changed to reflect the highest marking within its contents.

Core resources

HMG Security Policy Framework v.2.0
May 09

The criteria below provide a broad indication of the type of material at each level of protective marking. Detailed requirements, including specific details on definitions, protection, handling and disclosure instructions are contained in supplementary material within the framework.

Criteria for assessing **TOP SECRET** assets:
- threaten directly the internal stability of the United Kingdom or friendly countries;
- lead directly to widespread loss of life;
- cause exceptionally grave damage to the effectiveness or security of United Kingdom or allied forces or to the continuing effectiveness of extremely valuable security or intelligence operations;
- cause exceptionally grave damage to relations with friendly governments;
- cause severe long-term damage to the United Kingdom economy.

Criteria for assessing **SECRET** assets:
- raise international tension;
- to damage seriously relations with friendly governments;
- threaten life directly, or seriously prejudice public order, or individual security or liberty;
- cause serious damage to the operational effectiveness or security of United Kingdom or allied forces or the continuing effectiveness of highly valuable security or intelligence operations;
- cause substantial material damage to national finances or economic and commercial interests.

Criteria for assessing **CONFIDENTIAL** assets:
- materially damage diplomatic relations (i.e. cause formal protest or other sanction);
- prejudice individual security or liberty;
- cause damage to the operational effectiveness or security of United Kingdom or allied forces or the effectiveness of valuable security or intelligence operations;
- work substantially against national finances or economic and commercial interests;
- substantially to undermine the financial viability of major organisations;
- impede the investigation or facilitate the commission of serious crime;
- impede seriously the development or operation of major government policies;
- shut down or otherwise substantially disrupt significant national operations.

Criteria for assessing **RESTRICTED** assets:
- affect diplomatic relations adversely;
- cause substantial distress to individuals;
- make it more difficult to maintain the operational effectiveness or security of United Kingdom or allied forces;
- cause financial loss or loss of earning potential or to facilitate improper gain or advantage for individuals or companies;
- prejudice the investigation or facilitate the commission of crime;
- breach proper undertakings to maintain the confidence of information provided by third parties;
- impede the effective development or operation of government policies;
- to breach statutory restrictions on disclosure of information;
- disadvantage government in commercial or policy negotiations with others;
- undermine the proper management of the public sector and its operations.

Core resources

> Criteria for assessing **PROTECT** (Sub-national security marking) assets:
> - cause distress to individuals;
> - breach proper undertakings to maintain the confidence of information provided by third parties;
> - breach statutory restrictions on the disclosure of information;
> - cause financial loss or loss of earning potential, or to facilitate improper gain;
> - unfair advantage for individuals or companies;
> - prejudice the investigation or facilitate the commission of crime;
> - disadvantage government in commercial or policy negotiations with others.

Special handling

19. Supplementary markings may be applied to protectively marked material to indicate additional information about its contents, sensitivity and handling requirements. These markings can include national caveats (e.g. UK EYES ONLY), descriptors, codewords or compartmented handling regimes. In most cases, special handling requirements are only applied to highly sensitive material (e.g. intelligence material or material marked CONFIDENTIAL and above).

> **MANDATORY REQUIREMENT 20**
> Departments and Agencies must meet special handling arrangements where they apply and ensure that all staff handling such information understand these arrangements.

Breaches

20. Departments and Agencies must present their staff with a clear indication of the incremental penalties for breaching the rules regarding protectively marked material and the other mandatory requirements as laid out in this framework. This must include recourse to disciplinary and, where applicable, criminal proceedings.

MANDATORY REQUIREMENT 21
Departments and Agencies must have a breach system and give clear guidance to all staff that deliberate or accidental compromise of protectively marked material may lead to disciplinary and / or criminal proceedings.

Core resources

HMG Security Policy Framework   v.2.0
                                                                              May 09

Security Policy No.3: Personnel Security

1. This is the third of seven Security Policies within the HMG Security Policy Framework (SPF); outlining the mandatory security requirements and management arrangements to which all Departments and Agencies (defined as including all bodies directly responsible to them) **must** adhere.

Purpose

2. The purpose of personnel security is to provide a level of assurance as to the trustworthiness, integrity and reliability of all HMG employees, contractors and temporary staff. As a minimum requirement all staff are subject to recruitment controls known as the Baseline Personnel Security Standard (BPSS). For more sensitive posts there are a range of security controls, referred to as 'National Security Vetting' (NSV): these are specifically designed to ensure that such posts are filled by individuals who are unlikely to be susceptible, for whatever reason or motive, to influence or pressure which might cause them to abuse their position.

Risk management

3. Departments and Agencies must employ a risk management approach to Personnel Security in conformity with protective security principles, seeking to reduce the risk of damage, loss, or compromise of HMG assets by application of personnel security controls before and during employment. These controls do not provide a guarantee of reliability and must be supported by effective line management, nor should they be considered an alternative to the correct application of the 'need to know' principle or to access and information security controls.

> **MANDATORY REQUIREMENT 22**
>
> Departments and Agencies must, as part of their risk management approach to protective security, assess the need to apply personnel security controls against specific posts and

the access to sensitive assets.

Personnel security controls

Baseline Personnel Security Standard (BPSS)

4. The BPSS is the recognised standard for HMG pre-employment screening. It forms the foundation for National Security Vetting and seeks to address identity fraud, illegal working and deception generally. The BPSS comprises verification of four main elements: 1) identity; 2) employment history; 3) nationality and immigration status (including the right to work); and, if a formal NSV clearance is not required for the post, 4) unspent criminal records. In addition, prospective employees are required to account for any significant periods spent abroad. Satisfactory completion of the BPSS allows regular access to UK RESTRICTED and UK CONFIDENTIAL assets, and occasional access to UK SECRET assets, provided an individual has a 'need to know'.

> **MANDATORY REQUIREMENT 23**
>
> **Departments and Agencies must apply the requirements of the Baseline Personnel Security Standard (BPSS) to all HMG staff (including the armed forces), and contractors and temporary staff.**

5. In some cases, such as people taken on for very short periods of employment, or where local personnel are recruited overseas, it may not be practicable to meet the BPSS fully. In these instances the decision to accept the risk must be recorded. Verification of identity and right to work is a prerequisite that must be completed before the UK security clearance process is undertaken.

Core resources

HMG Security Policy Framework v.2.0
May 09

National Security Vetting

6. National Security Vetting is governed by HMG's statement of policy, made by the Prime Minister to Parliament on 15 December 1994. There are three levels of National Security Vetting: Counter-Terrorist Check (CTC), Security Check (SC) and Developed Vetting (DV). The need for vetting must be assessed against the requirements of each particular post. Vetting is required for those who have unescorted access to sites or work in close proximity to individuals assessed to be at risk of terrorist attack, who have access to information or assets which may be of value to terrorists, or have constant and frequent access to SECRET and /or TOP SECRET information or other assets, including the protectively marked assets of other nations and international organisations, the compromise of which could bring about the same degree of damage.

7. National Security Vetting involves a degree of intrusion into an individual's private life and must only be applied in accordance with HMG's statement of policy. For legal and policy reasons, it is not available on demand or on a speculative basis.

MANDATORY REQUIREMENT 24

Departments and Agencies must ensure that National Security Vetting is only applied where it is necessary, proportionate and adds real value.

National Security vetting procedures

MANDATORY REQUIREMENT 25

Departments and Agencies must follow the procedures for National Security Vetting as contained in supplementary material within the framework.

---

8. Permission for the relevant checks to be carried out is provided by an individual completing and signing a Security Questionnaire, indicating that they have read and understood HMG's policy statement on security vetting. It must be counter-signed by an appropriate member of staff from the sponsor organisation, indicating that checks are required for national security purposes.

All organisations undertaking security vetting must ensure that they are covered by the provisions of the Security Service Act 1989 (Section 2(3)).

National Security Vetting decisions

9. In making vetting decisions, judgement must be exercised taking into consideration all the information obtained during the clearance process. The existence of one or more factors of concern does not necessarily or conclusively demonstrate unreliability or present an unmanageable risk. Vetting officers must take into account the nature, likelihood and credibility of the threat, and the vulnerability, sensitivity and impact of compromise of the particular assets concerned, as well as any mitigating factors. They must also make every effort to establish the facts and resolve any apparent discrepancies which are revealed, or doubts which arise before making a clearance decision. When a security risk is identified the vetting authority must decide whether or not the risk is manageable, and if so, provide advice to line management, taking into account that information may have been revealed or obtained in confidence.

> **MANDATORY REQUIREMENT 26**
>
> **Only Government Departments and Agencies, or Police Forces can take security clearance decisions. They must make clear evidence based decisions taking into account all available information. They must be prepared to defend a decision if challenged.**

Refusal or withdrawal of clearance

10. If a clearance is refused or withdrawn for an existing HMG employee or a contractor, the Department or Agency must inform the individual of the fact and provide full reasons for that decision, unless there are demonstrable national security grounds for non-disclosure of the reasons. There is no requirement to inform applicants for employment (staff or contractors) of the fact or reasons for the refusal of a clearance, but this may be possible allowing for considerations of security and confidentiality, as it may impact on future employment applications.

Core resources

HMG Security Policy Framework

v.2.0
May 09

Ongoing personnel security management ('Aftercare')

11. Personnel security is an important element of an effective protective security regime as well as good overall management practice. The security clearance process only provides a snapshot of an individual at a particular time. The BPSS and National Security Vetting are the beginning of an ongoing and actively managed personnel security regime, which requires senior and line management support, awareness and education, and formal periodic reviews of security clearance.

MANDATORY REQUIREMENT 27

Departments and Agencies must have in place personnel security aftercare arrangements, including formal reviews of National Security Vetting clearances and the requirement to remind managers and individuals of their responsibility to inform the vetting authorities of any change in circumstance that may impact on the suitability to hold a security clearance.

Appeals

12. Existing employees must be made aware of the organisation's internal appeals process, and, if the decision to refuse or withdraw clearance is upheld, of the option to appeal to the independent Security Vetting Appeals Panel (SVAP). The Panel is available to all those, other than external applicants for employment, in the public and private sectors and in the Armed Forces who are subject to National Security Vetting, have exhausted existing internal appeal mechanisms within their organisations and remain dissatisfied with the result. Separate arrangements are available to staff and contractors of the Security and Intelligence Agencies through the Investigatory Powers Tribunal (IPT). Individuals must be provided with details of how to apply to the Panel and be informed that appeals must be received within 28 days of the individual being informed of the internal appeal decision. In all such cases Departmental legal advisers must be consulted. The Security Vetting Appeals Panel will make recommendations to

the Head of Department, who will take the final decision as to whether clearance is granted or not. Departments and Agencies must inform the Panel of subsequent action, but the Panel will not normally become involved in further examination of that action. The Panel is entitled to comment on the adequacy of any internal vetting appeals process.

13. External applicants for employment are not eligible to appeal against adverse vetting decisions either internally or to the SVAP, although applicants to the Security and Intelligence Agencies may apply to the IPT. Departments and Agencies should be aware that individuals may also seek to challenge vetting decisions through legal avenues.

MANDATORY REQUIREMENT 28

Departments and Agencies must have in place an internal departmental appeals process for existing employees wishing to challenge National Security Vetting decisions.

MANDATORY REQUIREMENT 29

Departments and Agencies must inform Cabinet Office Security Policy Division where an individual initiates a legal challenge in respect of a National Security Vetting decision.

Assurance

MANDATORY REQUIREMENT 30

Departments and Agencies must record how many, and what type of security vetting clearances (CTC, SC, DV) have been undertaken on an annual basis, and also the number, and the outcome of, internal and independent vetting appeals. This should be included in the annual report to your Head of Department / Management Board.

Core resources

HMG Security Policy Framework v.2.0
May 09

Security Policy No.4: Information Security and Assurance

1. This is the fourth of seven Security Policies within the HMG Security Policy Framework (SPF); outlining the mandatory security requirements and management arrangements to which all Departments and Agencies (defined as including all bodies directly responsible to them) **must** adhere.

Information security policy

> **MANDATORY REQUIREMENT 31**
>
> Departments and Agencies must have, as a component of their overarching security policy, an information security policy setting out how they, and their delivery partners (including offshore and nearshore (EU/EEA based) Managed Service Providers), comply with the minimum requirements set out in this policy and the wider framework.

Managing information risk

2. Information is a key asset to Government and its correct handling is vital to the delivery of public services and to the integrity of HMG. In striking the right balance between sharing and protecting data, Departments and Agencies must manage business impacts and risks associated with Confidentiality, Integrity and Availability (C, I & A) of all information. Information Assurance (IA) is the confidence that information systems will protect the information they carry and will function as they need to, when they need to, under the control of legitimate users. The IA functions that support the protection of Government Information and Communications Technology (ICT) Systems are risk management, accreditation, standards and compliance. The importance of IA to public service delivery has been demonstrated by the publication of a National IA Strategy; this policy supports this strategy. The International Standard for Information Security Management Systems (ISO/IEC 27001) is acknowledged as good practice and this policy is aligned to that standard.

HMG Security Policy Framework, Version 2.0, May 2009

> **MANDATORY REQUIREMENT 32**
>
> Departments and Agencies must conduct an annual technical risk assessment (using HMG IA Standard No.1) for all HMG ICT Projects and Programmes and when there is a significant change in a risk component (Threat, Vulnerability, Impact etc.) to existing HMG ICT Systems in operation. The assessment and the risk management decisions made must be recorded in the Risk Management and Accreditation Documentation Set (RMADS), using HMG IA Standard No.2 - Risk Management and Accreditation of Information Systems.

3. When handling personal data there is a further requirement to conduct a risk assessment every quarter, please refer to HMG IA Standard No.6 – Protecting Personal Data and Managing Information Risk.

Business impact

4. In assessing the level of impact likely to result from any compromise of information assets, Departments and Agencies must use 'Business Impact Levels', also known simply as Impact Levels (ILs). ILs provide a six-point scale which allows Departments and Agencies to make a balanced assessment of the countermeasures to meet risk management requirements for Confidentiality, Integrity and Availability. In addition, organisations must review where large amounts of data are aggregated, accumulated, or associated with other data, to determine whether a higher Impact Level, and therefore greater protection and specific handling, is required.

> **MANDATORY REQUIREMENT 33**
>
> Departments and Agencies must, in conjunction with the Protective Marking System, use Business Impact Levels (ILs) to assess and identify the impacts to the business through the loss of Confidentiality, Integrity and/or Availability of data and ICT systems should risks be realised. Aggregation of data must also be considered as a factor in determining ILs.

Core resources

HMG Security Policy Framework v.2.0
May 09

Personal data

5. HMG must handle, protect and share large amounts of personal data to maximise public service delivery. Departments and Agencies must comply with the data protection principles set out in the Data Protection Act to ensure a high level of confidence that personal data is handled correctly. There are specific requirements relating to handling personal data as defined in HMG IA Standard No.6 – Protecting Personal Data and Managing Information Risk – see Mandatory Requirement 14.

Roles and responsibilities

6. Accounting Officers (e.g. Head of Department/Permanent Secretary) have overall responsibility for ensuring that information risks are assessed and mitigated to an acceptable level. This responsibility must be supported by a Senior Information Risk Owner (SIRO) and the day-to-day duties may be delegated to the Departmental Security Officer (DSO), IT Security Officer (ITSO) or Information Asset Owners (IAOs).

> **MANDATORY REQUIREMENT 34**
>
> Information risk must be specifically addressed in the departmental annual Statement on Internal Control (SIC), which is signed off by the Accounting Officer.

> **MANDATORY REQUIREMENT 35**
>
> Departments and Agencies must have:
>
> a) A designated Senior Information Risk Owner (SIRO); a Board level individual responsible for managing departmental information risks, including maintaining and reviewing an information risk register (the SIRO role may be combined with other security or information management board level roles).
>
> b) A designated Information Technology Security Officer (ITSO); responsible for the security of information in electronic form.
>
> c) A designated Communications Security Officer (ComSO) if cryptographic material is

handled.

d) **Information Asset Owners**; senior named individuals responsible for each identified information asset.

7. It is advised that the ITSO reports to the DSO on information security matters. Where this is not the case, there should be clear mechanisms to ensure that IT security is considered as part of the overall approach to protective security. Smaller Departments and Agencies may wish to combine ComSO and ITSO roles, while larger ones may consider appointing Deputies and / or creating other specific IT/Communications security posts. It is also sufficient for Agencies to consider parent Departmental roles as their designated SIRO/ITSO/IAO/ComSO.

Accreditation and audit

8. Formal accreditation and audit processes provide important assurances that necessary standards are being met. As well as overall compliance arrangements for protective security (set out in Security Policy No.1: Governance, Risk Management and Compliance), there are specific and mandatory Information Assurance accreditation requirements.

MANDATORY REQUIREMENT 36

ICT systems that process protectively marked Government data must be accredited using H Standard No. 2 - Risk Management and Accreditation of Information Systems, an accreditation status must be reviewed at least annually to judge whether material changes occurred which could alter the original accreditation decision.

MANDATORY REQUIREMENT 37

Departments and Agencies must have the ability to regularly audit information assets and ICT systems. This must include:

a) Regular compliance checks carried out by the Accreditor, ITSO etc. (documented in the RM audit of the ICT system against configuration records).

Core resources

HMG Security Policy Framework   v.2.0
May 09

b) A forensic readiness policy that will maximise the ability to preserve and analyse data gen(
by an ICT system, that may be required for legal and management purposes.

MANDATORY REQUIREMENT 38

All ICT systems must have suitable identification and authentication controls to manage the
of unauthorised access, enable auditing and the correct management of user accounts.

Codes of connection and technical controls

MANDATORY REQUIREMENT 39

Departments and Agencies must follow the requirements of any codes of connection,
multilateral or bilateral international agreements and community or shared services security
policies to which they are signatories (for example Government Secure Intranet (GSI)).

Codes of connection should cover the following technical policies:

a) Patching policy, covering all ICT systems including Operating System and applications
reduce the risk from known vulnerabilities.

b) Policy to manage risks posed by all forms of malicious software ('malware'), inclu(
viruses, spyware and phishing etc.

c) Boundary security devices - (e.g. firewalls) must be installed on all systems with a connec
to untrusted networks, such as the Internet.

d) Content checking/blocking policy.

e) Lockdown policy to restrict unnecessary services and ensure that no user has more privile
(access and functionality) than required.

Where these are not covered by codes of connection, or Departments are not signatories,
separate policies covering these areas must be established.

Cryptography

MANDATORY REQUIREMENT 40

Departments and Agencies must comply with HMG IA Standard No.4 – Communications Security and Cryptography (parts 1-3) for the protection of protectively marked material. Paying particular attention to the circumstances when encryption is required, the requirement to only use CESG approved solutions, the control mechanisms for cryptographic items, and the requirement for specified levels of personnel security clearance for individuals handling cryptographic items.

Eavesdropping and Electro-Magnetic Countermeasures

MANDATORY REQUIREMENT 41

Departments and Agencies must follow specific Government procedures to manage the risk posed by eavesdropping and electro-magnetic emanations.

Remote working/mobile media

9. Home or remote working will introduce new vulnerabilities associated with off-site and portable ICT devices and media (e.g. laptops, PDAs, mobile phones, memory sticks, external drives, MP3s etc). Departmental standards and guidelines must be used for connecting to public (insecure) ICT systems such as the internet. Departments and Agencies should also, when handling personal data, avoid where possible the use of mobile media.

MANDATORY REQUIREMENT 42

Departments and Agencies must have a policy on remote working (e.g. home or mobile) that complies with the requirements in this framework.

Core resources

HMG Security Policy Framework
v.2.0
May 09

Procurement

MANDATORY REQUIREMENT 43

Departments and Agencies must ensure that security requirements are specified in ICT contracts and all new ICT contracts handling personal data must adhere to the Office of Government Commerce (OGC) ICT model terms and conditions.

Reporting incidents

MANDATORY REQUIREMENT 44

Departments and Agencies must have clear policies and processes for reporting, managing and resolving ICT security incidents. All security incidents must be reported to:

a) Appropriate departmental security authorities.

b) HMG incident management bodies: GovCERT for network incidents and CINRAS for communications security (involving cryptographic items).

c) The Information Commissioner's Office and the Cabinet Office Central Sponsor for Information Assurance for significant actual or possible losses of personal data.

Secure disposal

MANDATORY REQUIREMENT 45

Departments and Agencies must ensure that all media used for storing or processing protectively marked or otherwise sensitive information must be disposed of or sanitised in accordance with HMG IA Standard No. an 5 – Secure Sanitisation of Protectively Marked or Sensitive Information.

Personnel and physical security

10. Personnel and physical security are integral elements in mitigating information risk. Whilst the standards outlined in Security Policy No. 3 - Personnel security and Security Policy No. 5 –

Physical security deal with these, it should be noted that ICT and cryptographic posts (e.g. ITSO, Crypto-custodians, system administrators) must be specifically evaluated to assess the level of security clearances required. Moreover, the physical security of ICT hardware and infrastructures must be specifically addressed.

> **MANDATORY REQUIREMENT 46**
> Departments and Agencies must ensure that ICT users with higher levels of privilege and/or potentially wide access (e.g. system administrators, architects, programmers etc.), or those with responsibility for ICT security, must be subject to evaluation for National Security clearances appropriate to the protective marking of the information processed.

> **MANDATORY REQUIREMENT 47**
> Departments and Agencies must ensure that all locations where information and system assets (including cryptographic items) are kept must have an appropriate level of physical security as set out in this framework.

Education, training and awareness

> **MANDATORY REQUIREMENT 48**
> Departments and Agencies must ensure that all users of ICT systems are familiar with the security operating procedures governing their use, receive appropriate security training, and are aware of local processes for reporting issues of security concern. They must further ensure that staff who manage and maintain the secure configuration of ICT systems, and those with access to information assets, are appropriately trained, are aware of incident reporting, and the minimum standards relating to the handling of protectively marked data.

Core resources

Business Continuity and Disaster Recovery Planning

> **MANDATORY REQUIREMENT 49**
> Departments and Agencies must ensure that all locations where information and system assets (including cryptographic items) are kept must have appropriate Business Continuity and Disaster Recovery Plans.

11. These plans should form part of overall Business Continuity plans - see Security Policy No. 7 – Business Continuity and MR 70 for details.

Security Policy No.5: Physical Security

1. This is the fifth of seven Security Policies within the HMG Security Policy Framework (SPF); outlining the mandatory security requirements and management arrangements to which all Departments and Agencies (defined as including all bodies directly responsible to them) **must** adhere.

Purpose

2. Physical security involves the appropriate layout and design of facilities, combined with suitable security measures, to prevent unauthorised access and protection of HMG assets – people, information, materials and infrastructure. This means putting in place, or building into design, measures that prevent, deter, delay and detect, attempted or actual unauthorised access, acts of damage and/or violence, and triggers an appropriate response. For example, effective perimeter fencing and heightened access control measures may deter an attack because of the difficulties of gaining access; CCTV, intruder alarms and Radio Countermeasures might detect an attack in progress and trigger interception; whilst vehicle stand-off, blast proof glazing and postal screening can minimise the consequences of an attack. For detailed guidance on counter terrorist policy, please refer to Security Policy No. 6 – Counter-Terrorism.

Defence in depth

3. Physical security involves a number of distinct security measures which form part of a 'layered' or 'defence in depth' approach to security, which must take account of the balance between prevention, protection and response. Physical security measures, or products such as locks and doors, are categorised according to the level of protection offered.

4. The 'layered' approach to physical security starts with the protection of the asset at source (e.g. creation, access and storage), then proceeds progressively outwards to include the building, estate and perimeter of the establishment. Approach routes, parking areas, adjacent buildings

Core resources

HMG Security Policy Framework

v.2.0
May 09

and utilities/services beyond the perimeter should also be considered. To ensure appropriate physical security controls, departments must consider the following factors:
- The impact of loss of the site or asset.
- The level of threat.
- The vulnerability.
- The value, protective marking or amount of material held.
- The particular circumstances of the establishment, including considerations of environment, location and whether occupancy is sole or shared.

> **MANDATORY REQUIREMENT 50**
> Departments and Agencies must adopt a 'layered' approach to physical security, ensuring that their physical security policy incorporates identifiable elements of prevention, detection and response.

Storage of sensitive assets

5. Critical, sensitive or protectively marked assets should be located in secure areas, protected by a defined security perimeter, with appropriate security barriers and entry controls.

> **MANDATORY REQUIREMENT 51**
> Departments and Agencies must use the Physical Security Assessment Questionnaire and the Physical Security Baseline Controls Matrix to identify appropriate physical security measures.

Secure containers

> **MANDATORY REQUIREMENT 52**
> Departments and Agencies must ensure that protectively marked or valuable material is secured in appropriate security containers. Large amounts of protectively marked material or equipment, which cannot be stored in a security container, must be stored in a secure room.

Secure rooms

6. Where there is a need to store large amounts of inherently valuable removable items, a Strong Room should be used.

> **MANDATORY REQUIREMENT 53**
>
> **Departments and Agencies must ensure that windows, doors, locks and entry controls meet appropriate security standards in rooms holding protectively marked material or sensitive assets.**

Office areas

7. A clear desk policy is recommended in all office areas (particularly in open plan or shared office areas). This is primarily to ensure that sensitive material is not left unattended. Where it is not possible to implement a full clear desk policy, a risk-based approach should be adopted and the decision recorded in the appropriate Risk Register. The same principle should apply to computer screens and other office areas used to display potentially sensitive information, such as walls, pinboards etc. Computer screens should not be sited where they could be illicitly viewed (e.g. overlooked by windows or reflective surfaces).

> **MANDATORY REQUIREMENT 54**
>
> **In office areas (particularly open plan and shared areas); Departments and Agencies must put in place procedures to avoid access to protectively marked material by individuals who do not have a 'need to know'.**

Building security

8. For the purpose of assessing security risks to a building, buildings are rated according to their level of resistance to forced or surreptitious attack and blast protection. In any building in which protectively marked or other valuable assets are stored, there should be as few points of exit and

Core resources

entry as the functions of the site and safety will allow. Where these exist, physical security controls, such as window bars, grilles, shutters, security doors etc, should be installed. The effectiveness of such controls may be enhanced by the use of intruder detection systems or guard services.

9. When choosing from the many physical security measures available, Departments should ensure that security controls are able to mitigate violent acts and deter, detect or delay intrusion - those who are not deterred should be forced to use tools and methods that facilitate detection and delay.

> **MANDATORY REQUIREMENT 55**
> **Departments and Agencies must assess the security risks to their estate ensuring that security is fully integrated early in the process of planning, selecting, designing and modifying their facilities.**

Physical access control

10. Access control refers to the practice of controlling and monitoring access to a property or asset. Physical access control can be achieved through a combination of manned guarding, and mechanical or technical means. When deciding which access control measures to deploy, Departments must ensure that they consider the security measures in an integrated manner, such as combining automated access control systems with photo passes and CCTV.

11. Frontline staff such as security guards and receptionists play a vital role in controlling access, but to be fully effective, they may need to be supported by:
- Automatic Access Control System (AACS)
- Pass or ID system
- Visitor control
- Pass activated doors, turnstiles etc

- Entry and exiting searching
- CCTV

12. Frontline staff are likely to be exposed to a higher level of risk than others. This should be considered in the risk assessment and additional protections should be put in place as required.

MANDATORY REQUIREMENT 56

Departments and Agencies must control access to their estate using safeguards that will prevent unauthorised access.

MANDATORY REQUIREMENT 57

Departments and Agencies must have plans and procedures for dealing with and intercepting unauthorised visitors or intruders. Such plans must include the ability to systematically search the establishment if necessary.

MANDATORY REQUIREMENT 58

Departments and Agencies must ensure that access control policies are made available to all staff, and that staff are briefed on their personal responsibilities (e.g. wearing a pass at all times, escorting visitors and searching their work area if required).

Incoming mail and deliveries

13. Delivered items can include letters, packets and parcels and may contain:
- explosive or incendiary devices
- blades or sharp items
- offensive materials
- chemical, biological or radiological (CBR) materials or devices.

14. Anyone receiving a suspicious delivery is unlikely to know exactly which type it is, so procedures should cater for every eventuality.

Core resources

HMG Security Policy Framework
v.2.0
May 09

> **MANDATORY REQUIREMENT 59**
>
> Departments and Agencies must have appropriate procedures in place for screening incoming mail/deliveries for suspicious items.

Manned guarding

15. Manned guarding is a key element of integrated physical security. Guards provide deterrence against hostile activity and facilitate a rapid response to security incidents.

16. Guards may either be directly employed by a government department or agency, or be employed by a commercial guard force. Guard duties and the need for, and frequency of, patrols should be decided by considering the level of threat and any other security systems or equipment that might already be in place.

> **MANDATORY REQUIREMENT 60**
>
> Departments and Agencies must consider the use of guard forces to protect the assets they hold. Where guards are deployed the GSZ Manned Guarding Services Manual is considered best practice.

Perimeter security

17. A perimeter may be defined by a natural boundary, vehicle barriers such as bollards, by free-standing fences or walls, or by the outer walls of a building or divisions inside it. The security function of a perimeter is to provide a degree of physical, psychological and / or legal deterrence to intrusion, as well as providing a defined scope of physical responsibility.

> **MANDATORY REQUIREMENT 61**
>
> Departments and Agencies must establish a secure perimeter, with appropriate security

barriers and entry controls. Perimeters should offer physical protection from unauthorised access, damage and interference and allow for the quick identification of suspicious individuals or unusual items.

18. A perimeter's effectiveness as a security measure can be enhanced by the deployment of Perimeter Intruder Detection Systems (PIDS), Closed Circuit Television (CCTV), security lighting and / or guard forces. Perimeters can also be strengthened, particularly against vehicle borne threat, by installing more robust fencing or other barrier systems. In deciding which perimeter security measures to deploy, Departments and Agencies must ensure that they consider the security measures in an integrated manner. Security lighting is a relatively effective and low cost deterrent but the use of more expensive systems, such as PIDS and CCTV, should be considered when a higher level of protection and detection is required.

MANDATORY REQUIREMENT 62
Departments and Agencies must produce a detailed Operational Requirement before deciding to deploy a security measure, particularly when purchasing a system or security product. This should clearly define what the system is expected to achieve.

CCTV

MANDATORY REQUIREMENT 63
The deployment of CCTV must be in accordance with the Data Protection Act 1998.

19. Departments and Agencies should be particularly aware of the Data Protection Act Principles and the Information Commissioner's Code of Practice on CCTV, which is published under the Act.

Core resources

HMG Security Policy Framework v.2.0
May 09

Security Policy No.6: Counter-Terrorism

1. This is the sixth of seven Security Policies within the HMG Security Policy Framework (SPF); outlining the mandatory security requirements and management arrangements to which all Departments and Agencies (defined as including all bodies directly responsible to them) **must** adhere.

Introduction

2. Departments and Agencies are responsible for managing their assets – people, infrastructure and information. This includes reducing risk from terrorist attack to as low a level as is reasonably practicable. Here it is important to recognise that the visible level of security is a factor in terrorist targeting. Departments have legal obligations to protect employees and visitors. Departments must be resilient in the face of an attack and have in place physical security measures, proportionate to the threat and the assets to be protected and also contingency arrangements to facilitate the quick resumption of vital services (including contracted services). HMG is perceived by many terrorist groups as an attractive and 'legitimate' target, it is therefore of critical importance that Departments meet the obligations outlined in this framework.

CONTEST strategy

3. CONTEST is the Government's long term strategy for reducing the risk to the UK and its overseas interests from international terrorism. The strategy was published in July 2006 and more details can be found at: http://security.homeoffice.gov.uk/counter-terrorism-strategy/

Risk management

4. Departments must employ a risk management approach to Counter-Terrorism (CT) protective security, although it is recognised that for certain areas (for example the protection of nuclear

weapons and nuclear materials) CT security policy will be intentionally more prescriptive. It should be noted that CT measures are likely to complement other security measures and therefore should be considered in conjunction with general protective security risk management (please see Security Policy No. 5 – Physical Security and Security Policy No.7 – Business Continuity). However, there are some very specific baseline CT measures that all Departments must take and these are outlined in this Policy.

Categorisation of the government estate

5. All Departments should be considered a potential target for terrorist attack or hostile interest. Government establishments fall into three risk categories according to the likelihood of being a target of a terrorist attack. These risk categories are HIGH, MODERATE, and LOW.

> **MANDATORY REQUIREMENT 64**
> All Government establishments must be categorised according to the likelihood of being, or in close proximity to, a potential terrorist target.

Threat Levels

6. Threat Levels are designed to give a broad indication of the likelihood of a terrorist attack. The Threat Levels are LOW, MODERATE, SUBSTANTIAL, SEVERE and CRITICAL. The five levels reflect an assessment of probability of attack based on an analysis of terrorists' intentions, targeting priorities, capabilities and any evidence of current planning and timescales. Information on the national Threat Level is available on the Security Service website.

Threat information and briefings

7. If an establishment is identified as being at immediate threat, the police and security authorities will inform the Department and may take control of the scene. This can be either pre or post-incident depending on circumstances and may require careful handling to avoid compromising intelligence. In order to ensure Departments have current information on the terrorist threat, the

Core resources

HMG Security Policy Framework

v.2.0
May 09

Centre for the Protection of the National Infrastructure (CPNI) and Cabinet Office Security Policy Division (COSPD) produce regular threat updates, some of which can only be seen on a 'need to know' basis.

Government Estate Response Level system

8. The Cabinet Office operates a system of response giving Departments a broad indication of the level of protective security readiness required at any one time. The Response Level is informed by the level of threat as well as specific assessments of vulnerability and risk to HMG but Response Levels tend to relate to sites, whereas Threat Levels usually relate to broad areas of activity. The three Response Levels are: NORMAL, HEIGHTENED and EXCEPTIONAL.

Precise measures adopted for each individual site and at each Response Level are the responsibility of Departmental Security Officers (DSOs) in consultation with CPNI and specialist Counter-Terrorist Security Advisers, and must form part of CT planning. Measures are likely to include restricting access, increasing patrols and frequency of bag searching, however a more detailed description of incremental security measures is set out in the supplementary material within the framework.

> **MANDATORY REQUIREMENT 65**
> Department Security Officers must ensure that the Department and its Agencies have baseline Counter - Terrorist physical security measures and Counter - Terrorist incremental security measures in place at each Response Level. Further, at each Response Level, DSOs must ensure that the identified Counter - Terrorist incremental security measures are applied. Departments must be ready to impose or remove those measures with immediate effect when there is a change in Response Level and ensure that all staff are made clearly aware of the current Response Level and what Counter - Terrorist physical security measures must be adopted.

Counter-Terrorist protective security policy and plans

9. Departments are best placed to assess the risks they face, and must develop their own security policies in an integrated manner; this must include a CT policy and plans. These should be produced in accordance with national security authorities' advice and in consultation with local emergency services and should form part of business continuity plans.

MANDATORY REQUIREMENT 66

Departments and Agencies must, as part of their overall protective security policy, have a Counter-Terrorist protective security <u>policy</u> in place. This must seek to deter and minimise impact of an attack or hostile interest, and must include:

a) Application of central advice and guidance.
b) Departmental roles and responsibilities (including third parties, contractors etc).
c) Management controls and assurance that appropriate measures and plans are in place.
d) Communication arrangements including briefing of staff.
e) Arrangements for testing Counter-Terrorist plans.
f) Liaison with emergency services and any multi-agency contingency plans.

MANDATORY REQUIREMENT 67

Departments and Agencies must have a Counter-Terrorist protective security <u>plan</u> in place. This must seek to deter or minimise impact of an attack or hostile interest and must include:

a) Details of all protective security measures (including physical, personnel, information) to be implemented following an increase, or decrease, in the Government Response Level.
b) Instructions on how to respond to a specific threat, event or item (e.g. telephone bomb threat, a suspicious package or delivery, Vehicle Borne Improvised Explosive Device (VBIED), hostile reconnaissance or hostile individuals).
c) A search plan.
d) Evacuations plans, including details on securing premises in the event of full

Core resources

> evacuation.
> e) Business continuity plans.
> f) A communications and media strategy, including handling enquiries from concerned family and friends.
> g) Liaison with emergency services and any multi-agency contingency plans.

Protective security measures

10. This framework provides detailed policy and guidance on all aspects of protective security and DSOs must refer to these when developing CT policies and plans, but in broad terms they need to ensure:

   a. **Physical security** - That establishments (both new construction and existing), including non- government establishments which sustain HMG business, such as data centres, are suitably robust and offer an appropriate degree of protection against attack and hostile interest. Considerations may include protected spaces, glazing, stand-off, barriers, CCTV, public areas, internal communications, signage, Perimeter Intrusion Detection systems (PIDs), access points and control, building services (e.g. ventilation inlets) and parking areas.

   b. **Personnel security** - There is adequate protection for all staff, as well as personal protection arrangements required for high-threat personnel such as Ministers and VIPs. National Security Vetting is a core element of ensuring trusted individuals are employed in sensitive posts. The Counter-Terrorist Check (CTC) plays an important part in CT vetting measures but other aspects of personnel security must be considered equally important, such as the Baseline Personnel Security Standard (BPSS) and ongoing personnel security management.

c. **Information security** - That all ICT systems, as part of the formal ICT accreditation process, consider and mitigate potential physical and electronic terrorist attack, and that CT plans include the need to protect electronic and paper based information from unauthorised access, compromise or destruction.

Assurance

> **MANDATORY REQUIREMENT 68**
>
> The annual security report made by DSOs to their Head of Department must explicitly provide a statement of assurance on Counter-Terrorist protective security, including compliance with additional measures implemented after any increase in the Government Response Level.

Testing CT arrangements

11. Testing and exercises are essential elements in providing assurance – they ensure that staff are well versed in procedure, that equipment and communications are functioning and adequate and that arrangements with external bodies (e.g. emergency services, contractors, suppliers) are effective. They also provide an opportunity to identify and address problem areas. The testing of CT arrangements should form an important part of testing overall Business Continuity and emergency response plans.

> **MANDATORY REQUIREMENT 69**
>
> As part of Business Continuity and emergency response plans, Departments and Agencies must test their Counter-Terrorist protective security plans regularly, minimum requirements being:
> a) **HIGH risk** - at least annually
> b) **MODERATE risk** – at least once every two years
> c) **LOW risk** – at the Department's discretion
>
> Tests must be reported in the annual report to Heads of Department, demonstrating that plans are effective and potential problems are identified and remedied.

Core resources

HMG Security Policy Framework

v.2.0
May 09

Security Policy No.7: Business Continuity

1. This is the seventh Security Policy within the HMG Security Policy Framework (SPF); outlining the mandatory security requirements and management arrangements to which all Departments and their Agencies (defined as including all bodies directly responsible to them) **must** adhere.

What is Business Continuity Management?

2. The British Standard on Business Continuity Management (BCM), BS 25999 defines BCM as a: 'holistic management process that identifies potential threats to an organisation and the impacts to business operations that those threats, if realised, might cause, and which provides a framework for building organisational resilience with the capability for an effective response that safeguards the interests of its key stakeholders, reputation, brand and value-creating activities'.

3. Business Continuity Management (BCM) is the process through which Departments aim to continue their critical business activities following a disruption and effective recovery afterwards (return to 'normal'). It is an essential aspect of securing their business.

> **MANDATORY REQUIREMENT 70**
> Departments and Agencies must have robust, up to date, fit for purpose and flexible business continuity management arrangements that are regularly tested and reviewed and supported by competent staff that allow them to maintain, or as soon as possible resume provision of, key products and services in the event of disruption.

What should a BCM system look like?

4. An effective BCM programme will have the following features:
- A BCM strategy endorsed and supported by Board level management.
- A BCM programme appropriate to the size and complexity of the department.
- Planning to proportionately manage the impact of events and recover from them.

- BCM arrangements that are exercised, reviewed and renewed as appropriate for the organisation and supported by adequately trained staff.
- Communications that ensure that all staff are aware of the BCM arrangements and of their responsibilities within them.

What are the outcomes of a BCM programme?

5. The outcomes of an effective BCM programme are that:
- Key assets, products and services are identified and protected, ensuring their continuity.
- An incident management capability is developed to provide an effective response.
- The organisation's understanding of itself and its relationships with other departments and organisations to include Local Authorities and the Emergency Services is properly developed, documented and understood.
- Staff are trained to respond effectively to an incident or disruption.
- Stakeholder requirements are understood and able to be met.
- Staff and stakeholders receive adequate support and communications in the event of a disruption.
- The organisation's supply chain is secured.
- The organisation's reputation is protected.

6. Strong Business Continuity Management in Government Departments provides leadership to other public and private sector organisations; sending a message of reassurance to citizens and business, and demonstrating to international partners that the United Kingdom is a secure place to trade.

Core resources

The British Standard for Business Continuity Management: BS 25999

7. BS 25999 provides a basis for understanding, developing and implementing Business Continuity within an organisation. The standard comprises two parts:

- Part 1, the Code of Practice, provides BCM good practice recommendations.
- Part 2, the Specification, provides the requirements for a Business Continuity Management System (BCMS) based on BCM good practice and can be used to demonstrate compliance via an auditing and certification process.

8. It is recommended that Departments and Agencies work towards aligning their Business Continuity arrangements with BS 25999.

HMG Security Policy Framework, Version 2.0, May 2009

HMG Security Policy Framework

v.2.0
May 09

VERSION HISTORY

SPF VERSION	DATE PUBLISHED	SUMMARY OF CHANGES
V.1.0	DEC 08	N/A
V.2.0	1 MAY 09	Version History inserted. No other changes to Tier 1-3 text.

CONTACT DETAILS

The Cabinet Office is responsible for developing and communicating the Security Policy Framework.

E-mail : SPF@cabinet-office.x.gsi.gov.uk.

Publication date: May 2009

© Crown Copyright 2009

The text in this document site is subject to Crown copyright protection unless otherwise indicated. The Crown copyright protected material (other than the Royal Arms and departmental or agency logos) may be reproduced free of charge in any format or medium for research, private study or for internal circulation within an organisation. This is subject to the material being reproduced accurately and not used in a misleading context. Where any of the Crown copyright items on this site are being republished or copied to others, the source of the material must be identified and the copyright status acknowledged.

DATA HANDLING PROCEDURES IN GOVERNMENT: FINAL REPORT, JUNE 2008

CabinetOffice

Data Handling Procedures in Government: Final Report

June 2008

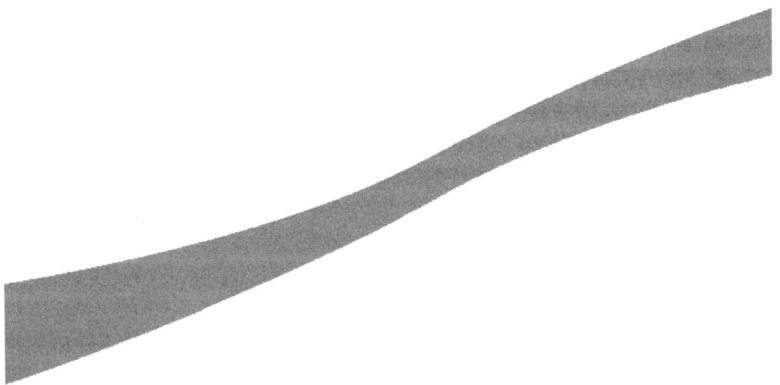

Making government work better

© Crown copyright. Reproduced by permission of Her Majesty's Stationery Office. Published by LexisNexis 2009.

Core resources

Contents

Foreword by Sir Gus O'Donnell	3
Summary	5
Section 1: Scene-setting	9
Report scope and relationship to other work	10
Government policy and use of information	11
Good practice	12
Future challenges	14
Section 2: Better data handling	16
Core measures to protect information	16
Culture	18
Stronger accountability	20
Stronger scrutiny	23
Section 3: Implementation	26
Central Government	26
The wider public sector	28
Reporting progress	28
Annexes	
I: Action taken in individual Departments	29
II: Implementation timeline	34
III: Conduct of the work	35
IV: Information charter	36
V: Cross-references to other work	37

Data Handling Procedures in Government: Final Report, June 2008

Foreword by Sir Gus O'Donnell

Effective use of information is absolutely central to the challenges facing the Government today – whether in improving health, tackling child poverty, or protecting the public from crime and terrorism. Those in public service need to keep that information secure, in order to build public confidence. This is essential to underpin greater data sharing to deliver personalised services and make us more effective.

Following the high profile loss of data by HM Revenue and Customs, the Prime Minister asked me to work with Departments and security experts to examine and improve data handling in Government.

This has involved intensive work across Departments and with their delivery bodies, which is summarised in this report.

Alongside the work in individual Departments, Government is improving the framework within which Departments manage information. This report sets out the action that is being taken to enhance consistency of protection, to get the right working culture in place, and to improve accountability and scrutiny of performance.

A lot has already been done, but there is more to do. This will inevitably be led largely in individual Departments, who are responsible for their own arrangements, but Cabinet Office will play its role in setting cross-Government standards and supporting Departments.

No organisation handling information can guarantee it will never experience losses. But people have a right to expect that their public services achieve and maintain high standards in this important area. Those involved in delivering those public services must work harder and be more effective to meet and exceed those expectations. Every loss or near miss must make us more determined. The action now underway will raise our game, but the task of improving information security will always be a continuing process.

GUS O'DONNELL

Core resources

Data Handling Procedures in Government: Final Report

Summary

1. All modern organisations handle and manage information, including personal data, as part of their business. Central Government Departments are no exception. Better use of information can improve public services. It can make access more convenient, ensure people get all the services to which they are entitled, or allow services to be personalised. It helps to protect the public and fight crime including fraud.

2. People want improved services, but they also want their privacy protected. Therefore, Departments have to make sure that the right people get the information they need, whether on paper or by electronic means, while protecting information from others.

3. Achieving this is never simple. It is particularly challenging against a background of changing services and technology. Even before recent high profile losses, there was work underway across Government to get arrangements right. The loss of two discs by HM Revenue and Customs (HMRC) started an intensive process as all Departments re-examined their practices.

4. This work has been conducted in parallel with a set of independent reviews: the Poynter Review into the HMRC loss; the Burton Review into the loss of a Ministry of Defence laptop; and the Walport / Thomas review of data sharing, commissioned before the losses.

5. An Interim Report, published on 17 December 2007, summarised action taken across Government. That work has continued and broadened, and further progress is set out in Annex I. All Departments have placed restrictions on their use of electronic removable media. These are designed to ensure that personal data are only stored or accessed remotely in cases where it is absolutely necessary to do so. All Departments have started a broader process of cultural change, for example raising awareness among staff about handling sensitive data responsibly and securely, as well as their responsibilities under Departmental arrangements.

6. Looking forward, the challenges in this area are going to get harder rather than easier. The pace of technological change is quickening. The level and sophistication of external threats, such as e-crime, is increasing. Plans to improve public services will mean greater use of data within organisations and more data sharing. Meanwhile, existing challenges around secure handling of other information, such as paper, will continue. Sir David Omand is looking at the handling of highly classified documents to learn lessons from the recent incident. Sir Gus O'Donnell is looking at implementation of rules for the handling of documents across Government, taking account of Sir David's findings.

7. In response, as well as improving individual Departmental arrangements, Government needs to reform the overall arrangements within which Departments manage information. This report sets out how it is doing so, through:

- core measures to protect information, including personal data, across

Government, to enhance consistency of protection and transparency of that protection to others;
- a culture that properly values, protects and uses data, both in the planning and delivery of public services;
- stronger accountability mechanisms, recognising that the individual Department or agency is best placed to understand and address risks to their information, including personal data; and
- stronger scrutiny of performance, to build confidence and ensure that lessons are learned and shared.

8. The Interim Report set out initial directions of reform:
- using the existing line of accountability through Accounting Officers to Parliament as a way to improve information handling;
- setting clear common standards and procedures, including tightening procedures for data stored overseas;
- increasing visibility of performance, with Departments publishing material in their annual reports, and a report on the issue as a whole to Parliament; and
- commitment by Government to provide the Information Commissioner with new powers to conduct "spot checks", and to introduce new sanctions under the Data Protection Act for the most serious breaches of its principles.

9. This report describes how Government has now put in place new measures to protect information, to apply across central Government. No organisation can guarantee it will never lose data, and the Government is no exception. But the actions in place:
- introduce obligatory use of protective measures (such as encryption and penetration testing) and controls (for example on use of mobile devices or on access to records). These will protect all personal data, while recognising that some data require a greater degree of protection than others;
- reinforce efforts to ensure that civil service working culture supports the proper use of information. This applies both at the planning stage through use of Privacy Impact Assessments and when services are being delivered. There will be mandatory training for those with access to protected personal information or involved in managing it, alongside new action to make clear that any failure to apply protective measures is a serious matter potentially leading to dismissal;
- standardise and enhance the processes by which Departments understand and manage their information risk, setting out the responsibilities for key individuals in doing so; and
- further enhance transparency of arrangements, through use of information charters, and greater publication of information on particular information assets and their use.

Core resources

10. The new actions in this report supplement and augment material provided to Departments in other ways, including through the Manual of Protective Security and the Civil Service Management Code. They set out minimum rules, in that individual Departments and agencies will continue to assess their own risk and often put in place a higher level of protection. The Government's guiding principle is that the protections outlined in this report, or their equivalent, should be in place and effective, no matter how information is held and processed for UK Government purposes. The same standards will be applied by contractors. Work is underway to develop equivalent material for the wider public sector.

11. Compliance will be assessed on an annual basis, and underpin the summary material in the Statement on Internal Control, and be the subject of peer review, through capability reviews and as requested by particular Departments. External scrutiny of performance and capability will be provided through:

- National Audit Office scrutiny of the Statement on Internal Control, using their knowledge of the organisation in question;
- spot checks by the Information Commissioner; and
- targeted intervention by Departments and CESG, the National Technical Authority for Information Assurance in GCHQ, to assess counterparts' systems and protections.

12. The Cabinet Office's responsibility is to review and update cross-Government standards in the future to accommodate lessons learned and new developments. Cabinet Office is adapting its resources to the new way of working set out in this report. Furthermore, to support implementation, cross-Government structures are being streamlined, with a particular emphasis on provision of support in areas like training and professional development, and on understanding cross-Government risks and what those mean for the overall Government framework.

13. The changes set out in this document are significant and, although much has already been done, there remains much to do. Progress will be overseen by the Cabinet Committee on Personal Data Security, chaired by Paul Murphy, the Secretary of State for Wales. Departments will report on progress made in their annual reporting. Cabinet Office will follow these with the first annual reporting on the issue as a whole following the end of 2008/09.

Data Handling Procedures in Government: Final Report, June 2008

Section 1: Scene-setting

This work was commissioned by the Prime Minister following high profile data losses in 2007. The aim was to assess and improve procedures for the use and storage of data in Government. It has been conducted alongside specific work into losses in HMRC and the Ministry of Defence, as well as more general work on data sharing being conducted by Richard Thomas and Dr Mark Walport.

Public service delivery relies on the right information being available to the right people. Better use of information can mean better services, through personalisation and by ensuring that people get all the services to which they are entitled. It helps to protect the public and fight crime. But services have to be planned and delivered while maintaining individual privacy.

The Data Protection Act and Human Rights Act provide the legal framework to safeguard privacy. Departments and their agencies are best placed to manage their own information, and are responsible for doing so. Cabinet Office, HM Treasury and the Ministry of Justice set the framework within which they manage information, and, with others, provide assistance. Government arrangements in this area have been the subject of on-going work, and action was underway to improve them before recent losses.

Good practice in managing information may be drawn from the public and private sectors. Technical and process measures need to be taken to minimise the scope for error or malicious action. Organisations need to achieve a culture that underpins the safe use of information, both when planning business and operating it. Clear accountability is vital, particularly at senior levels, to ensure that risks to information are considered from the start. Because no information handling system provides total protection, performance needs to be monitored and lessons learned on an ongoing basis.

Managing information risk in the public sector is likely to become harder in the future rather than easier. Technology and external threats both continue to change quickly, while the use of information in the public sector is likely to increase as services are improved.

A great deal of work has been done in Departments to improve data handling arrangements, and more is planned. But there must be continued vigilance to ensure the highest possible standard of information security.

Core resources

Data Handling Procedures in Government: Final Report

Report scope and relationship to other work

1.1. On 21 November, following the high-profile data loss from HM Revenue and Customs (HMRC) the Prime Minister announced that he had asked the Cabinet Secretary, with the advice of security experts, to work with Departments to ensure that they and their agencies check their procedures for the storage and use of data.

1.2. The terms of reference for the work were to examine:

- the procedures in Departments and agencies for the protection of data;
- their consistency with current Government-wide policies and standards;
- the arrangements for ensuring that procedures are being fully and properly implemented; and

    to make recommendations on improvements that should be made.

1.3. There are close links between personal data handling and information handling. The processes involved in successful management are similar. They involve understanding what is held, what the risks are to that information, and then mitigating them. As a result, while this work has focused on personal data, its conclusions are relevant to information more generally, whether held in paper or electronic form. In addition, Sir David Omand is looking at the handling of highly classified documents to learn lessons from the recent incident. Sir Gus O'Donnell is looking at implementation of rules for the handling of documents across Government, taking account of Sir David's findings.

1.4. This report examines information used by central government bodies and contractors to deliver central government objectives. It has not addressed data storage and use in the private sector, other than when they work as contractors, or by public sector bodies in other countries.

1.5. Within this focus, the work has concentrated on central Government bodies. Local government and other independent public sector organisations also play crucial roles in the delivery of public services. The aim has to be for consistent standards to be applied. The position for the wider public sector is considered in Section 3.

1.6. In examining data handling and use, the work considers both use of data within a given organisation and use when data are shared, but does not seek to explore issues specifically around data sharing. The work considers how data can be kept safe and how it should be handled, rather than whether sharing of particular data in a particular way is desirable. A review of data sharing in the UK public and private sectors is currently taking place, led by Richard Thomas, the Information Commissioner and Dr Mark Walport, Director of the Wellcome Trust. This will report shortly.

1.7. The work has been conducted alongside other detailed examinations of arrangements in specific Departments. The Poynter Review has examined the circumstances around the loss of data in HMRC[1], and the Burton Review has examined the circumstances around the loss of a laptop in the Ministry of Defence[2].

1.8. An interim report for this review was published on 17 December 2007. That report briefly summarised action being taken in each Department to examine and assess their arrangements for the handling of data. It also set out some initial reforms to the overall framework within which Departments manage their information, notably:

- building on the existing line of accountability through Accounting Officers to Parliament to improve the handling of information risk. Information assurance would be covered explicitly in annual Statements on Internal Control;
- setting clear common standards and procedures, including tightening procedures for data stored overseas;
- increasing visibility through Departments publishing material in their annual reports, and a report on the issue as a

---

[1] www.hm-treasury.gov.uk/independent_reviews/poynter_review/poynter_review_index.cfm
[2] www.publications.parliament.uk/pa/cm200708/cmhansrd/cm080207/wmstext/80207m0001.htm

Data Handling Procedures in Government: Final Report, June 2008

whole to Parliament; and

- greater scrutiny through "spot checks" conducted by the Information Commissioner, and the introduction of new sanctions under the Data Protection Act for the most serious breaches of its principles.

Government policy and use of information

1.9. The public sector depends on information to deliver public services, such as: paying benefits; delivering the National Heath Service; and managing the driving licence system. Organisations across the public sector collect, use and store a wide range of personal information, such as income, date of birth and health records, in order to carry out their work. Information is used to check identity and confirm eligibility and to detect and prevent fraud.

1.10. If Government is to deliver joined up services focused on the customer, it needs to know with whom it is dealing. This relies on information being available about the people being served. In the most extreme cases, failure to make information available can lead to serious harm to individuals, for example by failing to prevent crime. It can mean that vulnerable groups in society cannot be provided with the support they need.

1.11. As information and communications technology (ICT) systems become capable of storing and using more information faster, Government has the opportunity to design and develop better services using information from different sources. The difficulty and inconvenience caused to people trying to negotiate different parts of the public sector can be reduced considerably. The Government has set out a vision to ensure that information will be shared to expand opportunities for the most disadvantaged, fight crime and provide better public services for citizens and business, and in other instances where it is in the public interest.[3]

1.12. Some of the benefits in this area are already being realised. In the pension service, pensions and other benefits can now be obtained in one phone call, rather than filling in large amounts of paperwork.

1.13. While sharing information can offer new ways of delivering public services, it has to be done in a way that preserves individual privacy. The Data Protection Act (1998) and Human Rights Act (1998) set out the legal basis for the handling of information and the right of the individual to privacy. The need to use information to maintain security for society may be balanced, in some cases, against the rights of the individual, for example by sharing criminal records. The Freedom of Information Act (2000) set out the public 'right to know' in relation to public bodies.

1.14. The policy aim of the legal framework is to provide individuals with the assurance that their information will be protected and used only for legitimate purposes. As such, it supports the Government's intention to increase legitimate use of information, to increase public benefit and public protection. It is clear that there are sometimes difficult lines to draw about what is or is not a legitimate use of information. These are complex questions that are being explored in the Walport / Thomas review and are not further examined here.

1.15. Government has already introduced a new monetary penalty in the Data Protection Act (sections 55A to 55E). These ensure that data controllers who do not take reasonable steps to avoid the most serious breaches of Data Protection Act principles may be subject to a fine as well as to an enforcement notice.

1.16. There are also instances in which people deliberately and recklessly misuse personal data. The Information Commissioner has highlighted a lucrative and illegal trade in personal data. The Government takes this matter very seriously, and has amended the Data Protection Act to provide an order-making power to increase the maximum penalty for such offences. The maximum that could be specified in such an order would be two years imprisonment. This is intended as a strong signal that such action will not be tolerated.

1.17. Where Government holds or uses

---

[3] http://www.foi.gov.uk/sharing/information-sharing.pdf

Core resources

personal information, it must act as the custodian of that data and retain and build public confidence that information is held securely. This is particularly true where the law requires that Government be given information, such as in the case of financial information for tax records. Loss of public trust will mean that public services cannot be delivered efficiently or effectively. At the same time, the failure to make the right information available at the right time can have an adverse impact on public services.

1.18. Management of information is integral to the management of public services. Departments and their agencies are best placed to manage their own information and are responsible for its security. That is because they understand best what information they hold, how it has to be used, and the consequences of the risks they face.

1.19. Departments and their agencies exercise that responsibility within a number of frameworks:

- the law (discussed above) for which the Ministry of Justice is responsible;
- a strategic information assurance and security framework set by the Cabinet Office for Departments to implement;
- corporate governance and accountability requirements, promulgated by HM Treasury; and
- the Civil Service Management Code, promulgated by the Cabinet Office.

1.20. The Information Commissioner plays a statutory role in policing compliance with the Data Protection Act, and provides advice on relevant legislation and good practice.

1.21. In addition, there is a range of policy interests that are relevant to information use. Every Department constantly examines its services to seek to improve them, and many of the changes result in changes of information use.

1.22. In planning arrangements, Departments seek to maximise the impact of their activity while managing risks. As a result, they adopt a range of delivery mechanisms. Some services are delivered directly, some by arm's length or independent public bodies, and some by contractors.

1.23. When this work was commissioned in November 2007, there was already work underway to improve arrangements for data handling in Government. The Cabinet Office had commissioned an independent review to examine the Government's capacity to achieve information assurance in the era of Transformational Government. This work informed a refreshed National Information Assurance Strategy, published in June 2007. That Strategy set out an approach for improving information risk management through increased professionalisation and awareness raising, availability of information assurance products and services, and compliance and adoption of standards.[4]

Good practice

1.24. The challenges Government faces regarding information risk management are not unique to the UK or to the public sector. This section summarises good practice. The material is drawn from material made available by Departments, interviews with business, and input from external experts.

Specific measures

1.25. Organisations apply similar cycles of assessing their information, understanding the risks relating to that information, and planning mitigating action. This mitigation is then put in place and monitored.

> Company A adopts a risk-based approach to its staff, with regular vetting procedures for employees in accordance with their level of exposure and access to sensitive personal data. Staff are by default provided with minimum user access rights. Line managers are accountable for system access rights within their team and are required to evaluate the appropriate level of access rights for each role in their team, put forward a business case for additional access, and review and report on those access rights on a regular basis.

1.26. Strong common standards and controls are needed to control access to IT infrastructure. Business managers are

---

[4] www.cabinetoffice.gov.uk/csia

required to evaluate and declare appropriate access rights for each role in their areas and review those rights regularly. New members of staff are provided with access rights only on successful completion of training and minimum access rights are issued as a default.

1.27. Access to raw data are kept to a minimum in business areas with potential access to a high volume of data such as call centres, or areas with high staff turnover. Every information asset is classified and risk assessed by the relevant data owner.

1.28. Private sector organisations aim to use contractual terms to clarify ownership of data, allow regular due diligence checks, and preserve continuity, even where there is a changeover of contractors. They may assess contractors upfront to ensure they can meet the organisation's standards.

Culture

1.29. Strong organisations seek to foster a culture of individual accountability throughout the organisation, with targeted, relevant, role-based training to ensure that employees have a clear understanding of how to use and share information securely. At the same time as recognising the importance of cultural change, many commentators highlighted the difficulty of achieving it and the time taken to do so.

> Company B has initiated a concerted recruitment drive for information security staff who are able to communicate and present clearly how security risks affect the business, in the context of the organisation, and provide clear, relevant and practical guidance for senior management and staff. This is considered to be as important a skill as demonstrating technical expertise.

1.30. Information is seen as a key corporate asset and employees consider themselves 'trusted stewards' of sensitive data with an obligation to protect it. Data are valued throughout its lifecycle to ensure the maintenance of accurate and current records, with clear review, retention and disposal policies in line with relevant legal and regulatory frameworks.

1.31. Staff awareness and education programmes are often supported by regular, centrally monitored testing to assess employees' understanding and ability. When information security skills are included in the performance management framework they are underpinned by disciplinary measures. A learning system is needed, where people avoid mistakes where they can, but admit errors where they are made. This encourages continuous improvement by learning from mistakes, and enables the business to be honest with its customers about possible errors with their data.

> Company C has a bespoke e-learning training programme, tailored to role, which staff are required to complete on an annual basis. At the end of the training they complete a short test online, the results of which are sent to their line manager. New modules are rolled out in response to specific information security threats which staff are directed to when they log on.

1.32. However, it is important to set clear expectations about what constitutes an offence for which employees may be disciplined. Several interviewees commented that the rare occasions where an individual had been fired for misconduct, such as looking up the records of neighbours, served as strong deterrents.

Accountability

1.33. Senior level ownership of information risk is a key factor in success. Senior leadership demonstrates the importance of the issue and is critical in obtaining resource. A simple governance structure, with clear lines of ownership, is essential. Well defined roles and responsibilities are needed to follow up identified information security threats and managing incidents. Internal audit can play an important role in examining and assuring actions taken by others.

Scrutiny and transparency

1.34. Organisations work with the Information Commissioner's Office to ensure compliance with the legal and regulatory framework, and maintain open communication about the data they hold, how it is used, and consumers' rights with respect to the use of their information. Providing clear guidance on who to contact in the event of a query or complaint is key to maintaining customers' trust.

Core resources

Future challenges

1.35. Looking forward, the challenges of ensuring information security are likely to increase. This is as a result of changing technology and external threat. The greater use of information to improve services will add complexity to the problem.

1.36. The pace of technological change is likely to continue to accelerate. New technology to protect data in storage can be used to enhance security, but at the same time the pace of development, such as on wireless technology, adds complexity by creating new opportunities for exploitation.

1.37. Risks posed by deliberate action will remain significant. The threat from hacking and malicious software remains ever present and is becoming increasingly sophisticated.

1.38. Organised crime increasingly exploits the growth of the Internet, particularly in commerce and finance, to develop new crimes and transform traditional ones. The rapid growth of the Internet has resulted in the development of a criminal economy dedicated to the compromise, trade and exploitation of private data. The personal data held by Government are valuable to organised crime and, as a result are at risk from attack.

1.39. A number of countries continue to devote considerable time and energy seeking to obtain information on civilian and military projects in the UK, and political and economic intelligence. This results in attempts to penetrate Government information systems.

1.40. Meanwhile, as part of improving public services, more use will be made of information. This will mean greater connectivity and, therefore, new challenges to ensure that supporting controls and culture are consistent throughout the public sector. At the same time the Government must maintain its focus on protecting the large amount of information that continues to be handled in paper form.

1.41. The main responsibility for understanding and managing information risk should be discharged by the individual Department or agency. Managing information is integral to managing the business and should be handled accordingly.

1.42. Departments and their agencies have checked their procedures for the storage and use of data and their consistency with current cross-Government policies and standards, as well as arrangements for ensuring that procedures are being fully and properly implemented. An update on this work was provided through the Interim Report. A further update is provided in Annex I.

1.43. A wide range of work has taken place across Government. Many of the larger Departments who handle large volumes of personal data have initiated specific reviews into the management and handling of information throughout their organisation. Some have started designing and rolling out training and awareness programs for staff using a range of delivery methods. All Departments have been working with their delivery partners to roll out encryption for the laptops holding personal data where it was not previously in place.

1.44. In parallel, Government has developed its understanding of the need for reform to the overall standards within which Departments operate, building on the recommendations in the Interim Report.

1.45. It is clear that there will be demand for greater information sharing between public bodies, driven by the desire to improve public services or fight crime. Responding to this demand is likely to mean that common standards will become increasingly important.

1.46. Since the Manual of Protective Security[5] and other key documents are protectively marked, they are not published. This makes it difficult for others to understand and assess the approaches being adopted. While it will never be right to make the Government's security arrangements completely public, greater visibility can play a useful role in the public debate and in helping suppliers and partners anticipate key requirements that Departments will be looking to meet.

1.47. Government needs to recognise and

---

[5] The MPS is under revision and will be promulgated later this year as the Security Policy Framework in a more accessible form

respond to the need to nurture a culture that values, protects and uses information. UK public servants who inevitably handle information must understand the importance of privacy. However, there is a risk that service and technology changes may move faster than culture can adapt.

1.48. Following recent losses, Departments are working to test and where necessary to enhance their arrangements. Continued focus on the issue will be essential, particularly in light of future challenges. This means it makes sense to strengthen the accountability mechanisms for Departments, and scrutiny of their performance.

1.49. Government is therefore enhancing its arrangements through:

- core measures to protect information, including personal data, in place across Government;
- a culture that properly values, protects and uses data;
- stronger accountability mechanisms; and
- stronger scrutiny of performance.

1.50. Actions to achieve these aims are set out in the following section.

Core resources

Data Handling Procedures in Government: Final Report

Section 2: Better data handling

This section sets out how the Government is improving data handling, to achieve:

- core measures to protect information, including personal data, in place across Government, to enhance consistency of protection and transparency of that protection to others;
- a culture that properly values, protects and uses data, both in the planning and delivery of public services;
- stronger accountability mechanisms for Departments. The individual Department or agency is best placed to understand and address risks to their information, including personal data; and
- stronger scrutiny of performance, to build confidence and ensure that lessons are learned and shared.

Each topic is covered below.

Core measures to protect information

Departments are already provided with a wealth of security policy advice, guidance and information, notably in the Manual of Protective Security and the Civil Service Management Code. While these remain important parts of the regime, they need to be supplemented with a shorter set of core minimum requirements that are applied across the board. Departments will still determine the level of protection that is applied in particular circumstances, and will often go further than the minimum. But the new requirements in effect introduce a common level that they must meet.

The measures have been developed to reflect the wide range of activity by Departments and their delivery bodies. Some of these handle huge volumes of highly sensitive information, while others handle much less. The approach and material has been developed with the input and support of the Information Commissioner, and will be updated in the future in the light of experience.

Specific elements of the package relating to the transfer of data include:

- specifying personal data benefiting from higher levels of protection;
- where possible, not transferring such information, but accessing it on its home system or remotely via a secure channel;
- where transfer must occur, doing this through secure electronic transfer, so that discs are phased out where possible; and
- where data have to be put onto removable media such as discs or laptops, minimising the information transferred, and using encryption.

Departments are putting in place new controls to limit user rights to transfer data to removable media such as discs and to check the use of those rights.

858

> In addition, new core requirements cover:
>
> - securing disposal for paper or electronic records;
> - using independent penetration testing to test Departmental systems;
> - controls on access to information systems and logging and monitoring of use; and
> - increasing the use of the "accreditation" process, developed to provide assurance for systems holding national security information, for systems holding personal data.

2.1. The Data Protection Act defines "personal data" and "sensitive personal data". While the Government will continue to process all personal data in accordance with Data Protection Act requirements, neither is suitable for an administrative definition of information attracting certain technical protection. While all personal information is of value, the right technical level of protection varies significantly within the "personal data" category. "Sensitive personal data" is so specific as to exclude important aspects of information that require high levels of protection. As a result, this work has, with input from the Information Commissioner, specified an intermediate category of information, referred to as "protected personal information".

2.2. This definition relates to any material that links an identifiable individual with information that, if released, would put them at significant risk of harm or distress, or alternatively any source of information relating to 1000 or more individuals that is not in the public domain, even if the information about an individual is not considered likely to cause harm or distress. As in other areas, this is a minimum baseline. Departments will often wish to apply protection to smaller data sets depending on their risk assessment and the context in which information is kept.

2.3. Wherever possible, Government should keep such protected data within secure premises and systems. This means minimising the storage of, and, access to personal data on removable media, such as laptops, computer discs and memory sticks which may be lost or stolen. A hierarchy of options has been established with the accessing of data on secure systems in secure premises as the best method of handling and accessing personal data.

Where transfer must occur, Departments must consider whether it is possible to provide secure remote access so that data can be viewed without being permanently stored elsewhere.

2.4. Where the use of removable media is unavoidable, encryption will be used and the information transferred will be the minimum necessary to achieve the business purpose. There will remain some situations where encryption cannot be applied consistent with the business purpose – for example for back-up tapes that need to be accessible immediately – such material will be afforded physical protection using similar risk assessment processes as for large amounts of public money or precious objects. This is not an attempt to assign a monetary value to information, which can be complex and may be misleading, but to ensure appropriate secure arrangements for storage and transportation of what are key assets. Both paper and electronic records will be subject to secure disposal.

2.5. To test protections of IT systems against external attack, Departments whose delivery chain involves the handling of information relating to 100,000 or more identifiable individuals will use independent experts to conduct penetration testing.

2.6. To protect against misuse of information, access rights will be minimised, and arrangements put in place to log use of electronically held personal information. Both will be scrutinised by senior individuals.

2.7. Departments will make greater use of the accreditation process for IT systems. This process was developed to provide assurance to the senior business owners of systems holding national security information, and involves an expert assessor

Core resources

examining plans to ensure that information risk has been adequately addressed. New ICT systems containing protected information will be accredited to the Government standard and their accreditation status will be maintained throughout the life of the system.

2.8. The measures developed apply to situations when data are held or used within Government. High levels of data security are also important in citizen or industry-facing activity. Such activity can include both sending and receiving information, which can be sensitive. Departments cannot take responsibility for how others send information to them, although they can encourage good practice, and potentially refuse to accept material that is not handled safely. However, individual citizens may prefer to send or receive information in a way that is less secure, if it makes a service more convenient. Departments will seek to apply the same levels of protection when dealing with those outside Government as have been developed for use inside Government, while recognising that there may be a case to set other standards or make other arrangements. Where different standards are set, they will be clearly explained, along with alternative service routes.

Culture

High levels of data security must be underpinned by a culture that values, protects and uses information. This culture is important both when services are being planned and when they are being delivered.

Government is reinforcing its efforts to ensure that the right culture is in place. This has to be led from the top of Departments, and include all those involved in the management of and access to personal data. As in other areas, individual Departments are responsible for their own data security, and will need to lead the work, tailoring it to their circumstances. Departments will need to understand and actively manage any day-to-day operational processes that may, wrongly, lead staff to cut corners and expose information, in whatever form, to unacceptable risk.

Government should regard any data loss as a cause for concern, and take immediate action to improve matters for the future. When problems occur, however, the culture has to be one in which losses are identified and learned from. This should apply both to actual problems and "near misses". This is vital if Government is to avoid making the same mistakes, as well as allowing Government to be open with individuals who may be affected by problems.

All Departments will take the following action:
- introduce Privacy Impact Assessments, which ensure that privacy issues are factored into plans from the start, and those planning services are clear about their aims. Similarly, information risk management will be considered as part of the Government's "Gateway™" reviews that monitor progress of the most important projects;
- roll out a basic level of mandatory training to all data users and those involved in managing personal data, to be completed on appointment and annually;
- put in place processes by which individuals can bring concerns to the attention of senior management, anonymously if necessary; and

- amend HR processes where necessary to make clear that failing to apply controls in handling personal data could amount to gross misconduct.

Action will be taken by Cabinet Office with others to increase the professional qualifications of those involved in information assurance.

2.9. Most of those contributing to this work have stressed the importance of the right culture to underpin data security, if information risk is to be understood and efficiently handled in day-to-day operations as part of normal business. Any operational process that may, wrongly, lead staff to cut corners and thus expose information, in whatever form, to unacceptable risk must be identified and actively managed. Departments should put in place plans to lead and foster a culture that values, protects and uses information for the public good, and monitor progress, as a minimum through standardised civil service-wide questions in their people surveys.

2.10. The culture of an organisation affects its ability to protect its information in many ways. It affects the attitude to collecting information in the first place, and how systems are developed to do that. In recognition that collecting any sort of information potentially brings risk with it, good practice requires that privacy protection and data security are built into plans at the earliest stages.

2.11. The Information Commissioner has made a powerful case for Government to adopt Privacy Impact Assessments. These are structured assessments of a project's potential impact on privacy, carried out at an early stage.[6] They enable organisations to anticipate and address the likely impacts of new initiatives, foresee problems, and negotiate solutions. Risks can be managed through the gathering and sharing of information with stakeholders. Systems can be designed to avoid unnecessary privacy intrusion, and features can be built in from the outset that reduce any impact on privacy. The Privacy Impact Assessment adopts a risk management process approach, periodic reports from which (Privacy Impact Assessment Reports) may be published or distributed to stakeholders. The Government has accepted their value and they will be used in all Departments. Future "Gateway ™" reviews of ICT projects will check that they have been carried out as an integral part of the risk management assessment.

2.12. The OGC Gateway™ process is designed to examine the progress and likelihood of successful delivery of programmes and projects. Its use is mandatory in central Government for procurement, IT enabled and construction projects. An examination of project risk is an integral part of the Gateway™ Process, which will include information risk as well as privacy.

2.13. The operating culture of an organisation is also important. If staff understand the value of information and the potential threats to it, management and staff will find ways to deliver the services expected of them without exposing information, in whatever form, to unacceptable risk. They will keep alert to attempts by outsiders to gain illegitimate access to it, and can be an important source of ways to improve protections and arrangements.

2.14. Government will roll out at least a minimum level of information risk awareness training to all those with access to protected personal data. This will supplement training already in place to make staff and contractors aware of their responsibilities for safeguarding and handling information in accordance with the Manual of Protective Security and the Civil Service Management Code. Such training will, where possible, take the form of short, e-learning products including tests for understanding, and will be applied on appointment and annually.

2.15. To support a managerial culture that understands the importance of information and deals actively with risks to it, Government will roll out at least a minimum level of information management training to

---

[6] http://www.ico.gov.uk/upload/documents/pia_handbook_html/html/foreword.html

Core resources

all Information Asset Owners (see below under Accountability), on appointment and annually, and strategic information management training to Accounting Officers, Senior Information Risk Owners, and members of audit committees.

2.16. Cabinet Office will provide a minimum specification for this training, and seek views from Departments as to whether they would wish to use a standardised training product. The aim should be to develop training material that can be externally accredited and transferred between organisations, and integrate similar material into relevant courses run by external bodies.

2.17. Government needs to increase the professional qualifications of staff involved in information assurance work. The National Information Assurance Strategy set out the need to increase professional capacity. Cabinet Office will take this forward, working with others. The right links will need to be made with the closely related areas of IT and knowledge and information management, and with the work to develop professional capacity and capability in those areas.

2.18. HR processes in Departments will be amended where necessary to make clear that failing to apply controls in handling sensitive data is a serious matter, and could amount to gross misconduct.

Stronger accountability

The onus has to remain on Departments to plan and secure their own information. This is because protection and use of data are part and parcel of their business, and they are best placed to understand requirements and manage risks. The best mechanism to ensure that this happens is the chain of command from the Accounting Officer, who is ultimately responsible for having the appropriate controls in place in their Department.

However, more can and should be done to increase accountability, in particular to standardise and enhance the processes by which Departments understand and manage their information risk, setting out the responsibilities for key individuals in doing so. Departments are required to establish:

- a process by which information assets are identified and allocated to a responsible owner; and
- an annual assessment process to support the Accounting Officer's judgement for the Statement on Internal Control.

Simplified cross-Government structures will support this process, with Cabinet Office maintaining and updating the cross-Government requirements.

Responsibility in Departments

2.19. Most Government Departments are large, complex organisations. They can undertake very different tasks. In doing so, they draw on a wide range of expertise, including experts in knowledge management, ICT, information management, security and others. They approach their tasks in different ways. Different roles may be legitimately combined in different circumstances, so a single solution cannot be applied. But roles on information management and risk must be sufficiently standardised to drive responsibility and accountability. Similarly, it is necessary to balance the need to avoid unnecessary bureaucracy with the need to ensure that important decisions are considered, recorded and implemented.

2.20. Government has developed a set of specific actions to achieve these aims.

These build on good practice and international standards, and on established roles of the Accounting Officer and the Senior Information Risk Owner, who is a board level executive with particular responsibility for information risk. They are tailored to the circumstances of the UK central Government. Many Departments will, as now, work towards or achieve external ISO accreditation for some or all of their information systems, but independent input to this work suggested that systematic external accreditation would absorb effort that would be better used in a more targeted way.

2.21. Departments are now standardising and enhancing the processes by which they understand and manage their information risk, including by:

- defining their information risk policy, which says how information risk will be managed within the Department and by their delivery partners and how effectiveness will be assessed;
- identifying information assets, and giving senior individuals involved in running relevant businesses (Information Asset Owners - IAOs) clear responsibility for each in defined ways;
- assessing risks to the confidentiality, integrity and availability of information in their delivery chain at least quarterly, and putting in place responses to manage those risks as necessary; and
- specifying an annual process of assessment to provide an evidence base to support the judgement of the Accounting Officer, including written input from Information Asset Owners and the Senior Information Risk Owner.

2.22. The role of the Information Asset Owner is to understand what information is held and in what form, how it is added and removed, who has access, and why. They approve the level and extent of transfer of data to removable media, such as laptops, ensuring that it is the minimum necessary to conduct the business, and that it is properly protected. They ensure that access rights to IT systems are limited to the minimum needed, and that usage of information is monitored. Importantly, they are tasked with ensuring that best use is made of information, and receive and respond to requests from others for access to information.

2.23. In addition to these named roles, Departments will need to ensure that they have the right mix of professional advice and support, covering both risk and information issues specifically.

2.24. Putting in place these new arrangements represents a significant undertaking for most Departments, but they have committed to do so, and implementation has commenced. Departments' first full annual assessments will be completed for the year 2008/09 and reflected in Statements on Internal Control, the standard way of bringing risk management within an organised structure for reporting and internal use.

2.25. As Government bodies share more information, whether to improve services or to protect the public, they are increasingly developing information systems that reflect the interests of several different organisations. Contrary to some public perception, such systems may not be all-encompassing databases, but mechanisms to link together and make better specific use of information that is held separately.

2.26. Clear accountability and responsibility are crucial for effective operation of systems that cross Departmental boundaries, just as they are for systems operating within Departments. Government is learning to adapt established approaches to these new situations, in particular:

- ensuring that every system has a single Senior Responsible Owner[7] (SRO). The SRO is responsible for the business case and ensuring that the system achieves its aims. The SRO does this through management of the associated risks by ensuring that the right controls and protections are built in and monitored so that participating organisations can use it with confidence;

---

[7] The OGC definition of the SRO may be found at: http://www.ogc.gov.uk/User_roles_in_the_toolkit_senior_responsible_owner.asp

Core resources

Data Handling Procedures in Government: Final Report

- ensuring that information enters a system with the agreement of the owning Department, in effect that the controls provide sufficient protection; and

- the SRO, working with the IAO ensures that there is an individual responsible for the continued integrity of datasets, maintaining and enforcing application of policies and standards applicable to the system and scrutinising the system, remaining alert, for example, to the creation of new dataset combinations which raise new system challenges and, potentially, privacy concerns.

2.27. Cabinet Office will continue to set the overall standards for information assurance in Government, taking account of the need both for security and for knowledge and information management to assist in the delivery of public services. Responsibility for specific implementation of the regime in each Department lies within that Department. Cabinet Office will support the strengthened regime set out in this report by:

- setting the cross-Government mandatory standards. These will need to be updated in the light of experience, and of progress in Departments in implementation. Crucially they will need to continue to be informed by business experts, technical experts, and independent input from others;

- provision of practical support for implementation in Departments, for example developing and providing services of common interest, where it may be more efficient for Government to develop a single solution to a shared problem than to develop many different approaches. This will require the acceleration of the work to improve support to Departments foreseen in the National Information Assurance Strategy. Cabinet Office will provide support where it is best placed to do so, and co-ordinate others where that is a more effective approach;

- preparation of the annual report on information risk as a whole, including on the level of "common good" spending on information assurance needed for Government and specific policy issues as they arise.

2.28. In common with other policy areas, Cabinet Office can play a role in identifying and resolving issues that cannot be easily resolved between individual Departments. Experience shows that specific data sharing proposals can fall into this category. The network of Information Asset Owners provides a mechanism to identify such issues.

2.29. In addition, cross-Government functions will be reformed, in order to:

- understand information risk better across Government and, in particular, provide a central facility for sharing risk information. Cabinet Office will receive the annual assessments from Departments, and use those to develop a cross-Government view of the risks being faced by Departments, to inform work on updating the common standards, or other action; and

- simplify the complex array of groups active in the information risk area, which have developed over time in response to particular needs, but which can now be usefully consolidated.

2.30. Cabinet Office is committed to take forward these tasks, working with others. Cabinet Office is adapting its resources to the new ways of working set out in this report.

2.31. During the preparation of this report, the team benefited from input from a range of individuals and bodies, including industry and academia (see Annex III). The Government will maintain strong levels of engagement, in addition to the regular dialogue with potential suppliers that is already in place and seeking advice on best practice from independent experts.

2.32. Implementation of the action underway as a result of this report will be taken forward through a cross-Departmental programme, supported by a committee of senior officials. Collective Ministerial overview and approval of the report on information risk across Government will be provided by the Cabinet Sub-Committee on Personal Data Security, chaired by Paul Murphy, Secretary of State for Wales.

Stronger scrutiny

In publishing the Interim Report, the Government committed to enhanced transparency of actions. Departments will cover information assurance in their annual reports, and the Government will report annually to Parliament on information security as a whole. This commitment will now be reinforced through:

- the publication of Information Charters by all Departments. These set out the standards that people can expect from public bodies that request or hold their personal information, how they can get access to their personal data and what they can do if they do not think that these standards are being met;
- consideration by Departments of publication of material on specific information assets held, such as what information is contained and how it is used. This is to be considered with a presumption of openness, while recognising that there will always be some information and some uses of it (for example in the national security and law enforcement arenas) where transparency must rightly be limited; and
- publication by Cabinet Office of the new requirements on Departments[8].

Performance and capability will be monitored by a combination of specific controls, as well as by building information risk into existing mechanisms:

- reference to information assurance in the Statement on Internal Controls, which is subject to scrutiny by the National Audit Office (NAO), based upon their knowledge of the organisation in question;
- spot checks conducted by the Information Commissioner, or other more formal action, including application of existing sanctions of the Data Protection Act or new sanctions when they are in place; and
- inclusion of information risk issues in Whitehall "capability reviews".

In addition, given the greater connectedness of Departmental systems, Departments will be able to request on a peer basis additional assurance about their counterparts' systems and protections. Within this, CESG, the National Technical Authority for Information Assurance, will be an active and important source of expert scrutiny of performance.

---

[8] http://www.cabinetoffice.gov.uk/csia

Core resources

2.33. Following the requirements in this report, Departments will produce a range of internal material including:

- the information risk policy;
- quarterly risk assessments, including actions planned as a result;
- accreditation records; and
- an annual review against requirements, supported by evidence-based assessments from the SIRO and IAOs.

2.34. Together, these provide a clear audit trail between the detailed work to manage information risk and the judgement of the Accounting Officer in their Statement on Internal Control. This audit trail will be an important tool for those examining the performance of Departments in detail.

2.35. The NAO scrutinises Statements on Internal Control, using a process of "negative assurance". This means that they examine statements made to ensure they are not inconsistent with the information gathered during the course of their audit work. The new processes put in place in Departments will ensure that in their review of the work of the Board, the NAO will have access to material covering information risk.

2.36. The Information Commissioner has the power to carry out spot checks on Departments, with the first checks currently being planned. In future, such checks will be informed by the audit trail outlined above.

2.37. Government will incorporate greater scrutiny into its Whitehall processes by:

- building information risk handling into the Capability Review process, carried out on all Government Departments. Capability Reviews are conducted by a team of external reviewers drawn from the private sector, the wider public sector and Government Departments to examine how well equipped Departments are to meet their delivery challenges;
- increasing specific Department to Department scrutiny by widening existing practice under which Departments may request of others additional assurance about the protections that others have in place. This is currently carried out under the auspices of the Office of the Government Chief Information Officer and specifically related to ICT, but will be widened to cover broader information assurance issues; and
- increasing the focus and resource in CESG devoted to critical examination of Departmental systems, through the peer review processes mentioned above.

2.38. The work of the Information Commissioner and the NAO will mean that Parliament and others will be better able to monitor progress. To reinforce this, Government is introducing additional requirements on Departments to report directly on their actions and performance.

2.39. The public are entitled to understand how the information held about them is being handled and Parliament needs to be able to hold Government to account. At the same time, arrangements should not be so transparent as to help those seeking to exploit system vulnerabilities.

2.40. Similarly, there is a clear need for more robust performance monitoring, to reflect the seriousness of the issues. But a monitoring regime that was too draconian would bring its own problems. One risk is that staff and managers could become risk-averse in handling any data, meaning that innovation and even the conduct of ordinary business would be affected. A second risk could be that individuals may become unwilling to admit to errors. This would critically undermine the ability of organisations to recover from incidents, learn lessons, or to alert individuals whose information may be compromised.

2.41. In order to strike the appropriate balance the Government has committed to report on information breaches in summary form in Departments' annual reporting. The first such material will be included in annual reporting for 2007/08. There are two exceptions to this: when the interests of those affected are best served through public announcement, or when issues are so serious that Ministers judge that their immediate accountability to Parliament overrides other considerations.

2.42. For each financial year, Departments will report:

- a summary of protected personal data related incidents formally reported to the Information Commissioner;
- a summary of centrally recorded protected personal data related incidents not formally reported to the Information Commissioner; and
- a summary statement of actions to manage information risk.

2.43. In addition to the action already announced, Government will increase the information available externally in two ways:

- all Departments will issue an Information Charter, setting out the standards that people can expect from the public body when it requests or holds their personal information, how they can get access to their personal data and what they can do if they do not think that standards are being met. Model text is set out in Annex IV; and
- in addition, all Departments will consider the scope to publish material on specific information assets that it holds, such as what information is contained and how it is used. Departments will approach this with a presumption of openness, while recognising that there will always be some information and some uses of it (for example in the national security and law enforcement arenas) where transparency must rightly be limited.

Section 3: Implementation

> The conclusions from this report have been shared and acted upon by Departments as they have been developed. Implementation has started. All Departments have established new technical protections for information they hold directly. They have identified the protected personal data they hold, are rolling out encryption to protect it in transit, and have minimised the use of removable media. Departments are now working with their delivery partners to ensure that they apply the same protections.
>
> The Government's guiding principle is that the protections outlined in this report, or their equivalent, should be in place and effective, no matter how information is held and processed for central government purposes.
>
> Departments will work with all those involved in the delivery chain, whether they are public sector, private sector, or third sector. Progress will take time. Many public sector bodies are independent of central Government, and the material developed for central Government will need to be tailored so that it fits the audience and their requirements.
>
> No organisation can guarantee it will never lose data, and the Government is no exception. Some of the actions set out in this document – for instance around cultural change – will take time. The specific requirements and approach to rolling them out will continue to change as services, technology and threats change. It will always be possible to improve. This means that the development of processes for improved information security will never, in that sense, be "finished". This report is a new start in a continuous and evolving process.
>
> Departments have agreed a timetable for the initial steps for implementation over the coming year. These will be the subject of the first annual report to Parliament next year.

Central Government

3.1. As described in Annex I, Departments have worked to review and improve where necessary their own approaches to information risk and data handling. They have increased staff awareness of information risk, reminding them of their individual responsibilities as part of their organisation.

3.2. The action described in this report is being implemented as fast as possible. For Departments that deal with significant volumes of personal citizen data, this will involve working with complex and diverse delivery chains. These can include the Department, Non-Departmental Public Bodies (NDPB) and partners in the wider public or third sector, as well as contractors providing services for the Department.

3.3. The implementation approach will be phased to recognise this reality. Departments are moving fastest in respect of their own activity and the activity of those bodies where they are in a position to mandate certain ways of working. Where Departments can require the use of new measures, or higher standards where those are judged necessary, they will do so.

3.4. Where Departments cannot require the use of new measures throughout their area of responsibility immediately, they will seek to influence their delivery chain partners.

3.5. Many Government Departments engage with private sector companies to contract out elements of the services they provide, or to provide the Departments themselves with services which support their organisations. Contractors will, as part of their service provision, handle information belonging to the Department or to the public for whom the Department serves. Departments will build into new contracts the new requirements set out in this report. In addition, Departments are working with contractors under existing contracts to apply the same controls and to monitor their performance. Contact so far with contractors suggests that they recognise the shared interest in achieving high levels of data security.

3.6. The Office of Government Commerce (OGC) is updating the security clauses within its model ICT contract for services, which Departments will use to provide assurance that any contractor will have processes in place which comply with the new cross-Government requirements. In addition, Departments will set out their requirements where those go further.

3.7. Many of the specific controls to enhance protection for personal data are already in place in Departments themselves. All Departments have:

- formalised the role of SIRO;
- identified what personal data are held and used within the Department itself that falls into the new definition of "protected personal data";
- established procedures and policies to ensure such data are handled as if they are protectively marked;
- an encryption programme for such data, where it is on removable media, except where that is not possible, for example because of the need to access back-ups;
- where such data are stored electronically, minimised the use of removable media and the amount of data transferred to them, and minimised the user rights to copy files onto such media;
- introduced new arrangements where needed for secure disposal from the Department of paper and electronic records; and
- reviewed procedures for reporting information risk incidents.

3.8. Departments are undertaking a further set of activities, including:

- appointing Information Asset Owners;
- formalising their information risk policy, to reflect the actions in this report;
- rolling out protection for personal data beyond the Departments themselves to their delivery partners for which Departments can mandate use of specific measures;
- amending HR policies and guidance as necessary;
- introducing cultural change plans;
- publishing Information Charters; and
- compiling material on breaches for Departmental accounts, for 07/08 and previous years where possible.

3.9. From July:

- Information Asset Owners will review the position on their information assets, and perform their roles fully;
- new systems containing protected personal data will be subject to mandated accreditation, and build in greater access control and logging;
- standard contract clauses on information assurance will be incorporated into contracts; and
- Privacy Impact Assessments will be used and monitored.

3.10. Departments will have started their mandatory training by the end of October 2008. This timing is to allow them to develop and tailor materials as needed.

3.11. Other steps, including the deployment of penetration testing will take place during 2008/09. The first full annual assessments of progress will take place following the end of 2008/09 and be reflected in the first annual Cabinet Office Report on overall progress.

Core resources

3.12. As set out in the Interim Report, Government is putting in place a programme to tighten procedures for data held overseas. This will combine controls reflecting the actions set out in this report, and through case-by-case examination by experts from the CESG, and Office of Government Commerce, with support as necessary from the Ministry of Justice.

3.13. Ministerial overview of progress will be provided through:

- Ministerial action in individual Departments;
- the Minister with responsibility for Information Rights at the Ministry of Justice;
- the Minister for the Cabinet Office and Chancellor of the Duchy of Lancaster responsible for Cabinet Office functions; and
- Paul Murphy, Secretary of State for Wales, chairing the Cabinet Sub-Committee on Personal Data Security.

The wider public sector

3.14. The work underway by some central Government Departments will influence some practices in the wider public sector.

3.15. In parallel, recognising that data security challenges are real for other public sector bodies, Government wishes to encourage others to consider adopting similar approaches themselves. As a result, the material here has been shared as it has been developed with other interested parties.

3.16. The Devolved Administrations have taken forward action and will make their own announcements. The Government will continue to work with the Devolved Administrations as the work is taken forward.

3.17. Departments are working on specific issues with partners in the wider public sector, to apply the new measures.

3.18. The Local Government Association is producing equivalent material and approaches for local government as a whole. This work is expected to be completed by the end of summer 2008. The Information Commissioner has indicated his willingness to support the result of that work as good practice, meaning that implementation would be subject to monitoring by the Audit Commission.

3.19. The Government supports this work, while recognising the need for local government to find solutions that reflect their situation, and is grateful for the Information Commissioner's support.

Reporting progress

3.20. Because of the rapid changes both in technology and in the threat to Government-held data, this work has sought to consider not only how to respond to recent losses, but also to establish a strong position from which to tackle future challenges.

3.21. Some of the actions have been about establishing standards, roles and responsibilities, but above all, this requires a culture shift. Changing the way leadership and staff think about the value and handling of information in all forms will take time to set in place, although significant progress has already been made in establishing these changes.

3.22. Departments will be reporting on progress to date in their own annual reports. Cabinet Office will follow these with the first annual reporting on the issue as a whole from Government following the end of 2008/09.

Data Handling Procedures in Government: Final Report, June 2008

Annex I: Action taken in individual Departments

> The HMRC data loss started an intensive process as all Departments re-examined their data practices under the auspices of this work. The Interim Report, published in December, summarised action taken across Government. This work has continued and broadened. This Annex provides an updated summary.
>
> All Departments have initiated a program of cultural change in their organisations, looking at the current awareness of staff regarding data handling and information risk, and reminded staff of their responsibilities to handle information carefully. All Departments have undertaken the initial stages of implementation of the new technical and process measures to protect personal information.

I.1. The Cabinet Office (CO) has reviewed its internal security policies and procedures including those which specifically deal with the secure handling of information and protected personal data. The CO has ensured that these policies are compliant with the requirements of this report, specifically regarding limiting the use of removable media to the minimum necessary for business operation and providing encryption on any necessary non-encrypted media devices. A programme of encryption of all non-encrypted stand alone PCs used within the CO will be completed by the end of July 2008. Heads of business units in the Department have been asked to ensure and confirm that all their staff are aware of the existing policies and procedures which have been included in the Department's own security manual. CO departmental data copying continues to be audited by an automated software product. The CO continues to monitor that its procedures and systems remain compliant with the Manual of Protective Security and any other centrally provided advice. An additional exercise is being undertaken immediately (the Omand Review) to ensure that the CO's procedures, particularly concerning hard copy classified material, and the disposal of classified waste, are as effective as possible.

I.2. The Crown Prosecution Service (CPS) has reviewed and significantly changed write access to portable media. It is now only permissible to download data from the CPS system to portable media with the explicit permission of the IT Security Officer. An encryption programme for the hard drives of laptops containing personal data was completed by the end of May 2008. A review of back up tape procedures has taken place and written assurances that they are secure in transit and when stored has been provided by local managers. A Data and Information Integrity Audit has been completed with no significant issues being identified. Further work is on-going to assess and reduce risk and strengthen information risk governance, covering both personal data and other sensitive information. This will be completed during the next financial year utilising the ISO 27001 compliance programme.

I.3. The Department for Business Enterprise and Regulatory Reform (BERR) has undertaken an internal review to ensure best practice is understood across the BERR family and with delivery partners to ensure consistency and best practice in data handling security and management. Data governance arrangements have been strengthened with the appointment of senior civil service data owners. A network of Group Data Champions has also been established for liaison between the business, the data owners and BERR's delivery partners (including NDPBs).

I.4. The Department for Children, Schools and Families (DCSF) has completed a wide ranging review of security covering technology, culture, governance, data sharing procedures (including those of its

Core resources

delivery partners) and physical security. Deloitte has completed an independent review of the DCSF ContactPoint system. Both review reports show no obvious flaws in current systems and procedures, but have identified a number of opportunities for improvement. The new actions in this report are being implemented quickly in the Department. Strong controls remain in place covering the use of laptops and removable media. DCSF staff and partner organisations' security responsibilities continue to be reinforced by the Permanent Secretary and through management action, stronger guidance, and training. DCSF's governance framework is monitoring and ensuring progress and pace.

I.5. The Department for Communities and Local Government (CLG) has reviewed its processes and put in place a range of additional measures to further improve its data handling processes. Of particular note CLG has recently rolled out an updated Knowledge Management Strategy, including guidance on responsible data handling, to staff. Contractors and partners have been reminded of their responsibility in this area and the CIO has written to all his senior civil service colleagues. A new laptop solution has also been recently rolled out which is fully encrypted. Access policies to key systems with personal data on them have been reviewed and a code of conduct issued to all staff that have access to systems containing personal data. The wider Communities Group are carrying out similar activities with their staff and delivery partners. CLG will continue to lead and monitor this activity across the group to ensure that minimum requirements are always met or exceeded. Where potential risks have been identified either in the Group or with delivery partners remedial measures are being put in place. Communities and Local Government is working with the Local Government Association and the Cabinet Office to ensure local authorities have access to expert information assurance advice and best practice guidance is issued.

I.6. The Department for Culture, Media and Sport's (DCMS) information management strategy is still under review. The area will shortly be considered by both the Audit Committee and the Department's Board.

Draft principles for ensuring that information assurance and business risk form part of the Department's leadership culture have been published. Staff have been reminded of guidance and policies and an independent IT security audit has examined compliance. Encryption of laptops is underway, and completed for those that may be used for holding personal data. NDPBs have been informed of the new policy on the protection of data – DCMS will run a related seminar for NDPBs and delivery partners.

I.7. The Department for Environment, Food and Rural Affairs (DEFRA) has raised awareness of existing policies, procedures and good practice relevant to the use and storage of protected personal and other sensitive information. Staff across the DEFRA network have been reminded about their personal obligation to observe the existing guidance on handling information. This is being embedded through new information management accountabilities now being put in place, including a Board-level Senior Information Risk Owner and a network of Information Asset Owners. A Project on data handling procedures has been set up to deliver enhanced information assurance in DEFRA and its delivery network. A Project Board (consisting of representative key delivery bodies, business areas holding significant personal data and information risk experts) has been established to support the work to implement the requirements in the Data Handling Review. This includes ensuring appropriate accountabilities and responsibilities for information assurance; putting in place technical and other measures to ensure that protected personal and other sensitive information is adequately secured (including the roll out of a new fully encrypted laptop solution which will be completed by the end of 2008); and will also continue to review and improve, where necessary, existing security policies and procedures to ensure staff understand how data should be classified, stored, and handled.

I.8. The Department of Health (DH) has started implementation of the new actions in this report. Progress across the Department and its delivery bodies is being secured and monitored by a dedicated Programme Board. Reports on progress have been made to the Departmental Board and to the Audit Committee. Where the protections developed for use inside Government are not practicable for patient facing services within the NHS, work is in progress to ensure that equivalent safeguards are put in place. Full compliance will take some time, and must be achieved in a way that does not place patients at risk. For example the transmission of personal data to receiving A&E units by ambulance crews needs to be made more secure but prevention of transmission in the interim would have been detrimental to patient care. Individual NHS Trusts have been asked to make a local judgement on the balance of risk to patient care against risk to personal data security in determining whether existing data sharing for particular purposes should continue whilst the steps required to secure data transfers are taken.

I.9. The Department for Innovation, Universities and Skills (DIUS) adopted procedures from its two predecessor departments whilst developing its own approach. DIUS's IT policy is standardised on laptops with full disc encryption, which places the Department in a strong position regarding information security. But DIUS commissioned an independent review in support of its data handling procedures. An implementation plan has been formulated allowing the development of Department-wide policies and procedures to meet the outcomes for this report, and good progress is being made. The DIUS Audit and Risk Committee has met to discuss information assurance issues, and will continue to take an active interest in this area. Furthermore, DIUS has held the first in a series of information assurance forums to enable its delivery partners to hear and share best practice from each other and from other experts. This is part of an ongoing dialogue with delivery partners to ensure an appropriate level of information assurance throughout the DIUS delivery chain.

I.10. The Department for International Development (DfID) achieved accreditation to ISO 27001 in March 2008. The Department does not hold large amounts of personal data relating to members of the public, it does hold significant volumes of commercial and security data. It takes a risk-based approach to information security and is reviewing its decisions on the controls over the storage, retrieval and transmission of all sensitive data.

I.11. The Department for Transport (DfT) announced in December a series of measures to improve the security of the personal information it holds. Since then, further progress has been made, including encryption of laptops, further replacement of discs with electronic transfer, new procedures on bulk transfer of forms and letters containing personal data, and work with IT suppliers to ensure systems and processes are robust and secure. Existing procedures have continued to be reviewed and improved, reflecting both internal lessons and the conclusions of this report.

I.12. The Department for Work and Pensions (DWP) has introduced improved controls over the physical transfer of data on removable media. These include the introduction of new more stringent procedures for Departmental staff and Service Providers, including refreshed guidance and a secure same-day courier service. All laptops in the Department have been replaced with fully encrypted laptops and non-encrypted devices are electronically barred from connecting to the network. DWP has introduced a fast-track project for the encryption of data transfers that cannot be done electronically. The Department has set up a dedicated project, led by a senior executive, to implement a number of other actions to improve data handling.

I.13. The Foreign and Commonwealth Office (FCO) issued reinforced instructions on data security and data protection issues to UKvisas staff in December 2007. New instructions on data handling and data security, in particular laptops and drives containing personal data, were issued in January and have been updated since. A centralised system for reporting incidents involving personal data has now been put in place. Additional guidance on the Data Protection Act, to emphasise and advise on its practical implications, has been circulated to the key units. As part of the FCO role in providing a global network for Government, FCO are undertaking a review of its worldwide mail services and will be acting on its recommendations.

I.14. The Home Office (HO), before

Core resources

Data Handling Procedures in Government: Final Report: Annexes

the HMRC data loss, had already begun a review of its data security. This is being extended to take account of the issues arising from this report work. In parallel the HO has taken five further steps to tighten arrangements. New guidance has been issued to staff on the protective marking of documents and on their responsibilities under the Data Protection Act. Key data exchanges have been re-examined, with a view to increasing security. Data handling has been included in the compliance audit programme, to check that managers are following guidance. A new senior post has been created to support the SIRO and CIO on information management issues, including data handling procedures. Finally, the HO has established a new information assurance programme to ensure the implementation of the new mandatory minimum standards for the protection of personal data.

I.15. HM Revenue and Customs (HMRC) has continued to strengthen its data security arrangements since the Child Benefit data loss incident. It is co-operating fully with the external reviews, including the review by Kieran Poynter, and other investigations looking at the specifics of the incident, as well as wider data security issues. HMRC has taken significant steps to strengthen its data security arrangements in the short term and has now established and introduced a wide-ranging Departmental Data Security Programme to identify and drive forward delivery of further improvements in a structured way. This programme will incorporate any further work that may be required following receipt of the final Poynter Review report which is expected to be received in the first half of 2008 increased emphasis on compliance.

I.16. HM Treasury (HMT) is enhancing its staff education and training in security backed by senior management leadership and increased emphasis on compliance. In the light of the recent incident in which documents were lost, HMT has undertaken an immediate investigation and updated policies and procedures in light of the lessons learnt. The documents have been assessed to ensure that there was no breach of the Data Protection Act and there was no personal data associated with this incident.

I.17. The Ministry of Defence (MoD), following a loss of a laptop on 9 January 2008, commissioned an independent review by Sir Edmund Burton into the incident and lessons to be learned. Notwithstanding this review, the Chief of the Defence Staff and the Permanent Secretary have initiated a campaign across the Department to raise awareness as well as appointing a Departmental Head of Information Assurance and Data Protection. Further action has included: assigning responsibility for ensuring rigorous information assurance standards for systems outside the central accreditation and assurance system to the Departmental Security Officer; briefing information risk management to Integrated Project Team leaders; engaging with industry partners over the implications of this report; and putting in train the full-disc encryption of some 20,000 laptops across the Department. The Department is producing a consolidated programme to implement the recommendations of the Burton and Data Handling reviews.

I.18. The Ministry of Justice (MoJ) is continuing to make progress on all the actions identified in its December report. This includes ongoing communications to all staff about information management and security, launching a new Data Protection and Freedom of Information network, accompanied by new guidance about those Acts provisions and requirements, and work to review central induction and training programmes. Training delivery will reflect local solutions and included the roll-out from May 2008 of an on-line training package on security awareness and procedures in the National Offender Management Service (NOMS). A Ministry-wide information assurance programme is now in place to take forward implementation of the recommendations of this report.

I.19. The Northern Ireland Office (NIO) have completed a detailed review of their Data Handling and Information Assurance Policies and are satisfied that they comply with HMG policies/standards and ISO 27001. Policies will be continuously monitored to ensure compliance with any changes proposed or "lessons learnt" centrally. The Department has introduced new governance arrangements; an Accreditation Panel of key users and a

Senior Risk Owners Council under the chairmanship of the SIRO have been established. The Department is complying with central guidance vis-à-vis removable media unencrypted laptops holding personal or protectively marked material. All staff in the NIO and satellite bodies are receiving refresher training for Data Handling and Information Assurance.

Core resources

Data Handling Procedures in Government: Final Report: Annexes

Annex II: Timeline

II.1. By end April 2008, all Departments had completed initial measures for the protection of personal data.

II.2. Departments will include summary material on information risk in their annual reporting, through the Management Commentary to their resource accounts for 2007/08, as those are issued.

II.3. Departments are currently:

- completing roll-out of new protection through their delivery chains, where they can require the use of particular measures;
- putting plans in place to encourage use of protective measures where they cannot require their use;
- completing initial changes to Departmental HR policies;
- putting in place cultural change plans;
- allocating responsibility to Information Asset Owners;
- formalising their information risk policy in light of the material in this report; and
- publishing their Information Charter.

II.4. From July 2008 onwards:

- new systems containing protected personal data will be accredited;
- new contracts will include standard contract clauses including new protection;
- Privacy Impact Assessments will be completed;
- greater access control will be introduced; and
- penetration testing will be in place.

II.5. By October 2008:

- Information Asset Owners will have their controls operating for their information assets; and
- mandatory training for data users and senior managers will have commenced, with its first cycle to have been completed within 12 months, so that the current population will have been covered in that time.

II.6. During the 2008/09 reporting year, Departments will conduct their annual assessments, to inform their Accounting Officer's judgement in the Statement on Internal Control.

II.7. Following the end of the 2008/09 reporting year, Cabinet Office will provide to Parliament material on information risk as a whole.

Annex III: Conduct of the work

This work for this report was started in November 2007. An Interim Progress Report was published on 17 December 2007.

Governance

Members of the steering group for the work were: Gus O'Donnell (Chair); Natalie Ceeney, The National Archives; Alexis Cleveland, CO; James Crosby; Karen Dunnell, ONS; John Fiennes, CO; Robert Hannigan, CO; Helen Kilpatrick, HO; Leigh Lewis, DWP; David Pepper GCHQ; Ian Watmore, DIUS; Chris Wright, CO; and Tim Wright, DCSF.

In addition, a 'Red Team' was established to examine material. The team was: Charles Branch, BERR; Mara Broome, MoJ; Chris Bywater, DWP; David Chilver, HMRC; John Cook, MoD; Belinda Crowe, MoJ; Stephen Hickey, DfT; Colin Hurd, DCSF; Richard Jeavons, DH; Robin Pape, HO; Clive Porro, DEFRA; and Linda Wishart, DH.

Advice and expertise

The team are grateful for the help and support received from:

- Richard Thomas, the Information Commissioner, and his Office;
- The Local Government Association; and
- the Financial Services Authority.

The team benefited from input from:

- Professor John Beddington, Chief Scientific Advisor;
- Andy Clark, Head of Detica Forensics;
- Professor Brian Collins, DfT;
- Professor William Dutton, Oxford Internet Institute;
- Robert Ghanea-Hercock, BT;
- Professor Wendy Hall, School of Electronics and Computer Science, University of Southampton;
- Professor Keith Jeffery, Science and Technology Research Council;
- Professor Cliff Jones, Newcastle University;
- Professor John Pethica, Department of Materials, Oxford University;
- Professor Angela Sasse, University College London.

For their help in assessing private sector good practice, the team would like to thank:

- BT Group;
- Deloitte;
- Equifax plc;
- Experian Ltd;
- HBOS plc;
- Home Retail Group;
- Microsoft Corporation;
- Pfizer Ltd;
- Sapior Ltd; and
- Serco Consulting.

Core resources

Data Handling Procedures in Government: Final Report

Annex IV: Information charter

> This annex contains a standard information charter, which will be tailored by individual Departments and published.

We need to handle personal information about you so that we can provide better services for you. This is how we look after that information.

When we ask you for personal information, we promise:

- to make sure you know why we need it;
- to ask only for what we need, and not to collect too much or irrelevant information;
- to protect it and make sure nobody has access to it who shouldn't;
- to let you know if we share it with other organisations to give you better public services - and if you can say no;
- to make sure we don't keep it longer than necessary; and
- not to make your personal information available for commercial use without your permission.

In return, we ask you to:

- give us accurate information; and
- tell us as soon as possible if there are any changes, such as a new address.

This helps us to keep your information reliable and up to date.

You can get more details on:

- how to find out what information we hold about you and how to ask us to correct any mistakes;
- agreements we have with other organisations for sharing information;
- circumstances where we can pass on your personal information without telling you, for example, to prevent and detect crime or to produce anonymised statistics;
- our instructions to staff on how to collect, use and delete your personal information;
- how we check the information we hold is accurate and up to date; and
- how to make a complaint.

FOR MORE INFORMATION, PLEASE CONTACT: XXXXXX

When we ask you for information, we will keep to the law, including the Data Protection Act 1998. For independent advice about data protection, privacy and data-sharing issues, you can contact the Information Commissioner at: Wycliffe House, Water Lane, Wilmslow, Cheshire, SK9 5AF. Phone: 08456 30 60 60 or 01625 54 57 45 Fax: 01625 524510 Website: www.ico.gov.uk

Data Handling Procedures in Government: Final Report, June 2008

Annex V: Cross-references to other work

This annex provides a summary of recommendations from each of the following reports and how each of these recommendations has been or will be addressed.

Joint Committee on Human Rights, Data Protection and Human Rights Report (Fourteenth Report of Session 2007-08)

1. 'Government must show that any proposal for data sharing is both justifiable and proportionate, and that appropriate safeguards are in place to ensure that personal data is not disclosed arbitrarily but only in circumstances where it is proportionate to do so.' (paragraph 14 of JCHR)

   Agree. The provisions in this report should assist in this area. The use of Privacy Impact Assessments (www.ico.co.uk) should ensure that privacy issues are factored in at early stages of development. Issues around data sharing are also being considered in the Walport / Thomas review.

2. 'Where there is a demonstrable need to legislate to permit data sharing between public sector bodies, or between public and private sector bodies, the Government's intentions should be set out clearly in primary legislation.' (paragraph 20)

   Issues around data sharing are being considered in the Walport / Thomas review. (In some instances, Government does set out specific provisions in primary legislation.) Data protection safeguards are enshrined in the Data Protection Act. Whether data sharing provisions are best set out in primary or secondary legislation will depend on the context of the legislation and the data sharing involved. The efficient use of codes of practice may provide a more pragmatic and effective approach in the form of practical and detailed guidance to front line staff who manage and handle information than can be offered solely in the form of provisions set out in primary legislation.

3. 'There should be inter-departmental coordination to share best practice and help deal with the fall-out from significant breaches of data protection by Departments.' (paragraph 26)

   Agree. Cabinet Office has always sought to ensure that Departments are able to learn from each other, including when things go wrong. It will continue to do so. Departments will also be supported through peer review mechanisms.

4. 'The role of the data protection minister should be enhanced from just overseeing the data protection legislation to championing best practice and ensuring that lessons are learned from breaches.' (paragraph 26)

   The data protection minister and the Ministry of Justice already play this wider role. The data protection minister and others will participate in the collective work of the Committee on Personal Data Security, (DA(PDS)) to ensure that Government follows through its commitments in this report.

5. 'The Government should acknowledge the close connection between data protection and human rights; and explain how it proposes to ensure that a culture of respect for personal data is fostered throughout Government.'(paragraph 35)

   This report sets out actions to ensure that a culture of respect for personal data is fostered and valued, This will be achieved by greater transparency as Departments will report annually on information assurance issues but also throughout the whole of Government, through assessing privacy impacts at an early stage, through culture change and training, and through ensuring that HR systems support good performance.

6. 'Support proposals to enhance the Commissioner's powers and resources at his disposal to ensure that he can discharge his responsibilities more effectively.' (paragraph 39)

    The Government made clear in publishing the interim report for this work that it was committed to providing the Information Commissioner with the power to conduct spot checks and the Data Protection Act has been recently amended to confer, on the Information Commissioner, a power to impose a monetary penalty on a data controller where the Information Commissioner is satisfied that a serious contravention of the data protection principles has occurred. Spot checks by the Information Commissioner of government departments are due to commence over the coming months.

7. 'Government should take action to foster a positive culture for the protection of personal data by public sector bodies.' (paragraph 50)

    See the answer to recommendation 5 above. In addition, Government is improving accountability mechanisms, and strengthening scrutiny of performance.

Select Committee on Justice First Report, 3 January 2008

1. 'The introduction of new laws making significant security breaches, where reckless or repeated, a criminal offence.'

    Government introduced a new monetary penalty in the Criminal Justice and Immigration Act (2008) which will give the Information Commissioner the discretion to serve notice on a data controller who has seriously contravened the data protection principles. Government will take a considered view on what further measures are necessary to strengthen the protection of personal data in light of the recommendations of the various data protection reviews.

2. 'New reporting requirements that would require companies to report losses of data.'

    This issue relates to the wider legal framework, and Government will consider it in the light of the conclusions of the Walport / Thomas review due shortly.

3. 'Quick implementation of the new enforcement powers for the Information Commissioner to conduct unannounced spot checks on Government Departments' data systems.'

    No legislation is required to permit the Information Commissioner to conduct spot checks on Government Departments. Government has given its consent for such spot checks to be conducted. The Information Commissioner will lead on how and when such spot checks take place.

4. 'Proper resources for the Office of the Information Commissioner.'

    Government will take a considered view on what further measures if any are necessary to strengthen the protection of personal data in light of the recommendations of the various data protection reviews. This will include consideration of the funding arrangements for the Information Commissioner's Office.

Protecting Government Information: Independent review of Government information assurance, by Nick Coleman

Government accepts the thrust of each of the key recommendations in the report. Individual responses are set out below.

1. Government should create a vision for information assurance and that this vision should be incorporated into existing vision statements; laying out for citizens and other stakeholders what it considers are acceptable parameters for the sharing, managing and protecting of information held and managed by Government.

    A vision for information assurance was set out in the National Information Assurance Strategy, published in June 2007. In the course of this work, Government has specified a minimum definition of personal information that should be protected, and the minimum level of protection required for it. The establishment of Information Charters should also support transparency. Government will consider the need for further action in the light of the Walport / Thomas review due shortly.

2. Create a new approach for reviewing and managing information risks across Government. Enable new mechanisms to enhance the effectiveness of information risk management including a central facility for sharing risk information.

    This will be taken forward by Cabinet Office, working with Departments, as part of the work to embed information risk management practice across Government. Cabinet Office will receive annual assessments from Departments, and use those to develop a cross-Government view of the risks being faced by Departments, to inform work on common standards or other action. Departments will capture risk information for critical assets.

3. Mandate board owners to report quarterly on information risks and performance backed up by an annual audit of Department's capabilities. Within this, establish clear metrics for managing performance of suppliers.

    Quarterly reporting on information risk and annual assessment are part of the new approach in place for all Departments. As part of the development of their information risk policy, Departments will consider how best to ensure high levels of data security when working with suppliers. Cabinet Office will consider the case for further specific metrics, including for managing performance of suppliers, as part of work on future development of cross-Government requirements.

4. Provide the Prime Minister with a summary of information assurance across Government and associated spending required to deliver cross Government security associated with information assurance.

    The Prime Minister will be provided with a summary of information assurance across Government as part of the preparations for the annual report to Parliament on information risk. This will set out the level of "common good" spending.

5. Simplify the complexity of the twenty five plus working groups and structures in this area. Enable one central mechanism for developing coordinated joint working for sharing best practice and establishing information assurance priorities across Departments and agencies.

    While there will always be a significant range of groups with an interest in this area, this report recognises the need to simplify and streamline arrangements, and for Departments to learn from each other and co-operate where

Core resources

Data Handling Procedures in Government: Final Report

that makes sense.

6. Create clear mandatory policy rules on security across Government. Define minimum standards that Departments sign up to. Enable independent monitoring for compliance.

    The definition of clear mandatory policy and simple minimum standards has been taken forward by this report. Independent monitoring will be provided by the National Audit Office and Information Commissioner, in addition to peer review. The requirements for Departments will need to evolve in the future.

7. Tackle identity management challenges through mandating the use of Privacy Impact Assessments. Specify standards of protection for identity registration, management and use in Government and the wider public sector.

    Government is adopting Privacy Impact Assessments. Standards of protection for identity management will be the subject of on-going work. The use of Information Charters should improve transparency to the citizen.

8. Mandate professional certification for those working in information assurance in every Government Department across key defined roles. Ensure citizens, employees and other stakeholders are educated on information assurance and what is expected of them.

    Agree with the need for professional certification for individuals working in roles with technical information assurance content. Cabinet Office will take forward work to increase professional capacity, and ensure that the right links are made with the closely related areas of IT and knowledge and information management. Government has not mandated professional requirements for named roles, or additional remuneration, because of the widely different way in which Departments approach their business.

9. Measure security through audit and monitoring to a defined standard. Mandate the reporting of incidents to an independent organisation responsible for capturing incidents and ensuring investigations are conducted to a given standard and lessons are learned.

    Agree with the need to measure security through audit. This will be done against cross-Government standards. Reporting of incidents will take place to the Information Commissioner, who will take enforcement action where justified and appropriate. CESG, the National Technical Authority, will be one of a number of bodies able to trigger the peer review mechanism between Departments. The responsibility for ensuring investigations are carried out appropriately and lessons are learned should continue with the individual Department, subject to the scrutiny mechanisms set out in this report.

10. Have an independent oversight capability retained by Government who can be called upon to give independent oversight and advice on information assurance to give stakeholders confidence. Provide this capability in addition to the formal regulatory roles that exist outside Government.

    The formal regulatory role exercised by the Information Commissioner will remain important. Oversight will be provided by the NAO, in the course of their work. Additional independent input will be provided by CESG, through peer review, and other independent experts. Cabinet Office will continue to seek advice on best practice from independent experts.

Fifth Report from the House of Lords Science and Technology Committee, Session 2006-07, HL Paper 165, 24 July 2007

1. 'Government should ensure that the right incentives are in place to persuade businesses to take the necessary steps to act proportionately to protect personal data.'

   This relates to wider data sharing issues outside the scope of this review, and Government will consider it in the light of the conclusions of the Walport / Thomas review due shortly.

2. Government should introduce legislation, consistent with the principles enshrined in common law and, with regard to checks, in the Bills of Exchange Act (1882), to establish the principle that banks should be held liable for losses incurred as a result of electronic fraud.

   This issue relates to the wider legal framework, and Government will consider it in the light of the conclusions of the Walport / Thomas review due shortly.

3. Government should begin consultation on the scope of a data security breach notification law as a matter of urgency. The law should incorporate the following key elements:
   - workable definitions of data security breaches, covering both a threshold for the sensitivity of the data lost, and criteria for the accessibility of that data;
   - a mandatory and uniform central reporting system; clear rules on form and content of notification letters, which must state clearly the nature of the breach and provide advice on the steps that individuals should take to deal with it;

   This issue relates to the wider legal framework, and Government will consider it in the light of the conclusions of the Walport / Thomas review due shortly.

4. Government should examine as a matter of urgency the effectiveness of the Information Commissioner's Office in enforcing good standards of data protection across the business community. The Commissioner is currently handicapped in his work by lack of resources; a cumbersome "two strike" enforcement process; and inadequate penalties upon conviction.

   The Government introduced a new monetary penalty in the Criminal Justice and Immigration Act which will give the Information Commissioner the discretion to serve notice on a data controller who has seriously contravened the data protection principles. Government will take a considered view on what if any further measures are necessary to strengthen the protection of personal data in light of the recommendations of the various data protection reviews.

5. Government should reconsider the tariffs for the whole of the data protection regime, while also addressing resources and enforcement procedures as well. These should include the power to conduct random audits of the security measures in place in businesses and other organisations holding personal data.

   See above.

6. Government should introduce amendments to the criminal law, explicitly to criminalise the sale or purchase of the services of a 'botnet', regardless of the use to which it is put.

Core resources

The Computer Misuse Act (1990) has been amended through the Police & Justice Act (2006) to provide a legal base to tackle this problem. The Crown Prosecution Office has produced advice for courts to ensure that the legitimate use of such articles is not penalised. Work to implement the Police and Criminal Justice Act began in April 2008.

7. Government should, in partnership with the Association of Chief Police Officers and the Serious Organised Crime Agency, develop a unified, web-based reporting system for e-crime (including recommendations on reporting to banks of online fraud; establishment of computer forensic laboratories, HO to introduce Police Central e-crime Unit; ratify the Council of Europe CyberCrime Convention; issue guidance to courts on internet crime)

The Government takes the threat of e-crime seriously. The Government has provided £15m over the next three years to set up the National Fraud Reporting Centre, which will help identify and analyse electronic fraud. The Government will shortly be discussing with law enforcement agencies how best to tackle the issue of electronic fraud. The Government fully intends to ratify the CoE Cybercrime Convention, and work on this began in April 2008.

CROSS GOVERNMENT ACTIONS: MANDATORY MINIMUM MEASURES

Cross Government Actions: Mandatory Minimum Measures

Government has put in place a core set of mandatory minimum measures to protect information, to apply across central Government. They are minimum measures in that they oblige individual Departments and agencies to assess their own risk, and those organisations will often put in place a higher level of protection. They will be updated in the future to accommodate lessons and new developments.

1. Information is a key asset, and its proper use is fundamental to the delivery of public services. The public are entitled to expect that Government will protect their privacy and use and handle information professionally. Departments are best placed to understand their information and to protect it, but need to do so within a context of clear minimum standards ensuring protection of personal information.

2. This document sets out in Section I mandatory process measures to ensure that Departments identify and manage their information risks. In Section II it sets out mandatory specific minimum measures for protection of personal information. It does not cover physical and personnel security or business continuity, which are addressed in the Manual of Protective Security, which is under review. Departments must also comply with other obligations, such as those under contracts, codes of connection, and the law. The material in this document reflects good practice as set out in the ISO/IEC 27000 (Information Security Management System) series.

Section I: Process measures to manage information risk

General

3. Departments are responsible for managing their own information risks and ensuring proper management of information risks in their delivery chains, subject to meeting the mandatory rules set out in this document and its replacements. The Accounting Officer has overall responsibility for ensuring that information risks are assessed and mitigated to an acceptable level. They sign the annual Statement of Internal Control. From 08/09 onwards, this must explicitly cover information risk.

4. All Departments must:

4.1 have an information risk policy setting out how they implement the measures in this document in their own activity and that of their delivery partners, and monitor compliance with the policy and its effectiveness;

4.2 assess risks to the confidentiality, integrity and availability of information in their delivery chain at least quarterly, taking account of extant Government-wide guidance, and plan and implement proportionate responses, which must at least include implementation of the measures in Section II. At least once a year, the risk assessment must examine forthcoming potential changes in services, technology and threats;

4.3 accredit ICT systems handling protectively marked information to the Government standard, and to reaccredit when systems undergo significant change, or at least every five years;

4.4 conduct Privacy Impact Assessments so that they can be considered as part of the information risk aspects of Gateway Reviews, or while going through accreditation if no Gateway has been conducted for a particular system;

4.5 use the security clauses from the Office of Government Commerce's model ICT contract for services, with any changes relevant to information risk being approved by the SIRO (defined below);

4.6 consider whether each Section I measure needs to be

© Crown Copyright. Reproduced by permission of the Controller of Her Majesty's Stationery Office. Published by LexisNexis.

Core resources

applied to any organisation handling information on its behalf (whether public sector or private sector) to ensure appropriate information handling across the delivery chain, and apply those where there is a need to do so;

4.7 apply all Section II measures by organisations handling information on their behalf when they deal with Government data, and monitor the application of those measures. When seeking to apply Section I or Section II measures, Departments must insist on action where they can, and seek to influence others where necessary.

Roles

5. All Departments must:

5.1 name a board member as "Senior Information Risk Owner" (SIRO). The SIRO is an executive who is familiar with information risks and the organisation's response. The SIRO may also be the Chief Information Officer (CIO) if the latter is on the board. They own the information risk policy and risk assessment, act as an advocate for information risk on the board and in internal discussions, and provide written advice to the accounting officer on the content of their Statement of Internal Control relating to information risk;

5.2 identify their information assets, and name for each an "information asset owner". Asset owners must be senior individuals involved in running the relevant business. Their role is to understand what information is held, what is added and what is removed, how information is moved, and who has access and why. As a result they are able to understand and address risks to the information, and ensure that information is fully used within the law for the public good. They provide a written judgement of the security and use of their asset annually to support the audit process; and

5.3 identify and keep a record of those members of staff and contractors with access to or involved in handling individual records containing protected personal data (see attachment A), referred to below as "users". For simplicity, some Departments may wish to assume that all staff are users, or to conduct the exercise for their organisation piece by piece.

Maximising public benefit from information

6. Addressing information risk involves ensuring that information is used, as well as protecting it when it is used. Information Asset Owners must consider on an annual basis how better use could be made of their information assets within the law. Where they consider that public protection or public services could be enhanced through greater access to information held by others, they should submit a request to the relevant Information Asset Owner. Requests received must be logged and considered. Where it is decided that public access to information is in the public interest, Information Asset Owners should reflect this in their Departmental Freedom of Information Publication Scheme.

Audit

7. All Departments must:

7.1 share and discuss the information risk assessment (see 4.2) with their audit committee and main board;

7.2 conduct at least an annual review of information risk for the SIRO to support their written advice to the Accounting Officer. That review must cover the effectiveness of the overarching policy. It must be informed by the written judgement of the Information Asset Owners, and chair of the audit committee; and

7.3 once the Statement on Internal Control has been completed, share the relevant material and the supporting annual assessment with Cabinet Office.

Culture

8. All Departments must:

8.1 have and execute plans to

lead and foster a culture that values, protects and uses information for the public good, and monitor progress at least though standardised civil-service wide questions when conducting a people survey or equivalent;

8.2 reflect performance in managing information risk into HR processes, in particular making clear that failure to apply Departmental procedure is a serious matter, and in some situations amount to gross misconduct; and

8.3 maintain mechanisms that command the confidence of individuals through which they may bring concerns about information risk to the attention of senior management or the audit committee, anonymously if necessary, and record concerns expressed and action taken in response.

Incident management

9. All Departments must:

9.1 have a policy for reporting, managing and recovering from information risk incidents, including losses of protected personal data and ICT security incidents, defining responsibilities, and make staff aware of the policy; and

9.2 report security incidents to HMG's incident management schemes (GovCERTUK for network security incidents and CINRAS for incidents involving cryptographic items). Significant actual or potential losses of personal data should be shared with the Information Commissioner and the Cabinet Office.

Transparency

10. All Departments must:

10.1 publish an information charter setting out how they handle information and how members of the public can address any concerns that they have;

10.2 set out in the Departmental annual report summary material on information risk, covering the overall judgement in the Statement on Internal Control, numbers of information risk incidents sufficiently significant for the Information Commissioner to be informed, the numbers of people potentially affected, and actions taken to contain the breach and prevent recurrence.

Section II: Specific minimum measures to protect personal information

11. Government must be particularly careful to protect personal data whose release or loss could cause harm or distress to individuals. All Departments must:

11.1 determine what information they or their delivery partners hold that falls into this category. This must include at least the information outlined at A; and

11.2 handle all such information as if it were at least "PROTECT – PERSONAL DATA" while it is processed or stored within Government or its delivery partners, applying the measures in this document. Information should continue to be marked to a higher level where that is already done or where justified for example as a result of aggregation of data.

Preventing unauthorised access to protectively marked information

12. When PROTECT level information is held on paper, it must be locked away when not in use or the premises on which it is held secured. When information is held and accessed on ICT systems on secure premises, all Departments must apply the minimum protections for information set out in the matrix in the Annex, or equivalent measures, as well as any additional protections as needed as a result of their risk assessment. Where equivalent measures are adopted, or, in exceptional circumstances in which such measures cannot be applied, the SIRO must agree this action with the Accounting Officer and notify Cabinet Office.

13. Wherever possible, protected personal data should be held and

Core resources

accessed on paper or ICT systems on secure premises (see other documents within the MPS), protected as above. This means Departments should avoid use of removable media (including laptops, removable discs, CDs, USB memory sticks, PDAs and media card formats) for storage or access to such data where possible. Where this is not possible, all Departments should work to the following hierarchy, recording the reasons why a particular approach has been adopted in a particular case or a particular business area:

13.1 the best option is to hold and access data on ICT systems on secure premises;

13.2 second best is secure remote access, so that data can be viewed or amended without being permanently stored on the remote computer. This is possible at PROTECT level over the internet using products meeting the FIPS 140-2 standard or equivalent, or using a smaller set of products at RESTRICTED level. The National Technical Authority for Information Assurance, CESG, provides advice on suitable products and how to use them;

13.3 third best is secured transfer of information to a remote computer on a secure site on which it will be permanently stored. Both the data at rest and the link should be protected at least to the FIPS 140-2 standard or equivalent, using approved products as above. Protectively marked information must not be stored on privately owned computers unless they are protected in this way;

13.4 in all cases, the remote computer should be password protected, configured so that its functionality is minimised to its intended business use only, and have up to date software patches and anti-virus software.

14. Where it is not possible to avoid the use of removable media, all Departments should apply all of the following conditions:

14.1 the information transferred to the removable media should be the minimum necessary to achieve the business purpose, both in terms of the numbers of people covered by the information and the scope of information held. Where possible, only anonymised information should be held;

14.2 the removable media should be encrypted to a standard of at least FIPS 140-2 or equivalent in addition to being protected by a authentication mechanism, such as a password;

14.3 user rights to transfer data to removable media should be carefully considered and strictly limited to ensure that this is only provided where absolutely necessary for business purposes and subject to monitoring by managers and the Information Asset Owner; and

14.4 the individual responsible for the removable media should handle it – themselves or if they entrust it to others – as if it were the equivalent of a large amount of their own cash.

15. There are some exceptional situations in which the second condition of encryption cannot be applied consistent with business continuity and disaster recovery. For example, full system back-up tapes must contain all the relevant data and Departments may judge that encrypted data cannot be recovered with sufficient speed or certainty in the event of a disaster. Such unprotected data include some of the most valuable assets owned by a Department, and should be treated accordingly, being recorded, moved, stored and monitored with strong controls – equivalent to handling arrangements for very large amounts of public money in cash. There are also specific situations in which Departments hold removable media that they cannot encrypt for legal reasons, such as when such material is collected in evidence for a legal proceeding. In those situations, the legal obligation prevails.

16. All material that has been used for protected data should be subject to controlled disposal. All Departments must:

16.1 destroy paper records containing protected personal data by incineration, pulping or shredding so that reconstruction is unlikely; and

16.2 dispose of electronic media that have been used for protected personal data through secure destruction, overwriting, erasure or degaussing for re-use.

17. Decisions on handling on the issues in paragraphs 13 – 16 should be approved in writing by the relevant Information Asset Owner. In preparing for the annual assessment of information risk, all Departments must:

17.1 review compliance with the matrix in the Annex or equivalent measures and any SIRO decision to take other action agreed with the Accounting Officer;

17.2 review and test documentation relating to decisions made relating to paragraphs 13 – 16;

17.3 inspect a sample of the activities of those individuals with rights to transfer protected personal data to removable media, to ensure that there is still a business case for them to have those rights;

17.4 inspect a sample of those individuals who have left roles with access to protected personal data, to ensure that access rights have been removed;

17.5 inspect a sample of removable media to ensure that required safeguards are in place;

17.6 inspect unencrypted back-ups (see paragraph 15) and reconcile them with material that has been recorded;

17.7 monitor disposal channels for paper records containing protected personal data to ensure this has been properly handled; and

17.8 ask for sample electronic media to be processed as in 16.2 and testing to attempt data recovery.

18. All Departments whose delivery chain involves the handling of information relating to 100,000 or more identifiable individuals must engage independent experts to carry out penetration testing of their ICT systems and to make recommendations.

Minimising risk from authorised access to protectively marked information

19. All Departments must ensure that all data users must successfully undergo information risk awareness training on appointment and at least annually. In addition, all Information Asset Owners must pass information management training on appointment and at least annually, and accounting officers, SIROs, and members of the audit committee must pass strategic information risk management training at least annually.

20. All Departments must plan their business taking into account the information risks involved in different business models as well as their benefits. Once a business model is adopted, Departments must explicitly define and document the access rights granted to protected personal data that users enjoy, and minimise access rights within the adopted model. The Information Asset Owner must agree in writing that access rights permit the business to be transacted with an acceptable level of risk, and if not, an alternative must be identified. Access rights should be minimised in respect of each of the following:

20.1 pool of records accessible. The default should be that any member of staff has no access to protected personal information. If access is necessary, it should be to the smallest possible sub-set of records;

20.2 numbers of records viewed. The hierarchy should be no access / ability to view only aggregated data / ability to view only anonymous records / ability to view material from single identifiable records / ability to view material from many identifiable records simultaneously;

20.3 nature of information available. The hierarchy should be responses to defined queries (e.g. does X claim free school meals) without seeing the record / view of parts of the record itself / view of the whole record; and

20.4 functionality, including searching, alteration, deletion, printing, downloading or transferring information.

Core resources

21. All Departments must:

   20.5 put in place arrangements to log activity of data users in respect of electronically held protected personal information, and for managers to check it is being properly conducted, with a particular focus on those working remotely and those with higher levels of functionality. Summary records of managers' activity must be shared with the relevant Information Asset Owner and be available for inspection by the Information Commissioner's Office on request; and

   20.6 have a forensic readiness policy to maximise their ability to preserve, analyse and use evidence from an ICT system, should it be required.

Citizen-facing work

22. Departments and agencies need to ensure that citizen facing services are secure, while being easy for people or their representatives to use. Where possible, the same protective measures should be taken in transacting business with individuals as when information is stored or used within Government, but Departments should set their own proportionate standards in this area so long as those standards (and possible alternatives service routes) are clearly explained.

Cross Government Actions: Mandatory Minimum Measures

Minimum scope of protected personal data

Departments must identify data they or their delivery partners hold whose release or loss could cause harm or distress to individuals. This must include <u>as a minimum</u> all data falling into one or both categories below.

A. Any information that links one or more identifiable living person with information about them whose release would put them at significant risk of harm or distress.

1. one or more of the pieces of information which can be used along with public domain information to identify an individual	combined with	2. information about that individual whose release is likely to cause harm or distress
Name / addresses (home or business or both) / postcode / email / telephone numbers / driving licence number / date of birth [Note that driving licence number is included in this list because it directly yields date of birth and first part of surname]		Sensitive personal data as defined by s2 of the Data protection Act, including records relating to the criminal justice system, and group membership DNA or finger prints / bank, financial or credit card details / mother's maiden name / National Insurance number / Tax, benefit or pension records / health records / employment record / school attendance or records / material relating to social services including child protection and housing

These are not exhaustive lists. Departments should determine whether other information they hold should be included in either category.

B. Any source of information about 1000 or more identifiable individuals, other than information sourced from the public domain.

This could be a database with 1000 or more entries containing facts mentioned in box 1, or an electronic folder or drive containing 1000 or more records about individuals. Again, this is a minimum standard. Information on smaller numbers of individuals may warrant protection because of the nature of the individuals, nature or source of the information, or extent of information.

Core resources

"Suffolk Matrix" – external access by impact / e-GIF level

Business Impact Level / "Protective Marking"	Types of data/ system included in category	e-Gif/CSIA Registration Level	e-Gif/CSIA Authentication Levels	Network	External Access Gov PC To WWW WIFI	External Access WWW "café" 3G Data Card	External Access "PED" Blue Tooth	External Access Home Gov PC LAN Bootable USB
IL4 Confidential	Violent & Sex offenders Witness Protection	Level Three Full ID verification with appropriate vetting and need to know measures	Physical / personal / procedural protection with appropriate technical authentication mechanisms such as User Name + Password or Biometric / Certificate / Token	x GSi xCJX	Y[1]	N	N	Y[2]
IL3 Restricted "NHS Confidential"	Health record ContactPoint Crime Record/PNC	Level Two Cross checked ID verification with appropriate vetting and need to know measures	User Name Password / Biometric Digital Certificate	N3 GSi CJX	Y	N	Y[4]	Y[5]
IL2 Protect	General citizen data Finance Systems	Level One Basic ID verification	User Name Password & best commercial practice	GCSx Best Commercial	Y[6]	Y[7]	N	Y[8]
IL2 Protect					Y	N	Y	Y
IL1/IL0	Google search BBC News	anonymous	No authentication required	Any	Y	Y	Y[9]	Y

Arrangements for material at higher protective markings are dealt with separately

[1] Via 'Thin Client Internet Browse-down"
[2] Via hard-wired Government issue secure laptop (RAS)
[3] Requires a strong business case and CESG advice
[4] Via CESG approved product such as Blackberry. Ref. CESG Procedures for Blackberry Administrators and CESG Security Procedures for Blackberry Users
[5] Via CESG-approved VPN or validated Manual T or Manual V solutions
[6] Implementations must be compliant with CESG Manual Y
[7] Via Government issue secure laptop with software encryption (RAS)
[8] Using software-based cryptography
[9] Requires a strong business case and CESG advice

FSA REPORT 'DATA SECURITY IN FINANCIAL SERVICES: FIRMS' CONTROLS TO PREVENT DATA LOSS BY THEIR EMPLOYEES AND THIRD-PARTY SUPPLIERS', APRIL 2008

Financial Services Authority

Data Security in Financial Services

Firms' controls to prevent data loss by their employees and third-party suppliers

Financial Crime and Intelligence Division
Foreword by the Information Commissioner

April 2008

© Financial Services Authority. All Rights Reserved. Published by LexisNexis 2009

Core resources

Foreword by Richard Thomas, the Information Commissioner

I welcome this report on the protection of customer data within the financial services industry. It includes examples of good practice by some financial institutions which others could usefully learn from. However, I am disappointed – but not altogether surprised – that the FSA has found that financial services firms, in general, could significantly improve their controls to prevent data loss or theft.

The blunt truth is that all organisations need to take the protection of customer data with the utmost seriousness. I have made clear publicly on several occasions over the past year that organisations holding individuals' data must in particular take steps to ensure that it is adequately protected from loss or theft. There have been several high-profile incidents of data loss in public and private sectors during that time which have highlighted that some organisations could do much better. The coverage of these incidents has also raised public awareness of how lost or stolen data can be used for crimes like identity fraud. Getting data protection wrong can bring commercial, reputational, regulatory and legal penalties. Getting it right brings rewards in terms of customer trust and confidence.

The financial services industry needs to pay close attention to what its regulator is saying here. But this report is also relevant to organisations outside the financial services industry which hold data about private individuals. All organisations handling individuals' data, in both the public and private sectors, could benefit from the good practice advice it contains.

FSA report 'Data Security in Financial Services', April 2008

Core resources

Contents

1.	Executive summary		6
	1.1	Introduction	6
	1.2	Findings	7
	1.3	Conclusions	9
2.	Introduction		11
	2.1	Objectives	11
	2.2	Background	12
	2.3	Methodology	13
	2.4	How data loss occurs	14
	2.5	How lost data is used for identity fraud	15
	2.6	Firms' responsibilities	17
	2.6.1	Legal requirements	17
	2.7	Attitudes to data security and identity fraud	18
	2.7.1	Five fallacies	18
	2.7.2	Changing attitudes	20
	2.7.3	Changing behaviour	21
3.	Findings		22
	3.1	Governance – managing systems and controls	22
	3.1.1	Policies and procedures	23
	3.1.2	Benchmarking	24
	3.1.3	Risk assessment	24
	3.1.4	Organisation, monitoring performance and communication	25
	3.1.5	External liaison	26

3.1.6	Data loss reporting and response	27
3.1.7	Notifying customers of data loss	27
3.2	**Training and awareness**	30
3.2.1	Poor assumptions about risk awareness	31
3.2.2	Advantages of written guidelines	31
3.2.3	Effective training and awareness mechanisms	31
3.3	**Staff recruitment and vetting**	34
3.3.1	Initial Recruitment Process	35
3.3.2	Temporary staff	38
3.3.3	Ongoing vetting of staff	39
3.4	**Controls**	40
3.4.1	Controls in offshore operations	41
3.4.2	Access rights	42
3.4.3	Passwords and user accounts	47
3.4.4	Monitoring access to customer data	49
3.4.5	Authentication	51
3.4.6	Data back-up	53
3.4.7	Access to the internet and email	56
3.4.8	Key-logging devices	59
3.4.9	Laptops	60
3.4.10	Portable media including USB devices and CDs	63
3.5	**Physical security**	65
3.5.1	Access to firms' premises	66
3.5.2	Clear-desk policy	68
3.5.3	Storage of paper customer files	68
3.6	**Disposing of customer data**	70
3.6.1	Procedures for disposing of confidential paper	70

Core resources

	3.6.2	Procedures for disposing of obsolete computers and other electronic equipment	72
	3.7	**Managing third-party suppliers**	75
	3.7.1	Why do third parties matter?	75
	3.7.2	Firms' management of third-party suppliers	76
	3.7.3	Issues for firms to consider when using third-party suppliers	77
	3.8	**Internal audit and compliance monitoring**	80
	3.8.1	Internal audit	80
	3.8.2	Compliance monitoring	81
4.	Consolidated examples of good and poor practice		83
5.	Glossary		96
6.	References and useful links		99

FSA report 'Data Security in Financial Services', April 2008

1. Executive Summary

1.1 Introduction

1. This report describes how financial services firms in the UK are addressing the risk that their customer data may be lost or stolen and then used to commit fraud or other financial crime. It sets out the findings of our recent review of industry practice and standards in managing the risk of data loss or theft by employees and third-party suppliers.

2. We did not examine the threat of data theft by criminals seeking to infiltrate firms' systems by hi-tech means such as 'hacking' into computer systems.

3. Firms' responsibilities in this area are defined in our Principles for Businesses. Principle 2 requires that 'a firm must conduct its business with due skill, care and diligence' and Principle 3 that 'a firm must take reasonable care to organise and control its affairs responsibly and effectively, with adequate risk management systems'.

4. In line with these principles, firms' senior management are responsible for making an appropriate assessment of the financial crime risks associated with their customer data. Rule 3.2.6R in our Senior Management Arrangements, Systems and Controls sourcebook (SYSC) requires firms to 'take reasonable care to establish and maintain effective systems and controls for compliance with applicable requirements and standards under the regulatory system and for countering the risk that the firm might be used to further financial crime'. This is the minimum standard to meet the requirements of the regulatory system.

5. This report does not constitute formal guidance from the FSA. However, we expect firms to use our findings, to translate them into a more effective assessment of this risk, and to install more effective controls as a result. Small firms should consider the specific data security factsheets that we will make available to them on our website and monthly 'regulation round up' email. As in any other area of their business, firms should take a proportionate, risk-based approach to data security, taking into account their customer base, business and risk profile. Failure to do so may result in us taking enforcement action.

6. Firms should note that we support the Information Commissioner's position that it is not appropriate for customer data to be taken offsite on laptops or other portable devices which are not encrypted.[1] We may take enforcement action against firms that fail to encrypt customer data offsite.

---

[1] www.ico.gov.uk/about_us/news_and_views/current_topics/Our%20approach%20to%20encryption.aspx

Core resources

7. This report is based on a systematic review by our Financial Crime and Intelligence Division (FCID) to find out how firms are responding to this risk. We visited 39 firms, including retail and wholesale banks, investment firms, insurance companies, financial advisers and credit unions. Half of our sample was firms supervised by our Small Firms Division. We consulted other stakeholders including the Information Commissioner's Office, law enforcement, trade associations, forensic accountants and compliance consultants regarding industry practice and the risk to consumers arising from poor data security. We also spoke to CIFAS – the UK's fraud prevention agency – who have conducted significant research on the impact of identity fraud on consumers.[2] In addition, we took into account our experience of data loss incidents dealt with by our Financial Crime Operations Team. During 2007, the team dealt with 56 cases of lost or stolen customer data from financial services firms. Of course, these were only the losses which were reported to us by firms or identified by the team. We judge it to be highly likely that many data loss incidents go unreported.

8. The main purpose of the review was to gather information on current data security standards, identify good practice to share with the industry and highlight areas where improvement is required. The proactive identification of potential enforcement cases was not an objective of our review, but we have referred one firm to our Enforcement division as a result of our findings. However, we will be issuing guidance to supervisors to ensure data security is reviewed as part of normal supervision. If firms fail to take account of this report and continue to demonstrate poor data security practice, we may refer them to Enforcement. In addition, we are likely to repeat this project to see if standards have improved.

9. We would like to thank the firms that participated in the review for the information they supplied before and during our visits, and for meeting us.

10. A glossary of terms used in this report can be found in Section 5.

1.2 Findings

11. Many firms are failing to identify all aspects of the data security risk they face, for three main reasons. First, some do not appreciate the gravity of this risk; second, some do not have the expertise to make a reasonable assessment of key risk factors and devise ways of mitigating them; and third, many fail to devote or coordinate adequate resources to address this risk.

12. Large and medium-sized firms generally devote adequate resources to data security risk management but there is a lack of coordination among relevant business areas such as information technology, information security, human resources, financial crime, and

---

2 See: www.cifas.org.uk/default.asp?edit_id=577-73

13. Firms' risk assessment of their exposure to data loss incidents is often weak. Some make no risk assessment at all and only a few continuously monitor the effectiveness of their data security controls. In some medium-sized and small firms, there is a lack of awareness that customer data is a valuable commodity for criminals. As a consequence, systems and controls are often weak and sometimes absent. Now, with several well-publicised incidents of data loss during 2007, nobody in the UK can claim ignorance of the risk of customer data falling into the wrong hands. It is good practice for firms to conduct a risk assessment of their data security environment and implement adequate mitigating controls. If firms consider that their in-house resources or expertise are inadequate to perform a coherent risk assessment, they should consider seeking external guidance.

14. Our experience of dealing with data loss incidents shows that firms often fail to consider the wider risks of identity fraud arising from significant cases of data loss. Many firms appear more concerned about adverse media coverage than in being open and transparent with their customers about the risks they face and how they can protect themselves. However, some firms which suffer data loss are beginning to take a more responsible approach by writing to their customers to explain the circumstances, give advice and, in some cases, pay for precautions such as credit checking and CIFAS Protective Registration.[3]

15. Firms' vetting of staff is variable. In most firms, more-stringent vetting is applied to staff in senior positions – there is little consideration of the risk that junior staff with access to large volumes of customer data may facilitate financial crime. Consequently, very few firms conduct criminal record checks on junior staff. In addition, few firms repeat vetting to identify changes in an individual's circumstances which might make them more susceptible to financial crime.

16. Data security policies in medium-sized and larger firms are generally adequate but implementation is often patchy, with staff awareness of data security risk a key concern. Training for front-line staff (e.g. in call centres), who often have access to large volumes of customer data, is rarely relevant to their day-to-day duties and focuses more on legislation and regulation than the risk of financial crime. This means staff are often unaware of how to comply with policies and do not know that data security procedures are an important tool for reducing financial crime. In addition, many firms do not test that their staff understand their policies.

---

[3] CIFAS offers a service called Protective Registration which requires anyone applying for credit in that person's name to undergo additional checks. The product, supplied by the Equifax credit bureau, costs £12 plus VAT. CIFAS have recently launched a 'bulk' Protective Registration facility for firms to use in cases of mass data loss.

Core resources

17. Access to customer data via computer systems and databases is generally well controlled in large and medium-sized firms, with a general aim of only allowing staff to access information that they specifically require to do their job. In small firms, it is not unusual for all staff to have access to all customer data.

18. Firms' dealings with third-party suppliers are a major concern. Many firms, small and large, use third parties for IT maintenance, as well as the backing up of electronic files and archiving of paper documents. Firms generally rely too much on assumptions that contractual terms are being met, with very few firms proactively checking how third parties vet their employees or the security arrangements in place to protect customer data. In addition, some firms do not consider the risk associated with granting third-party suppliers such as cleaners and security staff access to their premises.

19. Large and medium-sized firms tend to transfer data to and from third parties using secure internet links but there are still occasions where data is transferred on CDs or mainframe cartridges. We observed that these items are not always encrypted. On rare occasions, firms are sending unencrypted customer data by unregistered post.

20. Large and medium-sized firms usually recognise the risks of data loss via laptops, USB devices and the internet. But few firms completely mitigate data security risks by locking down USB ports and CD writers, encrypting laptops and USB devices and blocking web-based communication facilities such as Hotmail and instant messaging. Small firms are very weak in this area, with few of them identifying or mitigating risks.

21. Disposal of confidential paper is generally very good, with most firms shredding sensitive documents either onsite or via a suitably-accredited supplier. This is likely to be the result of significant media attention on this subject (e.g. BBC Watchdog) as well as, in March 2007, the Information Commissioner's Office's public censure of firms disposing of customer data carelessly.

22. Compliance and Internal Audit of data security in large and medium-sized firms is variable. Some firms' compliance and audit staff lack the necessary understanding of the subject or technical expertise. As with firms' governance of data security in general, compliance and internal audit functions often lack coordination, do not examine data security holistically and do not pay adequate attention to the non-IT aspects of data security. Small firms are often wholly reliant on compliance consultants who we found do very little – if any – work on data security. So the standard of small firms' compliance checking – and their overall performance on data security – is very weak indeed.

1.3 Conclusions

23. This review and the incidents we have dealt with since the formation of our Financial Crime & Intelligence Division (FCID) at the beginning of 2007 has led us to conclude that poor data security is currently a serious, widespread and high-impact risk to our objective to reduce financial crime.

FSA report 'Data Security in Financial Services', April 2008

24. Recent incidents of data loss have brought many firms to consider data security for the first time. Some progress has been made: firms in general are beginning to understand more about this risk and are becoming more assertive in their efforts to contain it. However, there exists a very wide variation between the good practice demonstrated by firms committed to ensuring data security, and the weaknesses seen in firms that are not taking adequate steps to treat fairly the customers whose data they hold.

25. Overall, data security in financial services firms needs to be improved significantly. Many firms, particularly small firms, still need to make substantial progress to protect their customers from the risk of identity fraud and other financial crime.

This review was conducted by Robert Gruppetta, Stephen Oakes, Laura Covill and Emma Richardson.

This report is published for information; however, your comments are welcomed. Please contact:

Financial Crime Operations Team
Financial Services Authority
25 The North Colonnade
London
E14 5HS

Email: rob.gruppetta@fsa.gov.uk or stephen.oakes@fsa.gov.uk

Telephone: 020 7066 0140 or 020 7066 5530

Core resources

2. Introduction

2.1 Objectives

26. This report is the result of a significant effort during 2007 to examine how firms safeguard customer data. We investigated how financial services firms assess and manage their data security risks, how these risks are changing, and how they impact on our statutory objectives.

27. Our four statutory objectives are:

    - *market confidence*: maintaining confidence in the financial system;
    - *public awareness*: promoting public understanding of the financial system;
    - *consumer protection*: securing the appropriate degree of protection for consumers; and
    - *the reduction of financial crime*: reducing the extent to which it is possible for a business to be used for a purpose connected with financial crime.

28. Financial crime includes money laundering, market abuse and fraud or other dishonest practices. The risk of data loss and subsequent fraud is relevant to all four of our objectives for the following reasons:

    - *the reduction of financial crime* because poor controls over customer data present opportunities for thieves and fraudsters to steal data and commit identity fraud and other financial crime;
    - *consumer protection* because data loss, especially on a large scale, could cause significant detriment to individuals;
    - *market confidence* could be affected by large data loss which causes consumers to question the integrity or safety of the financial sector or service delivery channels, such as online banking; and
    - *consumer awareness* is also relevant, because people should take responsibility for keeping their own personal data safe.

29. We have highlighted data security as a significant issue in our Financial Risk Outlook in 2008 and the four previous years.[4]

> 'Personal data remains a high-value commodity for criminals, with both the market in consumer details and the technology used by criminals continuing to evolve.'
>
> FSA Financial Risk Outlook 2008

---

4   www.fsa.gov.uk/Pages/Library/corporate/Outlook/index.shtml

2.2 Background

30. In January 2007, we created a new Financial Crime and Intelligence Division (FCID). The division brings together financial crime experts that were previously spread throughout the organisation. It is equipped to address financial crime issues more intensively, in particular by checking firms' systems and controls for assessing and mitigating risk. The new centre of excellence provides advice and intelligence to the rest of the FSA, particularly firms' supervisors. FCID also undertakes thematic and case work on financial crime issues.

31. In 2007, FCID's Operations Team dealt with 56 cases of data loss by financial services firms. This accounted for just under a third of all financial crime cases dealt with by the team. In fact, data security was the most common type of financial crime incident dealt with during the year. These cases have revealed some serious weaknesses in firms' data security.

32. As a result of this developing trend, FCID reviewed data security in financial services firms, visiting 39 of them to find out how well they are identifying and tackling the risks of data loss. We examined how customer data is stored in electronic databases, paper files and with third-party suppliers; the controls in place to restrict access to customer data and prevent it from being lost or stolen; and how redundant customer data is disposed of securely.

33. We looked at some technical aspects such as passwords and encryption of laptops and other portable devices. However, we did not examine the threat of data theft by criminals seeking to infiltrate firms' systems by hi-tech means such as 'hacking' into computer systems.

34. This report describes the findings of the review and sets out examples of good and poor practice observed. It also describes some of the general trends we saw in the financial services industry, as well as risks that were specific to particular segments of it.

35. We discussed our intention to carry out this project when we gave evidence to the House of Lords Select Committee on Science and Technology in December 2006 and our Executive Committee approved the project on 2 March 2007.

36. We last published a detailed review of firms' information security controls in November 2004. It concluded that firms could be more active in managing relevant risks rather than being reactive to events and could protect better their own assets and those of their customers from the risk of fraudulent activity.[5]

37. We expect firms to use our findings, to translate them into a more effective assessment of this risk, and to install more-effective controls as a result. As in all areas of their business, firms should take a proportionate, risk-based approach to data security taking into account their customer base, business and risk profile. If firms fail to do this, we may take enforcement action.

---

[5] See www.fsa.gov.uk/pubs/other/fcrime_sector.pdf

Core resources

2.3 Methodology

38. We began the fieldwork for our review in April 2007 and continued it until December 2007. From April until June, we sought the views of 12 important stakeholders, including the Information Commissioner's Office, trade associations, law enforcement, forensic accountants and compliance consultants used by small firms. Overall, these meetings suggested that, while some firms were taking data security seriously and had good systems and controls in place, there was the need for significant improvement across the financial services industry.

> 'Firms do not understand the value to criminals of customer data.'
>
> 'Generally, firms are only concerned about data security risk if there is some risk to their own business – they are not concerned about protecting their customers from wider identity theft.'
>
> 'I have never seen a risk assessment which cuts across all aspects I would expect to be covered.'
>
> A 'big four' forensic accountant.

39. We visited 39 firms, including retail and wholesale banks, investment firms, insurance companies, financial advisers and credit unions. Half our sample comprised firms supervised by our Small Firms Division. We selected 20 small firms for visits by sending a simple questionnaire to 110 small firms and analysing the quality of their responses. We ensured that our review included firms that had given both good and poor responses to our questionnaire, and that it was focused on firms spread across the UK.

40. We interviewed staff with key roles in each firm to get a balanced view of how data security is handled, and identify at what level in the management structure it was dealt with. Where dedicated roles existed, we usually met managers responsible for information security, fraud, staff vetting, IT operations, compliance and internal audit. Where separate roles did not exist, for example in smaller firms, we met the individual with general responsibility for data security. We also met front-line staff to assess their understanding of policies and procedures, the quality of the training they received, whether their access to customer data was appropriate, and to conduct some limited testing of controls.

41. We also assessed:
    - firms' understanding of and attitude to data security risk and identity fraud (section 2.7);
    - the quality of risk assessment and related processes (section 3.1.3);
    - staff recruitment and vetting procedures (section 3.3);
    - IT controls, including those relating to laptops and other portable devices, and using the internet and email (section 3.4);

- staff access to electronic and paper-based customer data (section 3.4.2);
- physical security (section 3.5);
- disposing of paper records and redundant computers (section 3.6); and
- potential access to customer data by third-party suppliers of services such as IT consultancy, call centres and archiving firms (section 3.7.2).

Our sample

Type of firm	Total	FSA Supervisory Division			
		Major Retail Groups	Wholesale Firms	Retail Firms	Small Firms
Banks	6	2	3	1	
Building societies	2			2	
Credit unions	2				2
Insurance (Life and General)	7	1	1	4	1
Investment firms	22		1	4	17
Total	39	3	5	11	20

2.4 How data loss occurs

42. We have identified data security as a key risk because financial services firms, by the nature of their business, generally hold lots of data about their customers. Most firms hold an extensive stock of personal and financial data: names; addresses; dates of birth; contact details; national insurance numbers; passport numbers; bank account details; family circumstances; transaction records; passwords; PINs and so on.

43. There are many reasons for this. For example, the 'know your customer' (KYC) provisions of the anti-money laundering (AML) regime often require firms to gather documentary evidence of customers' identity. Firms must also gather information about their customers' personal circumstances to ensure they are offering appropriate products. Lenders ask their customers for details of employment, income and indebtedness, while life insurers require medical details.

44. Despite the Data Protection Act's requirement for firms holding customer data to keep it secure, data is sometimes lost, either though error – such as when an employee loses a company laptop – or theft. Firms are vulnerable to both types of loss.

Core resources

45. During 2007, FCID handled 187 financial crime cases and 56 of them involved data loss. This made data loss the most common type of financial crime incident reported to us last year. The most common reasons for the loss of data were the theft of a portable device such as a laptop or memory stick; data lost in the post and data lost by third-party suppliers. Only two cases reported to us involved malicious insiders. However, these were only the data losses reported to us by firms or identified by the team. We judge it to be highly likely that many data losses either are not identified or go unreported.

46. We have found that, in cases of data theft, firms often assume the thief was focused on the value of the equipment rather than the data on it. Although this may often be the case, there is a risk that criminals will use data for criminal purposes or sell the data on through criminal networks to specialist identity fraudsters.

2.5 How lost data is used for identity fraud

47. The implications of data loss are very serious. Criminals with access to lost or stolen data, particularly highly-confidential information such as national insurance numbers, payment card and banking information, can use it to commit identity and other frauds, according to the Serious Organised Crime Agency's (SOCA) Threat Assessment 2006/07. Firms have told us these frauds include false credit applications, fraudulent insurance claims, fraudulent transactions on a victim's account and even a complete account takeover.

48. These crimes are sometimes the work of opportunistic criminals but they are also carried out by organised criminal groups that possess expert knowledge of data technology. CIFAS has found that fraudsters often get help from insiders in financial services firms.

49. There is a mature and transparent international market for stolen customer data, including data belonging to UK citizens, according to PricewaterhouseCoopers, a consulting firm. Sets of data are bought and sold freely in social settings such as pubs and clubs and subsequently traded through criminal networks that often operate on the internet. Identity fraudsters use sophisticated technology to make full use of the stolen data, both by creating false documents and by making fraudulent transactions.

50. The proceeds of these crimes can be laundered within criminal networks and may be used to fund other criminal activities, including drug trafficking, human trafficking and terrorism. Indeed, identity fraud underpins a wide variety of serious organised criminal activities, according to the SOCA Threat Assessment 2006/07.

51. The impact on the consumer can be very serious, according to CIFAS. Victims of identity fraud suffer considerable inconvenience and possible financial detriment. They often need to spend substantial time and effort repairing their credit record, and repairing the damage done by fraudsters. In the meantime, their credit scores can be impaired, potentially affecting their ability to obtain a mortgage or find a new job. This stress and financial burden might continue for years, since identity fraudsters often strike

FSA report 'Data Security in Financial Services', April 2008

repeatedly. This is because customer data may be repackaged and re-sold many times over to criminals who are difficult to trace and prosecute, given the covert and often international nature of their activities.

> One firm we visited described how some job applicants discovered they had become victims of identity fraud only when their credit history was examined during pre-employment checks.

52. There is also evidence that consumers' fears about data loss affect their willingness to use new delivery channels; almost one in three internet users say they do not bank online because of concerns about security.[6]

> It can take between 3 and 48 hours of work for a typical victim of identity fraud to undo the damage done by fraudsters. In cases where a total identity hijack has occurred, perhaps involving 20 or 30 different firms, it may take the victim over 200 hours and cost them up to £8,000 before things are put right. They may suffer considerable (albeit temporary) damage to their credit status, which may then affect their ability to obtain finance, insurance or a mortgage.
>
> Source: CIFAS

53. Consumers have become much more aware in recent months of the dangers of identity fraud. No one in the UK can be ignorant of the potential harm of data loss following several well-publicised incidents. These included two compact discs holding data on all recipients of child benefit lost in transit from HM Revenue & Customs, a laptop containing a large amount of customer data stolen from a member of Nationwide Building Society staff; and the Information Commissioner's Office's public censure of 12 firms found to be disposing of customer data carelessly.

> We fined Nationwide Building Society £980,000 for failing to have effective systems and controls to manage its information security risks (see our Final Notice of 14 February 2007).[7]

54. These cases – and many campaigns to raise awareness of identity fraud – have encouraged consumers to keep their personal financial records safe, check their credit records for any unusual transactions, and exercise discretion in revealing any personal details to others. CIFAS, the UK Fraud Prevention Service, reports that, in 2006, 80,000 people applied for CIFAS Protective Registration – a protective measure to reduce the risk of identity fraud – compared with 24,000 people five years earlier.

---

6   Get Safe Online Report 2007, Get Safe Online
7   See www.fsa.gov.uk/pubs/final/nbs.pdf

Core resources

2.6 Firms' responsibilities

55. The safekeeping of customer data is a crucial responsibility for firms. We have emphasised the importance of data security for several years, and we currently regard poor data security controls as a serious, widespread and high-impact financial crime risk.

56. Firms' responsibilities in this area are defined in our Principles for Businesses. Principle 2 requires that 'a firm must conduct its business with due skill, care and diligence' and Principle 3 that 'a firm must take reasonable care to organise and control its affairs responsibly and effectively, with adequate risk management systems'.

57. Also relevant is FSA Rule SYSC 3.2.6R, which states that 'a firm must take reasonable care to establish and maintain effective systems and controls for compliance with applicable requirements and standards under the regulatory system and for countering the risk that the firm might be used to further financial crime'.

58. So firms have a responsibility to assess the risks of data loss and take reasonable steps to prevent that risk occurring. SYSC 3.2.6A says firms' relevant systems and controls must be 'comprehensive and proportionate to the nature, scale and complexity of their operations'. In essence, firms should put in place systems and controls to minimise the risk that their operations and information assets be exploited by thieves and fraudsters. Consumers are entitled to rely on firms to ensure their personal information is secure.

> Firms should note that we support the Information Commissioner's position that it is not appropriate for customer data to be taken offsite on laptops or other portable devices which are not encrypted. We may take enforcement action if firms fail to encrypt customer data taken offsite.

59. The secure handling of customer data is also part of the 'Treating Customers Fairly' standard that all firms must adhere to. Financial services firms, particularly banks, are often the first to be told when a customer becomes the victim of fraud. Indeed, the principal response to financial fraud in the UK is action by firms, mainly through anti-fraud systems and controls that must constantly evolve to counter the threat. So it is good practice for firms to have procedures in place to investigate fraud and help the customer where appropriate. For example, firms can place blocks or anti-fraud flags on an account, change details and passwords and provide advice to the consumer on how they can protect themselves from further fraud.

2.6.1 Legal requirements

60. The Data Protection Act 1998 (DPA) gives legal rights to individuals in respect of personal data processed about them by others. There are eight Principles in the DPA that apply to all data controllers who must comply with them, unless an exemption applies. A data controller is any person who determines the purpose for which personal data are to be processed and may include financial services firms. There is also a requirement for

FSA report 'Data Security in Financial Services', April 2008

a data controller to notify the Information Commissioner's Office (ICO) of their processing of personal data, so the ICO can maintain a public register. The ICO has certain powers and duties under the DPA to ensure that data controllers comply with this legislation. So it is important that firms are aware of their obligations under the DPA. The seventh DPA principle says that a data controller must take appropriate security measures against unauthorised or unlawful processing of personal data and against accidental loss, destruction of, or damage to, personal data. The DPA gives some further guidance on matters that should be taken into account in deciding whether security measures are 'appropriate'.

61. Many firms also pass on a customer's personal data to third-party suppliers. They do so usually because the firm has specific expertise, for example in sending bulk mailings to a large number of customers, or providing other services such as IT or archiving facilities. However, this does not absolve firms of responsibility for data security who, as the data controller, will still need to comply with the seventh principle. The DPA also introduces express obligations on data controllers when a data processor processes personal data on behalf of the data controller. In these circumstances, a data controller must choose a data processor providing sufficient guarantees in respect of the technical and organisational security measures they take. The data controller must also take reasonable steps to ensure compliance with those measures, and ensure the data processor carried out the processing under a contract containing certain terms and conditions. In addition, it is in the firm's own interest to comply with this legislation and protect their reputation, given increasing awareness of data loss and identity fraud in the media and among consumers.

2.7 Attitudes to data security and identity fraud

2.7.1 Five fallacies

62. This review – and the continuing series of data losses reported to us – has revealed misconceptions among many firms about the risk of data loss and identity fraud.

   i. The management of some firms believed the customer data they held was too limited or too piecemeal to be of value to fraudsters. This is misconceived: skilled fraudsters can supplement a small core of data by accessing several different public sources – telephone directories, the electoral roll and other public records, many of which are available on the internet. They also use impersonation, for instance during phone calls or in emails, to encourage the victim to reveal more. Ultimately, they build up enough information to pose as their victim and obtain credit and other advantages in the victim's name. In this way, a firm's customer data might complete a set of data extensive enough to commit fraud.

Core resources

ii. There is a perception that only individuals with a high net worth are attractive targets for identity fraudsters. In fact, people of all ages, in all occupations and in all income groups are vulnerable if their data is lost. Recent data published by CIFAS[8] shows the top ten postal districts affected by identity fraud are not all in affluent areas.

iii. A third fallacy is that only large firms with millions of customers are likely to be targeted. Even a small firm's customer database might be sold and re-sold for a substantial sum.

iv. Firms often assume the threat to data security is external – from burglars or computer hackers, for example. However, insiders have more opportunity to steal customer data and there are many examples of staff stealing customer data either to commit fraud themselves, or to pass it on to organised criminals.

v. Finally, some firms' believe that their firm is impervious to data breaches, because no customer has ever alerted them to identity fraud. The truth may be closer to the opposite: firms which successfully detect data loss do so because they have effective risk management systems. Firms with weak controls or monitoring are likely to be oblivious to any loss. Furthermore, when fraud does occur, the source of data loss is often impossible to trace. Data is held in so many places: by government, retailers, employers and many others besides financial services firms. A victim of identity fraud rarely has the means to identify where their data was lost.

63. These common misconceptions mean some firms are failing to recognise that data security is their responsibility. The result is that they often have weak systems and controls to prevent data loss or theft. Other firms recognise the risk, but rate it so low that it never attracts the attention of senior management, nor is it allocated adequate financial or human resources.

64. Some firms regard data security as the sole responsibility of IT staff, whose responsibilities include creating technical systems and controls to prevent data loss. In fact, many of the good practices highlighted in this report are simply common sense which require input from many areas of a firm's business.

65. Some firms which lose data recognise the risks to their own reputation and business but overlook the wider risks to their customers. Data stolen from a financial services firm might not be used to compromise accounts at that firm, but could, for instance, be abused to create a false passport. The personal risk to customers arising from data loss is very broad and is certainly not limited to their dealings with the firm which lost the data.

---

8 www.cifas.org.uk/default.asp?edit_id=789-57

FSA report 'Data Security in Financial Services', April 2008

2.7.2 Changing attitudes

66. These attitudes must change in the short term, for several reasons:

    i. Identity fraud is a growing financial cost for firms, because fraudsters make additional charges on credit cards, or debits on bank accounts. Credit card issuers and other lenders usually bear these costs. Loans and mortgages obtained fraudulently, using false identities, are rarely repaid in full.

    ii. Data security is an essential aspect of Treating Customers Fairly (TCF), and in particular relevant to the first of the six TCF outcomes, that consumers can be confident that they are dealing with firms where the fair treatment of customers is central to the corporate culture. By the end of March 2008, firms were expected to have appropriate management information or measures in place to test whether they are treating their customers fairly.

    iii. Firms suffer reputational damage if data entrusted to them is lost or stolen, particularly if they cannot demonstrate adequate preventative controls. We now regard it as good practice for firms to tell their customers of data loss, even if it is not demonstrably the firm's fault, unless there is law enforcement or regulatory advice to the contrary.

    iv. A firm's operations will be undermined by any successful attempt to infiltrate them and steal data. The firm must bear the costs of the disruption and repairs to the systems. A study by the Ponemon Institute[9] published in February 2008 found the average cost to UK firms of a data loss incident was £55 for each customer record.

    v. We are increasingly concerned and vigilant about data security and there is now a pattern of enforcement action to raise standards. Although the proactive identification of potential enforcement referrals was not an objective of our review, one firm has been referred to enforcement based on our findings.

67. So it is in firms' interest to have a good awareness of data security and to establish effective controls to prevent their customer data from being used for financial crime. We expect this report will help firms understand better their responsibilities for securing customer data, enable them to undertake more accurate risk assessments, and take more effective action to prevent data loss.

---

9   www.symantec.com/about/news/release/article.jsp?prid=20080225_02

Core resources

2.7.3 Changing behaviour

68. Our review found signs that firms are becoming more aware of the potential cost of losing customer data, both to themselves and their customers. But we found that firms could do much more to improve the systems and controls in place to protect customer data. Firms' internal controls are fundamental in ensuring customers' details remain as secure as they can be and, as technology evolves, firms should keep their systems and controls up to date to prevent lapses in security.

69. Despite the improvements, most firms still need more time and further public examples of good and poor practice to make improvements to their systems and controls to prevent data loss. This report provides many such examples – in Section 4, you will find consolidated examples of the good and poor practice we saw during our review.

FSA report 'Data Security in Financial Services', April 2008

3. Findings

3.1 Governance – managing systems and controls

70. Governance can be defined as the way a firm runs its business. It includes aspects such as strategy, objective setting and deciding risk appetite. It also encompasses the culture and values driven through the business by senior management.

71. During our visits to firms, we discussed with senior management what their policies, procedures and risk appetite were in relation to data security, how they performed data security risk assessments and how they communicated and monitored performance against those assessments.

72. It was evident from our review that the level of awareness of data security risks varied considerably across the industry. Many firms had not yet considered data security as a specific risk, so had not conducted a data security risk assessment. In addition, there was a lack of awareness in some firms that data security is an important aspect of fighting identity fraud and other financial crime. Firms that did not recognise this often had serious weaknesses in their systems and controls and, in some cases, controls were completely absent.

> A medium-sized insurance company, despite having a Fraud Committee, had never discussed data security at that committee. In addition, there was no IT representation on the committee – despite the fact that IT was the department with responsibility for data security.

73. This lack of awareness was sometimes demonstrated by poor pre-visit information provided by firms. Some firms, for example, did not suggest that we meet all staff with important roles to play in keeping customer data secure. Indeed, it appeared that some firms believed that only IT staff had a role to play in ensuring data security. In addition, a significant number of small firms did not consider the risk posed by insiders and focused their attention solely on external threats such as computer hackers.

> A financial adviser told us the main threat to customer data would arise from a fire or flood at the office. They had not considered the risk of data loss or theft.
>
> A medium-sized investment firm had not identified that high staff turnover and low staff morale might increase the risk of data loss or theft.

Core resources

74. Data security is not simply an IT issue. The responsibility for ensuring data security should be coordinated across the business. Senior management, information security, human resources, financial crime, physical security, IT, compliance and internal audit are all examples of functions that have an important role to play in keeping customer data safe.

75. With several well-publicised incidents of data loss during 2007, nobody in the UK can claim ignorance of the risks which arise from customer data falling into the wrong hands.

3.1.1 Policies and procedures

76. If a firm's management is committed to ensuring data security, it is likely to have specific written policies and procedures covering the subject. We were not convinced by firms that claimed to have detailed data security rules but were unable to produce written policies and procedures. Indeed, the existence or absence of an up-to-date, accurate and relevant data security policy can be a telling indication of whether the firm really understands the risk and takes it seriously.

> Some firms' written policies and procedures did not reflect their actual day to day practices.

77. Firms with large or complex operations tended to have detailed policies and procedures. Typically, the data security policy was a high-level document supplemented by more detailed procedures and guidance for different business areas relating to the specific risks they faced. Small firms, with their more-manageable risks, did not always have formal policy documents and used simple guides of 'Do's and Don'ts' as an effective way of setting out expectations and communicating them. However, in a worrying number of cases, firms failed to record policies and procedures at all. In these firms, senior management were effectively relying on the judgement of individual staff – often with little or no understanding of the risks – as their only data security control. This approach was typical of some small firms whose managers appeared to treat data security more as a matter of office administration than as a potentially significant risk that could affect their business, reputation and customers.

78. Good policies and procedures specify exactly what staff and contractors must do – and not do – to comply with expected standards and provide the means for enforcing them. Firms that do not set out or communicate clearly the standards they expect are running the risk that their staff do not understand what is expected of them; data security risk in these firms is likely to be high. The importance of training and awareness is covered in Section 3.2.

> A small financial adviser we visited did not have a dedicated data security policy. Some other internal policies covered the subject in a piecemeal fashion but some important aspects were not covered at all. Overall, the policies were inadequate.

Data Security in Financial Services   Page 23

FSA report 'Data Security in Financial Services', April 2008

3.1.2 Benchmarking

79. There is an international quality standard for data security: the ISO 27001 Security Management Standard which was introduced in 2005.[10] Some firms, particularly larger firms with dedicated information security officers, were aware of this code of practice and used it as a benchmark. However, it was interesting to observe that even some of the largest firms had not obtained certification to this standard.

3.1.3 Risk assessment

80. As in any other area of their business, firms should take a proportionate, risk-based approach to data security, taking into account their customer base, business and risk profile. Like any complex risk area, managing data security requires a systematic attempt to understand which risks are greatest and where a data loss is most likely.

81. Many firms are failing to identify all of the data security risks they face, for three main reasons. First, some do not appreciate the gravity of this risk; second, some do not have the expertise to make a reasonable assessment of the risks and devise ways of mitigating them; and third, many fail to devote or coordinate adequate resources to this risk.

> We found that some firms' staff could talk knowledgeably about data security risks facing their business, but the firm itself had never performed a data security risk assessment.

82. Very few firms had performed a risk assessment that identified and assessed all data security risks relevant to their business. We found that firms often had adequate resources across the business to manage data security risk effectively but failed to bring these resources together. Indeed, it was not unusual for many different departments to be working on different aspects of data security but not communicating with each other.

> It is good practice for firms to ensure that data security risk management is joined-up and that different departments are not working separately.

83. This lack of coordination, further weakened when firms do not allocate ultimate accountability for data security to a senior manager, can result in serious weaknesses in otherwise well-controlled firms. Firms that have not given a senior manager ultimate responsibility for data security may struggle to ensure effective communication between key stakeholders in the business. They may also fail to ensure that systems and controls are updated to take account of emerging or evolving risk.

---

10 www.17799.standardsdirect.org/

Core resources

> A small number of firms had drawn on expertise from across the business to perform a data security risk assessment and formed an Information Security Committee (or equivalent) with all relevant functions represented. This coordinated approach is good practice.

84. We appreciate that, for small firms, a single senior manager often has wide-ranging responsibilities and they might not have in-depth expertise in all of these areas. Despite this, the increasing coverage of data loss incidents means firms should now be aware of the risks to consumers that arise from data loss. So, if firms think their in-house resources or expertise are inadequate to perform an effective risk assessment, they should consider seeking external guidance.

> During our review, and when dealing with cases of actual data loss, we have observed that some firms have a reactive approach to data security risk assessment. It appears that some firms are willing to wait for a data loss to occur before considering data security risk.

85. Without a dedicated risk assessment, firms may allocate their resources inappropriately and expose themselves and their customers to unnecessary risk.

3.1.4 Organisation, monitoring performance and communication

86. The few firms which we judged to have effective systems and controls to mitigate the risk of data loss had usually set up a committee or working group with responsibility for data security. The committees and working groups monitored the effectiveness of data security controls in practice and ensured that weaknesses were escalated to the board as appropriate. In addition, the existence of a data security committee sent a very clear message to staff about the level of importance senior management gave to data security. This helped to embed a good data security culture across the firm.

87. Interestingly, although many firms had controls in place that addressed key aspects of data security, they had not always been put in place for this reason, and the firm did not always consider them to be a data security control.

> Effective and timely communication between line management, human resources, security and IT is essential in preventing unauthorised access to buildings and IT systems when staff leave firms. Despite this, line management and human resources were sometimes unaware about how the 'leavers process' was relevant to data security. Sometimes they believed it was there only to ensure staff were removed from the payroll or allocated to the correct cost centre in the business.

88. The example above highlights the importance of data security awareness and regular communication between key stakeholders in firms. It also demonstrates that an effective data security environment requires that management from across the business work in a coordinated way and assesses regularly the effectiveness of the firm's controls.

3.1.5 External liaison

The importance of sharing information about good practice

89. A good awareness of current and emerging data security threats is needed if firms are to assess risk properly and put in place effective systems and controls.

90. Many firms face similar data security risks, so it makes sense for them to share relevant knowledge and experience as widely as possible. Some firms recognised this and were networking extensively to discover and share best practice through professional and trade associations, networking meetings, conferences and online forums.

91. Our review found that IT managers who also had responsibility for data security tended to be the most active communicators. The professional groups and associations most commonly mentioned to us were the Jericho Forum, the British Bankers Association, APACS, CIFAS, the Information Risk Executive Council, the Security Institute, the North East Fraud Forum and the Information Systems Audit and Control Association. Managers of call centres focused on conferences and online message boards operated by the Customer Contact Association, which extends beyond financial services to other industry sectors.

> One firm reviewed was not taking obvious opportunities to learn about best practice. The firm was the UK arm of a large financial services corporation based in the United States. However, the firm had not discussed data security with its parent company and its overall performance on data security was weak.

92. We encourage firms to share information on data security for the benefit of the financial services sector as a whole. This is in line with our general fraud policy and complements our direct communication with firms on financial crime issues.

Difficulties for small firms

93. Many firms, particularly small firms, had no relevant contacts, nor were they aware of opportunities to learn more about data security; so their level of data security poor. While some admitted they did not see any need for any such communication, others did not take available opportunities to learn more about good practice. A third group did not know where to find the information they needed to improve their knowledge. Without adequate understanding of the risks or any means to gain that understanding, these firms may well fall further behind their more inquisitive and well-informed peers.

94. Small firms tended to rely on small networks of their peers. One small financial advice firm included in the review informed other members of their network about our interest in data security. The firm's managers told us that they would also pass on the knowledge and issues learnt during our visit.

Core resources

> One small firm commented that a SOCA officer went to speak to their staff about financial crime issues, after the firm's senior management made contact with the officer at a conference.

95. As noted in paragraph 22, small firms are often wholly reliant on compliance consultants who, we found, do very little – if any – work on data security. We would encourage compliance consultants to do more work with small firms on data security. We intend to contact the compliance consultancy firms most often used by small firms shortly after this report is published to update them on our findings and the importance we attach to good data security.

3.1.6 Data loss reporting and response

96. We expect senior management to encourage an open and honest culture of reporting data security incidents and issues. This may require transparent reporting mechanisms to be provided for staff and third parties. Reporting mechanisms do not need to be complicated. Staff must simply know that all data security breaches must be reported and who to report them to, and it is good practice for management to ensure the reporting process has been tested. An open culture where innocent mistakes or concerns can be reported by staff without fear of blame will help firms react quickly and appropriately both to control weaknesses and data losses.

> A medium-sized bank had a well-documented and tested incident response plan. They regularly tested the plan with spoof data security attacks to ensure that escalation to Board level and response by the business was timely and adequate. Improvements were made to the response plan as a result of the test.

97. Overall, few firms had a plan for reacting to a data loss. It was noticeable that firms that did not have data loss reporting mechanisms or response plans in place had generally not identified any data losses in the past. In other firms, senior managers believed that if a data loss occurred, an effective plan could be created spontaneously.

98. A well-defined response plan enables a firm to bring together quickly knowledge and expertise to assess the impact of the risks arising from a data loss. This is good practice for all firms, especially those with substantial relevant risks such as large customer databases and the extensive use of laptops, other portable devices and third-party suppliers.

3.1.7 Notifying customers of data loss

99. When customer data is lost, consumers that are affected have a right to know the enhanced personal risk they face so they can take adequate precautions. Even if there is

FSA report 'Data Security in Financial Services', April 2008

no evidence of theft or fraud, it is good practice for firms to inform affected customers of a data loss in writing, unless the data is encrypted or there is law enforcement or regulatory advice to the contrary. Firms should consider telling affected consumers exactly what data has been lost, give them an assessment of the risk and give advice and assistance to consumers at a heightened risk of identity fraud.[11]

100. Our experience of dealing with cases of data loss shows firms are still learning to communicate appropriately with customers affected by data loss. A financial adviser did the right thing by writing to a group of customers whose account-opening forms had accidentally been thrown away by cleaners. But the letter acknowledged the risk without helping customers take precautions against identity fraud. It said: 'We wish to apologise for this most unfortunate incident, and also to let you know that the cleaning company stated that it was a genuine mistake and that the account opening information was destroyed at the compressing plant. We understand that this event will be of considerable concern to you, as it is to us. We hope that by notifying you of this matter, you will have the opportunity to take whatever remedial steps you consider appropriate.'

101. It would have been better practice for the firm to assess the risk itself, rather than quoting the cleaners' assertion that the documents were destroyed. In addition, the firm could have suggested measures that their customers could take to protect themselves against identity fraud.

102. In a significant number of cases of data loss brought to our attention, firms have failed to consider the wider risks of identity fraud arising from data loss. Indeed, many firms appear more concerned about adverse media coverage than in being open and transparent with their customers about the risks they face. However, some firms are beginning to take a more responsible approach by writing to their customers to explain the circumstances, give advice and some are even offering to pay for precautions such as credit record checks and CIFAS Protective Registration.

> A building society sent a computer cartridge containing 6,500 customers' data to a government agency to fulfil legal reporting obligations. On arrival, the cartridge was missing from the package and could not be traced. Although the building society believed it was not at fault, it wrote to all customers concerned, explaining the circumstances, assessing the risk, and offering advice about how customers could safeguard their identities and credit records.

---

11 The government-backed Identity Fraud Consumer Awareness Group (IFCAG) gives consumers advice about how to protect themselves from identity fraud at: www.identity-theft.org.uk/protect-yourself.html

Core resources

Governance – examples of good practice

- Identifying data security as a key specific risk, subject to its own governance, policies and procedures and risk assessment.
- A senior manager with overall responsibility for data security, specifically mandated to manage data security risk assessment and communication between the key stakeholders within the firm such as: senior management, information security, human resources, financial crime, security, IT, compliance and internal audit.
- A specific committee with representation from relevant business areas to assess, monitor and control data security risk, which reports to the firm's board. As well as ensuring coordinated risk management, this structure sends a clear message to all staff about the importance of data security.
- Written data security policies and procedures which are proportionate, accurate and relevant to staff's day-to-day work.
- An open and honest culture of communication with pre-determined reporting mechanisms that make it easy for all staff and third parties to report data security concerns and data loss without fear of blame or recrimination.
- Firms seeking external assistance if they feel they do not have the necessary expertise to complete a data security risk assessment themselves.
- Firms liaising with peers and others to increase their awareness of data security risk and the implementation of good systems and controls.
- Detailed plans for reacting to a data loss including when and how to communicate with affected customers.
- Firms writing to affected customers promptly after a data loss, telling them what has been lost and how it was lost.
- Firms offering advice on protective measures against identity fraud to consumers affected by data loss and, where appropriate, paying for such services to be put in place.

Governance – examples of poor practice

- Treating data security as an IT issue and failing to involve other key staff from across the business in the risk assessment process.
- No written policies and procedures on data security.
- Failing to understand the need for sharing knowledge on data security
- Failing to take opportunities to share information with, and learn from, peers and others about data security risk and not recognising the need to do so.

- A 'blame culture' that discourages staff from reporting data security concerns and data losses.
- Failure to notify customers affected by data loss in case the details are picked up by the media.

3.2 Training and awareness

103. Many firms devote significant time and resource to creating and updating policies and procedures for ensuring data security. However, even the best policies and procedures have little value if front-line staff are not aware of them or do not understand what they mean in terms of their day-to-day responsibilities. Our experience shows that many instances of data loss occur because staff do not know or understand relevant policies and procedures. So it is good practice for senior management to put in place appropriate training and awareness mechanisms to ensure that their staff understand the relevance of policies and procedures to their roles.

> 'Staff were required to self-certify that they had read and understood Nationwide's procedures for information security. Staff received generic training on the application of the information security procedures; but no job-specific training was provided. Having designed and implemented its procedures for information security, Nationwide failed to establish controls adequate to ensure that its procedures were understood, and that staff adhered to these procedures.'
>
> FSA Final Notice of Enforcement action against Nationwide Building Society, 14 February 2007

104. Our review found that firms in general have substantial shortcomings in this important area. Many firms provided no training at all, and those that did often focused on the legal and regulatory aspects of poor data security rather than the financial crime risks that can arise from data loss. We found this approach often resulted in front-line staff being unaware of the importance of data security in reducing financial crime.

105. Many small firms tended to rely on a single staff member – often a secretary or administrator – to create data security procedures and communicate them to others. We noticed these individuals are often vigilant in reminding others of good practice such as locking filing cabinets and using complex passwords. However, their work was not usually based on a proper data security risk assessment and many important aspects of data security were often overlooked. This resulted in patchy and ineffective controls.

Core resources

> The 39 firms we visited were split into three broad groups:
> - Nearly half (17) offered no training at all.
> - Nine firms asked their staff to read their data security policy and certify that they had done so, but did not test staff's understanding of the policy.
> - The remaining firms offered formal training on data security; ten of them, including some small firms, repeated that training every six months or once a year.
>
> However, most firms did not test employees' understanding of the training received.

3.2.1 Poor assumptions about risk awareness

106. We found that, in some firms, senior management wrongly assumed their staff were aware of good data security practice even when there was no formal training in place to explain relevant policies and procedures. In addition, there was often an assumption that otherwise well-trained and honest staff would instinctively understand data security risk and know how to deal with it. These assumptions were misguided and we found that most front-line staff expected precise instructions from management about the procedures they should follow.

> The manager of a call centre at a medium-sized insurance firm was unaware of the risk of call centre staff being approached by fraudsters seeking to buy or extort customer data. This lack of relevant knowledge meant the manager was unable to warn his staff about a key risk.

107. If data security is left to individual judgement, standards will vary and policies and procedures will not be followed.

3.2.2 Advantages of written guidelines

108. Written policies, procedures and guidance are fundamental in ensuring that staff are aware of data security risks and the procedures to tackle those risks. Firms with no written policies, procedures or guidance are unlikely to be training their staff properly and ensuring proper awareness of data security risk throughout their business. The importance of written policies and procedures is covered in greater detail in Section 3.1.1.

3.2.3 Effective training and awareness mechanisms

109. Even where firms have detailed written policies, they often fail to train staff effectively. We have dealt with several cases of data loss that have demonstrated it is not realistic to expect staff to read and act on policies simply because they are available on the firm's intranet or in an employee handbook.

FSA report 'Data Security in Financial Services', April 2008

> A major insurance company relied on staff to read, understand and comply with a lengthy information security policy but took no steps to test staff's understanding of the policy.

110. We found that firms usually gave new recruits copies of lengthy data security policies and procedures, and sometimes asked them to sign to confirm they had read and understood them. In addition, some firms circulate policies and procedures regularly and ask staff to sign a declaration that they have read them. Firms must recognise there is a significant risk that staff will sign declarations without having read or understood policy documents, perhaps because they are too busy or, frankly, because they may find reading a data security policy boring.

> A senior manager at a major bank told us he did not expect staff or even branch managers to read the firm's data security policy. Instead, he said staff were guided into compliance with that policy through training, awareness campaigns and detailed procedural guidelines. 'The control process allows people to meet that process without having to understand the policy', he said.

111. Despite the risks of staff failing to understand policies and procedures, we found it was rare for firms – including some large ones – to provide staff with specific courses or coaching on the importance of data security, even on a risk-based approach. A small number of firms recognised this risk and, in some cases, offered incentives to increase staff interest in understanding policies.

> A data security quiz offering an iPod as the prize was the most popular staff competition ever at a large bank. The firm intends to repeat this successful initiative every six months.
>
> A major bank offered a flat-panel television as a prize in a data security competition designed to raise awareness of policies. There were over 20,000 entries from its staff.

112. When small firms provide staff training, it tends to be informal; this can be effective and proportionate for the type of business and risk the firm runs.

> A small financial advice firm's IT manager, who had a good understanding of data security, regularly reminded staff of good practice, checked the strength of staff passwords, and taught staff about the risk of customer data being used to commit fraud.

113. Although it is good practice for firms to assess staff understanding of data security policies and procedures regularly, we found it was rare for firms to require staff to repeat training or testing. In addition, training for front-line staff, such as those who work in call centres, tended to focus mainly on legislative and regulatory requirements. This

Core resources

approach does not teach staff about why data security is an essential tool in reducing the risk of financial crime. However, some firms did have some innovative (and inexpensive) training methods for demonstrating how customer data can be used to commit fraud.

> A medium-sized building society asked staff to identify items in a mocked-up handbag which could be used for identity fraud. The bag contained items such as credit cards, a driving licence and a utility bill. Once staff had picked out items that could be used by fraudsters, management reminded staff that the firm held similar customer data and emphasised the importance of keeping it secure.

114. Firms that are serious about ensuring good data security will try to raise awareness of relevant policies and procedures by bringing the subject to life and making it clear to employees what they need to do to protect customer data in their everyday work.

> In June 2007, we dealt with a case where a medium-sized investment administration firm had suffered from a spate of identity frauds. One way the firm reduced further fraud was to play recordings to call centre staff of suspected fraudsters' calls. Staff learned to recognise the fraudsters' voices and were able to alert their managers to further suspected frauds.

115. Some firms used posters, messages on screensavers, email reminders, or articles in staff newspapers to promote awareness of data security. Others took more imaginative approaches.

> A medium-sized investment firm set up a 'dodgy desk' that exposed all kinds of poor practice relevant to data security. For example, confidential information was left on-screen and confidential papers were left in open view. Staff were then asked to identity all the shortcomings.
>
> Another firm tested its employees' awareness of data security risk by targeting them with spoof 'phishing' attacks requesting username and password details.

116. We found the best good-practice guidance for staff was packaged in a simple, memorable format and was supplemented by controls to ensure that policies and procedures could not be ignored. We also observed that good awareness campaigns usually translated into good practice. For example, desks were clear, passwords were carefully guarded, and staff were generally careful in handling customer data. Simple but effective awareness campaigns can be achieved even in the largest firms. A major bank, for example, reduced its relevant policies to a few simple messages: keeping a clear desk, locking a PC when not in use, using the confidential waste bins and keeping passwords safe. In conjunction with the firm's strong controls, these messages helped to ensure a secure environment for customer data.

FSA report 'Data Security in Financial Services', April 2008

> A small firm produced a simple one-page list of 'Do's and Don'ts' for its employees that set out good data security practice.

Training and awareness – examples of good practice

- Innovative training and awareness campaigns that focus on the financial crime risks arising from poor data security, as well as the legal and regulatory requirements to protect customer data.
- Clear understanding among staff about why data security is relevant to their work and what they must do to comply with relevant policies and procedures.
- Simple, memorable and easily-digestible guidance for staff on good data security practice.
- Testing of staff understanding of data security policies on induction and annually thereafter.
- Competitions, posters, screensavers and group discussion to raise interest in the subject.

Training and awareness – examples of poor practice

- No training to communicate policies and procedures.
- Managers assuming that employees understand data security risk without any training.
- Data security policies which are very lengthy, complicated and difficult to read.
- Relying on staff signing an annual declaration saying they have read policy documents without any further testing.
- Staff being given no incentive to learn about data security.

3.3 Staff recruitment and vetting

117. One of the most important controls that firms can put in place to prevent data theft and other financial crime is a good standard of staff vetting. There have been many well-documented cases of staff either stealing customer data to use fraudulently or sell on to criminals who specialise in identity fraud. Other staff have been threatened, bribed or otherwise coerced by criminals into handing over customer data. So firms must be able to trust that their staff will handle and use customer data securely, in line with relevant policies and procedures.

Core resources

118. We examined firms' general recruitment and vetting policies and considered in particular whether vetting was appropriate for staff in roles that required access to large amounts of customer data, such as call centre, branch and IT staff.

> 'We know of organised crime groups who are placing people within the call centres so that they can steal customers' data and carry out fraud and money laundering.'
>
> DCI Derek Robertson, Strathclyde Police
>
> Source: BBC News online, October 2006

119. In addition, we examined whether firms conducted any ongoing vetting or monitoring of changes in employees' personal circumstances which could be an early indicator of susceptibility to financial crime. We also investigated whether recruitment standards for temporary and contract staff were equivalent to those applied to permanent staff, especially in higher-risk areas such as call centres.

3.3.1 Initial Recruitment Process

120. Many of the 39 firms we visited adopted a two-tier approach to recruitment. Higher vetting standards were generally applied to senior staff and those in 'controlled functions' – positions which require FSA approval of the relevant individual. For these roles, many firms carried out credit checks and, sometimes, criminal record checks. However, most firms did not conduct such a high level of vetting for junior staff (e.g. in call centres, administration and IT roles), despite the fact that they often had wider access to customer data than their senior colleagues.

> A small investment management firm's checks for non-FSA-approved staff were limited to references, right to work in the UK, and confirmation of academic qualifications. Only FSA-approved staff were subject to credit checks and no criminal record checks were carried out on any staff.
>
> Conversely, a major insurance firm applied consistent vetting to all staff regardless of rank. This included credit checks and criminal record checks.

121. Many firms had simply not considered that access to large amounts of customer data could make junior staff a higher risk in terms of data loss and financial crime. We were disappointed by this as it indicated that, in terms of their vetting standards, many firms were not adopting an appropriate risk-based approach to preventing financial crime, as required by our Handbook.

> A medium-sized insurance firm, that had high staff turnover in its call centre, employed staff solely on employment references. No credit or criminal records checks were carried out for reasons of cost. Furthermore, staff integrity was not routinely examined during the recruitment process.

122. However, we did identify a small number of firms who were applying a risk-based approach to staff recruitment and whose vetting standards were high.

> A large bank's financial crime team assisted its HR department to perform rigorous vetting of job applicants. Checks of address; employment references; academic certificates; credit records; financial sanctions lists; fraud intelligence databases; and criminal records databases were carried out for staff in 'higher risk' positions.
>
> The same firm also carried out an annual 'fit and proper' check for staff that included credit checks and financial sanctions list checks to identify changes in staff's personal circumstances which could increase data security or fraud risk.

123. Many small firms did not have a dedicated human resource function (this was mainly due to the low turnover in small firms generally) and recruitment would often be based on personal recommendation and references. Pre-employment checks such as credit references or criminal record checks were rarely carried out.

> A small financial advice firm employed all advisers as graduates and all administration staff based on personal recommendation. So the firm had no formal recruitment policies or procedures. Strong reliance was placed on the trust built up with staff over time.
>
> Another small financial advice firm's entire staff was made up of personal friends or recruits through personal recommendation to the manager.

124. Despite the low levels of staff turnover in many small firms, it is good practice for their senior management to consider the risk of customer data being stolen by staff employed on the basis of limited or no vetting. Several of the small firms we visited said we had raised their awareness of data security (and fraud) risks that could arise if a dishonest person was employed by the firm. In addition, many of them wished to be able to reassure their customers that their data was being handled by suitably-vetted staff.

125. Medium-sized and large firms tended to have higher rates of staff turnover than small firms. This was particularly true of firms with large call centres that sometimes had a relatively high number of temporary staff. We observed that high turnover in some firms often leads to conflicting priorities between different departments. For example, security and financial crime staff would wish to ensure that appropriate vetting was carried out on new recruits while line management were under pressure to fill vacancies quickly to maintain a good level of customer service. This was particularly evident in firms with call centre operations or large administration functions.

Core resources

> In a medium-sized insurance firm with high turnover, pressure to fill vacancies meant that call centre staff often had access to customer data for around two weeks before vetting was completed.

126. It is good practice for firms to manage work pressures without compromising the quality of their vetting. Some firms had in place measures to try and reduce pressures arising from high staff turnover. For example, several firms were training their staff in a number of disciplines (sometimes known as 'multi-skilling') to provide adequate cover if staff left suddenly. In addition, some firms were putting in place clear career development plans for call centre staff to increase staff morale and loyalty, and reduce turnover.

The importance of liaison between HR and Financial Crime in the vetting process

127. Some of the best practice we noted occurred in firms where there was close liaison between human resources and financial crime/anti-fraud departments. For example, a major bank assessed applicants against a 'traffic light' system of financial crime risk indicators, drawn up by HR and the firm's financial crime team. The table below gives examples of how this system worked.

Examples of 'red' criteria	Examples of 'amber' criteria	Examples of 'green' criteria
Five or more declared County Court Judgments (CCJs)	Fewer than five CCJs declared in excess of £100	A single declared CCJ for £100 or less
Two or more undeclared CCJs	A declared dismissal from previous employment	Adverse information received from previous employer not relating to a dismissal
Adverse employment references in connection with financial crime or serious misconduct	A declared criminal record	Criminal records for motoring offences
Non-discharged bankruptcy or Individual Voluntary Arrangements (IVAs)		

Note: This table is an example of what we saw at one firm; it is not exhaustive and firms should consider all risk factors relevant to their business if they choose to adopt a similar approach.

128. Any applicant meeting an element of red criteria would not be hired while an applicant meeting an amber criterion could only be recruited following an independent review and sign off by HR. In addition, the firm was trialling CIFAS staff fraud database[12] and

---

12 The CIFAS Staff Fraud Database is used by CIFAS Members specifically for staff vetting and security screening purposes. CIFAS members use the Staff Fraud Database to file data about their staff fraud cases and access staff fraud records filed by other CIFAS Members. For more information, visit: www.cifas.org.uk/default.asp?edit_id=718-87

criminal record checks on all staff meeting amber criteria (around a fifth of all applicants) regardless of role. The firm advised all new applicants of the possibility of criminal record checks, hoping that this would act as a deterrent to applicants with relevant criminal convictions. Importantly, the firm's financial crime team reviewed the traffic light indicators regularly and added new or emerging risk criteria to the system based on their own, and industry-wide, experience.

3.3.2 Temporary staff

129. For many firms, employment agencies are a key third-party supplier with relevance to data security. Although employment agencies are unlikely to handle customer data, they often play a key role in recruiting temporary staff with access to firms' customer data. So it is essential that firms have a clear understanding of the checks conducted by agencies on prospective staff and that regular checks are made to ensure agencies are complying with agreed vetting standards.

130. It is good practice for firms to ensure that temporary staff are not subject to less-rigorous vetting than permanent staff in similar roles. This is consistent with a risk-based approach to reducing financial crime because the risk to customer data does not decrease when a temporary member of staff handles it.

> A medium-sized investment firm did not tell their employment agencies the standard of vetting required for temporary staff. The firm's HR representative was unable to tell us what vetting was conducted by the agencies for temporary staff as he had never asked the agencies about their vetting standards.

131. The 20 small firms we visited very rarely employed temporary or contract staff because of their low levels of staff turnover. In contrast, the employment of temporary or contract staff was common in medium-sized and large firms, particularly in call centres or administrative roles. Many larger firms had contracts with 'preferred' employment agencies and used them to source temporary and contract staff. In general, larger firms relied on agencies to carry out relevant pre-employment checks on temporary and contract staff. However, a small number of firms chose not to rely on checks carried out by employment agencies and conducted their own vetting checks on staff put forward to them.

> Some firms arranged for agencies to put in place a pre-vetted panel of temporary staff to enable higher-risk vacancies to be filled quickly by suitable individuals.

132. Our findings on controls over third parties that handle customer data are detailed in Section 3.7.

Core resources

3.3.3 Ongoing vetting of staff

133. Although most firms recognise the risk of data theft by their employees, many firms had no formal process for identifying a change in an employee's personal circumstances. Bankruptcy, divorce and addictions to gambling, drugs or alcohol are all examples of lifestyle events that could affect an individual's financial soundness and make them more vulnerable to committing data theft and fraud.

134. Overall, we saw very few examples of formalised, repeated vetting of staff, even when individuals had access to large amounts of customer data. The exception was FSA-approved individuals, who were often subject to annual credit checks so that firms could satisfy themselves of the individual's continuing fitness and propriety.

> A large insurance firm that carried out credit checks on new recruits repeated them once a year as part of an individual's performance appraisal process.

135. The generally poor standard of vetting for new recruits, coupled with the relative rarity of ongoing vetting, gives rise to significant risk of data theft from financial services firms. For both initial and ongoing vetting, firms should take a risk-based approach and ensure that staff access to customer data is one of the factors considered.

136. Small firms often relied on the close-knit nature of their organisations, where staff were well-known to each other and often long-serving, and staff vigilance to identify unusual behaviour among their workforce. Their employees often sat in close proximity and were generally aware of what their colleagues' roles entailed. This may be a proportionate, risk-based approach in some small firms, but it is good practice for them to support it with a formal data security risk assessment covering the risk of corrupt staff.

137. In larger firms, there were usually clearly-defined management structures and line managers were generally responsible for continually assessing staff performance. Many large firms relied on the general performance management process as the main tool for identifying changes in employees' circumstances that could give rise to increased data security risk. We are not convinced this informal approach to ongoing vetting will always be appropriate, particularly for higher-risk roles. A more-structured approach incorporating tools such as regular credit or criminal record checks on a risk basis is likely to be far more effective in reducing data security risk in financial services firms.

Staff recruitment and vetting – examples of good practice

- A risk-based approach to vetting staff, taking into account data security and other fraud risk.

FSA report 'Data Security in Financial Services', April 2008

- Enhanced vetting – including checks of credit records, criminal records, financial sanctions lists and the CIFAS Staff Fraud Database – for staff in roles with access to large amounts of customer data.
- Liaison between HR and Financial Crime to ensure that financial crime risk indicators are considered during the vetting process.
- A good understanding of the level of vetting conducted by employment agencies during the recruitment of temporary and contract staff.
- Formal procedures to assess regularly whether staff in higher-risk positions are becoming vulnerable to committing fraud or being coerced by criminals.

Staff recruitment and vetting – examples of poor practice

- Allowing new recruits to access customer data before vetting has been completed.
- Temporary staff receiving less-rigorous vetting than permanently employed colleagues carrying out similar roles.
- Failing to consider whether staff in higher-risk positions are becoming vulnerable to committing fraud or being coerced by criminals.

3.4 Controls

138. Earlier in this report, we set out our findings on how policies and procedures are implemented and staff are trained about their responsibilities. While these factors are important in setting the tone for how a firm manages data security risk, it is essential that firms also have in place effective controls to prevent data loss if policies and procedures are not followed.

139. Without effective controls, data can be lost or stolen, even where policies, procedures and training are of a good standard. Examples of how this might happen include staff ignoring procedures because of a time constraint, other work pressure or perhaps being unaware of their responsibilities; perhaps they were sick when they were supposed to have been trained or they simply might not have been listening during a training session.

140. There is also the very real possibility of data theft by corrupt employees. This can occur when criminals or their associates infiltrate a firm or when existing staff are coerced by criminals – perhaps with the offer of a bribe, the threat of personal injury or blackmail – to give them customer data.

Core resources

> Examples of incidents of data theft brought to our attention during our review included:
> - a call centre employee in a major insurance firm who used a customer's credit card details to buy goods online; and
> - a call centre employee in a major bank who stole customer data for her boyfriend 'to prove her love'. This led to fraud on at least three customers' bank accounts before the theft was discovered.

141. During our visits, we examined in-depth the controls firms have in place to prevent data loss. Of the 39 firms we visited, we judged that only eight had good controls in place to minimise the risk of data loss. All of these firms were large or medium-sized firms in the banking and insurance industries. Interestingly, two of them offered identity theft insurance; one specifically stated that the potential reputational damage of a data loss to their identity theft insurance business was a key driver to ensure the best possible data security control environment.

142. The remaining 31 firms were split roughly into two groups. The first group (16 firms) had implemented a range of controls across their business but weaknesses in some areas gave rise to a significant risk of data loss. Worryingly, this group of firms included some very large firms that held, in some cases, millions of customers' details. The second group (15 firms) – the majority of which were small – had a poor control environment which gave rise to a high risk of data loss. This was often the result of a lack of awareness of data security risk at senior management level, but may also be attributable to a lack of financial or human resources.

> From our sample of 39 firms, just eight had good controls.
>
> Sixteen firms had some good controls in place but had significant weaknesses too.
>
> Fifteen firms had poor controls which gave rise to a high risk of data compromise.

3.4.1 Controls in offshore operations

143. A small number of the firms we visited had call centres both in the UK and in India. All of these firms believed the control environment in its India call centres, including physical security and recruitment, was at least equivalent to that of their UK call centres. These views are consistent with our previous work on offshore operations, published in 2005.[13]

144. One large firm told us its India call centre was subject to significantly higher physical security than the UK, including a 'paperless office'. This firm recognised the risk of data loss from its UK call centres but did not feel it could apply the rigorous security

---
[13] www.fsa.gov.uk/pubs/other/offshore_ops.pdf

arrangements in place in India. There were several reasons for this, including the potential detrimental effect on staff morale and possible trade union concerns.

3.4.2 Access rights

145. Properly-configured IT access rights and a well-defined joiners and leavers process are essential tools in ensuring data is appropriately secured. There are three main points at which it is good practice for firms to take appropriate steps to ensure that access rights are reviewed: on recruitment; when staff change roles; and when they leave the firm.

On recruitment

146. It is good practice for firms to ensure that, when recruited, staff are only given access to the information they require to do their job. This is often referred to as 'least privilege' access.

147. During our review, we found many examples of insufficient procedures to ensure least-privilege access. The most extreme examples included some firms that gave all staff access to all of their customer data, regardless of whether they needed the information to do their jobs. More often, access rights were determined on a case-by-case basis by line managers with no independent checking they were appropriate. There is a risk that, without an independent check, this could lead to some staff having inappropriate access to customer data.

> A medium-sized insurance firm had two main IT systems – a customer database and a workflow monitoring system. They contained a wide range of sensitive customer data, including financial and bank account details, scanned copies of customer signatures and detailed personal information required for life insurance applications. With the exception of medical information, access to this personal data was not restricted according to business need.

148. Some of the good practice we saw included detailed role profiles for each job – or type of job – that included a description of the access rights required to carry out the role, on a least-privilege basis. We observed this good practice in several firms of various sizes.

> Several investment firms restricted IT access so advisers could only access information about their own clients, not all clients of the firm. However, there were other firms that allowed unrestricted access to all customer data for all staff, regardless of business need.

Core resources

When a staff member changes jobs or is given new responsibilities

149. It is essential that firms have processes in place to ensure they review access rights when an individual changes roles or is given different responsibilities. Without such processes, staff can build up inappropriate access to large numbers of systems over time. This not only gives rise to data security risks, but also to more general fraud risks, as staff might be able to access information that has been segregated to prevent fraud.

150. Most firms had taken some steps to review the appropriateness of staff access rights in the event of a role change. Good practice we observed included:

    i. firms that had set up role-based access profiles for each role in their organisation that simply replaced the old role profile with the new one when an individual changed roles; and

    ii. firms that effectively treated staff changing roles as new joiners. All existing access rights would be deleted and the user would have their new access rights set up from scratch by the IT department.

151. However, we found some examples of firms of various sizes – including one major firm – that did not have effective controls to prevent staff building up inappropriate access to systems containing customer data.

When staff leave the firm

152. When a member of staff leaves employment, it is good practice for firms to ensure their IT access rights are permanently disabled or deleted. If this is not done, there is a risk of a corrupt member of staff using the vacant user account for criminal purposes, including the theft of customer data.

153. Some firms had appropriate controls to ensure that leavers' IT access rights were disabled. In many firms, this included the regular reconciliation of HR records against the IT department's log of user accounts. This would help to identify staff who had left the firm, but who, for some reason, had not had their user account disabled or deleted.

154. We did, however, find some poor practice in this area, with some firms failing to put in place effective controls to ensure that redundant user accounts were disabled on a timely and accurate basis.

> We spotted an example of very poor practice at a medium-sized insurance firm, which did not permanently disable redundant user accounts. Instead, their process was for IT support staff to change the user's password to a random string of letters and numbers 'which could not be guessed by anybody else'. The firm failed to recognise the risk that a corrupt member of IT support staff could note the new password and continue to use the user account to steal customer data and/or commit financial crime.

FSA report 'Data Security in Financial Services', April 2008

155. Three particular issues relating to access rights emerged during our review. In some cases, firms had failed to recognise the risk of data loss and weak access controls exposed the firm to a high level of data security risk.

Wide access to scanned copies of sensitive documents collected for 'know your customer' purposes

156. We noted during our visits a general shift in the financial services industry – including in small firms – from holding customer data in paper files to the electronic scanning and filing of correspondence. There are clear benefits in terms of efficiency and customer service for businesses that scan documents. However, we visited a significant number of firms and call centres where scanned correspondence containing customer data that could be used to commit fraud was accessible to too many staff without a genuine business need. The types of scanned correspondence typically included documents collected by firms to verify customers for anti-money laundering (AML) purposes, such as passports, driving licences, utility bills and bank/credit card statements.

> Several firms we visited – large and small – scanned 'know your customer' information on to their IT systems. In nearly all cases, access to this information was too wide. Sometimes, entire call centres could access scanned copies of documents like customers' passports, driving licences and bank statements. And in some cases, scans could be printed off, downloaded to USB devices or emailed externally.

157. It is good practice for firms to consider carefully the types of scanned documents that staff need to access to do their jobs when determining access rights. The findings of our review indicate it is rare for staff outside of firms' financial crime departments to need to see scanned copies of 'know your customer' information to do their job. Some staff in call centres told us they needed access to these documents to ensure that AML checks had been completed. However, when challenged, they conceded that a marker on the customer's record stating whether AML checks for the customer had been completed would enable them to do their job.

> A medium-sized insurance firm required customers to submit their credit card numbers and expiry details on their claim forms so that payments for the insurance excess could be taken. However, some customers (although not required to) also supplied their three digit security code. Copies of these claim forms – which included all of the information required to commit credit card fraud – were scanned onto the system and accessible to all call centre staff.

Core resources

Wide access to recordings of telephone conversations containing sensitive data

158. It is common industry practice for telephone conversations with customers to be recorded either for training purposes or in case of a dispute with the customer. However, it appears that access to call recordings is not always on a least-privilege basis, even when access to other IT systems is.

> One major firm – with several call centres in the UK and one in India – gave call centre team leaders and managers unrestricted access to recordings of every single call received by its many call centres. Many of these conversations included customers' names, addresses, dates of birth, policy details, and credit card/bank account details. The firm believed this was necessary for training purposes but we contended that training on good customer service could still be provided if access to call recordings was significantly restricted. Interestingly, the team leaders we spoke to did not believe that their access to these call recordings was ever monitored.

159. Call recordings often contain sensitive customer data such as passwords and financial information. As with other IT systems, it is good practice for firms to ensure that staff only have access to recordings needed for their particular role.

> A major bank authenticated its customers' identities via touch-tone telephone before customers were put through to call centre staff. This meant that call centre staff did not need to ask customers for sensitive data to confirm their identity, so this information was not recorded.

Full credit card numbers and bank account details available to large numbers of employees with no business need

160. We found that some firms – including large firms – made sensitive financial data such as credit card numbers and expiry dates, bank account details and sort codes available to a wide range of staff and sometimes entire call centres. Many call centre staff told us it would not affect their ability to do their job if the sensitive financial details were partially obscured on their systems.

> Some firms' databases only displayed partial credit card or bank account details to minimise the risk of data loss. For example, one firm displayed 16-digit credit card numbers in the following format: 1234 XXXX XXXX 5678. Another firm was halfway through a project to obscure such details on their databases.

FSA report 'Data Security in Financial Services', April 2008

Access rights – examples of good practice

- Specific IT access profiles for each role in the firm, which set out exactly what level of IT access is required for an individual to do their job.
- When a staff member changes roles or responsibilities, all IT access rights are deleted from the system and the user is set up using the same process as if they were a new joiner at the firm. The complexity of this process is significantly reduced if role-based IT access profiles are in place – the old one can simply be replaced with the new.
- A clearly-defined process to notify IT of forthcoming staff departures so IT accesses can be permanently disabled or deleted on a timely and accurate basis.
- A regular reconciliation of HR and IT user records to act as a failsafe if the firm's leavers process fails.
- Regular reviews of staff IT access rights to ensure there are no anomalies.
- Least-privilege access to call recordings and copies of scanned documents obtained for 'know your customer' purposes.
- Authentication of customers' identities using, for example, touch-tone telephone before a conversation with a call centre adviser takes place. This limits the amount of personal information and/or passwords contained in call recordings.
- Masking credit card, bank account details and other sensitive data like customer passwords where this would not affect staff's ability to do their job.

Access rights – Examples of poor practice

- Staff having access to customer data which they do not require to do their job.
- User access rights set up on a case-by-case basis with no independent check that they are appropriate.
- Redundant access rights being allowed to remain in force when a member of staff changes roles.
- User accounts being left 'live' or only suspended (i.e. not permanently disabled) when a staff member leaves.
- A lack of independent check of changes effected at any stage in the joiners, movers and leavers process.

Core resources

3.4.3 Passwords and user accounts

161. It is important that firms ensure access to IT systems, both through desktops and laptops, is controlled using individual user accounts (often referred to as 'user ID') and each user account is protected by a strong password. There is a risk that passwords can be easily guessed and studies have shown people often use the names of relatives, pets, their favourite football team and sometimes even the word 'password' to access their systems. In addition, password cracking software is now widely available.

> A senior manager of a small financial advice firm named Gill told us that her user ID was 'Gill' and her password was 'Gill' (name changed to protect identity).

162. During our review, we discovered many firms had poor password standards in place. This was mainly a problem in small firms but we also found examples of poor practice in some larger firms. In particular, several firms had policies in place recommending certain standards but had no controls in place to ensure these standards were met.

> A major bank allowed passwords that were only six characters long and did not need to contain a mix of upper and lower case letters, numbers or keyboard symbols. This is significantly below recommended standards on password strength. Get Safe Online – a government-backed campaign group – recommends that passwords should be a combination of letters, numbers and keyboard symbols; at least seven characters long; contain a mix of upper and lower case letters, numbers and keyboard symbols; and be changed regularly.[14]

163. It is essential that firms have individual user accounts in place so they can monitor users' activities to detect breaches of policies and procedures that could lead to data loss. However, we found some firms did not have individual user accounts in place and allowed all users to access their systems with the same password. This exposes firms to a significant risk of systems misuse, including data loss. For example, if a corrupt employee was systematically extracting customer data from a database using a generic password, the lack of an auditable, individual user account would make it difficult for the firm to find out – or prove – who was responsible.

Password sharing

164. In several small firms, we found examples of individual users' passwords being shared with or known to senior management and other employees; this could lead to user accounts being compromised. For example, one small firm told us senior management knew every staff member's password. The justification given was that some staff had particular software installed on their computers which senior management might need

---

14   http://www.getsafeonline.org/nqcontent.cfm?a_id=1127

Data Security in Financial Services

FSA report 'Data Security in Financial Services', April 2008

to use from time to time. Password sharing is poor practice and had arisen in this case because the firm had not ensured that each user had access to the systems and software they needed to do their jobs.

Multiple passwords

165. We noted during our visits that most firms had more than one system requiring a password. The proliferation of passwords required by individuals – both at work and in their everyday life – could have undesired results in terms of security. For example, a member of staff might use the same password for several systems or they might write down their passwords so they do not forget them.

> Two medium-sized firms – an insurer and a building society – had used password-cracking software on their staff's user accounts to check that passwords were robust enough. The building society did this regularly and, if a password could be cracked within an hour, they made staff change their password.

166. To reduce these risks, some larger firms said they were investigating moving to 'straight-through processing'. Straight-through processing allows users to log on to their computer with a single password and access all required databases or other software without the need for any more passwords. It is good practice for firms seeking to move to straight-through processing to have accurate, role-based access profiles in place (see paragraph 148) so staff only have access to the systems and data that they need to do their job. In addition, as only one password is required for straight-through processing, it is good practice for firms to ensure that each employee's password is strong.

> A major insurance firm was investigating 'straight-through processing' – a method that gives a user appropriate access to all databases and software with a single password. They acknowledged they would first need to ensure that accurate role-based access profiles were in place for all staff to reduce the risk of inappropriate access to some systems.

Passwords and user accounts – examples of good practice

- Individual user accounts – requiring passwords – in place for all systems containing customer data.
- Password standards at least equivalent to those recommended by campaign group Get Safe Online. At present, their recommended standard for passwords is a combination of letters, numbers and keyboard symbols at least seven characters in length and changed regularly.

Core resources

- Measures to ensure passwords are robust. These might include controls to ensure that passwords can only be set in accordance with policy and the use of password-cracking software on a risk-based approach.
- 'Straight through processing', but only if complemented by accurate role-based access profiles and strong passwords.

Passwords and user accounts – examples of poor practice

- The same user account and password used by multiple users to access particular systems.
- Names and dictionary words used as passwords.
- Systems which allow passwords to be set which do not comply with password policy.
- Password sharing of any kind.

3.4.4 Monitoring access to customer data

167. Even staff who have a legitimate need to access customer data can present risks. The most pertinent examples include corrupt staff who wish to use customer data to commit fraud themselves, staff who have been coerced by criminals to give them customer data and staff with links to criminal groups who have managed to get a job in a financial services firm.

168. For these reasons, it is good practice for firms to take a risk-based approach to monitoring employees' access to customer data to ensure that access is for genuine business reasons. An example of a simple check is to take a sample of when staff have accessed customer records in call centres and compare it with records of telephone calls the call centre has received from customers. This could highlight instances where customer data has potentially been accessed without a valid business reason and the firm can ask the relevant employee for an explanation. In addition, where databases record the time and date of changes made to customer records, these can also be cross-referenced to recordings of particular phone calls to ensure the changes made were actually requested by the customer.

> A medium-sized building society had software in place to track access, changes and other manipulation of data through exception reports, which the firm reviewed monthly. Importantly, the firm had invested significant time and resource to fine-tune the software from its 'off-the-shelf' format, so it would recognise genuine suspicious activity and reduce the number of false exceptions.

169. Few firms carried out proactive monitoring of their staff's access to data, even on a sample- or risk-based approach.

FSA report 'Data Security in Financial Services', April 2008

> A medium-sized investment firm had a database with an audit facility that could identify when customer data had been changed, who had changed it, and show the data before and after the change had been made. However, the firm failed to make routine use of the audit facility to ensure either that there were genuine business reasons for changes to customer data.

Superusers

170. 'Superusers' most often work in IT and are often responsible for database administration and creating staff access rights. Their technical knowledge means they often have the potential to access large amounts of customer data and sometimes to circumvent fraud controls. These factors are likely to make superusers attractive targets for organised criminals seeking to use an insider to steal customer data from a firm. So it is good practice for superusers to be carefully vetted and monitored.

> Most large and medium-sized firms had some measures in place to prevent staff from accessing bulk customer data. Many call centres, for example, only allowed staff to access one customer record at a time. However, it was not unusual for some staff – particularly in 'superuser' or other IT positions – to be able to extract bulk data.
>
> A major bank was unclear about the number of database administrators it employed and admitted these superusers had the capability to disable the audit trails used to monitor their activity.

171. We saw varied practice in larger firms in this area. Some had excellent controls including strict processes to prevent unauthorised changes to systems and data by database administrators. In other firms, superusers were not adequately controlled.

> A large bank had recently completed a project to put superuser passwords into a 'digital vault'. Superusers were required to complete a form stating the work they would carry out and get approval from independent staff before being able to 'unlock' the digital vault and access relevant systems with a single-use password. The superuser was then required to check the password back in to the digital vault within a given timeframe. At that point, the password would be automatically changed for its next use.

172. The monitoring of superusers poses real problems for small firms, as there is often a lack of technical knowledge, resource and understanding of the superuser's roles elsewhere in the firm. As a result, there is usually no independent check of superusers' work and trust is the main tool used to ensure a secure environment. Where this is the case, it is good practice for small firms to ensure the standard of vetting (see Section 3.3) is proportionate to the high risk posed by superusers' wide-ranging access to customer data. In addition, these firms may wish to ask their IT auditors or compliance consultants to conduct a regular review of superusers' activities.

Core resources

> A small investment firm did not conduct any independent check of the IT Director's work, even though he had completely unrestricted access to all IT systems in the firm. This risk was compounded as the firm did not check whether any of its staff, even in high-risk positions, had any criminal convictions. Situations like this were quite common in the sample of small firms we examined.

Monitoring access to customer data – examples of good practice

- Risk-based, proactive monitoring of staff's access to customer data to ensure that it is being accessed and/or updated for a genuine business reason.
- Using software designed to spot suspicious activity by employees with access to customer data. Such software may not be useful in its 'off-the-shelf' format so it is good practice for firms to ensure it is tailored to their business profile.
- Strict controls over superusers' access to customer data and independent checks of their work to ensure they have not accessed, manipulated or extracted data that was not required for a particular task.

Monitoring access to customer data – examples of poor practice

- Assuming that vetted staff with appropriate access rights will always act appropriately. Staff can breach procedures, for example by looking at account information relating to celebrities, be tempted to commit fraud themselves or be bribed or threatened to provide customer data to provide customer data to criminals.
- Failure to make regular use of management information about access to customer data.
- Failing to monitor superusers or other employees with access to large amounts of customer data.

3.4.5 Authentication

173. In August 2007, we published a special edition of our Financial Crime Newsletter which focused on the authentication and safeguarding of customer identity[15] (our 'Authentication Newsletter'). In it, we called on firms to take the following key steps to ensure customers' identities are effectively verified and protected:
    - establish a suitable and effective authentication process;
    - protect customer data, so it cannot be stolen and/or used to defraud consumers and firms; and
    - help customers be more security conscious.

---

15   www.fsa.gov.uk/pubs/newsletters/fc_newsletter8.pdf

FSA report 'Data Security in Financial Services', April 2008

174. The Authentication Newsletter contained good-practice guidance to help firms establish appropriate risk management systems. As this work was carried out recently, we did not focus on authentication during our review but, inevitably, the subject did arise from time to time. Our findings suggest there is still much for some firms to do if customers' identities are to be authenticated effectively.

175. Some of the medium-sized firms we visited asked customers to authenticate themselves by confirming details which were publicly available. For example, one firm's call-centre operators asked customers to confirm three random pieces of information about themselves to complete the authentication process. However, the firm had not considered the risk that call centre staff might ask for three pieces of publicly available information, such as name, address, and date of birth, creating significant opportunities for fraudsters to access customer accounts and/or data. Another firm had at least recognised the risk posed by the use of publicly-available data in the authentication process and was moving to a password-based system.

> One firm, which used a four-digit customer reference number as a tool for customer authentication, routinely included the reference number in mailings to customers. This mail could be intercepted by criminals seeking to gain access to customers' accounts and financial information.

176. It is good practice for firms using password-based systems to put in place measures to protect passwords and we observed that some larger firms had done so.

> Two banks had systems in place where call centre staff did not have access to entire customer passwords. Both firms asked customers to give two random letters from their passwords. Call centre staff then entered these random letters into the system to access account details.

177. In the worst cases we saw, two small investment firms had not considered any process at all for authenticating their customers. Instead, these firms told us they relied solely on advisers recognising their clients' voices. This could present significant opportunities for an identity fraudster to access or take over a customer account using impersonation.

> Two small investment firms had not established a suitable and effective authentication process for customers who telephoned the office to request or change information on their accounts. Instead, they relied solely on their advisers recognising their clients' voices. One of these firms had an adviser to client ratio of around 1:1,200; the other around 1:150. It is not possible for advisers to recognise the voices of such large numbers of clients, some of whom may contact the firm infrequently. Poor controls like this can lead to significant fraud.

Core resources

178. Interestingly, our Authentication Newsletter found that no firms routinely proved their own identity before asking the customer to authenticate themselves. During our review, we visited a medium-sized insurance firm whose products included mobile-phone insurance. The firm specifically instructed its call centre staff not to ask for customers' personal information until they had supplied the customer with basic information about their mobile phone and/or the call plan. While we were encouraged that the firm had thought about how they could prove their identity to customers before authenticating their identities, firms should take care they do not disclose customer data to somebody other than the customer. This would be a breach of the Data Protection Act and could expose customers to identity fraud.

179. As noted previously, our Authentication Newsletter contained good practice guidance for firms and highlighted areas for improvement.

3.4.6 Data back-up

180. Almost all firms with electronic systems back up their data on a regular basis to ensure that they would be able to continue operating after an adverse event such as a fire, flood or corruption of data held on IT systems. As part of this process, firms often take copies of all their data and store it offsite at one of their other offices, with a third-party supplier or at the home of a trusted employee.

181. Although the backing up of data is essential for disaster recovery purposes, the methods commonly used by firms give rise to several risks to data security that must be properly managed.

> The sheer volume and detail of customer data held on back-up tapes and servers makes them very attractive to criminals seeking to commit fraud. Put simply, if backed up data is not transferred or stored securely, all other controls to ensure data security at a firm are undermined.

182. However, we found that many firms simply did not recognise the risks associated with transferring and storing copies of all their data offsite. Others failed to examine all of the risks involved. For example, a firm might put in place good controls over the transfer of data to an archiving firm, but then have no understanding of – or fail to check – how securely the data is held at the archiving firm. Appropriate management of third-party suppliers is examined in depth in Section 3.7.

> A medium-sized insurance firm used a third-party supplier to store backed up data. Although the data – which included large amounts of customers' credit card and bank account data – was transferred to the third party using a secure, encrypted internet link, the data was held at the third party in plain text.
>
> The insurance firm admitted it had not conducted any due diligence of the third party's data security arrangements and later found out from the third party that a large number of their staff could potentially gain access to the data. This illustrates the importance of firms understanding how securely their data is held at third parties.

FSA report 'Data Security in Financial Services', April 2008

How do firms store their backed up data?

183. We found that major firms and other firms with multiple offices or branch networks either stored backed up data at alternative offices (often on a reciprocal basis) or used third-party storage firms to hold the back-up tapes. Medium-sized firms with single offices mainly used third-party storage firms to ensure timely access to data, while some small firms also used this method. However, many small firms relied on a trusted member of staff to hold tapes overnight.

> A building society had a dedicated back-up site with the same tight security arrangements as its head office. Designated staff at the firm personally transferred back up tapes to the storage site every day.

Appropriate encryption of back-up data both in storage and in transit

184. To minimise the risk of data loss, either in transit or at a third-party supplier, many firms ensured their back-up tapes were encrypted. However, we did see some examples of firms – including some quite large firms – that did not encrypt back-up tapes, leaving them vulnerable to compromise if they were lost or stolen either in transit or from the back-up site. It is good practice for firms to review the level of encryption applied to back-up tapes (and indeed other portable media) regularly to ensure it is appropriate.

> A medium-sized bank used a third-party storage firm to store its back-up tapes. However, it had not conducted any due diligence of the third party's security arrangements. In addition, the back-up tape was often left with the security guard at the bank's premises for passing on to an employee of the storage company. The security guard was not employed by the bank, nor had he been vetted by them.

Poor practice in small firms

185. Many small firms rely on a trusted member of staff to hold back-up tapes securely off-site. We encountered several instances where there had been very little or no consideration of the risks involved, resulting in a complete lack of formal process or security over backed-up data. The following are examples of poor practice that we observed in small firms.

Core resources

> A partner in a financial advice firm with around 16,000 customers took a weekly back-up tape off-site. He kept the tape in his car so he would not forget to bring it back to the office the following week. There had been no consideration of the risk to customer data if the car was stolen.
>
> The IT Director at a financial advice firm with over 6,000 customers did not know the name of the member of staff with responsibility for holding back-up tapes overnight. Back-up tapes were not encrypted and senior management had no idea about off-site security arrangements. In addition, the IT Director, who deputised as the holder of back-up tapes when the other member of staff was absent, told us that his storage arrangements were insecure.
>
> A credit union had very disorganised data back-up arrangements. The main backup was copied daily to another server held onsite. However, senior management at the firm also took irregular back-ups of the servers and some databases using external hard-drives, memory sticks and laptops, which were then taken off-site. Senior management were unsure about whether any of these portable storage devices were encrypted. We discuss the use of portable devices in greater depth in Section 3.4.10.

186. Despite these worrying examples of poor practice, some small firms had secure back-up arrangements in place, including encrypted tapes and safes installed at the home of the responsible member of staff. These measures are not expensive and are a clear message to other small firms that cheap yet secure arrangements are not impossible to achieve.

Data back-up – Examples of good practice

- Firms conducting a proper risk assessment of threats to data security arising from the data back-up process – from the point that back up tapes are produced, through the transit process to the ultimate place of storage.
- Firms encrypting backed-up data that is held offsite, including while in transit.
- Regular reviews of the level of encryption to ensure it remains appropriate to the current risk environment.
- Back up data being transferred by secure internet links.
- Due diligence on third parties that handle backed-up customer data so the firm has a good understanding of how it is secured, exactly who has access to it and how staff with access to it are vetted.
- Staff with responsibility for holding backed-up data off-site being given assistance to do so securely. For example, firms could offer to pay for a safe to be installed at the staff member's home.

FSA report 'Data Security in Financial Services', April 2008

- Firms conducting spot checks to ensure data held off-site is done so in accordance with accepted policies and procedures.

Data back-up – Examples of poor practice

- Firms failing to consider data security risk arising from the backing up of customer data
- A lack of clear and consistent procedures for backing up data, resulting in data being backed up in several different ways at different times. This makes it difficult for firms to keep track of copies of their data.
- Unrestricted access to back-up tapes for large numbers of staff at third party firms.
- Back-up tapes being held insecurely by firm's employees; for example, being left in their cars or at home on the kitchen table.

3.4.7 Access to the internet and email

187. The internet and email give firms the ability to communicate and access information quickly, easily and efficiently. However, they also present significant risks to data security if not properly managed and monitored. Most firms we visited gave internet and external email access to their staff, mainly by default, and many had not considered the risks of data loss or theft through these channels.

188. We would strongly encourage firms to consider whether there is a genuine business need for staff to have access to the internet and email and whether the benefits of giving internet access to staff handling large amounts of customer data outweigh the data security risks. A small minority of the firms we visited – mainly larger ones – had systems in place to restrict email and internet access only to staff with a genuine business need. Management sign-off was required for staff to have internet and email activated.

> One major insurance firm gave its many call centre staff access to external email and had a policy which allowed them to send a certain number of external emails every day. However, call centre staff told us they had no business need for external email. Indeed, they were specifically instructed by the firm not to give out their email addresses to customers or to communicate with customers via their personal email accounts.

Monitoring of internet/email use

189. Most firms – particularly large and medium-sized ones – produced management information on how their employees used the internet and email. However, this monitoring very rarely considered the risk of data loss through these channels. Instead, firms were mainly focused on whether staff were using the internet or email excessively or accessing/sending inappropriate content. Some firms had measures in place to block

Core resources

the sending of large attachments but this usually appeared to be for reasons of system performance, rather than to reduce the risk of data loss.

190. Several firms stated that, as a result of our visit, they would investigate whether the software they used to identify profanities or sexual language in emails could be adapted to search for strings of digits resembling credit card numbers or bank account details.

> One large bank had software in place that routinely scanned emails for 16-digit card numbers and PIN numbers. Another had plans in place to introduce sophisticated email monitoring software, specifically designed to prevent data loss.

Web-based communication facilities

191. Although the subject fell outside the scope of our project and we did not examine it in depth, many firms assured us that they had anti-virus and anti-spyware software in place to reduce the risk of hi-tech attacks by criminals.

192. We looked much more closely, however, at whether firms were blocking employee access to websites or other internet content which we judge currently give rise to a high risk of data loss. Examples of such content include:

- web-based email (popular providers include Hotmail, Gmail and Yahoo);
- social networking sites which allow users to exchange messages (eg Facebook);
- instant messaging facilities which allow messages to be sent externally (eg MSN); and
- 'peer-to-peer' file sharing software, such as Limewire, BitTorrent and eDonkey, which allow users to share and receive files – usually music and videos – over the internet.

> A 2007 study by researchers at the Center for Digital Strategies at Dartmouth College, New Hampshire, examined accidental data loss through peer-to-peer file sharing networks at a group of large financial firms. Sensitive customer data – including account information – was accidentally exposed when users searched for songs containing words which also appeared in firms' names. In addition, the study found indications that cyber-criminals are using peer-to-peer networks specifically to steal customer data. For example, a significant proportion of search terms appeared to be looking for databases, account information, passwords and PIN numbers.
>
> Many firms we visited were unaware of the data security risks posed by peer-to-peer file sharing. In addition, we spotted an adviser at a medium-sized investment firm with peer-to-peer file sharing software installed on his computer, potentially exposing the firm's customer data to other internet users.

950

FSA report 'Data Security in Financial Services', April 2008

193. One of the main risks of web-based communication facilities is firms' inability to detect when data is being lost or stolen. For example, if a corrupt member of staff was leaking information through a firm's email system, the firm would have the means – via its IT audit logs – to identify who was leaking the data and what data was lost. The firm could then put in place protective measures on its customers' accounts, alert its customers to the potential wider identity fraud risks and take appropriate action against the individual who leaked the data. However, if the data was leaked, for example, by web-based email, the firm would not be in a position to see what had been sent from the employee's computer and would not be able to establish whether a data loss had occurred at all.

> A medium-sized insurance firm allowed staff in its call centre – who had access to large amounts of sensitive customer data – access to web-based email.

194. We found that major firms blocked access to most web-based communication sites. This was usually achieved using software that allowed the firm to block categories of websites which they did not want their staff to access. Medium-sized firms also tended to block such websites but we found two that did not.

> In general, small firms had very poor or no controls in place to prevent staff accessing web-based communication sites. Thirteen of the 20 small firms we visited allowed their staff to use web-based email, putting their customer data at unnecessary risk.

Access to the internet and email – Examples of good practice

- Giving internet and email access only to staff with a genuine business need
- Considering the risk of data compromise when monitoring outbound email traffic, for example by looking for strings of numbers that might be credit card details.
- Where proportionate, using specialist IT software to detect data leakage via email.
- Completely blocking access to all internet content which allows web-based communication. This content includes web-based email, messaging facilities on social networking sites, external instant messaging and 'peer-to-peer' file sharing software.
- Firms that provide cyber-cafes for staff to use during breaks ensuring web-based communications are blocked and data cannot be transferred into the cyber-cafe, either in electronic or paper format.

Core resources

Access to the internet and email – Examples of poor practice

- Allowing staff who handle customer data to have access to the internet and email if there is no business reason for this.
- Allowing access to web-based communication internet sites. This content includes web-based email, messaging facilities on social networking sites, external instant messaging and 'peer-to-peer' file sharing software.

3.4.8 Key-logging devices

195. Key-loggers can pose a risk to the security of customer data, as well as other fraud risk. They work by recording each individual keystroke made by a computer user. So passwords to databases containing customer data, as well as encryption keys, can be compromised using key-loggers.

196. Key-loggers come in hardware and software forms. The risk of software key-loggers can be minimised by anti-spyware programmes and firewalls. However, it is more difficult for firms to protect themselves against hardware key-loggers, which can either be attached to a PC or inserted inside hardware such as keyboards and mice. The latter are particularly difficult to detect.

> In 2005, an organised crime group tried to defraud a major bank in London. They used key-logging devices to obtain the codes required to make large money transfers overseas. The fraud was detected and foiled but it is thought that the fraudsters, if successful, could have stolen £220m.

197. It is good practice for firms to consider on a risk basis whether it is appropriate to perform sweeps for key-logging devices. In terms of protecting customer data, a firm might consider it worthwhile to conduct regular sweeps in areas where staff handle or have access to large amounts of customer data, for example, IT super-users or call centres.

198. It is also good practice for staff to be made aware of the threat of key-logging devices in case their computers are targeted by criminals. One firm sent detailed guidance to staff about the risk of key-logging which included pictures of key-logging devices and an explanation of how they work. This raised staff awareness of how to report any suspicious devices attached to their computers.

199. Only two of the firms we visited (both medium-sized) told us they conducted sweeps for key-logging devices and, in both of these firms, these sweeps were on an ad-hoc or informal basis.

FSA report 'Data Security in Financial Services', April 2008

Key-logging devices – Examples of good practice

- Regular sweeping for key-logging devices in parts of the firm where employees have access to large amounts of, or sensitive, customer data. (Firms will also wish to conduct sweeps in other sensitive areas. For example, where money can be transferred.)
- Use of software to determine whether unusual or prohibited types of hardware have been attached to employees' computers.
- Awareness raising of the risk of key-logging devices. The vigilance of staff is a useful method of defence.
- Anti-spyware software and firewalls etc in place and kept up to date.

3.4.9 Laptops

200. Laptops are often used by firms whose staff work offsite regularly. If not properly managed or secured, customer data held on laptops can be lost or stolen very easily. This was demonstrated by the theft, in August 2006, of a laptop containing a large amount of Nationwide Building Society's customer data from the home of a Nationwide employee. This theft exposed weaknesses in Nationwide's data security systems and controls and we fined them £980,000 in February 2007.

201. Despite the widespread publicity the Nationwide case received, we were very disappointed to find some firms still had poor controls over laptops that resulted in a significant risk of data loss or theft.

> A medium-sized insurance firm had no policy on whether customer data should be held on laptops, had no means of establishing if customer data was being held on laptops, did not use laptop encryption and did not maintain a list of laptop users. So the firm may not have known if a laptop was lost or stolen and would not have been able to tell if customer data had been compromised. This is very poor practice.

Encryption of laptops – many firms are still exposed

202. As stated in paragraph 6, we support the Information Commissioner's position that it is not appropriate for customer data to be taken offsite on laptops or other portable devices that are not encrypted.

> In January 2008, the Information Commissioner's Office (ICO) found Marks & Spencer (M&S) in breach of the Data Protection Act following the theft of an unencrypted laptop which contained the personal information of 26,000 M&S employees. The ICO ordered M&S to ensure that all laptop hard drives are fully encrypted by April 2008.

Core resources

203. A significant number of firms – some of which were quite large – still allowed the widespread use of unencrypted laptops when they knew they contained customer data or when they had insufficient controls to prevent staff taking customer data offsite.

> A major bank with a large number of laptops – most of which were encrypted – was introducing software which could detect unencrypted laptops logging on to the network remotely.

204. It was clear from our review that several firms had put in place laptop encryption projects in light of the Nationwide case. While this is encouraging, it concerns us that, previously, these firms may not have been making an accurate assessment of the risks they faced.

> A medium-sized building society told us that encrypting their laptops was not an expensive exercise. A one-off payment of £1,500 was required for the encryption software, plus an extra £39 for each individual licence.

Over-reliance on staff complying with policies and procedures

205. Many firms had decided not to encrypt their laptops because they had policies and procedures in place that prohibited staff from taking customer data offsite. However, there was little consideration of the fact that staff can breach procedures due to work pressures, forget what policies are in place and, in some cases, steal data. It is good practice for firms to consider these risks and ensure they are appropriately mitigated.

> A major firm told us that, to ensure a tightly-controlled environment, they operated on the assumption that staff did not know what the firm's policies and procedures were.

The importance of accurate asset registers

> 'A laptop could go astray for a couple of weeks without being noticed' – Group Security Officer at a medium-sized bank.

206. Some firms we visited did not maintain asset registers that recorded who had been given laptops or other portable devices such as blackberries and USB sticks. This could expose firms to significant risk of data loss because:

   i. they would be unable to monitor all relevant employees' adherence to policies and procedures;

   ii. they would not be in a position to ensure that all relevant staff had received training on relevant policies and procedures;

FSA report 'Data Security in Financial Services', April 2008

    iii. they would not be able to ensure that all laptops and other portable devices had the most up-to-date security features in place; and

    iv. they might be unaware of the loss or theft of a portable device if an employee failed to report it. This would hinder the firm's ability to react appropriately if data was lost and could expose consumers to significant risk of identity fraud.

> A medium-sized building society that had spent a significant sum on a laptop encryption project did not maintain an accurate asset register. This meant that some of the firm's laptops might have gone unrecorded and therefore unencrypted.

Laptop sharing

207. Some firms allowed the sharing of laptops within teams or had a pool of laptops that could be loaned out to staff for short periods. Such arrangements give rise to the risk that customer data downloaded onto an unencrypted laptop by one user is passed to another without them being aware that customer data is on the laptop. It is good practice for firms to consider the risks to data security that arise from laptop sharing and put in place procedures and controls to mitigate them.

> A large bank had procedures in place to ensure that all shared laptops were returned to their IT department. The IT department then responsible for ensuring the laptop's hard drive was wiped before it was passed on to another user.

Laptops – examples of good practice

- The encryption of laptops and other portable devices containing customer data.
- Controls that mitigate the risk of employees failing to follow policies and procedures. We have dealt with several cases of lost or stolen laptops in the past year which arose from staff not doing what they should.
- Maintaining an accurate register of laptops issued to staff.
- Regular audits of the contents of laptops to ensure that only staff who are authorised to hold customer data on their laptops are doing so and that this is for genuine business reasons.
- The wiping of shared laptops' hard drives between uses.

Core resources

Laptops – examples of poor practice
- Unencrypted customer data on laptops.
- A poor understanding of which employees have been issued or are using laptops to hold customer data.
- Shared laptops used by staff without being signed out or wiped between uses.

3.4.10 Portable media including USB devices and CDs

USB devices and CD writers

208. In the same way that laptops are convenient for staff who work offsite regularly, USB devices and CDs are often used to transfer data quickly and efficiently, for example to employees' homes or to third-party suppliers. However, if not properly managed or secured, customer data held on portable devices can easily be lost or stolen.

209. We found that large and medium-sized firms generally recognised the risks of data loss arising from the use of portable media and most had locked down USB ports and CD writers. Others which had not locked them down had projects planned to do so. However, most of our total sample – particularly small firms – failed to mitigate the risks arising from portable media when staff had access to customer data.

> At least 26 of the 39 firms we visited – including one major bank – did not lock down USB ports when staff had access to customer data.
>
> None of the firms that allowed staff to use USB devices could assure us that all of the USB devices they had issued to staff were encrypted.
>
> Small firms were particularly weak in this area. We did not find a single small firm that locked down their USB ports. This was worrying considering that some small firms allowed all their staff to access all customer data.

210. In addition, very few of the firms that allowed the use of USB devices and CD writers had effective controls to ensure that:
    i. USB devices were encrypted;
    ii. they knew which staff had been issued USB devices and were authorised to use them;
    iii. personal USB devices capable of holding customer data – such as memory sticks, MP3 players and mobile phones – could not be used on their computers; and
    iv. the downloading of customer data onto USB devices and CDs was adequately controlled and monitored.

FSA report 'Data Security in Financial Services', April 2008

> A major bank had excellent controls in this area. Only staff who had made a strong business case had enabled USB ports. In addition, although USB devices were not encrypted when supplied, software installed on the bank's computers encrypted USB devices when they were used, regardless of whether they were owned by the firm or the individual. Specific types of USB device such as MP3 players could not be connected to any of the firm's computers, even if the USB port was enabled.

Encryption of portable devices

211. Where portable devices are used to store customer data, firms should ensure they are encrypted, as they are often and easily taken offsite.

> A medium-sized insurance firm had seven IT staff who could access bulk customer data including full credit card and bank account information. It was possible for these staff to download bulk amounts of data onto personal and/or unencrypted USB devices and there was no formal management or monitoring of their activities.

Increasingly sophisticated mobile phones and other personal technology

212. Several firms were becoming increasingly concerned about the possibility of data theft using high-end mobile phones. Downloading data through USB ports and taking photographs of customer data on-screen are two methods by which this can be achieved. Some firms – particularly with call centres – had taken steps to mitigate this risk or were considering doing so.

> Several firms prohibited call centre staff from having mobile phones on display at their workstations. In a mortgage firm, mobile phones had to be switched off in the call centre and staff were not allowed to take personal belongings to their desk. The firm provided storage facilities for their personal belongings.

213. Most of the 12 call centres we visited prohibited staff from using mobile phones at their desks and three gave staff lockers for personal belongings such as bags, mobile phones and MP3 players. However, it was unclear if these measures had been put in place to ensure data security, to increase productivity, or perhaps both. Of course, there are times when staff have a genuine and urgent personal need to use such equipment. Some call centres accommodated staff who needed emergency contact with, for example, their child's school or a sick relative by allowing line management to grant one-off approval for mobile phones to be switched on at the desk. However, such approval was usually time-limited and monitored closely by line management.

Core resources

> A medium-sized insurance firm's security staff used a device that could detect when a mobile phone had been switched on inside the firm's premises.

214. It is good practice for firms to assess continuously the risks posed by increasingly sophisticated mobile technology and put in place appropriate policies, procedures and controls to mitigate them.

Portable media including USB devices and CDs – examples of good practice

- Ensuring that only staff with a genuine business need can download customer data to portable media such as USB devices and CDs.
- Ensuring that staff authorised to hold customer data on portable media can only do so if it is encrypted.
- Maintaining an accurate register of staff allowed to use USB devices and staff who have been issued USB devices.
- The use of software to prevent and/or detect individuals using personal USB devices.
- Reviewing regularly on a risk-based approach the writing of customer data to portable media to ensure there is a genuine business reason for the activity.
- The automatic encryption of portable media attached to firms' computers.
- Providing lockers for higher-risk staff such as call centre staff and superusers and restricting them from taking personal effects to their desks.

Portable media including USB devices and CDs – examples of poor practice

- Allowing staff with access to bulk customer data – for example, superusers – to download to unencrypted portable media.
- Failing to review regularly the threats posed by increasingly sophisticated and quickly evolving personal technology such as mobile phones.

3.5 Physical security

215. Physical security over customer data should be a prime consideration for all firms, irrespective of their size, nature of business and number of customers. During our review, we discussed with senior management, and conducted some limited examination of, the physical security around access to firms' premises, the secure storage of customer data and the implementation and policing of clear desk policies.

FSA report 'Data Security in Financial Services', April 2008

3.5.1 Access to firms' premises

216. A firm's first line of defence in mitigating the risk of data loss is preventing unauthorised access to its premises. Nearly all firms had considered the physical security of their offices, and in 21 of the 39 firms visited we observed good physical security. This was often supplemented with either personal supervision around the office and/or authorised swipe access to areas of the business holding large amounts of customer data, such as call centres, IT areas and server rooms.

217. Many firms, particularly small firms located in vulnerable or run-down locations, had installed intruder deterrents such as buzzers or keypad entry doors, alarm systems, barred windows, and closed circuit television (CCTV) in strategic areas such as car parks and rear entrances. All of these measures gave some protection against the theft of customer data. However, small firms had a general lack of awareness of data security risk, which suggests such measures were in place primarily to prevent the theft of material items such as computer hardware.

> At a small financial advice firm, physical access to the building was well controlled with a buzzer to enter the building and an additional keypad code required to access the office. CCTV was used and monitored and the firm maintained a log of who had keys to the office.

218. Larger firms tended to have additional controls such as a reception area for registering visitors, visitor logs, and timed and dated visitor passes. In larger firms, we observed a better understanding than in small firms of data security and financial crime risks in general; this was often coupled with a conscious effort by some to instil a 'data security culture' throughout the business.

> In a medium-sized insurance broker, physical security was excellent. Controls included CCTV, tools to detect the unauthorised use of mobile phones and PDAs, strict visitors procedures, employee training regarding 'tailgating' and enforced stop and search procedures.

219. We would encourage firms to ensure that data security training and awareness programmes cover the more basic risks to customer data such as 'tailgating' to gain entry to offices. In some larger firms, we saw the innovative use of in-house magazines and poster campaigns to raise awareness of basic risks, along with the promotion of key security messages via email, screensavers, mouse mats, and 'post-it' note logos. Training and awareness is covered in more depth in Section 3.2.

Core resources

> A medium-sized investment firm made a conscious decision to use as few third-party suppliers as possible to ensure appropriate security. Security guards and staff in the firm's India call centre were employed directly by the firm and subject to the same vetting as other employees. In addition, the firm had a policy to limit the sharing of customer data with third parties as much as possible.

220. Two larger firms chose to employ security guards as direct employees of the firm, rather than through a third-party supplier. These firms believed that there was a clear benefit with this approach as they did not need to conduct due diligence of a third party and they were clear about the standard of vetting applied to the security guards. In addition, these firms believed that directly-employed staff were more likely to feel a commitment and loyalty to the firm than an employee of a third party. The management of the data security risks arising from the use of third-party suppliers is covered in Section 3.7.

221. In 10 of the 39 firms visited, we observed some alarmingly basic lapses in physical security, which gave rise to a significant risk to customer data and other assets. When we raised our concerns with senior management at these firms, they were generally accepting of the need to review and strengthen current procedures. Examples of these lapses included:

   i. A small financial advice firm located in an industrial estate, whose management considered the risk of burglary to be high, but had no basic security protections such as an alarm or CCTV. In addition, all staff had unrestricted access to the firm's premises outside of office hours.

   ii. A major insurance call centre where a door fault meant we could access the server room with a visitor's pass. In addition, the firm relied on staff (including a number of third parties not subject to equivalent vetting) to declare when they had accessed the server and communications rooms. There was no checking of electronic access records for undeclared access, despite a swipe-card facility being in place.

   iii. A small financial advice firm which allowed 12 people, including a security guard, to access their server room. The security guard was not employed by the firm and senior management had conducted no due diligence of the third-party supplier which provided the security guard; in fact, they did not even know the name of the third-party supplier.

   iv. A medium-sized investment firm, where the cleaners and main building receptionist had not been vetted but had full access to the firm's offices. We were told that the receptionist had no business need to access the offices but sometimes came in to use the microwave. The same firm did not operate a clear-desk policy.

FSA report 'Data Security in Financial Services', April 2008

v. A medium-sized insurance firm with a keypad entry system in place at its call centre, which left its main door wedged open for several hours during our visit.

3.5.2 Clear-desk policy

222. During our review, we observed some extreme examples of good and poor practice in terms of firms' implementation and policing of clear-desk policies. Small firms performed poorly. Eight of the 20 small firms either had no clear-desk policy whatsoever or a worrying lack of concern and understanding at senior management level. In several of these firms, the risk was exacerbated by poor physical security.

> A small financial advice firm did not enforce a clear-desk policy. Documents containing customers' personal details as well as staff's user account IDs and passwords were left on desks when the office was unattended.

223. To minimise the risks of data loss or theft, it is good practice for firms to implement and monitor an effective clear-desk policy, supported by good physical security in and around their premises.

> At another small financial advice firm, cleaners had unsupervised access to the firm's offices and alarm system. Despite this, the firm did not enforce a clear-desk policy.

3.5.3 Storage of paper customer files

224. Most firms, particularly small firms, kept paper-based customer records onsite in files. It is good practice for firms to ensure that, as far as possible, paper files are only accessible to staff with a genuine business need and that they are locked away overnight and protected from destruction by fireproof cabinets. Most firms used lockable filing cabinets to achieve this, although there were many occasions where filing cabinets were left unlocked all day, potentially allowing unauthorised staff to access customer data.

225. Seven firms displayed particularly poor and careless practice, such as customer records being stored overnight in unlocked cabinets or being left on the office floor due to a lack of storage facilities. In some firms, these factors combined with poor physical security, the absence of a clear-desk policy, and a poor understanding of the way that cleaners and security guards were vetted significantly increases the risk of data theft. Senior management at these firms gave no reasonable explanation as to why customer records were not stored securely.

Core resources

> At a medium-sized investment firm with high net worth customers, customer files – including copies of sensitive documents such as passports, driving licences and bank statements – were often left on desks or in unlocked cabinets overnight. During this time, third-party cleaners, who had not been vetted, had unsupervised access to the office area.

Physical security – examples of good practice

- Appropriately restricted access to areas where large amounts of customer data is accessible, such as server rooms, call centres and filing areas.
- The strategic use of robust intruder deterrents such as keypad entry doors, alarm systems, grilles or barred windows, and closed circuit television (CCTV) on a risk-based approach.
- Robust procedures for logging visitors and ensuring adequate supervision of them while on-site.
- Training and awareness programmes for staff to ensure they are fully aware of more basic risks to customer data arising from poor physical security.
- Employing security guards, cleaners etc directly to ensure an appropriate level of vetting and reduce risks which can arise through third-party suppliers accessing customer data.
- Use of electronic swipe card records to spot unusual behaviour or access to high-risk areas.
- Keeping filing cabinets locked during the day and leaving the key with a trusted member of staff.
- An enforced clear-desk policy.

Physical security – examples of poor practice

- Allowing staff or other persons with no genuine business need to access areas where customer data is held.
- Failure to check electronic records showing who has accessed sensitive areas of the office.
- Failure to lock away customer records and files when the office is left unattended.

FSA report 'Data Security in Financial Services', April 2008

3.6 Disposing of customer data

226. Every one of the firms we visited demonstrated an awareness of the risk that paper containing customer data could fall into the hands of criminals if disposed of carelessly. All were taking some steps to mitigate that risk by using shredders, locked bins for confidential waste or secure disposal companies. Even firms with poor systems and controls overall were taking some steps to dispose of customer data carefully. This encouraging finding suggests that, despite their failings in other areas, firms do have some awareness of the dangers of data loss, and will take steps to address those risks if there is a simple way to do so at reasonable cost.

227. This progress follows public censure in March 2007 by the Information Commissioner's Office (ICO) of 11 financial services firms which disposed of customer data carelessly.[16] Unannounced checks by the ICO found that customer data had been placed in waste bins or other receptacles on the firms' premises or outside the building. All 11 firms were found in breach of the Data Protection Act. This action received significant media coverage.

> 'It is unacceptable for banks and other organisations to carelessly discard their customers' information. It is vital that banks and other organisations take security seriously. If they do not, they not only risk further action from the Information Commissioner but also risk losing the trust of their customers. Individuals must feel confident that banks and other organisations are safeguarding their personal information.'
>
> David Smith, Deputy Information Commissioner, speaking after the public censure of 11 financial services firms.

3.6.1 Procedures for disposing of confidential paper

228. Firms in general appear to have learned from the ICO's Enforcement action and coverage of similar issues in the media (eg BBC Watchdog). All the firms we visited had processes in place to ensure the secure disposal of paper-based customer data.

229. Small firms – as well as branches of larger firms – tended to use shredders on their premises, while medium-sized and larger firms usually set up contracts with a specialist secure disposal company. These contractors usually provided locked confidential waste bins for the firm, the contents of which were collected periodically by the contractor. Some waste disposal firms brought a lorry to the premises, emptied each bin directly into the lorry, and shredded the contents onsite. Other contractors emptied the bins into their truck and returned to their own disposal site, where the waste was either shredded or incinerated. Several firms using contractors who shredded paper at the firm's premises ensured their own staff personally supervised the shredding process.

---

16 www.ico.gov.uk/upload/documents/pressreleases/2007/banks_in_unacceptable_data_protection_breach.pdf

Core resources

> Some firms combined disposal methods for added security. A medium-sized insurance firm, for example, shredded paper in their offices, stored the shredded paper in secure bins, and employed a secure disposal company to remove and incinerate the shredded paper.

230. Several firms recognised the risk that confidential waste might be placed into general waste bins by mistake. These firms usually mitigated this risk by treating all waste as confidential. Others relied on checks.

> A major bank required every one of its branch managers to search general waste bins at the end of the day and to certify that no confidential papers had been placed in them.
>
> Another firm, which had been censured by the ICO, told us it had since placed confidential waste bins in its branches' banking halls so that customers could dispose of their own waste securely.

231. Some firms were aware of an industry standard for secure disposal firms: accreditation by the British Security Industry Association (BSIA). This is awarded only to contractors which hold the BS7858 accreditation on staff vetting (which includes a five-year background check on employees within 16 weeks of joining) and the BS8470 accreditation on secure shredding procedures. Accredited firms are inspected at least once a year, a procedure that includes testing staff understanding of procedures and spot checks of vetting files. Accredited contractors usually give their client a certificate of secure disposal. Although some firms' contractors will be accredited by the BSIA, we noted that many firms had neither inquired about the security standards used by their waste disposal company, nor had they visited the disposal site to examine security.

> **Disposal methods for confidential paper**
> - Fifteen firms out of 39 shredded customer data themselves on their premises.
> - Twenty-four firms used confidential waste bins and a third-party secure disposal company instead.
> - In nine of these cases, the secure disposal company shredded paper on the firm's premises.
> - The other 15 firms used a secure disposal company that removed paper for shredding or incineration offsite.

232. Although firms' arrangements for secure disposal were generally sound, we noted some examples where a lack of adherence to procedures enhanced the risk of data loss.

FSA report 'Data Security in Financial Services', April 2008

> A medium-sized bank used shredders at its London head office, but did not enforce the same standard at its regional branches, where shredders were either broken or not used.
>
> A medium-sized insurance company left unsecured bags of confidential waste overnight in their car park, which could be accessed by climbing over a low wall.

233. Only a few firms, mostly large ones, had any guidelines or procedures covering the secure disposal of confidential waste for staff who worked offsite. In addition, onsite staff were rarely given guidance about the definition of 'confidential waste' and many firms had observed their own staff putting sensitive papers in general waste bins.

> In some firms, cleaners who were not vetted or monitored held keys to the confidential waste bins.

234. Despite these shortcomings, we were pleased that firms in general appeared to be continuing to improve the security of confidential waste disposal. Several firms stated they had recently made improvements to security arrangements even though generally satisfactory procedures were already in place. These improvements included:

- removing general waste bins so that all waste was treated as confidential;
- observing the disposal process to ensure that every bin was emptied into the secure disposal company's lorry;
- checking how secure disposal companies vetted their staff; and
- auditing adherence to waste disposal procedures.

235. In addition, several firms were aiming to create a 'paperless office' so that very little or no confidential waste is ever produced.

3.6.2 Procedures for disposing of obsolete computers and other electronic equipment

236. It is important that firms not only dispose of paper-based customer data securely, but also that electronic customer data held on computers and other devices is destroyed after use. This is because fraudsters might try to obtain computers and other devices that have been discarded by firms in the hope of finding customer data stored on them. It usually requires technical knowledge and appropriate software to erase all traces of data.

Core resources

> In August 2006, the BBC reported that fraudsters in West Africa were able to find internet banking data stored on recycled PCs sent from the UK to Africa.
>
> The ICO's Assistant Commissioner, Phil Jones, said 'It is essential that companies have appropriate procedures in place to ensure that personal records on computer hard drives are rendered unrecoverable when they dispose of computer equipment. Under the Data Protection Act, companies have a duty to store personal information securely and delete it when it is no longer required.'[17]

237. Although a user without technical expertise might delete files and believe that no files are visible on the hard-drive directory, fraudsters could use widely-available forensic software to retrieve, reconstruct and display files that have been erased. This risk can be mitigated, either by wiping the hard drive using specialist software or by removing or physically destroying the hard drive. The same applies to portable media such as USB sticks, CDs and cartridges.

238. We found that many firms showed some understanding of secure wiping techniques and technology. IT managers mentioned certain software products and explained the appropriate technical standard (stated simply, wiping and reformatting must be repeated many times). Others had been reassured by software providers that their software was used by UK and/or US government departments.

239. However, we found several cases where firms were not actually disposing of their obsolete electronic media. Several IT and Information Security managers with the knowledge and means to dispose of equipment securely were stockpiling old computers – in some cases for several years. This approach creates a new risk that obsolete computers might be stolen or copied. Other stockpiles of computers existed because firms recognised the risk of insecure disposal but did not know any methods of secure destruction.

> A medium-sized mortgage administration firm stored 'a couple of hundred' obsolete computer hard drives in an area which could be accessed by up to 20 members of staff. With no register of the drives stored there, it would be impossible for the firm to detect if a drive was accessed or removed. The firm's information security manager planned eventually to drill holes in them to destroy the contents.

240. Large and medium-sized firms often employed a BSIA-accredited third party supplier to wipe and then shred obsolete hard drives, and to certify that process. Some IT staff in medium-sized and small firms preferred to use a hammer, screwdriver or drill to destroy hard drives by brute force. However, some firms were stockpiling old hard drives as they had not considered how to destroy them.

---

17 http://news.bbc.co.uk/1/hi/business/4790293.stm

FSA report 'Data Security in Financial Services', April 2008

241. Small firms tended to rely on third parties to wipe their computers securely. A small financial advice firm donated its old computers to a charity which certified that the machines had been wiped and reformatted securely before recycling. Other firms were less rigorous and did not, in our view, display a due standard of care.

> The senior partner of a small investment firm relied on his teenage son to wipe a batch of computers before sending them to a charity in Africa. He did not know what software was used or whether it was effective.

Disposal of customer data – examples of good practice

- Procedures that result in the production of as little paper-based customer data as possible.
- Treating all paper as 'confidential waste' to eliminate confusion among employees about which type of bin to use.
- All customer data disposed of by employees securely, for example by using shredders (preferably cross-cut rather than straight-line shredders) or confidential waste bins.
- Checking general waste bins for the accidental disposal of customer data.
- Using a third-party supplier, preferably one with BSIA accreditation that provides a certificate of secure destruction, to shred or incinerate paper-based customer data. It is important for firms to have a good understanding of the supplier's process for destroying customer data and their employee vetting standards.
- Providing guidance for travelling or home-based staff on the secure disposal of customer data.
- Computer hard drives and portable media being properly wiped (using specialist software) or destroyed as soon as they become obsolete.

Disposal of customer data – examples of poor practice

- Poor awareness among staff about how to dispose of customer data securely.
- Slack procedures that present opportunities for fraudsters, for instance when confidential waste is left unguarded on the premises before it is destroyed.
- Staff working remotely failing to dispose of customer data securely.
- Firms failing to give guidance or assistance to remote workers who need to dispose of an obsolete home computer.

Core resources

- Firms stockpiling obsolete computers and other portable media for too long and in insecure environments.
- Firms relying on others to erase or destroy their hard drives and other portable media securely without evidence that this has been done competently.

3.7 Managing third-party suppliers

3.7.1 Why do third parties matter?

242. For reasons of efficiency, nearly all firms now use third-party suppliers for certain aspects of their business. It is common for firms to enable these suppliers to access their customer data directly, either on the firms' premises or by sending copies of the data to them. In addition, some firms grant individuals who are not employed by the firm indirect access to their customer data by allowing them to access their premises. As mentioned in Section 2.6.1, firms retain responsibility for customer data, even when it has been transferred to a third party for processing.

243. Examples of the types of third parties used by the firms who have direct or indirect access to customer data include:

- printers and mailing companies;
- marketing companies;
- providers of off-site storage facilities for archived files and back-up tapes;
- confidential waste disposal specialists;
- couriers;
- IT contractors and IT maintenance companies;
- cleaners;
- security;
- catering staff; and
- staff from other companies where offices and buildings are shared.

244. The type and number of third parties used by firms varied considerably. For example, a large bank outsourced all functions they deemed to be 'non-core' such as printing, marketing, cleaning, security and telephone sales. Each of these functions was carried out by a different third-party supplier and all required access to customer data. In contrast, a similar-sized insurance company retained nearly all functions in-house, with minimal reliance on third parties. Smaller firms tended to perform most operations in-house, simply due to the reduced scale of their business but nearly all firms relied on IT support from third parties.

FSA report 'Data Security in Financial Services', April 2008

245. It is therefore essential that firms are fully aware of the additional data security risks that arise from allowing third parties to access their customer data. As the number of third parties who have access to customer data increases, so does the risk of data loss.

246. It is good practice for firms to ensure that any individual or company with access to their customer data has appropriate data security standards. As discussed in Section 3.1.3, it is good practice for data security risk analysis to be embedded across the business, with all relevant business areas involved. In the same way, it is good practice for firms to assess the risks of allowing individual third-party suppliers to receive and handle customer data, as well as the risks arising from allowing third parties physical access to customer data on the firm's premises.

3.7.2 Firms' management of third-party suppliers

247. Nearly all firms had existing third-party relationships and most of them managed these relationships in different ways.

248. In general, we were disappointed to find that most firms – including some large ones – were over-reliant on third parties to comply with contractual obligations. There was little evidence that firms either performed data security due diligence on third parties before agreeing a contract or that they exercised audit rights to ensure that third parties were meeting agreed standards throughout the contract term.

> Most firms – including some large ones – were over-reliant on third parties to comply with contractual obligations covering data security.

249. For example, an important third-party relationship for many firms is with employment agencies who supply recruitment and staff vetting services. We were disappointed to find that firms rarely examined agencies' recruitment and vetting standards despite specific contractual rights to do so. Instead, firms' senior management often said that the mere existence of such clauses gave them comfort that the agencies would perform in line with the contract terms. Firms' use and management of employment agencies is discussed in more depth in Section 3.3.2.

250. We saw good practice at a medium-sized insurance firm that was conducting a rolling review of all third parties which had direct or indirect access to customer data. The firm was assessing all of the third parties' data security policies and procedures and working with them to improve systems and controls. Firms which audited third-party suppliers commented that comparing data security controls was beneficial both to them and their third party in ensuring that customer data was held securely.

> A major bank with over 50 third-party suppliers handling customer data had performed risk assessments on each supplier and visited them frequently to ensure that agreed data security standards were being met.

Core resources

3.7.3 Issues for firms to consider when using third party suppliers

Who has access to electronic customer data?

251. We noted during our visits that firms sometimes were not aware of which individuals at a third-party supplier had access to their customer data and they did not monitor when or why third parties had accessed their customer data. The most common examples of this were where firms used third-party suppliers to maintain their customer database or provide off-site data back-up facilities.

> Many small firms – and some larger firms – used third-party IT service providers to maintain their customer databases. In many cases, the firms did not know:
>
> - who at the third party had access to their customer database;
> - the vetting procedures used by the third party to screen their employees; or
> - whether the third-party supplier's staff were able to create copies of customer databases.
>
> In addition, most firms had no monitoring systems in place to track when or why IT service providers had accessed their customer data.

252. Firms that did not know which specific individuals at third-party suppliers had access to their customer data failed to recognise the risk of allowing third parties unrestricted, unmonitored access to their customer data. We were not satisfied that such firms had effective systems and controls in place to protect customer data.

Who has access to paper-based data?

253. It is essential that firms have robust controls in place to ensure that access to paper-based customer data is restricted. The need is exacerbated when firms allow third-party suppliers such as cleaners, contractors and security guards access to their offices, contact centres or storage facilities without vetting them in line with their own recruitment procedures. Physical security arrangements for paper-based customer data are covered in more depth in Section 3.5.3.

How do third-party suppliers vet their staff?

254. Section 3.3 covers staff recruitment and vetting, and includes analysis of firms' practices and good practice guidance. Where third-party suppliers have access to customer data, firms should ensure they have been vetted to an appropriate standard. Firms can achieve this by vetting third-party staff themselves or, perhaps more efficiently, regularly reviewing that the third-party firm has performed adequate vetting of its staff.

FSA report 'Data Security in Financial Services', April 2008

> A large investment firm relied on an external recruitment agency to perform all vetting checks on applicants. The firm ensured that the service level agreement set out clearly the types of vetting checks required. The firm also carried out monthly audits and performed sample checking for 10% of all recruits to ensure that vetting was performed in line with agreed standards.

255. In general, we were concerned that firms were often unaware of the vetting standards third party staff had been subject to. In some cases, firms simply did not know whether third-party staff had been vetted at all.

Due diligence

256. As mentioned in paragraph 248, we found that firms generally over-rely on third parties meeting contractual terms relating to data security. Therefore, perhaps unsurprisingly, we found that due diligence of third party suppliers' data security arrangements was not often performed by firms before a contract was agreed.

257. Firms were often unaware of what data security controls, if any, third-party suppliers had in place. Some firms had not even visited off-site storage locations to assess whether the facilities were secure. We do not think it is appropriate for firms to allow third parties access to their customer data when they have not assessed the third party's data security control environment.

> Many small firms selected third-party suppliers on recommendation or on the basis of personal relationships between senior members of the two firms. Due diligence was rarely performed.

258. As a minimum, it is good practice for firms to be clear about exactly which third party staff have access to their customer data and whether they have been vetted to an appropriate standard. This is because, even if a firm has conducted a thorough risk assessment of its own data security processes and procedures, data security will be severely weakened if relevant third parties do not have equivalent standards.

> A medium-sized mortgage firm had drawn up a list of 'preferred suppliers' and performed data security reviews on them. However, the firm's purchasing department had identified breaches in purchasing procedures which meant that only 70% of third parties being used by the firm were 'preferred suppliers'; this meant the firm had not reviewed the rest.

How is data protected in transit to third-party suppliers?

259. There are many methods that can be used to transfer data to third-party suppliers but they split into two broad groups:

Core resources

- electronic means such as email, shared access to networks or a secure internet link between the firm and the third party; and
- physical means such as tapes, cartridges, CDs, USB devices, laptops and paper. The transfer of physical media usually involves entrusting customer data to other third parties, such as couriers.

260. Over the past year, we have identified – during both our casework and this review – many examples of poor practice in this area. In general, large and medium-sized firms tend to transfer data to and from third parties using secure internet links but there are still occasions where data is transferred on physical media. These media are not always encrypted and, on rare occasions, unencrypted customer data has been sent by unregistered post.

> Wherever possible, it is good practice for firms to ensure that customer data is transferred to third parties using secure internet connections. If there is no alternative to posting encrypted data, some form of recorded delivery is the best option. In addition, it is good practice for the recipient to be notified in advance and for them to confirm receipt of the data. This should ensure that any data loss is identified and dealt with immediately.

261. It is appropriate here to repeat our support for the Information Commissioner's position that it is not appropriate for firms to allow customer data offsite on laptops or other portable media which are not encrypted.

Managing third-party suppliers – examples of good practice

- Conducting due diligence of data security standards at third-party suppliers before contracts are agreed.
- Regular reviews of third-party suppliers' data security systems and controls, with the frequency of review dependent on data security risks identified.
- Ensuring third-party suppliers' vetting standards are adequate by testing the checks performed on a sample of staff with access to customer data.
- Only allowing third-party IT suppliers access to customer databases for specific tasks on a case-by-case basis.
- Third-party suppliers being subject to procedures for reporting data security breaches within an agreed timeframe.
- The use of secure internet links to transfer data to third parties.

Managing third-party suppliers – examples of poor practice
- Allowing third-party suppliers to access customer data when no due diligence of data security arrangements has been performed.
- Firms not knowing exactly which third-party staff have access to their customer data.
- Firms not knowing how third-party suppliers' staff have been vetted.
- Allowing third-party staff unsupervised access to areas where customer data is held when they have not been vetted to the same standards as employees.
- Allowing IT suppliers to have unrestricted or unmonitored access to customer data.
- A lack of awareness of when/how third-party suppliers can access customer data and failure to monitor such access.
- Unencrypted customer data being sent to third parties using unregistered post.

3.8 Internal audit and compliance monitoring

3.8.1 Internal audit

262. A firm's internal auditors are there to give an independent assessment of risks and to report its findings to senior management. As part of our review, we sought to establish the quantity and quality of work on data security by internal audit departments.

263. As anticipated, during our visits to the 20 small firms, we saw little or no evidence either of an internal audit function or of an independent assessment of data security risk. As previously mentioned, if firms consider their in-house resources or expertise are inadequate to perform an effective risk assessment of data security, they should consider seeking external guidance.

264. We saw some evidence of good internal audit practice and awareness in larger firms, but many large firms did not treat data security as a separate issue. Instead, the subject tended to be addressed in parts; for example, relevant IT controls would be examined in an IT audit, physical security during a security audit and vetting during audits of HR. This perhaps reflects many firms' poor governance and lack of coordination when dealing with data security risk and could result in some risks not being considered.

> The head of internal audit at a large bank told us that data security had not been considered as a specific risk, and that audits considered processes rather than risks. Therefore, data security only featured in each audit as a risk to the process.
>
> Similarly, overall data security was not considered by internal audit at a major insurance firm; the overwhelming focus of any data security-related audit work was on IT.

Core resources

265. As noted in paragraph 82, it is good practice for firms to conduct a specific risk assessment of data security. It therefore follows that it is good practice for them to carry this through to their audit work by conducting general audits of data security. Some larger firms conducted specific data security audits and had also brought technical experts into their audit teams to focus on technical risk elements.

> A large investment firm had recently employed an experienced internal auditor who had identified the need for an audit of data security across the whole business.

3.8.2 Compliance monitoring

266. We interviewed the compliance officer (or equivalent) in every firm we visited and, although they were generally aware of high-profile incidents of data loss, we found little or no compliance focus on data security in 18 firms. Where compliance departments did conduct some monitoring of data security, this tended to be narrow in its focus and often concentrated only on IT or compliance with data protection legislation; it tended not to focus on compliance with relevant policies and procedures. It is good practice for compliance monitoring of data security to be risk based and consider adherence to relevant policies and procedures, as well as the regulatory and legislative responsibilities set out in Section 2.6.

> Following our enforcement action against Nationwide Building Society (see paragraph 53), a large insurance firm's compliance department conducted a gap analysis of its own data security standards. However, the focus was mainly on laptop encryption and access to laptop loss reporting procedures. It did not cover other important aspects of the case such as access to customer data and training and awareness.

267. Data security risk varies in different types and sizes of firm. In many small firms, the role of the compliance officer or external compliance consultant will be to assess, mitigate, and monitor those risks in the absence of a dedicated information security or risk officer. As previously noted, small firms were in practice often entirely reliant on external compliance consultants to provide a review of their business risks. We found evidence during our visits that some consultants may provide small firms with a 'one size fits all' solution to data security which does not take account of individual firms' risk profiles.

> We visited two small financial advice firms who used the same compliance consultant. The consultant gave each firm identical Data Protection Policy documents, which both firms regarded as being their data security procedures. This was despite the fact that the firms had different customer bases and therefore ran different risks. These firms' policy documents did not cover specific risks to their business and were therefore inadequate.

FSA report 'Data Security in Financial Services', April 2008

268. External compliance consultants were present during some of our visits to small firms and showed an interest in our review and potential outcomes. During our visit to a small financial advice firm, a representative from a large compliance consultancy said that he intended to alter compliance programmes for his clients as a result of what he learned during the visit.

269. As noted in paragraph 95, we would encourage compliance consultants to do more work with small firms on data security. We intend to contact the compliance consultancy firms most often used by small firms shortly after this report is published to update them on our findings and the importance we attach to good data security.

270. In general, Compliance professionals – both in-house and consultants – must widen their view of data security risk and play their part in ensuring good standards of data security across all areas of a firm's business.

Internal audit and compliance monitoring – examples of good practice

- Firms seeking external assistance where they do not have the necessary in-house expertise or resources.
- Compliance and internal audit conducting specific reviews of data security which cover all relevant areas of the business including IT, security, HR, training and awareness, governance and third-party suppliers.
- Firms using expertise from across the business to assist with the more technical aspects of data security audits and compliance monitoring.

Internal audit and compliance monitoring – examples of poor practice

- Compliance focusing only on compliance with data protection legislation and failing to consider adherence to data security policies and procedures.
- Compliance consultants adopting a 'one size fits all' approach to different clients' businesses.

Core resources

4. Consolidated examples of good and poor practice

Data security – consolidated examples of good and poor practice

Examples of good practice	Examples of poor practice
Governance	
• Identification of data security as a key specific risk, subject to its own governance, policies and procedures and risk assessment. • A senior manager with overall responsibility for data security, specifically mandated to manage data security risk assessment and communication between the key stakeholders within the firm such as: senior management, information security, Human Resources, financial crime, security, IT, compliance and internal audit. • A specific committee with representation from relevant business areas to assess, monitor and control data security risk, which reports to the firm's board. As well as ensuring coordinated risk management, this structure sends a clear message to all staff about the importance of data security. • Written data security policies and procedures that are proportionate, accurate and relevant to staff's day-to-day work. • An open and honest culture of communication with pre-determined reporting mechanisms which make it easy for all staff and third parties to report data security concerns and data loss without fear of blame or recrimination.	• Treating data security as an IT issue and failing to involve other key staff from across the business in the risk assessment process. • No written policies and procedures on data security. • Firms do not understand the need for knowledge-sharing on data security. • Failing to take opportunities to share information with, and learn from, peers and others about data security risk and not recognising the need to do so. • A 'blame culture' that discourages staff from reporting data security concerns and data losses. • Failure to notify customers affected by data loss in case the details are picked up by the media.

Data Security in Financial Services   Page 83

FSA report 'Data Security in Financial Services', April 2008

Data security – consolidated examples of good and poor practice

Examples of good practice	Examples of poor practice
Governance	
• Firms seeking external assistance if they feel they do not have the necessary expertise to complete a data security risk assessment themselves. • Firms liaising with peers and others to increase their awareness of data security risk and the implementation of good systems and controls. • Detailed plans for reacting to a data loss including when and how to communicate with affected customers. • Firms writing to affected customers promptly after a data loss, telling them what has been lost and how it was lost. • Firms offering advice on protective measures against identity fraud to consumers affected by data loss and, where appropriate, paying for such services to be put in place.	
Training and awareness	
• Innovative training and awareness campaigns that focus on the financial crime risks arising from poor data security, as well as the legal and regulatory requirements to protect customer data. • Clear understanding among staff about why data security is relevant to their work and what they must do to comply with relevant policies and procedures.	• No training to communicate policies and procedures. • Managers assuming that employees understand data security risk without any training. • Data security policies which are very lengthy, complicated and difficult to read.

Core resources

Data security – consolidated examples of good and poor practice

Examples of good practice	Examples of poor practice
Training and awareness	
• Simple, memorable and easily digestible guidance for staff on good data security practice. • Testing of staff understanding of data security policies on induction and once a year after that. • Competitions, posters, screensavers and group discussion to raise interest in the subject.	• Reliance on staff signing an annual declaration stating that they have read policy documents without any further testing. • Staff being given no incentive to learn about data security.
Staff recruitment and vetting	
• Vetting staff on a risk-based approach, taking into account data security and other fraud risk. • Enhanced vetting – including checks of credit records, criminal records, financial sanctions lists and the CIFAS Staff Fraud Database – for staff in roles with access to large amounts of customer data. • Liaison between HR and Financial Crime to ensure that financial crime risk indicators are considered during the vetting process. • A good understanding of vetting conducted by employment agencies for temporary and contract staff. • Formalised procedures to assess regularly whether staff in higher-risk positions are becoming vulnerable to committing fraud or being coerced by criminals.	• Allowing new recruits to access customer data before vetting has been completed. • Temporary staff receiving less-rigorous vetting than permanently employed colleagues carrying out similar roles. • Failing to consider continually whether staff in higher-risk positions are becoming vulnerable to committing fraud or being coerced by criminals.

FSA report 'Data Security in Financial Services', April 2008

Data security – consolidated examples of good and poor practice

Controls – Access rights

Examples of good practice	Examples of poor practice
• Specific IT access profiles for each role in the firm, which set out exactly what level of IT access is required for an individual to do their job.	• Staff having access to customer data that they do not require to do their job.
• If a staff member changes roles or responsibilities, all IT access rights are deleted from the system and the user is set up using the same process as if they were a new joiner at the firm. The complexity of this process is significantly reduced if role-based IT access profiles are in place – the old one can simply be replaced with the new.	• User access rights set up on a case-by-case basis with no independent check that they are appropriate.
	• Redundant access rights being allowed to remain in force when a member of staff changes roles.
• A clearly-defined process to notify IT of forthcoming staff departures in order that IT accesses can be permanently disabled or deleted on a timely and accurate basis.	• User accounts being left 'live' or only suspended (ie not permanently disabled) when a staff member leaves.
• A regular reconciliation of HR and IT user records to act as a failsafe in the event of a failure in the firm's leavers process.	• A lack of independent check of changes effected at any stage in the joiners, movers and leavers process.
• Regular reviews of staff IT access rights to ensure that there are no anomalies.	
• Least privilege access to call recordings and copies of scanned documents obtained for 'know your customer' purposes.	

979

Core resources

Data security – consolidated examples of good and poor practice

Examples of good practice	Examples of poor practice
Controls – Access rights	
• Authentication of customers' identitities using, for example, touch-tone telephone before a conversation with a call centre adviser takes place. This limits the amount of personal information and/or passwords contained in call recordings. • Masking credit card, bank account details and other sensitive data like customer passwords where this would not affect employees' ability to do their job.	
Controls – Passwords and user accounts	
• Individual user accounts – requiring passwords – in place for all systems containing customer data. • Password standards at least equivalent to those recommended by Get Safe Online – a government-backed campaign group. At present, their recommended standard for passwords is a combination of letters, numbers and keyboard symbols at least seven characters in length and changed regularly. • Measures to ensure passwords are robust. These might include controls to ensure that passwords can only be set in accordance with policy and the use of password-cracking software on a risk-based approach. • 'Straight-through processing', but only if complemented by accurate role-based access profiles and strong passwords.	• The same user account and password used by multiple users to access particular systems. • Names and dictionary words used as passwords. • Systems that allow passwords to be set which do not comply with password policy. • Password sharing of any kind.

980

FSA report 'Data Security in Financial Services', April 2008

Data security – consolidated examples of good and poor practice

Examples of good practice	Examples of poor practice
Controls – monitoring access to customer data	
• Risk-based, proactive monitoring of staff's access to customer data to ensure it is being accessed and/or updated for a genuine business reason.	• Assuming that vetted staff with appropriate access rights will always act appropriately. Staff can breach procedures, for example by looking at account information relating to celebrities, be tempted to commit fraud themselves or be bribed or threatened to give customer data to criminals.
• The use of software designed to spot suspicious activity by employees with access to customer data. Such software may not be useful in its 'off-the-shelf' format so it is good practice for firms to ensure that it is tailored to their business profile.	• Failure to make regular use of management information about access to customer data.
• Strict controls over superusers' access to customer data and independent checks of their work to ensure they have not accessed, manipulated or extracted data that was not required for a particular task.	• Failing to monitor superusers or other employees with access to large amounts of customer data.
Controls – Data back-up	
• Firms conducting a proper risk assessment of threats to data security arising from the data back-up process – from the point that back-up tapes are produced, through the transit process to the ultimate place of storage.	• Firms failing to consider data security risk arising from the backing up of customer data.
• Firms encrypting backed up data that is held offsite, including while in transit.	• A lack of clear and consistent procedures for backing up data, resulting in data being backed up in several different ways at different times. This makes it difficult for firms to keep track of copies of their data.
• Regular reviews of the level of encryption to ensure it remains appropriate to the current risk environment.	• Unrestricted access to back-up tapes for large numbers of staff at third-party firms.

Core resources

Data security – consolidated examples of good and poor practice

Examples of good practice	Examples of poor practice
Controls – Data back-up	
• Back up data being transferred by secure internet links. • Due diligence on third parties that handle backed-up customer data so the firm has a good understanding of how it is secured, exactly who has access to it and how staff with access to it are vetted. • Staff with responsibility for holding backed-up data off-site being given assistance to do so securely. For example, firms could offer to pay for a safe to be installed at the staff member's home. • Firms conducting spot checks to ensure that data held off-site is done so in accordance with accepted policies and procedures.	• Back-up tapes being held insecurely by firm's employees; for example, being left in their cars or at home on the kitchen table.
Controls – Access to the internet and email	
• Giving internet and email access only to staff with a genuine business need. • Considering the risk of data compromise when monitoring external email traffic, for example by looking for strings of numbers that might be credit card details. • Where proportionate, using specialist IT software to detect data leakage via email.	• Allowing staff who handle customer data to have access to the internet and email if there is no business reason for this. • Allowing access to web-based communication internet sites. This content includes web-based email, messaging facilities on social networking sites, external instant messaging and 'peer-to-peer' file sharing software.

Data security – consolidated examples of good and poor practice

Examples of good practice	Examples of poor practice
Controls – Access to the internet and email	
• Completely blocking access to all internet content which allows web-based communication. This content includes web-based email, messaging facilities on social networking sites, external instant messaging and 'peer-to-peer' file sharing software. • Firms that provide cyber-cafes for staff to use during breaks ensuring that web-based communications are blocked or that data cannot be transferred into the cyber-cafe, either in electronic or paper format.	
Controls – Key-logging devices	
• Regular sweeping for key-logging devices in parts of the firm where employees have access to large amounts of, or sensitive, customer data. (Firms will also wish to conduct sweeps in other sensitive areas. For example, where money can be transferred.) • Use of software to determine whether unusual or prohibited types of hardware have been attached to employees' computers. • Awareness raising of the risk of key-logging devices. The vigilance of staff is a useful method of defence. • Anti-spyware software and firewalls etc in place and kept up to date.	

Core resources

Data security – consolidated examples of good and poor practice

Examples of good practice	Examples of poor practice
Controls – Laptops	
• The encryption of laptops and other portable devices containing customer data.	• Unencrypted customer data on laptops.
• Controls that mitigate the risk of employees failing to follow policies and procedures. We have dealt with several cases of lost or stolen laptops in the past year that arose from staff not doing what they should.	• A poor understanding of which employees have been issued or are using laptops to hold customer data.
• Maintaining an accurate register of laptops issued to staff.	• Shared laptops used by staff without being signed out or wiped between uses.
• Regular audits of the contents of laptops to ensure that only staff who are authorised to hold customer data on their laptops are doing so and that this is for genuine business reasons.	
• The wiping of shared laptops' hard drives between uses.	
Controls – Portable media including USB devices and CDs	
• Ensuring that only staff with a genuine business need can download customer data to portable media such as USB devices and CDs.	• Allowing staff with access to bulk customer data – for example, superusers – to download to unencrypted portable media.
• Ensuring that staff authorised to hold customer data on portable media can only do so if it is encrypted.	• Failing to review regularly threats posed by increasingly sophisticated and quickly evolving personal technology such as mobile phones.

FSA report 'Data Security in Financial Services', April 2008

Data security – consolidated examples of good and poor practice

Examples of good practice	Examples of poor practice
Controls – Portable media including USB devices and CDs	
• Maintaining an accurate register of staff allowed to use USB devices and staff who have been issued USB devices. • The use of software to prevent and/or detect individuals using personal USB devices. • Firms reviewing regularly and on a risk-based approach the copying of customer data to portable media to ensure there is a genuine business reason for it. • The automatic encryption of portable media attached to firms' computers. • Providing lockers for higher-risk staff such as call centre staff and superusers and restricting them from taking personal effects to their desks.	
Physical security	
• Appropriately-restricted access to areas where large amounts of customer data is accessible, such as server rooms, call centres and filing areas. • Using robust intruder deterrents such as keypad entry doors, alarm systems, grilles or barred windows, and closed circuit television (CCTV). • Robust procedures for logging visitors and ensuring adequate supervision of them while on-site.	• Allowing staff or other persons with no genuine business need to access areas where customer data is held. • Failure to check electronic records showing who has accessed sensitive areas of the office. • Failure to lock away customer records and files when the office is left unattended.

Core resources

Data security – consolidated examples of good and poor practice

Examples of good practice	Examples of poor practice
Physical security	
• Training and awareness programmes for staff to ensure they are fully aware of more-basic risks to customer data arising from poor physical security.	
• Employing security guards, cleaners etc directly to ensure an appropriate level of vetting and reduce risks that can arise through third-party suppliers accessing customer data.	
• Using electronic swipe card records to spot unusual behaviour or access to high risk areas.	
• Keeping filing cabinets locked during the day and leaving the key with a trusted member of staff.	
• An enforced clear-desk policy.	
Disposal of customer data	
• Procedures that result in the production of as little paper-based customer data as possible.	• Poor awareness among staff about how to dispose of customer data securely.
• Treating all paper as 'confidential waste' to eliminate confusion among employees about which type of bin to use.	• Slack procedures that present opportunities for fraudsters, for instance when confidential waste is left unguarded on the premises before it is destroyed.
• All customer data disposed of by employees securely, for example by using shredders (preferably cross-cut rather than straight-line shredders) or confidential waste bins.	• Staff working remotely failing to dispose of customer data securely.

Data Security in Financial Services   Page 93

FSA report 'Data Security in Financial Services', April 2008

Data security – consolidated examples of good and poor practice

Examples of good practice	Examples of poor practice
Disposal of customer data	
• Checking general waste bins for the accidental disposal of customer data.	• Firms failing to provide guidance or assistance to remote workers who need to dispose of an obsolete home computer.
• Using a third-party supplier, preferably one with BSIA accreditation which provides a certificate of secure destruction, to shred or incinerate paper-based customer data. It is important for firms to have a good understanding of the supplier's process for destroying customer data and their employee vetting standards.	• Firms stockpiling obsolete computers and other portable media for too long and in insecure environments.
	• Firms relying on others to erase or destroy their hard drives and other portable media securely without evidence that this has been done competently.
• Providing guidance for travelling or home-based staff on the secure disposal of customer data.	
• Computer hard drives and portable media being properly wiped (using specialist software) or destroyed as soon as they become obsolete.	
Managing third-party suppliers	
• Conducting due diligence of data security standards at third-party suppliers before contracts are agreed.	• Allowing third-party suppliers to access customer data when no due diligence of data security arrangements has been performed.
• Regular reviews of third-party suppliers' data security systems and controls, with the frequency of review dependent on data security risks identified.	• Firms not knowing exactly which third-party staff have access to their customer data.
	• Firms not knowing how third-party suppliers' staff have been vetted.

987

Core resources

Data security – consolidated examples of good and poor practice

Examples of good practice	Examples of poor practice
Managing third-party suppliers	
• Ensuring third-party suppliers' vetting standards are adequate by testing the checks performed on a sample of staff with access to customer data.	• Allowing third-party staff unsupervised access to areas where customer data is held when they have not been vetted to the same standards as employees.
• Only allowing third-party IT suppliers access to customer databases for specific tasks on a case-by-case basis.	• Allowing IT suppliers unrestricted or unmonitored access to customer data.
• Third-party suppliers being subject to procedures for reporting data security breaches within an agreed timeframe.	• A lack of awareness of when/how third-party suppliers can access customer data and failure to monitor such access.
• The use of secure internet links to transfer data to third parties.	• Unencrypted customer data being sent to third parties using unregistered post.
Internal Audit and Compliance monitoring	
• Firms seeking external assistance where they do not have the necessary in-house expertise or resources.	• Compliance focusing only on compliance with data protection legislation and failing to consider adherence to data security policies and procedures.
• Compliance and internal audit conducting specific reviews of data security which cover all relevant areas of the business including IT, security, HR, training and awareness, governance and third-party suppliers.	• Compliance consultants adopting a 'one size fits all' approach to different clients' businesses.
• Firms using expertise from across the business to help with the more technical aspects of data security audits and compliance monitoring.	

FSA report 'Data Security in Financial Services', April 2008

5. Glossary

CIFAS Protective Registration	CIFAS offers a service called Protective Registration that requires anyone applying for credit in that person's name to undergo additional checks. The product, supplied by the Equifax credit bureau, costs £12 plus VAT. CIFAS have recently launched a 'bulk' Protective Registration facility for firms to use in cases of mass data loss.
CIFAS Staff Fraud Database	The CIFAS Staff Fraud Database is used by CIFAS Members specifically for staff vetting and security screening purposes. CIFAS members use the Staff Fraud Database to file data about their staff fraud cases and access staff fraud records filed by other CIFAS Members. For more information, visit: www.cifas.org.uk/default.asp?edit_id=718-87
Controlled function	A role that requires FSA approval of the individual performing it. Controlled functions include senior management, compliance and advisory roles. They are specified in SUP 10.4.5R in the FSA's Handbook.
Customer data	Customer data is any identifiable personal information about a customer held in any format. Customer data includes but is not limited to national insurance numbers, addresses, dates of birth, financial details and medical records.
Cyber-café	A small informal restaurant where you can pay to use the internet.
Data Protection Act	The UK's data protection legislation, which requires anyone who processes personal information to comply with eight principles, that ensure personal information is: • fairly and lawfully processed; • processed for limited purposes; • adequate, relevant and not excessive; • accurate and up to date; • not kept for longer than is necessary; • processed in line with your rights; • secure; and • not transferred to other countries without adequate protection.
Encryption	The process of changing electronic information or signals into a secret code that people cannot understand or use on normal equipment. Encryption software is widely available for computers and databases, USB devices and mobile telephones.

Core resources

Hacking	The hacking referred to in this report is where a malicious person infiltrates firms' computer systems in order to manipulate or steal data.
HR	Human Resources
Information Commissioner's Office	The UK's regulator for data protection, responsible for investigating breaches of, and enforcing, the Data Protection Act.
Instant messaging	Communication between two or more people, typed using computers or other electronic devices such as personal digital assistants. Instant messages can be relayed via the internet or inside another network.
IT	Information Technology
Key-loggers	Key-stroke logging or 'key-logging' is a method of capturing or recording a computer user's individual key-strokes. Therefore, passwords to databases containing customer data, as well as encryption keys, can be compromised using key-loggers. Key-loggers come in hardware and software forms. The risk of software key-loggers can be minimised by anti-spyware programmes and firewalls. However, it is more difficult for firms to protect against hardware key-loggers, which can either be attached to a PC or inserted inside keyboards.
Offshoring	The practice of relocating business operations overseas, usually to reduce costs or improve efficiency. IT services and customer call centres are two of the major operations relocated offshore by financial services firms.
Peer-to-peer file sharing	A means of sending and receiving files on the internet, most often used by individuals to exchange music files.
Phishing	A fraudulent attempt to acquire customer data by impersonating someone else. For example, some individuals are duped into revealing their personal data by emails purporting to come from a known and trusted organisation such as a bank. Firms become targets when fraudsters create fake websites or email communications using their name or corporate identity.
Spyware	Software installed surreptitiously on a computer to intercept or take partial control over the user's interaction with the computer. Spyware programmes can collect personal information and can also interfere in other ways, such as installing additional software and redirecting Web browser activity. Anti-spyware software is widely available.
'Straight-through' processing	An IT access model that allows users to log on to their computer with a single password and access all the databases or other systems that they need to do their job without the need for further passwords.

Data Security in Financial Services

FSA report 'Data Security in Financial Services', April 2008

Superuser	'Superusers' most often work in IT and are often responsible for database administration and creating access rights for other staff. Their technical knowledge means they often have the ability to access large amounts of customer data and sometimes to circumvent fraud controls.
Tailgating	Gaining unauthorised access to a restricted building or area by surreptitiously following an authorised person through a secure door or gate.
Third-party suppliers	A company or individual contracted to supply services to a regulated firm.
USB device	A device for storing data, readable by a computer that plugs into a computer's USB port. USB devices can hold large volumes of data and are generally very small and easily portable.
USB port	An outlet on a computer for connecting a USB device.

Core resources

6. References and useful links

The **Anti-Phishing Working Group** is an industry association focused on eliminating identity fraud resulting from phishing and email spoofing. www.antiphishing.org

APACS is the UK trade association for payments and the banking industry's voice on payments issues. www.apacs.org.uk

Bank Safe Online is the UK banking industry's initiative to help online banking users stay safe online. The site is run by APACS. www.banksafeonline.org.uk

The **British Bankers Association** is a trade association representing banks and other financial services firms operating in the UK. www.bba.org.uk

The **British Computer Society** is an industry body for IT professionals. It plays an important role in establishing standards and training needs for information security professionals. www.bcs.org

The **British Security Industry Association** is the trade association for the professional security industry in the UK which covers, among other things, information destruction. www.bsia.co.uk

British Standards is among the world's leading providers of standards and standards products. Through engagement and collaboration with its stakeholders, it develops standards and applies standardisation solutions to meet the needs of business and society. www.bsi-global.com

Business Link provides advice for businesses on implementing and managing information security. www.businesslink.gov.uk

Central Sponsor for Information Assurance (CSIA). The CSIA in the Cabinet Office works with partners across government and the private sector to help maintain a reliable, secure, and resilient national infrastructure. www.cabinetoffice.gov.uk/CSIA

The **Centre for the Protection of National Infrastructure** (CPNI) is the government authority which provides protective security advice to businesses and organisations across the national infrastructure. www.cpni.gov.uk/

CESG is the Information Assurance arm of GCHQ and is the UK government's National Technical Authority for information assurance. www.cesg.gov.uk

CIFAS is the UK's Fraud Prevention Service with 270 Members spread across banking, credit cards, asset finance, retail credit, mail order, insurance, savings and investments, telecommunications, factoring, and share dealing. Its website includes information for consumers and businesses about the risk of identity fraud. www.cifas.org.uk

The **Department of Trade and Industry** (DTI)) provides advice for businesses on protecting their information. www.dti.gov.uk/bestpractice/technology/security.htm

FSA report 'Data Security in Financial Services', April 2008

Get Safe Online is a site sponsored by leading businesses and the British government to promote security and safety on the internet. www.getsafeonline.org/

The **Home Office** is responsible for ensuring the UK's national infrastructure is protected as well as for policing for hi-tech crimes and gives internet crime prevention advice. www.homeoffice.gov.uk

We are a member of the **Home Office's Identity Fraud Steering Committee (IFSC)**. It has set up a website to educate consumers about identity fraud and the measures they can take to protect themselves from it. www.identity-fraud.gov.uk

The **International Information Integrity Institute** is a group of industry-leading organisations who share their expertise on managing information-related business risks. www.i4online.com

The **Information Assurance Advisory Council** (IAAC) brings together corporate leaders, public policy makers, law enforcement and the research community to address the challenges of information infrastructure protection. www.iaac.org.uk

The **Information Commissioner's Office** (ICO) is the UK's independent authority set up to promote access to official information and to protect personal information. www.ico.gov.uk

The **Information Systems Audit and Control Association** (ISACA) publishes on information governance, control and security matters for audit professionals. www.isaca.org

The **Information Systems Security Association** (ISSA) is an international organisation for information security professionals and practitioners that provides educational forums and publications to enhance the knowledge and skill of its members. www.issa.org

The **Information Security Forum** (ISF) is an international association of more than 250 leading organisations which fund and co-operate in the development of practical research about information security. www.securityforum.org

The **Jericho Forum** is an international IT security group which seeks to define methods to deliver secure IT operations in an increasingly internet-driven and networked world. www.opengroup.org/jericho/

The **National Computing Centre** is a membership and research organisation for IT professionals, which promotes information security best practice and guidance. www.ncc.co.uk

The **Ponemon Institute** promotes responsible information and privacy management practices in business and government. www.ponemon.org

The **Security Alliance for Internet and New Technologies** (SAINT) brings together industry leaders and government to exchange information and best practice. www.uksaint.org

Core resources

The Financial Services Authority
25 The North Colonnade Canary Wharf London E14 5HS
Telephone: +44 (0)20 7066 1000 Fax: +44 (0)20 7066 1099
Website: http://www.fsa.gov.uk
Registered as a Limited Company in England and Wales No. 1920623. Registered Office as above.

ICO 'GUIDANCE ON DATA SECURITY BREACH MANAGEMENT', MARCH 2008

Information Commissioner's Office
Promoting public access to official information and protecting your personal information

Guidance on data security breach management

Organisations which process personal data must take appropriate measures against unauthorised or unlawful processing and against accidental loss, destruction of or damage to personal data. Many organisations take the view that one of those measures might be the adoption of a policy on dealing with a data security breach.

This guidance note sets out some of the things an organisation needs to consider in the event of a security breach. This note is not intended as legal advice, nor is it a comprehensive guide to information security. It should, however, assist organisations in deciding on an appropriate course of action if a breach occurs.

A data security breach can happen for a number of reasons:

- Loss or theft of data or equipment on which data is stored
- Inappropriate access controls allowing unauthorised use
- Equipment failure
- Human error
- Unforeseen circumstances such as a fire or flood
- Hacking attack
- 'Blagging' offences where information is obtained by deceiving the organisation who holds it

However the breach has occurred, there are four important elements to any breach management plan:

1. Containment and recovery
2. Assessment of ongoing risk
3. Notification of breach
4. Evaluation and response

1. Containment and recovery

Data security breaches will require not just an initial response to investigate and contain the situation but also a recovery plan including, where necessary, damage limitation. This will often involve input from specialists across the business such as IT, HR and legal and in some cases contact with external stakeholders and suppliers. Consider the following:

© Information Commissioner. Published by LexisNexis 2009; this version was correct at time of going to press August 09.

Core resources

- Decide on who should take the lead on investigating the breach and ensure they have the appropriate resources
- Establish who needs to be made aware of the breach and inform them of what they are expected to do to assist in the containment exercise. This could be isolating or closing a compromised section of the network, finding a lost piece of equipment or simply changing the access codes at the front door.
- Establish whether there is anything you can do to recover any losses and limit the damage the breach can cause. As well as the physical recovery of equipment, this could involve the use of back up tapes to restore lost or damaged data or ensuring that staff recognise when someone tries to use stolen data to access accounts
- Where appropriate, inform the police

2. Assessing the risks

Some data security breaches will not lead to risks beyond possible inconvenience to those who need the data to do their job. An example might be where a laptop is irreparably damaged but its files were backed up and can be recovered, albeit at some cost to the business. While these types of incidents can still have significant consequences the risks are very different from those posed by, for example, the theft of a customer database, the data on which may be used to commit identity fraud. Before deciding on what steps are necessary further to immediate containment, assess the risks which may be associated with the breach. Perhaps most important is an assessment of potential adverse consequences for individuals, how serious or substantial these are and how likely they are to happen.

The following points are also likely to be helpful in making this assessment:

- What type of data is involved?
- How sensitive is it? Remember that some data is sensitive because of its very personal nature (health records) while other data types are sensitive because of what might happen if it is misused (bank account details)
- If data has been lost or stolen, are there any protections in place such as encryption?
- What has happened to the data? If data has been stolen, it could be used for purposes which are harmful to the individuals to whom the data relate; if it has been damaged, this poses a different type and level of risk
- Regardless of what has happened to the data, what could the data tell a third party about the individual? Sensitive data could mean very little to an opportunistic laptop thief while the loss of apparently trivial snippets of information could help a determined fraudster build up a detailed picture of other people

ICO 'Guidance on data security breach management', March 2008

- How many individuals' personal data are affected by the breach? It is not necessarily the case that the bigger risks will accrue from the loss of large amounts of data but is certainly an important determining factor in the overall risk assessment
- Who are the individuals whose data has been breached? Whether they are staff, customers, clients or suppliers, for example, will to some extent determine the level of risk posed by the breach and, therefore, your actions in attempting to mitigate those risks
- What harm can come to those individuals? Are there risks to physical safety or reputation, of financial loss or a combination of these and other aspects of their life?
- Are there wider consequences to consider such as a risk to public health or loss of public confidence in an important service you provide?
- If individuals' bank details have been lost, consider contacting the banks themselves for advice on anything they can do to help you prevent fraudulent use.

3. Notification of breaches

Informing people and organisations that you have experienced a data security breach can be an important element in your breach management strategy. However, informing people about a breach is not an end in itself. Notification should have a clear purpose, whether this is to enable individuals who may have been affected to take steps to protect themselves or to allow the appropriate regulatory bodies to perform their functions, provide advice and deal with complaints.

Answering the following questions will assist you in deciding whether to notify:

- Are there any legal or contractual requirements? At present, there is no law expressly requiring you to notify a breach but sector specific rules may lead you towards issuing a notification
- Can notification help you meet your security obligations with regard to the seventh data protection principle?
- Can notification help the individual? Bearing in mind the potential effects of the breach, could individuals act on the information you provide to mitigate risks, for example by cancelling a credit card or changing a password?
- If a large number of people are affected, or there are very serious consequences, you should inform the ICO
- Consider how notification can be made appropriate for particular groups of individuals, for example, if you are notifying children or vulnerable adults.
- Have you considered the dangers of 'over notifying'. Not every incident will warrant notification and notifying a whole 2 million strong customer

Core resources

base of an issue affecting only 2,000 customers may well cause disproportionate enquiries and work.

You also need to consider who to notify, what you are going to tell them and how you are going to communicate the message. This will depend to a large extent on the nature of the breach but the following points may be relevant to your decision:

- Make sure you notify the appropriate regulatory body. A sector specific regulator may require you to notify them of any type of breach but the ICO should only be notified when the breach involves personal data
- There are a number of different ways to notify those affected so consider using the most appropriate one. Always bear in mind the security of the medium as well as the urgency of the situation
- Your notification should at the very least include a description of how and when the breach occurred and what data was involved. Include details of what you have already done to respond to the risks posed by the breach
- When notifying individuals give specific and clear advice on the steps they can take to protect themselves and also what you are willing to do to help them
- Provide a way in which they can contact you for further information or to ask you questions about what has occurred – this could be a helpline number or a web page, for example.

When notifying the ICO you should also include details of the security measures in place such as encryption and, where appropriate, details of the security procedures you had in place at the time the breach occurred. You should also inform us if the media are aware of the breach so that we can manage any increase in enquiries from the public. When informing the media, it is useful to inform them whether you have contacted the ICO and what action is being taken. ICO will not normally tell the media or other their parties about a breach notified to us, but we may advise you to do so.

The ICO has produced guidance for organisations on the information we expect to receive as part of a breach notification and on what organisations can expect from us on receipt of their notification. This guidance is available on our website:

http://www.ico.gov.uk/Home/what_we_cover/data_protection/guidance/good_practice_notes.aspx.

You might also need to consider notifying third parties such as the police, insurers, professional bodies, bank or credit card companies who can assist in reducing the risk of financial loss to individuals, and trade unions.

4. Evaluation and response

It is important not only to investigate the causes of the breach but also to evaluate the effectiveness of your response to it. Clearly, if the breach was caused, even in part, by systemic and ongoing problems, then simply containing the breach and continuing 'business as usual' is not acceptable; similarly, if your response was hampered by inadequate policies or a lack of a clear allocation of responsibility then it is important to review and update these policies and lines responsibility in the light of experience.

You may find that existing procedures could lead to another breach and you will need to identify where improvements can be made. The following points will assist you:

- Make sure you know what personal data is held and where and how it is stored. Dealing with a data security breach is much easier if you know which data are involved. Your notification with the Information Commissioner will be a useful starting point.
- Establish where the biggest risks lie. For example, how much sensitive personal data do you hold? Do you store data across the business or is it concentrated in one location?
- Risks will arise when sharing with or disclosing to others. You should make sure not only that the method of transmission is secure but also that you only share or disclose the minimum amount of data necessary. By doing this, even if a breach occurs, the risks are reduced
- Identify weak points in your existing security measures such as the use of portable storage devices or access to public networks
- Monitor staff awareness of security issues and look to fill any gaps through training or tailored advice
- Consider whether you need to establish a group of technical and non-technical staff who discuss 'what if' scenarios – this would highlight risks and weaknesses as well as giving staff at different levels the opportunity to suggest solutions
- If your organisation already has a Business Continuity Plan for dealing with serious incidents, consider implementing a similar plan for data security breaches
- It is recommended that at the very least you identify a group of people responsible for reacting to reported breaches of security

This document was correct at the time of going to press. Please consult the ICO website to ensure that you are referring to the latest version.
http://www.ico.gov.uk/upload/documents/library/data_protection/practical_application/guidance_on_data_security_breach_management.pdf

ICO 'NOTIFICATION OF DATA SECURITY BREACHES TO THE INFORMATION COMMISSIONER'S OFFICE', MARCH 2008

Notification of Data Security Breaches to the Information Commissioner's Office

All data controllers have a responsibility under the Data Protection Act 1998 to ensure appropriate and proportionate security of the personal data they hold. (DPA 1998 7th Principle).

Although there is no legal obligation on data controllers to report breaches of security which result in loss, release or corruption of personal data, the Information Commissioner believes serious breaches should be brought to the attention of his Office. The nature of the breach or loss can then be considered together with whether the data controller is properly meeting his responsibilities under the DPA.

"Serious breaches" are not defined. However the following should assist data controllers in considering whether breaches should be reported:

The potential harm to data subjects:

> The potential harm to individuals is the overriding consideration in deciding whether a breach of data security should be reported to the Information Commissioner's Office.
>
> Ways in which harm can occur include:
>
> - exposure to identity theft through the release of non-public identifiers e.g. passport number
> - information about the private aspects of a person's life becoming known to others e.g. financial circumstances.
>
> The extent of harm, which can include distress, is dependant on both the volume of personal data involved and the sensitivity of the data.
>
> Where there is significant actual or potential harm as a result of the breach, whether because of the volume of data, its sensitivity or a combination of the two, there should be a presumption to report.
>
> Where there is little risk that individuals would suffer significant harm, for example because a stolen laptop is properly encrypted, or the information that is the subject of the breach is publicly available information, there is no need to report.

© Information Commissioner. Published by LexisNexis 2009; this version was correct at time of going to press August 09.

Core resources

The volume of personal data lost / released / corrupted:

There should be a presumption to report to the ICO where a large volume of personal data is concerned and there is a real risk of individuals suffering some harm. It is difficult to be precise what constitutes a large volume of personal data. Every case must be considered on its own merits but a reasonable rule of thumb is any collection containing information about 1000 or more individuals.

An example we would expect to be reported would be the theft / loss of an *unencrypted* laptop computer or other *unencrypted* portable electronic / digital media holding names and addresses, dates of birth and National Insurance Numbers of 1000 individuals.

An example we would not expect to be reported would be the theft / loss of a marketing list of 500 names and addresses or other contact details where there is no particular sensitivity of the product being marketed.

However it may be appropriate to report much lower volumes in some circumstances where the risk is particularly high perhaps because of the circumstances of the loss or the extent of information about each individual. If the data controller is unsure whether to report or not, then the presumption should be to report.

The sensitivity of the data lost / released / unlawfully corrupted:

There should be a presumption to report to the ICO where smaller amounts of personal data are involved, the release of which could cause a significant risk of individuals suffering substantial harm. This is most likely to be the case where that data is *sensitive personal data* as defined in section 2 of the DPA. As few as 10 records could be the trigger if the information is particularly sensitive.

An example we would expect to be reported would be a manual paper based filing system (or *unencrypted* digital media) holding the personal data relating to 50 named individuals and their financial records.

An example we would not expect to be reported would be a similar system holding the trade union subscription records of the same number of individuals where there were no special circumstances surrounding the loss.

ICO 'Notification of Data Security Breaches to the ICO', March 2008

Reporting

Serious breaches should be notified to the Information Commissioner's Office at mail@ico.gov.uk or at Address: *Wycliffe House, Water Lane, Wilmslow, Cheshire SK9 5AF.*

The notification should include:

- The type of information and number of records
- The circumstances of the loss / release / corruption
- Action taken to minimise / mitigate effect on individuals involved including whether they have been informed
- Details of how the breach is being investigated
- Whether any other regulatory body has been informed and their response
- Remedial action taken to prevent future occurrence
- Any other information you feel may assist us in making an assessment

Guidance on how to manage a data security breach can be found here:

http://www.ico.gov.uk/Home/what_we_cover/data_protection/guidance/good_practice_notes.aspx

What will the Information Commissioner's Office do when a breach is reported?

The nature and seriousness of the breach and the adequacy of any remedial action will be assessed and a course of action determined. We may:

- Record the breach and take no further action
- Investigate the circumstances of the breach and any remedial action which could lead to:

    1) no further action
    2) a requirement on the data controller to undertake a course of action to prevent further breaches
    3) formal enforcement action turning such a requirement into a legal obligation

It should be noted that the Information Commissioner does not have the power to impose a fine or other penalty as punishment for a breach. Our powers only extend to imposing obligations as to future conduct.

Will a reported breach be made public?

Core resources

We do not see it as our responsibility to publicise security breaches not already in the public domain or to inform any individuals affected. In so far as they arise these are the responsibilities of the data controller.

However, the ICO may recommend the data controller to make a breach public where it is clearly in the interests of the individuals concerned or there is a strong public interest argument to do so.

Where the Information Commissioner takes regulatory action, it is policy to publicise such action, unless there are exceptional reasons not to do so. This policy on publication extends to any formal undertakings provided to the Commissioner by a data controller.

However the Commissioner will not normally take regulatory action unless a data controller declines to take any recommended action, he has other reasons to doubt future compliance or there is a need to provide reassurance to the public. Such a need is most likely to arise where the circumstances of the breach are already in the public domain.

Further information on the ICO's regulatory action strategy can be found here:

http://www.ico.gov.uk/upload/documents/library/data_protection/detailed_specialist_guides/data_protection_regulatory_action_strategy.pdf

This document was correct at the time of going to press. Please consult the ICO website to ensure that you are referring to the latest version.
http://www.ico.gov.uk/upload/documents/library/data_protection/practical_application/breach_reporting.pdf

ICO 'DATA PROTECTION GUIDANCE NOTE: PRIVACY ENHANCING TECHNOLOGIES (PETS)', V2.0, MARCH 2007

Information Commissioner's Office
Promoting public access to official information and protecting your personal information

Data Protection Guidance Note:

Privacy enhancing technologies (PETs)

This technical note is intended to raise awareness of the concept of privacy enhancing technologies and is aimed at system designers and those commissioning them. It will give a brief description of privacy enhancing technologies but draws on the extensive information published elsewhere. It is not intended to be an exhaustive account; rather it is a point of entry for readers to further their own research.

Background

Individuals' use of the internet and email to communicate, research areas of interest and interact with businesses and government is at an all time high driven by the strong uptake of broadband services in the UK. At the same time the UK government and devolved administrations are committed to maximising the electronic interaction between the individual and the state at all levels and to sharing information across the databases that authorities control.

There is a growing move towards introducing computing power and/or information storage in everyday consumer products, which will redefine how we interact with our surroundings and could potentially generate information about the opinions, preferences and lifestyles of individuals at an as yet unknown level.

What are privacy enhancing technologies?

Technology can assist companies' compliance with the principles that protect individuals' privacy and can go further to empower individuals, giving them easier access to and control over information about them and allowing them to decide how and when it will be disclosed to and used by third parties.

The best protection for individuals is that their personal information is only collected where this is essential. Privacy enhancing technologies have traditionally been limited to 'pseudonymisation tools'. These are software and systems that allow individuals to withhold their true identity from those operating electronic systems or providing services through them, and only reveal it when absolutely necessary. These technologies help to minimise the information collected about individuals and include anonymous web browsers, specialist email services, and digital cash.

Core resources

Federated identity management systems potentially allow individuals to access the services of organisations without having to provide information to them. They involve one trusted organisation verifying the identity of an individual and then vouching for them using an electronic token that also specifies their particular entitlements. This allows the individual to access the services provided by third parties using the token without having to disclose their identity or other information necessary to prove their entitlement.

The Information Commissioner considers that privacy enhancing technologies are not limited to tools that provide a degree of anonymity for individuals but they are also any technology that exists to protect or enhance an individual's privacy, including facilitating individuals' access to their rights under the Data Protection Act 1998.

Examples of this wider approach to privacy enhancing technologies could include:
- encrypted biometric access systems that allow the use of a fingerprint to authenticate an individual's identity, but do not retain the actual fingerprint;
- secure online access for individuals to their own personal data to check its accuracy and make amendments;
- software that allows browsers to automatically detect the privacy policy of websites and compares it to the preferences expressed by the user, highlighting any clashes; and
- 'sticky' electronic privacy policies that are attached to the information itself preventing it being used in any way that is not compatible with that policy.

Why use privacy enhancing technologies?

They can save you money. The cost of including privacy at the system design stage is much less than the cost of having to amend a finished system to make sure it complies with legal requirements and respects individuals' privacy.

They help to reduce risks. Privacy controls that are incorporated into electronic information systems to supplement organisational procedures help to provide additional safeguards which better protect individuals' information from human error.

They help to build trust. The use of privacy enhancing technology in systems helps to signal the integrity and intention of organisations regarding the information that they hold, and encourages trust in those organisations by citizens and customers.

ICO 'Data Protection Guidance Note: PETs', V2.0, March 2007

The design philosophy

A system designer who starts from the position of trying to protect individuals' privacy by creating or implementing privacy enhancing technologies might ask the following questions as an essential part of the task.

- Do I need to collect any personal data at all?
- If so, what is the minimum needed?
- Who will have access to which data?
- How can accesses be controlled to allow only those which are for the purposes stated when the data was collected, and then only by those employees and processes that have an essential need?
- Can individuals make total or partial use of the system anonymously?
- How can I help individuals to exercise their rights securely?

In 2003, the HiSPEC team at the University of Manchester Institute of Science and Technology produced data protection best practice guidance for system designers in collaboration with the Information Commissioner's Office, which can be found on their website (see below).

Useful information sources

Data protection and privacy commissioners

Ontario data protection authority
Privacy enhancing technology testing and evaluation project (PETTEP) documentation
http://www.ipc.on.ca

Dutch data protection authority
Privacy enhancing technologies – a white paper for decision makers
http://www.dutchdpa.nl/downloads_overig/PET_whitebook.pdf?refer=true&theme=purple

Privacy-Enhancing Technologies – the path to anonymity. Revised edition (1998)
http://www.dutchdpa.nl/documenten/EN_av_11_Privacy-enhancing_technologies.shtml

Core resources

Researchers and academics

Rand Europe
Technology solutions to protect privacy in e-government
http://www.rand.org

Roger Clarke
Introducing PITs and PETS Technologies: technologies affecting privacy
http://www.anu.edu.au/people/Roger.Clarke/DV/PITsPETs.html

UMIST
Data protection best practice guidance
http://www.hispec.org.uk/public_documents/BPDMay02.pdf

Privacy enhancing technologies state of the art review (2002)
http://www.hispec.org.uk/public_documents/7_1PETreview3.pdf

Conferences
The workshop on privacy enhancing technologies
http://petworkshop.org

More information

If you need any more information about this or any other aspect of data protection, please contact us.

Phone: 01625 545745
Email: mail@ico.gsi.gov.uk
Website: www.ico.gov.uk

V2.0
29/03/2007

This document was correct at the time of going to press. Please consult the ICO website to ensure that you are referring to the latest version.
http://www.ico.gov.uk/upload/documents/library/data_protection/detailed_specialist_guides/privacy_enhancing_technologies_v2.pdf

1008

Index

[all references are to paragraph number]

ACPO/ACPOS Information Systems CSP
police service, and, 4.80
Advanced electronic signatures
based on qualified certificates
   certification-service-providers, 2.143
   definition, 2.140
   generally, 2.141
   liability for reliance on qualified certificate, 2.147
   qualified certificates, 2.142
   secure-signature creation devices, 2.144
certification-service-providers
   accreditation, 2.146
   generally, 2.143
   supervision, 2.146
creation, 2.141
definition, 2.140
generally, 2.141
legal effect, 2.145
types, 2.140
Article 29 Working party
compensation for breach of security obligation, 2.96
Electronic Communications Privacy Directive, and, 7.71–7.75
generally, 2.38
Assessment notices
code of practice, 6.147–6.148
editorial comment, 6.149–6.150
exempt materials, 6.143
generally, 6.138
designating private sector data controllers, 6.141–6.142
ICO proposals, 6.68
meaning, 6.139
monetary penalties, and, 6.158
recipients, 6.140
sanctions for non-compliance, 6.145

Assessment notices—*contd*
time for compliance, 6.144
use of material obtained, 6.146
Audit Directive
corporate governance, and, 3.8

Banking Consolidation Directive (2006/48/EC)
financial services, and, 3.14–3.15
'Banks in unacceptable data protection breach' (ICO, March 2007)
regulation and enforcement, and, 6.34–6.35
Barristers' Code of Conduct
secrecy laws, and, 5.29
Basel II
financial services, and, 3.14
Breach notification
Californian law, under
   computerised data, 7.108
   COPP guidance, 7.111–7.113
   early warning system, 7.112
   encryption, 7.109
   generally, 7.107
   seriousness threshold, 7.110
Coleman Report (June 2008), 7.51
Data Handling Review (June 2008)
   government's position, 7.52–7.55
   Information Commissioner's position, 7.44–7.45
Data Protection Act 1998, under
   fair processing, 7.4–7.6
   human rights issues, 7.13
   information notices, 7.11–7.12
   introduction, 7.3
   notification, 7.7–7.8
   registration, 7.7–7.8
   subject access, 7.9–7.10

Index

Breach notification—*contd*
Electronic Communications Privacy
  Directive (2002/58/EC)
  Article 29 Working Party opinion
    (February 2009), 7.71–7.75
  Commission amended proposal
    (November 2008), 7.68–7.70
  Commission Communication
    (February 2009), 7.83
  Commission proposal (November
    2007), 7.58–7.61
  Committee of the Regions opinion
    (June 2008), 7.63
  composite view, 7.86
  Council's Common Position
    (February 2009), 7.76–7.82
  EESC opinion (May 2008), 7.62
  generally, 7.57
  Parliament debate (September
    2008), 7.64–7.67
  Parliament debate (May 2009), 7.84–7.85
  Privacy Law and Business survey
    (May 2009), 7.87–7.88
electronic health information (US),
  for
  aims and objectives, 7.104
  generally, 7.103
  obligation to report, 7.105
EU's position
  Electronic Communications
    Privacy Directive
    (2002/58/EC), 7.57–7.88
fair processing, 7.4–7.6
Federal Trade Commission initiatives
  electronic health information, 7.103–7.105
  introduction, 7.98
  Red Flag Rules, 7.99–7.102
FSA's position, 7.89
government's position
  Coleman Report (June 2008), 7.51
  Data Handling Review, 7.52–7.55
  HMG Security Policy Framework, 7.56
  O'Donnell Report (June 2008), 7.52–7.55
  Personal Internet Security report
    (HoL, August 2007), 7.46–7.49
  *Protecting Government
    Information* report (Cabinet
    Office, June 2008), 7.51
  Protection of Private Data report
    (HoC, January 2008), 7.50
'Guidance on data security breach
  management' (ICO, March
  2008)
  content of reports, 7.24
  generally, 7.21

Breach notification—*contd*
'Guidance on data security breach
  management' (ICO, March
  2008)—*contd*
  initial considerations, 7.22
  introduction, 7.20
  reporting to other third parties, 7.23
HMG Security Policy Framework, 7.56
Home Affairs Committee inquiry
  (HoC, November 2007), 7.17
human rights issues, 7.13
Information Commissioner, and
  Data Handling Review, 7.44–7.45
  data security breach
    management, 7.21–7.24
  guidance (March 2008), 7.20–7.36
  Home Affairs Committee inquiry
    (HoC, November 2007), 7.17
  introduction, 7.15
  notification of security breaches, 7.25–7.36
  Personal Internet Security report
    (HoL, August 2007), 7.15–7.16
  Protection of Private Data report
    (HoC, January 2008), 7.18–7.19
  RSA Conference Europe speech
    (October 2008), 7.40–7.43
  Thomas-Walport Data Sharing
    Review (July 2008), 7.37–7.39
information notices, 7.11–7.12
introduction, 7.1–7.2
ISO 27000 series, under, 7.114
notification, 7.7–7.8
'*Notification of Security Breaches to
  the ICO*' (ICO, March 2008)
  causing harm, 7.27–7.29
  consequences of reporting, 7.34
  formal action, 7.35
  generally, 7.25
  incentivising non-reporting, 7.36
  informal action, 7.35
  information to be reported, 7.33
  introduction, 7.20
  potential for significant harm, 7.29
  presumption to report, 7.26
  rule of thumb approach, 7.30
  sensitivity of data affected, 7.32
  volume of data affected, 7.30–7.31
O'Donnell Report (June 2008)
  government's position, 7.52–7.55
  Information Commissioner's
    position, 7.44–7.45
online banking fraud, 7.47
overview, 2.42
Personal Internet Security report
  (HoL, August 2007)
  government's position, 7.46–7.49

Index

Breach notification—*contd*
  Personal Internet Security report (HoL, August 2007)—*contd*
    Information Commissioner's position, 7.15–7.16
  Protecting Government Information report (Cabinet Office, June 2008), 7.51
  Protection of Private Data report (HoC, January 2008)
    government's position, 7.50
    Information Commissioner's position, 7.18–7.19
  Red Flag Rules (US)
    financial institutions, 7.102
    introduction, 7.99
    management responsibility, 7.101
    warning signs, 7.100
  registration, 7.7–7.8
  RSA Conference Europe speech (October 2008), 7.40–7.43
  Science and Technology Committee report (HoL, August 2007), 7.15–7.16
  state (US) level, at
    form and content of reports, 7.95
    harm threshold to reporting, 7.92
    introduction, 7.91
    other laws, 7.97
    personal information, 7.94
    policies, 7.96
    rules for data processing, 7.93
  subject access, 7.9–7.10
  'Surveillance Society' inquiry (HoC, November 2007), 7.17
  Thomas-Walport Data Sharing Review (July 2008), 7.37–7.39
  transparency, and
    fair processing, 7.4–7.6
    human rights issues, 7.13
    information notices, 7.11–7.12
    introduction, 7.3
    notification, 7.7–7.8
    registration, 7.7–7.8
    subject access, 7.9–7.10
  US, in
    California, in, 7.107–7.113
    electronic health information, for, 7.103–7.105
    Federal Trade Commission initiatives, 7.98–7.105
    generally, 7.90
    other initiatives and federal rules, 7.106
    Red Flag Rules, 7.99–7.102
    state level, at, 7.91–7.97
Burton Report (April 2009)
  background, 4.92
  data protection, 4.100

Burton Report (April 2009)—*contd*
  encryption statistics, 4.96
  failure to encrypt, 4.99
  good practices at MoD, 4.102
  Information Commissioner's response, 4.104
  introduction, 4.93
  loss of TAFMIS laptop, 4.95
  management of data, 4.100
  recommendations, 4.101
  TAFMIS system, 4.97–4.98
  transformational government, and, 4.94

Caldicott Committee Report
  National Health Service, and, 4.72–4.73
Caldicott Guardian Manual 2006
  National Health Service, and, 4.74
Californian law (breach notification)
  computerised data, 7.108
  COPP guidance, 7.111–7.113
  early warning system, 7.112
  encryption, 7.109
  generally, 7.107
  seriousness threshold, 7.110
Capital Adequacy Directive (2006/49/EC)
  financial services, and, 3.14
CAPS
  CESG services, and, 4.12
'*Case for Amending the Data Protection Act*' (ICO, December 2007)
  regulation and enforcement, and, 6.66–6.73
Cayton Report
  National Health Service, and, 4.75
Central Sponsor for Information Assurance (CSIA)
  generally, 4.9
  National Information Assurance Strategy, 4.20–4.21
Centre for the Protection of National Infrastructure (CPNI)
  generally, 4.16
'*CEOs urged to raise their game following unacceptable privacy breaches*', (ICO, July 2007)
  regulation and enforcement, and, 6.45
Certification-service-providers
  accreditation, 2.146
  generally, 2.143
  supervision, 2.146
Civil Service Management Code
  generally, 4.61
Claims Tested Mark
  CESG services, and, 4.15
CLAS
  CESG services, and, 4.13

Index

Codes of practice
assessment notices, and, 6.147–6.148
Confidentiality Code, 4.71
Information Security Management Code, 4.70
Management of Police Information Code
  generally, 4.81
  guidance, 4.85
  Information Management Strategy, 4.83
  security, 4.84
  statutory basis, 4.82
National Archives Code, 4.6
National Health Service, and
  Confidentiality, 4.71
  Information Security Management, 4.70
  introduction, 4.69
police service, and
  Management of Police Information, 4.81–4.85
public sector records management, and
  international standards, 4.7
  National Archives, 4.6
Coleman Report
breach notification, and, 7.51
generally, 4.32
Combined Code
corporate governance, and, 3.10
Commissioners for Revenue and Customs Act 2005
secrecy laws, and, 5.19
Communications Act 2003
secrecy laws, and, 5.28
Communications Data Retention Directive (2006/24/EC)
data protection and data security regime, 2.104
generally, 2.101
Communications services
Communications Data Retention Directive (2006/24/EC)
  data protection and data security regime, 2.104
  generally, 2.101
Electronic Communications Privacy Directive (2002/58/EC)
  differences from 1997 Directive, 2.105
  exceptions from confidentiality obligations, 2.106
  generally, 2.101
  security and confidentiality regime, 2.103
  transposition in UK, 2.107
EU Directives, 2.101
human rights, and, 2.99

Communications services—*contd*
introduction, 2.99
Privacy and Electronic Communications (EC Directive) Regulations 2003
  generally, 2.123
  introduction, 2.107
Regulation of Investigatory Powers Act 2000
  'communication', 2.111
  decrypted information, 2.122
  encryption keys, 2.122
  exclusion of criminal liability, 2.117
  facilities for interception, 2.120–2.121
  generally, 2.108
  'in the course of transmission', 2.113–2.115
  'interception', 2.112
  interception in private systems, 2.117
  interception of business communications, 2.119
  introduction, 2.107
  'lawful authority', 2.116
  non-real time monitoring, 2.115
  'private telecommunication system', 2.110
  'public telecommunication system', 2.109
  stored e-mail and voicemail messages, 2.114
  supply of decrypted information and encryption keys, 2.122
  tort of unlawful interception, 2.118
regulators' obligation to ensure security, 2.100
right to respect for private and family life, and, 2.99
Telecommunications Privacy Directive (97/66/EC)
  differences from 2002 Directive, 2.105
  exceptions from confidentiality obligations, 2.106
  generally, 2.101
  security and confidentiality regime, 2.102
Companies
corporate governance
  Audit Directive, 3.8
  Combined Code, 3.10
  Company Law Directives, 3.8
  Financial Reporting Council guidance, 3.10
  FSA Handbook, 3.9
  introduction, 3.7
  meaning, 3.7
  SAS 70, 3.12
  statutory provision, 3.7
  Turnbull Guidance, 3.11

Index

Companies—*contd*
  corporate governance—*contd*
    UK rules, 3.9–3.12
  data controllers, as, 3.1
  directors' duties, 3.1–3.2
  financial services
    Banking Consolidation Directive, 3.14–3.15
    Basel II, 3.14
    Capital Adequacy Directive, 3.14
    Electronic Money Directive, 3.25
    EU Directives, 3.14–3.25
    Financial Services and Markets Act 2000, 3.26–3.27
    FSA Handbook, 3.28–3.35
    introduction, 3.13
    Market Abuse Directive, 3.19–3.20
    Market in Financial Instruments Directives, 3.16–3.18
    Money Laundering Directive, 3.22
    Payment Card Industry Data Security Standard (PCI DSS), 3.36–3.37
    Payment Services Directive, 3.23–3.24
    Principles for Business (PRIN), 3.29–3.30
    Prospectus Directive, 3.21
    reduction of financial crime, 3.27
    Senior Management, Arrangements, Systems and Controls, 3.31–3.33
    Supervision (SUP), 3.34
  record-keeping obligations, 3.2
  transparency
    EU Directive (2004/109/EC), 3.4–3.5
    FSA Handbook, 3.6
    introduction, 3.3
    statutory provision, 3.3
    UK rules, 3.6

Company Law Directives
  corporate governance, and, 3.8

Compensation
  breach of data security obligation, and
    Article 29 Working Party's views, 2.96
    'claims farming', and, 2.98
    damage and distress, 2.92–2.96
    consequences for data controllers, 2.97
    generally, 2.91
    Johnson v MDU decision, 2.93–2.95

Computer Misuse Act 1990
  introduction, 2.124
  offences
    unauthorised access to computer material, 2.127–2.133
    unauthorised access with intent to commit further offences, 2.134

Computer Misuse Act 1990—*contd*
  offences—*contd*
    unauthorised acts with intent to impair operation of computer, 2.135–2.137
  security controls, and, 2.138
  territorial scope
    generally, 2.125
    'significant links', 2.126
  unauthorised access to computer material
    causing a computer to perform a function, 2.128
    generally, 2.127
    intent to commit further offences, with, 2.134
    knowledge that access is unauthorised, 2.133
    purpose of offence, 2.127
    securing access, 2.129–2.130
    unauthorised, 2.131–2.132
  unauthorised access with intent to commit further offences, 2.134
  unauthorised acts with intent to impair operation of computer
    elements, 2.136
    generally, 2.135
    programs and data stored in moveable media, 2.137

'Confidential details lost by Revenue and Customs' (ICO, November 2007)
  regulation and enforcement, and, 6.57

Confidentiality
  duty of confidence
    creation, 2.6
    encryption, and, 2.7–2.10
    generally, 2.3
    information that has the necessary quality, 2.5
    liability of data controller for breach, 2.11–2.12
    liability of third party for misappropriation, 2.1
    parameters, 2.4
    types, 2.6
  encryption, and
    disclosure notices, 2.8–2.9
    generally, 2.7
    'protected information', 2.8
    Regulation of Investigatory Powers Act 2000, and, 2.8–2.10
  human rights, and
    generally, 2.14
    positive obligation, 2.15
  introduction, 2.3
  liability of data controller for breach, 2.11–2.12

Index

Confidentiality—*contd*
  liability of third party, 2.13
  misappropriation, and, 2.13
  negligence, and, 2.11–2.12
  right to respect for private and family life, 2.14
Confidentiality Code
  National Health Service, and, 4.71
Constitution Committee inquiry (HoL)
  oral evidence (November 2007), 6.51–6.56
  response (April 2009), 6.91
  written evidence (June 2007), 6.41–6.44
Contractual control mechanisms
  regulation and enforcement, and, 6.4
Coroners and Justice Bill
  additional commentary (February 2009), 6.89
  commentary (May 2009), 6.92–6.94
  effect on DPA 1998, and, 6.101
  memorandum (July 2009), 6.95–6.96
  memorandum and commentary (January 2009), 6.88
Corporate governance
  Audit Directive, 3.8
  Combined Code, 3.10
  Company Law Directives, 3.8
  Financial Reporting Council guidance, 3.10
  FSA Handbook, 3.9
  introduction, 3.7
  meaning, 3.7
  SAS 70, 3.12
  statutory provision, 3.7
  Turnbull Guidance, 3.11
  UK rules, 3.9–3.12
Council of Europe Data Protection Convention (1981)
  generally, 2.19
'Countering Financial Crime Risks in Information Security' (FSA, November 2004)
  regulation and enforcement, and, 6.26
Criminal proceedings
  action taken by the IC, 6.174
  generally, 6.159
Cross-border data flows
  data processors, and, 2.82
Cross Government Actions (December 2007)
  Data Handling Review, and, 4.24–4.26
CTAS
  CESG services, and, 4.14
Cyber Security Operations Centre
  generally, 4.17
Cyber Security Strategy
  generally, 4.58

Cybercrime Convention
  electronic signatures, and, 2.139

Data
  And see Data protection
  definition, 2.27
  introduction, 2.2
Data controllers
  And see Data protection
  companies, and, 3.1
  duty of confidence, and, 2.11–2.12
  generally, 2.34
Data Handling Review (June 2008)
  breach notification, and
    government's position, 7.52–7.55
    Information Commissioner's position, 7.44–7.45
  Cross Government Actions, 4.24–4.26
  data processors, and, 2.76
  Final Report, 4.28–4.29
  generally, 1.24
  Interim Report, 4.23
  introduction, 4.22
  political significance, 4.27
Data processors
  And see Data protection
  agreement with data processor, 2.67
  cross-border data flows, 2.82
  Data Handling Review, 2.76
  data processor as expert, 2.73
  data processor organisation as expert, 2.74
  discharge of duty via expert
    data processor organisations, and, 2.74
    expert, 2.72
    generally, 2.71
    processors, and, 2.73
  FSA Data Security in Financial Services report, 2.78
  government position
    Data Handling Review, 2.76
    Data Security in Financial Services report, 2.78
    ICO guidance, 2.79–2.81
    introduction, 2.75
    OGC Model Terms, 2.77
  Information Commissioner's Office guidance, 2.79–2.81
  introduction, 2.66
  OGC Model Terms, 2.77
  ostensibly competent independent contractors, 2.69
  practical steps, 2.83
  regulators position
    FSA Data Security in Financial Services report, 2.78
    ICO guidance, 2.79–2.81

Index

Data processors—*contd*
  regulators position—*contd*
    introduction, 2.75
    selection of data processor, 2.68
    self-monitoring by data processor, 2.73–2.74
    technical knowledge and experience, 2.70
    transborder data flows, 2.82
    vicarious liability, 2.69

Data protection
  aims, 2.20–2.21
  Article 29 Working party
    compensation for breach of security obligation, 2.96
    generally, 2.38
  assessment notices
    code of practice, 6.147–6.148
    editorial comment, 6.149–6.150
    exempt materials, 6.143
    generally, 6.138
    designating private sector data controllers, 6.141–6.142
    ICO proposals, 6.68
    meaning, 6.139
    monetary penalties, and, 6.158
    recipients, 6.140
    sanctions for non-compliance, 6.145
    time for compliance, 6.144
    use of material obtained, 6.146
  breach notification
    fair processing, 7.4–7.6
    human rights issues, 7.13
    information notices, 7.11–7.12
    introduction, 7.3
    notification, 7.7–7.8
    overview, 2.42
    registration, 7.7–7.8
    subject access, 7.9–7.10
  challenges to regulatory action
    effect of litigation, 6.166
    introduction, 6.165
    litigation strategies, 6.171
    understanding legal position, 6.167
    undertakings, 6.168–6.170
  compensation for breach of security obligation
    Article 29 Working Party's views, 2.96
    'claims farming', and, 2.98
    damage and distress, 2.92–2.96
    consequences for data controllers, 2.97
    generally, 2.91
    Johnson v MDU decision, 2.93–2.95
  Council of Europe Convention (1981), 2.19
  criminal proceedings, 6.159
  'data', 2.27
  data controllers, 2.34

Data protection—*contd*
  data processors, and
    agreement with data processor, 2.67
    cross-border data flows, 2.82
    Data Handling Review, 2.76
    data processor as expert, 2.73
    data processor organisation as expert, 2.74
    definition, 2.35–2.36
    discharge of duty via expert, 2.71–2.72
    FSA Data Security Financial Services report, 2.78
    government position, 2.75–2.81
    Information Commissioner's Office guidance, 2.79–2.81
    introduction, 2.66
    OGC Model Terms, 2.77
    ostensibly competent independent contractors, 2.69
    practical steps, 2.83
    regulators position, 2.75–2.81
    selection of data processor, 2.68
    self-monitoring by data processor, 2.73–2.74
    technical knowledge and experience, 2.70
    transborder data flows, 2.82
    vicarious liability, 2.69
  Data Protection Act 1998
    amendments, 6.101
    definitions, 2.26–2.32
    introduction, 2.16
    main actors, 2.33–2.39
    public sector records management, and, 4.5
    regulatory mechanisms, 2.40–2.45
  data subjects as regulators
    compensation claims, 6.163
    generally, 6.5
    introduction, 6.160
    proceedings for cessation of processing, 6.162
    requests for assessment, 6.161
    subject requests, 6.164
  definitions
    data, 2.27
    general structure, 2.26
    personal data, 2.28
    processing, 2.29–2.31
    protected personal information, 2.32
    sensitive personal data, 2.31
  employees, and
    discipline and dismissal procedures, 2.63
    employee monitoring, 2.61
    Employment Practices Code, 2.59–2.61
    forces subject access, 2.62

Index

Data protection—*contd*
  employees, and—*contd*
    introduction, 2.53
    justification for interference with
      privacy, 2.55
    monitoring of electronic
      communications, 2.56–2.58
    practical steps, 2.65
    pre-employment vetting, 2.60
    privacy within the workplace, 2.54–2.55
    security screening, 2.64
  enforcement, 2.45
  enforcement notices
    action taken by the IC, 6.172–6.173
    appeals, 6.116–6.118
    breach of principles, 6.107
    cancellation, 6.115
    compliance period, 6.114
    content, 6.113
    criminal breach, 6.119–6.120
    criteria, 6.106–6.111
    directors' criminal liability, 6.120
    discretion, 6.112
    form, 6.113
    generally, 6.102
    ICO proposals, 6.70, 6.72
    likelihood of damage or
      distress, 6.109–6.111
    obstacles to service, 6.106–6.111
    seriousness of breach of seventh
      principle, 6.105
    statutory purpose, 6.103–6.104
    steps required are reasonable to
      achieve compliance, 6.108
    time for compliance, 6.114
    variation, 6.115
  EU Directive (1995), 2.19
  European Commission, 2.39
  European law
    aims, 2.20–2.21
    development, 2.19
    introduction, 2.16
    main actors, 2.33–2.39
    objectives, 2.20–2.21
    personal data, 2.22–2.23
    processing, 2.24
    regulatory mechanisms, 2.40–2.45
    structured paper files, 2.25
  global processors, and, 2.21
  human rights, and
    breach notification, 7.13
    generally, 2.20
  information notices
    appeals, 6.127
    breach notification, and, 7.11–7.12
    criminal offences, 6.128

Data protection—*contd*
  information notices—*contd*
    data controller's obligations, 6.124
    generally, 6.121
    ICO proposals, 6.73
    method and timing of furnishing
      information, 6.125
    power to serve, 6.122
    time for compliance, 6.126
    timing of service, 6.123
  inspection powers
    assessment notice regime, 6.138–6.150
    generally, 6.129
    ICO proposals, 6.68
    introduction, 2.42
    report of a skilled person, 6.69
    search warrant regime, 6.130–6.137
  inspection powers (assessment notice
    regime)
    'assessment notice', 6.139
    code of practice, 6.147–6.148
    editorial comment, 6.149–6.150
    exempt materials, 6.143
    generally, 6.138
    designating private sector data
      controllers, 6.141–6.142
    ICO proposals, 6.68
    recipients, 6.140
    sanctions for non-compliance, 6.145
    time for compliance, 6.144
    use of material obtained, 6.146
  inspection powers (search warrant
    regime)
    action taken by the IC, 6.174
    control of power through notice
      requirements, 6.133
    criminal offences, 6.136
    failure to provide assistance, 6.136
    formalities, 6.135
    generally, 6.130
    ICO proposals, 6.68
    notice of intention to apply for
      warrant, 6.132
    notice of wish to gain access, 6.131
    obstruction of officers, 6.136
    powers granted by warrant, 6.134
    proposals to amend, 6.137
  international aspects, 2.18
  introduction, 2.16
  lawfulness
    data protection principles, and, 2.46
    generally, 2.43
  legitimacy
    data protection principles, and, 2.46
    generally, 2.43
  main actors
    Article 29 Working party, 2.38

Index

Data protection—*contd*
  main actors—*contd*
    data controllers, 2.34
    data processors, 2.35–2.36
    European Commission, 2.39
    introduction, 2.33
    regulators, 2.37
  monetary penalties
    amendments to DPA 1998, and, 6.100–6.101
    amount, 6.153
    assessment notices, and, 6.158
    enforcement, 6.156
    guidance, 6.155
    introduction, 6.151
    ICO proposals, 6.67
    notices, 6.155–6.157
    power to impose, 6.152
    procedural rights, 6.154
    Regulators' Compliance Code, and, 6.17
    statutory basis, 6.19
    supplemental provisions, 6.157
  non-automated processing, 2.25
  objections, 2.44
  objectives, 2.20–2.21
  personal data
    Durant v FSA decision, 2.23
    generally, 2.22
    processing, 2.24
    structured paper files, 2.25
    UK law, in, 2.28
  Privacy Enhancing Technologies (PETs), 2.90
  processing
    breach notification, and, 7.4–7.6
    EU law, in, 2.24
    generally, 2.29
    Johnson v MDU decision, 2.30
    special categories, 2.31
  protected personal information, 2.32
  public sector records management, and, 4.5
  regulation and enforcement, and
    action taken by ICO, 6.172–6.176
    amendments in Coroners and Justice Bill, 6.101
    assessment notices, 6.138–6.150
    challenges to regulatory action, 6.165–6.171
    criminal proceedings, 6.159
    data subject, by, 6.160–6.164
    enforcement notices, 6.102–6.120
    Information Commissioner's strategy, 6.98
    information notices, 6.121–6.128
    inspections, 6.129–6.137

Data protection—*contd*
  regulation and enforcement, and—*contd*
    introduction, 6.97
    monetary penalties, 6.151–6.158
    scheme summary, 6.99–6.100
  regulators, 2.37
  regulatory mechanisms
    breach notification, 2.42
    enforcement, 2.45
    inspections, 2.42
    introduction, 2.40
    lawfulness, 2.43
    legitimacy, 2.43
    objections, 2.44
    transparency, 2.41–2.42
  relevant filing system, 2.25
  reliability of data processors
    agreement with data processor, 2.67
    cross-border data flows, 2.82
    Data Handling Review, 2.76
    data processor as expert, 2.73
    data processor organisation as expert, 2.74
    discharge of duty via expert, 2.71–2.72
    FSA Data Security Financial Services report, 2.78
    government position, 2.75–2.81
    Information Commissioner's Office guidance, 2.79–2.81
    introduction, 2.66
    OGC Model Terms, 2.77
    ostensibly competent independent contractors, 2.69
    practical steps, 2.83
    regulators position, 2.75–2.81
    selection of data processor, 2.68
    self-monitoring by data processor, 2.73–2.74
    technical knowledge and experience, 2.70
    transborder data flows, 2.82
    vicarious liability, 2.69
  reliability of employees
    discipline and dismissal procedures, 2.63
    employee monitoring, 2.61
    Employment Practices Code, 2.59–2.61
    forces subject access, 2.62
    introduction, 2.53
    justification for interference with privacy, 2.55
    monitoring of electronic communications, 2.56–2.58
    practical steps, 2.65
    pre-employment vetting, 2.60
    privacy within the workplace, 2.54–2.55

1017

Index

Data protection—*contd*
  reliability of employees—*contd*
    security screening, 2.64
  remedy for breach of security obligation
    Article 29 Working Party's views, 2.96
    'claims farming', and, 2.98
    compensation for damage and distress, 2.92–2.95
    consequences for data controllers, 2.97
    generally, 2.91
    Johnson v MDU decision, 2.93–2.95
  right to respect for private and family life, 2.20
  secrecy laws, and, 5.22
  security principle
    appropriateness of measures taken, 2.49–2.52
    breach by controller, 2.48
    evolution, 2.19
    international aspects, 2.18
    introduction, 2.16
    relationship with other principles, 2.17
    reliability of data processors, 2.66–2.83
    reliability of employees, 2.53–2.65
    remedies for breach of obligation, 2.91–2.98
    safeguards against breaches and data loss, 2.47
    technological development, 2.84–2.90
  sensitive personal data, 2.31
  seventh data protection principle, 2.16
  structured paper files, 2.25
  technological development
    appropriate measure of sufficiency, 2.89
    'Bolam test', and, 2.87
    deployment of technology, 2.86
    generally, 2.84
    industry practice, 2.86
    Privacy Enhancing Technologies (PETs), 2.90
    professional negligence, 2.87–2.88
    state of technology deployment, 2.86
    'state of the art', 2.85
  transborder data flows, 2.82
  transparency, and
    fair processing, 7.4–7.6
    generally, 2.41–2.42
    human rights issues, 7.13
    information notices, 7.11–7.12
    introduction, 7.3
    notification, 7.7–7.8
    registration, 7.7–7.8
    subject access, 7.9–7.10
  vicarious liability, 2.69

'*Data Security in Financial Services*' (FSA, April 2008)
  foreword by Information Commissioner, 6.74
  generally, 6.28

Data security law
  custodial penalties, 1.35–1.44
  'data', 2.2
  'data theft' offence, 1.33–1.34
  development, 1.3–1.4
  HMRC/Child Benefit database case
    aftermath, 1.23
    chronological summary, 1.11–1.16
    conclusions, 1.23
    Data Handling Review, 1.24
    introduction, 1.9–1.10
    IPCC Report findings, 1.20
    IPCC Report recommendations, 1.22
    March 2007 audit, 1.12–1.14
    October 2007 audit, 1.16
    O'Donnell Review, 1.24
    Poynter Report findings, 1.17–1.19
    Poynter Report recommendations, 1.21
    reforms, 1.24
    regulatory consequences, 1.25
    removal of discs off-site, 1.15
  Information Commissioner's powers, 1.27–1.31
  introduction, 1.1
  'regulatory bear market', 1.5–1.8
  regulatory dynamic, 1.26
  sources, 2.1
  themes, 1.2
  '*What price privacy?*' (IC Report, May 2006), 1.32

Data subjects
  regulation and enforcement, and
    compensation claims, 6.163
    generally, 6.5
    introduction, 6.160
    proceedings for cessation of processing, 6.162
    requests for assessment, 6.161
    subject requests, 6.164

Decision Procedure and Penalties Manual
  consultation paper (CP09/19), 6.190
  financial penalties policy, 6.185–6.189
  introduction, 6.184

Decrypted information
  electronic communications privacy, and, 2.122

Digital Britain Report
  public sector, and, 4.59–4.60

Directors' duties
  generally, 3.1–3.2

Index

Disciplinary measures
    regulation and enforcement, and,   6.183
Disclosure notices
    encryption, and,   2.8–2.9
Duty of confidence
    creation,   2.6
    encryption, and
        disclosure notices,   2.8–2.9
        generally,   2.7
        'protected information',   2.8
        Regulation of Investigatory
            Powers Act 2000, and,   2.8–2.10
    generally,   2.3
    human rights, and
        generally,   2.14
        positive obligation,   2.15
    information that has the necessary
        quality,   2.5
    introduction,   2.3
    liability of data controller for
        breach,   2.11–2.12
    liability of third party for
        misappropriation,   2.1
    misappropriation, and,   2.13
    negligence, and,   2.11–2.12
    parameters,   2.4
    right to respect for private and
        family life
        generally,   2.14
        positive obligation,   2.15
    types,   2.6

Electronic Communications Act 2000
    electronic signatures, and,   2.148
Electronic Communications Privacy
    Directive (2002/58/EC)
    breach notification, and
        Article 29 Working Party opinion
            (February 2009),   7.71–7.75
        Commission amended proposal
            (November 2008),   7.68–7.70
        Commission Communication
            (February 2009),   7.83
        Commission proposal (November
            2007),   7.58–7.61
        Committee of the Regions opinion
            (June 2008),   7.63
        composite view,   7.86
        Council's Common Position
            (February 2009),   7.76–7.82
        EESC opinion (May 2008),   7.62
        generally,   7.57
        Parliament debate (September
            2008),   7.64–7.67
        Parliament debate (May 2009),   7.84–7.85
        Privacy Law and Business survey
            (May 2009),   7.87–7.88

Electronic Communications Privacy Directive
    (2002/58/EC)—contd
    differences from 1997 Directive,   2.105
    exceptions from confidentiality
        obligations,   2.106
    generally,   2.101
    security and confidentiality regime,   2.103
    transposition in UK,   2.107
Electronic communications services
    Communications Data Retention
        Directive (2006/24/EC)
        data protection and data security
            regime,   2.104
        generally,   2.101
    Electronic Communications Privacy
        Directive (2002/58/EC)
        differences from 1997 Directive,   2.105
        exceptions from confidentiality
            obligations,   2.106
        generally,   2.101
        security and confidentiality
            regime,   2.103
        transposition in UK,   2.107
    EU Directives,   2.101
    human rights, and,   2.99
    introduction,   2.99
    Privacy and Electronic
        Communications (EC Directive)
        Regulations 2003
        generally,   2.123
        introduction,   2.107
    Regulation of Investigatory Powers
        Act 2000
        'communication',   2.111
        decrypted information,   2.122
        encryption keys,   2.122
        exclusion of criminal liability,   2.117
        facilities for interception,   2.120–2.121
        generally,   2.108
        'in the course of transmission',   2.113–2.115
        'interception',   2.112
        interception in private systems,   2.117
        interception of business
            communications,   2.119
        introduction,   2.107
        'lawful authority',   2.116
        non-real time monitoring,   2.115
        'private telecommunication
            system',   2.110
        'public telecommunication
            system',   2.109
        stored e-mail and voicemail
            messages,   2.114
        supply of decrypted information
            and encryption keys,   2.122
        tort of unlawful interception,   2.118

Index

Electronic communications services—*contd*
  regulators' obligation to ensure
    security, 2.100
  right to respect for private and
    family life, and, 2.99
  Telecommunications Privacy
    Directive (97/66/EC)
    differences from 2002 Directive, 2.105
    exceptions from confidentiality
      obligations, 2.106
    generally, 2.101
    security and confidentiality
      regime, 2.102
Electronic health information (US)
  aims and objectives, 7.104
  generally, 7.103
  obligation to report, 7.105
Electronic Money Directive
  (2006/46/EC)
  financial services, and, 3.25
Electronic records
  National Health Service, and, 4.67–4.68
Electronic signatures
  advanced electronic signatures
    creation, 2.141
    definition, 2.140
    generally, 2.141
  advanced electronic signatures based
    on qualified certificates
    certification-service-providers, 2.143
    creation, 2.141
    definition, 2.140
    generally, 2.141
    liability for reliance on qualified
      certificate, 2.147
    qualified certificates, 2.142
    secure-signature creation devices, 2.144
  certification-service-providers
    accreditation, 2.146
    generally, 2.143
    supervision, 2.146
  Cybercrime Convention, 2.139
  definition, 2.140
  Electronic Communications
    Act 2000, 2.148
  EU Directive (1999/93/EC)
    generally, 2.139
    transposition, 2.148
  generally, 2.139
  legal effect, 2.145
  market access, 2.146
  Regulations 2002
    generally, 2.148
    introduction, 2.139
    secure-signature creation devices, 2.144
    types, 2.140

E-mail messages
  electronic communications privacy,
    and, 2.114
Employees
  data protection, and
    discipline and dismissal
      procedures, 2.63
    employee monitoring, 2.61
    Employment Practices Code, 2.59–2.61
    forces subject access, 2.62
    introduction, 2.53
    justification for interference with
      privacy, 2.55
    monitoring of electronic
      communications, 2.56–2.58
    practical steps, 2.65
    pre-employment vetting, 2.60
    privacy within the workplace, 2.54–2.55
    security screening, 2.64
Encryption
  disclosure notices, 2.8–2.9
  generally, 2.7
  'protected information', 2.8
  Regulation of Investigatory Powers
    Act 2000, and, 2.8–2.10
Encryption keys
  electronic communications privacy,
    and, 2.122
Enforcement notices
  action taken by the IC, 6.172–6.173
  appeals, 6.116–6.118
  breach of principles, 6.107
  cancellation, 6.115
  compliance period, 6.114
  content, 6.113
  criminal breach
    directors' liability, 6.120
    generally, 6.119
  criteria
    breach of principles, 6.107
    introduction, 6.106
    likelihood of damage or
      distress, 6.109–6.111
    steps required are reasonable to
      achieve compliance, 6.108
  directors' criminal liability, 6.120
  discretion, 6.112
  form, 6.113
  generally, 6.102
  ICO proposals, 6.70, 6.72
  likelihood of damage or distress, 6.109–6.111
  obstacles to service
    breach of principles, 6.107
    introduction, 6.106

1020

Index

Enforcement notices—*contd*
  obstacles to service—*contd*
    likelihood of damage or
      distress, 6.109–6.111
    steps required are reasonable to
      achieve compliance, 6.108
  seriousness of breach of seventh
    principle, 6.105
  statutory purpose, 6.103–6.104
  steps required are reasonable to
    achieve compliance, 6.108
  time for compliance, 6.114
  variation, 6.115

EU Directives
  breach notification, and
    Article 29 Working Party opinion
      (February 2009), 7.71–7.75
    Commission amended proposal
      (November 2008), 7.68–7.70
    Commission Communication
      (February 2009), 7.83
    Commission proposal (November
      2007), 7.58–7.61
    Committee of the Regions opinion
      (June 2008), 7.63
    composite view, 7.86
    Council's Common Position
      (February 2009), 7.76–7.82
    EESC opinion (May 2008), 7.62
    generally, 7.57
    Parliament debate (September
      2008), 7.64–7.67
    Parliament debate (May 2009), 7.84–7.85
    Privacy Law and Business survey
      (May 2009), 7.87–7.88
  data protection, and, 2.19
  electronic communications, and, 2.101
  electronic signatures, and
    generally, 2.139
    transposition, 2.148
  financial services, and
    Banking Consolidation, 3.14–3.15
    Capital Adequacy, 3.14
    Electronic Money, 3.25
    Market Abuse, 3.19–3.20
    Market in Financial Instruments, 3.16–3.18
    Money Laundering, 3.22
    Payment Services, 3.23–3.24
    Prospectus, 3.21
  transparency, and, 3.4–3.5

European Commission
  data protection, and, 2.39

European law
  breach notification, and
    Electronic Communications
      Privacy Directive
      (2002/58/EC), 7.57–7.88
  data protection, and
    aims, 2.20–2.21
    development, 2.19
    introduction, 2.16
    main actors, 2.33–2.39
    objectives, 2.20–2.21
    personal data, 2.22–2.23
    processing, 2.24
    regulatory mechanisms, 2.40–2.45
    structured paper files, 2.25

Fair processing
And see Processing
  breach notification, and, 7.4–7.6

Federal Trade Commission (breach notification)
  electronic health information
    aims and objectives, 7.104
    generally, 7.103
    obligation to report, 7.105
  introduction, 7.98
  Red Flag Rules
    financial institutions, 7.102
    introduction, 7.99
    management responsibility, 7.101
    warning signs, 7.100

Financial Crime newsletter (October 2007)
  regulation and enforcement, and, 6.27

Financial Reporting Council (FRC) guidance
  corporate governance, and, 3.10

Financial services
  Banking Consolidation Directive
    (2006/48/EC), 3.14–3.15
  Basel II, 3.14
  Capital Adequacy Directive
    (2006/49/EC), 3.14
  Electronic Money Directive
    (2006/46/EC), 3.25
  EU Directives
    Banking Consolidation, 3.14–3.15
    Capital Adequacy, 3.14
    Electronic Money, 3.25
    Market Abuse, 3.19–3.20
    Market in Financial Instruments, 3.16–3.18
    Money Laundering, 3.22
    Payment Services, 3.23–3.24
    Prospectus, 3.21
  Financial Services and Markets
    Act 2000, 3.26–3.27

Index

Financial services—*contd*
FSA Handbook
  introduction, 3.28
  other, 3.35
  Principles for Business (PRIN), 3.29–3.30
  Senior Management,
    Arrangements, Systems and
    Controls (SYSC), 3.31–3.33
  Supervision (SUP), 3.34
introduction, 3.13
Market Abuse Directive, 3.19–3.20
Market in Financial Instruments
  Directives, 3.16–3.18
Money Laundering Directive, 3.22
Payment Card Industry Data
  Security Standard (PCI DSS), 3.36–3.37
Payment Services Directive, 3.23–3.24
Principles for Business (PRIN), 3.29–3.30
Prospectus Directive, 3.21
reduction of financial crime, 3.27
Senior Management, Arrangements,
  Systems and Controls, 3.31–3.33
Supervision (SUP), 3.34

Financial Services and Markets Act 2000
action taken by FSA, 6.191
Decision Procedure and Penalties
  Manual 6.184–6.190
disciplinary measures, 6.183
FSA Financial Crime Sector Team, 6.178
FSA Handbook, 6.180
general rule making power, 6.180
introduction, 6.177
investigations, 6.181–6.182
statutory scheme, 6.179–6.180

Financial Services Authority (FSA)
And see Financial services
And see FSA Handbook
breach notification, 7.89
Data Security in Financial Services
  report, 2.78
regulation and enforcement, and
  'Countering Financial Crime Risks
    in Information Security', 6.26
  creation of regulatory bear
    market, 6.24
  '*Data Security in Financial
    Services*', 6.28
  differences from ICO's role, 6.23
  Financial Crime newsletter, 6.27
  generally, 6.22
  introduction, 6.20
  overview, 6.2
  public statements, 6.25–6.29

Financial Services Authority (FSA)—*contd*
regulation and enforcement, and—*contd*
  'Review of financial crime
    controls in offshore centres', 6.29
Freedom of Information Act 2000
public sector records management,
  and, 4.4
FSA Data Security in Financial Services report
data processors, and, 2.78
FSA Financial Crime Sector Team
regulation and enforcement, and, 6.178
FSA Handbook
corporate governance, and, 3.9
financial services, and
  introduction, 3.28
  other, 3.35
  Principles for Business (PRIN), 3.29–3.30
  Senior Management,
    Arrangements, Systems and
    Controls (SYSC), 3.31–3.33
  Supervision (SUP), 3.34
regulation and enforcement, and, 6.180
secrecy laws, and
  Audit Directive, 5.27
  introduction, 5.23
  MiFID, 5.26
  Payment Services Directive, 5.24
  Transparency Directive, 5.25
transparency, and, 3.6

General Medical Council's guidance
secrecy laws, and, 5.29
Google
National Health Service, and, 4.79
GovCERTUK
CESG services, and, 4.11
'*Guidance on data security breach
  management*' (ICO, March 2008)
  content of reports, 7.24
  generally, 7.21
  initial considerations, 7.22
  introduction, 7.20
  reporting to other third parties, 7.23

Hampton Report (HMT, March 2005)
consequences, 6.13
generally, 6.9
recommendations and principles, 6.10
HMG Security Policy Framework
access controls, 4.38
access rights, 4.39
accountability, 4.40–4.41
accreditation of technology, 4.42
audits, 4.43
awareness programmes, 4.54
breach notification, and, 7.56

Index

HMG Security Policy Framework—*contd*
  business continuity, 4.44
  contractual control, 4.45
  core security principles, 4.37
  disaster recovery, 4.44
  employee-worker due diligence, 4.46
  encryption, 4.47
  introduction, 4.35
  outsourcing, 4.52
  physical security, 4.48
  security policy, 4.49–4.50
  third party assurance, 4.52
  threat assessment, 4.51
  training programmes, 4.54
  transparency, 4.53
  use of data processors, 4.52
  vulnerability assessment, 4.51
  waste, 4.55

HMRC/Child Benefit database case
  aftermath, 1.23
  chronological summary, 1.11–1.16
  conclusions, 1.23
  Data Handling Review, 1.24
  introduction, 1.9–1.10
  IPCC Report findings, 1.20
  IPCC Report recommendations, 1.22
  March 2007 audit, 1.12–1.14
  October 2007 audit, 1.16
  O'Donnell Review, 1.24
  Poynter Report findings, 1.17–1.19
  Poynter Report recommendations, 1.21
  public sector, and, 4.1
  reforms, 1.24
  regulatory consequences, 1.25
  removal of discs off-site, 1.15

Home Affairs Committee inquiry (HoC)
  breach notification, and, 7.17
  oral evidence (May 2007), 6.36–6.40
  written evidence (November 2007), 6.47–6.50

House of Lords Constitution Committee inquiry
  oral evidence (November 2007), 6.51–6.56
  response (April 2009), 6.91
  written evidence (June 2007), 6.41–6.44

Human rights
  breach notification, and, 7.13
  confidentiality, and
    generally, 2.14
    positive obligation, 2.15
  data protection, and, 2.20
  electronic communications, and, 2.99
  public sector, and, 4.1

Human rights—*contd*
  transparency, and, 7.13

Identity Cards Act 2006
  secrecy laws, and, 5.20

Identity theft warnings
  regulation and enforcement, and, 6.46

Independent contractors
  data processors, and, 2.69

Information Commissioner
  action taken, 6.172–6.176
  '*Banks in unacceptable data protection breach*', 6.34–6.35
  breach notification, and
    Data Handling Review, 7.44–7.45
  data security breach management, 7.21–7.24
  guidance (March 2008), 7.20–7.36
  Home Affairs Committee inquiry (HoC, November 2007), 7.17
  introduction, 7.15
  notification of security breaches, 7.25–7.36
  Personal Internet Security report (HoL, August 2007), 7.15–7.16
  Protection of Private Data report (HoC, January 2008), 7.18–7.19
  RSA Conference Europe speech (October 2008), 7.40–7.43
  Thomas-Walport Data Sharing Review (July 2008), 7.37–7.39
  '*Case for Amending the Data Protection Act*', 6.66–6.73
  '*CEOs urged to raise their game following unacceptable privacy breaches*', 6.45
  '*Confidential details lost by Revenue and Customs*', 6.57
  Constitution Committee inquiry (HoL)
    oral evidence (November 2007), 6.51–6.56
    response (April 2009), 6.91
    written evidence (June 2007), 6.41–6.44
  Coroners and Justice Bill
    additional commentary (February 2009), 6.89
    commentary (May 2009), 6.92–6.94
    effect on DPA 1998, and, 6.101
    memorandum (July 2009), 6.95–6.96
    memorandum and commentary (January 2009), 6.88
  data processors, and, 2.79–2.81
  foreword to 'Data Security in Financial Services', 6.74

1023

Index

Information Commissioner—*contd*
'*Guidance on data security breach management*' (March 2008)
- content of reports, 7.24
- generally, 7.21
- initial considerations, 7.22
- introduction, 7.20
- reporting to other third parties, 7.23

Home Affairs Committee inquiry (HoC)
- oral evidence (May 2007), 6.36–6.40
- written evidence (November 2007), 6.47–6.50
- identity theft warnings, 6.46

Joint Committee on Human Rights response (February 2009), 6.90

Justice Committee inquiry (December 2007), 6.63–6.65

memorandum and commentary on Coroners and Justice Bill, 6.88–6.89, 6.92–6.96

Ministry of Defence, and, 4.10
National Health Service, and, 4.77–4.78

'*Notification of Security Breaches to the ICO*' (ICO, March 2008)
- causing harm, 7.27–7.29
- consequences of reporting, 7.34
- formal action, 7.35
- generally, 7.25
- incentivising non-reporting, 7.36
- informal action, 7.35
- information to be reported, 7.33
- introduction, 7.20
- potential for significant harm, 7.29
- presumption to report, 7.26
- rule of thumb approach, 7.30
- sensitivity of data affected, 7.32
- volume of data affected, 7.30–7.31

'*Our approach to encryption*', 6.58–6.62

regulation and enforcement, and
- action taken, 6.172–6.176
- '*Banks in unacceptable data protection breach*', 6.34–6.35
- '*Case for Amending the Data Protection Act*', 6.66–6.73
- '*CEOs urged to raise their game following unacceptable privacy breaches*', 6.45
- '*Confidential details lost by Revenue and Customs*', 6.57
- Constitution Committee inquiry (June 2007), 6.41–6.44
- Constitution Committee inquiry (November 2007), 6.51–6.56
- creation of regulatory bear market, 6.24
- differences from FSA's role, 6.23

Information Commissioner—*contd*
regulation and enforcement, and—*contd*
- foreword to 'Data Security in Financial Services', 6.74
- generally, 6.21
- Home Affairs Committee inquiry (May 2007), 6.36–6.40
- Home Affairs Committee inquiry (November 2007), 6.47–6.50
- identity theft warnings, 6.46
- introduction, 6.20
- Justice Committee inquiry (December 2007), 6.63–6.65
- memorandum and commentary on Coroners and Justice Bill, 6.88–6.89, 6.92–6.96
- '*Our approach to encryption*', 6.58–6.62
- overview, 6.2
- public statements, 6.30–6.96
- response to Constitution Committee inquiry, 6.91
- response to Joint Committee on Human Rights, 6.90
- RSA Conference speech, 6.75–6.81
- '*Taking stock, taking action*', 6.82–6.87
- '*What Price Privacy?*', 6.31–6.33
- RSA Conference speech, 6.75–6.81
- '*Taking stock, taking action*', 6.82–6.87

'*What price privacy?*' (IC Report, May 2006)
- generally, 6.31
- imprisonment for unlawfully obtaining personal data, 6.32
- *News of the World* case, 6.33

'*Information Governance in the DoH and NHS*'
National Health Service, and, 4.75

Information notices
- appeals, 6.127
- breach notification, and, 7.11–7.12
- criminal offences, 6.128
- data controller's obligations, 6.124
- generally, 6.121
- ICO proposals, 6.73
- method and timing of furnishing information, 6.125
- power to serve, 6.122
- time for compliance, 6.126
- timing of service, 6.123

Information Security Management Code
National Health Service, and, 4.70

Injunctions
regulation and enforcement, and, 6.70

Index

Inspection powers
assessment notice regime
  'assessment notice', 6.139
  code of practice, 6.147–6.148
  editorial comment, 6.149–6.150
  exempt materials, 6.143
  generally, 6.138
  designating private sector data controllers, 6.141–6.142
  ICO proposals, 6.68
  recipients, 6.140
  sanctions for non-compliance, 6.145
  time for compliance, 6.144
  use of material obtained, 6.146
data protection, and, 2.42
generally, 6.129
ICO proposals, 6.68
report of a skilled person, 6.69
search warrant regime
  action taken by the IC, 6.174
  control of power through notice requirements, 6.133
  criminal offences, 6.136
  failure to provide assistance, 6.136
  formalities, 6.135
  generally, 6.130
  ICO proposals, 6.68
  notice of intention to apply for warrant, 6.132
  notice of wish to gain access, 6.131
  obstruction of officers, 6.136
  powers granted by warrant, 6.134
  proposals to amend, 6.137

Institute of Chartered Accountants Handbook
secrecy laws, and, 5.29

Interception of communications
Communications Data Retention Directive (2006/24/EC)
  data protection and data security regime, 2.104
  generally, 2.101
Electronic Communications Privacy Directive (2002/58/EC)
  differences from 1997 Directive, 2.105
  exceptions from confidentiality obligations, 2.106
  generally, 2.101
  security and confidentiality regime, 2.103
  transposition in UK, 2.107
EU Directives, 2.101
human rights, and, 2.99
introduction, 2.99

Interception of communications—*contd*
Privacy and Electronic Communications (EC Directive) Regulations 2003
  generally, 2.123
  introduction, 2.107
Regulation of Investigatory Powers Act 2000
  'communication', 2.111
  decrypted information, 2.122
  encryption keys, 2.122
  exclusion of criminal liability, 2.117
  facilities for interception, 2.120–2.121
  generally, 2.108
  'in the course of transmission', 2.113–2.115
  'interception', 2.112
  interception in private systems, 2.117
  interception of business communications, 2.119
  introduction, 2.107
  'lawful authority', 2.116
  non-real time monitoring, 2.115
  'private telecommunication system', 2.110
  'public telecommunication system', 2.109
  stored e-mail and voicemail messages, 2.114
  supply of decrypted information and encryption keys, 2.122
  tort of unlawful interception, 2.118
regulators' obligation to ensure security, 2.100
right to respect for private and family life, and, 2.99
Telecommunications Privacy Directive (97/66/EC)
  differences from 2002 Directive, 2.105
  exceptions from confidentiality obligations, 2.106
  generally, 2.101
  security and confidentiality regime, 2.102

Investigations
regulation and enforcement, and, 6.181–6.182

ISO 27000 series
breach notification, and, 7.114

Joint Committee on Human Rights
response (February 2009), 6.90

Justice Committee inquiry (HoC)
December 2007 oral evidence, 6.63–6.65

Lawful authority
electronic communications privacy, and, 2.116

1025

Index

Lawfulness
  data protection, and
    data protection principles, and,   2.46
    generally,   2.43
Legislative and Regulatory Reform Act 2006
  generally,   6.14
  Statutory Code of Practice for Regulators,   6.15–6.18
Legitimacy
  data protection principles, and,   2.46
  generally,   2.43

Macrory Report (BRE, November 2006)
  consequences,   6.13
  generally,   6.11
  sanction regime design,   6.12
Management of Police Information Code
  generally,   4.81
  guidance,   4.85
  Information Management Strategy,   4.83
  security,   4.84
  statutory basis,   4.82
Market Abuse Directives
  financial services, and,   3.19–3.20
Market in Financial Instruments Directives (MiFID)
  financial services, and,   3.16–3.18
Ministry of Defence
  Burton Report
    background,   4.92
    data protection,   4.100
    encryption statistics,   4.96
    failure to encrypt,   4.99
    good practices at MoD,   4.102
    Information Commissioner's response,   4.104
    introduction,   4.93
    loss of TAFMIS laptop,   4.95
    management of data,   4.100
    recommendations,   4.101
    TAFMIS system,   4.97–4.98
    transformational government, and,   4.94
  Information Commissioner's actions,   4.104
  introduction,   4.92
  MoD Action Plan,   4.103
Misappropriation
  duty of confidence, and,   2.13
Misuse of systems and data
  police service, and,   4.91
Monetary penalties
  amendments to DPA 1998, and,   6.100–6.101
  amount,   6.153

Monetary penalties—*contd*
  assessment notices, and,   6.158
  enforcement,   6.156
  guidance,   6.155
  introduction,   6.151
  ICO proposals,   6.67
  notices,   6.155–6.157
  power to impose,   6.152
  procedural rights,   6.154
  Regulators' Compliance Code, and,   6.17
  statutory basis,   6.19
  supplemental provisions,   6.157
Money Laundering Directive (2005/60/EC)
  financial services, and,   3.22

National Archives
  public sector records management, and,   4.6
National Health Service (NHS)
  Caldicott Committee Report,   4.72–4.73
  Caldicott Guardian Manual 2006,   4.74
  Cayton Report,   4.75
  codes of practice
    Confidentiality,   4.71
    Information Security Management,   4.70
    introduction,   4.69
  Confidentiality Code,   4.71
  electronic records,   4.67–4.68
  Google, and,   4.79
  Information Commissioner's actions,   4.77–4.78
  '*Information Governance in the DoH and NHS*',   4.75
  Information Security Management Code,   4.70
  information systems and technology,   4.65–4.66
  introduction,   4.64
  other polices and advice,   4.75
  Patient-Identifiable Information Review,   4.72–4.73
National Information Assurance Strategy
  public sector, and,   4.20–4.21
National Policing Improvement Agency
  police service, and,   4.90
National Risk Register
  public sector, and,   4.33–4.34
National Security Strategy
  general,   4.30
  update,   4.56–4.57
National Technical Authority for Information Assurance (CESG)
  CAPS,   4.12
  Claims Tested Mark,   4.15
  CLAS,   4.13

Index

National Technical Authority for Information Assurance (CESG)—*contd*
  CTAS, 4.14
  generally, 4.10
  GovCERTUK, 4.11

Negligence
  duty of confidence, and, 2.11–2.12

News of the World case
  regulation and enforcement, and, 6.33

Non-automated processing
  data protection, and, 2.25

Non-real time monitoring
  electronic communications privacy, and, 2.115

'Notification of Security Breaches to the ICO' (ICO, March 2008)
  causing harm, 7.27–7.29
  consequences of reporting, 7.34
  formal action, 7.35
  generally, 7.25
  incentivising non-reporting, 7.36
  informal action, 7.35
  information to be reported, 7.33
  introduction, 7.20
  potential for significant harm, 7.29
  presumption to report, 7.26
  rule of thumb approach, 7.30
  sensitivity of data affected, 7.32
  volume of data affected, 7.30–7.31

O'Donnell Report (June 2008)
  breach notification, and
    government's position, 7.52–7.55
    Information Commissioner's position, 7.44–7.45
  Cross Government Actions, 4.24–4.26
  data processors, and, 2.76
  Final Report, 4.28–4.29
  generally, 1.24
  Interim Report, 4.23
  introduction, 4.22
  political significance, 4.27

OFCOM
  regulation and enforcement, and, 6.2

Office of Fair Trading
  regulation and enforcement, and, 6.2

'Our approach to encryption' (ICO, November 2007)
  regulation and enforcement, and, 6.58–6.62

Press Complaints Commission
  regulation and enforcement, and, 6.3

Privacy enhancing technologies (PETs)
  Constitution Committee inquiry (HoL, June 2007), 6.43
  Constitution Committee inquiry (HoL, November 2007), 6.55

Privacy enhancing technologies (PETs)—*contd*
  Home Affairs Committee inquiry (HoC, November 2007), 6.47
  memorandum and commentary on Coroners and Justice Bill, 6.96
  '*Our approach to encryption*' (ICO, November 2007), 6.59
  '*Taking stock, taking action*' (ICO, November 2008), 6.85

Privacy impact assessments
  Constitution Committee inquiry (HoL, June 2007), 6.44
  Constitution Committee inquiry (HoL, November 2007), 6.56
  Home Affairs Committee inquiry (HoC, May 2007), 6.40
  Home Affairs Committee inquiry (HoC, November 2007), 6.50
  memorandum and commentary on Coroners and Justice Bill, 6.96
  '*Taking stock, taking action*' (ICO, November 2008), 6.84

Private investigators
  regulation and enforcement, and, 6.3

Office of Cyber Security
  public sector, and, 4.17

Official secrets
  See also Secrecy laws
  information entrusted in confidence to other states etc, 5.15
  information relating to country's defence, 5.11
  information relating to crime
    generally, 5.13
    special investigation powers under statutory warrant, 5.14
  information relating to international relations, 5.12
  information relating to national security and intelligence
    damaging disclosures, 5.9
    disclosure, 5.8
    members of security and intelligence services, 5.7
    Shayler case, 5.10
  information resulting from unauthorised disclosures, 5.16
  introduction, 5.2
  members of security and intelligence services, 5.7
  Official Secrets Act 1911, 5.3
  Official Secrets Act 1920, 5.4
  Official Secrets Act 1989
    Clive Ponting case, 5.6
    information entrusted in confidence to other states etc, 5.15

Index

Official secrets—*contd*
  Official Secrets Act 1989—*contd*
    information relating to country's
      defence, 5.11
    information relating to crime, 5.13–5.14
    information relating to
      international relations, 5.12
    information relating to national
      security and intelligence, 5.7–5.10
    information resulting from
      unauthorised disclosures, 5.16
    introduction, 5.5
    return of information, 5.17
    overview, 5.1
    special investigation powers under
      statutory warrant, 5.14
OGC Model Terms
  data processors, and, 2.77
Online banking fraud
  breach notification, and, 7.47

Patient-Identifiable Information Review
  National Health Service, and, 4.72–4.73
Payment Card Industry Data Security
  Standard (PCI DSS)
  financial services, and, 3.36–3.37
Payment Services Directive
  (2997/64/EC)
  financial services, and, 3.23–3.24
Personal data
  And see Data protection
  Durant v FSA decision, 2.23
  generally, 2.22
  processing, 2.24
  structured paper files, 2.25
  UK law, in, 2.28
Personal Internet Security report (HoL,
  August 2007)
  breach notification, and
    government's position, 7.46–7.49
    Information Commissioner's
      position, 7.15–7.16
Police service
  ACPO/ACPOS Information Systems
    CSP, 4.80
  Management of Police Information
    code
    generally, 4.81
    guidance, 4.85
    Information Management
      Strategy, 4.83
    security, 4.84
    statutory basis, 4.82
  misuse of systems and data, 4.91
  National Policing Improvement
    Agency, 4.90
  processes for date sharing, 4.86

Police service—*contd*
  secure disposal of data, 4.89
  worker education, 4.88
Poynter Report (June 2008)
  findings, 1.17–1.19
  introduction, 1.9
  recommendations, 1.21
Press Complaints Commission
  secrecy laws, and, 5.30
Principles for Business (PRIN)
  financial services, and, 3.29–3.30
Privacy and Electronic
  Communications (EC Directive)
  Regulations 2003
  generally, 2.123
  introduction, 2.107
Privacy Enhancing Technologies (PETs)
  And see Data protection
  accreditation scheme, 8.28–8.29
  Commission's definition, 8.20
  Commission's objectives, 8.21–8.24
  compliance with data protection
    principles, 8.11
  control mechanisms in data
    protection law
    contractual control mechanism, 8.5
    generally, 8.3
    geographical control mechanism, 8.4
    refocusing on the technological
      control mechanism, 8.6
  Date Protection Guidance Note, 8.14–8.15
  data protection principles, 8.19
  definitions, 8.10
  development of data security law,
    and, 1.4
  economic benefits, 8.25
  EU position, 8.18
  examples
    encryption, 8.8–8.9
    generally, 8.7
  generally, 2.90
  introduction, 8.1–8.2
  legal effect, 8.27
  PETs – Your New Best Friends, 8.12–8.13
  Privacy By Design (Information
    Commissioner), 8.30
  risks to personal data, 8.19
  use by consumers, 8.24
  use by data controllers, 8.23
  White Paper for Decision-Makers, 8.16–8.17
Private telecommunication system
  electronic communications privacy,
    and, 2.110

Index

Processing
And see Data protection
  breach notification, and,   7.4–7.6
  EU law, in,   2.24
  generally,   2.29
  Johnson v MDU decision,   2.30
  special categories,   2.31
Prospectus Directive (2003/71/EC)
  financial services, and,   3.21
Protected information
  encryption, and,   2.8
Protected personal information
  data protection, and,   2.32
Protecting Government Information (June 2008)
  breach notification, and,   7.51
  generally,   4.32
Protection of Private Data report (HoC, January 2008)
  breach notification, and
    government's position,   7.50
    Information Commissioner's position,   7.18–7.19
Public sector
  application of laws and rules,   4.1
  Burton Report (2005),   4.2
  Central Sponsor for Information Assurance (CSIA)
    generally,   4.9
    National Information Assurance Strategy,   4.20–4.21
  Centre for the Protection of National Infrastructure,   4.16
  CAPS,   4.12
  Civil Service Management Code,   4.61
  Claims Tested Mark,   4.15
  CLAS,   4.13
  CTAS,   4.14
  codes of practice for records management
    international standards,   4.7
    National Archives,   4.6
  Coleman Report,   4.32
  contracting with public sector,   4.62
  Cross Government Actions,   4.24–4.26
  Cyber Security Operations Centre,   4.17
  Cyber Security Strategy,   4.58
  Data Handling Review
    Cross Government Actions,   4.24–4.26
    Final Report,   4.28–4.29
    Interim Report,   4.23
    introduction,   4.22
    political significance,   4.27
  Data Protection Act 1998,   4.5
  Digital Britain Report,   4.59–4.60
  Freedom of Information Act 2000,   4.4
  GovCERTUK,   4.11

Public sector—*contd*
  HMG Security Policy Framework,   4.35
  HMRC/Child Benefit database case,   4.1
  human rights, and,   4.1
  introduction,   4.1
  Ministry of Defence
    Burton Report,   4.93–4.102
    Information Commissioner's actions,   4.104
    introduction,   4.92
    MoD Action Plan,   4.103
  model contract terms,   4.62
  National Archives,   4.6
  National Health Service (NHS), and
    Caldicott Committee Report,   4.72–4.73
    Caldicott Guardian Manual 2006,   4.74
    Cayton Report,   4.75
    codes of practice,   4.69–4.71
    Confidentiality Code,   4.71
    electronic records,   4.67–4.68
    Google, and,   4.79
    Information Commissioner's actions,   4.77–4.78
    'Information Governance in the DoH and NHS',   4.75
    Information Security Management Code,   4.70
    information systems and technology,   4.65–4.66
    introduction,   4.64
    other polices and advice,   4.75
    Patient-Identifiable Information Review,   4.72–4.73
  National Information Assurance Strategy,   4.20–4.21
  National Risk Register,   4.33–4.34
  National Security Strategy
    general,   4.30
    update,   4.56–4.57
  National Technical Authority for Information Assurance (CESG)
    CAPS,   4.12
    Claims Tested Mark,   4.15
    CLAS,   4.13
    CTAS,   4.14
    generally,   4.10
    GovCERTUK,   4.11
  Office of Cyber Security,   4.17
  police service, and
    ACPO/ACPOS Information Systems CSP,   4.80
    Management of Police Information code,   4.81–4.85
    misuse of systems and data,   4.91
    National Policing Improvement Agency,   4.90

Index

Public sector—*contd*
  police service, and—*contd*
    processes for date sharing, 4.86
    secure disposal of data, 4.89
    worker education, 4.88
  Protecting Government Information (June 2008), 4.32
  reports and policy statements
    Coleman Report, 4.32
    consequences for public sector, 4.19
    Cyber Security Strategy, 4.58
    Data Handling Review, 4.22–4.29
    Digital Britain Report, 4.59–4.60
    HMG Security Policy Framework, 4.35–4.55
    introduction, 4.18
    National Information Assurance Strategy, 4.20–4.21
    National Risk Register, 4.33–4.34
    National Security Strategy, 4.30
  responsible authorities
    Central Sponsor for Information Assurance, 4.9
    Centre for the Protection of National Infrastructure, 4.16
    Cyber Security Operations Centre, 4.17
    introduction, 4.8
    National Technical Authority for Information Assurance, 4.10–4.15
    Office of Cyber Security, 4.17
  security considerations
    codes of practice for records management, 4.6–4.7
    Data Protection Act 1998, 4.5
    Freedom of Information Act 2000, 4.4
    introduction, 4.3
  Security Policy Framework
    access controls, 4.38
    access rights, 4.39
    accountability, 4.40–4.41
    accreditation of technology, 4.42
    audits, 4.43
    awareness programmes, 4.54
    business continuity, 4.44
    contractual control, 4.45
    core security principles, 4.37
    disaster recovery, 4.44
    employee-worker due diligence, 4.46
    encryption, 4.47
    introduction, 4.35
    outsourcing, 4.52
    physical security, 4.48
    security policy, 4.49–4.50
    third party assurance, 4.52
    threat assessment, 4.51
    training programmes, 4.54

Public sector—*contd*
  Security Policy Framework—*contd*
    transparency, 4.53
    use of data processors, 4.52
    vulnerability assessment, 4.51
    waste, 4.55
  'Transformational Government' (Cabinet Office, 2005), 4.2

Public telecommunication system
  electronic communications privacy, and, 2.109

Record-keeping obligations
  companies, and, 3.2

Red Flag Rules (US)
  financial institutions, 7.102
  introduction, 7.99
  management responsibility, 7.101
  warning signs, 7.100

Regulation
  assessment notices
    code of practice, 6.147–6.148
    editorial comment, 6.149–6.150
    exempt materials, 6.143
    generally, 6.138
    designating private sector data controllers, 6.141–6.142
    ICO proposals, 6.68
    meaning, 6.139
    monetary penalties, and, 6.158
    recipients, 6.140
    sanctions for non-compliance, 6.145
    time for compliance, 6.144
    use of material obtained, 6.146
  'Banks in unacceptable data protection breach' (ICO, March 2007), 6.34–6.35
  'Case for Amending the Data Protection Act' (ICO, December 2007), 6.66–6.73
  'CEOs urged to raise their game following unacceptable privacy breaches', (ICO, July 2007), 6.45
  challenges to regulatory action
    effect of litigation, 6.166
    introduction, 6.165
    litigation strategies, 6.171
    understanding legal position, 6.167
    undertakings, 6.168–6.170
  'Confidential details lost by Revenue and Customs' (ICO, November 2007), 6.57
  Constitution Committee inquiry (HoL)
    oral evidence (November 2007), 6.51–6.56
    response (April 2009), 6.91

Regulation—*contd*
  Constitution Committee inquiry
    (HoL)—*contd*
    written evidence (June 2007), 6.41–6.44
  contractual control mechanisms, and, 6.4
  Coroners and Justice Bill
    additional commentary (February 2009), 6.89
    commentary (May 2009), 6.92–6.94
    effect on DPA 1998, and, 6.101
    memorandum (July 2009), 6.95–6.96
    memorandum and commentary (January 2009), 6.88
  '*Countering Financial Crime Risks in Information Security*' (FSA, November 2004), 6.26
  criminal proceedings
    action taken by the IC, 6.174
    generally, 6.159
  Data Protection Act 1998, under
    action taken by ICO, 6.172–6.176
    amendments in Coroners and Justice Bill, 6.101
    assessment notices, 6.138–6.150
    challenges to regulatory action, 6.165–6.171
    criminal proceedings, 6.159
    data subject, by, 6.160–6.164
    enforcement notices, 6.102–6.120
    Information Commissioner's strategy, 6.98
    information notices, 6.121–6.128
    inspections, 6.129–6.137
    introduction, 6.97
    monetary penalties, 6.151–6.158
    scheme summary, 6.99–6.100
  '*Data Security in Financial Services*' (FSA, April 2008)
    foreword by Information Commissioner, 6.74
    generally, 6.28
  data subjects, by
    compensation claims, 6.163
    generally, 6.5
    introduction, 6.160
    proceedings for cessation of processing, 6.162
    requests for assessment, 6.161
    subject requests, 6.164
  Decision Procedure and Penalties Manual
    consultation paper (CP09/19), 6.190
    financial penalties policy, 6.185–6.189
    introduction, 6.184
    disciplinary measures, 6.183

Regulation—*contd*
  enforcement notices
    action taken by the IC, 6.172–6.173
    appeals, 6.116–6.118
    breach of principles, 6.107
    cancellation, 6.115
    compliance period, 6.114
    content, 6.113
    criminal breach, 6.119–6.120
    criteria, 6.106–6.111
    directors' criminal liability, 6.120
    discretion, 6.112
    form, 6.113
    generally, 6.102
    ICO proposals, 6.70, 6.72
    likelihood of damage or distress, 6.109–6.111
    obstacles to service, 6.106–6.111
    seriousness of breach of seventh principle, 6.105
    statutory purpose, 6.103–6.104
    steps required are reasonable to achieve compliance, 6.108
    time for compliance, 6.114
    variation, 6.115
  Financial Crime newsletter (October 2007), 6.27
  Financial Services and Markets Act 2000, under
    action taken by FSA, 6.191
    Decision Procedure and Penalties Manual 6.184–6.190
    disciplinary measures, 6.183
    FSA Financial Crime Sector Team, 6.178
    FSA Handbook, 6.180
    general rule making power, 6.180
    introduction, 6.177
    investigations, 6.181–6.182
    statutory scheme, 6.179–6.180
  Financial Services Authority, and
    '*Countering Financial Crime Risks in Information Security*', 6.26
    creation of regulatory bear market, 6.24
    '*Data Security in Financial Services*', 6.28
    differences from ICO's role, 6.23
    Financial Crime newsletter, 6.27
    generally, 6.22
    introduction, 6.20
    overview, 6.2
    public statements, 6.25–6.29
    '*Review of financial crime controls in offshore centres*', 6.29

Index

Regulation—*contd*
  foreword to '*Data Security in Financial Services*' (IC, April 2008),   6.74
  FSA Financial Crime Sector Team,   6.178
  FSA Handbook,   6.180
  general principles
    Hampton Report,   6.9–6.10
    introduction,   6.8
    Legislative and Regulatory Reform Act 2006,   6.14–6.18
    Macrory Report,   6.11–6.13
    Regulatory Enforcement and Sanctions Act 2008,   6.19
  Hampton Report (HMT, March 2005)7
    consequences,   6.13
    generally,   6.9
    recommendations and principles,   6.10
  Home Affairs Committee inquiry (HoC)
    oral evidence (May 2007),   6.36–6.40
    written evidence (November 2007),   6.47–6.50
  House of Lords Constitution Committee inquiry
    oral evidence (November 2007),   6.51–6.56
    response (April 2009),   6.91
    written evidence (June 2007),   6.41–6.44
  identity theft warnings,   6.46
  Information Commissioner, and
    action taken,   6.172–6.176
    '*Banks in unacceptable data protection breach*',   6.34–6.35
    '*Case for Amending the Data Protection Act*',   6.66–6.73
    '*CEOs urged to raise their game following unacceptable privacy breaches*',   6.45
    '*Confidential details lost by Revenue and Customs*',   6.57
    Constitution Committee inquiry (June 2007),   6.41–6.44
    Constitution Committee inquiry (November 2007),   6.51–6.56
    creation of regulatory bear market,   6.24
    differences from FSA's role,   6.23
    foreword to 'Data Security in Financial Services',   6.74
    generally,   6.21
    Home Affairs Committee inquiry (May 2007),   6.36–6.40
    Home Affairs Committee inquiry (November 2007),   6.47–6.50
    identity theft warnings,   6.46

Regulation—*contd*
  Information Commissioner, and—*contd*
    introduction,   6.20
    Justice Committee inquiry (December 2007),   6.63–6.65
    memorandum and commentary on Coroners and Justice Bill,   6.88–6.89, 6.92–6.96
    '*Our approach to encryption*',   6.58–6.62
    overview,   6.2
    public statements,   6.30–6.96
    response to Constitution Committee inquiry,   6.91
    response to Joint Committee on Human Rights,   6.90
    RSA Conference speech,   6.75–6.81
    '*Taking stock, taking action*',   6.82–6.87
    '*What Price Privacy?*',   6.31–6.33
  information notices
    appeals,   6.127
    criminal offences,   6.128
    data controller's obligations,   6.124
    generally,   6.121
    ICO proposals,   6.73
    method and timing of furnishing information,   6.125
    power to serve,   6.122
    time for compliance,   6.126
    timing of service,   6.123
  injunctions,   6.70
  inspection powers
    assessment notice regime,   6.138–6.150
    generally,   6.129
    ICO proposals,   6.68
    report of a skilled person,   6.69
    search warrant regime,   6.130–6.137
  inspection powers (assessment notice regime)
    'assessment notice',   6.139
    code of practice,   6.147–6.148
    editorial comment,   6.149–6.150
    exempt materials,   6.143
    generally,   6.138
    designating private sector data controllers,   6.141–6.142
    ICO proposals,   6.68
    recipients,   6.140
    sanctions for non-compliance,   6.145
    time for compliance,   6.144
    use of material obtained,   6.146
  inspection powers (search warrant regime)
    action taken by the IC,   6.174
    control of power through notice requirements,   6.133

Index

Regulation—*contd*
inspection powers (search warrant regime)—*contd*
  criminal offences, 6.136
  failure to provide assistance, 6.136
  formalities, 6.135
  generally, 6.130
  ICO proposals, 6.68
  notice of intention to apply for warrant, 6.132
  notice of wish to gain access, 6.131
  obstruction of officers, 6.136
  powers granted by warrant, 6.134
  proposals to amend, 6.137
introduction, 6.1
investigations, 6.181–6.182
Joint Committee on Human Rights response (February 2009), 6.90
Justice Committee inquiry (HoC) December 2007 oral evidence, 6.63–6.65
Legislative and Regulatory Reform Act 2006
  generally, 6.14
  Statutory Code of Practice for Regulators, 6.15–6.18
Macrory Report (BRE, November 2006)
  consequences, 6.13
  generally, 6.11
  sanction regime design, 6.12
monetary penalties
  amendments to DPA 1998, and, 6.100–6.101
  amount, 6.153
  assessment notices, and, 6.158
  enforcement, 6.156
  guidance, 6.155
  introduction, 6.151
  ICO proposals, 6.67
  notices, 6.155–6.157
  power to impose, 6.152
  procedural rights, 6.154
  Regulators' Compliance Code, and, 6.17
  statutory basis, 6.19
  supplemental provisions, 6.157
News of the World case, 6.33
OFCOM, and, 6.2
Office of Fair Trading, and, 6.2
'*Our approach to encryption*' (ICO, November 2007), 6.58–6.62
Press Complaints Commission, and, 6.3
privacy enhancing technologies (PETs)
  Constitution Committee inquiry (HoL, June 2007), 6.43

Regulation—*contd*
privacy enhancing technologies (PETs)—*contd*
  Constitution Committee inquiry (HoL, November 2007), 6.55
  Home Affairs Committee inquiry (HoC, November 2007), 6.47
  memorandum and commentary on Coroners and Justice Bill, 6.96
  '*Our approach to encryption*' (ICO, November 2007), 6.59
  '*Taking stock, taking action*' (ICO, November 2008), 6.85
privacy impact assessments
  Constitution Committee inquiry (HoL, June 2007), 6.44
  Constitution Committee inquiry (HoL, November 2007), 6.56
  Home Affairs Committee inquiry (HoC, May 2007), 6.40
  Home Affairs Committee inquiry (HoC, November 2007), 6.50
  memorandum and commentary on Coroners and Justice Bill, 6.96
  '*Taking stock, taking action*' (ICO, November 2008), 6.84
private investigators, and, 6.3
professions, and, 6.3
regulators, 6.2–6.3
Regulators Compliance Code
  compliance and enforcement actions, 6.18
  generally, 6.15–6.16
  inspections and visits, 6.17
Regulatory Enforcement and Sanctions Act 2008, 6.19
report of a skilled person, 6.69
'*Review of financial crime controls in offshore centres*' (FSA, April 2009), 6.29
RSA Conference speech (IC, October 2008), 6.75–6.81
search warrants
  action taken by the IC, 6.174
  control of power through notice requirements, 6.133
  criminal offences, 6.136
  failure to provide assistance, 6.136
  formalities, 6.135
  generally, 6.130
  ICO proposals, 6.68
  notice of intention to apply for warrant, 6.132
  notice of wish to gain access, 6.131
  obstruction of officers, 6.136
  powers granted by warrant, 6.134
  proposals to amend, 6.137
self-regulation, 6.4

Index

Regulation—*contd*
  state's obligation, 6.6
  Statutory Code of Practice for Regulators
    compliance and enforcement actions, 6.18
    generally, 6.15–6.16
    inspections and visits, 6.17
  statutory undertakings
    action taken by the IC, 6.172–6.173
    generally, 6.168–6.170
    ICO proposals, 6.70–6.71
  'Surveillance Society' inquiry (HoC)
    oral evidence (May 2007), 6.36–6.40
    written evidence (November 2007), 6.47–6.50
  'Surveillance Society' inquiry (HoL)
    oral evidence (November 2007), 6.51–6.56
    response (April 2009), 6.91
    written evidence (June 2007), 6.41–6.44
  'Taking stock, taking action' (ICO, November 2008), 6.82–6.87
  undertakings
    action taken by the IC, 6.172–6.173
    generally, 6.168–6.170
    ICO proposals, 6.70–6.71
  'What price privacy?' (IC Report, May 2006)
    generally, 6.31
    imprisonment for unlawfully obtaining personal data, 6.32
    News of the World case, 6.33
Regulation of Investigatory Powers Act 2000
  'communication', 2.111
  decrypted information, 2.122
  encryption, and
    disclosure notices, 2.8–2.9
    generally, 2.7
    'protected information', 2.8
    summary, 2.10
  encryption keys, 2.122
  exclusion of criminal liability, 2.117
  facilities for interception, 2.120–2.121
  generally, 2.108
  'in the course of transmission', 2.113–2.115
  'interception', 2.112
  interception in private systems, 2.117
  interception of business communications, 2.119
  introduction, 2.107
  'lawful authority', 2.116
  non-real time monitoring, 2.115
  'private telecommunication system', 2.110

Regulation of Investigatory Powers Act 2000—*contd*
  'public telecommunication system', 2.109
  stored e-mail and voicemail messages, 2.114
  supply of decrypted information and encryption keys, 2.122
  tort of unlawful interception, 2.118
Regulators
  data protection, and, 2.37
Regulators Compliance Code
  compliance and enforcement actions, 6.18
  generally, 6.15–6.16
  inspections and visits, 6.17
  Regulatory Enforcement and Sanctions Act 2008, 6.19
Relevant filing system
  data protection, and, 2.25
Remedies
  breach of data security obligation, and
    Article 29 Working Party's views, 2.96
    'claims farming', and, 2.98
    compensation for damage and distress, 2.92–2.95
    consequences for data controllers, 2.97
    7generally, 2.91
    Johnson v MDU decision, 2.93–2.95
Report of a skilled person
  regulation and enforcement, and, 6.69
'Review of financial crime controls in offshore centres' (FSA, April 2009)
  regulation and enforcement, and, 6.29
Right to respect for private and family life
  data protection, and, 2.20
  duty of confidence, and
    generally, 2.14
    positive obligation, 2.15
  electronic communications, and, 2.99
RSA Conference Europe speech (IC, October 2008)
  breach notification, and, 7.40–7.43
  regulation and enforcement, and, 6.75–6.81

SAS 70
  corporate governance, and, 3.12
Science and Technology Committee report (HoL, August 2007)
  breach notification, and, 7.15–7.16
Search warrants
  action taken by the IC, 6.174
  control of power through notice requirements, 6.133
  criminal offences, 6.136
  failure to provide assistance, 6.136

Index

Search warrants—*contd*
  formalities, 6.135
  generally, 6.130
  ICO proposals, 6.68
  notice of intention to apply for
    warrant, 6.132
  notice of wish to gain access, 6.131
  obstruction of officers, 6.136
  powers granted by warrant, 6.134
  proposals to amend, 6.137
  self-regulation, 6.4
  state's obligation, 6.6
Secrecy laws
  See also Secrecy laws
  Barristers' Code of Conduct, 5.29
  Commissioners for Revenue and
    Customs Act 2005, 5.19
  Communications Act 2003, 5.28
  Data Protection Act 1998, 5.22
  FSA Handbook
    Audit Directive, 5.27
    introduction, 5.23
    MiFID, 5.26
    Payment Services Directive, 5.24
    Transparency Directive, 5.25
  General Medical Council's guidance, 5.29
  Identity Cards Act 2006, 5.20
  Institute of Chartered Accountants
    Handbook, 5.29
  official secrets
    And see Official secrets
    introduction, 5.2
    Official Secrets Act 1911, 5.3
    Official Secrets Act 1920, 5.4
    Official Secrets Act 1989, 5.5–5.17
    overview, 5.1
  other examples, 5.18
  Press Complaints Commission, 5.30
  professionals, 5.29
  regulators
    Communications Act 2003, 5.28
    Data Protection Act 1998, 5.22
    FSA Handbook, 5.23–5.27
    introduction, 5.21
  Solicitors' Code of Conduct, 5.29
Secure-signature creation devices
  electronic signatures, and, 2.144
Security Policy Framework
  access controls, 4.38
  access rights, 4.39
  accountability, 4.40–4.41
  accreditation of technology, 4.42
  audits, 4.43
  awareness programmes, 4.54
  breach notification, and, 7.56
  business continuity, 4.44
  contractual control, 4.45

Security Policy Framework—*contd*
  core security principles, 4.37
  disaster recovery, 4.44
  employee-worker due diligence, 4.46
  encryption, 4.47
  introduction, 4.35
  outsourcing, 4.52
  physical security, 4.48
  security policy, 4.49–4.50
  third party assurance, 4.52
  threat assessment, 4.51
  training programmes, 4.54
  transparency, 4.53
  use of data processors, 4.52
  vulnerability assessment, 4.51
  waste, 4.55
Security principle
  And see Data protection
  appropriateness of measures taken, 2.49–2.52
  breach by controller, 2.48
  evolution, 2.19
  international aspects, 2.18
  introduction, 2.16
  relationship with other principles, 2.17
  reliability of data processors, 2.66–2.83
  reliability of employees, 2.53–2.65
  remedies for breach of obligation, 2.91–2.98
  safeguards against breaches and data
    loss, 2.47
  technological development, 2.84–2.90
Self-monitoring
  data processors, and, 2.73–2.74
Senior Management, Arrangements,
  Systems and Controls (SYSC)
  financial services, and, 3.31–3.33
Sensitive personal data
  data protection, and, 2.31
Solicitors' Code of Conduct
  secrecy laws, and, 5.29
Statutory Code of Practice for
  Regulators
  compliance and enforcement actions, 6.18
  generally, 6.15–6.16
  inspections and visits, 6.17
Statutory undertakings
  action taken by the IC, 6.172–6.173
  generally, 6.168–6.170
  ICO proposals, 6.70–6.71
Structured paper files
  data protection, and, 2.25
Subject access
  breach notification, and, 7.9–7.10
Supervision (SUP)
  financial services, and, 3.34

Index

'Surveillance Society' inquiry (HoC)
 breach notification, and, 7.17
 oral evidence (May 2007), 6.36–6.40
 written evidence (November 2007), 6.47–6.50
'Surveillance Society' inquiry (HoL)
 oral evidence (November 2007), 6.51–6.56
 response (April 2009), 6.91
 written evidence (June 2007), 6.41–6.44

'Taking stock, taking action' (ICO, November 2008)
 regulation and enforcement, and, 6.82–6.87
Technological development
 And see Data protection
 appropriate measure of sufficiency, 2.89
 'Bolam test', and, 2.87
 deployment of technology, 2.86
 generally, 2.84
 industry practice, 2.86
 Privacy Enhancing Technologies (PETs), 2.90
 professional negligence, 2.87–2.88
 state of technology deployment, 2.86
 'state of the art', 2.85
Technical knowledge and experience
 data processors, and, 2.70
Telecommunications Privacy Directive (97/66/EC)
 differences from 2002 Directive, 2.105
 exceptions from confidentiality obligations, 2.106
 generally, 2.101
 security and confidentiality regime, 2.102
Telecommunications services
 Communications Data Retention Directive (2006/24/EC)
  data protection and data security regime, 2.104
  generally, 2.101
 Electronic Communications Privacy Directive (2002/58/EC)
  differences from 1997 Directive, 2.105
  exceptions from confidentiality obligations, 2.106
  generally, 2.101
  security and confidentiality regime, 2.103
  transposition in UK, 2.107
 EU Directives, 2.101
 human rights, and, 2.99
 introduction, 2.99
 Privacy and Electronic Communications (EC Directive) Regulations 2003
  generally, 2.123

Telecommunications services—*contd*
 Privacy and Electronic Communications (EC Directive) Regulations 2003—*contd*
  introduction, 2.107
 Regulation of Investigatory Powers Act 2000
  'communication', 2.111
  decrypted information, 2.122
  encryption keys, 2.122
  exclusion of criminal liability, 2.117
  facilities for interception, 2.120–2.121
  generally, 2.108
  'in the course of transmission', 2.113–2.115
  'interception', 2.112
  interception in private systems, 2.117
  interception of business communications, 2.119
  introduction, 2.107
  'lawful authority', 2.116
  non-real time monitoring, 2.115
  'private telecommunication system', 2.110
  'public telecommunication system', 2.109
  stored e-mail and voicemail messages, 2.114
  supply of decrypted information and encryption keys, 2.122
  tort of unlawful interception, 2.118
 regulators' obligation to ensure security, 2.100
 right to respect for private and family life, and, 2.99
 Telecommunications Privacy Directive (97/66/EC)
  differences from 2002 Directive, 2.105
  exceptions from confidentiality obligations, 2.106
  generally, 2.101
  security and confidentiality regime, 2.102
Thomas-Walport Data Sharing Review (July 2008)
 breach notification, and, 7.37–7.39
Transborder data flows
 data processors, and, 2.82
'Transformational Government' (Cabinet Office, 2005)
 public sector, and, 4.2
Transparency
 breach notification, and
  fair processing, 7.4–7.6
  human rights issues, 7.13
  information notices, 7.11–7.12
  introduction, 7.3
  notification, 7.7–7.8

Index

Transparency—*contd*
  breach notification, and—*contd*
    registration, 7.7–7.8
    subject access, 7.9–7.10
  companies, and
    EU Directive (2004/109/EC), 3.4–3.5
    FSA Handbook, 3.6
    introduction, 3.3
    statutory provision, 3.3
    UK rules, 3.6
  data protection, and, 2.41–2.42
Turnbull Guidance
  corporate governance, and, 3.11

Unauthorised access to computer material
  causing a computer to perform a function, 2.128
  generally, 2.127
  intent to commit further offences, with, 2.134
  knowledge that access is unauthorised, 2.133
  purpose of offence, 2.127
  securing access, 2.129–2.130
  security controls, and, 2.138
  territorial scope
    generally, 2.125
    'significant links', 2.126
    unauthorised, 2.131–2.132
Unauthorised acts with intent to impair operation of computer
  elements, 2.136
  generally, 2.135
  programs and data stored in moveable media, 2.137
  security controls, and, 2.138
  territorial scope, 2.125–2.126
Undertakings
  action taken by the IC, 6.172–6.173
  generally, 6.168–6.170
  ICO proposals, 6.70–6.71
Unlawful interception
  electronic communications privacy, and, 2.118

US (breach notification)
  Californian law
    computerised data, 7.108
    COPP guidance, 7.111–7.113
    early warning system, 7.112
    encryption, 7.109
    generally, 7.107
    seriousness threshold, 7.110
  electronic health information
    aims and objectives, 7.104
    generally, 7.103
    obligation to report, 7.105
  Federal Trade Commission initiatives
    electronic health information, 7.103–7.105
    introduction, 7.98
    Red Flag Rules, 7.99–7.102
  generally, 7.90
  other initiatives and federal rules, 7.106
  Red Flag Rules
    financial institutions, 7.102
    introduction, 7.99
    management responsibility, 7.101
    warning signs, 7.100
  state level
    form and content of reports, 7.95
    harm threshold to reporting, 7.92
    introduction, 7.91
    other laws, 7.97
    personal information, 7.94
    policies, 7.96
    rules for data processing, 7.93

Vicarious liability
  data processors, and, 2.69
Voicemail messages
  electronic communications privacy, and, 2.114

'What price privacy?' (IC Report, May 2006)
  generally, 6.31
  imprisonment for unlawfully obtaining personal data, 6.32
  introduction, 1.32
  News of the World case, 6.33

1037